Executive Editor: *Carolyn Merrill*
Editorial Assistant: *Carolyn Mulloy*
Marketing Manager: *Wendy Gordon*
Editorial Production Service: *Chestnut Hill Enterprises, Inc.*
Manufacturing Buyer: *JoAnne Sweeney*
Cover Administrator: *Linda Knowles*
Text Designer: *Carol Somberg*
Electronic Composition: *Omegatype Typography, Inc.*

For related titles and support materials, visit our online catalog at
www.ablongman.com

Between the time Website information is gathered and published, some sites may
have closed. Also, the transcription of URLs can result in typographical errors.
The publisher would appreciate notification of any problems with URLs so that
they may be corrected in subsequent editions.

Library of Congress Cataloging-in-Publication Data

Carver, Charles S.
    Perspectives on personality / Charles S. Carver, Michael F. Scheier.—5th ed.
        p.   cm.
    Includes bibliographical references and index.
    ISBN 0-205-37576-6 (alk. paper)
    1. Personality.   I. Scheier, Michael.   II. Title.

BF698.C22 2004
155.2—dc21

2003044325

Printed in the United States of America

10   9   8   7   6   5   4   3   2   1   08   07   06   05   04   03

For Sheri Lou — *CSC*

For Karen Ann — *MFS*

Contents

Preface   xxi

Acknowledgments   xxiii

About the Authors   xxv

PART ONE:
An Introduction   1

1   What Is Personality Psychology?   2

Defining Personality   3
Why Use Personality as a Concept?   3
A Working Definition   5
Two Fundamental Issues in Personality Psychology   6

Theory in Personality Psychology   7
What Do Theories Do?   7
Evaluating Theories: The Role of Research   8
What Else Makes a Theory Good?   8

Perspectives on Personality   10
Groupings among Theories   10
How Distinct Are the Perspectives?   12
Another Kind of "Perspective"   12

Organization within Chapters   13
Assessment   13
Problems in Behavior, and Behavior Change   14

SUMMARY   15

2   Methods in the Study of Personality   16

Gathering Information   17
Sources: Observe Yourself and Observe Others   17
Seeking Depth: Case Studies   17
Seeking Generality: Studies of Many People   19

Establishing Relationships among Variables   20
Correlation between Variables   21
Two Kinds of Significance   25
Causality and a Limitation on Inference   25
Search for Causality: Experimental Research   27
Recognizing Types of Study   30
What Kind of Research Is Best?   30
Multifactor Studies   31
Reading Figures from Multifactor Research   32

SUMMARY   33

3 | Issues in Personality Assessment   35

Sources of Information   36

Reliability of Measurement   38
Internal Consistency   38
Inter-Rater Reliability   40
Stability across Time   40

Validity of Measurement   41
Construct Validity   42
Criterion Validity   43
Convergent Validity   43
Discriminant Validity   44
Face Validity   44
Culture and Validity   45
Response Sets and Loss of Validity   45

Two Rationales behind the Development of Assessment Devices   47
Rational, or Theoretical, Approach   47
Empirical Approaches   48

Better Assessment: A Never-Ending Search   49

SUMMARY   50

PART TWO:
The Dispositional Perspective   53

Prologue: The Dispositional Perspective: Major Themes
and Underlying Assumptions   54

4 | Types, Traits, and Interactionism   56

Types and Traits   57
Nomothetic and Idiographic Views of Traits   58

What Traits Matter?   59
A Key Tool: Factor Analysis   59
Let Reality Reveal Itself: Cattell's Approach   62

Start from a Theory: Eysenck's Approach   63
Another Theoretical Starting Point: The Interpersonal Circle   65

The Five-Factor Model: The Basic Dimensions of Personality?   **67**
What *Are* the Five Factors?   67
Reflections of the Five Factors   70
The Five-Factor Model in Relation to Other Models   71
Cautions and Some Further Variations   72
Are Superordinate Traits the Best Level to Use?   73

Traits, Situations, and Interactionism   **73**
Is Behavior Actually Traitlike?   73
Situationism   74
Low Reliability in Measuring Behavior   74
Interactionism   76
Individual Differences in Consistency   77
Beyond Analysis of Variance in Interactionism   78
Was the Problem Ever Really as Bad as It Seemed?   79

Interactionism Becomes a New View of Traits: Context-Dependent Expression of Personality   **79**
Fitting the Pieces Together: Views of Traits and Behavior   81

Assessment   **82**
Comparing Individuals: Personality Profiles   82

Problems in Behavior, and Behavior Change   **84**
The Five-Factor Model and Personality Disorders   84
Interactionism in Behavior Problems   84
Behavior Change   85

Trait Psychology: Problems and Prospects   **86**

SUMMARY   **87**

5 **Needs and Motives**   **89**

Basic Theoretical Elements   **90**
Needs   90
Motives   92
Press   93

Needs, Motives, and Personality   **94**
Motivational States and Motive Dispositions   94
Murray's System of Needs   95
Measuring Motives: The Thematic Apperception Test   96

Individual Differences in Specific Needs   **98**
Need for Achievement   98
Divergent Motives Underlying Achievement Behavior   101
Need for Power   103
Need for Affiliation   105
Need for Intimacy   106
Patterned Needs: Inhibited Power Motive   108

Further Determinants of Behavior   **108**
Incentive Value   109
Expectancy and Skill   110

The Methods of Personology   **110**

Assessment   **111**
Self-Reports and the TAT May Not Measure the Same Thing   111
Motives and the Five-Factor Model   112
Traits and Motives as Distinct   113

Problems in Behavior, and Behavior Change   **113**
The Need for Power and Alcohol Abuse   114
Focusing On and Changing Motivation   114

Need and Motive Theories: Problems and Prospects   **115**

SUMMARY   **117**

PART THREE:
The Biological Perspective   121

Prologue: **The Biological Perspective: Major Themes and Underlying Assumptions**   **122**

6 Inheritance, Evolution, and Personality   124

Determining the Role of Inheritance in Personality   **125**
Twin Study Method   125
Adoption Research   128

What Personality Qualities Are Inherited?   **128**
Temperaments: Activity, Sociability, and Emotionality   129
Are There Other Temperaments?   131
Inheritance of Traits   132
Temperaments and the Five-Factor Model   133
Genetics of Other Qualities: How Distinct Are They?   134
Inheritance and Sexual Orientation   134
Molecular Genetics and New Sources of Evidence   135

Environmental Effects   **136**
The Size of Environmental Influences   136
The Nature of Environmental Influences   137

Evolution and Human Behavior   **138**
Sociobiology and Evolutionary Psychology   138
Genetic Similarity and Attraction   141
Mate Selection and Competition for Mates   142
Mate Retention and Other Issues   145
Aggression and the Young Male Syndrome   146

Assessment   **147**

Problems in Behavior, and Behavior Change   **148**

Behavior Genetics and Disorders   149
Evolution and Problems in Behavior   150
Behavior Change: How Much Is Possible?   151

Inheritance and Evolution: Problems and Prospects   **151**

SUMMARY   **153**

---

7   **Biological Processes and Personality**   **155**

Eysenck: Extraversion, Neuroticism, and Brain Functions   **156**

Extraversion and Cortical Arousal   156
Biological Basis of Neuroticism   160

A Contemporary View of Brain Functions:
Approach and Inhibition   **160**

Behavioral Approach, Activation, Engagement, or Facilitation   160
Neurotransmitters and the Approach System   162
Behavioral Inhibition, Withdrawal, or Avoidance   162
Neurotransmitters and the Withdrawal System   163
Relating These Systems to Temperaments or Traits   164
Two Areas of Disagreement   165

Sensation Seeking: A Third Biological System?   **166**

Function of Sensation Seeking   167
Sensation Seeking, Impulsiveness, and Other Systems   169
One More Angle on Impulsivity   169

Impulsiveness: Further Issues   **169**

What Does Serotonin Function Mean?   170
What Are the Personality Scales Measuring?   171

Hormones and Personality   **172**

Hormones, the Body, and the Brain   172
Early Hormonal Exposure and Behavior   173
Testosterone and Adult Personality   174
Cycle of Testosterone and Action   177
Testosterone, Dominance, and Evolutionary Psychology   178
Responding to Stress: Men, Women, and Oxytocin   178

Assessment   **180**

Electroencephalograms   180
Neuro-Imaging   180

Problems in Behavior, and Behavior Change   **181**

Biological Bases of Anxiety, Depression,
     and Antisocial Personality   182
Medication in Therapy   183

Biological Processes and Personality: Problems and Prospects   **184**

SUMMARY   **185**

PART FOUR:
The Psychoanalytic Perspective   187

Prologue: The Psychoanalytic Perspective: Major Themes and Underlying Assumptions   188

8   Psychoanalytic Structure and Process   190

The Topographical Model of Mind   193

Aspects of Personality: The Structural Model   195
Id   195
Ego   196
Superego   198
Balancing the Forces   199

Motivation: The Drives of Personality   200
Cathexes and the Use of Energy   202
Two Classes of Drives: Life and Death Instincts   203
Coming Together of Libidinal and Aggressive Energies   204
Catharsis   204
Displacement and Sublimation of Motive Forces   207

Psychosexual Development   208
The Oral Stage   208
The Anal Stage   210
The Phallic Stage   211
The Latency Period   214
The Genital Stage   215

Psychoanalytic Structure and Process: Problems and Prospects   215

SUMMARY   217

9   Anxiety, Defense, and Self-Protection   220

Anxiety   221

Mechanisms of Defense   222
Repression   222
Denial   224
Projection   226
Rationalization   226
Intellectualization   227
Reaction Formation   227
Regression   228
Displacement and Sublimation   228
Research on Defenses   229
Evidence of Unconscious Conflict   230

Exposing the Unconscious   231
The Psychopathology of Everyday Life   231
Dreams   234
Humor   236

Projective Techniques of Assessment   237
Rorschach Inkblot Test   238

Problems in Behavior, and Behavior Change   240
Origins of Problems   240
Behavior Change   241
Does Psychoanalytic Therapy Work?   245

Psychoanalytic Defense: Problems and Prospects   245

SUMMARY   247

PART FIVE:
The Neoanalytic Perspective   249

Prologue: **The Neoanalytic Perspective: Major Themes and Underlying Assumptions   250**

10 | Ego Psychology   252

Principles of Ego Psychology   253
Shifting the Emphasis from Id to Ego   255
Adaptation and Autonomy   256
The Ego, Adaptation, and Competence Motivation   256
Is Competence Striving Automatic, or Is It Done to Remedy Inferiority?   259
Ego Control and Ego Resiliency   262
Ego Control, Ego Resiliency, and the Five-Factor Model   264

Ego Development   265
Early Ego Development   266
Middle Stages of Ego Development: Control of Impulses   267
Advanced Stages of Ego Development: Taking More into Account   268
Research on Ego Development   269
Ego Development and the Five-Factor Model   271

Assessment   271
Assessment of Lifestyles   272
Assessment of Level of Ego Development   274

Problems in Behavior, and Behavior Change   275
Inferiority and Superiority Complexes   275
Overcontrol and Undercontrol   275
Behavior Change   276

Ego Psychology: Problems and Prospects   276

SUMMARY   278

11 Psychosocial Theories   280

Object Relations Theories   281
Self Psychology   283
Basic Anxiety   283

Attachment Theory and Personality   285
Attachment Patterns in Adults   287
How Many Patterns?   289
Stability and Specificity   289
Other Reflections of Adult Attachment   290
Attachment Patterns and the Five-Factor Model   291

Erikson's Theory of Psychosocial Development   292
Ego Identity, Competence, and the Experience of Crisis   292
Infancy   294
Early Childhood   295
Preschool   295
School Age   296
Adolescence   297
Young Adulthood   300
Adulthood   301
Old Age   302
The Epigenetic Principle   304
Identity as Life Story   304
Linking Erikson's Theory to Other Psychosocial Theories   305

Assessment   305
Object Relations, Attachment, and the Focus of Assessment   305
Play in Assessment   306

Problems in Behavior, and Behavior Change   307
Narcissism as a Disorder of Personality   307
Neurotic Needs   307
Attachment and Depression   308
Behavior Change   309

Psychosocial Theories: Problems and Prospects   310

SUMMARY   310

PART SIX:
The Learning Perspective   313

Prologue: **The Learning Perspective: Major Themes and Underlying Assumptions   314**

12 Conditioning Theories   316

Classical Conditioning   317
Basic Elements   317
Classical Conditioning as Anticipatory Learning   320

Discrimination, Generalization, and Extinction
in Classical Conditioning   320
Emotional Conditioning   322

Instrumental Conditioning   324
The Law of Effect   325
Reinforcement and Punishment   326
Discrimination, Generalization, and Extinction
in Instrumental Conditioning   327
Altering the Shape of Behavior   329
Schedules of Reinforcement and the Issue of Persistence   330
Learning "Irrational" Behavior   332
Reinforcement of Dimensions of Behavior   334

Assessment   334
Techniques   335

Problems in Behavior, and Behavior Change   336
Classical Conditioning of Emotional Responses   337
Classical Conditioning of Aversion   339
Conditioning and Context   340
Instrumental Conditioning and Maladaptive Behaviors   341
Instrumental Conditioning of Conflict   341
Instrumental Conditioning and Token Economies   342
Instrumental Conditioning and Biofeedback   342

Conditioning Theories: Problems and Prospects   343

SUMMARY   344

13 Social-Cognitive Learning Theories   347

Elaborations on Conditioning Processes   348
Social Reinforcement   348
Vicarious Emotional Arousal   350
Vicarious Reinforcement   352
Semantic Generalization   352
Rule-Based Learning   353
Expectancies concerning Outcomes   354
Locus-of-Control Expectancies   356
Efficacy Expectancies   357

Observational Learning   359
Acquisition versus Performance   361

Manifestations of Cognitive and Social Learning   363
Modeling and Sex Role Acquisition   364
Modeling of Aggression and the Issue of Media Violence   366

Assessment   367

Problems in Behavior, and Behavior Change   368
Conceptualizing Behavioral Problems   368
Modeling-Based Therapy for Skill Deficits   369

Modeling and Responses to Fear   371
Therapeutic Changes in Efficacy Expectancy   372
Self-Instructions and Cognitive Behavioral Modification   373

**Social-Cognitive Learning Theories:
Problems and Prospects   374**

SUMMARY   376

PART SEVEN:
The Phenomenological Perspective   379

Prologue: **The Phenomenological Perspective: Major Themes
and Underlying Assumptions   380**

14 Humanistic Psychology: Self-Actualization
and Self-Determination   382

Self-Actualization   383
The Need for Positive Regard   384

Self-Determination   387
Introjection and Identification   387
Need for Relatedness   388
Self-Concordance   389
Free Will   389

The Self and Processes of Defense   390
Incongruity, Disorganization, and Defense   391
Self-Esteem Maintenance and Enhancement   392
Self-Handicapping   393

**Self-Actualization and Maslow's
Hierarchy of Motives   394**
Characteristics of Frequent Self-Actualizers   397
The Peak Experience   400

Existential Psychology: Being and Death   400
The Existential Dilemma   401
Emptiness   402
Terror Management   402

Assessment   404
Interviews in Assessment   404
Measuring the Self-Concept by Q-Sort   404
Measuring Self-Actualization   406
Measuring Autonomy and Control   406

Problems in Behavior, and Behavior Change   407
Client-Centered Therapy   408
Beyond Therapy, to Personal Growth   409

Humanistic Theories: Problems and Prospects   410

SUMMARY   411

15   Personal Constructs   414

Personal Constructs and Personality   416
Using Constructs   417
Constructs Are Bipolar   418
The Role of Recurrences   419
Range and Focus of Convenience   419
Elaboration and Change in Construct Systems   420
Organization among Constructs   422
Individuality of Constructs   423
Similarities and Differences between People   425
Role Taking   426
Personal Constructs and Behavioral Consistency   428

Assessment   429
Kelly's Role Construct Repertory Test   429

Problems in Behavior, and Behavior Change   431
Personal Constructs and Psychological Distress   431
Dealing with Anxiety and Threat   433
Fixed Role Therapy   434

Personal Construct Theory: Problems and Prospects   435

SUMMARY   436

**PART EIGHT:
The Cognitive Self-Regulation Perspective**   439

Prologue: **The Cognitive Self-Regulation Perspective: Major Themes
and Underlying Assumptions**   440

16   Contemporary Cognitive Views   442

Representing Your Experience of the World   443
Schemas and Their Development   443
Effects of Schemas   444
Semantic Memory, Episodic Memory, and Scripts   445
Socially Relevant Schemas   446
Self-Schemas   447
Entity and Incremental Schemas   448
Attribution   449
Activation and Use of Memories   450

Connectionist Views of Mental Organization   **453**
Dual Process Models   456

Pulling the Pieces Together   **458**
Cognitive Person Variables   458
Personality as a Cognitive–Affective Processing System   460

Assessment   **462**
Think-Aloud, Experience Sampling, and Self-Monitoring   462
Contextualized Assessment   463
Diagnostic Categories as Prototypes   464

Problems in Behavior, and Behavior Change   **464**
Information-Processing Deficits   464
Depressive Self-Schemas   465
Cognitive Therapy   466

Contemporary Cognitive Theories: Problems and Prospects   **467**

SUMMARY   **468**

17   **Self-Regulation**   **471**

From Cognition to Behavior   **472**
Schemas for Action   473
Automaticity in Action   475
Intentions   475
Implementation Intentions, and Deliberative
    and Implemental Mindsets   477
Goals and Goal Setting   478

Self-Regulation and Feedback Control   **479**
Feedback Control   479
Self-Directed Attention and the Action of the Comparator   481
Hierarchical Organization   482
Issues concerning Hierarchical Organization   485
Research on Hierarchies of Behavior   486
Emotion   486
Effects of Expectancies: Effort versus Disengagement   488

Assessment   **490**
Assessment of Self-Regulatory Qualities   491
Assessment of Goals   492

Problems in Behavior, and Behavior Change   **492**
Problems as Conflicts among Goals, and Lack of Goal Specifications   493
Problems from an Inability to Disengage   494
Self-Regulation and the Process of Therapy   495
Therapy Is Training in Problem Solving   495

Self-Regulation Theories: Problems and Prospects   **496**

SUMMARY   **498**

PART NINE:
Personality in Perspective   501

18 Overlap and Integration   502

Similarities among Perspectives   504
Psychoanalysis and Evolutionary Psychology: The Structural Model   504
Psychoanalysis and Evolutionary Psychology:
   Fixations and Mating Patterns   505
Psychoanalysis and Conditioning   505
Psychoanalysis and Self-Regulation: The Structural Model   506
Psychoanalysis and Cognitive Processes   507
Social Learning and Cognitive Self-Regulation Views   510
Neoanalytic and Cognitive Self-Regulation Perspectives   512
Maslow's Hierarchy and Hierarchies of Self-Regulation   512
Self-Actualization and Self-Regulation   513
Dispositions and Their Equivalents in Other Models   513

Recurrent Themes, Viewed from Different Angles   514
Impulse and Restraint   514
Individual versus Group Needs   515

Combining Perspectives   516
Eclecticism   516
An Example: Biology and Learning as Complementary
   Influences on Personality   517

Which Theory Is Best?   518

SUMMARY   519

References   521

Name Index   589

Subject Index   601

*P*erspectives on Personality, Fifth Edition, examines one of the most engaging and mysterious topics in all of life: human personality. As the book's title implies, there are many perspectives a person might take on personality, many ways to think about how people function in life. This book describes a range of viewpoints that are used by personality psychologists today.

What's the Same in This Edition?

As in the four earlier editions, the book's content reflects two of our strongly held beliefs. The first is that *ideas* are the most important part of a first course on personality. For this reason, we stress concepts throughout the book. Our first priority has been to present as clearly as we can the ideas that form each theoretical viewpoint.

The second belief is that research is important in personality psychology. Ideas and intuitions are valuable, but an idea shouldn't lie around too long before someone checks to see whether it actually works. For this reason, along with each theory we discuss research that bears on the theory. This emphasis on the role of research stresses the fact that personality psychology is a living, dynamic process of ongoing scientific exploration.

As in previous editions, we present the theories in groups, which we've labeled *perspectives*. Each group of theories depends on a particular sort of orienting viewpoint, an angle from which the theorists proceeded. Within a given perspective there often are several theories, which differ from one another. In each case, however, the theories of a given perspective share fundamental assumptions about human nature.

Each perspective on personality is presented in a pair of chapters, introduced by a prologue. The prologue provides an overview of that perspective's orienting assumptions and core themes. By starting with these orienting assumptions, you'll be right inside the thought processes of the theorists as you go on to read the chapters themselves. Each chapter concludes with a discussion of current problems within that theoretical viewpoint and our own best guess about its future prospects.

The perspectives are presented in an order that makes sense to us, but they can easily be read in other orders. Each theoretical section of the book is intended to stand on its own, with no assumptions about previous exposure to other parts of the book. Thus, instructors can move through the perspectives in whatever order they prefer.

As in the previous editions, the final chapter takes up the question of how different views relate to each other. The main goal of this chapter is to tie together ideas from theories discussed separately in earlier chapters. A second goal is to consider the usefulness of blending theoretical viewpoints, treating theories as complementary to each other rather than as competitors.

This edition also continues our use of the feature "The Theorist and the Theory." These boxes focus on how the personal experiences of some of the theorists have influenced the form their theories took. In several cases, theorists almost literally took events from their own lives as models of human events more generally, and went on to derive an entire theory from those personal experiences. Not all cases are quite this striking, but personal experience does appear to have played a role in the development of several views on personality.

In this revision we've continued to try very hard to make the content accessible. We use an informal, conversational style throughout, to try to draw you into the ideas. We've also included examples of how the ideas can apply to your own life. We hope these qualities make the book engaging and enjoyable, as well as informative.

What's Different about This Edition?

This edition retains the prior structure (the same chapters, in the same perspectives). However, the content of this edition differs in several ways from that of the fourth edition. These changes reflect four years of rapid change in the continually evolving research literature of personality psychology. Updates have been made to every substantive chapter. In fact, we used information from over 400 new sources. Although updates have been made everywhere, several areas of change are major enough that we should note them explicitly.

First, work has continued at a rapid rate on the trait structure of personality and the implications of that structure for behavior. Most of this work is taking place within the framework of the five-factor model. This has resulted in considerable change in Chapter 4 (Types, Trait, and Interactionism). It's also resulted in the inclusion of additional material bearing on the five-factor model in several other chapters.

Second, there continue to be *incredibly* rapid advances in work concerning behavioral genetics, molecular genetics, temperament, neurotransmitters, and other biological processes and how they relate to aspects of personality. Theorists have approached these processes and their relations to personality from several directions. As a result, Chapters 6 and 7 have both undergone major updates.

Another area of rapid expansion is work on adult attachment patterns and their implications for personality and social behavior. This explosion of work has resulted in major changes in the chapter dealing with psychosocial theories (Chapter 11).

Rapid expansion has also taken place in work on self-actualization and related models. Research deriving from self-determination theory, terror management theory, and related theories has been very active over the past four years. The information produced by this work has reinvigorated interest in this view of personality, causing major changes in Chapter 14.

Finally, we've included a good deal of new material in the chapters of the Cognitive Self-Regulation perspective. This new material includes a discussion of connectionist models of cognitive processes, expanded information on contextual models of behavior, and a broader discussion of the process by which intentions are implemented. These two chapters have changed substantially from the previous edition.

Despite adding a great deal of new information, we've also been able to shorten several of the book's longer chapters. We did this by simplifying and tightening the writing. We hope the result is more readable, but with no loss of clarity.

For more information on *Perspectives on Personality*, Fifth Edition, consult its Web page: www.ablongman.com/carver5e.

Acknowledgments

We would both like to express our thanks to some of the people who were important in the creation of this edition, starting with Carolyn Merrill, our editor at Allyn and Bacon, and her assistant, Carolyn Mulloy. We also thank Steve Manuck and Tom Kamarck for comments on Chapter 7 and the following reviewers for comments and suggestions on the previous edition: Brian Burke, University of Arizona; Douglas Davis, Haverford College; Aubrey Immelman, St. John's University; and Mary Jo Litten, Pittsburg State University.

We also have some more personal acknowledgements:

From Coral Gables, my thanks to those who've been part of my life during this period, particularly Linda Cahan, Sheri Johnson, André Perwin, Rod Gillis, Pati Arena, Jenifer Culver, Susan Alferi, Bonnie McGregor, Chris Beevers, Roselyn Smith, Vida Petronis, Mike Antoni, and Rod Wellens. A particular bow to Linda Cahan, who (yet again) exerted Herculean efforts to keep everything organized, accurate, and on track at all stages of the process. The revision was done while I was on a sabbatical leave in Berkeley, California, and I am grateful to Shawn and Diane Johnson for their generosity and friendship, and to Barbara Johnson, Monique Leary, and Alex Krummenacher who provided a congenial workplace during that year. My thanks also to my family: Jeff, Allysen, Alexandra, and Julia; Carol; Nancy Lorey; all the Sherricks; and Mike, Karen, Meredith, and Jeremy. Finally, a very special thank-you goes to my shag terrier Calvin, who continues to amaze me with his deep insights about life and his ability to sleep upside down.

From Pittsburgh, thanks go first to my partner in life, Karen Matthews, and to our two children, Jeremy and Meredith. Thanks also to the following group of friends and colleagues: Chuck Carver, Peggy Clark, Sheldon Cohen, Ed Gerrard, Vicki Helgeson, David Klahr, Ken Kotovsky, Rich Schulz, and Jim Staszewski. I'd also like to express my gratitude to Ginger Placone, for her help in proofreading portions of the text. Finally, I'd like to thank the remaining members of my research group: Suzanne Colvin, Amanda Ciotti, Mary Alberth, and Dara Stern. Their dedication and effort made it a lot easier for me to attend to the task of creating this fifth edition.

Coral Gables, Florida

Pittsburgh, Pennsylvania

About the Authors

T he authors met in graduate school at the University of Texas at Austin, where they both earned Ph.D. degrees in personality psychology. After graduation, they took jobs at the University of Miami and Carnegie Mellon University, respectively, where they have remained throughout their careers. They've collaborated for nearly three decades in work that spans personality, social, motivational, clinical, and health psychology, with a particular emphasis in recent years on personality and coping as influences on well-being under stress. In 1998, they received awards for Outstanding Scientific Contribution (Senior Level) from the Division of Health Psychology of the American Psychological Association. Mike is the 2003–2004 President of APA's Division of Health Psychology. Chuck is currently editor of APA's *Journal of Personality and Social Psychology: Personality Processes and Individual Differences.* Along with five editions of *Perspectives on Personality,* the authors have published two books on self-regulation (the more recent being *On the Self-Regulation of Behavior,* in 1998) and over 220 articles and chapters. Mike is an avid outdoorsman, hunter, and fisherman. Chuck keeps intending to take up painting but always gets distracted by things that need fixing.

www.psy.miami.edu/faculty/ccarver/

www.psy.cmu.edu/~scheier/mscheier/html

PART one

An Introduction

chapter

1 | *What Is Personality Psychology?*

■ **Defining Personality**
Why Use Personality as a Concept?
A Working Definition
Two Fundamental Issues in Personality Psychology

■ **Theory in Personality Psychology**
What Do Theories Do?
Evaluating Theories: The Role of Research
What Else Makes a Theory Good?

■ **Perspectives on Personality**
Groupings among Theories
How Distinct Are the Perspectives?
Another Kind of "Perspective"

■ **Organization within Chapters**
Assessment
Problems in Behavior, and Behavior Change

SUMMARY

■ Sue met Rick in a philosophy class when both were starting their sophomore year of college. They started to date casually soon afterward and their relationship gradually deepened. Now, two years later, they're talking seriously of marriage. Here's Sue describing Rick: "He's attractive to me in so many ways. He's good-looking, and athletic, and smart—and he likes the same music I like. He knows how to do lots of things you don't expect a guy to know, like cooking and even sewing. But the best part I don't even know how to put into words, except to say he has a really wonderful personality."

Every now and then someone does a survey of the qualities people value in a potential husband or wife. The surveys usually find that most people want their mate to have a sense of humor, good looks, and a streak of romance. Almost always, though, a high priority concerns the person's personality. If you're like most people, you want someone who has a "good personality."

A good personality. What does that phrase mean to you? If you were to describe a friend of yours who *does* have a good personality, what would you say about that person? "Rick has a wonderful personality. . . ." But then what?

Describing someone's personality means trying to capture the person's essence. It involves crystallizing something from the bits of knowledge you have about the person. It means taking a large pile of information and reducing it to a smaller set of qualities. Evidence about personality comes partly from what people do and say, but it's partly a matter of *how* people do what they do—the style that brings a unique and personal touch to their actions.

Defining Personality

You may not have thought of it this way, but trying to describe someone's personality is an exercise in being a psychologist. Everyone is a psychologist part of the time, because everyone spends part of his or her life trying to understand what other people are like. When you think about what qualities describe someone, and what reveals those qualities to you, you're doing informally part of what personality psychologists do more formally.

There's a difference in focus, though, between what you do in your daily life and what personality psychologists do. Everyday use of the word *personality* tends to focus on the *specific* personalities of specific persons (Rick, for instance). Psychologists are more likely to focus on personality as an abstraction. When psychologists use the word *personality,* they usually are referring to a conception of personality, in the abstract, that can apply to everyone.

What *is* personality, viewed this way? This question is hard to answer. Psychologists have disagreed for a long time about exactly how to define personality. Many definitions have been offered, but none is universally accepted. Personality, in fact, is quite an elusive concept.

Why Use Personality as a Concept?

In trying to define the concept of personality, one way to start is to think about why the word is used. Understanding why people use it should help us decide what it means. The reasons for using the word converge on an implicit definition for it.

When *you* use the word personality, why do you use it? What makes you use that word instead of another one?

One reason for using the word personality appears to be the desire to convey a sense of *consistency* or *continuity* about a person. There are several kinds of consistency. All of them bring the concept of personality to mind. You may see consistency in a person across time (Sue talked a lot when you first met her, and years later she still dominates conversations). You may see consistency across similar situations (André is very polite to waiters in restaurants and has been so every time you've had dinner with him). You sometimes even see consistency across situations that are very different from each other (Barbara tends to order people around—in stores, at work, even at *parties*). In each of these, there's the sense that it's undeniably the same person from one instance to another, because the person acts (or talks, or thinks, or feels) in consistent ways from time to time and from setting to setting. One reason for using the word *personality*, then, is to imply this consistency or continuity within the person.

A second reason people use the word *personality* is to convey the sense that whatever the person is doing (or thinking or feeling) is *coming from within*. The idea that behavior arises from inside the person may seem so obvious that it hardly deserves mention, but not everyone sees it that way. There are philosophical and theoretical disagreements on this issue. Still, using the term *personality* conveys the sense of a causal force *within* the person, influencing how the person acts.

These two reasons for using the term *personality* join with each other when you try to predict and understand people's behavior (even your own). Predicting behavior can be important. When you choose a new roommate for next year, you're pre-

Personality produces consistencies in behavior across different contexts. Although this woman finds herself in different situations, her warm and caring nature comes through in all of them.

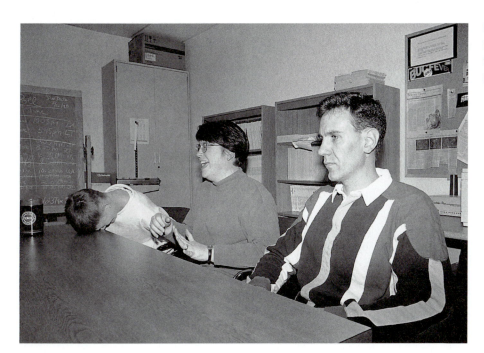

Individual differences in behavior and reactions are an important part of personality.

dicting you'll get along well. When you tell a chronically late friend that the movie starts at 8 when it really starts at 8:30, you're predicting that this will get her to arrive more or less on time. An important source of information behind these predictions is your judgment about what the other person's personality is like.

The term *personality* is also used for another reason. It often conveys the sense that a few characteristics can summarize what a person is like because they are prominent in that person's behavior. Saying that Karen has an outgoing personality implies that she seems outgoing much of the time. Saying that Tanya has a hostile personality implies that hostility influences many of her actions. The qualities that first come to mind when you try to describe someone are the ones that you think seem central to that person. The more central the quality is, the more useful it is for predicting the person's behavior. Thinking about the highly prominent characteristics of a person brings to mind the concept of personality.

These are some reasons why people use the term *personality*. This patchwork of reasons for using it moves us closer to having a definition for it. That is, the word *personality* conveys a sense of consistency, internal causality, and personal distinctiveness. As it happens, these qualities are built into almost all definitions of personality.

A Working Definition

Here's one definition. We're not saying that this is the "right" one, but we think it comes close. We've adapted it slightly from one given decades ago by Gordon Allport (1961): *Personality is a dynamic organization, inside the person, of psychophysical systems that create the person's characteristic patterns of behavior, thoughts, and feelings.*

This definition makes several points:

- Personality isn't just an accumulation of bits and pieces; it has *organization*.
- Personality doesn't just lie there; it's active, with *processes* of some sort.
- Personality is a *psychological* concept, but it's tied to the *physical* body.

- Personality is a *causal force* that helps determine how the person relates to the world.
- Personality shows up in *patterns*—recurrences and consistencies.
- Personality is displayed not just one way but *many ways,* in behaviors, thoughts, and feelings.

This definition covers a lot of ground. It points to several elements that ought to be part of any conceptualization of personality. As good as it is, though, it isn't perfect. Even this careful definition seems to let something about the concept slip through your fingers. This elusiveness is something that personality psychologists have struggled with for many years.

Two Fundamental Issues in Personality Psychology

From what we've said so far, two core issues stand out in thinking about personality. One issue is the existence of **individual differences.** Each person who ever lived is different from everyone else. No two personalities are quite alike—not even those of identical twins. Some people are happy, some are sad. Some people are sociable, some are shy and reclusive. As we said earlier, one reason to use the word *personality* in the first place is to capture central features of a person. This couldn't happen if the features didn't differ from one person to another. Thus, the notion of individual differences is key to everyday use of the term *personality.*

Individual differences are also important to the theorist who tries to understand personality. To be useful, any approach to personality has to have something to say about these differences. A complete account of personality must devote some attention to where the differences come from. A complete account should also consider the questions of why these differences matter.

The other issue concerns what we'll call **intrapersonal functioning.** By this phrase we mean a set of processes within the person, the processes Allport called a "dynamic organization" of systems. The idea here is that personality isn't like a rubber stamp that you pound onto each situation you enter. Instead, there are processes that go on inside you, leading you to act the way you do. Such processes can create a sense of continuity within the person, even if the person acts differently in different circumstances. That is, the same processes are engaged, even if the results differ in different situations.

Here's an example. Some psychologists believe that people's behavior is a product of their motives. Motivational tendencies rise and fall over time and across changes in situations. Which motive is strongest at any given time determines what the person does at that time. A person may work in isolation for several hours, then spend a couple of hours socializing, then go eat dinner, followed by some reading. Although the behaviors differ, they all stem from motives within the person that vary in strength over the course of the day. In this view of personality, the motives are key variables. The processes by which motives vary in strength are some of the processes of intrapersonal functioning.

This is just one example of a theorized intrapersonal process. It's not the only kind of process people have assumed. Regardless of what processes you assume, though, the idea of process is important. A complete account of personality should say what kinds of processes underlie personality and how they work.

Different approaches to personality place different amounts of emphasis on these two issues. Some approaches emphasize process and consist largely of a view of intrapersonal functioning, with little attention to differences among people. Other approaches treat individual uniqueness as the most important aspect of personality and are more vague about what processes occur inside. These differences of emphasis contribute to the diversity among personality theories.

Why have we gone on so long in describing what personality psychology is about? In the words of Salvatore Maddi, "theorizing about the nature of personality without keeping in mind just what you want to understand about human behavior is like building a boat in the absence of knowledge of what water is like" (1980, p. 645). He's right. Theorists have to keep in mind what aspects of human experience they want to understand. If you're going to understand the theories, you'll have to do so too.

Theory in Personality Psychology

Much of this book is a series of statements of theoretical principles. Because theories are so important, let's devote a little attention to what they are, what they do, and how to evaluate them.

What Do Theories Do?

What *is* a theory? A **theory** is a summary statement, a general principle or set of principles about a class of events. A theory can apply to a very specific class of events, or it can be broader. Some theories in psychology are about processes in a single nerve cell. Others concern more complex behaviors, such as maintaining close relationships, playing chess, or living all of life.

Theories are used for two purposes (no matter what the theory is about). The first purpose is to *explain* the phenomena it addresses. A theory always provides a way to explain some things that are known to be true. For example, some biological personality theories hold that heredity influences personality. This idea provides a way to explain why children often resemble their parents in how they act or react to events.

Every theory about personality provides an account of at least some phenomena. This first purpose of the theory—explanation—is absolutely fundamental. Without giving an explanation for at least some of what's already known, a theory would be useless.

Theories also have a second purpose, though. A theory should also suggest possibilities you don't yet know for sure are true. To put it differently, a theory should allow you to *predict new information.* A theory of personality should allow you to predict things about people you haven't thought to look for yet—maybe things *nobody* has thought to look for yet. For the psychologist, this is where much of the excitement lies.

The psychologist generally wants to make predictions about large numbers of people, but the same principle holds when you make predictions in your own life. It's exciting to take an idea about personality and use it to predict how your roommate will react to a situation you haven't seen her in before. It's particularly exciting when your prediction turns out to be right!

The predictive function of theories is more subtle and more difficult than the explanatory function. The difficulty lies partly in the fact that most theories have a little ambiguity. This often makes it unclear exactly what the prediction should be. In fact, the broader the theory (the more things it has to account for), the more likely it is to be ambiguous. As you've seen, personality is a very broad concept, covering a wide range of phenomena. This forces theories of personality to be complex. As a result, it's sometimes hard to tell what they should predict.

Evaluating Theories: The Role of Research

How do psychologists decide whether a theory is any good? In describing the predictive function of theories, we've revealed a bias held by many personality psychologists: Theories should be *testable* and they should be *tested*. It's important to find out whether a theory makes predictions that receive support.

We want to be very clear about what we're saying here. Personality is such an important part of life that lots of people besides psychologists think about it. Theologians, philosophers, artists, poets, novelists, and songwriters have all written about personality, and many of them have had important insights about it. We don't mean to diminish the value of these insights. But are they enough?

People have different opinions on this question. Some believe that insight stands on its own and requires nothing further. Even some personality theorists have believed this. Sigmund Freud, who's often thought of as the father of personality psychology, wasn't much interested in whether his ideas were supported in research by others. He saw his own insights as sufficient in themselves.

The view that dominates today's psychology, however, is that ideas—even brilliant ideas—have to be tested before they can be trusted. Too often things that *seem* true turn out not to be true after all. Unfortunately, unless you test them, you never know which ideas are brilliant and right—and which are brilliant but wrong. Because of this, today's personality psychology is a scientific field, in which research counts for a lot. Studies of personality provide information about how accurate or useful a theory is. The information from these studies can either confirm or disconfirm predictions, and thereby support or undermine the theory.

When theories are used to generate predictions for research, a continuous interplay arises (Figure 1.1). If a theory makes predictions, the result is research—scientific studies—to test the predictions. Results often support the predictions. Sometimes, however, the result either fails to support the theory or supports it only partly. The outcome may suggest a limit on the theory—perhaps it predicts accurately under some conditions but not others. Such a finding leads to revision of the theory.

Once modified, the theory must be tested again because it's no longer quite the same theory as before. Its new elements must be examined for other predictions they might make. The cycle of prediction, testing, revision or refinement, and additional prediction and testing can be virtually never-ending.

What Else Makes a Theory Good?

To the scientist, then, an important basis for deciding whether a theory is good is the extent to which it does what a theory's supposed to do: explain and predict. But this

Figure 1.1

In a scientific approach to personality psychology, there is a continuous cycling between theory and research. Theory suggests predictions to be tested; the results of studies suggest the need for new or modified theory.

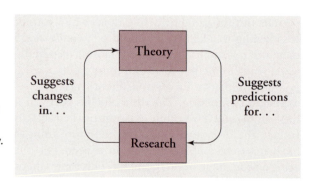

isn't the only way people evaluate theories. There are several other reasons why one theory may be preferable to another.

One reason concerns the breadth of the information behind the theory (Maddi, 1980). Some theories are criticized because they're based heavily on the theorists' experiences in conducting therapy. Other theories are criticized because they rely on the behavior of laboratory animals in highly artificial situations. Others are criticized because they rest largely on information from long sets of rating scales. None of these sources of information is bad in itself. But to base a theory on just one source of information weakens the theory.

A theory should also have the quality of **parsimony.** That is, it should use as few assumptions (or concepts) as possible. To put it differently, things should be as simple as possible. This criterion is important, but there's a danger in applying it too rigidly to personality theories. Knowledge about personality is far from complete. A theory that looks parsimonious today may be unable to account for something that will be discovered tomorrow. A theory that looks too complex today may be the *only* one that can handle tomorrow's discovery. Nevertheless, excess theoretical baggage is a cause for concern.

Another basis for evaluating theories is highly subjective. To put it bluntly, some theories just "feel" better than others. Some theories you'll read about will fit your personal worldview better than others. You're not the only one who reacts this way. So do psychologists. There's even evidence that behavioral scientists prefer theories that fit with their images of *themselves* (Johnson, Germer, Efran, & Overton, 1988). William James, an important figure in the early years of psychology, said people will prefer theories that "are most interesting, . . . appeal most urgently to our aesthetic, emotional, and active needs" (James, 1890, p. 312). Which theories will feel best to

Like a good work of art, a good theory should evoke some sort of reaction, either good or bad, but not indifferent.

you, then, will depend partly on how you see the world. This shouldn't be the only criterion you rely on, but it can be an important one.

Finally, a theory should be *stimulating* (Maddi, 1980). Being stimulating may mean provoking enthusiasm, interest, or excitement. A theory can also be stimulating by provoking outrage and efforts to show how wrong it is. Provoking either reaction is good, because the reaction leads to efforts at finding out whether the theory is useful or not. Theories so dull they provoke no reaction at all are less useful, because no one bothers to study their implications.

Perspectives on Personality

That's a little about the nature of theory. Now let's preview the kinds of theories people have created to talk about personality. The theories range considerably in their starting points, which can make matters a little confusing. To sort out the confusion a little, let's back up one more step and consider how various theorists decided *where to start*.

The starting point, in some sense, is always a vague conception of human nature. How often have you heard the expression, "It's just human nature"? Use of the phrase "human nature" implies a way of viewing what people are like. But what *is* human nature? *In what terms* should we think about people? As you will see, different theorists have had very different answers to these questions, ranging from human nature as primitive beast to human nature as robot.

Groupings among Theories

Theories bearing on personality form groups. Each group is characterized by a general viewpoint on how best to think of human nature. Each group's view of human nature differs (sometimes slightly, sometimes radically) from those of the other groups. Throughout the book we refer to each of these orientations as a "perspective" on personality.

Another term that means much the same as this is *metatheory*. A metatheory is a set of orienting assumptions *within which* theories are devised. These orienting assumptions are more general than are the assumptions of a particular theory. Metatheories are guides to what kinds of concepts make sense to think about using in theories. For example, the view that life involves competition among energy systems is a metatheory. There are lots of ways to think about energy systems, which could lead to many theories. But all of them would be grounded in the idea that life is about energy systems. Each perspective, or metatheory, thus provides a core metaphor for human nature. The metaphor becomes a guide for developing specific theories.

In this book we discuss seven perspectives on personality. We've given them the labels dispositional, biological, psychoanalytic, neoanalytic, learning, phenomenological, and cognitive self-regulation. In almost every case, a given perspective is reflected in several theories. The theories of a given perspective sometimes differ substantially from one another. However, they seem to share a set of orienting assumptions.

Each perspective is described in a separate section of the book, organized as follows: A brief prologue describes the basic themes and core assumptions of that section's metatheory. This is the metaphor of human nature that represents the bedrock for that perspective on personality. This prologue is followed by content chapters, each covering a theoretical view of personality within that perspective. Each of these chapters ends with a statement on the problems that area of theory faces, and our guesses about its prospects for future development. Here are brief characterizations of the perspectives you'll be reading about.

The *dispositional* perspective is based on the idea that people have fairly stable qualities (dispositions) that are displayed across diverse settings. These dispositions are shown outwardly in different ways, but they're deeply embedded in the person. Human nature, from this point of view, is a set of relatively permanent qualities built into the person. Theorists of this perspective vary in how they view dispositions. Some simply emphasize that dispositions exist, and don't say much about how they influence behavior. Others focus on the idea that dispositions pertain to motive forces, which influence behavior. These two sets of ideas are described in separate chapters in the dispositional section.

Another way of thinking about human nature, the *biological perspective,* emphasizes the fact that humans are biological creatures. One biological view resembles dispositional theories, but with a different emphasis. This approach says personality is genetically based: dispositions are inherited. Indeed, some theorists take this idea a step further, to suggest that many qualities of human behavior exist precisely because long ago they had evolutionary purposes. Another part of the biological perspective stems from the idea that personality reflects the workings of the body we inhabit. This biological view focuses on how the nervous system and hormones influence the kind of person you become.

The *psychoanalytic perspective,* taken up next, is a very different view of the world. It's based on the idea that personality is a set of internal forces that compete and conflict with one another. The dynamics of these forces (and the way they influence behavior) are the focus of this perspective. Human nature, from this viewpoint, entails a set of pressures inside the person that sometimes work with each other and sometimes are at war with each other. This perspective is perhaps the most tightly focused of all, in the sense that one theory dominates it—the theory of Sigmund Freud.

The next perspective we've termed *neoanalytic.* In a sense, neoanalytic theories aren't really a distinct perspective: they all derive in one way or another from psychoanalytic theory (thus the name "neoanalytic"). One might argue that this makes them all variations on the psychoanalytic perspective (indeed, we said that in the first edition of this book). On the other hand, the theories evolved in ways that make them very different from Freud's theory. For this reason, we believe they no longer share the worldview assumed in Freud's theory. The ideas that form the core of the neoanalytic perspective concern the ego and its development, and the importance of social relationships in personality.

The next perspective, the *learning perspective,* begins with a view of human nature in which *change,* rather than consistency, is paramount. That is, the key quality of human nature, from this perspective, is that behavior changes systematically as a result of experience. Because there are several views of how learning takes place, several theories link learning to personality. Though they differ, they share a single metatheory, holding that a person's personality is the integrated sum of whatever the person has learned up till now.

Next comes the *phenomenological perspective.* The roots of this perspective trace to two ideas. The first is that everyone's subjective experience is important, valuable, meaningful—and unique. The second is that people tend naturally toward self-perfection and that all people can move themselves in that direction by exercising their free will to do so. The sense of self-determination is central to this view

of human nature. A person's personality, in this view, is partly a matter of the uniqueness hidden within, and partly a matter of what the person chooses to make of that
uniqueness.

We've labeled the final perspective with the phrase *cognitive self-regulation.* This
view holds that cognitive processes are the underpinnings of personality. The nervous system is a huge matrix of buzzing neurons, all sending messages to other
neurons. Somehow the nervous system manifests systematic sets of decision rules.
It uses information in organized, coherent, patterned ways, rather than randomly.
In this view, these patterns give rise to personality. Another aspect of this perspective is that people are self-regulating systems, setting goals and progressing toward those goals. Again there is an assumption of organization, coherence,
patterning.

How Distinct Are the Perspectives?

This brief description makes it clear that each perspective on personality starts with
a different view of human nature. There are also links among the perspectives, however. For example, phenomenological theories emphasize the concept of self and
the need for the self to grow and develop naturally. The concept of self isn't too different from the concept of ego, which is a focus of neoanalytic theories. Thus, there's
a link between neoanalytic and phenomenological theories. As another example,
George Kelly, a phenomenological theorist, developed ideas that were reflected in
later cognitive theories. This creates a link between the phenomenological and cognitive self-regulation views.

Is the linking of each theory to a perspectives arbitrary, then? No, but it's im-
perfect. Here's an analogy. Think of theories as hot-air balloons (perhaps a dangerous metaphor). All are attached by mooring ropes to posts in the ground. Each post
represents a metatheory. Each balloon is tied quite firmly to one post, with a board-
ing ramp for passengers. However, most also have second ropes (and sometimes third
and fourth ones) tied to other posts. Some posts have many balloons tied to them,
others have only one or two. Some of the mooring ropes are thick and heavy, some
are lighter. In an analogous way, each theory in this book is placed according to the
metatheory it's tied to most firmly, but they often have secondary ties to other
metatheories.

Another Kind of "Perspective"

One more thing about our use of the term *perspective:* There was a time when personality psychologists created grand theories aimed at the total complexity of personality. Freud's theory is the clearest example (some would say the only good
example). However, this has become less common over time. More common today
are theories that deal with some *aspect* of the subject of personality. Most of these theories weren't really intended to be full models of personality, and it's somewhat misleading to present them (and judge them) as though they were.

The fact that they aren't grand-scale theories doesn't mean they have nothing
important to say about personality. It does mean, though, that such a theory won't
say *everything* about personality. It gives us a particular viewing angle on the subject
(a more literal meaning of the word *perspective*). This viewing angle may be special
and may yield insights you can't find from other angles. But it illuminates only part
of the picture. This limitation is important to keep in mind as you think about the
various theories and what they have to say.

Today's approach to theory development also has another implication. Many people who have contributed to today's understanding of personality have made contributions to *several* points of view. Don't be surprised when you see the same names show up in two or three different places. In today's personality psychology, people whose work informs us about psychoanalytic concepts may also have had useful things to say about principles of self-regulation. People who have helped us to understand learning may also have contributed to trait psychology.

This is one reason why, in general, we haven't focused the book's chapters on particular individuals. Rather, in each chapter we've emphasized conceptual *themes* emphasized by a given theoretical viewpoint.

Organization within Chapters

Each chapter within a given perspective addresses a specific type of theory. Most of the content of each chapter is a description of the basic elements and processes of personality, as viewed from that theoretical vantage point. Each chapter thus tells you something about individual differences and intrapersonal functioning as seen by that theory.

Each chapter also addresses two more subjects. One is the process of measuring personality, called *assessment*. The other is the potential for problems to arise in human experience, and the processes by which behavior is changed for the better through therapy. Here's a brief preview of what these sections will be like.

Assessment

Personality psychologists give considerable attention to the process of measuring personality, for at least three reasons. First, psychologists want to be able to portray the personalities of specific individuals, in much the same way as you characterize the personalities of people you know. To be confident these pictures are accurate, psychologists need good ways to measure personality.

A second reason for assessing personality concerns the effort to conduct research on personality. To study qualities of personality, psychologists have to be able to measure those qualities. Without good ways to assess individual differences or intrapersonal functioning, it's impossible to study them. Good assessment, then, lies at the heart of personality research.

A third important reason to measure personality strays a bit from the main focus of this book. Specifically, determining the personality characteristics of individuals is an important part of applied psychology. For example, organizational psychologists use personality as a basis for making hiring decisions (you might want to be sure, for example, that you're hiring someone with a desired pattern of motives). Clinical psychologists also use personality assessment in making a diagnosis of pathology (it can be important to know whether a person's personality shows signs of poor functioning).

Assessment is a goal that's important throughout personality psychology. This goal is viewed somewhat differently, however, from different perspectives on personality (though some issues, addressed in Chapter 3, are shared by all). As a result, the theoretical viewpoints often differ in the assessment techniques they emphasize. In discussing assessment in each later chapter, we focus on how assessment from that viewpoint has its own special character.

Personality does not always function smoothly. Each perspective on personality has its own view about why problems occur.

Problems in Behavior, and Behavior Change

The other topic incorporated into each theory chapter concerns the fact that people's lives don't always go smoothly. Each viewpoint on normal personality functioning also suggests a way to think about the nature of problems (more formally, psychopathology). Indeed, it can be argued that a theory of personality gains in credibility from saying useful things about problems. To clarify how each approach to personality views problems, we briefly take up this issue in each chapter, from that chapter's viewpoint. As with assessment, our emphasis is on the special contribution made by that theoretical orientation to thinking about problems.

Finally, we address the contributions that the theoretical orientation under discussion makes to understanding the therapeutic management of problems. If each view has a way of thinking about normal processes and about how things can go wrong, each viewpoint also has a way of thinking about how to try to deal with the problems. Each suggests ways to turn problematic functioning back into effective and satisfying functioning.

SUMMARY

Personality is a difficult concept to define. Even the best definitions are quite abstract. Thinking about how people use the concept, however, suggests three reasons for its use. People use it to convey a sense of consistency or continuity within a person, to convey the sense that the person is the origin of behavior, and to convey the sense that the essence of a person can be summarized or captured in a few salient qualities.

The field of personality addresses two fundamental issues. One is the existence of differences among people. The other is how best to conceptualize intrapersonal functioning—the processes that take place within all persons, giving form and continuity to behavior.

Much of this book deals with theories. Theories are summary statements, sets of principles that pertain to some class of events. Theories have two purposes: to explain things that are known and to predict possibilities that haven't yet been examined. One way to evaluate the worth of a theory is to ask whether research supports its predictions. Scientific psychology represents a continuing cycle between theory and research, as theories are tested, modified on the basis of results, and tested again.

Theories can be evaluated on several grounds other than research. For example, a theory shouldn't be based on a single kind of information. Theories also benefit from being parsimonious—from needing relatively few assumptions (or concepts). Apart from these considerations, theories are given greater weight when they fit well with one's intuitions, and they have a greater impact if they stimulate interest (and thus efforts to test them).

The theories addressed in this book are based on seven different perspectives, or viewpoints, on human nature. They are identified with the terms *dispositional, biological, psychoanalytic, neoanalytic, learning, phenomenological,* and *cognitive self-regulation.* Each theory chapter focuses on the assumptions about the nature of personality within a particular theoretical framework. Also included are a discussion of assessment from the viewpoint of the theory under discussion, and a discussion of problems in behavior and how they can be remedied.

GLOSSARY

Individual differences Differences in personality from one person to another.

Intrapersonal functioning Psychological processes that take place within the person.

Metatheories Sets of orienting assumptions about reality, which provide guidelines for what kinds of ideas to use to create theories.

Parsimony The quality of requiring few assumptions; simplicity.

Personality A dynamic organization, inside the person, of psychophysical systems that create the person's characteristic patterns of behavior, thoughts, and feelings.

Theory An abstract statement that summarizes a set of principles pertaining to a class of events.

chapter

2 Methods in the Study of Personality

■ **Gathering Information**
Sources: Observe Yourself and Observe Others
Seeking Depth: Case Studies
Seeking Generality: Studies of Many People

■ **Establishing Relationships among Variables**
Correlation between Variables

Two Kinds of Significance
Causality and a Limitation on Inference
Search for Causality: Experimental Research
Recognizing Types of Study
What Kind of Research Is Best?
Multifactor Studies
Reading Figures from Multifactor Research

SUMMARY

■ Sam and Dave are at the cafeteria taking a break from studying. Sam says "My roommate got a letter yesterday from his girlfriend at home—breaking up with him. People around here better watch out 'cause he's gonna be looking for some serious partying to help him forget her."

"What makes you think so?"

"What kind of question is that? I thought it over. It's obvious. That's what *I'd* do."

"Oh? I know lots of guys who've been dumped by their hometown girlfriends, and *none* of them did that. In fact, it was the opposite. They just lay around for a few weeks moping. I think you're wrong about how people react to this kind of thing."

W hen people try to understand the nature of personality, where do they start? When people form theories, where do the theories come from? How are theories confirmed or disconfirmed? How do personality psychologists decide what to believe and not believe? These are questions about the methods of science. They can be asked in all areas of study, astronomy to zoology. They are particularly challenging, though, when applied to the subject of personality.

Gathering Information

Sources: Observe Yourself and Observe Others

One simple way to gather information about personality is to look inward to your own experience (a process called introspection). This technique (used by Sam in the opening example) is available to everyone. Try it. After all, you have a personality. If you want to understand personality in general, perhaps you should take a look at yours as an example. Sit back and think about recent events in your life. Think about what you did and how you felt, and try to pull from those recollections a thread of continuity. From this might come the start of a theory—a set of principles to explain your thoughts, feelings, and actions.

Examining your own experience is an easy beginning, and it can be a useful one, but it has a drawback. Specifically, your own consciousness has a special relationship to your memories (and to your present actions). It's hard to be sure that this special relationship doesn't distort what you're seeing. For instance, you can misrecall something you experienced, yet feel sure your memory is correct.

This problem diminishes when you look at someone else instead of yourself (as did Dave in the opening example). This is the second method of gathering information: observation of someone else. This method has its own problem, though, the opposite of introspection's problem. Specifically, it's impossible to be "inside another person's head," to really know what that person is thinking and feeling. This difference in perspective can create vast differences in understanding (cf. Jones & Nisbett, 1971). It can lead to misinterpretation.

Which starting point is better? Most psychologists would agree that each of them has a place in the search for truth, though each also has problems. Each can lead to theories and research.

Seeking Depth: Case Studies

Some psychologists interested in personality seek explicitly to understand the entire person at once, rather than just part of the person. Henry Murray (1938), who strongly emphasized the need to study persons as coherent entities, coined the term **personology** to refer to this effort. Many other early personality theorists took a similar view.

This view leads to the use of a technique called the **case study.** A case study involves repeated, in-depth examination of one person. It usually entails a long period of observation, and typically uses unstructured interviews as well as more standardized procedures. Sometimes it involves spending a day or two interacting with the person, or just being around the person to see how he or she interacts with others. The repeated observations allow the observer to confirm initial impressions or to correct impressions that were misleading. Confirming or disconfirming an impression is hard to do if you make only one brief observation. The depth of probing that's possible in a case study can reveal detail about the person's life that otherwise wouldn't be apparent. This, in turn, can yield important insights.

Case studies are rich in detail and can create vivid descriptions of the persons under study. Particularly compelling incidents or examples are often viewed as illustrating broader themes in the person's life. There are other advantages to case studies, as well. Because they examine the person in his or her life situation instead of settings created by the researcher, the information pertains directly to normal life. Because they're open-ended, the observer can follow whatever leads seem interesting, rather than asking only questions chosen ahead of time.

Many case studies (though not all) are also clinical studies. That is, people who do case studies often focus on persons who have some kind of problem. Often these are therapists studying people they're treating. Clinical case studies give information about ways personality goes awry, as well as information about the normal workings of the person. Indeed, several theories of personality arose largely from case-study observations in the context of therapy.

As an illustration of how a case study might be used to generate broader ideas about personality, consider this excerpt from the brief case study of a college student who's having personal difficulties: John is nineteen years old, slender, and of medium height. His typical manner of dress conveys no particular style other than "average college student." The middle of three sons, John grew up in a small city in the midwest. His father is a factory worker, and his mother works as an aide in a nursing home. Their combined income provides a modest living and lets the sons plan to attend the state university, but does not permit many luxuries. John's older brother (by four years) had been a stellar athlete in high school, but his college career ended with an injury, and he now works in the same factory as his father. John's younger brother (by three years) shows a talent for math and science, and his father refers to him as "the engineer," clearly reflecting his hope for the boy's future.

Asked to talk about what his high school years were like, John said that he felt they had been mostly good, but maybe not as good for him as for others. Asked to clarify this, he related several minor disappointments in high school, none of which seemed to carry much weight by itself. Then he described an incident in which he had done poorly on a test for which he'd felt fully prepared. He shrugged, as if to suggest that the event wasn't important, but he seemed more tense than at other times during the conversation (or in other interviews).

John has had consistent academic difficulties at the university, despite having higher than average SAT scores. Academic Services referred him to the university's counseling center in the hope of resolving the difficulties. At first John was the picture of bravado with his counselor, but he didn't maintain that stance for long. In their second meeting, John said to his counselor that he didn't want to disappoint his parents, but he had doubts about whether he belonged in college. Although other people in his dorm never seemed to question their abilities, John felt a constant nagging sense that he wasn't up to the challenge.

After just a few discussions it became apparent to his counselor that John is lacking in self-esteem. As the counselor updated her notes on his case, she thought again about an idea that had crossed her mind more than once before: students low in self-esteem don't seem to perform up to their potential in college. This is an idea that has many implications, and the counselor made some more notes on it.

Thus, a series of observations—even brief observations—made in the course of examining one person's life situation can lead an observer to conclusions about how personality is involved in important categories of events.

Seeking Generality: Studies of Many People

Case studies can provide insights into the human experience. They provide useful information for researchers and often serve as an important source of ideas. But currently they aren't the main source of information about personality. In large part, this is because a case study, no matter how complete, is lacking in an important respect. It deals with just one person. When you're forming theories or drawing conclusions from observations, you want them to apply to many people—if possible, to *all* people.

The breadth of applicability of a conclusion is called its **generality,** or its **generalizability.** If a conclusion is to be generalizable, it must be based on the observation of many people, not just one or two. The more people you look at, the more convinced you can be that what you see is true of people in general, instead of only a few people. In most research on personality done today, researchers look at tens— even hundreds—of people to increase the generality of their conclusions.

The generality of a conclusion can be established only by studying a mix of people from different backgrounds.

To truly ensure generality, researchers should study people of many ages and from all walks of life—indeed, from all cultures. For various reasons, however, this isn't always done. As a matter of convenience, much research on personality over the last several decades has examined only college students.

Do college students provide a reasonably good cross-section of the processes that are important in personality? Maybe yes, maybe no. College students differ from older adults in several ways, including having a less fully formulated sense of self (Sears, 1986). This may make a difference in the research findings. How big a difference is a matter of conjecture. It does seem clear, though, that we should be cautious in assuming that conclusions drawn from research on college students are always applicable to "people in general."

Similarly, most observations on personality come from research done in the United States and western Europe. Most of the research has been done with middle- to upper-middle-class people. Some of it has used only men or only women. One must be cautious in assuming that the conclusions of a study are applicable to people from other cultures, other socioeconomic groups, and (sometimes) both genders.

Generalizability, then, is a kind of continuum. Rarely does any study range broadly enough to ensure total generalizability. Some are better than others, however. How broadly a conclusion can be generalized is an issue that must always be kept in mind in evaluating results of studies.

The desire for generality and the desire for in-depth understanding of a person represent competing pressures for observers of personality. They thus lead to a trade-off. That is, given the same investment of time and energy, you can know a great deal about the life of one person (or a very few people), or you can know a little bit about the lives of a much larger number of people. It's nearly impossible to do both at once. As a result, researchers tend to choose one path or the other, according to which pressure they find more important.

Establishing Relationships among Variables

Insights gained by introspection, observation, or systematic examination of a person by a case study can suggest relationships between variables. A **variable** is a dimension along which variations exist. There must be at least two values or levels on that dimension, though some variables have an infinite number of values. For example, "sex" is a variable with values of male and female. Self-esteem is a variable that has a virtually limitless number of values (from very low to very high) as you make finer discriminations among people.

It's important to see the difference between a variable and the values it comprises, because conclusions about relationships involve the entire dimension, not just one end of it. For this reason, researchers always examine at least two levels of the variable they're interested in. For example, you can't see the effects of low self-esteem by looking only at people with low self-esteem. If there's a relationship between self-esteem and academic performance, the only way you can find out is to look at people with *different levels* of self-esteem (Figure 2.1). If the relationship does exist, people with very low self-esteem should have poor grades and people with higher self-esteem should have better grades.

The last part of that statement is every bit as important as the first part. Knowing that people low in self-esteem have poor grades isn't informative if it turns out that people high in self-esteem also have poor grades. It can be hard to keep this in mind. In fact, people often fail to realize how important this issue is. If you don't

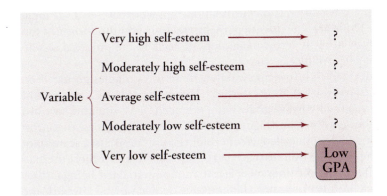

Figure 2.1

Whether or not a relationship exists between variables can be determined only by looking at more than one value on each variable. Knowing that people low in self-esteem have poor academic performances leaves open the question of whether everyone else has performances that are just as poor. This question is critically important in establishing a relationship between the two variables.

keep it in mind, though, you can make serious errors in the conclusions you reach (for illustrations see Chapman, 1967; Crocker, 1981).

The need to examine people across a range of variability before drawing conclusions is another reason why it's important to go beyond case studies (recall that the issue of generality was the first reason). Indeed, the importance of examining a range of variability is what leads to the methods on which we focus for the remainder of this chapter.

Correlation between Variables

There are two kinds of relationship that can be found between variables. The first is called **correlation.** A correlation between two dimensions means that as you examine them across many examples or instances, the values tend to go together in a

A correlation between two variables means they covary in some systematic way. Here there is a correlation between height and place in line.

systematic way. There are two aspects of this relationship, which are entirely separate from each other. These are the *direction* of the correlation and the *strength* of the correlation. To clarify what these terms mean, let's go back to the question of self-esteem and academic performance.

Suppose you've decided to investigate whether these two variables go together. You've gone out and found forty students to study. They've completed a measure of self-esteem and given you their current grade point average (GPA). You now have two pieces of information for each person (Figure 2.2, A). One way to organize this information is to create a kind of graph called a scatterplot (Figure 2.2, B). In a scatterplot the two variables are represented by lines placed at right angles to each other (the axes of the graph). The point where the lines meet is zero for both variables. Being farther away from zero on each line means having a higher value on that variable. Because the two lines are at right angles, the combination of any score on one variable and any score on the other variable can be portrayed as a point in a two-dimensional space. For example, in Figure 2.2, Tim has a self-esteem score of 42 (thus being to the right side on the horizontal line) and a GPA of 3.8 (thus being toward the top on the vertical line). The scatterplot for your study would consist of the points that represent the combinations of self-esteem scores and GPA for each person in the study.

To ask whether the two variables are correlated means (essentially) asking the following question about the scatterplot: When you look at points that represent low versus high values on the *horizontal* dimension, do they differ in how they line up regarding the *vertical* dimension? If low values tend to go with low values and high values tend to go with high values (as in Figure 2.3, A), the two variables are said to be *positively* correlated. If people low in self-esteem tended to have low GPAs, and peo-

Figure 2.2

Thinking about the meaning of correlation (with hypothetical data): (A) For each person, there are two pieces of information, a self-esteem score and a grade point average (GPA). (B) The data can be arranged to form a scatterplot by plotting each person's self-esteem score along the horizontal dimension and GPA along the vertical dimension, thereby locating the combination in a two-dimensional space.

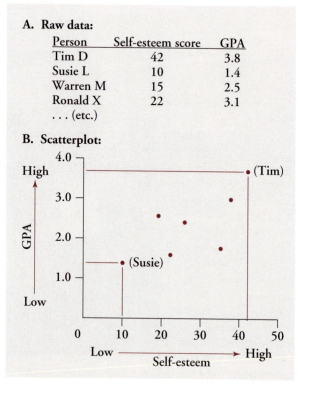

A. Raw data:

Person	Self-esteem score	GPA
Tim D	42	3.8
Susie L	10	1.4
Warren M	15	2.5
Ronald X	22	3.1
. . . (etc.)		

B. Scatterplot:

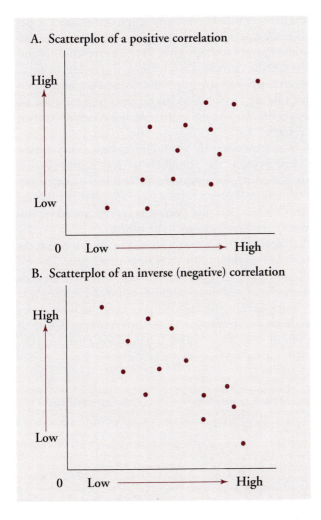

A. Scatterplot of a positive correlation

B. Scatterplot of an inverse (negative) correlation

Figure 2.3

(A) If high numbers on one dimension tend to go with high numbers on the other dimension (and low with low), there is a positive correlation. (B) If high numbers on one dimension tend to go with low numbers on the other dimension, there is an inverse, or negative, correlation.

ple high in self-esteem tended to have high GPAs, you would say that self-esteem correlates positively with GPA. This finding has, in fact, emerged from actual studies of these variables (for reviews see Scheirer & Kraut, 1979; Wylie, 1979).

Sometimes, however, a different kind of correlation occurs. Sometimes high values on one dimension tend to go along with low values on the other dimension (and vice versa). When this happens (Figure 2.3, B), the correlation between the variables is termed *inverse*, or *negative*. This kind of correlation might have emerged if you had studied the relationship between GPA and the frequency of going to parties. That is, you might have found that students who party the most tend to have lower GPAs, whereas those who party the least tend to have higher GPAs.

The *direction* of the association between variables (positive versus negative) is one aspect of correlation. The second aspect—entirely separate from the first—is the *strength* of the correlation. Think of strength as the "sloppiness" of the association between the variables. More formally, it refers to the degree of accuracy with which you can predict values on one dimension from values on the other dimension. That is, assume a positive correlation between self-esteem and GPA. Suppose that you knew that Victoria had the second highest score on self-esteem in your study. How accurate a guess could you make about Victoria's GPA?

The answer to this question is determined by how strong the correlation is. Because the correlation is positive, knowing that Victoria is on the high end of the self-esteem dimension would lead you to predict a high GPA. If the correlation is also *strong*, you're very likely to be right. If the correlation is weaker, you're less likely to be right. A perfect positive correlation—the strongest possible—means that the person who has the very highest value on one variable also has the very highest value on the other, the person next highest on one is also next highest on the other, and on so, throughout the list (see Figure 2.4, A).

The strength of a correlation is expressed by a number called a **correlation coefficient** (often labeled with a lowercase *r*). An absolutely perfect positive correlation (as in Figure 2.4, A) is expressed with the number 1.0. This is the largest numerical value a correlation can take. It indicates a totally accurate prediction from one dimension to the other. If you know where the person is on one variable, you can tell with complete confidence where he or she is on the other.

The scatterplot of a somewhat weaker correlation is shown in Figure 2.4, B. As you can see, there's more "scatter" among the points than in the first case. There's still a noticeable tendency for higher values on one dimension to match up with higher ones on the other, and for lows to match up with lows, but the tendency is less exact. As the correlation becomes weaker, the number representing it becomes smaller (thus, virtually all correlations are decimal values). Correlations of .6 to .8 are regarded as strong. Correlations of .3 to .5 are weaker but moderately strong. Be-

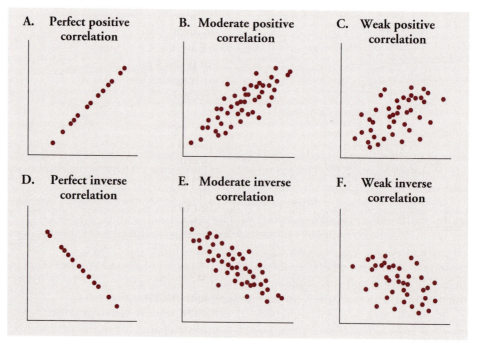

Figure 2.4

Six correlations: (A) A perfect positive correlation. (B) A moderately strong positive correlation. (C) A weak positive correlation. (D) A perfect inverse correlation. (E) A moderately strong inverse correlation. (F) A weak inverse correlation. The weaker the correlation, the more "scatter" in the scatterplot.

low .3 or .2, the prediction from one variable to the other is getting poorer. As you can see in Figure 2.4, C, weak correlations have even more scatter. The tendency toward a positive relation is discernable, but it definitely isn't strong. A correlation of .0 means the two variables aren't related to each other at all. A scatterplot of a zero correlation is random dots.

As we said before, a correlation's strength is entirely separate from its direction. Strength refers only to degree of accuracy in prediction. Thus, it is eminently sensible to talk about a perfect inverse (negative) correlation as well as a perfect positive correlation. A perfect inverse correlation (Figure 2.4, D) means that the person who had the highest value on one variable also had the very lowest value on the other variable, the person with the next highest value on one had the next-to-lowest value on the other, and so on.

Negative correlations are expressed in numbers, just as are positive correlations. But to show that the relationship is an inverse one, a minus sign is placed in front. Thus an *r* value of −.75 is precisely as strong as an *r* value of .75. The first represents an inverse correlation, though, whereas the second represents a positive correlation.

Two Kinds of Significance

We've been describing the strength of correlations in terms of the size of the numbers that serve as their statistical representation. Although the size of the number gives information about its strength, the size of the number by itself doesn't tell a researcher whether the correlation is believable or meaningful. This is true, in fact, for all statistics. You can't tell just by looking at the statistic, or by looking at a graph, whether the result is real. Instead, you need to know whether the result is **statistically significant.**

Significant in this context has a very specific meaning: it means the correlation (or whatever) is large enough to be unlikely to have been a product of chance factors. When the probability that it was an accident is small enough (just under 5 percent), the correlation (or whatever statistic it is) is said to be statistically significant (see also Box 2.1). At that point, the researcher concludes that the relationship is a real one rather than a random occurrence.

A second use of the word *significant* has also become common in psychology. This use more closely resembles the use of the word in day-to-day language. An association is said to be **clinically significant,** or **practically significant,** if the effect is both statistically significant (so it's believable) and large enough to have some practical importance. How large it must be varies from case to case. It's possible, though, for an association to be statistically significant but to account for only a tiny part of the behavior under study. The practical significance of such an association usually isn't very great.

Causality and a Limitation on Inference

Correlations tell us whether or not two variables go together (and in what direction and how strongly). But they don't allow us to know *why* the variables go together. The "why" question takes us beyond the realm of correlation into a second kind of relationship. This relationship is called **causality**—the relationship between a cause and its effect. Correlational research isn't able to provide evidence on this second kind of relationship. A correlational study often gives people strong *intuitions* about causality, but it can't be definitive.

Why? The answer is illustrated in Figure 2.5 on page 27. Each arrow there represents a possible path of causality. What this figure shows is that there are always

BOX 2.1

TWO KINDS OF STATISTICS
Description versus Inference

When people think of statistics, they often think of the statistics that portray a set of people or events, for example, "The average American earns $37,000 a year," or "She averaged 21.6 points per game over the last three years." These figures are called **descriptive statistics** because their purpose is to give a description.

Psychologists also use statistics in a different way, as indicated in the body of the chapter. This second kind of statistics is called **inferential statistics** because they allow the researcher to make inferences. The information they convey guides the scientist in deciding whether or not to believe something is true. Interestingly enough, it isn't possible to *prove* that something is true. What statistics do is show how likely it is that an effect occurred by chance, or randomly. If it can be shown that the effect was very *unlikely* to have been random, the researcher infers that it's real.

An interesting example of the ability of inferential statistics to reveal patterns, and the limitations on what they can say, took place immediately after the 2000 presidential election in the United States. Voters in Palm Beach county in Florida had encountered an unfamiliar and confusing ballot format on election day. Many later reported accidentally voting for one candidate (Buchanan), meaning to vote for another

one (Gore). The election, won by Bush, was extremely close! Its outcome might have turned on such errors! Were these people just complaining because their candidate lost? Or did this actually happen?

Social scientists Greg Adams and Chris Fastnow (2000) used inferential statistics to test whether the pattern of votes in Palm Beach county differed from those in other Florida counties. In every county but Palm Beach, the more votes cast for Bush, the more votes there also were for Buchanan. If Palm Beach had been like every other county in Florida, Buchanan would have gotten around 600 votes instead of 3407. The inference was clear: the chances were extremely small that this difference in pattern could have been random. Something apparently was throwing off the voting pattern in Palm Beach.

We say "apparently" to emphasize something about the nature of inferential statistics. Whenever you use them to make a judgment, the conclusion is always probabilistic. The odds that the inference was wrong in this case were *extremely* small. But the possibility does exist. Inferential statistics thus are best viewed as procedures that allow us to attach "confidence units" to our judgments, rather than procedures that lead infallibly to correct choices.

---

three ways to account for the results of a correlational study. Consider the correlation between self-esteem and academic performance. What causes that association? Your intuition may say the best explanation is that having bad academic outcomes causes people to develop lower self-esteem, whereas good outcomes cause people to feel good about themselves (arrow 1 in Figure 2.5). Or maybe you think the best explanation is that having low self-esteem causes people not to try as hard in their courses, thus resulting in poorer performances (arrow 2). Both of these explanations are plausible, though they represent opposite cause–effect relationships.

It could also be, however, that a third variable—not measured, perhaps not even thought of—actually exerts a causal influence over both variables that were measured (the pair of arrows labeled 3). Perhaps having a high level of intelligence causes a positive sense of self-esteem and also causes better academic performance. In this scenario, both self-esteem and academic performance are effects, and something else is the cause.

The possible involvement of another variable underlying a correlation is sometimes called the **third variable problem.** It's a problem that can't be handled by cor-

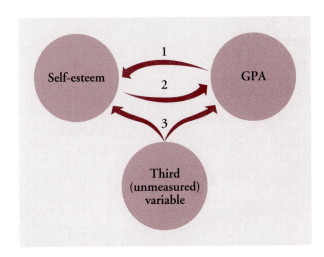

Figure 2.5

Correlation does not imply cause and effect, because there are always three possibilities: (1) variations in one variable (academic performance) may be causing variations in the second (self-esteem); (2) variations in the second may be causing variations in the first; or (3) a third variable may actually be causing both observed effects. Knowing only the single correlation between self-esteem and GPA doesn't allow you to distinguish among these possibilities.

relational research. These methods cannot tell which of the three possibilities shown in Figure 2.5 is actually correct.

Search for Causality: Experimental Research

There *is* a method that allows one to demonstrate cause and effect, however. It's called the **experimental method.** Think of it as having two defining characteristics. The first is that in an experiment the researcher "manipulates" one variable—that is, creates the existence of at least two levels of it. The one the experimenter is manipulating is called the **independent variable.** It's the one the experimenter is testing as the possible *cause* in a cause–effect relationship. When we say the experimenter is "creating" two (or more) levels of this variable, we mean exactly that. There's some kind of event that *actively creates* a difference between the experience of some people and that of other people.

Sometimes researchers do experiments in order to better understand what they've seen in correlational studies. Let's illustrate the experimental method by doing just that, pursuing the example of a correlational finding just discussed. Suppose you have a hunch that variations in academic performance have a causal effect on self-esteem (unlike John's counselor, you think poor performances make people get down on themselves and good performances make them happy with themselves). To study this possibility, you conduct an experiment, in which you hypothesize (predict) that academic outcomes cause an effect on self-esteem.

You can't really manipulate GPA in this experiment, but it's fairly easy to manipulate other things with overtones of academic performance. For instance, you could arrange to have some people experience a success and others a failure (using a task rigged to be easy or impossible). By arranging this, you would be *creating* the difference between success and failure. You'd be manipulating it—not measuring it. You're sure that a difference now exists between the two sets of people in your experiment, because you *made* it exist.

As in all research, you'd do your best to treat every participant in your experiment exactly the same in all ways other than that one. Treating everyone the same—in fact, making everything be exactly the same except for what you manipulate—is called **experimental control.** Exerting a high degree of experimental control is important to the logic of the experimental method, as you'll see momentarily.

Random assignment is an important hallmark of the experimental method. The experimenter randomly assigns participants to a condition, much as a roulette wheel randomly catches the ball in a black or red slot.

Although control is important, you can't control everything. It's rarely possible to have every person participate in the research at the same time of day or on the same day of the week. More obviously, perhaps, it's impossible to be sure the people in the experiment are exactly alike. One of the main points of this book, after all, is that people differ. Some people in the experiment are just naturally going to have higher self-esteem when they walk in the door than are others. How can these differences be handled?

This question brings us to the second defining characteristic of the experimental method: Any variable that can't be controlled—such as individual differences—is treated by **random assignment.** In your experiment, you would deal with individual differences by randomly assigning each participant to either the success experience or the failure experience. Random assignment is often done by such means as tossing a coin or using a list of random numbers to determine assignment.

The use of random assignment rests on a specific assumption: that if you study enough people in the experiment, any important differences between people (and from other sources as well) will balance out between the groups. Each group is likely to have as many tall people, fat people, depressed people, and confident people as the other group—*if* you have a fairly large number of participants and use random assignment. Anything that matters should balance out.

So you've brought people to your research laboratory one at a time, randomly assigned them to the two conditions, manipulated the independent variable, and exerted experimental control over everything else. At some point in the experiment, you would then measure the variable you think is the effect in the cause-and-effect relationship. This one is termed the **dependent variable.**

In this experiment your hypothesis was that differences in success and failure cause people to differ in their self-esteem. Thus, the dependent measure would be a measure of self-esteem (for example, self-report items asking people how they feel about themselves). After getting this measure for each person in the experiment, you would compare the groups to each other (by statistical procedures that need not concern us here). If the difference between groups was statistically significant, you could confidently conclude that the experience of success and failure *causes* people to differ in self-esteem.

What would make you so confident in that cause-and-effect conclusion? The answer, despite all the details we've gone through, is really quite simple. The logic is displayed graphically in Figure 2.6. At the beginning of the experiment, you separated people into two groups. (By the way, the reasoning applies even if the independent variable has more than two levels.) If the assumption about the effect of random assignment is correct, the two groups don't differ from each other at this point. Because you exercise experimental control throughout your procedures, the groups still don't differ as the experiment unfolds.

At one point, however, a difference between groups is introduced—when you manipulate the independent variable. As we said before, you know there's a difference at this point, and you know *what* the difference is, because you created it yourself. For this reason, if you find that the groups differ from each other on the dependent measure at the end, you know there's only one thing that could have caused the difference (Figure 2.6). It *had* to come from the manipulation of the independent variable. That was the only place where a difference between groups was introduced during the experiment. It was the only thing that could have been responsible for causing the effect.

This reasoning is straightforward. We should note, however, that this method isn't entirely perfect. Its problem is this: when you do an experiment, you show that the *manipulation* causes the difference on the dependent measure—but you can't always be completely sure *what it was* about the manipulation that did the causing. Maybe it was the aspect of the manipulation that you were focused on, but maybe it was something else.

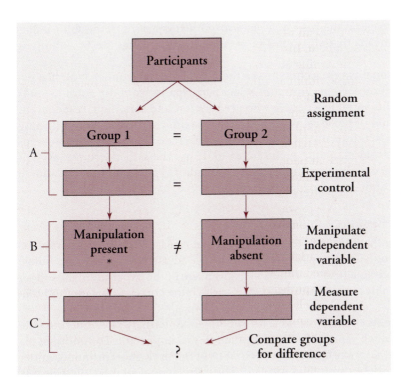

Figure 2.6

The logic of the experimental method: (A) Because of random assignment and experimental control, there is no systematic difference between groups at first; (B) The experimental manipulation creates—for the first time—a specific difference; (C) If the groups then are found to differ in another fashion, the manipulation must have caused this difference.

For example, in the experiment we've been considering, low self-esteem may have been caused by the failure and the self-doubt to which it led. But it *might* have been caused by other things about the manipulation. Maybe the people were worried that they had spoiled the results of your experiment by not solving the problems. They didn't feel a sense of *failure* but were unhappy with themselves for creating a problem for you. This interpretation of the result wouldn't mean quite the same thing as your first interpretation of it. This issue requires us always to be a bit cautious in how we view results, even from experiments.

Recognizing Types of Study

When you read about correlational studies and experiments in later chapters of this book, how easy is it going to be for you to tell them apart? At first glance, it seems simple. An experiment involves a comparison between groups, and a correlational study gives you a correlation, right? Well, no. Results of correlational studies aren't always reported as correlations. Sometimes the study compares two (or more) groups with each other on a dependent measure, and the word *correlation* is never even mentioned.

Suppose you studied some people who were 40 percent overweight and some who were 40 percent underweight. You interviewed them individually and judged how sociable they were, and you found that heavy people were more sociable than thin people. Would this be an experiment or a correlational study? The way to tell is by recalling the two defining characteristics of the experiment: manipulation of the independent variable, and random assignment of people to groups. You didn't randomly assign people to be heavy or thin (and didn't *create* these differences). Therefore, this is a correlational study. The limitation on correlational research (the inability to conclude cause and effect) applies to it.

A good rule of thumb is that any time groupings reflect *naturally occurring differences* or are formed on the basis of a *characteristic that you measure,* the study is correlational. This means that all studies of personality differences are by definition correlational.

Why do personality researchers make their correlational studies look like experiments? Sometimes it's because they select participants from the extreme ends of some personality variable—people who are very low and very high, respectively, on some dimension of personality. This strategy maximizes the chances of finding differences. That is, removing the people who are average on that dimension helps to remove clutter and make the picture clearer. It has the side effect, however, of making it hard to express the finding as a correlation. The result is correlational studies that look at first glance like experiments.

What Kind of Research Is Best?

Another question that's often asked is which kind of research is better, experiments or correlational studies? The answer is that both have advantages, and the advantage of each is the disadvantage of the other. The advantage of the experimental method, of course, is its ability to show cause and effect, which the correlational method cannot do.

But experiments also have drawbacks. For one (as noted), there's sometimes uncertainty about which aspect of the manipulation was important. For another, experiments on people are usually limited to events of relatively short duration, under conditions that must be carefully controlled. The correlational method, on the other hand, lets you examine events that take place over long periods (even decades) and events that are much more elaborate. Correlational studies also let us get information about events in which experimental manipulation would be unethical—for example, the effects of being raised by a divorced parent or the effects of cigarette smoking.

Many personality psychologists also criticize experiments on the grounds that the kinds of relationships they reveal often have little to do with the central issues of personality. Even experiments that seem to bear on important issues in personality may tell less than they seem to. Consider the hypothetical experiment described earlier, in which you manipulated success and failure and measured self-esteem. Assume for the moment that participants given a failure had lower self-esteem afterward than participants given a success. You might be tempted to infer from this experiment that having poor academic outcomes over the course of one's life causes people to develop low self-esteem.

This conclusion, however, may not be justified. The experiment dealt with a brief task outcome, manipulated in a particular way. The broader conclusion you're tempted to draw deals with a basic quality of personality. This latter quality may differ in many ways from the momentary state you manipulated. The "reasoning by analogy" you're tempted to engage in is dangerous, and it can be misleading.

To many personality psychologists, the only way to really understand personality is to look at naturally occurring differences between people (see Underwood, 1975). These psychologists are willing to accept the limitation on causal inference that's inherent in correlations; they regard it as an acceptable price to pay. On the other hand, many of these psychologists are comfortable *combining* the correlational strategy with experimental techniques, as described in the next section.

Multifactor Studies

We've been talking about studies as though they always involved predicting a dependent variable from a single predictor variable (either an experimental manipulation or an individual difference). In fact, however, studies often look at the effects of several predictors at once, by using multifactor designs. In this sort of study, two (or more) variables are varied *separately*, which means creating all combinations of the various levels of the predictor variables (Figure 2.7). The study shown in Figure 2.7 involves two factors, but more than two can be used. The more factors in a study, of course, the larger is the resulting array of combinations, and the trickier it is to keep track of things.

Sometimes the factors in a multifactor study are all experimental manipulations. Sometimes they're all personality variables. Often, though, studies involve designs in which experimental manipulations are crossed by individual-difference variables.

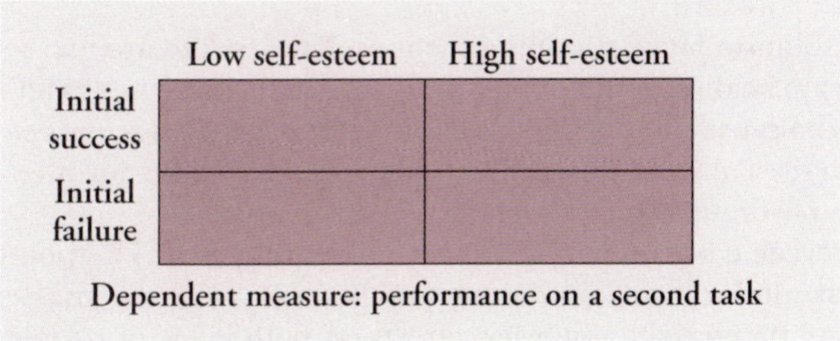

Figure 2.7

Diagram of a hypothetical two-factor study. Each square represents the combination of the value listed above it and the value listed to the left. In multifactor studies, all combinations of values of the predictor variables are created in this fashion.

The example shown in Figure 2.7 is a such a design. The self-esteem factor is the level of self-esteem people had when they came to the research session. This is a personality dimension (thus correlational). The success–failure factor is an experimental manipulation, which takes place during the session. In this particular experiment, the dependent measure is performance on a second task, which the participants work on after the experimental manipulation.

These designs allow researchers to examine how different types of people respond to variations in situations. They thus offer a glimpse into the underlying dynamics of the individual difference variable. Because this type of study combines experimental procedures and individual differences, it is often referred to as **experimental personality research.**

Reading Figures from Multifactor Research

Because multifactor designs are more complex than a single-factor study, what they can tell you is also more complex. Indeed, people who do experimental personality research use these designs precisely for this reason.

You don't *always* get a complex result from a multifactor study. Sometimes you find only the same outcomes you would have found if you had studied each predictor variable separately. When you find that a predictor variable is linked to the outcome variable in a systematic way, completely separate from the other predictor, the finding is referred to as a **main effect.** For example, the study outlined in Figure 2.7 might find only that people of both self-esteem levels perform worse after a failure than after a success.

The complexity in multifactor research occurs when a study finds what's termed an **interaction.** Figure 2.8 portrays two interactions, each a possible outcome of the hypothetical study of Figure 2.7. In each case, the vertical dimension portrays the dependent measure, performance on the second task. The two marks on the horizontal line represent the two values of the manipulated variable, initial success versus failure. The color of the line depicts the other predictor variable: the green line represents participants high in self-esteem, the black line represents those low in self-esteem.

We emphasize that these graphs show *hypothetical* outcomes. They are intended only to give you a clearer understanding of what interactions are about. Figure 2.8, A portrays a finding that people who are low in self-esteem perform worse after an initial failure than after a success. Among people high in self-esteem, however, this doesn't occur. The failure apparently has no effect on them. Thus, the effect of one variable (success vs. failure) differs across the two levels of the other variable (degree of self-esteem). That is the meaning of the term *interaction*. In the case in Figure 2.8, A, a failure has an effect at one level of the second variable (among the low self-esteem group) but has no effect at the other level of the second variable (the high self-esteem group).

There are two more points to make about interactions. First, to find an interaction, it's *absolutely necessary* to study more than one factor at a time. You simply can't find an interaction unless both contributors to it are studied at once. This is one reason why researchers often use complex designs: they allow the possibility for interactions to emerge.

The second point is revealed by comparing Figure 2.8, A with 2.8, B. This point is that interactions can take many forms. In contrast to the interaction we just described, the graph in panel B says that failure has effects on both kinds of people,

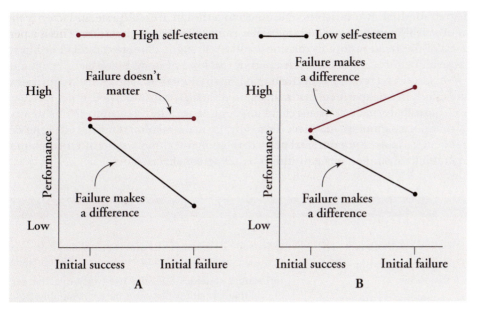

Figure 2.8

Two hypothetical outcomes of a two-factor study looking at self-esteem and an initial success-versus-failure experience as predictors of performance on a second task. (A) This graph indicates that experiencing a failure causes people low in self-esteem to perform worse later on than if they had experienced a success, but that the failure does not have any effect at all on people high in self-esteem. (B) This graph indicates that experiencing a failure causes people low in self-esteem to perform worse later on, but that the failure causes people high in self-esteem to perform *better* later on. Thus, the failure influences both kinds of people but does so in opposite ways.

but opposite effects. People low in self-esteem perform worse after failure (as in the first graph), but people high in self-esteem actually perform better after a failure, perhaps because the failure motivated them to try harder.

These two graphs aren't the only forms of interactions. Exactly what an interaction means always depends on the form it takes. Thus, exploring interactions always requires checking to see in what way each group was influenced by the other variable under study.

SUMMARY

Research in personality relies on observations of both the self and others. The desire to understand a person as an integrated whole led to case studies, in-depth examinations of specific persons. The desire for generalizability—conclusions that would apply to many rather than to a few people—led to studies involving systematic examination of many people.

Gathering information is only the first step toward examining relationships between and among variables. Relationships among variables are examined in two ways, corresponding to two kinds of relationships. Correlational research determines the degree to which two variables tend to go together in a predictable way when measured at different levels along the dimensions. This technique determines two aspects of the relationship: its direction and its strength. The special relationship of cause and effect cannot be determined by this kind of study, however.

A second technique, called the experimental method, allows testing for cause and effect. In an experiment, an independent variable is manipulated, other variables are controlled (made constant), and anything that cannot be controlled is treated by random assignment. An effect caused by the manipulation is measured in the dependent variable. Experimental and correlational techniques are often combined in multifactor studies, termed experimental personality research.

GLOSSARY

Case study An in-depth study of one individual.

Causality A relationship such that variation in one dimension produces variation in another.

Clinically significant An association that is large enough to have some practical importance.

Correlation A relationship in which two variables or dimensions covary when measured repeatedly.

Correlation coefficient A numeric index of the degree of correlation between two variables.

Dependent variable The variable measured as the outcome of an experiment; the "effect" in a cause–effect relation.

Descriptive statistics Statistics used to describe or characterize some group.

Experimental control The holding constant of variables that are not being manipulated.

Experimental method The method in which one variable is manipulated to test for causal influence on another variable.

Experimental personality research A study involving a personality factor and an experimental factor.

Generality (generalizability) The degree to which a conclusion applies to many people.

Independent variable The variable manipulated in an experiment, tested as the "cause" in a cause–effect relation.

Inferential statistics Statistics used to judge the likelihood that a relationship exists between variables.

Interaction A finding in which the effect of one predictor variable differs, depending on the level of another predictor variable.

Main effect A finding in which the effect of one predictor variable is independent of other variables.

Personology The study of the whole person, as opposed to studying only one aspect of the person.

Practical significance An association being large enough to have practical importance.

Random assignment The process of putting people randomly into groups of an experiment so that their characteristics balance out across groups.

Statistical significance An effect being unlikely to have occurred by chance, and thus being believable as real.

Third variable problem The possibility that an unmeasured variable caused variations in both of two correlated variables.

Variable A dimension along which two or more variations exist.

Issues in Personality Assessment

3

■ **Sources of Information**

■ **Reliability of Measurement**
Internal Consistency
Inter-Rater Reliability
Stability across Time

■ **Validity of Measurement**
Construct Validity
Criterion Validity
Convergent Validity
Discriminant Validity
Face Validity

Culture and Validity
Response Sets and Loss of Validity

■ **Two Rationales behind the Development of Assessment Devices**
Rational, or Theoretical, Approach
Empirical Approaches

■ **Better Assessment: A Never-Ending Search**

SUMMARY

■ On the first day of personality class, Jeff saw a woman he didn't know, and he's been trying ever since to get an idea of what she's like. He watches how she acts and dresses, listens to what she says to people. He asks friends if they know anything about her. After a while he starts to wonder how "good" the information is he's gathering. Pat always sees things in a slanted way, so what she says has to be taken with a grain of salt. Jennifer hardly notices things that are right in front of her, so who knows what to make of what she says? When the stranger raises her hand and gives opinions in class, do they reflect who she is, or is she just trying to convince the teacher she's an intellectual? When she turned down a date with Chris after class the other day, was that a trace of scorn in her voice? Or was she just flustered?

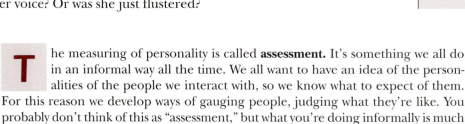

T he measuring of personality is called **assessment.** It's something we all do in an informal way all the time. We all want to have an idea of the personalities of the people we interact with, so we know what to expect of them. For this reason we develop ways of gauging people, judging what they're like. You probably don't think of this as "assessment," but what you're doing informally is much the same—in principle—as what psychologists do more formally.

Forming impressions of what other people are like can be difficult. It's easy to get misleading impressions. Personality assessment is also difficult for psychologists. All the problems you have, they have too. But personality psychologists work hard to deal with those problems (for a more extensive discussion, see Anastasi, 1988).

Sources of Information

Informal assessment takes information from many sources, and so does formal assessment. In fact, as you'll see momentarily, each way of getting information mentioned in the opening example has a counterpart in a formal assessment technique.

Many measures of personality come from someone other than the person being assessed (e.g., Funder, 1991; Paunonen, 1989). The broad name for this technique is **observer ratings.** There are many kinds of observer ratings. Sometimes observers make judgments about the person being assessed without interacting directly with the person. In some cases the judgments are based on observing the person's actions. In other cases, the judgments are opinions, ratings made by people who know the person well enough to say what he or she is like.

In contrast, some observer assessments involve interviews. People being assessed may talk in their own words about themselves and the interviewer draws conclusions from what's said and how it's said. Sometimes the people being interviewed talk about something *other than* themselves. In so doing, they reveal something indirectly to the interviewer about what they're like.

Though many techniques of assessment rely on the impressions of outside observers, not all do. A great many measures of personality—indeed, the vast majority—are **self-reports.** In self-reports people themselves indicate what they think they're like or how they feel or act. Self-reports thus resemble the process of introspection described in the last chapter. Although self-reporting can be done in an unstructured descriptive way, usually it's not. Most self-reports ask people to respond to a specific set of items.

There are many different types of observer ratings. Here an observer is directly rating a research participant's overt behavior.

Self-report scales can be created in many formats. An example is the true–false format. In this one you read statements and decide whether each one is true or false for you. Another common format is a multipoint rating scale. In this one a wider range of response options is available, for example, ranging from "strongly agree" to "strongly disagree."

Some self-reports focus on a single quality of personality. Often, though, people who develop tests want to assess *several* aspects of personality in the same test (as distinct scales). A device that assesses several dimensions of personality is termed an **inventory.** The process of developing an inventory is no different from the process of developing a single scale. The only difference is that in developing an inventory, you must go through each step of development for *each scale of the inventory,* rather than just one.

As you can see, the arsenal of possible assessment techniques is large. All incorporate two processes, though. First, in each case, the person who's being assessed produces a sample of "behavior" of some sort. This may literally be action, which someone else observes, it may be internal behaviors such as changes in heart rate, or it may be the behavior of answering some self-report items. Second, someone then uses the behavior sample as a guide to some aspect of the person's personality.

Some measures are termed **subjective,** whereas others are termed **objective.** Subjective measures are those in which an interpretation is part of the measure. An example would be an observer's judgment that the person being watched looks nervous. The judgment renders the measure subjective, because it is an *interpretation* of the behavior. If the measure instead focuses on a concrete physical reality that requires no interpretation, it's said to be objective. For example, you could count the number of times the person stammers while talking. This would involve no interpretation yet. Although this count might later be used to infer nervousness (an interpretation), the measure itself is objective.

To some extent, this issue cuts across the distinction between observer ratings and self-reports. An observer can make objective counts of acts, or can develop a subjective impression of the person. In the same way, a person making a self-report can report counts of specific events, or can give a subjective impression of what he or she is like as a person. It should be apparent, though, that self-reports are particularly vulnerable to incorporating subjectivity. Even reports of specific events, if they're retrospective, permit unintentional interpretations to creep in.

Reliability of Measurement

All techniques of assessment confront several kinds of problems, or issues. One issue is termed **reliability** of measurement. The nature of this issue can be conveyed by putting it as a question: Once you've made an observation about someone, how confident can you be that if you made the same observation a second or third time you'd see about the same thing? When an observation is reliable, it has a high degree of *consistency*, or *repeatability*. Low reliability means the observation is less consistent. The measure isn't just reflecting the person being measured. It's somehow also including a lot of randomness, termed **error.**

All measurement procedures have sources of error (error can be reduced, but not eliminated). When you use a telescope to look at the moon, a little dust on the lens, minor imperfections in the glass, flickering lights from the city nearby, and swirling air currents can all contribute error to what you see. When you use a rating scale to measure how "independent" people think they are, the way you phrase the item can be a source of error, because it can cue different interpretations. When you have an observer watching a child's behavior, the observer is a source of error, because of variations in how closely he's paying attention, thinking about what he's seeing, or being influenced by a thousand other things.

How do you deal with the issue of reliability in measurement? The general answer is to repeat the measurement, make the observation more than once. Usually this means measuring the same quality from a slightly different angle or using a slightly different "measuring device." This lets the diverse sources of error in the different devices cancel each other out.

Reliability actually is a family of problems (not just a single problem), because it crops up in several different contexts. Each version of the problem has a separate name, and the tactic used to treat each version differs slightly from the tactics used on the others.

Internal Consistency

The simplest case of assessment is the single observation or measurement. How can you be sure it doesn't include too much error? Let's take an illustration from ability assessment. Think about what you'd do if you wanted to know how good someone was at a particular type of problem, for example, math problems or word puzzles. You wouldn't give the person just a *single* problem to solve, because whether he or she solved it easily or not might depend too much on some quirk of that particular problem. If you want to know (reliably) how well the person solves that kind of problem, you'd give a *series* of problems.

The same strategy applies to personality assessment. If you were using a self-report to ask people how independent they think they are, you wouldn't ask just once. You'd ask several times, using different items that all reflect independence, but in different words. In this example, *each item* is a "measuring device." When you shift to a new item, you're shifting to a different measuring device, trying to measure the same quality in the same person. In effect, you're putting down one telescope and

Human judges are not infallible. They sometimes perceive things inaccurately.

picking up another. The reliability question is whether you see about the same thing through the different telescopes.

This kind of reliability is termed **internal reliability** or **internal consistency.** This is reliability within a set of observations of the same aspect of personality. Because different items have different sources of random error, using many items should tend to balance out the error. The more observations, the more likely it is that the random error will cancel out. Because people using self-report scales want good reliability, most scales contain fairly large numbers of items. If the items are reliable enough, they're then used together as a single index of the personality quality.

How do you find out whether the items you're using have good internal reliability? Having a large number of items doesn't guarantee it. Reliability is a question about the correlations among people's responses to the items. Saying that the items are highly reliable means that people's responses to the items are highly intercorrelated.

In practical terms, there are several ways to investigate internal consistency. All of them examine correlations among people's responses across items. Perhaps the best way (although it's cumbersome) is to look at the average correlation between each pair of items taken separately. A simpler approach is to separate the items into two subsets (often odd- versus even-numbered items), add up people's scores for each subset, and correlate the two subtotals with each other. This correlation provides an index called **split-half reliability.** If the two halves of the full set measure the same quality of personality, people who score high on one half should also score high on the other half, and people who score low on one half should also score low on the other half. Thus, a strong positive correlation between halves is evidence of internal consistency.

Inter-Rater Reliability

As noted earlier, personality isn't always measured by self-reports. Some observations are *literally* observations, made by one person watching and assessing someone else. Use of observer ratings gives rise to a slightly different reliability problem than occurs in self-report scales. In an observer rating, the *person making the observation* is a "measuring device." There are sources of error in this device, just as in other devices. How can you judge the extent of reliability in this case?

Conceptually, the answer is the same as it was in the preceding section. You need to put down one telescope and pick up another. In the case of observer ratings, you need to check this observer against another observer. To the extent that both see about the same thing when they look at the same event, reliability is high. This double observation is logically the same as using two questionnaire items rather than one. Raters whose judgments correlate highly with each other across many ratings are said to have high **inter-rater reliability.**

In many cases, obtaining high inter-rater reliability requires the judges to be thoroughly trained in how to observe what they're observing. Judges of Olympic diving competitions, for example, have witnessed many thousands of dives and know precisely what to look for. As a result, their inter-rater reliability is high. Similarly, when observers assess qualities of personality, they often receive considerable instruction and practice before turning to the "real thing," so their reliability will be high.

Stability across Time

There's one more kind of reliability that's important in the measurement of personality. This type of reliability concerns stability across time. That is, assessment at one time should agree fairly well with assessment done at a different time.

Why is this important? Remember, personality is supposed to be stable—that's one reason people use the word, to convey the sense of stability. If personality is really *stable*—doesn't fluctuate from minute to minute or from day to day—then *measures*

If all judges are seeing the same thing when they rate an event, then inter-rater reliability will be high.

of personality should be reliable across time: people's scores should stay roughly the same when measured a week later, a month later, or four years later.

This kind of reliability is termed **test-retest reliability.** It's determined by giving the test to the same people at two different times. A measure with high test-retest reliability will yield scores the second time (the retest) that are fairly similar to those from the first time. People with high scores the first time will have high scores the second time, those with lower scores at first will have lower scores later on. (For a summary of these three types of reliability, see Table 3.1.)

Validity of Measurement

Reliability is a starting point in measurement, but it isn't the only issue that matters. It's possible for measures to be highly reliable but completely meaningless. Another important issue here is termed **validity.** This issue concerns whether what you're measuring is what you *think* you're measuring (or what you're *trying* to measure) when you make an observation. Earlier the concept of reliability was illustrated in terms of random influences on the image in a telescope as you look through it at the moon. To extend the same analogy, the validity issue is whether the image you're seeing is really the moon, or just a street light (see also Figure 3.1).

How do you decide whether you're measuring what you want to measure? There are two ways to answer this question. One is an "in-principle" answer, the other is a set of tactics. The in-principle answer is that people decide by comparing two kinds of "definitions" with each other. When you hear the word *definition,* what probably comes to mind is a conceptual, or dictionary, definition. This is an abstract spelling out of the word's meaning in terms of conceptual qualities or attributes. It tells us the information that the users of a language have agreed is conveyed by the word. Psychologists also talk about another kind of definition, however, called an **operational definition.** This is a description of some kind of physical event.

To illustrate the difference between the two kinds of definition, consider the concept of love. The conceptual (dictionary) definition of the word *love* might be something like "a strong affection for another person." There are many ways, however, to define love operationally. For example, you might ask the person you're assessing to indicate on a rating scale how much she loves someone. You might measure how often she looks into that person's eyes when interacting with him. You might measure how willing she is to give up events she enjoys in order to be with him. These

Table 3.1

Three Kinds of Reliability. Each assesses the consistency or "repeatability" of an observation by looking a second time, either with the same "measuring device" or with a slightly different one.

Type of reliability	"Measuring device"	Type of consistency
Internal reliability	Test item	Consistency within the test
Inter-rater reliability	Rater	Agreement between raters
Test-retest reliability	Entire test	Consistency across time

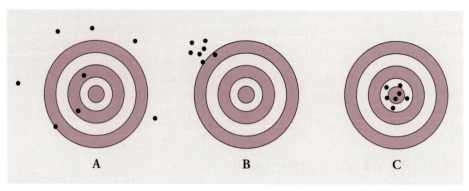

Figure 3.1

A simple way to think about the difference between reliability and validity uses the metaphor of target shooting. (A) Sometimes when people shoot at a target their shots go all over. This result corresponds to measurement that's neither reliable nor valid. (B) Reliability is higher as the shots are closer together. Shots that miss the mark, however, are not valid. (C) Good measurement means that the shots are close together (reliable) *and* near the bull's-eye (valid).

three measures differ considerably from one another. Yet each might be taken as an operational definition (or operationalization) of love.

The essence of the validity issue in measurement is summarized in this question: How well does the *operational* definition being used (the event) match the *conceptual* definition (the abstract quality that you have in mind to measure)? If the two are close, the measure has high validity. If they aren't close, validity is low.

How do you decide whether the two are close? Usually psychologists poke at the conceptual definition until it's clear what the critical elements are and then look to see whether the same elements are in the operationalization. If they aren't (at least by strong implication), the validity of the operationalization is questionable.

The validity issue is important, and also tricky. It's the subject of continual debate in psychology, as researchers try to think of better and better ways to look at human behavior. The reason this issue is important is that conclusions about personality are going to be formed in terms of what researchers and assessors *think* they're measuring. If what they're measuring isn't what they think they're measuring, researchers will draw false conclusions. Likewise, a clinician may draw the wrong conclusion about a person being assessed if the device isn't measuring what the clinician thinks it's measuring.

Validity as an issue is important whenever anything is being observed. In personality assessment, however, the validity question is so important that it's been examined closely for a long time. In trying to be sure that personality tests are valid, theorists have come to distinguish several aspects of validity from one another. These distinctions have also influenced the practical process of establishing validity.

Construct Validity

The idea of validity you have in mind at this point is technically called **construct validity** (Campbell, 1960; Cronbach & Meehl, 1955). Construct validity is an all-encompassing validity. It thus is the most important kind (cf. Hogan & Nicholson,

1988; Landy, 1986). Construct validity means that the measure (the assessment device) accurately reflects the construct (the conceptual quality) that the psychologist has in mind. Although the word *construct* sounds abstract, a construct is just a concept. Any trait quality, for example, is a construct.

Establishing construct validity for a measure is a long and complex process. It requires several kinds of information, each treated as a separate aspect of the validation process. For this reason, the various qualities that contribute to construct validity have separate names of their own. They are described in the following paragraphs.

Criterion Validity

A particularly important part of showing that an assessment device has construct validity is showing that it relates to other manifestations of the quality the device is supposed to measure (Campbell, 1960). This usually means using a behavioral index (or the judgment of a carefully trained observer) as an external *criterion* (a standard of comparison) and seeing how well the assessment device correlates with it. This aspect of validity is sometimes referred to as **criterion validity** (because it uses an external criterion) or **predictive validity** (because it tests how well the measure predicts something it's supposed to predict).

As an example, suppose you wanted to establish criterion validity for a measure of dominance you were developing. One way to approach this problem would be to select people who score high and low on your measure and bring them to a laboratory (one at a time) to work on a task with two other people. You could tape each group's discussion and score the tape for the number of times each person made suggestions, gave instructions, took charge of the situation, and so on. These behaviors would represent criteria of dominance. If people who scored high on your measure did these things more than people who scored low, it would indicate that the measure had a kind of criterion validity.

Another way to approach the problem would be to have a trained interviewer spend twenty minutes with each of the people who completed your scale and rate each person's level of dominance after the interview. The interviewer's impression of the person would be a different kind of criterion of dominance. If the impressions proved to be related to the scores on your measure, it would indicate a different kind of criterion validity for the measure.

Criterion validity is usually regarded as the most important indicator of construct validity. In recent years, though, a controversy has arisen over the process of establishing it. Howard (1990; Howard et al., 1980) has pointed out that people often assume the behavioral criterion chosen is a perfect reflection of the construct. In reality, though, this is almost never true. In fact, far too often researchers choose criterion measures that are *poor* reflections of the construct. We raise this point to emphasize how critical it is to be careful in deciding what criterion to use. Unless the criterion is a good one, associations with it are meaningless. Despite this issue, however, criterion validity remains the keystone of construct validation.

Convergent Validity

Another aspect of trying to show construct validity involves showing that the measure relates to characteristics that are similar to, but not the same as, what it's supposed to measure. How is this different from criterion validation? In this case, you know the second measure aims to assess something a little different from what your measure assesses. Because getting this sort of evidence often proceeds from several directions, it is often termed **convergent validation** (Campbell & Fiske, 1959). That is, the findings "converge" on the construct you're interested in, even though any single finding by itself won't clearly reflect the construct.

For example, a scale intended to measure dominance should be somewhat related to measures of characteristics such as leadership (positively) or shyness (inversely). The correlations should be far from perfect because these aren't quite the same constructs, but the correlations shouldn't be zero. If you developed a measure intended to assess dominance and it didn't correlate at all with measures of leadership and shyness, you'd have to start wondering whether your measure was really assessing dominance.

Discriminant Validity

It's important to show that an assessment device measures what it's intended to measure. But it's also important to show that it does *not* measure qualities it's *not* intended to measure—especially qualities that don't fit with what the researcher had in mind as a construct (Campbell, 1960). This aspect of the overall construct validation process is termed **discriminant validation** (Campbell & Fiske, 1959).

The importance of discriminant validation can be easy to overlook. However, discriminant validation is a major line of defense against the "third variable" problem in correlational research, discussed in Chapter 2. That is, you can't be sure why two correlated variables correlate. It may be that one has an influence on the other. But it may also be that a third variable, correlated with the two you've studied, is really responsible for their correlation. In principle, it's always possible to attribute the effect of a personality dimension on behavior to some other personality dimension. In practice, however, this can be made much harder by evidence of discriminant validity. That is, if research shows that the dimension you're interested in is unrelated to another variable, then that variable can't be invoked as an alternative explanation for the effect of the first.

To illustrate this, let's return to an example used in discussing the third variable problem in Chapter 2, a correlation between self-esteem and academic performance. This association *might* reflect the effect of an unmeasured variable, for instance, IQ. Suppose, though, that we know this measure of self-esteem isn't correlated with IQ, because someone checked that possibility during the process of its validation. This information would make it difficult to claim that IQ is what really underlies the correlation between self-esteem and academic performance.

The process of discriminant validation is never-ending because new possibilities for third variables always suggest themselves. Ruling out alternative explanations thus is a challenging task, but it's also a necessary one.

Face Validity

Establishing construct validity is a long-term process that's of great importance. There is, however, one more kind of validity that should be mentioned. It is much simpler, a little more intuitive, and less important. It's called **face validity.** Face validity means that the assessment device appears, on its "face," to be measuring the construct it was intended to measure. It *looks* right. A test of sociability made up of items such as "I prefer to spend time with friends rather than alone" and "I would rather socialize than read books" would have a high degree of face validity. A test of sociability made up of items such as "Green is my favorite color" and "I prefer imports to American-made cars" would have a low degree of face validity.

Face validity is regarded as a convenience by researchers, for two reasons. First, some researchers believe that face valid measures are easier for people to respond to than measures that have less face validity. Second, researchers sometimes focus on distinctions between qualities of personality that differ in subtle ways. It often seems as though there's no other way to separate these qualities from each other than to use instruments that are high in face validity.

On the other hand, face validity can occasionally be a detriment. This is true when the assessment device is intended to measure something that the person being assessed would find threatening or undesirable to admit. In these cases, the test developer usually tries to obscure the purpose of the test by reducing its face validity.

Whether face validity is good, bad, or neither, it should be clear that it is less important than other kinds of validity. If an assessment device is to be useful in the long run, it must undergo the laborious process of construct validation. The "bottom line" is always construct validity.

Culture and Validity

Another important issue in assessment is cultural differences. In a sense this is a validity issue; in a sense it's an issue of generalizability. The issue might be framed as a question: Do the scores on a personality test have the same meaning for a person from an Asian culture or a Latino culture or an African American culture as they do for a middle-American European culture?

There are at least two aspects to this question. The first is whether the psychological construct *itself* has the same meaning from one culture to another. This is a fundamental question about the nature of personality. Are the elements of personality the same from one human group to another? Many people assume the basic elements of personality are universal. That may, in fact, be a dangerous assumption.

The second aspect of the question concerns how the items of the personality measure are interpreted by people from different cultures. If an item has one meaning or implication for middle-income Americans, but a different meaning in some other culture, people's responses to the item will also have different meanings in the different cultures. A similar issue arises when a measure is translated into a different language. This actually involves translation into the new language, then translation back into the original language by someone who's never seen the original items. This process sometimes reveals that items contain idiomatic or metaphorical meaning that's hard to translate to an equivalent form. The process of adapting a measure developed in one culture for use in another culture is a complex one with many difficulties (Butcher, 1996). It must be done very carefully, if the measure is to be valid in the new culture.

Response Sets and Loss of Validity

Any discussion of validity must also include the fact that there are problems in self-report assessment that can interfere with the validity of the information collected. We've already mentioned the fact that biases in recall of information can distort the picture. This can render the information invalid. In the same way, people's motivational tendencies can also get in the way of accurate reporting.

There are at least two biases in the way people respond in assessment. These biases are called **response sets.** A response set is a psychological orientation, a readiness to answer in a particular way (Berg, 1967; Jackson & Messick, 1967; Rorer, 1965). Response sets create distortions in the information assessed. Personality psychologists want their assessments to provide information that's free from contamination. Thus, response sets are problems.

Two response sets are of particular importance in personality assessment. One of them emerges most clearly when the assessment device is a self-report instrument that in one fashion or another asks the person questions that require a yes-or-no response (or a response on a rating scale with *agree* and *disagree* as the opposite ends of the scale). This response set, called **acquiescence,** is nothing more than the tendency to say "yes" (Couch & Keniston, 1960).

Everyone presumably has this tendency to a degree, but people vary greatly on it. That's what causes the problem. If the set isn't counteracted, the scores of people who are highly acquiescent become inflated. Their high scores reflect the response set instead of their personality. People who have extreme personalities but not much acquiescence will also have high scores. But you won't know whose scores are from personality and whose are from acquiescence.

Acquiescence is usually viewed as an easy problem to combat. The way it's handled for self-reports is to write only half the items so that a *yes* response indicates being high on the personality characteristic. Write the other half of the items so that a *no* response means the person is high on the personality characteristic. In the process of scoring the test, then, any bias coming from the simple tendency to say "yes" is canceled out.

Although this procedure takes care of the problem of overagreement, not everyone is convinced it's a good idea. Negatively worded items often turn out to be harder to understand or more complicated to answer than positively worded items. The result can be responses that are less accurate (Converse & Presser, 1986; Schriesheim & Hill, 1981). For this reason, some people feel it's better to live with the acquiescence problem than to introduce a different kind of error by complex wordings.

There's a second response set that's perhaps more important than acquiescence and also more troublesome. It's called **social desirability,** reflecting the fact that peo-

The tendency to provide socially desirable responses can sometimes mask a person's true characteristics or feelings.

ple tend to portray themselves in a good light (in socially desirable ways) whenever possible. Once again, this tendency is stronger among some people than others (see Crowne & Marlowe, 1964; Edwards, 1957). As with acquiescence, if it isn't counter-acted, people with strong concerns about social desirability will produce scores that reflect the response set rather than their personalities.

For some personality dimensions this is not much of a problem. This is because some personality qualities imply no social approval or disapproval at either end of the dimension. In other cases, though, there's a consensus that it's better to be one way (for example, honest or likable) than the other (dishonest or unlikable). In these cases assessment becomes tricky.

In general, psychologists deal with this problem by trying to phrase questions (or whatever the assessment device uses) so that the issue of social desirability isn't salient. As much as anything else, this is a process of trying to avoid even bringing up the idea that one kind of person is better liked than the other. Sometimes this means phrasing the undesirable response in a way that makes it more acceptable. Sometimes it means looking for ways to let people admit the undesirable quality indirectly. A different way to deal with the problem is to include items that assess the person's degree of concern about social desirability and to use this information as a correction factor in evaluating the person's responses to other items. In any event, it should be clear that this problem is one that personality psychologists must be constantly aware of and constantly guarding against in trying to measure what people are like.

Two Rationales behind the Development of Assessment Devices

Thus far, this chapter has considered issues that arise in attempts to measure any quality of personality. What hasn't been taken up yet is how people decide what qualities to measure in the first place. This question won't be answered completely here, because the answer depends partly on the theoretical perspective from which the assessor is proceeding. There is, however, a general issue to address. In particular, development of personality measures usually follows one of two paths. Each path has a certain kind of logic, but the logics differ from each other.

Rational, or Theoretical, Approach

One strategy is termed a **rational,** or **theoretical, approach** to assessment. This strategy is based on theoretical considerations from the very beginning. The psychologist first develops a rational basis for believing that a particular dimension of personality is important. The next task is to create a test in which this dimension is reflected validly and reliably in people's answers. This approach to test development often leads to assessment devices that have a high degree of face validity.

It's important to recognize that the work doesn't stop once a set of items has been developed. Instruments developed from this starting point must be shown to be reliable, to predict behavioral criteria, and to have good construct validity. Until these steps are taken, the scale shouldn't be considered a useful measure of anything.

It's probably safe to say that the majority of personality measurement devices that now exist were developed using the theoretical path. Some of these measures are single scales, others are inventories. Most of the measures that are discussed in later chapters were created by first deciding *what* to measure and then figuring out *how* to measure it.

Empirical Approaches

The theoretical approach isn't the only way to start in scale development, though. A second strategy is usually characterized as an **empirical,** or data-based, approach. The basic characteristic of this approach is that it relies on data rather than on theory to decide what items make up the assessment device.

There are two important variations on this theme. One of them is an inductive approach whereby the person developing the measure uses the data to decide what qualities of personality even exist to measure (Cattell, 1947, 1965, 1979). Because this line of thought is an important contributor to trait psychology, we're going to defer our discussion of it until the chapter on trait psychology. We'll focus here on another empirical approach. This one reflects a very pragmatic orientation to the process of assessment. It's guided less by a desire to understand personality than by a practical aim of sorting people into categories. If a quick or inexpensive technique can be found to do this, the technique provides an important benefit.

Instead of developing the test first and then validating it against a criterion, this approach works in the opposite direction. The groups into which people are to be sorted represent the criteria for the test. Developing the test is a matter of starting out with many possible items and finding out which items are answered differently by members of one criterion group than by other people. This is termed the **criterion keying** approach to test development. This label comes from the fact that the items that are retained are those that empirically distinguish between the *criterion* group and other people. If such an item set can be found for each criterion group, then the entire test (all the item sets together) can be used to tell who belongs to which group.

In the point of view reflected in this approach, it doesn't matter at all what the items of the assessment device look like. It only matters that they distinguish persons who fit a criterion from those who don't. The items in a scale reflecting this approach were chosen because members of a specific group (defined on some other basis) tend to answer them differently than other people.

The best illustration of the use of this method is the Minnesota Multiphasic Personality Inventory, better known as the MMPI (Hathaway & McKinley, 1943) and revised in 1989 as the MMPI-2 (Butcher, Dahlstrom, Graham, Tellegen, & Kaemmer, 1989). The MMPI was a very long true–false inventory developed as a measure of abnormality. The first step in its development was to collect a large number of self-descriptive statements. The statements then were given to a group of normal persons and to groups of previously diagnosed psychiatric patients—people already judged by a clinician to have a specific disorder. Thus, the criterion already existed. The next step was to test the usefulness of each item. Do people with one psychiatric diagnosis agree or disagree with the item more often than normal people and people with different diagnoses? If so, that item was included in the scale pertaining to that psychiatric diagnosis.

The original MMPI was developed long ago, on a sample that was narrow ethnically and geographically (largely from Minnesota), and had a narrow age range. Concern arose that scores from other populations might not be interpreted properly. In addition, many items were out of date, and some were hard to understand. The people developing the MMPI-2 reworded about 20 percent of the original items for clarity, wrote 154 new ones, and distilled the total to 567. They collected data from people who varied more widely in ethnicity, age, and gender. Thus, the interpretation of responses has been made more consistent with the contemporary U.S. populace.

As did the original, the MMPI-2 has ten basic content scales (Table 3.2). It also has six validity scales. The content scales indicate how similar a person's responses are to those of patients with a particular diagnosis. The validity scales provide an estimate of how meaningful the person's entire response profile is. For example, the Lie scale measures people's tendencies to present themselves too favorably to be true. As another example, frequent "cannot say" responses—an inability to choose the true or false option—may mean that the person is being evasive. If too many of these responses are made, the meaning of the other responses is called into question.

Better Assessment: A Never-Ending Search

As described in the preceding section, even one of the most widely used tests in the world wasn't considered "finished" just because it was being widely used. It was subjected to further refinement, further data gathering, and a continuing examination of how people respond to its items. The result was an improvement in what the test can tell the people who use it.

The MMPI isn't the only measure to be reexamined and revised in this way. Most personality scales in widespread use have been revised once or more and restandardized periodically. The process of establishing construct validity requires not just a single study but many. It thus takes time. The process of establishing discriminant validity is virtually never-ending. A tremendous amount of effort is invested in the process of creating and improving tests of personality. This investment of effort is necessary if people are to feel confident of knowing what the tests are measuring. Having that confidence is an important part of the assessment of personality.

The characteristics of personality tests discussed in this chapter distinguish these tests from those you see from time to time in newspapers, magazines, on TV, and so forth. In some cases, the items in a magazine article were written specifically for that

Table 3.2

Content scales of the MMPI-2 and interpretation of each scale's meaning.

Clinical scales	Interpretation
Hypochondriasis	High scorers are cynical, defeatist, overconcerned with physical health
Depression	High scorers are despondent, distressed, depressed
Hysteria	High scorers report frequent symptoms with no apparent organic cause
Psychopathic deviate	High scorers are adventurous, have disregard for social or moral standards
Masculinity/femininity	Scores provide indication of level of "traditional" male/female interests
Paranoia	High scorers are guarded and suspicious, feel persecuted
Psychasthenia	High scorers are anxious, rigid, tense, and worrying
Schizophrenia	High scorers exhibit social alienation, bizarreness in thinking
Hypomania	High scorers are emotionally excitable, impulsive, hyperactive
Social introversion	High scorers are shy, withdrawn, uninvolved in social relationships

article. It's unlikely that anyone checked on their reliability. It's even less likely that anyone checked on their validity. Even if the items were taken from a carefully developed instrument, the entire set of items usually doesn't appear; it can be hard to be sure how well the ones that do appear reflect the entire scale. Unless the right steps have been taken to create an instrument, you should be careful about putting your faith in the results that come from it.

SUMMARY

Assessment (measurement of personality) is something that people constantly do informally. Psychologists formalize this process into several distinct techniques. Observer ratings are judgments made about people who are being assessed by an observer—an interviewer, someone who just watches, or someone who knows the people well enough to make ratings of what they are like. Observer ratings often are somewhat subjective, involving interpretations of the person's behavior. Self-reports are made by the people being assessed, about themselves. Self-reports can be single scales or multiscale inventories. Assessment devices can be subjective or objective. Objective techniques require no interpretation as the assessment is made. Subjective techniques involve some sort of interpretation as an intrinsic part of the measure.

One issue for all assessment is reliability (the reproducibility of the measurement). Reliability is determined by checking one measurement against another (or several others). Self-report scales usually have many items (each a measurement), leading to indices of internal reliability, or internal consistency. Observer judgments are checked by inter-rater reliability. Test-retest reliability assesses the reproducibility of the measure over time. In all cases, high correlation among measures means good reliability.

Another important issue is validity (whether what you're measuring is what you want to measure). The attempt to determine whether the operational definition (the assessment device) matches the concept you set out to measure is called construct validation. Contributors to construct validity are evidence of criterion, convergent, and discriminant validity. Face validity is not usually taken as an important element of construct validity. Validity is threatened by the fact that people have response sets (acquiescence and social desirability) that bias their responses.

Development of assessment devices proceeds along one of two paths. The rational path uses a theory to decide what should be measured and then figures out the best way to measure it. Most assessment devices developed this way. The empirical path involves using data to determine what items should be in a scale. The MMPI was developed this way, using a technique called criterion keying, in which the test developers let people's responses tell them which items to use. Test items that members of a diagnostic category answered differently from other people were retained.

GLOSSARY

Acquiescence The response set of tending to agree, to say "yes" in response to any question.

Assessment The measuring of personality.

Construct validity The accuracy with which a measure reflects the underlying concept.

Convergent validity The degree to which a measure relates to other characteristics that are conceptually similar to what it's supposed to assess.

Criterion keying The developing of a test by seeing which items distinguish between groups.

Criterion validity The degree to which the measure correlates with a separate criterion of the same concept.

Discriminant validity The degree to which a scale does *not* measure unintended qualities.

Empirical approach (to scale development) The use of data instead of theory to decide what should go into the measure.

Error Random influences incorporated in measurements.

Face validity The scale "looking" as if it measures what it's supposed to measure.

Internal reliability (internal consistency) The agreement among responses made to the items of a measure.

Inter-rater reliability The degree of agreement between observers of the same events.

Inventory A personality test measuring several aspects of personality on distinct subscales.

Objective measure A measure that incorporates no interpretation.

Observer ratings An assessment in which someone else produces information on the person being assessed.

Operational definition The defining of a concept by the concrete events through which it is measured (or manipulated).

Predictive validity The degree to which the measure predicts other variables it should predict.

Rational approach (to scale development) The use of a theory to decide what you want to measure, then deciding how to measure it.

Reliability Consistency across repeated measurements.

Response set A biased orientation to answering.

Self-report An assessment in which people make ratings pertaining to themselves.

Social desirability The response set or style of tending to portray oneself favorably.

Split-half reliability One way of assessing internal consistency among responses to items of a measure.

Subjective measure A measure incorporating personal interpretation.

Test-retest reliability The stability of measurements across time.

Theoretical approach See **Rational approach.**

Validity A measure's "truthfulness," or the degree to which it actually measures what it is intended to measure.

The Dispositional Perspective

prologue to
PART *two*

THE DISPOSITIONAL PERSPECTIVE:
Major Themes and Underlying Assumptions

A key theme of the dispositional perspective on personality is the idea that people display consistency or continuity in their actions, thoughts, and feelings. A human being's dispositional nature doesn't shift aimlessly from moment to moment—it endures across changes in time and place. Indeed, the very concept of disposition is a way of conceptualizing the fact that people remain the same people, even through passage of time and even as they move from situation to situation. Dispositions are qualities that people carry around with them, that belong to them, that are part of them.

Certainly we all experience occasional periods in which we're unpredictable, in which we may feel buffeted by the psychological winds around us. But for most people that experience of unpredictability is the exception rather than the rule. It certainly isn't the essence of personality. Rather, personality implies stability, constancy, something that doesn't vary much from one time to another. You—like most

people—undoubtedly feel within yourself a sense of coherence, a kind of permanence across time, events, and experiences. You're the person you are, and you'll still be that person tomorrow, and next week, and next year. This is the meaning of dispositions.

A second theme of the dispositional perspective derives from the fact that people differ from each other in many ways. As indicated in Chapter 1, the entire field of personality psychology is guided in part by an emphasis on differences among people. This emphasis is particularly central to the dispositional perspective. From this perspective, each person's personality consists of a pattern of dispositional qualities, and the composition of the pattern differs from one person to another. The intersection among these dispositions in any given person constitutes the defining nature of that person's personality.

These assumptions are important throughout the dispositional perspective. They're dealt with differently, however, by different kinds of theorists.

One approach emphasizes the mere existence of dispositions. It focuses primarily on trying to measure and catalog them in better ways, to reach a clearer understanding of what dimensions are most important in personality and to find better ways to place people on those dimensions. This "trait and type" approach is discussed in Chapter 4. This trait approach most clearly exemplifies the dispositional perspective.

This isn't the only way to approach the concept of disposition, though. A second way is to think of dispositions as enduring motivational characteristics that vary in strength from person to person. These differences in the motive tendencies that underlie people's actions are reflected in differences in the qualities that the people display in their behavior. This "needs and motives" approach to dispositions is examined in Chapter 5.

chapter

4 *Types, Traits, and Interactionism*

■ **Types and Traits**
Nomothetic and Idiographic Views of Traits
What Traits Matter?
A Key Tool: Factor Analysis
Let Reality Reveal Itself: Cattell's Approach
Start from a Theory: Eysenck's Approach
Another Theoretical Starting Point:
    The Interpersonal Circle

■ **The Five-Factor Model: The Basic Dimensions of Personality?**
What *Are* the Five Factors?
Reflections of the Five Factors
The Five-Factor Model in Relation to Other Models
Cautions and Some Further Variations
Are Superordinate Traits the Best Level to Use?

■ **Traits, Situations, and Interactionism**
Is Behavior Actually Traitlike?
Situationism
Low Reliability in Measuring Behavior
Interactionism

Individual Differences in Consistency
Beyond Analysis of Variance in Interactionism
Was the Problem Ever Really as Bad as It Seemed?

■ **Interactionism Becomes a New View of Traits: Context-Dependent Expression of Personality**
Fitting the Pieces Together: Views
    of Traits and Behavior

■ **Assessment**
Comparing Individuals: Personality Profiles

■ **Problems in Behavior, and Behavior Change**
The Five-Factor Model and Personality Disorders
Interactionism in Behavior Problems
Behavior Change

■ **Trait Psychology: Problems and Prospects**

SUMMARY

■ "I want you to meet a friend of mine from high school. He's really outgoing. He's friendly, but he doesn't go along with the crowd all the time. You might say he's sociable, but he's also independent."

■ "My psychology professor is *so* predictable. He's smart, but he's *such* a geek. He must spend all his time locked up in his office. I can't imagine him doing anything interesting or fun. He can't help it, I guess. It's just his personality."

These quotes illustrate a central theme in personality psychology. It's common to assume that each person has a set of dispositions that a little observation reveals to you fairly easily. When you find out what people are like, you can rely on that as a guide for what to expect of them in the future. This theme, of course, applies to all of personality psychology. But it's particularly prominent in the trait and type view of personality. The words *trait* and *type* convey slightly different meanings. They converge, though, on the idea that people have stable characteristics that they exhibit across different circumstances and over time.

Types and Traits

The idea that people could be divided into different types, or categories, goes back at least to the time of Hippocrates (about 400 B.C.), whose ideas were later embellished by Galen (about A.D. 150). In those times, people were thought to form four groups: *choleric* (irritable), *melancholic* (depressed), *sanguine* (optimistic), and *phlegmatic* (calm). Each personality type was thought to reflect an excess of one of four basic bodily fluids.

A typology of more recent origin is Carl Jung's (1933) argument that people are either introverts or extraverts. An **introvert** tends to be alone a lot, may seem shy, and prefers solitary activities. When facing stress, they tend to withdraw into themselves. An **extrovert** is a person who isn't at all shy, and who prefers to spend time with others rather than alone. When facing stress, extraverts are likely to seek out other people.

In typologies, the **types** are usually regarded as categories that are distinct and discontinuous. An example of a discontinuous category is gender, with people being either male or female. Jung often portrayed the categories of introvert and extravert as discontinuous in the same way, so that a person is either one or the other (Figure 4.1). Any appearance to the contrary simply reflects a distortion of the person's basic personality.

In contrast, discussions of **traits** usually assume that people differ along continuous variables or dimensions (Figure 4.1). For this reason, this sort of theory is sometimes called a "dimensional" approach. In trait theories, people differ from each other in the *amounts* of various characteristics they have in their personality. This view treats differences among people as *quantitative* rather than qualitative.

Type theories have generally fallen from favor. Even Jung wasn't really a type theorist; he used type labels as a convenience. Today it's far more common to think of people in terms of continuous trait dimensions (for differing opinions, however, see Gangestad & Snyder, 1985; Meehl, 1992; Robins, John, Caspi, Moffitt, & Stouthamer-Loeber, 1996; Strube, 1989; York & John, 1992; and for a typology that's widely used in the world of business, see Blake & Mouton, 1980).

Figure 4.1

(A) Early type theories assumed a discontinuity between or among categories of people.
(B) Trait theories assume that traits are continuous dimensions of variability on some character-istic and that the degree of presence versus absence of the characteristic is distributed across a population.

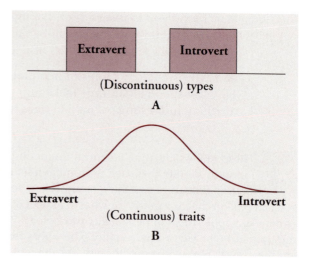

As true typologies faded, the term *type* began to be used in a way that differed from earlier usage. This second use comes from Hans Eysenck (1967, 1970, 1975). He used the word not to indicate discontinuity, but to suggest a "supertrait"—a trait that's very broad and important.

Nomothetic and Idiographic Views of Traits

Thus far, we've implied that traits are qualities of personality that are relevant to every person. People just vary in how much of each quality they have. Is this assumption reasonable?

The idea that traits exist in the same way in every person is known as a **nomothetic** view of personality (Allport, 1961). The term *nomothetic* derives from the Greek word meaning 'law.' This view emphasizes comparisons among people, and you can't compare people unless a trait has the same meaning for everyone. The nomothetic view has dominated trait psychology for at least the past forty-five years, right up to the present.

In contrast is the **idiographic** view (Allport, 1961), which emphasizes that each person is unique (see also Lamiell, 1981). The term *idiographic* has the same source as *idiosyncratic*. This view holds that traits are individualized. A trait may be possessed by only one person. Indeed, there may be as many traits as there are people. This view suggests there are times when people can't be compared, because everyone is on a different scale. Even if the same trait term applies to two people, its connotations will differ between people (Dunning & McElwee, 1995). Even if the connotations are the same, the trait may differ so much in importance between people that the people can't be compared meaningfully (Britt & Shepperd, 1999).

Does the nomothetic view deny individual uniqueness? No, psychologists who favor the nomothetic view do believe everyone is unique. To them, however, uniqueness reflects unique *combinations* of levels on many trait dimensions. The dimensions themselves are the same for everyone. As Eysenck once put it, "To the scientist, the unique individual is simply the point of intersection of a number of quantitative variables" (1952, p. 18).

Even psychologists who emphasize the idiographic don't entirely reject the nomothetic. Allport, for example, was nomothetic in most of his work. He believed, though, that nomothetic views always yield an approximation or oversimplification. In his opinion, personality psychologists should never lose sight of that fact: Even the traits that people seem to share always have a personal flavor (maybe from differences in how the trait is expressed) that varies from person to person (Allport, 1961).

Most trait psychologists do keep this point in the back of their minds. But most tend to disregard the strong version of the idiographic approach: the idea that the traits themselves differ from person to person.

What Traits Matter?

Thinking of personality in terms of traits quickly leads to a question: *What are the traits that make up personality?*

This is a hard question to answer. In fact, there have been serious disagreements about where to *start* in answering it. This led different people to approach it in two different ways. Before we turn to these approaches, let's consider a logical problem that all trait theorists share and a tool that helps deal with it.

A Key Tool: Factor Analysis

Personality is reflected in many ways—for example, in descriptive words. If each word describing personality meant a different trait, a psychologist would go crazy trying to organize things. That, in a nutshell, is a problem every trait psychologist faces: bringing order to such diversity. A solution to this problem derives from the idea that the many words reflect a small number of underlying dimensions. But how do you figure out what the dimensions are?

A tool that's often used for this is a statistical technique called **factor analysis.** The basic idea is simple: if two or more characteristics covary (vary along with each other) when assessed across many people, they may reflect a shared underlying trait. *Patterns* of covariation, then, may reveal the trait dimensions that lie beneath the measured qualities.

Recall from Chapter 2 that covariation between two variables is computed as a correlation. Factor analysis is a more complex version of a correlation. Instead of looking at one correlation between *two* variables, a factor analysis uses a matrix of correlations among *many* variables. Because the process is very complex, factor analysis has been widely used only since computers were easily available. Indeed, the rise in computing power over the years has led to increasing sophistication in these procedures (Bentler, 1990; Jöreskog & Sörbom, 1979).

You start the process by collecting measurements on many variables, across large numbers of people. The measurements can take any form, for example, self-reports or observer ratings. Different kinds of measures can even be mixed. The same measures must be taken for all the people, though (you can't use self-reports for some people, behavioral observations for others).

Once the data are collected, correlations are computed between every pair of variables (see also Box 4.1). The set of correlations is then put through a procedure called *factor extraction.* This procedure distills the correlations to a smaller set of **factors.** Each factor represents shared variations among several of the measures in the data set (underlying commonalities).

Once the factors are extracted, each can be described by a set of **factor loadings.** Think of these as correlations between the factor and each item (or measures) that contributes to its existence. Items that correlate strongly with the factor (usually higher than .30 or so) are said to "load on" that factor. Items that don't correlate with

BOX 4.1

A CLOSER LOOK
Factor Analysis

The process of factor analysis is complex, but its logic is fairly simple. It's an attempt to find regularities or patterns of association in a set of variables.

The process has several steps. The first step is collecting data. This is more complicated than it might seem. First you have to decide what *kinds* of data to collect. Should you use self-reports, observer ratings, or both? Even more fundamentally, what aspects of behavior do you want to measure? Should your analysis be guided strictly by "what's out there," or do you want theory to play a role? As you can see, the first step—"collecting data"—entails many decisions.

Let's use an example in which we let theory play a role. Imagine you're interested in how people cope with stress (Lazarus & Folkman, 1984). You've decided to use self-reports: people's ratings of how much they did particular things during the most stressful event they experienced in the past two months. To "collect data," get 300 or so of your friends to recall their stressful event and respond to each of a set of twenty-eight items (which list things that people sometimes do when under stress). Among the items are things like these:

1. Took action quickly, before things could get out of hand.
2. Refused to believe that it was real.
3. Did something concrete to make the situation better.

4. Tried to convince myself that it wasn't happening.
5. Went on thinking things were just like they were.
6. Changed or grew as a person in a new way.
7. Tried to look on the bright side of things.

The second step is to compute the correlation of every item with every other item (panel A, right). Each individual correlation reflects the degree to which the 300 people tended to answer one item the same way as they answered the other item. As you can see, there are strong correlations between items 1 and 3, between items 6 and 7, and between item 2 and items 4 and 5 (which are also strongly related to each other). The other correlations are very weak.

Because you had people respond to twenty-eight items (instead of just these seven), your correlation matrix is huge (each item with each other item). Interpreting the pattern of correlations from that matrix would be a real chore. The size of the chore is diminished by the third step in the analysis, called factor extraction. Through a small mathematical miracle, your matrix is reduced to a smaller number of underlying dimensions (for example, the associations among items 2, 4, and 5 would contribute to one dimension). These dimensions of underlying commonality are called **factors.** Factors are hazy entities you can imagine but can't see.

Now that the factors are extracted, the next step is to compute the **factor loadings** of each item on

the factor are said not to load on it. The items that load on the factor tell you what the factor is about.

The final step in the factor analysis—the most delicate part of the process—is labeling the factors. Because a factor is defined by items that load on it, you choose a label to characterize as closely as possible the content of those items, particularly those with the highest loadings. In factor analyses bearing on personality, the factor is being viewed as the statistical reflection of a trait. When you name the factor, you are naming the trait.

The act of naming the factor is very subjective. Several names might seem equally good. Which name is chosen, however, can have important consequences. People often forget that the label is an inference from the pattern of data. They rely on the label to tell them what the trait is. If the label you choose is at all misleading, it can create problems of interpretation later.

each factor. Factor loadings tell you the relations between each item and the factors (panel B, right). Each loading indicates the degree to which the item reflects the underlying dimension. As with any correlation, factor loadings can range from +1.00 to –1.00, and larger numbers mean stronger associations. Thus, a large number (a high loading) means the item is related to that dimension, a small number means it's not. As shown in panel B, items 1 and 3 load on factor A (but no other factor), items 6 and 7 load on factor B (but no other factor), and items 2, 4, and 5 load on factor C (but no other factor). Similar loadings are produced for all the twenty-eight items you began with, letting you know which items go together.

Once it's clear which items form which factors, you've reached the final step: naming the factors. This is tricky. You want to convey the essence of the underlying dimension, but your only guide is the items loading on it. Often the items are ambiguous or have mixed content, clouding the picture. In this example, a couple of factors are easy. The items loading on Factor A reflect a tendency to take action to try to resolve the problem. This might be called "problem-focused coping." Given the content of Items 2, 4, and 5, Factor C might be labeled "denial." Factor B seems to reflect "positive reinterpretation" or "post-traumatic growth" or "looking on the bright side," but it's hard to be sure which is best. It's important to be careful, though, because the name you call the factor will guide your future thinking.

A. Hypothetical Correlation Matrix

Item	1	2	3	4	5	6	7
1	*	.10	.75	–.05	.03	.12	.00
2		*	–.02	.52	.61	–.07	–.08
3			*	.17	.00	.09	.15
4				*	.71	.11	.08
5					*	.06	–.04
6						*	.59
7							*

B. Hypothetical Factor Loadings

Factor	A	B	C
Item 1	.62	.15	.01
Item 2	.03	–.08	.49
Item 3	.54	.04	–.20
Item 4	.10	.11	.56
Item 5	.07	.08	.50
Item 6	–.02	.72	.12
Item 7	.08	.48	.08

Factor analysis as a tool in trait psychology does three things. It reduces the multiple reflections of personality to a smaller set of traits (tells you what traits underlie the reflections). Second, it provides a basis for arguing that some traits matter more than others. That is, if a factor accounts for a lot of variability in the data, it reflects an important trait; if it accounts for less variability, it's less important. Third, factor analysis helps in creating assessment devices. You keep items (or ratings) that load strongly (reflect the factor to a great degree) and discard items that don't load well. Through repeated item creation and analysis, items that don't do a good job of measuring a particular trait are replaced by better ones.

Factor analysis is a very useful tool. It's only a tool, though. What we've told you has a major hole in it. We haven't said anything about *what measures to collect in the first place*. A factor analysis can tell you only about what you put into it. Thus, the decision about what to measure has a huge impact on what emerges as traits.

How do you decide what measures to collect? As we said earlier, different people have answered this question differently. Let's now return to that question.

Let Reality Reveal Itself: Cattell's Approach

One answer given was that researchers must determine *empirically* what traits make up personality, not impose preconceptions. If you start with preconceptions, you'll lead yourself astray. This was the argument of Raymond Cattell, an early contributor to trait psychology and one of the first users of factor analysis (Cattell, 1947, 1965, 1978; Cattell & Kline, 1977). This reasoning had a strong influence on many other trait researchers (Goldberg, 1993b).

How do you determine the structure of personality empirically? One source of information is language (see Goldberg, 1982), based on the following reasoning. A language that's evolved over thousands of years has words to describe many human qualities. Presumably any trait that matters is reflected in words that describe it. In fact, the more words that apply to a quality of personality the more it probably matters. This is called the **lexical criterion** of importance.

Using this idea, Cattell (1947, 1965) took a set of 4,500 trait terms (already reduced from a larger number by Allport & Odbert, 1936) and removed obvious synonyms, leaving 171 trait names. He then collected ratings on these words and factor-analyzed the ratings. The resulting factors were the traits he believed are important.

After many analyses on various kinds of data, Cattell came to believe that personality is captured in a set of sixteen dimensions (Table 4.1). These dimensions reemerged in analyses across the various types of data he was using, and he saw them as the primary traits in personality. These sixteen primary factors provide a name for the inventory that resulted: the 16 Personality Factor inventory, or 16PF (Cattell, Eber, & Tatsuoka, 1977).

Recall the statement earlier that labeling of factors is subjective and difficult. Cattell tried to deal with this by making up names (such as *alaxia, praxernia, threctia,* and *parmia*). Because these words had no connotations, they were not likely to be misleading. Eventually, though, he shifted to the labels in Table 4.1, which convey better the psychological sense of the factors.

Whereas extraverts prefer exciting activities involving other people, introverts like to be alone.

Table 4.1

The sixteen factors in Cattell's view of personality, as defined by the characteristics of high and low scorers on each trait dimension. The factors are listed in order of variance accounted for by each factor. The labels listed are the currently used verbal approximations for the content of each factor.

1. Reserved	versus	Warm
2. Concrete-reasoning	versus	Abstract-reasoning
3. Reactive	versus	Emotionally stable
4. Deferential	versus	Dominant
5. Serious	versus	Lively
6. Expedient	versus	Rule-conscientious
7. Shy	versus	Socially-bold
8. Utilitarian	versus	Sensitive
9. Trusting	versus	Vigilant
10. Practical	versus	Imaginative
11. Forthright	versus	Private
12. Self-assured	versus	Apprehensive
13. Traditional	versus	Open to change
14. Group-oriented	versus	Self-reliant
15. Tolerates disorder	versus	Perfectionist
16. Relaxed	versus	Tense

Start from a Theory: Eysenck's Approach

Though many believe an empirical starting point is best, not all agree. Another argument is that we should begin with well-developed ideas about what we want to measure. Then we should set about measuring those qualities well. Another major contributor to trait psychology, Hans Eysenck, used this approach (e.g., 1967, 1970, 1975, 1986; Eysenck & Eysenck, 1985).

In framing his theory, he relied on observations made by others over many centuries. He began with the typology of Hippocrates and Galen and related observations made by Jung and Wundt (Eysenck, 1967). He set out to investigate the idea that the four types identified by Hippocrates and Galen (and re-identified by others) could be created by combining high and low levels of two supertraits.

The two supertraits Eysenck posed as the underlying dimensions of personality are introversion-extraversion and emotionality-stability (or neuroticism). The extraversion dimension concerns tendencies toward sociability, craving excitement, liveliness, activeness, and dominance. All of these characterize the extravert. The emotional stability dimension concerns the ease and frequency with which the person becomes upset and distressed. Greater moodiness, anxiety, and depression reflect greater neuroticism.

These dimensions can create more diversity than you might guess. Table 4.2 portrays four sets of people, with combinations of highs and lows on these dimensions.

The ancient type label for each group described is printed in color. In considering the nature of these groups, keep two things in mind: First, although the form of Table 4.2 suggests discontinuity, both dimensions are continuous. Second, the descriptions apply to fairly extreme and clear-cut cases. Most people are closer to the midpoint on both dimensions and thus have less extreme characteristics.

Look first at the introvert groups. As Table 4.2 indicates, people who are both introverted *and emotionally stable* tend to be careful, controlled, calm, and thoughtful in their actions. The combination of introversion and emotional *instability*, on the other hand, tends to create a more moody sense of unsociable reserve, a pessimistic and anxious quality. Thus introverts can differ substantially, depending on their levels of emotional stability or instability. So can extraverts. When extraversion is combined with emotional stability, the result is an easygoing, carefree sociability. Emotional *instability* in an extravert introduces an excitable aggressive quality. Thus the impact of one dimension (extraversion) can differ as a result of which other trait the person has (high versus low neuroticism).

Eysenck assessed these two dimensions by a self-report measure called the Eysenck Personality Questionnaire, or EPQ (Eysenck & Eysenck, 1975). He used factor analysis to help create it, but he had a different goal in mind than Cattell had. Cattell used factor analysis to find out what dimensions *exist*. Eysenck used factor analysis to refine his scales, by selecting items that loaded well, and to confirm that the scales measure two factors, as he intended.

Eysenck and Cattell started out very differently, but the trait structures that emerged have distinct similarities. The two dimensions Eysenck saw as supertraits re-

Table 4.2

Traits that are common among four categories of people deriving from the two major personality dimensions proposed by Eysenck. Each category results from combining introversion or extraversion with either a high or a low level of emotional stability (adapted from Eysenck, 1975).

	Emotionally stable	Emotionally unstable
Introvert	Passive, careful, thoughtful, peaceful, controlled, reliable, even-tempered, calm — **Phlegmatic**	Quiet, pessimistic, unsociable, sober, rigid, moody, anxious, reserved — **Melancholic**
Extravert	Sociable, outgoing, talkative, responsive, easygoing, lively, carefree, leaderly — **Sanguine**	Active, optimistic, impulsive, changeable, excitable, aggressive, restless, touchy — **Choleric**

semble two of the first three factors of Cattell's 16PF (Table 4.1). The similarities are even stronger in **second-order factors** from the 16PF. A second-order factor analysis tells whether the factors *themselves* form factors (correlate in clusters). One second-order factor from the 16PF is virtually identical to extraversion (Cattell & Kline, 1977). Another is similar to neuroticism.

Another reflection of the resemblance can be seen in Eysenck's view that the dimensions of extraversion and neuroticism are at the top of an unfolding hierarchy of qualities that combine to form personality (Figure 4.2). Each supertrait is made of component traits (which resemble Cattell's primary traits). Component traits are specific qualities that contribute to the supertrait. Component traits, in turn, reflect habits, which derive from specific responses. Eysenck believed all levels are involved in behavior, but he saw the type level as the most important.

Two more points about Eysenck's view: First, he believed that extraversion and neuroticism link to aspects of nervous system functioning. That part of his theory comes up in Chapter 7. Second, there's a third dimension in Eysenck's view, which gets less attention than the others. Called *psychoticism* (Eysenck & Eysenck, 1976), it involves a predisposition toward psychological detachment from other people. It's been studied less than the other dimensions, so less is known about it. But people high in this trait tend to be hostile, manipulative, impulsive, and tend to seek out unusual experiences (Eysenck, 1992).

Another Theoretical Starting Point: The Interpersonal Circle

Eysenck's is the best known theoretically based approach to traits. But it isn't the only one. Another theoretical starting point emphasized interpersonal issues. Based on early work by Leary (1957) and others, Jerry Wiggins and his colleagues (Wiggins, 1979; Wiggins, Phillips, & Trapnell, 1989) argued that the core human traits are those that influence interpersonal life. Wiggins proposed a set of eight patterns, which he calls the **interpersonal circle,** arrayed around two dimensions that underlie human relations (Figure 4.3). The core dimensions in this view are dominance (or status) and love.

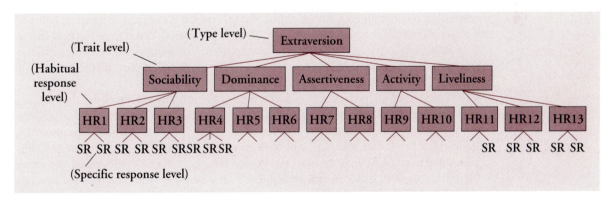

Figure 4.2

Eysenck's hierarchical view of personality. The superordinate level of the model (types) subsumes the elements represented at the next-lower level (traits). These elements, in turn, are made up of yet lower-order qualities (habits), which are made up of associations between stimulus and response. Adapted from *The Biological Basis of Personality* (1967, p. 36) by H. J. Eysenck. Reprinted courtesy of Charles C Thomas, Publisher, Springfield, IL.

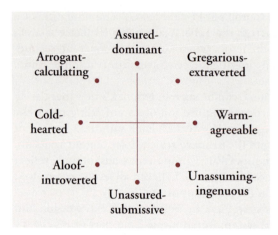

Figure 4.3

The interpersonal circle, a set of personality patterns portrayed in terms of their relative prevalence of two traits: love (the horizontal dimension) and dominance (the vertical dimension). The midpoint of each trait is the point where the lines cross. Adapted from Wiggins, Phillips, and Trapnell (1989).

Wiggins argued (as did Eysenck) that diverse personalities arise from combinations of values on the two core dimensions. For example, a person who's high in dominance and toward the cold-hearted end of love will seem arrogant and calculating. Put the same degree of dominance together with warmth on the love dimension, though, and you get a person who's gregarious and extraverted. Introversion and extraversion appear on this interpersonal circle (in lower left and upper right corners), but here they aren't a fundamental dimension. Instead, they are seen as resulting from the intersection of two other qualities.

The Five-Factor Model: The Basic Dimensions of Personality?

Despite the different starting points taken by different people, a remarkably strong consensus has begun to emerge about what traits are basic. The emerging consensus has overtones of several ideas we've already presented, but it goes beyond them. The emerging consensus is that the basic structure of personality may incorporate five superordinate factors. These are often referred to as the "five-factor model," or the "big five" (Goldberg, 1981; Wiggins, 1996).

Evidence in support of a five-factor view of personality structure has been accumulating for over fifty years (Digman, 1990). Early evidence appeared in 1949, when D. W. Fiske reported being unable to reproduce Cattell's 16-factor structure. Instead, he found a five-factor solution. Those findings sat in obscurity until the early 1960s, when Norman (1963), Borgatta (1964), and Smith (1967) all addressed the same general issue with different measures. Each reached the same conclusion: five factors provided the best account of the data.

During the decades of the 1980s and 1990s, there was an explosion of work on this topic, which has continued to the present. Diverse samples have been collected, including teachers' ratings of children (Digman & Inouye, 1986) and peer ratings (McCrae & Costa, 1987). Some studies used a kind of self-rating called a *Q-sort* (Lanning, 1994; McCrae, Costa, & Busch, 1986); others assessed frequencies with which people engage in particular kinds of actions (by self-report and observer reports [Botwin & Buss, 1989]); others conducted nonverbal assessments (Paunonen et al., 1992). Yet others tested the model against measures developed from entirely different lines of thought (Costa & McCrae, 1988a; McCrae & Costa, 1989a). Peabody and Goldberg (1989; Peabody, 1984) used scales that were chosen to be sure there were enough *common* trait words instead of terms that mean more to psychologists than to people at large. Haas (2002) has even explored the idea that proverbs capture the five factors.

Data have now been collected from many cultures and languages. The findings as a group suggest that the five factors may transcend boundaries of language and culture (e.g., Benet-Martínez & John, 1998; Church, 2001; Katigbak, Church, Guanzon-Lapeña, Carlota, & del Pilar, 2002; McCrae & Costa, 1997; McCrae et al., 1996; Paunonen et al., 1992; Saucier & Ostendorf, 1999; Somer & Goldberg, 1999; Stumpf, 1993). The cultures examined in this work are as diverse as those of Turkey (Somer & Goldberg, 1999) and the Philippines (Katigbak et al., 2002). It has even been argued that the factors (or at least some of them) apply to lower animals (Gosling, 2001)!

There have been some failures to find the five-factor pattern (e.g., Benet & Waller, 1995; Zuckerman, Kuhlman, & Camac, 1988) and some imperfections in the findings (Church & Burke, 1994; Di Blas & Forzi, 1991; Lanning, 1994). Yet the body of literature as a whole is impressive in the extent to which it fits the five-factor model (Digman, 1990; John, 1990; McCrae & Costa, 1997; McCrae & John, 1992; Ozer & Reise, 1994).

What *Are* the Five Factors?

Given the emerging consensus on the five-factor model, what comes next may surprise you. There's still a fair amount of disagreement as to exactly what the five dimensions *are* (Briggs, 1989; John, 1990; Johnson & Ostendorf, 1993; Pytlik Zillig, Hemenover, & Dienstbier, 2002; Saucier, 1992).

The disagreement has at least two sources. First, recall that naming factors can be difficult. You do it by looking at the items that load on the factor and trying to extract what underlying thread connects them. But words have several connotations, and trait terms often represent blends of factors rather than one factor per word (Hofstee, de Raad, & Goldberg, 1992). Naturally, then, there are disagreements in interpretation.

Second, exactly what a factor looks like depends on what measures are in the study. If a particular quality is left out or isn't well represented in the items, its involvement in a trait will be missed (Peabody & Goldberg, 1989). Thus, studies with slightly different measures can lead to different conclusions about the meaning of the factors, even when there's agreement that more or less the same factors have appeared.

Table 4.3 displays the five traits, using a variety of names for each. Peabody and Goldberg (1989) suggested that the big-five factors are the metaphorical equivalent of a piece of classical music in which there's a theme and a series of variations on it. That's pretty much what you see in Table 4.3. The labels listed under each factor all share a theme, but there are also variations. Some of the basis for the variation is displayed in Table 4.4, which lists examples of the descriptive terms that loaded on the five factors in one study or another.

The first factor is usually called *extraversion,* but there's a good deal of variation in what it includes (McCrae & Costa, 1987). This helps account for the different

Table 4.3

Labels used by various authors to refer to the big–five factors in personality. Labels in the rows are from (in order) Fiske (1949), Norman (1963), Borgatta (1964), Digman (1990), and Costa and McCrae (1985). The final row provides a characterization by Peabody and Goldberg (1989) of the life domain to which the trait pertains.

1	2	3	4	5
Social adaptability	Conformity	Will to achieve	Emotional control	Inquiring intellect
Surgency	Agreeableness	Conscientiousness	Emotionality	Culture
Assertiveness	Likeability	Responsibility	Emotionality	Intelligence
Extraversion	Friendly compliance	Will to achieve	Neuroticism	Intellect
Extraversion	Agreeableness	Conscientiousness	Neuroticism	Openness to experience
Power	**Love**	**Work**	**Affect**	**Intellect**

labels. Sometimes this factor seems grounded in assertiveness, an open expression of impulses. Sometimes it's based in a kind of dominance and confident assurance, sometimes a quality of happiness. Extraversion is often thought of as implying a sense of sociability (Watson, Clark, McIntyre, & Hamaker, 1992), but some argue that that's actually a by-product of other features of extraversion (Lucas, Diener, Grob, Suh, & Shao, 2000).

The second factor is most commonly called *agreeableness*. This trait is often characterized as being concerned with the maintaining of relationships. Digman and his colleagues (Digman, 1990; Digman & Inouye, 1986; Digman & Takemoto-Chock, 1981) have argued that it isn't just a quality of being warm and likeable versus being cold. Some see it as including a kind of docile compliance. It can also imply a sense of nurturance and emotional supportiveness, requiring inhibition of negative affect (Graziano & Eisenberg, 1999). Disagreeableness (the opposite pole) has an oppositional or antagonistic quality verging toward hostility (Digman, 1990). Fitting this, there's evidence that people low in agreeableness choose displays of power as a way of resolving social conflict more than people higher in agreeableness (Graziano, Jensen-Campbell, & Hair, 1996). There's also evidence that they actually *experience* more conflicts (Asendorpf & Wilpers, 1998).

The essence of the third factor is also a little hard to capture. The most commonly used label is *conscientiousness*. However, this label doesn't fully reflect its qualities of planning, persistence, and purposeful striving toward goals (Digman & Inouye, 1986). (Indeed, because the word *conscientious* itself has two shades of meaning, that word loads on both this factor and agreeableness, suggesting that conscientiousness may not be the perfect name for this factor.) Digman (1990), noting that several studies have linked this quality to educational achievement (see also Dollinger & Orf, 1991), has suggested that it be thought of as will to achieve, or simply *will*. Other suggested names include *constraint* and *responsibility*.

There's more agreement (though still not unanimity) about the meaning of the fourth factor. *Neuroticism,* or *emotionality,* is regarded by most as being what Eysenck referred to with those terms. But Digman and Takemoto-Chock (1981) wanted to call it emotional disorganization, because the items contributing to it convey more than the mere presence of emotion. What's at the heart of this factor, though, seems to be the subjective experience of anxiety.

Table 4.4

Bipolar and unipolar adjective scales reflective of the five major personality factors. Taken from Digman and Inouye (1986), McCrae and Costa (1987), Norman (1963), Peabody and Goldberg (1989).

Factor	Item	
Extraversion	Bold–timid	Gregarious
	Forceful–submissive	Outspoken
	Self-confident–unassured	Energetic
	Talkative–silent	Happy
	Spontaneous–inhibited	Seclusive (inverse)
Agreeableness	Friendly–unfriendly	Jealous (inverse)
	Warm–cold	Considerate
	Kind–unkind	Spiteful (inverse)
	Polite–rude	Touchy (inverse)
	Good-natured–irritable	Complaining (inverse)
Conscientiousness	Cautious–rash	Neat
	Serious–frivolous	Persevering
	Responsible–irresponsible	Planful
	Thorough–careless	Careful
	Hardworking–lazy	Eccentric (inverse)
Emotionality	Nervous–poised	Concerned
	Anxious–calm	Nervous
	Excitable–composed	Fearful
	Relaxed–high strung	Tense
Intellect	Imaginative–simple	Knowledgeable
	Intellectual–unreflective	Perceptive
	Polished–crude	Imaginative
	Uncurious–curious	Verbal
	Uncreative–creative	Original

The largest disagreement may be about factor five. The disagreement stems at least partly from differences in measures. Early on, Cattell measured qualities relevant to intelligence; then he stopped doing so, and started using the term *culture* to refer to the qualities that remained. The label stuck. Peabody and Goldberg (1989) point out, though, that when intelligence-related measures are reintroduced, they join with culture. They suggest the factor should more properly be labeled *intellect*. Costa and McCrae (1985) favor yet another label: *openness* to experience.

Peabody and Goldberg (1989) argued that Costa and McCrae's measure of this factor taps one aspect of intellect (the imaginative side) but misses the other side (the logical side). They said that when both sides are measured they merge, thus implying that this factor is really intellect. McCrae and Costa (1987) disagreed. They argued that intelligence just provides a basis for the broader sense of openness. The concept of openness to experience is newer to psychology than is intelligence. However, McCrae (1996) has reviewed a wide range of ways in which openness is relevant to human social experience, suggesting that it may be far more important than most people realize.

Reflections of the Five Factors

Until recently, most work on the five-factor model was aimed at the factors themselves: that is, showing that they occur in diverse cultures and using many ways of assessing them. More recently, however, some have turned to looking at how these five traits are reflected, or expressed, on the broader canvas of people's lives.

Here's a rundown of a few recent findings, starting with conscientiousness. More conscientiousness predicts avoidance of unsafe sex (Trobst, Herbst, Masters, & Costa, 2002); in a sample of prisoners it related to lower numbers of arrests (Clower & Bothwell, 2001). Being more conscientious relates to less likelihood of trying to steal someone else's romantic partner and less responsiveness to such overtures by others (Schmitt & Buss, 2001). Conscientiousness has also been linked to more responsive parenting of young children (Clark, Kochanska, & Ready, 2000), and to more use of negotiation as a conflict-resolution strategy (Jensen-Campbell & Graziano, 2001). In a study of life goals, conscientiousness related to a desire for a career, but not necessarily a high standard of living (Roberts & Robins, 2000). Interestingly enough, conscientiousness did not relate strongly to any other kinds of goals.

Conscientiousness also seems to have health implications. In a study of cancer risk, conscientiousness led to more restrictive household bans on smoking (Hampson, Andrews, Barckley, Lichtenstein, & Lee, 2000). People who are high in conscientiousness even seem to live longer, presumably because they take better care of themselves (Christensen et al., 2002; Friedman et al., 1995).

Openness to experience has been found to predict greater engagement with the existential challenges of life (Keyes, Shmotkin, & Ryff, 2002). Others found that people high in openness desire artistic expression, and devalue traditional marriage and the possibility of an easy, lazy life (Roberts & Robins, 2000). On the other hand, openness has also been found to predict more prior arrests among prisoners (Clower & Bothwell, 2001).

Several projects have focused on the idea that extraversion and agreeableness are both relevant to social situations, but can have very different effects in those situations. As Jensen-Campbell and Graziano (2001) put it, extraversion seems to relate to *having social impact,* whereas agreeableness seems to relate to *maintaining positive relations* with others.

Thus, for example, extraversion predicts greater prominence in groups such as fraternities and sororities (Anderson, John, Keltner, & Kring, 2001), whereas agreeableness does not. In a study of adolescent peer relations (Jensen-Campbell et al., 2002), extraversion and agreeableness both related to peer acceptance, but agreeableness also protected against peer victimization. This makes sense, if agreeableness is largely about maintaining good relations. Consistent with this idea, agreeableness has also been found to predict more empathy and responsiveness in parenting (Clark et al., 2000), less seeking of revenge after being harmed (McCullough & Hoyt, 2002), and greater attempts to control negative emotions (Tobin, Graziano, Vanman, & Tassinary, 2000). Agreeableness also predicts less poaching of romantic partners and less responsiveness to poaching attempts by others (Schmitt & Buss, 2001), whereas extraversion related to neither of these.

Extraversion generally is helpful socially. Extraverted men interact better with women they don't know than introverts (Berry & Miller, 2001), and extraverts have the firm handshake that conveys confidence (Chaplin, Phillips, Brown, Clanton, & Stein, 2000). But there can be a dark side to the desire for social impact. There's evidence that extraverts are less cooperative when facing a social dilemma over re-

People high in agreeableness care about maintaining positive relations with others.

sources than introverts, whereas agreeableness relates to being more cooperative (Koole, Jager, van den Berg, Vlek, & Hofstee, 2001).

Studies have also found that these two traits relate in consistent ways to personal values and life goals. Extraversion has been related to valuing achievement and stimulation, whereas agreeableness related to valuing benevolence and tradition (Roccas, Sagiv, Schwartz, & Knafo, 2002). Extraversion relates to the desires for a high-status career, political influence, an exciting lifestyle, and children; agreeableness relates to desires for goals pertaining to group welfare and harmonious family relations, and actually relates inversely to desires for wealth, political influence, and an exciting lifestyle (Roberts & Robins, 2000).

The question of how the five traits are reflected has also been asked in a second, more abstract way. This question concerns the "channels" through which traits are expressed. Most people agree, in principle, that traits can influence behavior, thoughts, and feelings. There seem to be striking differences among the five factors, though, in how they are reflected (Pytlik Zillig et al., 2002). At least, there are big differences in the content of measures of the big five.

Measures of neuroticism are almost entirely focused on affect (neuroticism is mostly about distress). In sharp contrast, measures of conscientiousness deal largely with behavior, plus a little cognition, with hardly any affect implied at all. Openness tends to be reflected mostly in cognition, though it has both behavioral and affective overtones. Measures of extraversion blend behavior and affect, but don't say much about thoughts. Agreeableness is the most balanced, with reflections in all three channels. Why are the five factors reflected in such different ways? What are the implications of the differences? These questions presently have no clear answers.

The Five-Factor Model in Relation to Other Models

The five-factor model has similarities to several other trait models. Let's consider some of those similarities. The easiest comparison is to Eysenck's theory. It's obvious from Table 4.3 that two of the big five resemble Eysenck's supertraits, extraversion and emotional stability. It's also been suggested that Eysenck's third dimension, psychoticism, is a blend of agreeableness and conscientiousness (Goldberg, 1993b; Zuckerman, Kuhlman, Joireman, Teta, & Kraft, 1993).

A second similarity to Eysenck is also noteworthy. Specifically, the five factors are superordinate traits, incorporating narrower traits. For example, Paul Costa and Robert McCrae (1985, 1992) developed a measure called the NEO Personality Inventory (NEO-PI; NEO stands for neuroticism, extraversion, and openness; agreeableness and conscientiousness were added after the name had been coined). The NEO-PI includes measures of six narrow traits for each domain of the five-factor model. The six narrow traits combine into a score for that supertrait. Thus, people using the five-factor model share with Eysenck the idea that the core traits are supertraits, which in turn are composed of more specific facet traits.

Another useful comparison is with the interpersonal circle of Wiggins and his colleagues. The basic dimensions there are dominance and love (agreeableness). If dominance were taken as roughly equivalent to the first factor of the big five, then the interpersonal circle would comprise the first two factors of the five-factor model (McCrae & Costa, 1989b; Peabody & Goldberg, 1989). Trapnell and Wiggins (1990) expanded the measure of the interpersonal circle to include additional scales, providing an even better fit to the five-factor model (see also Saucier, 1992).

This comparison with the interpersonal circle, however, also raises a question. As noted earlier (Figure 4.3), Wiggins sees extraversion as a combination of two qualities in the circle, not as a basic dimension. Whether that conflicts with the five-factor model may depend on how you define *extraversion*. Remember that there are also differences of opinion on how to think about that first factor. Is it about dominance and assertiveness, or is it about social involvement?

To summarize some of the points made in this part of the chapter, the five-factor model of personality structure has emerged as a candidate to integrate a variety of earlier models. The data make this set of broad traits look very much as though they represent universal aspects of personality (McCrae & Costa, 1997). Remember, though, that what comes out of a factor analysis depends on what goes into it. It can be dangerous to draw solid conclusions too fast. At present, however, the five-factor model seems to offer the best promise of a consensus about the dimensions of personality that trait psychology has ever seen.

Cautions and Some Further Variations

Consensus is not the same as unanimity, however. Several people have disagreed with this view for a variety of reasons (e.g., Block, 1995, 2001; Eysenck, 1992, 1993; Zuckerman, 1992). One line of dissent claims that work from the lexical approach omitted a set of words that shouldn't have been left out, words that are purely evaluative (e.g., *excellent, evil*). When these words are included, two more factors emerge: *positive valence* and *negative valence* (Almagor, Tellegen, & Waller, 1995; Benet & Waller, 1995).

Another point is that the five-factor model can be distilled further, into two dimensions (Digman, 1997). That is, using the five factors in a higher-order analysis yields two higher-order factors. The first is defined by agreeableness, conscientiousness, and emotional stability. Digman characterized it as reflecting *socialization,* because all these qualities influence whether people get along in social units. The second is defined by extraversion (surgency) and intellect (openness). Digman characterized it as reflecting *personal growth,* because these qualities influence whether people expose themselves to new things, thereby fostering growth. Block (2001) has argued that these characterizations are so broad as to be applicable to any model of personality at all, and thus have no special relevance to the five-factor model.

Others have objected that exclusive reliance on the five-factor model may cause important traits to be left out. This possibility has been viewed differently by different people. Saucier and Goldberg (1998) found evidence of several dimensions beyond the five factors, but argued that those dimensions are outside personality. Examples are height, religiousness, employment status, and attractiveness. Paunonen and Jackson (2000) looked at the same evidence and saw instead nine to ten dimensions that they thought ought to be seen as traits, albeit narrow ones. Examples are religiousness, dishonesty, seductiveness, humorousness, and conventionality. They argued further that some of these narrow traits might even coalesce to form *honesty,* which might represent a sixth supertrait (see also Ashton, Lee, & Son, 2000).

In sum, the emerging consensus is strong but not complete. There still remain a number of issues to be resolved.

Are Superordinate Traits the Best Level to Use?

There remains at least one more question to raise, even if you accept the five-factor model. As we said, this is a model of superordinate traits. Supertraits have facets. As noted earlier, Costa and McCrae's NEO-PI measures six different facets of each factor. Those who use the five-factor model sometimes point to the utility of examining patterns of traits within each factor (Costa & McCrae, 1995; Goldberg, 1993a), but this strategy is not used very often.

Is anything lost when lower-level traits are combined to form the supertraits? This is essentially what Cattell asked Eysenck when they disagreed about the meaning of second-order factors in the Cattell data (see also Briggs, 1989; H. Cattell, 1993; Funder, 1991; John, 1990). The question has now received some attention, and the evidence suggests that something is indeed lost when facet traits are merged.

Paunonen and Ashton (2001a) compared the big-five factors to specific facets scales. They were tested as predictors of forty different behaviors, measured by self-report and peer ratings. The behaviors were chosen to be of some social significance (e.g., altruistic behavior, smoking, alcohol consumption, religiosity). The evidence revealed that on a substantial number of these behaviors, facet scales added significantly to prediction after all five factors had been used as predictors. Thus, something is lost if only the big five were used. Conceptually similar findings have come from a number of other studies (Mershon & Gorsuch, 1988; Paunonen, 1998; Paunonen & Ashton, 2001b; Wolfe & Kasmer, 1988).

Better prediction from specific narrow traits comes at a cost, though. The cost is that to understand the findings you have to hold a larger number of traits in mind at once. In general terms, that's the tradeoff: using supertraits creates a picture that's more intuitive and easier to hold in mind. Using the narrower traits may often give greater accuracy.

Traits, Situations, and Interactionism

We turn now to a very different part of the trait approach. Trait psychology experienced an important controversy over a period of two decades, from about 1970 to about 1990. The ways researchers reacted to this controversy had a big impact on today's views of traits, although this impact is separate from anything we've discussed so far.

Is Behavior Actually Traitlike?

The issue that shook the foundations of trait psychology in the early 1970s is whether behavior actually shows traitlike consistency. Traits are assumed to be *stable* aspects of personality that influence behavior in a *wide range of settings*. The reason for assuming traits in the first place was to account for consistency in people's thoughts and actions across time and circumstances. Differences on a trait should predict differences in trait-related behaviors.

It was somewhat surprising, then, that trait measures and behavior often didn't correlate well (Mischel, 1968; P. E. Vernon, 1964). Walter Mischel (1968) coined the phrase **personality coefficient** to characterize the modest correlations between trait self-reports and actual behavior, which often were around .30. This correlation means that the trait accounts for less than 10 percent of the variation in the behavior, with the remaining 90 percent unaccounted for. Later estimates ranged a little higher (around .40). Even so, the proportion of variance accounted for isn't so high.

What, then, are we to think about traits? If traits don't predict people's actions, then why should the trait concept be considered useful? (Indeed, some people went so far as to ask why the concept of *personality* should be considered useful.)

Situationism

An extreme form of the attack on traits was called **situationism.** This is the idea that situational variables determine behavior, not personality. This view was held by some social psychologists, who traditionally emphasize the impact of the social environment rather than personality as a cause of actions. This view assumed that correlations between traits and behavior were low because situational variables overwhelmed the effect of personality. This, in fact, turned out to be quite wrong.

Funder and Ozer (1983) pointed out that effects of situations and effects of traits usually are reported with different statistics. This makes it hard to compare them. Funder and Ozer returned to several famous studies of the impact of situations on behavior and converted the original statistics to correlations. To the astonishment of many, these correlations were *about the same size* as the personality coefficients that had been criticized so sharply.

Low Reliability in Measuring Behavior

Well, if situations are not overwhelming traits, what's going on? Epstein (1979, 1980) took the position that the apparent problem is really only an issue of measurement. Measurement error can be large when something is measured only once. That's why personality scales use more than one item, to increase reliability (Chapter 3). But people don't think about this issue as fully when they measure behavior. A single measurement of a person's action is, in effect, a one-item test. Maybe correlations are poor because there's so much error in the one-item test.

Epstein (1979) argued that correlations between trait measures and behavior would go up if the behavior were measured more than once and the measures were combined, a process called **aggregation.** To test this, he had students complete trait scales, then keep detailed records of relevant feelings and behaviors for two weeks. The feelings and actions varied a lot from day to day. When they were aggregated over a longer period, however, differences between people became quite stable. More important, the aggregated indices (but not the separate reports) related closely to the traits measured earlier. Similar findings have been reported by others (Cheek, 1982; Rushton, Brainerd, & Pressley, 1983).

There's a good deal of stability in behavior, then, once it's aggregated across measurements. This idea has not always been well received, though (Mischel & Peake, 1982). When people think of consistency, they usually are thinking of consistency across day-to-day events. If traits really do have a big influence on behavior, you shouldn't have to condense a week's events to be able to see it (see also Box 4.2).

BOX 4.2

HOW STABLE IS PERSONALITY OVER *LONG* PERIODS OF TIME?

Discussions of consistency in personality often focus on fairly short periods or across a few situations. However, the trait concept also implies stability over much longer periods. As we consider consistency, we should also ask what evidence exists that people's personalities are the same years later as they used to be.

Several projects on this issue are noteworthy. Helson and Moane (1987) described women who were first studied as college seniors, then at age twenty-seven, and again at age forty-three. During each span, the trait scales showed high test-retest correlations. The women did change over the years as a group, becoming more dominant and independent from age twenty-seven to forty-three. Assessment at age fifty-two (Wink & Helson, 1993) found that the change toward more competence and self-confidence continued over the next nine years as well (see also Agronick & Duncan, 1998). There was also evidence that women with the most change were those who'd begun families or had career development during this period—activities that changed role demands, which changed how the women saw themselves.

Several recent studies investigated how people change and stay the same, in moving from adolescence to young adulthood. Robins, Fraley, Roberts, and Trzesniewski (2001) examined personality reports across the college years and found some change in mean levels, but large correlations over time. Similarly, Roberts, Caspi, and Moffitt (2001) found overall changes from ages eighteen to twenty-six that were consistent with a group shift toward greater maturity. For the most part, though, correlations of traits across time were quite strong.

One interesting project focused on two specific qualities of childhood personality—shyness and temper—and how they predict adult behavior (Caspi, Elder, & Bem, 1987, 1988). This study started with mothers of eight- to ten-year-old children describing what the children were like. The children themselves were interviewed when they were thirty and forty, along with their spouses and their own children. The study found that boys with frequent temper tantrums in childhood grew up to be ill-tempered men. Girls with frequent tantrums didn't seem that way when interviewed as adults, but their *families* saw them as ill-tempered mothers. Effects of childhood shyness also occurred later on. Shy boys married late and were slow to establish stable careers. Shy girls weren't slower to marry but they were more likely to follow a conventional pattern of family and homemaking than were less-shy girls.

On the whole, research seems to confirm two ideas. They may seem at first glance to be contradictory, but they really aren't. First, people change as they age. For example, they become more conscientious and more agreeable (Helson, Kwan, John, & Jones, 2002). Second, there is a great deal of rank-order stability within any given cohort over long periods of time. Even as the cohort may become (for example) more conscientious as they all grow older and wiser, the ones who were most conscientious at eighteen are still the most conscientious at thirty, and at sixty. Indeed, a review of the evidence from 152 longitudinal studies found that correlations of personality grow increasingly strong from college, through mid-adulthood, to later adulthood (Roberts & Del Vecchio, 2000; see also Costa & McCrae, 1988b, 1989; McCrae, 1993). This kind of consistency is one more reason to believe that traits are real.

Interactionism

Another approach to the inconsistency between traits and actions is called **interactionism** (e.g., Ekehammer, 1974; Endler & Magnusson, 1976; Magnusson & Endler, 1977; Ozer, 1986; Pervin, 1985). Interactionism is the idea that traits and situations interact to influence behavior. Neither the setting alone nor the person alone provides a complete account.

The term *interactionism* is tied in part to an "analysis of variance" understanding of how two variables (or in this case, two classes of variables) influence an outcome. To make this clear, we return to an idea from Chapter 2. We described there how experimental personality research often combines two variables as factors in a single study. We now state that point again, in terms of persons and situations.

When a situation and a trait are examined in the same study, there are three systematic sources of influence on behavior. Sometimes variations in the *situation* have an effect on all persons—for example, stressful situations may induce depression. Sometimes variations on a *trait* have an effect in all situations—for example, people who are susceptible to depression may be generally more depressed than people who are less susceptible. It's also possible, however, for the situation and trait to *interact* (Figure 4.4).

An interaction means that variations in situation affect some people in one way and others in a different way. For example, stress may cause an increase in depression among people who are prone to depression but not among other people. This interaction may occur in addition to one or both of the overall effects, or it may occur *instead of* them, thereby creating a picture of weak overall effects for both the trait and the situation.

In this "analysis of variance" view, situations and dispositions can interact in several ways to determine behavior. Perhaps most obvious (the case shown in Figure 4.4) is that a situation may influence one kind of person but not others. Sometimes a situational variable induces one behavior in one person and a *different* behavior in another person. For example, a stressful situation may cause extraverts to seek out others and introverts to withdraw from others.

Here's another way to describe such interactions, which creates a different feel for what the interaction is: Some situations permit easy expression of personality. Other situations force behavior into channels, thus preventing expression of personality (Monson, Hesley, & Chernick, 1982; Schutte, Kenrick, & Sadalla, 1985). The first set are called *weak* situations, the second set are called *strong* situations (Mischel,

Figure 4.4

Sometimes there is an interaction between a situation and a trait variable, such that variations in the situation affect some people but not others. This particular interaction is one that has, in fact, been hypothesized by Abramson, Seligman, and Teasdale (1978). The type of interaction displayed here is only one type of potential interaction between people and situations (see text).

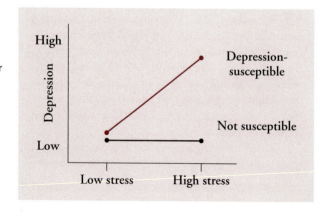

Some situations act to constrain behavior and hide individual differences. Other situations allow personality free expression.

1977). As an example, the lawns of a college campus on a Sunday afternoon are a weak situation. Individual differences can be expressed easily; in fact, the situation seems to invite it. An army boot camp is a strong situation. It dampens any expression of individual differences.

Individual Differences in Consistency

Apparently dispositions can also be strong and weak, in the same sense. That is, some people overwhelm the situations they're in and thus are very consistent. Other people let situational influences guide them and thus are less consistent.

Some of the evidence pertains to a personality quality called self-monitoring (Snyder, 1974, 1987). People high in self-monitoring like to fit smoothly into situations they encounter. They look to others for cues about what actions are appropriate, and they bend to the needs of the situation. People low in self-monitoring behave the way they think they *are,* no matter the situation. It follows that high self-monitors should be less consistent from one situation to another than low self-monitors. This turns out to be true (see Snyder, 1987).

There is also evidence that people vary in consistency on *specific* traits. Bem and Allen (1974) found that people who saw themselves as being inconsistent on a trait acted in ways that didn't relate well to their trait self-reports. Among those who reported being consistent, however, the self-reports predicted their actions quite well. Similar results have been reported by others (Kenrick & Stringfield, 1980; Woodruffe, 1985; Zuckerman et al., 1989; Zuckerman, Koestner, et al., 1988).

Beyond Analysis of Variance in Interactionism

The body of thought known as interactionism also has further aspects. The analysis of variance model derives from lab research, a context in which researchers put people into identical situations. It tends to imply that people outside the lab also enter identical situations. This, of course, is wrong—a point made by a number of researchers (e.g., D. M. Buss, 1984; Emmons & Diener, 1986; Emmons, Diener, & Larsen, 1986; Magnus, Diener, Fujita, & Pavot, 1993; Plomin, DeFries, & Loehlin, 1977; Scarr & McCartney, 1983; Snyder & Gangestad, 1982). In life outside the lab (and rarely, but occasionally, even in the lab), people exercise considerable choice over which environments they enter.

Some people choose to go to church, others choose not to. Some people choose to go to basketball games, some to rock concerts, some to country meadows. By exercising choice over the settings they enter, people thereby influence the behaviors they engage in. Indeed, there's even evidence that people choose their *marriage partners* partly by whether the partner lets them be who they are (Caspi & Herbener, 1990). The choices that people make about what situations to enter depend partly on personality differences (Brandstätter, 1983; Emmons & Diener, 1986; Emmons et al., 1986).

Another way persons and situations interact is that people differ in the kinds of responses they elicit from others (Scarr & McCartney, 1983). Some people naturally bring a smile to your face, others can make you frown just by entering the room. Introverts tend to steer conversations in one direction, extraverts in another (Thorne, 1987). Indeed, people actively manipulate each other, using such tactics as charm, coercion, and silence (Buss, Gomes, Higgins, & Lauterbach, 1987). All these effects serve to change the situation, so that *the situation is actually different for one person than it is for another.* This reciprocal influence is another way persons and situations interact.

People exercise choice over the settings they enter, which influences the behaviors they engage in. Some people choose to go to football games, other people do not.

Was the Problem Ever Really as Bad as it Seemed?

Attempts to understand weak links from trait to behavior have provided a wealth of information about how they relate. We should note, however, that doubt has arisen that the weakness of the link was actually as bad a problem as it seemed to be.

After Mischel (1968) said that personality correlated with behavior around .30, others pointed out that the studies leading to that conclusion weren't the best of studies (Block, 1977; Hogan, DeSoto, & Solano, 1977). There seems to have been some truth to this argument. More recent studies, more carefully designed (e.g., Conley, 1985; Deluty, 1985; Funder & Block, 1989; Funder & Colvin, 1991; Moskowitz, 1994; Woodruffe, 1985), have found much stronger relationships than those Mischel had summarized.

There also turn out to be statistical reasons why a correlation of .30 isn't really so bad. Many actions are influenced by more than one trait. For example, when you get to a party where you don't know anyone, what you'll do next will depend on how extraverted you are, but it will also depend on how anxiety prone you are. As it happens, whenever a behavior is influenced by several traits at once, the *mere fact of multiple influence* puts limits on how strong a correlation can be for any single trait (Ahadi & Diener, 1989). This limit looks, in fact, very nearly the same as the much maligned personality coefficient.

Maybe the core problem really wasn't ever as bad as it seemed to be in 1968. But the work addressing it has been very informative about how behavior emerges. Indeed, this work has led many people to hold a more elaborate view of the trait construct than they might otherwise hold. We consider this view next.

Interactionism Becomes a New View of Traits: Context-Dependent Expression of Personality

Psychologists put a lot of effort into developing the ideas known collectively as interactionism. Nonpsychologists, however, seem naturally to approach traits with what seems an interactionist mentality. That is, people seem to recognize intuitively that whether a trait influences behavior varies from setting to setting. A given trait shouldn't be expected to operate all the time—only in situations to which it's relevant.

This is reflected in the fact that people often use verbal "hedges" in discussing personality (Wright & Mischel, 1988). A hedge (in this context) means a word or phrase that limits a trait's applicability. As examples, you might describe someone as "shy *with strangers*" or "aggressive *when teased*." The ultimate hedge for traits is the word *sometimes*. Use of a hedge implies you think the trait-based behaviors occur only in particular kinds of situations (see also Shoda, Mischel, & Wright, 1989).

Such evidence, along with the insights of interactionism more generally, led Mischel and Shoda (1995) to a more elaborated analysis of how traits influence behavior (see also Cervone, 1997; Mischel, Shoda, & Mendoza-Denton, 2002). They argued that traits are not freestanding tendencies to act, but patterns of linkages between situation and action. Given situation *x*, action *y* is likely. A key implication of this idea is that the action shouldn't be expected to occur all the time, because the situation that brings it out isn't always present. Thus, a person's behavior may look inconsistent across situations.

Another key point in this theory is that the pattern of linkage between situation and behavior is different from one person to another. This is the source of individuality, indeed uniqueness: the pattern of situation–behavior links the person has established over time and experience. Even if two people tend toward the same kind of behavior, the situations that elicit that behavior may differ from one person to the other. If so, these two people will act differently from each other in many situations, even though they have the same trait. This, in fact, may be a way in which idiographic traits can exist. Each person's unique pattern of links from situation to action creates a trait that is just a little different from that of any other person.

We noted earlier that aggregating behavior across time creates better correspondence between traits and behavior (Epstein, 1979, 1980). The error of measurement is reduced when the acts are aggregated. Yet many continued to wonder about the *source* of that short-term measurement error. Mischel and Shoda (1995) held that the error isn't random. It comes from the fact that the behavior is context-dependent. The behavior emerges only when you encounter a relevant situation. The context may not be there every day, but if you aggregate over a long enough period it will show up eventually, and the trait-related behavior will occur.

The idea that traits represent patterns of situation–action linkages opens other possibilities as well. For example, imagine a person who is mostly an introvert, but occasionally acts in ways befitting an extravert—for example, by becoming talkative. From the perspective of the linkage model, this would simply mean that there are classes of situations (perhaps infrequent in their occurrence) that link to those actions for this person. From this way of thinking, there would be no contradiction in the idea that a person can display qualities from one end of a trait dimension in one situation and qualities from the opposite end of the dimension in another.

Considerable support for this argument has been reported by Fleeson (2001). Indeed, he found that most people regularly experience the full range of variability on a trait dimension, even while they differ in behaviors pertaining to that trait they do most often (Figure 4.5). More recent research (Fleeson, Malanos, & Achille, in press) shows that the positive emotions that are tied to extraversion also vary from hour to hour, right along with the degree of extraverted behavior the person is engaged in.

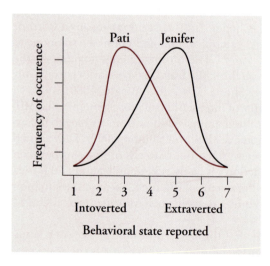

Figure 4.5

Traits as situation-linked frequency distributions of states. People occasionally act extraverted, even if they are essentially introverts (such as Pati); people occasionally act introverted, even if they are essentially extraverts (such as Jenifer). The person's generalized trait is reflected in the fact that particular sorts of behavioral states are most frequent (after Fleeson, 2001).

The linkage viewpoint seems to deal well with some problems people have had in thinking about traits. It doesn't distort the trait concept, but it clearly adds something to the concept as it was discussed in the first part of this chapter. This theory has other elements that are considered in Chapter 16. For now, the point is that the impact of traits seems to be context-dependent. This conclusion is very much of a piece with an interactionist view of personality.

Fitting the Pieces Together: Views of Traits and Behavior

Let's pull these ideas together with what came earlier. If you had read only the first half of this chapter, you might have been tempted to assume that most trait theorists hold the view in Figure 4.6, panel A or B, in which traits have a relatively *constant* influence on behavior. People who discuss the five-factor model tend not to talk much about how traits and situations interact. It can be easy to infer from their statements that that's what they are assuming.

But traits don't really work that way. Research described in the previous sections makes that clear. Rather, traits sometimes influence behavior a lot, and sometimes not at all. Whether the trait matters depends on the situation (Figure 4.6, C). This dynamic approach to the role of traits in the constantly varying social environment recognizes complexities in the creation of behavior.

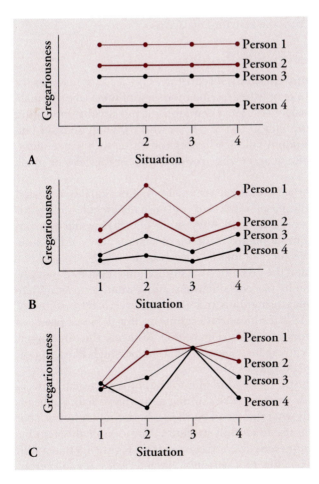

Figure 4.6

Three models of the effects of traits on behavior (portrayed for the trait of gregariousness). (A) A naive model, in which people are assumed to display their traits at a relatively constant level, no matter what situation they're in (what Magnusson & Endler, 1977, called absolute consistency). (B) A model in which situations influence the *overall* levels at which the trait is displayed, but people retain the same ordering (relative consistency). (C) An interactionist model, in which some situations (2 and 4) permit or even elicit individual differences, whereas others (1 and 3) don't do so.

This picture is certainly more compelling than the simple ones. Interestingly enough, the core idea isn't all that new. Some trait theorists of earlier years said much the same thing. They didn't say it in as much detail as it's being said today, however.

As early as 1937 Gordon Allport wrote that "traits are often aroused in one situation and not in another" (p. 331). His conception of a trait explicitly included the assumption that the trait doesn't influence all behaviors and that it may not influence a given category of behavior at all times (see Zuroff, 1986). Rather, the effect of the trait depends on whether it's evoked in that situation. Allport even believed that people have *contradictory* traits. The fact that the different traits are aroused by different situations keeps this from being a problem (as Fleeson, 2001, also found). Allport also anticipated another contemporary theme when he pointed out that people choose the situations they enter and actively change the situations they're in (Zuroff, 1986). Thus, the essence of the ideas that would become known as interactionism has roots that go back a long way.

Assessment

More than is true of most viewpoints on personality, the trait approach focuses a great deal on the process of assessment. Indeed, the first part of this chapter incorporated discussion of how various theorists developed assessment instruments. In this section we consider briefly how the instruments are used.

Comparing Individuals: Personality Profiles

The trait approach makes extensive use of self-report inventories as an assessment technique. These self-reports ask people to describe their view of themselves by making ratings of one kind or another. The most common ratings involve indicating whether a descriptive adjective applies to you or not, or where on a dimension (anchored by opposing adjectives) you'd fall, or whether you agree with a statement. The ratings may be made as yes–no or agree–disagree decisions, or they may be made on multipoint scales.

Recall that traits are thought of as fundamental qualities of personality, reflected in diverse behaviors. For this reason, self-reports of traits usually include ratings for several reflections of each trait being measured. A test using adjectives would have several adjectives for each trait; a questionnaire made up of statements would include statements suggesting diverse ways the trait might be expressed.

Regardless of the exact form of the inventory, the nomothetic version of trait psychology assumes that anyone can be placed somewhere along whatever trait dimensions are assessed. Inventories measuring these traits are used to create "profiles" of individuals. A personality profile is a summary description of a person's place on each trait dimension the inventory measures (Figure 4.7). Knowing the dimensions and the person's place on each can create a sense of what the person is like and how the person is likely to behave in a variety of situations.

The profile in Figure 4.7 illustrates the kind of information a personality inventory gives. At first glance, a profile can seem like nothing more than a string of beads (Allport, 1961, said that's exactly what they are). Perhaps a better metaphor is a bar code, like the ones supermarkets use to identify products. Nomothetic theorists believe that the profile is where uniqueness lies. You can see from Figure 4.7 that a shift on any single trait changes the balance of a person's characteristics. It can thereby change how the person will act in various settings and how the person will seem to

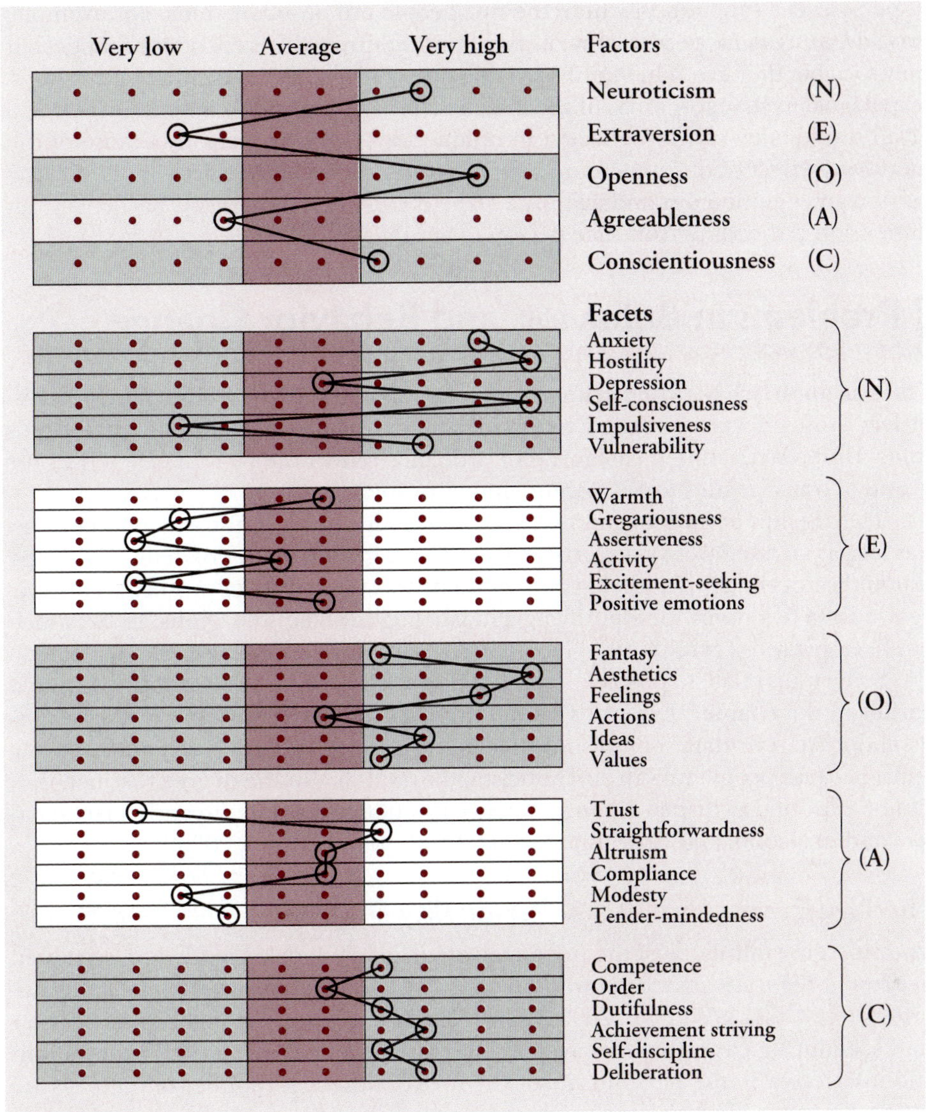

	Very low	Average	Very high	Factors	

Figure 4.7

someone else. Since everyone has a unique combination of trait levels, everyone is different from everyone else.

Further, most trait theorists believe traits can *interact* with one another. To put it differently, how a given level of a specific trait is expressed may differ from person to person, as a function of where the two people are on other traits. For example, two adventuresome people may display their boldness differently as a function of how sociable they are. The highly sociable one may engage in exciting and risky interpersonal exchanges, whereas the less sociable one may climb mountains. Thus, a given trait quality can be reflected in unique ways for each person because of the modifying effect of differences on *other* traits (recall the earlier discussion of extraversion and emotionality and Table 4.2). This is true even though any particular trait dimension is the same from one person to another.

Problems in Behavior, and Behavior Change

The trait approach was the starting point for some of the earliest efforts to assess disorder. Those efforts were based on the idea that problems directly reflect a person's traits. Differences among categories of problems reflect the fact that each trait (or group of traits) relates to a different kind of problem.

The attempt to understand psychopathology from this trait-based point of view was largely an attempt to categorize it. Categorizing was a matter of determining the trait indicators in people's behavior that relate to a given class of problem. This process led to a taxonomy for identifying and labeling problems (Wiggins, 1973), which has been revised several times.

Some traits relate to problems because the trait itself *defines* abnormality. As noted earlier in the chapter, Eysenck's model includes a dimension termed *psychoticism*. Psychoticism is virtually a predisposition toward certain kinds of psychological problems. Because people vary in psychoticism, they will vary in the degree to which they can be expected to display those problems. Psychoticism relates to antisocial behaviors and to alcohol and drug abuse (Sher, Bartholow, & Wood, 2000).

The Five-Factor Model and Personality Disorders

The emerging influence of the five-factor model of personality has led to a renewed interest in the traits associated with one particular class of disorder: personality disorders (see Costa & Widiger, 2002; Watson & Clark, 1994). Personality disorders are stable, enduring patterns of behavior that deviate from normal cultural expectations and interfere with the person's life or the lives of others. A number of theorists are interested in whether personality disorders are essentially rigid and extreme manifestations of several of the big-five traits (see Larstone, Jang, Livesley, Vernon, & Wolf, 2002; Widiger, Trull, Clarkin, Sanderson, & Costa, 2002).

Recent research indicates this might be the case. For example, Connor and Dyce (2001) reported finding that all personality disorders are represented within the five-factor model. Reynolds and Clark (2001) similarly found that the big five did a good job of representing personality disorder, and that the facet scales (the narrow scales within the five domains) did even better. An edited volume containing diverse reviews of relevant evidence, and theoretical statements on the relation between the big five and the personality disorders has recently appeared in a second edition (Costa & Widiger, 2002). This area of work is likely to continue to be an important focus for further exploration in future years.

Interactionism in Behavior Problems

As described earlier in the chapter, evidence of a poor relationship between traits and actions led to development of a position termed *interactionism*. The logic of interac-

Even a person prone to experiencing fear will not experience fear unless a fear-producing situation is encountered.

tionism is useful not just for understanding normal behavior, but also for understanding problems.

A basic idea of interactionism is that individual differences are important in some situations but not in others. As applied to problems, the idea takes on slightly different connotations. The connotations are easiest to understand if you think of a trait as a *vulnerability* or *susceptibility* to a problem. Saying a person is susceptible to a problem doesn't mean that the person *has* the problem. It means the problem will occur more easily for this person than for someone else. To put it in terms of interactionism, there are situations in which the susceptibility matters and others in which it doesn't (recall Figure 4.4).

Situations in which the susceptibility matters usually are those in which the person is under a lot of stress. Therefore, this approach to problems is called a **diathesis-stress model.** (The word *diathesis* means a predisposition or susceptibility.) In this model, an interaction is required between the diathesis and a stress before the problem will develop (Meehl, 1962). Diathesis-stress models have been quite common in thinking about psychological problems.

Behavior Change

What of the process of therapeutic behavior change? The trait approach is inherently a little pessimistic about change. If traits define a person's personality, how much can problems be resolved without changing the person's personality? Traits are stable. Any change that therapy produces is likely to be in how traits are displayed, rather than in the traits themselves.

On the other hand, the interactionist approach also has an implication regarding this issue. If problems arise through an interaction between susceptibilities and difficult situations, it should be helpful for the susceptible person to avoid entering situations in which the relevant stresses are likely to occur. Avoiding such situations should prevent the problems from arising.

This, of course, is something that people often do on their own. As we said earlier in the chapter, people exercise some degree of control over the situations they choose to enter. Just as some people choose to go to church and some do not, some people choose to avoid situations in which their vulnerabilities place them at risk. Shy people may avoid singles bars. People with short tempers may try to avoid arguments. Avoidance as a strategy isn't always possible. Yet, if people learn which stressors they can and cannot handle, this knowledge should make them more effective in managing their lives.

Trait Psychology: Problems and Prospects

The trait view is in many respects the most basic approach to personality of all. The very concepts of type and trait arose literally thousands of years ago, to account for consistency in behavior across time and circumstances. The concepts have been elaborated and embellished over the years, but in some ways their core remains the same.

Although the trait view on personality is the most basic, some people find it unsatisfying. It's been criticized on several grounds in recent years (for opinions on both sides, see Pervin, 1994, and the commentaries that follow it). One problem is that trait theories have had extraordinarily little to say about how personality works (Block, 1995) or how it influences behavior, how the person gets from trait to action (Pervin, 1994). A clear exception to this characterization is the more recent work of Mischel and Shoda (1995), their colleagues, and others pursuing their ideas. This work is not at all typical of the trait approach of years past, but it may represent the trait approach of the future.

To put it differently, until the recent past, the trait approach has had little to say about intrapersonal functioning. This has resulted in a picture of personality that feels static and empty. McAdams (1992) called trait psychology the "psychology of the stranger," because it provides information that would be important if you knew nothing about a person, but it doesn't portray the dynamic aspects of personality. Labeling a person as friendly, or sociable, or dominant provides a name for what you see. But it doesn't tell you anything about how or why the person acts that way. This is a major criticism of the trait concept.

The idea that the trait viewpoint has had little to say about the process side of personality is often made jointly with a second, related criticism. This second criticism is that trait theories sometimes resort to circular explanation in trying to deal with causality. As an example, imagine a woman who acts in a dominant manner—not just occasionally, but often; not just in one situation, or with one set of people, but in many situations, with whoever else is around. You might conclude from this that she has a high level of the trait of dominance.

But that can be a hollow conclusion. Ask yourself two questions and think about your natural responses. Question: Why does she behave that way? (Answer: Because she's dominant.) Question: How do you know she's dominant? (Answer: Because she behaves that way.) The problem here is that the information about behavior is being used to infer the existence of a trait, which is being used in turn to explain the behavior. This is called circular reasoning, because it can go around and around in an endless circle. There's no point here at which the presumed trait is used to predict anything but the evidence that was used to presume it initially. The circularity can be broken if the trait is used to predict something new, and sometimes trait theorists do that. However, this view on personality is more vulnerable than most to the criticism of circularity.

A final problem that was raised in years past concerns the issue of consistency. As noted earlier, the concepts of trait psychology were developed to account for stability in behavior across time and situations. The discovery that people's behavior sometimes fails to display this consistency created a crisis for trait theorists. There have been many creative and thoughtful responses to this discovery, however. Thus, this problem served as a basis for evolution in this viewpoint. There has been a growing awareness among trait theorists that to view traits as having a constant impact on behavior is too simple. This view is being replaced by approaches in which situational forces and the interaction between situations and dispositions are taken into account. These insights hold further promise for the possibility of linking the trait approach to other views that have a more prominent place for process.

A final point in support of the future of the trait approach is this: no matter how hard various people have tried over the years to dispense with the use of traits as explanatory mechanisms, the trait concept has retained an active place in the working vocabulary of the personality psychologist. The long history of these concepts attests to their hardiness. Somehow it appears as though the personality psychologist needs them (A. H. Buss, 1989). The fact that they've endured the test of time seems to imply a fundamental correctness that is difficult to deny.

SUMMARY

The trait and type approach begins with the assumption that personality consists of stable inner qualities, which are reflected in behavior. Types are discontinuous categories of personalities, with each person falling into one category or another. This concept has largely, though not entirely, disappeared from use. Traits are continuous dimensions of variability, along which any person can be placed. Most trait approaches are nomothetic, emphasizing how people differ but assuming that the trait dimensions are the same for everyone. The idiographic approach emphasizes persons' uniqueness and treats some dimensions as unique to specific persons.

Factor analysis is a tool used by many trait psychologists. Factor analysis tells what items (or ratings, etc.) go together. Further, the more variability in ratings a factor accounts for, the more important the factor. Factor analysis also lets you tell which observations do and don't reflect a factor well, thus helping refine scales.

An important question in trait psychology is what traits are basic and important. Cattell, who believed we must let reality tell us the structure of personality, saw personality as having sixteen primary dimensions. Eysenck, who believed we must start with a theory, saw two major factors as critically important in personality: extraversion and emotional stability. Other views have also been developed, including one that emphasizes traits that are relevant to social interaction (the interpersonal circle).

Attention is increasingly being given to the idea that there are five major factors in personality. Evidence to that effect is strong, and a relatively successful attempt has also been made to fit these five factors to the models of personality structure already mentioned. There is disagreement about the precise nature of the five factors, but commonly used labels for them are extraversion, agreeableness, conscientiousness, emotionality, and openness. Recent research has examined how these traits relate to behaviors and experiences in people's lives.

A question about the usefulness of the trait concept was raised by the finding that people's behavior often wasn't well predicted from trait self-reports. This led some to question whether traits actually influence behavior. Situationism, the idea that behavior is controlled by situational influences instead of dispositions, was an inadequate alternative. Trait differences in behavior do seem to become consistent over time if measures are aggregated. Interactionism holds that personality and situations interact in several ways to determine behavior. For example, some situations permit or even elicit individual differences, whereas other situations don't. People also choose which situations to enter, and then they influence the nature of situations by their own actions. Indeed, people also vary in how consistent they are. Those who know they're inconsistent don't act consistently, those who say they are consistent act more consistently.

The idea that the influence of traits on behavior is dependent on situations has been expanded into a broader view of personality structure, in which traits are individualized linkages between situations and actions. This view accounts for stability over time within the person as well as for variability across situations. This view of the nature of traits provides a sense of process for trait models.

Personality assessment from the viewpoint of trait psychology is a matter of developing a personality profile of the person being assessed—a description of where the person falls on all the dimensions being measured by the inventory. To these psychologists, the profile holds the key to understanding the person's uniqueness.

Regarding problems in behavior, trait theorists say that some problems result from having a trait that is intrinsically problematic, such as psychoticism. Other kinds of problems stem from having an extreme position on some trait dimension. Interest in the relation between personality disorder and the five-factor model is growing. The interactionist position suggests the following possibility (termed a *diathesis-stress model*): certain dispositions may create a susceptibility to some kind of problem, but the problem occurs only under certain conditions, usually involving stress. Therapeutic behavior change, from the trait perspective, may mean changing how a trait is reflected in behavior, because a person's traits are not easily altered. Alternatively, it may mean avoiding situations in which the problem behavior arises.

GLOSSARY

Aggregation The process of combining a variable across several measurements.

Diathesis-stress model Theory holding that a vulnerability plus stress creates problems in behavior.

Extravert A person who prefers social and outgoing activities.

Factor A dimension that underlies a set of interrelated ratings.

Factor analysis A statistical procedure used to find basic dimensions underlying a set of measures.

Factor loading A correlation between a single measure and the factor to which it is being related.

Idiographic Pertaining to an approach that focuses on an individual person's uniqueness.

Interactionism The idea that situations and personality interact to determine behavior.

Interpersonal circle Personality patterns deriving from varying levels of dominance and love.

Introvert A person who prefers solitary activities.

Lexical criterion An index of the importance of a trait from the number of words that refer to it.

Nomothetic Pertaining to an approach that focuses on norms and on variations among persons.

Personality coefficient A stereotypic correlation between personality and behavior of about .30.

Second-order factor A factor that emerges from a factor analysis performed on a set of previously found factors.

Situationism The idea that situations are the primary determinants of behavior.

Traits The dimensions of personality on which people vary.

Types Distinct and discontinuous categories of persons.

Needs and Motives

5

■ **Basic Theoretical Elements**

Needs
Motives
Press

■ **Needs, Motives, and Personality**

Motivational States and Motive Dispositions
Murray's System of Needs
Measuring Motives: The Thematic
   Apperception Test

■ **Individual Differences
in Specific Needs**

Need for Achievement
Divergent Motives Underlying
   Achievement Behavior
Need for Power
Need for Affiliation
Need for Intimacy
Patterned Needs: Inhibited Power Motive

■ **Further Determinants of Behavior**

Incentive Value
Expectancy and Skill

■ **The Methods of Personology**

■ **Assessment**

Self-Reports and the TAT May Not
   Measure the Same Thing
Motives and the Five-Factor Model
Traits and Motives as Distinct

■ **Problems in Behavior,
and Behavior Change**

The Need for Power and Alcohol Abuse
Focusing On and Changing Motivation

■ **Need and Motive Theories:
Problems and Prospects**

SUMMARY

■ I'm in the pre-med program here, and I really want to get into a good medical school. The courses aren't that easy for me, so I have to study more than some people. I can't even take time off on weekends because I'm taking an extra heavy load. I don't mind, though, because I'm really motivated to go to med school, and that makes it worth the effort.

■ I've been going with my boyfriend for over two years now. I care for him a lot, really I do. But lately I've been wondering if this is really the right relationship for me. It's hard to describe what's wrong. It's not anything about *him,* exactly, but it's like the relationship isn't meeting my needs. I don't know how else to put it.

T hink for a moment about the major concerns of your life. One concern that stands out in the minds of many college students is what to do after graduation. Some people have ambitions they're already pursuing full speed (as the pre-med student quoted above). Others know some qualities they want their work to have, but they aren't sure exactly what the work will be. To some people, in contrast, what they'll do doesn't seem a big deal one way or another.

Another topic that may occupy a place in your thoughts is relationships. Some college-age people are thinking about marriage and trying to decide whether the person they're with is the right one. Some don't have this kind of relationship but wish they did. For some people, this is the most demanding issue of their lives. For others, it matters less.

These sets of concerns are probably familiar to you. Work and love as aspects of existence are part of everyone's life. They aren't everything, of course, and some people have other things on their mind. Some are trying to find order and meaning in life's experiences. Some seek truth, some seek beauty. For others, what really matters isn't truth *or* beauty but having the laundry done, the kitchen clean, or new high-performance tires on their SUV.

Look at the concerns we've touched on and you'll see a lot of diversity. Despite the diversity, these concerns (and others) have something in common. They imply the existence of needs and motives behind people's thoughts and actions. Think about how people describe their preoccupations. I *need* to find a lover. I *need* to have a direction for my future. I *want* to do well in school. I *need* to find a sense of purpose in life. I *want* to get caught up on my chores. I *need* to get an A on this test. And there are individual differences. For any aspect of life you might imagine, some people feel a deep need within it, others don't.

If needs and motives influence people's thoughts and actions this way, they must be important. It might even be argued that they define who a person is. This idea forms the basis for the approach to personality examined in this chapter.

Basic Theoretical Elements

Needs

The fundamental principle of this approach is the idea that human behavior is best understood as a reflection of needs. A **need** is an internal state that's less than satisfactory, a lack of something that's necessary for well-being. Henry Murray (1938), who began this approach to personality (see Box 5.1), defined a need as an internal directional force that determines how people seek out or respond to objects or situations in the environment.

Some needs are based in our biological nature (needs for food, water, air, sex, and pain avoidance). Murray called them **primary needs.** Others, such as the need for power and the need for achievement, either *derive* from biological needs or are inherent in our *psychological* makeup. Murray called them **secondary needs,** or **psychogenic needs.**

BOX 5.1

THE THEORIST AND THE THEORY
Henry Murray and Human Motives

The history of Henry Murray, the father of the motive view of personality, contains tantalizing suggestions about how his theory drew on his life's experiences, but clear links are harder to make. Murray was born into a wealthy family in New York in 1893. He got on well with his father but had a poor relationship with his mother. He reports feeling that his mother gave him less attention than his sister and brother. The emotional separation he felt created a deep-seated need to stand on his own. This became central to his personality. It's tempting to speculate that this experience led Murray to be especially aware of social needs, and may have led his thinking toward the idea that such needs are the underlying determinants of personality.

Murray's education was varied. Oddly enough, however, none of it was in psychology (he disliked his only psychology course). He majored in history, but shifted to biomedical studies. He finished medical school, got a master's degree in biology, did an internship in surgery, and then a Ph.D. in biochemistry. A theme past college was his focus on the biology of human functioning. This biological emphasis is also apparent in Murray's thinking about personality. As noted elsewhere, the ideas behind his theory are most easily illustrated by biological motives. Indeed, Murray believed that even psychological motives have biological roots.

Murray's medical background also influenced his approach to research. The program he led at the Harvard Psychological Clinic was very much a team approach. This seems to reflect the view that personality is best assessed by a team of specialists working together, much as a team of physicians collaborates on diagnosing patients.

A turning point in Murray's life occurred seven years into his marriage, when he fell in love with Christiana Morgan. This was a turning point in at least two ways. First, Murray was faced with a serious conflict. He didn't want to leave his wife, but neither did he want to give up his lover. He wanted both women in his life, which surely made Murray acutely aware of the conflicting pressures that differing motives exert on a person.

The experience was a turning point in a second way, as well. Morgan had been fascinated by the psychology of Carl Jung. At Morgan's urging, Murray visited Jung in Switzerland. Jung, it turned out, was living in much the same situation as Murray, but with no discomfort. Jung's advice was to continue with both relationships, which Murray proceeded to do for forty years (for biographies of Murray and Morgan, see Robinson, 1992, and Douglas, 1993). The experience of bringing a problem to a psychologist and receiving an answer that seemed to work had a great impact on Murray, leading him to seriously consider psychology as a career (J. W. Anderson, 1988). When given the opportunity to assist in founding the Harvard Psychological Clinic, which was being set up specifically to study personality, he jumped at the chance.

When you start to examine need theories, it's easiest to start with biological needs, because biology is a good model for how needs work. Biological needs must be satisfied repeatedly over time. As time passes, needs gradually become more intense, and the person comes to act in a way that causes the need to be satisfied. For example, as time passes your body starts to need food. Eventually, when the need gets strong enough, you'll do something to get some food. That reduces the need.

The strength of a need influences the intensity of the related behavior. The stronger the need, the more intense the action. The concept of intensity covers several qualities: vigor, enthusiasm, and thoroughness. But intensity can also be expressed in less obvious ways. For example, need strength can help set priorities—which action you take first versus put off until later. The stronger the need, the sooner it's reflected in action. Figure 5.1 shows how this prioritizing can create a continually changing stream of actions as need strengths build and subside. The need that's greatest at any given point is the one that appears in behavior.

Needs are directive, helping determine which of many possible actions occurs at a given time. They are directive in two senses. First, when you have a need, it's a need for something in particular. When you need water, you don't just *need,* you need *water.* Needs thus pertain to classes of goal objects or events. Needs are also directive in specifying movement *toward* the object or *away* from it. A need is a need to get something or to avoid something. Thirst reflects a water-related need, but it's more than just water-*related.* After all, fear of swimming also reflects a water-related need. Thirst reflects a need to *get* water. Moving toward versus moving away is part of the directionality of all needs.

Motives

Many theorists assume that needs operate through **motives.** Motives take the underlying need and move it a step closer to behavior. David McClelland (1984), an important contributor to this view of personality, said motives are clusters of *cognitions with affective overtones, organized around preferred experiences and goals.* Motives appear in your thoughts and preoccupations. The thoughts pertain to goals that are either desired or undesired, thus are affectively toned. Motives are eventually reflected in actions.

To illustrate, the need for food occurs in the tissues of the body. But it gives rise to a motivational state called hunger. Unlike the need for food, hunger is experi-

Figure 5.1

A graphic display of how changes in behavior over time can be explained by variations in the relative strengths of several motives over the same time. The letters at the top of the diagram indicate which of three activities the person is engaged in at any given time (shifting from one to the other). The three lines indicate the levels of the three motives related to these three activities. As one motive rises above the other two, the behavior changes (adapted from Seltzer, 1973).

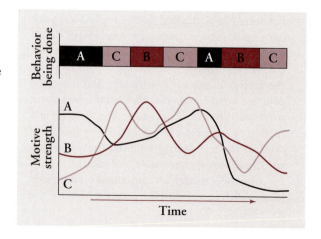

Every need has associated with it some category of "goal objects." When thirsty, you need water, not food.

enced directly. It creates mental preoccupation and it leads to behavior that will reduce the hunger (and the need for food). Thus, people who distinguish needs from motives do so partly by whether there is a subjective experience. The need is a physical condition you don't sense directly. It creates a motivational state that you *do* experience subjectively.

Press

Motives aren't influenced just by internal needs. They're also influenced by external events. Murray (1938) used the term **press** to refer to such external influences. A press (plural is also *press*) is an external condition that creates a desire to obtain (or avoid) something. It thus exerts a motivational influence, just as does an internal need (Figure 5.2).

It's probably easiest to get a feel for the effects of need and press using a biological motive. Imagine your need for food created a hunger motive. You responded by eating lunch. Your peanut butter sandwich, though dry and crumbly, satisfied the need for food. But now, just as you finish, someone walks in with an extra-large pizza (or whatever you find irresistible). Suddenly you don't seem as satisfied as you did a moment before. The motive to eat has been rekindled—not by a need, but by a press.

The concept of press also applies to motives stemming from secondary needs. Seeing someone else receive an honor can increase your motive for recognition. Being around someone who's in a close relationship may increase your motive to be with someone. A student once told us that being around new mothers brings out caretaking motives, and she finds herself wishing she had a baby to care for. These are all examples of motive states induced by environmental press. Table 5.1 has examples of press that Murray saw as important influences in childhood.

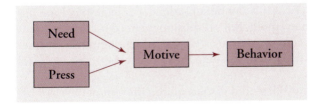

Figure 5.2

Internal need states and external press can both influence motives to engage in particular kinds of action, which in turn become realized in overt behavior.

Table 5.1

Examples of press during childhood that can influence motives and thereby behavior (adapted from Murray, 1938).

Press	Resulting motive
Lack of companionship	Desire to make new friends
Family discord	Desire to be comforted
Lack of variety	Desire to seek out new experiences
Betrayal of trust	Desire for revenge
Inconsistent discipline	Desire for predictability
Friendships	Desire to be nurturant
Confinement	Desire for freedom

Although needs and motives clearly *can* be distinguished from each other, people don't always do so. One reason is that it's harder to make the distinction for psychological needs than biological needs. A need for achievement involves no deficit in the body. It's hard to say how the need to achieve differs from the motive to achieve. For this reason, it's common for people writing about needs and motives in personality to use the two terms interchangeably. In general, that's what we'll do here.

Needs, Motives, and Personality

When needs and motives are strong, they're reflected in behaviors we commonly think of as relating to personality. The effects have two facets, because people have both temporary variations in needs and deeper, more permanent patterns of needs.

Motivational States and Motive Dispositions

Everyone's needs vary across time and circumstances. People also vary in their *dispositional* needs. That is, some people just naturally have more of a particular need pretty much all the time than do other people. Just as some people are always hungry, some are always motivated to achieve, or to be close to others.

We've already shown how to think about temporary fluctuations of needs (Figure 5.1, earlier). People shift from doing one thing to doing something else, as one need is satisfied and others build up. Ongoing behavior reflects whichever need is now greatest. This model provides a sensible portrayal of how people shift from one action to another over time.

Now add the idea that people differ from each other in their dispositional levels of needs. This might be portayed as differences in the overall heights of the lines. Moment-to-moment consequences of this can be substantial. For example, John has a high dispositional need for achievement, Bill's dispositional need for achievement is lower. Assume both have the same experiences, so the achievement motive goes up and down in the same pattern for both. Assume further that they have identical patterns in all their other needs.

As Figure 5.3 shows, John and Bill would display quite different patterns of behavior over time. Why? Because *even when John's other needs are also up, his need for*

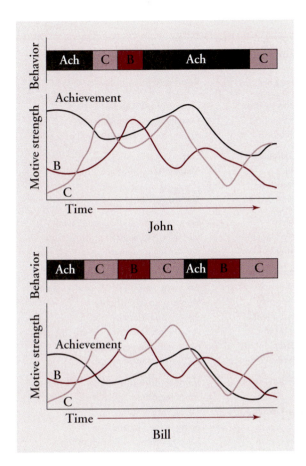

Figure 5.3

John has a high dispositional need for achievement; Bill's is lower. Assume this need fluctuates for both of them in the same pattern across time. John's and Bill's levels of two other needs are identical (and also fluctuate). The difference in the dispositional need for achievement creates a great difference in the overt actions John and Bill display (the bars above the lines).

achievement is so high it tends to remain above the others. As a result, he tends to do achievement-related things a lot of the time. For Bill, the achievement motive rarely gets high enough to be the strongest motive. Thus, Bill doesn't display achievement-related behavior very often.

Murray's System of Needs

Murray (1938) developed a theory of personality that was organized in terms of needs, press, and motives. He and his colleagues developed a catalog of needs, emphasizing the secondary ones. Part of his list of secondary needs is in Table 5.2. These, to Murray, are the motives that underlie important human behavior. They are the needs that describe personality. Murray believed everyone has all these needs. He also believed everyone has a dispositional tendency toward having *a particular level* of each need.

Each need stands on its own, but Murray argued that needs can also be interrelated in several ways. Needs sometimes *fuse,* and are expressed in the same act. For example, Sarah's mother has a high need to dominate and a high need to nurture. She often acts toward Sarah in a caring manner (nurturing) but in such a way that Sarah's wishes and preferences are disregarded (dominating). A single action thus satisfies two needs for her at the same time.

Needs can also act *in the service of* one another. For instance, a person may have a need for order, which works to the benefit of a more general need for achievement. As another example, there's evidence that sexual activity, which is motivating in its own

Table 5.2

Partial list of psychological needs (adapted and abridged from Murray, 1938)

Domain	Need for . . .	Representative behavior
Pertaining to ambition	**Achievement***	Overcoming obstacles
	Recognition	Describing accomplishments
	Exhibition	Attempting to shock or thrill others
Pertaining to inanimate objects	Acquisition	Obtaining things
	Order	Making things neat and orderly
	Retention	Hoarding things
	Construction	Building something
Pertaining to defense of status	Infavoidance	Concealing a handicap or a failing
	Defendance	Giving an explanation or excuse
	Counteraction	Retaliating for something
Pertaining to human power	**Dominance**	Directing others' behavior
	Deference	Cooperating with or obeying someone
	Autonomy	Standing up to authority
	Contrariance	Being oppositional
	Aggression	Attacking or belittling others
	Abasement	Apologizing or confessing
	Blame avoidance	Stifling blameworthy impulses
Pertaining to affection between people	**Affiliation**	Spending time with others
	Rejection	Snubbing others
	Nurturance	Taking care of someone
	Succorance	Being helped by another
	Play	Seeking diversion through others
Pertaining to exchange of information	Cognizance	Asking questions of others
	Exposition	Delivering information to others

*Needs printed in boldface are those that have received the most research attention from other psychologists.

right, can serve and support a variety of other motives (Cooper, Shapiro, & Powers, 1998). Needs can *conflict* with one another, as well. For instance, the need for autonomy can conflict with the need for intimacy. Someone with a strong need to be independent and also a strong need to share experiences with someone else may feel conflicted in social relations.

Just as needs can interrelate in complex ways, needs and press can interrelate. As one need can operate in the service of another, a press can operate in the service of a need. For example, Jane, who has a high need for achievement, works at an advertising firm. Her office surrounds her with challenging tasks, each of which is a press for achievement. Having this constant press at work facilitates and supplements her already high motive to achieve.

Measuring Motives: The Thematic Apperception Test

To study the motive view on personality, researchers have to measure motives. Motives turn out to be tricky to measure, because people don't always show their needs openly. **Manifest needs** can be seen in overt actions. These are easy to assess. **Latent needs** are those that aren't being displayed. This doesn't mean they aren't there. In fact, often it's the pattern of latent needs you really want to know about.

How do you measure latent needs? Morgan and Murray (1935) suggested that a strong latent need will be "projected" into a person's fantasy, just as the image of a movie is projected onto a screen. (This idea derives from psychoanalytic theory; we'll say more about it in Chapter 9.) Murray applied the term **apperception** to the process of projecting imagery onto an outside stimulus. The assumption that people naturally engage in apperception provided the rationale behind the **Thematic Apperception Test,** or **TAT** (Morgan & Murray, 1935; Murray, 1938; Smith, 1992). This is the technique that's most frequently used to assess latent needs.

When your motives are being assessed by TAT (see Box 5.2), you view a set of pictures in which it isn't clear what's going on. You're asked to create a story about each one. Your story should describe what's happening, the characters' thoughts

BOX 5.2

THE PROCESS BEHIND THE TAT

Take a good look at the picture on the right. Something's happening in the minds of these people, but what? Decide for yourself. Make up a story that fits the picture. Include the following specific information (and whatever else you want to include): *What's just happened to these people? What's the relationship between them? What are their present thoughts and feelings? What will be the outcome of the situation?* Take your time, and make your story as long and detailed as you wish.

What you've just done is similar to what people do when completing the Thematic Apperception Test, or TAT (Morgan & Murray, 1935). The idea is that people's needs will show up in the thoughts they generate from their imaginations when they try to make sense out of ambiguous stimuli such as this picture. The picture's ambiguity makes it less likely that environmental press will determine your story's content and more likely that your needs will influence what you write. When people complete the TAT, they write stories for several pictures, including one that's completely blank (the ultimate in ambiguity!).

Scoring people's responses can be complex, but here's a simple version of what happens. Look to see what kinds of events take place in your story and what themes and images are in it. Events that involve overcoming obstacles, attaining goals, and positive feelings about these activities reflect the achievement motive. Events in which people choose to be with other people or emphasize relationships among people reflect the affiliation motive. Stories with images of one person controlling another reflect the power motive. The themes in your story can be scored separately, so the story can be used to assess several different motives. If you're interested in the motives of your own personality, look for evidence of each of the motives listed in Table 5.2.

Different pictures do tend to elicit stories with different themes. Some pictures naturally elicit achievement-related stories; others are more amenable to stories with affiliation themes. Over the course of several pictures, however, dispositional tendencies emerge in the fantasy narratives that people compose. Presumably these storytelling tendencies reflect the motives that characterize the person's personality.

Illustration by Stephen P. Scheier. Reproduced by permission.

and feelings, the relationship among characters (if there's more than one), and the outcome of the situation. The idea of apperception is that the themes in your stories reflect your latent motivations. To put it another way, people put into their stories the motivational concerns that occupy their minds.

Do fantasy responses really reflect people's needs? Yes. Several initial validation studies were done. One of them looked at a biological need, the need for food. Subjects were deprived of food for varying lengths of time, so they'd have different needs for food. They proved to differ in food-related TAT imagery (Atkinson & McClelland, 1948).

Other research manipulated people's achievement motive, by giving some a success and others a failure. A failure should cause a temporary increase in the achievement need, because it creates an achievement deficit, just as the passage of time creates a deficit for food. A success should reduce the achievement motive because it satisfies the need. As predicted, after these experiences subjects differed in TAT achievement imagery (McClelland, Atkinson, Clark, & Lowell, 1953). In the same way, people led to be concerned about their social acceptability displayed heightened affiliation imagery (Atkinson, Heyns, & Veroff, 1954).

Individual Differences in Specific Needs

Once validated by such studies, the TAT was used extensively to measure individual differences in *dispositional* needs. Because the TAT was responsive to experimentally created differences, it should also be sensitive to personality differences. Using this method, researchers have studied several dispositional needs in detail.

Need for Achievement

Of the various needs identified by Murray, the first to receive research attention was the **need for achievement.** This motive plays a role in many human pursuits. It's been studied for several decades by David McClelland, John Atkinson, and many others (e.g., Atkinson & Birch, 1970; Atkinson & Raynor, 1974; Heckhausen, 1967; Heckhausen, Schmalt, & Schneider, 1985; McClelland et al., 1953).

Achievement motivation is *the desire to do things well, to feel pleasure in overcoming obstacles.* Need for achievement is reflected in TAT responses that mention performing well at something, reaching goals or overcoming obstacles to goal attainment, having positive feelings about success, or negative feelings about failure.

Studies of people who differ in achievement motivation have found they differ in several ways regarding achievement-related situations. Consider, for instance, the very act of choosing a task. Tasks (or problems within a task) can be easy, hard, or somewhere in-between. Given a choice, which would you prefer? (When you set up your course schedule for next semester, do you choose easy courses and professors, hard ones, or ones in between?)

People low in need for achievement prefer tasks that are either very easy or very hard (Atkinson, 1957). It's easy to see why they might like easy ones. There isn't much achievement pressure in an easy task, and it's nice to get something right, even if everyone else gets it right too. Why, though, would people with low achievement needs choose a hard task? Apparently it's not for the challenge. It seems to have more to do with the fact that doing poorly on a hard problem doesn't reflect badly on you. And there's always the possibility (however remote) that you'll get lucky and succeed.

People high in need for achievement, in contrast, tend to prefer tasks of moderate difficulty. Consistent with this, people high in achievement motivation take up

Persons high in achievement motivation have a strong need to succeed.

occupational goals that are challenging but realistic, given their capabilities (Mahone, 1960; Morris, 1966). People high in need for achievement also work harder on moderately difficult tasks than on very hard or very easy tasks (Clark & McClelland, 1956; French, 1955).

Why do people high in need for achievement prefer tasks of intermediate difficulty? These tasks provide the most information about ability (Trope, 1975, 1979). If you do well at an easy task, you don't learn much about your ability, because everyone does well. If you *fail* at a *hard* task, you don't learn much about your ability, because almost *no one* does well. In the middle, though, you can find out a lot. Perhaps people high in achievement motivation want to find out about their abilities. Trope (1975, 1980) tested this by having people choose test items. He figured out a way to manipulate (separately) the items' difficulty and their **diagnosticity** (how much they tell about ability). People with high achievement needs had a strong preference for diagnostic items (Figure 5.4), whereas difficulty in itself turned out not to be important.

Effects of achievement motivation have been studied in a variety of domains. For example, need for achievement relates to persistence in the face of failure (e.g., Feather, 1961). It relates to task performances (e.g., Lowell, 1952) and even to grades in school (Schultz & Pomerantz, 1976; see Atkinson & Birch, 1978, for a more complete treatment). This variable thus plays an important role in a variety of achievement-related behaviors.

Indeed, it's even been suggested that the need for achievement plays a major role in the economic rise and decline of entire cultures. This idea led to studies examining literature from several civilizations, at several distinct points in their history. The literature is interpreted for its themes, in much the same way as TAT responses are interpreted. The economic growth and decline of that civilization are then plotted over the same period.

Figure 5.4

Participants in this study chose items to work on that they expected to be either highly diagnostic of their abilities or not diagnostic. This figure divides participants into four levels of achievement motive, ranging from very low to very high. There is an increasingly strong preference for highly diagnostic items among those with higher levels of achievement motivation (adapted from Trope, 1975).

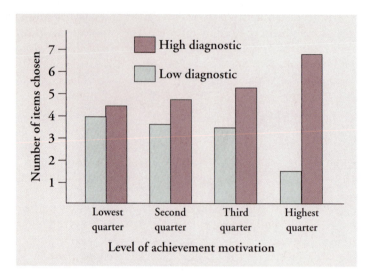

One impressive study of this sort was done by Bradburn and Berlew (1961), who examined the literature and economic history of England from 1500 to just after 1800. They divided this period into fifty-year segments and coded achievement imagery and economic development in each. Achievement imagery was stable for about one hundred years, fell off, and then rose sharply. The index of economic development followed a nearly identical pattern of falling then rising—but fifty years later. This suggests that shifts in achievement needs had economic consequences.

Another, even more complex study of this sort was done by McClelland (1961). This study focused on a much narrower period (1925 to 1950) but looked at twenty-three cultures across the world. McClelland coded achievement imagery from children's schoolbooks at both points in history. He developed two measures of economic growth over the intervening period, and compared the achievement imagery to economic growth. A moderately strong association emerged between achievement imagery in 1925 and economic growth from 1925 to 1950. As in the Bradburn and Berlew study, there was virtually no relation between economic growth and later achievement imagery. This pattern suggests that motivation (reflected in the imagery) produced the economic achievement, instead of vice versa.

Achievement motivation predicted economic success in these studies, but in some situations the need for achievement can work against people. For example, those who serve in high-level managerial or political positions don't have opportunities for personal achievement. Their task is to mobilize others (which depends on a different need altogether). If people in this situation try to do too much themselves, it can backfire, producing worse outcomes rather than better. Consistent with this idea, Spangler and House (1991) found that need for achievement related inversely to the effectiveness of U.S. presidents.

An interesting aspect of the literature on the achievement motive is that, until recently, far more was known about its effects among men than among women because most early research studied only males. Eventually, however, researchers looked more closely at achievement needs among women. Much of this work suggests that achievement needs are expressed in varying ways among women, depending on the direction in which they see their lives going.

Elder and MacInnis (1983) recruited two sets of seventeen- to eighteen-year-old girls. One group was family oriented, the other group had a mix of family and career interests. Achievement motives, assessed at the same time, predicted different outcomes in the two groups as they moved into adulthood. Among family-oriented women, those with high achievement needs invested energy in activities leading to marriage and family. In effect, they defined achievement as creating and sustaining a family. Among career-minded women, high achievement motivation led to putting off marriage and families. Presumably this was because they were focusing on their careers. In a similar vein, Stewart (1980) found that achievement needs predicted women's career persistence across fourteen years, but only among women with no children. Thus, what the woman values as an achievement goal seems to determine what behaviors follow from achievement needs.

Another way of portraying these findings is to say that women with achievement needs pursue achievement in ways that fit their views of themselves and the world they live in. It seems reasonable that this principle also influences what careers women consider. Jenkins (1987) looked at career choices made by women who were college seniors in 1967. Those high in need for achievement were likely to become teachers, but not to go into business. Why? Teaching provided an outlet for their achievement needs but didn't conflict with traditional women's roles. Business careers didn't fit as well with those roles. Thus, the achievement needs of these women were channeled by other aspects of their social environments.

These studies raise questions about whether achievement behavior promotes social acceptance for women, as it seems to do for men. Some have argued it doesn't (French & Lesser, 1964; Horner, 1973; Lesser, 1973; Tresemer, 1977). High-achieving women may risk being seen as losing their femininity. This can create conflict for a woman motivated to achieve. She may even develop a motive to *avoid* success (Horner, 1973), as a way to avoid the adverse consequences of high levels of the achievement motive. The fear of success appears to be more rare than was once thought (Peplau, 1976), but the idea that women are threatened by achievement is still under investigation (Pollak & Gilligan, 1982).

Divergent Motives Underlying Achievement Behavior

It seems straightforward to speak of achievement behavior as motivated by the desire to attain goals. But whenever there's an achievement task, the possibility of *failing* is always present. As mentioned earlier, a motive is either a readiness to approach something or a readiness to avoid something. Thus far, we've talked about achievement only in terms of approach: people who desire to achieve try to move toward success. It seems likely, though, that the desire to avoid failure also plays a role in achievement-related behavior.

There are several ways this can happen. For example, people who want to avoid failing may avoid achievement-related situations altogether. Never trying allows you to avoid failing. Another way to avoid failing, though, is *by the very act of succeeding*. It may well be that some of the people who try hard to achieve don't care so much about gaining success as they do about the fact that by gaining success they thereby avoid failure.

Much early research on achievement actually included measures of both these motives. Much of that research derived from Atkinson's (1957) theory of achievement behavior. That theory makes its clearest predictions for people who are only motivated to approach success and people who are only motivated to avoid failure. Predictions are less clear for people who are high in both motives and people who are low in both motives. For that reason, studies often included only the two groups who were high in one motive and low in the other.

This strategy was based in theory, but it has a problematic side effect: it creates a perfect confounding between the two motives. This causes ambiguity in interpretation (see Chapter 2). If the groups act differently from each other, is it because of the difference in the motive to approach success, or because of the difference in the motive to avoid failure? There is no way to know, though most interpretations focus on the motive to approach success.

In recent years the distinction between approach and avoidance motivation has reemerged as a focus for research on achievement, much of it by Elliot and his colleagues (e.g., Elliot & Harackiewicz, 1996; Elliot & McGregor, 2001). Part of their theory is that achievement can reflect either of these motives (see also Box 5.3). Which motive is central, however, will influence many aspects of the person's experience. Elliot and McGregor (2001) found that the motive to succeed in mastering course material (approach) related to study strategies involving thoughtfully elaborating on the material. The avoidance motive related to memorization and to reports of having problems organizing study time effectively. Elliot and Sheldon (1997)

BOX 5.3

APPROACH AND AVOIDANCE MOTIVES

As indicated in the main text, there is renewed interest in the idea that some achievement behaviors reflect approach motives, whereas other achievement behaviors derive from the motive to avoid failure. Although we addressed this issue with regard to achievement in the main text, the issue actually applies much more widely. Once you grasp the idea of separate approach and avoidance motives, you realize that the idea has implications for *every* motive you can think of (see also Carver, Lawrence, & Scheier, 1999; Higgins, 1997; Ogilvie, 1987).

Pick any motive in Table 5.2 (or think of one that's not in the table) and try it out. Identify a behavior that seems to reflect that motive. Then see if you spot the alternate motive that might influence the same behavior. Acts of affiliation, for example, can be based in the desire to *be with others* (need for affiliation), but they can also be based in a desire to *avoid being alone* (Boyatzis, 1973; Pollak & Gilligan, 1982). These two motives aren't identical. One is a motive to approach; the other is a motive to avoid. In the same way, the need to dominate is paralleled by a need to avoid being dominated. The same point can be made for any need you can think of.

Just as with achievement behavior, evidence is beginning to accumulate that approach and avoidance motives have different consequences in other domains. A powerful example is a study of commitment among romantic partners (Frank & Brandstätter, 2002). This study found that commitment based in approach predicted greater relationship satisfaction six and thirteen months later. However, commitment based in avoidance (i.e., avoiding the process of breaking up or ending the commitment) predicted lower relationship satisfaction at those follow-ups.

The idea that a given behavior can be based on either an approach motive or an avoidance motive (or some combination of the two) raises very broad questions about why people do the things they do. Are people generally moving toward goals, or are they trying to avoid or escape from things? Do people's actions differ, depending on which motive is more prominent? Do the feelings that result from the actions differ? (These questions, interestingly enough, will also come up in Chapters 7 and 14.) The general idea that any approach motive has a corresponding avoidance motive is one that has very broad implications. It complicates the picture of human behavior enormously. Despite the fact that we will put this idea aside for the remainder of this chapter, you should keep in mind that it's always in the background.

found that the two motive tendencies also have different effects on subjective experiences. People who spend their effort trying to avoid failure report poorer well-being and less satisfaction with their performances than do people who are trying to approach success.

Need for Power

Another motive that's been studied extensively is the **need for power.** Need for power, studied by David Winter (e.g., 1973) and others, is *the motive to have impact on other people, to have prestige, to feel strong* compared to others. TAT responses that reflect the need for power have images of forceful, vigorous action—especially action that evokes strong emotional responses in others. Responses showing concern about status or position also reflect need for power.

What kinds of behavior express the power motive? Not surprisingly, people high in need for power seek out positions of authority and influence. Students high in the power motive are likely to be officeholders in student organizations (Greene & Winter, 1971). The power motive seems to enhance organizational effectiveness. For example, among U.S. presidents, those high in the power motive were more effective than those lower in this motive (Spangler & House, 1991).

When in positions of authority or responsibility, people with different levels of the power motive also differ in how they respond to problems. One study examined supervisors of work groups that were either efficient or inefficient (Fodor, 1984). The question was how they'd respond to others' inefficiency. People high in the need for power reported becoming more aroused or activated when things went poorly. Thus, encountering leadership difficulties seems to engage the energies of people high in the need for power.

A different—and much less obvious—effect of the power motive occurs in friendship patterns. It's been found that people with high need for power tend to form

The need for power is often expressed in the tendency to acquire high-status possessions and to surround oneself with symbols of power.

friendships with others who aren't especially popular or well-known (Winter, 1973). At first this doesn't sound right. Wouldn't power-minded people seek each other out? After a little more thought, though, it makes sense. If your friends aren't popular, they won't compete with you for power. If what you want is power and influence, influential friends can get in the way.

A finding similar to this is that men with high power needs are more likely than those with lower power needs to say that the ideal wife is a woman who's dependent (Winter, 1973). An independent woman is a potential threat. A dependent woman allows a man to feel superior. A later study confirmed that the wives of men high in power needs were less likely to have careers of their own than wives of men lower in this need (Winter, Stewart, & McClelland, 1977).

This isn't to say that the need for power is something that matters only among men. Women vary in this need as well, and it has proved to predict important outcomes among women. One study (Jenkins, 1994) found that women high in the need for power have more power-related job satisfactions than women lower in this need, but also more *dis*satisfactions. These women also made greater strides in career development over a fourteen-year period, but only if they were in power-relevant jobs.

The level of a person's need for power can influence how the person relates to others. In one study (McAdams, Healy, & Krause, 1984) participants described peer interactions, and the descriptions were analyzed. Need for power related strongly to indications that the person had taken an active, assertive, controlling orientation in the interaction. Another study (Mason & Blankenship, 1987) found evidence of a more extreme exercise of power, with more ominous overtones. This study found that men high in power needs were more likely than men with lower power needs to physically abuse their female partners during arguments.

There are many other ways the power motive can be manifest in behavior. People high in the need for power surround themselves with symbols of power, including credit cards (Davis, 1969) and high-prestige possessions (Winter, 1972). This occurs even among college students (Winter, 1973). Power-motivated students are also more argumentative in class and eager to convince others of their point of view (Veroff, 1957). This may be why they do particularly well in courses requiring classroom participation (McKeachie, 1961).

Many of these findings fit the idea that people with a high need for power are concerned about controlling the self-images they present to others around them (see McAdams, 1984). They're motivated to enhance their reputations. They want to create in others' minds images of themselves as authoritative and influential. It will be no surprise that they tend to be somewhat narcissistic, absorbed in their own importance (Carroll, 1987). People high in the power motive are less likely to make concessions in diplomatic negotiations than those lower in this motive (Langner & Winter, 2001).

Winter has suggested that the power motive is manifested in different ways, depending on whether socialization has created a sense of responsibility (Winter, 1988; Winter & Barenbaum, 1985). For those high in responsibility, the power motive is reflected in "conscientious" pursuit of prestige. In such cases, power is expressed in socially accepted ways. For those lower in responsibility, though, the need for power can lead to more problematic ways of influencing others—what Winter calls "profligate, impulsive" power. This includes aggressiveness, sexual exploitation, and alcohol and drug use.

Winter and Barenbaum (1985) found considerable support for this argument. For example, in one sample of men who were coded as low responsible, need for power related to drinking, fighting, and sexual possessiveness. Among men coded as high responsible, need for power related inversely to all these tendencies. Similar findings emerged from other samples. Others have since found that men with high need for power without the sense of responsibility also had a rise in testosterone when imagining and experiencing a power-related success (Schultheiss, Campbell, & McClelland, 1999; Schultheiss & Rohde, 2002).

Need for Affiliation

Another motive that's received a good deal of attention is the motive to affiliate (Boyatzis, 1973). The **need for affiliation** is *the motive to spend time with others*. This isn't a need to dominate others but to be in social relationships, to interact with others. These interactions aren't a means to some other end; they're a goal in their own right. In TAT responses, need for affiliation is reflected in concern over acceptance by others, or active attempts to establish or maintain positive relations with others (Shipley & Veroff, 1952).

Studies have uncovered several implications of this motive. For example, people who want to affiliate should want to be seen as agreeable. If a group exerts pressure on them, they should go along—compared to people with lower affiliation needs—and they do (Hardy, 1957). People high in need for affiliation also display concern with being accepted and liked by other people in other ways. They get nervous if they think others are judging their interpersonal skills (Byrne, McDonald, & Mikawa, 1963). They show a strong preference for interaction partners who are warm compared to those who are reserved (Hill, 1991). They're also more likely to initiate contacts and to try to establish friendships (Crouse & Mehrabian, 1977), and more likely to make concessions in negotiations (Langner & Winter, 2001).

Actively making social contacts suggests that affiliative needs go further than worrying about acceptance from others. These needs can also lead to active participation in social events. For example, Sorrentino and Field (1986) studied the emergence of leadership in discussion groups, which met in five weekly sessions. At the end, group members were asked to indicate whom they viewed as group leaders. As can be seen in Figure 5.5, people high in need for affiliation were nominated more often than people lower in need for affiliation.

As suggested by Sorrentino and Field's research, people with a strong affiliation motive spend more time actively engaged in social activities than people lower in this motive. They make more phone calls (Lansing & Heyns, 1959), and when paged

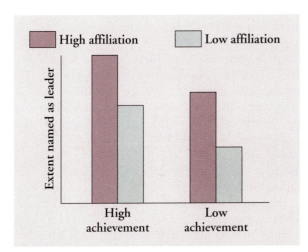

Figure 5.5

Participants interacted informally in groups for five weeks, then indicated who they thought were the leaders in the group. Those with higher affiliation motivation were rated as showing more leadership, and a similar tendency also appeared for the achievement motive (adapted from Sorrentino & Field, 1986).

they're more likely to be engaged in social activities—conversing or letter writing (Constantian, 1981; McAdams & Constantian, 1983). When they're alone, they're more likely to express a wish to be interacting with others (McAdams & Constantian, 1983; Wong & Csikszentmihalyi, 1991).

Another study suggests that the affiliation motive influences relationship satisfaction (Meyer & Pepper, 1977), though in a complex way. Happiness depends partly on the balance of affiliation needs between partners. That is, well-adjusted husbands and wives had affiliation needs that *correlated* with each other. Poorly adjusted couples had affiliation needs that were unrelated. To put it concretely, if you have low affiliation needs, you're best off with someone else with low affiliation needs. If your affiliation needs are high, you're best off with someone whose affiliation needs are also high.

We noted in Chapter 4 a difference of opinion about whether traits should be measured as broad supertraits or as more narrow traits. A similar question has been raised about affiliation motivation, and by implication about the entire motive approach to personality. Hill (1987) pointed out that affiliation can occur for several reasons. Perhaps the reasons for affiliation should be considered as separate motives.

To do this, Hill developed self-report scales for four affiliation needs: social comparison, emotional support, positive stimulation, and attention from others. The scales correlated only moderately with each other. Of more interest is how they predicted behavior. Hill created four hypothetical situations, each eliciting a particular sort of affiliation need. One involved a job interview that was confusing and ambiguous, which should target a need for social comparison but not other affiliation motives. As expected, the social comparison scale predicted responses to this situation better than any other scale. The same pattern held for each situation: in each case, the theoretically relevant scale was the best predictor of responses.

These findings suggest, more generally, that there is merit in focusing on specific rather than on global needs. As with traits, however, the question seems to be whether the better prediction is worth the trade-off of having to hold more variables in mind.

Need for Intimacy

Another motive that's emerged as a research focus is the **need for intimacy.** It's been studied intensively by Dan McAdams (1982, 1985, 1989) and his collaborators. Intimacy motivation is *the desire to experience warm, close, and communicative exchanges with another person, to feel close to another person.* Carried to an extreme, it's the desire to merge with another person. Intimacy motivation shares with affiliation motivation a wish to be with others as an end rather than as a means to an end. It goes beyond the need for affiliation, though, in its emphasis on closeness and open sharing with another person.

Interestingly enough, intimacy motivation wasn't on Murray's list. McAdams proposed it partly because he felt the need for affiliation didn't focus enough on the positive, affirmative aspects of relationships. Additionally, the need for affiliation is an active, striving, "doing" orientation, whereas the need for intimacy as McAdams views it is a more passive, noncontrolling, "being" orientation (McAdams & Powers, 1981). The two aren't entirely distinct, of course. McAdams and Constantian (1983) reported a correlation between them of .58.

What kinds of behaviors derive from the intimacy motive? In one study, people higher in the need for intimacy reported having more one-to-one exchanges with other people, though not more large-group interaction (McAdams, Healy, & Krause, 1984). The interactions reported by intimacy-motivated subjects involved more self-disclosure, as well. To put it differently, people with high intimacy needs are more

Need for intimacy is the desire to experience warm, close, and meaningful relationships with others.

likely to share with friends their hopes, fears, and fantasies. The sharing goes both ways: people with high intimacy needs report doing more *listening* than people with low intimacy needs, perhaps because they are more concerned about their friends' well-being. Indeed, intimacy seems to entail both self-disclosure and partner disclosure (Laurenceau, Feldman Barrett, & Pietromonaco, 1998).

Because close interactions are important to people with high intimacy needs, it should be no surprise that they define their lives partly in terms of such interactions. McAdams (1982) collected autobiographical recollections among students high and low in intimacy needs. They were asked to report a particularly joyful or transcendent experience from their past and then an important learning experience. The content of each was coded several ways. For instance, some events involved considerable psychological or physical intimacy with another person; others did not. Analysis revealed that intimacy motivation was strongly correlated with memory content that also implied intimacy.

How do people high in the intimacy motive act when they're with others? They laugh, smile, and make more eye contact when conversing than do people with lower intimacy needs (McAdams, Jackson, & Kirshnit, 1984). They don't try to dominate the social scene (people with the need for power do that). Instead, they seem to view group activities as chances for group members to be involved in a communal way (McAdams & Powers, 1981).

There's evidence that the desire for intimacy may be good for people (McAdams & Vaillant, 1982). Men in this study wrote narrative fantasies at age thirty and were assessed for psychosocial adjustment seventeen years later. Men with higher intimacy motivation at thirty had greater marital and job satisfaction at forty-seven than did those with less intimacy motivation. Another study found that women high in the intimacy motive reported greater happiness and gratification in their lives than those low in the intimacy motive—unless they were living alone (McAdams & Bryant, 1987).

On the other hand, intimacy needs (needing to be close) don't coexist well with power needs (needing to influence or dominate others). Persons high in both needs are often poorly adjusted (Zeldow, Daugherty, & McAdams, 1988).

Some have suggested that strong intimacy needs may threaten men's sense of masculinity (Helgeson & Sharpsteen, 1987; Pollak & Gilligan, 1982; Wong & Csikszentmihalyi, 1991). This idea has a logical parallel to the idea, mentioned earlier in the chapter, that achievement threatens the sense of femininity. Both ideas are controversial (Benton et al., 1983); both surely will be investigated further.

Patterned Needs: Inhibited Power Motive

Thus far, for the most part, we've discussed needs individually. Indeed, for many years that's how researchers examined needs—one at a time. However, some have also examined patterns involving several needs at once, sometimes in combination with other characteristics. One well-known pattern combines a low need for affiliation with a high need for power, in conjunction with the tendency to inhibit the expression of the latter. This pattern is called **inhibited power motivation** (McClelland, 1979). Why this pattern is of interest depends on the context in which it's examined.

One context is leadership. The theory goes as follows: a person high in need for power wants to influence people. Being low in need for affiliation lets the person make hard decisions without worrying about being disliked. Being high in self-control (inhibiting the use of power) means the person will want to follow orderly procedures and stay within the organizational framework. Such a person should do very well in the structure of a business organization.

This pattern does seem to relate to managerial success (McClelland & Boyatzis, 1982). Those with the inhibited power pattern moved to higher levels of management in a sixteen-year period than others, but only those who were nontechnical managers. Among managers whose jobs rested on engineering skills, personality didn't matter. This is understandable, because the managerial value of those people depends heavily on their particular skills.

There is also evidence that people with this pattern are especially effective at persuasion (Schultheiss & Brunstein, 2002). Their persuasiveness stems both from greater verbal fluency and from an effective use of nonverbal cues such as gesturing. Presumably greater persuasion helps contribute to effectiveness in mobilizing others.

The pattern of high power motivation and low affiliation motivation may be good for getting others mobilized, but even this may be a mixed blessing. Winter (1993) has argued that this pattern is actually conducive to starting wars. Historical data has revealed that high levels of power imagery and low levels of affiliation imagery in the statements of politicians predicted going to war. For example, speeches made by the sovereigns of Great Britain contained more power than affiliation imagery in the year before Britain entered a war, whereas the reverse was true during years preceding a no-war year (Figure 5.6). In another case (the Cuban missile crisis of 1962), greater affiliation than power imagery preceded the *avoidance* of a war.

Further Determinants of Behavior

It should be clear that no single motive—no matter how interesting—is the only determinant of personality. From the motivational point of view, personality is a *system of multiple needs*. In this section we briefly reconsider how the continually changing stream of human behavior reflects the waxing and waning of many needs.

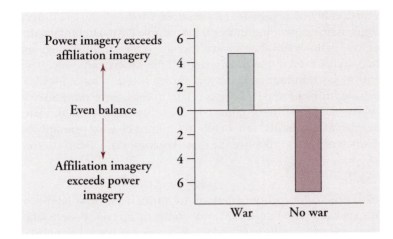

Power imagery exceeds affiliation imagery

Even balance

Affiliation imagery exceeds power imagery

War   No war

Figure 5.6

Balance of power motive imagery versus affiliation motive imagery in sovereign's speeches during the year before Great Britain entered a war (eighteen cases) compared to the year before Britain did *not* enter a war (thirty-six cases; adapted from Winter, 1993, Table 3).

As indicated earlier, every human motive exists in every person. The behavior that takes place at a given time is determined partly by how *intense* various motives are. As one need becomes so intense that it outweighs the others, it's reflected in activity. As that need is satisfied and others grow more intense, the balance changes and the person shifts to another activity. The result is a flow of continually changing behavior (Atkinson & Birch, 1978).

Winter (1996) has suggested that needs for achievement, affiliation–intimacy, and power are the fundamental dimensions underlying Murray's more elaborate list. In his view, although many needs wax and wane, they form three broad domains of needs. One might think of each domain as a superordinate need within which facets needs can vary somewhat independently.

Incentive Value

This analysis is reasonable, but it's missing something. If your need for affiliation is now more intense than your other needs, this analysis predicts you'll engage in an affiliative act. But what act in particular? Here the theory must use additional concepts (e.g., McClelland, 1985).

Another determinant is **incentive,** the degree to which a given action can satisfy a need for you. It's sort of a personalized weighting of how relevant the act is to the need. Incentive values determine how a motive is expressed in behavior. For example, a person with a high need for affiliation who likes long conversations with special friends but dislikes impersonal crowds will avoid parties. Avoiding parties may appear strange for a person with a high need for affiliation. But people don't engage in all conceivable types of need-related behavior. They choose ways to satisfy their needs, based partly on the incentive values that various activities have for them.

We didn't point to the role of incentives earlier in the chapter. It should be clear, however, that something like it is needed to account for behavior's diversity. People differ considerably in the activities they engage in, even when trying to satisfy the same need. As noted earlier, some women seem to satisfy a need for achievement through careers, others do so by achieving strong family lives. These activities differ, yet each can satisfy the need to achieve.

This principle relates to a point made in Chapter 4 regarding interactionism: we said that people choose for themselves which situations to enter and which to avoid, thus creating an interaction between person and situation. We didn't say *why* different people choose different situations. One answer is that people have different needs, which relate to different situations. Another answer, though, is that various situations have different *incentive* values, even if the situations fulfill the same need.

Needs and incentives both influence behavior, but in different ways. McClelland (1985) held that measures of need strength relate to long-term *frequencies of need-relevant actions of any type.* Measures of values, on the other hand, should relate to *choices within a domain of action.* In his view, needs influence behavior primarily at a nonconscious level, whereas values influence the more conscious process of choice.

Expectancy and Skill

McClelland (1985) also noted that people's actions are influenced by at least two other factors. One is **expectancy:** the perceived probability of success. People who expect an action to succeed will continue to engage in it, even if it's going poorly. People who are doubtful are more likely to think about other ways to satisfy the need. The second additional factor, which is a partial determinant of expectancy, is the presence or absence of skills needed to do the action.

These additional variables obviously are important. To consider them all at once, however, creates a description that becomes very complex (for broader treatment see, e.g., Atkinson & Birch, 1978; McClelland, 1985). This is why we've focused this chapter on the central concepts of this approach: needs and motives.

The Methods of Personology

Research examining the effects of motive patterns has tended to take one of two forms. Some studies examine how people respond to particular events, in the laboratory or in the field. Other studies collect evidence of a dispositional motive (or set of motives) in stories composed at one time and relate the motive to some outcome that occurs considerably later.

These two ways of studying motives differ greatly from the approach favored by Murray, the father of this viewpoint. Murray believed the way to understand personality is to study the *whole person,* and to do so over an extended period. The work on which he based his theory was an intensive study of fifty-one college men (Murray, 1938). Each was tested in many ways and also interviewed by a staff of professionals. These people then presented their impressions to what Murray called the Diagnostic Council, the most experienced members of the team. This group came to know each participant's personality quite thoroughly.

This approach was idiographic in nature, focusing on the pattern of qualities that made each person unique. Murray disliked nomothetic methods. He thought their focus on comparison prevents them from probing deeply into a person's life. To Murray, the nomothetic approach yields only a superficial understanding.

In fact, Murray's concern about the inadequacies of nomothetic approaches led him to coin the term **personology** to refer to the approach he preferred. He defined personology as the study of individual lives and the factors that influence their course. He believed that personology was more meaningful than other approaches because of its emphasis on the person's life history. According to Murray (1938, p. 604), "the history of a personality *is* the personality."

Murray was not alone in this belief. One who agreed was Erik Erikson, a member of the research team that Murray assembled. However, Erikson (whose ideas are discussed in Chapter 11) is usually seen as a neoanalytic theorist, partly because of that focus on the role of personal history. The emphasis Murray placed on this particular issue thus seems to align more with the neoanalytic perspective than with the dispositional perspective.

Recent years have seen a resurgence of interest in this way of thinking about personality. For example, Dan McAdams, whose work on intimacy motivation was described earlier, has written extensively on the idea that identity takes the form of an extended narrative, a life story that each of us writes and lives out over time (McAdams, 1985). This narrative has chapters, heros, and thematic threads that recur and permeate the story line (see also Rabin, Zucker, Emmons, & Frank, 1990). Whether this approach will become more prominent in personality psychology in the future remains to be seen, but it surely is a development that Murray would have applauded.

Assessment

Assessment of personality from this viewpoint is a matter of determining the dispositional levels of a person's needs. This approach to personality uses several techniques, including self-reports and interviews. The assessment technique most distinctly associated with assessment of needs, however, is the TAT (Smith, 1992; Winter, 1996).

Though the TAT is widely used to measure motives, it has also been criticized. Questions have been raised about its relatively low internal consistency and test-retest reliability (Entwisle, 1972; Lilienfeld et al., 2000). Defenders reply that there are good reasons for both of these to be low. The pictures in the TAT vary considerably in content. It's not surprising that they bring out different kinds of stories. This reduces internal consistency. It is also arguable that being instructed to tell several stories creates implicit pressure to avoid repetition. This can reduce both internal consistency and test-retest reliability (e.g., Atkinson & Raynor, 1974). There's evidence, though, that the reliability of the TAT may not have to be as low as was once believed (Lundy, 1985).

Another criticism of the TAT is more pragmatic: it takes a lot of time and effort to give and score it. This is an important reason why self-report measures of motives were developed.

There have been several attempts to develop self-reports of the needs Murray saw as basic to personality. An early effort was the Edwards Personal Preference Schedule (Edwards, 1959). A more recent one is the Personality Research Form, or PRF (Jackson, 1984). It measures twenty needs derived from Murray's list. As with any inventory, it can be used to create personality profiles. In this case, however, the traits measured are motivational traits.

Self-Reports and the TAT May Not Measure the Same Thing

Although researchers such as Edwards and Jackson intended their self-report scales to measure motives, questions have been raised about whether they really do so. The reason for concern is that the self-reports usually correlate poorly with TAT assessment (McClelland, Koestner, & Weinberger, 1989; Schultheiss & Brunstein, 2001). The question is why.

McClelland and his colleagues have argued that the two kinds of assessments are, in fact, measuring different things (McClelland, Koestner, & Weinberger, 1989).

They used the term *implicit motive* to refer to what the TAT measures. They called the motives implicit because the person may or may not be aware of them. They used the term *self-attributed motive* to refer to what's measured by self-reports.

McClelland et al. argued that implicit motives are basic. They are the recurrent preferences for classes of affective experiences that McClelland believed lie at the heart of motives (the feeling of "doing better" for the achievement motive, the feeling of "being strong" for the power motive, the feeling of "being close" for the intimacy motive). Implicit motives may be primitive and automatic (Schultheiss, 2002). Because these are basic, they are good predictors of broad behavioral tendencies over time.

In contrast, self-attributed motives tie to specific action goals. They may relate more closely to incentives than to needs. They tell how a person will act in a particular situation. For this reason, they're better at predicting responses in structured settings.

Further evidence that these qualities are distinct comes from research in which subjects completed TAT and self-report measures, then kept records of memorable experiences over sixty days (Woike, 1995). The records were coded for motive relevance and for feelings. Implicit motive strength (from the TAT) related to the frequency of reporting feelings relevant to that motive (but self-report motive strength did not). Self-report motives related to the frequency of reporting motive-related events that had no feelings (but TAT scores did not). It seems, then, that the two aspects of motivation link to different aspects of memory.

McClelland believed that both qualities are important, but that they should be viewed separately. Sometimes it makes sense to expect an implicit motive to predict an outcome, but not a self-attributed motive. Sometimes the opposite is true. For this reason, it's important to be sure which one you want to measure, and to measure it right (McClelland, 1989).

Motives and the Five-Factor Model

The PRF derived from Murray's list of needs. Do the qualities it measures resemble those measured by scales with different starting points? Chapter 4 described the idea that the basic traits of personality largely fall within the framework of five supertraits. Can the five-factor model absorb the qualities Murray saw as important?

Several researchers have addressed this question. As a starting point, several analyses of the PRF have yielded five factors (Stumpf, 1993). Stumpf concluded that all of the big five except neuroticism were captured in the PRF. Costa and McCrae (1988a) looked at associations of PRF scales with the NEO-PI, a big-five measure. Their findings suggested that many PRF scales reflect underlying qualities of the five-factor model. For example, scales measuring needs for affiliation, play, and exhibition all load on extraversion. Scales measuring needs for change, sentience, understanding, and (inversely) harm-avoidance load on openness to experience.

On the other hand, several prominent PRF scales loaded on two or more factors rather than one. This appears to indicate that those motives are tied to several traits. For example, the need for dominance related to extraversion, openness, and (inversely) agreeableness. It seems, then, that the five-factor model doesn't perfectly absorb the needs reflected in the PRF. This general pattern of loadings has been replicated by Paunonen et al. (1992). In contrast, somewhat better support for the five-factor model has been found using the Edwards measure of needs (Piedmont, McCrae, & Costa, 1992).

Traits and Motives as Distinct

The attempt to fit the motives identified by Murray and others to the five-factor model is viewed by some as an effort to integrate across theoretical boundaries. Some believe, however, that the effort is misguided, that traits and motives are fundamentally different from each other (Winter, John, Stewart, Klohnen, & Duncan, 1998). In taking this position, Winter et al. noted that all the evidence just reviewed dealt with self-attributed motives, not TAT-derived motives. The fact that self-attributed and TAT-derived motives aren't strongly related is reason enough to be cautious about concluding that traits and motives are the same. In fact, there is evidence that TAT-derived motives relate poorly to the five-factor model (Schultheiss & Brunstein, 2001).

Winter et al. (1998) proposed a different sort of integration: that motives represent fundamental desires, and that traits channel how those desires are expressed. Thus, they argued, motives and traits interact to produce behavior. In some respects, this resembles the argument described earlier about implicit motives and incentive values. In the view taken by Winter et al., traits may represent patterns of incentive preferences.

In support of their argument, Winter et al. presented two studies of the trait of extraversion and (TAT-derived) needs. The studies examined women's lives across many decades. Winter et al. predicted that intimacy needs would have different effects among introverts and extraverts (Table 5.3). For women with low intimacy needs, it should hardly matter whether they are introverts or extraverts. Intimacy just isn't a big need for them.

For women with high intimacy needs, though, the picture is more complex. An extravert with intimacy needs should do fine in relationships, because extraverts are comfortable with and good at various kinds of interaction. In contrast, introverts with high intimacy needs should have more problems. Their inner-directed orientation should create interference with relationships (their partners may see them as remote or withholding), and they should be more likely to have marital problems. This is exactly what Winter et al. (1998) found.

Problems in Behavior, and Behavior Change

People working within the motive approach to personality have been interested in specific domains of human activity (e.g., achievement, affiliation, power, intimacy)

Table 5.3

Sample hypothesis about the interaction between the Affiliation–Intimacy motive and the trait of Introversion–Extraversion (adapted from Winter et al., 1998)

	Affiliation–Intimacy Motive	
	Low	*High*
Extravert	Intimate relationship not salient as a desire	Desire for intimate relationship leads to single stable relationship
Introvert	Intimate relationship not salient as a desire	Desire for intimate relationships, but difficulty maintaining them, because being focused on inner world is disruptive

and in the more general idea of motivation as a concept. They haven't addressed the question of problems in behavior in great detail, nor have they suggested a particular approach to therapy. Nevertheless, the literature in this area has at least tentative links to certain problems in behavior and to the processes of behavior change.

The Need for Power and Alcohol Abuse

It's been suggested that the need for power can play a role in developing drinking problems (McClelland, Davis, Kalin, & Wanner, 1972). This idea stems partly from the finding that drinking alcohol leads to feelings of power. Thus, a person with a need for power can satisfy that need, at least somewhat, by drinking. This doesn't satisfy the need for long, of course, because in this case the feeling of power is illusory. It goes away when the person sobers up.

The idea that alcohol abuse may reflect a need for power leads to some recommendations for treatment. In particular, it suggests that people who are using alcohol this way aren't aware of doing so. They'd probably benefit from realizing what they're doing. By encouraging other ways to satisfy the power motive, therapists can treat the issue productively, rather than simply treating a symptom. Evidence from one study (Cutter, Boyatzis, & Clancy, 1977) indicates that this approach can be more effective than traditional therapies, yielding nearly twice the rate of rehabilitation at one-year follow-up (see also McClelland, 1977).

Focusing On and Changing Motivation

Theorists who've contributed to the motive approach to personality have also had relatively little to say about therapeutic behavior change. Murray, the father of this approach, was a therapist, but he didn't develop new therapy techniques. In general, he tended to apply the currently existing psychodynamic techniques to people's problems.

It would seem, however, that one of the studies just discussed makes some suggestions for the process of behavior change. As indicated, some people appear to use alcohol as a way of temporarily satisfying a desire for power. A treatment program developed for these people had two focuses. It made them more aware that this motive was behind their drinking. It also helped them to find other ways to satisfy the need for power, thus making drinking unnecessary.

A broader implication of this discussion is that people may *often* be unaware of the motives behind their problem behaviors. Many problem behaviors may reflect needs that are being poorly channeled. If so, taking a close look at the person's motive tendencies might tell something about the source of the problem. Knowing the source may make it easier to make changes.

Another program of work with indirect implications for therapy has been conducted by McClelland and his colleagues. This research concerns a training program developed to raise people's levels of achievement motivation (McClelland, 1965; McClelland & Winter, 1969). It's been used mostly among business people (see also Lemann, 1994). The program has its roots in the idea that thinking a lot about achievement-related ideas increases your motive to achieve.

This program begins by describing the nature of the achievement motive and instructing people on how to score TAT protocols for achievement imagery. People then are taught to use achievement imagery in their thoughts as much as possible. By teaching themselves to think in terms of achievement, they increase the likelihood of taking an achieving orientation to whatever activity they engage in.

Motivation seminars are often used to enhance achievement motivation among people in business.

Achievement-related thinking is important. By itself, however, it isn't enough. A second purpose of the training is to link these thoughts to specific concrete action patterns. It's also important to be sure the patterns work outside the training program. The person is encouraged to think in achievement terms everywhere—not just in the training sessions—and to put the action patterns into motion. People who complete the course write down the plans they have for the next two years. They're encouraged to plan realistically and to set goals that are challenging but not out of reach. This description is a way of turning the achievement orientation they've learned into a self-prescription for a course of activity. This prescription then can be used in guiding actual achievement later on.

Is the course effective? The answer seems to be "yes." In a two-year follow-up, participants had higher business achievements, were more likely to have started new business ventures, and were more likely to be employing more people than before, compared to control participants (McClelland & Winter, 1969).

This program shows it's possible to change people's achievement-related behavior, though a question remains as to whether the underlying needs have changed (see also Box 5.4). It also remains uncertain how much these results can be generalized to the broader domain of therapy. Nonetheless, the studies do seem to provide intriguing suggestions about behavior change.

Need and Motive Theories: Problems and Prospects

The previous chapter dealt with trait theorists. As a group, those theorists are more concerned about describing the structure of personality than in describing the mechanics by which personality traits are expressed. The theorists of this chapter, in contrast, look to motivational processes and the pressures they place on people as a way to specify how dispositions influence actions. By providing a way to think about how dispositions create behavior—by specifying a type of intrapersonal functioning—this approach to dispositions evades one of the criticisms of trait theories.

A criticism that's less easily evaded is that decisions about what qualities to study have been arbitrary. Murray developed his list of needs from his own intuition, and

BOX 5.4

THEORETICAL CONTROVERSY
Are Motives Biologically Based or Are They Rooted in Cognition?

As we've noted, McClelland and his colleagues developed a training program to increase people's achievement motive. This program seemed to produce the desired results. But its success raises fundamental questions about the nature of the achievement motive—indeed, about all psychological motives.

Early motive theorists such as Murray assumed that even psychological or social needs derive from biological processes. Biology is used here more as a metaphor than an explanatory device. Still, it's generally been assumed that individual differences in need profiles are stable, determined by the person's basic nature.

McClelland (1965), on the other hand, came to believe that psychological motives are learned. Thus they can be altered fairly easily. The success of his program stands as a testament to this idea. The program is very simple. Participants get a clear understanding of what the motive is and how it shows up in behavior and thought. They're then taught to think and act that way. Because McClelland knew a lot about how need for achievement is manifested, it was easy for him to tell people what to do.

Though these procedures produced the intended changes, they raise questions. If motives are so easily altered—if motives are learned—why not discard the concept of motive altogether? There are, after all, psychologists from other perspectives who see concepts

such as motive as being useless and even misleading (Chapters 12 and 13). Isn't this, then, a case in which a motivational theorist is turning around and embracing a competing approach?

Another question is raised by the training program's emphasis on cognitive processes. The program entails elaborately coding in memory the nature of the motive the people are trying to acquire. It also includes drawing explicit mental associations between that motive and concrete actions, and an emphasis on monitoring outcomes. These processes look suspiciously like the things that would be emphasized by people who take a cognitive or self-regulation approach to personality (Chapters 16 and 17). Are the effects of the program, then, really motivational?

One possible response to these questions is that the program developed by McClelland may change people's motives but not their needs. That is, recall from earlier in the chapter, theorists sometimes distinguish needs from motives, and that motives are influenced by both needs and press. It's possible to think of McClelland's training program as teaching people how to surround themselves with situational press to evoke the achievement motive. This way of thinking would account for the fact that the motive seems to change, while still allowing the assumption that needs are enduring dispositions.

others working in that tradition accepted it uncritically. Yet one omission from that list that McAdams noted later—the need for intimacy—is strikingly obvious as a human motive. This omission in itself suggests that Murray's intuitive list was somewhat arbitrary. A response to this criticism is that the motives that have been examined most closely in research are those that fit with ideas also appearing elsewhere in psychology, including trait psychology. This convergence across views suggests that the needs in question really are fundamental.

Another criticism that's sometimes made bears less on the theory than on its implementation. Murray was very explicit in his view that the dynamics of personality can be understood only by considering multiple needs at the same time. However, research from the motive approach to personality has rarely done that. More often people have studied one motive at a time, to examine its dynamics. Occasionally researchers have stretched to the point of looking at particular clusters of two or three needs, but this is rare. On the other hand, it's important to keep in mind that, despite Murray's wishes, the motive view of dispositions is not the same as the practice of personology. It is certainly possible to investigate the former without adopting the latter.

Despite these limitations, work on personality from the point of view of motive dispositions has continued from Murray's time into the present. Indeed, such work has enjoyed a resurgence in the past decade or so. The idea that people vary in what motivates them has a good deal of intuitive appeal. Further appeal derives from the fact that this idea can be joined to the idea that motive states wax and wane across time and circumstances. This approach thus has a built-in way of incorporating both situational influences and dispositional influences in an integrated way. Given these strengths, and a growing interest in the relation between motive theories and trait theories, the future of this approach seems assured.

SUMMARY

The motive approach to personality assumes that behavior reflects a set of underlying needs. As a need becomes more intense, it is more likely to influence what behavior is done. Behavior is also influenced by press: external stimuli that elicit motivational tendencies. Needs (and press) vary in strength from moment to moment, but people also differ from each other in patterns of chronic need intensities. According to this viewpoint, this difference is the source of individual differences in personality.

Murray made an ambitious attempt to catalog human needs, listing both biological (primary) and psychogenic (secondary) needs. Several of the psychological motives later received systematic study by others. The first studied (by McClelland, Atkinson, and others) was the need for achievement: the motive to overcome obstacles and to attain goals. People with high levels of the achievement motive behave differently from those with lower levels in several ways: the kinds of tasks they prefer, the level of task difficulty they prefer, their degree of persistence, and their performance levels. Early research on achievement tended to disregard how approach and avoidance motives might separately influence behavior. More recent work, however, has begun to examine those distinct influences.

The need for power—the motive to be strong compared to other people—has also been studied extensively. People who score high in this need tend to seek out positions of influence, to surround themselves with the trappings of power, and to become aroused when the groups they are guiding experience difficulties. People with high levels of the power motive tend to choose as friends people who aren't influential or popular, thereby protecting themselves from undesired competition. Power-motivated men prefer wives who are dependent, and these wives tend not to have their own careers. The power motive can lead to unpleasant forms of social influence unless it's tempered by a sense of responsibility.

The need for affiliation, another need from Murray's list, is the desire to spend time with other people, to develop and maintain relationships. People who score high in this need are responsive to social influence, spend a relatively large proportion of their time communicating with other people, and when alone often think about being with others. A related motive that isn't represented in Murray's list but has received research attention in recent years is the need for intimacy. People high in this need want warm, close, and communicative relationships with other persons. People with strong intimacy needs tend to spend more time in one-to-one interaction and less in groups. They tend to engage in interactions that involve lots of self-disclosure and are especially concerned about their friends' well-being.

Recent research has also begun to investigate patterns of motives, such as inhibited power motive. This pattern is defined by having more of a need for power than a need for affiliation and by restraining the power need. People with this pattern do well in managerial careers, but the pattern has also been linked to political orientations preceding wars.

Most of the emphasis of this view on personality concerns needs and motives, but the theorists of this view also use other concepts in talking about behavior. Incentive value, the extent to which a given action will satisfy a given need for a person, helps to explain why people with the same need express the need in different ways. Expectancy, the apparent likelihood of success, helps determine whether people pursue incentives.

Although somewhat distinct from his emphasis on needs and motives in behavior, Murray also emphasized the study of individual lives over extended periods of time. He coined the term *personology* to refer to the study of the whole person, and he viewed personology as his goal. This emphasis has reemerged more recently in the work of several other researchers.

Although many kinds of assessment devices are used in the motivational approach to personality, the contribution to assessment most identified with this approach is the Thematic Apperception Test (TAT). The TAT is based on the idea that individuals' motives are reflected in the imagery that they "apperceive," that is, read into an ambiguous stimulus—in this case, a set of pictures depicting people in ambiguous situations. Although there are also self-report measures of needs, they appear to measure something (self-attributed motives) different from what the TAT measures (implicit motives). Some people have suggested that the five-factor model can be fit to the motives that Murray listed. Others point out that the evidence comes only from self-report measures, and view traits and motives as different.

The motivational approach to personality has largely ignored the issue of analyzing problems in behavior, although at least some evidence links the need for power to the misuse of alcohol. It's possible to infer from this evidence, however, that many problems in behavior may stem from inappropriate channeling of motives. It's also reasonable that people can be helped by increasing their awareness of the motive that underlies the problem, so the motive can be channeled in alternative ways. Research on increasing the need for achievement suggests that it may be possible to alter people's dispositional levels of the motives that make up personality.

GLOSSARY

Apperception The projecting of a motive as imagery onto an ambiguous external stimulus.

Diagnosticity The extent to which a task provides information about something.

Expectancy The anticipated probable outcome of an action.

Incentive The degree to which an action can satisfy a particular need for a person.

Inhibited power motivation The condition of having more need for power than for affiliation, but restraining its use.

Latent need A motive that exists but presently isn't being openly displayed.

Manifest need A motive that presently is influencing a person's actions.

Motive Cognitive–affective clusters organized around readiness for a particular kind of experience.

Need An unsatisfactory internal condition that motivates behavior.

Need for achievement The need to overcome obstacles and attain goals.

Need for affiliation The need to form and maintain relationships and to be with people.

Need for intimacy The need for close communication with someone else.

Need for power The need to have influence over other people.

Personology Study of the entire person.

Press An external stimulus that increases the level of a motive.

Primary need A biological need, such as the need for food.

Secondary (psychogenic) need A psychological or social need.

Thematic Apperception Test (TAT) A method of assessing the strength of a motive through narrative fantasy.

PART three

The Biological Perspective

prologue to
P A R T *three*

THE BIOLOGICAL PERSPECTIVE:
Major Themes and Underlying Assumptions

Human beings are biological creatures, members of the animal kingdom. We carry around all of the characteristics implied by citizenship in that kingdom. We eat, drink, breathe, void wastes, and engage in sexual activities that ensure the continuation of our species. We're also influenced by a number of more subtle forces reflecting our animal nature.

How deeply rooted are these biological pressures? How pervasive is their influence? Are the qualities of personality determined by genes? Is the existence of personality itself a product of evolution? How much of an influence do biological processes have on personality? What adaptive functions do these influences serve? These are some of the questions that underlie the biological perspective on personality.

Biological approaches to personality have varied widely in focus over the years. Some theories of this group are only vaguely biological. Others are tied to specific biological processes and structures.

The nature of the research also varies widely, from studies examining the nature of biological functions to studies of inheritance. In some ways, the biological perspective is a scattered approach to personality. There are, however, threads of thought that underlie the fragmented surface, linking many of the pieces together.

The biological orientation to personality has two thrusts, and people working from this point of view tend to have two somewhat separate sets of interests. Theorists of the first group focus on the idea that personality characteristics are genetically determined. The biological mechanisms by which inherited differences influence behavior aren't well understood. Until recently, they were rarely explored. That is changing fast, however. The interest of this group lies largely in knowing what characteristics of personality and social behavior are influenced by heredity. These theorists are something of a cross between the biological perspective and the dispositional perspective.

Many of these same people are also interested in the broader idea that the qualities of personality resulted from the evolutionary pressures that produced the human species. This view has grown rapidly in recent years. It's now suggested that far more of human social behavior is a product of our evolutionary heritage than anyone would have guessed two decades ago. These two ideas—that many personality characteristics are genetically determined and that human behavioral tendencies derive from our evolutionary history—form the basis of Chapter 6.

The second focus of the biological perspective is the idea that human behavior is produced by a complex biological system. The processes that make up this system reflect the way we're organized as living creatures. In this view, many biological processes have systematic influences on people's behavior and experience. To understand these influences, theorists first try to follow the biological systems that exist, to see exactly what they're about and how they work. They then think about how the workings of these systems might influence the kinds of phenomena that are identified with personality.

This idea has its roots in antiquity, but it's been revolutionized by methodological advances of the recent past. The component processes of the nervous system are becoming better understood. We're also coming to understand how hormones affect behavior. The viewpoint represented in this work is a "process" approach to personality, looking at how biological functions influence human action. As you'll see, however, this focus on process doesn't mean ignoring individual differences. That is, the processes often operate to different degrees in different people, thereby creating the patterns of uniqueness we know as personality. This type of biological approach to personality is considered in Chapter 7.

chapter

6 Inheritance, Evolution, and Personality

■ **Determining the Role of Inheritance in Personality**
Twin Study Method
Adoption Research

■ **What Personality Qualities Are Inherited?**
Temperaments: Activity, Sociability, and Emotionality
Are There Other Temperaments?
Inheritance of Traits
Temperaments and the Five-Factor Model
Genetics of Other Qualities: How Distinct Are They?
Inheritance and Sexual Orientation
Molecular Genetics and New Sources of Evidence

■ **Environmental Effects**
The Size of Environmental Influences
The Nature of Environmental Influences

■ **Evolution and Human Behavior**
Sociobiology and Evolutionary Psychology
Genetic Similarity and Attraction
Mate Selection and Competition for Mates
Mate Retention and Other Issues
Aggression and the Young Male Syndrome

■ **Assessment**

■ **Problems in Behavior, and Behavior Change**
Behavior Genetics and Disorders
Evolution and Problems in Behavior
Behavior Change: How Much Is Possible?

■ **Inheritance and Evolution: Problems and Prospects**

SUMMARY

■ Two three-day-old babies are lying in cradles behind the glass window. One of them lies peacefully for hours at a time, rarely crying, and moving only a little. The other thrashes his arms and legs, screws up his face, and rends the air with piercing yowls. What could possibly have made two children be so thoroughly different from each other so soon in life?

■ A group of young men, sixteen to eighteen years old, have been hanging around the pool hall–bar all afternoon, acting cool, eyeing women who pass by, and trying to outdo one another with inventive insults. Occasionally tempers flare, the lines of faces harden, and there's pushing and taunting. This time, though, the one doing the taunting went too far. There's a glint of dark steel, and the hot air is shattered by gunshots. Later, the dead one's grieving mother cries out, "Why do men do these things?"

P art of who you are is the body you walk around in. Some people have big bodies, some have small ones. Some bodies are strong, some are frail. Some bodies are coordinated, some are klutzy. Some bodies turn toward dolls at a certain stage of life, others turn instead to Legos.

Your body is not your personality. But does it influence the personality you have? The idea that our bodies determine our personalities goes back at least to Hippocrates and Galen. As we said in Chapter 4, Hippocrates proposed four personality types; Galen added the idea that each type reflects an excess of some bodily fluid. The idea that people's physical makeup determines their personalities has reemerged repeatedly ever since.

"Physical makeup" has meant different things to theorists at different times, however. In the early and mid-twentieth century, it meant physique, or body build (see Box 6.1). Today, physical makeup means genes. Many people now believe most qualities of personality are partly—maybe even largely—inherited.

Determining the Role of Inheritance in Personality

How do researchers decide whether a given quality is inherited? From family resemblances? That's a starting point, but it has a serious problem. Family members could be similar for two reasons: They may be similar because of inheritance. Or they may be similar because they're around each other a lot and learned to act like each other (see Chapter 13).

To get a clearer picture requires better methods. Psychologists turned to the discipline of genetics for ideas. The result was a mix of psychology and genetics called **behavioral genetics.** This is the study of genetic influences on behavioral qualities, including personality qualities, abnormalities, and even cognitive and emotional processes (Plomin, 1997; Plomin, DeFries, & McClearn, 1990; Plomin & Rende, 1991).

Twin Study Method

A method that's widely used in behavioral genetics is the **twin study.** It takes advantage of two accidents in reproduction, which produce two types of twins. One accident occurs shortly after conception. A fertilized egg normally divides into two cells,

BOX 6.1

EARLY BIOLOGICAL VIEWS
Physique and Personality

The idea that people's bodies relate to their personalities is reflected in popular stereotypes: the easygoing, jolly fat man; the adventurous, strong hero; the frail intellectual. Is there any truth to it? Several theorists have thought so over the years. Kretschmer (1925) classified people as thin, muscular, or obese, and found that each group was prone to a different set of disorders. William Sheldon (1942) expanded the idea from categories to dimensions of variability, and examined normal personality. What he called a person's **somatotype** is defined by placing the person on three dimensions corresponding to Kretschmer's categories. It is designated by three numbers, each from 1 to 7, indicating the degree to which the person has that body quality. Sheldon believed each quality reflects an emphasis on one of three layers of the embryo. For that reason, he named the characteristics after the layers.

Endomorphy is the tendency toward plumpness (reflecting an emphasis on digestion). Endomorphs are soft and round. **Mesomorphy** is the tendency toward muscularity (reflecting a predominance of bone, muscle, and connective tissue). Mesomorphs are hard and rectangular, strong, and suited to hard exertion. **Ectomorphy** is the tendency toward thinness (reflecting predominance of the skin and nervous system). Ectomorphs are delicate and frail, easily overwhelmed by stimulation and not suited to physical labor. Most people have a little of each quality. Someone who's generally muscular but a little pudgy might be a 4-6-2 (endomorphy-mesomorphy-ectomorphy). A person who's frail but has a potbelly might be a 6-1-7. A person who's absolutely average would be a 4-4-4.

In parallel with the physical dimensions, Sheldon proposed three aspects of "temperament." **Viscerotonia** implies qualities such as relaxation, tolerance, sociability, love of comfort, good will, and easygoingness. **Somatotonia** is qualities such as boldness, assertiveness, and a desire for adventure and activity. **Cerebrotonia** includes avoidance of social interaction, restraint, high pain sensitivity, and a mental intensity approaching apprehensiveness. As with somatotypes, most people have some of each of these three sets of qualities.

As he'd predicted, Sheldon found that temperaments and somatotypes go together. Mesomorphy was related to somatotonia, endomorphy to viscerotonia, and ectomorphy to cerebrotonia. Later studies also supported this view, in ratings of children (Walker, 1962), in self-reports (e.g., Cortes & Gatti, 1965; Yates & Taylor, 1978), and in other ways (Davidson, McInnes, & Parnell, 1957; Glueck & Glueck, 1956; Parnell, 1957).

These studies all indicated that body types relate to personality. But why? Does physique cause personality? Is the link more roundabout? The body types reflect well-known stereotypes, which include expectations about how people act. If we have such expectations, we may induce people to act as "expected" (Gacsaly & Borges, 1979). This can produce an association between physique and behavior. It would stem from social pressure, though, not body type per se.

It's hard to know why associations exist between body type and personality. Partly for this reason, many people were skeptical of the theory, and interest in it waned. Sheldon's ideas as such are no longer influential, but he stressed a theme that reemerged only a couple of decades later. He believed that personality, along with body type, was inherited. He didn't test this belief. Indeed, in his time it wasn't widely understood *how* to test it. Others found ways to do so, however, leading to the findings presented in the first half of this chapter.

---

then four, then eight, eventually forming a person. Sometimes, though, the first two cells become separated, and each grows *separately* into a person. These persons are identical twins, or **monozygotic (MZ) twins.** Because they came from what was a single cell, they are 100 percent alike genetically.

The second kind of accident occurs in conception itself. Usually only one egg is released from the mother's ovary, but occasionally two are. If both happen to be fer-

Comparisons between identical and fraternal twins can provide information about the heritability of characteristics.

tilized and begin to develop simultaneously, the result is fraternal twins, or **dizygotic (DZ) twins.** Genetically, DZ twins are like any pair of brothers, pair of sisters, or brother and sister. They just happen to be born at the same time rather than separately. As with any pair of **siblings** (brothers or sisters), they are, on the average, 50 percent alike genetically (though the overlap of specific pairs ranges from zero to 100). Interestingly enough, many twins are wrong about which kind they are, and errors are just as common for MZ as DZ twins. One study found that in about 30 percent of pairs one twin was wrong; in about 12 percent of pairs *both* twins were wrong (Scarr & Carter-Saltzman, 1979).

In a twin study (Figure 6.1), pairs of identical twins are related to each other on the characteristic of interest by a correlation; the same is done with pairs of same-sex fraternal twins. The two *correlations* are then compared. If identical twins are more similar to each other than fraternal twins, it must be because of the difference in genetic similarity.

The index of genetic influence on personality is termed a **heritability** estimate. This index is considered to be the amount of variance accounted for by inheritance in the trait under study. The higher the heritability, the stronger the evidence that genes matter.

The twin study method is based on the assumption that co-twins who are raised together are exposed to much the same life experiences as each other, *whether they are identical or fraternal twins.* This is critically important (Figure 6.1). You couldn't conclude that a difference between correlations comes from heredity if parents treated DZ twins differently from MZ twins. The difference in genetic overlap would be confounded with the difference in treatment.

Are the two kinds of twins treated more or less the same? The answer seems to be a cautious "yes." MZ twins are more likely than DZ twins to be dressed alike, but the differences are slight (Plomin et al., 1990). MZ twins also don't seem to resemble each other more in personality if they were treated alike than if they were not (Loehlin & Nichols, 1976). On the other hand, one study found that DZ twins who thought they were MZ twins were more alike than other DZ twins (Scarr & Carter-Saltzman, 1979). A more recent study found that MZ pairs recalled somewhat more similar experiences than DZ twin pairs, but these similarities were not related to personality similarity (Borkenau, Riemann, Angleitner, & Spinath, 2002).

Figure 6.1

A basic twin study method examines pairs of identical and same-sex fraternal twins raised together. Members of each twin pair are assessed on the variable of interest, and a separate correlation is computed for each type of twin. The correlation for fraternal (DZ) twins is subtracted from the correlation for identical (MZ) twins. Multiplying this difference by 2 gives an index of the heritability of the characteristic, an estimate of the proportion of variance in that characteristic that is accounted for by inheritance.

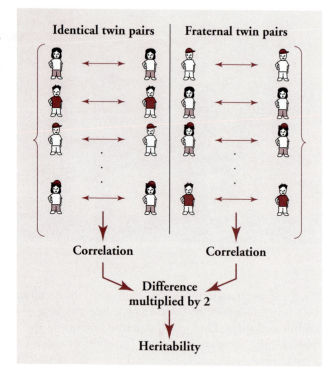

Adoption Research

The twin study isn't the only way to study inheritance. Another method, termed the **adoption study,** is also used. An adoption study looks at how the adopted child resembles the biological parents and the adoptive parents. Resemblance to biological parents is viewed as genetically based, whereas resemblance to the adoptive parents is environmentally based.

Another method combines features of the twin study with features of the adoption study. It's sometimes possible to study MZ twins who were adopted and raised separately (see Box 6.2). Because they grew up in different homes, environmental impacts should cause *differences* rather than similarities. Similarity between these pairs can be contrasted with MZ twins raised together and DZ twins raised together. If heredity is important to the trait under study, MZ twins—even if they were raised apart—should be more similar than DZ twins. If heredity's *really* important, MZ twins raised apart should be nearly as similar as MZ twins raised together.

What Personality Qualities Are Inherited?

These methods have been used for three decades to study genetic influences on personality. One body of work focuses on **temperaments.** This term has been used in several ways. Some have used the singular *temperament,* rather than the plural, to refer to a person's overall "emotional nature" (e.g., Allport, 1961; Gallagher, 1994; Kagan, 1994). Today's use of the word may be best exemplified in the work of Arnold Buss and Robert Plomin (1984, p. 84). They used the plural *temperaments* to refer to "inherited personality traits present in early childhood." What distinguishes temperaments from other traits, in their view, is that temperaments are genetically based.

BOX 6.2

TWINS SEPARATED AT BIRTH, REUNITED AS ADULTS
Some Startling Similarities

Our emphasis here is on systematic studies of genetics and personality. However, some of the most striking indications that personality can be inherited are more anecdotal. The information comes from the experiences of identical twins who were separated early in life and raised in different homes, and were reunited later on (Segal, 1999).

This combination of circumstances occurs when identical twins are put up for adoption separately as newborns, a practice that once was fairly common, but no longer is. In many cases, the infants grew into adults who had no idea they were twins. In some cases, though, they were reunited as adults. Imagine the surprise of discovering someone else who looks just like you!

What's it like to discover your identical twin after you're both grown? Reunited twins sometimes discover astonishing similarities (Rosen, 1987; Segal, 1999). Fascinating stories have emerged from projects studying twins raised apart, such as the Minnesota Center for Twin and Adoption Research. Two of their participants, brothers from New Jersey, didn't meet—didn't even know the other existed—until they were adults. At that time both were volunteer firefighters, both held their beer bottles in the same unusual way, both drank the same brand, and both tended to make the same remarks and gestures when joking, which both did frequently. Another pair of twins discovered that they both smoked the same brand of cigarettes, drove the same kind of car, and did woodworking as a hobby.

A pair of women from Finland provide another amazing example. They were raised in economic circumstances that were very different from each other, but both grew up to be penny pinchers. Each had a fear of heights, each had had a miscarriage, then three healthy children. Not long after they first met, they were so in tune with each other that they began finishing each other's sentences—all this despite being raised totally separated from each other.

Examples such as these are striking, but it's hard to say how much they capitalize on chance. That is, although reunited twins do tend to be similar in many ways, not every pair of twins displays such dramatic patterns of unlikely similarities. Nonetheless, dramatic examples such as these do tend to stick in people's minds and influence their thinking about the nature of personality. Such illustrations convey the impression that inheritance not only influences broad qualities such as activity level and emotionality but also affects personality in more subtle ways.

They see temperaments as more pervasive in influence than other traits (A. Buss, 1995). They affect *what* people do, and *how* people do what they do.

Temperaments: Activity, Sociability, and Emotionality

Buss and Plomin (1984) argued that three normal personality qualities deserve to be called temperaments. These are *activity level, sociability,* and *emotionality.* Each of these is a dimension of individual differences.

Activity level is the person's overall output of energy or behavior. This temperament has two aspects that differ conceptually, but are highly correlated. One is *vigor:* the intensity of behavior. Vigorous acts involve a lot of energy. People high in vigor prefer high-intensity action (e.g., they may prefer tennis over shuffleboard). The second facet is *tempo:* speed. People whose tempo is high prefer fast-paced activities. They tend to do quickly whatever they're doing. Those whose tempo is lower take a more leisurely approach to things.

Sociability is the tendency to prefer being with other people rather than alone. Sociability is a desire for other people's attention, sharing activities, and the responsiveness and stimulation that are part of social interaction. According to Buss and Plomin,

Temperaments influence many kinds of behavior; for example, activity level expresses itself through the kinds of leisure activities people choose to engage in. Some activities are more laid back, others are more fast paced and require lots of energy.

sociability is *not* a matter of desiring social rewards such as praise, respect, or sympathy. Rather, to be sociable is to value intrinsically the process of interacting with others.

Emotionality is defined by Buss and Plomin as the tendency to become physiologically aroused—easily and intensely—in upsetting situations. They see this temperament as pertaining to three emotions: distress, anger, and fear. In their view, other emotions don't involve enough arousal to be relevant to this temperament. Their measure of temperament for adults has three subscales, measuring proneness to these three emotions. It's of interest that anger proneness isn't highly correlated with the other two (Buss & Plomin, 1984). Perhaps the temperament of emotionality is actually two distinct traits.

The temperaments proposed by Buss and Plomin resemble those of Sheldon (Box 6.1) more than is usually recognized. Indeed, these resemblances are quite intriguing. Activity level, and the impact on the world this concept implies, resembles somatotonia. Sociability was part of viscerotonia. Emotionality (apprehensiveness) was part of cerebrotonia.

What's the evidence that these temperaments are inherited? Consider twin studies of parents' ratings of their children (Buss & Plomin, 1975; Plomin, 1974; Plomin & Rowe, 1977; Plomin, described in Plomin & Foch, 1980). Correlations between parent ratings of activity, emotionality, and sociability were strong for MZ twins (average correlations are shown in Figure 6.2). They were next to nonexistent and sometimes even inverse for DZ twins. Thus, the data indicate a powerful role for heredity in these three characteristics (see also Thomas & Chess, 1977).

Concerns have been raised, though, about rater bias when parents rate their children (Neale & Stevenson, 1989; Saudino, McGuire, Reiss, Hetherington, & Plomin, 1995). Parents of DZ twins that don't much resemble each other tend to contrast the two, amplifying differences. Parents of MZ twins, seeing more similarity, don't do this. Further, there's evidence that mothers of very young children aren't very good reporters of their children's behavior (Seifer, Sameroff, Barrett, & Krafchuk, 1994).

It's important, then, that other sources of evidence exist. Several studies have examined heritability of emotionality using Eysenck's self-report scales. These stud-

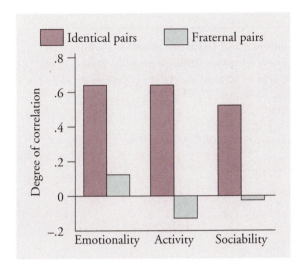

Figure 6.2

Average correlations for parental ratings of identical and fraternal twins on temperaments of emotionality, activity level, and sociability. (Correlations are averaged across four samples, totaling 228 pairs of identical twins and 172 pairs of fraternal twins, with an average age of 5 years 1 month; adapted from Buss & Plomin, 1984).

ies uniformly found that MZ twins are more alike by self-report than DZ twins (Floderus-Myrhed, Pedersen, & Rasmuson, 1980; Loehlin & Nichols, 1976; Viken, Rose, Kaprio, & Koskenvuo, 1994; Young, Eaves, & Eysenck, 1980; see also Loehlin, Willerman, & Horn, 1985; Eysenck & Eysenck, 1985). One study found the same relation when using co-twin ratings rather than self-reports (Heath, Neale, Kessler, Eaves, & Kendler, 1992). These findings give added weight to the conclusion that emotionality is genetically influenced.

Adoption research (Loehlin et al., 1985) also supports a genetic influence for activity level and sociability. This study compared adopted children with their biological parents and their adoptive parents. The measures were two self-report inventories, the California Psychological Inventory (CPI) and the Thurstone Temperament Schedule (TTS). The CPI has two scales that reflect sociability (sociability and social presence), and the TTS also has a sociability scale. The TTS also has scales that reflect activity level (called active and vigorous).

Table 6.1 shows some of the correlations from this study. Although the children had spent their lives with their adoptive parents (from a few days after birth), there was remarkably little resemblance between them (column A). On the other hand, despite the separation from their biological parents, there was a pattern of moderate correlations between them (column B).

The data also allowed comparisons between the adopted children and both biological and adoptive siblings (columns C and D). The pattern is less consistent than for parents, but the same general picture emerges: the adopted children are more like their biological brothers and sisters than their adoptive brothers and sisters.

Are There Other Temperaments?

Two other dimensions merit mention in discussing temperaments: impulsivity and intelligence. In the earliest statement of their theory, Buss and Plomin (1975) saw impulsivity as a possible temperament. Evidence between then and 1984 was inconclusive, and they dropped it. Later on, a new study found a genetic influence on impulsiveness (Pedersen et al., 1988). This study was unusual in that it examined older adults (average age fifty-eight), whereas Buss and Plomin had relied mostly on parent

Table 6.1

Correlations between adopted children and (A) their adoptive parents, (B) their biological parents, (C) their adoptive siblings, and (D) their biological siblings, on three measures of sociability and two measures of activity (data adapted from Loehlin, Willerman, & Horn, 1985)*

Measure	(A) Adoptive parent	(B) Biological parent	(C) Adoptive siblings	(D) Biological siblings
Sociability (CPI)[†]	.04	.17	.04	.22
Social presence (CPI)	.12	.34	−.08	.70
Sociable (TTS)[††]	.02	.18	−.13	.38
Active (TTS)	.02	.16	−.12	.06
Vigorous (TTS)	.06	.33	.18	.42

*Parent correlations are averages of child–father and child–mother correlations; sibling correlations are also averaged.

[†]CPI is the California Psychological Inventory.

[††]TTS is the Thurstone Temperament Schedule.

ratings of children. Pedersen et al.'s finding may reopen the question of whether impulsiveness should be seen as a temperament.

Intelligence is a different case. Intelligence is not usually regarded as a *personality* trait (for a dissenting opinion see Eysenck & Eysenck, 1985). It has the characteristics Buss and Plomin used to define temperaments, however. It's genetically influenced (Bouchard, Lykken, McGue, Segal, & Tellegen, 1990; Loehlin et al., 1988; Plomin, 1989), and its effects on behavior are broad, manifest early in life, and continue throughout the life span. Perhaps intelligence should also be viewed as a temperament.

Inheritance of Traits

We began this discussion with temperaments: broad, pervasive qualities that underlie a wide range of behaviors. Are other traits influenced by inheritance?

Twin studies have looked at heritability of many traits, using personality inventories. An early twin study (Loehlin & Nichols, 1976) found correlations among MZ twins were higher than among DZ twins on a wide range of characteristics (an average of about .50 versus an average of about .30). Other studies (reviewed by Carey, Goldsmith, Tellegen, & Gottesman, 1978) found similar results, as did a study of twins raised apart (Bouchard & McGue, 1990).

Many of these studies were done before trait theorists began to converge on the idea that personality is described by five basic factors. With the emergence of the five-factor model, researchers have begun to ask whether those five dimensions are genetically influenced. The answer appears to be "yes."

A number of twin studies have now explicitly studied the five-factor model (Bergeman et al., 1993; Jang et al., 1996; Jang et al., 1998) or elements of the big five (Tellegen et al., 1988). The studies all found evidence of heritability for conscientiousness. Agreeableness was found heritable in the three studies in which it was measured. With respect to both neuroticism and extraversion (which have been studied over a far longer period), the evidence of heritability is quite strong and consistent (e.g., Heath et al., 1992; Jang et al., 1996; Tellegen et al., 1988; Viken et al., 1994).

As noted in Chapter 4, the last of the big five is the one that's been the hardest to characterize and name. Some call it openness to experience, others call it intellect, culture, and even intelligence. As indicated earlier, there's lots of evidence of a genetic contribution to intelligence. There's now also evidence of a genetic contribution to openness to experience (Bergeman et al., 1993; Jang et al., 1996; Jang et al., 1998; see also Loehlin, 1992).

Most twin studies of adult personality use self-reports or reports of people close to the twins. This leads to the same criticism as was made of studies in which mothers rated their infants. That is, the potential exists for contrast effects that exaggerate differences between twins that are slightly dissimilar. To deal with this possibility, Borkenau, Riemann, Angleitner, and Spinath (2001) did a twin study in which participants were videotaped then rated by people who didn't know them. They also found evidence of genetic contribution to all five factors.

Temperaments and the Five-Factor Model

The supertraits that make up the five-factor model are broad and pervasive in influence. In that respect they're actually a lot like temperaments. Indeed, some have suggested that no distinction should be made between traits and temperaments (McCrae, Costa, Ostendorf et al., 2000). This suggests more questions, which may have already arisen in your mind. What's the relationship between the five-factor model and the temperaments discussed earlier in this chapter? Do the big five *derive from* those temperaments? Are they *the same* as the temperaments?

Let's consider how the big five relate to those temperaments (for broader discussion, see Digman & Shmelyov, 1996; Halverson, Kohnstamm, & Martin, 1994; Loehlin, 1992). An obvious similarity is that Buss and Plomin's (1984) emotionality closely resembles neuroticism, or emotional instability. The labels emotionality and emotional instability are more neutral than neuroticism, but the dimension clearly focuses on *negative* emotions, particularly anxiety. Thus, this temperament–trait pair are quite similar.

Another of the big five is extraversion. This trait has overtones of not one but two temperaments (plus some other qualities). Extraversion suggests a preference for being with others, implying a possible link to sociability. Eysenck (1986) also included a quality of activity in his portrayal of extraversion. This suggests extraversion may blend sociability with activity. On the other hand, extraversion has come to be viewed partly in terms of social dominance, which isn't directly implied either by sociability or by activity.

Another of the five factors—agreeableness—also has overtones of sociability, although again not being identical to it. Agreeableness suggests liking to be with people. It goes beyond that, however, in having connotations of being easy to get along with. Whether agreeableness derives from sociability is something of an open question.

What of conscientiousness? Examination of this supertrait suggests that it's defined partly by the absence of impulsiveness. That is, conscientiousness is a planful, persistent, focused orientation toward life's activities. Given the possibility that impulsivity is a temperament (Pedersen et al., 1988), this would suggest another link between temperaments and the five-factor model.

The last of the big five is openness to experience, or intellect, culture, or intelligence. Given the diverse labels for this factor, it's unsure whether this is the same quality as intelligence, mentioned earlier as a potential temperament. (Indeed, it's not entirely clear exactly what intelligence is, cf. Sternberg, 1982.) But if this part of the five-factor model did reflect what intelligence tests measure, there'd be yet another link between temperament and trait models.

In sum, although the fit is not perfect, the set of qualities proposed as biologically based temperaments bears a good deal of resemblance to the five-factor model. The places where the resemblance is less clear serve partly to raise interesting questions. For example, why should activity and sociability be considered fundamental, rather than extraversion? There are many ways to divide up the qualities of behavior, and it's hard to know which is best.

It is likely that these questions will continue to be of interest. More specifically, it seems likely that the five-factor model will continue to have an increasing influence on how behavioral genetics researchers decide which qualities of personality to study in their research.

Genetics of Other Qualities: How Distinct Are They?

Studies of traditional traits aren't the only evidence that inheritance influences personality. A number of other effects have emerged, some of which relate fairly readily to personality.

An example is evidence of a genetic influence on risk of divorce (McGue & Lykken, 1992). There's now evidence that the effect operates through personality (Jockin, McGue, & Lykken, 1996). A particularly unlikely finding is a genetic influence on the likelihood of experiencing impactful life events. It's true, though. Again, evidence indicates that it operates via personality (Saudino et al., 1997). Heredity also influences how much social support people have (Kessler, Kendler, Heath, Neale, & Eaves, 1992), which probably reflects personality differences (Brissette, Scheier, & Carver, 2002; Kendler, 1997). There's also a genetic contribution to people's attitudes on various topics (Eaves, Eysenck, & Martin, 1989; Olson, Vernon, Harris, & Jang, 2001; Tesser, 1993). This also seems likely to reflect broader personality qualities.

Findings such as these raise a question: To what extent are the effects distinct and separate? The temperaments discussed earlier are broad, relating to many traits. When evidence is found that a quality is genetically influenced, it raises a question. Is this a *separate* effect? Or is the effect there only because the quality under study relates to a temperament?

The question of how many distinct qualities are *separately* influenced by inheritance is one that hasn't been explored much. However, it's an important question in understanding how inheritance affects personality. A recent study began to explore it, within the framework of the five-factor model (Jang et al., 1998). This study found that not only were the five supertraits heritable, so were most of their facet traits. Indeed, the latter genetic influences were separate from the genetic influences on the overall traits. This suggests that many distinct qualities may be genetically influenced, rather than just a few broad ones.

Inheritance and Sexual Orientation

A topic about which there's been much discussion in recent years is the possible role of genetics in determining a person's sexual orientation. Some people would regard this topic as outside the realm of personality, but others would say it's very much a part of personality.

Evidence regarding the possibility of a genetic role in sexual orientation goes back forty years, with the report of a higher incidence of homosexuality among men whose MZ twin was gay than men whose DZ twin was gay (Eysenck, 1964a). Later twin studies also looked at homosexual men (Bailey & Pillard, 1991) and homosexual women (Bailey, Pillard, Neale, & Agyei, 1993). In each case, a co-twin was more than twice as likely to be homosexual if the twins were MZ than if they were DZ (similar findings were also reported by Whitam, Diamond, & Martin, 1993). Not all results have been that clear. A recent twin study found substantially weaker effects (Bailey, Dunne, & Martin, 2000). On the other hand, that study did find evidence that a likely precursor of homosexuality is genetically influenced. That variable is childhood gender nonconformity (feelings of gender identity and participation in gender-typed activities).

Another article reported evidence of a genetic basis for male homosexuality using an entirely different approach (Hamer, Hu, Magnuson, Hu, & Pattatucci, 1993). This team examined families of gay men for patterns of similarity. They found more gay relatives on the mother's side of the family (maternal uncles and sons of maternal aunts) than on the father's side. This suggested to them that the homosexual gene might be on the X chromosome (which a son always receives from his mother).

Examination of genetic material revealed a region of the X chromosome that was similar among most of the gay participants. This suggests a genetic basis for at least some instances of homosexuality. The evidence also suggests that other instances have a different basis, because this region *wasn't* similar for some gay men (see also Pool, 1993). It's long been wondered why homosexuality hasn't died out over generations, because gay men don't reproduce at the same rate as other men. If the gene is on the X chromosome, that would account for it. That is, the X chromosome is carried by women as well as men. The gene can be passed on without being reflected in behavior. All involved in this research caution that the finding must be replicated before its implications are pursued too far, but the finding does have far-reaching implications.

Molecular Genetics and New Sources of Evidence

The preceding paragraph raised a new issue. There now are ways to study genetic influences that weren't available even a short time ago. The effort to map the human **genome**—the genetic blueprint of the body—has been wildly successful. A first draft was completed in 2000, years ahead of schedule. It's increasingly possible to identify specific genes that cause differences among people. The differences range from vulnerability to physical and psychological disorders to normal personality. Many believe the ability to identify genes linked to such differences will revolutionize medicine, psychiatry, and psychology (Plomin, 1995; Plomin & Crabbe, 2000; Plomin, DeFries, Craig, & McGuffin, 2003).

A huge proportion of the human genome is identical for everyone. Interest focuses on the parts that vary. The different forms of DNA that occur at a particular location are termed **alleles.** Any genetic difference between persons means they have different alleles at some location. The first question is which locations influence a given personality quality. Plomin and Crabbe (2000) suggested that we are likely to find many genes related to a given personality quality. Indeed, different genes may be involved in different aspects of behavior related to the trait.

The first discoveries in this area have mostly been single genes relating to broad outcomes, such as disorders. A few genes have also been identified that have clear relevance to normal personality. For example, a gene has been identified that relates to the use of dopamine in the brain. This gene has several versions (alleles), one of which is longer than the others. Two research teams (Benjamin et al., 1996; Ebstein et al., 1996) found almost simultaneously that people with the long allele have high scores on personality scales that relate to novelty seeking. Others have not always been able to repeat this, but some have (Wahlsten, 1999).

Another gene has been identified that relates to use of serotonin in the brain. Several research groups have found a link between the short allele of that gene and high scores on personality scales assessing anxiety and avoidance of harm (e.g., Katsuragi et al., 1999; Lesch et al., 1996; Osher et al., 2000). Again, not everyone has been able to repeat the effect (Jorm et al., 1998), but some have. There is even evidence that this gene is partly responsible for the moderately high inverse correlation between neuroticism and agreeableness (Jang et al., 2001).

Despite the prominence that these single-gene discoveries have received, it's likely that most genetic influences on behavior will involve small contributions from many genes (Plomin & Crabbe, 2000). News programs and magazines may trumpet every new discovery as "the" gene for something, but that's almost sure to be misleading. Nonetheless, it's clear that the tools of molecular genetics have changed greatly the way in which researchers pursue the genetic contributions to many aspects of the human experience, including personality.

Environmental Effects

There are two more issues to raise in this part of the chapter. They concern the "other" effects in twin and adoption studies, the part we haven't emphasized. Specifically, these studies always find that nonhereditary factors contribute to personality. The issues are how great a contribution they make and what kind of contribution they make.

The Size of Environmental Influences

A topic that's been debated as long as twin and adoption studies have been conducted is the size of genetic versus environmental influence. The argument seems easy enough to resolve. That is, the statistics of the study tell you the effects. But that's not the end of it. There are reasons why the statistics themselves may have built-in biases. The arguments are subtle and complex. Here are two of them.

Dickens and Flynn (2001) said that there often are unrecognized correlations between genetic influences and environmental influences on the same outcome. The example they used is intelligence. People with high intelligence gravitate to environments that foster learning, more than do people with less intelligence. In those environments, they learn more. Their IQs go up. The environment had an effect on their IQ. But the possibility for that to happen derived indirectly from their genetic makeup. Thus, the two influences are correlated.

Why does this matter? The size of an environmental effect on an outcome is judged by how much variability is not explained by the genetic effect. If an environmental effect is mistaken to be a genetic effect (because they're correlated), the genetic effect gets the credit for what the environment is doing. The genetic statistical effect from the study is larger than it should be, and the environmental statistical effect is smaller than it should be.

Dickens and Flynn made this argument in the context of IQ. It also can be applied to personality. As was said in Chapter 4, people gravitate to environments that suit their interests, that let them be who they are. Maybe those environments even induce people to have more of the quality that first led them there. Someone who's slightly introverted who starts reading more or keeping a diary may discover the joys of solitary pursuits and become even more introverted. Someone who's slightly extraverted who gets involved in group activities may discover she likes being in charge of groups, and develop greater extraversion.

Another argument begins with the fact that influences on societies as a whole change over extended periods of time. These broad influences may have an impact on personality. There is evidence, for example, that people in the United States of a given age were more anxious in 1993 than in 1952 (Twenge, 2000). Indeed, in that study the average child in the 1980s reported more anxiety than did children who were psychiatric patients in the 1950s! Age-cohort effects have also been found for extraversion (Twenge, 2001) and self-esteem (Twenge & Campbell, 2001).

Why does this matter? It matters because these seem to be environmental influences on personality (perhaps across the entire population). But this very broad environmental influence never gets included in the computations of genetic and environmental effects in twin studies. It's controlled out of the entire analysis (Twenge, 2002). Again, this would mean the genetic effects seem larger in the studies than they are in reality.

The Nature of Environmental Influences

The studies that establish a powerful role for inheritance in personality also show an important role for nonhereditary factors. Surprisingly, however, the evidence on the whole suggests that families don't make children alike, as you might assume. The environment has an impact on personality, but primarily at an *individual* level (Plomin & Daniels, 1987).

What might be the sources of nonshared environmental influence? There isn't a lot of information on the question. Several guesses sound reasonable, though (Dunn & Plomin, 1990; Plomin & Daniels, 1987; Rowe, 1994). For example, siblings often have different sets of friends, sometimes totally different. Peers have a big influence on growing children—some think even stronger than the influence of parents (Harris, 1995). Differences in peer groups may cause children's personalities to become different. If that happens, it's an environmental influence, but it's one that's not shared by the siblings.

Another point is that siblings in families don't exist side by side. In their interactions, they develop roles that play off each other (e.g., Daniels, 1986; Hoffman, 1991). For example, if one child often helps another child with schoolwork, the two are developing styles of interacting that diverge. As another example, parents sometimes favor one child over another. This can affect the children's relationship, perhaps inducing differences between them. Again, the effects would be environmental, but they would differ from one child to the other.

The exact manner in which the environment influences personality development remains to be fully explored. And questions remain about the impact of the shared environment versus the unshared environment. When behavior measures are used instead of rating scales, the shared environment seems more important (Turkheimer, 1998). For example, in the study described earlier in which videotaped behavior was rated by strangers, Borkenau et al. (2001) found a much larger effect for shared environment than is typically found. It seems clear that this set of issues will continue to receive attention in the future.

Evolution and Human Behavior

Evidence that inheritance plays a role in personality is one contributor to the emergence of a broader current of thought. The broader current is the idea that evolutionary processes have a major influence on present-day human behavior. This line of thought is tied to several labels, including behavioral ecology, sociobiology, and evolutionary psychology (Barkow, Cosmides, & Tooby, 1992; Bjorklund & Pellegrini, 2002; D. Buss, 1991, 1995; Caporael, 2001; Heschl, 2002; Segal, 1993; Tooby & Cosmides, 1989, 1990). Work deriving from this group of ideas has grown explosively in recent years.

Sociobiology and Evolutionary Psychology

Sociobiology (Alexander, 1979; Barash, 1977, 1986, 2001; Crawford, 1989; Crawford, Smith, & Krebs, 1987; Dawkins, 1976; Lumsden & Wilson, 1981; Wilson, 1975) was defined as the study of the biological basis of social behavior. The core assumption is that many—perhaps all—of the basic elements of social interaction in humans are products of evolution. That is, the patterns were retained genetically because at some point in prehistory they conferred an adaptive advantage.

In some respects this view resembles that presented earlier by a group working in **ethology,** the study of animals' behavior in their natural environment. Two topics in ethology are often mentioned in psychology. One is imprinting, in which the young of many species attach to their mothers (Hess, 1973). Another is the idea that animals mark and defend territories (cf. Ardrey, 1966). Ethologists suggested humans have similar patterns. For example, things in your room can be seen as territorial markers. It may be a mess, but it's *your* mess. Attachment of infants to mothers may entail the same processes as imprinting. Psychologists have been wary of adopting such ideas too quickly. Drawing parallels to other animals gets risky when the animals aren't closely related to people, for example, the birds in which imprinting is so clear.

Ethologists influenced thinking about human behavior mostly by making analogies. Sociobiologists, in contrast, focused on evolutionary genetics and the question of how behavior patterns might get built in (see also Box 6.3). This view is more radical than that of ethologists. To a sociobiologist, a behavior pattern might exist in humans *but in no other species,* because of a unique adaptation among humans.

This reasoning led in some surprising directions. For example, it's led to a way to account for altruism, a tendency that seems very hard to explain in evolutionary terms. Altruism is acting for the welfare of others, to the point of sacrificing one's own well-being (potentially one's life) for someone else. Altruism would seem to confer a biological *dis*advantage. That is, being altruistic may help someone, but it also might get you killed. This prevents your genes from being passed on to the next generation. If the genes aren't passed on, a genetically based tendency toward altruism should disappear very quickly.

Sociobiologists point out, however, that the process of evolution isn't really a matter of individual survival. What matters concerns a "gene pool," distributed across a population. If one *group* in a population survives, prospers, and reproduces at a high rate, its genes move onward into subsequent generations more than other groups' genes.

This means there are ways to get your genes carried forward besides reproducing on your own. Your genes are helped into the next generation by anything that

BOX 6.3

THEORETICAL ISSUE
Species-Wide Adaptations and the Existence of Individual Differences

The basic concepts of natural selection and population genetics are simple. If a characteristic differs from person to person, it means the gene (or genes) behind that characteristic has several potential forms, or alleles. Some people have one allele, some have another one. (Actually, it's even more complicated, because everyone has two of each chromosome, so you can also have mixed alleles, even if there are only two versions available.)

Selection means one form of the gene is more likely to show up in the next generation because it's been helpful in survival or reproduction, or is less likely to show up because it's *interfered* with survival or reproduction. This is **directional selection.** It means a shift toward greater proportion of the adaptive allele in the population's next generation. If it goes on long enough, directional selection reduces or even eliminates individual differences. Over many generations, those without the adaptive allele fail to reproduce, and a larger proportion of the next generation have the adaptive one. In principle, this is how a characteristic can become universal in the population.

Many characteristics might influence survival. For example, in a world where strength matters (which probably was true during human evolution), strength makes you more likely to survive long enough to reproduce. That sends genes for strength into the next generation. As long as these genes are well represented in the population, the population will tend to survive and create yet another generation.

But wait. If some characteristics are more adaptive than others, why are there individual differences? Why aren't we all large and strong and smart and stealthy and whatever else is a good thing to be? A

tricky thing about selection is that whether a particular value is adaptive or not depends on the setting. Sometimes a value that's useful in one environment is not just useless—but fatal—in another. In the long run, genetic variability in the population is necessary for it to survive in a changing world. Thus, the importance of another kind of selection, termed **stabilizing selection,** which maintains genetic variability (Plomin, 1981). Stabilizing selection occurs when an intermediate value of some characteristic is more adaptive than the value at either extreme. Presumably, intermediate values reflect combinations of alleles, rather than a specific allele, and maybe even multiple genes. Predominance of intermediate values thus implies genetic variability.

How can an intermediate value of a characteristic be more adaptive than an extreme value? Consider this example. It's important for people to have some sociability, given that we are such a social species. Having too little sociability isn't adaptive. But neither is it adaptive to have too *much* sociability. A person with extremely high sociability can hardly bear to be alone, and life sometimes requires people to be alone.

Intermediate values are especially adaptive in many of the domains that are relevant to personality. That's why personality traits vary from person to person. There is genetic diversity on those traits. Otherwise, there'd be only a single personality, which everyone would have. Sociobiology and evolutionary psychology tend to emphasize the idea that certain behavioral adaptations are part of everyone. An interesting question is whether they are part of everyone, or whether they instead represent dimensions of variability, present in some and absent in others.

helps *your part of the gene pool* reproduce, an idea called **inclusive fitness** (W. D. Hamilton, 1964). If you act altruistically for a relative, it helps the relative survive. If an extremely altruistic act (in which you die) saves a great many of your relatives, it helps aspects of your genetic makeup be passed on because your relatives resemble you genetically. This process is sometimes called "kin selection."

Evolutionary psychologists believe that even acts of altruism, such as doing disaster relief work for the Red Cross, may have a genetic basis.

Thus, it's argued, the tendency to be altruistic may be genetically based. This argument also implies that people will be more altruistic toward those in their kinship group than strangers (especially competitors). This seems to be true (Burnstein, Crandall, & Kitayama, 1994). Also fitting this view, there seems to be a genetic contribution to empathic concern for others, which may underlie altruism (Burnstein et al., 1994; Matthews, Batson, Horn, & Rosenman, 1981; Rushton, Fulker, Neale, Nias, & Eysenck, 1986). Indeed, there is evidence that emotional closeness, which increases with genetic relatedness, partly underlies the effect of relatedness on altruism (Korchmaros & Kenny, 2001).

The idea that altruistic tendencies are part of human nature has been extended to suggest an evolutionary basis for cooperation even among nonrelatives. The idea is essentially that our far ancestors survived better by cooperating than by being individualists. Thus, they acquired a tendency toward being helpful more generally. One person helps the other in the expectation that the help will be returned, an idea termed **reciprocal altruism** (Trivers, 1971).

Can this possibly have happened? Wouldn't people cheat, and take without giving? Sometimes. But those who do get punished (Fehr & Gächter, 2002). From an evolutionary view, the issue is whether cooperation leads to better outcomes for the group. There's evidence that it does, at least in the cooperative situations studied by psychologists (Axelrod & Hamilton, 1981). This has led some to conclude that a tendency to cooperate is part of human nature (Guisinger & Blatt, 1994; Kriegman &

Knight, 1988). There's also evidence that punishing those who fail to cooperate leads to better group outcomes (Fehr & Gächter, 2002). Maybe punishing those who don't go along is also genetically built into human nature.

Genetic Similarity and Attraction

The idea that people act altruistically toward relatives has been extended by Philippe Rushton and his colleagues (Rushton, 1989a; Rushton, Russell, & Wells, 1984) to what he calls **genetic similarity theory.** The basic idea is what we've said before: a gene "survives" (is represented in the next generation) by any action that brings about reproduction of any organism in which copies of itself exist. That may mean being altruistic to your kinship group, but Rushton says it means other things as well.

Rushton and his colleagues (1984) argued that genetic similarity has an influence on who attracts you. Specifically, you're more attracted to strangers who resemble you genetically than to those who don't. How does this help the survival of the gene? If you're attracted to someone, you may become sexually involved, which may result in offspring. Offspring have genes from both parents. By making you attracted to someone with genes like yours, your genes increase the odds that genes like themselves will be copied (from one parent or the other) into a new person, surviving into the next generation.

Are people attracted to others whose genes resemble their own? Maybe so. Rushton (1988) had couples take blood tests that give a rough index of genetic similarity. He found that sexually involved couples had in common 50 percent of the genetic markers. When he took the data and paired people randomly, the pairs shared only 43 percent of the markers, significantly less. Rushton went on to compare couples who'd had children with those who hadn't. Those with a child shared 52 percent of the genetic markers; those with no child shared only 44 percent. Thus, among sexually active couples, those most similar were also most likely to have reproduced.

This attraction effect isn't limited to the opposite sex. People also tend to form friendships with others who are genetically similar to them. Rushton (1989b) repeated his study with pairs of men who were close friends (all heterosexual). The pairs of friends shared 54 percent of the genetic markers, random pairs shared only 48 percent. Again, it appears that genetic similarity related somehow to attraction.

How would friendships with genetically similar people of the same sex be adaptive? The point is to get the genes into offspring. Having same-sex friends won't do that directly. There are two ways it can help, though. The first is similar to the idea discussed earlier about altruism and kin selection. You're more likely to be altruistic for a close friend than a stranger, making the friend more likely to live to reproduce. The second possibility is that you may meet the same-sex friend's opposite-sex sibling. If the sibling is also genetically similar to you, an attraction may develop, with potential sexual activity, resulting in offspring.

How do people detect genetic similarity in others? It's hard to say. One possibility is that we are drawn to others who share our facial and body features. People who look like you seem like family and therefore attract you. Another possibility is that genetic similarity is conveyed by smell. Consistent with this, there is evidence that women prefer the odor of men who are genetically similar to their fathers (Jacob, McClintock, Zelano, & Ober, 2002). Outside your awareness, you may recognize those who are like you by subtle physical cues.

It's also likely that culture plays a role here. If you are descended from eastern Europeans, you may feel more comfortable around people who share your (eastern

Both men and women are in competition for desirable mates.

European) traditions. It might be the familiar traditions that bring you close, but the result is that you are drawn to people who come from your part of the gene pool.

The general idea that people choose mates on the basis of particular character-istics is called **assortative mating** (Thiessen & Gregg, 1980). It's clear that mating isn't random. People select their mates on the basis of a variety of characteristics, though there are limitations on how fine-grained this selection is (Lykken & Tellegen, 1993). Often the features that influence mate selection are similarities to the self (Buss, 1985).

Mate Selection and Competition for Mates

We've talked at some length about the importance of getting genes to the next gen-eration. (From this view, it's sometimes said, a person is a gene's way of creating an-other gene, cf. Barash, 2001.) Obviously, then, the evolutionary view on personality focuses closely on mating (Gangestad & Simpson, 2000). Indeed, from this view, mat-ing is what life's all about (although other issues do arise when you think about the complexities of mating). Just as certain qualities confer survival advantage, certain qualities also confer reproductive advantage.

Mating involves competition. Males compete with one another; females com-pete with one another. But what's being competed for differs between sexes. Trivers (1972) has argued that males and females evolved different strategies, based on their roles in reproduction. Female humans have greater investment in offspring than males: they carry them for nine months, and they're more tied to caring for them after birth. The general rule across species is that the sex with the greater investment can generate fewer offspring over the life span because of the commitment of time and energy to each. It thus is choosier about a mate (though not everyone agrees on this point; see Small, 1993). The sex with less investment can generate more off-spring, and thus is less discriminating.

Given the difference in biological investment, the strategy of women is to tend to hold back from mating until they identify the best available male. "Best" here is defined as quality of genetic contribution, parental care, or material support for the mate and offspring. In contrast, the strategy of males is to maximize sexual opportunities, copulating as often as possible. This means seeking partners who are available and fertile (Buss, 1994a, 1994b). In this view, men tend to view women as *sex objects*, whereas women tend to view men as *success objects*.

These differences in orientation should produce different strategies for trying to get the opportunity to mate (which both males and females want). David Buss and David Schmitt (1993) examined differences in how men and women compete for and select mates, and how the strategies differ from short term to long term (see also Buss, 1994a, 1994b; Feingold, 1992; Schmitt & Buss, 1996). Because men are interested in finding fertile partners, women should compete by emphasizing their attributes that relate to fertility—youth and beauty. Because women want to find partners that will provide for them and their babies, men should compete by emphasizing their status, personal dominance and ambition, and wealth or potential for wealth (Sidanius, Pratto, & Bobo, 1994; Sprecher, Sullivan, & Hatfield, 1994).

What do men and women actually *do* to compete for mates? College students report doing pretty much that (Buss, 1988). Men brag about their accomplishments and earning potential, display expensive possessions, and flex their muscles. Women enhance their beauty through makeup, jewelry, clothing, and hairstyles. Women also play hard to get, to incite widespread interest among many males. This permits the women to be choosy once candidates are identified (see also Kenrick, Sadalla, Groth, & Trost, 1990).

Buss (1989) also examined aspects of mate preferences in thirty-seven different cultures around the world. Cultural differences were relatively rare. The preferences of U.S. college students didn't differ much from those of people elsewhere. Males (more than females) are drawn to cues of reproductive capacity. Females (more than males) are drawn to cues indicating availability of resources (see also Singh, 1995). This may not be a case of "more is better"; it may just be that men who aren't at an acceptable level are out of the running (Kenrick, Sundie, Nicastle, & Stone, 2001). Females are also drawn to cues of dominance and high status (Cunningham, Barbee, & Pike, 1990; Feingold, 1992; Kenrick et al., 1990; Sadalla et al., 1987), especially dominance expressed in socially positive ways (Jensen-Campbell, Graziano, & West, 1995).

Despite these gender differences, the qualities just listed don't always rank high in people's lists of desired characteristics. This has led some to be skeptical of their importance. It appears, however, that rankings can be deceiving. Other research gave people tight "budgets" for getting what they want in a partner (Li, Bailey, Kenrick, & Linsenmeier, 2002). In this situation, men treated physical attractiveness as a necessity rather than an option, women treated status and resources as necessities, and both treated kindness and intelligence as necessities. That is, given that they couldn't be choosy about everything, they went for these qualities first.

People have investigated implications of the evolutionary model in several ways. For example, research shows that men prefer younger women, especially as they themselves grow older, consistent with the seeking of reproductive capacity. This comes from a study of the age ranges specified in singles' ads (Kenrick & Keefe, 1992). As can be seen in Figure 6.3, men past age twenty-five specified a range that extended increasingly below their own age. Women, in contrast, tended to express a preference for men slightly older than themselves.

Figure 6.3

Singles' ads placed by men and women often specify age ranges of persons of the opposite sex whom the placer of the ad would like to meet. In this sample of ads, men expressed an increasing preference for younger women. Women tended to prefer men slightly older than they were, and the extent of that preference didn't change over time (adapted from Kenrick & Keefe, 1992).

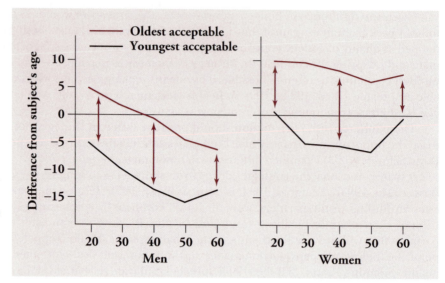

Also consistent with predictions from the evolutionary model are results from several other studies of gender differences (see also Table 6.2). Men are more interested in casual sex than are women (Bailey, Gaulin, Agyei, & Gladue, 1994; Buss & Schmitt, 1993; Clark & Hatfield, 1989; Oliver & Hyde, 1993) and less selective in their criteria for one-night stands (Kenrick, Groth, Trost, & Sadalla, 1993). Men are more readily excited by visual erotica than are women (Bailey et al., 1994). Men's commitment to their relationship is shaken by exposure to a very attractive woman, whereas women's commitment is shaken by exposure to a very dominant man (Kenrick, Neuberg, Zierk, & Krones, 1994). Similarly, men's confidence in their value as a mate is shaken by exposure to a very dominant man (but not an attractive one), and women's confidence in their value as a mate is shaken by exposure to a very attractive woman (but not a dominant one; Gutierres, Kenrick, & Partch, 1999). Men over-interpret women's

Table 6.2

Summary of predictions from evolutionary psychology for sex differences in mating tendencies

Issue	Females	Males
Reproductive constraints	Can produce only a limited number of children over life	Can reproduce without limit through life
Optimal reproductive strategy	Locate and hold onto best quality mate	Mate as widely and often as possible
Desired quality in potential mate	Resources to protect and support them and offspring	Childbearing capability
Basis for evaluating mate potential	Earning capacity, status, possessions, generosity	Physical attractiveness, health, youth
Prime basis for jealousy	Partner's emotional attachment to another	Partner's sexual infidelity

smiles and touches as implying sexual interest, and women are overly conservative in judging men's actual commitment in relationships that are forming (Buss, 2001).

Both men and women experience jealousy, but there may be a difference in what creates this emotion. In theory, it's evolutionarily important for men to be concerned about paternity (they want to support their *own* children, not someone else's). Thus, men should be especially jealous about sexual infidelity. In theory, women are most concerned about whether the man will continue to support her and her children. Thus, women should be jealous about a man's having emotional bonds with another woman, rather than sex per se. Data from several studies fit this view: men were more disturbed by thoughts of sexual infidelity, and women were more disturbed by thoughts of emotional infidelity (Buss, Larsen, Westen, & Semmelroth, 1992; see also Bailey et al., 1994). This particular finding has been challenged, however, in part because asking the question in a slightly different way erases the gender difference (DeSteno, Bartlett, Braverman, & Salovey, 2002; Harris, 2002).

Jealousy is partly about what your partner may have done, but it's partly about the presence of rivals. Again there is evidence of a gender difference in what qualities matter. Men are more jealous when the potential rival is dominant than when he is physically attractive; women are more jealous when the potential rival is physically attractive (Dijkstra & Buunk, 1998).

Mate Retention and Other Issues

The first challenge in mating is attracting a potential mate. The next challenge is *keeping* the mate. Men and women both have the potential to stray, and other people make efforts to induce straying (Schmitt & Buss, 2001). People use various tactics to prevent this (Buss & Shackelford, 1997). Some of these tactics are used by men and women alike, others differ by gender. For example, men report spending a lot of money and giving in to their wives' wishes. Women try to make themselves look extra attractive and let others know their mate is already taken.

Use of retention tactics also relates predictably to other factors in the relationship, but differently for men and women. Men use their tactics more if they see their wife as physically attractive. Men also devote more effort to retention if the wife is young, an effect that's independent of the man's age and the length of the relationship. In contrast, women work harder at retention when their husbands have higher incomes. They also make more efforts if their husbands are striving for high status (independent of current income).

Although mating strategies are the starting point for much of this research on gender differences, others have applied the theme more broadly. (As noted earlier, issues involved in mating lead to several other complexities in life.) Several have suggested that evolutionary differences cause men and women to have very different styles—indeed different *needs*—in communication (e.g., J. Gray, 1992; Tannen, 1990). Men are seen as having an individualistic, dominance-oriented, problem-solving approach. Women are seen as having an inclusive, sharing, communal approach. The argument is also made that these differences in goals and patterns of communication lead to a good deal of misunderstanding between men and women.

We should note that our discussion has emphasized gender differences, not similarities. There are, of course, many similarities. Both genders are looking for partners who have a good sense of humor and a pleasing personality (Feingold, 1992), who are agreeable and emotionally stable (Kenrick et al., 1993), intelligent (Li et al., 2002), and kind and loving (Buss, 1994b). Both also seem to prefer partners whose faces are symmetrical (Grammer & Thornhill, 1994). The way men and women look at each other goes far beyond seeing each other as sex objects and success objects (Buss, 1994b). Nevertheless, gender differences also seem important.

Aggression and the Young Male Syndrome

Competition for mating opportunities leads to posturing on the part of males. It has been blamed for many problem aspects of young men's behavior, including their risky driving compared to any other group (Nell, 2002). But it can also lead to more. When males face hard competition for scarce resources (females), the result sometimes is confrontation and potentially serious violence of several sorts (Hilton, Harris, & Rice, 2000).

This pattern has been referred to as the "young male syndrome" (Wilson & Daly, 1985). It's viewed as partly an effect of evolutionary pressures from long ago and partly a response to situations that elicit the pattern. That is, although the pattern of behavior may be coded in every man's genes, it's most likely to emerge when current situations predict reproductive failure. The worst case would be single men who are unemployed and thus poor candidates as mates.

In line with this analysis, there's clear evidence that homicide between competitors is primarily a male affair (Daly & Wilson, 1990). Figure 6.4 displays the homicide rates in Chicago during a sixteen-year period, omitting cases in which the person killed was a relative. Males are far more likely to kill one another than are females. It's also obvious that the prime ages for killing are the prime ages for mating. According to Daly and Wilson, these killings come largely from conflicts over "face" and status (see also Wilson & Daly, 1996). Trivial events escalate into violence, and someone is killed.

Why killing instead of ritualized displays of aggressiveness? No one knows for sure. One guess rests on the easy access to guns in the United States. When weapons aren't there, the same pressures are more likely to result in pushing and shouting. Deadly violence certainly is possible without weapons. But when weapons are present, death is far more likely.

We should point out explicitly that the theory underlying this area of study is very different from ideas about aggression and human nature of only a few years

Figure 6.4

Homicide rates for males and females killing nonrelatives of the same sex in Chicago during the period 1965–1981 (adapted from Daly & Wilson, 1990).

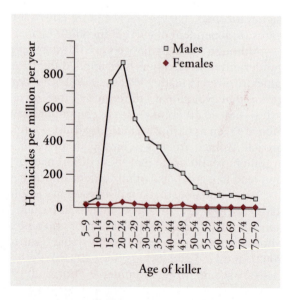

ago. This view isn't that aggression is part of human nature, expressed indiscriminately. Rather, aggression is seen as largely a male phenomenon, which occurs specifically as a result of sexual selection pressures in the competition for mates.

Our focus here is on violence by young men toward their genetic competitors. It's worth noting that genetic competition also appears to play a role in violence within family units. In particular, children—especially very young children—are far more likely to be killed by stepparents than by genetic parents (Daly & Wilson, 1988, 1996). The overall frequency of this event is low; most parents don't kill children. Yet if it happens, a stepparent is far more likely to be the perpetrator than a biological parent. As is true of the young male syndrome, this finding may reflect a deep-rooted desire to help one's own genes into the next generation instead of a competitor's genes.

We noted earlier that part of mating is retaining one's mate. People have a variety of tactics for doing this. Most of them are quite benign. Some can even be viewed as efforts at solidifying the relationship to make it resistant to temptation. However, some tactics of mate retention are coercive. Some men are so concerned about losing their mates—or unknowingly supporting a rival's child—that they become quite controlling. Tactics to control the woman sometimes escalate to violence against her (Hilton et al., 2000; Wilson & Daly, 1996). Sometimes that violence is a warning: don't stray. Sometimes the violence is murder, ending all possibility of straying. When killings occur *within* families, most victims are wives.

Although male violence against women is cause for great concern, you should also be aware that it is not just men who do this. Aggression against partners also occurs among women (Hilton et al., 2000).

Assessment

The orientation to personality that was discussed in the first part of this chapter developed as a branch of the dispositional perspective. In general, its ways of assessing personality reflect the dispositional view. What it offers primarily is content—ideas about which traits to assess. As we said earlier, theorists who take the genetic view on personality feel that certain dispositions are inherited as biological substrates of personality. By implication, these are the qualities to assess.

A second point made by this approach to personality concerns a more general issue regarding assessment in research. The issue is what kind of data to collect to measure the trait you want to study (an issue also discussed in Chapter 3). For example, in some twin studies, the data were self-report scales. In other studies, children were rated by their parents or by teachers. Occasionally, but not often, behavioral observations have been made of children at play.

It turns out that it may matter considerably which of these sources of data is used in the research, because different types of data don't always give the same answers about degree of genetic influence (Plomin & Foch, 1980). In general, parent ratings of children and self-ratings indicate genetic influence more reliably than do behavioral observations (in fact, they may well overestimate the size of genetic effects, Saudino et al., 1995). This raises questions about which kind of data to have most confidence in. The importance of deciding which kind of measure to use is not unique to the biological approach. But it may be particularly important here because of the fact that twin studies are difficult and expensive.

Given the rise in influence of molecular genetics, some have raised the possibility that gene assessment will eventually be done as a better way of determining personality. Although it is too soon to be sure, many people prominent in this area see this as unlikely (e.g., Plomin & Crabbe, 2000). The reason is the belief that personality traits are influenced by many, many genes, each exerting a small effect. It will be hard enough to identify those genes, never mind use them as convenient personality tests.

Problems in Behavior, and Behavior Change

Let's turn now to problems in behavior. The genetic approach has made a major contribution here. Behavior geneticists have examined the possibility that several kinds of vulnerabilities to problems may be influenced by inheritance (see also Box 6.4).

BOX 6.4

LIVING IN A POSTGENOMIC WORLD

The human genome is decoded. Researchers today know more than ever about the makeup of the human body and the functions of some of our genes (Plomin et al., 2003). The technology behind these advances is continuing its rapid development, with no signs of slowing down.

Mapping the human genome will surely yield benefits. Some disorders are caused by single genes. Knowing the map makes it easier to locate the genes. (For example, the gene for cystic fibrosis is in the middle of chromosome 7.) This information can be used in genetic counseling. People can be warned if they carry a gene for a disorder they may pass on to a child. Another benefit is genetic therapies, which now exist for some disorders, for example, to correct defects in producing blood cells. Researchers also hold out the possibility of altering genes prior to conception to eliminate defects. Some say the map of the genome, by allowing identification of genetic weaknesses, will usher in a new era of preventive medicine, dramatically changing the way we deal with disease (Lewin, 1990).

The mapping of the genome excites imaginations, but it also raises concerns (Buchanan et al., 2000; Fukuyama, 2002; Lynn, 2001; Stock, 2002). Knowing what genes control body and behavior raises serious moral and ethical issues. For example, a great deal of pressure would doubtlessly arise to modify genes to create specific characteristics in new children, creating "designer babies" (Plomin & Crabbe, 2000; Stock, 2002). Should this happen? Who is to decide which characteristics should be created? What happens to

people whose genetic characteristics are viewed by society as inferior?

Knowledge about disorders also raises ethical issues. Will social and employment discrimination befall people with particular genetic profiles? What happens to the cost of medical insurance when it's possible to know who is susceptible to what diseases? Will insurance even remain *available* to people with disease susceptibilities? This isn't an idle question. Already, insurance policies have been cancelled for entire families because of genetic problems in specific family members (Stolberg, 1994).

The same issue arises with respect to psychological disorders. If it's known that your genes render you vulnerable to mania or depression, will you be able to get a job? Will you be able to have insurance coverage against the possibility of needing treatment? The other side of this issue, however, is that it may be discovered that many patterns now known as disorders are simply extremes of normal personality (Plomin & Crabbe, 2000). Clarity on this issue would follow from knowing what genes are involved in both the problem patterns and normal patterns. Such a realization might go a long way toward removing stigma from disorders.

In short, the project to map the genome holds out much promise, but it also raises very difficult issues that will have to be addressed (Hubbard, 1995). You may want to start thinking about them, because they're issues that are in your future—and the future of your children.

Behavior Genetics and Disorders

Inheritance of pathology has been studied in the same ways as inheritance of normal personality traits (for a broad review see Vandenberg, Singer, & Pauls, 1986). For many years, research on the behavior genetics of problems focused mainly on schizophrenia and bipolar disorder. Most of the research is on schizophrenia, which is characterized by disorientation, confusion, cognitive disturbances, and a separation from reality.

A well-known early study of genetic influence on schizophrenia was conducted by Gottesman and Shields (1972). Their study began by recruiting twins who'd been admitted to a hospital with a diagnosis of schizophrenia. They then sought out each such person's co-twin and independently evaluated the co-twin's psychiatric status.

The term **concordance** is used to describe similarity of diagnosis. A pair of twins were concordant if they were both diagnosed as schizophrenic. Gottesman and Shields (1972) found a concordance rate of 50 percent among identical twins and a rate of 9 percent among fraternal twins. They also found an association (among identical twins) between severity of the initial case and the likelihood that the co-twin was also schizophrenic. It appears from this that inheritance plays an important role in developing schizophrenia. Indeed, this conclusion follows from over a dozen studies similar to this one. A recent study has even isolated a gene location that seems to be related to schizophrenia (Straub et al., 2002).

Nevertheless, the twin-study data also indicate that life circumstances play a role in determining who shows schizophrenic symptoms openly (Plomin & Rende, 1991). Some people have the genetic susceptibility but don't develop the disorder. This interaction between a susceptibility and a context that touches it off reflects the diathesis-stress view of disorder (discussed in Chapter 4).

A second disorder that may be influenced by heredity is called bipolar (manic-depressive) disorder. It is characterized by episodes of frenetic, hyperactive, grandiose, and talkative behavior, accompanied by a rush of ideas. Often the manic pattern is accompanied by elevated mood, but if the person becomes frustrated, anger is also common. The onset of this disorder is usually sudden. As with schizophrenia, twin studies reveal a tendency toward a genetic contribution (M. G. Allen, 1976; Loehlin et al., 1988; Tsuang & Faraone, 1990).

One study also linked bipolar disorder to a specific dominant gene on chromosome 11 in a group of Amish families (Egeland et al., 1987). Two other studies, however, found no link from the disorder and that chromosome. That means this gene can't always be responsible for the disorder (Detera-Wadleigh et al., 1987; Hodgkinson et al., 1987). Scientists continue to look for genetic markers of bipolar disorder, using techniques of molecular genetics.

Although most research on the genetics of problems has focused on schizophrenia and bipolar disorder, some studies have gone beyond these boundaries (Rowe, 1994; Segal, 1999; Vandenberg et al., 1986). These studies have taken people in at least two directions. One of them relates to abuse of alcohol and other substances.

Quite some time ago, Eysenck (1964b) found that MZ twins were more likely to share tendencies toward alcoholism than DZ twins. Similar findings, with information about the metabolic processes that underlie the difference, were reported by Schuckit and Rayses (1979). A later Swedish adoption study found 22 percent of the biological sons of alcohol-abusing men were alcoholic, again indicating a genetic role (Bohman et al., 1987). Another finding provides an interesting reflection of the interweaving of genetic and environmental influences (Dick & Rose, 2002). Genetic contributions to drinking in this study increased from about a third of the variance at age sixteen to half the variance—in the same sample—at age eighteen.

Recent research has also implicated a specific gene in the craving for alcohol that some people experience after having a little (Hutchison, McGeary, Smolen, Bryan, & Swift, 2002). The gene turns out to be the long allele of the dopamine-related gene described earlier in the chapter. That was the gene that was related to measures of novelty seeking. That allele has also been linked to heroin addiction (Kotler et al., 1997; Li et al., 1997).

Another direction work has headed concerns antisocial behavior. Eysenck (1964a) reported higher concordance rates among MZ than DZ twins on antisocial characteristics: childhood behavior problems and adult crime. Other research has also supported the idea that antisocial personality may be genetically influenced (Rowe, 1994; Vandenberg et al., 1986; Willerman, Loehlin, & Horn, 1992). Further research on adult criminality tends to fit the picture of a genetic influence (DiLalla & Gottesman, 1991; Wilson & Herrnstein, 1985), though studies of juvenile delinquency have sometimes not (Gottesman, Carey, & Hanson, 1983). After reviewing the accumulated evidence, Rhee and Waldman (2002) concluded there are clear genetic influences on antisocial behavior.

Evolution and Problems in Behavior

A somewhat different view of certain behavior problems is suggested by sociobiology. Barash (1986) argued that many difficulties in human life stem from the fact that two kinds of evolution influence people. There is biological evolution, a very slow process that occurs over millenia. There is also cultural evolution, which is much faster. Your experiences of life stem partly from what biological evolution shaped humans to be during prehistory, and partly from the cultural circumstances in which you live.

According to Barash, the problem is that biological evolution prepared us for life in a world very different from the one we live in now. Cultural evolution has raced far ahead. Biological evolution can't keep up. Being in a world to which we don't

Some people believe that our cultural evolution has outstripped the ability of our biological evolution to keep up.

quite belong, we are conflicted and alienated. Barash's point is a general one, not specific to a particular disorder, but it's an interesting one: that is, problems emerge when behavioral tendencies that have been built in as part of human nature conflict with pressures that are built into contemporary culture.

Behavior Change: How Much Is Possible?

A major question about therapeutic behavior change is raised by the view under discussion in this chapter. Biologically based personality qualities—whether temperaments or not—are by definition firmly anchored in the person's constitutional functioning. How easy can it be to alter these aspects of personality in any major way, through *whatever* therapeutic processes are used? Psychotherapy may change the person to some extent. But how far against their biological nature can people be expected to bend?

This is an interesting issue, about which little is known. It's been suggested that even true temperaments can be modified, within limits (Buss & Plomin, 1984). But what are the limits? It seems likely that some kinds of therapeutic change are more difficult to create and sustain for some people than for others. For example, it will be harder for a therapy aimed at reducing emotional reactions to be effective for someone with high emotionality than for someone lower in that temperament. In fact, there may be some people whose constitutions make certain kinds of therapy so difficult as to be impractical.

On the other hand, it should also be recognized that the heritability of personality, though strong, is not overwhelming. There's a good deal of influence from experiences. Thus, the data that establish a genetic influence on personality also indicate that genetic determination is not total. How much behavior change is hampered by genetically coded tendencies is an important issue raised by this view on personality. Unfortunately, little is thus far known about it.

Inheritance and Evolution: Problems and Prospects

The biological view on personality has roots that go far back in the history of ideas. Yet today's views are in many ways quite new. Research on heritability of personality is still fairly recent in origin. Application of the ideas of evolutionary psychology is even more recent. With the advent of advances in molecular genetics, people are now trying to link particular genes with qualities of personality, an approach that's newer still.

In considering the usefulness of these biological ideas in thinking about personality, several issues arise. For example, temperaments are broad tendencies reflected in fundamental aspects of behavior. The fact that temperaments are so basic, however, raises a question about how to view their role in personality. It's clear that activity level, emotionality, and sociability are important. By themselves, though, they don't constitute a very complete picture of personality. The question, then, is this: Does it make more sense to think of temperaments as all of personality, as part of personality, or perhaps as the bedrock on which personality is constructed?

It's hard to answer this question, partly because there hasn't been much research on how temperaments influence people's day-to-day lives. That is, do combinations of high and low activity, emotionality, and sociability have direct influences on the kinds of experiences that are thought of as implying personality? Or is the effect of temperaments more indirect? Perhaps they provide a basis for developing more-specialized traits, which then influence behavior more directly.

Another important question for clarifying the picture of heredity and personality concerns the fact that many personality traits seem to be at least somewhat heritable. Many of the traits relate conceptually to temperaments. It's not clear how to think about relations between the specific traits and temperaments. The general question is "how many traits are genetically influenced, and how many *look like* they're heritable because they derive from the first group?" Recent evidence suggests that facets of the five supertraits are separately heritable. This puts a different twist on the question. Now maybe we should be asking whether the temperaments are really unitary, broad qualities, or whether instead they are aggregates of separate traits.

A final question concerns the methods of behavioral genetics as a discipline. Although we didn't address this point in discussing the research, questions have been raised about whether the methods used in this research really tell the investigators what they believe they are being told (e.g., Haviland, McGuire, & Rothbaum, 1983; Wahlsten, 1990). The issues here are very technical, and it's difficult to know how they will be resolved. But until they *are* resolved, there will remain at least a small cloud on the horizon of the behavioral genetics approach to personality.

Another aspect of the viewpoint discussed in this chapter is sociobiology and evolutionary psychology. This view on personality has been controversial during its relatively brief existence and has been criticized on several grounds (e.g., Miller, Putcha-Bhagavatula, & Pedersen, 2002). The early arguments of sociobiology were very theoretical, with little supporting evidence. Sociobiology was seen by some as a game of speculation rather than a serious science. More than a few people scorned the ideas under discussion as unfalsifiable and, indeed, untestable.

In the past decade and a half, however, this situation changed dramatically. As more precise ideas were developed about the implications of evolutionary theory, this way of thinking led to a surge of studies. Evolutionary psychology is now an area of vigorous research activity. It seems clear that evolutionary thinking provides a wealth of hypotheses for researchers. Moreover, the hypotheses are becoming more and more sophisticated.

Nevertheless, there remains concern about whether the hypotheses being studied by these researchers really *depend on* evolutionary theory, as opposed to merely being *consistent* with it. One challenge evolutionary psychology faces today is that of making clear predictions that resist alternative interpretations. This issue, of course, is faced by all views on personality, not just the evolutionary one. The issue, however, seems likely to remain an important one for this approach for some time. (Those interested in this problem may be interested in an article by Rushton, 1989a, and the commentaries that follow it.)

Sociobiology and evolutionary psychology have also been criticized because their statements have disturbing political and social overtones. Some regard arguments about how human nature evolved as thinly veiled justifications for unfair social conditions in today's world (Kitcher, 1987, and the succeeding commentaries; see also Lewontin, Rose, & Kamin, 1984). That is, these ideas explain why men are bullies, why there's a double standard of sexual behavior for men and women, and why race and class differences exist. These explanations provide a basis for considering such conditions to be natural. This is only a small step from saying they should continue to exist (see Pratto & Hegarty, 2000). These overtones of evolutionary thinking are seen by some as racist and sexist, and have prompted considerable hostility toward the theories among some people.

One response to this sort of criticism is to point out that evolution is a natural force that works dispassionately, based on the principles of reproduction and survival. In the arena of evolution, issues of equal rights and equal opportunities have no meaning. It may well be that in today's world some of the results of evolution work against some people because evolution prepared us to fit not this world but the world of prehistory. If people are disadvantaged by the consequences of evolution, though, it's something that must be dealt with by the cultures that people have built. The fact that the theory explains why inequity exists can't be used as an argument that the theory is wrong. As you might expect, this response is not entirely satisfying to critics.

Despite controversies such as these, there remains a huge interest in evolutionary ideas in today's personality psychology. These ideas will not go away any time soon.

SUMMARY

The approach to personality rooted in inheritance and evolution has two facets. One of them emphasizes that your personality is tied to the biological body you inherit. This idea goes far back in history, but today's version of the idea is quite different, emphasizing the role of genes.

Behavior genetics provides ways to find out whether personality differences are inherited. In twin studies, correlations among identical twins are compared with correlations among fraternal twins; in adoption studies, children are compared with their biological and adoptive families. Studies of identical twins raised apart provide yet a different look at the effects of inheritance and environment.

Twin research has been used to look at genetic contributions to a variety of dispositions. Recent theorists define temperaments as broad inherited traits that appear early in life. At least three seem to be genetically influenced: activity level, emotionality, and sociability. There also is evidence of genetic influence in the big-five supertraits and other variables. It's unclear whether the big five derive from (or duplicate) the temperaments studied under other names. It is also unclear whether other hereditary influences depend on associations between the other variable and a temperament. Recent developments in molecular genetics provide a new tool in the search for genetic influences on personality. Now there is evidence of specific genes playing roles in traits, including novelty seeking and neuroticism.

The idea that dispositions are genetically influenced can be extended a step further, to the suggestion that many aspects of human social behavior are products of evolution. This idea is behind an area of work termed sociobiology or evolutionary psychology. Sociobiologists propose ways to account for various aspects of human behavior, even behavior that on the face of it seems not to provide an evolutionary advantage. Altruism, for example, is understood as people acting for the benefit of their family groups, so that the family's genes are more likely to be continued (kin selection). This idea has been extended to the notion that people are attracted to other people who share their genetic makeup.

The evolutionary view also has implications concerning mate selection, including the idea that males and females use different strategies. The male strategy is to mate whenever possible, and males are drawn to signs of reproductive capability. The female strategy is to seek the best male available, and females are drawn to signs of resources. People use the relevant strategies and act in ways that make them seem better candidates as mates. Mating pressures also may lead to aggression among young men. Theory suggests that violence is most likely among men of reproductive age who are in poor reproductive circumstances. Evidence seems to bear this out, along with the idea that much violence concerns conflicts over status.

The genetic approach to personality says little about assessment except to suggest what dispositions are particularly important to assess—those that have biological links. Assessment directly from genes seems unlikely, due to the probable involvement of many genes in any given trait. With regard to problems in behavior, there is substantial evidence that schizophrenia and manic-depressive disorder are affected by heredity. As elsewhere, this area is beginning to use the tools of molecular biology to search for genetic influences.

With regard to therapeutic behavior change, this approach raises a question on the basis of studies of temperament: how much can people be expected to change, even with therapy, in directions that deviate from their biological makeup?

GLOSSARY

Activity level The overall output of a person's energy or behavior.

Adoption study A study of resemblances between children and their adoptive and biological parents.

Allele Some version of a particular gene.

Assortative mating Mating based on choice of specific characteristics rather than randomly.

Behavioral genetics The study of inheritance of behavioral qualities.

Cerebrotonia A mental overintensity that promotes apprehensiveness and social inhibition.

Concordance Agreement on some characteristic between a twin and a co-twin.

Directional selection Evolution in which one extreme of a dimension is more adaptive than the other.

Dizygotic (DZ) twins Fraternal twins (overlapping genetically 50 percent, on average).

Ectomorphy A tendency toward frail thinness.

Emotionality The tendency to become emotionally aroused easily.

Endomorphy A tendency toward obesity.

Ethology The study of animals in their natural environment.

Genetic similarity theory The idea that people work toward reproduction of genes similar to their own.

Genome The sequence of the genes contained in the full complement of chromosomes.

Heritability An estimate of how much variance of some characteristic is accounted for by inheritance.

Inclusive fitness The passing on of genes through the survival of relatives.

Mesomorphy A tendency toward muscularity.

Monozygotic (MZ) twins Identical twins (overlapping genetically 100 percent).

Reciprocal altruism Helping others with the expectation the help will be returned.

Siblings Brothers and sisters.

Sociability The tendency to prefer being with people over being alone.

Sociobiology The study of the evolutionary basis for social behavior.

Somatotonia Energetic desire for adventure and physical activity.

Somatotype The description of a person's body configuration along three dimensions.

Stabilizing selection Evolution in which intermediate values of a dimension are most adaptive.

Temperaments Inherited traits that appear early in life.

Twin study A study comparing similarity between MZ twins against similarity between DZ twins.

Viscerotonia A relaxed sociability and love of comfort.

Biological Processes and Personality

■ **Eysenck: Extroversions, Neuroticism, and Brain Functions**

Extroversions and Cortical Arousal
Biological Basis of Neuroticism

■ **A Contemporary View of Brain Functions: Approach and Inhibition**

Behavioral Approach, Activation, Engagement, or Facilitation
Neurotransmitters and the Approach System
Behavioral Inhibition, Withdrawal, or Avoidance
Neurotransmitters and the Withdrawal System
Relating These Systems to Temperaments or Traits
Two Areas of Disagreement

■ **Sensation Seeking: A Third Biological System?**

Function of Sensation Seeking
Sensation Seeking, Impulsiveness, and Other Systems
One More Angle on Impulsivity

■ **Impulsiveness: Further Issues**

What Does Serotonin Function Mean?
What Are the Personality Scales Measuring?

■ **Hormones and Personality**

Hormones, the Body, and the Brain
Early Hormonal Exposure and Behavior
Testosterone and Adult Personality
Cycle of Testosterone and Action
Testosterone, Dominance, and Evolutionary Psychology
Responding to Stress: Men, Women, and Oxytocin

■ **Assessment**

Electroencephalograms
Neuro-Imaging

■ **Problems in Behavior, and Behavior Change**

Biological Bases of Anxiety, Depression, and Antisocial Personality
Medication in Therapy

■ **Biological Processes and Personality: Problems and Prospects**

SUMMARY

■   Louise craves adventure. She always seems to be widening her circle of friends and activities. It's as though she needs the stimulation to keep her alive and happy. Her boyfriend Leo shies away from it. He doesn't dislike Louise's friends, but all the noise and action seem too much for him. He's just more comfortable when things are less intense. Oddly enough, both of them feel their bodies are telling them what's best for them, even though "what's best" is so different from the one to the other.

T he idea that people's personalities are somehow embedded in the makeup of their bodies was the starting point for Chapter 6. There we focused on the idea that genetics play a big role in what people are like. That idea accounts for why people are different from one another (they inherit different traits). It also accounts for why people are the same (evolution shaped certain tendencies into the human species as a whole).

The ideas in Chapter 6 are definitely biological. If something is genetically caused, the influence must occur through a biological process. But the ideas in Chapter 6 say little about how the effects are *exerted*. That is, knowing that traits are inherited says nothing about the process by which genes influence the behaviors that eventually emerge.

In this chapter, we take the same starting point: the idea that personality is embedded in people's bodies. This time, though, we focus on the idea that personality is influenced by the *workings* of the body. Now we consider aspects of physiology. The point of view considered here is that personality is a manifestation of these physiological processes.

As in the last chapter, there's room for similarities among people and also differences. The similarities reflect the fact that everyone has a nervous system and an endocrine system. The systems have the same basic structure and functions from one person to another. Differences reflect the fact that parts of the nervous system and endocrine system are more active or more responsive in some people than in others.

Eysenck: Extroversions, Neuroticism, and Brain Functions

One of the first modern attempts to link personality to biological functions was that of Hans Eysenck (see also Box 7.1). Recall from Chapter 4 that Eysenck saw personality as composed largely of two supertraits: neuroticism and extroversions. He saw these as rooted in the body.

Extroversion and Cortical Arousal

Introverts are quiet and introspective; extroverts are outgoing, uninhibited, dominant, and immersed in social activity. Eysenck (1967) argued that this difference derives from a part of the brain called the **ascending reticular activating system** (**ARAS**). The ARAS activates and deactivates the cerebral cortex. It's involved in maintaining alertness and concentration and in controlling the sleep cycle. When it's functioning at a high level, the person is sharp and alert. When it's functioning at a low level, the person is sluggish and drowsy.

Eysenck proposed that the typical (resting) level of ARAS activity in introverts is higher than in extroverts (Eysenck, 1981). Thus, when nothing's going on, introverts

BOX 7.1

THE THEORIST AND THE THEORY
The Many-Faceted Contributions of Hans Eysenck

Hans Eysenck was one of the most eclectic theorists in psychology. As described in Chapter 4, he played a major role in the dispositional view of personality. He also studied inheritance and tried to understand how the nervous system relates to personality. Nor did his interests stop there. Eysenck wrote about topics as diverse as intelligence, politics, links between personality and health, parapsychology, and astrology. He published more than fifty books and hundreds of articles and has often been embroiled in controversy (which he appeared to relish).

Eysenck would seem to have been destined for the stage. His parents were successful actors in Germany, where he was born in 1916. This theatrical background may have contributed to his enjoyment of public appearances. If so, it happened quickly, because his parents divorced when he was two, and he lived with his grandmother for years afterward. Given his theoretical views, Eysenck would probably ascribe his personality more to biology. The fact that his parents were actors may say something about their genetic makeup; this then was passed on to him.

Regardless of the source of his temperament, Eysenck grew quickly into a self-confident and strong-willed young man. Two anecdotes illustrate his tenacity (Gibson, 1981). When he was about eight, he was called on during singing class to sing a solo passage. He declined on the grounds that his voice wasn't any good, but the teacher insisted. He finally went ahead, but sang so poorly the teacher thought he was mocking the lesson. The teacher was about to punish him for this, but Eysenck struck first, taking the teacher's thumb in his teeth and holding on like a bulldog, not letting go until the headmaster intervened.

The second incident occurred as the Nazis were seizing power, when Eysenck was in high school. His teacher once said that Jews were known to be lacking in military valor. Eysenck set off to explore this question and returned with the fact that Jewish soldiers had earned an extra-high proportion of military honors during World War I. This incident didn't endear him to his teacher, but it illustrates Eysenck's tendency to take on controversy willingly. It also illustrates his dedication to scientific evidence.

Eysenck later went to England for university studies. He had decided to study physics and astronomy, but in starting out he made an error that changed the path of his life. Prospective students had to take a set of exams in the areas of their intended study. Eysenck inadvertently took the wrong exams, making himself eligible to major only in subjects other than his chosen ones. Because psychology was the most scientific of the majors available to him at that point, he decided to study psychology. One wonders how much this series of events provoked his later interests in astrology and parapsychology.

In short, the qualities that mark Eysenck's contributions to personality psychology include an extremely diverse range of interests, a tenacity about sticking with what he believes, and an enjoyment of controversy and of being the center of attention. All those qualities were apparent early in his life. These same qualities also play a role in the central construct of his theory: extraversion.

---

are more alert than extroverts. Because introverts have higher base arousal levels, they're easily overaroused. They may withdraw from social interaction because they're sensitive to being overstimulated. Extroverts, with lower base levels, seek stimulation to bring their arousal up.

This influences the kinds of situations introverts and extroverts prefer. People should be comfortable when the situation has just the right amount of stimulation.

Figure 7.1

Comfort and discomfort theoretically experienced by introverts and extroverts in situations of varying stimulation. If introverts naturally are more aroused cortically than are extroverts, introverts are more likely to be overwhelmed by too much stimulation than are extroverts. The result is that introverts should feel more comfortable at lower levels of stimulation (up to a point) than at higher levels. The low level of arousal of extroverts should lead them to be more comfortable at higher levels of stimulation (again, up to a point) than at lower levels (after Eysenck, 1971).

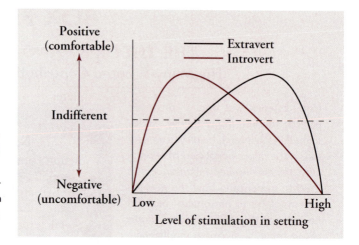

Situations add arousal to your baseline. If everyone's comfortable at the same level, and if introverts begin with more arousal, they should prefer different situations (Figure 7.1). Introverts should prefer lower levels of stimulation—but not *too* low, or it gets boring even to them. Extroverts should prefer higher levels—but not *too* high, or it gets overwhelming even to them.

This seems to be the case. Geen (1984) told participants he was looking at effects of noises on a task. Some people could choose the intensity of noise they'd hear. Others were assigned intensities. Each of the latter group got a level chosen by someone in the former group. When choosing, extroverts spontaneously chose louder noise than introverts. When getting the levels they'd chosen (which were different), introverts and extroverts had comparable heart rates (the unconnected diamonds in Figure 7.2). This suggests that being at the preferred stimulation level (which differed between groups) led to the same level of arousal in the two groups.

Figure 7.2

Heart rate among six groups of participants working on a task while being exposed to random noises. On the left are groups hearing the quieter noises chosen by introverts; on the right are groups hearing the louder noises chosen by extroverts. Introverts and extroverts who chose freely (the two diamonds) don't differ in their arousal. Arousal goes up among introverts who have to hear louder noise (dark line), and arousal goes down among extroverts who have to hear quieter noise (lighter line). The findings fit the picture that introverts are more aroused than extroverts at lower levels of stimulation (adapted from Geen, 1984).

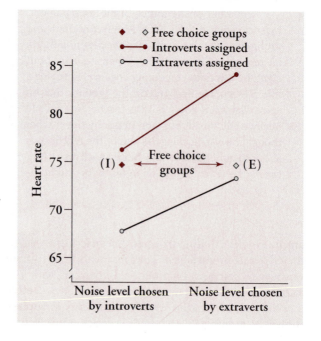

Recall that some participants had no choice: they got the level chosen by introverts or the level chosen by extroverts. Introverts hearing noise chosen by introverts had heart rates the same as those of free-choice introverts. Those forced to listen to the louder noise chosen by extroverts had higher heart rates. Extroverts assigned to hear the noise level chosen by other extroverts had heart rates that matched free-choice extroverts. Those assigned to hear the quieter noise chosen by introverts had lower heart rates.

Finally, introverts did best on the task at the level chosen by introverts (even if it had been assigned). Extroverts performed best at the level chosen by extroverts. It seems, then, that the two groups really do function better with different levels of stimulation.

It's easy to relate these findings to life outside the lab. Imagine the university's housing office assigns an introvert and an extrovert to room together. The extrovert always wants the stereo louder than the introvert. Each thinks life is right when the stereo's set the way he likes it. When the extrovert sets the volume, the introvert is keyed up and can't study. When the introvert sets the volume, the extrovert can't get going. Each one knows what level is "right," but each one's "right" is different from the other's (as in the chapter opening).

Other evidence also fits the idea that introverts and extroverts differ in alertness. In boring, repetitive tasks, you eventually pause, from loss of alertness. Extroverts pause more often than introverts (Eysenck, 1964b). Also relevant are vigilance tasks, which require you to be alert for specific stimuli. For example, you might have to listen to a long series of numbers and press a button whenever you hear three odd ones in a row. If your mind wanders, you miss some of what you're listening for. Introverts miss less (Claridge, 1967). Then there are drug effects. If introverts are highly alert, they shouldn't need as much of a stimulant to reach a given level of arousal. On the other side, introverts should need more of a depressant drug to reach a given index of "unalertness." This seems to be the case (Claridge, 1967; Eysenck, 1983).

Laboratory studies suggest that introverts may do better then extraverts at tasks that require the monitoring of slowly changing visual displays, as is required in the work of air traffic controllers.

Biological Basis of Neuroticism

Eysenck also proposed a neural basis for neuroticism (emotionality). He said people who are high on this trait are easily aroused in the brain's emotion centers. Eysenck thought this had two implications. First, emotional arousal causes the behavioral reflections of both extroverts and introverts to emerge more fully. It makes both of them become "more what they are."

Second, emotional arousal can set the stage for conditioning, because conditioning sometimes follows from emotional reactions (see Chapter 12). Eysenck said that introverts, being cortically aroused, condition easily. If they also happen to be emotional, they'll have emotions in many settings, and thus have many opportunities for conditioning. Much of the conditioning during childhood arises from punishment and frustration. Thus the emotions that get conditioned are mostly negative. As a result, Eysenck argued, neurotic introverts should be vulnerable to development of anxiety and depression.

What happens when neuroticism combines with extroversions? Here the effects are different. Extroverts don't condition well, because they're less aroused cortically. Thus they don't learn from punishment. Extroverts who happen also to be highly emotional respond to the emotions especially impulsively, showing a lack of socialization.

A Contemporary View of Brain Functions: Approach and Inhibition

Eysenck's attempt to link these two personality dimensions to specific aspects of brain function is often praised as a pathbreaking effort. However, when he wrote, brain functioning was not as well understood as it is now. Given the changes in knowledge, some of the people who applaud Eysenck's effort also believe his ideas were wrong.

Within the past fifteen years or so, several theorists have proposed newer ideas about how the nervous system relates to personality. The ideas vary in focus. Some ideas concern what parts of the brain are involved in certain kinds of actions. Some concern what brain chemicals are involved in certain kinds of activities. All of them use what might be called a functional approach. That is, they ask "What *functions* do particular actions serve?" The various kinds of behavior that emerge from this analytic effort then are linked back to ideas about brain processes. Both sets of ideas are also linked back to personality.

Many people are working hard on this topic. The good news is that there are broad areas of agreement. The bad news is that there are also disagreements. The situation resembles that of trait views ten years ago. There's a lot of agreement about major elements in the personality "pie." But there are lots of ways to slice the pie. People differ in where they draw the lines for slicing. They also differ in what they think is contained in a given piece of the pie.

Behavioral Approach, Activation, Engagement, or Facilitation

Most theorists of this group believe there's a set of brain structures that cause animals to move toward **incentives:** things they desire. Several theorists have made assertions about which parts of the brain are involved in this system, though they're not in full agreement (for discussions see Cloninger, 1988; Davidson, 1992, 1995; Davidson, Jackson, & Kalin, 2000; Depue & Collins, 1999; Depue & Iacono, 1989; J. A. Gray, 1982, 1991).

This set of structures has several names: the activation system (Cloninger, 1987; Fowles, 1980), behavioral engagement system (Depue, Krauss, & Spoont, 1987), behavioral facilitation system (Depue & Iacono, 1989); we will refer to it here as the **BAS,** for **behavioral approach system** (J. A. Gray, 1987, 1990, 1994a, 1994b). You might think of this system as regulating the psychic gas pedal, moving you toward what you want. It's a "go" system. Fowles (1980) described it as reward-seeking.

Theorists of this group assume that this set of brain structures is involved when a person is pursuing an incentive. Certain parts of the brain are involved in the pursuit of food, others in the pursuit of sex, and others in the pursuit of shade on a hot summer day. But the assumption is that the separate parts also link up to a BAS. Thus, the BAS is a general mechanism to go after things you want. BAS doesn't rev you up "in neutral," though, with no incentive in mind (Depue & Collins, 1999). It's relevant only to the active pursuit of an incentive.

The BAS is also held to be responsible for positive emotions (e.g., hope, eagerness, and excitement). These emotions reflect anticipations of attaining incentives. Researchers have also pursued this idea in studies of brain activity in emotions. Richard Davidson and his colleagues study emotions by recording the electrical activity from people's brains (Davidson, 1988, 1992, 1995; Davidson & Sutton, 1995). While that's happening, the people are exposed to stimuli such as video clips chosen to create specific kinds of emotional reactions. The question is which parts of the brain become more active in various situations.

A variety of evidence suggests that positive feelings involve activity in the left prefrontal cortex. More left prefrontal activity occurs in adults presented with an incentive (Sobotka et al., 1992) or with positive emotional adjectives (Cacioppo & Petty, 1980). Similar effects arose when ten-month-olds viewed their approaching mothers (Fox & Davidson, 1988). Higher *resting* levels in that area predict positive responses to happy films (Wheeler, Davidson, & Tomarken, 1993). They also relate to self-reported BAS sensitivity (Harmon-Jones & Allen, 1997; Sutton & Davidson, 1997). Findings such as these led Davidson and his colleagues to two conclusions: first, the tendency to experience positive emotion relates to a behavioral approach system. Second, that system is based partly in the left prefrontal cortex.

Another project has linked BAS sensitivity to conditioning. Recall that Eysenck argued introverts condition more easily than extroverts. Thinking in terms of BAS activity, however, leads to a different hypothesis. The BAS responds to incentives. Thus, BAS should relate to conditioning involving *positive* outcomes, but not conditioning involving negative outcomes. Work by Zinbarg and Mohlman (1998) supports this idea. A BAS-based self-report measure predicted speed at learning cues of reward in a conditioning task. This scale did not relate to speed at learning cues of punishment.

A theory that had different origins than the BAS model, but has important similarities to it, was developed by Auke Tellegen (1985), David Watson, Lee Anna Clark, and their colleagues (Watson & Clark, 1984; Watson & Tellegen, 1985). This theory focused first on emotions, and more recently has been applied to motives (Watson, Wiese, Vaidya, & Tellegen, 1999). This theory holds that some people are predisposed to have frequent positive emotions, others less so. This dimension of individual differences is termed **positive emotionality.** Measures of positive emotionality are sometimes used in research intended to bear on the approach system.

To sum up, people with reactive approach systems are highly sensitive to incentives, or cues of good things about to happen. Those whose approach systems are less reactive don't respond as much (either behaviorally or emotionally) to such cues. As an example, consider two people with tickets to an upcoming concert by a band they like. Melanie gets excited whenever she thinks about the concert (although it isn't until next week). Every time she thinks about it she's ready to jump in the car. Melanie is very high in incentive reactivity, or BAS sensitivity. Barbara, on the other hand, is more calm about it. She knows she'll enjoy the concert, but she's not so responsive to thoughts of potential reward. Barbara has less incentive reactivity.

Neurotransmitters and the Approach System

Operation of the approach system has been tied to a specific **neurotransmitter** in the brain. A neurotransmitter is a chemical involved in sending messages along nerve pathways. There are many neurotransmitters, which seem to have different roles. Several theorists have argued that a neurotransmitter called **dopamine** is involved in the system that pursues incentives and creates positive feelings (Cloninger, 1988; Depue, in press; Depue & Collins, 1999; Zuckerman, 1994).

As we noted in Chapter 6, dopamine has been linked to a specific gene. Researchers (Benjamin et al., 1996; Ebstein et al., 1996) found that people with one version of that gene score higher than other people on personality scales assumed to relate to approach (novelty seeking). This finding links a biological *process* variable (dopamine function) with *inheritance* (variation in a particular gene). The common interpretation is that people with the long allele don't have enough dopamine activity in the brain, and they seek novelty to increase it (Plomin & Caspi, 1999). Others have failed to find such a link, however, and this aspect of the evidence remains controversial (e.g., Burt, McGue, Iacono, Comings, & MacMurray, 2002).

Another research team used a very different method to study dopamine. Depue, Luciana, Arbisi, Collins, and Leon (1994) looked at individual differences in dopamine reactivity, using biomedical indicators of response to drug challenges. Dopamine reactivity related to positive emotionality. Others used such procedures to relate dopamine to novelty seeking (Hansenne et al., 2002). Monkey research also links dopamine to greater social dominance (Kaplan, Manuck, Fontenot, & Mann, 2002).

Behavioral Inhibition, Withdrawal, or Avoidance

The last section dealt with an approach system. Most theorists of this group (though not all; see Depue & Collins, 1999; Depue & Iacono, 1989) also assume a separate system that responds to punishers. Gray (1987, 1990, 1994a, 1994b) calls it the **behavioral inhibition system** (**BIS**). It's sometimes called an avoidance system (Cloninger, 1987) or a withdrawal system (Davidson, 1988, 1992, 1995). Activity in this system causes people to *inhibit* movement, or pull back from whatever they just encountered. You might think of the BIS as a psychic brake pedal. It's a "stop" system (sometimes more a "stop-and-throw-it-into-reverse" system).

The BIS is responsive to cues of punishment or danger. It's involved any time a person displays an avoidance or inhibition tendency. When the BIS is operating, the person may stop and scan the environment for further cues. The person may also pull back. As a system that's responsive to threat or danger, the BIS is also responsible for feelings such as anxiety.

Once again, research on cortical activity fits this conclusion. We said earlier that left prefrontal areas are more active when people are happy. There's an increase in activity in *right* prefrontal areas when people are feeling anxiety or aversion. Right prefrontal activity goes up when people view film clips that induce fear and disgust (Davidson, Ekman, Saron, Senulis, & Friesen, 1990). Higher resting levels in that area predict more negative feelings when seeing such films. Higher resting levels in that area also relate to greater self-reports of BIS sensitivity (Harmon-Jones & Allen, 1997; Sutton & Davidson, 1997). Findings such as these led Davidson and his colleagues to argue that the experience of anxiety relates to a behavioral withdrawal system, which involves the right prefrontal cortex.

Research on conditioning has also examined BIS sensitivity. The BIS is reactive to punishments, not incentives. Thus, BIS sensitivity should relate to conditioning for *negative* outcomes, not positive ones. This was found by Zinbarg and Mohlman (1998). A self-report measure of BIS sensitivity predicted speed at learning cues of punishment (but not cues of reward). Conceptually similar results were reported by Corr, Pickering, and Gray (1997).

We noted earlier that Tellegen, Watson, and Clark have pursued the idea that some people are predisposed to have frequent positive emotions, others less. At the same time, they've also pursued the idea that some people are predisposed to frequent *negative* emotions, others less so. This dimension is termed **negative emotionality.**

To sum up this section, people with reactive inhibition systems are sensitive to threat. It's apparent that this dimension reflects the trait of anxiety proneness. As an example of how it influences experiences, think of two people who just took a psychology test and suspect they did badly. Anxiety-prone Randy is almost in a panic about it. Jessica, less anxiety-prone, is bothered hardly at all. One of them is reacting emotionally to the sense of threat, the other isn't.

Threat sensitivity and incentive sensitivity are thought to be separate. People presumably differ from each other on both. As a result, all combinations of high and low BAS and BIS sensitivity probably exist. As an example, it might be intuitive to think of sociability as the opposite of shyness, but that's too simple (L. A. Schmidt, 1999). It's possible to be both very sociable (drawn to social incentives) and very shy (fearful of social interaction).

Neurotransmitters and the Withdrawal System

As with the BAS, there have been efforts to link the BIS to a particular neurotransmitter. Cloninger (1987) argued that harm avoidance, his BIS-equivalent system, is mediated by **serotonin.** Gray (1987, 1990) also sees a link from the BIS to serotonin, but he thinks its role is more minor. Depue thinks serotonin has a different role (e.g., Depue et al., 1994; Zald & Depue, 2001), which we'll come to a bit later.

As we noted in Chapter 6, a gene involved in serotonin functioning has been identified. Some have found a link between one allele of that gene and high scores on measures of anxiety proneness and harm avoidance (e.g., Katsuragi et al., 1999; Lesch et al., 1996; Osher et al., 2000). Others have failed to find such associations, however (Herbst, Zonderman, McCrae, & Costa, 2000; Jorm et al., 1998), so again this aspect of the evidence is controversial.

Several studies have also been done using biochemical challenges to the serotonin system and relating responses to personality measures (see Box 7.2). Some of these studies have found that serotonin function relates inversely to harm avoidance (Peirson et al., 1999; Weijers, Wiesbeck, Jakob, & Böning, 2001).

BOX 7.2

RESEARCH QUESTION

How Do You Assess Neurotransmitter Function?

Researchers are now examining the role of neurotransmitters in a wide range of behavior. All the techniques for studying this require some way to assess neurotransmitter functions in research participants. How is this done? It's more complicated than assessing how much of that particular neurotransmitter is lying around in the person's brain. What's at issue is how the neurotransmitter is being used.

Serotonin is a particularly interesting case. Serotonin receptors can vary in sensitivity (as can all receptors for neurotransmitters). If someone has chronically low serotonin (call him Eddie), the receptors adjust to become more sensitive. If someone has chronically high serotonin (call him Phil), the receptors adjust to become less sensitive. Because Eddie's receptors are very sensitive, they can do their work with relatively little serotonin. Because Phil's receptors are relatively insensitive, they respond less to the same amount of serotonin. Phil needs more serotonin to have the same "processing" effect. Eddie has very responsive serotonin functioning, whereas Phil's is less responsive.

The responsiveness of a neurotransmitter system in humans is often assessed by a biochemical "challenge." This means challenging the system's ability to regulate itself, by administering an agent that perturbs its stable state. The drug that's administered stimulates the system, to see how big a response occurs.

For example, a drug called fenfluramine causes the release of serotonin from presynaptic storage areas and also inhibits its reuptake. Thus, it causes an increase (that lasts several hours) in the levels of serotonin available for use in serotonergic neural transmission. Receptors in the hypothalamus sense this increase in serotonin, and cause the pituitary gland to release prolactin into circulation. Presumably this eventually helps bring the serotonin level back down, but it takes a while. Prolactin concentrations are fairly easy to assess. Researchers track the prolactin level, and determine its peak increase over a period of three to five hours after the fenfluramine is taken. That peak prolactin response (the increase over baseline) is an index of the responsiveness of the serotonin system (e.g., Manuck et al., 2000). A large rise in prolactin means a sensitive or responsive serotonin system.

Because high levels of available serotonin imply an unresponsive serotonin system, it turns out that people who experience more negative affect actually have more serotonin for use than people who have less negative affect. Then why are anxiety and depression treated by serotonin reuptake inhibitors? Those kinds of drugs would seem to raise the levels of available serotonin. The answer is that no one actually knows exactly what those drugs do. One possibility (which is suggested by the fact that they typically take weeks to have an effect) is that they ultimately act because they readjust receptor sensitivity, rather than because they change how much serotonin is available for use. At present, however, the exact mechanism is unclear.

Relating These Systems to Temperaments or Traits

Let's stop and consider what we've said thus far. Many theorists converge on the idea that one brain system manages approach of incentives and another manages withdrawal from threats (Cacioppo, Gardner, & Berntson, 1999; Watson et al., 1999). The one that manages approach also creates excitement and positive feelings. The one that manages withdrawal creates anxiety. How do these principles fit with ideas from previous chapters?

The easiest link to make is from BIS sensitivity to the temperament of emotionality, or the trait of neuroticism. As noted in Chapter 6, despite the fact that some labels for this trait are neutral, anxiety is always at its core. Consistent with this, Larsen and Ketelaar (1991) found that neuroticism predicts susceptibility to a manipulation of anxiety. Carver and White (1994) found the same for their measure of BIS sensitivity. In sum, neuroticism and anxiety proneness have a great deal in common (Elliot & Thrash, 2002, also provide support for this idea). In fact, there's little doubt that the brain system we've been calling the BIS is critical to neuroticism.

Theorists have also suggested a link between the BAS and extroversions. The fit between these two is a little trickier than that between neuroticism and BIS. It's trickier partly because theorists differ about what defines extroversions. Definitions of extroversions usually include a sense of activity and agency (Morrone, Depue, Scherer, & White, 2000). Most include a sense of sociability. Sometimes there's a quality of social dominance or potency. Sometimes there's a quality of impulsiveness. Most definitions include a tendency to experience positive emotions.

How well do these various extroversions packages relate to the BAS? Pretty well, especially regarding positive feelings. Extroversions relates closely to positive emotionality, as measured by Tellegen (Costa & McCrae, 1980; Diener, Sandvik, Pavot, & Fujita, 1992), and to a measure of BAS sensitivity (Carver & White, 1994). Extroverts respond to positive mood manipulations (Larsen & Ketelaar, 1991). BAS sensitivity relates to positive feelings to cues of impending reward (Carver & White, 1994). Zelenski and Larsen (1999) found measures of extroversions and BAS constructs all related to each other, and as a set they predicted positive feelings.

Two Areas of Disagreement

There are, however, a couple of areas of disagreement. Table 7.1 lists several theorists who have written about extroversions, or traits resembling it. The table also lists some qualities the theorists see as belonging to these traits. As you can see, there are two places where questions arise.

One disagreement concerns the social quality that's part of extroversions. That quality is missing from Gray's view of the BAS, but then Gray ignores sociability altogether. One way to fit things together might be to think of BAS sensitivity as sensitivity

Table 7.1

Several theorists and qualities that they believe belong to extraversion (and alternative traits closely related to extraversion). All incorporate pursuit of incentives and a tendency to experience positive emotions. Many, though not all, include a quality of sociability. A few, but again not all, include impulsiveness.

Theorist	Preferred term	Pursuit of incentives	Sociability	Impulsivity	Positive emotions
Eysenck	Extraversion	x			x
Costa & McGee	Extraversion	x			x
Depue	Extraversion	x			x
Zuckerman	Sociability	x			x
Tellegen	Positive emotionality	x			x
Cloninger	Novelty Seeking	x			x
Gray	BAS-Impulsivity	x			x

to *social* incentives. Given that humans are a very social species, it might make sense to think of human approach primarily in terms of approaching social interaction.

Several recent studies suggest, however, that the social aspect of extroversions is not its core quality. One of these projects, mentioned in Chapter 4, was by Lucas, Diener, Grob, Suh, and Shao (2000). Their studies led them to conclude the core of extroversions is *reward sensitivity* and the tendency to experience *positive affect*. They inferred that the social tendencies of extroverts stem from the fact that social interaction is one source of positive experiences. Lucas and Diener (2001) reported further support for this idea. They found extroverts were drawn to situations that offered opportunities for pleasant experiences, whether social or nonsocial.

Other evidence also fits this picture. Lieberman and Rosenthal (2001) were perplexed by findings that introverts and extroverts don't differ in decoding nonverbal cues. Social sensitivity seems so obviously part of extroversions that it didn't make sense. But in studies showing no difference, people had the task of decoding cues *and only that task*. Lieberman and Rosenthal found that extroverts are better at multitasking than introverts. Consequently, they're better at decoding social cues while pursuing other goals. Introverts are less able to split their attention that way. This ability to multitask seems important to the pursuit of incentives (Carver, 2003).

The second issue on which theories differ concerns the role of impulsivity. Gray uses the word *impulsivity* for incentive sensitivity, but he doesn't seem to have issues of impulse control in mind. Eysenck included it in his view of extroversions for years, but later moved it to his third supertrait. This fits the views of those who see impulsivity as the flip side of conscientiousness or constraint, rather than part of extroversions (Tellegen, 1985; Watson & Clark, 1997). Depue and Collins (1999) have the most complex view. They think impulsivity with positive affect (the key to extroversions) belongs in extroversions but impulsivity without it doesn't.

Relevant to this issue is a study by Zelenski and Larsen (1999). They factor-analyzed several personality measures, including measures of BIS and BAS sensitivity and impulsivity. They found that measures of impulsivity loaded on a different factor than extroversions (which loaded on the BAS factor). Also relevant is evidence from monkey research (Fairbanks, 2001). This study found that social dominance, which many see as part of extroversions, relates to moderate impulsivity—not high or low. On the whole, the evidence suggests that impulsivity may not belong in extroversions.

This issue—where to place impulsivity—begins to raise another very broad question. Is there perhaps another biological dimension besides BAS and BIS? Many believe the answer is "yes" and that impulsiveness is an important reflection of it.

Sensation Seeking: A Third Biological System?

Another long-standing effort to link personality with the functioning of the nervous system is represented in the work of Marvin Zuckerman (e.g., 1971, 1985, 1991a, 1991b, 1992, 1993, 1994). The variable that he and his colleagues have studied is **sensation seeking.**

People high in sensation seeking are in search of new, varied, and exciting experiences. Compared to people lower on this trait, they're faster drivers (Zuckerman & Neeb, 1980). They are more likely to use drugs (Zuckerman, 1979), to increase alcohol use over time (Newcomb & McGee, 1991), to do high-risk sports such as skydiving (Hymbaugh & Garrett, 1974), and to engage in risky antisocial behaviors (Horvath & Zuckerman, 1993). They are more sexually experienced and sexually responsive (Fisher, 1973), and when in relationships they're more dissatisfied (Thron-

Sensation seekers like to seek out new, varied, and exciting experiences.

quist, Zuckerman, & Exline, 1991). In the army, they're more likely to volunteer for combat units (Hobfoll, Rom, & Segal, 1989).

Is there a particular brain chemical for sensation seeking or constraint? Opinions and evidence are both mixed. Zuckerman (1994, 1995) has suggested a role for an enzyme called monoamine oxidase (MAO). MAO regulates several neurotransmitters, including serotonin and dopamine. Sensation seeking relates to MAO levels (Zuckerman, 1994). MAO also relates to social dominance, sociability, and aggression (Rowe, 2001; Zuckerman, 1995). A gene related to MAO levels has been linked to aggression and impulsivity (Manuck, Flory, Ferrell, Mann, & Muldoon, 2000). Maybe MAO is one key, then, to this system.

Function of Sensation Seeking

Earlier we said theorists of this group tend to use a functional approach—that is, to look for the purpose that a given biological system might serve. What might be the point of a sensation-seeking system? One view is that it regulates exposure to stimulus intensity (Zuckerman, 1979, 1991a, 1991b, 1994). People high in sensation seeking open themselves to stimulation. Low sensation seekers protect themselves from stimulation (see also Aron & Aron, 1997). This produces the behavioral differences between them.

Some of the evidence underlying this view concerns reactions to unexpected stimuli. The **orienting response** is a shift of attention to the stimulus, increasing sensory intake. People high in sensation seeking show stronger orienting responses than people low in sensation seeking (Feij, Orlebeke, Gazendam, & van Zuilen, 1985; Neary & Zuckerman, 1976).

Another source of evidence is the brain activity that occurs when a person is exposed to a series of stimuli varying in intensity. Some people (called augmenters) increase in brain-wave response as the stimuli get more intense. Other people (reducers) decrease in response as the stimuli get more intense. As shown in Figure 7.3, high sensation seekers tend to be augmenters, low sensation seekers reducers (e.g., Coursey, Buchsbaum, & Frankel, 1975; Zuckerman, 1991a; Zuckerman, Murtaugh, & Siegel, 1974). The inference is that high sensation seekers open themselves to the stimulation, whereas low sensation seekers protect themselves from it.

Both of these patterns have advantages and disadvantages (Zuckerman, 1991a). People high in sensation seeking should function well in overstimulating conditions such as combat. But they can display antisocial and even manic behavior when the situation is less demanding. People lower in sensation seeking are better adapted to most circumstances of life, but they may "shut down" psychologically when things get too intense.

Another view of the function of this trait relates it to the demands of social living. Zuckerman (1991a, 1991b, 1993) found a higher-order factor he calls **impulsive unsocialized sensation seeking** (**IUSS**). He thinks IUSS concerns a capacity to inhibit behavior in service of social adaptation. People high on IUSS don't do this well. Consistent with this, IUSS relates inversely to sociability and positively to aggressiveness (Zuckerman et al., 1993). It also relates inversely to conscientiousness from the five-factor model (Zuckerman, 1996). Finally, it relates positively to the third trait in Eysenck's model—psychoticism—which concerns disregard of social restraint in pursuit of intense sensations. Eysenck once placed impulsiveness in extroversions, but later moved it to psychoticism. This shift fits Zuckerman's view.

Tellegen's (1985) theory also deserves mention in this context. Recall that his positive emotionality and negative emotionality are roughly equivalent to extroversions and neuroticism. Tellegen also assumes a third trait, called *constraint*. Constraint is the opposite of IUSS. It's the holding back of impulses. It has facets called control, harm avoidance, and traditionalism. This sounds like a reverse description of

Figure 7.3

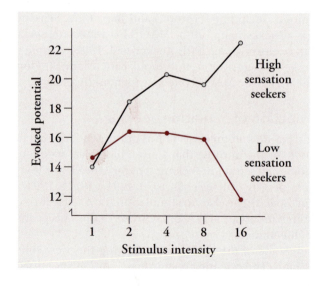

Average evoked potential (cortical activity in response to stimuli) among persons who scored high versus those who scored low on a subscale of the Sensation Seeking scale. Low evoked potentials are sometimes interpreted as a screening out of the stimulation. This difference between high and low sensation seekers suggests that the lows are acting (at some level) to screen away stimulation (adapted from Zuckerman, Murtaugh, & Siegel, 1974).

the dimension Zuckerman assumes. Some see this as a third major aspect of temperament (Clark & Watson, 1999).

Sensation Seeking, Impulsiveness, and Other Systems

How does this view of a third system relate to what we said earlier about the first two systems? High IUSS involves seeking events that are expected to be positive (e.g., Zuckerman, 1985). This sounds a little like high BAS. High IUSS also involves lack of inhibition. This sounds a little like low BIS. But Zuckerman doesn't see high IUSS as just a combination of high BAS and low BIS. He sees it as another system that's distinct from both of them.

Think of it like this: If you have a sensitive BIS, cues of impending punishment cause you distress. But if you're also high in IUSS, any distress you experience doesn't stop you from doing what you're about to do. Furthermore, if you're high in IUSS, you may not think ahead to the *possibility* of punishment until it's already there.

One More Angle on Impulsivity

As if things weren't already confusing enough, here's one more possibility. People other than personality psychologists are interested in impulsivity versus constraint, under slightly different names and for different reasons. Some of them are also interested in the idea that spontaneous and controlled behavior involve different parts of the nervous system (Lieberman, Gaunt, Gilbert, & Trope, in press; Poldrack & Gabrieli, 2001).

Evidence on this is sketchy (a lot of research is now ongoing), but Lieberman et al. (in press) examined the evidence and concluded this: There's reason to think there are two separate processes involved in "knowing the world." There's a global pattern-recognition system that processes events early and fast. It uses one set of brain structures (we'll spare you the details). Farther along (past this system) comes another system that processes sequentially, more slowly, and in more of a rule-based way. This takes place in a second set of structures (involving the prefrontal cortex).

Here's why this is of interest: Responses that are triggered by the first system would be impulsive. Responses generated by the second system would be more constrained. Presumably people vary in which set of structures they rely on most in acting. Perhaps the tendency to rely on one versus the other represents the dimension of impulsivity versus constraint. This would be consistent with the idea that the critical issue in impulsivity is whether the person stops and thinks before acting (Patterson & Newman, 1993).

It's of interest that the brain structures in this model exist in both sides of the brain. Thus its distinction between impulsive and constrained seems separate from that between BAS and BIS (if the ideas about BAS and BIS being localized in left versus right prefrontal areas are correct). This would have a couple of implications. For one, in this view constraint versus impulsivity could, in principle, be reflected both in approach and in avoidance. For another, it would mean that impulsivity is not a product of the balance between BAS and BIS functioning.

Impulsiveness: Further Issues

The idea that behavior sometimes is spontaneous and impulsive, and sometimes is controlled, constrained, and thought-over comes up at several points in this book. It's not just here that it matters. It's a core issue in psychoanalysis (Chapter 8). It also emerges in a neoanalytic ego theory (Chapter 10), and yet again in cognitive theories (Chapter 16).

The question of how to account for impulsiveness is a hard one. It's a major source of disagreement among biological theorists (Avila, 2001; Nigg, 2000). Some see impulsiveness as deriving from two systems, some from a third one (see also Box 7.3). Let's consider more closely some of the issues that underlie this question.

Evidence bearing on the question has several interwoven facets. One facet concerns serotonin. We said earlier that some theorists believe serotonin is important to BIS functioning. For example, there's evidence linking neuroticism and harm avoidance to genes that pertain to serotonin. However, others see these associations a little differently. There's also some evidence that doesn't fit that picture so clearly.

What Does Serotonin Function Mean?

Depue argues that serotonin relates not to BIS, but to constraint. Most studies of serotonin functioning in humans relate it to negative emotion. But usually the rela-

BOX 7.3

THEORETICAL CONTROVERSY
Is Impulsiveness a Basic Property or a Resultant Property?

There is wide consensus that impulsivity is an important dimension of human behavior. Issues of impulse control emerge throughout personality psychology in various forms, as you will see in many chapters. Both ends of this dimension can relate to problems. People who have lives of total constraint fail to open themselves to experiences from which they might profit. Those who are completely unable to control their impulses are a threat to society. Understanding how this aspect of personality is managed would seem to be a high-priority goal.

Although everyone agrees it's important to understand impulsiveness, there's far less agreement on how to understand it (Nigg, 2000). As described in the main text, some theorists assume a third system behind this quality. However, it can be hard to disentangle the workings of that system from the workings of BAS and BIS. Indeed, some think there's no third system at all. Rather, they see impulsive behavior as emerging from the joint actions of the BAS and BIS (Depue & Collins, 1999).

Indeed, there are several different ways to conceptualize impulsiveness as a resultant of BIS and BAS sensitivities. A person with a highly active BAS pursues incentives with great vigor. Maybe that's the real source of impulsiveness (Arnett, Smith, & Newman, 1997;

Avila, 2001). Alternatively, a person with a weak BIS doesn't experience much anxiety in the face of threats (Avila, 2001). Maybe this interferes with punishment-based learning, leading to a person who hasn't learned to restrain the pursuit of incentives.

Or maybe impulsiveness derives from a *combination* of BIS and BAS qualities. Maybe both a strong BAS and a weak BIS are required to produce impulsivity. Maybe there's no third *system*, but another factor (a hormone or a neurotransmitter or an enzyme) that causes the balance of influence between BIS and BAS to shift. Maybe that's the function of MAO (Zuckerman, 1996).

From a personality point of view (as opposed to a neurological one), separating these possibilities from each other will require inventive research. An attempt must be made to assess personality on BIS and BAS sensitivities (in some form) along with the dimension that's believed to be the third system. If the third dimension really matters in impulsive behavior, it will predict that behavior when BIS, BAS, and their interaction are all taken into account. Such work remains yet to be done. In the meantime, however, most observers continue to argue for a more complex path to impulsiveness, involving a third biological system.

tion isn't to anxiety, the core emotion of the BIS. It's to anger. Lower serotonin function has been linked to a history of fighting and assault (Coccaro, Kavoussi, Cooper, & Hauger, 1997) and to impulsive aggression more generally, particularly in men (Cleare & Bond, 1997). Monkey research has found low serotonin function relates to dominance. This was distinct from the link between dopamine and dominance (Kaplan et al., 2002), suggesting that there are two pathways to dominance.

Early studies used very small samples, often patients. Another study looked at the issue in a large community sample (Manuck, Flory, McCaffery, Matthews, Mann, & Muldoon, 1998). It found low serotonin response related to aggression, and also to impulsiveness, neuroticism, and the neuroticism facet of angry hostility. High serotonin responses in this sample related to conscientiousness. Manuck and colleagues have also found evidence of a link between hostility and aggression and a gene believed to relate to serotonin functioning (Manuck, Flory, Ferrell, Dent, Mann, & Muldoon, 1999). Monkey research has also linked serotonin to impulsiveness (Fairbanks et al., 2001).

We said earlier that serotonin function has been related inversely to harm avoidance (Peirson et al., 1999; Weijers et al., 2001). But in one of these studies it also related positively to responsibility and resourcefulness (Peirson et al., 1999). Other research has found a measure of persistence, rather than harm avoidance, related to serotonin genes (Comings et al., 2000).

As a group, these findings suggest support for the constraint hypothesis. There's also one more twist to the evidence. Zald and Depue (2001) argued that serotonin should inhibit positive emotions as well as negative. To test this, they had men track their emotions for two weeks. They computed averages separately for positive and negative feelings. They then related these data to the men's levels of serotonin function. Higher serotonin function related to less negative affect, consistent with findings linking serotonin to lower trait neuroticism. However, higher serotonin function also related to lower levels of *positive* feelings (interested, active, attentive, and enthusiastic). Zald and Depue concluded that serotonin provides a constraining influence over the biological systems that manage affects of both sorts.

This group of findings suggests there is a sound basis for thinking of impulsiveness as deriving from a third biological system. The findings also suggest that the third system, rather than the BIS, may be managed at least partly by serotonin. Clearly, the role that is played by serotonin in the regulation of behavior is far from resolved at this point.

What Are the Personality Scales Measuring?

As just described, part of the puzzle here is figuring out what the function of serotonin is. Another part of the puzzle is knowing what qualities of behavior the personality scales are assessing. This turns out to be harder than it might seem. The constructs different people use—and the scales they use to measure them—don't match up perfectly. As we said earlier, different people slice the pie at different angles, and they assume different elements in the slices. That was true for extroversions, and it's also true here.

Consider Cloninger's measures. Harm avoidance is his BIS-equivalent construct. But Cloninger (1987) sees people low in harm avoidance as being uninhibited and prone to risk-taking and aggression. This sounds like constraint versus impulsivity. Novelty seeking is Cloninger's BAS-equivalent construct. But Zelenski and Larsen (1999) found that novelty seeking loaded on a factor of impulsiveness and sensation seeking, not on approach. Fitting the idea that novelty seeking reflects impulsivity rather than approach, another study linked novelty seeking more to serotonin genes than to dopamine genes (Comings et al., 2000). Cloninger's measures are in use in many medical studies bearing on personality. Some would say, however, that studies using these measures can be difficult to interpret.

This is far from the only problem in fitting assessment devices to each other and to the concepts they share. We said earlier that Tellegen and his colleagues have a theory in which positive emotionality resembles extroversions, negative emotionality resembles neuroticism, and constraint resembles conscientiousness. These factors resemble those of the five-factor model but don't quite duplicate them. The relationships between Tellegen's scales and measures of that model are in fact more complex than that (Church, 1994).

Although one can criticize measures for including qualities that should not be included, it's hard to know what should be included and what should not. When we began this discussion of impulsivity, we noted that it's possible to think of impulsivity as deriving entirely from the balance between go and stop—BAS and BIS (recall Box 7.3). If you held that view, you'd incorporate the sense of impulse and restraint in your scales for BAS and BIS. This is essentially what Cloninger's scales do.

Hormones and Personality

We turn now to a different aspect of biology and personality: hormones. An important group is sex hormones. They determine a developing embryo's physical sexual characteristics. They also influence physical characteristics at other stages of development. We won't explore all the ways sex hormones influence behavior (see, e.g., Le Vay, 1993; Rubin, Reinisch, & Haskett, 1981; Tavris & Wade, 1984), but we'll examine a few of them, focusing on testosterone.

Hormones, the Body, and the Brain

Sex hormones are important in a variety of ways from very early in life. Normal males have higher testosterone than normal females from week eight to week twenty-four of gestation, from about the first through the fifth month after birth, and again after puberty (Le Vay, 1993). Testosterone differences in gestation appear essential to changes in the nervous system that create normal male and female physical development. Many believe the hormones also change the brain in ways that result in behavioral differences (Breedlove, 1994; Le Vay, 1993).

The basic template for a human body is female. Only if hormones cause specific changes to occur does a body emerge that looks male. If a genetic male isn't exposed to androgen ("male-making") hormones at critical points in development, the result is an exterior that looks female. If a genetic female is exposed to testosterone at the same points, the result is an exterior that looks male (Breedlove, 1994). During typical fetal development, of course, only males are exposed to enough androgen to be masculinized.

The hormones that guide the body in its sexual development also affect nerve cells (Breedlove, 1992; Le Vay, 1993). They organize the developing brains of males and females differently, in subtle ways. Animal research suggests there aren't just two patterns, but a broad range of variation, with male and female patterns as the extremes (Panksepp, 1998). The genders tend to differ in linkages among synapses and in the size of some brain structures. For example, the two sides of the cortex are more fully interconnected in women than men (Le Vay, 1993). Men are more visually dominated than women (Panksepp, 1998). Interestingly, there's evidence that the brains of gay men structurally resemble those of women more than those of heterosexual men (Allen & Gorski, 1992; Le Vay, 1991).

How might these differences in the nervous system relate to personality? We said earlier that exposure to androgens may "masculinize" the nervous system. Several things may follow from this.

Early Hormonal Exposure and Behavior

Early exposure to hormones—even prenatal exposure—can influence later behavior. One study (Reinisch, 1981) looked at children whose mothers had received synthetic hormones that act like testosterone during treatment for complications in their pregnancies. Each child thus was exposed to the hormones prenatally (an average of eleven years earlier), during a critical phase of development. The other group was their same-sex siblings (to match as closely as possible on genetic and environmental variables).

Each child completed a self-report measure in which six situations are described, each involving interpersonal conflict. The children made decisions about what they would do in each situation. The measure was the likelihood of responding with physical aggression, verbal aggression, withdrawal, and nonaggressive coping.

The study yielded two separate effects, both bearing on the choice of physical aggression as a response to conflict (Figure 7.4). The first was a sex difference: boys chose this response more than girls. There was also an effect of prenatal exposure to the hormone. Children who'd been exposed chose physical aggression more than did those who hadn't been exposed. This was true both for boys and for girls.

This study is intriguing for a couple of reasons. It's clear that a biological variable—the hormone—influenced the behavior. It's less clear *how* it did so. Animal

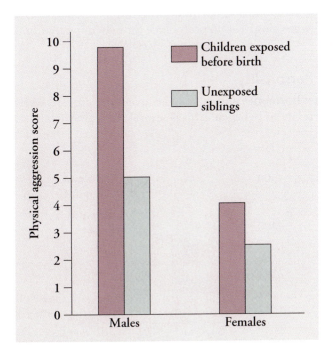

Figure 7.4

Average (self-report) physical aggression scores during childhood for boys and girls who had been exposed to synthetic hormones before birth and for their sex-matched siblings who had not been exposed. Exposure to the hormone produced elevated aggression scores for both boys and girls (adapted from Reinisch, 1981).

research indicates that exposure to male hormones during early development increases aggressive displays (Reinisch, 1981). But that wasn't the behavior measured here. Reinisch measured no aggressive acts, just self-reports indicating the choice of aggressive acts. Thus, any masculinizing influence on the nervous system had to filter through a lot of cognition to be displayed.

In another project, Berenbaum and Hines (1992) studied children with a genetic disorder that causes high levels of androgens (masculinizing hormones) prenatally and soon after birth. Years later (ages three to eight), these children (and unaffected same-sex relatives) were observed as they played individually. Available were toys that had been determined to be generally preferred by boys and by girls. The question was who played with which toys.

The androgen-exposed girls spent more time with the boys' toys and less time with the girls' toys than did unexposed girls (Figure 7.5). In fact, they displayed a preference pattern like that of boys. Preferences among the boys were unaffected by exposure. These findings suggest that a masculinizing hormone can influence the activities children engage in much later in life.

Androgens come from several sources. Exposure through a mother's medical treatment during pregnancy is one. Another is the adrenal glands, which secrete androgen normally. High levels of natural androgen in girls has been related to greater involvement in sports that involve rough body contact (Kimura, 1999), activities that are more typical of boys.

Other research also suggests that hormones influence play styles. Jacklin, Maccoby, and Doering (1983) found that hormone levels at birth were related to boldness versus timidity in infant boys over the next eighteen months. Boldness was assessed by exposing children to novel (and thus somewhat scary) toys. Higher testosterone among boys at birth predicted more boldness. In contrast, higher estradiol (an estrogen) related to more timidity. No association with a hormone was significant among the girls in the study, however.

The findings thus are somewhat mixed, but they appear generally consistent with the idea that early exposure to masculinizing hormones can influence behavior. It can increase the potential for aggression, lead to preference for masculine toys, and enhance boldness.

Testosterone and Adult Personality

A good deal of research on sex hormones and personality examines current levels of testosterone and how they relate to behavior. This is several steps away from the

Figure 7.5

Amount of time two groups of girls played in a free-play setting with toys generally preferred by boys and toys generally preferred by girls. Some of the girls had been exposed to masculinizing hormones before birth and shortly afterward, the others had not been exposed (adapted from Berenbaum & Hines, 1992).

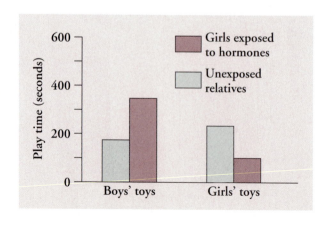

idea that testosterone masculinizes the nervous system. Yet it shares with it the theme that testosterone is involved in regulating important qualities of human behavior. Much of the research in this area has been conducted by James Dabbs and his colleagues (see Dabbs & Dabbs, 2000).

Testosterone is a sex hormone, but research on testosterone focuses more often on dominance and antisocial behavior than sexual behavior. One study of men in prison (Dabbs, Frady, Carr, & Besch, 1987) found inmates high in testosterone had violated prison rules more often and were more dominant than inmates lower in testosterone. They were also more likely to have committed violent crimes. Similar results have come from female inmates (Dabbs et al., 1988) and adolescent males (Dabbs, Jurkovic, & Frady, 1991). In a recent sample of men who had committed murders, those high in testosterone were more likely to have planned the act ahead of time and to have killed people they knew (Dabbs, Riad, & Chance, 2001).

Another study examined testosterone and antisocial behaviors in a noncriminal population (Dabbs & Morris, 1990). Participants were military veterans. They were asked questions about antisocial behaviors during childhood and in the recent past. Men higher in testosterone had larger numbers of sex partners and were more likely to abuse alcohol and other drugs. They were more likely to have gone AWOL in the military and to have assaulted others. They were also more likely to have had trouble with parents, teachers, and classmates while growing up (see also Box 7.4). These effects were far stronger among men of low socioeconomic status (SES) than among men of higher SES.

Being low-SES can increase the ill effects of high testosterone, and research also suggests that high testosterone tends to lead men *into* lower-SES occupations (Dabbs, 1992a). This seems to be because high testosterone promotes antisocial behavior and disruption of education. Both of these factors then lead people away from white-collar occupations.

Recent research suggests a link between testosterone level and aggression.

BOX 7.4

STEROIDS
An Unintended Path to Aggression

Discussing the effects of testosterone on behavior brings up a related topic: body building and its excesses. The appeal of body building comes partly from the result: a body that looks as though it's chiseled from rock. Cultural expectations of men's bodies (as reflected in *Playgirl* photos) have shifted over the past two decades, becoming increasingly dense and muscular (Leit, Pope, & Gray, 2001). These expectations create pressure on men to look that way.

The desire for a well-formed body has led many people into the use of **anabolic steroids.** The word *anabolic* means "building up." Anabolic steroids are chemicals that mimic the body's tendency to rebuild muscle tissues that have been stressed or exercised. Your body gives you small doses of such chemicals, producing growth in muscle size. Using steroids gives you a much bigger dose. Steroids thus let you speed up and exaggerate the building of muscles in ways that exercise alone can't do. That's why people use them.

Indeed, some people are using steroids and steroidlike substances without fully realizing it. So-called "dietary supplements," which many use, are often potent drugs. A recent survey of gym users found that 18 percent of men said they used adrenal hormones, 25 percent used ephedrine, and another 5 percent used anabolic steroids (Kanayama, Gruber, Pope, Borowiecki, & Hudson, 2001). An even more recent survey by the National Institute on Drug Abuse found that steroid use more than doubled among high-school sophomores from 1992 to 2000.

Many users don't realize that steroids are synthetic hormones. Their effects go far beyond the building of muscles. Steroids are related to testosterone (that's why men's muscles tend to be larger than women's). Testosterone is involved in many things, not just building

muscle tissue. Consequently, people who use steroids for larger muscles are in for a surprise: there can be unintended and unpleasant side effects.

Some of these effects are physical. If you're a man, part of your body sees the steroids as testosterone. It reacts to what looks like too much testosterone by shutting down production of more. The results are a lowered sperm count and a decreased sex drive (the steroids don't act like testosterone in these respects). If you're a woman, steroids cause masculinizing effects: shrinking breasts, deepening voice, and growth in facial and body hair (Gruber & Pope, 2000).

Steroids also have behavioral effects, which are of particular interest here. As you've read in the main text, studies link testosterone to dominance and aggressiveness. Steroids produce much the same effects. Because the doses tend to be large, so are the effects. Heavy steroid use can yield irrational bursts of anger that are popularly referred to as "roid rages." Adverse behavioral and psychological responses are not limited to men, either. In a sample of women users, 56 percent reported hypomanic symptoms during steroid use and 40 percent reported depressive symptoms during steroid withdrawal (Gruber & Pope, 2000). Ominously, there is evidence from animal research that steroid use during adolescence can create aggressive tendencies that remain after the steroid is withdrawn (Harrison, Connor, Nowak, Nash, & Melloni, 2000).

These effects are bad enough in the average person, but body building and steroid use aren't limited to the average person. Body building has considerable appeal for people who already have a strong streak of dominance and aggressiveness. Add steroids to an already aggressive personality, and the result is a potential for serious violence.

Differences in testosterone relate to occupations in other ways, as well, fitting a link between testosterone and social dominance (Mazur & Booth, 1998). For example, trial lawyers (of both genders) are higher in testosterone than nontrial lawyers (Dabbs, Alford, & Fielden, 1998). Actors and NFL football players have high testosterone (Dabbs, de La Rue, & Williams, 1990), ministers have low levels (college professors, if you must know, are intermediate).

Why are actors so different from ministers? After all, they're both on stage. Dabbs et al. (1990) suggested that actors must be dominant constantly, because their reputation is only as good as their last show. Ministers operate in a framework that tolerates more variability. Further, the actor's role is to seek and hold onto glory, whereas a minister's role is to be self-effacing.

Effects of testosterone occur in many small ways that are related to social potency and dominance. In one study testosterone related to deeper voices among men (Dabbs & Mallinger, 1999). In studies of brief interactions with strangers, participants higher in testosterone entered more quickly, focused more directly on the other person, and displayed more independence and confidence than those with less testosterone (Dabbs, Bernieri, Strong, Campo, & Milun, 2001). Even young children high in testosterone are more independent on the playground than those with less testosterone (Strong & Dabbs, 2000).

The dominance that's linked to high testosterone is useful in many contexts, but it can interfere with relationships. Booth and Dabbs (1993) found that men with higher testosterone were less likely to have married. If they did marry, they were more likely to divorce. They were also more likely to have had extramarital sex and to commit domestic abuse. Men high in testosterone have smiles that are less friendly than men lower in testosterone, and they express more dominance in their gaze when in conversation (Dabbs, 1992b, 1997). Members of low-testosterone fraternities are friendly and smile a lot, whereas members of high-testosterone fraternities are wilder and more unruly (Dabbs, Hargrove, & Heusel, 1996).

Several studies have related testosterone to personality measures. In two studies, personality data and testosterone data were factor-analyzed, forming a factor around testosterone (Daitzman & Zuckerman, 1980; Udry & Talbert, 1988). In both cases, the factor had overtones of impulsiveness, sensation seeking, and dominance. Udry and Talbert's (1988) factor included these self-ratings: cynical, dominant, sarcastic, spontaneous, persistent, and uninhibited. These findings may relate back to work on brain functions and impulsivity, earlier in the chapter.

Cycle of Testosterone and Action

It may be most obvious to think about testosterone in terms of stable individual differences. However, testosterone is also part of a dynamic system that changes over time and events (Dabbs, 1992b). Levels of testosterone shift in response to social situations of several types. These shifts may, in turn, go on to influence the person's later behavior.

Testosterone levels rise after certain kinds of positive experience, and the experience doesn't have to involve great exertion. As shown in Figure 7.6, testosterone rises after success at a competitive event (Mazur, Booth, & Dabbs, 1992) and falls after a failure or humiliation. It rises when your team wins and falls when your team loses (Bernhardt, Dabbs, Fielden, & Lutter, 1998). It rises when you are confronted with the challenge of an insult (Nisbett & Cohen, 1996). And it rises (for both men and women) after sexual intercourse (Dabbs & Mohammed, 1992).

Such changes in testosterone also have implications for subsequent behavior. Increases in testosterone make people more sexually active (Dabbs, 1992b). An increase in testosterone can also make a person more assertive—may lead him to seek out new competitive challenges and opportunities to be dominant (Mazur, 1985; Mazur et al., 1992). Decreases in testosterone after a failure may cause a person to be less assertive and to avoid new competition. Thus, in either case (success or failure) there's a tendency toward a spiraling effect: a given outcome tends to promote more of the same outcome.

Figure 7.6

Testosterone levels among chess players who won or lost close matches in a citywide tournament (adapted from Mazur et al., 1992).

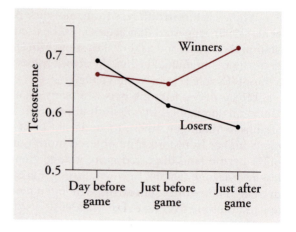

Testosterone, Dominance, and Evolutionary Psychology

Let's step back from these studies to consider a broader implication. The findings as a group seem to fit with one of the themes of evolutionary psychology, discussed in Chapter 6.

Recall that evolutionary thinking includes the idea that selection pressures led to certain gender differences. These differences stem from the fact that human females have greater investment than males in offspring (through the long period of pregnancy and mothering). Females are believed to be choosy about mates for this reason, trying to find one who will provide resources for her children. A gender difference in dominance and aggression is also believed to follow from the differing selection pressures.

In that view, aggression can increase males' opportunities to mate. Aggressiveness helps males establish dominance and status. Overt aggressiveness in females doesn't confer the same advantage and may even be a disadvantage. It can create the potential for damage to an unborn or young child. It also interferes with her more important activities (bearing and raising children). Research discussed in this second part of the chapter suggests that this difference in the behavior of men and women occurs partly via differences in levels of testosterone.

Dabbs (1992b, 1998) notes an interesting irony here. In the evolutionary view, males are high in testosterone and dominance, because physical domination over other males brought access to mates. In recent millenia, however, the rules have changed somewhat. Success is now defined partly in socioeconomic terms, rather than by physical dominance. A man who's too preoccupied with displays and posturing may have difficulty acquiring the skills needed for economic and social power. Thus, a quality that was important in prehistory may actually interfere with success in today's world.

Responding to Stress: Men, Women, and Oxytocin

Another important hormonal influence concerns responses to stress, but extends far beyond. A phrase that's well known in psychology, coined long ago by Cannon (1932) is "the fight or flight response." It refers to the fact that when an animal confronts a predator or competitor, it has two obvious adaptive choices: attack (hoping to overcome the adversary) or flee (hoping to escape). Presumably the flight response connects in some way to the BIS, discussed earlier in the chapter. Apparently there's a link between the fight response and the system of impulsivity–constraint, also discussed earlier in the chapter.

It's often been assumed that these are the only important responses to threat. Shelley Taylor (2002) and her colleagues (Taylor, Klein, Lewis, Gruenewald, Gurung, & Updegraff, 2000) have argued that this assumption is wrong. As they point out, most of the evidence for that view comes from studies of males (and mostly male rats, at that). Females have been studied in a few stressful contexts, but the behavior examined in those studies hasn't been about fight or flight. Rather, the behavior has concerned affiliation, particularly affiliation with other women.

Taylor et al. argued that focusing on male behavior caused an important set of responses to stress to be widely ignored. They refer to these responses, which are stronger in females than in males, with the phrase "tend and befriend." Taylor et al. think the existence of these responses reflects a difference in evolutionary pressures on males and females, due to differing investment in offspring. That is, as noted just earlier, attacking and fleeing may make good sense for males, who aren't carrying offspring (or pregnant). It makes less sense for females. Females thus may have evolved strategies that benefit both themselves and their offspring.

Tending refers to calming of offspring. You protect them from harm in part by calming them and thus fading into the background, where the threat is less. By extension, you do the same for adults you're close to who are stressed. Befriending means affiliating and bonding with others. This reduces certain kinds of risk (there's greater safety in numbers) and increases the chances of receiving tending from each other when needed (Taylor, 2002).

This pattern of response is believed to derive from the system that produces attachment between infant and caregiver. Attachment is often discussed from the perspective of the infant's bond to a caregiver (see Chapter 11). It's less often discussed the other way around. Yet there's a good deal of research on this topic (mostly with lower animals), and aspects of the biological mechanism that creates it have been identified (Panksepp, 1998).

This system involves a hormone called oxytocin. It acts to relax and sedate (e.g., Light et al., 2000), and it reduces fear. Both males and females have this hormone, but females seem to have more of it. Further, androgens inhibit its release under stress, and estrogen increases its effects (see Taylor et al., 2000). Thus, men and women react somewhat differently to stress. Men tend to remove themselves from social interaction; women immerse themselves in nurturing those around them (Repetti, 1989).

The idea that oxytocin is involved (along with endogenous opioids) in mother–infant bonding is a starting point. But it's also argued that oxytocin is involved in social bonding more generally (Carter, 1998; Panksepp, 1998; Taylor et al., 2000; Turner, Altemus, Enos, Cooper, & McGuinness, 1999). Oxytocin is released during orgasm, childbirth, massage, and breast-feeding (Matthiesen et al., 2001; Turner et al., 1999). Animal research shows it plays a key role in adult pair-bonding in some species.

And what of personality? There definitely are individual differences in oxytocin release to particular stimuli. But thus far there's no clear link between these differences and personality traits. This reflects the fact that human research on oxytocin is just getting momentum, in part because it's harder to study than some other hormones. If oxytocin is important in the formation of social bonds, though, it's a key biological influence on human experience. Undoubtedly, its influence on personality will be the subject of further work in years to come.

Assessment

The biological view on personality discussed in this chapter assumes that personality derives from events in the nervous system and hormonal system. If personality is biological, then why not just assess the biological characteristics?

There are a couple of problems with this. In many cases no one's quite sure how the biological influences are exerted, so it's hard to know what to measure. It's also hard to assess biological functions in a way that doesn't require a sensor in the body or the drawing of blood. Despite these problems, some biological methods of assessment are now in use.

Electroencephalograms

An indirect indication of what's going on in the brain can be obtained by recording electrical activity from the skin over the skull. The record is called an **electroencephalogram,** or **EEG.** The reasoning behind it is that neurons throughout the brain fire at various intervals, creating continuous fluctuations in voltage. Electrodes on the scalp sense these changes. This gives a view of aspects of the activity in the cerebral cortex. Cortical activity is very complex, but it forms patterns that relate to different subjective states.

EEGs are now used as a way of investigating normal personality processes. In fact, some of the work discussed earlier in the chapter used EEGs. Various regions of the cortex are active to different degrees when people are in various psychological states. Mapping EEG activities in different locations shows what areas of the brain are involved in what kinds of mental activity. For example, it's possible to identify a person who's dominated by incentive motivation or by avoidance motivation by looking at left versus right frontal activation levels at rest (Harmon-Jones & Allen, 1997; Sutton & Davidson, 1997).

Neuro-Imaging

Mapping of brain activities has also moved further inside the brain. One technique is called **positron emission tomography** (**PET**). PET derives a picture of brain functioning from metabolic activity. The person receives a radioactive form of glucose (the brain's energy source). Later, radioactivity in different brain areas are recorded. Presumably more active areas use more glucose, resulting in higher radioactivity there. A computer color-codes the intensities, producing a brain map in which colors represent levels of brain activity.

One application of the PET procedure is measuring neurotransmitter function. To do this, a radioactively labeled drug with known effects is given. The person's brain activity is then compared to its activity when in a nondrugged condition. Differences between the PET scans provide information about the receptor systems involved in the drug's effects.

Another technique, called **magnetic resonance imaging** (**MRI**), relies on a very subtle property of nerve activity. Functioning nerve cells create magnetic fields. With a good deal of computer assistance, the magnetic resonances of a person's brain can be translated into a visual image. Typically, the image is of slices across the brain, as seen from above. Different slices give different information, because they show different parts of the brain.

At first, MRI images were used primarily to look for structural problems in the brain. For example, if you were having blackouts after an auto accident, you might

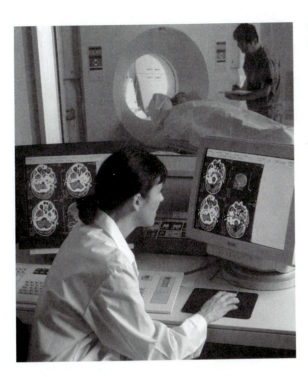

MRIs create an image of the inside of the brain.

be asked to have an MRI to look for possible damage. MRIs are also now being used in a different way. People are being studied to assess levels of activation in the cortex and other brain structures, both at rest and in other mental states. The picture from this sort of study, called **functional MRI** (**fMRI**), is much more detailed than what comes from EEG recordings. Of particular importance is that it lets the brain be viewed in slices at different levels. The result is a very detailed three-dimensional picture about what brain centers are active. As with PET scans, the images are usually created in multiple colors, with each color representing a different level of activity.

Use of fMRI as a tool to understand how the brain works has increased at an incredible rate over the past decade. It's very expensive (it requires a giant, very powerful magnet). But the fact that it can provide a three-dimensional picture means it can show very precise locations of increases and decreases in neural activity as a function of what the person is doing. People can be placed in different motivational and emotional states while in the device, and can engage in diverse mental activities. This enables researchers to determine which parts of the brain are involved in those various experiences. More and more researchers are thinking of possible uses for this tool. This is an area that unquestionably will grow enormously in the years to come.

Problems in Behavior, and Behavior Change

Let's now consider problems in behavior. The biological process approach has made large contributions to the understanding of disorders. A full treatment is well beyond the scope of this chapter. We focus here on contributions that relate to the ideas discussed earlier in the chapter.

Biological Bases of Anxiety, Depression, and Antisocial Personality

Recall that a basic assumption of these models is that two motivational systems in the brain manage the approach of incentives and avoidance of threats, respectively. People presumably vary in the strength or sensitivity of these systems. Being too extreme on one or the other system may set a person up for problems.

Perhaps the easiest problem to link to this view is anxiety disorders. The BIS creates anxiety to cues of impending punishment. A person with a very sensitive BIS will experience anxiety easily and frequently. This creates fertile ground for an anxiety disorder to develop. If these people are exposed to frequent punishments during childhood socialization, they learn anxiety responses to many stimuli. The result may be the development of such clinical symptoms as phobias, anxiety attacks, and obsessive-compulsive disorders.

A related problem is depression. There's less consensus on biological roots of depression than those of anxiety (Davidson, Pizzagalli, Nitschke, & Putnam, 2002). Some see depression as a variant of anxiety, reflecting an oversensitive BIS. Others tie depression instead to a weak BAS (e.g., Allen, Iacono, Depue, & Arbisi, 1993; Henriques & Davidson, 1990, 1991). In this view, a person with weak BAS activation has little motivation to approach incentives. The result is the leaden behavioral qualities that typify depression.

Another problem that's often discussed in terms of biological systems is **antisocial personality.** As noted earlier, it involves impulsivity and an inability to restrain antisocial urges. It's sometimes argued that these people have an overactive BAS (Arnett et al., 1997). Thus, they pursue whatever incentive comes to mind. It's sometimes argued that they have BIS deficits (Fowles, 1980). Thus, they fail to learn from punishment or aren't motivated to avoid it. Some think the failure to learn from punishment stems not from deficient BIS, but from failure to stop and think before plowing ahead in pursuit of some incentive (Bernstein, Newman, Wallace, & Luh, 2000; Patterson & Newman, 1993; Schmitt, Brinkley, & Newman, 1999).

Some views of the antisocial personality involve a third system, the one underlying sensation seeking (Krueger et al., 1994; Rowe, 2001; Zuckerman, 1994). Indeed, insufficient MAO (associated with this system) may be a vulnerability, interacting with the environment (Caspi et al., 2002). In this study, boys with genes causing low MAO engaged in more antisocial behavior—but only if they also received maltreatment while growing up (Figure 7.7). The authors reported that, although men hav-

Figure 7.7

Scores on an index of antisocial behavior, among men with a gene causing low MAO and men with a gene for normal MAO, who had experienced either no maltreatment (abuse) during childhood, probably some maltreatment, or severe maltreatment (adapted from Caspi et al., 2002).

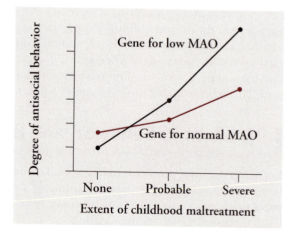

ing the combination of low MAO gene and severe maltreatment were only 12 percent of the male birth cohort studies, they accounted for 44 percent of the cohort's violent convictions. Indeed, a full 85 percent of this group developed some sort of antisocial behavior.

Not all discussions of antisocial behavior involve these neural systems. Recall that high levels of testosterone relate to various kinds of violent and antisocial behavior (Dabbs & Dabbs, 2000; Dabbs et al., 2001). There's even evidence that high testosterone relates to disruptive behavior in boys as young as five to eleven years of age (Chance, Brown, Dabbs, & Casey, 2000). Thus, this set of problems seems to relate to both hormonal and neural processes.

Medication in Therapy

The biological process approach to personality also has a relatively straightforward implication for therapy. Many manifestations of problems in personality reflect biological functions. It follows that changing these biological functions should change the manifestation of the disorder. There are several disorders for which this approach seems effective. Because the treatments typically involves administering drugs, they are often termed **pharmacotherapy.**

It has long been known that manic-depressive, or bipolar, disorder can be relieved by lithium. About 80 percent of people with bipolar disorder respond to lithium (Depue, 1979). Besides treating existing symptoms, repeated doses can ward off new symptoms. Unfortunately, lithium has serious unpleasant side effects. Nevertheless, its effectiveness supports two ideas: that the disorder is biological and that its treatment should be biologically based (at least in part).

A similar case has also been made for treatment of schizophrenia. Research on the biological basis of schizophrenia has looked for ways to treat its symptoms. One hypothesis is that the symptoms reflect too much dopamine (see Walker & Diforio, 1997). As we said earlier, dopamine is a neurotransmitter. With too much dopamine, transmission in certain parts of the nervous system is too easy. With too many messages being sent, communication is disrupted.

This hypothesis is speculative. But it is supported by studies of biochemical treatments for schizophrenic symptoms. Drugs that remove the symptoms of schizophrenia also turn out to lower the levels of usable dopamine in the brain. Apparently the effectiveness of these drugs is related to their ability to block the use of dopamine. Once again, this finding suggests that the disorder is biological and that treatment should also be biologically based (at least in part).

Pharmacological treatments are also used for disorders that are far less extreme than the two just discussed. Antianxiety drugs are among the most often prescribed of all medications. Current antidepressants—selective serotonin reuptake inhibitors (SSRIs)—are used by many people with moderate to mild depression. Indeed, development of this set of antidepressants (such as Prozac) has led to a far wider use of mood-altering medication than ever before.

The widespread use of these drugs raises a number of questions and issues, many discussed in a book called *Listening to Prozac* (Kramer, 1993). One issue concerns the fact that responses to these medications often are much broader than the mere lifting of a depressed mood. People's personalities undergo changes that are subtle but profound and pervasive. People become more confident, more resilient, more decisive—almost more dominant—than they were before. In a sense, they aren't quite the same people as they were before taking the medication. Their very personalities have changed.

Seeing these changes in personality take place as a function of a slight alteration in brain chemistry caused Kramer to question for himself (as a psychiatrist) where personality resides. No longer was it obvious that the personality is a stable entity apart from the symptoms that brought people to him. Personality, in the form of the person's biological processes, now seemed the *source* of the symptoms. No longer was it obvious that the medication was treating an illness. In the view Kramer began to hold, treating an illness had become treating personality. In the view that was emerging, personality may *be* the person's biological functioning and the experiences to which it gives rise.

The descriptions in Kramer's book were anecdotal, from his experiences with people in therapy. Since then, however, researchers have asked whether drugs such as Prozac have an influence on people who don't have a disorder. One study (Knutson et al., 1998) gave people either an SSRI or a placebo for four weeks, and assessed them before and afterward. Those given the medication later reported less hostility and negativity (but not greater positive feelings). They also displayed more positive social behavior while working on a cooperative task. Another study (Tse & Bond, 2001) found an increase on a measure of self-direction, which assesses such qualities as purposefulness and resourcefulness.

The availability of drugs with these broad effects on personality raises more questions. How widely should they be prescribed? Should people whose problems are not severe be given medication if it will make their lives more enjoyable? Should all people have the option of changing their personalities by taking a pill? These questions are associated with considerable controversy that is a long way from being resolved.

Biological Processes and Personality: Problems and Prospects

This chapter has discussed the idea that patterns of biological processes have important things to tell us about personality. We wouldn't blame you if you came away feeling that the presentation was a little fragmented. In truth, the ideas themselves are somewhat fragmented. The pieces are coming together, but they're not there yet. As a result, this way of thinking about personality has something of a disjointed feel.

One reason for this is that theories about how the nervous system and hormones influence behavior rely in part on knowledge from other sciences. Ideas in those sciences are continually evolving, causing changes in these ideas about personality. Further, work on these topics is as new as the methodological advances that permit closer looks at how the biological systems function. These methodological advances continue to march forward (Davidson et al., 2000; Lane & Nadel, 2000; Posner & DiGirolamo, 2000). The result is a kaleidoscope of new looks at biological functioning that sometimes have unexpected implications for personality.

For example, psychologists now have access to PET scans and fMRIs that illuminate brain functioning in ways only dreamed of a few years ago. The findings generated from these techniques have raised as many new questions as have been answered. There is likely to be a good deal of complexity in sorting out the picture that such methods reveal.

It's clear that there's been progress in these areas of research and thought. To a large extent the theorists agree about what they're trying to account for. There's general consensus that approach and avoidance (and positive and negative feelings) are important focal points for biological theory building. Almost everyone seems to feel the need to include something more than that, but there's been less consensus about what else to include. Partly for this reason, this way of thinking doesn't yet stand as a fully developed personality theory. It's more of a vantage point, a place from which to look at and consider the nature of personality.

Lest you be tempted to conclude from the disagreements that these theorists aren't doing their homework carefully enough, let us point out that it's not easy to tell what's going on in the nervous system. To really know what connects to what in the brain means tracing neural pathways, which can't be done in human subjects. The animals used as subjects in these studies can't report directly on the psychological effects of what the researcher is doing. Thus, information often is indirect, and progress can be slow. The functions of the nervous system are being sorted out by research of several types, but there's a long way to go. Until the nature of the organization of the nervous system becomes clearer, personality psychologists of this orientation won't have definitive models.

Although criticisms can be made of various aspects of this way of thinking about personality, this line of work is one of the most active areas of personality psychology. Many people believe that the mysteries of the mind will be revealed by a better understanding of the brain. They are committed to unraveling those mysteries and their implications for personality. At present, the prospects of this viewpoint seem quite bright indeed.

SUMMARY

The idea that personality is tied to the biological functions of the body leads to a variety of possibilities involving the functions of the nervous system and the endocrine (hormone) system. An initial approach of this sort was Eysenck's theory that brain processes underlie extroversions. He argued that introverts are more cortically aroused than extroverts. Thus, introverts avoid overstimulation, whereas extroverts seek out stimulation.

Others have taken issue with this, arguing that personality rests on an approach system (BAS) that responds to incentives and an inhibition system (BIS) that responds to threats. Work on emotions suggests that the approach system, which produces positive feelings, involves the left prefrontal cortex, and that the withdrawal system, which produces feelings such as fear, involves the right prefrontal cortex. The BIS seems to represent the biological basis for the trait of neuroticism. Some suggest that the BAS represents the biological basis for extroversions. Differences of opinion about extroversions relate to the involvement of sociability (which isn't intrinsically part of BAS theories) and the placement of impulsivity.

Questions about impulsiveness introduce another biological variable: sensation seeking, the tendency to seek out novel, complex, and exciting stimuli. Sensation seeking relates to Eysenck's dimension of psychoticism and Tellegen's dimension of constraint. Research suggests that sensation seeking relates to biological systems that regulate exposure to stimulation (as a defense process), with people scoring low in sensation seeking being those who show defense responses.

Another aspect of the biological view on personality focuses on the role in behavior played by male hormones. Exposure to such substances before birth can cause people years later to choose more aggressive responses to conflict; it can also increase girls' preference for boys' toys. Testosterone in adults relates to dominance behavior, sometimes expressed in antisocial ways. Testosterone also fluctuates, increasing with challenges and victories, decreasing with failures.

An emerging area of work examines the possibility that another hormone, called oxytocin, is important in human social behavior. Oxytocin appears to relate to female responses to stress, termed a "tend and befriend" response. The roots of this response may be in the attachment system, and it may relate to social bonding more generally.

This approach to personality suggests it may be possible to assess personality through biological functions. Although the attempt to do this is in its infancy, some believe recordings of brain activity—particularly fMRIs—hold great promise for the future.

With regard to problems in behavior, high levels of BIS activity promote disorders involving anxiety. Either high BIS or low BAS may contribute to depression. High BAS function, or low BIS, can yield symptoms of antisocial personality, which also relates to sensation seeking and testosterone. This orientation to personality also suggests that therapy based on medication is a means to bring about behavioral change. The idea is that medication can influence the underlying biological system, thereby altering the person's behavior and subjective experience.

GLOSSARY

Anabolic steroids Chemicals that mimic the body's tendency to rebuild muscle tissues.

Antisocial personality A person who displays impulsive action with little thought to consequences.

Ascending reticular activating system (ARAS) The part of the brain that activates the cerebral cortex into alertness.

Behavioral approach system (BAS) The part of the brain that regulates pursuit of incentives.

Behavioral inhibition system (BIS) The part of the brain that regulates anticipation of punishment.

Dopamine A neurotransmitter believed to be especially important to approach regulation.

Electroencephalogram (EEG) A record of overall electrical activity in higher regions of the brain.

Functional magnetic resonance imaging (fMRI) Use of MRI to create a picture of activity inside the brain in different mental states.

Impulsive unsocialized sensation seeking (IUSS) Trait involving the capacity to inhibit behavior in the service of social adaptation.

Incentives Things that people desire.

Magnetic resonance imaging (MRI) A picture of activity inside the brain based on the brain's electromagnetic energy.

Negative emotionality The predisposition to experience negative feelings frequently.

Neurotransmitter A chemical involved in sending messages along nerve pathways.

Orienting response The shift of attention to a stimulus that suddenly appears.

Pharmacotherapy A therapy based on use of medication.

Positive emotionality The predisposition to experience positive feelings frequently.

Positron emission tomography (PET) A picture of activity in the brain based on the brain's metabolism.

Sensation seeking The tendency to seek out varied, unusual, and exciting stimuli.

Serotonin A neurotransmitter that some believe is involved in behavioral inhibition.

The Psychoanalytic Perspective

THE PSYCHOANALYTIC PERSPECTIVE:
Major Themes and Underlying Assumptions

The psychoanalytic perspective originated in the writings of Sigmund Freud. His impact on thought in personality psychology was so strong that his ideas form the essence of a distinct perspective on personality, although others have contributed to it. The psychoanalytic view on personality is the subject of Chapters 8 and 9.

One theme of this perspective, which gave rise to the term *psychodynamic*, is the idea that personality is a dynamic set of processes, always in motion. They sometimes work in harmony with one another and sometimes against one another, but rarely or never are they still. Personality is a dynamo—or a bubbling spring—from which emerge forces that can be set free, channeled, modified, or transformed. As long as you're alive, these forces never come to rest.

An important implication of this dynamic quality in personality is that the forces sometimes work against each other. The processes of personality sometimes compete or wrestle for control over the person's behavior. The assumption that pressures within the personality can *conflict* with each other is another theme that's very prominent in the psychoanalytic perspective.

An additional assumption goes hand in hand with this one. Specifically, psychoanalytic thinking emphasizes the role of the unconscious in determining behavior. The conflicts that take place among the elements of personality are often outside awareness. Many of the motivations that people have are also unconscious. The emphasis on unconscious influence wasn't unique to Freud, but it is a theme that permeates this perspective on personality.

Another theme in the psychoanalytic perspective is the idea that human experience is suffused with qualities of lust and aggression, sexuality and death. These assumptions tie psychoanalytic thinking to Darwin's theory of evolution (for more detail see Ritvo, 1990). They serve as a reminder that humans are, first of all, animals whose purpose in life is reproduction. Although this idea doesn't seem so odd today, the extent to which Freud emphasized the role of sexuality in human life was very unusual at the time.

Indeed, Freud's emphasis on sexuality even extended to his ideas about the development of personality. A fifth theme of the psychoanalytic perspective is that personality is greatly influenced by early experiences. Freud argued more specifically that human sexuality must be taken into account at all stages of development, even infancy. Many people found the idea of infantile sexuality either absurd or shocking. Nevertheless, the idea that the fundamentals of personality emerge from the crucible of early experience is deeply embedded in psychoanalytic thought.

Another theme that characterizes psychoanalysis is the idea that defense is an important aspect of human functioning. This idea rests on the assumption that there are things about every person that are threatening to him or her. Maybe you have what you regard as shameful desires or impulses; maybe you secretly feel you're unworthy or inadequate as a human being; or maybe you're afraid the social world will reject you. Whatever it is that most threatens you, psychological processes operate to keep these impulses or elements of self-knowledge from overpowering you. The notion of defense is an important aspect of psychoanalytic thought.

The psychoanalytic perspective on personality is extremely metaphorical in nature. Oddly enough, given this emphasis on metaphor and analogy, it's difficult to point to a single metaphor for human

nature that dominates this perspective. Rather, it uses multiple metaphors. Freud was a physician, and the idea of biological processes underlying mental processes often appeared in his writing. Similarly, his concepts of life instincts and death instincts resemble the dual processes of metabolic functioning, continually tearing down and building up.

Freud didn't limit himself to the biological metaphor, however, but used many others as well. Sometimes he likened the human psyche to a sociopolitical system, making reference to censors, economics, compromises, and repression. Sometimes his analogies were from physics, with personality described as an energy system, and the competition among forces compared to hydraulic systems in which energy focused at one point had an inevitable consequence at another point. At other times, he treated psychological phenomena almost as though they were the products of artistic or literary efforts.

Despite the lack of a single orienting point, or perhaps because of it, the psychoanalytic viewpoint on personality may be characterized fairly as one in which the *quality* of analogy or metaphor figures prominently. Human behavior is to be understood not as the product of any one process but as a reflection of multiple processes whose functioning can be captured only imperfectly by any one metaphor.

A final theme of the psychoanalytic perspective is the idea that mental health depends on a balance of forces in one's life. It's good to express your deep desires, but it's not good to let them control your life. It's good to act morally, but a constant effort to be perfect cripples your personality. It's good to have self-control, but not to be overcontrolled. Moderation and balance among these forces provide the healthiest experience of life.

8 Psychoanalytic Structure and Process

■ **The Topographical Model of Mind**

■ **Aspects of Personality:**
  The Structural Model
Id
Ego
Superego
Balancing the Forces

■ **Motivation: The Drives of Personality**
Cathexes and the Use of Energy
Two Classes of Drives: Life and Death Instincts
Coming Together of Libidinal and Aggressive Energies
Catharsis
Displacement and Sublimation of Motive Forces

■ **Psychosexual Development**
The Oral Stage
The Anal Stage
The Phallic Stage
The Latency Period
The Genital Stage

■ **Psychoanalytic Structure and Process:**
  Problems and Prospects

SUMMARY

■ John and his girlfriend Ann go to different colleges, a thousand miles apart. It's been hard for them to be separated for long periods of time, and John has finally decided he can't go on this way. He's decided to call Ann and break up. He picks up the phone, dials a number, and hears a voice on the other end of the line say hello—at the dorm where Ann lived last year, before she moved off campus. "Now why'd I dial *that* number?" John wonders to himself.

Why did you do that? Most people, most of the time, find it easy to answer this question with no doubt that their answer is correct. Most of us assume a direct link between our intentions and our actions. Accidents may interfere with those intentions, but accidents are just random events.

There's a viewpoint on the nature of personality that sharply challenges these assumptions. It sees behavior as determined partly by inner forces that lie outside your awareness and control. As for accidents, this view holds that accidents rarely happen. What seems accidental, you've usually done on purpose—you just aren't *aware* of the purpose.

The approach to personality that takes this view is psychoanalytic theory, or psychoanalysis. Psychoanalytic theory is closely identified with a single theorist (although it rests more on historical precedents than is widely realized; Ellenberger, 1970; Erdelyi, 1985). The theorist was an Austrian physician named Sigmund Freud. The theory, which evolved over the period from 1895 to 1940, stunned the scientific world when it was proposed (Box 8.1). Since then, it's been one of the most influential views ever developed. Its effects have been felt not just in psychology but in anthropology, political science, sociology, and even art and literature. Indeed, it's hard to think of a single aspect of modern-day thought in Western civilization that hasn't been touched in some way by psychoanalytic ideas.

One testament to the impact of psychoanalytic ideas is the extent to which they've crept into everyday language and experiences. For example, people often use the phrase "Freudian slip" to refer to errors in speech that seem to suggest hidden (unconscious) feelings or desires. Such slips imply that behavior is caused by forces outside our awareness, an idea that traces directly to psychoanalysis.

Before describing the elements of the theory, we note two features that make it different from any other in personality psychology. First, Freud was fascinated by symbols, metaphors, and analogies. This fascination is reflected both in the form of the theory and in its content. In its form, the theory uses many analogies. Freud constantly sought new metaphors. He used different ones at different times, and the metaphor in use often had an impact on the form the theory took. As a result, it can be hard to be sure which ideas are basic and which are only metaphors (Erdelyi, 1985).

Freud's fascination with symbol and metaphor is also reflected in the theory's content. Specifically, Freud came to believe that human behavior itself is highly symbolic. People's acts are rarely quite what they seem to be. Instead, qualities of each act symbolize other, more hidden qualities. This is an idea that permeates psychoanalytic theory.

A second feature is that it's hard to separate Freud's theory from the therapy procedures on which he based it or from the assessment that occurs continually within that therapy. Indeed, the very word *psychoanalysis* is applied to Freudian therapy,

BOX 8.1

PSYCHOANALYSIS IN HISTORICAL CONTEXT

The concepts of psychoanalytic theory were developed earlier than any other theory in this book (starting before the turn of the twentieth century). The cultural and scientific context in which the theory was created differed greatly from that of today, and the context had a big impact on the theory's form. To get a better idea of why Freud's ideas took the form they did (and why they had the impact they had), consider the world in which he lived.

Freud did his early writing during the latter part of the Victorian era (late 1800s), a time in which middle- and upper-class society had come to view humans as having reached a lofty state of rational self-control, civilization, and even near perfection. It was a smug and self-satisfied society. By today's standards it would be seen as stuffy and hypocritical. For example, human sexuality was rarely even acknowledged publicly, never mind openly discussed.

Into this calm society, Freud dropped a cultural bomb. Instead of seeing people as rational, he argued that people are driven by forces of which they are unaware. Instead of godlike, people are primitive animals. Instead of intellectual beings, people—even in infancy—are driven by sexual and aggressive urges.

Freud observed that humanity's admiration of itself had suffered three traumatic shocks: the first was the discovery by Copernicus that the earth is not the center of the universe. The second was the assertion by Darwin that humans evolved as animals, just as other animals. The third was Freud's own assertion that people are at the mercy of forces that are unconscious and uncontrollable. For good measure, the horror of World War I showed conclusively that the veneer of civilization was far thinner than most assumed at that time.

Freud's ideas jolted the scientific world when they were proposed, partly because they conflicted so sharply with widely held assumptions. Another reason was Freud's emphasis on sexuality, particularly infantile sexuality. This caused many to view him as a pervert, obscene and wicked. The fact that he was

a Jew in an anti-Semitic society raised additional suspicion. Further, he presented his theories without much evidence, which didn't sit well in the scientific community. All these factors raised controversy. Ironically, the controversy only brought his ideas more attention.

Although Freud's ideas sharply contradicted the assumptions of Victorian society, they didn't arise in an intellectual vacuum. Darwin's earlier assertion that humans were just one sort of animal carried several other assumptions. Darwin saw all creatures as driven by instincts to survive and reproduce. Freud's sexual and life instincts are similar to these. Although society at large viewed humanity as rational, philosophers such as Schopenhauer and Nietzsche argued that human behavior is often impelled by unconscious and irrational forces. This idea is also echoed in Freud's work.

Freud was also influenced by the ideas of scientists in other areas, and he often assimilated these ideas into his own theories (Ellenberger, 1970). For example, Freud's view of the human being as an energy system drew directly from then-current ideas in physics and chemistry. Nineteenth-century physicists had also developed the principle of conservation, the idea that matter and energy can be transformed but not destroyed. This led many scientists to ponder how systems could be viewed in terms of transformations of energy. Among them was Freud. This conservation principle is reflected in his belief that impulses must eventually be expressed, in one form or another.

If Freud had lived in a different time, his metaphors may well have been different. But psychoanalysis lives on in the terms Freud used. As you read this chapter, keep in mind the cultural and scientific context in which the theory was constructed. We've tried to present the theory as it applies to you, in today's world. If aspects of the concepts seem out of date metaphorically, try to keep in mind the world in which they were conceived.

Freud's method of research, and his theory of personality. The entanglement of theory with therapy is far greater here than in any other approach to personality, and this tends to color all aspects of the theory.

When viewed in its entirety, psychoanalytic theory is very complex. Underlying this complexity, however, is a fairly small number of principles. The theory can be confusing, because its concepts are deeply interwoven. For this reason it's hard to talk about any aspect of the theory separate from other aspects. Perhaps the best place to start, though, is Freud's view of how the mind is organized. This is often termed Freud's **topographical model** of mind.

The Topographical Model of Mind

A common description of the mind says it has two regions. One region holds conscious experience: the thoughts, feelings, and behaviors you're aware of at the moment. The other contains memories, now outside awareness but able to come to awareness easily. Drawing on the work of other theorists of his time (Ellenberger, 1970), Freud added a third region to this list. Taken together, the three regions form what Freud thought of as the mind's topography, or its surface configuration.

Freud used the term **conscious** in much the way we use it today, to mean the part of the mind that holds what you're now aware of. People can verbalize their conscious experience and think about it in a logical way. The part of the mind that represents ordinary memory is termed **preconscious.** Elements in the preconscious, although now outside awareness, can be brought to awareness easily. For example, if you think of your phone number or the name of the last movie you saw, you're bringing that information from the preconscious to consciousness.

Freud used the term **unconscious** in a way that's considerably different from the way it's used in everyday language. He reserved this word to stand for a portion of the mind that's not directly accessible to awareness (see also Box 8.2). Freud viewed the unconscious as being (in part) a repository for urges, feelings, and ideas that are tied to anxiety, conflict, or pain (e.g., Rhawn, 1980). Being unconscious doesn't mean they're gone, though. *They exert a continuing influence* on later actions and conscious experience.

Freud compared the mind to an iceberg (an idea he borrowed from Theodor Lipps, see Ellenberger, 1970). The tip of the iceberg corresponds to consciousness. The much larger part, the part below water, is outside awareness. Part of that submerged portion (the part you can see through the water) is the preconscious. The vast majority of it, however—the part you can't see—is the unconscious. Although the conscious and preconscious influence behavior, Freud saw them as less important than the unconscious. The unconscious is where Freud thought the truly important operations of personality take place.

The three levels of consciousness constitute the topographical model of the mind (Figure 8.1). Material passes easily from conscious to preconscious and back again. Material from both of these can slip into the unconscious. Truly unconscious material, however, can't be brought voluntarily to awareness, because of psychological forces that keep it hidden. These regions of the mind constitute the theater in which the dynamics of personality are played out.

BOX 8.2

TODAY'S VIEWS ON THE UNCONSCIOUS

Psychologists have long had an interest in the nature of consciousness. It was apparent almost immediately that events outside awareness influence what happens in awareness. Hardly anyone has gone on to assume an unconscious as contentious and conflicted as Freud assumed. But many have found it necessary to make assumptions about what's going on in the unconscious.

In recent years, interest in how the mind works has grown dramatically, along with the field of cognitive psychology (more about cognitive processes comes up in Chapter 16). Theorists now use the concept of the unconscious with different connotations than Freud did (Bargh, 1997; Brody, 1987; Epstein, 1994; Kihlstrom, 1987; Loftus, 1992). The unconscious is still seen as part of the mind to which we don't have ready access, but for different reasons than Freud assumed. Reflecting this difference, today's theorists sometimes talk of the *cognitive unconscious,* as opposed to the psychodynamic unconscious.

From today's point of view, consciousness is viewed as a sort of workspace where you consider information and make judgments, come to decisions, and form intentions. If these processes become sufficiently routine, they begin to occur automatically, outside awareness. What makes things routine? Some processes are innately routine. You don't have to think about making digestive juices flow or having your heart beat, and you'd have trouble bringing into consciousness the processes by which those events take place.

Other processes become routine from practice. As you practice anything (a tennis stroke, a new recipe, typing, forming a first impression), what happens changes over repetitions. The first few times, you devote lots of attention to it. As you do it over and over, it starts to feel more fluid and go more smoothly. The more you practice, the less attention it requires. When you've practiced it enough, you disregard it almost totally. When an activity is *very* automatic, the processes that underlie it have become unconscious. You no longer have access to them as you did when you were just starting out. One well-

known study, for example, showed that people couldn't accurately report the basis of a decision they'd just made; instead they fell back on stereotypes (Nisbett & Wilson, 1977). The automation seems to occur even for higher mental processes (Bargh & Ferguson, 2000). Even goals can become activated and pursued without the person being aware of it (Bargh, Gollwitzer, Lee-Chai, Barndollar, & Trötschel, 2001).

Other evidence of an unconscious part of mind comes from studies of hypnosis (Hilgard & Hilgard, 1983; Kihlstrom, 1987). Hypnotic suggestion can cause people not to experience subjective discomfort from a normally painful stimulus. At the same time there's evidence that the stimulus has registered on the person's perceptual system, and that part of the person's mind is aware of the pain. Although the hypnotist can reach that part of the mind to verify the pain, the hypnotized persons themselves apparently can not.

Seymour Epstein (1994) argues that all these phenomena and more are reflections of what he calls an *experiential* mode of processing. This mode of processing occurs in parallel to, but distinct from, rational processing. The experiential system is emotional and nonverbal, rather than deliberative and verbal. Its functioning is fast and largely out of awareness. Epstein argues that an unconscious as chaotic as the one Freud assumed would have been unlikely to evolve. Being so poorly fit to reality, it couldn't possibly have survived. On the other hand, an unconscious such as Epstein argues for has much more adaptive value.

In sum, researchers have found that many aspects of people's experience are influenced by processes that occur outside awareness. Such influences occur when you form perceptions and impressions of other people, and when you make judgments about how likely something is to happen. Such influences can also affect your mood states and your actions. Whether you agree with Freud about what defines the *contents* of the unconscious, it's clear that he was right about its existence.

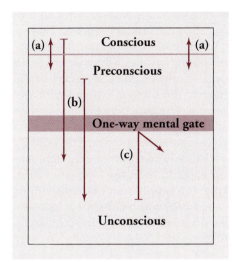

Figure 8.1

Graphic representation of Freud's topographical model of the mind. (a) Material can pass easily back and forth between the conscious and preconscious portions of the mind. (b) Material can also move from the conscious and preconscious into the unconscious. But once material is in the unconscious, the person is prevented from having conscious access to it because (c) a mental gate prevents retrieval.

Aspects of Personality: The Structural Model

Freud (1962/1923) also developed a **structural model** of personality, which complements the topographical model. He came to see personality as having three aspects, which work with each other to create the complexity of human behavior. They aren't physical entities in the body, but rather labels for three aspects of functioning. They are known as id, ego, and superego.

Id

The **id** is the original component of personality, the only one present at birth. Id (the Latin word meaning 'it') encompasses all the inherited, instinctive, primitive aspects of personality. The id functions entirely in the unconscious. It's closely tied to basic biological processes, from which it draws energy. Indeed, Freud believed that *all* psychic energy comes through the id. Thus the id is the "engine" of personality.

The id follows what's called the **pleasure principle.** The pleasure principle is that needs should be satisfied immediately (Freud, 1949/1940). Unsatisfied needs constitute an aversive tension state. Thus, there is a reason to gratify needs whenever they arise. Under the pleasure principle, any increase in hunger should cause an attempt to eat. Any twinge of sexual desire should cause the person to try to obtain sexual gratification.

At first glance, this looks great. Who wants to walk around with unmet needs? There's a problem, though. The pleasure principle doesn't concern *how* needs are to be met. It doesn't imply that needs should be met in a way that takes into account risks or potential problems. It just implies that needs are to be met at once.

Acting totally by the pleasure principle would soon get you into a lot of trouble. There's a complex and often threatening world out there. A hungry person can't just rush across a street filled with zooming cars to get to food. Social reality also presents problems. For example, if you grab your roommate's pizza before he can get to it (or if you get too friendly with his girlfriend), you may find yourself with an angry roommate on your hands.

Nonetheless, the pleasure principle means that when any tension arises, id tries to discharge it. Id's mechanism for doing this is called the **primary process.** This entails forming a mental image (fantasy, dream, hallucination, or delusion) of an object or event that would satisfy the need, and becoming involved with that image. In the case of a hungry infant, the primary process might produce an image of the mother's breast or a bottle. When you're separated from someone you love, the primary process produces fantasy images of that person. The experience of having such an image is called **wish fulfillment.**

Tension reduction by primary process has a drawback, however. The primary process can't distinguish between an image and reality. Primary-process thought may reduce tension in the short run, but it can't by itself do so in the long run (Zern, 1973). The hungry infant that imagines sucking at a nipple won't be satisfied for long. The person who misses a loved one won't be content with fantasies of being together, no matter how vivid. This illustrates once again how the id doesn't take reality into account. It's in a world of its own wishes.

Ego

Because the id and its primary process can't deal with reality, a second set of functions develops, termed **ego** (the Latin word for 'I'). The ego evolves from the id and harnesses part of id's energy for its own use. Ego focuses on making sure id impulses are expressed *effectively*, by taking into account the external world. Because of this engagement with the outside world, most ego functioning occurs in the conscious and preconscious. Given the ego's ties to the id, however, it also functions in the unconscious.

The ego is said to follow the **reality principle** (G. S. Klein, 1972). This is the taking into account of external reality in addition to internal needs and urges. The reality principle brings a sense of rationality to behavior (Zern, 1973). Because it orients you toward the world, it leads you to weigh the risks associated with an action before acting. If the risks seem too high, you'll consider another way to meet the need. If there's no safe way to reduce tension immediately, you'll delay it to a later, safer, or more sensible time.

Thus, a goal of the ego is to *delay the discharge* of id's tension until an appropriate object or activity can be found (Box 8.3). The ego tries through what's called the **secondary process** to match the primary-process image of a tension-reducing object to a real object. Until such an object can be found, ego keeps the tension in check. Ego's goal is *not* to block the id's desires permanently. The ego wants the id's urges to be satisfied. But the ego wants them satisfied at a time and in a way that's safe, that won't cause trouble because of some danger in the world (Bergmann, 1980).

The ego, functioning under the reality principle and using secondary-process thought, is the source of intellectual processes and problem solving. The capacity for realistic thought allows the ego to form plans of action to satisfy needs and test them mentally to see whether they'll work. This is called **reality testing.** The ego is often described as having an "executive" role in personality, mediating between the desires of the id and constraints of the external world.

It's easy to see how the pleasure and reality principles, and thus id and ego, conflict (Figure 8.2). The pleasure principle dictates that needs be met *now;* the reality principle leads to delay. The pleasure principle orients to the press of internal tensions; the reality principle orients to external constraints. The ego's function, in the short run, is to prevent the id from operating—to hold it up, so its needs can be met

BOX 8.3

EGO CONTROL AND DELAY OF GRATIFICATION

A major function of the ego is to delay gratification of impulses and urges until a later time (Block & Block, 1980). Delay of gratification is a mark of a mature personality; it's a major goal of socialization. Children must learn to wait for rewards (e.g., to work now but be paid later), if they're to become contributing members of society. The *inability* to delay gratification predicts greater involvement with cigarettes, alcohol, and marijuana among high school students (Wulfert, Block, Santa Ana, Rodriguez, & Colsman, 2002) and may play an important role in development of criminal behavior. For all these reasons, delay of gratification has been studied from a variety of angles (in fact, it comes up several more times in this textbook). Much of the research was prompted by ideas other than psychoanalytic theory, but the findings are relevant to psychodynamic processes.

In most laboratory studies of this phenomenon, children are given the following choice. They can have a smaller, less desired reward now, or they can wait for a while and then get a larger, more desired reward. One focus of research using this paradigm is on the determinants of delay of gratification (for reviews, see Mischel, 1966, 1974). It's harder for children to delay when the desired objects are right in front of them (Mischel & Ebbesen, 1970). Delay is easier if the children can mentally transform the situation to make it seem the objects aren't really there. For example, they might imagine the objects are only "color pictures in

their heads" (Mischel & Baker, 1975; Moore, Mischel, & Zeiss, 1976). More generally, delay of gratification seems to be easiest when children distract themselves, shifting attention away from the desired rewards (Mischel, Ebbesen, & Zeiss, 1973). In effect, the ego tricks the id by getting it involved in something else.

A second line of research on delay of gratification concerns personality correlates of the ability to delay. Ability to delay relates to certain aspects of intelligence (Mischel & Metzner, 1962). Maybe this is because brighter children can more easily transform the situation mentally. Children who are better able to delay also seem more concerned with achievement and social responsibility (Mischel, 1961), fitting the idea that they have well-defined egos.

More recent longitudinal research by Funder, Block, and Block (1983) suggests that the basis for delay differs slightly from boys to girls. Among boys, delay seems to be closely related to the ability to control emotional and motivational impulses, to concentrate deeply, and to be deliberate in action. This fits the idea that delay of gratification is an ego function, aimed at control over id impulse expression. Delay among girls, in contrast, seems most strongly related to intelligence, resourcefulness, and competence. According to Funder et al. (1983), these gender differences stem from differences in the manner in which boys and girls are socialized (see also Block, von der Lippe, & Block, 1973; Block, 1973, 1979).

in a realistic way. Given all this, there is a vast potential for conflict within the personality. This theme runs deep in psychoanalytic theory.

Freud (1933) used the metaphor of a horse and rider to refer to this pulling of forces within personality. The id is the horse, providing power for movement; the ego is the rider, trying to direct the movement. Often the rider is successful in directing the horse's energy in appropriate ways. Sometimes, though, the rider can only guide the horse in small ways, as the horse goes in the direction it wants to go.

The ego can appear to be a positive force, because it exercises restraint over the id. That's somewhat misleading, however. The ego has no moral sense. It's entirely pragmatic, concerned with getting by, given the constraints of reality. The ego wouldn't be bothered by cheating or stealing, or giving free rein to the pleasure principle, as long as there's no danger involved. The moral sense resides in the third and final part of personality.

Figure 8.2

Graphic representation of the basis of conflict between the id (which follows the pleasure principle) and the ego (which follows the reality principle).

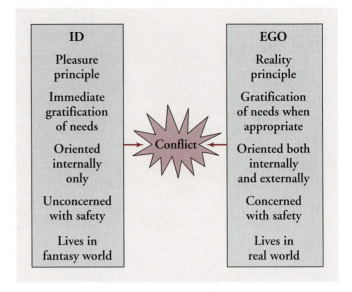

ID		EGO
Pleasure principle		Reality principle
Immediate gratification of needs	Conflict	Gratification of needs when appropriate
Oriented internally only		Oriented both internally and externally
Unconcerned with safety		Concerned with safety
Lives in fantasy world		Lives in real world

Superego

The final aspect of personality—the last to develop—is the **superego** (a joining of two Latin words meaning 'over-I'). Freud held that the superego develops while the person resolves a particular conflict during development (a process discussed later in the chapter).

The superego is the embodiment of parental and societal values. It holds an image of what's right and wrong and strives for perfection rather than pleasure. The values in your superego stem from the values of your parents. To obtain its parents' love, the child comes to do what the parents think is right. To avoid pain, punishment, and rejection, the child avoids what its parents think is wrong. The process of "taking in," or incorporating, the values of parents (and wider society) is called **introjection.** Although other authority figures can influence the superego, Freud saw it as deriving largely from parents.

The superego is further divided into two subsystems. The **ego ideal** consists of rules for good behavior, standards of excellence toward which the person must strive. What the parents approve of, or value, is in the ego ideal. Conforming to those values makes you feel proud. The **conscience** consists of rules about what behaviors are bad. Prohibitions against actions that parents disapprove of, and punish, are in the conscience (Sederer & Seidenberg, 1976). Bad actions or thoughts causes the conscience to punish you with guilt feelings.

The superego has three interrelated goals. First, it tries to inhibit completely (rather than just postpone) any id impulse that would be frowned on by your parents. Second, it tries to force the ego to act morally, rather than rationally. Third, it tries to guide the person toward perfection in thought, word, and deed. The superego surely exerts a "civilizing" influence on the person, but its perfectionism is quite removed from reality.

Like the ego, the superego operates at all three levels of consciousness. This has important implications for how you experience the superego's effects. When superego processes are conscious, you're aware of your feelings and where they're coming from. For example, if you're aware you've just insulted someone, despite your

DENNIS THE MENACE

"MOM TELLS ME THE STUFF I SHOULDN'T DO AND
MY DAD TELLS ME THE STUFF I *SHOULD* DO!"

The superego has two parts. The conscience holds an image of undesirable behavior, and the ego-ideal holds an image of desirable behavior.

DENNIS THE MENACE® used by permission of Hank Ketcham and © by North America Syndicate.

belief that insulting people is inexcusable, the source of your guilt is obvious. However, when the superego operates unconsciously to punish an urge of the id (also unconscious), the experience is different. You feel guilty but you don't know why. Because guilt can be set off by primary-process thought (an id fantasy that doesn't really occur), the guilt itself may even be completely irrational.

Balancing the Forces

Once the superego develops, the ego has a hard road (see Stolar & Fromm, 1974). It must deal simultaneously with the desires of the id, the moral dictates of the superego, and the constraints of reality (Figure 8.3). To satisfy all these demands, the ego would have to find a way to release all tension immediately in a way that's both socially acceptable and realistic. This, of course, is highly unlikely. It's much more likely that repeated conflicts will occur among these forces. In the psychoanalytic view, such conflicts are an intrinsic part of life.

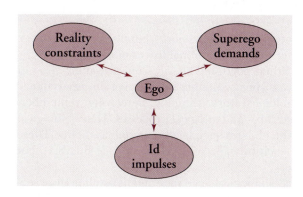

Figure 8.3

Graphic representation of how the ego must mediate among the often conflicting demands of the id, the superego, and the constraints of outside reality.

Ego strength refers to a person's ability to deal effectively with competing demands and taxing situations.

The term **ego strength** refers to the ego's ability to function effectively despite these conflicting forces (Barron, 1953). With little ego strength, the person is torn among competing pressures. With more ego strength, the person can manage the pressures without problems. It's possible, however, for the ego to be too strong. A person whose ego is too strong is very rational and efficient but may also be very boring, or cold and distant.

In fact, there's a more general point here. Freud didn't hold that any aspect of personality is "better" than the others. Rather, there should be a balance among them. A person whose superego is too strong may feel guilty all the time or may act in an insufferably "saintly" way. A person whose id is too strong may be busy with self-gratification and completely uninterested in other people. The healthiest personality is one in which the influences of the three aspects are well-balanced.

Motivation: The Drives of Personality

At several points we've talked in general terms about energy, impulses, tension states, drives, and urges. Let's now consider these motivational forces more explicitly.

In thinking about motivation, Freud borrowed heavily from prevailing views in the biological and physical sciences. He saw people as complex energy systems, in which the energy used in psychological work (thinking, perceiving, remembering, planning, dreaming) is released through biological processes. These biological processes, which operate through the id, have been labeled *instinct* and *drive*. These two terms are differentiated from each other in other contexts (see Box 8.4), but they are used interchangeably here.

A drive has two related elements: a biological need state and its psychological representation (or wish). For example, the need state underlying the experience of thirst

BOX 8.4

HAVE FREUD'S IDEAS BEEN DISTORTED BY TRANSLATION AND CULTURAL DISTANCE?

Freud wrote in German and lived in a culture different from ours. His ideas were later translated into English. Translation of any complex or subtle idea from one language into another is hard, and there is great potential for error. Even less than perfect word choices can greatly distort meaning. It's hard for any translator to know precisely what the original writer intended to convey, and it's likely that no translation is entirely faithful to the original.

How faithful are the translations of Freud's writings? Not very, according to Bruno Bettelheim (1982), an important analyst in his own right. Bettelheim had the background to judge. He came from a Jewish family of Vienna, spoke German from childhood, and lived in exactly the same cultural context as Freud. Fluent in English and German, he was distressed by many aspects of the English translations of Freud. Here are some examples.

Whenever possible, Freud tried to communicate his ideas in words that his readers had used since childhood, adding new insights to those common words. Two names he chose for aspects of personality are among the first words learned by every German-speaking child. In the original, the words are personal pronouns. In the pronoun *I* (*Ich*), Freud chose a word that virtually forces you to think of yourself, eliciting the emotional qualities associated with your assertive affirmation of your own existence. The translated *ego*, in contrast, is lifeless and sterile. Why use such an empty word?

In the pronoun *it* (*Es*), Freud made an allusion that's completely lost to people who speak only English. In German, the word meaning 'child' is neuter. For this reason, during early childhood virtually every German child is referred to as an "it." This word, as applied to a part of the self, has clear emotional overtones: it's what you were called when you were so young you hadn't learned to stifle your impulses or to feel guilty about them. A sense of personalized infancy is conveyed in the original, whereas the translated *id* has no intrinsic associations at all.

Another common word used by Freud was *Trieb*, which is commonly translated as *instinct*. Bettelheim says *drive* is better, because Freud used a different word when he wanted to refer to inborn instincts of animals.

Thus, Freud distinguished between the concepts. By *Trieb*, he meant to convey an inner propulsion, a basic urge, an impulse, but not the sense that the drive was the same as an animal instinct, inborn and unalterable.

Among the few non-German terms Freud used in his theory are *Eros* and *Psyche*. These are the names of two characters in a Greek myth. They were characters Freud knew intimately, as did most of the people to whom he was writing (educated people at that time read the classics). When Freud wrote of "erotic" qualities, he meant to evoke these characters and their qualities: Eros's charm and cunning, and the deep love he had for Psyche. Psyche had at first been tricked into believing that Eros was disgusting, and the message of the myth is that this is an error. For sexual love to be true erotic pleasure, it must be imbued with beauty (symbolized by Eros himself) and also express the longings of the soul (symbolized by Psyche). These are some of the connotations Freud wanted to convey with the word *erotic*. When those connotations are stripped away (because readers don't know the myth), the word not only loses its true meaning, but even takes on connotations opposite to Freud's intention.

Indeed, Bettelheim argued that the word *psyche* itself has also been misrepresented. We're accustomed to think of the psyche as the mind, because that's how it's been translated. The German word for psyche, however, is *Seele*, which means soul. Thus, said Bettelheim, Freud's focus was on the metaphysical, but this has been misread as a focus on the mental.

In sum, Bettelheim argued that much of the sense of Freud's ideas has been misportrayed. Freud chose his language to evoke responses not just at an intellectual level but at an emotional level. This is lost in translation. Because we don't live in the cultural context in which Freud wrote, we also miss many of his nods to ideas that were common at the time.

Bettelheim also argued, however, that Freud was aware of the distortions and chose to let them go. Why? Freud, never an admirer of the United States, was annoyed at the U.S. medical establishment, which seemed intent on making psychoanalysis part of medicine, which Freud opposed. Apparently he simply didn't care enough to correct them.

is a lack of sufficient water in the body's cells. This results in the psychological state of thirst, the desire for water. These elements combine to form a drive to drink water. (This portrayal isn't much different from the picture of motives presented in Chapter 5.)

These processes operate continuously. Drive states build up until an action causes their tension to be released. If a drive isn't expressed, its pressure continues to build. This view of motives is called a "hydraulic" model. In this view, trying to prevent a drive from being expressed only creates greater pressure toward its expression. This idea has important implications a little further along.

Cathexes and the Use of Energy

Freud believed that psychic energy is generated continuously, but gradually. Only so much is available at any given time. The idea that there's only a limited amount available within a given time has received support in recent research (Baumeister, 2002; Baumeister, Bratslavsky, Muraven, & Tice, 1998; Muraven & Baumeister, 2000; Muraven, Tice, & Baumeister, 1998). If you expend effort at controlling one thing, there's not as much left to control something else.

Given a limited energy supply at any given time, how energy gets distributed becomes an important issue. The three aspects of personality—id, ego, and superego—compete for the energy. Each gains power only at the expense of the other two.

Early in life, of course, the id has all the energy. The energy is used to satisfy the id's needs and to operate the primary process. Investing energy in an activity or an image is called forming a **cathexis.** The more important an object or activity, the more energy invested (cathected) in it. As we said earlier, the id doesn't distinguish reality from unreality. As far as the id is concerned, cathecting an image is as good as cathecting the object. This limitation lets the ego capture part of the id's energy for its own use.

The ego uses secondary-process thought to identify objects in the world that match the id's images. Because real objects satisfy needs better than images, the ego gradually comes to control more and more of the id's energy. Over time and experience, the ego controls enough energy that a surplus is available for uses other than gratifying id urges. The ego uses this surplus to bring intellectual functioning to a higher level and to form cathexes of its own. These **ego cathexes** form with objects and activities *associated with* satisfying needs. Regarding hunger, for example, ego cathexes might form with reading *Gourmet* or restaurant reviews, shopping for food, or watching cooking shows on TV.

The ego also has to use energy to restrain the id from acting irrationally or immorally. The restraining forces are called **anticathexes,** because they prevent cathexes from being expressed. The clearest illustration of an anticathexis is **repression.** Repression is investing energy to keep an upsetting idea or impulse in the unconscious. Doing this prevents the cathexis from being expressed. The harder it pushes to emerge, the more energy must be used in the anticathexis that keeps it hidden.

In the short run, anticathexes are useful because they prevent troubling urges from being expressed. They create problems in the long run, though, because they continue to drain energy from the ego that could be used in other ways. Remember, there's only so much energy to go around at any given time (Baumeister, 2002; Muraven & Baumeister, 2000). If too much of it is tied up in anticathexes, the ego has little energy left for anything else. When resources are lacking, behavior becomes less flexible and accommodating (Finkel & Campbell, 2001).

The superego also gathers energy from the id, through a process of *identification*. It goes like this: young children depend on parents for need satisfaction. This leads the child into id-based cathexes toward the parents. As parents impose rules of conduct—punish bad behavior and reward good behavior—the child determines which behaviors maximize need satisfaction. The child's affection for the parents (its cathexis to them) leads the child to act in ways the parents value and to *hold* those values. Cathected parental ideals thereby become part of the ego ideal, and cathected prohibitions become part of the conscience.

The competition for psychic energy among the three aspects of personality is never-ending. It's yet one more way the aspects conflict with one another. Energy, after all, is the power to exert control. As one aspect of personality gains control, the influence of the others diminishes.

Two Classes of Drives: Life and Death Instincts

As with many aspects of Freud's work, his ideas about the nature and number of drives changed over time. Ultimately, he contended that all the basic instincts form two classes (Freud, 1933). The first class is termed **life** or **sexual instincts** (collectively called **Eros**). Eros is a set of drives that deal with survival, reproduction, and pleasure. Despite the label Eros, not all life instincts deal with erotic urges per se. Hunger and pain avoidance, as well as sex, are life instincts. Collectively, the energy produced by the life instincts is known as **libido.**

Although not all life instincts are explicitly sexual, sexuality plays an important role in psychoanalytic theory (Freud, 1953/1905). According to Freud, there's not one sex drive, but many. Each is associated with a different area of the body, called an **erogenous zone.** The erogenous zones are the mouth, anus, and genitals. Erogenous zones are potential sources of tension. Manipulating these areas relieves the tension and produces pleasure. Thus, sucking or smoking produces oral pleasure, emptying the bowels produces anal pleasure, and rubbing of the vagina or penis produces genital pleasure.

A second set of instincts is **death instincts** (also termed **Thanatos**). Freud's view of these instincts is reflected in his statement that "the goal of all life is death" (Freud, 1955/1920). He believed that life provides a vehicle for death and that people desire (unconsciously) to return to the inanimate state from which they came. The expression of death instincts is usually held back by the life instincts, however. Thus the effects of the death instincts aren't always visible.

Freud never coined a specific term for the energy associated with death instincts, and the death drive has received less attention than Eros. Today's biology, however, holds that a death instinct does exist in human physiology. That is, there is an active gene-directed suicide process that occurs in human cells in certain circumstances. This suicide process is termed *apoptosis*. It is a critical element in human development (e.g., Clark, 1996). It also may be involved in the body's defense against cancer (Tyner et al., 2002). The cell-death machinery is part of your cells (Hopkin, 1995). This all suggests that death is an ultimate goal for parts of the body. Perhaps the principle extends more broadly into the personality as well.

One aspect of the death instinct that *has* received attention from psychologists concerns aggression. Freud believed that aggression isn't a basic drive, but stems from the thwarting of the death drive. That is, if Eros blocks expression of the death drive, tension remains—energy is left unspent. It can be dissipated in aggressive or destructive actions against others. In this view, acts of aggression express *self*-destructive urges, but turned outward onto others.

Coming Together of Libidinal and Aggressive Energies

Usually libidinal and aggressive energies are released in separate activities. Sometimes, however, sexual and aggressive drives exist side by side, with one expressed, then the other. This pattern is termed *ambivalence*. Sometimes the two even fuse and jointly energize a single activity (Freud, 1933). This merging of sex and aggression is termed *sadism*.

Several research areas bear on Freud's ideas concerning the interplay between sexual and aggressive energies. One of the more interesting ones aimed to examine effects of pornography on aggression, rather than to test psychoanalytic theory per se (for reviews, see Donnerstein, 1983, or Malamuth & Donnerstein, 1984). Nevertheless, some of the findings are instructive regarding the competition between these energies and their possible blending.

The major point in this literature is that sexual arousal can facilitate or inhibit aggression, depending on other factors. When a person is angry, exposure to *mild* sexual stimuli typically reduces aggression (e.g., Baron, 1974a, 1974b, 1979; Baron & Bell, 1977; Donnerstein, Donnerstein, & Evans, 1975; Frodi, 1977). In one study (Baron, 1974a), men were angered (or not) and later retaliated. Before retaliation, half viewed pictures of nude women, and the rest saw a set of neutral stimuli (pictures of scenery, furniture, and abstract art). As can be seen in Figure 8.4, exposure to erotica significantly reduced aggression among the angry subjects.

In contrast to this, creation of *intense* sexual arousal *increases* aggression among angry persons. In one study (Zillmann, 1971), male subjects were angered (or not) and later retaliated. Just beforehand, they viewed either a neutral film or a highly erotic, explicitly sexual film. The highly erotic film increased the aggression of angry subjects to a level even higher than was created by watching a violent fight film. Other research found that highly erotic material increases aggression toward women (Donnerstein & Hallam, 1978), especially when the erotic stimuli are themselves aggressive (Donnerstein, 1980) and regardless of whether the material has a pleasant or an unpleasant ending (Donnerstein & Berkowitz, 1981). In sum, the evidence suggests that sexual and aggressive urges are sometimes antagonistic to each other but sometimes combine with each other (for broader discussion see Zillmann, 1998).

Catharsis

We said earlier that if a drive's tension isn't released, the pressure of the drive remains and even grows. At some point, the buildup of energy may become so great

Figure 8.4

Influence of mild sexual arousal on aggression. Exposure to mildly erotic pictures reduced aggressiveness among men who had previously been angered but had no effect on men who had not been angered (adapted from Baron, 1974a).

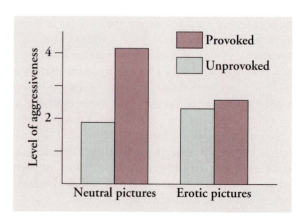

that it can't be restrained any longer. At this point, control is lost and the impulse is unleashed. The term **catharsis** is used to refer to the release of emotional tension that occurs in such an experience. (The term also has a second use that's discussed in Chapter 9.)

The concept of catharsis in the context of motive forces has been studied mostly with respect to aggression. The principle of catharsis leads to two predictions there. First, engaging in aggression should reduce tension, because the aggressive drive is no longer being stifled. Second, because this act dissipates the drive's energy, the person should be less likely to aggress again in the near future.

This view of aggressive energy and its release is echoed in the ideas of more recent theorists. For example, Megargee analyzed acts of extreme violence (1966, 1971; Megargee, Cook, & Mendelsohn, 1967). He argued that people with strong inhibitions against aggressing rarely blow off steam, even when provoked. Over time, though, their feelings build until their restraints can no longer hold. Because so much energy has built up, the aggression released may be quite brutal. Ironically, the final provocation is often trivial, "the straw that broke the camel's back." Once the aggressive episode is over, these people (whom Megargee terms *overcontrolled aggressors*) tend to revert to overcontrolled, passive patterns.

This portrayal is consistent with the psychoanalytic view of aggression, if one assumes the id impulses of these people are overcontrolled by ego and superego processes. The dynamics of overcontrolled aggression have also received a fair amount of verification (see, e.g., Blackburn, 1968a, 1968b; Megargee, 1966). Note, though, that overcontrolled aggressors are a rather select group of people.

How accurate is the catharsis hypothesis for aggression in *most* people? People seem to *think* aggression will make them feel better (Bushman, Baumeister, & Phillips, 2001), but the evidence is mixed (Baron & Richardson, 1994). Aggression can help dissipate arousal (Geen, Stonner, & Shope, 1975; Hokanson & Burgess, 1962a, 1962b; Hokanson, Burgess, & Cohen, 1963), but it's not clear why. For example, in one study (Hokanson & Burgess, 1962b) subjects working on a task were harassed by the experimenter. That raised their blood pressure. Later, some could retaliate physically, others verbally, others in fantasy (writing an aggressive story in response to a TAT picture), and some not at all. As shown in Figure 8.5, the results supported the idea that true retaliation produces emotional catharsis. Subjects who retaliated physically or verbally showed decreases in blood pressure, though fantasy aggression had little effect.

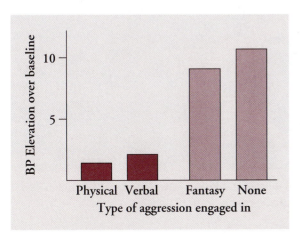

Figure 8.5

Tension-reducing effects of aggressive acts. This figure portrays elevations in systolic blood pressure after being provoked and then engaging in various kinds of aggression, in comparison with levels before provocation. Both physical and verbal aggression were relatively effective in returning participants to their initial levels, whereas fantasy aggression was not (adapted from Hokanson & Burgess, 1962b).

Although this general pattern of effects has been obtained many times, there are important limiting conditions. The target of the aggression can't be high in status (Hokanson & Burgess, 1962a; Hokanson & Shetler, 1961) and must either be the instigator or linked to the instigator (Hokanson, Burgess, & Cohen, 1963). Moreover, tension reduction doesn't require aggression per se. Virtually *any* response that stops a provocation can reduce arousal (e.g., Hokanson & Edelman, 1966; Hokanson, Willers, & Koropsak, 1968; Stone & Hokanson, 1969). There's even evidence that, for women, responding to provocation in a friendly fashion reduces arousal more than does responding aggressively (Hokanson & Edelman, 1966). This finding isn't very consistent with the catharsis hypothesis.

What about the other reflection of catharsis? Does aggression make the person less aggressive in the near future? The findings here are even more mixed. Baron and Richardson (1994) concluded that such effects occur only under very specific conditions. Aggression reduces later aggression only if it's a response to an instigation (e.g., Bramel, Taub, & Blum, 1968; Doob, 1970; Konecni, 1975) and the retaliation is both toward the instigator and roughly equivalent to the instigation (e.g., Berkowitz & Alioto, 1973; Ebbesen, Duncan, & Konecni, 1975; Goldstein & Arms, 1971; Goranson, 1970; Mallick & McCandless, 1966). Interestingly enough, the retaliation itself may be done by someone else and still reduce aggression (E. J. Murray, 1985). On the other hand, sometimes engaging in aggression actually *increases* later aggression (Geen, Stonner, & Shope, 1975), contradicting the catharsis hypothesis. Fantasy aggression can also increase later aggression (Bartholow & Anderson, 2001; Bushman, 2002).

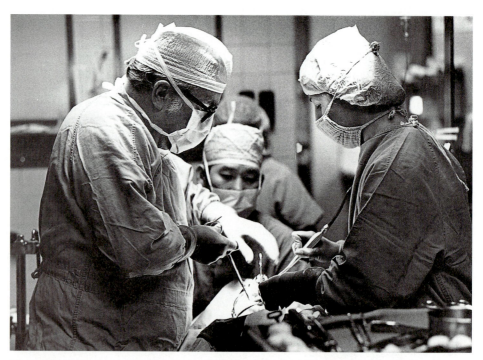

One view of surgery is that it allows unacceptable aggressive energy to be sublimated and released through a more socially acceptable form of activity.

In sum, although some evidence is consistent with catharsis effects, the effects occur only under very specific circumstances. Moreover, other evidence seems to contradict the principle of catharsis. Taken together, this body of evidence doesn't seem easy to reconcile with psychoanalytic theory.

Displacement and Sublimation of Motive Forces

The life and death instincts provide for a wide range of behavior. Behavior is rendered even more diverse by two additional processes that influence how these drives are expressed. One, called **displacement,** is a change in how energy is used or in the object toward which it's used. As people grow or circumstances change, old ways of satisfying desires may no longer be available or acceptable. Displacement lets the blocked energy be released in another way or toward another object. For example, a hostile impulse toward your boss might be displaced and vented toward your apartment mate.

Strictly speaking, the word *displacement* applies to any shift in object choice. There's a special kind of displacement, however, that's important enough that it has a special name: **sublimation.** In sublimation, a shift occurs from a socially unacceptable form of action to an acceptable or even praiseworthy form of action.

As an illustration, consider two students who are angry over criticisms a professor wrote on their term papers. Both want to hit the professor with a baseball bat. Neither does, though. One goes home, kicks his dog, and yells at his roommates. The other writes a letter to the editor of the campus newspaper, criticizing a policy of the university's administration. In both cases, aggressive energy is released through an activity that substitutes for the desired act (hitting the professor). The one who wrote the letter, however, did a more acceptable activity than the one who took out his anger on the dog and roommates. The one who kicked the dog was displacing. The one who wrote the letter was both displacing and sublimating.

As another example, consider two women who are experiencing sexual urges toward their best friend's boyfriend. One of them displaces this impulse by acting out the sexual impulses toward the person she happens to be dating. The other one sublimates the sexual energy by composing a poem.

Although displacement presumably occurs for both sexual and aggressive energy, most research on displacement looks at aggression. A good deal of research makes it absolutely clear that displacement of aggression happens (e.g., Fenigstein & Buss, 1974; Holmes, 1972; Marcus-Newhall, Pedersen, Carlson, & Miller, 2000; Twenge, Baumeister, Tice, & Stucke, 2001). Fenigstein and Buss (1974), for example, found that people who'd been provoked acted more aggressively in the context of a research task, even though the person on the receiving end was just an innocent bystander.

The concepts of displacement and sublimation are very important in psychoanalytic theory. They provide it with the flexibility needed to account for the diversity of human behavior. From the psychoanalytic view, such wide-ranging phenomena as works of art and music, altruism, creativity, critical thinking, and excellence in sports can all be attributed to patterns of displaced and sublimated sexual and aggressive energy.

Indeed, the concept of sublimation is even more important than that. It's sublimation that permits humans to be civilized. Freud believed that, without this transformation, people would act wholly from greed and their own basic desires. Thanks to sublimation, people are capable of acts of altruism and cooperation. Sublimation, then, is the path by which humans are able to transcend their animal nature and form societies.

Psychosexual Development

Freud derived his ideas primarily from a few case histories of adults in therapy. Despite this, he wrote a great deal about how personality develops during childhood. He believed that early experiences play a critical role in determining what a person's adult personality is like. To understand the difficulties of adulthood, one must know the difficulties of childhood. Indeed, Freud thought that personality is largely determined by age five. During later life, personality stabilizes further, and its expression becomes more symbolic and less literal.

Freud viewed personality development as movement through a series of stages. Each stage reflects a body area through which libido, or sexual energy, is discharged during that period. For this reason, they're called *psychosexual stages*. In Freud's view, the child confronts conflicts at three stages. If the conflict isn't well resolved, too much libido gets permanently invested in that stage, a process termed **fixation.** This means less energy is then available to handle conflicts in later stages. As a result, it's harder to successfully resolve the conflict in the later stages. In this sense, each stage builds on previous ones.

Fixation can occur for two reasons. A person who is overindulged in a stage may be reluctant to leave it and move on. A person whose needs are deeply frustrated *can't* move on until the needs are met. In either case, personality becomes partly stuck at this stage, as a portion of the libido becomes invested in that cathexis. The stronger the fixation, the greater the amount of libido invested in it. In a very strong fixation, one is so preoccupied—unconsciously—that one has little energy left for anything else.

The Oral Stage

The **oral stage** extends from birth to roughly eighteen months. During this time, much of the infant's interaction with the world occurs through the mouth and lips, and gratification focuses in that area. The mouth is the source of tension reduction (eating) and pleasurable sensations (tasting, licking, and sucking). At the same time, infants are completely dependent on others for their security and survival. The basic conflict of this stage concerns the ending of this arrangement: the process of weaning—literal and figurative. That is, toward the end of this stage, children are under increasing pressure to let go of their mother and become less reliant on her.

The oral stage has two substages. During the first phase (lasting roughly six months) the baby is particularly helpless and dependent. Because the infant is more or less limited to taking things in (both food and other experiences), the first part of the oral stage is called the *oral incorporative phase.* Freud thought that several traits develop during this time. These traits include a general sense of optimism versus pessimism, trust versus mistrust, and dependency on others. Recall Freud's fascination with symbolism and the idea that literal events become transformed into symbolic versions. This fascination extended to his ideas about traits. He believed that the trait of gullibility—the tendency to "swallow" everything you're told—arises from events during the oral incorporative phase.

The second part of the oral stage starts with teething. It's called the *oral sadistic phase.* Sexual pleasure now comes from biting and chewing (and even inflicting pain—

Although oral gratification may be most important during infancy, the pleasure of oral stimulation continues throughout life.

thus sadistic). During this time the infant is weaned from the bottle or breast and begins to bite and chew food. Traits arising during the oral sadistic phase can be traced to this newly acquired ability. This phase is thought to determine who is verbally aggressive later in life, and who tends to use "biting" sarcasm in conversation.

In general terms, oral characters should relate to the world orally. They should be more preoccupied than others with food and drink. When stressed, they should be more likely than others to reduce tension through activities involving the mouth, such as smoking, drinking, or nail biting. When angry, they should engage in verbal aggression. Oral characters should be concerned with receiving support from others, and should do things to ease interactions with people rather than alienate them.

Is this characterization accurate? Perhaps. Joseph Masling and his colleagues have found that tests of oral imagery relate to both obesity (Masling, Rabie, & Blondheim, 1967; Weiss & Masling, 1970) and alcoholism (Bertrand & Masling, 1969). Orality has also been related to measures of interpersonal interest and social skills. For example, use of oral imagery was correlated with the need to nurture others (Holt, 1966) and with interpersonal effectiveness (Masling, Johnson, & Saturansky, 1974). Persons high in oral imagery also volunteer readily for interpersonal tasks (Bornstein & Masling, 1985; Masling, O'Neill, & Jayne, 1981) and rely on other people's judgments during ambiguous tasks (Masling, Weiss, & Rothschild, 1968).

More generally, people who display oral imagery seem to be highly motivated to gain closeness and support from others and are sensitive to how others react to them. They have greater physiological reactivity to social isolation (Masling, Price, Goldband, & Katkin, 1981) and to subtle cues of rejection (Masling, O'Neill, & Katkin, 1982) than do people who display less oral imagery. They also use more physical contact during social interaction (Juni, Masling, & Brannon, 1979) and are more self-disclosing (Juni, 1981) than less oral people (see also Blum & Miller, 1952; Fisher & Greenberg, 1977).

We should point out that you don't have to be an extremely oral character to seek oral gratification. Lots of people chew gum. Nor is the expression of sexual energy through oral contact limited to early childhood. Indeed, there's evidence all around you that seeking of oral pleasure continues into adulthood. After all, what is serious kissing but an oral expression of sexuality? Nor is that the only way sexuality is expressed orally among adults. In sum, it seems true that the mouth is an important part of the body through which the human's sexual nature is expressed and pleasure is obtained.

The Anal Stage

The **anal stage** of psychosexual development begins at about eighteen months and continues into the third year of life. During this period the anus is the focal erogenous zone, and sexual pleasure comes from the stimulation that occurs when defecating. The major event of this period is the start of toilet training. For many children, toilet training is the first time that external constraints are systematically imposed on satisfaction of internal urges. When toilet training starts, children can't relieve themselves whenever and wherever they want, but must learn instead that there's an appropriate time and place for everything.

The personality characteristics said to arise from fixations during this period depend on how toilet training is approached by parents and caretakers. Two orientations are typical. One involves urging the child to eliminate at a desired time and place and praising the child lavishly for success. This approach places a lot of attention on the elimination process and reward for the child. The child is thereby convinced of the value of producing "things" (in this case urine and feces) at the "right" time and place, by whatever means possible. To Freud, this experience provides a basis for adult productivity and creativity.

The second approach to toilet training is harsher. Rather than praise for a job well done, emphasis is on punishment, ridicule, and shame for failures. These practices yield two patterns of characteristics, depending on how the child reacts. If the child adopts an active pattern of rebellion, eliminating forcefully when the parents least want it, a set of *anal expulsive traits* develop. These are tendencies to be messy, cruel, destructive, and overtly hostile.

An anal retentive personality might be displayed in an excessively neat and tidy workplace.

If the child attempts to get even by withholding feces and urine, a set of *anal retentive* traits develops. The anal retentive personality is a rigid, obsessive style of interacting with the world (Shapiro, 1965). The personality characteristics that make up this pattern are sometimes known as the *anal triad*: stinginess, obstinacy, and orderliness or cleanliness. Stinginess stems from the desire to retain feces. Obstinacy stems from the struggle of wills over toilet training. Orderliness is a reaction against the messiness of defecating. Such a pattern does seem to exist. In one study (Rosenwald, 1972), male students assessed as having the greatest anal anxiety were also the most obstinate and compulsively neat (see also Juni & Fischer, 1985; Juni & Lo Cascio, 1985).

The Phallic Stage

The **phallic stage** begins during the third year and continues through the fifth year. During this period the focus of libidinal excitation shifts to the genital organs. This is also the period when most children begin to masturbate, as they become aware of the sensory pleasure that arises from genital manipulation.

At first the awakening sexual desires are completely *autoerotic* in nature. That is, sexual pleasure is totally derived from, and satisfied by, self-stimulation. Gradually, however, libido begins to shift toward the opposite-sex parent, as boys develop an interest in their mothers and girls develop an interest in their fathers. At the same time the child becomes hostile toward the same-sex parent because of perceived competition between them over the affection of the other parent.

The desire on the part of boys to possess their mothers and replace their fathers is termed the **Oedipus complex** (after the character in Sophocles' play, *Oedipus Rex*, who unwittingly marries his mother after killing his father). Comparable feelings in girls are sometimes called an Oedipus complex and sometimes an *Electra* complex (after the Greek character Electra, who persuades her brother to kill both their mother and their mother's lover in revenge for the death of their father). These complexes reflect forces that are similar in many ways. But the forces are manifested differently for boys and girls. With this shift, the developmental pattern for boys and girls diverges.

Let's consider first what happens to a boy. Two changes take place. His initial love for his mother transforms into a strong sexual desire. His feelings for his father shift toward hostility and hatred, because his father is a rival for his mother's affection. Over time, the boy's jealousy and competitiveness toward his father may become so extreme that he may want the father out of the family, or even dead. Such thoughts may induce feelings of guilt. At the same time, the boy is threatened by fear that his father will retaliate against him for his desire toward his mother. In traditional psychoanalytic theory, the boy's fear is quite specific: he fears that his father will castrate him to eliminate the source of his lust. Freud termed this **castration anxiety.**

Ultimately, castration anxiety causes the boy to push his sexual desire for his mother into the unconscious. Castration anxiety also causes the boy to **identify** with his father, a term that takes on a somewhat different meaning here than earlier in the chapter. *Identification,* as used here, means to develop feelings of similarity to and connectedness with someone else. This serves several functions. First, it gives the boy a kind of "protective coloration." Being like his father makes it seem less likely that his father will harm him. Second, by identifying with desirable aspects of the father, the boy reduces his ambivalence toward him. The process of identification thus paves the way for the development of the superego, as the boy introjects his father's values.

Finally, by identifying with the father, the boy gains a vicarious outlet for his sexual urges toward his mother. That is, he gains symbolic access to his mother *through* his father. Presumably, the more the boy resembles the father, the more easily the boy can unconsciously fantasize himself in his father's place.

For girls, the conflict of the phallic stage is more complicated. As we said earlier, girls abandon their love relationship with their mother for a new one with their father. This shift occurs when the girl realizes she has no penis. She withdraws love from her mother because she blames her mother for her castrated condition (after discovering that her mother has no penis either). At the same time, the girl's affection is drawn to her father, who does have a penis. Ultimately the girl comes to wish that her father would share his penis with her through sexual union or that he would provide her with the symbolic equivalent of a penis—a baby.

Freud referred to these feelings as **penis envy** (though see Box 8.5). Penis envy is the female counterpart of castration anxiety in boys. As for boys, the emotional con-

BOX 8.5

PENIS ENVY OR VAGINA ENVY?

As discussed in the body of the chapter, Freud assumed that developing girls eventually confront the fact that they don't have a penis. He believed this discovery has shattering implications. Girls feel castrated—betrayed—and they blame their mothers for it. This feeling of castration and incompleteness haunts them for the rest of their lives. In his view, the envy women develop for men—penis envy—motivates much of their later behavior, both directly and symbolically.

Examples come from many domains. Women try to recover their lost penises symbolically, by incorporating one into their bodies through sexual intercourse and by giving birth to male children. In today's society, they also seek to obtain the power the penis confers by entering business, law, and other power-related pursuits. Manifestations of penis envy aren't limited to efforts to regain the missing organ. Envy can also be expressed by desiring others to share the same fate. Thus, some women try to reduce men to the same pitiful state as they themselves occupy, castrating men symbolically by being "sharp" and "cutting" in social interactions.

This characterization is entirely compatible with psychoanalytic thought. And a case can be made that at least some girls experience in their childhood a sense that they're missing something boys have, something that may be important. But the idea that penis envy is a prime source of women's motivation is not exactly calculated to win friends among women. To many, this position is condescending and demeaning toward women and presents a gross distortion (Horney, 1939, 1967).

To point out the arbitrariness of Freud's assumptions, Peterson (1980) set forth a different hypothesis. According to her, Freud was on the right track, but he got things backward (perhaps because the truth was too threatening to him). It's not women who are envious of men; it's men who are envious of women. Young boys, growing up, sooner or later confront the fact that they have no vagina. This shattering discovery leads to an envy from which they never recover. The resentment that stems from this envy influences all male behavior.

As did Freud, Peterson assumed that the manifestations of this envy are primarily symbolic. This, suggested Peterson, is why men insist on having pockets in their pants. Lots of pockets. Indeed, the three-piece suit (worn by businessmen and others making vain, pathetic attempts to convey an image of power) is a virtual orgy of symbolic wish fulfillment. It has pants pockets, vest pockets, jacket pockets, even an *internal* jacket pocket—symbolism on top of symbolism!

It should be obvious that Peterson's argument was made tongue in cheek (although we're not about to tell you which of us requires four pockets in every pair of pants he buys). However, she also was making a more serious point about psychoanalytic theory, and about theory more generally. There are places in psychoanalytic theory (as in any theory) where assumptions are made that are arbitrary, seemingly based on societal preconceptions rather than theoretical necessity. It's always important to think about the basis for assumptions in order to decide for yourself whether or not they're sensible.

flict is resolved through identification. By becoming more like her mother, the girl gains vicarious access to her father. She also increases the chances that she'll marry someone just like him.

Several studies have sought evidence of penis envy among girls and castration anxiety among boys. Hall and Van de Castle (1963) found that women's dreams have more symbols of penis envy, whereas men's dreams include more symbols of castration anxiety. Johnson (1966) studied penis envy by seeing whether or not subjects returned a pencil (a penis symbol) after borrowing it for an exam. Women kept the pencils more often than did men. Of course, this measure is pretty far removed from the concept of penis envy. The results may simply reflect an automatic tendency to return pencils to purses.

Fixations that develop during the phallic stage result in personalities that, in effect, continue to wrestle with Oedipal conflicts. Men may go to great lengths to demonstrate that they haven't been castrated, seducing as many women as they can or fathering many children. The attempt to assert their masculinity may also be expressed symbolically by attaining great success in their career. Alternatively, they may fail in their sexual and occupational lives (purposely, but unconsciously so) because of the guilt they feel over competing with their father for their mother's love.

Among women, the continuation of the Oedipal conflict results in a way of relating to men that is excessively seductive and flirtatious, but with a denial of the underlying sexuality. This style of relating first develops toward the woman's father. She was drawn to him first, but by this point has repressed the sexual desire that first drew her. The pattern is then carried over to her later social interactions. This is a woman who excites men with her seductive behavior and then is surprised when the men want sexual contact with her.

Freud felt that identifying the Oedipus complex was one of his most significant theoretical contributions. This brief span involves considerable emotional turmoil filled with love, hate, guilt, jealousy, and fear. He believed that how children negotiate the conflicts and difficulties of the phallic stage determines their fundamental attitudes toward sexuality, interpersonal competitiveness, and personal adequacy (see also Box 8.6).

Fixations that develop during these first three stages of development presumably form much of the basis of adult personality. Some of the traits deriving from fixations during these stages are summarized in Table 8.1.

Table 8.1

Personality qualities that follow from fixations in the first three stages of psychosexual development.

Stage of fixation	Personality qualities
Oral	Incorporative: Dependent, gullible, jealous Sadistic: Sarcastic and verbally aggressive
Anal	Expulsive: messy, cruel, destructive Retentive: obstinate, neat and orderly, stingy
Phallic	Among males: macho aggressive sexuality, excessive striving for career power; alternatively, sexual and occupational impotence Among females: flirtatious, seductive behavior that doesn't lead to sexual interaction

BOX 8.6

THE THEORIST AND THE THEORY
Freud's Own Oedipal Crisis

The idea that personal experiences of personality theorists influenced the very form taken by their theories is vividly illustrated by the life of Sigmund Freud. In fact it's widely believed that several aspects of Freud's life had a direct impact on his theories.

Freud's father Jakob, a merchant, was forty years old at the time of Sigmund's birth (1856). By all accounts he was a strict and authoritarian father. Given this, it would be no surprise that Freud's feelings about his father were ambivalent. Freud's memories later in life were, in fact, of hating his father as well as loving him. A hint of scandal concerning Sigmund's birth may also have had a bearing on his relationship with his father. Two different dates are indicated in various places as his birthdate. This may have been a clerical error. Some believe, however, that the later date was an effort to disguise the fact that Freud's mother was pregnant when she and his father married (Balmary, 1979).

Jakob Freud had had two sons in a prior marriage and was himself a grandfather when Sigmund was born. His wife Amalie, on the other hand, was only twenty. Sigmund was her first child and her special favorite. Sigmund responded to this maternal affection by developing a highly idealized image of his mother and a strong affection for her. By all accounts, they had a very close relationship throughout her life.

In short, the relationships of Freud's childhood had all the elements of what he would later call the Oedipal conflict. There was a deep attachment to his mother, which some have said had sexual overtones. There was also a strong ambivalence toward his father (the depths of which are reflected in the fact that Freud was late for his father's funeral, an act he later saw as having been unconsciously motivated). It seems hard to ignore the possibility that Freud used his own experiences as a model for what he came to argue were universal aspects of development.

Nor was the Oedipal crisis the only aspect of Freud's thinking to be influenced by events in his own life. The experience of World War I, in which 10 million people were killed, deeply disillusioned Freud, along with many other Europeans. Newspapers were filled with accounts of the slaughter, which seemed truly purposeless. Two of Freud's sons fought in the war, and his fears for their safety must have been a great strain on him. Shortly after the end of the war Freud wrote his view of the death instinct: that people have an unconscious wish to die, which they turn outward toward others in murderous actions such as war. It seems likely that this view was partly Freud's attempt to understand how the atrocities of that war could have come to happen. Thus, once again, the elements of the theory seem formed by the experiences of the theorist.

The Latency Period

At the close of the phallic stage, the child enters a period of relative calm, termed the **latency period.** This period, from about age six to the early teens, is a time when sexual and aggressive drives become less active. The lessening of these urges results partly from changes in the body and partly from the emergence of ego and superego aspects of personality. During this period, children turn their attention to other pursuits, often intellectual or social in nature. Thus, the latency period is a time when the child's experiences broaden, rather than a time when new conflicts are confronted and new traits emerge. As an example, parental identifications adopted during the phallic stage may be supplemented by identifications with other figures of authority, perhaps religious figures or teachers.

With the onset of puberty (toward the end of this period), libidinal and aggressive urges again intensify. In addition, conflicts of previous periods may be reencountered. This is a time when the coping skills of the ego are severely taxed. Although adolescents have adult sexual desires, the release of sexual energy through intercourse isn't socially sanctioned. As a result, sexual gratification is sought in other ways—for instance, through masturbation.

The Genital Stage

In later adolescence and adulthood the person moves into the final stage of psychosexual development, the **genital stage.** If earlier psychosexual stages have been negotiated well, the person enters this stage with libido still organized around the genitals, and it remains focused there throughout life. The sexual gratification during this stage differs, however, from that of earlier stages. Specifically, earlier attachments were narcissistic. The child was interested only in his or her own sexual pleasure. Others were of interest only insofar as they furthered the child's own pleasure. In the genital stage, a desire develops to share mutual sexual gratification with someone else. Thus the person becomes capable of loving others not only for selfish reasons but also for altruistic reasons.

Ideally, the person is able to achieve full and free orgasm on an equal basis. Indeed, this ability to share with others in a warm and caring way, and to be concerned with their welfare, is the hallmark of the genital stage. Persons in this stage also have more control over impulses, both sexual and aggressive, and are able to release them in smaller amounts (but more frequently) in sublimated, socially acceptable ways. In this manner the person becomes transformed from a self-centered pleasure-seeking infant into a well-socialized caring adult.

Freud believed that people don't enter the genital stage automatically and that this transition is rarely achieved in its entirety (see Fenichel, 1945). Most people have less control over their impulses than they should, and most have difficulty in gratifying sexual desires in a completely satisfying and acceptable way. In this sense the genital personality is an ideal to strive for, rather than an end point to be taken for granted. It is the perfect culmination of psychosexual development from the analytic point of view.

Psychoanalytic Structure and Process: Problems and Prospects

The psychoanalytic view on how personality is organized and how it functions has been influential since its development, but it has also been controversial. From the start, people were reluctant to accept aspects of the theory. Many were incensed by the prominence of its sexual themes. They were shocked that anyone could suggest that the behavior of young children is sexually motivated. It also was difficult for many to believe that behavior is determined largely by forces outside awareness.

The scientific community faulted psychodynamic theory on other grounds. The primary problem from a scientific standpoint is that the theory is very hard to test. One reason is that many psychoanalytic concepts are defined ambiguously. An example of this is provided by the term *libido*. Freud used this term to refer to sexual energy, a psychological quality that arises from physiological processes. We know lit-tle else about it. Where does it come from? What is it that makes it sexual in nature? Most important, how do you measure it? Without some way to measure it, you can't study it. By implication, other ideas to which libido is linked (e.g., psychosexual de-velopment, fixation) are also hard to examine.

Nor is this problem limited to the concept of libido. Other psychoanalytic concepts—cathexis, the death wish, id, ego—are also problematic from a research point of view. When a theory's concepts can't be defined operationally, the theory can't be tested.

Part of the ambiguity of psychoanalytic concepts comes from Freud's tendency to describe concepts differently from one time to another. Even more ambiguity comes from the fact that Freud thought about personality in such metaphorical ways. This metaphorical approach is deeply embedded in descriptions of the theory. As a result, it's difficult to know when Freud should be read literally and when he should be read metaphorically.

Consider, for example, his description of the Oedipal complex. Should we take Freud to mean literally that he thought every boy comes to desire his mother sexu-ally at around age four? Or should we take it metaphorically and assume he was us-ing the Oedipal theme as a graphic way to describe the conflict between young children and their parents? Freud wrote at one point that many of the specific ex-planatory devices he used could be replaced or discarded without damaging the the-ory (see Silverman, 1976). Clearly, then, parts of what he wrote shouldn't be taken literally. Unfortunately, he didn't specify which parts.

As a metaphorical statement, the Oedipal theme makes a good deal of sense. As a literal statement, it doesn't hold up so well. Sears (1943, p. 136) wrote, "Freud's no-tion of the universal Oedipus complex stands as a sharply etched grotesquerie against his otherwise informative description of sexual development."

Scientific psychologists also criticize the evidence on which psychoanalytic the-ory rests. One focus of this criticism is Freud's heavy reliance on case studies in de-veloping his ideas, particularly ideas involving infantile sexuality. The case study method has several problems. It's inherently subjective, influenced as much by what the researcher brings to the situation as by what's brought by the object of study. It's hard to be sure whether the insights gained by one researcher would be gained by another person, even looking at the same case.

The problem of reliability is even further compounded in this instance. Freud acted both as theorist–researcher and as therapist. Thus, he took an active role in the development of the case history, becoming involved in the interpretation of what was said and done. Freud's actions as a participant–observer may have biased the kinds of things his patients said even more than usual (Powell & Boer, 1994). For example, more sexually toned material came from patients across the course of therapy. Was this because repression was weakening, or because patients learned over time that this was the kind of information Freud was interested in? Indeed, there is evidence that Freud was sometimes highly directive with patients (Esterton, 1998).

Freud allowed himself to be biased in another way, as well, by relying so much on patients. He carefully screened potential patients and allowed into therapy only those he thought were very good candidates. Thus, he developed his ideas from observa-tions of a biased set of cases. We can't be sure how much or in what ways these peo-ple differed from the overall population, but they certainly weren't chosen randomly.

Moreover, the number of cases Freud relied on for a database was distressingly small. In fact, in all his writings and works Freud described case histories of only a dozen or so people. Yet, from this very narrow database—a dozen or so people, all of whom he had carefully chosen and all of whom were in therapy—he went on to formulate what he regarded as universal rules about personality functioning in general. Many find this very problematic.

Another criticism of psychoanalytic ideas is the tendency to confuse facts with inferences. For example, certain observations led Freud to infer the existence (and universality) of an Oedipal complex. He then went on to discuss the Oedipal complex as though its existence were a fact, with no need to test the inference. A general tendency to mix fact with inference has contributed to an intellectual climate in psychoanalytic circles in which basic concepts have gone untested—because it apparently was thought they didn't *need* to be tested (Crews, 1996; Esterson, 1993).

Despite these problems, there's been a resurgence of interest in the ideas that make up both the topographic model of mind and the structural model of personality (Bargh, 1997; Carver, 1996). With respect to the topography of the mind, many people who start from different perspectives now argue that important aspects of memory cannot be brought to consciousness voluntarily. In some cases, this is because the elements are too small, or too hard to locate. Sometimes it apparently is because the thing we're looking for (by its very nature) can be "used" but not "viewed." Sometimes it's because the thing we might be looking for has become so automatic that, in effect, it's fallen out of our mental address book and become lost. Although these aren't quite the same as the unconscious phenomena Freud emphasized, they represent new interest in the idea that the mind has more than two regions.

With respect to the structural model, observers have begun to reemphasize that we shouldn't get distracted by the idea that the mind has three components. Think of them instead as three modes of functioning (Grigsby & Stevens, 2000). Take the descriptions less literally. The id is simply the psychological nature of the infant. Infantile qualities are overlaid in all of us by effects of socialization. But those infantile qualities remain in some sense the basic structure from which we grew. Id is the part that *wants*—wants as the one-year-old wants, without regard to dangers or disapprovals. We still have that part, and it still makes its presence known. Ego is the set of restraints we learn, restraints that diminish the pain we experience from grabbing too fast for what we want without looking for danger. Superego is the abstract rules we learn, to become part of a society in which we can't always have our way, even if we wait patiently.

The idea that humans begin life grabbing for what they want when they first want it, and only gradually learn to restrain themselves, makes a lot of sense. The idea that people later learn abstractions concerning morality also makes sense. So does the idea that those abstractions can conflict with the wants. In sum, the structural model expresses a fair amount of truth about the human experience.

What is the future of these ideas? Some see them as being of historical interest only. Others see them as valuable. They remain an important part of the course you're taking. We suspect they'll remain there for a long time.

SUMMARY

Freud's topographical model holds that there are three regions of mind: the conscious, the preconscious (ordinary memory), and the unconscious (a part of mind that isn't accessible to consciousness). The unconscious is a repository for threatening or unacceptable ideas and urges.

Freud also assumed that personality has three component structures. The id (the original part of personality) is the source of all psychic energy. It follows the pleasure principle (that all needs should be immediately gratified), exists wholly in the unconscious, and uses primary-process thinking (which is primitive and separate from reality). The ego eventually develops from the id because the id ignores the demands of the external world, and they cannot be ignored. The ego follows the reality principle (that behavior must take into account external reality), operates in all three regions of the mind, and tries to see that id impulses are gratified in a realistic manner. The ego uses secondary-process (reality-based) thought. The third aspect of personality, superego, is a representation of rules by which parents reward and punish the child. It has two parts: ego ideal is standards of moral perfection. Conscience holds a representation of behaviors that are considered reprehensible. Both function in all three regions of the mind. Once the superego develops, the ego must mediate among id, superego, and reality.

The investment of energy in a need is called a cathexis. Restraining forces (from the ego) are called anticathexes. Id impulses form two categories: life instincts (Eros) aim for self-preservation and sexual pleasure. Death instincts (Thanatos) are self-destructive and may be turned outward as aggression. Catharsis in aggression is the releasing of an aggressive desire, which leads to tension reduction and a decreased need to aggress. Impulses can be displaced, released onto a different target from that initially intended. Impulses can also be sublimated, that is, transformed into socially acceptable acts.

Freud argued that child development proceeds through psychosexual stages and that adult personality is influenced by how crises are resolved at each stage. In the oral stage, sexuality centers on the mouth, and the crisis involves being weaned from the mother. In the anal stage, sexuality centers on the anus, and the crisis involves toilet training. In the phallic stage, sexuality centers on the genitals, and the crisis (creating Oedipal and Electra complexes) involves lust for the opposite-sex parent and fear of or hatred for the same-sex parent. The latency period is a calm interval with no serious conflict. The genital period is maturity, in which genital sexuality shifts from selfish narcissism to mutual sharing.

GLOSSARY

Anal stage The second stage of development, in which anal needs create a crisis over toilet training.

Anticathexis The investment of energy in suppressing an impulse or image.

Castration anxiety A boy's fear (from the phallic stage) that his father will perceive him as a rival and castrate him.

Catharsis The release of emotional tension.

Cathexis The investment of psychic energy in a desired activity or image.

Conscience The part of the superego that punishes violations of moral standards.

Conscious The part of the mind that holds what one is currently aware of.

Death instincts (Thanatos) Self-destructive instincts, often turned outward as aggression.

Displacement The shifting of an impulse from its original target to a different target.

Ego The rational part of the personality that deals pragmatically with reality.

Ego cathexis Binding psychic energy in an ego-guided activity.

Ego ideal The part of the superego that represents perfection and rewards for good behavior.

Ego strength The ability of the ego to function despite competing demands of id, superego, and reality.

Erogenous zone A sexually responsive area of the body.

Fixation The condition of being partly stuck in some early stage of psychosexual development.

Genital stage The final stage of development, mature and mutual sexual involvement with another.

Id The original, primitive component of personality, the source of all energy.

Identify Develop feelings of similarity to, and connectedness with, another person.

Introjection Absorbing the values of one's parents into one's superego.

Latency period The period in which the crises of the phallic stage give way to a temporary calm.

Libido The collective energy of the life instincts.

Life instincts or **sexual instincts (Eros)** Survival and sexual instincts.

Oedipus complex The mix of desire for the opposite-sex parent and fear of or hatred for the other parent.

Oral stage The first stage of psychosexual development, in which oral needs create a crisis over weaning.

Penis envy A girl's envy of males, from feelings of having been castrated.

Phallic stage The third stage of development, in which a crisis occurs over sexual desire for the opposite-sex parent.

Pleasure principle The idea that impulses should be gratified immediately.

Preconscious The region of the mind that corresponds to ordinary memory.

Primary process The id process that creates an unconscious image of a desired object.

Reality principle The idea that actions must take into account the constraints of external reality.

Reality testing The ego's checking to see whether plans will work before they are put into action.

Repression Preventing an idea or impulse from becoming conscious.

Secondary process The ego process of rationally seeking an object to satisfy a desire.

Structural model Freud's model of three components of personality.

Sublimation Altering an unacceptable id impulse to an activity that's more socially acceptable.

Superego The component of personality that seeks moral perfection.

Topographical model Freud's model of three regions, or areas, of the mind.

Unconscious The region of the mind that's not accessible to consciousness.

Wish fulfillment The creation of an unconscious image of a desired object.

9 Anxiety, Defense, and Self-Protection

■ **Anxiety**

■ **Mechanisms of Defense**

Repression
Denial
Projection
Rationalization
Intellectualization
Reaction Formation
Regression
Displacement and Sublimation
Research on Defenses
Evidence of Unconscious Conflict

■ **Exposing the Unconscious**

The Psychopathology of Everyday Life
Dreams
Humor

■ **Projective Techniques of Assessment**

Rorschach Inkblot Test

■ **Problems in Behavior, and Behavior Change**

Origins of Problems
Behavior Change
Does Psychoanalytic Therapy Work?

■ **Psychoanalytic Defense: Problems and Prospects**

SUMMARY

■   Dan and Jamie are talking about a party they'd been to last weekend, at which one of their friends had gotten flagrantly, ostentatiously drunk—something she's done weekly for the past year. "Man, I can't believe how much Robin *drinks,*" says Jamie. "She soaks it up like a sponge." At this moment Robin rounds the corner, practically running into them. "Hey Robin, are you still high from last weekend?" Jamie asks. "What are you talking about?" replies Robin, "I didn't drink that much." "Seriously, Robin," Dan throws in, "aren't you concerned about how much you've been drinking?" Robin's face takes on an offended look. "Look, guys, I don't have a problem, so just stay off my back," she says, as she turns and walks away. Dan and Jamie look at each other and shrug.

■   Roselyn and Roy, who have been dating for several months, are at a party. Also there is Tim, a very good-looking guy they both know. At the end of the evening after Tim and his date have left, Roselyn is talking about him with Roy and several friends. "Didn't you see the way he was coming on to me? I wish he wouldn't do it, but he does it all the time." Later, on the way home, Roy says to her, "Roselyn, you just made a fool of yourself—and me—in front of all those people. Tim didn't come on to you at all. I can't imagine where you got such an idea."

C hapter 8 described the basic elements of the psychoanalytic view of human nature. In this chapter we consider more deeply some of the ways in which human nature is reflected in behavior. In many respects the points made here are direct extensions of the logic of Sigmund Freud's theory. Some of the ideas, however, were developed by people other than him. Most prominent among them was his daughter, Anna Freud (1966).

Anxiety

Much of the process within personality—in people who are perfectly normal, as well as people with problems—is linked to **anxiety.** Anxiety is an aversive inner state that people seek to avoid or escape. Freud (1936/1926) saw anxiety as a warning signal to the ego that something bad is about to happen.

Freud (1959/1926) distinguished among three different types of anxiety, which reflect three different categories of bad things. The most basic is **reality anxiety.** It arises from a threat or danger in the world. It's the kind of fear you experience when you realize you're about to be bitten by a dog, crash your car, be yelled at for a big mistake at work, or fail an exam. As its name implies, reality anxiety is rooted in reality. One way to deal with it is to fix, avoid, or escape from the situation that's producing the feeling.

The second type of anxiety is **neurotic anxiety.** This is unconscious fear that your id impulses will get out of control and make you do something that will get you punished. The person experiencing a lot of neurotic anxiety is constantly worried about the id's escaping from the ego's control (though the worry is unconscious). This anxiety isn't a fear of expressing id impulses per se. It's a fear of the punishment that may result from expressing them.

Because people are often punished for impulsive behavior, particularly if it's behavior that society disapproves of, this type of anxiety has a sort of basis in reality. Unlike reality anxiety, however, the danger arises from within the person, from the urges of the id. For this reason, neurotic anxiety is harder to deal with than reality anxiety. You can drive carefully, prepare for exams, and avoid dangerous dogs, but you can't escape from your id. It always has the potential to get out of control.

The third type of anxiety is called **moral anxiety.** This is the fear people have when they've violated (or are about to violate) their moral codes. If your moral sense forbids cheating and you're tempted to cheat, you feel moral anxiety. If your moral sense forbids sex before marriage and you're just about to have sex with someone, you experience moral anxiety. Subjectively, moral anxiety is felt as guilt or shame.

Moral anxiety arises from the conscience that's part of your superego. The stronger your superego, the more likely you'll have moral anxiety. As with neurotic anxiety, it's important to be clear about the difference between this and reality anxiety. People are often punished by society for transgressing moral standards, but the threat of punishment from society isn't the basis of moral anxiety. Its source is internal, in your conscience. As with neurotic anxiety, it's hard to deal with. Just as you can't escape your id, you can't run away from your conscience.

Mechanisms of Defense

If your ego were doing its job perfectly, you'd never feel any anxiety. External dangers would be avoided or dealt with, thereby preventing reality anxiety. Id impulses would be released in degrees at appropriate times, preventing neurotic anxiety. You'd never let yourself do anything (or even *want* to do anything) that your superego prohibits, thereby preventing moral anxiety. No one's ego works this well, however. As a result, most people experience some anxiety, and many people experience a lot. This is a part of all normal human lives.

When anxiety occurs, the ego responds in one of two ways. First, it increases rational problem-oriented coping efforts. It tries to deal (consciously) with the source of the threat. This works best for reality anxiety. Second, it engages **defense mechanisms.** These are tactics the ego develops to help it deal with anxiety. When defenses work well, they prevent anxiety from arising. Defense mechanisms share two characteristics: first, they all can operate unconsciously. Second, they all distort, transform, or falsify reality in one way or another.

Various theorists have postulated varying numbers of defense mechanisms. Anna Freud (1966), whose work on ego defenses was very influential, identified ten mechanisms available to the ego. The following sections outline several of them.

Repression

The fundamental mechanism of defense is called **repression.** Indeed, Sigmund Freud often used the terms *defense* and *repression* interchangeably. Repression can be done consciously (thereby being equivalent to *suppression*), as the person tries to force something out of consciousness (see also Box 9.1). Most discussions of repression, however, focus on its unconscious operation.

We said in Chapter 8 that repression can mean forming an anticathexis with an id impulse. By doing this, the ego restrains it from being expressed. If you have the impulse to fondle the person next to you in class, your ego (presumably) takes action to keep the impulse out of your awareness.

BOX 9.1

UNINTENDED EFFECTS OF THOUGHT SUPPRESSION

People sometimes exert conscious effort to try to keep particular thoughts out of their minds. If you're trying to quit smoking, you want to avoid thinking about cigarettes. If you're trying to lose weight, you want to avoid thoughts of food. If you've just broken up with someone, you want to avoid thinking about the things you used to do together. So you try to keep these ideas out of your consciousness.

Sometimes this thought suppression works. But trying not to think of something can have unintended side effects. Dan Wegner and his colleagues have conducted a program of studies on thought suppression (Wegner, 1989, 1994; Wenzlaff & Wegner, 2000), and their conclusions may surprise you. Trying not to think about something can actually make that thought become more likely later on, especially if the thought's an emotionally arousing one (Wegner, Shortt, Blake, & Page, 1990).

The idea of conscious thought suppression contains a paradox. Thought suppression requires two steps: deciding to suppress the thought, and then getting rid of all manifestations of the thought—including the plan to suppress it. This seems to require you to be conscious of your intent and not conscious of it, all at once. (If repression occurs unconsciously, of course, this problem is avoided, because the plan to get rid of the thought is unconscious.)

So what happens when people try to suppress a thought? Initial research (e.g., Wegner, Schneider, Carter, & White, 1987) taught people a think-aloud technique in which they report in a stream of consciousness all thoughts that come to mind. They were then asked to do this for periods of five minutes under two different conditions. In one condition they're to try not to think of a white bear. Every time a white bear comes to mind, they're to ring a bell in front of them. In the other condition they're to *think* of a

white bear and to ring the bell when they do. For some people the suppression came first, then the thinking. For others the order was reversed.

Two findings emerged from this study. First, it was hard to avoid thinking of a white bear (the most effective strategy used was to focus on something else). Interestingly, most intrusions of the unwanted thought occurred when the person had just finished a sentence or thought and was silent. It was as though the thought could be kept out as long as the mental machinery was fully occupied, but when an opening came up the thought leaped in. The authors argued that suppression is hard unless you have a distractor to think of instead (additional evidence supports this idea). To put this idea in psychoanalytic terms, it's apparently easier to form an alternative cathexis than to form an anticathexis.

The second finding was that people who suppressed showed a rebound effect. That is, when they were later asked to think of the bear, they did so more frequently and consistently than did the other people. Their reports of the white bear were stable over the five-minute period. In contrast, those who'd started by thinking of the bear wore out fairly quickly, and their reports fell off over the five-minute period.

In practical terms, what are the implications of findings such as these? What should you do when you want not to think about something? Wegner (1989) argues that, as odd as it may sound, the best medicine is to let the thoughts in. Experience the feelings associated with the intrusion and let the experience run its course. Only by relaxing our mental control, he says, can we regain it. By lowering your defenses, you eventually reduce the pressure of the unwanted thought, and it will go away on its own (perhaps through the mechanisms of the unconscious).

Repression is important for restraining id impulses. But it also applies to information in the mind that's painful or upsetting. Sometimes that information represents the memory of impulses that have already been expressed. If you did something last week you're utterly ashamed of, you try not to think about it and eventually may be unable to recall doing it. However, painful and threatening thoughts have many sources, not all of which stem from id impulses.

Threat can come from personal lapses—for example, forgetting to lock your apartment, thereby letting someone steal your TV. It can come from things about yourself you think are inadequate—for example, the fact that you're unpopular, or the fact you can't dance. It can come from being part of a group that others disparage (Steele, 1997) or from the realization you will eventually die (Pyszczynski, Greenberg, & Solomon, 2000). Threat can even come from situations in life that conflict with your superego's standards—for example, the fact that people in the world are starving and you're not doing anything about it, or the thought that your parents have an active sex life with certain preferred positions for intercourse.

Some people, of course, do think about their parents' sex lives (or the fact that they can't dance or the fact that they let somebody steal their TV). This illustrates two more points about repression. First, what's repressed depends partly on what values are in your superego and what acts are likely to get you punished. What gets people punished varies across cultures. In the same way, the values in people's superegos also presumably vary. When Freud began writing, society was very conflicted about sex. That's less true today, and the values absorbed into superegos today may focus less on sex than was true one hundred years ago. As the values of societies shift, what's repressed also shifts. Instead of repressing sexual feelings, perhaps you repress memories of actions you took that harmed the environment.

The second point is that repression need not be total. It's easiest to talk about defenses in all-or-nothing terms, but this can be misleading. You can partly repress a moderately distressing memory, so you don't think about it often. You haven't forgotten it. If reminded of it, you're still aware it's there. But you'd just as soon not be reminded of it. This would be a partial repression (for more on repression see Box 9.2).

Denial

Another fairly simple defense occurs when people are overwhelmed by a threatening reality. This defense is **denial:** refusal to believe an event took place or a condition exists. An example is the mother who refuses to believe the message that her son has been killed in combat and acts as though he's still alive. Another is a child abused by a parent who goes on as if nothing is wrong (Freyd, 1996). A less extreme case is a college student who refuses to believe the grade posted by her name and assumes

Denial prevents us from becoming aware of unpleasant things in our lives.

BOX 9.2

RECALL OF TRAUMATIC CHILDHOOD MEMORIES
Breakdown of Repression, or Events That Never Happened?

Repression can keep memories of past traumas from reaching awareness. If the events can't be recalled, the person is spared any anxiety, anguish, or guilt associated with the experience. It's possible, however, for repression to break down. If that happens, people will recall episodes from their lives they might prefer not to recall.

Consider, for example, the following case reported by Elizabeth Loftus (1997). Nadean Cool sought psychiatric help to deal with her reactions to a trauma experienced by her daughter. Through hypnosis and other techniques, she recalled repressed memories of abuse she herself had endured. She became convinced she had repressed memories of having been in a satanic cult, eating babies, being raped, having sex with animals, and being forced to watch the murder of her eight-year-old friend.

In fact, none of these events ever happened. The therapist's procedures induced her to think they had. When she realized this, she sued the psychiatrist for malpractice and eventually won a $2.4 million settlement. Nor is this the only case of "memories" being inadvertently planted by therapists (see Loftus, 1997, for other examples).

Indeed, evidence suggests that false memories are surprisingly easy to induce. In one method of study, researchers ask people to recall childhood events mentioned by relatives (e.g., Loftus, Coan, & Pickrell, 1996; Loftus & Pickrell, 1995). A few events that weren't mentioned—because they never happened—are embedded among the real ones. Not surprisingly, most people (80 percent or so) recall something about the real events. More surprising is the percent-age who report memories about the events that never happened. Twenty to 30 percent of people typically report memories of nonexistent events, and the rate sometimes exceeds 60 percent!

False memories seem to depend partly on the event's being plausible. However, even events that are unusual or highly unlikely can produce false recall (Hyman, Husband, & Billings, 1995; Spanos, 1996). Another important variable seems to be the extent to which the events are verifiable. False memories are more likely for events that can't be easily verified (Lynn, Myers, & Malinoski, 1997).

Interest in "recovered" memories runs high today, partly because the memories often lead to accusations of terrible acts that had been repressed. Many persons have been accused of acts of physical and sexual abuse on the basis of such newly recovered memories. Some of them have been shown to be innocent. Yet they've undergone public humiliation in ways that permanently changed their lives.

It's very important to bear in mind that the occurrence of false memories doesn't mean that the spontaneous recall of traumatic events is never true. Children are sometimes the victims of sexual, physical, and emotional abuse. Sometimes those events are repressed, to avoid distress associated with them. However, it does seem clear that not all cases of recalled trauma are real. Sometimes people are misled into remembering things that never happened. It can be very hard to tell whether a vivid memory is true or false. But given the consequences of such memories, a great deal can depend on deciding which it is.

there's been some sort of mistake. Denial also is implicit when a young boy assumes a role of power while playing, thereby hiding the reality of his weakness.

As people mature and the ego gets better at assessing reality accurately, denial becomes harder. That is, reality stares you in the face more clearly as you get more experienced. Denial remains possible at any age, though. It's common for people who have serious problems with alcohol or drugs to deny the problem (as in the example opening the chapter). It's common for someone whose lover is straying to deny it. Many victims of Nazi persecution failed to flee to safe havens while there was still time, apparently because of denial. Indeed, it's been argued that self-report measures of well-being can be untrustworthy because some people deny to themselves the distress that they're experiencing (Shedler, Mayman, & Manis, 1993).

Denial is similar in many ways to repression. Both keep out of awareness things the person feels unable to cope with. They differ from each other in the source of the threat. Repression deals with threats that originate within the dynamics of the mind. Denial deals with threats that have other sources.

Everyone uses repression and denial, because they work. They save you from pain or anxiety. But too much repression or denial has a cost. These anticathexes (keeping unacceptable things from consciousness) require energy. Energy tied up this way is unavailable for other uses. If an act of repression continues, the investment of energy is more or less permanent. Thus, despite the fact that repression and denial are sometimes needed, they can eventually work against you.

Perhaps for this reason, other defenses also develop. These other mechanisms operate in combination with repression (and in combination with one another). They free some of the energy from anticathexes, while still keeping unacceptable impulses, thoughts, or feelings from registering on consciousness. How they do so varies from one defense to another.

Projection

In **projection,** anxiety is reduced by ascribing your own unacceptable impulses, desires, or qualities to someone else. Projection thereby provides a way to hide your knowledge of a disliked aspect of yourself, while still expressing that unacceptable quality, though in a highly distorted form (Mikulincer & Horesh, 1999).

For example, if you have feelings of hostility toward others, you remove the feelings from awareness through repression. The feelings are still there, however. In projection, you develop the perception that others hate you or are out to get you. In this way, your hostile impulse gains expression, but in a distorted way that's not threatening to you. Another example is a woman who has sexual urges toward someone she shouldn't feel that way about, and accuses him of being seductive toward her (as in the second example opening the chapter). The impulse gets out in a distorted form, while the woman remains unaware of her own desires.

Thus, projection serves two purposes, as do all the more elaborate ego defenses. It helps to get the id's desires into the open in one form or other, releasing some of the energy required to repress them. When you project, you're recognizing that the threatening quality exists, because you're seeing it. Just as importantly, though, the desire emerges in such a form that the ego and superego don't recognize it. Thus, the power of the threat is side-stepped (see Figure 9.1).

Rationalization

Another important defense mechanism is **rationalization.** In rationalization the person reduces anxiety by finding a rational explanation (or excuse) for a behavior that really was done for unacceptable reasons. For example, the man who cheats on his income tax may rationalize his behavior as reducing the amount of money spent on weapons in the world.

Rationalization also protects against other kinds of threats. For example, after a failure, rationalization maintains self-esteem. If you don't get into medical school, you may convince yourself that you really didn't want to be a doctor anyway. A man who's snubbed when asking for a date may convince himself that the woman really

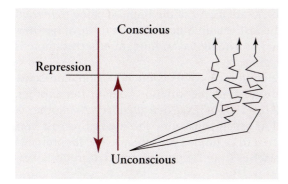

Figure 9.1

Defenses begin with repression, removing threatening material from the conscious region of the mind to the unconscious. What has been repressed cannot be brought out directly because it's too anxiety-provoking. Repressed material can sneak around the barrier, however, by being transformed so as to make it less recognizable. Though these distortions permit the repressed urges to gain expression, the expression is weaker and less effective than the initial urge. Thus, pressure to express the urge remains.

wasn't so great after all. Rationalization is very common in people's responses to success and failure. It's been shown repeatedly that people tend to take credit for good performances and blame bad performances on forces outside their control (e.g., Ross & Fletcher, 1985).

Intellectualization

Another defense is the tendency to think about threats in cold, analytical, and detached terms. This process is called **intellectualization.** Thinking about events in such a clinical fashion allows people to dissociate their thoughts from the feelings involved. This insulates them from anxiety. Through this process the threatening event is separated and isolated from the feeling that normally would accompany it (Feldman Barrett, Williams, & Fong, 2002).

For example, the woman who finds out that her husband is dying of cancer may try to learn as much about cancer and its treatment as she can. By focusing on the disease intellectually and compartmentalizing that information, she shields herself from distress. A man who is sexually aroused by a coworker may analyze in detail the qualities that make her attractive, considering her from the point of view of an uninvolved connoisseur of beauty. Doing this lets him distance himself from his desires.

Freud (1915/1961) made a more general point about this aspect of defense when discussing the separation of the unconscious from the conscious part of the mind. He suggested that an idea can exist in both parts of the mind at once, but in different forms. The intellectual aspect of the idea can exist in consciousness, even if it's a potentially threatening idea such as hating your father. This can be managed if the emotional quality attached to the idea, the deeply personal part that makes the idea psychologically meaningful, remains repressed. This sounds like a perfect description of intellectualization.

Reaction Formation

One way to guard against the release of an unacceptable impulse is to make a point of stressing its *opposite*. Doing this is called **reaction formation.** For example, a child may deal with hostile feelings toward a new baby in the family by repressing her hostile feelings and replacing them with effusive positive displays.

Freud believed that it's often hard to tell whether an act stems from its apparent motivation or from the opposite impulse. Reaction formation is sometimes inferred from the size of the response. If the person seems to "go overboard" or the response seems out of proportion to the context, you may be seeing reaction formation.

Another clue is that the act may incorporate tinges of the impulse being defended against. For example, the child in the last example may attempt to "love her new brother to death" by hugging him so hard he begins to hurt. Another example is "friendly advice" that is subtly disparaging.

It's also possible to point to more adult forms of reaction formation. For example, a man who appears to be a super-stud, sleeping with one woman after another, may be doing so to hide from himself fears about his sexual adequacy. As another illustration, cases have been reported in which legislators who worked to pass laws against homosexual rights were rumored to be homosexual themselves. It's arguable that they were trying to prevent themselves from facing their true nature by behaving in a way that was its opposite.

You can also display reaction formation in interpreting the behaviors of people close to you. For example, people confronting evidence that their romantic partners have important faults may distort their perceptions of the evidence. The result is to turn the faults into virtues (Murray & Holmes, 1993).

Regression

In Chapter 8 we described the stages of psychosexual development and indicated how people can become fixated in them. The fixation means that energy remains bound up in the cathexes of that stage. Anna Freud believed that stress often causes people to abandon mature coping strategies and instead use patterns of the stages in which they are fixated. She called this **regression,** because it means giving up a more advanced form of coping in favor of one that's more primitive and infantile.

For example, an adult who's fixated at the oral stage might smoke more or eat or drink more when stressed at work. Someone with an anal fixation may respond to stress by becoming even more obstinate and compulsive than usual. The stronger a fixation, the more likely is the person to regress under stress to the mode of functioning that characterizes that stage. Recall that fixations can develop because needs were gratified well in an early stage of development. Thus, regression often is a return to a way of relating to the world that used to be very effective (A. Freud, 1966).

Regression can occur at any point in development. An older child can regress to patterns of earlier childhood. Adults can also regress. It should be clear that in adult regression people don't always behave literally as they did during the earlier stage of development (although this may occur). Rather, the person's thoughts and actions become permeated with the concerns of the earlier stage. The manifestation of these concerns is often symbolic rather than literal.

Displacement and Sublimation

Two final defense mechanisms were introduced in Chapter 8: displacement and sublimation. These defenses are generally considered less neurotic than the others we've described and more adaptive. **Displacement** is shifting an impulse from one target to another. This often (though not always) happens when the intended target is threatening. Displacement is a defense mechanism in such cases because substituting a less threatening target for the original one reduces anxiety.

For example, the student who's angry with her professor and takes out her hostility on her very understanding boyfriend avoids the anxiety that would arise from attacking her professor. The person with an inappropriate lust who displaces that urge onto a permissible target avoids the anxiety that would arise from expressing the desires toward the true target.

People often express impulses in symbolic form. Sometimes people live out their impulses through their children—or even their pets!

Sublimation also allows impulses to be expressed, by transforming the impulse to a more acceptable form. In this case it's not something about the target that creates the threat, but something about the impulse. Sublimation is a defense because anxiety goes down when a transformed impulse is expressed instead of the initial one. Freud felt that sublimation, more than any other mechanism, reflects maturity. Sublimation is a mechanism that keeps problems from occurring, rather than a tactic that people turn to after anxiety is aroused.

Research on Defenses

What's the scientific status of the defense mechanisms? A fair amount of research has been done on this topic and, after a quiet period, interest is growing again (Cramer, 2000). Consider a study of projection by Halpern (1977). People who did or did not seem sexually defensive (by a self-report scale) either were or were not exposed to erotic photos before making ratings of someone else. Those classed as sexually defensive rated the other person as more "lustful" if they'd seen erotic photos than if they hadn't. Those who weren't defensive about sexual issues didn't display this projection. This pattern makes sense from a psychodynamic perspective. You project only about things that threaten you.

More recent research has investigated the idea that projection occurs when people actively try to suppress thoughts about something they don't like about themselves (Newman, Duff, & Baumeister, 1997). This active attempt to suppress seems to cause thoughts about the unwanted trait to push back and become even more accessible. This in turn causes the thoughts to be ready for use when someone else's behavior even remotely fits the trait.

These studies seem supportive of the idea of defense. But the literature as a whole is ambiguous, and alternative interpretations are often easy to construct. As a result, different readers draw different conclusions. To Sherwood (1981) there was substantial evidence of projection, whereas to Holmes (1981) there wasn't. Many people are convinced that repression occurs in the short term (e.g., Erdelyi, 1985; Paulhus & Suedfeld, 1988), although in the longer term there are more questions.

Recent research has begun to take a different angle on the study of repression. This research looks at individual differences in the tendency to repress and asks whether repressors differ in important ways from people who repress less. In one study, subjects did a task that required them to make associations to phrases with sexual and aggressive content (Weinberger, Schwartz, & Davidson, 1979). Repressors reported the lowest level of distress during this task, but they also showed the most physical arousal. In other research, repressors were less able to recall emotional memories from childhood and from their day-to-day experiences than were other subjects (Davis, 1987; Davis & Schwartz, 1987). These findings suggest that the search for evidence of repression may be coming closer to fruition.

Evidence of Unconscious Conflict

Much of the preceding discussion of ego defenses assumes that conflicts are buried in the unconscious through repression, to avoid neurotic or moral anxiety. Although unconscious, the conflicts presumably continue to influence behavior. Some of those influences are reflected in the defenses we've been discussing. That is, repressed desires leak out through such processes as projection, reaction formation, or sublimation.

Sometimes, though, the conflicts emerge through symptoms, such as depression. The idea that unconscious conflicts influence symptoms has received support from research by Lloyd Silverman and his colleagues (Silverman, 1976, 1983; Weinberger & Silverman, 1987). This idea is hard to test experimentally, because it requires arousing the conflict in the unconscious but not letting it reach consciousness. The solution was to present material subliminally, at exposures so brief people couldn't tell what they were seeing.

Subliminal stimuli apparently do register. When susceptible people were shown material designed to stir up their unconscious conflicts, their symptoms increased. One susceptible group is depression-prone people. In the psychoanalytic view, depression reflects an unconscious death wish. Such wishes can be stirred up by words (e.g., *Cannibal eats person*) or pictures (e.g., one person stabbing another). In several studies (reviewed by Silverman, 1976), showing such material subliminally to depression-prone people caused them to have deeper feelings of depression. This did *not* happen if the stimuli were allowed to enter consciousness, by using longer exposures. This supports the idea that it's the unconscious producing the symptoms.

Other research in this series involved arousing or diminishing Oedipal feelings in college men (Silverman, Ross, Adler, & Lustig, 1978). Participants first did a competitive dart-throwing task. Then they viewed subliminal stimuli. In one condition a message read "Beating Dad is wrong"; in another condition the message read "Beating Dad is OK"; in a third condition the stimuli weren't related to Oedipal issues. Finally, the men repeated the dart-throwing task. Stirring up Oedipal feelings (Beating Dad is OK) led to improved scores (Figure 9.2). Presumably the Oedipal feelings translated into stronger competition. Pushing the Oedipal desires down (Beating Dad is wrong) led to poorer scores.

In sum, there's evidence that surface displays of psychological characteristics can be influenced by arousing a conflict at an unconscious level. There are limitations. Some effects occur reliably only among people in whom the conflict is already well established. In the last study described, in contrast, the effect was more general, presumably because *everyone* has experienced the Oedipal conflict.

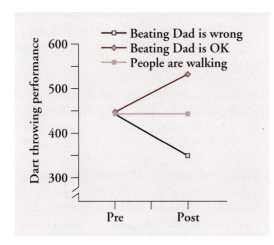

Figure 9.2

Effects of subliminal activation (or deactivation) of Oedipal feelings on competitive dart throwing. Participants threw darts for one score before exposure to the subliminal stimuli (pre) and threw again afterward (post). Subjects exposed to "Beating Dad is wrong" got lower scores the second time. Those exposed to "Beating Dad is OK" got higher scores the second time. Those exposed to "People are walking" were not affected (adapted from Silverman et al., 1978).

We should also note that Silverman's research has been controversial, partly because others have found it hard to obtain the same effects (e.g., Heilbrun, 1980). Another problem is a lack of evidence for processes assumed to underlie the effects (Weinberger & Hardaway, 1990). Despite the controversy—or perhaps even because of it—it seems likely that this research technique will continue to be explored as a way to study unconscious conflict.

Exposing the Unconscious

We've been focusing on how the ego handles conflicts. To guard against neurotic and moral anxiety, the ego represses desires that are threatening. This material, now unconscious, continues to influence behavior through the operation of further ego defenses.

Freud believed that the unconscious is where the vital forces of human life are at work, influencing people in complex ways. There is where the true motives lie. Gaining access to the conflicts and desires of the unconscious seems a daunting task. Freud believed, though, that it's not as hard as it seems. He thought unconscious impulses are revealed constantly in everyday events. You just have to look for them. In this section, we discuss some ways in which unconscious motives are revealed to the careful observer.

The Psychopathology of Everyday Life

One way such motives are revealed is in people's mistakes. We all make mistakes from time to time. We forget things, get our words jumbled, and have accidents. Freud (1960b/1901) referred to such events as the *psychopathology of everyday life* (a phrase that also conveys his belief that all normal life contains a little of the abnormal). He believed such events, far from being random, stem from urges in the unconscious. The urges emerge in a distorted form, as mistakes. Thus memory lapses, slips of speech, and accidents provide indirect insights into a person's true desires (for a contrasting opinion, however, see Reason & Mycielska, 1982).

Collectively, these events are termed **parapraxes** (a literal translation from the German term is "faulty achievement"; Bettelheim, 1982). Perhaps the simplest parapraxis is forgetting. From the psychoanalytic perspective, forgetting reflects repression, an attempt to keep something from consciousness. Sometimes it's easy to see why for-getting occurs (e.g., the student who forgets to return an important book to some-one he doesn't like). At other times, it's harder to see the motive. Yet a motive can often be found, if enough is known about the situation.

A simple example comes from a psychology professor we know. He was heading off to a small conference of eminent psychologists, including some he had profes-sional disagreements with. He arrived at the airport only to discover he'd left his wal-let at home. As a result, he was unable to board the plane (and would have been unable to pick up his rental car at his destination). The delay caused him to miss the first half-day of the conference.

A more elaborate example was reported by Brenner (1957), from a case history of a patient. He had been unable to bring to mind the name of a friend when the two met at a social event. As the patient talked, it became clear that his friend had the same name as someone else the patient disliked. It also became clear that he felt guilty about the dislike. Finally, the patient mentioned that his friend was disabled, which reminded him of his wish to harm the disliked person.

Why, then, did the patient forget his friend's name? Brenner believed that the sight of the disabled friend had unconsciously reminded him of the other man, whom he wished to hurt. To prevent this hostile impulse from becoming conscious—and bringing the guilt with it—the patient repressed the name that would have estab-lished the link between the two. Because the motive for the repression and the re-pression itself were both unconscious, the patient was unable to identify the cause of the memory lapse.

If forgetting is a successful act of repression, slips of the tongue and pen are par-tially *un*successful acts of repression. That is, the person inadvertently expresses all or part of the unconscious thought or wish, despite the effort to keep it hidden. As with forgetting, the hidden meaning is sometimes obvious to observers. Consider the woman who reveals her ambivalent feelings toward her lover by telling him he's exactly the kind of person she'd like to "bury" (instead of "marry"). At other times the hidden meaning is hard to decipher and can be established only with the help of the person who makes the slip.

There's evidence that these verbal slips are related to anxiety, although the evi-dence falls short of indicating that the anxiety is unconscious. Motley (1985) and his colleagues have done studies inducing people to make a certain kind of slip. In this slip a pair of words is read as a different word pair (for example, saying "flute fry" in-stead of "fruit fly"). The research requires creating specific pairs that are easy to mis-read into slips with particular overtones. The studies involve creating specific anxieties and seeing whether those anxieties increase relevant slips.

For example, in one case males were made to feel anxious about receiving elec-tric shocks. In another, the session was run by a provocatively dressed woman, to arouse anxiety over sexual issues. Both conditions included word pairs that could be misread as shock-related (e.g., "damn shock" instead of "sham dock") and pairs that could be misread as sex-related (e.g., "happy sex" instead of "sappy hex"). As can be seen in Figure 9.3, men led to be nervous about shocks made more shock-related slips than anyone else; men led to be thinking about sex made more slips with sexual con-notations than anyone else. Another study found that sexual slips were most frequent among men high on a measure of sex guilt (Motley, 1985).

When accused of making a slip, most people attribute it to factors such as fa-tigue, distraction, or haste. Freud held that such factors facilitate but don't cause slips. The real cause always comes from the unconscious. A person is more likely to

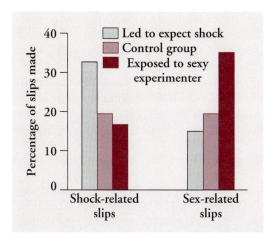

Figure 9.3

Freudian slips induced in the laboratory. When participants expected to receive electric shocks, they made more shock-related slips (left side). When participants had been exposed to a provocatively dressed experimenter, they made more sex-related slips (right side) (adapted from Motley, 1985).

make a slip of the tongue or pen when tired or inattentive, but the form of the slip depends on unconscious forces.

Accidents, on the other hand, are more complicated. Accidents that are most interesting from a psychoanalytic point of view are those that stem from the carelessness of the person involved. To decide whether something is an accident, you must look at the circumstances. If you learn a man was struck by a motorboat while scuba diving,

Freud believed that accidents often result from an unconscious desire to cause harm.

you might think it an accident. But if you learn that the man, an experienced diver, failed to put out a diving marker and didn't pause to listen for motors before surfacing, you might be more inclined to conclude that (for whatever reason) he had an unconscious desire to do himself harm.

Accidents are complicated for another reason as well. Because they can involve injury, accidents can serve several functions at once. In harming yourself, you can also harm someone else—someone who cares for you. In this sense, an accident can serve both as crime (causing someone else to feel bad) and as punishment (causing you to suffer an injury).

Dreams

Freud (1953b/1900) believed the unconscious also reveals itself through dreams. Indeed, he referred to dreams as "the royal road to the unconscious." Freud began by distinguishing two kinds of dream content. **Manifest content** is the sensory images of the dreamer, what most of us think of as the dream. More interesting, to Freud, was the **latent content,** the unconscious thoughts, feelings, and wishes that give rise to manifest content. Latent content tells why a dream takes the form it takes (see Box 9.3 for another view).

Freud believed that latent content derives from three sources. The first is the *sensory stimulation* that bombards us as we sleep: a thunderstorm, a passing siren, or the barking of a dog. These sounds can prompt dreams and be incorporated into them. When this happens, the stimulation is part of the dream's latent content. Dreams are said to be "guardians of sleep," because bringing an outside stimulus into a dream prevents the stimulus from awakening the sleeper.

The second source of latent dream content is thoughts, ideas, and feelings connected to the sleeper's waking life—**current concerns**—which remain active in the unconscious while you sleep. For example, during the day you may have been thinking about an upcoming exam, an unfinished project, an interesting person you'd just met, or a financial problem you've got. Incorporating thoughts about that topic into dreams prevents them from waking you, just as with sensory stimuli.

The third source of latent dream content is unconscious *id impulses* that the ego has blocked from expression while you're awake. Often these impulses relate to childhood conflicts. For this reason, the impulse is often infantile in form and primitive in content. Freud believed that every dream incorporates some unconscious impulse or urge.

Manifest content consists of conscious sensory impressions (usually visual). Manifest content is a fantasy in which the latent wish or impulse is expressed. To use a term from Chapter 8, the dream is *wish fulfillment* on the part of the id.

During early childhood, the tie between latent and manifest content is quite transparent. Consider the dream of a two-year-old boy a few days after his mother brought home a new baby from the hospital (Brenner, 1957). The boy reported as manifest content, "See baby go away." It takes little imagination to infer the latent content, especially as the mother felt the boy had been hostile toward the new baby's arrival from the moment he learned of the impending event. In this case, then, the dream's manifest content was a direct translation of the latent content—the boy's wish to have the new baby no longer a part of his life. The manifest content simply fulfilled this wish in the form of visual images.

During later childhood and adulthood, the relationship between latent and manifest content becomes less obvious. Indeed, dreams sometimes seem complete

BOX 9.3

FUNCTIONS OF SLEEP AND DREAMS

Sleep has long been a source of wonder and mystery. Each of us, willing or not, spends a substantial part of each twenty-four-hour day in a state suspended somewhere between life and death. And what are dreams? Fragmented recollections of journeys to other dimensions? Bits of truth whispered by gods (on the condition we not remember them for long)? Are dreams reflections of the primary process, visual echoes of the snarling and lurid passions of the id? Or are they just a jumble of nonsense, mutterings of a brain left to idle like a car at a red light?

In Freud's time, little was known about sleep and dreams. It seemed natural to him to think of dreams as the pathway to the unconscious, given their surreal and symbolic qualities. In later years, though, scientists have studied sleep and dreaming, and at least a little more is now known about them (e.g., Hobson, 1988; Winson, 1985, 1990).

What do we know? For starters, everybody dreams, although many people don't remember them. A breakthrough was the discovery of a sleep state in which people's eyes move rapidly, breathing becomes irregular, heart rate increases, and movement is suppressed (Aserinsky & Kleitman, 1953). Because rapid eye movement (REM) seems to be a key feature of the state, it is known as REM sleep. People awakened from REM sleep almost always report that they were dreaming. People awakened from non-REM sleep rarely say that. REM sleep occurs four or five times a night for adults; infants spend nearly eight hours a day in REM sleep.

Several other things about REM sleep: first, it occurs in other mammals as well as humans. Second, it seems not to occur in animals *other than* mammals. Third, whatever's going on in REM sleep apparently is necessary. When people are kept out of REM (by being awakened whenever it starts), they show a stronger tendency to enter it.

Why is REM sleep necessary? And if REM sleep is dreaming, what in the world are *infants* dreaming so much about? After piecing together evidence from several sources, Winson (1985) made the following argument: a basic problem in biological adaptation is how to integrate new experiences with old ones. Winson argued that, among mammals, this takes place during REM sleep. If this were so, a single set of neuronal structures could serve two purposes: guiding action when you're awake, and consolidating and integrating knowledge when you're asleep. Thus, we can get the most out of our nervous system, since it's being used round the clock rather than just when we're awake.

Why then do infants dream so much? Perhaps the processes that produce consolidation also are involved in the final stage of cortical development. Perhaps it's because the almost complete absence of a personal history means that infants have to do more consolidation than adults.

Winson (1985) argued that the paths of symbolic association that fascinated Freud reflect a more prosaic fact. Consolidation is a process of following mental associations, even associations that are odd and tangential. In this view, the brain is simply doing its homework in the dreaming state, linking the experiences of the day (and the week) to all the various categories to which they relate. Symbolic associations are just one more set of links.

Recent work adds yet a little more information: it turns out that during REM sleep two important areas of the brain are essentially shut down (Braun et al., 1998). One of them is the part of the cortex that handles visual input from the eyes. Whatever is forming visual aspects of the dream is apparently coming from memory, with no help from the regions that create vision "on line." The other area shut down is the frontal lobes, which provide working memory, among other things. If there's no workspace for sorting through things, any consolidation that's being done in REM sleep is probably subtle and low-level. The absence of frontal activity would help account, however, for why dreamers seem to accept uncritically bizarre events in their dreams.

gibberish. How can such dreams relate to wish fulfillment? The answer is that with age it becomes more important to distort or disguise the dream's latent content. The ego and the superego must remain unaware that an unacceptable impulse is being expressed. Keeping them unaware gets harder as people grow. Thus, even in dreams the defense mechanisms remain at work.

Two processes allow forbidden impulses to be represented in the manifest content of dreams. One is called **symbolization.** In symbolization, unacceptable latent content is expressed in manifest content directly but symbolically. The symbol is a form that's less recognizable to the ego and the superego and is thereby less threatening. Symbolization might be considered the dreaming equivalent of sublimation.

The second way in which latent content is translated into manifest content is called **dream work.** In dream work, latent content is disguised in other ways to make it more acceptable to the ego and the superego. It involves several mechanisms. In **condensation,** separate thoughts are compressed and combined into a single unified thought. The combination is less threatening than the separate thoughts. When several thoughts are jumbled, it's harder to tell what's what, and the threat is reduced.

In the **mechanism of opposites** an unacceptable element of latent content is expressed manifestly as the opposite of its latent form. For example, a boy who fears his dog will run away might dream of the dog's returning to him from a journey. A woman who secretly wishes her husband dead may dream of holding a celebration for him. This distortion resembles the defense mechanism of reaction formation, employed during waking hours.

Because dream work operates according to primary-process thought, resulting manifest content is often chaotic. To cause it to make better sense, a dreamer will often fill in missing elements or build up a sketchy part of a dream (Freud, 1933). This part of the dream is actually unrelated to the latent content. The process of making dreams more understandable is called **secondary elaboration.** Secondary elaboration also diminishes threat by further disguising the urges and desires that underlie the dream.

Interpretation of dreams involves examining manifest content, seeking its unconscious meaning. Freud believed many symbols that appear in dreams are unique to the dreamer. He also believed, however, that there are certain categories of shared symbols that have shared meanings (Box 9.4). The universality of some symbols makes dream analysis easier.

Humor

A final way in which the unconscious reveals itself is humor (Freud, 1960a/1905). Humor often rests on threatening desires or impulses that are transformed in amusing ways. Much humor, for example, reflects underlying hostility. This hostility is blunted by its distortion into something ludicrous. Many jokes depend on an underlying inhibited thought. The joke-telling slips around the inhibition, diverts attention, and permits the internal censor of the ego to relax. When the punch line comes, the forbidden thought is abruptly expressed, too fast for the censor to recover. The energy previously devoted to restraining the forbidden thought is released in laughter.

Humor is similar to dreams in some respects, for example, in use of condensation and symbolism. They differ, though, in important ways. Dreams permit the urges of the unconscious to emerge only in a symbolic and unrecognizable form. Humor, in contrast, is communicated from one person to another. Whereas dreams conceal their latent content, joking tends to expose the underlying content more completely (Oring, 1984). There's protection from threat in the symbolism and the laughter, but the latent content is far closer to the surface than in dreams.

BOX 9.4

DREAM ANALYSIS

As noted in the main text, Freud believed insights about personality could be gained by dream analysis. One step in dream analysis is translating manifest content into latent (unconscious) content. Some symbols in dreams are idiosyncratic: to understand them you need to know something about the meaning the *dreamer* attaches to them. Others are more universal.

Freud believed that latent content concerns a relatively small number of things, which are symbolized in dreams in a wide variety of ways. The important elements underlying dreams are the human body, parents, children, siblings, birth, death, nakedness, and sexual activity. Here are some common dream symbols and their psychoanalytic interpretations:

- Authority figures—kings, queens, police officers, and so on—represent parents.
- Small animals—mice, squirrels—symbolize children.
- Reference to water signifies birth; going on a journey symbolizes dying.
- Uniforms and clothes stand for nakedness (through the mechanism of opposites).
- A house symbolizes the human body. If it has plain walls, it's a man. If there are ledges, balconies, or other kinds of projections outward, it's a woman.

In keeping with other aspects of psychoanalytic theory, sexual activity is seen as most richly represented of all. There are many symbols of male and female genitalia. For example, the number 3 stands for male genitals as a group (penis and testicles). The penis itself is symbolized by a wide range of images, some by their shape (e.g., sticks, umbrellas, poles, golf clubs), others by their penetrating function (e.g., knives, daggers) or by their function as devices through which things flow or erupt (e.g., hypodermic needles,

fire hoses, faucets, pistols, rifles). Yet others symbolize the penis by their capacity to lengthen or to rise up in defiance of gravity (e.g., airplanes, blimps, balloons, and expanding telescopes).

Female genitals are symbolized by objects that enclose spaces or serve as receptacles (e.g., pits, caves, bottles, jars, pockets, shoes). Rooms, cupboards, and ovens are symbols of the uterus. Things that can be opened and closed (e.g., gates, doors, windows) are symbols for the vagina. Breasts are symbolized by fruits (e.g., peaches, melons, apples). Lush landscapes and gardens also represent female genitals. Other female symbols include wood and paper, snails, oysters, clams, churches, and chapels.

Sexual pleasure is often symbolized by candy or sugar-covered fruit. Play—for example, playing musical instruments or group games—symbolizes masturbation. Masturbation is also represented by activities such as sliding or gliding or pulling something off something else. Sexual intercourse is implied in any kind of rhythmic activity—for example, dancing, riding, and jogging. It can also be symbolized by the image of being threatened by a weapon or by being the victim of violence—for example, being run over by a car or train.

A word of caution is in order here. We've listed common symbols and their typical interpretations to give you a look at how dreams may give insight into unconscious processes. We emphasize, though, that dreams aren't interpreted strictly on the basis of "typical" meanings. Because some of the meaning is unique to the dreamer, it's also essential to know what personal significance the dream has for the dreamer. If you're tempted to try out these symbols on your own dreams, keep this in mind.

Projective Techniques of Assessment

The preceding sections focused on ways in which the unconscious reveals itself in everyday life. We now turn to ways in which the unconscious reveals itself in formal assessment, as practiced from the psychoanalytic perspective.

Formal methods of assessing unconscious processes are called **projective techniques** (Frank, 1939). These tests confront people with ambiguous stimuli. Because there's no obvious response, people's responses are determined primarily by their own feelings, attitudes, desires, and needs (recall our discussion of the TAT as a projective technique in Chapter 5). These tests allow people to apply the defense mechanism of projection to their hidden feelings and put the feelings into their interpretations of what they see. What's projected presumably is beyond the person's conscious control and thus reflects the unconscious.

Several projective techniques exist. In *associative* techniques, people respond to a stimulus with the first word or thought that comes to mind. *Constructive* techniques involve creating stories. *Completion* techniques involve completing a thought begun in an incomplete stimulus, such as a sentence that begins, "I wish. . . ."

Although the techniques differ in format, they share several features. They all use stimuli that are ambiguous. The test taker is never told the purpose of the test. Instructions stress that there are no right or wrong answers and that the test takers can respond in whatever way they wish. Finally, because of the open-ended and ambiguous nature of the technique, scoring relies heavily on subjective clinical judgments.

We focus for the rest of this section on one device that's often used to assess unconscious processes: the **Rorschach inkblot test.**

Rorschach Inkblot Test

Swiss psychiatrist Hermann Rorschach is usually credited with systematizing the use of inkblots for assessment (Rorschach, 1942). He tried geometric patterns but found them too structured. He began to experiment with inkblots. He finally arrived at a set of ten blots, chosen for their ability to evoke different responses from different groups of psychiatric patients. (His strategy thus made use of the criterion-keying approach to test development, described in Chapter 3.)

The ten inkblots in the Rorschach set are all bilaterally symmetrical, meaning that they are approximately the same on both sides of an imaginary center line (Figure 9.4). The ink on five of them is all black, but the intensity is uneven, ranging

Figure 9.4

Example of inkblot similar to those used in the Rorschach test. (Courtesy of Jeremy Matthews Scheier and Meredith Matthews Scheier.)

from solid black to light gray. Two have both black and red ink. The remaining three are composed of diverse pastel colors, including blue, green, yellow, and orange.

The Rorschach usually is administered to one person at a time in a two-stage procedure. First the person views the inkblots in a predetermined order and indicates what he or she sees in them, or what the inkblot resembles or suggests, while the examiner records what's being said. Then the person views all ten cards again. The examiner provides reminders of what was said earlier about the card and asks what it was about the card that made the person say that.

Several systems have been devised for scoring the Rorschach. The most popular by far is that of John Exner (1974, 1993). In Exner's system the responses are first compared against those of people with known personality characteristics. Then the person's responses are examined as a progression from one card to the next. Finally, content is analyzed in terms of location, determinants, and content. *Location* is where in the blot the response focuses (the whole blot, a commonly noted detail, an unusual detail, the space surrounding the blot). *Determinants* of the response include form, color, shading, or perceived movement in the location that prompted the response. The *content* of the response is its subject matter. Table 9.1 has examples of common interpretations of specific responses. Be aware, however, that a given response is interpreted only in the context of the entire test profile.

Although it's interesting as a technique, the Rorschach has serious psychometric problems. Its internal consistency is low, its test-retest reliability and inter-rater reliability are low, and its validity has been hard to establish (Anastasi, 1988; Lilienfeld,

Table 9.1

Rorschach Inkblot Responses. Here are three categories in which responses to the Rorschach are placed. In the left column is the category name, followed by its definition in the second column. The third column gives examples of responses that would be placed into each category. The right column gives an interpretation for each example and an indication of why this interpretation is made.

Name of Category	Nature of Category	Example Response	Possible Interpretation (with critical feature identified)
Location	Place on blot from which response arose	"Overall, it reminds me of a cornstalk."	Suggests ability to think conceptually (response is based on whole blot)
		"That thing there looks like a hammer."	Suggests need to be exact and precise (response is based on a commonly noted detail)
Determinant	Quality of blot that led to response	"It's a whale bleeding."	Suggests high degree of emotionality (response is based on color)
		"It's a bat flying."	Suggests high degree of imagination (response is based on perceived movement)
Content	Subject matter of response	"It's a man about to be beaten up by others."	Suggests anxiety over hostile feelings (response involves aggression)
		"It's a person diving into the ocean waves."	Suggests strong fantasy life (response involves *human* movement)

Wood, & Garb, 2000). Exner and his collaborators have tried to improve these qualities. Recently, however, their efforts came under fire. Wood, Nezworski, and Stejskal (1996a, 1996b) criticized Exner's work on several methodological grounds bearing on issues of reliability and validity (see also Lilienfeld et al., 2000). On the other side, Ganellen (1996a, 1996b) has reported that the Rorschach does better at identifying depressed and psychotic persons than does the MMPI-2. Some of the issues raised in the critiques of Exner's scoring system are technical, some are not (for example, the fact that so much of the relevant evidence is unpublished). Wood et al.'s conclusions have been disputed by Exner (1996). It seems clear that this argument is not over.

Many who favor projective tests respond to the criticisms by saying that psychometric criteria are irrelevant to the Rorschach's usefulness. In their view, its value is in the insights it gives the examiner. Perhaps psychologists should stop treating the Rorschach as a test and think of it instead as a clinical tool. From this perspective the Rorschach would be a supplementary interview aid in the hands of a trained clinician, giving clues and suggesting hypotheses worthy of further investigation.

It's too early to say how the Rorschach (and instruments like it) will come to be viewed. Continued efforts to standardize scoring procedures may yield better psychometric properties. Even if the Rorschach is viewed only as a clinical aid, though, it is not likely to be discarded soon as part of the psychoanalytic assessment battery.

Problems in Behavior, and Behavior Change

This chapter has emphasized two ideas: first, people use ego defenses to protect themselves against anxiety. Second, repressed urges and memories continue to influence behavior via these defenses. Psychoanalytic theorists believe that everyone uses defense mechanisms. Merely using defense mechanisms is not a sign that the person has a problem.

On the other hand, this is a viewpoint on personality in which normalcy shades easily into abnormality, with no clear boundary. Psychoanalytic theorists tend to distinguish normal from abnormal functioning by how much defense mechanisms dominate the person's life. Too much use of defenses is a sign of problems. Heavy use of defenses can save the person from dealing with conflicts, but it ties up too much energy in anticathexes. This leaves little energy for the person to use in dealing with new challenges. As the person's level of functioning begins to deteriorate, it becomes clearer that this is someone with a problem.

Our discussion of problems and how they can be dealt with emphasizes the themes stressed all along. Freud believed the unconscious holds the secrets of people's difficulties in life. Only by delving into the unconscious can those difficulties be identified and resolved. This section begins by considering the psychoanalytic perspective on ways in which problems arise.

Origins of Problems

Problems have several possible origins. One origin is experiences in childhood. As stated in Chapter 8, Freud believed adult personality is determined by early psychosexual development. If the person handles early stages successfully, relatively little residue is carried into adulthood. However, it's rare for a person to enter the later stages of development unmarked. Most persons are partly fixated at earlier stages. If fixations are strong, a great deal of energy is invested in them. In a very strong fixation, the preoccupation—albeit unconscious—leaves the person with little energy for anything else. This is one source of problems: overinvestment of energy in a fixation. This prevents flexible adult functioning by depleting energy the ego requires (Baumeister, 2002).

Another source of problems is a broad repression of basic needs and urges. If an overly punitive superego or a harsh environment causes too many urges to be buried, the person's fundamental nature is distorted and denied. The person is cramped and can't function in the way he or she is supposed to function. The repressed needs can squeeze their way past the repression only in distorted forms. This isn't really effective in meeting the needs. Again, the repression required to keep the needs hidden is a constant drain on energy available to the ego.

A third source of problems is buried trauma. Although traumatic incidents can occur at any point in life, most discussion of trauma focuses on early childhood. Indeed, at one point early in the evolution of his thinking, Freud believed the majority of his patients had suffered childhood sexual abuse. The "seduction theory," as it came to be known, was later abandoned when Freud decided the seductions hadn't actually taken place.

It was this change in his thinking that led to his theory of the Oedipal conflict (Chapter 8), in which children deal with a sexual attraction to their opposite-sex parent. The Oedipal theory accounted for sexual imagery among patients, and it did so in a way that didn't require Freud to conclude that large numbers of parents had seduced their children (though see Box 9.5).

Despite this change, Freud's theory clearly holds a place for traumatic experiences such as sexual or physical abuse. His altered view simply reflects his conclusion that such experiences aren't the norm. Still, a child who experiences physical abuse, especially repeated abuse, has a deeply unpleasant part of reality to deal with. The same is true of a child who is sexually abused. Indeed, many events that objectively are far less traumatic can loom large in the experience of a child: rejection by a parent, death of a person (or a pet) close to the child, exposure to fighting parents. Children who experience traumas such as these have large threats to deal with. They're dealt with first and foremost by repression—always the first response to overwhelming anxiety. Once again, the energy invested in forgetting is a constant drain on resources.

These three points of origin for problems differ, and the problems that result may also differ. All three paths, however, share one mechanism. In each case the original fixation, urge, or trauma is repressed. This repression may protect the person, but it does so at a cost.

Behavior Change

What to do about this situation? The therapeutic methods of psychoanalysis developed through a period of trial and error in Freud's practice. His understanding of how to deal with problems evolved along with his views on the *bases* of those problems. Early on, he found that symptoms could be reduced by hypnotically inducing the person to relive highly emotional (and thus repressed) events—relive them fully and emotionally. The release of energy seemed to free the person from the problem by diminishing the energy investment in the repressed event. This experience is often referred to as a *catharsis*, because of the release of emotional energy.

Two discoveries radically changed Freud's approach. First, he found it wasn't necessary to hypnotize people. If the person simply said aloud whatever came to mind—a procedure called **free association**—the secrets of the unconscious would gradually emerge. In free association the person is encouraged not to censor any

BOX 9.5

SEDUCTION FANTASIES, CHILD MOLESTATION, OR NEITHER?

A controversy arose in the 1980s about Freud's abandonment of his seduction theory of the origin of psychological disorder. As indicated in the main text, Freud eventually "realized" that the accounts he heard from patients weren't literally true. The women hadn't been seduced as children. Rather, they had unconsciously distorted their own sexual desires for their parents into a symbolic form and projected it outward.

That's the way Freud put it: he'd realized the truth. In 1984, however, Jeffrey Masson challenged that statement. Drawing from previously unpublished letters, he argued that the seductions were in fact real, that Freud knew it, and that he'd chosen to back away from their reality. Masson said Freud lacked the courage to stand by the shameful truth that child sexual abuse was widespread.

Why would Freud lack the courage to stand up for what he believed? Masson argued that a possible reason concerns Freud's professional reputation. His first presentation of the seduction theory, in a speech to a professional society, was met with utter silence. Masson said Freud was later urged not to publish it (though others contradict this assertion, Ellenberger, 1970; Esterson, 2002; McCullough, 2001). Perhaps Freud needed a way out, to salvage his career prospects.

Masson also argued that *seduction* is an extremely unfortunate label and that the word is not at all typical of Freud's first statement of the theory, in which he also used the terms *rape, abuse, attack, assault, aggression,*

and *trauma.* Even as the theory was being set aside, Masson suggested, use of the term *seduction* made the theory's implications seem more benign. Perhaps the terminology was one last defense against the truth.

Not everyone found Masson's account convincing. Some criticisms of his account are even less flattering to Freud than was Masson's own view. Esterson (1993, 2001) has argued that the seduction theory was a sham from the very start, that the so-called evidence of molestation in patient accounts simply did not exist. Esterson argues, in effect, that Freud projected his own preconceived ideas onto what his patients said. Freud himself even wrote that patients assured him they did not believe their recollections were of sexual contact (Esterson, 2001). Thus, to Esterson, the issue is not whether patient reports were recollection or fantasy. The important issue is that it wasn't the patients themselves who generated that material, but Freud himself (see also Schimek, 1987).

What really *is* the truth? We can't return to Freud's era to investigate the rate of child abuse. If Freud was aware of high rates of abuse, he might have interpreted any hint of sexual contact—even a symbolic hint—in such terms. But even more damaging is the implication of the assertion that he let himself be guided by his preconceptions, letting his interpretations stand in place of patient reports, as Esterson argues. If so, there would be little reason to believe either his seduction theory *or* its successor.

---

thoughts but to say immediately whatever thoughts arise, even if they seem trivial, illogical, or embarrassing. The therapist stays out of view during this procedure, to minimize the person's inhibitions against speaking.

Freud's second discovery was that what emerged from free association (and hypnotherapy) often wasn't literally true. As noted earlier, early cases had led him to believe patients had experienced childhood seductions. Eventually he decided those encounters had not taken place. This led to a reorganization in how Freud viewed not only the content of free association but also childhood sexuality. Free association was producing something important, but it wasn't quite what it had seemed to be.

In Freud's newer view, unconscious material emerges through free association in *symbolic* form. The symbolism renders it less threatening to the person, thus letting it emerge. Images of seduction are less threatening than images of one's own carnal desires. Free association often creates a jumble of symbols that make no sense on the surface. Yet, as in a crossword puzzle, they provide a partial context from which missing elements may be inferred (Erdelyi, 1985).

As noted above, many problems serious enough to produce behavioral manifestations stem from repressed conflicts and urges and from suppressed libidinal energy. The goal of therapy is to uncover the conflicts and unleash the restrained energy (see also Box 9.6). Free association is a first step to this, because it allows symbolic

BOX 9.6

REPRESSION, DISCLOSURE, AND HEALTH

Our main discussion focuses on the idea that repression has a psychological cost. Evidence is accumulating, however, that holding back thoughts and feelings can also have a *physical* cost. One example is a study of women undergoing breast biopsies (Greer & Morris, 1975). Women who reported suppressing their emotions (most notably anger) were more likely to have cancer than those who didn't (see also Jensen, 1987). Another study looked at atherosclerosis over a ten-year period (Matthews, Owens, Kuller, Sutton-Tyrrell, & Jansen-McWilliams, 1998). Women who reported in an initial interview that they held their anger in had greater atherosclerosis ten years later. Not all evidence supports the view that suppression relates to disease (O'Donnell, Fisher, Rickard, & McConaghy, 2000; Price et al., 2001). But enough support exists to make the possibility worth further study.

The flip side of this idea is that releasing threatening thoughts and feelings can have physical benefits. James Pennebaker and his colleagues have been at the forefront of research on disclosure of suppressed thoughts and feelings (Pennebaker, 1989, 1993; Pennebaker & Graybeal, 2001; see also Smyth, 1998). Participants in this research are asked to describe (with complete anonymity, in most studies) their deepest thoughts and feelings either about a specific nontraumatic event, or about "the most upsetting or traumatic experience of your entire life." Ideally, the event the participant is to talk about (or write about) is one that he or she hasn't talked about much with other people. Thus, it's more likely to be something that's been repressed, at least partially. The disclosure of thoughts and feelings typically takes place for about twenty minutes at a time on four successive days.

The short-term effect of disclosing traumatic events is that people feel more distress. In the longer term, however, self-disclosure seems to have health benefits. In one study, students who disclosed about traumatic events were less likely to visit the health center in the next six months than those not asked to disclose (Pennebaker & Beall, 1986). Results of another study suggest that disclosure has an influence on the functioning of the immune system (Pennebaker, Kiecolt-Glaser, & Glaser, 1988). In a study of Holocaust survivors, those who seemed to "let go" the most during disclosure were least likely to visit their physicians later (Pennebaker, 1989).

Why might disclosure of painful memories and the thoughts and feelings that accompany them have health benefits? Pennebaker is pursuing the idea that the mechanism lies in the cognitive changes that occur during and after the disclosures. He's found evidence that people who come to organize their experiences into causal narratives benefit more than people who do not (Pennebaker & Graybeal, 2001). Interestingly enough, it apparently isn't *having* a coherent story that helps, but the process of *creating* the story.

Pennebaker (1993) suggested that the body expresses itself linguistically and biologically at the same time. As we struggle to create meaning from trauma, we create beneficial changes in our biological functions as well. The result is better biological functioning and ultimately better health. This perspective on the consequences of emotional expression is one that surely will evoke controversy and interest in the coming years. It is a viewpoint with many important implications. If it continues to be supported by research evidence, it will change the way many people think about therapy, and even about such activities as keeping a diary!

access to the problem. It rarely reaches the heart of the problem, though, because of the threat value of the repressed material.

Indeed, people in therapy sometimes actively fight against becoming aware of repressed conflicts and impulses. This struggle is termed **resistance.** Resistance may be conscious, for instance when a person has an association that arouses anxiety but doesn't report it. Resistance also may occur unconsciously. Unconscious resistance reflects an automatic use of ego defenses against the possibility of anxiety. Its occurrence is usually a sign that something important is nearby, that the person is close to revealing something sensitive.

Whether conscious or unconscious, resistance provides an illustration of how emotionally wrenching the psychoanalytic therapy process can be. The person in therapy is trying to uncover distressing truths, truths that have been buried in the unconscious precisely *because* they're too painful to acknowledge. It's no wonder that the process of uncovering them is hard.

An important element in psychoanalytic therapy is **transference.** Transference is a set of *displacements*. Feelings toward people in the patient's conflicts and repressed desires are displaced (transferred) onto the therapist. The feelings can be love or hatred, depending on the underlying issue. Transference serves as another defense, in that the therapist provokes less anxiety than do the original objects of the feelings.

Transference can interfere with therapy because the patient may become caught up in what's being felt toward the therapist. These feelings themselves don't reveal the real conflict, because the conflict pertains to someone else. On the other hand, transference can point out the significance of the feelings that are being displaced. When transference occurs, then, its interpretation is an important part of the therapy process.

The goal of psychoanalytic psychology is **insight,** which is defined from this theoretical view as an emotional experiencing of previously unconscious parts of one's personality. Insight in therapy isn't an intellectual understanding. Rather, this term implies the reexperiencing of the emotional reality of repressed conflicts, memories, or urges (see also Table 9.2). Intellectual understanding has no power to change the person. For a cognitive reorganization to be useful, it must come in the context of an emotional catharsis. On the other hand, emotional release by itself is not helpful either (Kelly, Klusas, von Weiss, & Kenny, 2001).

The development of true insight allows the person to see how the conflicts and urges have influenced his or her functioning for years. The insight provides a basis to work from so that the person can attain greater acceptance of these previously unacceptable parts of the self. One result is that the person can get by with less defense in the future.

Table 9.2

Three origins of problems in personality and the goal of psychoanalysis in treating each.	
Origin	Goal
Fixation	Relive prior conflict to work through
Repressed trauma	Relive experience for catharsis of feelings
Repressed basic needs	Gain emotional insight into the needs and their acceptability

Does Psychoanalytic Therapy Work?

Psychoanalytic therapy is long (literally years) and usually painful. Given the costs, financial and emotional, an important question is whether it's effective. Even Freud's view changed over the years. Initially he was optimistic about psychoanalysis as therapy. He believed that patients, particularly those who were bright and well educated, could benefit from the insights they gained from therapy. He expected them to become better, and ultimately happier, people.

During the middle of his career, however, his thinking on this matter began to shift. He became more and more convinced that the real value of his work was in his theory of the mind, not the therapy. By the end of his career he'd become pessimistic about the effectiveness of psychoanalysis. He'd come to believe that most of what happens to a person is due to biological factors that are beyond anyone's control.

How effective *is* psychoanalytic therapy? Early reviews concluded that therapy in general, including psychoanalysis, isn't much help (Eysenck, 1961; Feldman, 1968; Wolpe, 1981). Other reviews, however, found that therapy works and that analytic therapy does about as well as other techniques (Smith & Glass, 1977; Smith, Glass, & Miller, 1980).

A problem in interpreting the studies stems from the fact that there are several ways to define success. Whether therapy is successful depends on how success is defined. It could be defined by a therapist's judgment of improvement. It could be defined by the patient's reports of less distress (symptoms such as anxiety or depression). These are, in fact, the ways in which success is typically defined in outcome research.

Psychoanalysts, however, tend to use different criteria of success. Although it's hard to find complete consensus, success in psychoanalysis is often defined by how much insight patients gain into their conflicts and dynamics (a judgment that can be made from the perspective of either patient or therapist). This insight may or may not yield less distress. Some believe, however, that the goal of psychoanalysis should be insight per se rather than reduced distress. Given this different goal, it's hard to be sure what negative findings say about the success of psychoanalytic therapy (for a more detailed discussion see Fisher & Greenberg, 1977).

This discussion also makes it more understandable why people continue to seek out and endure the painful effort of psychoanalysis. People who undergo this treatment must think that they're getting something out of it, or they wouldn't continue. It seems likely that people will find value in psychoanalysis if they believe the psychoanalytic perspective and believe insight is of value. Perhaps the hope of a better life that this conviction can bring is a sufficient benefit in itself to warrant undertaking the therapy process.

Psychoanalytic Defense: Problems and Prospects

The ideas presented in this chapter extend and elaborate on those in Chapter 8, adding complexity to the theory with respect to its problems and it prospects. These ideas also can be evaluated on their own merits. How do these ideas fare in today's personality psychology? What are their implications for the broader usefulness of psychoanalytic theory?

We said at the end of Chapter 8 that a problem with psychoanalysis is that its concepts are hard to test. The ideas in this chapter create an even larger problem in that respect. Specifically, defense mechanisms provide limitless flexibility. They can be used to explain virtually any pattern of behavior that might occur. Flexibility is good, because it allows a theory to account for a lot. However, it also makes prediction hard. If a theory is too flexible, you can reconcile *any* finding with it. To the extent that findings contrary to prediction can be "explained away" after the fact, the ideas being tested aren't tested at all.

Suppose, for example, you were interested in the idea that anal fixation is related to neatness. If the data show that neatness and anality are positively related, the idea is supported. But if the data show the opposite, that anal characters are the messiest of people, you just add a twist. You assume that the messiness is a defensive reaction formation, protecting these people against the anxiety that's created by their underlying need to be neat.

Given the defense mechanisms assumed by psychoanalytic theory, such a twist can always be invoked. If a desire is too threatening, it's repressed. It emerges from the unconscious in a disguised or distorted form, even completely opposite to its original form. If this is too threatening (perhaps because a reversal doesn't hide the threat well enough because it's too "obvious"), then a different distortion occurs. Thus, the theory is amenable to virtually any outcome. As a result, predictions from it can never be disconfirmed. Unfortunately, when a theory can never be disconfirmed, it can never really be confirmed, either.

Despite these criticisms, the basic idea that humans have defenses and self-protective tendencies has been absorbed deeply into the fabric of today's understanding of personality. This principle has been widely accepted, even by people who accept nothing else of the psychodynamic viewpoint.

Other criticisms of the elements of the psychoanalytic perspective introduced in this chapter concern the techniques for assessing personality and for therapy. Assessment in this perspective relies largely on projective techniques. As we said earlier, these techniques have been subjected to serious criticism. It's not clear that projective tests will ever live up to the psychometric standards set by most personality psychologists.

Regarding psychoanalytic therapy, disagreement about its efficacy reflects disagreement on its goals. A further difficulty in evaluating psychoanalysis as therapy is that information isn't always available to verify insights that emerge during therapy. If someone experiences a sudden realization that she's always resented her mother, who died five years ago, is this a "realization" or a self-deception? If you free associate long enough, eventually you'll recall bad feelings about almost anyone. But in many cases it's hard to tell how important the bad feelings actually were.

Given the various problems associated with psychoanalytic theory, why has it been so popular? Indeed, there's been a resurgence of interest in psychoanalytic theory in recent years, after a period of diminished influence (the American Psychoanalytic Association accredits twenty-two institutes and centers throughout the United States). There seem to be at least three reasons for this enduring popularity. One is that Freud's was the first comprehensive theory of personality. Whenever something comes first, its influence persists for a long time. Second, Freud spoke to questions and issues that lie at the heart of personality: how does childhood influence later life? What is mental health? To what extent are people's motives accessible to them? The questions he posed began to stake out the territory of what would become personality psychology.

A final reason for the theory's popularity concerns the intuitive appeal of its major themes. Any metaphor that's incorporated into a language is adopted because it captures an element of reality in a striking and vivid way. Psychoanalytic theory uses many images and metaphors. Their scientific status aside, notions such as libido, unconscious motivation, psychosexual development, and the intrapsychic tug-of-war of conflicting pressures from id, ego, and superego have an emotional appeal. The ideas are novel, exciting, and interesting. In a word, they are seductive. Freud's theory undoubtedly established its foothold in part because it portrayed personality in a way that people found—and continue to find—interesting.

SUMMARY

Anxiety is a warning signal to the ego. Reality anxiety is fear of a threat in the world. Neurotic anxiety is fear that id impulses will get out of control and get you in trouble. Moral anxiety is fear of violating the superego's moral code. The ego deals with anxiety (and sometimes prevents it from arising) by employing defense mechanisms.

The basic defense is repression—forcing id impulses and other threatening material out of consciousness. Repression is useful, but it ties up energy. Denial is a refusal to acknowledge the reality of something that lies outside the mind. Other defenses, which typically operate along with repression, are projection (attributing your unacceptable impulse to someone else), rationalization (developing a plausible and acceptable but incorrect explanation for your action), intellectualization (separating your thoughts from your feelings and allowing the thoughts but not the feelings to enter awareness), reaction formation (behaving in a way opposite to the initial impulse), regression (returning to a mode of behavior characteristic of an earlier stage of development), displacement (shifting an impulse from one target to another, usually a safer one), and sublimation (transforming an unacceptable impulse to an acceptable one).

The psychoanalytic orientation holds that the unconscious is the key to personality. Freud believed that the unconscious reveals itself in many ways in day-to-day life. Parapraxes are slips of the tongue and pen that occur when unconscious desires cause you to act in a way other than you consciously intend. Similar processes are believed to underlie many accidents. Unconscious processes are also revealed in humor and in dreams. Dreams have manifest content (what's in the dream) and latent content (the determinants of the dream, many of which are unconscious). Manifest content usually is symbolic of latent content, which also may be distorted through other mechanisms termed *dream work*.

The unconscious can also be revealed more formally, through projective assessment techniques such as the Rorschach inkblot test. Projective techniques allow the person's unconscious to release symbolic versions of threatening material while describing ambiguous stimuli. The Rorschach is somewhat controversial in that its reliability and validity have not been strongly supported by research evidence.

In the psychoanalytic view, behavioral problems reflect an overuse of defenses. Problems may derive from fixations (unresolved conflicts at a pregenital stage of psychosexual development), from a general repression of libido, or from repressed traumas. In any case, too much energy is spent in confining the threatening material within the unconscious. The goal of therapy is to release some of the repression, thereby freeing some of the energy.

Psychoanalytic therapy begins with free association, saying whatever comes to mind without censoring it in any way. This approach typically produces an incomplete matrix of symbolic meanings from which other elements can be inferred. People in therapy often display resistance, which implies that the ego is trying to defend itself against something that the therapy is beginning to touch on. Eventually the person in therapy displays transference, displacing onto the therapist the feelings associated with the person about whom the conflicts exist. The goal of the therapy is insight, an emotional experiencing of previously unconscious parts of one's personality.

Freud came to believe that psychoanalysis was not as beneficial as he had first thought. This pessimistic view also emerged from some evaluation studies of the therapy process, although more recent studies have been more encouraging. Even in the absence of strong support for the usefulness of psychoanalytic therapy, many people continue to engage in it because they believe it provides benefits that are not adequately assessed by the measures used in outcome research.

GLOSSARY

Anxiety An aversive feeling warning the ego that something bad is about to happen.

Condensation The compression and combination of several thoughts in a dream.

Current concerns Preoccupations in one's current waking life.

Defense mechanism An ego-protective strategy to hide threats from yourself and thereby reduce anxiety.

Denial A refusal to believe that some real condition exists.

Displacement The shifting of an impulse from its original target to a different one.

Dream work Processes that distort latent dream content and transform it into manifest content.

Free association A therapy procedure of saying without hesitation whatever comes to mind.

Insight An emotional reexperiencing of earlier conflicts in one's life that occurs during therapy.

Intellectualization The process of thinking about something clinically and without emotion.

Latent content The underlying sources of symbolic dream images.

Manifest content The images that make up the dream experience as it is recalled.

Mechanism of opposites Dreaming the opposite of what you fear.

Moral anxiety The fear of behaving in conflict with the superego's moral code.

Neurotic anxiety The fear that your id impulses will get out of control and get you into trouble.

Parapraxis A slip of the tongue, behavior, or memory.

Projection Ascribing a threatening urge or quality in yourself to someone else.

Projective techniques An assessment in which you project from the unconscious onto ambiguous stimuli.

Rationalization Finding an acceptable but incorrect explanation for an action or event.

Reaction formation Doing the opposite of what your impulses are.

Reality anxiety The fear of danger in the world.

Regression A return to a mode of coping from an earlier developmental stage.

Repression The process of keeping an idea or impulse in the unconscious.

Resistance An attempt to avoid becoming conscious of threatening material in therapy.

Rorschach inkblot test A projective test that uses inkblots as ambiguous stimuli.

Secondary elaboration The filling out of the content of a dream to make it somewhat sensible.

Sublimation The alteration of an id impulse into a socially acceptable act.

Symbolization The transformation of unacceptable latent dream content into less threatening symbols.

Transference The displacement onto your therapist of feelings that are tied to an object of conflict.

The Neoanalytic
Perspective

THE NEOANALYTIC PERSPECTIVE:
Major Themes and Underlying Assumptions

As the term *neoanalytic* implies, this perspective on personality derives in part from the psychoanalytic perspective. Freud attracted many followers and colleagues. All of them adopted aspects of his viewpoint, but they also differed from him in important ways. They dealt with their ambivalence about psychoanalysis by recasting and embellishing Freud's ideas in their own terms. In doing so, they deemphasized aspects of his theory they disliked, and they expanded those they liked. Their disagreements with Freud are basic enough that their views seem distinctly different from Freud's. For this reason, we've chosen to treat them as a distinct perspective on personality.

These "post-Freudian" psychodynamic theorists were fairly diverse in their thinking. As a result, there are as many different post-Freudian theories as there were theorists. Treatment of each theory by itself can create a jumble of ideas that's hard to keep straight. On the other hand, although the theories are distinct in some ways, there are at least two themes that many of them share. As a result, the two chapters in this section of the book don't simply discuss each theory in isolation from the others. Rather, the focus is on several of the theories which most clearly reflect the two themes that are most salient in post-Freudian psychodynamic thinking. Points made by other theorists that supplement these core ideas are introduced where they seem most relevant.

The theorists who form the neoanalytic group differed from Freud on several grounds. Some neoanalytic theorists were bothered by Freud's emphasis on the importance of sexuality and the idea that sexual issues are important even in infancy. Others took issue with Freud's strong emphasis on the importance of unconscious processes. Perhaps the most frequent criticism among Freud's followers, however, was that he didn't give enough attention to the ego. As a result, many neoanalytic theories focus on the ego and how it functions. As a group, these theories emphasize the existence of certain ego processes and how they come to be. This line of thinking is the focus of Chapter 10.

Theorists who emphasize ego functioning and ego development tend to focus more on how the ego works than on the content of the problems and situations it confronts. However, a second group of neoanalytic theories focuses on the question of what kinds of situations are central in the ego's transactions with the world. In general, the theorists of this second group have held that the ego's primary tasks revolve around the quality of the person's relations with other people. The theories deriving from this assumption focus on how the ego interacts with, and is affected by, other individuals and the broader social and cultural matrix. The theories with this emphasis on social interaction are described in Chapter 11.

10 | *Ego Psychology*

■ **Principles of Ego Psychology**
Shifting the Emphasis from Id to Ego
Adaptation and Autonomy
The Ego, Adaptation, and Competence Motivation
Is Competence Striving Automatic,
    or Is It Done to Remedy Inferiority?
Ego Control and Ego Resiliency
Ego Control, Ego Resiliency,
    and the Five-Factor Model

■ **Ego Development**
Early Ego Development
Middle Stages of Ego Development:
    Control of Impulses
Advanced Stages of Ego Development:
    Taking More into Account
Research on Ego Development
Ego Development and the Five-Factor Model

■ **Assessment**
Assessment of Lifestyles
Assessment of Level of Ego Development

■ **Problems In Behavior,
    and Behavior Change**
Inferiority and Superiority Complexes
Overcontrol and Undercontrol
Behavior Change

■ **Ego Psychology:
    Problems and Prospects**

SUMMARY

■   Jeremy has an apparently irresistible attraction to video and computer games. He will sit transfixed for hours at a time in front of any challenging game. When he isn't pumping quarters into an arcade machine, he's parked in front of his computer, trying out whatever new game has just come out. His scores are so high that most of his friends have stopped playing with him. It's just Jeremy and the machine, locked in combat. Why? It's obviously not that he wants to be best in his group, or even the best in town (he's long since been that). When asked, Jeremy shrugs and replies that he simply feels a desire to be better than he already is. "It's hard to explain—I just want to be as good at it as I can be."

W hy do people spend large amounts of time becoming good at things that have no practical significance? Name an activity, and people somewhere spend countless hours perfecting their skills at it: bowling, golf, cow-chip tossing, ballet, hog calling, and—yes—video games. Why? Psychoanalysis said there's an explanation for everything. You just need to find a symbolic meaning behind the activity. But how do you feel about the idea that getting good at video games is, for example, a symbolic reflection of Oedipal urges?

This question raises a more general point. If you're like most people, you had a mixed reaction to psychoanalytic theory. Most people find some aspects of the theory reasonable. For example, many agree that early experience has a big effect on personality. Many agree that conflict is inherent in personality functioning. Most agree that behavior is usually aimed at gaining pleasure and avoiding pain. Probably, though, there were aspects of the theory you found less convincing. Maybe you don't agree with Freud's stress on the unconscious. Maybe you're put off by his insistence that so much of human behavior is sexually motivated.

Even Freud's close followers were ambivalent. There were several areas of disagreement. Perhaps the most frequent criticism was that Freud didn't give enough attention to the ego and what it does (see Box 10.1 for another disagreement). Interestingly enough, toward the end of his career Freud felt the same way himself. He began to wonder whether the ego might have a more important and autonomous status than he'd earlier believed.

Freud died before he could openly indicate his gradually changing position on this matter. Even his last publication (Freud, 1949/1940) gives no hint of this shift in thinking. Others knew of Freud's informal statements, though, and found his shifting views more compatible with their own thinking. Encouraged by his change, they began to develop a set of ideas that collectively came to be called **ego psychology.** As the name implies, ego psychology is a psychodynamic framework in which ego functioning has more status than Freud gave it.

The emergence of ego psychology was a subtle and gradual process that began well before Freud's death. Indeed, many would say that some of the ideas described in Chapter 9 are just as relevant to ego psychology as to psychoanalysis. It was Anna Freud who analyzed the process of defense so carefully, and her ideas weren't identical to those of her father. Recall that the defenses are used *by the ego* to protect itself. Thus, they're easily seen as ego functions and a part of ego psychology.

Principles of Ego Psychology

Anna Freud's analysis of defense mechanisms is a transitional statement. That is, it can be applied either to traditional psychoanalysis or to ego psychology. But other

BOX 10.1

ANOTHER KIND OF PSYCHODYNAMICS
Jung's Analytical Psychology

This chapter focuses on people who modified Freud's ideas by emphasizing the ego and deemphasizing the unconscious. We should, however, note another theorist of the time whose ideas moved in the other direction: Carl Jung (e.g., 1960/1926, 1968). Jung was less a follower of Freud than a *contemporary* of Freud (though twenty years younger) who was influenced by many of the same currents of thought as molded Freud's work. Thus, similarities in some of the ideas they advanced seemed initially to give them common ground.

Freud and Jung associated professionally and personally for six years, during which Freud began to view Jung as his "crown prince" and eventual successor (McGuire, 1974). However, two factors drove a wedge between them. The first was a series of theoretical differences. The second was a growing interpersonal difficulty. Freud saw himself as a father figure to Jung, and he began to suspect that Jung wished to usurp his power and authority (note the Oedipal overtones). Jung found this attitude hard to tolerate, and he eventually broke away from Freud.

Jung's theory differs from Freud's in many ways. It's a theory of great complexity, and we can make only a couple of points about it here. Jung agreed with the neoanalysts that Freud overemphasized sexuality as a motive. He differed, however, in holding that Freud had too limited a view of spirituality. Unlike Freud, for whom spirituality reflected sublimation of sexual drives, Jung considered it a fundamental aspect of human existence.

Jung's thinking was also dominated by the **principle of opposites,** the idea that the human experience consists of polarities—qualities that oppose and tend to balance each other. He proposed a set of dichotomies in human functioning, each of which has some resemblance to what others would view as aspects of ego functioning. Jung believed that people are dominated by one of two attitudes: introversion or extraversion. People dominated by extraversion are absorbed by external experiences and spend their time engaged with the world around them.

People dominated by introversion are preoccupied by their inner experiences and tend to be less outgoing. Both tendencies can facilitate adaptation. And even though you're dominated by one of them, the other remains inside you as well, opposing and balancing it.

Jung also assumed two more pairs of opposed functions. One pair, *thinking* and *feeling,* are both rational, in that each involves a kind of judgment. Thinking is a judgment of which ideas are true; feeling is a judgment about whether you like or dislike something. The other pair, *sensing* and *intuiting,* are nonrational, in that they don't rely on thought. Both are ways of perceiving, one using senses, the other using the unconscious. Each of these pairs also forms a polarity, with one of each pair tending to dominate the other. Indeed, a further polarization exists between the rational and irrational. Jung believed that combinations of dominance of these functions (plus introversion-extraversion) produce the range of individual differences in personality. Today these tendencies are measured by an instrument called the Myers-Briggs Type Indicator (Myers & McCaulley, 1985), which is widely used for assessment in settings such as businesses and career counseling (DeVito, 1985).

Although Jung's theory has certain similarities to ego psychology, there are also great differences. For example, instead of deemphasizing the unconscious, Jung emphasized it even more. Jung believed human beings share a **collective unconscious,** or "racial memory," a set of memories from our human and even prehuman ancestors. He believed that these memories, which aren't recalled consciously, go back for countless generations. They provide the basis for images called **archetypes,** aspects of the world that people have an inherited tendency to notice. Jung described many archetypes, including birth, death, power, magic, unity, God, and the self, which he believed are experienced by everyone. Each of these, in Jung's view, exists in the person because it's been part of the experience of human and prehuman life for millenia.

aspects of ego psychology depart more clearly from psychoanalysis. Freud emphasized that the ego's primary task was to mediate among the id, the superego, and external reality. From the vantage point of ego psychology, the ego does far more than that. It's involved in the process of *adaptation,* of fitting better into the world. This view holds that adaptation and the conscious processes by which it occurs are more important than is unconscious behavior (Wolberg, 1967).

Nor is this the only break from Freud. Ego psychologists widely assumed that the ego exists at birth and has its own energy source. One ego psychologist (Fairbairn, 1952) even went so far as to suggest that there is no id—only ego—and that what were seen as id functions are simply reflections of an ego at a primitive stage of development. All these ideas follow from the core assumption of the ego psychologists: that ego processes are important in their own right.

Shifting the Emphasis from Id to Ego

Because many of the people who became known as ego psychologists began as followers of Freud, they faced a dilemma. They wanted to construct theories that emphasized the ego, but many also wanted to avoid undermining the core ideas of psychoanalysis. How could this be done? This was a hard problem because psychoanalysis had given the ego a specific role—to help the impulses of the id gain expression.

Heinz Hartmann (1958/1939, 1964) had an inventive and simple solution to this dilemma: he ignored it. More specifically, he proposed that the ego serves two roles simultaneously. On the one hand it reduces conflict between the id and superego and between the id and external reality, as Freud had said. On the other hand it acts through its cognitive processes to adapt the person better to the environment.

Hartmann held that the ego acts in two different modes to handle these different functions (see Figure 10.1). When it acts to reduce conflict, it's operating in what he called the *conflict sphere* of personality. When it acts to promote adaptation, it's operating in the *conflict-free sphere.* Thus, said Hartmann, Freud's view of the ego was right and so was the emerging view of ego psychology. Each view simply emphasizes different aspects of what the ego does.

How can the ego function in two spheres? Hartmann assumed that ego and id have the same biological source. Thus, part of the ego stays in contact with the id throughout life. This part of the ego operates in the conflict sphere and tries to satisfy the id's needs. The rest develops more independently and operates in the conflict-free sphere.

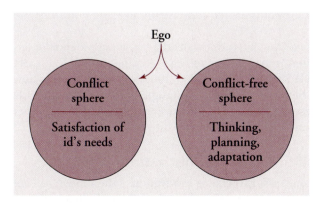

Figure 10.1

Hartmann assumed that the ego can operate in either of two modes. In the conflict sphere, it acts to see that the id's impulses are satisfied. In the conflict-free sphere, it engages in activities for its own purposes, aimed at better adaptation.

There it works for its own purposes. The latter aspect of the ego is what Hartmann and (other ego psychologists) were interested in.

Having said that Freud was partly right (that the ego functions in the conflict sphere), Hartmann then proceeded to ignore that aspect of the ego almost entirely. In that way he managed to remain connected to psychoanalysis while heading off in a new direction.

Adaptation and Autonomy

In Hartmann's view, adaptation to the environment is the ultimate goal of behavior. This became an important theme throughout ego psychology. Adaptation occurs on several levels. Physically, people must learn to move their bodies to get where they want to go and do what they want to do. Psychologically, people must learn to gain control over their impulses, modifying them and channeling them into appropriate actions.

Hartmann agreed with Freud that sexual and aggressive energies provide the foundation of much of human behavior. He differed, however, in how he interpreted people's attempts to deal with their impulses. Freud saw the struggle to inhibit impulses in terms of avoiding anxiety (by avoiding punishment or danger). Hartmann (and others) saw the effort to inhibit as part of a broader process of adaptation. The difference isn't so much in *what* happens as in *why* it happens. To Hartmann, the reason for impulse control is rooted in the ego's own goals.

Hartmann talked about two kinds of autonomy in describing the ego. First, ego processes exist on their own from birth and can function apart from the id (a principle called **primary ego autonomy**). An implication of this is that people get satisfaction from using ego processes to think, plan, imagine, integrate information, and so on (see also Box 10.2). In this view, being effective is pleasurable in itself. As you exercise your ego, you become more adept, and thereby more efficient (better adapted) in dealing with the world.

The phrase **secondary ego autonomy** refers to the idea that an ego function originally done for one purpose may continue to be done long after that purpose has been satisfied. The original purpose may have been to fill some other need (even an id need). But the ego function is now gratifying in its own right. The meaning of the term *secondary ego autonomy* is similar to what Allport (1961) called **functional autonomy.** When a behavior that was originally done for one reason continues to occur after the original reason no longer applies, the behavior is said to have acquired functional autonomy. It's as though the behavior has now become an end in itself. As an illustration, think of a person who began an exercise program to lose weight. Even after she's lost the weight she continues to exercise because she now finds the exercise itself satisfying.

The idea of an autonomous ego that has the goal of adaptation was widely adopted by other theorists, who extended it in a variety of ways. Among others, Rapaport (1960), Gill (1959), G. S. Klein (1970), and White (1959, 1963) were interested in how the ego goes about fitting itself better to the world. Although many ego psychologists view the exercise of ego processes as a source of pleasure and satisfaction, this idea was perhaps elaborated most compellingly by Robert White (1959, 1963).

The Ego, Adaptation, and Competence Motivation

White used two motivational concepts. **Effectance motivation** is the motive to *have an effect* or an impact on one's surroundings. White believed effectance is a basic hu-

BOX 10.2

THE JOY OF THINKING

Explorations in the Need for Cognition

The idea that ego processes are gratifying in their own right is consistent with a literature on a topic called the **need for cognition.** This is the need to think about and impose meaningful structure on experiences (Cohen, 1957; Cohen, Stotland, & Wolfe, 1955). People high in the need for cognition are likely to evaluate, organize, and elaborate spontaneously on information to which they're exposed. They're less easily bored than people lower in the need (Watt & Blanchard, 1994). They attend more to the details of others' behavior (Lassiter, Briggs, & Bowman, 1991) and think more about its meaning (Lassiter, Briggs, & Slaw, 1991). People high in this need also are flexible and tend to explain events in complex ways (Fletcher et al., 1986). They aren't necessarily smarter than people lower in this need—they just like to think things over (Cacioppo, Petty, Kao, & Rodriguez, 1986; Cacioppo, Petty, & Morris, 1983).

This ego function is reflected in several ways (for a review see Cacioppo, Petty, Feinstein, & Jarvis, 1996). Consider, for example, what happens when people try to persuade each other of something. It's known that persuasion affects people in two different ways. When people get a persuasive message, some evaluate it and even *elaborate* on it in their minds. Others just take it at face value. Cacioppo and Petty (1982, 1984) argued that this difference in responses rests on the need for cognition. People high in the need for cognition evaluate and elaborate; people low in the need for cognition accept what they're given.

Cacioppo and associates examined this idea by finding people who held the same attitudes on a target issue but differed in their need for cognition (Cacioppo et al., 1983; Cacioppo et al., 1986, Experiment 1). They received an essay trying to persuade them to change their opinion. Either the essay was full of weak arguments (which people resist), or it was full of strong arguments (which are more persuasive). As you might expect, people with high cognition needs reported thinking harder about the message than those with lower needs. They also remembered more of the arguments in it.

Does thinking harder and remembering more result in more persuasion? Not always. Thinking about strong arguments produced more persuasion. Thinking about weak arguments, however, caused people to be more resistant to persuasion. In sum, people high in the need for cognition thought more about the value of what they'd read, and they used the value of the arguments as a guide for deciding whether to change their attitudes. Later research found that once the attitude changed, the change was also more persistent for those high in the need for cognition (Haugtvedt & Petty, 1992; Verplanken, 1991). This overall pattern seems much in line with the functions the ego psychologists emphasized, as people try to deal effectively and adaptively with external reality.

man motive. During early childhood it's the major outlet for the ego's energies. This motive gradually evolves into the more complex **competence motivation.** This is a motive *to be effective* when dealing with the environment. Because the goal of the competence motive is to be more effective, this motive underlies adaptive ego functioning. Competence motivation is limitless in its impact. There are always new competencies (and higher levels of competence) to attain. The competence motive thus moves the person toward ever-new masteries (recall Jeremy and his video games from the chapter opening).

White pointed out that there are important differences between attaining goals and satisfying the competence motivation. Attaining a goal satisfies the desire to reach that goal, but the goal itself may or may not pertain to your competence. If you

Children often seem driven to figure things out on their own. Successful mastery of the environment is important in developing feelings of competence.

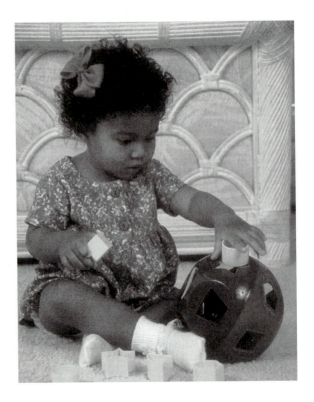

get a perfect exam score in a course you think is pointless, or too easy, it won't enhance your sense of competence.

Consider for a moment how effectance and competence motives might be expressed in a child's behavior. Imagine an infant, surrounded by toys in her crib, who lunges at a dangling mobile and gives it a good whack with her fist. As the mobile jangles and bounces, the child has visible evidence of her impact on the environment. This gratifies her desire for effectance. Knocking things over, moving toys around, spreading stewed carrots all over her table tray—each of these actions has an effect on the world around her. Each satisfies the effectance motive. Infants clearly do these things, and they do seem to obtain pleasure from them.

What about competence? Suppose the child is just learning how to stand up. She struggles over and over to pull herself up against the wall of her crib. She does it even though every effort meets with failure and no one's there to encourage her. When success finally comes, she giggles and shrieks with pleasure. She's manifested a mastery over the environment, a new competence in dealing with it. The motive to develop increasing mastery over the environment will continue to be an important part of her life.

In White's view, effectance and competence motives reflect the way the brain is organized. He held that people inherently seek stimulation from exploring the environment. This biological urge can be shown in many ways, but its most advanced form is the desire to be competent and feel competent in dealing with the world. This is an adaptive urge because it causes people to be engaged in effective commerce with their environment to the greatest extent possible.

This theme has had reverberations in other perspectives on personality, as well as in ego psychology. As you'll see in Chapter 13, some learning theorists have come

Feelings of inferiority can produce strivings for superiority.

to believe that the sense of personal efficacy is a major determinant of people's actions. It can easily be argued that that line of thought traces to White's emphasis on an intrinsic desire to master the environment. An additional theoretical similarity will become apparent when you read about humanistic views on personality in Chapter 14.

Is Competence Striving Automatic, or Is It Done to Remedy Inferiority?

White considered the desire for greater competence to be the major force behind people's attempts to be effective. This position differs from the view taken by another ego psychologist, Alfred Adler (1927, 1929, 1931). Adler also believed that people strive for greater competence, but he saw this as occurring for different reasons.

Adler began his line of theory with an interest in a medical question—why one person develops heart trouble, a second has respiratory problems, and a third gets ulcers. Adler's hypothesis was that people have an inferiority in some region of the body, which makes them vulnerable to illness at that site. He called this weakness an **organ inferiority** (Adler, 1917). He also argued that people try to *compensate* by strengthening the weak organ through exercise and training. He termed this effort a *striving for superiority*. No doubt Adler's belief in this principle of compensatory striving was influenced by his own life. He was a sickly child who nearly died in childhood. Through considerable effort, however, he overcame his health problems.

Support for this idea about compensatory striving comes from a study of the performances of undersea divers engaged in a demanding task (Helmreich, LeFan,

Bakeman, Wilhelm, & Radloff, 1972). This study found that the divers who performed best had had a serious illness during childhood. From Adler's perspective, these divers were compensating behaviorally for their earlier body inferiority.

Adler went on to expand his thinking to include *all* feelings of inferiority and to extend the principle to personality. He proposed that whenever a person has **feelings of inferiority** (any sense of inadequacy), a compensatory process is activated and the person strives for superiority (Adler, 1927, 1929, 1931). For example, consider a sprinter who feels inferior because she can't run 100 yards in ten seconds. Because she feels inferior, she trains until she breaks the ten-second barrier. Her satisfaction, however, is relatively short-lived. Feelings of inferiority set in again as she realizes she could be even faster, and the struggle to improve begins anew.

Consider another example: a college freshman who arrives for his first semester knowing no one. He's a little shy, and in a few minutes he feels a sense of inferiority because people all around him are engaged in conversations with one another. What does he do? He grits his teeth and approaches a group of three people to introduce himself. Within a month, new friendships are sprouting like summer weeds. By now, though, just having friends isn't enough. He feels inferior because the friendships are a little superficial. He thinks he should know some people better than he does. To overcome that, he gets involved in a church group that meets once a week to talk with others about personal reactions to the experience of college life.

There are many ways of responding to a feeling of inferiority. Adler coined the term **lifestyle** to refer both to a person's concerns over inferiority and to the person's preferred way of striving for superiority. Healthy lifestyles move the person forward in an adaptive path of development in important domains of life. They allow people to attain meaningful goals and to get along well with others.

But there are also what Adler called **mistaken lifestyles.** Some people respond to feelings of inferiority by trying to dominate others, or becoming dependent and taking things from others instead of attaining them on their own. Other people respond to feelings of inferiority by trying to avoid situations in which such feelings can arise. They attempt to avoid a sense of inferiority by never trying. Other people respond to such feelings by being as useful as they can to others, thereby drawing their own attention away from their inferiorities. These people almost deny the validity of their own ego and their own feelings. Consistent with this view, people who are *excessively* concerned with the needs of others have been found to be lower in self-esteem and more likely to neglect their own needs than people whose concern with others is more moderate (Fritz & Helgeson, 1998; Helgeson & Fritz, 1998, 1999).

Adler believed that inferiority feelings and superiority strivings continue to cycle with each other constantly. The result, unless the person has a mistaken lifestyle, is that people continually work to get better, more proficient at whatever they do (see also Box 10.3). Adler thus viewed the struggle for increased competence to be an important part of healthy ego functioning. He called it the "great upward drive," and he believed that healthy people continue to work in this way throughout life toward ever-greater integration and perfection.

To Adler, effort toward improvement begins with and stems from feelings of inferiority. He believed everyone confronts these on a recurring basis. These feelings are part of being human. Because a major consequence of inferiority feelings is an effort to better oneself, the behavior that results is exactly the same as the pattern White described. But the two theorists proposed very different mechanisms for it. To White, competence strivings are simply an intrinsic part of the ego's activity. To Adler, they're a reaction to, and an attempt to replace, feelings of inferiority.

BOX 10.3

BIRTH ORDER AND PERSONALITY

There are many influences on the development of a person's lifestyle. Adler saw birth order as one such influence. He believed every child in a family is treated differently from every other child. The differences in treatment produce different adaptations, different personalities, and different choices of lifestyle (Adler, 1964/1933).

Adler argued that *firstborn* children begin life as the focus of the family's attention. Their parents place great expectations on them. This can motivate them to high achievement. The firstborn is vulnerable to feelings of being "dethroned," however, if a second child comes along. This loss of attention and power can be deeply distressing, and may give the firstborn a lifelong sensitivity to issues of power. If the first child isn't old enough to have begun developing a cooperative lifestyle, the firstborn may resent the second-born forever.

Some firstborns are also *only children*. Only children are never dethroned and thus spend all of their lives as the center of family attention. As a result, they often develop an exaggerated sense of their importance. This can be threatened when the child heads off to school, where a different sort of dethroning occurs. Adler thought only children were likely to fail to develop a true interest in others. Rather, they would continue to expect others to attend to their needs. They're often affectionate, but in a way that facilitates their remaining the center of attention.

Second-born children are in a very different situation. They enter a family with a rival already in place. They've never occupied a position of power, so they tend to be less sensitive to power issues. On the other hand, they have to "hit the ground running," because their lives will be a constant effort to catch up with the firstborn. Adler thought of second as the best place in the birth order, and his reasoning fits with his views on life in general. He saw the second-born as like a long-distance runner who's a few yards behind the leader. The sense of inferiority is there all the time because the firstborn is always a little ahead. The result is a constant striving for superiority. This can work to your advantage if your striv-

ing produces good results. But second-borns sometimes develop the sense that they'll never be as good as the firstborns.

The other place in the birth order that interested Adler was at the other end of the line: the *youngest child*. Adler believed this is the worst position. The youngest child tends to be spoiled. That may be fun, but it can have bad effects. Adler (1958/1931) argued that it undermines the child's desire to strive. There's irony here, in that the youngest child (by definition) has many of the same cues as the second-born (by having an older rival) and thus should have strong striving for superiority. Adler argued, though, that the sense of attaining goals through your own efforts is damaged by having things given to you too easily. Thus, youngest children sometimes break from the family mold to seek an identity in a different area. If the father is a lawyer and the older siblings are all taking up law, the youngest may decide to become an artist or musician.

What evidence is there for the effects of birth order? There's much anecdotal evidence that firstborns are overrepresented in positions of power and prestige. For example, twenty-one of the first twenty-three American astronauts were firstborns. There's also evidence that firstborn and only children in the United States have higher levels of educational goals and achievements than later children (e.g., Belmont & Marolla, 1973; Breland, 1974; Falbo, 1981; Paulhus, Trapnell, & Chen, 1999), though there are exceptions. This pattern is consistent with the idea that the firstborn is the center of attention and that parents place the highest expectations on their first child (see Sulloway, 1996). But the evidence doesn't seem to support the idea that it's the second-born who has the greatest urge to strive for superiority. Effects on other aspects of personality are less common. Ernst and Angst (1983) reviewed a large literature on birth order and found little support for the idea that birth order matters for most aspects of personality. More recent studies are similarly inconsistent in their results (Michalski & Shackelford, 2002; Sulloway, 1996).

Ego Control and Ego Resiliency

The theorists named thus far all emphasized the idea that the primary goal of the ego is better adaptation to the world. Let's consider this concept a little more closely. Adaptation can be seen as having two aspects. Part of adaptation is learning to *restrain impulses*. This lets you gain better command of your transactions with the world. It prevents mistakes that would arise from acting impulsively. Part of successful adaptation, though, is being *flexible* in dealing with the world. This is a matter of knowing when to restrain yourself and when to behave more freely. These issues surrounding restraint of impulses in the service of better adaptation lie at the heart of the work of contemporary ego psychologists Jeanne and Jack Block (1980; J. Block, 2002). They and their colleagues have examined these two distinct aspects of ego functioning.

Block and Block called one aspect **ego control.** This is the extent to which the person tends to inhibit the expression of impulses. At one extreme are people who undercontrol, people who can't delay gratification, who express their feelings and desires immediately. Block and Block described these impulsive people as having many-but-brief enthusiasms and interests, as being distractible and exploratory, non-conforming and unconventional, and comfortable with ambiguity and inconsistency. They live an impromptu life.

At the other end are people who overcontrol, people who delay gratification endlessly, who inhibit their actions and feelings, and who insulate themselves from outside distractions. Block and Block describe them as conforming rather than exploratory, planful and organized, uneasy in ambiguous or inconsistent situations, and having narrow and unchanging interests. From their description of what these people are like, it's clear that the Blocks believed great restraint doesn't necessarily mean better adaptation.

In the middle of the dimension are people who inhibit and control impulses to a degree, but who don't overdo it. These people are less organized than those high in ego control, but they're less impromptu and chaotic than those low in ego control. The people in the middle seem better adapted than are those at either extreme.

The other aspect of ego functioning that Block and Block focused on is called **ego resiliency.** This is flexibility. It's *the capacity to modify your usual level of ego control*—in either direction—to adapt to the demands of a given situation. People low in ego resilience can't break out of their usual way of relating to the world, even when it's temporarily good to do so. People who are ego-resilient are resourceful and adapt well to changing circumstances. If there's a situational reason to be organized, they can do it without trouble. If there's a reason to be crazy and impulsive, they can be that way too. As Block and Kremen (1996) put it, the ego-resilient person's goal is to be "as undercontrolled as possible and as overcontrolled as necessary" (p. 351). This means being responsive to what's possible and what's necessary in a given situation.

Not surprisingly, there's evidence that people who are high in ego resilience are better adjusted than people who are low (Klohnen, 1996). For example, in two samples of women, those higher in ego resiliency did better at negotiating menopause than those who were ego-brittle. They were more likely to continue their education or career building, and had fewer health problems (Klohnen, Vandewater, & Young, 1996). Another project found that children high in ego resilience were faster to develop in their understanding of friendships and moral reasoning than children lower in ego resilience (Hart, Keller, Edelstein, & Hofmann, 1998).

It might be tempting to conclude that people with high ego resilience are just smarter than people with less ego resilience. Thus they're quicker to recognize what a situation calls for. Although these variables are related, there are also important differences (Block & Kremen, 1996). Pure ego resilience—controlling for effects of IQ—relates to competence in the world of interpersonal interaction.

Ego control and ego resilience have both been related to restraint, in the form of delay of gratification (Funder & Block, 1989). Participants were fourteen-year-olds being paid $4 for each of six sessions. After each session, they were given the choice of being paid then or deferring payment until the end. Each time they deferred payment, they'd get a small bonus in "interest." The question was how often (from five opportunities) they chose to delay. Decisions to delay related to ego control, as expected ($r = .45$, controlling for both ego resiliency and intelligence). Ego resiliency also played a role. Recall that delay is sometimes a good policy, sometimes not. This situation was set up so that delay produced extra payoff, so delay was good. Flexible people pick up on this and choose to delay, even if that's not their usual style. Thus, ego resiliency related to delay choices ($r = .41$, controlling for both ego control and intelligence).

These ego qualities have also been related to other kinds of behavior. One program of research has found that greater ego control related to longer delays before engaging in sexual intercourse (Jessor & Jessor, 1975; Jessor, Costa, Jessor, & Donovan, 1983). Other studies found that ego control has a similar relation to drinking: undercontrol relates to problem drinking and overcontrol relates to total abstinence (M. C. Jones, 1968, 1971). Shedler and Block (1990) reported similar results with respect to drug use (see Table 10.1).

Table 10.1

Observer-rating items that distinguished among three groups of eighteen-year-olds. Those of one group were total abstainers from drug use, those of the second group were occasional experimenters, and those of the third group were frequent users (adapted from Shedler & Block, 1990).

Items distinguishing frequent users from occasional experimenters

Is self-indulgent

Gives up and withdraws in the face of frustration, adversity

Thinks and associates to ideas in unusual ways

Is unpredictable and changeable in behavior, attitudes

Undercontrols needs and impulses; unable to delay gratification

Tends to be rebellious and nonconforming

Characteristically pushes and tries to stretch limits

Items distinguishing total abstainers from occasional experimenters

Is moralistic

Favors conservative values in a variety of areas

Prides self on being "objective," rational

Overcontrols needs and impulses; delays gratification unnecessarily

Is facially and/or gesturally expressive (lower score)

Is unpredictable and changeable in behavior, attitudes (lower score)

Enjoys sensuous experience (touch, taste, smell, physical contact) (lower score)

In theory, ego control and ego resilience are distinct. However, there's evidence that things are more complex than that (Eisenberg, Fabes, Guthrie, & Reiser, 2000). It may be intrinsically harder for someone who's at an extreme in ego control to be resilient, compared with someone with moderate ego control. If so, there would be low ego resilience at both extremes of the ego control dimension. Several recent studies (Asendorpf & van Aken, 1999; Robins, John, Caspi, Moffitt, & Stouthamer-Loeber, 1996) have found exactly that.

These studies found three clusters of people (see Figure 10.2). Overcontrolled people are high in ego control and low in ego resilience. Undercontrolled people are low in ego control and low in ego resilience. Resilient people are moderate in ego control and high in ego resilience. The overcontrolled and undercontrolled groups have the characteristics described above for highs and lows in ego control. The resilient group has the characteristics described above for highs in ego resilience. Future research on this topic may focus more on these three patterns.

Ego Control, Ego Resilience, and the Five-Factor Model

We've noted in earlier chapters that interest in the five-factor model of trait structure (Chapter 4) has led people to ask how other views of personality fit with that model. Several studies have looked at this question regarding the view just described (Asendorpf & van Aken, 1999; Robins et al., 1996). The results are very similar across studies. Idealized profiles of three groups of people are shown in Figure 10.3.

The easiest to characterize is the resilient group: They're at the "good" end of all the scales. The undercontrolled group is as extraverted as the resilients, but they're low in agreeableness and conscientiousness and moderately low in emotional stability and openness. This gives a picture of someone who is impulsive and cares little about other people's opinions, which fits other descriptions of them. In contrast to both of these, the overcontrolled group is introverted, but they are as agreeable as the resilient group. They're also the lowest in emotional stability (i.e., highest in neuroticism) and only moderately open and conscientious. Consistent with the

Figure 10.2

Approximate locations in two-dimensional space of three clusters of persons. Two clusters are at the extremes in ego control. The third cluster is identified by being high in ego resilience. (Based on information from Robins et al., 1996, and Asendorpf & van Aken, 1999).

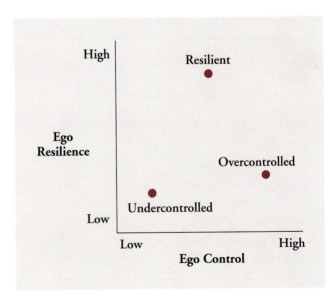

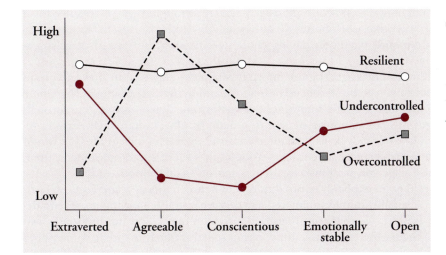

Figure 10.3

Idealized five-factor profiles of people who are resilient, undercontrolled, and overcontrolled. (Based on information from Robins et al., 1996, and Asendorpf & van Aken, 1999).

Blocks' portrayal, they seem withdrawn, conforming, and anxious. It seems, then, that there's a fairly easy integration between the qualities in the Blocks' model and the five-factor model.

Ego Development

Thus far we've emphasized the idea that a primary function of the ego is to establish better adaptation to the world. Now we turn to a slightly different viewpoint on this function. Though different, it's fully compatible with the themes we've emphasized thus far.

Jane Loevinger (1969, 1976) has argued that the ego is primarily a synthesizer and integrator of experience. This function certainly fits the overall goal of enhancing adaptation. In her view the ego adapts to the world by making sense of the experiences the world supplies it. She argues that this synthesizing function isn't just one of many things the ego does. Rather, this function is what the ego *is*. To Loevinger, the process of synthesis and integration is the essence of the ego.

Loevinger has proposed a detailed account of the ego's development (Loevinger, 1966, 1976, 1987; Loevinger & Knoll, 1983). By ego development, she doesn't mean a process by which the ego comes to *exist*. Rather, she's referring to how the ego's synthesizing function evolves across life. Her theory rests on ideas about cognitive development from theorists such as Piaget. A basic idea is that as cognitive capabilities grow, people organize and structure their experience in more elaborate ways. As a result, the integrating function of the ego must also act in more elaborate ways.

Loevinger's is a stage theory. She believes each shift in the nature of ego functioning derives from, and thus depends on, the nature of ego functioning in the preceding stage. Thus the person moves through the stages in a particular order. As you move to higher stages, the ego's syntheses become more differentiated and complex but also more integrated.

What makes people move forward into a different stage? It's generally assumed that both cognitive development and ego development emerge because existing functions don't quite fit reality. That is, if an ego function works perfectly, there's no reason to change it. If it doesn't work perfectly, though, there's pressure for it to evolve in ways that work better (Baumeister, 1994; Block, 1982). Thus, ego development depends partly on having challenge in one's life (see also Helson & Roberts, 1994).

According to Loevinger, people move through the stages until they can go no further. How far you go is influenced by heredity and by life circumstances (Newman, Tellegen, & Bouchard, 1998). Loevinger does *not* assume that everyone goes through all the stages. It's possible for a person to remain fixed in even a fairly early stage. Such an adult would not be well adapted to certain complexities in life, but would get along adequately in many contexts. Your adult level of ego development, then, is the highest stage you're able to attain as you grow to adulthood.

We should point explicitly to two differences between this view and Freud's. First, Freud saw personality development as occurring early in life. Loevinger sees ego development as a process that continues well into adulthood. Second, in Freud's psychoanalytic theory the ego's basic functioning remains much the same, though the issues it deals with change over the years. Loevinger, however, argues that the nature of the synthesizing process that *defines* the ego actually changes over the course of life.

Early Ego Development

The stages Loevinger identified are summarized in Table 10.2. At first the ego is primitive. Its major task is to acquire the ability to distinguish self from nonself. This ability emerges during the first stage of ego development, called the *Symbiotic* stage. This name comes from the fact that a young child's tie to the mother is so strong the

Table 10.2

Summary of Loevinger's portrayal of the stages of ego development (adapted from Loevinger, 1987).

Stage name	Behavioral manifestations
Symbiotic	Working to acquire sense of separation between self, nonself
Impulsive	Assertion of self through impulse expression; relationships with others are exploitive, for own needs
Self-protective	Begins to grasp rules, but only as guides to avoid punishment; no moral sense; personal expediency, opportunism
Conformist	Rules adopted because they are accepted by group; concerned with appearing properly to the social group
Self-aware	Realization that rules have exceptions; increased introspection, with increased awareness that own behavior isn't perfect
Conscientious	Use of self-evaluated standards rather than group's norm; realization that events have multiple meanings
Individualistic	Clearer sense of individuality; greater tolerance for individual differences
Autonomous	Realization of interdependence among people; awareness of conflicts among one's own needs; recognition of others' need for autonomy
Integrated	Conflicting demands have been resolved; not just tolerance, but intense appreciation of others' viewpoints

child has trouble distinguishing itself from mother. The process of consolidating a sense of being a separate person is assisted greatly by the emergence of language.

The next period of ego development is the *Impulsive* stage. Loevinger says that children of this stage release impulses purposely, as a way of affirming their existence. In effect, the ego is acting to have an impact on the world. (This seems similar to exercising what White called effectance motivation.) This is a time when phrases such as "*I* do" and "by *myself*" emerge often (and often loudly) from the child. The child is oriented to the present time, with little consideration of the future or broad implications of behavior. Children's need for other people is high, because they can't do everything for themselves. But the relationships are exploitive: others are valued only for what they can give the child.

It's of some interest that the behaviors of this period are behaviors that a traditional psychoanalytic view would see as caused by the id. Behavior is impulsive and demanding, and the child doesn't *relate* to other people so much as *use* them. Loevinger argues, though, that the actions reflect not an id, but a not-very-well-developed ego struggling to assert itself. These very different views of the same qualities of behavior illustrate a way in which the ego psychologists' perspective differs from the psychoanalytic perspective.

Middle Stages of Ego Development: Control of Impulses

The intentional releasing of impulses eventually gives way to a different way of relating to the world. The *Self-protective* stage marks the first step toward self-control of impulses. During this stage children start to grasp the idea that there are rules about how to act, and that breaking the rules leads to punishment. Children still lack full appreciation of the meaning of rules, however. At this stage, rules simply give information about how the world works—what you have to do to avoid punishment. As Loevinger (1976) put it, the main rule is "Don't get caught." The child's only morality at this stage is expediency.

The self-protective quality of this stage is reflected in the fact that children use the rules they learn mostly for their own advantage. Behavior thus remains exploitive. On the other hand, Loevinger (1987) says this isn't a calculated opportunism. It's just an open expression of self-interest. In Loevinger's view, the best indicator of the self-protective mode of ego functioning isn't exploitiveness, but the absence of long-term goals and purposes.

Once again it seems useful to point to the relation between this theory and Freud's theory. This stage is where the theories bear the greatest resemblance in their views of the ego. Recall that to Freud the ego is amoral; it acts to satisfy the desires of the id as expeditiously as possible, without concern about right or wrong. The behavioral result looks much like what Loevinger describes happening at the self-protective stage. Yet once again, there's a difference. Loevinger doesn't see this as reflecting the emergence of a new structure in personality. Rather, it reflects a change in how the ego synthesizes and integrates, in its efforts to adapt to the world.

The next stage of ego development is called the *Conformist* stage. Children attain it by starting to link their own welfare and security to that of a group (family or peers). This is when rules start to be truly internalized. This change requires developing a sense of trust in the group. Rules no longer are seen as ways to avoid punishment. They're used because they reflect social consensus about how to act. Conformists obey rules precisely because the group has them. Little distinction is made between rules that matter and social norms that don't. Rules are rules. The power of rules comes from their social basis. Thus, punishments that are most effective during this stage involve social disapproval ("You let us down," or "We don't like what you did").

At this stage the ego is preoccupied with issues of reputation and social appearance. The appearances are one-dimensional, though. Life is seen in stereotypes and clichés. People at the conformist level of ego development often seem very conventional. That's not a reliable clue to being at the conformist level, however. Indeed, real conformists often appear radically different from "most" people. At the same time, though, they're conforming quite closely to the norms of their own social group. Many adolescents display this pattern, and some people never outgrow it. Control of impulses is regulated by shame (a sense of looking bad to the group) more than in previous stages (Einstein & Lanning, 1998).

The next stage (Loevinger, 1987) seems to be the most common level of ego development in the population of Americans between ages sixteen and twenty-six (Holt, 1980). This stage is called the *Self-aware* level. Its name reflects the fact that the person in this stage is seeing—for the first time—multiple possibilities for the self.

Loevinger describes this stage by asking what pressures might move a person beyond conformity. She suggests that people move on when they come to perceive they don't fit the perfect-person stereotype held out to them by conformist thinking. Coming to such a perception seems to depend on developing a greater capacity for (or tendency toward) introspection. Loevinger says that during this stage the person begins to differentiate "what I am" from "what I ought to be." People at this level realize that rules of conduct often have qualifications or exceptions. You can do this "if you're old enough." You can't do this "until you're married." Despite a developing inner complexity, however, people at this stage are still basically conformists in their actions.

One more cognitive change seems to be needed for movement into the *Conscientious* stage: an awareness of the fact that events have multiple meanings. This change makes it possible to understand and assimilate abstract moral rules. Abstract rules eventually seem more important than group-consensus rules. The weakening influence of consensus means that morality now is truly internalized. During this stage and from now on, shame becomes less important a factor in keeping people from breaking moral codes. Loevinger (1987) holds that the distinctive mark of this stage is self-evaluated standards. That is, you approve or disapprove of your conduct because of what you personally feel, not because of the wishes of some social group.

The life of the person at the conscientious stage is richer and more complex than was possible at earlier stages. Instead of seeing other people as just good or bad, you see them as complicated, with good and bad qualities. Achievement is valued for its own sake rather than as a way to gain advantage over someone else (as in the self-protective stage) or as a way to gain social recognition (as in the conformist stage). Fitting this, there's evidence that women who reach the conscientious stage by middle age also increase in the qualities of *achievement via independence* and *tolerance* during that period (Helson & Roberts, 1994).

Advanced Stages of Ego Development: Taking More into Account

A transitional level comes between the Conscientious stage and the next full stage of development. This transition is called the *Individualistic* level of ego development. The person at this level has a heightened sense of individuality and of style of life. There's an emerging tolerance for differences among people concerning these matters. People at the individualistic level also have more appreciation of the fact that a given person is different when in different roles (e.g., wife, mother, daughter, lover, career woman, tennis partner).

These themes are elaborated even more fully as the person moves into the *Autonomous stage*. Now the ego is preoccupied with the interdependency among people and the search for self-fulfillment (as opposed to achievement). The person has the capacity to recognize and cope with conflicts among differing needs, differing duties, and combinations of needs and duties. For example, you may need to study all evening for an exam tomorrow, but you also have the duty to "be there" for your friend who's taking the recent death of her father very badly. At the Individualist stage, you'd view this conflict as being between your own need and an unyielding environment. In the Autonomous stage, you accept the fact that many such conflicts occur intrinsically, even among your own wishes and needs.

The term *autonomous* can be a confusing label for this stage, because the key isn't a desire for one's own autonomy. It's an awareness of *others'* need for autonomy. Along with the ability to deal effectively with your own turmoil comes a greater tolerance for others dealing with their conflicts. Parents who recognize their children's need to learn from their own mistakes display this quality when they let the children make mistakes without stopping them. Loevinger believes that full attainment of this level of ego development (i.e., the ability to use this mode of relating to the world in all of one's interactions) is relatively rare.

The final stage of ego development, which is even more rare (1 percent of the population), is called *Integrated*. Entry into this stage means the person has come to grips with internal conflict and has found a way to satisfy conflicting demands. If necessary, goals that are unattainable or unrealistic are abandoned. In the Integrated stage, tolerance for others' viewpoints goes beyond mere tolerance to become an intense appreciation of those viewpoints. A conscious attempt is made in this stage to weave the threads of previous stages into an integrated whole.

In summary, Loevinger holds that as the ego passes through these stages of evolution, it acquires greater complexity in its functioning and in its ability to relate and adapt to the world around it. Loevinger also argued that the ego plays the major role in acquiring moral character, impulse control, and internalization of rules of conduct. The ego gradually develops these capabilities over time and experience.

It seems useful to make one last comparison between Loevinger's theory and Freud's. Many qualities that the ego displays in later stages of Loevinger's theory resemble the functions of the superego in Freud's theory. Recall that Loevinger attributes the *lack* of impulse control at an early age to the ego rather than to id. Similarly, she attributes a moral sense to the ego rather than superego. From theories such as this, it's clear that ego psychologists elevated the status of the ego partly by ascribing functions to it that Freud had assigned to the id and superego.

Research on Ego Development

Loevinger's analysis of ego development has been studied in research, but the work is hard to do. One reason is that her model doesn't predict many clear relationships between ego development and overt behavior (Hauser, 1976). Its predictions are more about the mental dynamics that underlie a given behavior. Consequently, much of the research on this theory has been descriptive.

It's known, for example, that older adolescents score higher on a measure of ego development than younger adolescents, and adults score higher than adolescents (Avery & Ryan, 1988). This fits the idea that the characteristics have a developmental progression. Girls seem to develop faster during middle and late childhood, though boys catch up by adulthood (Cohn, 1991). Ego development also relates to development of moral-reasoning capabilities (Lee & Snarey, 1988). This finding establishes convergent validity for both concepts, because there are certain logical similarities between changes in moral reasoning and changes in how the ego deals with reality. In a similar way, ego development has been related to increasing maturity in thinking about interpersonal intimacy (White, Houlihan, Costos, & Speisman, 1990).

Another study obtained evidence on other psychological qualities that should be tied to variations in ego development. Rozsnafszky (1981) studied hospitalized veterans, collecting both self-ratings and observer ratings (made by nurses and therapists) of the participants' traits. These ratings then were related to participants' levels of ego development (Table 10.3). Those at the impulsive or self-protective level showed poor socialization and limited self-awareness. Those at the conformist and self-aware levels were seen as valuing rules, possessions, physical appearance, and social conventions. Those at higher levels displayed greater insight into their own personality and motives. All of these findings are just as would be expected theoretically.

Although studies of behavioral reflections of ego development are somewhat rare, they aren't entirely lacking. There's evidence, for example, that social conformity is greatest among people who are at the conformist and self-aware stage of development. It falls off among people whose development attains higher stages (Hoppe, 1972; Westenberg & Block, 1993). Research has also found that higher ego development relates to higher peer ratings of mature functioning in careers and

Table 10.3

Observer-rating items that were found to distinguish among three groups of male research participants. People of one group were at the impulsive or self-protective level of ego development, those of the second group were at the conformist or self-aware level, those of the third group were at higher levels (adapted from Rozsnafszky, 1981).

Impulsive / Self-protective

Exploitive; sees people as sources of supply; "good" seems to mean "good for me"

Sees what he can get away with; follows rules only to avoid punishment

Is self-defensive, manipulative, opportunistic

Impulsive; when he doesn't get what he wants, he may be self-destructive in an impulsive way

Self-aware

Tends to feel guilty if he has not done his duty

Behaves in a sympathetic, considerate, and helpful manner

Is concerned with the impression he makes on others; self-aware

Compares self to others; wants to be like others, i.e., "normal"

More advanced stages

Has insight into own motives and behavior

Behaves in an ethically consistent manner; is consistent with own behavior

Is comfortable with uncertainty and complexities; resists seeing the world as black-and-white

Values his own and others' individuality and uniqueness

community involvement (Adams & Shea, 1979). Finally, there's evidence that adolescent inner-city delinquents have lower levels of ego development than nondelinquents (Frank & Quinlan, 1976).

Other research has examined variables that may influence advancement through the stages. It's been found that progress is tied to having a clearer sense of identity (Adams & Shea, 1979) and to being psychologically minded (Helson & Roberts, 1994; Westenberg & Block, 1993). Life challenge (in the form of successful careers) predicted progression to higher levels of ego development in adult women (Helson & Roberts, 1994). Indeed, even the successful handling of marital separation and divorce seems to promote ego development (Bursik, 1991). It's also of interest that ego resiliency (flexibility in degree of ego control), discussed earlier in the chapter, relates to attaining higher ego development (Westenberg & Block, 1993).

Ego Development and the Five-Factor Model

Does this theory of ego development relate in any way to the five-factor model? The available information suggests there's not a lot of connection. Einstein and Lanning (1998) found higher ego development related to greater conscientiousness in men but not women. Higher ego development related to greater openness in women but not men. The authors concluded that the two models are best thought of as complementary, as was also suggested by Loevinger (1993).

However, differences in the measures may play a role. Any of the five traits is likely to be manifested differently at different stages of ego development (Hogansen & Lanning, 2001). The five traits are measured by self-reports that don't permit that diversity to emerge. That is, you get to answer only the items you're given, and the items may or may not relate well to how that trait is reflected at your stage of ego development. Hogansen and Lanning figured out a way to measure the five factors from the sentence completions used to assess ego development. With the five factors scored this way, level of ego development related strongly to openness (r = .59) and more modestly to introversion and emotional stability. Whatever constitutes openness to experience seems to go along well with ego development. For the rest of the traits, the earlier conclusion may be right: these are better thought of as complementary models.

Assessment

Throughout this chapter we've pointed to ways in which ego psychology differs from Freudian psychoanalysis. It's also useful to consider that issue with respect to assessment. Assessment in ego psychology differs from psychoanalytic assessment in two ways. First, ego psychologists are interested more in the ego than in unconscious conflict. As a result, the techniques they've developed focus on assessing qualities of the ego.

A second difference (which goes hand in hand with the first) is a general difference in technique. Given the de-emphasis in the role of the unconscious, it didn't seem so important to try to ease information from the unconscious by projective techniques. Thus, ego psychology shifted away from reliance on projective tests. Some ego psychologists moved all the way to self-report instruments, although most blend projective and self-report methods.

One similarity does remain, however. Ego psychologists are willing (as was Freud) to draw on a wide range of formal and informal sources to obtain clues about personality.

Assessment of Lifestyles

Some assessment in ego psychology is highly informal. Recall Adler's belief that people develop lifestyles. Your lifestyle leads you to be especially attuned to certain kinds of inferiorities and to deal with them in a characteristic way. A reasonable question is how to identify a person's lifestyle.

Adler believed a person's lifestyle can be identified by asking the person about his or her earliest memories from childhood or infancy. Adler thought the nature of these memories gives a clue to the themes playing themselves out in the person's life. This idea has been borne out in research (Bruhn & Schiffman, 1982). In this research, people who see themselves as having control over events in their lives reported early memories of mastery over the environment. People who see themselves as having little control tended to recall experiences in which they were passive and events were beyond their control.

Interestingly enough, Adler didn't think it important that the memories be accurate. What's important is how you view the experiences you recall. It's *how the person looks at the event* that tells you the person's concerns, the nature of the inferiority feelings, and the domains in which the person is striving for superiority. Adler believed, in fact, that memories are very likely to be distorted by lifestyle (cf. Ross, 1989). For example, if your lifestyle is organized around the idea that others don't give you enough credit, your memories will tend to reflect that idea. Although any memories can be revealing, Adler felt that a person's earliest memories reveal the most, because they reflect the person's fundamental view of life. "It offers us an opportunity to see at one glance what he has taken as the starting point for his development" (Adler, 1956, p. 351).

Adler collected interesting illustrations of links between early memories and lifestyle. An example is a man whose life was filled with anxiety and jealousy over the possibility that others would be preferred to him. His earliest memory was of being held by his mother and then being put down so she could pick up his younger

Many psychologists believe that birth order plays a significant role in the development of personality.

brother. Adler's own first memories were of illness and death, and his lifestyle oriented around pursuit of a career in medicine (see also Box 10.4). Indeed, Adler found that among a group of medical doctors, memories of serious illness or a death in the family were frequently reported as first memories.

BOX 10.4

THE THEORIST AND THE THEORY
Adler's Lifestyle and the Ideas to Which It Led

The work of Alfred Adler provides an excellent illustration of how the elements of a theory often stem from the life experiences of the theorist (for detail on Adler's career see Hoffman, 1994). Several themes that Adler contributed to ego psychology drew directly from his own life, something of which he was very well aware (Bottome, 1939). Let's consider a couple of them.

Perhaps the easiest point to make pertains to what we've just said in the main text about early memories. Adler's lifestyle, including his theory, was organized partly around his interest in medicine and the body, and his earliest memories were of illness. Adler's lifestyle also reflected personal anxiety and fear of inferiority, and for good reason. As noted earlier, he was seriously ill as a child, and his parents were once told it was futile to try to educate him. Yet he struggled against these obstacles.

This aspect of his lifestyle is deeply symbolized in another of his early memories. He recalled being about five years old and being frightened over the fact that the path to school led through a cemetery (Adler, 1927). The other children weren't afraid, which only exaggerated his feelings of inferiority. One day, in an effort to rid himself of his fear, he ran back and forth through the cemetery, over and over. From then on he was able to walk through it on his way to school without difficulty.

This memory neatly captures Adler's lifelong tendency to combat his fears by deliberately forcing himself to stand up to them. There's something else, though, that makes this example even more interesting. Many years later Adler met a former

schoolmate and asked him something about the cemetery. The man was bewildered by the question, replying that there hadn't *been* a cemetery. After seeking out other former schoolmates and getting the same reply, Adler finally realized that his memory was wrong. This experience doubtlessly played a role in his view that it doesn't matter whether memories are accurate or not—they're still revealing.

As another illustration of how personal experience influenced Adler's views, consider his analysis of birth order (described in Box 10.3). Adler saw the second-born as someone with a constant sense of inferiority by virtue of being developmentally behind the firstborn. This can work in the second-born's favor, because it serves as a constant spur to strivings. But it can also lead to lifelong competitiveness and jealousy. Of considerable interest is the fact that Adler was second-born (1870) and throughout his life felt overshadowed by his older brother, who was a wealthy businessman (his name, ironically, was Sigmund). It seems likely that this experience led Adler to argue more generally for the impact of birth order on personality.

Finally, and most generally, recall how Adler's theory focuses on how people experience repeated feelings of inferiority and engage in compensatory strivings for superiority. This pervasive theme reflects virtually all of the experiences of Adler's life. His feelings of inferiority in several domains—physical and psychological—led to a great upward drive in his own behavior. This experience, in turn, helped lead Adler to believe that these same processes characterize everyone.

Assessment of Level of Ego Development

Another aspect of ego functioning that can be useful to assess is level of ego development. Loevinger's analysis of the stages of ego development has been used to create a systematic measure called the Sentence Completion Test for Ego Development (Loevinger & Wessler, 1970; for a more recent manual see Hy & Loevinger, 1996). It consists of a series of partial sentences to which the person writes an ending. Thus, its format is projective. Unlike most projective tests, though, it has good reliability and validity (Lilienfeld et al., 2000).

Each response is classified as reflecting one of the stages in Loevinger's model, from the impulsive stage onward (primitive earlier stages can't be measured with this test). Examples of responses reflecting various stages are in Table 10.4. The codings given to each response are entered into a formula, yielding an index of the person's overall ego development. Scorers who've been trained carefully show high interjudge reliability, and there's evidence of high internal consistency and test-retest reliability as well (Redmore & Waldman, 1975). This test was used to assess stage of ego development in the research done on Loevinger's theory discussed earlier in the chapter.

Table 10.4

Examples of responses to a sentence-completion item and the stage that they reflect. The item stem, "The thing I like about myself is—," is from the Washington University Sentence Completion Test (adapted from Hy & Loevinger, 1996).

Stage name	Response	Theme
Presocial	[not assessed]	
Symbiotic	[not assessed]	
Impulsive	. . . that I'm nice	Self-gratification
Self-protective	. . . that people like me . . . my grade in math	Exploitiveness
Conformist	. . . that I'm athletic . . . that I don't hate other people	Stereotypic thinking
Self-aware	. . . I'm very considerate of others . . . that I'm a straightforward person	Modified stereotype
Conscientious	. . . that I can forgive and maintain caring feelings . . . my ability to look for the good in most things	Events in social context
Individualistic	. . . that I'm different, but that's OK—I don't want to be like everyone else . . . that I'm really aware of others and how they relate to me	Multiple viewpoints
Autonomous	. . . my personality, my constant striving to become more competent, and yet my ability to be patient . . . my outlook on life, the fact that I can take people for who they are, and that I can stand by them while they deal with their problems	Recognition of mutual autonomy needs
Integrated	. . . the fact that I try to be honest with myself, even though I'm aware that that perception may be delusional . . . that I can think independently and creatively, that I don't judge people I meet, and that I can still be a child when I feel like it	Fully integrated

Problems in Behavior, and Behavior Change

Different ego psychologists emphasized different aspects of ego functioning, but one theme runs through them all: the key role of the ego's ability to adapt itself to the world. In line with this theme, problems in behavior are seen as reflecting deficiencies in this adaptation.

Ego psychologists view the process of adaptation as never-ending. In a sense, then, problems are part of life. People struggle to make themselves better, and difficulties in that struggle are inevitable. Problems become serious only if deficiencies are extreme. Thus well-being is defined not by whether you confront difficulties, but by how well you cope.

Inferiority and Superiority Complexes

Adler exemplifies this view. Recall his belief that inferiority feelings and superiority strivings cycle throughout life. The result usually is that people continue trying to get more proficient at what they do. The issue of inferiority is confronted repeatedly. Problems arise only if feelings of inferiority are so strong as to be overwhelming, preventing you from striving. When feelings of inferiority are that strong, the person is said to have an **inferiority complex.**

Adler believed inferiority complexes have two sources. One source is neglect or rejection during development. Being neglected may cause a person to feel unworthy and inferior in ways too large to overcome. This person may develop a lifestyle involving dependency or avoidance. Another source is pampering during childhood. As indicated earlier (Box 10.3), spoiling can undermine the child's desire to strive for superiority, again producing a mistaken lifestyle.

Sometimes an inferiority complex leads to passivity or avoidance. Sometimes, though, strong feelings of inferiority lead a person to *over*compensate, strive for superiority in inappropriate ways or to an exaggerated degree. Inappropriate striving is seen in a lifestyle that involves efforts to dominate others. Sometimes a lifestyle involves a driven way of striving in which the person has to excel at all costs. Such exaggerated strivings are sometimes called a **superiority complex.**

Adler also believed that people with problems tend to use certain strategies to protect whatever small sense of superiority they're able to hold onto. These strategies are aimed at diminishing the sense of inferiority. One strategy is to blame others for your shortcomings or failures. People using this strategy may spend all their time seeking revenge instead of making up the failure. Another strategy is to deprecate accomplishments or qualities of other people. This implies that your own qualities are better than they actually are. This strategy is obviously applied when others are competing with you, but it can also apply elsewhere. For example, having very high standards for a mate (you wouldn't consider someone who's not good looking, intelligent, a successful professional, and rich) may mean you're just trying to ease your own sense of inferiority. If no one out there is good enough for you, you must be *really* good.

Overcontrol and Undercontrol

Another way of thinking about problems returns us to the concept of ego control (Eisenberg et al., 2000). Specifically, being extreme on that dimension (along with the low ego resilience that seems to come along with it) can create problems (Block,

2002). Overcontrollers are prone to problems such as anxiety and depression (Robins et al., 1996). Undercontrollers, as their label suggests, are out of control. They are more likely to have school problems as adolescents, and to have symptoms of conduct disorders (Robins et al., 1996). As noted earlier in the chapter, they are also more prone to socially problematic behavior such as drug use, aggression, and sexual impulsiveness. Both overcontrollers and undercontrollers lack the flexibility that would help them adapt to the world.

Behavior Change

The process of therapeutic change from the viewpoint of ego psychology reflects the overall themes of this line of thought. Therapies practiced by ego psychologists place more emphasis on current problems than on factors in the past that might have led to the problems. The emphasis on current problems fits with a point about assessment in ego psychology. Ego psychologists are more likely than Freudian psychoanalysts to take the person's behavior at face value and not look for symbols and hidden meaning.

The therapist who operates from this viewpoint is more supportive than one who operates from the psychoanalytic viewpoint. On the other hand, the therapist is also clear about where the source of change must lie. That is, problems are viewed as something patients have let emerge in their own lives. The patient thus must take responsibility for dealing with the problems. This tendency to be direct with the patient is another way in which the therapeutic approaches differ.

One consequence of this shift in emphasis is to draw the patient into the therapeutic process as a collaborator. This increased emphasis on patient involvement can be seen as evolving directly from the core idea of ego psychology. That is, the major task of the ego is to promote adaptation to the world. If behavioral problems arise, it's because the ego isn't doing its job. For the ego to alter what it's doing, the patient has to become involved.

Ego Psychology: Problems and Prospects

The group of neoanalysts who came to be known as ego psychologists includes a large number of people. As a group they proposed a fairly diverse set of ideas. In all cases, however, the ideas reflect the theme that the ego is the most important aspect of personality. This theme is one of two that stand at the forefront of neoanalytic thinking.

Although ego psychology has had its adherents, it's fair to stand back and ask some questions about it. One reasonable question is whether these ideas really have anything at all to do with the psychoanalytic theory from which they evolved. Are these neoanalytic ideas really "analytic"? Or, despite the absorption with psychoanalytic traditions, do these ideas actually have more in common with concepts from other areas of personality psychology?

Keep in mind the angle from which the neoanalysts proceeded. Most of them wanted to develop their own ideas, but at the same time they wanted not to stray too far from Freud. After all, these people were *analysts*. That was their professional identity, to themselves, to one another, and to the world at large. As analysts, they thought of their ideas as amendments to Freud's theory rather than as separate and distinct theories.

All this orienting toward Freud, however, produced what was in some respects a very narrow view. As a result, the ideas can seem more revolutionary (to analysts) than they are. For example, it's widely believed that Freud created the concept of ego. Ego psychologists certainly saw themselves as building on a Freudian idea. But according to Loevinger (1976), Freud's theory was itself partly a reaction *against an already existing nineteenth-century ego psychology*. She also notes that her own theory of ego development was strongly foreshadowed in the writings of people who came before Freud (e.g., Bain, 1859; Mill, 1962/1859; Smith, 1969/1759).

Another comparison is also instructive. Aspects of ego psychology resemble ideas from a group of theorists (discussed later in the book) called humanistic. Though the latter group had a starting point very different from that of the neoanalysts, many themes in humanistic theories resemble themes of ego psychology. Despite this, analytically oriented people tend to ignore humanists. Again, the analytically oriented have tended to view their ideas in relation to Freud's theory, rather than in relation to the broader spectrum of ideas in personality psychology.

It's easy to understand why the writings of the ego psychologists disregard nineteenth-century ideas. *Most* psychologists don't know much about nineteenth-century ideas. However, the failure to note other literatures may say something more about ego psychology per se. In particular, psychoanalysis in the United States has long been identified with medicine. Nearly all psychoanalysts begin their training with an MD degree and then do a psychoanalytic specialization. This also was true for early ego psychologists (Adler and Hartmann, for example, were MDs). There's a natural tendency to use ideas that are discussed within one's professional circle and to disregard ideas from outside. Because analytically oriented theorists were mostly medical people, it was the ideas of medical people that they took seriously.

To some extent, ego psychology began relatively apart from the rest of psychology. It was a branch of psychoanalysis that was growing in the direction of psychology. This has changed over the years, as psychologists became more prominent in this group. Theorists such as the Blocks and Jane Loevinger have helped pull ego psychology toward academic personality psychology. This shift has served to integrate neoanalytic ideas more into the mainstream of academic thought. This integration has also yielded an increase in the tolerance and regard that academic psychologists in general have had for psychodynamic conceptualizations.

The evolution of ego psychology appears, however, to carry with it the seeds of a more complete break with traditional psychoanalytic theory. What's unique about psychoanalysis is its emphasis on the dynamics of the unconscious and on the importance of powerful primitive impulses. In large part, ego psychologists have abandoned this conceptual heritage. Although the theories are often still called psychodynamic, the dynamics that remain are very, very different from those that Freud asserted. In moving toward greater harmony with the rest of psychology, ego psychology is at the same time leaving Freud behind.

What are the prospects, then, for this view of human behavior? Some of the ideas of this group already have a permanent place in personality psychology—for example, White's ideas about effectance and competence. We are also certain that Loevinger's theory and that of the Blocks will continue to stand as influential views of human development and behavior. If these two theories in particular continue to inspire active research activities, as they do now, ego psychology will continue to remain an essential part of personality psychology.

SUMMARY

Neoanalytic theorists differed from Freud on several points. Many shared a feeling that Freud hadn't given enough emphasis to the ego and its functions. Accordingly, they devised ideas in which the ego plays a more central role. For this reason, they are termed ego psychologists.

Hartmann argued that the ego can function to facilitate the id's impulses but can also function autonomously in the service of better adaptation to the environment. He believed that the ego has a separate existence at birth (primary ego autonomy) and that ego functions often continue long after their initial purposes are served (secondary ego autonomy). Others, such as White, emphasized that the ego strives for competence and mastery over the environment. The motive to become more competent serves the goal of better adaptation.

Adler also proposed that people strive for better adaptations, but he assumed a different underlying reason. Adler argued that people repeatedly experience feelings of inferiority in one or another aspect of life and that they respond to those feelings with a compensatory striving for superiority, that is, movement toward greater perfection. Adler used the term *lifestyle* to refer to the person's characteristic constellation of inferiority feelings and preferred way of dealing with them. Some lifestyles are effective, but others (called mistaken lifestyles) are not.

Block and Block examined the effects of two other kinds of individual differences: differences in ego control (impulse control) and ego resiliency (flexibility in ego control). Too much ego control is bad; so is too little. Ego resiliency fosters better adaptation. Both qualities relate to behaviors that reflect restraint or impulsiveness, and ego resilience relates to better social development. Evidence suggests that ego control and ego resiliency may combine to form three clusters of persons— overcontrolled, undercontrolled, and resilient. The nature of these clusters converges in an interesting way with the five-factor model from Chapter 4.

Loevinger has examined how the ego's abilities grow and become more complex through a series of stages that extend into adulthood. In early stages the ego is focused on differentiating itself from others and on affirming its separate existence through expression of impulses. Later, the person begins to learn rules of conduct and to follow them to avoid group censure. Still later, the person begins to appreciate the diversity of viewpoints on existence and experience. People develop through these stages until they exhaust their ability to move further; not everyone goes through all stages. This approach to personality does not connect well at all to the five-factor model, except that ego development seems related to openness to experience.

Assessment in ego psychology partly shifts away from projective techniques toward more objective techniques (though Loevinger's test of ego development is projective). The content of assessment from this viewpoint focuses on the ego and how it's functioning.

From the viewpoint of ego psychology, problems in behavior always are a matter of degree, because no one is perfectly adapted to the world. Struggle is an intrinsic part of life, but serious feelings of inferiority can produce an inferiority complex (paralyzing inability to strive) or a superiority complex (overcompensatory strivings), either of which is disruptive. Another view of problems is that they derive from being either too high or too low in ego control, both of which represent patterns that are too rigid for successful adaptation.

The approach that ego psychologists take to therapy is similar in some ways to the psychoanalytic approach, but it also differs in important ways. For one, it focuses on the here-and-now problems that the person has, rather than on buried fixations. There is much less of an attempt to probe for deep meanings and a stronger tendency to accept statements at face value. The person seeking treatment is also brought more into the treatment process, as a collaborator in the attempt to produce behavior change.

GLOSSARY

Archetypes Aspects of the world that people have an inherited tendency to notice or perceive.

Collective unconscious Memories everyone has from human and even prehuman ancestors.

Competence motivation The motive to be effective or adept in dealing with the environment.

Effectance motivation The need to have an impact on the environment.

Ego control The extent to which a person modifies or inhibits impulse expression.

Ego psychology The neoanalytic theories that give ego functions central importance.

Ego resiliency The capacity to modify one's usual level of ego control to adapt to new situations.

Feelings of inferiority The realization that one is deficient in some way, minor or major.

Functional autonomy The continuance of an act even after its initial purpose no longer exists.

Inferiority complex Feelings of inferiority bad enough to suggest an inability to solve life's problems.

Lifestyle A person's pattern of inferiority feelings and manner of striving for superiority.

Mistaken lifestyle A lifestyle that isn't effective in adapting or attaining superiority.

Need for cognition A need to think about and impose meaningful structure on experiences.

Organ inferiority A weakness in an area of the body, making one vulnerable to illness there.

Primary ego autonomy The idea that the ego exists independently from the id from birth onward.

Principle of opposites The idea that life consists of polarities that oppose and balance each other.

Secondary ego autonomy The idea that an ego function can become satisfying in its own right.

Superiority complex Exaggerated strivings to excel to compensate for deep inferiority feelings.

■ **Object Relations Theories**
Self Psychology
Basic Anxiety

■ **Attachment Theory and Personality**
Attachment Patterns in Adults
How Many Patterns?
Stability and Specificity
Other Reflections of Adult Attachment
Attachment Patterns and the Five-Factor Model

■ **Erikson's Theory of
   Psychosocial Development**
Ego Identity, Competence,
   and the Experience of Crisis
Infancy
Early Childhood
Preschool
School Age
Adolescence
Young Adulthood
Adulthood

Old Age
The Epigenetic Principle
Identity as Life Story
Linking Erikson's Theory to Other
   Psychosocial Theories

■ **Assessment**
Object Relations, Attachment,
   and the Focus of Assessment
Play in Assessment

■ **Problems in Behavior,
   and Behavior Change**
Narcissism as a Disorder of Personality
Neurotic Needs
Attachment and Depression
Behavior Change

■ **Psychosocial Theories:
   Problems and Prospects**

SUMMARY

■   Ever since she was in high school, Christina has had a particular pattern in her love relationships with men. She tends to be close and clingy as the relationship is first being established, wanting almost to be joined to him. Later on, an ambivalent quality emerges. She wants closeness, but at the same time she does things that drive her lover away; she gets upset with him, gets into arguments over nothing, and isn't satisfied by anything he does to calm her. As he gets more and more irritated by this, and their relationship is more and more strained, she makes her final move—she breaks up. Even afterward there's ambivalence. Sometimes she recalls a former lover as being too good for her. Sometimes she thinks of them as no good at all. None of this makes her optimistic about her future. "Why can't I ever find the right kind of man?" she cries.

A s the ego became more prominent in neoanalytic theories and as its functions were examined in more detail, another change was also taking place. There was an increasing emphasis on the idea that personality is inherently social. Theorists began to stress that many of the issues in personality concern one's relationships with other people.

This is a considerable change of direction. As described in Chapters 8 and 9, Freud's ideas focused within the person. To him, people deal with outside reality only to satisfy impulses better. Even many ego psychologists tended to share this focus on the internal. They were more interested in how the ego works than in the interplay between it and the outside world. This wasn't true of all ego psychologists. For example, Adler (1930), who stressed striving for superiority, also noted the importance of caring for other people, which he saw as necessary to a complete person.

Adler's ideas about the social nature of personality were relatively simple. Ideas that others put forward on this theme were more complex, however. Those ideas form the basis of this chapter.

Object Relations Theories

We begin with a group of theories that have diverse origins and terminologies but are strikingly similar to one another. This group is referred to by the phrase **object relations** (for overviews see J. Klein, 1987; Masling & Bornstein, 1994; St. Clair, 1986). In the phrase *object relations* the "object" is another *person*. Thus these theories focus on the individual's relations to others.

The concept of object relations derives from an idea of Freud's (Eagle, 1984). Freud saw an ego cathexis as the creation of a bond from the ego to an external "object." It forms to release id energies effectively. Object relations theories focus on such bonds, but only for people as objects. Here the point isn't to satisfy the id. Instead, the bond is a *fundamental ego function*. It's the main focus for personality. As in other neoanalytic theories, the emphasis is on the ego (e.g., Fairbairn, 1954).

Object relations theories were developed by several people in the neoanalytic movement. They differ in many ways (J. Klein, 1987; St. Clair, 1986), but share two broad themes. First, they all emphasize that a person's pattern of relating to others is laid down in early childhood. Second, they all assume that patterns formed at that time tend to recur over and over throughout later life.

One influential object relations theory is that of Margaret Mahler (1968; Mahler, Pine, & Bergman, 1975; see also Blanck & Blanck, 1986). She believed that newborns begin life in a state of psychological fusion with others. In her view personality development is a process of breaking down this fusion, of becoming an individual who's separate and distinct from others.

The period when the infant is fused with its mother is called **symbiosis.** Boundaries between mother and self haven't been built yet (e.g., the infant doesn't distinguish its mother's nipple from its own thumb). Around six months of age, a shift begins. The child starts acquiring an awareness of its separate existence, a process Mahler termed **separation-individuation.** This process involves exploration away from mother, but this must be gradual. Remember that unity with the mother is all the infant has ever known. If movement away from fusion comes too fast or goes too far, the child will experience *separation anxiety.* This renews the desire to be with mother. Thus, there's a back-and-forth quality to the child's behavior, first moving away, then drawing close again.

There's a built-in conflict here between two pressures in the child at this time. The first is a wish to be taken care of by, and reunited with, the love object (mother). The second is a fear of being overwhelmed in a merger with the love object, and a desire to establish one's own selfhood. Thus, the child strives for individuation and separation but also wants the earlier sense of union. This conflict is important in adult behavior, as well.

How the mother acts during this period determines the child's later adjustment. She should combine emotional availability with a gentle nudge toward independence. If the mother is too present in the child's experience, the child can't establish a separate existence. If there's too much push toward individuation, the child will experience a sense of rejection and loss.

Eventually (at about age three), the child develops a stable mental representation of its mother. Now she will be with the child all the time symbolically. The "object relation" is internalized. In the future the child will use this image in two ways. First, it will be a lens through which the child will view mother in the future. Second, this internal image will be generalized to other people. In many respects the child will act toward other people as though they were its mother (and father).

Often the early years include some stresses—a sense of rejection from a parent or too much smothering fusion. If so, those stresses are carried by your internal object representations into your later life. Because this internalization derives from infant experiences, there's a lot of potential for distortion. Object representations don't always reflect the experiences accurately. What matters, though, isn't what *happens* in childhood, but what the child *experiences* as happening.

You may not be very persuaded by the idea that you relate to others as though they were your mother and father. You think you treat everyone uniquely. An object relations theorist would reply that you think that because you're looking at yourself from *inside* your patterns (see also Andersen & Chen, 2002). Being inside them, you don't notice them. You notice only variations within the patterns. You think the variations are big, but in some ways they're really quite minor.

In this view, the pattern of relating to others that you develop in early childhood forms the core of your way of relating to others for the rest of your life. Indeed, this pattern forms the very core of your personality. As such, you take it for granted as much as any other aspect of your personality. It's the lens through which you view not just your parents but the entire world.

Self Psychology

Another important neoanalyst was Heinz Kohut. Kohut felt that relationships create the structure of the self. Thus, his theory is called **self psychology** (e.g., A. Goldberg, 1985). Despite this different label, his theory focuses on experiences that others termed object relations.

Kohut began with the idea that people have narcissistic (self-centered) needs that have to be satisfied through others. He used the term **selfobject** to refer to someone who's important in satisfying your needs. In early childhood, selfobjects (parents) are experienced as extensions of the self. Later the term *selfobject* means any person *as he or she is experienced within the structure of the self.* Selfobjects still exist from the self's point of view and to serve the self's needs.

Kohut thought the child acquires a self through interaction with parents. Parents engage in **mirroring:** responding to the child in an empathic, accepting way. Mirroring gratifies the child's narcissistic needs, because it makes the child temporarily the center of the universe. The child's sense of self at first is grandiose. The illusion of all-importance must be sustained to a degree throughout development, to create a sense of self-importance to be carried into adulthood. It also must be tempered, though, so the child can deal with difficulties and frustrations later in life.

In a healthy personality the grandiosity is modified and channeled into realistic activities. It turns into ambition and self-esteem. If there are severe failures of mirroring, though, the child never has an adequate sense of self. This child will grow with deeper narcissistic needs than other people, because the needs have been unmet. Thus, he will continue relating to selfobjects (other people) immaturely. A delicate balance is required here: parents must give the child enough mirroring to nurture development, but not too much. This is similar to the balance between forces in Mahler's theory, regarding separation-individuation and fusion with the other.

Mirroring continues to be important in relationships throughout life (see Tesser, 1991). Later mirroring involves **transferences** from parents to other selfobjects. This use of that term means you transfer the orientation you've developed to your parents to other people, using it as a frame of reference for them (Andersen & Chen, 2002). In effect, other people become parent substitutes and you expect them to mirror you as your parents did. This parallels Mahler's idea that the internal object relation regarding a parent is used in forming later relationships.

Kohut's conception of love illustrates adult mirroring. He thought of a love relationship as one in which two people are selfobjects for each other. They mirror each other and enhance each other's self-esteem (Kohut, 1977). Thus, a healthy narcissism in normal adults, which Kohut saw as part of life, is satisfied and nurtured properly through mutual mirroring.

Basic Anxiety

Several of these themes were foreshadowed in the writings of Karen Horney (pronounced 'horn-eye'), another post-Freudian (see Box 11.1). Horney (1937, 1945) argued that, from childhood on, people have a sense of insecurity she called **basic anxiety.** This is a feeling of being abandoned, of being isolated and helpless in a hostile world. Basic anxiety can be minimized by being raised in a home where there's security, trust, love, warmth, and tolerance, but it remains there for everyone.

Horney (1937) said people develop strategies to combat basic anxiety. A child may try to strike back against the people who've abandoned it. A person may try to

BOX 11.1

THE THEORIST AND THE THEORY
Karen Horney's Feminism

Although much of Horney's work concerned such general themes as the role of basic anxiety in behavior, she also had much to say regarding the psychoanalytic view of women. Horney was a vocal critic of Freud, believing that he'd managed to get nearly everything wrong.

Recall that, to Freud, a woman's life is deeply affected by the fact that she has no penis. According to him, women feel castrated and inferior, and they envy and resent men throughout their lives because of it. Horney came to a very different view (for a biographical account see Quinn, 1987). Her great feelings of pleasure and pride in childbirth and motherhood led her to realize how shallow were the comparable experiences of men. Men play a minor role in creating and nurturing new life, and Horney came to think that this leads to a deep sense of inferiority. This idea was also confirmed in her therapy experiences with men, who gave considerable evidence of envying women's ability to have children.

One result of men's feelings of inferiority is an attempt to compensate through achievement. The world of business is an attempt to *create,* although such creations can never compare to creating a baby. Besides these achievement efforts, men try to hide their inferiorities by disparaging and devaluing women. By denying women equal rights, men are able to hide from themselves the fact that they can never be as valuable to human society as women.

Horney argued forcefully that the tendency of women to feel inferior arises not from penis envy but from the cultural context in which they live. If women regard themselves as unworthy, it's only because men have treated them that way for so long. It isn't penises that women want, but the ability to participate as full members of society (Horney was born in 1885, so keep in mind that the culture in which she lived was more restrictive than that of the present).

How did Freud feel about all this? He never responded directly to her arguments, but late in life he wrote something that probably was aimed in her direction. He wrote, "We shall not be very greatly surprised if a woman analyst who has not been sufficiently convinced of the intensity of her own wish for a penis also fails to attach proper importance to that factor in her patients" (Freud, 1949/1940). To Freud, the source of Horney's theory was her own penis envy.

Horney took many positions that anticipated and foreshadowed later developments in psychological theory and in Western culture more broadly. Her feminist stance was no exception. She did much to create the outlines of a feminist agenda for the future. She argued that a woman's identity is not to be found in the mere reflection of her husband. Rather, women should seek their own identities by developing their abilities and pursuing careers. Truly, Karen Horney was a woman ahead of her time.

win back love by being submissive, never doing anything that could antagonize others. A third possibility is to develop an inflated self-concept to compensate for insecurity. A child who considers it impossible to win back a parent's love may try to gain power over others, to compensate for the feelings of helplessness.

Horney coined the term **vicious cycle** to refer to a pattern that can follow from basic anxiety. Feeling insecurity leads to an enhanced awareness of the need for love. If the need isn't met through whatever strategies are available (and often it isn't), the result is a further increase in the sense of anxiety and insecurity. Only if the need for affection is met is the cycle broken.

Attachment Theory and Personality

The ideas discussed thus far fit in many ways with ideas proposed by theorists interested in the infant's **attachment** to its mother (e.g., Ainsworth, Blehar, Waters, & Wall, 1978; Bowlby, 1969, 1988; Sroufe & Fleeson, 1986). Attachment is an emotional connection. The need for such a connection is a basic element of the human experience (see Baumeister & Leary, 1995). The first attachment theorist was John Bowlby. He believed the clinging and following of the infant serve an important biological purpose: they keep the infant close to the mother, increasing the infant's chances of survival.

A basic theme in attachment theory is that mothers (and others) who are responsive to the infant create a secure base for the child. The infant needs to know that the major person in his or her life is *dependable*, is there whenever needed. This sense of security gives the child a base from which to explore the world. It also provides a place of comfort (a safe haven) when the child is threatened (Figure 11.1).

Attachment theorists also assume that the child builds implicit mental "working models" of self, others, and the nature of relationships. These working models are later used to relate to the world (Bowlby, 1969). This is similar both to Mahler's idea about internalized object representations guiding future experiences and to Kohut's idea of selfobjects.

To assess attachment Mary Ainsworth and her colleagues devised a procedure called the **strange situation** (Ainsworth et al., 1978). This is a series of events involving the infant's mother and a stranger. Of special relevance are two times when the infant is left alone with the stranger, then the mother returns. Assessors observe the infant throughout, paying special attention to its responses to the mother's return.

This procedure has identified several patterns. *Secure attachment* is reflected by normal distress when mother leaves and happy enthusiasm when she returns. There are also three types of *insecure attachment*. An *ambivalent* (or *resistant*) baby is clingy and becomes unusually upset when mother leaves. The response to mother's return mixes approach with rejection and anger. The infant seeks contact with its mother but then angrily resists all efforts to be soothed. In the *avoidant* pattern, the infant stays calm when mother leaves and responds to her return in an avoiding, rejecting way. It's as though this infant expects to be abandoned and is retaliating in kind.

Observations made in the home suggest a basis for variations in attachment (Ainsworth, 1983; Ainsworth et al., 1978). Mothers of securely attached infants

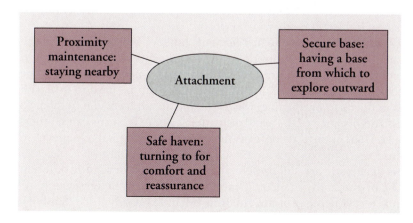

Figure 11.1

Three defining features of attachment and three functions of attachment: Attachment provides a secure base for exploration, keeps the infant nearby and safe, and provides a source of comfort (adapted from Hazan & Shaver, 1994).

Early attachment patterns can influence the quality of later social relationships.

respond to their infants' crying and quickly return their smiles. They also show "synchronous" behavior—making appropriate replies to a variety of infant actions (Isabella, Belsky, & von Eye, 1989). Mothers of ambivalent babies are inconsistent, sometimes responsive and sometimes not. Mothers of avoidant babies are distant, radiating a kind of emotional unavailability and sometimes being outright rejecting or neglectful.

Interestingly enough, it's not always the mothers' actions that differ between groups. For example, mothers of secure and avoidant infants don't differ in how much total time they spend holding their babies. Mothers of avoidant babies, however, are less likely to hold the baby *when it signals it wants to be held.* Timing apparently can be very important.

On the basis of findings such as these, Hazan and Shaver (1994) characterized the secure, ambivalent, and avoidant attachment patterns as reflecting three possible answers to the question "Can I count on my attachment figure to be available and responsive when needed?" The possible answers—yes, no, and maybe—correspond to the secure, avoidant, and ambivalent patterns.

At first it was believed that all infants fell into the three groups just described. Later a rarer group was identified, called *disorganized/disoriented* (Main & Solomon, 1986). Some of these act in contradictory ways (e.g., approaching but with its head turned away). Some appear disoriented (freezing, as if dazed). This child's behavior often differs greatly between the two parents (Main & Solomon, 1986), seeming secure with one parent but not the other.

In theory, it's possible to get past an insecure attachment by forming a better one with someone later on. This is hard, however, because insecure attachment leads to actions that alienate others. This interferes with creating a new attachment. The clinginess mixed with rejection in the ambivalent pattern can be hard to deal with (recall Christina in the chapter opening, who displayed an adult version of this). So can the aloofness and distance of the avoidant pattern. These patterns cause others to react negatively. That, in turn, reconfirms the perceptions that led to patterns in the first place. Insecure patterns thus have a self-perpetuating quality.

The patterns of age one are still present at age six, though in slightly different form (Table 11.1). In one study, infant attachment could be identified by current responses to parents for 84 percent of the children (Main & Cassidy, 1988, Study 1).

Table 11.1

Four forms of attachment related behavior, viewed at one year and six years of age (adapted from Main & Cassidy, 1988).		
Name of pattern at 1 year	**Behavior at 1 year**	**Behavior at 6 years**
Secure	Seeks interaction, closeness, contact with returning parent. Readily soothed by parent and returns to play.	Initiates conversation with returning parent or responds to parent's overture. Remains calm throughout.
Avoidant	Actively avoids and ignores returning parent, looks away, remains occupied with toys.	Minimizes opportunity for interaction with returning parent, looking and speaking only briefly, returns to toys.
Ambivalent	Distress over separation isn't soothed by parent. Child wants contact, but shows overt to subtle signs of anger.	Posture and voice exaggerate sense of intimacy and dependency. Shows some resistance, subtle signs of hostility.
Disorganized/disoriented*	Shows one or several signs of disorganization (contradictory cues) or disorientation (freezing). Usually shows these cues to one parent only.	Assumes partial parental role toward parents. Attempts to control and direct parent behavior, by either humiliating parent or being overly solicitous.

*At age six, this pattern is relabeled as Controlling

Secure children were still acting secure, avoidant ones were still withdrawn, and ambivalent ones were still being both dependent and sullen. A change had occurred in the disorganized/disoriented children, who were now controlling their parents in an almost adult way, sometimes being embarrassing, sometimes doing caregiving.

Attachment Patterns in Adults

Attachment behavior in childhood is interesting, but more relevant to our goals is how these ideas relate to adult personality. Research on this question began with the idea that the working models of relationships developed in childhood are carried into adulthood (with modifications along the way). These working models influence the adult's social relationships. In that way, they represent the core of personality.

During the past decade and a half, research on adult attachment patterns has exploded (see Cassidy & Shaver, 1999; Hazan & Shaver, 1994; Simpson & Rholes, 1998; Sperling & Berman, 1994). The first study was done by Cindy Hazan and Phillip Shaver (1987). Participants classified themselves from descriptions as being secure, ambivalent, or avoidant. They then described the most important romance of their life (past or current) on several scales (see Figure 11.2).

Secure adults described their most important love relationship as more happy, friendly, and trusting, compared with the other two groups. Their relationships also had lasted longer. Avoidant adults were less likely than the others to report accepting their lovers' imperfections. Ambivalents experienced love as an obsessive

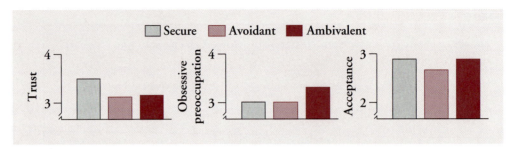

Figure 11.2

Adults with a secure attachment pattern report higher levels of trust in their romantic partner than do other groups, those with an ambivalent pattern report greater obsessive
preoccupation, and those with an avoidant pattern report lower levels of acceptance of
their partners' imperfections (adapted from Hazan & Shaver, 1987).

preoccupation, with a desire for reciprocation and union, extreme emotional highs
and lows, and extremes of both sexual attraction and jealousy. These people were also
more likely than others to report that the relationship had been love at first sight.

Hazan and Shaver also investigated the mental models these people held on the
nature of relationships (see Table 11.2). Secure adults said, in effect, love is real and
when it comes it stays. Avoidants were more cynical, saying that romantic love doesn't
last. Ambivalent subjects showed their ambivalence. They said falling in love is easy
and happens often to them, but they also agreed that love doesn't last. Other research suggests that ambivalent college students are most likely to have obsessive and
dependent love relationships (Collins & Read, 1990). Avoidants are the least likely
to report being in love either presently or in the past (Feeney & Noller, 1990). Secures show the most interdependence, commitment, and trust (Mikulincer, 1998b;
Simpson, 1990).

Table 11.2

Mental models of love held by adults of three attachment groups
(adapted from Hazan & Shaver, 1987).

Endorsed *more* often by secure adults than others:

   In some relationships, romantic love really lasts; it doesn't fade with time.

Endorsed *less* often by secure adults than others:

   The kind of head-over-heels romantic love depicted in novels and movies doesn't exist
   in real life.

Endorsed *more* often by avoidant adults than others:

   Intense romantic love is common at the beginning of a relationship, but it rarely lasts forever.

   It's rare to find someone you can really fall in love with.

Endorsed *more* often by ambivalent adults than others:

   It's easy to fall in love.

   I feel myself beginning to fall in love often.

How Many Patterns?

The proliferation of work on adult attachment has raised many issues, complicating the picture. Early studies used the three main categories from the infancy work, but another approach has also emerged. Bartholomew and Horowitz (1991) started with Bowlby's notion of working models, but focused on models of self and other rather than a model of the relationship. They argued for two dimensions. One is a positive versus negative model of self (the self is lovable or not). The other is a positive versus negative model of others (others are trustworthy or not). The dimensions are often termed anxiety and avoidance, respectively (Brennan, Clark, & Shaver, 1998). With this approach, hypotheses sometimes are tested using the two dimensions, and sometimes people are grouped by their models of self and other (Figure 11.3). Two of these groups are equivalent to the secures and ambivalents from the other approach. However, avoidants from the other approach are two groups here, which are called dismissive and fearful, depending on whether anxiety is involved.

The literature of adult attachment research is divided on which of these approaches to use. Each has a conceptual strength. The three-category approach nicely conveys the sense that a significant other can be either available, unpredictable, or unavailable. The two-dimensional (or four-category) approach nicely conveys the sense that two separate issues are involved in the attachment response. This issue doubtlessly will continue to be debated in the years to come.

Stability and Specificity

Two more questions about this view of personality concern its stability and its generality. If the attachment pattern is part of personality, it should remain fairly stable. Does it? If attachment concerns key figures in one's life, are the same patterns used in casual interactions or groups?

First, consider stability. Although findings are mixed, attachment seems to be moderately stable over fairly long periods of time. Fraley (2002) has concluded from a review of studies that a prototype for close relationships arises in infancy, and it doesn't go away, despite new experiences. On the other hand, moderate stability is not total stability. Some people change, and some change more than others. There is evidence that people who vary in self-portrayal over time are insecure at core, but periodically feel more secure (Davila, Burge, & Hammen, 1997).

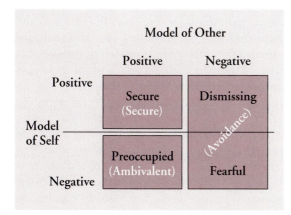

Figure 11.3

Combinations of positive and negative views of self and other, yielding four types of attachment patterns. In white are shown the names of the comparable patterns from the three-category model (adapted from Bartholomew & Horowitz, 1991).

What about specificity? Does each person have one pattern of relating to others, or do people have many patterns for different relationships? The answer seems to be many patterns. We've already mentioned that even infants sometimes display one pattern to one parent and a different pattern to the other parent. This diversity in relational behavior also appears in adults (Baldwin, Keelan, Fehr, Enns, & Koh-Rangarajoo, 1996; Bartholomew & Horowitz, 1991; Cook, 2000; La Guardia, Ryan, Couchman, & Deci, 2000; Pierce & Lydon, 2001). For example, one study had participants define each of their ten closest relationships in terms of the three categories. Across the ten descriptions, almost everyone used at least two patterns and nearly half used all three (Baldwin et al., 1996). There's also evidence that people display particular patterns of attachment to groups, distinct from their patterns for close relationships (Smith, Murphy, & Coats, 1999). There's even evidence that religious beliefs involve yet another pattern of attachment (Kirkpatrick, 1998).

Thus, the ways people relate to others in their lives—even significant others—does seem to have variability. There may be a "general" orientation for starting new relationships, or a "central tendency" among the various orientations that a person takes (Crittenden, 1990; Pierce & Lydon, 2001). And these may well derive from early childhood experiences. But adult behavior definitely has more complexity than would occur if each person had just a single way of relating to others.

Other Reflections of Adult Attachment

A surprising range of behaviors has been tied to the attachment patterns that people report for close relationships. Hazan and Shaver (1990) studied relations between attachment and people's orientations to work. Recall that ambivalence involves a sense of insecurity. Consistent with this, ambivalents report unhappiness with the recognition they get at work and their degree of job security. They're also most likely to say their work is motivated by a desire for others' approval. Avoidants report a desire to keep busy with work, and they socialize less during leisure time. Hazan and Shaver suggested that avoidants use work as a way to escape from their lack of relationships.

A good deal of research has looked at how attachment patterns relate to comfort seeking and caregiving in stressful situations. In one study (Simpson, Rholes, & Nelligan, 1992), women were told they were going to do a task that creates anxiety. They then waited for five minutes with their boyfriends, who were to do a different task. The women's responses depended on their attachment pattern. As anxiety increased, secure women sought support from their partners, talked about being nervous, and so on. Avoidant women did the opposite: the more anxious they got, the *less* they sought support. The men also varied. Among secure men, the more anxiety their partners showed, the more reassuring they were. Among avoidant men, the more anxiety their partners showed, the *less* they offered reassurance (see also Kobak & Hazan, 1991). Others have found avoidant men even get angry when their partners show signs of distress (Rholes, Simpson, & Oriña, 1999).

This pattern of results has been confirmed and extended in several ways. The tendency to give less support to partners under stress has been observed among avoidant women, as well as men (Simpson, Rholes, Oriña, & Grich, 2002). These patterns of support giving have also been confirmed by Feeney and Collins (2001) using different methods. They found that avoidance related inversely to a measure of responsive caregiving; avoidance also related inversely to reports of prosocial orientation, trust, and interdependence. Anxiety related to higher levels of compulsive caregiving, and also to higher levels of egoistic motivation and lower levels of trust.

Seeking and supplying support has also been looked at in other situations. For example, Fraley and Shaver (1998) observed couples at an airport where one was leaving on a flight. They found that avoidant women sought contact less, did less caregiving, and displayed more behavioral avoidance than more secure women. Westmaas and Silver (2001) studied a nonromantic situation. They looked at how students reacted to a stranger they thought was being treated for cancer. Those with more avoidance were less supportive in interacting with her.

Those findings are about how people behave in dyads. Another study examined differences in individual coping responses to stress. This study looked at people dealing with threats of missile attacks in Israel (Mikulincer, Florian, & Weller, 1993). Avoidants used more "distancing" coping (trying not to think about the situation) than did other people. Ambivalents had higher levels of a wide range of ineffective emotion-focused reactions (self-criticism, wishing they could change how they felt). Secure people used their social support more than did the other groups.

Recall that one aspect of secure infant attachment is the sense of a secure base. This aspect of attachment in adults has also been examined in several studies. Security relates to an exploratory orientation (Green & Campbell, 2000), perhaps because the sense of security causes people to react more positively to neutral stimuli (Mikulincer, Hirschberger, Nachmias, & Gillath, 2001). Security also reduces the typical negative reactions to out-groups (Mikulincer & Shaver, 2001), also suggesting willingness to explore. On the other side of the coin, there's evidence that the avoidant pattern leads people to perceive hostile intent underlying others' behavior (Mikulincer, 1998).

Also of interest is how people with the various attachment patterns relate to one another. Unsurprisingly, secure partners are most desired, and they tend to wind up with each other (Collins & Read, 1990). Both partners are less satisfied in relationships where the man is avoidant and in relationships where the woman is ambivalent. On the other hand, there's evidence that avoidant men with ambivalent women tend to be stable pairings (Kirkpatrick & Davis, 1994), despite the dissatisfactions. Why? Avoidant men also avoid conflict, which may help the relationship run smoothly. Ambivalent women may work harder at holding things together.

Pairings of avoidants with avoidants and of ambivalents with ambivalents are rare (Kirkpatrick & Davis, 1994). This fits with the idea that people with insecure attachment patterns steer away from partners who would treat them as they were treated in infancy. Avoidants avoid partners who will be emotionally inaccessible, and ambivalents avoid partners who will be inconsistent (Collins & Read, 1990; Kirkpatrick & Davis, 1994; Pietromonaco & Carnelley, 1994; Simpson, 1990).

This pattern of findings also suggests more generally that people are sensitive to the issue that was critical to them earlier. Perhaps in holding the mental model that people will let them down, avoidants consider only people who display more closeness than they'd had earlier. Perhaps in holding the mental model that people are inconsistent, ambivalents consider only people who provide consistency—even if the consistency is consistent distance.

Attachment Patterns and the Five-Factor Model

The research on adult attachment has also raised a question from another part of personality psychology. Recall that many people are interested in how various views of personality relate to the five-factor model of trait structure. This has also been examined with attachment patterns in adults. At least two groups have found substantial correlations between measures of adult attachment and two traits from the five-factor model (Carver, 1997a; Shaver & Brennan, 1992). These studies used the three-category view of attachment. They found that avoidants are introverted, secures are extraverted, and ambivalents are high in neuroticism or anxiety proneness.

An even stronger correspondence seems implied by the alternate approach to attachment. Recall that it rests on two dimensions. As noted earlier, the dimensions are sometimes termed avoidance (of close social ties) and anxiety (about social relations). Although the focus there is on relationships as a context, the dimensions strongly resemble introversion–extraversion and neuroticism. Maybe avoidants are simply not that interested in social connections because they're introverts. This would be consistent with the finding that avoidants encode less when listening to a tape about relationships than do secures (Fraley, Garner, & Shaver, 2000)

If one added the twist of viewing extraversion as a desire for social incentives (from Chapter 7) and the idea that neuroticism is essentially anxiety proneness, the fit is even closer. Given the focus on relationships as a context, it might even be argued that the attachment patterns represent focused versions of extraversion and neuroticism. Alternatively, they might represent ways in which extraversion and neuroticism are displayed in particular classes of settings.

Do these patterns in personality arise from patterns of parenting (as held by psychosocial theorists)? Or are they manifestations of genetically determined traits, manifestations that simply happen to be social (as held by others)? One study of a very large national adult sample found that reports of interpersonal trauma (from abuse, to threat with a weapon, to parental violence) related to insecure adult attachment (Mickelson, Kessler, & Shaver, 1997). So did a history of parental depression and anxiety. These findings suggest a social origin to the patterns. Simpson et al. (2002) reported that measures of extraversion and neuroticism did not duplicate the effects of attachment patterns. So even though there is overlap, the attachment dimensions seem not to be identical with the big-five traits. Nonetheless, much more information on this issue is needed.

Erikson's Theory of Psychosocial Development

We turn now to what is probably the most elaborate of psychosocial theories, that of Erik Erikson (1950, 1963, 1968). Erikson adopted Freud's view that personality develops in a series of stages. However, whereas Freud's is a theory of psychosexual development, Erikson's is a theory of psycho*social* development. It describes the impact of social phenomena across life.

Another difference pertains to the age span involved. The stages that Freud described unfold in the first few years of life. In contrast, Erikson believed that personality evolves throughout life, from birth through maturity to death. He also believed no part of life is intrinsically more important than any other. Erikson thus was one of the first to propose the idea of **life-span development.** Many consider this to be one of his most important contributions to psychology.

Ego Identity, Competence, and the Experience of Crisis

The central theme of Erikson's theory is **ego identity** and its development (Erikson, 1968, 1974). Ego identity is the consciously experienced sense of self. It derives from transactions with social reality. A person's ego identity changes constantly in response to events in the social environment. To Erikson, forming and maintaining a strong sense of ego identity is critical.

According to the principle of life-span development, all periods of a person's life are important, infancy through adulthood—even old age.

A second major theme in Erikson's theory concerns competence and personal adequacy. As you'll see shortly, his stages focus on aspects of mastery. If a stage is managed well, the person emerges with feelings of competence. If not, the person has feelings of inadequacy. This theme in Erikson's theory—that a desire for competence is a motivating force behind people's actions—is similar in some ways to White's ideas about competence, discussed in Chapter 10.

Erikson viewed development as a series of periods in which some issue is prominent. In his view, people experience a **psychosocial crisis,** or **conflict,** during each stage. The terms *crisis* and *conflict* are interchangeable here. They have a special meaning, though, that differs from the use of either word in day-to-day speech. Here a crisis is a *turning point:* a period when potential for growth is high but when the person is also quite vulnerable. Each crisis is relatively long (none is shorter than about a year) and some are quite long (perhaps thirty years). Thus, Erikson's use of the word conveys the sense of crucial importance more than the sense of time pressure.

The "conflict" in each crisis isn't a confrontation between persons, nor is it a conflict within personality. Rather, it's a struggle between attaining some psychological quality versus failing to attain it. To Erikson, the conflict never ends. Even handling it in the period when it's most intense doesn't mean you've mastered it once and for all. The conflict is always there to a degree, and you confront it repeatedly in different forms throughout life.

Erikson identified eight psychosocial stages. The first four parallel periods of psychosexual development outlined by Freud. Each focuses on some aspect of transactions with social reality. Each has a conflict, or crisis. Each conflict pits two possibilities against each other, as a pair of opposed psychological qualities. One of the pair is obviously adaptive, the other appears less so. The labels that Erikson gave to the two qualities indicate the nature of the crisis.

People negotiate each stage by developing a balance between the qualities for which the stage is named. The point isn't just to acquire the "good" quality. In fact, it's important that the ego incorporate *both* sides of the conflict, at least a little. Having too much of the quality that seems good can create problems. For example, if you had only "basic trust" and absolutely no sense of "basic mistrust," you'd be unable to deal effectively with a world that's sometimes *not* trustworthy.

Nonetheless, successful negotiation of a stage does imply that the balance is weighted more toward the positive value than the negative one. If this occurs, the person emerges from the crisis with a positive orientation toward future events relevant to that conflict. Erikson used several terms to refer to this positive orientation, for example, **ego quality, ego strength,** and **virtue** (Erikson, 1964; Stevens, 1983). Once established, these qualities remain a part of your personality.

Erikson was very reluctant to specify age norms for stages. He believed people pass through the stages in order, but that each person has a unique timetable. Thus, it's hard to say when each stage will begin and end for a person. The ages given here are only rough approximations.

Infancy

The first stage (see Figure 11.4) is infancy, roughly the first year. The conflict at this stage—the most fundamental crisis of life—is between a sense of *basic trust versus basic mistrust*. In this stage the infant is totally dependent on others to meet its most basic needs. If the needs are met, the infant develops a sense of security and trust. This is reflected by the infant's feeding easily, sleeping well, and eliminating regularly. Caretakers can leave the infant alone for short periods without causing too much

Figure 11.4

Erikson's eight psychosocial stages, the approximate age range in which each occurs, and the crisis that dominates each stage.

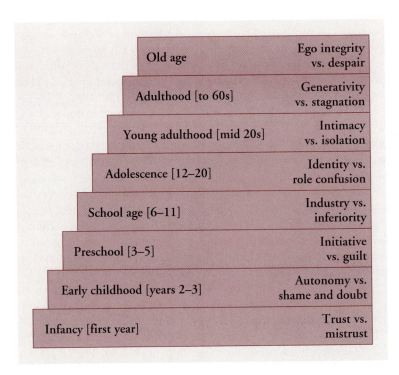

Old age	Ego integrity vs. despair
Adulthood [to 60s]	Generativity vs. stagnation
Young adulthood [mid 20s]	Intimacy vs. isolation
Adolescence [12–20]	Identity vs. role confusion
School age [6–11]	Industry vs. inferiority
Preschool [3–5]	Initiative vs. guilt
Early childhood [years 2–3]	Autonomy vs. shame and doubt
Infancy [first year]	Trust vs. mistrust

distress, because the infant has learned to "trust" that they'll return. Mistrust is reflected by fitful sleep, fussiness in feeding, constipation, and greater distress when the infant is left alone.

The sense of trust is extremely important. It provides a basis for believing that the world is predictable, especially relationships. Trust is enhanced by interactions in which caregivers are attentive, affectionate, and responsive. A sense of mistrust is created by inconsistent treatment, emotional unavailability, or rejection. This portrayal closely resembles ideas concerning object relations, basic anxiety, and attachment patterns seen several times already in this chapter. A predominance of trust over mistrust gives rise to the ego strength of *hope*. Hope is an enduring belief that wishes are attainable. It is a kind of optimism about life.

Early Childhood

The second stage is early childhood (the second and third years of life). The focus of children's efforts begins to shift to gaining control over their actions. The crisis of this stage concerns these efforts. It's about creating a sense of *autonomy* in actions *versus shame and doubt* about being able to act independently.

Erikson followed Freud in assuming that toilet training was an important event here, but for different reasons. To Erikson, acquiring control over bladder and bowels is a way to gain feelings of autonomy (self-direction, independence). Achieving control over these functions gives a sense of control, as opposed to being at the mercy of your body's impulses. But this is just one way to gain these feelings. When children interact effectively with people and objects, feelings of autonomy and competence are strengthened. If the efforts lead to failure, ridicule, or criticism—or if parents don't let the children act on their own—the result is feelings of shame and self-doubt. Management of this conflict properly leads to the ego quality of *will:* the determination to exercise free choice.

Much of the research bearing on Erikson's theory focuses on the idea that successful management of the crisis of one stage prepares you to deal with the next crisis. Let's consider how this idea applies to the first two stages. The sense of basic trust is reflected in secure attachment. In one study, attachment was assessed at one year; then at two-and-a-half years the children and their mothers came to a laboratory where they could explore a play area (Hazen & Durrett, 1982). Observers coded how many times the child went alone (or led the mother) to a new part of the area—action that reflects autonomy and self-initiation of behavior. They also coded how often the child was *led by* the mother into new parts of the area—action that's *not* autonomous.

As can be seen in Figure 11.5, children who'd been securely attached a year and a half earlier explored more than those who'd been less securely attached. Further, a higher percentage of the exploration was self-initiated (autonomous) among the securely attached. Conceptually similar results have been reported by several others (e.g., Matas, Arend, & Sroufe, 1978). Thus, a sense of basic trust seems to promote more autonomy later on.

Preschool

The next period is the preschool stage (from about three to five). Being autonomous and capable of controlling your actions is an important start, but it's only a start. An ability to manipulate objects in the world leads to an increasing desire to exert influence, to make things happen—in short, a desire for *power* (McAdams, 1985). This

Figure 11.5

Children with a greater sense of basic trust and security at one year explore more at two and a half years of age than do less securely attached children, and a higher proportion of their exploration is self-initiated, or autonomous. This finding suggests that successful management of the first crisis prepares the child to do better with the second crisis (adapted from Hazen & Durrett, 1982).

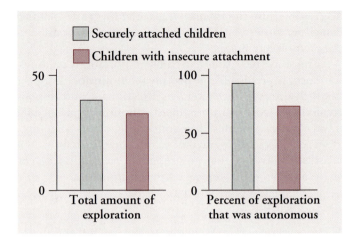

period corresponds to Freud's genital stage. Freud saw Oedipal conflicts emerging here. As we said earlier, people who are skeptical about the Oedipal conflict tend to treat Freud's depiction as a metaphor for a more extensive power struggle between parents and child, who by now has become willful. It's this power struggle on which Erikson focused.

The conflict at this stage concerns *initiative versus guilt*. Children who take the initiative are seeking to impose their newly developed sense of will on their surroundings. They express and act on their curiosity as they explore and manipulate their world and ask about things going on around them. (This pattern resembles the impulsive stage in Loevinger's theory, described in Chapter 10.)

Acts and words can also be perilous, however. Action that's too powerful can cause others pain (grabbing a toy you want can distress another child). Asking too many questions can become tiresome to adults. If taking the initiative too often leads to disapproval, feelings of guilt will result. Because constantly exerting power does tend to produce some disapproval, initiative eventually must be tempered by restraint. If this crisis is managed well, the child emerges with the ego quality of *purpose:* the courage to pursue valued goals without fear of punishment.

Research has asked whether attaining a sense of basic trust during the first year fosters later initiative. In one study (Lütkenhaus, Grossmann, & Grossmann, 1985), attachment was assessed at age one and the children were studied again (at home) at age three. Those who'd been securely attached were quicker to show initiative in interacting with a stranger than those who'd been insecurely attached. During a game involving a failure, securely attached children responded by increasing their efforts, but the other children decreased their efforts. Thus, the sense of basic trust seems to provide groundwork for the sense of initiative and purpose.

School Age

The next stage corresponds to Freud's latency period (from about five to eleven). Unlike Freud, Erikson held that this period also has a conflict. He called it *industry versus inferiority*. The term *industry* reflects the fact that the child's life remains focused on doing things that have an impact. But now the nature of those efforts acquires a different shade of meaning. In particular, it's no longer enough just to take the initiative and assert power. Now there's pressure to do things that others judge to be *good*, in two senses. Industriousness isn't just *doing* things, it's doing things that others *value*. It's also doing things in ways that others regard as *appropriate* and *commendable*.

The crisis over this sense of industry begins about when the child enters elementary school. The school experience is aimed at teaching children to become productive and responsible members of society. School years are also the period when intellectual skills are first tested. Children are urged to do well in school, and the adequacy of their performance is explicitly evaluated.

The school experience also involves learning social roles. Children are beginning to learn about the nature of adult work. They're also being exposed to some of the tools of adult work. In former times, these were tools of farming, carpentry, and homemaking; today it's more likely to be computers. Another role children are acquiring is that of citizenship. Thus, the child's sense of industry is being judged partly by the acceptability of his or her behavior to the social group.

Children with a strong sense of industry differ in several ways from children with less of this sense (Kowaz & Marcia, 1991). They tend to prefer reality-based activities over fantasy. They're more able to distinguish the role of effort from that of ability in producing outcomes. They get better grades. And they agree more with statements that are socially desirable.

To emerge from this stage successfully children must feel they're mastering the tasks set for them, in a fashion that's acceptable to those around them. The danger at this stage is feelings of inferiority. Such feelings can arise when children are led by others (parents, teachers, or peers) to view their performances as inadequate or as morally wrong. Managing the conflict between industry and inferiority results in an ego quality that Erikson termed *competence:* the sense that one can do things that are valued by others.

Adolescence

Next comes adolescence, a period that begins with the physical changes of puberty and lasts until roughly age twenty. This stage is a larger break with the past than any stage up to this point. Part of the sense of separation comes from the physical changes of puberty. Your body doesn't just get larger during this period but also changes in other ways. You have desires you never had before. You're not quite the same person you used to be. But who *are* you?

Part of the break with the past reflects the fact that you're now beginning to think explicitly about yourself and your life in relation to the adult world. You'll have to find your place in that world, and doing so requires you to decide what roles fit your identity. This, in turn, means knowing who you are.

The crisis of this stage is between *identity versus role confusion*. Identity reflects an integrated sense of self. It's the answer to the question "who am I?" The phrase *role confusion* reflects the fact that every self has many facets that sometimes seem incompatible. The greater the incompatibility, the harder it is to pull the facets together and the more confused you are. Worse yet, you can even be in a position where *no* role feels as though it's part of your identity.

To emerge from adolescence with a strong sense of identity requires the person to evolve in two ways. First, you must consolidate the self-conceptions from the previous stages, merging them in a way that's sensible. Second, this integrated self-view must be integrated with the view of you that others hold. This reflects the fact that identity is something you develop in a consensus with the people you relate to. Only by considering both views does a full sense of identity emerge.

Thus, from Erikson's perspective, identity derives from a blending of private and social self-conceptions. The outcome of this integration is a sense of personal continuity or inner congruence. Erikson placed great emphasis on the importance of developing a sense of identity. In many ways, he saw this as each person's major life task (see also Box 11.2).

BOX 11.2

THE THEORIST AND THE THEORY
Erikson's Lifelong Search for Identity

Erikson's life had a distinct impact on the form of his theory, particularly his emphasis on the importance of attaining a sense of identity (for a biographical account see Friedman, 1999). Erikson was born in Germany in 1902, of Danish parents. His father abandoned his mother before he was born, and three years later she married Theodor Homburger, a Jewish physician. Erik wasn't told for years that Homburger wasn't his real father, which he later referred to as an act of "loving deceit."

He grew up as Erik Homburger, a Jew with the appearance of a Scandinavian. Jews saw him as a gentile, gentiles saw him as a Jew. For this reason he wasn't accepted by either group and he began to form an image of himself as an outsider. By adolescence he'd been told of his adoption, and his identity confusion was further complicated by the realization that his ancestry was Danish rather than German.

As he wandered around Europe during his early twenties, his feelings of a lack of identity deepened. He worked as a portrait painter, but the work was sporadic and not conducive to developing a clear sense of identity as an artist. Homburger interrupted periods of formal training in art to continue wandering, in search of his identity. Eventually he took a teaching job in Vienna, at a school created for children of Freud's patients and friends. There he became familiar with a number of psychoanalysts, including Anna Freud, with whom he went on to train as an analyst. In 1933 he moved to the United States, where he established a practice as a child analyst. As Erik Homburger, he was also in the research team that Henry Murray brought together, which led to development of the motive approach to personality described in Chapter 5.

In 1939 Homburger became naturalized as a U.S. citizen. At that time he took the name Erikson. This was an event—and, indeed, a choice of name—that unquestionably had much personal meaning, symbolizing his full attainment of the sense of identity.

In later years Erikson spent time studying methods of child rearing and other aspects of cultural life among the Sioux of South Dakota and the Yurok of northern California. These studies were important for two reasons. First, they led to themes that would permeate Erikson's thinking, concerning the importance of culture and society in identity. Second, they revealed to him symptoms of dislocation, feelings of having been uprooted and separated from cultural traditions. The members of these tribes appeared to have lost their sense of identity, much as Erikson himself had done earlier in his life. Erikson also observed similar qualities in the lives of veterans of World War II who returned with emotional difficulties.

From all these experiences Erikson came to believe that the attainment and preservation of a sense of identity—not wholly separate from but rather embedded in one's own society—was the critical task of growing up. This idea was to stand as one of the major themes of his viewpoint on personality.

If the person fails to form a consolidated identity, the result is role confusion, an absence of direction in the sense of self. Role confusion is reflected in an inability to select a career (or a major in college that will take you toward a career). Role confusion can also lead people to identify with popular heroes or groups (or even antiheroes), to try to fill the void. The virtue associated with successful identity formation is *fidelity*. Fidelity means truthfulness. It's the ability to live up to who you are, despite the contradictions that inevitably occur among the values you hold.

A good deal of research has evolved from Erikson's ideas about the development of identity during adolescence. Much of this work has been conducted by James Marcia (1966, 1976, 1980) and his colleagues. He began by expanding on Erikson's ideas. He argues that the development of an identity requires the person to experience an **identity crisis,** and to form a commitment to an identity. Marcia's use of the word *crisis* here is similar to Erikson's use of the word. An identity crisis is actively exploring different ways of viewing oneself and giving serious thought to the implications of those views.

Marcia (1966) developed an interview method to measure ego identity. It applies the criteria of crisis and commitment to the person's occupation (intended work role), ideology (beliefs and values), and sexuality. He distinguishes among four **identity statuses** (see Table 11.3).

Identity achievement is the status of a person who's experienced a period of crisis and made a commitment. *Moratorium* applies to a person who's now in crisis (exploring alternatives) but has no commitment. *Foreclosure* is the status of a person who's made a commitment, but with little evidence of a crisis, for example, a young man committed to becoming a surgeon because his father and grandfather were surgeons. In *identity diffusion,* there's no crisis and no commitment. Not surprisingly, either achieving or foreclosing on an identity has a benefit. People in these two groups feel better about themselves than people who haven't made commitments (Prager, 1982).

The existence of these four identity statuses is now well established, and researchers are beginning to learn what these people are like and how they come to exist (Bourne, 1978a, 1978b; Marcia, 1980; Waterman, 1982). Foreclosed persons have closer relationships with their parents than other groups. Foreclosed men also are more willing than others to involve their families in life decisions. These close ties seem to prevent an identity crisis. Instead the person makes identity commitments without actively struggling to determine the kind of person he or she wants to be.

People who've had identity crises (identity achievers and those in moratorium) are more critical of their parents and less concerned with living up to their wishes.

Table 11.3

Four identity statuses defined by Marcia. This matrix of possibilities is derived by applying two criteria in the form of questions. Each possible pair of answers defines an identity status.

		Has an identity crisis been experienced?	
		Yes	*No*
Has a commitment been made?	Yes	Identity achievement	Foreclosure
	No	Moratorium	Identity diffusion

They tend to turn inward rather than to family when life decisions have to be made (this presumably facilitated their identity crises). Although these groups are not closely tied to family (both are autonomous in that respect), they differ in how they see their parents. Compared with identity achievers, people in moratorium feel ambivalent about parents, sometimes viewing them as examples of identities they want to avoid. Presumably the ambivalence reflects the fact that the crisis is ongoing for these people.

Identity diffusers are the hardest group to characterize. They seem almost to have withdrawn from pursuing an identity (e.g., Berzonsky & Neimeyer, 1994). They report feeling out of place and isolated (Donovan, 1975), which doesn't bode well for the next stage. They report seeing their parents as distant from them, which hints they may have had problems with basic trust.

Young Adulthood

The next stage in Erikson's theory is young adulthood (through the mid-twenties). The conflict here concerns the desire for *intimacy, versus isolation.* Intimacy is a close, warm relationship with someone, with a sense of commitment to that person. Erikson saw intimacy as an issue in relationships of all kinds, nonsexual as well as sexual.

True intimacy requires you to approach relationships in a caring and open way and to be willing to share the most personal aspects of yourself with others. You also must be open and receptive to others' disclosures. Intimacy requires the moral strength to live up to commitments, even when it requires sacrifice. Erikson believed people are capable of intimacy only if they have a strong sense of identity.

The opposite pole at this stage is isolation, feeling apart from others and unable to make commitments to them. A person can drift into isolation if conditions aren't right for intimacy—if no one's there who fills your needs. Sometimes, though, people withdraw into isolation on their own—for instance, if they feel a relationship threatens their sense of separate identity. Withdrawing can have other consequences, however. People can become self-absorbed to the point that they aren't able to establish intimate relationships in the future (Erikson, 1982). The ego quality associated with the ability to be intimate is *love*. This is a mutuality that subdues the antagonisms of separate identities.

The theme that handling one crisis prepares you for the next one continues here. Erikson said people need a strong sense of identity to be able to attain intimacy. Is this true? One study looked at identity strength in college and intimacy in middle age (Kahn, Zimmerman, Csikszentmihalyi, & Getzels, 1985). Intimacy was assessed in terms of whether subjects had married and, if so, whether the marriage had been disrupted by divorce. There was a clear link between a strong identity and a later capacity for intimacy. The effect differed slightly, however, between men and women (Figure 11.6). Men with stronger identities were more likely to have married during the eighteen years. Identity didn't predict whether the women married, but among those who *had* married, those with strong identity were less likely to divorce. Conceptually similar findings have been reported by others (e.g., Orlofsky, Marcia, & Lesser, 1973; Schiedel & Marcia, 1985; Tesch & Whitbourne, 1982).

The other pole of the conflict of this stage—isolation—has drawn interest in its own right (e.g., Peplau & Perlman, 1982; Shaver & Rubenstein, 1980; Weiss, 1973). Two aspects of it are distinguishable from each other. *Social isolation* is a failure to be integrated into a society. People who stand apart from social groups fail to develop a sense of belonging. In contrast, the failure to have intimacy in your life is termed *emotional isolation*—more simply, loneliness.

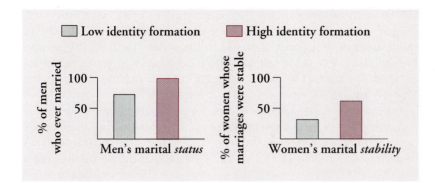

Figure 11.6

Percentage of men who had ever been married during the eighteen-year period after art school and percentage of women who had married and whose marriages remained intact during the same period, as a function of preassessed identity formation (adapted from Kahn et al., 1985).

Emotional isolation feeds on itself. Recall that to experience intimacy requires self-disclosing, opening oneself to others. Lonely people don't do this (Jones, Hobbes, & Hockenberg, 1982; Mikulincer & Nachshon, 1991). They're also less responsive, ask fewer questions, and seem less interested in what the other person is saying. As a result, they're hard to get to know and are likely to remain lonely.

Adulthood

Young adulthood is followed by adulthood, the longest of the psychosocial stages, typically lasting into the mid-sixties. The crisis of adulthood centers around being able to generate or nurture. For this reason the central conflict in this stage is termed *generativity versus stagnation.*

The desire for generativity is the desire to create things in the world that will outlive you (Kotre, 1984)—children, for example. By creating new lives tied to yours,

One way in which feelings of generativity are displayed is by helping the next generation learn about life.

you symbolically ensure your continuation into the future. Consistent with this idea, McAdams and de St. Aubin (1992) found that men who'd had children scored higher on a self-report measure of generativity than did childless men. Generativity has also been found to relate to a view of the self as a role model and source of wisdom for one's children (Hart, McAdams, Hirsch, & Bauer, 2001) and to a parenting style that fosters autonomy (Pratt, Danso, Arnold, Norris, & Filyer, 2001).

Although generativity is partly a matter of creating and guiding the growth of the next generation, the concept is broader than that. It includes creating ideas or objects, teaching young people who aren't your own children, anything that influences the future in a positive way (Table 11.4). Erikson believed that the desire for generativity reflects a shift in focus from one close relationship (intimacy) to a broader concern with society as a whole.

Consistent with this idea, highly generative persons express high levels of commitment to assisting the next generation; they also reveal an integration between that commitment and the sense of agency in the self (Mansfield & McAdams, 1996; see also McAdams, Diamond, de St. Aubin, & Mansfield, 1997). Sometimes this experience of commitment also has overtones of redemption, the turning of something bad into something good (McAdams, Reynolds, Lewis, Patten, & Bowman, 2001). Once the sense of generativity is developed, it may continue through the rest of one's life (Zucker, Ostrove, & Stewart, 2002).

Adults who fail to develop this sense of generativity drift into stagnation. Stagnation is an inability or unwillingness to give of oneself to the future. These people are preoccupied with their own concerns. They have a self-centered or self-indulgent quality that keeps them from deeper involvement in the world around them. There's also evidence that an absence of generativity is related to poorer psychological well-being (Vandewater, Ostrove, & Stewart, 1997).

If there's a positive balance of generativity, the ego quality that emerges is *care*. Care is a widening concern for whatever you've generated in your life, be it children, something in your work, or something that emerged from your involvement with other people.

Old Age

The final stage is maturity, or old age. This is the closing chapter of people's lives. It's a time when people look back and review the choices they made and reflect on

Table 11.4

Aspects of generativity (adapted from Kotre, 1984, p. 12).	
Aspect	**Description**
Biological	Creating, bearing, and nursing an infant
Parental	Raising, nurturing, shaping, and socializing children, providing them with family traditions
Technical	Teaching the skills that make up the "body" of a culture, training a new generation in techniques for doing things
Cultural	Creating, changing, and maintaining a symbol system that represents the "mind" of a culture, passing it on to the next generation

their accomplishments (and failures) and on the turns their lives have taken (see also Box 11.3). The crisis here is termed *ego integrity versus despair.* If you come away from this review feeling that your life has had order and meaning, accepting the choices you made and the things you did, a sense of ego integrity emerges. This is a feeling of satisfaction, a feeling that things went about the way you wanted them to, that you wouldn't change much.

BOX 11.3

IS THERE A "MIDLIFE CRISIS"?

From Erikson's point of view, the last years of life are spent in review, examining choices that were made, values that were pursued, and passions that were abandoned. Erikson saw this review as coming late in life, after the opportunity to make changes has passed.

Others have also talked about a life review (Gould, 1980; Levinson, 1978; Stewart & Vandewater, 1999; Vaillant, 1977), but one that occurs earlier, around age forty or so. Given its timing, the phenomenon is popularly referred to as the "midlife crisis." It's a questioning of the decisions you've made over your adult years, the validity and worth of your goals, the adequacy of your life situation—nearly everything about your existence. It's a time of reevaluation, but it's also a chance to change the way things are before it's too late. If you don't like your life, change it. Remake decisions, rearrange your priorities, change careers, change your marriage (or perhaps leave it altogether).

The notion of a midlife crisis rests partly on the typical course of life's major events in Western cultures. It's common in the United States to finish college and take a job in one's early twenties, marry, and start raising a family in one's twenties and thirties. Depending on when the children are born, they're growing up and leaving home when you're in your forties or early fifties. Around this time it's also common to experience the death of one or both of your parents. Many of the changes of midlife are profound ones. Is it any wonder that they seem to cry out for reevaluation of your life?

Another contributor to such a crisis is cultural assumptions about the timing of these events. As a result, people do a certain amount of checking to see whether their lives are "on schedule." If you're in your

mid-thirties, are you making as much money as you're supposed to be? Are you in line for the career advancement you planned on? If you're nearing forty with no children, you can hear the biological clock ticking, telling you that you'll never have that experience if you don't hurry up. Comparing your life against these markers of "normal" life can produce a lot of soul-searching.

Is there a midlife crisis? As two people well on the far side of forty, we're inclined to feel there's some truth to the idea. We know the feelings we've just written about (we also know why one of us bought a motorcycle a few years ago). People do experience regrets at midlife, and that does cause some (though not all) to make life changes (Stewart & Vandewater, 1999).

Yet the evidence doesn't indicate that a real midlife crisis is all that common. Two longitudinal studies found little support for the idea in fairly large samples (Clausen, 1981; Haan, 1981). On the other hand, the participants in those studies lived through some very difficult times—the Great Depression and World War II—and it's possible that having survived those experiences made them less likely to reevaluate their choices and goals at midlife. Perhaps the midlife crisis is actually a "baby boomer" phenomenon.

Alternatively, it may be that the midlife crisis isn't so much a matter of midlife as it is a manifestation of a more consistent tendency to be worried. This conclusion would fit with findings obtained by Costa and McCrae (1980) concerning life satisfaction over time. They found that satisfaction was relatively stable across a period of ten years and that dissatisfaction related to the broad trait of neuroticism. Maybe, then, people who are inclined to worry do so throughout life, and it just happens to be more obvious at midlife.

The opposite pole of this conflict is despair: the feeling that your life was wasted. It's a sense of wishing you'd done things differently, but knowing that it's too late. Instead of acceptance of your life's story as a valuable gift, there's a bitterness that things turned out as they did.

Emerging from this life review with a sense of integrity results in the ego quality of *wisdom.* Wisdom involves meaning-making and benevolence (Helson & Srivastava, 2002). It is a detached yet active concern with life, even as one confronts the impending reality of death (see also Baltes & Staudinger, 1993).

The Epigenetic Principle

One more issue to address in Erikson's theory is the idea that a given conflict exists outside the stage in which it's focal. Erikson adopted the concept of **epigenesis** from embryology. Epigenesis is the process by which a single cell turns into a complex organism. For this process to occur requires a "blueprint" at the beginning, with instructions for all the changes and their sequencing. As applied to Erikson's theory, this idea means there's a readiness for each crisis at birth. The core issue of each crisis is especially focal during a particular stage, but all of the issues are always there.

The principle of epigenesis has several implications. It means your orientation to a particular crisis is influenced by the outcomes of all the earlier ones. It also means that in resolving the core crisis of any particular stage, you're preparing solutions (in rudimentary form) for the ones coming later. As you deal in adolescence with the conflict between ego identity and role confusion, you're also moving toward handling the crisis of intimacy versus isolation. Finally, the epigenetic principle means that crises aren't resolved once and for all. Your resolutions of previous conflicts are reshaped at each new stage of life (Whitbourne, Zuschlag, Elliot, & Waterman, 1992).

Identity as Life Story

The sense of the epigenetic principle is well conveyed in some of the work of Dan McAdams. His work focuses partly on motivations that underlie personality (discussed in Chapter 5) and partly on the idea that people construct their identities as narratives, or life stories (McAdams, 1985, 1993, 2001). In his view, your story is never completed until the end of your life. It is constantly being written. Indeed, it is constantly under revision, just as your identity is constantly evolving.

As in any good book, the opening chapters of your narrative begin setting the stage for things that happen much later. Sometimes future events are foreshadowed, sometimes things that happen in early chapters create conditions that have to be reacted to later on. As chapters pile up, characters reinterpret events they experienced earlier, or understand them in different ways. All the pieces will eventually come together into a full and integrated picture, and the picture that results has taken on qualities from everything that's happened throughout the story. McAdams thus sees the broad crisis of identity as one that continues to occupy each person throughout life (see McAdams, 2001).

Of interest is how categories of narrative themes show up in many people's lives. McAdams and his colleagues have found, for example, that highly generative midlife adults often report life stories in which they had early advantages, became aware of the suffering of others, established a personal belief system that involved prosocial values, and committed themselves to benefiting society. McAdams calls these commitment stories. These stories often contain *redemption* themes, in which a bad situation somehow is transformed into something good (McAdams et al., 2001).

Particularly unlikely in adults high in generativity (but more likely in adults lower in generativity) are stories involving *contamination* themes, in which a good situation somehow turns bad.

Linking Erikson's Theory to Other Psychosocial Theories

Now let's look back to the theories discussed earlier in this chapter, to make a final point. Those theories surely represent contributions of their own. Yet, in a sense, the fundamental theme of each is the same as that of the first crisis in Erikson's theory: basic trust versus basic mistrust. That's a big part of what security in attachment is about. It seems implicit in object relations theories. It's at the heart of Horney's concept of basic anxiety. This issue is also the core of Erikson's own theory, providing the critical foundation on which the rest of personality is built.

We humans seem to need to be able to trust in the relationships that sustain our lives. In the minds of many theorists, that trust is necessary for adequate functioning. People who are deeply mistrustful of relationships, or are constantly frightened about possibly losing relationships, have lives that are damaged and distorted. The damage may be slight or it may be significant. Avoiding such mistrust and doubt (or recognizing and overcoming it, if it's already there) seems a central task in human existence.

Assessment

Let's turn now to assessment from the psychosocial viewpoint. In general, assessment here is similar to that of the ego psychologists. There are two aspects of assessment, however, that are specific to this view.

Object Relations, Attachment, and the Focus of Assessment

One difference concerns what's being assessed. Specifically, the psychosocial approach places a greater emphasis than do other approaches on assessing the person's view of relationships.

There are several ways in which a person's mental model of relationships might be assessed. Relevant measures range from some that are open-ended in nature (e.g., Blatt, Wein, Chevron, & Quinlan, 1979) to structured self-reports (e.g., Bell, Billington, & Becker, 1986). Some measures assess a range of issues pertaining to relationships (Bell et al., 1986). Others focus specifically on the attachments that you have to other people (e.g., Bartholomew & Horowitz, 1991; Carver, 1997a; Collins & Read, 1990; Griffin & Bartholomew, 1994; Simpson, 1990).

The object-relations measure of Bell et al. (1986) provides a good illustration of the content assessed from this viewpoint. It has four scales. The *alienation* scale measures a lack of basic trust in relationships and an inability to be close. People high on this scale are suspicious, guarded, and isolated, convinced that others will fail them. This resembles avoidant attachment. A second scale measures *insecure attachment,* in a manner that resembles the ambivalent pattern. This is sensitivity to rejection, and concern about being liked and accepted. People who score high on this scale enter relationships in a painful search for security, and are hypersensitive to signs of abandonment. The third scale, *egocentricity,* assesses narcissism, a self-protective and exploitive attitude toward relationships. Those high on this scale tend to view others only in relation to their own needs and aims. The final scale measures *social incompetence,* as reflected in shyness and uncertainty about how to engage in even simple social interactions. People high on this scale have trouble making friends and are interpersonally unresponsive and emotionally blunted.

A different approach to assessment is the open-ended measure of Blatt et al. (1979). It has a coding system that assesses the developmental maturity of people's perceptions of social relations. This measure asks you to describe your mother and father. If you're at a low level of maturity you tend to focus on how parents acted to satisfy your needs. Higher-level descriptions focus more on parents' values, thoughts, and feelings, apart from your needs. At a very high level, the description takes into account internal contradictions in the parent, and change over time. This measure reflects a person's level of separation and individuation from the parent.

Play in Assessment

Another aspect of the psychosocial view on assessment reflects the fact that this view emphasizes experiences of childhood as determinants of personality. As a result, this view emphasizes child assessment more than other views. Assessment of children here tends to emphasize the use of play as an assessment tool. It is often said that children's play reveals their preoccupations (e.g., Axline, 1947, 1964; Erikson, 1963; M. Klein, 1935, 1955a, 1955b). Play lets them express their concerns in a way they can't do in words. Erikson (1963) devised a standardized play situation, using a specific set of toys on a table. The child is to imagine that the table is a movie studio and the toys are actors and sets. The child is to create a scene and describe what's happening. Other techniques use less structured play settings, but the elements almost always include a variety of dolls (e.g., mother, father, older person, children, baby). This permits children to choose characters that are relevant to their own concerns or preoccupations.

Children often reveal their feelings through play.

The play situation is projective, because the child imposes a story on ambiguous stimuli. It often has two objective characteristics, however. First is a *behavioral record*. This includes what the child says about the scene and a description of the scene and the sequence of steps taken to create it. Second, the face value of the child's behavior receives more attention than is usual in projectives. It isn't automatically assumed that the child's behavior has deeply hidden meanings.

Problems in Behavior, and Behavior Change

Given that psychosocial theorists focus on the nature of people's relationships, it's natural that they see problems as reflecting relationship difficulties. Here are three examples of how this approach applies to problems in behavior.

Narcissism as a Disorder of Personality

One psychosocial view focuses specifically on **narcissism** as a disorder. Indeed, this disorder was the starting point for Kohut's work on the self. Pathological narcissism involves a sense that everyone and everything is an extension of the self or exists to serve the self. There's a grandiose sense of self-importance and need for constant attention. Narcissists display a sense of *entitlement,* of deserving others' adulation. As a result, they often exploit others.

Research supports this view. Narcissists may seem agreeable at first, but opinions of them get worse when they're around for a while (Paulhus, 1998). They are very responsive to opportunities for self-enhancement (Wallace & Baumeister, 2002). They love to take credit for successes, but respond to failure or criticism with anger (Rhodewalt & Morf, 1998). Indeed, narcissists may erupt in extremes of rage when their desires are thwarted (Bushman & Baumeister, 1998; Stucke & Sporer, 2002), and they can be disruptive in the infantile demands they make on others.

Recall that Kohut said everyone begins life with a grandiose narcissism, which is tempered during development. Some people never escape it, however. To Kohut, this stems from inadequate mirroring by parents. That frustrates the narcissistic needs and prevents formation of an adequate self structure (Kohut, 1977). Similarly, Kernberg (1976, 1980) said that narcissism arises from parental rejection. The child comes to believe that the only person who can be trusted (and therefore loved) is himself or herself. Fitting this picture, narcissists prefer romantic partners who will be admiring over those who offer intimacy (Campbell, 1999). They're also less committed in their relationships, always on the lookout for someone better (Campbell & Foster, 2002).

A person in whom this narcissism isn't satisfied may distort reality in several ways to serve the narcissistic needs. For example, narcissistic people are more likely to inflate their judgments of their own performances in various arenas of life than are less narcissistic people (John & Robins, 1994). If threatened by being told that someone else has outperformed them, they're more likely to put the other person down (Morf & Rhodewalt, 1993).

Neurotic Needs

Another way of thinking about problems comes from Horney's ideas about basic anxiety. She believed the strategies people use to combat basic anxiety can become a fixed part of personality if they're used too much. Horney (1942) made a list of ten needs that can be acquired by attempts to deal with problem relationships

Table 11.5

> **Horney's list of neurotic needs (and a brief description of each), which arise from overuse of various strategies of coping with anxiety** (adapted from Horney, 1942, 1945).
>
> *Neurotic need for affection and approval.* Indiscriminate wish to please others and live up to their expectations. Extreme sensitivity to any sign of rejection or unfriendliness
>
> *Neurotic need for a partner who will take over one's life.* Feeling extremely afraid of being deserted and left alone
>
> *Neurotic need to restrict one's life within narrow borders.* Being extremely undemanding, content with little, preferring to remain inconspicuous
>
> *Neurotic need for power.* Craving power for its own sake, adoration of strength and contempt for weakness. May also be reflected in intellectual exploitation
>
> *Neurotic need to exploit others.* Using others to your own advantage
>
> *Neurotic need for prestige.* Basing your self-evaluation on public recognition
>
> *Neurotic need for personal admiration.* Having an inflated picture of yourself and wishing to be admired for that, not for what you really are
>
> *Neurotic ambition for personal achievement.* Wanting to be the very best, and driving yourself to greater and greater achievements as a result of basic insecurity
>
> *Neurotic need for self-sufficiency and independence.* Setting yourself apart from others, becoming a "loner," refusing to be tied down to anyone or anything because of disappointment in attempts to find warm, satisfying relationships with people
>
> *Neurotic need for perfection and unassailability.* Trying to make yourself impregnable and infallible. Constantly searching for flaws in yourself so that they can be covered up before becoming obvious to others

(Table 11.5). She called them **neurotic needs** because they aren't effective solutions to the problem. Instead they often lead into vicious cycles.

Horney argued that neurotic needs give rise to three styles, depending on whether the need moves you *toward* others, *away* from others, or *against* others (Horney, 1945, 1950). Neurotic needs such as those for love and approval move you toward others, but in clingy dependency (as in the ambivalent attachment pattern). Neurotic needs for independence and self-sufficiency move you away from others (as in the avoidant attachment pattern). Needs such as power and exploitation move you against others. As with all defenses, each style can be useful but is problematic if it is used to an extreme. Indeed, extremes of the styles relate to measures of personality disorders (Coolidge, Moor, Yamazaki, Stewart, & Segal, 2001).

Well-adapted people usually take one style at a time and shift from one to another flexibly as needed. Although there may be a preference for one style over the others, all three can be used. This flexibility is the hallmark of good adaptation. People with problems more often rigidly adopt a single orientation, even in situations where one of the other styles might be more useful.

Attachment and Depression

Another window on the nature of problems comes from the suggestion that an important cause of depression is interpersonal rejection (Blatt & Zuroff, 1992). This cause resembles the presumed cause of the avoidant attachment pattern. That is, avoidance is believed to be a product of neglectful or rejecting parenting, which results in sadness, despair, and eventual emotional detachment (Hazan & Shaver, 1994; see also Carnelley, Pietromonaco, & Jaffe, 1994). The idea that interpersonal rejection can lead to depression has received a good deal of support (Blatt & Zuroff, 1992).

The avoidant attachment pattern has also been linked to development of elevated emotional distress when under stress (Berant, Mikulincer, & Florian, 2001). Participants were women who had found out two weeks earlier that their newborns had congenital heart disease. Those with avoidant (and those with anxious) attachment patterns were more distressed. Avoidant patterns also predicted further deterioration in emotional well-being a year later.

It's been suggested that both the avoidant attachment pattern and the depression to which it's linked can be passed from one generation to another. The argument is based on behavior rather than genetics. The pattern you acquire as a child is the working model you bring to bear when you have children of your own. If you're an avoidant adult (due to parental rejection), and especially if you're a *depressed* avoidant adult, what kind of parent will you be? An emotionally distant one. You may be experienced as a rejecting parent—not because you dislike your child, but because you're so distant. Being emotionally unavailable, you may then create an avoidant child, just like you.

Thus, parents may transfer to the next generation precisely the attachment qualities that made them unhappy themselves. There's support for this line of reasoning on rejection and depression (Whitbeck et al., 1992). There's also evidence of transmission of an erratic pattern of adult behavior that may be tied to the ambivalent attachment pattern (Elder, Caspi, & Downey, 1986).

Behavior Change

The process of therapeutic behavior change from the viewpoint of psychosocial theories reflects many of the themes we discussed for ego psychology. The techniques tend to focus on the here and now, and the person with the problem is seen as a collaborator in the therapeutic process.

Nevertheless, a few additional techniques were developed by people in the psychosocial tradition. For example, psychologists such as Erikson (1963), Virginia Axline (1947), and Melanie Klein (1955a, 1955b) developed **play therapy** techniques for use with children. These techniques give the child the opportunity to do as he or she wishes, without pressuring, intruding, prodding, or nagging from an adult. Under these conditions children can have distance from others (if they are worried about being smothered by a too ever-present parent) or can play out anger or the wish for closeness (if they're feeling rejected or unwanted). The playroom is the child's world. In it children have the opportunity to bring their feelings to the surface, deal with them, and potentially change their working models of relationships and of the self in positive ways (Landreth, 1991).

Because object relations and self theories emphasize the role of relationships in problems, they also emphasize relationships as part of the therapeutic process. Therapists try to provide the kind of relationship the patient needs so the patient can reintegrate problematic parts of the self. Healing is brought about by providing a successful experience of narcissism or attachment (almost a kind of re-parenting), replacing the earlier emotional failure.

These therapy techniques can be seen as representing a way of restoring to the person's life a sense of connectedness to others. By modifying the representations of relationships that were built in the past, they permit the developing of more satisfying relationships in the future. The optimism that this approach holds about being able to undo problematic experiences from the past is reflected in the saying, "It's never too late to have a happy childhood."

Psychosocial Theories: Problems and Prospects

As was true of ego psychology, the psychosocial neoanalytic approach is home to many theorists. Although they had different starting points, there's a remarkable consistency in the themes behind their work. Each assumes that human relationships are the most important part of human life, and that how relationships are managed is a core issue in personality. Each tends to assume that people develop working models of relationships from early experience, which then are used to frame new ones. Also implied is the idea that health requires a balance between being separate and autonomous and being closely connected to someone (see also Helgeson, 1994; Helgeson & Fritz, 1999).

A strength of psychosocial theories is that they point us in directions that other theories don't. Thinking about personality in terms of attachment patterns, for example, suggests hypotheses that aren't readily derived from other viewpoints. Work based in attachment theory is leading to a better understanding of how personality plays out in social relations. This picture of this aspect of personality would very likely not have emerged without the attachment model as a starting point. Furthermore, linking the themes of attachment to models of greater complexity, such as Erikson's, creates a picture of change and evolution across the life span that would be nearly impossible to derive from other viewpoints. The psychosocial viewpoint clearly adds something of great importance to our understanding of personality.

This is not to say that no unresolved issues remain for this approach. One important issue concerns a rather sharp clash between this view and the view of trait psychologists and behavior geneticists. Manifestations of adult attachment patterns correspond well to genetically influenced traits. Avoidants are essentially introverts, secures are extraverts, and anxious-ambivalents are high in neuroticism. Do these patterns result from parenting, or are they genetically determined? There are strong opinions on both sides of this question. It's a question that will surely be examined more closely in the years ahead.

Indeed, in considering the prospects of this viewpoint for the future, we should note explicitly that research on psychosocial approaches is continuing. Indeed, adult attachment and related ideas represent one of the most active areas of research in personality psychology today. The recent flood of research on this topic shows no sign of abating. Research on the implications of attachment patterns for the life of the child—and the adult—promises to yield interesting new insights into the human experience. The prospects of this area of work for the immediate future seem very bright, as do the prospects for the approach more generally.

SUMMARY

Psychosocial theories emphasize the idea that personality is intrinsically social and that the important issues of personality concern how people relate to others. Several psychosocial theories focus on early life. Mahler's object relations theory proposes that infants begin life merged psychologically with their mothers and that they separate and individuate during the first three years of life. How this takes place influences later adjustment.

Kohut's self psychology resembles object relations theory. He said humans have narcissistic needs that are satisfied by other people, represented as selfobjects. If the child receives enough mirroring (positive attention) from selfobjects (chiefly the mother), the sense of self develops appropriately. If there's too much mirroring, the child won't be able to deal with frustrations. If there's too little, the development of the self is stunted.

Many of the themes of object relations and self psychology were anticipated by Horney, who wrote that people suffer from basic anxiety, a feeling of being abandoned, isolated, and alone. People develop strategies to cope with this. If the strategies aren't successful in obtaining affection, they lead to a vicious cycle of increased anxiety.

Some of these ideas are also echoed in the work of attachment theorists such as Bowlby and Ainsworth. Secure attachment provides a solid base for exploration. There are also patterns of insecure attachment (ambivalent and avoidant), which stem from inconsistent treatment, neglect, or rejection. There's increasing interest in the idea that infant attachment patterns persist and influence adult personality. There is now a great deal of work on this topic, assessing adult attachment in several ways. Although people do display diverse ways of relating across their social connections, a core tendency seems to exist. Adult attachment patterns influence many aspects of behavior, including how people relate to work activities and how they seek and give emotional support, as well as how they relate to romantic partners.

Another important theory of the psychosocial group is Erikson's theory of psychosocial development. Erikson postulated a series of crises from infancy to late adulthood, giving rise to ego strengths that influence one's ego identity: the consciously experienced sense of self. Erikson assumed that each crisis becomes focal at one stage but that each is present in a less obvious form throughout life.

The first crisis concerns the development of a sense of *basic trust*. The child then becomes concerned with control over its body and the sense of *autonomy* that goes along with that. The next issue is *initiative,* as the child seeks to exercise its power. As children enter the school years, they begin to realize that the social environment demands that they be *industrious*. With adolescence, the child enters a new stage of life and a crisis over *identity*. In young adulthood, identity issues give way to concern over *intimacy*. In adulthood, the person moves to a concern over *generativity*. Finally, in the last stage of life, people confront the *integrity* of their lives as a whole.

Assessment techniques from the psychosocial view are similar to those of ego psychology, but focus more on people's relationships. This approach also leads to use of play as an assessment method with children. The psychosocial view of problems focuses on the idea that problems are rooted in relationship issues. Kohut suggested that pathological narcissism stems from inadequate childhood mirroring. Horney suggested that people's strategies for dealing with basic anxiety involve moving toward, away from, or against other people. Adaptive functioning involves flexibly shifting from one strategy to another as needed. Poor adjustment comes from rigid reliance on one strategy. It has also been suggested that insecure attachment creates a risk for depression.

These theories approach therapy in ways similar to those of ego psychology, but there are additional variations. One of them is play therapy for children. Object relations and attachment theories also suggest that a relationship with a therapist is critical, in permitting reintegration of the sense of self or establishing a sense of secure attachment.

GLOSSARY

Attachment An emotional connection to someone else.

Basic anxiety A sense of insecurity, a feeling of being abandoned and isolated.

Ego identity The overall sense of self that emerges from transactions with social reality.

Ego quality (ego strength or **virtue)** The quality that becomes part of one's personality through successful management of a crisis.

Epigenesis The idea (adopted from embryology) that an internal plan for future development is present at the beginning of life.

Identity crisis A time of intense exploration of alternative ways of viewing oneself.

Identity status The condition of whether an identity crisis has occurred and whether an identity has been attained.

Life-span development The idea that developmental processes continue throughout life.

Mirroring The giving of positive attention and supportiveness to someone.

Narcissism Grandiose self-importance and sense of entitlement.

Neurotic needs Maladaptive needs that emerge from overuse of strategies to combat anxiety.

Object relations An individual's symbolized relations to other persons (such as parents).

Play therapy The use of play as a procedure for conducting therapy with children.

Psychosocial crisis (or conflict) A period when some interpersonal issue is being dealt with and growth potential and vulnerability are both high.

Selfobject The mental symbol of another person who serves functions for oneself.

Self psychology Kohut's theory that relationships create the structure of the self.

Separation-individuation The process of acquiring a distinct identity; separating from fusion with mother.

Strange situation A procedure used to assess the attachment pattern of infant to mother.

Symbiosis A period in which an infant experiences fusion with mother.

Transference The viewing of other people through selfobject representations originally developed for parents.

Vicious cycle A cycle of needing affection, failing to obtain it, and the need thereby increasing.

The Learning
Perspective

prologue to

PART six

THE LEARNING PERSPECTIVE:
Major Themes and Underlying Assumptions

The experiences of life change us, and they do so in ways that are lawful and predictable. This is the central assumption of the learning perspective on personality. People have been interested in the processes of learning for a long time. At first, this interest was confined largely to those who studied lower animals. At first, this interest also focused primarily on small bits of behavior.

As knowledge grew, however, a tantalizing possibility began to take shape. The suspicion grew that the principles of learning might constitute the basic building blocks of behavior. All behavior. Not just the actions of rats in laboratory cages, but also the more complex actions of human beings in the world. Personality, from this point of view, is an accumulated set of learned tendencies. It's all the tendencies a person has learned over the course of a lifetime's experiences.

It's sometimes said that the basic metaphor of the learning perspective is the human being as a white rat. In a sense this is true, because many who take this perspective on behavior assume that learning processes are "universal," that is, they are the same in virtually all animals. In that sense, a human being is nothing more than a very complex version of the rats and mice that occupy the attention (and the cages) of many scientists who study the learning process. This metaphor has been accepted by many of the learning theorists who've applied their findings to personality. The principles that they've focused on are discussed in Chapter 12.

Although this metaphor was useful as a starting place, many learning theorists ultimately came to believe that it's too simple. The processes of human learning began to appear more complex than they'd seemed at first. The result was the need for a more elaborated metaphor, along with more elaborate theories of learning. In the new metaphor, the human being is still a learner, but now a more self-directive learner and a learner whose knowledge can accumulate in great leaps rather than just small increments. The learning is also seen as involving a set of cognitions, which play an important role themselves in behavior. The theories that draw on that expanded metaphor are discussed in Chapter 13.

The learning perspective on personality has also sparked something of a philosophical argument, which evolved and shifted as did the learning approach itself. In simple terms, the argument is about where behavior is "controlled." Is behavior controlled from within the person, or is it controlled by events and processes outside the person? The analysis of behavior offered by the earliest learning the-orists argued that behavior is shaped by external events, by stimuli and outcomes imposed from the environment. This assumption wasn't viewed with enthusiasm by everyone, perhaps partly because it doesn't offer a very flattering portrayal of human nature. More recently, many learning theorists have backed away from this assumption.

Nevertheless, one theme remains constant within the framework of the learning perspective across its two variants: changes in behavior occur in predictable ways as a result of experience. By extrapolation, personality must also be susceptible to molding, grinding, and polishing by the events that form the person's unique and individual history.

12 Conditioning Theories

■ **Classical Conditioning**

Basic Elements
Classical Conditioning as Anticipatory Learning
Discrimination, Generalization, and
    Extinction in Classical Conditioning
Emotional Conditioning

■ **Instrumental Conditioning**

The Law of Effect
Reinforcement and Punishment
Discrimination, Generalization, and
    Extinction in Instrumental Conditioning
Altering the Shape of Behavior
Schedules of Reinforcement and
    the Issue of Persistence
Learning "Irrational" Behavior
Reinforcement of Dimensions of Behavior

■ **Assessment**

Techniques

■ **Problems in Behavior,
    and Behavior Change**

Classical Conditioning of Emotional Responses
Classical Conditioning of Aversion
Conditioning and Context
Instrumental Conditioning and
    Maladaptive Behaviors
Instrumental Conditioning of Conflict
Instrumental Conditioning and Token Economies
Instrumental Conditioning and Biofeedback

■ **Conditioning Theories:
    Problems and Prospects**

SUMMARY

■ Lisa has a fondness for pastels. When asked why, she looks sort of blank and says she doesn't know, except she's felt that way at least since her eighth birthday, when she had the most wonderful surprise party, decorated all in pale pink, green, and violet.

■ Cindy works hard at her job at the library. She bustles from meeting to meeting, smoothing disagreements among the people she works with and making it easier for them to get their projects done. People express their appreciation in many ways—smiles, thank-yous, and last month a promotion to staff coordinator. The more signs she gets that she's doing a good job, the more enthusiasm she puts into each new morning.

Why are these people the way they are? Why do people have the preferences they do? What makes one person put so much effort into her work when someone else doesn't? One answer is that these aspects of behavior, which contribute so much to the individuality of personality, are acquired through learning.

The beginnings of what would become the learning perspective on personality go back a long way. The puzzle of just how learning takes place, what the elements of the process are, intrigued scientists from all over the world. The puzzle wasn't solved all at once, but a little at a time. Indeed, it isn't fully solved even yet. For example, there remain disagreements about whether learning is a single process with several manifestations or whether there are several distinct processes (e.g., Locurto, Terrace, & Gibbon, 1980; Rescorla, 1987; Staats, 1996).

From the learning perspective, personality consists of all the tendencies a person has learned during the experiences of his or her life. If personality is the residue of learning, then it's clearly important to know how learning works. In this part of the chapter we focus on broad principles of learning (for deeper discussion see, e.g., B. Schwartz, 1989).

For ease in presentation, we've adopted the view implicitly taken by most people: that there are distinct types of learning with their own rules. This chapter focuses on two forms of learning called *conditioning*: classical conditioning and instrumental conditioning. Much of the work on these processes has used animals other than humans. Nonetheless, many theorists think these processes underlie the human qualities we know as personality.

Classical Conditioning

One of the earliest findings in the effort to understand learning was that responses could be acquired by associating one stimulus with another. This type of learning is called **classical conditioning.** It's sometimes also called Pavlovian conditioning, after the Russian scientist Ivan Pavlov, whose efforts opened the door to understanding it (e.g., Pavlov, 1927, 1955).

Basic Elements

At least two things are required for classical conditioning to occur. First, the organism must already respond to some class of stimuli reflexively. That is, the response must occur *reliably and automatically whenever the stimulus occurs*. A **reflex** thus is an existing connection between a stimulus and a response, such that the one causes the other.

Consider some examples of reflexes from day-to-day experience. When you put something dry, acidic, or sour in your mouth (lemonade, tart candy) you start to salivate. When you see an object suddenly increase in size, as though it's approaching rapidly, you reflexively draw back. When skin near sexual organs is rubbed, you feel sexual excitement. When you put your hand on a hot stove or touch a hot car door, you automatically yank your hand away. When someone smiles warmly at you, you automatically feel good. These reactions happen reflexively for most people. Some are innate, some are learned, but in each case a stimulus leads directly and reliably to a particular response.

The second condition required for classical conditioning is that the stimulus in the reflex response must become associated in time and place with another stimulus. This second stimulus is usually (though not always) "neutral" at first. That is, by itself it causes no particular response beyond being noticed. There aren't any special requirements for this stimulus. It can be pretty much anything—a color, a sound, an object, a person.

For clarity, people often describe the process of classical conditioning in terms of several stages (Figure 12.1). The first stage is the situation *before* conditioning. At this point, only the reflex exists: stimulus causing automatic response. This stimulus is termed the **unconditioned** or **unconditional stimulus (US).** The response it touches off is called the **unconditioned** or **unconditional response (UR).** The word *unconditional* here means there's no special condition required for the response to occur. It's automatic when the stimulus occurs (Figure 12.1, A).

The second stage is when conditioning takes place. This involves the neutral stimulus occurring along with, or slightly before, the US (Figure 12.1, B). The neu-

Figure 12.1

The various stages of a typical classical conditioning procedure (time runs left to right in each panel): (A) There is a preexisting reflexive connection between a stimulus (US) and a response (UR). (B) A neutral stimulus (CS) is then paired repeatedly in time and space with the US. (C) The result is the development of a new response, termed a conditioned response (CR). (D) Once conditioning has occurred, presenting the CS by itself will now lead to the CR.

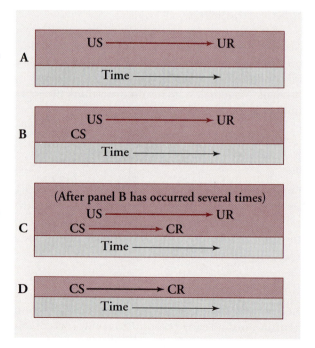

tral stimulus now gets a technical name: **conditioned** or **conditional stimulus (CS).** Here are two easy ways to keep track of what that means. First, this is the stimulus that's becoming "conditioned." Second, a response occurs in the presence of this stimulus only under the specific condition that the US be there as well. When the US comes, the UR follows automatically, reflexively (and remember that it does so *whenever* the US is presented, whether something else is there or not).

When the US and the CS are paired frequently, something gradually starts to change (Figure 12.1, C). The CS starts to acquire the ability to produce a response *of its own.* This response is termed the **conditioned response (CR).** The CR is often very similar to the UR. Indeed, in some cases they look identical (Table 12.1, row A), except that the CR is less intense than the UR. In other cases, the two can be distinguished (e.g., Hall, 1966). There is, however, a key similarity: specifically, if the UR has an unpleasant quality, so will the CR (Table 12.1, row B). If the UR has a pleasant quality, so will the CR (Table 12.1, rows C and D).

How does any of this apply to your life? Let's go back to the examples used earlier to illustrate reflexes. Suppose you've taken to squandering your late evenings at a bar specializing in Italian wines and Sicilian folk music. Every time you take a sip of the extremely dry Chianti (US), your salivary glands ooze like crazy (UR) because of the acidity. This reflexive event is surrounded by the strains of Sicilian folk songs (CS). Eventually you may come to develop a salivation response (CR) to the music itself.

As another example, suppose that while in that little bar you meet someone (US) who induces in you an astonishingly high degree of sexual arousal (UR). As you bask in candlelight, surrounded by green wine bottles, crimson wallpaper, and the soft strains of a Sicilian love song (all CSs), you may be acquiring a conditioned sexual response (CR) to those previously neutral features of the setting. Candlelight, for you, may never be the same again. The song you're hearing may gain a special place in your heart.

If you know that a US has occurred repeatedly along with a neutral stimulus, how do you know whether conditioning has taken place? To find out, present the CS by itself, without the US (Figure 12.1, D). If the CS (alone) gets a reaction, conditioning has occurred. If there's no reaction, there's been no conditioning. Generally speaking, the more frequently the CS is paired with the US, the more likely it is to lead to conditioning. If a US is very strong, however—if it causes a very intense

Table 12.1

Illustrations of the elements of classical conditioning in two common research procedures, in one common childhood experience, and in one common adult experience. (Note that the elements are arranged here in terms of stimulus and associated response, not in time sequence.)

	US	UR	CS	CR
(A)	Lemon juice in mouth	Salivation	Tone	Salivation
(B)	Shock to foot	Pain	Light	Fear
(C)	Ice cream in mouth	Pleasant taste	Sight of ice cream	Happiness
(D)	Romantically enticing partner	Sexual arousal	Mood music	Sexual arousal

UR—conditioning may occur with only one pairing. For example, cancer patients undergoing chemotherapy often experience extreme nausea from the medication and develop very strong CRs to surrounding stimuli.

Classical Conditioning as Anticipatory Learning

It has been suggested that CRs represent anticipatory reactions (Zener, 1937; see also Rescorla, 1972). That is, CRs, though involuntary, seem to reflect anticipation of, or preparation for, an impending US. Think back to earlier examples. If a tone sounds before lemon juice hits your mouth, the tone is a signal that the lemon will be arriving shortly. The CR (salivation) prepares the surface of your mouth for the acidity of the lemon. As another example, if a child hears his father's steps coming up the stairs just before he gets a spanking, the steps signal the spanking and the reflexive pain. The CR (fear, and perhaps trembling) reflect anticipation of the pain.

Another clue that CRs may be anticipatory is that they develop more easily in some situations than others. We said earlier that conditioning occurs through the more-or-less simultaneous presentation of the US and the CS. But classical conditioning is actually most effective if the CS slightly precedes the US (as in Figure 12.1). It's less effective if the two are simultaneous. It's even *less* so if the CS comes *after* the US (e.g., Schneiderman & Gormezano, 1964; Spetch, Wilkie, & Pinel, 1981; Spooner & Kellogg, 1947). This also makes it look as though an anticipatory reaction is being developed.

Don't necessarily assume that the anticipatory reaction is a *conscious* anticipation of the US. In theory, the tone needn't evoke the image of lemon juice. The sound of steps needn't lead to the inference that a spanking is coming. According to a strict conditioning analysis, the CR is connected *to the CS itself, not to an image of the US* that comes to mind. The CS and reaction to it are assumed to be bound together at this point, so the one reflexively produces the other (but see Box 12.1 for a more complex view).

Once conditioning has taken place, the CS-CR combination can go on to function just as any other reflex. That is, once it's solidly there, this combination can serve as US and UR for another case of classical conditioning (Figure 12.2). For example, once soft candlelight leads to sexual arousal, candlelight can be used to condition arousal to other things, such as particular *meals* you eat by candlelight. This process is termed **higher-order conditioning.**

Given this extension to new cases, classical conditioning can be very pervasive. There are limitations, of course. The most potent USs are those that elicit very intense URs. The farther away you get from biological reflexes, the weaker the reflexes are, and the weaker is the conditioning that results.

Discrimination, Generalization, and Extinction in Classical Conditioning

Classical conditioning provides a mechanism for new responses to become attached to neutral stimuli. Yet the CS almost never recurs later on in precisely the same form as it did earlier. On the other hand, you run across many stimuli later on that are somewhat similar to the CS. What happens in these cases?

Learning theorists address this question with the concepts **discrimination** and **generalization.** Discrimination means telling things apart. More formally it means

BOX 12.1

WHAT'S GOING ON IN CLASSICAL CONDITIONING?

Classical conditioning has been a staple of psychology courses for decades. In most accounts, it's a process that was well mapped out early in the development of learning theory, and there's been little new to add since then. Not everyone agrees with this, however, and there's been a new surge of interest in questions that lie just beneath the surface.

Classical conditioning is usually portrayed as a low-level process in which control over a response gets transferred from one stimulus to another by their being together at about the same time. Robert Rescorla (1988) said that's not the way it really is. He said conditioning concerns *relations* among events in the world. In his view, organisms use their experiences of relations between parts of the world to represent reality. Rescorla went on to say that association in time and place isn't what makes conditioning take place. Rather, what's important is the information one stimulus gives about the other. To Rescorla, learning is a process by which the organism's representation of the world is brought into line with the actual state of the world. Organisms learn only when they're "surprised" by something that happens to them.

As a result, two stimuli experienced together sometimes don't become associated. For example (Kamin, 1968), consider two animals. One has had a series of trials in which a light (as a CS) has been paired with a shock (as a US). The other hasn't had this experience. Both then get a series of trials in which both the light and a tone (as *two* CSs) are paired with the shock. What's interesting is that the second animal acquires a CR to the tone, but the first one doesn't. Apparently the earlier experience with the light (alone) has made the tone redundant. That is, because the light already signals that the US is coming, there's no need to condition to the tone, and the learning doesn't happen.

In the same way, studies have found that cancer patients undergoing chemotherapy can be induced to form conditioned aversions to very specific foods, if an unusual food is given before chemotherapy (Bernstein, 1985). Doing this can make that specific food a "scapegoat," and prevent the conditioning of aversions to other foods, which otherwise is very common.

Rescorla also challenges other aspects of the traditional view. He argues against the assumption that classical conditioning is a slow process requiring many pairings of stimuli. He says, in fact, that learning in five to six trials is common. In summarizing his stance, Rescorla said that classical conditioning "is not a stupid process by which the organism willy-nilly forms associations between any two stimuli that happen to co-occur. Rather, the organism is better seen as an information seeker using logical and perceptual relations among events, along with its own preconceptions, to form a sophisticated representation of the world" (1988, p. 154).

Rescorla is not alone in believing that internal events are more important in conditioning than previously realized. An analysis with somewhat similar characteristics (but even more cognitive in certain respects) was proposed by Holyoak, Koh, and Nisbett (1989). Their model is based in part on ideas from cognitive psychology identified with the term *connectionism* (McClelland & Rumelhart, 1986). The most important characteristic of that model for the issue we're raising here is that it treats classical conditioning as *rule* learning.

The positions taken by Rescorla and by Holyoak et al. are clearly at odds with the point of view that's expressed in the body of this chapter. The views they express also herald a broad issue that becomes more prominent in the next chapter: the role of cognition in the phenomena of learning.

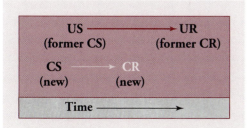

Figure 12.2

Once a link has been created between a stimulus and a response by classical conditioning, that new reflex can serve as a US-UR pair for additional conditioning, termed *higher-order conditioning*.

responding differently to different stimuli. For example, suppose your experiences in the Sicilian wine bar have led you to associate candlelight, muted crimson wallpaper, and wine bottles (as CSs) with sexual arousal (as CR). If you entered a room that closely resembled the bar (all other things being equal), you'd begin to feel a mellow glow (your CR). If you walked instead into a room with fluorescent lights and blue walls, that glow would surely not emerge. You *discriminate,* in your conditioned reactions, between the two classes of stimuli.

Now a harder question: what would happen if you walked into a room with muted lamplight, walls painted burgundy, and green glass vases? These aren't quite the stimuli that got linked to sexual arousal, but they're close. Here's where the process of generalization comes in. In all probability, you'd begin to feel the glow, although it might not be as strong as in the first room. As shown in Figure 12.3, generalization from conditioned stimuli definitely takes place. The intensity of the reaction falls off, though, as the stimulus gets farther and farther removed from the original CS (Hovland, 1937; Moore, 1972). To put it differently, generalization begins to give way to discrimination, as the stimuli become more different from the initial CS. Discrimination and generalization thus are complementary.

One more question: do conditioned responses ever go away? Discussions of conditioning don't use terms such as *forgetting.* CRs do weaken, however, by a process called **extinction.** Extinction occurs when a CS comes repeatedly without the US (Pavlov, 1927). At first, the CS leads reliably to the CR (Figure 12.4). Gradually, over repeated presentations, the CR grows weaker. The CR doesn't actually disappear, however. Even when a response stops in a given session, there's a "spontaneous recovery" the next day (e.g., Wagner, Siegel, Thomas, & Ellison, 1964). It is now believed that classical conditioning leaves a permanent record in the nervous system, and that its effects can be muted but not erased (see Bouton, 1994, 2000).

Emotional Conditioning

As you may have realized already, much of the classical conditioning in humans involves responses with emotional qualities. That is, stimuli that most clearly lead to reflexive reactions are those that elicit good feelings (hope, delight, excitement) or bad feelings (fear, anger, pain). The term **emotional conditioning** is sometimes used to refer to classical conditioning in which the CRs are emotional reactions.

Figure 12.3

An illustration of generalization of a classically conditioned response to stimuli that are similar to the CS, and of discrimination regarding stimuli that are less similar to the CS. The CS is a tone of 1200 Hz. Tones that are similar to it (800, 1600 Hz) elicit CRs—generalization. Tones that are less similar (400, 2000 Hz) elicit fewer CRs—discrimination (data from Moore, 1972, combined across two groups).

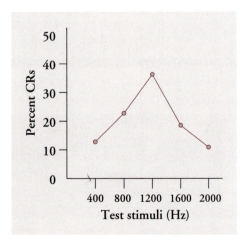

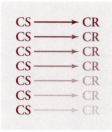

Figure 12.4

Extinction in classical conditioning. When a CS appears over and over without the US, the CR becomes progressively weaker and eventually disappears (or nearly does).

Conditioning of emotional responses is important in the learning view on personality. It's argued that the likes and dislikes, the preferences and biases that help define personality, arise through emotional conditioning (De Houwer, Thomas, & Baeyens, 2001). Preferences reflect associations between neutral stimuli and events that reflexively caused good or bad feelings. Linking a neutral stimulus to a pleasant event creates a like (Razran, 1940; Staats & Staats, 1958). Linking a stimulus to an upsetting event creates a dislike (Watson & Raynor, 1920; see also Cacioppo & Sandman, 1981; Riordan & Tedeschi, 1983; Staats, Staats, & Crawford, 1962). In fact, just hearing someone describe a good or bad trait in someone else can link that trait in your mind to the person who's talking (Skowronski, Carlston, Mae, & Crawford, 1998).

Different people experience different bits of the world and thus have different patterns of emotional arousal. Different people also experience even the same event from the perspective of their unique "histories." As we noted in Chapter 6, children from the same family experience the family differently (Daniels & Plomin, 1985). Given these variations, people can wind up with remarkably different patterns of likes and dislikes (Box 12.2). Thus emotional conditioning may play a major role in creating the uniqueness of personality (Staats & Burns, 1982).

One purpose of the business lunch is to associate your company and its products (as CSs) with the positive feelings produced by a good meal in a nice restaurant (as USs).

BOX 12.2

CLASSICAL CONDITIONING AND ATTITUDES

Where do attitudes come from? One answer to this question is that you develop attitudes by classical conditioning. This chapter describes how a neutral stimulus (CS) begins to produce an emotional reaction (CR) if it's paired with a stimulus (US) that already creates an emotional reaction. The conditioning approach holds that people come to have emotional responses to attitude objects (classes of things, people, ideas, or events) in exactly that way. If the attitude object is paired with an emotion-arousing stimulus, it comes to evoke the emotion itself. This emotional response, then, is the basis for an attitude.

One of the first experiments on classical conditioning of attitudes was conducted over sixty years ago (Razran, 1940). In an initial phase of the study, he presented several political slogans to people and had them rate how much they approved of each. Later he presented the slogans again, under one of three conditions: while the people were eating a free lunch, while they were inhaling noxious odors, or while they were sitting in a nondescript, neutral setting. Later on, they rated their approval of the slogans a second time. Slogans paired with a free lunch were now rated more positively than before. Slogans paired with unpleasant odors were now rated more negatively than before. Slogans presented in the neutral room weren't rated differently than before. (Similar results were obtained by Nunnally, Duchnowski, & Parker, 1965.) These findings are exactly what one would predict from the principle of classical conditioning.

This approach was later extended to conditioning of attitudes toward words (Staats, Staats, & Crawford, 1962). One group of words was presented with electric shocks. After several pairings, the words were presented without the shocks, and subjects rated how much they liked each. The ratings were more negative than ratings of words that hadn't been paired with shocks (for similar findings see Berkowitz & Knurek,

1969; Zanna, Kiesler, & Pilkonis, 1970). Even the *threat* of shock has been shown to produce conditioning, in this case to another person who happened to be present (Riordan & Tedeschi, 1983).

It's not just artificial stimuli such as those that lead to attitudes. Walther (2002) found that pairing photos of neutral persons with liked or disliked persons led to positive and negative attitudes respectively toward the neutral persons. These attitudes were also found to be resistant to extinction.

There's also the potential for higher-order conditioning here. Negative attitudes formed by associating a neutral person with a disliked person can produce further conditioning from that one to another neutral person (Walther, 2002). And think about the fact that words such as *good* and *bad* are tied in most people's experience to positive and negative events (Staats & Staats, 1957, 1958) and thus probably yield an emotional response themselves. People use such words all the time around others, creating opportunities for higher-order conditioning.

A large number of studies have shown that classical conditioning *can* be involved in development of attitudes (De Houwer et al., 2001), but they don't tell us whether attitudes *are* usually acquired this way. But events that arouse emotions are common in day-to-day life, which provides opportunities for conditioning to take place. For example, the "business lunch" is remarkably similar to Razran's experimental manipulation. Certainly we are all exposed repeatedly to people who are presently neutral, in conjunction with others whom we like and dislike. It seems not at all unreasonable that classical conditioning processes may underlie many of people's preferences for persons, events, things, places, and ideas. Given that these preferences are important aspects of personality, conditioning would appear to represent an important contributor to personality.

Instrumental Conditioning

A second form of conditioning is called **instrumental conditioning.** (This phrase is often used interchangeably with *operant conditioning*, despite slight differences in meaning.) Instrumental conditioning differs in several ways from classical conditioning. For one, classical conditioning is passive. When a reflex occurs, conditioning doesn't require you to *do* anything—just be there and aware of other stimuli. Instrumental conditioning is active (Skinner, 1938). The events that define it begin with a behavior on your part (even if the "behavior" is the act of remaining still).

The Law of Effect

Instrumental conditioning is a simple process, although its ramifications are widespread. The process goes like this: if a behavior is followed by a better or more satisfying state of affairs, the behavior is more likely to be done again later on in a similar situation (Figure 12.5, A). If a behavior is followed by a worse or less satisfying state of affairs, the behavior is less likely to be done again later (Figure 12.5, B).

This simple description—linking an action, an outcome, and a change in the likelihood of future action—is the "law of effect" deduced by Thorndike a century ago (Thorndike, 1898, 1905). The law of effect is simple but profound. It provides a way to account for regularities in behavior. That is, any situation permits many potential acts (Figure 12.5, C). Some acts come to occur with great regularity, others happen once and disappear, never to return. Others turn up occasionally, but only occasionally. Why? Because some have been followed by satisfying outcomes, and others haven't.

Think of all the behaviors that a person might do in a given situation as forming a **habit hierarchy,** a list of response potentials (Miller & Dollard, 1941). The list derives from prior conditioning. Some responses are very likely, because they've often been followed by more satisfying states of affairs. Others are less likely, and others even less so. For example, when you're in the cafeteria at noon, getting and eating lunch are very likely behaviors, working on coursework is less likely (although maybe not too far down the list), and taking off all your clothes and reciting Shakespeare are very *un*likely. As another example, if you need to ask your parents for money, there are some tactics you'll use because they've worked in the past and others you've

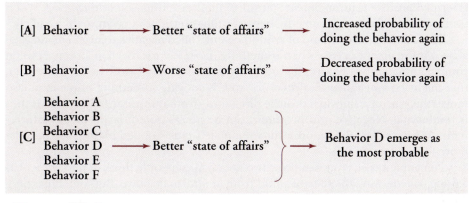

Figure 12.5

Instrumental conditioning: (A) Behavior that is followed by a more satisfying state of affairs is more likely to be done again. (B) Behavior that is followed by a less satisfying state of affairs is less likely to be done again. (C) This principle accounts for the fact that (over time and experiences) some behaviors emerge from the many possible behaviors as habitual responses that occur in specific situations.

given up because they haven't worked. Habit hierarchies continually evolve, as the various actions you engage in are followed by either more or less satisfying states of affairs.

Reinforcement and Punishment

The term **reinforcer** quickly replaced the cumbersome "satisfying state of affairs." The word reinforcer conveys the sense that it *strengthens* the tendency to do whatever act came before it.

A reinforcer is anything that strengthens a behavioral tendency. Reinforcers may reduce biological needs (e.g., food or water) or satisfy social desires (e.g., smiles and acceptance). Some have acquired their reinforcing quality indirectly (e.g., money). There's even evidence that visual sensations (seeing something you like) can act as reinforcers (Hayes, Rincover, & Volosin, 1980). Different kinds of reinforcers have different names. A *primary reinforcer* is one that diminishes a biological need. A *secondary reinforcer* has acquired reinforcing properties by association with a primary reinforcer (through classical conditioning) or by virtue of the fact that it can be used to *get* primary reinforcers (Wolfe, 1936; Zimmerman, 1957).

The term **punisher** refers to unpleasant or aversive outcomes. Punishers reduce the tendency to do the behavior that came before them, although there's been controversy about how effective they are (Rachman & Teasdale, 1969; Solomon, 1964; Thorndike, 1933). As with reinforcement, punishment can be primary or secondary. That is, some events are intrinsically aversive (e.g., pain). Others are aversive because of associations with primary punishers.

There's another distinction that's also important. When you think of reinforcement, what probably comes to mind is things you find desirable—gifts, money, trips to fun places, CDs, and so on. When you think of punishment, you probably think of pain—of being slapped, yelled at, or frowned at. In reality, however, both concepts are broader and more subtle than that.

Reinforcement always implies moving the person's "state of affairs" in a positive direction. But this can happen in two ways. The more obvious way is receiving the good things that come to mind as reinforcers (gifts, money). Receiving these things is termed **positive reinforcement.** "Positive" implies adding something good. When positive reinforcement occurs, the behavior that preceded it becomes more likely.

There's also a second kind of reinforcement, called **negative reinforcement.** Negative reinforcement occurs when something *aversive* is *removed*. For instance, when your roommate stops playing his annoying tape of "Polka Favorites" over and over, that might be a negative reinforcer for you. Removing something unpleasant also moves the state of affairs in a positive direction—from unpleasant to neutral. It thus is reinforcing. Negative reinforcement can be just as potent as positive reinforcement. Whatever you did before your roommate's tape stopped playing will become more likely in the future.

Punishment also comes in these two forms. Most people think of punishment as adding pain, moving the state of affairs from neutral to negative. But sometimes punishment involves removing something good, changing from a positive to a neutral (thus less satisfying) state of affairs. This principle—punishing by withdrawing something desirable—underlies a tactic that's widely used to discourage unwanted behavior in children. It's called a **time out,** short for "time out from positive reinforcement" (Drabman & Spitalnik, 1973; Risley, 1968). A time out removes the child from whatever activity is going on to a place where there's nothing fun to do. Many find this practice appealing because it's more humane than painful punish-

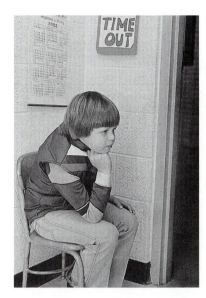

Time out is an effective way of discouraging unwanted behavior in children.

ments such as spanking. In principle, however, a time out creates a "less satisfying state of affairs" for the child and thus should have the same effect on behavior as any other punishment.

A final issue concerning reinforcement is that it's hard to specify how "satisfying" an outcome is (and thus how reinforcing it is). An outcome's value is determined partly by your situation. If you're starving, being handed a box of stale Cheez puffs is a good outcome. If you've just had a great meal, the Cheez puffs won't do much for you. In the same way, a truly starving man may not be impressed by a beautiful woman's offer of sex, which in other circumstances would seem to him an *extremely* satisfying state of affairs.

This issue has led many people (though not all) to think of instrumental conditioning as a process that occurs primarily when the person has a motivation to which the reinforcer relates (see Box 12.3). Indeed, many people use the term *instrumental* more broadly, going beyond the conditioning process per se. This broader use of the word implies "goal-directed," conveying the sense that the behavior is the instrument or tool by which a desired outcome is obtained.

Discrimination, Generalization, and Extinction in Instrumental Conditioning

Several ideas introduced in the context of classical conditioning also apply to instrumental conditioning, with slight differences in connotation. For example, discrimination still means responding differently in the presence of different stimuli. Here, however, the difference in response results from variations in prior reinforcement.

To understand how a discrimination develops, imagine that a stimulus is present whenever a behavior is followed by a reinforcer. Further, when the stimulus is absent, the behavior is *never* followed by a reinforcer. Gradually the presence or absence of the stimulus gains an influence over whether the behavior takes place. It becomes a **discriminative stimulus,** a stimulus that turns the behavior on and off. You use the stimulus to discriminate among situations, and thus among responses. Miller and Dollard

BOX 12.3

THEORETICAL CONTROVERSY
Do Motives Play a Role in Instrumental Conditioning?

As pointed out in the main text, you have to know an organism's present state to know what's reinforcing to it. There are, however, several ways to think about this. Neal Miller and John Dollard (1941; Dollard & Miller, 1950), the first theorists to try to portray the full breadth of human personality in terms of learning, held that the nature of reinforcement is intimately related to motivation.

Their view of the nature of reinforcement relied on Clark Hull's (1943) theory of motivation. Hull said that when an organism is deprived of a needed substance (e.g., food or water), it experiences an increase in **drive.** When drive goes up, it increases the tendency to emit behaviors high in the habit hierarchy. Sooner or later, you get what you've been deprived of. That causes drive to go back down. According to Miller and Dollard, *drive reduction constitutes reinforcement.* In this view, to know what will be reinforcing to a person, you need to know the person's needs or motives.

Not all conditioning theorists have agreed that motivational concepts are helpful. An alternative view was posed by B. F. Skinner (e.g., 1953, 1974), who argued that the effort to explain behavior doesn't benefit from guessing about what's going on inside the organism. He was quite outspoken about his belief that concepts like motive, wish, desire—not to mention cognition—serve more to confuse the picture than to clarify it.

Skinner argued that use of terms such as *motive* or *wish* is often circular. That is, we often infer that people are motivated to do something by whether they do it. Skinner asked why not forget about the motive and simply analyze the acts. Indeed, Skinner felt that terms such as *drive* and *motive* are actually misleading, because they create the impression of an explanation while not really explaining anything.

Rather than talk about drives or needs, Skinner said, you should simply describe the stimulus conditions of *deprivation* versus *satiation*. Deprivation is a period of the absence of a consummatory behavior (for example, eating or drinking). Satiation is the end of a period of intense consummatory behavior. Both events are observable. Along with knowledge of prior reinforcement contingencies, they provide all the information necessary to predict behavior. This theoretical position is often called **radical behaviorism** because it represents a strict (thus radical) application of the idea that one shouldn't invent imaginary mechanisms when behavior can be accounted for by observable events (O'Donohue & Kitchener, 1999).

In sum, these two theoretical models agree in one respect and disagree in another. Both assume it's important to take the organism's "present condition" into account. But they take very different views on how to think about the organism's present condition.

(1941) called this a *cue* function. Behavior that's cued by discriminative stimuli is said to be *under stimulus control.*

Here's an illustration of discriminative stimuli that may resonate with your own memories. Imagine a high school class whose regular teacher is stiff and formal and doesn't tolerate play during class. The teacher sometimes misses class due to illness. The substitute is more relaxed and easygoing. In truth, he'd rather have a good time with the class than stick to the lesson plan. When he's there, cutting up is followed by more reinforcement than when the regular teacher's there. The highly predictable result is that quiet prevails for the regular teacher, but the class turns into a party when the substitute's there. Because the shift occurs as a function of the teacher (the discriminative stimuli), the students' behavior is under stimulus control.

Earlier in this section we mentioned the idea of a habit hierarchy (an ordering of the likelihood of doing various behaviors). We noted that your hierarchy shifts constantly because of the ongoing flow of reinforcing (and nonreinforcing) events. It shifts constantly for another reason as well: every change in situation means a change in cues (discriminative stimuli). Because the cues suggest what behaviors are reinforced in that situation, the shift in cues rearranges the list of behavior probabilities.

The concept of discriminative stimulus is important to reinforcement views of personality. It accounts for complexity in behavior. Very slight changes in the stimulus field dramatically alter the behaviors that occur. As traffic lights turn green, people drive forward; as the lights turn red, they stop. As the clock reads 12, people leave their desks and go to lunch; as the clock reads 1, the same people return and start to work again. These differences in behavior are large in scope, but they're caused by extremely small changes in the surrounding array of stimuli.

The principle of generalization is also important here. It contributes a sense of continuity in behavior. As you enter new settings and see objects and people you've never seen before, you respond easily and automatically. There are similarities between the new settings and previous discriminative stimuli. You generalize behaviors from the one to the other, and action flows smoothly forward. You may never have seen a particular style of spoon before, but you won't hesitate to use it on the soup. You may never have driven a particular make of car before, but if that's what the rental agency gives you, you'll probably be able to handle it.

The principle of generalization gives conditioning theorists a way to talk about traitlike qualities. A person should behave consistently across time and circumstances if discriminative stimuli stay fairly similar across the times and circumstances. Because key stimulus qualities often *do* stay the same across settings (even if other qualities differ greatly), the person's action tendency also stays the same across the settings. The result is that, to an outside observer, the person appears to have a set of internal traits, or dispositions. In this view, however, consistency of behavior depends on similarities of environments (an idea that's not too different from the discussion of consistency late in Chapter 4).

Extinction in instrumental conditioning occurs when a behavior that once led to a reinforcer does so no longer. As the behavior is done over and over—with no reinforcer—its probability drops. Eventually it dies out to the point where it's barely there at all (though just as in classical conditioning there's a tendency for spontaneous recovery, causing some to believe that it hasn't gone away; Bouton, 1994; Rescorla, 1997, 1998). Thus, extinction is a way in which behavioral tendencies fade.

Altering the Shape of Behavior

The concepts of reward and punishment provide a way of talking about how behaviors become more or less likely to occur. Thus far, however, we haven't dealt with how a behavior changes in its form. Still missing is the concept of **shaping.**

Let's look first at shaping in the laboratory. Many times it's not practical to wait for a desired act and then reinforce it. Instead, reinforcement is first given for a rough *approximation* of the behavior, which then begins to occur more often. Gradually you reinforce only closer and closer approximations of the desired act. This method is called **successive approximation.** Through it, the behavior of the organism comes to be very specific; that is, behavior is "shaped" in a particular direction. To characterize the process differently, the organism is learning a continually changing discrimination.

One might think of this as simply a convenient laboratory tactic, but much the same thing happens all the time outside the lab. Whether by chance or by design, general tendencies (e.g., going to school) are reinforced at first. These general tendencies then are channeled into more specific tendencies (e.g., studying political science) by shifts in patterns of reinforcement. This shaping can ultimately result in specific and highly specialized tendencies (attending law school, becoming a state representative). Shaping, then, provides a way to understand how behavior (indeed, personality) evolves continuously, with changing reinforcement patterns.

Schedules of Reinforcement and the Issue of Persistence

The issue of whether behavior tendencies stay or disappear is important in thinking about personality, especially growth and change. Extinction helps us understand which behaviors persist and which do not, but it's not the only principle that matters. The persistence of an action tendency is also influenced by the *pattern* with which it's been reinforced in the past.

In reading about instrumental conditioning, people often assume that a reinforcement occurs every time the behavior occurs. But common sense and your own experience should tell you life's not like that. Sometimes reinforcements are frequent, but sometimes not. Variations in frequency and pattern are called *schedules of reinforcement.* A simple variation in schedules is between continuous and partial (or intermittent) reinforcement. In **continuous reinforcement** the behavior is followed by a reinforcer *every single time.* In **partial reinforcement,** the behavior is followed by a reinforcer less often than every time.

There are many patterns of partial reinforcement. The reinforcer can come after a certain *number of occurrences* of the behavior (your teacher smiles and says "good" every fifth time you contribute to class discussion). This pattern is called a ratio schedule. The number involved can be large (every tenth time) or small (every second time). The numbers can be fixed (every sixth time exactly) or variable (randomly varying, but every sixth time on the average). The reinforcer may depend on the passage of a period of time as well as the occurrence of the behavior (a week has to pass since your teacher last smiled and said "good," but then he does it the next time you contribute to class). This pattern is called an interval schedule. Intervals can also be fixed (exactly one week has to pass before your next contribution is rewarded) or variable (on the average, one week has to pass before your next contribution is rewarded).

Different schedules of reinforcement lead to different behavior tendencies across time. Figure 12.6 shows the tendencies associated with each type of schedule just described (adapted from Reese, 1966; see also Lundin, 1961). The tendencies are de-

Figure 12.6

Behavioral tendencies created by four different types of reinforcement schedules, in which the total reinforcement across a long span of time is equivalent. Behavior is portrayed as "cumulative frequencies" of response, responses summed across time. Each small mark on the line represents the occurrence of a reinforcer. As you can see, some reinforcement schedules produce higher and more consistent rates of behavior than others (adapted from Reese, 1966).

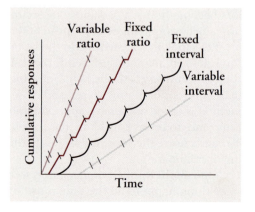

scribed in this figure in terms of cumulative frequencies of response—responses added up across time. Each small mark on the line represents the occurrence of a reinforcer.

A *fixed ratio* schedule causes a high rate of responding, with a brief pause immediately after reinforcement. This schedule is reflected in "piecework," in which a person is paid a fixed amount per unit of work (object assembled, basket of vegetables picked, and so on). A *variable ratio* schedule creates an even higher rate of response, without pauses after reinforcement. An example of a variable ratio is gambling, which pays off occasionally but unpredictably.

The *fixed interval* schedule produces a pronounced and reliable "scalloping" of the curve, a complete absence of behavior immediately after reinforcement, followed by a gradual renewal, which accelerates until the next reinforcer occurs. A good illustration of this schedule is the study behavior of a student whose psychology course has tests at predictable intervals, who studies most just before tests. This pattern also describes the behavior of the U.S. Congress, which passes most of its bills just before it adjourns (Weisberg & Waldrop, 1972).

Scalloping isn't apparent at all in the last schedule, the *variable interval* schedule. This one is characterized by consistent activity, as with the variable ratio schedule, but (in general) at a lower level of activity. An example of this schedule is the behavior of the student whose instructor gives pop quizzes unexpectedly, rather than tests at predictable intervals.

As you see, reinforcement patterns can get complicated. What's most important, though, is that infrequent and unpredictable reinforcement affects behavior differently than reinforcement that's frequent and predictable. There are two differences. The first is that you acquire a new behavior faster when reinforcement is frequent than when it's not. Eventually, even infrequent reinforcement results in high rates of the behavior, but it may take a while.

The other effect is less intuitive but more important. It's often called the **partial reinforcement effect.** It shows up when reinforcement stops (Figure 12.7). Take away the reinforcer, and a behavior built in by continuous reinforcement goes away quickly. A behavior built in by partial (less frequent) reinforcement remains longer—it's more *resistant to extinction* (Amsel, 1967; Humphreys, 1939).

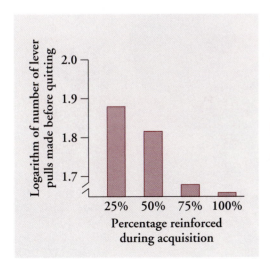

Figure 12.7

Effect of partial reinforcement and continuous reinforcement on persistence. Participants first played on a slot machine that paid off 25 percent, 50 percent, 75 percent, or 100 percent of the time. Then they were allowed to continue playing for as long as they liked, but they never again won. As can be seen, partial reinforcement leads to greater resistance to extinction. That is, the groups initially rewarded less than 100 percent of the time persist longer when all reward is removed. Moreover, the lower the percentage of partial reinforcement initially given, the greater the persistence (adapted from Lewis & Duncan, 1956).

Apparently this effect isn't simply a matter of how easy or hard it is to tell when the extinction period is starting (Jenkins, 1962; Theios, 1962). Rather, there seems to be a subtle difference in what's conditioned in the first place (Amsel, 1967). In intermittent reinforcement, a nonreinforcement is actually becoming a discriminative stimulus that cues *persistence* (because, if you keep trying, you eventually get a reinforcement). Nonreinforcement continues to act as a discriminative stimulus for a long time, even when the reinforcer's gone for good. When you start with continuous reinforcement, though, the link between nonreinforcement and persistence never gets made. When the reinforcer goes away, nothing remains to keep the behavior going.

In the same vein, it has been argued that people learn to be industrious by receiving patterns of reinforcement that cause sensations of effort to become a cue for persistence (Eisenberger, 1992). Thus, instead of finding the experience of effort aversive, people find it rewarding. One can imagine a situation in which even a very aversive experience, such as fear, can become a discriminative stimulus for persistence. Such a case would represent a kind of "conditioned courage."

The partial reinforcement effect carries an important message. If you want a behavior to remain relatively persistent in someone, don't reinforce it all the time. In fact, the lower the rate of reinforcement (if it's enough to sustain the behavior), the stronger is the link between the cue of nonreinforcement and persistence. Ironically, although this view emphasizes the importance of reinforcement in producing behavior, it also emphasizes the importance of *non*reinforcement during conditioning in *sustaining* the behavior.

Learning "Irrational" Behavior

People who use conditioning principles often emphasize that the behavior need not *cause* the reinforcer for conditioning to occur. The behavior needs only to be *followed by* the reinforcer. Whatever behavior preceded the reinforcer is strengthened by the reinforcer's occurrence.

Many personal superstitions are learned through a schedule of random partial reinforcement.

This relationship can lead to rather strange effects, which Skinner (1948) pointed out in a study of pigeons. Picture a pigeon in a cage, which gets a reinforcer (a bit of food) at a regular interval, regardless of what it's doing. Every reinforcer strengthens the behavior that preceded it. At first, because behavior is somewhat random, several behaviors are strengthened. Eventually, though, one action is reinforced often enough that it starts to predominate. Because it's more common, it gets reinforced even more. The result is that the bird is now doing an entirely arbitrary behavior quite regularly.

Because the pigeon acts as though these specific actions are causing the reinforcer, Skinner called this *superstitious behavior.* He argued that seemingly irrational or senseless behaviors in people develop exactly the same way. Reinforcers occurred for reasons unrelated to the behavior, and they built the behavior in and shaped it into its present form. Skinner didn't assume, by the way, that the pigeon was thinking about what caused the reinforcement, only that its behavior gave that outward appearance (see Box 12.4).

There's no difference between the process by which superstitious behaviors are acquired and the process by which any other behavior is acquired. To call a behavior

BOX 12.4

BEHAVIORISTS' VIEW OF THE ROLE OF THOUGHT IN CONDITIONING

Conditioning theorists hold that behavior tendencies are determined by reinforcement patterns. Most of them assume thought processes are irrelevant to this process (Rachlin, 1977). Although Skinner's pigeons may have acted *as though* they thought a particular action was producing the reinforcer, the appearance is illusory. Even if pigeons could think (which is questionable), their thoughts aren't behind the behavior. The reinforcement pattern is behind the behavior.

It's undeniable that people (unlike pigeons) talk and think. To conditioning theorists, however, these tendencies among humans simply reflect the fact that verbal behaviors (both overt speech and covert thought) become conditioned in particular ways (e.g., Miller & Dollard, 1941). That is, people are conditioned to think in particular patterns and to talk in certain ways. Nevertheless, the real causes of all three phenomena—the behavior, the talk, and the thoughts—are the patterns of reinforcement.

Behaviorists try to avoid as much as possible using words such as *intention, thought, cognition,* and *consciousness* because they see them as unnecessary in explaining how people act and perhaps even mis-

leading (Skinner, 1987). Many behaviorists see the mental events that occur along with behavior and reinforcement as **epiphenomena,** phenomena with no causal role. They just happen alongside the behavior, or may even be caused by the behavior as subjective offshoots (cf. Rachlin, 1977). Skinner (1989) pointed out, in this regard, that many words now used to describe mental states had their origins in descriptions of behavior. This history fits his contention that the behavior is what really matters.

This point of view has been more than a little controversial over the years. It hasn't been well received at all by people outside the behaviorist camp (see Catania & Harnad, 1988, for a wide-ranging discussion). Critics of the behaviorist position point out that a conditioning view has difficulty in accounting for a number of phenomena, including the emergence of language in children (Chomsky, 1959). This criticism has led some people to regard the conditioning view as incorrect. It led others more sympathetic to the learning perspective to modify the theories, a response that is taken up in the next chapter.

irrational versus adaptive is an observer's value judgment. To the conditioning theorist, all behavior is acquired the same way (through reinforcement). On the other hand, there's an important difference between the situation just described and situations people normally encounter. Skinner had full control over the birds' environment. He could easily ensure that reinforcers had a completely arbitrary pattern. In contrast, for people, reinforcers more often result from some particular behavior for nonarbitrary reasons. These contingencies shape most human behavior into orderly patterns that only more rarely appear to be superstitious or irrational.

Reinforcement of Dimensions of Behavior

One final point about learning through instrumental conditioning: It's most intuitive to think that the reinforcer makes a particular *act* more likely in the future. However, it often seems that what becomes more likely isn't a concrete act, but rather some *quality* of action (Eisenberger & Selbst, 1994). For example, reinforcing *effort* in one setting can increase *effortfulness* in other settings (Mueller & Dweck, 1998). Reinforcing accuracy on one task increases accuracy on other tasks. Reinforcing speed on one task increases speed elsewhere. Reinforcing creativity yields more creativity (Eisenberger & Rhoades, 2001), whereas reinforcing focused thought produces more focused thinking elsewhere (Eisenberger, Armeli, & Pretz, 1998).

Thus, reinforcement can change not just particular behaviors, but whole dimensions of behavior. This idea broadens considerably the ways in which reinforcement principles may act on human beings. It suggests that reinforcers act at many levels of abstraction. Indeed, perhaps many aspects of behavior at many different levels are reinforced *simultaneously* when a person experiences a more satisfying state of affairs. This possibility creates a far more complex picture of change through conditioning than was apparent in earlier parts of the chapter.

▌Assessment

From the view of conditioning theories, personality is the accumulation of a person's conditioned tendencies (Ciminero, Calhoun, & Adams, 1977; Hersen & Bellack, 1976; Staats, 1996). By adulthood you have a wide range of conditioned emotional responses to various stimuli, which you experience as attitudes and preferences. You also have tendencies to engage in various kinds of actions in various kinds of settings. These tendencies differ from person to person in probability, resistance to extinction, and the discriminative stimuli that cue them.

This viewpoint has at least three implications for the process of personality assessment. Most simply, it suggests that assessment should focus on behavioral qualities, rather than cognitions. The assessment procedures suggested by this approach focus on observable aspects of emotional reactions or action tendencies, rather than trying to obtain a general sense of what the person is "like" (Kanfer & Saslow, 1965).

A second implication stems from the idea that emotional responses are linked to specific CSs and that actions depend on discriminative stimuli (stimuli associated with reinforcement of the actions). This means that feelings and actions are tied to specific classes of situations or to cues within those situations. Thus, assessment should focus on specific classes of situations and specific responses rather than on creating broad generalizations about the person.

A final implication is that there's no better form of assessment than direct observation. People can give self-reports of feelings and self-reports of act tendencies, but these may or may not be reliable or accurate. A better way of assessing people's responses is to observe. Put the person in the situation you're interested in and let the person do or feel what comes naturally. Then measure what happens, as directly as possible, with as little interpretation as possible.

Techniques

This view of personality relates to two kinds of assessment techniques. One focuses on assessment of emotional responses, the other is broader in scope. The first, sometimes called **physiological assessment,** relies on the fact that emotional responses have several components. Besides subjective qualities, emotions also have physiological aspects (Cacioppo & Petty, 1983; Greenfield & Sternbach, 1972). When you experience an emotion (especially if it's intense) changes take place in your body: changes in muscle tension, heart rate, blood pressure, brain waves, sweat-gland activity, and more. The changes can be thought of as internal behaviors.

These responses can be measured by devices called physiographs. The reactions thus are observable aspects of emotional experiences. More specifically, the degree of response can be taken as an index of the *intensity* of an emotional reaction. To illustrate, imagine yourself wired to a physiograph, which is collecting your body's responses. As you sit there, you are shown a series of stimuli that are possible sources of fear reactions: snakes, spiders, a view downward from a tall building, and so on. Your body's responses reflect the intensity of any fear you have. An observer could conclude, for example, that you're scared of heights but not by snakes. All this can be assessed without a word from you. Your internal behavior gives all the information. Some believe that these procedures are quite useful in assessment of problems such as posttraumatic stress disorder (Keane et al., 1998; Orr et al., 1998).

Physiological assessment is direct and objective, but it's also elaborate and technical. It tends to be used more in research than in clinical applications. A second technique can also be used to assess emotional responses. It's called **behavioral assessment** (Barlow, 1981; Haynes & O'Brien, 2000; Staats, 1996). It entails observing the person's overt behavior in situations of interest. Emotions such as fear can be

Physiological responses provide one index of the intensity of emotional reactions.

assessed by behavioral indicators—trembling, paleness, avoidance, and so on. This technique can also be applied more broadly. It can be used to assess what kinds of activities people undertake, for how long, and in what patterns.

Behavioral assessment varies widely in how it's actually done. Sometimes the observer simply counts acts of specific types, checks possibilities from a prearranged list, or watches how far into a sequence of action a person goes before stopping (Lang & Lazovik, 1963; O'Leary & Becker, 1967; Paul, 1966). In other cases the procedure is more elaborate, using automated devices to record how long the person being assessed engages in various behaviors.

For example, behavioral assessment of children often uses recorders with separate channels to keep track of the frequency and duration of activities such as talking, running, and sitting alone (Lovaas, Freitag, Gold, & Kassorla, 1965). The observer in this research pushes a separate button that corresponds to each behavior category and continues holding for as long as that kind of behavior is being performed by the child whose behavior is being assessed.

These various techniques are useful but they have their problems. Most obviously, they're elaborate and thus hard to use. Another problem is that different techniques don't always give the same results. The amount of behavioral avoidance in a situation—an index one might expect to be highly correlated with fear—doesn't always correspond well with self-reports of fear (Bernstein, 1973). Physiograph records may not fit well with either of these measures. Given this kind of disagreement, it's hard to know which measure represents the "real" fear level.

Problems in Behavior, and Behavior Change

If personality derives from classical and instrumental conditioning, so does maladaptive behavior. People sometimes learn things that interfere with their lives. They sometimes fail to learn things that make life easier. This view suggests a basis for several kinds of personality problems along with ways of treating such problems. As a group, the treatment techniques are termed **behavior modification** or **behavior therapy** (Craighead, Kazdin, & Mahoney, 1981). These terms reflect the fact that the emphasis is on changing the person's actual *behavior*.

Table 12.2

Names of some common and less common phobias and the stimulus that is the focus of each.

Name of Phobia	Feared Stimulus	Name of Phobia	Feared Stimulus
Acrophobia	Heights	Cynophobia	Dogs
Agoraphobia	Open spaces	Murophobia	Mice
Claustrophobia	Enclosed spaces	Trichophobia	Hair
Mysophobia	Dirt, germs, contamination	Anthophobia	Flowers
		Astraphobia	Lightning
Xenophobia	Strangers	Brontophobia	Thunder
Arachnophobia	Spiders	Thanatophobia	Death
Ophidiophobia	Snakes		

Classical Conditioning of Emotional Responses

One class of problems is emotional reactions that interfere with effective functioning. For example, people sometimes have intensely unpleasant anxiety when exposed to specific kinds of stimuli. Sometimes the anxiety is also inappropriate, because the same stimuli don't provoke comparable anxiety in other people.

Intense irrational fears are called **phobias.** The phobic person experiences fear whenever a particular stimulus is present and often becomes anxious just from thinking of it. Although a phobic reaction can become tied to virtually any stimulus, some phobias are more common than others (Table 12.2 lists some of them). Common focal points for phobias are animals such as dogs, snakes, and spiders; closed-in spaces such as elevators; open or exposed spaces such as railings on high balconies; and germs and the possibility of infection.

The conditioning view assumes that phobic reactions are classically conditioned (though see Box 12.5). At some point (in this view) the person must have experienced intense fear while in the presence of what's now the phobic stimulus (cf. Watson &

BOX 12.5

ANOTHER VIEW ON PHOBIAS AND RESPONSES TO ANXIETY

A somewhat different view on the development of phobic behavior was suggested by Miller and Dollard. Their view also uses *instrumental* conditioning, rather than just classical conditioning. Miller and Dollard assumed that people acquire new drives by classical conditioning from biologically built-in drives (Miller, 1948, 1951). Fear was seen as a learned drive that develops from the experience of pain. Once a fear drive is acquired, cues that arouse fear engage a drive to escape the fear. Remember that they equated drive reduction with reinforcement. If you avoid or escape from whatever has cued fear, the drive goes down. This reinforces the avoidance or escape behavior, making the same behavior more likely next time.

Consider an example: imagine there are two ways to get to class in the morning. The shorter, faster route requires you to go over a high, scary bridge, which makes you anxious. As you approach the bridge, fear mounts—and so does the drive to escape the fear. One day you abruptly decide to go the long way and avoid the bridge. As you head away from the bridge, your drive level goes down. The avoidance behavior is reinforced. As a result, you're more likely to avoid the shorter route in the future. If this avoidance occurs often, you'll have a phobia concerning that bridge.

Some stimuli that cause anxiety can't be avoided through overt behavior because the stimuli are internal—your thoughts. How can you reduce the fear if your own thoughts are creating the fear? The answer is simple. Just *don't think of whatever it is that's threatening you.* Successful "not-thinking" gets rid of the fear. It thereby causes a reduction in the drive, which reinforces the not-thinking tendency. In this way, Miller and Dollard accounted in conditioning terms for the psychoanalytic phenomenon of repression. Repression is not-thinking. It occurs because doing it reduces the fear drive. Eventually, not-thinking happens before the threatening thought even comes to mind. Thus, the thought never becomes conscious.

The fact that Miller and Dollard's theory was able to deal with this psychoanalytic phenomenon wasn't just a curious sidelight of their thinking. In fact, their theory was intended more generally as an explicit attempt to address psychoanalytic concepts through the principles of learning. This analysis of phobic behavior and repression is just one example of their efforts in that direction (see also J. S. Brown, 1948, 1957; Miller, 1944). As suggested by this example, it proved to be possible to use the language of learning to understand events that Freud and others had viewed in very different terms.

Raynor, 1920). The previously neutral stimulus thereby took on the ability to provoke anxiety. The same principle presumably applies no matter what the feared stimulus is.

As an example, consider the plight of Allison, who nearly drowned in a boating accident three years ago. The intense fear she experienced in that incident became tied to a wide range of stimuli that previously had been neutral (even positive) for her—stimuli such as her father's boat, the lake she was on, and other aspects of the surroundings. Since this experience, Allison has been unable to walk out on a dock or step onto a boat without trembling violently and turning ghostly pale. She can't even drive near the lake without getting upset.

The conditioning view also leads to suggestions about how to treat phobias (M. C. Jones, 1924). Two ideas are important here. The first is extinction. The anxiety reaction should weaken if the CS (the phobic stimulus) is presented repeatedly without the US (whatever caused the fear during conditioning). Oddly enough, by actively avoiding the phobic stimulus in their day-to-day activities, people such as Allison are actually preventing extinction from taking place.

The second important idea is that a *different* emotion can become conditioned to the *same* stimulus. If the new emotion is incompatible with fear, it will gradually come to predominate in place of the fear (a process termed **counterconditioning**). Although these ideas—extinction and counterconditioning—differ slightly from each other, in practice they lead to the same general sorts of therapeutic procedures (e.g., Davison & Wilson, 1973; Wolpe, 1961).

One important technique is **systematic desensitization.** People are first taught how to relax themselves thoroughly. This relaxation response is the incompatible "emotion" that's intended to take over for the anxiety. The therapist and the phobic person create an anxiety hierarchy, a list of situations with the feared stimulus, ranked by how much anxiety each creates (Table 12.3). This hierarchy varies from person to person in what situations create the greatest fear.

In the desensitization process you relax as fully as you can, then visualize a scene from the least-threatening end of the hierarchy. Anxiety aroused by this image is al-

Table 12.3

An anxiety hierarchy such as might be used in systematic desensitization for one type of acrophobia (fear of heights). Each scene is carefully visualized while the person relaxes completely, working from the least threatening scene (at the bottom) to those that produce greater anxiety (toward the top).

Looking down from the top of the Empire State Building

Walking around the top floor of the Empire State Building

Looking out the window of a 12-story building

Looking over the balcony rail of a 4-story building

Looking out the window of a 4-story building

Looking up at a 30-story building from across a small park

Reading a story about the construction of a skyscraper

Reading a story that mentions being on top of the Statue of Liberty

Hearing a news story that mentions the tall buildings of a city

Seeing a TV news story in which tall buildings appear in the background

lowed to dissipate. Then, while you continue to relax, you imagine the scene again. Do this sequence repeatedly, until the scene provokes no anxiety at all. Then move to the next level. Gradually, you're able to imagine increasingly threatening scenes without anxiety. Eventually, the imagined scenes are replaced by the actual feared stimulus. As the anxiety is countered by relaxation, you're able to interact more and more effectively with the stimulus that previously produced intense fear.

Systematic desensitization has proven very effective in reducing fear reactions, particularly fears that focus on a specific stimulus (e.g., Brady, 1972; Davison & Wilson, 1973). It works far more quickly than do many other therapies, and thus is less expensive. The technique has been of enormous benefit to people with debilitating anxieties. How disruptive a phobia is, of course, depends on its focus. A fear of elephants wouldn't have too big an impact on most people's lives, but anxiety over entering stores with crowds of people can cripple your very existence.

Procedures such as this also have secondary benefits. First, they've gone a long way to minimize the shame that people feel when their emotions hamper their actions. The learning perspective teaches people that having fear is no reason for being ashamed. Fear isn't a sign of a diseased personality. To the contrary, even irrational fears can result from ordinary events of life through the mechanism of classical conditioning.

Additional benefit can also come from learning a technique such as relaxation. These techniques are tools that people can apply more broadly, any time they feel anxious or upset (Goldfried, 1971; Goldfried & Merbaum, 1973). The techniques thus promote effective functioning far beyond the therapy setting in which they're first learned.

Although phobias provide a clear example of how the concepts of classical conditioning can be applied to problems, there are other examples. People often have conditioned responses of other emotions that they don't want to have, such as anger. Such undesired responses can be treated in the same way as fear: by extinguishing or counterconditioning the response.

It's hard to emphasize strongly enough how much the conditioning approach to dealing with phobias differs from approaches suggested by some of the other theoretical perspectives. For example, a psychoanalytic therapist (Chapter 9) wouldn't account for a phobia by looking for an instance of classical conditioning, but would try instead to uncover hidden conflicts from childhood. To the psychoanalyst, if it mattered at all what stimuli now elicit anxiety (and it might not matter), it would only be to suggest in a symbolic way what the real problem is. These approaches are indeed quite different.

Classical Conditioning of Aversion

Classical conditioning in therapy is usually aimed at getting rid of conditioned responses. Sometimes, however, people want to *acquire* conditioned responses. These are cases in which people now have positive responses to stimuli they'd be better off disliking and avoiding. This would be a way to portray the situation of people who are trying to stop smoking or drinking (Cannon, Baker, Gino, & Nathan, 1986; Hackett & Horan, 1979) or who are trying to stop sexual practices they view as inappropriate (Feldman & MacCulloch, 1971). The stimuli related to those behaviors (liquor, cigarettes, and so on) are now tied to pleasant emotions. They would be easier to avoid if they provoked *un*pleasant emotions.

Application of conditioning to this kind of situation is called **aversion therapy** (Rachman & Teasdale, 1969). The logic is much the same as that of systematic desensitization, but with a different goal. The goal now is to condition a *negative* emotional response (rather than a neutral one) to stimuli that now cause a positive response. Doing this requires presenting the stimulus as a CS along with a US that produces a negative reaction. For example, nausea-inducing drugs are sometimes used as a US to be related to the taste of liquor and settings for drinking (Cannon et al., 1986). As another example, electric shocks are sometimes used as a US to be associated with the touch of a cigarette (Powell & Azrin, 1968).

Aversive conditioning isn't as widely used as systematic desensitization, partly because some find the procedures objectionable. Partly it's because questions have been raised about whether it's as effective as other procedures (Lichtenstein & Danaher, 1976; Powell & Azrin, 1968). Nevertheless, it does appear useful in some contexts (Cannon et al., 1986; Rachman & Teasdale, 1969).

Conditioning and Context

The point of procedures based on extinction and counterconditioning is to replace an undesired response with a neutral response, or a response opposite to the original one. However, there are some issues that complicate things. For one, it's now believed that extinction doesn't remove the original conditioning (Bouton, 1994, 2000). Rather, it creates a second conditioned response that can dominate the original one. Sometimes, though, the original response comes back. How can that be made less likely?

An important role is played by context. That is, the context of the original conditioning often differs from the context of the therapeutic effort to extinguish (or countercondition). In effect, each context is a set of discriminative stimuli. People acquire a neutral response (via extinction) to the target stimulus in the therapy room. But when they return to the setting where the original response was learned, the old response may reappear (Bouton, 2000). Why? Because the stimuli of the original setting *weren't there during the extinction.* Thus, they still link to CRs.

For the new neutral response to predominate in the person's experience, one of two things must happen. First, the person can acquire the neutral response in a setting that resembles the setting where the old response was acquired. This will cause the new response to generalize to the original setting. Alternatively, the person can avoid the original setting. That's why many approaches to avoiding relapse emphasize staying away from settings resembling those where the original response was acquired.

As a concrete example, consider work on smoking relapse. Withdrawal from nicotine isn't the sole problem in quitting (Perkins, 1999). Relapse rates are as high as 60 percent, even if smokers get nicotine other ways (Kenford et al., 1994). Similarly, many who quit smoking return to it well past the end of nicotine withdrawal (e.g., Brandon et al., 1990). Why? The answer is that the smoking has been conditioned to particular contexts (after meals, after sex, or when drinking at social gatherings). The context itself remains a discriminative stimulus for smoking, long after the craving for nicotine is gone (Carter & Tiffany, 1999).

Programs to quit smoking now emphasize efforts to extinguish responses to the contextual cues linked to smoking. The contextual cues are presented alone, with no smoking. The hope is that the nonsmoking response will condition to those cues, and the person will thereby become resistant to relapse. Such programs have had only limited success (Conklin & Tiffany, 2002). Perhaps that's because they've used "normative" smoking cues rather than personalized ones. Because everyone has a unique smoking history, individualizing the cues may promote better success (Conklin & Tiffany, 2001).

Instrumental Conditioning and Maladaptive Behaviors

Another set of problems relates to the concepts of instrumental conditioning. The reasoning here stems from the idea that behavioral tendencies are built in by reinforcement. Further, tendencies can be acquired in ways that make them resistant to extinction.

How might this reasoning be applied to problems? Imagine that a certain behavior or class of behavior—throwing tantrums when you don't get your way—was reinforced at one period of your life, because your parents gave in to them. The reinforcement strengthened the tendency to repeat the tantrums. If reinforced often enough, and in the right pattern of partial reinforcement, the behavior becomes both frequent and persistent.

Later on (when you grow older), the behavior becomes less appropriate. It isn't reinforced as often now, although people do give in to it occasionally. (It's surprising how often people reinforce the very behaviors they wish would stop.) Although the reinforcement is rare, the behavior continues (thanks to the partial reinforcement effect). The behavior seems irrational to observers, but from the conditioning view it's just showing resistance to extinction.

The principles of instrumental conditioning suggest that the way to change the undesired behavior is to change the patterns of reinforcement. The best approach would be to increase reinforcements after a desired (alternative) action. At the same time, (if possible) reduce even further any reinforcement of the undesired action. This should shape behavior in the direction of greater adaptiveness or suitability. This approach is sometimes called **contingency management.**

An example comes from the literature of health psychology. Childhood obesity is a risk factor for serious health problems later on. It stems partly from sedentary habits, such as watching TV instead of being active, and partly from poor diet. Recent research has shown that reinforcing less sedentary activities causes both an increase in those activities and a decrease in the sedentary activities (Epstein, Saelens, Myers, & Vito, 1997). Similarly, reinforcing choices of fruits and vegetables over snack foods causes an increase in the tendency to choose those healthy foods (Goldfield & Epstein, 2002).

Contingency management programs have also been used in efforts to keep people from drug and alcohol abuse. It can be used to shape undesired behavior in the direction of abstinence over time before quitting (Preston, Umbricht, Wong, & Epstein, 2001). It also can be useful in treating alcohol dependence (Petry, Martin, Cooney, & Kranzler, 2000) and in supporting abstinence from cocaine use (Higgins, Wong, Badger, Haug, Ogden, & Dantona, 2000).

Instrumental Conditioning of Conflict

Another potential contributor to problems in personality is inconsistency in reinforcement. That is, a given act can be reinforced at some times and punished at other times. If the reinforcement and punishment occur in different settings, the person will learn a discrimination. But if they occur in the same setting (or if the cues for discrimination are hard to tell apart), the person experiences a **conflict** (Dollard & Miller, 1950; Miller, 1944). That is, the reinforcement produces a tendency to do the behavior, the punishment produces a tendency to not do it.

Whichever tendency is stronger is presumably the one that will dominate. The fact that the other tendency is there, however, means there will be discomfort as the behavior is being done (or not done). If the situation is conflicted enough, the person may even learn to treat punishment as a discriminative stimulus for *doing* the behavior (if persistence is eventually followed by reinforcement). This person's behavior will appear especially irrational, and can even be self-destructive, but it's a predictable result of inconsistent outcomes.

This issue is of special concern in child rearing, because parents can easily fall into the pattern of mixing reinforcement and punishment for the same behavior. It's interesting that many of the transitions of childhood that can be difficult for that reason are the transitions noted by Freud many years ago: weaning, toilet training, establishing power relationships between parent and child. Freud saw these situations as conflicted due to sexual pressures. The same situations seem open to analysis in terms of inconsistent treatment by the parents.

Instrumental Conditioning and Token Economies

The principles of instrumental conditioning apply to the behavior of anyone. The principles have even been used to shape the behavior of persons with serious mental disorders. The goal of these efforts is to produce patterns of behavior that are more "normal" and, thus, more adaptive. A longer-range goal is to bring the person back into the flow of human events, reinstating the ordinary reinforcement contingencies that shape the behavior of most people, and reducing the person's dependency on caretakers for the necessities of life.

These projects are usually undertaken in institutions, where close control can be maintained over response-reinforcement relationships (although they're also used in other highly structured settings such as classrooms). The strategy involves creating a small-scale economy within the institution. Because it's usually based on tokens, rather than dollars, it's often called a **token economy** (e.g., Ayllon & Azrin, 1965, 1968; Kazdin, 1977; Krasner, 1970). The tokens act as secondary reinforcers, the same as money. That is, they're exchanged for special foods or special privileges (in some programs, they're needed even for ordinary foods and privileges).

The patients are given these tokens as reinforcers for socially desirable behaviors, such as making their beds or engaging in normal conversations with other patients or staff members. Consistent with the principles of instrumental conditioning, the reinforcement tends to increase desired behaviors and decrease undesired ones. Such programs have been effective in shaping the behavior of hospitalized schizophrenics, whose behavior is extremely hard to change (e.g., Ayllon & Azrin, 1968; Krasner, 1970).

This technique isn't entirely free of problems, though. For example, behavior reinforced with tokens in the institution is unlikely to be reinforced as often outside the institution. Thus, the adaptive behavior may not persist outside that sheltered environment, unless steps are taken to make the transition a gradual one. Despite such limitations, token economies are an important weapon in the arsenal of therapeutic behavior change.

Instrumental Conditioning and Biofeedback

Another use of instrumental conditioning concepts in therapy focuses on changing internal behaviors. The behaviors are usually small in scale, for example, muscle tensing that creates headaches or influences blood pressure, muscle cramping that produces pain in one's neck or lower back, or small muscle movements in areas that are paralyzed. As these examples imply, this therapy deals primarily with problems of pain or other conditions of ill health.

It was long thought that most internal behaviors of this type are outside voluntary control. Eventually, however, it was discovered that people could learn to control the internal actions through procedures thought to involve instrumental conditioning. The procedures as a group are called **biofeedback.**

Biofeedback training requires an internal behavior that's specific in one sense but vague in another. For example, you might be asked to raise the temperature of your hand, reduce muscle tension in your forehead, or lower your pulse rate. You aren't told *how* to do this, just to do it. While you try, you're attached to a machine that continuously tells you whether or not you're successful, by a signal light or tone. The light or tone (the "biofeedback") acts as a reinforcer for whatever you did just before. The result is that people can learn to do very subtle internal behaviors through such training. Presumably, once the behavior is well learned, it will continue to occur even without the biofeedback.

This technique has been proposed as a way to treat physical problems that involve subtle muscle activity (Blanchard & Epstein, 1978). Many people, for example, can change their blood pressure during biofeedback, although it doesn't generalize well outside the training setting (Shapiro & Surwit, 1979). Biofeedback is also used as a treatment for many kinds of pain (Elmore & Tursky, 1981). It's even been suggested that biofeedback provides a way to retrain muscles after paralyzing events such as strokes (Fernando & Basmajian, 1978; Runck, 1980). Clearly this is an area of investigation in which more work is likely in the years to come.

Conditioning Theories: Problems and Prospects

The conditioning view on personality is influential among two groups of psychologists: researchers who are actively involved in the experimental analysis of behavior in the laboratory, and clinicians who received their training during the heyday of the behavior therapies. The conditioning view is attractive to these two groups for two different reasons, which in turn represent two strengths of this view of personality.

First, the conditioning viewpoint emerged—as had no other perspective before it—from the crucible of experimental research. The ideas that form this approach to behavior were intended to be subjected to close scrutiny, to be either upheld or disconfirmed through research. Many of the ideas have been tested thoroughly, and the evidence that supports them is substantial. This empirical base is important. Having a viewpoint on the nature of personality that can be verified by careful, objective observation is very satisfying to the researcher.

The second reason for the impact of conditioning ideas is the effectiveness of behavioral therapy techniques. Clinical psychologists found that many of people's problems in life can be treated with fairly simple procedures. With this realization, the clinicians began to look carefully at the principles that seemed to underlie the procedures. The learning perspective has taken on an aura of importance and credibility among this group of psychologists because of its good fit with these effective techniques of behavior change.

Although many psychologists find this viewpoint congenial, it also has its share of problems and criticisms. Some of the criticisms derive from a virtue we just named: the emphasis on research. More specifically, conditioning theorists have emphasized the utility of studying laboratory animals. If the laws of learning are the same across different species, it makes no difference which animal they study. Many people, however, are wary of the assumption that underlies that strategy—that learning is the same across species. Indeed, skepticism on this point helped foster the development of a second generation of learning theories, discussed in Chapter 13.

A more subtle criticism concerns the researchers' tendency to simplify the situation under study. Simplification ensures experimental control. Having control helps clarify the relation of cause and effect. But it sometimes results in experimental situations that seem to offer extremely few options for behavior. There's sometimes a nagging suspicion that the behavior occurred because there were so many pressures in its direction and so little chance to do anything *else*. What happens to behavior when the person leaves the laboratory? With more options, will the regularities still hold up?

This question turns out to be a very important one for many species, not just people. Breland and Breland (1961) tried to use operant procedures to train animals. They were distressed to discover that reinforcers often were less powerful than animals' natural tendencies. For example, they tried to train a raccoon to pick up coins and put them into a "bank," but found he had a strong tendency to hold the coins and rub them together. He looked like a miser, but he was only trying to do what he would do with crayfish in his normal environment, rub them together to remove their shells. In the same way, pigs being trained to deposit wooden coins into a bank preferred to drop the coins, root them along the ground, and toss them into the air. The Brelands eventually questioned whether lab studies of conditioning really provide an accurate picture of behavior in normal environments. Perhaps the picture being conveyed is actually quite distorted.

Another problem with this view is that it isn't really a theory of personality. Rather, it's a view of the determinants of behavior. Some people believe this view is too simplistic to ever provide a meaningful view of personality. The processes of learning presumably operate continuously, in a piecemeal and haphazard fashion. The human experience, on the other hand, seems highly complex and orderly. How do the haphazard learning processes yield such an orderly product?

To put it another way, conditioning theories tell us a lot about how a specific behavior becomes more probable or less probable, but it doesn't tell us much about the person who is doing the behavior. The processes in the theories are cold and mechanistic. There seems to be little place here for the subjective sense of "personhood," little focus on the continuity and coherence that characterize the sense of self. In sum, to many people this analysis of personality doesn't convey the subjective experience of what it means to *have* a personality. Perhaps the greatest challenge to the conditioning approach, then, is to convince skeptics that it accounts for the subjective qualities that seem so important to personality.

SUMMARY

The conditioning approach to personality emphasizes two types of learning. In classical conditioning, a neutral stimulus (CS) is presented along with another stimulus (US) that already elicits a reflexive response (UR). After repeated pairings, the CS itself comes to elicit a response (CR) that's similar to the UR. The CR appears to be an anticipatory response that prepares for the US.

This basic phenomenon is modified by discrimination (with different stimuli leading to different responses) and extended by generalization (with different stimuli leading to similar responses). CRs decrease in intensity if the CS is presented repeatedly without the US, a process termed extinction. Classical conditioning is important to personality primarily when the responses being conditioned are emotional reactions (emotional conditioning). Classical conditioning thus provides a basis for understanding people's unique preferences and aversions, and it provides a way of analyzing certain psychological problems, such as phobias.

In instrumental conditioning (a more "active" process), a behavior is followed by an outcome that's either positively valued or aversive. If the outcome is positively valued, the tendency to perform the behavior is strengthened. Thus, the outcome is called a reinforcer. If the outcome is aversive (a punisher), the tendency to perform the behavior is reduced. Discrimination in instrumental conditioning is responding in different ways to different situational cues; generalization is responding in a similar way to different cues; and extinction is the reduction of a behavioral tendency through nonreinforcement of the behavior. Behavior is shaped in new directions by reinforcing successively better approximations of the behavior you want eventually to occur. Reinforcers can occur in many patterns, termed schedules. The most important effect of variations in reinforcement schedules is that behavior learned by intermittent (partial) reinforcement is more persistent (under later conditions of nonreinforcement) than is a behavior learned by continuous reinforcement.

The conditioning approach holds that personality is the sum of the person's conditioned tendencies. Assessment, from this point of view, emphasizes the observation of various aspects of behavior tendencies as they occur in specific situations. Assessment can focus on people's physiological responses, their overt behaviors, or their reports of emotional reactions in response to different kinds of stimuli.

The conditioning approach assumes that problems in behavior are the result of the same kinds of conditioning processes as result in normal behavior. Classical conditioning can produce intense and irrational fears, called phobias; instrumental conditioning can produce behavior tendencies that persist even when they are no longer adaptive. These various problems can be treated by means of conditioning procedures, which collectively are termed behavior therapy or behavior modification. Systematic desensitization counterconditions fear reactions with relaxation. Aversion therapy conditions negative reactions in the place of positive reactions. The principles of instrumental conditioning underlie a variety of therapy techniques. In a token economy (usually in an institutional setting), people receive secondary reinforcers (tokens) for engaging in desirable behaviors. In biofeedback training, people learn to engage in certain kinds of internal behavior for such goals as controlling pain.

GLOSSARY

Aversion therapy The conditioning of an aversive reaction to what's now a positive stimulus.

Behavioral assessment An assessment made by observing a person's overt behavior.

Behavior modification (or **behavior therapy**) The changing of behavior therapeutically through conditioning processes.

Biofeedback The technique of learning to control an internal behavior by instrumental conditioning.

Classical conditioning The pairing of a neutral stimulus with an unconditioned stimulus.

Conditioned (or conditional) stimulus (CS) A neutral stimulus that's paired with a US to become conditioned.

Conditioned (or conditional) response (CR) A response to the CS that's acquired by classical conditioning.

Conflict The simultaneous arousal of two incompatible behavioral tendencies.

Contingency management Programs in which reinforcement is increased for desired behaviors and withheld after undesired behaviors.

Continuous reinforcement A schedule in which reinforcement follows each instance of the behavior.

Counterconditioning The linking of an emotion to a stimulus that differs from the emotion the stimulus now causes.

Discrimination Responding in a different manner to different stimuli.

Discriminative stimulus A cue that controls the occurrence of behavior.

Drive A motivational state that increases behaviors that are high in the habit hierarchy.

Emotional conditioning Classical conditioning in which the CR is an emotional reaction.

Epiphenomena Phenomena that occur along with behavior but have no causal role in behavior.

Extinction In classical conditioning, the reduction of a CR by repeating the CS without the US; in instrumental conditioning, the reduction of a behavioral tendency by removing reinforcement.

Generalization Responding in a similar manner to somewhat different stimuli.

Habit hierarchy The ordering of a person's potential responses by their likelihood.

Higher-order conditioning Event in which a former CS now acts as a US in a new instance of conditioning.

Instrumental conditioning Conditioning in which a behavior becomes more likely because it is followed by a desirable event, or less likely because it is followed by an undesirable event.

Negative reinforcement The removal of an aversive stimulus.

Partial reinforcement A schedule in which the behavior is reinforced less often than every time it occurs.

Partial reinforcement effect The fact that a behavior acquired through partial reinforcement is resistant to extinction.

Phobia An inappropriately intense fear of some specific class of stimuli.

Physiological assessment The measuring of physiological aspects of emotional reactions.

Positive reinforcement A reinforcement involving addition of a desired stimulus.

Punisher An undesired event that weakens the behavior that came before it.

Radical behaviorism The position that behavior should be explained solely on the basis of observable events.

Reflex An event in which a stimulus produces an automatic response.

Reinforcer An event that strengthens the behavior that came before it.

Shaping Changing the nature of ongoing behavior by reinforcing a specific aspect of the behavior.

Successive approximation Shaping by reinforcing closer approximations of the desired behavior.

Systematic desensitization A therapeutic procedure intended to extinguish fear.

Time out A disciplinary technique in which a child is temporarily removed from an enjoyable activity.

Token economy The shaping of behavior in institutions by using tokens as reinforcers.

Unconditioned (or unconditional) response (UR) A reflexive response to an unconditioned stimulus.

Unconditioned (or unconditional) stimulus (US) A stimulus that causes a reflexive (unconditioned) response.

Social-Cognitive Learning Theories

13

■ **Elaborations on Conditioning Processes**

Social Reinforcement
Vicarious Emotional Arousal
Vicarious Reinforcement
Semantic Generalization
Rule-Based Learning
Expectancies concerning Outcomes
Locus-of-Control Expectancies
Efficacy Expectancies

■ **Observational Learning**

Acquisition versus Performance

■ **Manifestations of Cognitive and Social Learning**

Modeling and Sex Role Acquisition
Modeling of Aggression and the
    Issue of Media Violence

■ **Assessment**

■ **Problems in Behavior, and Behavior Change**

Conceptualizing Behavioral Problems
Modeling-Based Therapy for Skill Deficits
Modeling and Responses to Fear
Therapeutic Changes in Efficacy Expectancy
Self-Instructions and Cognitive
    Behavioral Modification

■ **Social-Cognitive Learning Theories: Problems and Prospects**

SUMMARY

■ I was watching my two-year-old the other day in the kitchen, when he reached in and popped open the childproof latch on one of the cabinet doors, just like that, and reached in for a pan. I was so surprised I thought my teeth were gonna fall out. How do you suppose he figured out how to do that? Must've been from watching me, I guess.

■ My job has changed a lot in the last year. The business has expanded really fast. In fact, they haven't always had time to create new procedures for everything we do. We've been having to make our own guesses about what would work best. It hasn't been too bad, though. We seem to be guessing right most of the time. Sometimes you don't know if a decision was right until way later on, but that just makes it more interesting.

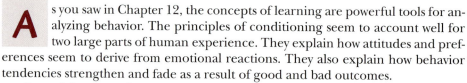

A s you saw in Chapter 12, the concepts of learning are powerful tools for analyzing behavior. The principles of conditioning seem to account well for two large parts of human experience. They explain how attitudes and preferences seem to derive from emotional reactions. They also explain how behavior tendencies strengthen and fade as a result of good and bad outcomes.

Powerful as those theories are, however, they haven't been completely accepted, not even by everyone who believes learning is the key to personality. Some became disenchanted with conditioning theories because they ignore aspects of behavior that seem obvious outside the lab. For example, people often learn by watching one another. People often decide whether to do something by thinking about what would happen if they did it.

How can conditioning theories account for a baby's suddenly doing something complex that he'd never done before? How can they deal with decision processes of a person trying to guess what to do in a specific situation at work? The conditioning theories don't seem wrong, exactly, but they seem incomplete. They explain some things well, but they don't cover it all.

From these dissatisfactions—and from the work to which they led—came what might be seen as another generation of learning theories. They provide a learning view of personality, but they emphasize mental events more than do earlier theories. For this reason, they're often called *cognitive* learning theories. They also emphasize social aspects of learning more than was done before. Thus, they're often called *social* learning theories.

Elaborations on Conditioning Processes

The theorists of the newer learning approach didn't abandon conditioning principles. Instead, they began by elaborating on them. The easiest way to start a discussion of the newer theories is with those elaborations.

Social Reinforcement

As social learning theory began to evolve, its theorists began to reconsider the usefulness of studying lower animals. Can human behavior be analyzed by studying laboratory rats, or is it wiser to focus on people? What variables matter most in *human* learning? Asking these questions led to a different view of reinforcement.

Many of the important reinforcers affecting human behavior are social in nature.

Many came to believe that reinforcement in human experience (at least, beyond infancy) has little or nothing to do with physical needs. Rather, people are most affected by **social reinforcers:** acceptance, smiles, hugs, praise, approval, interest, and attention from others (Rotter, 1954, 1982; see also Bandura, 1978; Kanfer & Marston, 1963). The idea that most reinforcers for people are social is one of several senses in which these learning theories are social (Brokaw & McLemore, 1983; A. H. Buss, 1983; Turner, Foa, & Foa, 1971).

As an example of the power of social reinforcement, consider a study by Hall, Lund, and Jackson (1968). It focused on children who spent little time studying. After assessing baselines, the researchers gave social reinforcement in the form of attention and praise whenever a child engaged in studying. Figure 13.1 shows the impact of this procedure on one child. This child studied more than twice as much when social reinforcement was given than when it was not.

Emphasizing social reinforcement has a secondary theoretical implication. In particular, social learning theorists see no need to appeal to drives in order to discuss reinforcement (e.g., Bandura, 1977a; Rotter, 1954, 1982). They take this position partly because social reinforcers don't seem to act via physical need states. It

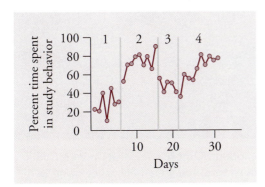

Figure 13.1

The effect of social reinforcement. This third-grade boy, whose baseline level of studying in class was quite low (period 1), was systematically given attention and approval for studying. This greatly increased his study behavior (period 2). To see whether the effect depended on social reinforcement, attention was removed, which caused a decrease in studying (period 3). Reinstituting the social reinforcement (period 4) caused a return to a high rate of studying (adapted from Hall et al., 1968).

isn't usually necessary, for example, that the person being reinforced be in a state of deprivation.

A description of social reinforcement should also mention **self-reinforcement.** This term actually has two meanings. The first is the idea that people may award themselves reinforcers after doing something they've set out to do (Bandura, 1976; Goldiamond, 1976; Heiby, 1982). For example, you might reward yourself with a pizza for studying six straight hours, or you may get yourself a new piece of stereo equipment after a semester of good grades.

The second meaning of self-reinforcement derives more directly from the concept of social reinforcement. It's the idea that you react to your own behavior with approval or disapproval, much as you react to someone else's behavior. In responding to your actions with approval, you reinforce yourself. In responding with disapproval, you punish yourself. This sort of internal self-reinforcement and self-punishment plays an important role in social-cognitive learning theories of behavior and behavior change (Bandura 1977a, 1986; Kanfer, 1977; Kanfer & Hagerman, 1981; Mischel, 1973, 1979).

Vicarious Emotional Arousal

Another elaboration on conditioning comes from the fact that people can experience events vicariously—indirectly through someone else. Vicarious processes represent a second sense in which learning among humans is social. That is, vicarious processes involve two people, one to experience something directly, a second to experience it indirectly.

Empathy causes us to experience others' emotions. Others' grief elicits sadness from us, and happiness elicits joy. As you look at this picture, you are probably beginning to feel the same emotions that the people in the picture are experiencing.

One type of vicarious experience is **vicarious emotional arousal,** or empathy. This occurs when you observe someone feeling an intense emotion and you experience the same feeling yourself (usually less intensely). Empathy isn't the same as sympathy, a feeling of concern and unhappiness when someone else is suffering (Gruen & Mendelsohn, 1986; Wispé, 1986). In empathy, you feel the same feeling, good or bad, as the other person (Stotland, 1969a). Everyone can have this experience, but there are individual differences in its intensity (Eisenberg et al., 1994; Levenson & Ruef, 1992; Marangoni et al., 1995).

Examples of empathy are easy to point to (see also Box 13.1). When something wonderful happens to a friend, putting her in ecstasy, you feel happiness yourself. Being around someone who's frightened makes most people feel jumpy. Laughter is often contagious, even when you don't know what the other person is laughing at. There's even evidence that being around someone who's embarrassed can make you feel embarrassed too (Miller, 1987).

Experiencing vicarious emotional arousal doesn't *constitute* learning, but it creates an opportunity for learning. Recall from Chapter 12 the process called emotional conditioning. In emotional conditioning, feeling an emotion in the presence of a neutral stimulus causes that stimulus to become capable of evoking a similar emotion. It doesn't matter how the emotion is created. It's only necessary that it be *present*. The emotion can be caused by something you experience directly, but it can

BOX 13.1

EMPATHY AND ALTRUISM

The focus of this part of the chapter is the idea that vicarious processes influence learning. While we're talking about empathy, though, we'd like to point to another aspect of human behavior to which empathy is relevant: altruism, or helping. One general view on helping is that when you see someone else suffering, your empathy response causes you to help. There are, however, different theories about *why* this happens.

A theory developed by Robert Cialdini and his colleagues (e.g., Cialdini, Schaller, et al., 1987) holds that empathy in this situation causes you to experience distress. One way to escape from those feelings is to do something to reduce the other person's suffering. In this view empathy leads to helping as a way to reduce your *own* distress. The benefit to the other person is a side effect. A competing theory by Daniel Batson and his colleagues (Batson, 1990, 1991; Batson, Dyck, et al., 1988) holds that empathy creates a desire to relieve the suffering of the other person, plain and simple.

Which explanation is right? The answer actually may be that both are right. There's evidence that ex-posure to someone else's distress provokes several different emotions, not just one (Batson, Fultz, & Schoenrade, 1987; Fultz, Schaller, & Cialdini, 1988). The feelings include distress, sadness, and sympathy for the other person. These different feeling qualities may well lead to very different motivations.

Research on this question must wrestle with that and other subtle issues. Despite some contradictory evidence (Batson, Bolen, Cross, & Neuringer-Benefiel, 1986; Smith, Keating, & Stotland, 1989), the data seem to suggest that empathic concern for someone else arouses a desire to ease that person's suffering, and that this desire is separate from a desire to reduce one's own distress (Batson, 1990). The desire to reduce one's own distress also plays an important role, though, and that may turn out to be the most important one (Maner, Luce, Neuberg, Cialdini, Brown, & Sagarin, 2002). No matter which pathway predominates, it's clear that empathy plays an important role in bringing people to each other's aid.

also arise vicariously. Thus, vicarious emotional arousal creates a possibility for classical conditioning. Such an event is called **vicarious classical conditioning.**

Consider, for example, research in which participants watched a second person. A tone sounded (a neutral stimulus), then the second person received an electric shock and grimaced. After a series of pairings of tone and shock, the observers themselves began to react emotionally when the tone was sounded by itself (Berger, 1962; see also Bandura & Rosenthal, 1966; Craig & Weinstein, 1965; Vaughan & Lanzetta, 1980). This was true even though the observers never experienced pain directly. This change appears to represent vicarious classical conditioning.

Vicarious Reinforcement

Another vicarious process may be even more important. This one, called **vicarious reinforcement,** is very simple: if you observe someone do something that's followed by reinforcement, you become more likely to do the same thing yourself (Kanfer & Marston, 1963; Liebert & Fernandez, 1970). If you see a person punished after doing something, you're less likely to do it. The reinforcer or punishment went to the other person, not to you. But your own behavior tendencies are affected as though you'd received it yourself (Figure 13.2).

This process is very important. It permits a lot of the trial and error of instrumental conditioning to take place secondhand. You don't have to "behave" all the time—just watch others behave and see what follows. Learning this way lets you learn about a lot of situations that other people are in, including some you'd rather not experience firsthand. Taking advantage of this can save wear and tear on self-esteem, because you learn from other people's mistakes as well as from their successes. Sometimes vicarious reinforcement even produces better learning than direct reinforcement does. Apparently the vicarious situation lets you give "learning" some of the attention you'd normally devote to "behaving" (Berger, 1961; Hillix & Marx, 1960).

How do vicarious reinforcement and punishment influence people? Presumably seeing someone else reinforced after a behavior leads you to infer you'd get the same reinforcer if you acted the same way (Bandura, 1971). If someone else is punished, you conclude the same thing would happen to you if you acted that way (Bandura, 1973; Walters & Parke, 1964). Often the effects involve more extensive inferences. For example, you may limit your conclusion to situations resembling the one you observed. To put it differently, you may learn *discriminations* vicariously. For instance, you may learn from observing others that talking in class leads to a scolding, but only in certain classes.

Figure 13.2

Effect of vicarious reinforcement. Participants are asked to say any word at random into a microphone whenever a signal is given. They also hear someone they think is a co-participant say words periodically. In one condition, the experimenter reinforces the other voice by saying "good" every time it says a human noun. The measure of interest is how often the real participant says human nouns. As can be seen here, the reinforcement given to the other person causes a steady increase in the participants' tendency to do the same, despite the fact that they were never reinforced themselves (adapted from Kanfer & Marston, 1963).

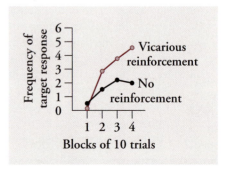

Note that the effect of vicarious reinforcement appears to involve developing an implicit (or even explicit) expectancy—that is, a mental model of links between acts and reinforcers. This is one instance of a more general theme in the social-cognitive learning approach: the involvement of expectancies in learning. This theme comes up again later in the chapter.

Semantic Generalization

We said that the newer theories are more social and more cognitive than the earlier theories. So far we've considered ways they're more social. Now let's consider ways they're more cognitive.

Another elaboration on the basic principles of conditioning came from looking more closely at the phenomenon of generalization—responding in a similar way to stimuli that are similar to (but not the same as) those in which conditioning has already taken place. Most animals can generalize in response to varying lights or tones, but people can generalize in more interesting ways. They can do **semantic generalization,** generalization along a dimension of *meaning.* It's something people do often, and take completely for granted.

Semantic generalization, just as any other generalization, can occur in both classical conditioning and instrumental conditioning (Diven, 1936; Maltzman, 1968). As an illustration of how it happens in classical conditioning, imagine a person who's been through a nasty divorce and now has a negative emotional reaction (anger and anxiety) to the mere mention of the word *divorce.* This person might well generalize this emotional reaction to semantically related words such as *courtroom, settlement, alimony,* and *breakup.*

Semantic generalization is explained by assuming that conditioning doesn't take place to a stimulus itself. Rather, it occurs toward cognitive elements representing aspects of the stimulus. Semantic generalization occurs when there are mental associations to other words with related meanings. The theories discussed in this chapter assume this kind of elaborate mental structure. This is one of several senses in which they are "cognitive" learning theories.

Rule-Based Learning

Another elaboration on conditioning is suggested by the idea that people use instrumental learning to learn *rules* rather than just to learn behaviors. Conditioning principles suggest that behavior tendencies build incrementally. Each reinforcer strengthens the tendency slightly. The longer the history of reinforcement, the stronger the tendency to behave in a certain way.

There are cases, though, that simply don't fit this picture. Perhaps the easiest illustration of how rules are used in human behavior comes from studies of language acquisition. Language uses a large set of rules. For example, there are rules that specify how the parts of a sentence are ordered and rules concerning the formation of verb tenses and noun forms.

Early in life, children don't pay much attention to rules. They're preoccupied with learning what specific words mean. As children get older and say things that are more complicated, they begin to use new word forms (e.g., new verb tenses), which they acquire word by word. At some point, though, they seem to realize that there are regularities to language, and they begin to use those regularities in their speech. The child may not be able to tell what the rule is, but the rule gets used when the child speaks. How do you know the child's learned a rule? Because at this stage the child sometimes *overregularizes*—uses the rule even where it doesn't apply (Marcus, 1996).

Consider the English rule for specifying past tense, which is to add *-ed* at the end (e.g., *cook* becomes *cooked*). There are many exceptions to this rule, verbs whose past tense is created a different way (*go* becomes *went, take* becomes *took, break* becomes *broke*). Children use these irregular verb forms perfectly well when they first learn them, apparently because they memorize the words (which may entail an incremental conditioning process). The words are used correctly right up to the point where the rule begins to be used. At that point, the child applies the rule to every verb, even the irregular ones. As a result, the child now begins to make errors. A child who said "I went into the back yard" only a few weeks ago now sometimes says "I goed into the back yard." This suggests that the child is acquiring a rule.

Once rule-based learning begins to take place, it becomes a pervasive feature of human learning. Past infancy, humans seem to respond to the outcomes they experience by learning implicit rules and conceptual principles. When you learn how to study for a psychology test, you're learning principles of preparing for tests in general. When you learn to drive, you're learning not just a set of movements, but a set of rules for creating forward motion, stopping, distancing from other cars, and so on. Whenever you've learned a rule, you can apply it to widely divergent new situations (e.g., preparing for an exam in a new course or driving in unfamiliar territory).

What, then, is the role of incremental conditioning in behavior? It may be that incremental learning influences how a rule or principle first emerges. That is, reinforcement processes may nudge you a little bit at a time in the right direction until you begin to identify the rule. When the rule comes into focus, concept learning takes over and the rate of learning increases.

Expectancies concerning Outcomes

The learning theories in this chapter include a facet that can be viewed in either of two ways. It can be seen as an elaboration on conditioning theories, or as a step away from conditioning. This facet provides another sense in which these theories are cognitive. Specifically, the theories assume that people hold expectancies about whether a behavior will lead to desired outcomes (Rotter, 1954). This expectancy, then, is an important determinant of what the person does.

This concept is often discussed along with a view on motivation termed expectancy-incentive theory (we touched on this view in Chapter 5). **Incentives** are values that goals have for the person. Incentives don't necessarily depend on deprivation. The concept thus differs in important ways from the concept of drive. **Expectancies,** here, are implicit judgments about the likelihood that a given behavior will result in attainment of the goal. Predicting behavior, from this view, requires you to take into account both incentives and expectancies (Feather, 1982).

The idea that people hold expectancies and that expectancies influence action wasn't new when it became part of social learning theory (e.g., Brunswik, 1951; Lewin, 1951b; Postman, 1951; Tolman, 1932). But an emphasis on expectancies (in one form or other) is a cornerstone of this approach to personality (Rotter, 1954; see also Bandura, 1977a, 1986; Kanfer, 1977; Mischel, 1973).

Let's be clear about how this view differs from the conditioning approach (see also Box 13.2). Conditioning theorists assume reinforcement has a direct influence on the probability of the behavior. They *don't* assume that mental representations (expectancies) matter. In the social-cognitive theories, people are seen as thinking over the available evidence—past outcomes, the situation they now confront—and

BOX 13.2

THEORETICAL CONTROVERSY
How Does Learning Take Place?

We've treated the principles of the social-cognitive learning theories as elaborations on earlier conditioning theories. Our aim has been to show how the various changes can be inserted into the picture of the learning process that was drawn in Chapter 12. Some of the modifications, however, raise serious questions about the concepts that they seem at first to embellish. This box briefly explores two aspects of this question (see also Brewer, 1974).

The Role of Awareness

The first issue concerns the role of awareness in conditioning. It's long been assumed that conditioning—particularly classical conditioning—is automatic (cf. Skinner, 1953). There's reason to suspect, though, that it actually involves cognition. For example, several studies seem to indicate that people show little or no classical conditioning from repeated pairings of stimuli unless they realize the stimuli are correlated (e.g., Chatterjee & Eriksen, 1962; Dawson & Furedy, 1976; Grings, 1973). On the other side of the coin, sometimes just expecting an aversive event (as a US) can produce conditioned responses to other stimuli (Bridger & Mandel, 1964; Spacapan & Cohen, 1983). There's also evidence that people change their behavior in response to reinforcers only when they've become aware of what's being reinforced (Dulany, 1968; Spielberger & DeNike, 1966).

Extinction may also involve cognition. After classical conditioning of a fear response, a statement that the painful US will no longer be given sometimes eliminates fear of the CS (Bandura, 1969; Grings, 1973). Classical conditioning is supposed to be automatic, independent of thought. It's supposed to link stimuli directly with responses. But effects such as these suggest that expectations may play an even more central role than do external stimuli (Bandura, 1986).

The Concept of Reinforcement

The second issue concerns the concept of reinforcement—and, by implication, the very nature of instrumental conditioning. Conditioning theorists say reinforcers are events that strengthen the tendency to do the behavior that preceded them. Yet Bandura (1976, 1977a), a prominent social learning theorist, explicitly rejected this sense of the reinforcement concept, while continuing to use the term *reinforcement* (see also Bolles, 1972; Brewer, 1974; Rotter, 1954).

If reinforcers don't strengthen action tendencies, what do they do? Bandura's answer is they do two things: in providing information about outcomes, they lead to hypotheses (expectancies) about what actions are useful in what settings. They also provide the potential for future motivational states through mental anticipation of the reinforcer in the future. In the same way, Henderlong and Lepper (2002) argued that praise enhances motivation by linking outcomes to causes that are controllable. Many people would agree that these various functions are important. But do the functions really constitute "reinforcement" in any meaningful sense? If not, do they actually belong in the process of instrumental conditioning?

The two issues addressed here—the nature of reinforcement and the role of awareness in conditioning—raise a far broader question: if reinforcement doesn't strengthen response tendencies, and if conditioning isn't really conditioning, then just how strong a conceptual connection remains between the social-cognitive learning theories and the conditioning theories from which they grew?

---

judging the likelihood of the desired outcome. These expectancy judgments then have a causal influence on behavioral choices (e.g., Kirsch, 1985).

There are disagreements among theorists about exactly what kinds of expectancies matter. Major theories have been proposed concerning two specific types of expectancies. These ideas are described, in the order they were developed, in the next two sections.

Locus-of-Control Expectancies

The first idea was developed by Julian Rotter (1954, 1966) from his observations of people in therapy. Rotter's observations led him to this conclusion: Different people learn different things from the same event. More specifically, some people react to reinforcement just as the principle of instrumental conditioning says. Others seem not to learn anything at all.

As an illustration, imagine two college freshmen, Bert and Ernie, who are shy and have trouble making conversation with women. Each goes to the university guidance center for help, and the therapist provides suggestions concerning topics of conversation, ways to make the conversation move along, and so on. After some practice, the therapist asks each young man to go out and have a conversation with an attractive young woman who works in the next office.

In each case, the woman's response is pleasant and positive. Bert returns to the therapist and says, "I did what you suggested and she seemed to like me. I'm going to remember those suggestions from now on, because they really seem useful." Ernie returns and says, "I did what you suggested. She acted friendly, but I don't know why. It couldn't have been anything to do with me." Bert's response looks like instrumental learning: if something works well enough to be reinforced, it tends to be done again. But what sense does Ernie's response make?

Rotter became convinced that people differ from each other in the extent to which they see a cause-and-effect link between their behaviors and the reinforcers that follow. Rotter believed, as do most social learning theorists, that perceiving that connection is necessary for instrumental learning to occur. Because some people (like Bert) see a link between behavior and reinforcer, the reinforcer affects their behavior. People who don't see a link (like Ernie) react haphazardly to reinforcers. Instrumental conditioning, for these people, isn't straightforward at all.

The phrase used in discussing this idea is **locus of control** (Rotter, Seeman, & Liverant, 1962; Rotter, 1966, 1990). *Locus* means place. People termed *internals* (internal locus of control) see reinforcers as controlled from within, by their own actions. Those termed *externals* (external locus of control) see reinforcers as controlled by something outside themselves, something other than their own actions. Although locus of control is a continuous dimension, it's often described by its endpoints. Because the terms *internal* and *external* are so commonly used to refer to the two orientations, the concept is referred to with the letters *I-E*.

This dimension has been studied both in experiments and in individual-difference research. In experiments, temporary variations in locus of control are created by telling some people that task outcomes are caused by skill (internal) and telling others they're caused by chance (external). In one early study, Phares (1957) found that subjects with skill instructions used their outcomes as a guide to likely future outcomes. This is just what should occur from instrumental conditioning. It didn't occur, though, among those told their outcomes were based on luck (see also Holden & Rotter, 1962; Walls & Cox, 1971).

A large body of evidence has also accumulated (hundreds of studies) concerning individual differences in locus of control (for reviews see Lefcourt, 1976; Phares, 1976). People who report an internal locus of control adjust their expectancies upward after success and downward after failure. Externals, in contrast, often shift their expectancies in the direction *opposite* to the prior outcome (which also occurs when an outcome is ascribed to chance, Battle & Rotter, 1963; Feather, 1968; Lefcourt & Ludwig, 1965). These differences in how people learn have important implications for other, more elaborate behaviors, including such areas as academic achievement (reviewed by Findley & Cooper, 1983).

Most research on this topic has used Rotter's measure (1966) of locus of control, but this scale has been criticized on several grounds. For one, it measures only generalized expectancies, not specific ones. It also mixes perceptions of control over personal outcomes with perceptions of control over government and so on (cf. Gurin, Gurin, Lao, & Beattie, 1969; Mirels, 1970). Finally, there is more diversity among externals than internals, because there are many different ways to have an external control orientation (Hersch & Scheibe, 1967).

These criticisms led to new measures (Lefcourt, 1981). Several groups, for example, created measures that focus selectively on one domain of behavior at a time (Lefcourt, Martin, Fick, & Saleh, 1985; Lefcourt, Von Baeyer, Ware, & Cox, 1979; Paulhus, 1983; Paulhus & Christie, 1981; Wallston & Wallston, 1978, 1981). Another effort has been to separate causal influences from one another. For example, Levenson's (1973, 1981) scale distinguishes between chance factors and powerful others as external causes of outcomes.

Although the locus-of-control concept has been very influential, a theoretical question has been raised about it. Recall the underlying rationale: instrumental learning requires seeing a link between action and outcome. Rotter (1966) assumed that this link depends on having an internal locus of control. Others, however (e.g., Weiner, Heckhausen, Meyer, & Cook, 1972), have challenged that view, noting that much of the relevant evidence confounds two qualities.

Consider the experiments described earlier in which task outcomes were said to be based on either luck or skill. These two labels differ in the locus of the cause, but they also differ in other ways. Skill is a *stable* causal force, whereas chance is more *variable*. Which dimension influences change in expectancy, locus or stability? Research tends to favor stability (e.g., Diener & Dweck, 1978; McMahan, 1973; Meyer, 1980; Weiner et al., 1972; Weiner, Nierenberg, & Goldstein, 1976).

This raises broader questions about the meaning of the locus-of-control literature more generally. For example, does the I-E personality scale similarly confound locus with stability? This question hasn't been answered. More recently, though, it's been suggested that the I-E scale confounds locus with confidence about the outcomes, with internals being more confident than externals (Carver, 1997b). This would suggest the possibility that expectancies about good outcomes in the future may be what matters rather than perceived locus of cause.

Efficacy Expectancies

A second variation on the broad theme of expectancies also derives partly from clinical experience. Albert Bandura (1977b) argued that people with problems generally know exactly what actions are needed to reach the outcomes they want. Just knowing what to do, however, isn't enough. You must also be confident of your ability to *do* the behavior. This perceived ability to carry out a desired action is what Bandura terms **efficacy expectancy,** or **self-efficacy.** To Bandura, when therapy works, it's because the therapy restored the person's sense of efficacy, or confidence in the ability to carry out actions that earlier were troublesome.

The concept of efficacy expectancy draws conceptually on a variety of earlier sources, including White's discussion (1959) of competence motivation (outlined in Chapter 10). White believed the competence motive is central to human behavior. Bandura argues more specifically that a sense of personal efficacy is needed for people to strive consistently (see also Box 13.3).

Efficacy expectancy differs from internal locus of control, despite superficial similarities. In principle, people with internal locus of control see both good and bad outcomes as depending on their own actions. But they don't necessarily feel they

BOX 13.3

THE THEORIST AND THE THEORY
Bandura Stresses Personal Agency, but Also Appreciates the Role of Chance

Albert Bandura has made many contributions to the learning perspective on personality, having done pioneering work on observational learning and the effects of social reward. More recently he has argued forcefully for the importance of feelings of personal efficacy. Yet this theorist who places such emphasis on personal agency has also been outspoken in pointing to the role of chance encounters in people's lives, including his own.

Bandura was born in 1925 in a small town in northern Alberta, Canada, the son of wheat farmers of Polish descent. His town's school had only two teachers and a handful of students, but it was good enough to send him to college at the University of British Columbia. There, sharing a ride to class with several other students, he had a chance encounter that would change his life. His friends, mostly premed and engineering students, had very early classes. Lacking anything better to do at that early hour, Bandura decided to kill time by taking a psychology course. He liked it so much he decided to make psychology his career (Evans, 1989).

A similar chance encounter helped Bandura find a special interest in *clinical* psychology. During a summer spent as a laborer, filling potholes in the Alaskan highway in the Yukon, he found himself in

the company of an odd assortment of characters, people who had fled to the remote North for a variety of unsavory reasons. This chance exposure to a range of bizarre individuals caused Bandura to develop an appreciation for the minor "psychopathology of everyday life," which continued to spark his interest for years thereafter.

A third chance encounter is also notable. Bandura himself has marked its importance in the course of his life (Bandura, 1982b). While a graduate student, he went one day to play golf with a friend. By chance they found themselves playing behind two attractive young women. The two twosomes became a foursome for the rest of the round, and one of the women later became Bandura's wife. As Bandura (1982b) wrote, without this chance encounter "it is exceedingly unlikely" the two of them would ever have met.

Surely this story isn't unique. Many lifelong relationships begin with improbable and unforeseen encounters. Indeed, Bandura's point was how often life is influenced in dramatic and critical ways by chance events. It's somewhat ironic, though, that chance encounters played such an important role in determining the life goals of this theorist whose belief in human self-agency came to be so strong.

have the competence to act in effective ways. In theory, they're just as likely to view bad outcomes as indicating they're bad at what they're trying to do. For example, Joe has an internal locus of control. This is reflected in his belief that getting good grades is directly related to his preparing for exams. He also believes he doesn't know how to prepare for exams. Thus, it's possible for people with an internal locus of control to have low expectancies of personal efficacy.

What of the person with an external locus of control? This one is a little trickier. In a sense, the concept of self-efficacy seems less relevant to these people at all. If their outcomes depend on the whims of fate or powerful people around them, efficacy isn't much of an issue. One might argue that the absence of a sense of personal control implies a low sense of personal efficacy. On the other hand, Bandura sometimes treats a belief in the efficacy of external agents such as medications as equivalent to belief in one's own personal efficacy. This suggests even externals can have high efficacy expectancies if they see themselves as lucky or well connected.

Research on Bandura's concept began by focusing on behavioral and cognitive changes associated with therapy. The work expanded to examine a wide range of other topics (reviewed by Bandura, 1986, 1997). For instance, Brown and Inouye (1978) found that people with perceptions of high self-efficacy are more persistent on problems than people with lower efficacy perceptions. Wood and Bandura (1989) found that efficacy beliefs influenced the performances of business students in a simulation of a management task. Manning and Wright (1983) found that efficacy perceptions predicted the ability to control pain during childbirth (see also Litt, 1988). Cozzarelli (1993) found that efficacy perceptions predicted adjustment to the experience of abortion. Bauer and Bonano (2001) found that self-efficacy perceptions predicted less grief over time among persons adapting to bereavement. There's even evidence that acquiring a sense of efficacy can have a positive influence on immune function (Wiedenfeld et al., 1990).

Beyond these direct associations, perceptions of efficacy seem to be embedded in the positive effects of other variables. For example, there's evidence that efficacy perceptions are a pathway by which social support gives people a sense of well-being (Major et al., 1990). There's also evidence that self-esteem and optimism operate through perceptions of efficacy (Major, Richards, Cooper, Cozzarelli, & Zubek, 1998).

Observational Learning

As we said earlier, many aspects of social learning theory can be viewed as elaborations on the concepts of classical and instrumental conditioning. There is, however, at least one part of social learning theory that leaves the conditioning concepts behind, suggesting a completely different basis for learning. This part is called **observational learning.** Two people play roles in this process, providing yet another basis for the term *social learning theory.*

Observational learning takes place when one person performs an action, and another person observes and thereby acquires the ability to repeat the act (Bandura, 1986; Flanders, 1968). For such an event to represent observational learning unambiguously, the behavior should be one the observer doesn't already know. At a minimum, the behavior should be one the observer hadn't associated with the context in which it's now occurring.

Observational learning allows people to pack huge amounts of information into their memories quickly. This makes it very important. Observational learning takes place as early as the first year of life (Meltzoff, 1985). What's most remarkable about it is how simple it is. It seems to require little more than the observer's noticing and understanding what's going on.

This last statement requires several qualifications, which help to give a better sense of what observational learning is (Table 13.1). First, observational learning requires the observer to pay *attention* to the model (the person being observed). If attention isn't given to the right aspect of the model's behavior, the behavior won't be encoded well enough to be remembered.

This principle has several implications. For example, it means that observational learning will be better with some models than others. Models that draw attention for

Table 13.1

Four categories of variables (and specific examples of each) that influence ob-servational learning and performance (adapted from Bandura, 1977a, 1986).

Attention for Encoding

Characteristics of model:

Is the model attractive, powerful, or an expert?

Characteristics of behavior:

Is the behavior distinctive, clear, and simple?

Characteristics of the observer:

Is the observer motivated to attend and capable of attending?

Retention

Use of imagery as an encoding strategy

Use of language as an encoding strategy

Use of mental rehearsal to keep in memory

Production

Observer's capacity to produce necessary responses

Observer's prior experience with overall behavior

Observer's prior experience with components of behavior

Performance

Consequences to model:

Is the model rewarded or punished, or are there no consequences?

Consequences to observer:

Is the observer rewarded or punished, or are there no consequences?

---

some reason—such as their power or attractiveness—are most likely to be effective. The role of attention also means that some *acts* are more likely to be encoded than others. Acts that are especially salient have more impact than acts that aren't (cf. McArthur, 1981; Taylor & Fiske, 1978). Other variables that matter here are the observer's capabilities, intentions, and concentration. For instance, if an observer is distracted by music while viewing a model, he may miss entirely what she's doing.

A second important set of processes in observational learning concern *retention* of what's observed (Zimmerman & Rosenthal, 1974). In some way or other, what's been observed has to be represented in memory (which makes this a cognitive as well as a social sort of learning).

Two strategies of coding predominate. One is *imaginal coding,* creating images, mental pictures of what you're seeing. The other is *verbal coding,* creating a description to yourself of what you're seeing. Either strategy can produce a memory that can later be used to repeat the behavior (Bandura & Jeffery, 1973; Bandura, Jeffery, & Bachicha, 1974; Gerst, 1971). Mental rehearsal is also an aid to retention (Jeffery, 1976).

Once an action's in memory, there's one more requirement for the act to actually occur. Specifically, you have to translate what you observed into a form you can

Having readily available summary labels for action sequences greatly simplifies the task of storing things in memory. Reprinted by permission: Tribune Media Services.

produce in your own actions. How successfully that's done depends partly on whether you already know some of the components of the act. It's easier to reproduce a behavior if you have skills that underlie it or know bits of action involved in it. That's why it's often so easy for experienced athletes to pick up a new sport. They typically already know movements similar to those the new sport requires.

The importance of having components available also applies to the encoding process (see Johnson & Kieras, 1983). For example, if you already know names (or have good images) for components of the modeled activity, you have to put less into memory. If you have to remember every little thing, it gets more complicated and harder to keep straight. Think of the difference in complexity between the label "sauté one onion" (or "remove the brake pad assembly") and the set of physical acts the label refers to. Now think about how much easier it is to remember the label than the sequence of actions. Using the label as mental shorthand simplifies the task for memory. But you can do this only if you know what the label refers to (see cartoon above).

Acquisition versus Performance

Observational learning permits fast learning of complicated behaviors. Given what we've just discussed, it also seems to be a case of "the more you already know, the easier it is to learn." There's an important distinction to be made, however, between *acquisition* of a behavioral potential and the *performance* of the behavior. People don't always repeat the actions they see others display. People learn a great deal that they never do.

To know whether observational learning will result in behavior, we need to know something else. We need to know the person's incentives (Bandura, 1977a, 1986)— what reinforcement or punishment the person expects the behavior to lead to. A good illustration of the distinction between acquisition and performance comes from a study of children by Bandura (1965). Children saw a five-minute film in which an adult model performed a series of distinctive aggressive acts toward an inflated doll. The model accompanied each act with statements to himself, each associated with one aggressive behavior. For example, as he pounded the doll on the head with a mallet, he said, "Sockeroo—stay down."

At this point three experimental conditions were created, using three versions of the film. In one condition, another adult entered the picture and praised the model as a "strong champion" and said his excellent performance deserved a special treat.

Many complex behaviors are acquired by children through observational learning.

He then gave the model some candy, making it clear that it and the social approval were both consequences of the aggressive acts.

In a second condition (the no-consequence control group), this final scene was simply omitted. In a third condition, this scene was replaced by one in which the second adult came in and punished the model for the aggressive actions. In this condition the model was called a "big bully" and was spanked by the other person, who made it clear that the punishment resulted from the aggressive acts.

After seeing one of these three films, the child in the study was taken to an observation room that held a wide range of toys. Among the toys was an inflated doll identical to the one in the film. The child was left alone for ten minutes, and hidden assistants noted whether the child did any of the previously modeled aggressive acts. The number of acts the child did was the measure of spontaneous *performance*.

Ten minutes later, the experimenter returned. At this point the child was offered an incentive (fruit juice and picture stickers) to show the experimenter as many of the previously viewed aggressive acts as the child could remember. The number of behaviors that were correctly shown was the measure of *acquisition*.

The results of this study are very instructive. The top line in Figure 13.3 shows how many acts children reproduced correctly in the three experimental conditions, when given an incentive to do so (the measure of acquisition). It's obvious there isn't a trace of difference in acquisition. Reinforcement or punishment for the model had no impact here.

Spontaneous performance, though, shows a different picture. The outcome for the model influenced what the observers did spontaneously. As in many studies (Thelen & Rennie, 1972), the effect of punishment was greater than that of reward, al-

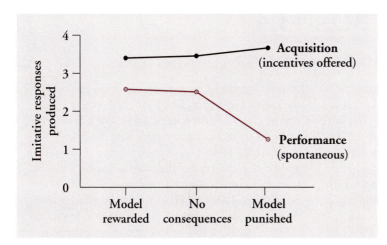

Figure 13.3

Acquisition and performance. Participants observed a model display a series of aggressive acts that led to either reward, no consequences, or punishment. Participants then had an opportunity to imitate the model spontaneously (performance). Finally, they were asked to demonstrate what they could remember of the model's behavior (acquisition). The study shows that reinforcement of the model plays no role in acquisition but does influence spontaneous performance (adapted from Bandura & Walters, 1963).

though there's other evidence that both can be effective in this sort of situation (e.g., Kanfer & Marston, 1963; Liebert & Fernandez, 1970; Rosekrans, 1967).

In conclusion, vicarious reinforcement influences whether people spontaneously do behaviors that they acquired by observation. This effect is the same as any instance of vicarious reinforcement. It thus reflects vicarious instrumental learning. In contrast, reinforcement to the model has no influence on acquisition of the behavioral potential. Thus, observational learning and instrumental learning are distinct processes.

Although reinforcement doesn't influence observational learning directly, it can have an indirect effect. Recall that encoding requires attention to the act being modeled. Don't forget that paying attention is itself a behavior, similar in principle to other behavior. Its probability can be influenced by reinforcement. If you think that paying careful attention to something will be reinforced (for instance, if you were offered $50 to remember what a model is doing), you'll pay careful attention. Thus, reinforcement can influence a function on which acquisition depends.

Observational learning is a powerful process in human learning (and in the learning of some other animals, Zentall, Sutton, & Sherburne, 1996). Its power and its value to personality development lie in the fact that it allows huge amounts of information to be added to a person's behavioral repertoire quickly. It's much faster than shaping through instrumental conditioning or even vicarious instrumental conditioning. On the other hand, this process doesn't determine which acts occurs in which situations (motivational and reinforcement variables seem to do that). Rather, it's a way for diverse behavior potentials to be acquired for use. To paraphrase Bandura (1977a), once the ability to engage in observational learning emerges (in infancy), it's virtually impossible to prevent people from learning what they see.

Manifestations of Cognitive and Social Learning

The processes described thus far provide a set of tools for analyzing behavior. To indicate how broadly they can be used, the next sections describe two areas in which the processes play central roles (see also Box 13.4). The processes get tangled up with one another in both areas. Nevertheless, they can be distinguished conceptually, and we'll do so as we go along.

BOX 13.4

MODELING AND DELAY OF GRATIFICATION

Social-cognitive learning theories emphasize that people's acts are determined by cognitions about potential outcomes of their behavior (Kirsch, 1985). This emphasis fits with the concept of **self-control,** the idea that people can regulate and restrain their own actions.

Self-control is an idea we considered at length in Chapter 10. As noted there, people often face the choice of getting a desired outcome immediately or getting a better outcome later on. The latter choice—delay of gratification—isn't all that easy to make. Imagine that after saving for four months, you have enough money to go to an oceanside resort for two weeks. You know that if you saved for another ten months, you could take the trip to Europe you've always wanted. One event is closer in time. The other is better, but getting it requires more self-control. Ten more months with no vacation is a long time.

As we noted earlier, many variables influence people's ability to delay. Of relevance to this chapter is the role played by modeling (Mischel, 1974). Consider a study by Bandura and Mischel (1965) on fourth and fifth graders who (according to a pretest) preferred either immediate or delayed reward. Children of each preference were put into one of three conditions. In one, the child saw an adult model make a series of choices between desirable items that had to be delayed and less desirable ones that could be had imme-

diately. The model consistently chose the opposite of the child's preference. Children in the second condition read about the model's choices. In the third condition (a control group), there was no modeling.

All the children were given a series of delay-of-gratification choices just afterward and again a month later. Exposure to a model who chose immediate rewards increased the tendency of delay-preferring children to choose immediate reward, too. In the same manner, exposure to a model who chose delayed rewards increased the tendency of immediate-preferring children to delay. These tendencies were maintained a month later. Similar effects were shown among eighteen- to twenty-year-old prison inmates who'd had only weak tendencies to delay gratification before being exposed to models showing strong preference for delay (Stumphauzer, 1972).

How do models exert this influence on self-control? Presumably through vicarious reinforcement. In the Bandura and Mischel study (1965), for example, the model vocalized reasons for preferring one choice over the other. The statements imply that the model felt reinforced by his choices (see also Bandura, Grusec, & Menlove, 1967; Mischel & Liebert, 1966; Parke, 1969). Thus, people obtain information from seeing how others react to experiences and use that information to guide their own actions.

Modeling and Sex Role Acquisition

Sex roles are behavior patterns that people in a given culture see as more appropriate in one sex than the other (cf. Bussey & Bandura, 1999; Deaux & Lewis, 1984; Eagly, 1987; Eagly & Wood, 1999). As with all roles, sex roles are expectations about how to act. American society has a fairly stereotyped set of sex roles, though their content is always evolving somewhat.

Children learn about sex roles early in life. This knowledge is acquired by several processes discussed in this chapter. Some information comes from explicitly stated rules ("Little girls don't play tackle football" or "Little boys don't wear dresses"). Observational learning also plays a role (Sears, Rau, & Alpert, 1965). Sons who watch their fathers shaving and working with wrenches encode aspects of the activities. Daughters who watch their mothers do housework and cook encode aspects of those activities.

But wait a minute. Don't children watch both parents? Shouldn't boys and girls learn the same things by observational learning? Yes and no. Certainly both boys and girls do encode a lot of information about activities of both genders. But there's some evidence that a discrimination is made even in encoding. A study by Maccoby and Wilson (1957) suggests that children encode more from same-sex models than they do from opposite-sex models (although other research has found no such difference, e.g., Bussey & Bandura, 1984).

Why would there be a difference in encoding? Subjects in the Maccoby and Wilson study reported liking and identifying with same-sex characters more than opposite-sex ones. Other research shows that children prefer same-sex adults (Stevenson, Hale, Hill, & Moely, 1967; see also Mischel, 1970). People presumably attend more to models they like than to models they don't like, which means more encoding.

A far greater contributor to gender-role behavior is the subtle web of social reinforcement, both direct and vicarious. Children are rewarded for attending to, and acting like, adults and children of their own sex. Little Tommy gets more smiles and affection when watching Daddy change the oil in the car than when watching Mommy put on her makeup. Little Suzy is treated the opposite way. Given these patterns of reinforcement, Tommy and Suzy spend more time watching the activities of one adult than the other. They also probably see those activities differently in terms of relevance to themselves.

Despite having a preference for models of their own sex, children undoubtedly learn a lot of opposite-sex-role behavior. But remember the acquisition—performance distinction. At an early age, children see which actions are gender-appropriate and tend to spontaneously perform only gender-appropriate ones (Bussey & Bandura, 1984). Why? Because of the reward and punishment contingencies they've been led to anticipate (Fagot, 1977; Raskin & Israel, 1981). Suzy may be praised and cuddled after putting on makeup, but if Tommy does that it won't lead to the same result (nor will the message be lost on Mikey, if he happens to be watching).

One question about gender roles has been debated, leading to divergent conclusions about what's going on. The question is, why these qualities? One answer is given by the evolutionary view (discussed in Chapter 6). Another answer is that what qualities form the roles (and thus are learned) depends on the cultural contexts. Wood and Eagly (2002) summarized evidence that where cultures differ in pressures, the nature of gender roles also differs across cultures.

Live models are important in the acquisition of sex roles and other behavior. In the modern world **symbolic models** are also important. Indeed, they exert a pervasive influence. Symbolic models are figures on TV, in movies, magazines, books, and so on. The actions they portray and the patterns of reinforcement around those actions can have a big impact on both acquisition and performance tendencies of observers. If TV portrays women as weak and powerless, observers learn that weakness is feminine behavior. If TV portrays men as hiding their emotions, observers learn that masculinity means not showing feelings.

Concern over the power of media to shape conceptions of sex roles is one facet of a broader interest in the nature of sex roles themselves. It's implicit in the social learning view that there's nothing magic about what behaviors define these roles. Indeed, this point of view would see all role definitions as a little arbitrary. Given that there's something of value in each sex role, many wonder whether there might be virtue in encouraging people to develop the positive qualities of both roles. Having both "masculine" qualities (e.g., assertiveness, competitiveness) and "feminine" qualities (e.g., gentleness, sympathy) has been called **androgyny** (S. L. Bem, 1974, 1975; Kaplan & Bean, 1976; Kaplan & Sedney, 1980). It's been suggested that such diversity makes people more adaptable and flexible (for a review, see Taylor & Hall, 1982).

Modeling of Aggression and the Issue of Media Violence

Another topic to which social-cognitive learning theories have been applied is symbolic models in aggression. This topic is particularly sensitive, given the levels of violence in TV programs and movies (by a 1992 estimate the average child has watched 40,000 murders on TV by age eighteen, and the number is steadily increasing). All the ways models influence observers are implicated here, to one degree or another. At least three processes are proposed, and there is substantial support for all of them (though Freedman, 1986, raised a cautionary note).

First, people who observe innovative aggressive techniques (live or on film) can and do acquire the techniques as behavior potentials by observational learning. That is, observational learning *does* occur wherever it *can* occur. This is clear (Geen, 1998; Heller & Polsky, 1975). This principle looms large as producers strive to make movies "new and different" every year. Among the sources of novelty inevitably are new methods for inflicting pain on others.

Second, observing violence that is permitted, condoned, or even rewarded helps promote the belief that aggression is an appropriate way to deal with conflicts or disagreements. Vicarious reinforcement thus increases the likelihood that viewers will use such tactics themselves. (By implication, at least, this is also why some people worry about sex on TV and in movies.)

When it's suggested that violence is reinforced in the media, a common reply is that "bad guys" in TV and movie stories get punished. Note two things, though. First, punishment usually comes late in the story, after aggression has produced a lot of short-term reinforcement. Thus, aggression is linked more closely to reinforcement than to punishment. Second, the actions of the heroes usually are also aggressive, and these actions are highly reinforced. Thus, the portrayal sends a clear message that aggression is a good way to deal with problems.

Does viewing "acceptable" aggression make people more likely to use aggression in their own lives when they're annoyed? The overwhelming majority of the evidence says "yes." Whether the model is live (e.g., Baron & Kempner, 1970) or symbolic (e.g., Bandura, 1965; Liebert & Baron, 1972), exposure to aggressive models increases the aggression of observers.

The final point to be made here is more diffuse. It's that repeated exposure to violence *desensitizes* observers to human suffering. The shock and upset that most people would associate with acts of extreme violence become extinguished by repeated instances of violent stimuli. Washington, D.C.'s police chief was quoted in 1991 as saying "When I talk to young people involved with violence, there's no remorse, . . . no sense that this is morally wrong."

Evidence that desensitization occurs comes from several sources (e.g., Cline, Croft, & Courrier, 1973; Geen, 1981; Thomas, Horton, Lippincott, & Drabman, 1977). Results of one study are shown in Figure 13.4 (Thomas et al., 1977, Experiment 1). Participants were attached to a machine that measured emotional reactions, as "bumps" of arousal. They first watched a videotape of either an exciting volleyball championship or a violent program. As can be seen in Figure 13.4, A, the tapes were (overall) equally arousing. Later, they briefly viewed what they thought was a real confrontation resulting in physical violence. As Figure 13.4, B shows, those who'd seen the violent TV show reacted less to this than did the other group. Watching the TV violence apparently made them less sensitive to "real life" violence.

This process has long-term consequences that are profoundly worrisome. As people's emotional reactions to violence extinguish, being victimized (and also victimizing others) is coming to be seen as an ordinary part of life. It's hard to study the

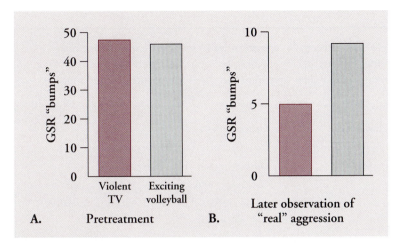

Figure 13.4

Habituation to aggression by viewing aggression. (A) Participants watched a videotape of either an exciting volleyball championship or a violent TV program, which were equally arousing (as measured by GSR bumps). (B) When seeing an apparently real confrontation that resulted in physical violence, participants who had watched the violent TV reacted less to this aggression than did the other group. Presumably watching the TV violence made them less sensitive to later "real life" violence (adapted from Thomas et al., 1977, Experiment 1).

impact of this process in its full scope. The effects are pervasive enough, however, that they represent a real threat to society.

Assessment

Let's turn now to assessment in the social-cognitive learning approach to personality. This section addresses the social-cognitive learning view on assessment in general terms. The point is to make explicit some of the logical threads that underlie it.

Three issues are important. The first is that self-report devices are widely used to assess personality from this view, as opposed to behavioral observation. Recall that the cognitive view of learning emphasizes the role of thoughts in behavior. Given that, it's only natural to take people's reports of their tendencies to act in various ways and to experience various kinds of thoughts and feelings as being appropriate and useful sources of information.

The second issue concerns what variables are measured. Given the assumption that cognitive processes influence behavior, assessment from this view tends to focus on *experiential* variables. That is, rather than charting actions, assessments frequently ask people how they feel in certain situations or what kinds of thoughts go through their minds in those situations (see Table 13.2). Particularly important are people's expectancies: expectancies of control, expectancies of coping, and expectancies of personal efficacy. This emphasis should be no surprise, because expectations are regarded as so important in this view of behavior.

Table 13.2

Assessing people's psychological experiences in difficult exam situations.
The first set of items (answered on five-point scales) examines emotional reactions to the exam; the second set examines cognitions that can interfere with test performance.

Emotionality	Worry
I feel my heart beating fast.	I feel regretful.
I am so tense that my stomach is upset.	I am afraid that I should have studied more for this test.
I have an uneasy, upset feeling.	I feel that others will be disappointed in me.
I am nervous.	I feel I may not do as well on this test as I could.
I feel panicky.	I do not feel very confident about my performance on this test.

Items from Morris, Davis, & Hutchings, 1981.

Copyright 1981 by the American Psychological Association. Reprinted by permission of the author.

A third issue is also implicit in the last paragraph. Assessment in the social-cognitive learning view tends to emphasize responses to *specific* categories of situations. This emphasis actually applies throughout the learning perspective on personality. It reflects the fact that behavior can vary greatly from one situation to another. The social-cognitive learning view differs from the conditioning view, however, in its emphasis on *personal* views of situations rather than *objective* definitions of situations (e.g., Mischel, 1973). One person may see a philosophy class as a chance to learn something new; another person may see the same class as a threat to his grade-point average. This approach says it's people's own representations that determine how they act. This must be taken into account in assessment.

Problems in Behavior, and Behavior Change

We now turn to problems in behavior as conceptualized by the social-cognitive learning view and treatment procedures that derive from this view. Again, the discussion combines concepts from conditioning theories with concepts that are more cognitive and social in nature.

Conceptualizing Behavioral Problems

Principles of conditioning suggest that inappropriate emotions such as fear result from classical conditioning. Similarly, inappropriate behavioral tendencies can result from prior reinforcement patterns. The social-cognitive learning approach suggests further contributors, using three key principles: vicarious conditioning, expectancies, and observational learning.

Thinking about vicarious processes suggests two changes to earlier analyses. First, you don't have to have direct experience with a stimulus to develop an emotional response (such as fear) toward it. You can acquire emotional responses vicariously. Second, your patterns of action can be influenced by watching outcomes that other people experience. Vicarious reinforcement can build in behavior, even if the behavior isn't desirable. Vicarious punishment can reduce your tendency to do a behavior, even if it's a behavior that's actually adaptive.

All these effects may be viewed as mediated in part by expectancies (see Bandura, 1986). If you *expect* to experience strong fear in high places (even if the expectation is baseless), you'll avoid high places. If you *expect* to get social approval for bullying someone else, you may do it. If you *expect* to be rejected by an attractive person, or to do badly on an exam, or even to do badly at "life" (Scheier & Carver, 1992), you may not try. These expectations can develop from direct experience, from vicarious experience, from things that other people tell you, or from putting two and two together in your own head.

No matter how expectations are acquired, they can have powerful effects on your actions and feelings. Negative expectations can cause you to stop putting out effort, thereby preventing the possibility of success. The conviction that success won't come leads to a pattern of low motivation and reduced effort that's sometimes called **learned helplessness** (see also Box 13.5).

A final source of behavior problems, in the social learning view, is more specific. Problems sometimes reflect **skill deficits.** A person with a skill deficit is literally unable to do something that's necessary or desirable. Some skill deficits reflect deficits in observational learning. That is, when people have inadequacies in certain areas, it's often because they never had good models to learn from. Without being able to learn how to do important things (such as cooking, taking notes in class, dancing, and many others), people can have gaps in the ability to function.

Note that having a skill deficit can influence the development of expectations. People who know they lack particular skills come to anticipate bad outcomes where the skills are relevant. (For example, people who see themselves as lacking social skills come to expect the worst in social situations.) People who do have skills may come to view the situations as being under their personal control (Lefcourt et al., 1985).

Modeling-Based Therapy for Skill Deficits

It will be no surprise to discover that modeling plays an important role in the therapy techniques identified with the social-cognitive learning viewpoint. Techniques involving modeling have been used in two areas: skill deficits and emotion-based problems.

When people lack specific types of adaptive behaviors, the skills can often be added through good models. The model is put in the situation for which the skill is lacking and makes an action appropriate to the situation. The observer (the person in therapy) is then encouraged to repeat the action. This repetition can be overt (action), or it can be covert (mentally practicing the action). Indeed, the modeling can also be covert, with the subject told to imagine someone else doing a particular behavior within a particular scenario (Kazdin, 1975).

In principle, modeling can be used to supply missing skills any place there are deficits. Research on this subject, however, commonly focuses on such behaviors as basic social skills (e.g., La Greca & Santogrossi, 1980; La Greca, Stone, & Bell, 1983; Ross, Ross, & Evans, 1971) and assertiveness (Goldfried & Davison, 1976; Kazdin, 1974, 1975; McFall & Twentyman, 1973; Rosenthal & Reese, 1976). Assertiveness is acting to make sure your rights aren't violated, while at the same time not violating someone else's rights. It can be difficult to know just how to respond to hard situations in a manner that's properly assertive. But models who provide specific illustrations of appropriate responses (combined with a little practice, to make sure you can do the same thing) can make a big difference.

BOX 13.5

HELPLESSNESS
Case Study of a Theory

The concept of learned helplessness originated in the finding that exposure to painful and unavoidable shocks made it harder for dogs to learn an avoidance or escape response when that response became possible (Overmier & Seligman, 1967; Seligman & Maier, 1967). This finding led to a flood of research on humans. The typical procedure in human research looks at effects of prolonged failure on later performances. Extensive failure often has an adverse—sometimes devastating—impact on later performance (e.g., Hiroto & Seligman, 1975; Miller & Norman, 1979; Roth, 1980). This has implications for analyzing problems such as depression (Abramson, Metalsky, & Alloy, 1989; Abramson et al., 1978).

The evolution of theories of helplessness makes an interesting case study. It's particularly interesting when viewed in combination with the issue discussed in Box 13.2: the relationship between conditioning theories and social-cognitive learning theories. The first explanation for the effect was based, somewhat loosely, on conditioning principles. Exposure to unavoidable shock results in learning that an outcome (removal of pain) isn't contingent on behavior (avoidance effort). The result is reduction in effort, to the point where the animal no longer tries at all. Indeed, the term *learned helplessness* was coined because the animal looked as though it had learned it was helpless to avoid the shocks. In conditioning terms, the pretreatment extinguished the attempt to escape. Thus, the animal doesn't do any escape behavior when it actually would work.

As analogous research was done on people, however, the theory became progressively more cognitive in nature. Explanations of helplessness in humans typically rely on expectations of future noncontingency (Abramson et al., 1978) or expectations of being unable to control outcomes (Wortman & Brehm, 1975). In simple terms, the person develops (temporarily) the

idea that good outcomes can't be obtained because they're not related to his or her actions.

More recent analyses of helplessness have included additional cognitive processes. Several analyses emphasize attributional variables as a way of discussing how the expectation of bad outcomes develops (Abramson et al., 1978; Miller & Norman, 1979; Roth, 1980). Vicarious and verbal-symbolic processes also appear to play an important role here. For example, watching someone else experience noncontingency (particularly someone you think has the same ability level as you) can produce behavioral impairments in you (Brown & Inouye, 1978; DeVellis, DeVellis, & McCauley, 1978). These various effects appear to indicate that the *cognition* of uncontrollability is critical to helplessness, rather than actual uncontrollability.

As if these weren't cognitive enough, another approach added yet another layer of thought processes. This approach (Frankel & Snyder, 1978; Snyder, Stephan, & Rosenfield, 1978) holds that people do poorly after prolonged failure because the failure threatens self-esteem. Rather than risk looking foolish on a later task, they stop trying. The withdrawal of effort creates a face-saving attribution while at the same time (ironically) causing the poor outcome they'd been afraid of in the first place (Frankel & Snyder, 1978).

Thus, a phenomenon identified in the animal conditioning lab was extended to human behavior. In doing this, however, theorists who pursued the phenomenon have increasingly invoked cognitive processes as a way of accounting for it. Doing so raises questions. Do the same processes apply to human helplessness as apply to helplessness in other species? One probably wouldn't want to argue that dogs stop trying to escape because they're concerned about their self-esteem. But what about the other processes—expectancies and attributions? At the moment, there's no clear answer to this question.

In therapies dealing with skill deficits, observational learning is often intermingled with vicarious reinforcement. There are cases, though, in which one or the other seems most relevant. In some cases, people literally don't know what to do in a given situation. Observational learning is most relevant here, because it provides new responses. In other cases, it's not so much that people don't know what to do, but rather that they have doubts about whether doing it will work. In these cases vicarious reinforcement would seem to play a larger role.

Modeling and Responses to Fear

In discussing modeling and fear-related behavior problems, a distinction is made between two kinds of models: those who exhibit mastery and those who exhibit coping (e.g., Meichenbaum, 1971). A **mastery model** seems to be completely without fear regarding what the person in therapy fears. This model presumably creates vicarious extinction of the conditioned fear, as the observer sees that the model experiences no distress (M. C. Jones, 1924; see also Denney, 1974).

In contrast, a **coping model** is one that initially displays fear, but overcomes the fear and eventually handles the situation. The effect of this model presumably depends on the fact that the model is in the *same situation* as the observer but is (noticeably) able to overcome the fear by active effort. This effect seems more cognitive than that of the mastery model. Although the evidence isn't entirely consistent, coping models seem more effective than mastery models in therapy for fears (Kornhaber & Schroeder, 1975; Meichenbaum, 1971). This effectiveness attests to the powerful role that cognitive processes can play in coping with fear.

Another distinction to be made here is between modeling in which the observer just observes and **participant modeling,** in which the model (often the therapist) performs the behavior in front of the other person, who then repeats it. Participant modeling usually involves a lot of verbalization, instruction, and personalized assurance from the model. It takes more of the therapist's time, but it's more powerful as a behavior-change technique (e.g., Bandura, 1982a; Bandura, Adams, & Beyer, 1977).

In a typical modeling therapy for a specific fear, a model approaches, engages, and deals with the feared stimulus. While doing so, the model describes the feelings

Seeing someone else cope successfully with something that you fear can help you develop the ability to cope successfully yourself.

that develop and the mental strategies that are being used to cope. Then the observer tries to do the same thing, first with the therapist's help, then alone. This procedure is effective at reducing fear and increasing coping in a variety of domains. These include fears aroused by animals such as dogs and snakes (Bandura, Adams, & Beyer, 1977; Bandura, Grusec, & Menlove, 1967; Bandura & Menlove, 1968), by surgery, injections, and dental work (Melamed & Siegel, 1975; Melamed, Weinstein, Hawes, & Katin-Borland, 1975; D. T. A. Vernon, 1974), and by test taking (Cooley & Spiegler, 1980; Malec, Park, & Watkins, 1976; Sarason, 1975).

Therapeutic Changes in Efficacy Expectancy

The research just outlined indicates that models who display an ability to cope with difficulties can help people to overcome their own fears. But how does it happen? Bandura (1977b) says these effects illustrate a broader principle behind behavior change. He says that, when therapy is effective (through whatever technique), it works by increasing the person's sense of efficacy for a given class of situations. In his view, when a model shows an ability to overcome fear, it helps give observers a sense that they can also overcome their fear. This enhanced perception of personal efficacy, then, results in greater effort and persistence.

These ideas, which were introduced earlier in the chapter, have been tested in many studies of the therapy process (e.g., Avia & Kanfer, 1980; Bandura et al., 1977; Bandura, Adams, Hardy, & Howells, 1980; Bandura & Schunk, 1981; DiClemente, 1981; Gauthier & Ladouceur, 1981). As an illustration, consider an experiment by Bandura et al. (1977) in which people with intense fear of snakes were given one of three treatments. In a participant-modeling condition, they saw a therapist perform a series of increasingly threatening actions with a live snake. Then, with the therapist's assistance, they tried the same actions. In a modeling-only condition, they saw a model but didn't practice the activities. Those in a control condition had no therapy at all.

Participants were tested both before and after therapy on a behavioral avoidance test. This required trying a range of actions with the snake without assistance. Participants also rated their expectations for being able to perform each of the acts in the avoidance test. They made these ratings at three times: after the behavioral pretest and both before and after the behavioral posttest. This self-report constituted a measure of perceived self-efficacy.

Figure 13.5, A shows that participant modeling had a more beneficial impact on behavior than did modeling without practice, which had a more beneficial impact than no treatment. These differences in behavior were paralleled by differences in efficacy statements (Figure 13.5, B). Moreover, both approach outcomes generalized (particularly for the participant-modeling group) to a snake that looked distinctly different from the snake used during treatment.

In Bandura's view, results such as these make several points (see Bandura, 1986, 1997). The broadest is that change in efficacy expectancy can mediate behavior change. That is, the behavior changes *because* there's a change in the expectancy. Two other points concern factors that determine efficacy perceptions. Notice that expectancy ratings in this study changed most among people who had an opportunity to show themselves that they could cope (the participant-modeling group). This fits with Bandura's belief that *performance accomplishments* are the strongest influence on efficacy perceptions.

The study also demonstrates a second influence on efficacy perceptions, however: *vicarious experiences*. That is, the modeling-only group outperformed the con-

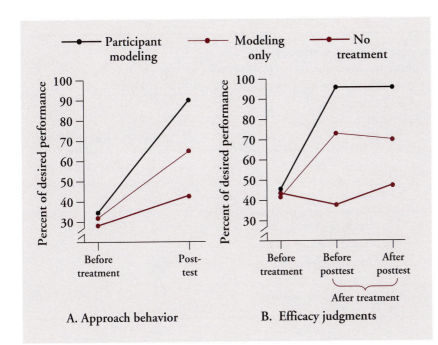

Figure 13.5

(A) Level of approach toward a feared stimulus and (B) self-efficacy judgments. Both behavior and efficacy perceptions were assessed before therapy (left side of each panel) and afterward (right side of each panel). Efficacy perceptions were assessed both before and immediately after the behavioral posttest (adapted from Bandura, Adams, & Beyer, 1977).

trol group and also reported greater efficacy. Vicarious consequences don't have as strong an impact as personal outcomes, but they definitely play a role. Bandura (1977b) also holds that *verbal persuasion* and *emotional arousal* can influence efficacy perceptions, although neither was examined in this study.

Bandura's view is very influential, though it's also had some criticism (commentaries, both pro and con, can be found in Rachman, 1978). Most of the discussion bears on whether efficacy perceptions are causes or consequences of behavior, but there are also other issues. For example, increasing efficacy perceptions is not useful for everyone—some prefer that responsibility for changing their behavior lie elsewhere (Burger, 1989; Chambliss & Murray, 1979). This leads to the question of which is critical: perceptions of personal efficacy, or expectations that desired outcomes will occur (Carver & Scheier, 1986, 1998).

Self-Instructions and Cognitive Behavioral Modification

One last approach to therapy we'll note here is called **cognitive behavioral modification** (Meichenbaum, 1971, 1972, 1977; Meichenbaum & Goodman, 1971). This approach assumes that problems stem from ineffective and disruptive cognitions that slip into people's minds unnoticed. People often tell themselves that problems are bigger or less resolvable than they really are—even tell themselves they can't cope. The expectation of a bad outcome causes them not to try. The goal of cognitive behavioral therapies is to get the person to recognize cases of maladaptive thinking and make suitable adjustments.

This process involves teaching the person to identify stimuli that bring out negative cognitions. Then the therapist and client develop substitute cognitions designed to be adaptive and functional (Table 13.3). These cognitions usually emphasize the following strategy: (1) break the situation you're confronting into concrete components, each of which can be mastered by itself; (2) acknowledge that problem emotions

Table 13.3

Examples of coping statements used in cognitive therapy. The purpose of the therapy is to train people to engage in effective self-instructions such as these rather than fill their minds with negative thoughts when engaged in a stressful or fear-inducing activity (from Meichenbaum, 1974).

Preparing for the Stressor

What exactly do you have to do?

You can develop a plan to deal with it.

Don't worry—worry won't help anything.

No negative self-statements—just think rationally.

Confronting and Coping with the Stressor

One step at a time—you can handle the situation.

This anxiety is what the doctor said you would feel. It's a reminder to use your coping exercises.

Don't try to eliminate fear totally—just keep it manageable.

When fear comes, just pause.

Keep the focus on the present—what is it you have to do?

After the Coping Attempt

It's getting better each time you use the procedures.

You can be pleased with the progress you're making.

(e.g., anxiety or anger) may exist, but be determined not to let them overwhelm you; and (3) redirect yourself to the actions that have to be done to manage the situation effectively, instead of worrying about how well you'll do.

One more set of self-statements is used after the coping attempt is done. These statements emphasize that progress is incremental: if you didn't do as well as you hoped this time, you'll do better next time. This sort of self-statement helps prevent people from becoming discouraged (from developing negative expectations). Once these mental statements have been laid out and learned, the person practices using them when confronting the problem that's being dealt with.

Cognitive-behavioral therapies often focus on specific problems such as test anxiety (Meichenbaum, 1972), anger (Novaco, 1978), physical pain (Turk, 1978), and children's impulsiveness (Meichenbaum & Goodman, 1971). It should be obvious, though, that it's easy to generalize to other kinds of stressful experiences. For example, one study found that teaching coping skills to handle test anxiety resulted in lowered anxiety, improved academic performance, and higher levels of a generalized sense of self-efficacy (Smith, 1989). The term **stress inoculation** is sometimes used to refer to the process of training people to use these techniques not just for one problem but for a broad range of stressful events (Meichenbaum, 1985).

Social-Cognitive Learning Theories: Problems and Prospects

The social-cognitive learning view on personality has been influential in personality psychology over a period of several decades. Some reasons for its influence are the same as those noted earlier for the conditioning view. That is, the concepts of this approach have been tested extensively in research settings and have generally been supported. Similarly, cognitive-behavioral therapy techniques have been shown to be very effective for many kinds of problems.

The social-cognitive learning approach also benefits further from having addressed problems confronted by the conditioning approach. A criticism of the conditioning approach mentioned in Chapter 12 was that research on conditioning usually involves drastically simplified laboratory situations. This criticism is far less applicable to the social-cognitive learning approach. People doing research within its framework have examined human behavior in very diverse settings and contexts. People have studied locus of control and efficacy perceptions in situations as varied as have been studied for any view of personality.

Another criticism of the conditioning view was that it seemed to have little place for the sense of "personhood," the continuity and coherence that characterize the sense of self. This criticism is also less applicable to the social-cognitive learning theories. Concepts such as the sense of personal efficacy have a great deal to do with that sense of personhood, even if the focus is on only a limited part of the person at any given time. The idea of evaluating oneself with respect to the attainment of desired incentives also evokes the sense of personhood.

A problem remaining for both learning viewpoints concerns the relationship between the two. The two approaches to learning that are described in Chapters 12 and 13 are split by a disagreement so fundamental that it's hard to know how a single perspective can be welded from the pieces. We minimized this issue while presenting the theoretical principles, but it deserves reexamination.

The problem is this: in explaining behavior, the conditioning approach restricts itself to events that are observable. Behavioral tendencies are explained from patterns of prior experiences and present cues. Nothing else is needed. If cognitions exist, they are irrelevant—foam on the stream of behavior, shaped by the same forces as shape behavior, but not important in understanding behavior. The social-cognitive learning approach is in direct opposition to this view. Expectations cause behavior. Actions follow from thinking, rather than occurring in parallel with thinking.

This latter characterization fits more with the introspections that most people have about their own lives. As noted earlier, however, treating cognitions as causes of behavior may mean rejecting some of the most fundamental tenets of the conditioning approach. In the more cognitive view, classical and instrumental conditioning aren't incremental processes occurring outside awareness; they depend on expectancies and mental models. Reinforcement is seen as providing information about future incentives, instead of acting directly to strengthen behavioral tendencies.

Nor is the emphasis on expectancies and other cognitions the only area of conflict between the approaches. Social-cognitive learning theorists agree with conditioning theorists that reinforcement is necessary to maintain behavior (despite holding a view of reinforcement that differs drastically from that of conditioning theorists). But sometimes a behavior occurs with no obvious reinforcer. In such a case, theorists may assert that the behavior is being supported by self-reinforcement. The appeal to self-reinforcement is far from satisfying, both to conditioning theorists and to people who stand outside the learning perspective. If self-reinforcement accounts for behavior *sometimes*, why isn't it enough *all the time*? Why is external reinforcement *ever* necessary? How do you decide when it's needed and when it isn't?

One challenge for the evolution of the thinking of the social-cognitive learning theorists is to determine how—or whether—their ideas can be reconciled with the principles of conditioning. Are the newer theories extrapolations from the previous theories, or are they fundamentally different? Can they be merged, or are they competitors for the same theoretical niche? That is, some people would say that the newer version of the learning perspective should simply *replace* the conditioning version—that the conditioning view was wrong, that human learning simply doesn't occur that way.

Some people have abandoned the attempt at integration, and simply stepped away from the issue altogether. For example, in recent years Bandura has dropped the word *learning* from the phrase he uses to characterize his theory. He now calls it social-cognitive theory (Bandura, 1986). This raises the question of whether his current ideas (as opposed to his earlier ideas) should be seen as belonging to the learning perspective on personality at all.

Bandura's change of label reflects a more general trend among people who started out within the social learning framework. Many of these people have been influenced in the past twenty-five years by the ideas of cognitive psychology. Many people who used to call their orientation a social learning view now would hedge. Some of them would give their orientation a different label today, which would be more likely to include terms such as *cognitive* and *self-regulation*. There has been a gradual fraying of the edge of the social learning approach, which blends with the newer cognitive self-regulation theories. This overlap will become more apparent in later chapters.

This blurring and shifting between bodies of thought raises a final question for the social-cognitive learning approach. Will this approach retain its identity as an active area of work in the years to come, or will it disperse, its themes absorbed by other viewpoints?

SUMMARY

Dissatisfactions with the conditioning approach led to development of another generation of learning theories. They're called cognitive because they emphasize the role of thought processes in behavior, and social because they emphasize the idea that people often learn from one another. Several aspects of these theories can be thought of as elaborations on conditioning principles, although close examination of the elaborations raises questions about the validity of those conditioning principles.

These elaborations include an emphasis on the role of social reinforcement (rather than other sorts of reinforcement) in shaping behavior. Social reinforcers such as acceptance and approval can also be applied to oneself. Because humans have the capability for empathy (vicariously aroused emotions), we can experience classical conditioning vicariously. We also experience reinforcement and punishment vicariously, causing shifts in action tendencies on the basis of someone else's outcomes. Functions such as discrimination and generalization are broadened in these theories to include such phenomena as semantic generalization. This view also holds that human learning is not always incremental. That is, we often learn rules and then apply them to new situations.

A fundamental principle that seems to underlie many aspects of human learning is that expectancies concerning upcoming events and outcomes play an important part in determining our responses. Specific theorists have also focused on two additional kinds of expectancy. Rotter holds that people who expect their outcomes to be determined by their actions (internals) learn from reinforcers, but that people who expect their outcomes to be unrelated to their actions (externals) do not. Bandura holds that perceptions of personal efficacy or competence determine whether a person will persist when in stressful circumstances.

One portion of this approach to personality stands as completely distinct from conditioning principles: the process of acquiring behavior potentials through observational learning. This process requires only that an observer attend to a model (who is displaying a behavior), retain some memory of what was done (usually a visual or verbal memory), and have the component skills to be able to reproduce what was modeled. This process of acquisition is not directly influenced by reinforcement contingencies, although reinforcement can have an indirect effect by influencing how much attention is paid to the model. On the other hand, spontaneous performance of the acquired behavior is very much influenced by perceptions of reinforcement contingencies.

It's easy to see the importance of the various processes of social-cognitive learning in many domains, including the acquisition of sex role behavior, the tendency to be aggressive, and strategies that are used to delay gratification.

Personality assessment within this framework emphasizes the use of self-report devices. Many of these instruments are designed to measure subjective qualities such as feelings, cognitions, and expectancies (consistent with the emphasis placed on these qualities as determinants of behavior). There is also a growing emphasis on assessment within the context of the person's own definitions of situations.

Problems in behavior can develop through both vicarious and direct learning. Problems also result when people haven't had the opportunity to learn needed behaviors from models. Therapy techniques based on the social-cognitive learning approach often involve modeling procedures, whether as an attempt to remedy skill deficits through observational learning or as an attempt to show the utility of coping skills through vicarious reinforcement. Such techniques seem most effective when subjects overtly engage in the behaviors under the therapist's guidance, which led Bandura to suggest that improvement is mediated by a growing sense of efficacy. Other therapies emphasize the idea that people often hurt themselves by saying things to themselves that are negativistic. These therapies teach people to stop these negative self-statements and substitute self-statements that emphasize active, effective coping.

GLOSSARY

Androgyny The condition of having both masculine and feminine qualities.

Cognitive behavioral modification A therapeutic technique that attempts to change behaviors by changing thought patterns.

Coping model A model that displays fear but ultimately handles it.

Efficacy expectancy Confidence of being able to do something successfully.

Expectancy Judgment about how likely a specific behavior is to attain a goal.

Incentive The desirability of an outcome.

Learned helplessness A state of low motivation and effort following extensive exposure to lack of control.

Locus of control A dimension of believing that your outcomes are caused by yourself or by external forces.

Mastery model A model that displays no fear.

Observational learning The acquisition of the ability to do a new behavior by watching someone else do it.

Participant modeling The act of practicing a behavior that's hard for oneself while using the therapist as model.

Self-control The regulation and sometimes restraint of one's own activities.

Self-efficacy Confidence of being able to do something successfully.

Self-reinforcement The approval one gives to oneself for one's own behavior.

Semantic generalization Generalization along a dimension of meaning.

Sex role The behaviors associated more with members of one sex than the other.

Skill deficit The absence or insufficiency of a needed behavior or skill.

Social reinforcement Praise, liking, acceptance, or approval received from someone else.

Stress inoculation A therapy to develop the ability to cope with a broad range of stressors.

Symbolic models Models in print, movies, TV, and so on.

Vicarious classical conditioning Conditioning in which the UCR occurs via empathy.

Vicarious emotional arousal The tendency to feel someone else's feelings along with them; also called *empathy*.

Vicarious reinforcement Event in which a reinforcement experienced by someone else has a reinforcing effect on one's own behavior.

The Phenomenological Perspective

prologue to

PART *seven*

THE PHENOMENOLOGICAL PERSPECTIVE:
Major Themes and Underlying Assumptions

Every person who ever lived has been unique. No two people have ever had quite the same orientation to life. In fact, no two people ever experience any event precisely the same way. This is true whether the event is perceptual (seeing or hearing something), cognitive (thinking about something or coming to a conclusion), or behavioral (acting in one way or another). Each of us has a slightly different physical perspective on every event we witness. Each of us also has a unique psychological view, causing us to interpret in slightly personalized ways all the information we take in from the world.

The phenomenological perspective on personality has its roots in the uniqueness of each person's frame of reference. One major theme underlying this perspective is that the subjective experience of reality is extremely important. The personal frame of reference that makes each of us different from everyone else has a very powerful influence on

every bit of our lives. Indeed, the word *phenomenology* literally means "the subjective experiences of an individual." Pressed to its logical extreme, this emphasis on the subjective and personal implies that "objective" reality is unimportant. All that really matters is the subjective frame of reference that the individual takes toward the *experience* of reality.

Another theme of the phenomenological perspective is that people can determine for themselves (indeed, *must* determine for themselves) what their lives are to be like. Self-determination—free will—is part of human nature, to be exercised by each person who chooses to do so. Unfortunately, some people let themselves slip into thinking they don't have this capacity. Some people let regrets over the past or worries about the future blind them to opportunities of the present. In the phenomenological view, this happens only when people lose sight of the freedom of self-determination that's actually theirs.

A final assumption that underlies much of this perspective on personality is that human beings are intrinsically good and self-perfecting. According to this view, it's human nature to be drawn consistently toward greater health, self-sufficiency, and maturity, unless there are strong pressures to the contrary. The theories that make up this perspective thus are optimistic ones, focused on possibilities and potentials rather than on constraints and limitations. If there's a metaphor that characterizes the phenomenological perspective, it may be the human being as an opening flower or growing tree, evolving naturally toward greater beauty and completeness.

The phenomenological perspective on personality is represented by theories of two types. They are treated separately from each other, based on which of these themes they emphasize. Some contributors to this perspective place greatest emphasis on self-determination and the intrinsically positive nature of the human being. This aspect of the approach is discussed in Chapter 14. Another theorist who's contributed to this perspective emphasized more strongly the subjective nature of people's perceptions and cognitions. He argued that we literally create for ourselves a unique and personal world of experience. This aspect of the phenomenological perspective is discussed in Chapter 15.

14 Humanistic Psychology: Self-Actualization and Self-Determination

■ **Self-Actualization**

The Need for Positive Regard

■ **Self-Determination**

Introjection and Identification
Need for Relatedness
Self-Concordance
Free Will

■ **The Self and Processes of Defense**

Incongruity, Disorganization, and Defense
Self-Esteem Maintenance and Enhancement
Self-Handicapping

■ **Self-Actualization and Maslow's Hierarchy of Motives**

Characteristics of Frequent Self-Actualizers
The Peak Experience

■ **Existential Psychology: Being and Death**

The Existential Dilemma
Emptiness
Terror Management

■ **Assessment**

Interviews in Assessment
Measuring the Self-Concept by Q-Sort
Measuring Self-Actualization
Measuring Autonomy and Control

■ **Problems in Behavior, and Behavior Change**

Client-Centered Therapy
Beyond Therapy, to Personal Growth

■ **Humanistic Theories: Problems and Prospects**

SUMMARY

■ Julia spends most of her waking hours doing things for others. She talks often with her mother, whose life never goes smoothly and who always wants more from Julia than she has to give. When dealing with her mother Julia sometimes feels as though she's being drawn into quicksand, but she never complains. Then there's Eric, a guy she used to date. Eric's life is a mess, and he often calls Julia late at night for advice. Although she needs her sleep, she never refuses him a sympathetic ear. Julia always seems to be setting her own life aside for the benefit of others. It's as though she thinks she's unworthy as a person unless she does so. Deep inside, a small voice says she's wrong about that (although she's usually too busy to hear). And sometimes, just sometimes, she has the feeling that a different destiny awaits her, if she could only free herself to find it.

T he experience of being human is mysterious and challenging. You are living a pattern of events, feelings, thoughts, and choices that are different from those of any other person who ever has lived or ever will live. You are continuously "becoming," evolving from a simpler version of yourself into a more complex version of the same self. It's sometimes mystifying, because you don't always understand why you feel what you're feeling. But the fact that the life you're living is your own—a set of sensations that belongs to you and nobody else—makes the experience also vivid and compelling.

How does your self know *how* to "become"? As you evolve over your lifetime, how do you still remain yourself? Why do you sometimes feel as though part of you wants to grow in one direction and another part wants to grow in another direction? Why is it that even when things are pulling in different ways inside you, you still have the sense of being an integrated person? What qualities make this experience of being human so different and so special? These are among the questions asked by those whose ideas form the phenomenological perspective on personality. In this chapter, we examine some of the answers these theorists have provided.

The subject of this chapter is sometimes referred to with the phrase **humanistic psychology,** or the *human potential movement* (Schneider, Bugental, & Pierson, 2001). These terms reflect the idea that everyone has the potential for growth and development. No one—absolutely no one—is inherently bad or unworthy. A goal of humanistic psychology is to help people realize this about themselves, so they'll have the chance to grow.

Self-Actualization

An important figure in humanistic psychology was Carl Rogers. His ideas provide a way to talk about how potential is realized, and what can keep that from happening. In Rogers's view the potential for positive, healthy growth naturally expresses itself in everyone if there are no strong opposing influences. This growth process is termed **actualization.** Actualization is a tendency to develop capabilities in ways that *maintain or enhance the organism* (Rogers, 1959). It's assumed to exist within every living creature.

In part, the actualizing tendency is reflected physically. For example, your body actualizes as your immune system works to kill disease organisms. Your body actualizes when it grows bigger and stronger. The actualizing tendency also applies to personality. When actualization promotes maintenance or enhancement of the self, it's called **self-actualization.** Self-actualization moves you toward greater autonomy and self-sufficiency. It expands or enriches your life experiences, and it enhances creativity. It promotes **congruence,** *wholeness* or *integration* within the person, and it minimizes disorganization or incongruence.

Rogers believed that the actualizing tendency is part of human nature. This is also reflected in another term he used: the **organismic valuing process.** This phrase refers to the idea that the organism automatically evaluates its experiences and actions to tell whether they're actualizing. If they aren't, the organismic valuing process creates a nagging sense that something isn't right.

Rogers used the term **fully functioning person** to describe someone who is self-actualizing. Fully functioning people are open to experiencing their feelings, aren't threatened by them, no matter what the feelings are. They trust the feelings rather than question them. Fully functioning people are also open to experiencing the world. Rather than hide from it, they immerse themselves in it. The result is that the fully functioning person lives a life filled with meaning, challenge, and excitement, but also a willingness to risk pain. The fully functioning person isn't a particular *kind of person*. Rather, it's a *way of functioning* that can be adopted by anyone who chooses to live that way (see Box 14.1).

The Need for Positive Regard

As important as self-actualization is, it's not the only important influence on human behavior. People also have a strong motive to be accepted and to have the love, friendship, and affection of others—particularly others who matter to them (called *significant others*). Rogers referred to this acceptance with the term **positive regard.**

Positive regard can come in two different ways, and the difference is important. Affection given without special conditions—with no "strings" attached—is termed **unconditional positive regard.** Sometimes, affection is given only if certain condi-

We all have a strong need to experience positive regard from others, to feel wanted, appreciated, and respected.

BOX 14.1

THE THEORIST AND THE THEORY
Carl Rogers as a Fully Functioning Person

Although Carl Rogers apparently didn't consciously draw on his own life in developing his theory, his life certainly embodied all the theory's principles. Rogers lived a life characterized by a willingness to change, and openness to experience. Several times he left the security of the familiar and moved in new directions, using only his intuitions and feelings as guides. Rogers was very much the fully functioning, self-actualizing person his theory describes.

Rogers was born in Oak Park, Illinois, in 1902, the middle child in a large family. His parents were conservative and devoutly Christian. During college he decided to pursue a life in the ministry. At the same time he also participated in a six-month-long religious conference in China. This trip had a profound effect on him. The exposure to religious leaders from different cultures changed his thinking about religious issues. He began to entertain the possibility that all he had believed might be wrong—that Jesus may have been only a man, rather than divine. At this point, Rogers wrote to his parents announcing his independence from their religious views, fully realizing the emotional cost that such an act would incur.

Rogers took his degree in history, then continued pursuing his remaining interest in religion, while also taking courses in psychology. After a period of dividing his efforts this way, he abandoned the path of religion forever and focused on psychology full-time. Having received his doctorate, Rogers took his first job in Rochester, New York. Here two experiences greatly influenced his thinking. First, clinical experience made it apparent to him that psychoanalytic therapy, which dominated the group in which he worked, was often ineffective. Second, he realized that there were vast disagreements among his senior colleagues about how to deal with specific cases. In short, conventional wisdom didn't seem to be working, and the authorities couldn't agree about what to do. To Rogers, it was time to go it alone and develop his own way of treating problems.

In 1939, Rogers published the first of his books on the therapy technique he'd developed. This led to a series of academic appointments at several universities. In his later years, he left the familiar confines of academia and set out once again to make a change. The latter part of his career took place at the Western Behavioral Sciences Institute in California—where he pursued his developing interest in group therapies of various kinds—and at the Center for Studies of the Person.

tions are satisfied. The conditions vary from case to case, but the principle is the same: I'll like you and accept you, but only *if* you act in a particular way. This is called **conditional positive regard.** Much of the affection that people get in their day-to-day lives is conditional.

Another phrase used in this context is **conditions of worth.** Conditions of worth are the conditions under which the person is judged to be worthy of positive regard. When people change their actions to conform to a condition of worth, they're doing so not because the act is *intrinsically* desirable, but to get positive regard from other people (see Cartoon 14.1).

Rogers argued that, after years of having conditions of worth applied to us by people around us, we start to apply them to *ourselves* (Sheldon & Elliot, 1998). We

SHOE by Jeff MacNelly

**People sometimes attempt to impose conditions of worth on other people.
Reprinted by permission: Tribune Media Services.**

give ourselves affection and acceptance only when we act to satisfy those conditions. This pattern of self-acceptance (and self-rejection) is called **conditional self-regard.** Conditional self-regard makes you behave so as to fit the conditions of worth you're applying to yourself (Crocker & Wolfe, 2001).

Conditions of worth and conditional regard have an important effect. *Altering your behavior, values, or goals to gain acceptance can interfere or conflict with self-actualization.* Because self-actualizing is more important than fulfilling conditions of worth, it should get first priority. But the need for positive regard is so salient that its influence is often felt more keenly.

Let's consider a couple of examples to see how these motives can conflict with each other. Joel is a young man who's decided to give up a possible career in music because his father needs help in the family business. In doing this, Joel is responding to conditions of worth imposed by his family. Bowing to those conditions of worth, however, may mean denying something that's important inside him, something that's truly a part of who he is.

The same kind of conflict is experienced to some degree by Julia, the woman described in the chapter opening. Recall that Julia spends much of her time and energy giving of herself to others. Her actions, however, seem driven by a need to prove she's worthy as a human being. She seems to be applying conditions of worth to herself. By trying to live up to them, Julia prevents herself from hearing the voice of self-actualization and from growing in her own way.

Finally, Jayne feels a strong desire for a career, but her parents want her to marry and raise a family. If her parents won't fully accept her unless she bends to their wishes, they're creating a condition of worth for her. Accepting this condition may interfere with her self-actualization. Remember, though, that conditions of worth aren't always imposed from outside. It's possible that Jayne's desire for a career may itself be a condition of worth, a self-imposed condition (just like Julia's need to prove her worthiness by giving to others). Jayne may have decided she won't accept herself as a complete person unless she has a career.

It can be very hard to distinguish a true desire from a condition of worth (Janoff-Bulman & Leggatt, 2002). What defines a condition of worth is that it's a *precondition for acceptance,* whether self-acceptance or acceptance by others. A condition of worth is always coercive: it pushes you into doing what it requires of you. Whenever there are such conditions, they can prevent self-actualization from taking place.

Self-Determination

The ideas of Rogers are echoed in a more recent theory of **self-determination** proposed by Ed Deci (Deci, 1975) and expanded on by Deci and Richard Ryan (1980, 1985, 1991, 2000; Ryan, 1993; Ryan & Deci, 2001; see also Vallerand, 1997). Deci and Ryan believe that three needs must be satisfied to have a life of growth, integrity, and well-being. The needs are for autonomy (self-determination), competence, and relatedness. Evidence has recently been found that people in general also see these needs as most important (Sheldon, Elliot, Kim, & Kasser, 2001).

This work began with the idea that behavior can reflect several underlying dynamics. Some actions are *self-determined,* done because the actions have intrinsic interest or value to you. Other actions are *controlled,* done to gain payment or to satisfy someone's pressures. A behavior can be controlled even if the control occurs entirely inside your own mind. If you do something because you know you'd feel guilty if you didn't, you're engaging in controlled behavior.

Whether behavior is controlled or self-determined can have several consequences. One of them concerns how long you'll stay interested in the activity. People stay interested longer when their actions are self-determined. There's a great deal of evidence that promising rewards for working on activities can undermine people's interest in them (Deci, Koestner, & Ryan, 1999). The effect has been found in children as well as adults. In children it's been called "turning play into work" (Lepper & Greene, 1975, 1978).

Apparently it's not the reward itself that does this. What matters is whether people see their actions as self-determined. Telling people they're going to be paid for working often seems to make them infer that their behavior isn't self-determined. As a result, they lose interest.

Sometimes, though, the presence of reward increases motivation instead of undermining it (Elliot & Harackiewicz, 1994; Harackiewicz, 1979; Henderlong & Lepper, 2002). Why? Because reward has two aspects (Deci, 1975). It has a *controlling* aspect, telling you your actions aren't self-determined. It can also have an *informational* aspect, telling you something about yourself. If a reward tells you you're competent, it increases motivation (Eisenberger & Rhoades, 2001; Koestner, Zuckerman, & Koestner, 1987). It's even possible for a reward to promote a sense of autonomy, given the right conditions (Henderlong & Lepper, 2002). If the reward implies a condition of worth, however, or if it implies you're engaged in the activity only for the reward, the controlling aspect stands out and motivation falls off.

Deci and Ryan hold that people want to feel a sense of autonomy in everything they do. In this view, accomplishments, such as doing well in your courses, are satisfying only if you feel a sense of self-determination in them. If you feel you're forced to do those things, or pressured to do them by others, you'll have less satisfaction and less motivation (Flink, Boggiano, & Barrett, 1990; Grolnick & Ryan, 1989). Indeed, pressuring *yourself* to do well can also reduce motivation (Ryan, 1982). This fits the idea that people can impose conditions of worth on themselves.

Introjection and Identification

Deci and Ryan and their colleagues have used several more terms in describing controlled and self-determined behavior. *Introjected regulation* happens when a person uses a value pertaining to behavior, but treats it as a "should" or an "ought." That is, the person does the behavior to avoid guilt or to get self-approval. If you try to do well in a class so you won't feel guilty about wasting your parents' money, that's introjected behavior. Introjected behavior is controlled, but the control is being exerted from inside the person. If you try to do well in a class so your parents won't look down on you, that's also controlled, but it's not introjected.

In *identified regulation* the person has come over time to hold the behavior as personally meaningful and valuable. If you try to do well in a class because you believe the information in it is important to your growth, that's identified regulation. Identified regulation is self-determined. It's not quite as self-determined as intrinsically motivated behavior (for which the interest is naturally there already), but it's close.

These ideas have many applications. For example, what do you want out of life? Research has found that aspiring to financial success (which generally reflects controlled behavior) relates to poorer mental health, whereas aspiring to community involvement relates to better mental health (Kasser, 2002; Kasser & Ryan, 1993). Of course, *why* the person has the aspiration is what really matters (Carver & Baird, 1998). Thus, wanting community involvement for controlling reasons (because it will make people like you) is bad. Wanting financial success for truly self-determined reasons (because the process itself is intrinsically enjoyable) can be good.

The pressures that lead to introjected regulation stem from the desire to be accepted by others or to avoid a sense of guilt over doing things you think others won't like. This fits with Rogers's belief that the desire for positive regard can disrupt self-actualization. A lot depends on whether significant others place conditions of worth on you. For example, restrictive parenting produces adults who value conformity instead of self-direction (Kassner, Koestner, & Lekes, 2002).

Having a sense of autonomy also seems to foster further autonomy. In one research project, medical students who thought their professors were supportive of their own autonomy became even more autonomous in their learning over time (Williams & Deci, 1996). They also felt more competent in the skills they were learning. Finally, they acted toward others in ways that were supportive of the others' autonomy.

Need for Relatedness

Deci and Ryan also hold that people have an intrinsic need for relatedness (Baumeister & Leary, 1995). At first glance it might seem that the need for relatedness must conflict with the need for autonomy. However, Deci and Ryan's view of autonomy doesn't mean being independent from others—and thus low in relatedness. It means having the sense of free self-determination (Deci & Ryan, 1991, 2000). Real relatedness doesn't conflict with this.

Several studies have confirmed that autonomy and relatedness can exist side by side. One project found across several studies that autonomy and relatedness were complementary: each related independently to well-being (Bettencourt & Sheldon, 2001). Another study found that a measure of behaving autonomously related to *more* relatedness, in the form of having open and positive communication with significant others. People who regulated their lives in a controlled way were the ones who interacted defensively with others (Hodgins, Koestner, & Duncan, 1996). Yet another study found that an autonomy orientation related to use of relationship-maintaining coping strategies and positive responses in discussing the relationships (Knee, Patrick, Vietor, Nanayakkara, & Neighbors, 2002).

The need for relatedness has some resemblance to the need for positive regard. Accordingly, we might also ask whether the need for relatedness can interfere with self-actualization. The answer seems to be "no." Deci and Ryan's conception of relatedness implies a genuine connection to others, an unconditional acceptance rather than a connection based on pressure and demand. It might be more accurate to equate this need to a need for *unconditional* regard.

Self-Concordance

Another implication of self-determination theory concerns people's goals. Elsewhere in this book you will read about personality being expressed in the goals people take up (for example, Chapter 17). But goals are not equal in what they're about or in their contributions to well-being. The key is that it's good to pursue goals that are consistent with your core values, a situation termed **self-concordance** (Sheldon & Elliot, 1999). You're more invested in such goals. You'll also benefit more from attaining them than from attaining goals that aren't connected to your core values. Support for this reasoning comes from several sources (Brunstein, Schultheiss, & Grässmann, 1998; Sheldon & Elliot, 1999; Sheldon & Kasser, 1998).

There's even evidence that pursuit of self-concordant goals can create a longer-term spiral of benefit (Sheldon & Houser-Marko, 2001). When you try to reach self-concordant goals, you try harder, you have more satisfying experiences, and you attain better well-being. Moreover, this experience promotes greater motivation for the next self-concordant goal, and the cycle continues.

Free Will

Humanistic psychologists emphasize the idea that people have freedom to decide for themselves how to act, what to become. For example, Rogers believed that people are free to choose whether to act in self-actualizing ways or to accept conditions of worth. Deci and Ryan believe that people are exerting their will when they choose to act in self-determined ways.

The concept of free will is interesting and controversial. It's nearly impossible to know for sure whether we have free will, but people certainly seem to *think* they do.

When we are prevented from doing something that we want to do, our desire to do that activity increases even more.

Figure 14.1

Time pressure makes decisions harder. Participants in this research were to choose between two people, one of whom would interview them about a series of sensitive topics (except for a control group who didn't expect to make a decision). Each was given written descriptions of the two people and then was asked for an initial opinion about each. If they thought the decision was farther away (fifteen minutes), they reported opinions of the two that differed considerably, suggesting an initial preference. If they thought the decision would have to be made soon (three minutes), the ratings became similar to each other. Thus, as people come closer to decisions, they display increasing indecision (adapted from Linder & Crane, 1970).

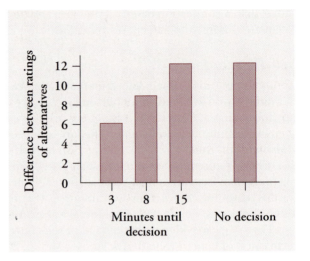

One reflection of this belief is called **reactance** (Brehm, 1966; Brehm & Brehm, 1981). Reactance occurs when you expect to have a particular freedom and something causes you to see the freedom as being threatened. The result is an attempt to regain or reassert that freedom. There are lots of examples. Young children who've been told they can't do something want to do it all the more. In the same way, "playing hard to get" can create more attraction. The best illustration of reactance, however, may be what's often said when one person is pressuring another: "Don't tell me what to do!"

You can also threaten a freedom yourself. Just having an initial preference for something can be a threat to freedom. Imagine being at dinner at a nice restaurant. You've been thinking about shrimp all day, so you have an initial preference. *This preference interferes with your freedom to choose something else.* The result is indecision. People in this situation step back from the initial preference and get interested in alternatives (e.g., Linder & Crane, 1970; Linder, Wortman, & Brehm, 1971). The closer to decision time, the more the indecision (see Figure 14.1).

Although people think they have free will, research by Wegner and Wheatley (1999) raises questions about it. They set up a situation in which pairs of people together moved a computer mouse (as if using a Ouija board). One person (who was actually part of the experiment) caused the mouse to stop at particular moments, so the cursor fell on specific objects on the computer screen. Through complicated procedures, the researchers caused the actual participants to think of the object on which the cursor stopped, either just before or after the stop occurred. If they thought about the object just before the stop (which, remember, was caused by the other person), they reported they had stopped there intentionally. This and other evidence led Wegner (2002) to suggest that free will is an illusion. This issue, of course, will continue to be debated.

The Self and Processes of Defense

Let us now turn to the concept of self. Rogers is sometimes called a *self theorist,* because he stressed the importance of this concept. As many theorists, he assumed that the self doesn't exist at birth but that infants gradually differentiate self from nonself. As the person grows, the self becomes more elaborate and complex. It never reaches an end state but continues to evolve.

Rogers used the term *self* in several ways. Sometimes he used it to refer to the subjective awareness of being (Rogers, 1965). At other times he used it interchangeably with *self-concept*. The self-concept is the set of qualities a person views as being part of himself or herself (much like the concept of ego identity, Chapter 11). Many distinctions can be made among the elements that form the self-concept. One of them is between the actual (or real, or experienced) self and the ideal self. The **ideal self** is an image of the kind of person you want to be. The **actual self** is what you think you're really like as a person right now.

Recall that self-actualizing is supposed to promote congruence. Congruence means fitting closely together. One kind of congruence relates to this distinction between actual and ideal selves. In particular, as self-actualization takes place, it creates a closer fit between the actual and the ideal. It leads you to become more like the self you want to be.

There's a second kind of congruence that's also important: between the actual self and experience. That is, the experiences you have in life should fit with the kind of person you think you are. For example, if you think you're a kind person and you find yourself doing something that's insensitive and unkind, there's an incongruity between self and experience. If you think you're a smart person but find yourself doing poorly in a course, there's an incongruity between self and experience. Self-actualization should tend to promote a closer congruence here, as well.

Incongruity, Disorganization, and Defense

Incongruence is disorganization, a breakdown in the unitary sense of self. You don't always know it consciously, but the organismic valuing process notes it automatically. According to Rogers, incongruence (whether a perception of a gap between real and ideal or experiencing something that doesn't fit your self-image) leads to anxiety.

The experience of incongruence can also make people vulnerable to yet further problems. Low self-esteem (incongruity between the actual and ideal self) leads people to underestimate greatly how much significant others care for them (Murray, Holmes, & Griffin, 2000; Murray, Holmes, Griffin, Bellavia, & Rose, 2001). This misperception can cause them to react poorly to their partners. They feel pessimistic about the relationship, may act in ways that are not genuine, and ultimately the relationship is less likely to flourish.

It isn't always possible to have complete congruence. Rogers assumed, though, that people defend themselves against even the *perception* of incongruence to avoid the anxiety it creates. Defenses against perceptions of incongruity form two categories, which aren't so different from some of the defenses addressed by psychoanalytic theory (Chapter 9).

One kind of defense involves *distortion of experience.* An example is rationalization: creating a plausible but untrue explanation for why something is the way it is. Another distortion occurs when you perceive an event as being different from the way it really is. For instance, if you say something that makes someone else feel bad, you may protect yourself by believing that the other person wasn't really bothered.

The second kind of defense involves *preventing threatening experiences from reaching awareness.* Denial—refusal to admit to yourself that a situation exists or an experience took place—serves this function. A woman who ignores overwhelming evidence that her boyfriend is unfaithful to her is engaged in denial.

You can also prevent an experience from reaching awareness indirectly, by not letting yourself be in a situation where the experience would be *possible*. By taking steps to prevent it from occurring, you prevent its access to consciousness. This is a subtle defense. For example, a person whose self-image is threatened by sexual feelings among strangers may avoid going to the beach or to nightclubs, thereby preventing the experience from occurring.

Self-Esteem Maintenance and Enhancement

Defenses act to maintain and enhance the congruity or integrity of the self. Another way to put it is that defenses protect and enhance self-esteem (though see Box 14.2). The idea that people go out of their way to protect self-esteem has been around for a long time. It's been an active area of study under several labels, including self-evaluation maintenance, self-affirmation, ego-defensiveness, and egotism (e.g., Darley & Goethals, 1980; M. L. Snyder, Stephan, & Rosenfield, 1976, 1978; Steele, 1988; Tesser, 1986, 1988; Tesser & Campbell, 1983).

It's often said that two conditions are required for concerns to arise about maintaining (or enhancing) self-esteem (Snyder et al., 1978). First, an event must take place that's attributable to you. If events are outside your control, they're not relevant to you. Second, the event must be good or bad, thereby having potential connotations for self-esteem.

What happens when there's a threat to self-esteem? Just as Rogers argued, people either distort perceptions or keep them out of awareness. If self-esteem is threatened, people minimize the negativity of the event, thus distorting their perceptions. Alternatively, they try to prevent the event from being attributed to permanent qualities of the self, thereby denying its relevance.

Let's consider a couple of examples. A common threat to self-esteem is failure. Failure (academic, social, or in another domain) can make most of us feel inadequate. What do people do when they fail? They make excuses (C. R. Snyder & Higgins, 1988). They blame the failure on things beyond their control. They attribute the failure to task difficulty, to chance, to other people, or (in a bind) to a lack of effort (e.g., Bradley, 1978; Snyder et al., 1976, 1978). This happens whether the event is as trivial as failure on a laboratory task, or as profound as the experience of divorce (Gray & Silver, 1990). Blaming something else creates distance between the failure and yourself. Given enough distance, the failure doesn't threaten your self-esteem.

When you experience success, on the other hand, you have the chance to *enhance* self-esteem. You can do this by attributing the success to your abilities (Agostinelli, Sherman, Presson, & Chassin, 1992; Bradley, 1978; Snyder et al., 1976, 1978; Taylor & Brown, 1988). Indeed, there's even evidence that people think that their positive personal qualities are under their own control, allowing them to claim credit for being the way they are (Alicke, 1985).

A person can also protect self-esteem after a failure by distorting perceptions another way. As we said earlier, an event is relevant to self-esteem only if it has an impact that's either good or bad. You can be self-protective, then, by distorting your perceptions to minimize the event's impact. An academic failure isn't a failure if the course doesn't matter to you. Making a bad impression on someone isn't a problem if that person isn't worth bothering with. This sort of distortion also seems to occur. For example, in one study people were told they'd done well or done poorly on a test (Greenberg, Pyszczynski, & Solomon, 1982). They then were asked how valid they thought the test was and how important it had been for them to do well on it. Those who believed they'd done poorly saw the test as less valid and less important.

BOX 14.2

HOW CAN YOU MANAGE TWO KINDS OF CONGRUENCE SIMULTANEOUSLY?

This section of the chapter discusses how people protect or enhance their self-images, to defend against perception of incongruence between the actual self and the ideal self. Don't forget, though, that another kind of incongruence—between the self and experience—is also distressing. Unfortunately, there are circumstances when the desire to avoid one kind of incongruity can plunge you right into the other.

What kind of circumstance would do that? An example is suggested by the work of William Swann and his colleagues on what they call self-verification (e.g., Swann, 1987, 1990). The principle behind this research is that once people have an idea of what they're like, they want to have that self-concept confirmed by other people's reactions to them. That is, people want their experience to be congruent with their self-concept. For example, if you think you're a good athlete, you want others to think so too. If you think you're shy, you want others to realize it. It may seem odd, but the desire to verify beliefs about yourself extends even to beliefs that are unflattering (Swann, Wenzlaff, & Tafarodi, 1992). If you think you're not good looking, you'd rather have someone else agree than say the opposite.

But there's a problem. For a person who holds a negative self-view, there's a built-in conflict between self-verification and self-protection. Self-verification is trying not to have incongruity between one's self and one's experience. Self-protection is trying not to be aware of incongruity between a desired self and one's actual self. Unfortunately, attempts to diminish the two incongruities can pull a person in opposite directions.

Swann and his colleagues argue that both of these forces operate in everyone. Which one dominates at a given moment depends on your options. Keep in mind that most people's self-concepts contain both positive and negative qualities (Swann, Pelham, & Krull, 1989). Suppose, then, you had the chance to obtain information about yourself (from another person or from a personality test). Would you prefer to get information about what you view as your best quality, or about what you view as your worst? Given this option, most people prefer to learn about something they view as desirable. This fits the self-protection tendency.

But suppose you know that the quality about which you can get information is one you think you're bad on. Would you rather get information about how you're good in that quality, or about how you're bad? The answer obtained by Swann et al. (1989) is that people tend to seek unfavorable information, if the information is about a quality they think they're bad on.

In sum, the self-protection and self-enhancement tendency seems to influence where you look (and where you don't look) when you consider relations between your actual and desired selves. You prefer to look at favorable self-aspects. Once you're looking at some self-aspect in particular, though, the self-verification tendency influences the kind of information you focus on. You want information that confirms your view of who you are—fits your experienced self to your actual self. In each case, the effect is to enhance perceptions of congruence, consistent with the ideas proposed by Rogers.

Self-Handicapping

Distorting perceptions of bad outcomes maintains self-esteem. But there's also another way: denial to awareness. Consider what's called **self-handicapping** (e.g., Arkin & Baumgardner, 1985; Higgins, Snyder, & Berglas, 1990; Jones & Berglas, 1978; Jones & Pittman, 1982). Self-handicapping is acting to create the very conditions that tend to produce a failure. If you have a test tomorrow, it's self-handicapping to party all night instead of studying. If you want to make a good impression on someone, it's self-handicapping to show up drunk or drenched in sweat.

Why would you do this to yourself? If you want to reach a goal, why create conditions that make it harder? The theory is that a hard goal is a threat to self-esteem, because there's substantial risk of failure. You can't really fail, though, if success is prevented by circumstances beyond your control. If such conditions exist, the stigma of failing goes away. If you fail the test or make a poor impression, well, *no one* could do well under those conditions. So it wasn't really a failure. Thus, you've prevented the awareness of failing. Note that for this strategy to be successful you need to be *unaware of using it.* If you realize you're setting up barriers for yourself, the barriers won't have the same psychological meaning.

Self-handicapping may be more common than people realize (see Higgins et al., 1990). The idea has even been extended to phenomena that are usually viewed differently, for example, test anxiety. Everyone knows people who say they freeze up during tests, even though they know the material. Claiming to be test anxious can have a self-handicapping function, helping protect self-esteem (Greenberg, Pyszczynski, & Paisley, 1984; Smith, Snyder, & Handelsman, 1982). That is, being test anxious gives an explanation for a failure that doesn't reflect on your ability.

Although self-handicapping may be common, it's not a good thing to do. People who tend to self-handicap cope poorly with stress (Zuckerman, Kieffer, & Knee, 1998). Let us also point out explicitly that self-handicapping often helps create the very failure it was intended to protect against (Zuckerman et al., 1998).

Self-Actualization and Maslow's Hierarchy of Motives

Rogers wasn't the only theorist to emphasize the importance of self-actualization. Another who did so was Abraham Maslow (1962, 1970). Maslow was interested in the qualities of people who seem to get the most out of life—the most fully functioning of persons, the healthiest, and the best adjusted. He spent most of his career trying to understand how these people were able to be so complete and so well adapted (see Box 14.3).

As part of this effort, Maslow looked closely at how people live life. He eventually came to examine motivation and how motives are organized. Although Maslow thus was a motivational theorist, his view of motivation was very different from the view discussed in Chapter 5.

Maslow came to view the various human needs as forming a hierarchy (Maslow, 1970), which is often portrayed as a pyramid (Figure 14.2). Maslow pointed out that needs vary in their immediacy and power. Some are extremely primitive, basic, and demanding. Because they're so fundamental, they form the base of the pyramid. These needs are *physiological*—pertaining to air, water, food, and so on—things obviously necessary for survival. The qualities at the next higher level of the hierarchy are also necessary for survival, but are less demanding. These are *safety and* (physical) *security* needs: shelter from the weather, protection against predators, and so on.

Maslow considered this second class of needs to be less basic than the first class because safety needs require satisfaction less frequently than do physiological needs. When satisfied, they usually remain so for longer periods. You need to get oxygen every few seconds, water every few hours, food once or twice a day. But once you've found a house or apartment, you have physical shelter for quite a while (as long as you pay the rent). If both your apartment and your air supply became inaccessible, you'd surely try to regain the air first and worry about the apartment later.

BOX 14.3

THE THEORIST AND THE THEORY
Maslow's Focus on the Positive

Abraham Maslow focused his work almost exclusively on the positive side of human experience. He was interested in what caused some people to achieve greatness in their lives and to succeed where others failed. He cared about issues of growth and the realization of human potential. It's clear that these interests were influenced by events in his own life.

Maslow was born in 1908 in Brooklyn, the oldest of seven children of Russian-Jewish immigrants. His home life definitely did not foster personal growth. His father thought little of him and even publicly ridiculed his appearance. This experience led young Maslow to seek out empty cars whenever he rode the subway, to spare others the sight of him. If Maslow's father treated him badly, his mother's treatment was worse. Because the family was poor, she kept a lock on the refrigerator to keep the children out, feeding them only when she saw fit. Maslow once characterized her as a "cruel, ignorant, and hostile figure, one so unloving as to nearly induce madness in her children" (Hoffman, 1988, p. 7).

Maslow was later to say that his focus on the positive side of personality was a direct consequence of his mother's treatment of him. It was a "reaction formation" to the things his mother did and the qualities she represented (Maslow, 1979, p. 958). Thus, from a life begun in hardship came a determination to understand the highest and best in human experience.

Maslow entered college intending a career in law, but he quickly became disenchanted, because law focuses so much on evil and so little on good. He turned to psychology. According to Maslow, that was when his life really started. His doctoral work, done under the direction of well-known primate researcher Harry Harlow, focused on how dominance is established among monkeys. Thus, even while conducting animal research, Maslow was interested in what sets exceptional individuals off from others who are less special.

Maslow shifted this research interest to humans during the period surrounding World War II. New York in the 1930s and 1940s was a gathering place for some of the greatest intellectuals of Europe, who were escaping from Nazi Germany. Maslow was quite taken with several of them and tried to find out everything he could about them. In this search to understand how these people came to be the way they were, Maslow was sowing the seeds of more formal work to come later. The formal research was prompted in part by the eruption of war. That is, Maslow was deeply moved by the suffering and anguish that the war caused, and he vowed to devote his life to proving that humans were capable of something better than war, prejudice, and hatred. He proceeded to do just that, by studying the process of self-actualization.

At the next level of the hierarchy, the needs begin to have more social qualities. The level immediately above safety needs is the category of *love and belongingness.* Here the needs are for companionship, affection, and acceptance from others (much like the need for positive regard posited by Rogers). Needs of this type are satisfied through interaction with other people.

Higher yet on the pyramid are *esteem* needs, needs bearing on evaluation (and self-evaluation). Esteem needs include the need for a sense of mastery and power and a sense of appreciation from others (Leary & Baumeister, 2000). Notice that this

Figure 14.2

Maslow's theoretical hierarchy of needs. Needs lower on the hierarchy are more demanding and animalistic. Needs higher on the hierarchy are more subtle, but more distinctly human.

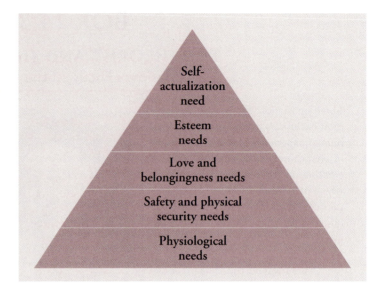

differs from acceptance and affection in the last paragraph. *Acceptance* may not be evaluative. *Appreciation* is. You're appreciated and esteemed for some quality or qualities that you possess. The need for appreciation thus is more elaborate than the need for acceptance.

At the top of this hierarchy stands *self-actualization*. Maslow used this term much as Rogers did, to mean the tendency to become whatever you're capable of becoming, to extend yourself to the limits of your capacities. Self-actualization, to Maslow, is the highest of human motives.

This hierarchical organization has several implications. The pyramid is a visual analogue for Maslow's core assumption. He assumed that low-level needs are more primitive and more demanding than needs higher on the hierarchy. As we said earlier, the need for air is more demanding than the need for shelter. Maslow's assumption was broader than that, however. He also assumed that the need for physical shelter is more demanding than the need to have a sense of being accepted, and that the need for a sense of belonging is more demanding than the need to be appreciated or powerful. Maslow thus held that the power of the motive force weakens as you move step by step up the pyramid.

On the other hand, as you move up the hierarchy, the needs are also more distinctly human and less animalistic. Thus, Maslow saw a trade-off between the constraints of biology and the uniqueness of being human. We have needs that make us different from other creatures. Self-actualization is the highest and most important. But we can't escape the motives we share with other creatures. Those needs are more powerful when they're unsatisfied than the needs that make us special.

In general, then, people must deal with the needs they have at lower levels of the pyramid before they can attend to needs that are higher. There are two further implications of this. First, if a need begins to develop at a lower level while you're trying to satisfy a higher one, *the developing lower-level need can cause you to be pulled away from the higher-level one.* Your attention, in effect, is pulled downward, and you're forced to do something about the more basic need (see Wicker, Brown, Wiehe, Hagen, & Reed, 1993).

The second implication concerns how people move up through this set of needs. It may be precisely the freeing of your mind from the demands of low-level needs that lets you be attuned to the quiet voice of self-actualization. Remember, the farther up the pyramid you go, the more subtle and less survival-related is the motive. Self-actualization, the highest motive, is the last to be taken into account. Only when the other needs are quieted can this one be attended to.

The steps on the hierarchy also differ from each other in one more sense. Maslow said that motives low on the pyramid are **deficiency-based motives,** whereas the high levels (particularly self-actualization) are **growth-based motives** (Maslow, 1955). That is, lower needs arise from deprivation. Satisfying such needs means escaping unpleasant conditions. Self-actualization, in contrast, is more like the distant call of your still-unrealized potential as a person. Satisfying this need isn't a matter of avoiding an unpleasant state. Rather, it's the seeking of growth (see also Markus & Nurius, 1986; Sheldon et al., 2001).

Finally, we make a point about the relation between Maslow's ideas and those of Rogers. Rogers emphasized two motives. The first was the self-actualizing tendency, which he saw as most important. The second was the need for positive regard: affection and acceptance. This need is also important, and very powerful.

It's possible to see a commonality between these ideas and the more elaborate structure laid out by Maslow (Figure 14.2). The bottom two levels of Maslow's pyramid refer to needs that Rogers ignored. Rogers focused on social needs, which for Maslow begin at the third level. Maslow assumed, as did Rogers, that the need for acceptance could be more demanding than the need for self-actualization. The structure of this hierarchy clearly implies that people can be distracted from self-actualization by the need for positive regard.

The intermediate level of Maslow's pyramid—esteem needs—can be viewed as an elaboration on the need for positive regard. Esteem needs seem similar in many ways to Rogers's conditions of worth. The two theorists differed somewhat in how they viewed this motive. To Rogers, bowing to conditions of worth is bad. To Maslow, esteem needs are part of being human, although less important than the need to self-actualize. The two agreed, however, that this need can get in the way of self-actualization. In sum, despite the fact that each theorist had unique ideas about personality, their theoretical views also have much in common.

Characteristics of Frequent Self-Actualizers

The concept of self-actualization is, in many ways, the most engaging and intriguing of all the ideas generated by these theorists. Although Maslow painted a broad picture of human motives, it was self-actualization that most fully absorbed his interest and imagination. As noted earlier, he devoted much of his career to studying it.

According to Maslow, everyone has the potential to self-actualize, and everyone has an intrinsic desire to become more and more the person that he or she is capable of being. Because self-actualization is so diffuse a quality, it can appear in virtually any kind of behavior. It isn't just the painter, musician, writer, or actor who can be self-actualizing—it's any person who's in the process of becoming more congruent, more integrated, more complete as a person.

Despite the belief that every person has this potential, Maslow also recognized that some people self-actualize more often than others. To better understand self-actualizing, he sought out people who displayed self-actualizing properties often. He worked hard to describe these people, in part because self-actualization is such a hard concept to grasp. By describing them he hoped to help others recognize self-actualizing experiences in their own lives.

Maslow came to believe that frequent self-actualizers share several characteristics (Maslow, 1962, 1968). Here are a few of them (for a more complete list, see Table 14.1):

Table 14.1

Characteristics of self-actualizers (based on Maslow, 1968).

Self-actualizing people . . .

are *efficient* and accurate *in perceiving* reality

are *accepting* of themselves, of other people, and of nature

are *spontaneous* in thought and emotion, natural rather than artificial

are *problem–centered*, concerned with eternal philosophical questions

are *independent* and *autonomous* when it comes to satisfactions

have a continued *freshness of appreciation* of ordinary events

often experience "*oceanic feelings*," a sense of oneness with nature that transcends time and space

identify with all of *humanity*, are democratic and respectful of others

form *deep ties*, but *with only a few persons*

appreciate, for its own sake, the *process* of doing things

have a *philosophical*, thoughtful, nonhostile *sense of humor*

have a childlike and fresh *creativity and inventiveness*

maintain an inner *detachment from* the *culture* in which they live

are sufficiently *strong*, independent, and guided by their own inner visions that they sometimes
      appear *temperamental* and even *ruthless*

self-actualizers are *efficient* in their perception of reality. That is, their experience is in extra-sharp focus. Self-actualizers can spot the confused perceptions of others and cut through tangles. People who frequently engage in self-actualization are also *accepting*. They accept themselves and others. Their self-acceptance isn't smug self-assurance. Self-actualizers realize they're not perfect. They accept themselves *as they are,* imperfections and all. The same is true of their reactions to people around them. The frailties of others are accepted as a part of who they are.

Another characteristic of the self-actualizer is a mental *spontaneity*. This is reflected in a creativity without artificiality. This is often linked to a *freshness of appreciation* of life, an excitement in the process of living. The idea that creativity relates to self-actualization has received support (Amabile, 1985). In this research, writers were led to think about the act of creation either from the view of extrinsic incentives (thus lower on Maslow's hierarchy) or from qualities intrinsic to the act itself (by implication, self-actualization). They then wrote a poem. Judges later rated the creativity of the poems. Those written after thinking about external incentives were lower in creativity than those written from the self-actualizing orientation.

The self-actualizing person is often said to be *problem-centered*, but this phrase is a little misleading. The word *problem* here refers to enduring questions of philosophy or ethics. Self-actualizers take a wide view, concerning themselves with universal issues. Along with this goes an independence from their own culture and immediate environment. The self-actualizer lives in the universe, and only incidentally in this apartment, city, or country. Frequent self-actualizers (who generally have satisfied relationship needs) know that relationships require effort. They have deep ties, because relationships matter to them, but the ties are often limited to a very few others.

Toward the end of his life, Maslow made a distinction between two kinds of self-actualizers (Maslow, 1971). One of them we've already described. Maslow called the others **transcendent self-actualizers.** These people are so invested in experiences of self-actualization that it becomes the most precious aspect of their life. They are more consciously motivated by universal values or goals outside themselves (such as beauty, truth, and unity). They're more holistic about the world, seeing the integration of all its elements. There's a greater transcendence of the self, so that self-actualization almost becomes "universe-actualization." All of experience seems sacred to them. They see themselves as instruments by which capabilities are expressed, rather than the owners of those capabilities. From this characterization comes the term *transpersonal* (beyond the person), which is sometimes used to refer to this way of viewing human potential (see also Box 14.4).

BOX 14.4

SELF-ACTUALIZATION AND *YOUR* LIFE

By now you've read a lot about the concept of self-actualization, and it may all sound pretty abstract. To get a more concrete feel for the idea, try spending a few minutes thinking about how it applies to your own life.

For example, think about how Maslow's hierarchy of needs pertains to your current existence. Which level of the hierarchy dominates your day-to-day experiences? Are you mostly concerned with having or maintaining a sense of belonging to a social group (or perhaps feeling a sense of acceptance and closeness with a particular person)? Is the need to feel valued and respected what you're currently focused on? Or are you engaged in trying to grow as close as possible to the blueprint hidden inside you holding the secret of your possibilities?

Now think back to your junior year of high school and what your life was like back then. What were your needs and concerns during that period? Since then has your focus moved upward on the hierarchy, or downward, or are you focused at about the same level?

Here's another question: think about your current "mission" in life, the goal that gives your life focus and provides it meaning. Where did it come from? Did it get passed down to you by your parents (or someone else)? Or does it come from deep inside you? How *sure* are you that your goal is your own and not someone else's assignment for you, a condition of worth? How sure are you it isn't an assignment you've given *yourself*? What would it feel like to spend the rest of your life doing assignments?

Another question: You can't always do what you want. Everyone knows that. Sometimes you have to do things you *have* to do. But how much of the time? How much of your time—how much of your *self*—should be used up doing your duty, being obedient to conditions of worth, before you turn to your other needs? How dangerous is it to say to yourself that you'll do these assignments—these duties—for a while, just for a little while, and that after a few weeks or months or years you'll turn to the things you really want? How sure are you that you won't get in a rut and come to see the assignments as the only reality in life? How sure are you that you'll be able to make the decision to turn to your own self-actualization, years down the road, when it's become such a habit to focus on fulfilling conditions of worth?

Not every experience in life is self-actualizing. Even people who self-actualize extensively sometimes get stalled and have trouble with it. When *you* find yourself unable to self-actualize, what's preventing it? What barriers to growth do you confront from time to time? Are they the demands of other needs? Do they stem from your relationships with your parents and family? With your friends? Are they barriers you place in front of yourself?

Obviously, these questions aren't easy to answer. You can't expect to answer them in just a few minutes. People spend lifetimes trying to answer them. But these questions are important, and thinking about them for a little while should give you a more vivid sense of the issues the phenomenological approach raises.

Peak experiences occur when a person is deeply engaged in a demanding activity and fully caught up in the moment. Imagine how this football player feels while scoring this touchdown.

The Peak Experience

In trying to describe the process of self-actualization, Maslow also focused on moments in which self-actualization was clearly occurring. Remember, not every act involves self-actualization, even for a person who self-actualizes a great deal. Maslow used the term **peak experience** to refer to moments of intense self-actualization.

In peak experiences, people have a sense of being connected with the elements of their surroundings. Colors and sounds seem crisper. There's a sharper clarity in perceptions (see Privette & Landsman, 1983). There's also a loss of the sense of time as the experience flows by. The feelings associated with the peak experience are often those of awe, wonder, or even ecstasy. The peak experience is something that tends to take you outside yourself. You aren't thinking about yourself but rather are experiencing whatever you're experiencing as fully as possible.

Peak experiences *can* occur in a passive way (for instance, in examining a great work of art). Usually, though, they occur when people are engaged in action of some kind (Czikszentmihalyi, 1975; Privette & Landsman, 1983). Indeed, there's evidence that they happen more during work than during leisure (Czikszentmihalyi & LeFevre, 1989). The person having a peak experience is so immersed in an activity that the activity seems to "become" the person. The term **flow** is also used for such experiences (Czikszentmihalyi, 1990; Czikszentmihalyi & Czikszentmihalyi, 1988).

We should reemphasize that it's not necessary that the activity involve artistic creation or any such thing. What's important isn't *what*'s being done, but rather how it takes place. If you're completely immersed in it, if it's stretching you as a human being, it can be a peak experience.

Existential Psychology: Being and Death

Thus far we've focused on several themes of the humanistic perspective. These include the idea that people have a natural tendency toward growth, that people can exert free will to change the course of their lives, that people defend against perceptions of incongruence and try to prevent them from arising, and that the motive to grow is at the summit of a hierarchy of motives.

However, there's another side to talk of growth and human potential: the possibilities of self-actualization have a cost. They bring responsibilities. This is a message of another group of phenomenological psychologists called **existential psychologists.** The term *existential* is related to the word *existence*. It's tied to a philosophical view that stresses the idea that existence is all anyone has. Each person is alone in an unfathomable universe. This view stresses the idea that each person must take responsibility for his or her choices in life. In emphasizing the importance of the individual's personal experience of reality, this view fits the phenomenological orientation.

The Existential Dilemma

A concept that's central to the existentialist view is **dasein.** This German word is often translated as "being-in-the-world." This phrase is used to imply the totality of a person's experience of the self as an autonomous, separate, and evolving entity (Binswanger, 1963; Boss, 1963; May, 1958). The term *dasein* also emphasizes that humans have no existence apart from the world and that the world has no meaning apart from the people in it.

To the existentialists, the basic issue in life is that life inevitably ends in death, which can come at any time (Becker, 1973). Death is the one event no one escapes, no matter how self-actualizing your experiences are. Awareness of the inevitability of death provokes *angst*—dread, anguish far deeper than the anxiety experienced over incongruity. There exist only being and not-being, and we constantly face the polarity between them.

How should you respond to this realization? To the existentialists, this is the key question in life. The choice is to retreat into nothingness or have the courage to *be.* At its extreme, the choice is whether or not to commit suicide, thus avoiding the absurdity of a life that will end in death anyway. But nothingness can also be chosen in less extreme ways. People can choose not to act authentically, not to commit themselves to the responsibilities and goals that are part of who they are. They can drift, go along with one or another crowd. When people fail to take responsibility for their lives, they're choosing nothingness.

What's involved in the choice to be? To the existentialists, life has no meaning unless you create it. Each person with the courage to do so must assign meaning to his or her existence. You assign meaning to your life by acting authentically, by being who you are. The very recognition of the existential dilemma is an important step to doing this. As May (1958, p. 47) put it, "To grasp what it means to exist, one needs to grasp the fact that he might not exist."

Exercising this freedom isn't easy. It can be hard to find the way to knowing who you are, and it can be hard to stare death in the face. It's often easier to let other people decide what's right and proper, and just go along. Existential psychologists believe, though, that all persons have the responsibility for making the most of every moment of their existence and fulfilling that existence to the best of their ability (Boss, 1963; see also Frankl, 1969; May, 1969). This responsibility is inescapable, and it's not to be taken lightly.

Although people are responsible for their choices, even honest choices won't always be good ones. You won't always deal perfectly with people you care about. You'll sometimes lose track of your connection to nature. Even if your choices are wise, you'll still have **existential guilt,** over failing to fulfill your possibilities. This guilt is strongest when a person who's free to choose fails to choose. But a person who's aware is never completely free of existential guilt, because it's impossible to fulfill every possibility. In realizing some of your capabilities, you prevent other ones from being expressed. Thus, existential guilt is inescapable. It's part of the cost of being.

Emptiness

The existentialists also focus on the problem of emptiness in life. They are concerned that people have lost faith in values (May, 1953). Many no longer have a sense of worth and dignity. This is partly because they've found themselves powerless to influence forces such as government and big business. The planet warms and we do nothing to stop it. Our banks and businesses need multibillion dollar bail-outs, and we're stuck with the bill. The leaders of our country commit us to wars without justifying them, or even declaring them as wars, and we must bear the consequences.

Existentialists point out that when people lose their commitment to a set of values, they experience a sense of emptiness and meaninglessness. When people feel this way, they turn to others for answers. The answers aren't there, however, because the problem is really within the person. This illustrates once again the existentialist theme that you must be responsible for your own actions and that truth can come only from within and from your actions.

Terror Management

Some of the ideas of existential psychology are reflected in terror management theory (Greenberg, Pyszczynski, & Solomon, 1986). This theory begins with the idea that an awareness of one's eventual death creates existential angst, or terror (Becker, 1973). People respond to the terror by trying to live lives of meaning and value. This much matches what we've already said about existential psychology.

Terror management theory goes on to suggest, however, that most people don't define the meaning of life on their own. Rather, they use a process of social and cultural consensus. This means that group identity plays an important role in how people confirm the value of their lives. Reminders of mortality lead people to be more protective of their own cultural values (Greenberg, Solomon, & Pyszczynski, 1997). By weaving themselves tightly into a meaningful cultural fabric, a fabric that will last long after they're gone, they affirm their own value as human beings.

This theory has led to a great deal of research over the past two decades (summarized by Greenberg et al., 1997). Some of these studies have shown that making mortality salient causes people to become more favorable toward those who uphold their worldview and more negative toward those who don't. Mortality salience also makes people adhere more to cultural norms themselves. Americans become more patriotic, jihadists become more devoted to their cause (Pyszczynski, Solomon, & Greenberg, 2002). Mortality salience can make people act more altruistically—supporting charities (Jonas, Schimel, Greenberg, & Pyszczynski, 2002)—but only if the charities connect to their own culture.

Mortality salience doesn't always cause support for one's own group. It does if the group is viewed in a positive way. But what happens if there's a reason to be concerned about the group's adequacy? In that case, mortality salience may instead cause people to disidentify with, and even derogate, their own group (Arndt, Greenberg, Schimel, Pyszczynski, & Solomon, 2002).

Most research in this area examines how people affirm cultural worldviews after being reminded of their mortality. However, at least one study has looked at how

People respond to reminders of mortality by holding more closely to their social fabric.

people affirm values of the self (McGregor, Zanna, Holmes, & Spencer, 2001, Study 4). After a mortality salience manipulation, participants completed a measure of identity seeking and an assessment of their goals for the immediate future. Those whose mortality had been brought to mind stood higher on the measure of identity seeking than others. They also reported intending to work at projects that were more self-consistent than were the projects reported by others.

Terror management theory leads to a number of other interesting ideas. One of them is that viewing ourselves as separate from other animals also reflects terror management. To think of yourself as an animal is to be reminded of your death, because all animals die. Consistent with this idea, making mortality salient causes people to have more disgust in response to animals, and to favor more strongly the position that humans are distinct from other animals (Goldenberg, Pyszczynski, Greenberg, Solomon, Kluck, & Cornwell, 2001).

This view also has implications for sexuality (Goldenberg, Pyszczynski, Greenberg, & Solomon, 2000). Sex is one more reminder of your animal nature. That may be one reason many people are nervous about sex, because it reminds them of their mortality. People sidestep this reminder in many ways. They ascribe aesthetic value to the sex act. They create romance around it, to distract themselves from its animal qualities (Florian, Mikulincer, & Hirschberger, 2002). They create cultural standards of beauty that are idealized and symbolic. In doing so, the animal is transformed to the spiritual.

As we said, this theory has prompted a great deal of research, extending in many directions. For present purposes, however, let's link it back to the existentialist view. The research makes it clear that reminding people of their eventual death makes them try to affirm the value of their lives. People do this mostly by embracing the values of the culture in which they live. Only a little evidence indicates that people try to create their own personal meanings. Does this mean that for most people the response to existential angst is to "let other people decide what's right, and just go along"? Surely this would dismay the existential psychologists. It may simply mean, though, that values are naturally defined more consensually than the earlier existentialists realized.

Assessment

A basic issue in personality assessment is how to go about it. Various views suggest different approaches to the process. This view suggests yet another one.

Interviews in Assessment

Phenomenological psychologists are less tied than other psychologists to the structure of specific measuring instruments. To them, assessment isn't a process of having a person respond to a set of stimuli. It's a process of finding out *what the person is like*. Given this view, they are very much at home with interviews as an assessment technique. The interview offers maximum flexibility. It lets the person being assessed say whatever comes up. It lets the interviewer follow stray thoughts and ask questions that might not otherwise occur. It lets the interviewer get a subjective sense, from *interacting* with the other person, of what that person is like.

Finding out what a person is like in this way requires empathy. After all, the interviewer is trying to enter the other person's private world. Empathy isn't automatic. It requires sensitivity to small changes. You must repeatedly check the accuracy of your sensing, to make sure you haven't taken a wrong turn. (Empathy isn't important just for interviewing, by the way. In Rogers's view, it's important to doing therapy, and it's part of being a fully functioning person.)

An extensive interview produces a lot of information, which can be treated by **content analysis.** This involves grouping the person's statements in some way and seeing how many statements fall into each group. For example, in an interview Susan said two things about herself expressing self-approval, eighteen expressing self-disapproval, and fifteen that were ambivalent. One might infer from this that Susan isn't very satisfied with herself.

This tactic can also be used to assess progress in therapy. For example, in a second interview after three months of therapy, Susan made five statements that expressed approval of herself, five that expressed disapproval, and eight that were ambivalent. One implication might be that Susan is now less negative about herself than before.

The flexibility that makes interviews useful also creates problems. Unless an interview is highly structured, it's hard to compare one with another. If Jane expresses more self-disapproval than Sally, is it because Jane dislikes herself more than Sally? Or did the interviewer just happen to follow up a particularly bothersome aspect of Jane's self-image? If Susan expresses less self-disapproval after therapy than before, is it because she's more satisfied with herself afterward, or because the interviewer failed to get into self-critical areas in the second interview?

It's also clear that what a person says in an interview can differ widely as a function of other variables. For example, people are more self-disclosing if the interviewer has good rapport with them (Jourard, 1974). In fact, small differences in an interviewer's verbal behavior can produce large differences in what people say (Matarazzo & Wiens, 1972). Thus, many see the interview as primarily a tool for getting informal impressions rather than for full assessment.

Measuring the Self-Concept by Q-Sort

The other core issue in assessment is what qualities to assess. The theorists discussed in this chapter suggest several answers. One answer is that the self-concept is a very

Table 14.2

Statements commonly used in Q-sort procedures.

I am intelligent.	I am ambitious.
I often feel guilty.	I am an impulsive person.
I am optimistic.	I get anxious easily.
I express my emotions freely.	I make strong demands on myself.
I understand myself.	I get along easily with others.
I am lazy.	I often feel driven.
I am generally happy.	I am self-reliant.
I am moody.	I am responsible for my troubles.

important aspect of personality. Accordingly, one focus for assessment is how people view themselves.

A technique Rogers preferred for assessing self-concept is called the **Q-sort** (e.g., Block, 1961; Rogers & Dymond, 1954). There are many variations on this procedure, but the basic process is the same. It always involves giving the person a large set of items, printed on cards. The items often are self-evaluative statements as in Table 14.2, but they can be phrases, words, or other things. The person doing the Q-sort is asked to sort the cards into piles (Figure 14.3). At one end are piles with statements that are *most like you,* at the other end are piles with statements that are *least like you,* and piles in-between represent gradations between the extremes.

There are rules about how many statements can go in a given pile (Figure 14.3). Usually people start by sorting very generally (like me, not like me, neither) and then sorting further. By the time you're done, you've had to look hard at the statements and decide which one or two are *really* like you, and which ones are less so. The technique thus forces you to decide what you're like, by comparing qualities to each other. The Q-sort differs in this way from rating scales in which each response is separate. The latter scales allow you to say that all the descriptors apply equally well. This can't possibly happen in a Q-sort.

In the most basic Q-sort, you sort the statements according to how you think you *actually are.* Q-sorts can also be used, though, to get more complex information. Sometimes people sort the statements again according to what they were like earlier

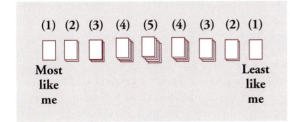

Most like me ... Least like me

(1) (2) (3) (4) (5) (4) (3) (2) (1)

Figure 14.3

In the Q-sort procedure, you sort a set of items (printed on cards) into a row of piles. At one end of the row is the single item that's most like you; at the other end is the single item that's least like you. The other piles represent gradations between these two points. As you can see from the numbers in parentheses, the piles toward the middle are permitted to have more cards in them than the piles closer to the end points. Thus, you're forced to decide which items really are very much like and unlike yourself.

in their lives. It's then possible to look at how well the two match. Differences between the two reflect changes in the self-concept over time. It's also possible to sort for the ideal self (the kind of person you want to be). Then you can look to see how much difference or similarity there is between the ideal and the actual. Similarity here reflects *congruence,* the closeness between your ideal self and your perceived self.

Measuring Self-Actualization

A second content for personality assessment is suggested by the emphasis placed on the tendency toward self-actualization. Given this emphasis, it would seem desirable to measure the degree to which people have characteristics of frequent self-actualization.

The Personal Orientation Inventory (POI) was developed for this purpose (Shostrom, 1964, 1974; see also Knapp, 1976). The POI consists of paired statements. People choose the one from each pair they agree with more. The POI has two major scales. One is called *time competence.* It reflects in part the degree to which the person lives in the present, as opposed to being distracted by past and future. As the word *competence* hints, though, it also has a more complex meaning. Time-competent people are able to tie the past and future with the present effectively. They sense continuity among these three aspects of time.

The second scale assesses a tendency to be *inner-directed* in the search for values and meaning. Self-actualizers are believed to have a stronger tendency toward inner direction in determining their values than people who are less self-actualizing. It's been found that scores on the POI improve after group therapy (Dosamantes-Alperson & Merrill, 1980).

Jones and Crandall (1986) developed another measure of self-actualization. Their scale has four factors, reflecting self-direction, self-acceptance, acceptance of emotions, and trust and responsibility in interpersonal relations. As with the POI, there's evidence that scores on this scale change after group therapy (Crandall, McCown, & Robb, 1988).

Measuring Autonomy and Control

Yet another quality that's important to the viewpoints presented in this chapter is the extent to which a person's actions tend to be autonomous versus controlled. A number of self-report measures exist to assess this difference among people. One measure assesses the extent to which people generally tend to function in a self-determined way in their lives (Sheldon, Ryan, & Reis, 1996). This measure of general self-determination can give a broad sense of the person's behavior across multiple domains. It's been used, for example, to show that people high in general self-determination have harmony between their needs and goals (e.g., Thrash & Elliot, 2002).

Several other measures focus on how people behave in some specific domain of life. For example, Ryan and Connell (1989) developed a measure of children's academic behavior and prosocial behavior. The items ask children why they do various things, and provide potential reasons that had been chosen to reflect controlled or autonomous motivation. In another project, Black and Deci (2000) developed a measure to ask college students their reasons for learning things in their courses. Again, options are provided for reasons that are controlled and reasons that are autonomous. Another such measure was devised to assess the motives underlying religious behavior (Ryan, Rigby, & King, 1993).

Problems in Behavior, and Behavior Change

How are problems in living and the process of behavior change conceptualized in this view? Recall that fully functioning people are attuned to the actualizing tendency, and are experiencing a sense of coherence and consistency. They're not trying to live up to conditions of worth. They're being who they are. To Rogers (and others), lack of congruity within the self results in psychological problems (for supporting evidence of various kinds see Deci & Ryan, 1991; Higgins, 1987, 1990; Ryan, Sheldon, Kasser, & Deci, 1996).

To Rogers, incongruity (between experience and self-concept, or within the self-concept) is experienced as anxiety (though see Box 14.5 for a more complex view).

BOX 14.5

SELF DISCREPANCIES AND EMOTIONS

Rogers believed that incongruity of any sort results in anxiety. This belief is challenged by work done by Tory Higgins (1987) and his colleagues. They say the situation is more complicated. Higgins says that three self-aspects need to be taken into account, not just two: the *actual,* the *ideal,* and the *ought* self. To Higgins, the ideal self is what you wish for yourself, the self to which you aspire. The ought self is defined by duty or obligation. An ought is something you feel compelled to be rather than desire to be. An ought sounds very much like a condition of worth. Higgins refers to the ideal and the ought as **self guides,** because they serve as comparison points for the actual self and as guides for behavior.

Higgins assumes, as did Rogers, that incongruities between these self guides and the actual self produce negative feelings. Unlike Rogers, however, Higgins distinguishes between two feelings, which come from two different kinds of incongruities. Specifically, Higgins holds that discrepancies between actual and *ideal* self cause feelings of depression and dejection. Discrepancies between actual and *ought* self cause feelings of anxiety.

Higgins and his colleagues have done several studies to investigate predictions made by this theory. The studies have consistently supported his reasoning (e.g., Higgins, Bond, Klein, & Strauman, 1986; Strauman, 1989; Strauman & Higgins, 1987). In most studies, self-concepts are assessed by having people list ten attributes they think contribute to their actual selves, then ten they think contribute to their ideal selves, and finally ten they think contribute to their ought selves. The extent of discrepancy between actual and ideal is computed by seeing how many matches there are on the two lists and how many opposites there are. A similar procedure is used to assess discrepancy between actual and ought. Either in the same session or at another time, subjects also report their moods, including feelings of depression and feelings of anxiety.

The usual finding is that the extent of actual–ideal discrepancy is uniquely related to depression but not anxiety. Extent of actual–ought discrepancy is uniquely related to anxiety but not depression. These results are especially impressive in light of the fact that depression and anxiety tend to occur together. In fact, many psychologists have viewed them as different facets of the same thing. Being able to distinguish between them is no small feat.

It's also of interest that the ought self seems to be linked conceptually to the notion of conditions of worth. That is, an ought is an obligation, a duty. The ideal self, in contrast, isn't tied to conditions of worth. This body of research, then, suggests a variation on the position taken by Rogers. Incongruities that derive from failures to meet *conditions of worth* lead to anxiety. Incongruities that derive from a failure to self-actualize are reflected in dejection.

Anxiety is a signal from the organismic valuing process that the holistic self is disorganized. Although we have ways to protect the self from such threats (discussed earlier in the chapter), anxiety can intrude. This is especially likely if the person focuses too much on conditions of worth and acts in ways that interfere with self-actualization. If incongruities become large, the person will act in ways that are labeled *neurotic*. If the disorganization is extreme enough, the person may be labeled *psychotic*.

When the holistic self is threatened by uncertainty, the person becomes not just more distressed, but more rigid (McGregor et al., 2001). This seems to be an effort to hold onto the self that existed before. People faced by an incongruity in one self-aspect stress their certainty about other things, apparently trying to compensate for what's threatened. They become more zealous or extreme in their beliefs and personal values. In fact, McGregor et al. (2001) have suggested that this is what happens in the terror management responses discussed earlier in the chapter.

The process of therapy, to Rogers, is essentially the process of reintegrating a partially disorganized self. In part, this involves reversing the processes of defense, to confront the discrepancies between the elements of the person's experience. Doing so isn't easy, however. Rogers believed that an important condition must be met before such changes can occur.

Specifically, the conditions of worth that distorted the person's behavior in the past must be taken away. The person still needs positive regard. But it must be *unconditional.* Only then will the person feel able to confront the discrepancies. Removing the conditions of worth will allow the person to focus more fully on the organismic valuing process, the quiet inner voice that knows what's good and what's bad for you. This in turn allows a reintegration of the self. Consistent with this is evidence that being accepted for who they are makes people less defensive than being accepted in an evaluative, conditional way (Arndt, Schimel, Greenberg, & Pyszczynski, 2002; Schimel, Arndt, Pyszczynski, & Greenberg, 2001).

Unconditional positive regard, then, is a key to therapy. But it's a complex key. For unconditional regard to be effective, it must be given *from the person's own frame of reference.* That is, acceptance from someone who knows nothing about you or your feelings is hardly acceptance at all. This is a second reason why it's important for a therapist to be empathic. The first was that empathy is necessary to get an adequate sense of what the client is like. The second is that it's necessary if the therapist is to show unconditional positive regard for the client in a way that will facilitate reintegration of the client's personality.

There's one more potential problem here. Sometimes people undertake therapy to *satisfy* someone's conditions of worth for them. It stands to reason that people who are trying to make changes for autonomous reasons will do better than people trying to make similar changes to satisfy conditions of worth. In at least one domain of change—weight loss—there's evidence that this is so. Those losing weight for autonomous reasons lost more and kept it off longer than those doing it for less autonomous reasons (Williams, Grow, Freedman, Ryan, & Deci, 1996).

Client-Centered Therapy

There are several humanistic approaches to therapy (Cain & Seeman, 2002). The one that's best known, developed by Rogers (1951, 1961; Rogers & Stevens, 1967), is called **client-centered therapy,** or person-centered therapy. As the phrase implies, the client takes responsibility for his or her own improvement. Recall that Rogers assumed people have an intrinsic tendency toward actualizing. If people with problems can be put in a situation in which distractions and conditions of worth are removed, they should reintegrate themselves through this natural tendency. This is much like the rationale for putting a bandage on a wound. The bandage doesn't heal you, but by maintaining a sterile environment, it helps the natural healing process to take place.

In person-centered therapy, the therapist displays empathy and unconditional positive regard. This lets the client escape temporarily from conditions of worth and begin exploring aspects of experience that are incongruent with the self. Throughout, the therapist remains nondirective and nonevaluative, showing no emotion and giving no advice. The therapist's role is to *remove* the pressure of conditions of worth. By avoiding evaluative comments (e.g., saying that something is good or bad), the effective therapist avoids imposing additional conditions of worth.

Rather than being evaluative, the therapist tries to help clients gain a clear perspective on their own feelings and experiences. In general, this means reflecting back to the client, in slightly different ways, things the client is saying, so the client can reexamine them from a different angle. There are two variations on this procedure.

The first is called **clarification of feelings.** Part of what the client does in the therapy session is emotional, expressing feelings about things, either directly in words or indirectly in other ways. As feelings are expressed, the therapist repeats those expressions in different words. The purpose here is to make clients more aware of what their true feelings are. Simply being reminded of the feelings can help this to happen.

The usefulness of this technique should come as no surprise. Feelings are often fleeting. When people express feelings in their words or actions, they often fail to notice them. Moments later they may be unaware of having had them. If the feelings are threatening, people actively defend against recognizing them. The process of reflecting feelings back to the client allows the nature and the intensity of the feelings to become more obvious to the client. This puts the client into closer touch with the experience.

The second kind of reflection in person-centered therapy is more intellectual and less emotional. It's called **restatement of content.** This procedure is equivalent to what we just described, but it operates in terms of the *ideas* contained in the client's statements, the cognitive content of what the client says.

Is client-centered therapy effective? It can be (Smith & Glass, 1977). Studies of this technique focus primarily on changes in self-image, and there's evidence that people do change their pictures of themselves after client-centered therapy, so that their perceived self becomes more congruent with their ideals (e.g., Butler & Haigh, 1954; Truax & Mitchell, 1971).

Beyond Therapy, to Personal Growth

To humanistic psychologists, therapy isn't a special process of fixing something that's wrong and then forgetting about it. Rather, it's on a continuum with other life experiences. In this view, a person who's living life to the fullest should always engage in more or less the same processes as occur in therapy. These processes provide a way for people who have average lives—or even very good lives—to further enrich their experiences and to self-actualize even more completely.

Rogers's view of the ideal way of life is captured in the phrase *fully functioning person.* He believed that personal growth throughout life should be a goal for everyone. Growth requires the same conditions as those needed for effective therapy. Growth requires that people with whom you interact be genuine and open, with no holding back and no false fronts. It requires empathic understanding, together with unconditional positive regard. This view on growth is similar to Maslow's view on self-actualization: growth isn't a goal that's reached once and cast aside. It's a way of living, to be pursued throughout your lifetime.

Humanistic Theories: Problems and Prospects

The humanistic view is regarded by many as an intuitively "accessible" approach to personality. The intuitive appeal of this view derives partly from its emphasis on the uniqueness and validity of each person's experience. Indeed, this view treats each person's subjective experience as being of primary importance. This emphasis on personal experience fits well with what many people bring to mind when they think of the word *personality*, especially when they think of their *own* personality. For this reason this viewpoint feels comfortable and commonsensical to many people.

This viewpoint also has at least two other virtues. First, it takes a generally optimistic and positive view of human nature. Humanistic psychologists such as Rogers, Maslow, Deci, and Ryan have argued strenuously that people are intrinsically good—are naturally motivated to be the best they can be. According to this view, that motive will be expressed in everyone, as long as other circumstances don't interfere too much.

This optimistic outlook on humanity is also reflected in a "practical" virtue of the humanistic view. It has emphasized the importance of fully experiencing and appreciating your own reality and of maintaining close contact with your feelings. This emphasis provides a strategy for living that many people have used to enrich their lives. The benefits sometimes have come through formal therapy experiences. But remember that many phenomenologists assume there's no real distinction between therapy and the more ordinary "course corrections" that are part of normal living. Thus, the move toward personal enrichment has come for many people in informal ways. It's been sort of a self-guided exploration of how to make one's life better.

Although humanistic psychology certainly has virtues, it has problems as well. One problem historically has been a lack of precision. It's sometimes been hard to generate easily tested research hypotheses from the theories. For example, consider self-actualization. To study self-actualization, you need to know the areas of life to which the actualizing tendency is relevant for each person you're studying. Remember that actualization occurs in different ways within different people. In theory, it might be necessary to study as many types of behavior as there are people being studied. This makes it hard to evaluate any observations you make.

This difficulty is a serious one, and it should not be minimized or taken lightly. On the other hand, more recent psychologists have taken many steps to overcome it. Deci and Ryan and their coworkers, who share many orienting assumptions with earlier humanists, have devised hypotheses that can be tested very straightforwardly. This is apparently because these people have a somewhat narrower focus than did people such as Rogers and Maslow. Findings from research on topics such as self-determination provide powerful support for many assumptions of the humanistic viewpoint.

A second set of criticisms of humanistic psychology aims at a quality we just described as a virtue: its optimistic, positive view of human nature. This view is sometimes criticized as arbitrary, naïve, sentimental, and romantic. Some believe it has no basis other than the theorists' conviction that people are inherently good. And not everyone believes that all people are inherently good (Baumeister & Campbell, 1999).

The assumption that there's a self-actualizing tendency is also criticized as being arbitrary. Some say that if this assumption were carried to its extreme, it would require that each person be permitted—indeed, be encouraged—to live life to the fullest, regardless of the consequences for anyone else. The result of such unrestrained self-expression would be chaos. Such a way of life would create serious conflict whenever one person's self-actualization somehow interfered with someone else's self-actualization, which certainly would happen.

It's also worth noting that the optimistic overtones that permeate so much of humanistic psychology are largely missing from the writings of the existentialists. Whereas humanists such as Rogers and Maslow emphasized the fulfilling quality that can come from making your own way in the world, the existentialists emphasize that doing this is hard and can be very painful. Living honestly means confronting harsh realities and absurdities and rising above them. This picture is very different from the one painted by Rogers and Maslow. It can be difficult to reconcile the warm and glowing optimism of the one view with the angst of the other.

Another point of contention about this view on personality concerns the concept of free will (Carver & Scheier, 2000). Humanists tend to assume that people can decide for themselves what to do at any point in their lives. Others regard this conception of free will as a convenient fiction, an illusion that is misleading at best. Surely people act as though they *think* they have free will. But how to demonstrate the *existence* of free will has never been an easy problem to solve. Indeed, there's now evidence for the position that the perception of will is illusory (Bargh & Ferguson, 2000; Wegner, 2002).

What, then, are the prospects for this approach to personality? Although many questions remain to be answered, the future of this way of thinking seems substantially brighter than it did two decades ago. Several areas of vigorous and enthusiastic research activity have opened up seams of knowledge bearing on assumptions made years earlier by pioneers of humanism. Work on topics such as self-determination continues to be very active, as does work on various self-discrepancies and the associated emotional reactions. The development and exploration of these sorts of ideas is a source of considerable encouragement for the future prospects of this approach.

SUMMARY

The theorists of this chapter emphasize that people have an intrinsic tendency toward self-actualization. Self-actualization is the tendency to develop your capabilities in ways that maintain or enhance the self. This tendency promotes a sense of congruence, or integration, within the person. Its effectiveness is monitored by the organismic valuing process.

People also have a need for positive regard, acceptance and affection from others. Positive regard may be unconditional, or it may be conditional on your acting in certain ways. These conditions of worth mean that the person is held "worthy" only if he or she is acting in the desired manner. Conditions of worth, which can be self-imposed as well as imposed by others, can cause you to act in ways that oppose self-actualization.

Self-determination theory focuses on the difference between behavior that's self-determined and behavior that's controlled in some fashion. People enjoy activities more if they feel they're doing them from intrinsic interest instead of extrinsic reward. People whose lives are dominated by activities that are controlled are less healthy than people whose lives are self-determined.

Many theorists of this group assume that people have free will. This is a very hard idea to test, but people do seem to think they have free will. Studies of reactance show that people resist threats to freedoms they expect to have. Other research questions whether will is illusory, though.

Behavior that opposes the actualizing tendency creates disorganization in the sense of self. Disorganization can be reduced by two kinds of defenses. You can distort perceptions of reality to reduce the threat, or you can act in ways that prevent threatening experiences from reaching awareness, for example, by ignoring them. Use of these defenses is seen in the fact that people blame failures on factors outside themselves while taking credit for successes. People also engage in self-handicapping strategies, creating esteem-protective explanations for the possibility of failure before it even happens. Use of self-handicapping is paradoxical because it increases the likelihood of failure.

Maslow elaborated on the idea of self-actualization by proposing a hierarchy of motives, ranging from physical needs (most basic) to self-actualization (at the top). Basic needs are more demanding than higher needs, which (being more subtle) can affect you only when the lower needs are relatively satisfied. Maslow's intermediate levels appear to relate to the need for positive regard, suggesting why it can be hard to ignore the desire for acceptance from others.

Existential psychologists point out that with freedom comes the responsibility to choose for yourself what meaning your life has. The basic choice is to invest your life with meaning or to retreat into nothingness. When people are reminded of their own mortality, they try harder to connect to cultural values. Even if you try to find meaning, you can't escape existential guilt. No life can reflect all the possibilities it holds, because each choice rules out other possibilities.

This view on personality uses many assessment techniques, including both interviews and self-reports. Regarding content, it emphasizes the self-concept, self-actualization, and self-determination. One way to assess self-concept is the Q-sort, in which a set of items is sorted into piles according to how much they apply to oneself. Different "sorts" can be compared with each other for additional information.

From this perspective, problems derive from incongruity. Large incongruity is reflected as neurosis; when even more extreme, the result is psychosis. Therapy is a process of reintegrating a partly disorganized self. For reintegration to occur, the client must feel a sense of unconditional positive regard. In client-centered therapy, people are led to refocus on their feelings about their problems. The (nonevaluative) therapist simply helps clients to clarify their feelings. In this viewpoint, the processes of therapy blend into those of ordinary living, with the goal of experiencing continued personal growth.

GLOSSARY

Actualization The tendency to grow in ways that maintain or enhance the organism.

Actual self One's self as one presently views it.

Clarification of feelings The procedure in which a therapist restates a client's expressed feelings.

Client-centered therapy (also called person-centered therapy) A therapy that removes conditions of worth and has clients examine their feelings.

Conditional positive regard Affection that's given only under certain conditions.

Conditional self-regard Self-acceptance that's given only under certain conditions.

Conditions of worth Contingencies placed on positive regard.

Congruence An integration within the self, and a coherence between the self and one's experiences.

Content analysis The grouping and counting of various categories of statements in an interview.

Dasein "Being-in-the-world," the totality of one's autonomous personal existence.

Deficiency-based motive Motive reflecting a lack within the person that needs to be filled.

Existential guilt A sense of guilt over failing to fulfill all of one's possibilities.

Existential psychology The view that people are responsible for investing their lives with meaning.

Flow Experience of being immersed completely in an activity.

Fully functioning person A person who's open to the experiences of life and who's self-actualizing.

Growth-based motives Motives reflecting desires to extend and elaborate yourself.

Humanistic psychology A branch of psychology emphasizing universal capacity for personal growth.

Ideal self The personal values to which one aspires.

Organismic valuing process The internal signal that tells whether self-actualization is occurring.

Peak experience A subjective experience of intense self-actualization.

Positive regard Acceptance and affection.

Q-sort An assessment technique in which descriptors are sorted as applying to oneself or not.

Reactance A motive to regain or reassert a freedom that's been threatened.

Restatement of content A procedure in which a therapist rephrases the ideas expressed by a client.

Self-actualization A process of growing in ways that maintain or enhance the self.

Self-concordance Pursuing goals that are consistent with your core values.

Self-determination Deciding for oneself what to do.

Self guides Qualities of the self one desires to be (ideal) or feels compelled to be (ought).

Self-handicapping The creating of situations that make it hard to succeed, thus enabling avoidance of self-blame for failure.

Transcendent self-actualizers People whose actualization goes beyond the self to become more universal.

Unconditional positive regard Acceptance and affection with "no strings attached."

■ **Personal Constructs and Personality**
Using Constructs
Constructs Are Bipolar
The Role of Recurrences
Range and Focus of Convenience
Elaboration and Change in Construct Systems
Organization among Constructs
Individuality of Constructs
Similarities and Differences between People
Role Taking
Personal Constructs and Behavioral Consistency

■ **Assessment**
Kelly's Role Construct Repertory Test

■ **Problems in Behavior,
and Behavior Change**
Personal Constructs and Psychological Distress
Dealing with Anxiety and Threat
Fixed Role Therapy

■ **Personal Construct Theory:
Problems and Prospects**

SUMMARY

■ Rachel and Jerry are sitting in the lounge taking a break from studying. They're talking about a new movie they've both just seen, and they're disagreeing loudly about how good it was (or wasn't). Rachel thinks the plot was subtly intricate and that there was a delicate tension throughout. Jerry thinks there wasn't any plot at all and that the film could not possibly have moved more slowly. At this point Susan joins them and chimes in with her opinion. She didn't see the nuances of plot that Rachel saw, but she points out that the film had a lot of symbolism. Jerry just shakes his head in wonder.

T he world that surrounds us is the same for everyone. An oak tree growing across the street is the same physical object when *you* look at it as when anyone else looks at it. A building stands there—brick and mortar—and no matter who's inside, or in front of it, or driving by it, its nature doesn't change. Physical reality is, after all, physical reality.

But people's experience of the world isn't based entirely on physical reality. Rachel, Jerry, and Susan saw the same film, but their experience wasn't even remotely the same. The same is potentially true of all experiences. For example, consider again that oak across the street. *You* might look at it and sense a graceful product of nature's mysteries. Someone else may glance at the same tree and see a source of shade on a hot day. Another person sees a nuisance, a tall thing covered with leaves that soon will have to be raked. A fourth person may see a source of hardwood for furniture. The physical reality is the same for all, but the *experience* of it varies widely from person to person.

This is true in experiencing ourselves, the people around us, the actions we engage in, and the events of our lives. Consider John, a college student who works extrahard at his studies, spending weekends in the library instead of partying. John sees his actions as an effort to learn as much as he can, about as many things as he can, while he has the chance. John's father sees his son's actions as an effort to establish a good record, thereby getting a good start toward a high-paying job. To one of John's professors, the pattern is an effort to compensate for feelings of inferiority. Dan, a casual friend, sees a sort of mindless compulsiveness. Susan, an even more casual friend, thinks it's silly to study so much, and she sees John as an incredibly dull person.

How is it that people have such different experiences when exposed to the same realities? Where do these differences in interpretation come from? Some psychologists answer these questions by saying that physical reality isn't the essence of human experience. It's merely the raw material. No one can examine all the raw material available—no one has the time. No one can deal with *just* raw material, either. You have to impose organization on it, create order from the chaos. So each person *samples* the raw material and constructs a personal vision of how reality is organized. These mental representations then provide the basis for future perceptions, interpretations, and actions (Jussim, 1991).

It can be argued that personality consists of the organization of mental structures through which the person views reality (or which the person imposes on reality). This is essentially the position taken by George Kelly, whose ideas are the subject of this chapter (Kelly, 1955; for reviews, see Adams-Webber, 1979; Bannister, 1970, 1985; Bonarius, Holland, & Rosenberg, 1980; Mancuso & Adams-Webber, 1982).

Kelly is discussed as part of the phenomenological perspective, because he emphasized the uniqueness of each person's subjective worldview. As you read about his ideas, you'll see some similarity to themes of Chapter 14, such as the idea that people choose for themselves how to think and act. But in many ways Kelly's ideas also foreshadow a cognitive viewpoint that began to form nearly two decades later (discussed in Chapter 16). It may be useful to think of Kelly's theory as creating a bridge between the phenomenological perspective and a newer perspective that hadn't yet come into being.

Personal Constructs and Personality

Kelly argued that the best way to understand personality is to think of people as scientists. This view was also being promoted at about the same time by Fritz Heider (1958), an early cognitive theorist in social psychology. Just as do scientists, all of us have a need to predict events and to understand things that take place around us. Just as scientists, all of us develop theories about reality.

The need for prediction is basic to life. It shows up in every aspect of behavior. You may not realize it until you think about it, but you're making a prediction about the nature of the world every time you turn on a faucet and expect to see water come out. You test a prediction whenever you do something as simple as turn a doorknob (expecting the door to open) or eat (expecting not to get sick). In truth, it's hard to think of any action that doesn't involve an implicit prediction about how reality is organized. Most of these predictions are made automatically and unconsciously, but they're predictions nonetheless.

Because so much of human life is social, the desire for predictability is especially important in social events. Every time you look at someone's expression and use it as a guide to his or her feelings, you're predicting social reality. Virtually all social encounters—even those as simple as buying something at a store—involve many implicit assumptions and predictions. In order to choose our own actions we need to understand or interpret other people's actions.

Each person responds to this need to predict by constructing a personal view of the world and how it works. This personal view, or theory, is a guide to predicting and interpreting future events. In Kelly's terms, people generate a set of **personal constructs** and then impose those constructs on reality. In his view, people don't experience the world directly. Rather, they know the world through the lens of their constructs. This is the essence of Kelly's "fundamental postulate" of human behavior: that *people's behavior, thoughts, and feelings are determined by the constructs they use to anticipate or predict events.*

Kelly saw constructs as important because he believed all events in life are open to multiple interpretations (see also Box 15.1). Kelly used the term **constructive alternativism** as a label for this idea and for the further assumption that people decide for themselves what constructs to apply to events. Kelly held that people can always alter their experiences, even looking back on them, by construing them in different ways.

We should perhaps say something about the meaning of the word *event* before going on. Kelly used this word to refer broadly to virtually anything in a person's experience. We'll use it the same way here. *Event* can refer to objects, people, feelings, experiences, or physical events. We should also say something about the word *construe.* This word refers to mental processes that range from perception to understanding and interpretation. It's a broader word than any of these, encompassing all of them. It's also a more specific word, in the sense that it more strongly implies actively taking a point of view.

BOX 15.1

APPRAISAL AND STRESS

Kelly's assertion that personal constructs determine how people see the world is echoed in a number of other theories. An example is a theory of psychological stress developed by Richard Lazarus, Susan Folkman, and their colleagues (e.g., Lazarus, 1966; Lazarus & Folkman, 1984). You certainly have an intuitive understanding of what the word *stress* means. However, the precise nature of stress has been hard for psychologists to agree on. Lazarus took a very "cognitive" view of it, which fits nicely with many of the ideas discussed in this chapter.

Lazarus argues that the experience of stress involves three processes. The first, **primary appraisal,** is the process of perceiving an impending threat. The next, **secondary appraisal,** is the process of determining what to do (of the many things that might be done) to deal with the threat. The third element, **coping,** is the effort to do whatever's been chosen. It should be obvious that this analysis of stress relies extensively on the concept of appraisal. Appraisal is weighing and evaluating the meaning of the raw material of one's perceptions. The word *appraisal*, in fact, is similar in meaning to the word *construal*.

Lazarus has always emphasized that the two appraisal processes rely heavily on the person's internal representation of reality. As a result, many kinds of "stress" can easily be said to be in the mind of the beholder rather than in the outside world. That is, per-

ceiving a threat (versus no threat) is largely a matter of how people construe the situations they're in. A bustling city street may seem absolutely harmless to one person, may seem enticing to another, but the same street may appear fraught with peril to someone else.

Similarly, how people choose to respond to a threat will depend partly on how they construe various actions. For one person, walking away from a threat means losing face or looking foolish. For another person, the same response means being efficient and not wasting energy. In both cases personal interpretations are crucial determinants of what people experience and how they act in response to a given event.

It's also assumed that people often *reinterpret* the meanings of events, either while they are taking place or afterward. These reappraisals can be induced by changes in the situation or by changes in the constructs the person brings to bear on the situation (e.g., Holmes & Houston, 1974). In some cases, called **defensive reappraisal,** the act of reappraising seems calculated to produce the best possible construal, even if it's unrealistic. In other cases, however, the reappraisal seems to be more a matter of finding an interpretation that fits the event well. This emphasis on people's ability to reorganize their interpretations of stressors is similar to the philosophical orientation that Kelly called *constructive alternativism*.

Using Constructs

Applying a construct to an event is slightly more complex than it might seem at first. The process is similar to the way a scientist uses a theory. That is, when you apply a construct, you hypothesize (implicitly) that it will fit an event. Then you *test* the hypothesis by applying the construct and predicting a consequence. If your prediction is confirmed, the construct applies and you retain it as useful. If your prediction is *dis*confirmed, you may rethink when to apply the construct, you may revise the construct, or you may even abandon it. Constructs that successfully predict events most of the time have a high degree of **predictive efficiency.**

To illustrate, consider Ann's view that some men see women as unique individuals with their own distinct qualities, whereas other men see women as stereotypes. When meeting and first talking with Jim, she construes him as a man who views women as individuals. She's about to test this hypothesis by making the implicit prediction that he'll be interested in her weekend activity, motocross racing. If Jim is interested or impressed, her prediction is confirmed. If he recoils in horror, the prediction is disconfirmed. If so, something about how Ann applies the construct, or something about the construct itself, may require revision.

Kelly's starting point was that people use their constructs to predict and anticipate events. He expanded on this basic idea by making a set of more focused statements, called *corollaries,* about constructs and how they're used. Several of them are discussed in the following sections.

Constructs Are Bipolar

Kelly assumed that constructs are bipolar. That is, a construct consists of a pair of opposing characteristics. Examples are "friendly versus unfriendly" and "stable versus changeable." The pole that you're applying to the event you're construing is the **emergent pole** of the construct. If you view a person as friendly, you're applying your friendliness construct, with "friendly" as the emergent pole.

The end of the construct that's *not* being actively applied to the event is the **implicit pole.** The implicit pole is just as important as the emergent pole in defining the construct's nature. It's meaningless to think of someone as friendly unless you have an implicit recognition that it's possible for people to be *un*friendly. Thus, both ends are involved in the mere existence of the construct, even though it's easy to lose track of that when you're using the construct.

Kelly believed that constructs are dichotomous as well as bipolar. That is, he believed that people use constructs in a yes-or-no manner, not as varying on a continuum. Kelly admitted that people see gradations, but he had a way to deal with that (Kelly, 1955). He assumed gradations arise from an array of interrelated dichotomous constructs. The array makes finer and finer distinctions, as one dichotomous decision leads to another one, at a lower level (Figure 15.1).

For example, consider the construct "long versus short." You can use it as a dichotomy, then repeat the process over and over again. It's as though you decide how long something is in a quick series of steps. First you decide if it's basically long or short. Assume you decided it's long. That throws out half the scale (the right half of Figure 15.1). Then you decide whether it's long or not among the generally long. That decision then reduces the range by half again, and you make another decision within whichever part is left. If you do this often enough, the decisions become so fine-grained that the result is equivalent to a continuum.

Figure 15.1

A dichotomous decision, repeated several times across ever-finer units, creates a set of possibilities that duplicates the range of variation along a continuum. The simple set of decisions illustrated here yields sixteen gradations. Given a few more decisions, the result would be indistinguishable from a continuously varying scale.

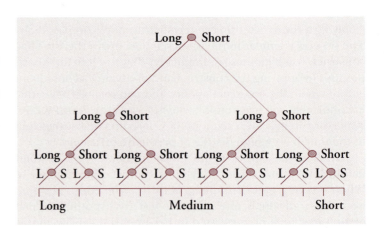

Consistent with Kelly's general view, there's evidence that people tend to polarize their perceptions—particularly social perceptions—seeing the world in black-and-white terms. For example, when people are in different groups, they tend to think of the two groups in terms of "us versus them" (Tajfel & Turner, 1986). In the same way, people who are very committed to a partner in a close relationship tend to polarize their perceptions by devaluing potential alternative partners (Johnson & Rusbult, 1989).

The Role of Recurrences

Constructs reflect qualities that *recur* in the person's experience, that show up repeatedly. It's rare for a construct to emerge on the basis of a single event. Constructs evolve over time and across repeated experiences. Developing a construct from a series of events is complicated by the fact that no two events are exactly alike, even if they're from the same "family" of events. Think, for instance, of filling your car at a gas station. The experience is somewhat the same each time, but it's not identical from one time to another.

The fact that constructs are based on recurring elements makes good sense from the view we began with—that people try to anticipate events according to a personal theory. The kind of theory that's most sensible to invent would be one that's been useful in construing *many* events, not just a few. It follows, then, that constructs should be based on *recurring* themes or qualities.

Range and Focus of Convenience

Although recurrences are important, it's also important to recognize that most constructs won't be useful *everywhere* in your experience. A few can be used widely, for instance, "good versus bad." But most are more limited in scope, and some apply only narrowly. For example, the construct "friendly versus unfriendly" can be applied to fewer events than "good versus bad," "supportive versus not supportive" can be applied to even fewer, and "willing to lend class notes versus unwilling to lend class notes" to still fewer. The set of events for which a construct is useful is called its **range of convenience.** The range of convenience is wide for some constructs, narrow for others.

When people try to apply a construct to events outside its range of convenience, there's usually a loss of predictive efficiency. For example, the range of convenience of the construct "happy versus sad" includes people, some animals, songs, many social events, and possibly such things as skies and flowers. It would be harder to apply the same construct to events such as stones or spaghetti. The result of *trying* to make such an application is likely to be a lack of predictive efficiency. In general, it's not too often that people try to apply a construct to events that fall outside its range of convenience.

A construct's range of convenience isn't permanently fixed, however, because sometimes you *do* apply it outside its range of convenience and it works. The **permeability** of a construct is the degree to which its range of convenience can be spread to include new events. A construct that's permeable allows new types of events to be added into its range of convenience fairly easily. A construct that's impermeable is more rigid and is less likely to let new events be added to its range of convenience.

Another aspect of a construct's applicability is its **focus of convenience:** the events for which the construct is *most* predictive. Focus and range of convenience are related, but they aren't the same. A construct's focus of convenience is some *portion* of its range of convenience.

To illustrate the difference, consider the constructs "sociable versus unsociable" and "polite versus impolite," and situations where you might apply them. If you wanted to guess how many people Jane will talk to at a party, you'd probably be better off using the construct of sociability than politeness. This event falls within the range of convenience of both, but talking to people at a social event is almost the essence of sociability. It's clearly within its focus of convenience. If you were predicting how Jane would reply to a surly store clerk, the sociability construct might work. But you'd probably be better off predicting from politeness. Its focus of convenience is events involving role-based behavior and specific social conventions. Both the party and the interaction with the store clerk are within the *range* of convenience of each construct. But differences in *focus* of convenience make one construct more useful than the other for each type of event.

Elaboration and Change in Construct Systems

As indicated previously, people's constructs evolve across time and experience. Change can come in several ways. If a construct continues to predict events well, it becomes more refined. If it predicts in new and interesting ways, it grows.

Kelly gave names to these two kinds of changes in a construct system. **Definition** occurs during ordinary use of a construct. It involves applying the construct in a familiar way to an event it's very likely to fit. Applying it this way allows it to become more explicit or possibly more refined and precise. For example, people often squeeze avocados to tell whether they're ripe. The construal "ripe" implies a prediction of what you'll find when you cut the avocado open. Repeated application of this technique lets you refine your sense of how much softness implies perfect ripeness.

The other kind of elaboration, called **extension,** involves using the construct to predict or construe an event it hasn't been applied to before. This use has more potential for predictive error, given the unfamiliarity. But it also provides the potential for elaboration. If the construct predicts well in unfamiliar territory, it thereby proves more broadly useful than was obvious before. This outcome adds more information than does definition. As an example, a person who's familiar with avocados but not cantaloupes may apply the squeeze technique to decide whether a cantaloupe is ripe. If the prediction made this way is accurate, the ripeness construct has been extended. The principle of extension relates to the concept of permeability, which we just discussed. Constructs that are permeable are applied to new events more easily than are those that are less permeable. Thus, they're more capable of being modified by the extension process.

Both extension and definition are important processes. Indeed, both are necessary. They differ in important ways, however. In general terms, definition is the "safer" of the two, whereas extension is potentially the more "informative" of the two. Which process is more likely to occur depends on several factors. Some people are chronically more likely than others to go out on a limb and apply a construct in new ways, as extension requires. Indeed, some people make a habit of seeking out opportunities to engage in extension (see also Box 15.2). On the other hand, it's rare for people to do this throughout their construct systems at once. That is, employing definition in some domains is a way of creating a sense of security. You then can feel more at ease trying extension (which is psychologically more risky) in some other domain.

BOX 15.2

THE THEORIST AND THE THEORY
George Kelly, Conceptual Pioneer

Just as individuals must elaborate and extend their construct systems, so must theorists. George Kelly was a theorist who was always willing to shift his construct system in directions that felt right to him, no matter what anyone else thought. His ideas moved along paths not yet traveled by personality theorists of his age. He displayed a true pioneering spirit in his work, a pioneering spirit that had a counterpart in his personal history.

Kelly was born in 1905 on a farm in Kansas. When he was four, his parents uprooted the family to move to Colorado to homestead a parcel of land (Thompson, 1968). Homesteading was a risky and adventurous life in the best of circumstances, and the circumstances the Kellys confronted weren't the best—the land they'd claimed had no water. As a result, they soon moved back to Kansas. Still, their westward migration reflected considerable independence of spirit. This spirit is also shown in Kelly's theoretical independence.

Two other experiences in Kelly's life also appear to be reflected directly in the theory he developed. The first occurred while he was teaching at a junior college in Iowa. His duties there included being drama coach. The fact that Kelly held this role is interesting for two reasons. First, it may well have helped sensitize him to the elusive nature of objective reality and the importance of the person's private understanding in creating a personal reality. This theme permeates his theory. Second, Kelly later developed a novel form of therapy, in which the client is asked to enact a role, as if in a play. It seems

likely that the idea for this technique, which is described later in the chapter, derived in part from Kelly's experiences with acting.

The other noteworthy experience occurred when Kelly was on the faculty at Fort Hays State College in Kansas. While there he developed a traveling clinic to serve public schools by helping teachers deal with problem children. Kelly made two observations during this period that influenced his later thinking. First, he discovered that inventing an unusual explanation for a client's problem often caused improvement. It didn't seem to matter what the explanation was, as long as it had two qualities. It had to account for the facts as the client understood them, and it had to suggest the usefulness of looking at the situation in a different way. If people could be made to look at their situation differently, they seemed to improve. Second, Kelly discovered that the problems teachers were reporting often said more about the teachers than the students. That is, it was the way the teacher was construing the child's behavior that defined the problem, not the child's behavior itself. Both observations were strongly reflected in Kelly's theory.

Finally, by all evidence Kelly was a practical man (he'd originally planned to be an engineer). If something worked for him either as a clinician or as a theorist, he kept it. If it didn't, he got rid of it. To a practical man, this is just common sense. That simple idea went on to become an important element in his vision of human mental life: if a construct works—if it predicts events—it stays. If it doesn't, it goes.

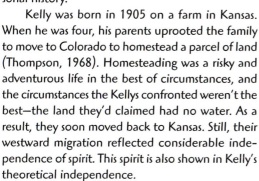

Temporary situational factors probably also influence whether definition or extension occurs. For instance, being upset or anxious (maybe because of a wrong prediction) may inhibit extension. Having been made uncertain about one thing may make you want to be very certain about other things (McGregor, Zanna, Holmes, & Spencer, 2001). In contrast, boredom may lead to extension (Sechrest,

1977). Knowing which of these will occur at any moment may require knowing whether the person is motivated toward security or adventure at that moment.

Evolution of a construct system through definition and extension represents growth. By implication at least, both of these stem from people's choices about how to use their constructs. Both are fairly gradual. Sometimes, though, circumstances *force* changes on people. Such changes can be disruptive. When people experience a very unusual event, they don't have constructs readily available for interpreting it. If an existing construct is used and fails badly, or if the person feels an absence of *any* construct to apply, the result can be abrupt change in the construct system. We'll consider the question of forced change later in the chapter, when we take up the question of how to think about problems in adjustment.

Organization among Constructs

The personal construct is the basic unit of analysis in this theory. But constructs don't rattle around loose in people's minds, to be applied piecemeal. Kelly assumed that each person's constructs are interrelated in an organized and coherent fashion. Specifically, he argued that constructs form a hierarchy, with some constructs at low (subordinate) levels of abstraction, and others at higher (superordinate) levels, subsuming or taking in the more basic ones (see also Epstein, 1983). For example, "good versus bad" may subsume "generous versus stingy," "friendly versus unfriendly," and "broken versus unbroken." Good versus bad thus is superordinate to the others (see Meyers & Berscheid, 1997, for another good example).

Earlier in the chapter we described how a hierarchy of constructs could create a sense of continuous variability on a dimension. In the example we used to illustrate that idea (construal of length), the same fundamental quality was dichotomized at each decision point. What we're talking about now is a little different. The qualities at the different levels relate to one another, but they aren't the same as each other.

The hierarchical arrangements that people have among their constructs aren't assumed to be permanent. The organization is retained only if it has predictive efficiency, just as is true of the constructs themselves. One change that can occur is in what specific subordinate constructs a superordinate construct includes. For example, Alice's "friendly versus unfriendly" construct used to subsume "polite versus impolite." She eventually grew to see these two as not related. In her new organization, politeness relates instead to constructs such as "manipulative versus not manipulative."

Organizations among constructs can be even more fluid than that. It's possible in principle for two constructs to *reverse* their places, so that the subordinate one becomes superordinate and vice versa. For instance, Judy's "loving versus not loving" used to be a broad construct that encompassed a number of others such as "accepting versus rejecting," which was more specific. Over time and experience, though, she came to see the sense of "acceptance" as broader. Her viewpoint shifted so that "loving" was encompassed by "acceptance." She now has a different organization, in which the relationship between constructs has reversed (see Figure 15.2).

Organizations among constructs play a role in creating individual differences in personality. Assume for a moment that two people have similar sets of constructs but different *organizations* among them (Figure 15.2). These two people would be quite different from each other in how they view and relate to the world.

There's one last point to be made about these hierarchies of constructs. Although the organization can change over time, at any given moment the organization constrains your construals and actions. In particular, using a particular su-

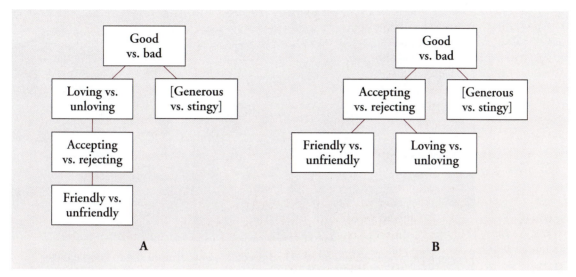

Figure 15.2

Two potential hierarchies of constructs held by two different people (or by one person at two different times) incorporating the same constructs but organized differently. In organization A, loving versus unloving subsumes accepting versus rejecting, which in turn subsumes friendly versus unfriendly. In B, accepting versus rejecting subsumes both friendly versus unfriendly and loving versus unloving. Someone with organization B would hold acceptance as fundamental and as implicit both in friendliness and in loving, which are distinct from each other. Someone with organization A would treat loving as fundamental and as implicit in acceptance, which in turn is implicit in friendliness.

perordinate construct dictates which subordinate constructs you're most likely to use in more fine-grained construals of the event. That is, any superordinate construct subsumes some lower-level ones but not others. Using a superordinate construct will channel you toward subordinate constructs that fall under it, and away from those that don't. This, in turn, will greatly influence the character of your subsequent impressions.

For example, Julie walks up to David after class, converses for a few minutes, and then asks him whether he wants to study with her for their upcoming test. If David initially construes Julie as a "student," he's likely to apply constructs that fall under "student" in his hierarchy as he further construes her behavior. He may evaluate her conversation to gauge how much she knows, and may decide from that whether the proposed study session would be helpful. If David initially construes Julie as an "attractive woman," he'll apply different constructs to the same aspects of her behavior. He may see her conversation as a sign of interest, the offer to study together as a ploy to get to know him better, and the study session as a step toward intimacy.

Individuality of Constructs

Thus far our discussion of constructs and their organization has largely disregarded the word *personal*. However, the word *personal* was every bit as important to Kelly as the word *construct*. Kelly emphasized that each person creates an understanding of reality that's separate from everyone else's. Each person's construct system is unique.

People have a need to understand and predict events around them. People differ greatly from each other, however, in how they interpret any given event.

It's easy to be misled on this point by the fact that people typically have no difficulty using words to refer to many constructs. However, words don't always mean precisely the same thing to one person as to another. Perhaps the easiest illustration is the deceptively simple statement "I love you." This sentence can have a vast number of meanings, depending on who's saying it to whom and the psychological context in which it's being said.

Indeed, even when two people think they agree about the meaning of a single word, it's impossible to be sure they do. For example, you say something is red, and I agree with you: it's red. But is your experience of redness, your construal of it, exactly the same as mine, or even close to mine? Who can know? In principle, the same problem occurs in all experience. And that is precisely Kelly's point about people's constructs. Even if the words are the same, the constructs are probably not. Indeed, Kelly emphasized that constructs are "preverbal." People can have a hard time representing their constructs, even to themselves, except as raw experience (Kelly, 1969; see also Riedel, 1970).

If everyone's constructs are potentially so different from those of other people, how do we ever communicate? How do we ever get along with one another? The answer in part is that your constructs don't *totally* diverge from those of other people. Remember, constructs are retained only if they have predictive efficiency. If they fail to predict events adequately, you modify or discard them and form new ones. By the time you're an adult, you've tested your constructs quite a bit. So has everyone else. There's got to be *some* similarity between your construct system and those of other people, or the systems wouldn't have been maintained for so long.

Nevertheless, construct systems do differ enough that there's plenty of potential for disagreement. How then do people find a sense of harmony with each other? How do they even get to know each other? In Kelly's view, the process of getting to know other people is partly (perhaps largely) one of testing your constructs against theirs. If you find you agree about what constructs apply to various events, you feel comfortable with each other. To put it another way, people with similar construct systems see the same things when they look at the world. That similarity of views is reassuring and forms the basis of a friendship. From this view, you feel your way toward relationships with other people by jointly assessing similarities in construct systems (see Duck, 1973, 1977; Duck & Allison, 1978; Klion & Leitner, 1991; Tesser, 1971).

Both the use of constructs in forming impressions of other people and the fact that different people use different constructs are nicely illustrated in research by Higgins, King, and Mavin (1982). Participants were asked to write down the traits of several specific friends (Study 1) or the traits of several specific types of people (Study 2). The traits that a given person wrote down frequently (Study 1) or wrote down first (Study 2) were taken by the researchers as representing important constructs for that person, because they were so "accessible" in memory.

Several days later, in what was portrayed as a separate study, the participants read a description of a target person written specially for each participant. The description included some of the participant's important (accessible) constructs and some that were less important (less accessible). After doing another task (to interfere with memory), participants wrote their impressions of the target person. Then they tried to recall the description they'd read. As expected, their impressions were influenced by the constructs that were important to them personally, and they tended to disregard the other ones (Figure 15.3). Indeed, they had a harder time even recalling the unimportant ones. Apparently, then, different people do rely on different mental dimensions in construing others.

Similarities and Differences between People

In Kelly's view, people are psychologically similar to each other if their systems of constructs are similar. Two people need not have gone through the same set of events

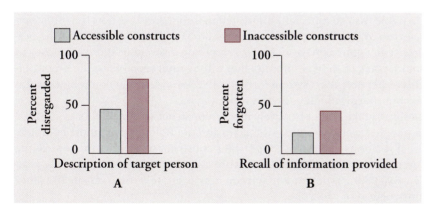

Figure 15.3

Participants received a description of a person that was made up of several accessible constructs (ones that the participant used spontaneously) and several inaccessible constructs (ones they didn't use spontaneously). (A) In writing their impressions of this person later on, participants gave a lot of weight to the accessible constructs that had been mentioned and tended to disregard the others. (B) Indeed, they were even less able to remember the inaccessible constructs when asked to recall the initial description of the target person (adapted from Higgins, King, & Mavin, 1982, Experiment 1).

to have similar constructs. Nor will two people who do experience the same set of events necessarily have similar constructs. A given construct can emerge from a thousand different events, and any event can be construed in many different ways. What makes people resemble each other is similarity in their *patterns of construals*—however the patterns arise—not similarity in their "learning histories" (see also Gilovich, 1990).

To Kelly, this principle applies to differences and similarities between persons and also to those between cultures. People from a given culture typically share a physical environment and manner of upbringing, but to Kelly this is of secondary importance. To him the essence of a culture is a similarity in how people construe experiences (Kelly, 1962).

Recent research appears to support the idea that cultural differences do relate to variations in people's constructs (Triandis et al., 1984). Each participant in this research made judgments about what kinds of behavioral elements occur in different kinds of social interactions. Analysis of judgments made by each participant revealed something of the constructs applied by that person to social situations. Comparisons from one person to another indicated that people from the same culture shared elements of their construct systems. These similarities were *not* shared as widely across the different cultures.

Role Taking

According to this theory, a true social interaction entails an elaborate set of cognitive processes. It involves an attempt by each person to construe some part of the construct system held by the other. In other words, to really interact with someone else requires you to try to understand and anticipate how that person is understanding and anticipating reality. This is what Kelly meant by **role taking** with respect to another person.

When in a role, you're especially interested in understanding how the other person views *your* role. What does the person expect of you? What constructs is the person using to predict your behavior? If you can create answers to these questions in your own mind, you can then act in ways that will be interpretable to the other person within his or her construct system (see Box 15.3 for a view that complements this in some ways but sharply challenges it in other ways).

Is it possible to take roles effectively if your construct system differs from those of the other people involved? The answer is yes and no. Role taking is more complete and effective if you construe the other person's construct system in more or less the way that it actually exists. But it's not the entire construct system that matters. How effective your role taking is depends mainly on how accurately you construe the other person's construction of *your* role.

Evidence that people work to get pictures of each other's roles when interacting comes from research on how people try to establish common ground in a conversation. As an example, when an expert talks with a novice, the expert has to use different terms than when talking with another expert. The expert also must decide how much detail to convey. But this decision isn't made just once. The expert has to continue to judge whether the novice is following the expert, and adjust further, if necessary. Research indicates that this continued adjustment does occur in people's conversations (Isaacs & Clark, 1987). Furthermore, it's an interactive process between those conversing. People who overhear the conversation don't grasp the common ground as clearly as do the people in it (Schober & Clark, 1989).

BOX 15.3

DOES THE SELF CREATE REALITY, OR DOES SOCIETY CREATE THE SELF?

The major theme of Kelly's orientation to personality is that people develop personalized systems of constructs. They then impose these internally generated constructs on events to interpret them. From this point of view, the self is the architect of its own experience. All understanding ultimately comes from within.

How accurate is this view? Where do people's constructs really come from? There's another view that suggests a different origin for people's understanding of reality. This view, called **symbolic interactionism,** holds that the self isn't an intrinsic part of the person. Instead it develops from repeated social interactions. From this point of view, people don't impose self-generated construals on social reality. Rather, people's construals are created *for* them by their social relations. The major theorists of this viewpoint (Baldwin, 1902; Blumer, 1969; Cooley, 1902; Mead, 1934; Shibutani, 1961) were sociologists and social psychologists rather than personality psychologists. Nevertheless, their ideas have intriguing implications for personality (see Lauer & Handel, 1983, for a review).

Symbolic interactionists point out that human life is communal rather than solitary and that communication (through symbols) plays a central role in interactions (thus the term *symbolic interactionism*). Symbolic interactionists assume that a self emerges through social interaction in the following way. You can't communicate effectively with someone else (or understand someone else's communication to you) without taking on the other person's perspective or role. It's particularly important in many kinds of communication to understand the other person's perspective on *yourself*. This part of the symbolic interactionist position sounds a lot like Kelly's assumptions about the nature of role taking.

The symbolic interactionists proposed, however, that early in life you don't have the ability to take an other person's perspective on you. Nor does this ability appear automatically as you get older. Rather, it's acquired only *through the process of interacting with other people.* Only when you try to interact with others do you realize that they have their own perspectives. As you begin to realize this, you try to take those perspectives. Through perspective taking, the self comes to exist. According to Mead (1934), repeatedly trying to adopt the perspective that other people hold on you causes you to develop a mental representation of their view. This view is called the **perspective of the generalized other** because it derives from many other people's vantage points on you, rather than just one. According to the symbolic interactionists, it's only when you've acquired the perspective of the generalized other that a self can be said to genuinely exist.

The perspective of the generalized other is important in the symbolic interactionist view of social behavior. Once you're capable of taking that perspective, you're capable of regulating your behavior as part of a social unit. When you consider possible actions, you consider this internalized sense of the social matrix and evaluate the actions from that viewpoint. You use that viewpoint to decide how to act, which in turn can influence how you see yourself in the future (Schlenker, Dlugolecki, & Doherty, 1994).

Thus, to the symbolic interactionists the self evolves from society rather than vice versa. Here this idea is interesting because it suggests a different origin for people's constructs than is implicit in Kelly's theory. In particular, it suggests that many (perhaps all) of the constructs we apply to ourselves, and perhaps many of the constructs we apply to other entities, are acquired from *other people* rather than being generated from our own points of view.

We enact many roles in the course of our lives. Not all are important or have more than superficial impact. The "store customer" role, for instance, matters little to most of us most of the time. Other roles, however, are extremely important, even central to our lives. These roles, which Kelly termed **core roles,** are major determinants of our sense of identity. Examples are occupational and professional roles, the roles of parent and child, close friend, lover, and so on. Whether any of these actually *is* a core role depends on the person, of course.

Because core roles are important, failing to perform them adequately can have adverse consequences. Kelly said that failing to enact a core role in the way it's construed by another person produces guilt. **Guilt** thus is an awareness of a disparity between your actions and the actions you see as fitting the other's expectations for your role. This definition of guilt is similar in some respects to Rogers's discussion of "conditions of worth" (Chapter 14), in which people feel uncomfortable when they fail to live up to others' expectations for them.

Personal Constructs and Behavioral Consistency

Back in Chapter 4 we addressed in some detail the issue of behavioral consistency. We noted there that people are apparently less consistent in their actions than seems implied by early trait views of personality. This evidence led to the emergence of an "interactionist" position, in which personality and situational forces are seen as joint determinants of behavior.

The personal construct viewpoint allows us to address this issue in a way that's very similar to the "context-dependent" view of traits presented toward the end of Chapter 4 (and is also discussed in Chapter 16). It suggests that to predict a person's behavior in any given situation we need to know how the person *construes* the situation. An individual will act in a consistent way across situations *to the degree that the situations are construed in similar ways.*

This idea sounds a little like the principle of generalization from the learning perspective. Where it differs from generalization is its emphasis on the personal. It doesn't matter whether the situations look the same or different to an outside "objective" observer. What matters is whether the person who's behaving perceives the situations as similar. Similar construals of situations should yield cross-situational consistency. Divergent construals should yield less consistency. This is directly implied by Kelly's theory.

An effective communicator presents ideas in terms the listener can understand.

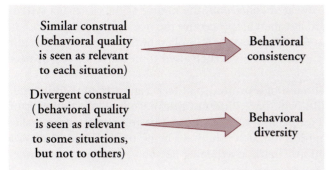

Figure 15.4

When people construe several situations as involving similar qualities of behavior, their behavior tends to be consistent across those situations. When people construe situations as involving qualities that differ across the situations, their behavior tends to diverge across those situations.

Research by Lord (1982) found support for this idea. Participants described what characteristics would go into being "conscientious" in each of six common situations (e.g., keeping good lecture notes, keeping an orderly closet). These descriptions were done using a variation on the Q-sort method described in Chapter 14. These Q-sorts produced profiles of how the participant viewed the characteristics of each situation. The profiles then could be compared with one another (for each participant) to assess their similarity.

Participants' actual conscientiousness then was rated by an observer who appeared at unannounced times in six situations corresponding closely to those the participant had rated. Comparisons revealed that participants' level of conscientiousness was most consistent across the situations that they'd construed in similar terms (see also Figure 15.4). Behavior was less consistent across situations that they'd construed in divergent terms.

Assessment

We've focused in this chapter on the idea that personality is defined by the constructs that a person uses in dealing with the world. Personality assessment from this viewpoint likewise emphasizes assessment of the constructs the person uses.

Kelly's Role Construct Repertory Test

In thinking about how to get an accurate view of another person's system of constructs, Kelly confronted a dilemma. It's useless to do behavioral observation, because a given behavior might stem from the use of any of several constructs. On the other hand, asking people to describe their constructs isn't satisfactory either, for several reasons.

First, although we've been giving names to constructs throughout the chapter, constructs aren't always easy to label. As noted earlier, many are intuitive or preverbal. They exist in a private experiential language that can't be expressed. Second, people aren't used to describing their constructs. As a result, they may not do a good job at communicating what they mean, even if they can pin it down. Finally, the words that people choose to describe constructs are often so general that it's hard to get clear, specific meaning from what's being said.

Faced with these problems, Kelly tried to devise a strategy for getting at people's constructs indirectly. Rather than have them verbalize constructs, he had them engage in active construals. Across repeated construals, the nature of the construct system should begin to reveal itself. Kelly called his procedure the *Role Construct Repertory Test,* a name that's usually shortened to **Rep Test.** As is implied by the longer title, this test often (although not always) focuses on constructs used to perceive aspects of people and their roles.

The Rep Test involves the use of a printed grid (see Figure 15.5). In this grid, significant people in your life (who have different roles) are listed at the heads of columns. The rows are used to specify a set of comparisons and construals to make. You begin by reading a definition for each role that's being used and deciding *who in your life* best fits that definition. Then you write that person's name on the grid next to the role label, not using any person's name twice.

Then you start with the construals. For each row, you're asked to think about the people listed in three specific columns (marked by circles in the figure). More precisely, think of an important characteristic that makes two of those three people similar to each other and different from the third. Once you've decided, mark the two that are similar and write a word or phrase in the column headed "emergent pole" to indicate how the two are alike. In the column headed "implicit pole," indicate how the third person is different. Then look at the people (roles) in the other columns. Decide whether they fit the emergent pole of the construct or the implicit pole, and mark each accordingly.

When you've done one row, go to the next. Repeat the whole process row by row. As you go through the rows, you're generating a list of constructs. These aren't

Sort no.	Yourself 1	Mother 2	Father 3	Spouse 4	Pal 5	Rejecting person 6	Pitied person 7	Attractive person 8	Emergent pole	Implicit pole
1						O	O	O		
2	O			O	O					
3	O						O	O		
4				O	O		O			
5	O	O	O							
6		O	O				O			
...										
n		O		O		O				

Figure 15.5

Example of the sort of grid used in the Rep Test. You begin by placing the names of the people who play various roles in your life in the slanted sections at the top. Then you conduct a series of comparisons among sets of three people at a time, deciding how two of them are similar to each other in a way that makes them different from the third (see text for more complete description). From Kelly, 1955. Reproduced with permission of Gladys Kelly.

the only constructs you have. But since the people listed across the top are people who play important roles in your life, the constructs that emerge are probably fairly important in your construals of people. Several of the comparisons in the Rep Test are of interest in their own right. Consider line 3 in Figure 15.5, where you're asked to think about yourself, an attractive person, and a pitied person. Which of the two will you see as more like yourself, and why? This comparison reveals something about your feelings toward yourself and also what aspect of yourself comes easily to mind.

The roles listed in Figure 15.5 represent only a few of the roles in the full Rep Test. Furthermore, people doing this test also usually do many construals, thus providing a much larger base of information. This procedure has also been adapted to assess construals of other sorts of events, for instance, social issues (Epting, 1972), occupations (Shubsachs, 1975), and situations (Krieger, Epting, & Leitner, 1974; Neimeyer & Neimeyer, 1981).

Though the Rep Test is useful and interesting, it also has limitations. As noted earlier, people's constructs can't always be verbalized. The Rep Test tries to get around this by asking people to actively construe other people and to use whatever construct naturally comes to mind to say what makes people similar or different. This strategy only partly handles the problem, though, because the person still has to provide a label for the construct that was used.

This requirement of the test creates two potential problems. The first is the ordinary problem of knowing whether the word used to identify the construct means the same thing to one person as to another. The second problem stems from the fact that being asked repeatedly to label your constructs may create a bias concerning what constructs you use while doing the test. Specifically, you may be inclined to report *only constructs that are easy to verbalize,* even if those aren't the most important constructs in your mind (cf. Shubsachs, 1975). Thus, even the Rep Test may be susceptible to the problems inherent in just asking people to describe their construct systems.

Problems in Behavior, and Behavior Change

The focus on the importance of personal constructs in personality is also maintained in considering the nature of psychological problems and what's involved in the process of therapy (see also Neimeyer, 1985).

Personal Constructs and Psychological Distress

Recall that in Kelly's view normal human functioning involves successfully anticipating and interpreting events through a system of constructs. A direct extension of this view is that problems in behavior involve problems in interpreting or predicting events.

Such difficulties can arise for several reasons. One possibility is you may confront events that differ drastically from any previously experienced. Because of this lack of experience, you may not have constructs that seem relevant. The event, in effect, is beyond your ability to grasp it. Another possibility is that you may be trying to construe the event with a construct whose predictive efficiency has fallen off.

Kelly said that when people don't have adequate constructs, they feel uncertain and helpless. He labeled this experience **anxiety.** If the event is outside the available construct system, people sometimes even have trouble grasping why they're experiencing anxiety.

How often do people experience events that differ greatly from their prior experiences? Perhaps more often than you might imagine. Think back to your first week at college, for example. That period was probably filled with new experiences that differed enough from what you'd known before to make you wonder what was going on. Perhaps you even felt concern or apprehension. The same feelings can occur for someone entering a new job (Van Maanen, 1973, 1975), being hospitalized for an illness, or having her first child (Deutsch et al., 1988). In fact, anytime you do *anything* for the very first time, it can be unsettling, just because it's the first time and you don't know just what to expect.

As more extreme cases, consider the experiences of people involved in disasters such as hurricanes, fires, or earthquakes. It's often said that such experiences are traumatic precisely because they are so unlike anything the people have ever gone through before. Consequently, the people have no constructs for interpreting the event or anticipating its consequences. Think about people in the midst of a divorce, victims of crime, or those who unexpectedly win huge sums of money. These people are suddenly experiencing things that events in their lives haven't prepared them for. Part of the difficulty in living through these events is the very lack of constructs available for use in anticipating their consequences and implications.

It's unpleasant to discover that your constructs are inadequate to deal with events. Even worse, however, are events which suggest that important aspects of your construct system may be completely *wrong*, and that major change may be necessary (cf. Leitner & Cado, 1982). The more central the construct that's challenged, the more extensive is the change that's necessary, and the greater is the problem. The awareness of an imminent comprehensive change in one's fundamental construct system is termed **threat.** The experience of threat is much the same as that of anxiety, but more extreme. Both arise from poor prediction from the construct system. In threat, however, the failure is more massive and fundamental than in anxiety.

Experiences unlike any you have had before are hard to absorb, because you lack constructs for them.

Dealing with Anxiety and Threat

It's straightforward in principle to reduce anxiety (or even threat) from inadequate constructs, though it can be more difficult in practice. One way to do so is to generate a new construct. This response to poor prediction is probably the major source of new constructs across a person's lifetime (see also Box 15.4). The other way is to modify an existing construct so the experience can be successfully construed through

BOX 15.4

RECONSTRUING YOUR WORLD AFTER A TRAUMATIC EVENT

Minor adversity strikes almost everyone occasionally—getting a test score that falls a point short of the grade you wanted, finding a ticket on your car window after shopping just a little too long, or coming down with the flu just before spring break. Most people's constructs allow them to interpret and understand such minor inconveniences (e.g., "stuff happens"). But what about traumatic events—being diagnosed with a life-threatening illness, hearing that members of your family were just killed in a car accident, being raped or beaten?

Common sense suggests that truly traumatic events are harder to integrate into one's worldview than minor events. There are many reasons for this. For one thing, traumatic events often are sudden and unexpected. Traumatic events often create irreversible, long-lasting problems for the future. By their very nature, traumatic events suggest a world that's unpredictable and uncontrollable (Tedeschi & Calhoun, 1995). They can undermine the most basic assumptions people hold about themselves and their world (e.g., Horowitz, 1986; Janoff-Bulman, 1992).

Kelly's theory suggests that people in this situation will struggle to create new constructs for interpreting the traumatic event. That's also what more recent theorists suggest. Tedeschi and Calhoun (1995) argue that a traumatic event partly destroys the person's worldview. They also say that the event thereby initiates a potential for growth. The shattering of one worldview prompts an effort to construct a new, more meaningful one. Others have taken similar positions (e.g., Davis, Nolen-Hoeksema, & Larson, 1998; Taylor, 1983; Thompson & Janigian, 1988).

Research has even begun to show that making sense of traumatic events helps people adjust and move forward. For example, Thompson (1985) studied people whose homes were severely damaged by fire. Those who found a positive meaning in the event coped best with it. She has found similar effects among people who had suffered strokes (Thompson, 1991). Mendola, Tennen, Affleck, McCann, and Fitzgerald (1990) examined women diagnosed with infertility. Those who better adapted cognitively to this news also showed more psychological well-being. Finding positive aspects of having cancer seems to help people cope with the experience (Andrykowski, Brady, & Hunt, 1993; Stanton et al., 2002; Taylor, Lichtman, & Wood, 1984; Tomich & Helgeson, 2002).

These and other studies have helped establish a link between psychological well-being and the capacity to understand and find meaning in traumatic events. Finding meaning may even promote physical health. Bower, Kemeny, Taylor, and Fahey (1998) examined immune functioning and mortality among HIV-positive gay men who had recently experienced an AIDS-related death of a partner or close friend. Men who found meaning in the death showed better immune functioning during the months afterward, compared to those less able to find meaning. Those who found meaning also had a lower rate of AIDS-related mortality during that period. Conceptually similar results have been reported by Tomich and Helgeson (2002) in a study of physical functioning among breast cancer patients. Thus, finding meaning may not only enhance well-being after a traumatic event, it may also help keep people alive.

it. If the event can now be construed with predictive efficiency, the anxiety or threat should evaporate.

As noted earlier in the chapter, sometimes you can modify a construct by extending its range of convenience. Doing this means saying, in effect, that the new experience really isn't totally new. It has similarities to other experiences you've had; you just didn't notice it before.

Sometimes this doesn't work, though, and you have to change the construct in a bigger way. One change may even require more changes. To see why, recall that your construct system forms a hierarchy. Subordinate constructs contribute to and help define high-level constructs. When you change your sense of what one construct means to you, you're rearranging some of the connections in your hierarchy, maybe even a lot of connections.

Sometimes the problem isn't that you don't have a construct to apply but that you're continuing to use a construct that's outlived its usefulness. Sometimes you're treating a construct as though it has a broader range of convenience than it actually has. The result in each of these cases is unsuccessful anticipation of new events. Again the solution is to reorganize your construct system. In the latter case, the reorganization just means making the range of convenience more restricted than it had been. If your construct has really outlived its usefulness, though, you're back to having to come up with a new one.

From the personal construct view on personality, the dissatisfaction that goes with poor prediction of events is the primary symptom of problems. This dissatisfaction is what leads a person to seek help. Keep in mind that the construct system is the essence of personality, from this point of view. The process of therapy is one of assisting people in elaborating or altering their construct system to improve its predictive efficiency (see Epting, 1980; Fransella, 1972). Better prediction will result in less anxiety, distress, and dissatisfaction.

Fixed Role Therapy

What kinds of therapeutic procedures help attain this goal? It's important to keep in mind that Kelly didn't believe there's some "perfect" construct system that people should adopt to be better adjusted to reality. Everyone has a personal view of the world. Each person must evolve an arrangement of constructs that will be functional from that personal viewpoint. The goal of the therapy procedure is to facilitate evolution of the construct system in its own way.

Kelly believed the best way to facilitate evolution of the construct system is to induce the person to change outward behavior. This will force the person to generate unusual construals of events that result. The procedure Kelly developed for doing this is called **fixed role therapy.** In this procedure the client enacts the role of a hypothetical person. This person is carefully structured to have certain characteristics that the client wants. This fixed role character is even given a name, to provide a sense of identity to the role.

The therapeutic process begins with an assessment in which the client completes a variety of instruments, including a self-characterization or self-description. On the basis of this, the therapist develops a role for the client to enact. The role is a composite of some of the client's positive characteristics and of some characteristics the client feels unable to display. These are characteristics for which constructs presumably are lacking.

The use of a composite role has several benefits. Building in some familiar characteristics helps make the role easier to adopt because it keeps the role from being entirely alien. Building preexisting *positive* qualities into it helps to create a sense of confidence in your ability to enact the role, and it strengthens the use of constructs that contribute to those positive qualities.

When the fixed role has been established, you're asked to enact it for a while. The idea is not to adopt the role as a permanent part of your personality, but just to enact it for some period. This instruction means there's little risk involved, which takes some of the pressure off. If you aren't happy with how something goes, the experience can be viewed as just a bit of acting that needs more polishing, not a failure. It often happens, however, that after a while clients stop thinking of the role as a role and start to think of it as a natural part of themselves.

Enacting this fixed role forces the client to construe events in ways that differ from those used previously. For example, consider Luke, a man who sees himself as shy and passive and interpersonally inadequate. Luke might be asked to take on the role of a person who's quiet but "deep," a person others find interesting and stimulating, but who doesn't always show those characteristics openly because he's more interested in learning something from others than in showing his own strengths; he's a person who has a pronounced but subtle influence on others, so that people don't always realize they're being influenced until later on.

Notice that this role (which is adapted from Kelly, 1955, p. 121) is a composite of Luke's self-image and characteristics that he sees himself as lacking. The role incorporates quietness (which Luke now has) but recasts it within a general effectiveness in interpersonal interaction. In order to enact this role, Luke must see his behavior in ways that differ from his previous view of himself. He must construe his quietness as a positive act of benefiting from others rather than as a sign of passivity and inadequacy. In that way, he's rearranging his system of constructs. As he enacts this role over time, he should gradually reorganize his construct system, modifying constructs at some points and perhaps developing new ones at other points. The result should be a system with a high degree of predictive efficiency that permits him to live a more satisfying life than he did before.

Personal Construct Theory: Problems and Prospects

Personal construct theory shares a couple of strengths with the humanistic theories described in Chapter 14. Its emphasis on the uniqueness and validity of each person's experience fits with the emphasis those theories place on the importance of subjective experiences. Similarly, the principle of constructive alternativism suggests a basis for assuming that people tend toward being better over time. That is, people can always reconstrue events in more and more functional ways.

The personal construct view places less of an emphasis on will than did the theorists of the humanistic orientation. Although in principle you're free to determine for yourself how to construe the present, past experiences have a big influence on present construals. When people make drastic reorganizations of how they view the world, they don't do so easily or without strain. It remains an open question, then, how free people actually are from their past.

Perhaps the greatest strength of this view on personality is one that was wholly unanticipated by its author. As you'll see in the next chapter, Kelly's intuitions foreshadowed several themes that would emerge again, later on, from very different sources. The reemergence of these ideas came from cognitive psychology, rather than personality. The ideas returned to personality only through a circuitous path. Kelly's view, however, was much more idiographic than the newer cognitive view (recall the emphasis on the idea that constructs are personal). This idiographic emphasis "humanizes" the ideas in a way that the newer views don't usually do.

One problem that personal construct psychology historically has had is that it's not terribly conducive to research. There is a cadre of personality psychologists who are devoted to personal construct psychology, and there are journals devoted to personal construct psychology. But the group who take this view is relatively small in number.

What are the prospects for this view on personality? We've continued to include it in this book largely because of its status as a forerunner of cognitive theories. The extent to which this is true is quite remarkable. Some of Kelly's principles are strikingly similar to those emerging from the newer literature. In some ways, it is this convergence of lines of thought that provides a continuing basis for interest in personal construct psychology. Lacking an active research literature of its own, however, personal construct psychology is beginning to acquire the patina of ideas that are primarily of historical interest. It appears to be on its way to fading from the scene, perhaps becoming a footnote to the newer cognitive models.

SUMMARY

Kelly believed that people have a fundamental need to predict the events that they experience. They do so by developing a system of personal constructs, which they use to interpret or construe new events. Constructs are derived from recurring elements in one's experience, but because they're developed separately by each person, each person's system of constructs is unique. Constructive alternativism is the idea that any event for any person is open to multiple interpretations and that people decide for themselves how to construe each event.

People implicitly evaluate their constructs over time in terms of predictive efficiency, or the degree to which the constructs allow the person to interact successfully with the world. Kelly treated constructs as bipolar and dichotomous. Each construct under use has an emergent pole, the end of the conceptual dimension that is being applied to the event being construed. The implicit pole of the construct is the end not being applied. A construct's range of convenience is the range of events to which it can be applied meaningfully. Its focus of convenience is the range of events for which it is optimally predictive.

Constructs can be refined by actively using them in familiar ways (a process called definition) and can be elaborated by using them in unfamiliar ways (a process called extension). Changes in one's construct system can also be induced by situations in which one finds oneself without adequate constructs to interpret an event. Constructs are organized in a hierarchical system of inclusiveness. This organization is not permanent, however, just as the constructs themselves are not permanent. How long any aspect of the construct system remains stable depends on its predictive efficiency.

Kelly held that constructs are unique to each person, despite the fact that they're often illustrated by familiar words. The fact that each person's constructs are potentially different from those of other people raises questions about how people can interact effectively. In Kelly's view, getting to know other people means testing one's own constructs against theirs. People are similar to the extent their construct systems are similar. Interpersonal interaction in this viewpoint involves the taking of a role with respect to some other person. Role taking entails construing how the other person is construing yourself in your role. Core roles are those roles that are particularly important to one's sense of identity.

Assessment from Kelly's viewpoint is done by the Rep Test, which assesses the constructs that people use in construing their role relations and other aspects of their experience. Kelly's viewpoint on problems in self-management was that people experience anxiety when events fall outside the range of convenience of their construct systems, and they experience threat when they anticipate a major reorganization of important aspects of their construct systems because of poor predictive efficiency. Kelly developed fixed role therapy as a way of getting people to engage in behaviors that they would not ordinarily engage in, for the purpose of developing different ways of construing events in their lives.

GLOSSARY

Anxiety The response to inability to impose a construct adequately on an event you're experiencing.

Constructive alternativism The idea that any event can be construed in many ways.

Coping The effort to handle a threat by executing whatever response has been chosen.

Core roles The roles that are central to one's life, contributing to one's identity.

Defensive reappraisal The process of defining a threat out of existence.

Definition The applying of a construct in a familiar way, causing refinement of the construct.

Emergent pole The end of a construct that's being applied to the event being construed.

Extension The applying of a construct to an unfamiliar event in an attempt to increase its range of convenience.

Fixed role therapy A therapy in which clients enact roles that differ somewhat from their current self-perceptions.

Focus of convenience The range of applicable events for which a construct has the best prediction.

Guilt The sensing of a discrepancy between one's acts and another's role expectations for oneself.

Implicit pole The end of the construct that isn't being applied to the event being construed.

Permeability The degree to which a construct extends to events it hasn't been applied to yet.

Personal construct A mental representation used to interpret events.

Perspective of the generalized other An integrated sense of others' views of you.

Predictive efficiency The degree to which a construct can be applied successfully to events.

Primary appraisal The process of perceiving a threat in the environment.

Range of convenience The range of events for which a construct is useful.

Rep Test A test used to identify a person's major constructs.

Role taking The process of construing how another person construes you.

Secondary appraisal The process of determining how to respond to a threat.

Symbolic interactionism A theory in which the self arises from the process of social interaction.

Threat The perception of an impending reorganization of one's construct system.

PART eight

The Cognitive
Self-Regulation
Perspective

THE COGNITIVE SELF-REGULATION PERSPECTIVE:
Major Themes and Underlying Assumptions

The human nervous system is a vast and elaborate network of tiny cells that communicate continuously with each other. They relay information from one place to another throughout your life, whether you're awake or asleep. This network has been compared to many things over the decades, including an organization of hydraulic tubes, a network of telephone lines, a paper-shuffling bureaucracy, and (in the last thirty years) a computer.

The computer metaphor appeals to some cognitive psychologists because of a similarity between certain mental processes—organizing experiences and storing them in patterns—and certain computer functions. The metaphor also has some appeal for people who analyze motor control, because computer-driven robots display many complex behaviors. Indeed, the *robot* metaphor may actually be better than the computer, because our lives are filled with actions aimed at reaching goals (Batson, 1990). To some psychologists, it doesn't seem outlandish to ask

whether human beings, pursuing those goals, are not perhaps the ultimate "guided missiles."

Theories that relate these metaphors to personality aren't as well developed as theories with longer histories. Nonetheless, this way of thinking does seem to have at least a few implications for personality. Those implications are described in Chapters 16 and 17.

The ideas presented in these chapters can be seen as resting on three assumptions. The first is that understanding behavior means understanding how people deal with the information that surrounds them. *Information* is a pretty vague term, but it's easy to get a sense of what it means. Look around the room you're in. You're surrounded by visual stimulation, probably auditory stimulation as well (especially if you study with the stereo on), and maybe other people doing various things. Each of these is a source of information. The information comes to you in tiny bits, but you don't experience it that way. You see *walls,* not just patches of color. You hear a *song,* not unconnected bits of noise. You have an *impression* of your roommate, not just a collection of facts. To have these broader experiences, you integrate and organize the bits of information the world provides you. From these functions comes the term *information processing.*

A second assumption is that the flow of life consists of an elaborate web of decisions. Some of them are made consciously, but far more are made implicitly, outside awareness. Your personality is reflected partly in how decision making flows in your mind, what biases are introduced by the mental organization you have and how you use it. The idea that life is a flow of decisions relates to the computer metaphor. Digital computers are decision-making devices. Their smallest elements are electronic switches that embody one of two possible qualities (yes or no, on or off, open or shut). Each element thus is continuously manifesting a decision. Some theorists think that human thought is a similar stream of implicit decisions at many levels.

These two assumptions underlie some of the ideas presented in Chapter 16. Chapter 16 describes cognitive theories about how the mind is organized and how personality thus is structured. The ideas described there focus on how events are represented in memory and how the memories guide your experience of the world. How all this complexity is or-ganized and used is an important issue, from the cognitive vantage point.

A third assumption behind this perspective on personality is that human behavior is goal directed. This idea represents a view of motivation, somewhat different from the motive view we considered in Chapter 5. The idea that goals underlie behavior is important in robotics. A robot has a purpose (or several) that it's trying to fulfill. It often has some kind of representation of its goal, and it tries to move toward that representation.

One view on personality assumes that people do much the same: take up (or create) goals and try to move toward them. To be sure they're moving in the right direction, people monitor their progress. From this idea comes the term *self-regulation.* In this view, human action is continually aimed at attaining some goal or other. Life is a never-ending stream of sensing, checking, and adjusting—an ever-continuing process of moving within a network of self-defined goals. This idea provides part of the basis of Chapter 17.

These two chapters are more interconnected than were the pairs of chapters on any other perspective other than psychoanalysis. The ideas in them aren't so much alternative views as inter-related views. One set of ideas tends to flow into the other. Chapter 16 focuses on the person's mental world; Chapter 17 focuses on how this mental world is reflected in actions.

Contemporary Cognitive Views

■ **Representing Your Experience
of the World**

Schemas and Their Development
Effects of Schemas
Semantic Memory, Episodic Memory, and Scripts
Socially Relevant Schemas
Self-Schemas
Entity and Incremental Schemas
Attribution
Activation and Use of Memories

■ **Connectionist Views
of Mental Organization**

Dual Process Models

■ **Pulling the Pieces Together**

Cognitive Person Variables
Personality as a Cognitive–Affective
Processing System

■ **Assessment**

Think-Aloud, Experience Sampling,
and Self-Monitoring
Contextualized Assessment
Diagnostic Categories as Prototypes

■ **Problems in Behavior,
and Behavior Change**

Information-Processing Deficits
Depressive Self-Schemas
Cognitive Therapy

■ **Contemporary Cognitive Theories:
Problems and Prospects**

SUMMARY

■ Don and Sandy have been shopping for a house. Some they've looked at were easy to discard: one was way too much money, one was right next to a gas station, one was hideously ugly. Others have been harder. They're getting to be good at noticing things they care about and categorizing houses quickly. They've started making a brief list of the pros and cons of each, sure that that will lead them to a rational choice. Last month, though, they went by the house on Forest Hills Drive. It's smaller than they wanted, needs more work than they wanted, doesn't have the pool they wanted. But something about it seemed exactly right. Almost at once they decided to buy it, and now it's their home.

O ne focus of cognitive psychology is how people represent their experiences. Another is how people make decisions. Hundreds of studies have examined these processes, and several theories have been proposed to account for them. The picture of how these processes work has also begun to influence how theorists think about personality.

Aspects of the picture are startlingly similar to ideas presented much earlier by George Kelly, described in Chapter 15. Kelly never saw himself as a cognitive theorist. In fact, he actively tried to dissociate himself from that idea (Neimeyer & Neimeyer, 1981). Work on cognitive processes in personality stemmed mostly from other lines of thought (e.g., Bruner, 1957; Heider, 1958; Koffka, 1935; Köhler, 1947; Lewin, 1951a). In fact, in what came to be called the "cognitive revolution" in psychology, Kelly was pretty thoroughly ignored. Yet many of today's ideas about cognition in personality greatly resemble his ideas.

For example, today's cognitive theorists view people as implicit scientists who try to predict the world. But today there's a different slant on *why* this is so. Today's view is that you're surrounded by more information than you can possibly use. You can't check every bit, so you don't try (Gigerenzer & Goldstein, 1996). Instead, you impose an organization, and use partial information to make inferences about the rest (Anderson, 1991; Nisbett & Ross, 1980). This saves mental resources (Macrae, Milne, & Bodenhausen, 1994). That's important, because you usually have several things on your mind at once, and you *need* those resources. You can save resources in this way, however, only if you can predict events well.

Representing Your Experience of the World

Cognitive theorists are interested in how people organize, store, and retrieve memories of their experiences. How *do* we do these things?

Schemas and Their Development

People impose order based on recurrences of similar qualities across repeated events. This "order" takes the form of **schemas.** A schema is a mental organization of information, a knowledge structure. Schemas are (roughly) categories. They can incorporate many kinds of elements, including perceptual images, abstract knowledge, feeling qualities, and information about time sequence (Schwarz, 1990).

Most views assume that schemas include information about specific cases (**exemplars** of the category) and also information about the more general sense of what the category is. Thus, for any given category (e.g., college football players), you can bring to mind specific examples. You can also bring to mind a sense of the category as a whole (a "typical" football player).

There are several views of the form schemas take (Anderson, 1985; Newell, 1990; Suppes, Pavel, & Falmagne, 1994). Some people think they form around the category's "best member," its **prototype.** In some theories this is the best *actual* member you've found so far. In other theories it's an *idealized* member, an average of those you've found so far.

It's also been argued that categories don't have definitions. The features of the category all contribute to its nature, but aren't *necessary.* For example, your bird schema probably includes the idea that birds fly. But some birds don't fly, such as chickens and penguins. This means flying can't be a *defining* feature of birds, though flying does make an animal more likely to fit the bird schema. The term **fuzzy set** has been used to describe this situation (Zadeh, 1965; see also Lakoff, 1987; Medin, 1989). That is, the schema is defined in a fuzzy way by a set of criteria that are relevant but not necessary. The more criteria met by an exemplar, the more likely it is to be seen as a category member. But if there's no *defining* criterion, members can differ a lot from one another in the attributes they do and don't have.

These theories differ, but in all of them schemas have an organizing quality. They provide an integration of meaning. An event is a collection of elements, people, movements, objects in use, and so on. But unless you have a sense of what the event's *about,* it might just as well all be random. In the same way, the attributes of an object are just a collection of bits, unless you have an overriding sense of what the object *is.* The schema, in effect, is the glue that holds the bits of information together.

Once schemas are developed, they're used to recognize new experiences. You identify new events by quickly (and mostly unconsciously) comparing them to the schemas (Anderson, 1976, 1985; Medin, 1989; Rosch & Mervis, 1975; Smith, Shoben, & Rips, 1974). If the features of the new event resemble a schema, the new stimulus is identified as "one of those." This seems to be how we recognize objects and events. Each new perception is based partly on incoming information and partly on what you've got for schemas (Jussim, 1991).

Effects of Schemas

Schemas have several effects. First, they make it easier to code new information in memory. It's as though the schema were made of flypaper or Velcro. New information sticks to them.

An as illustration, here are some statements to remember: "Arrange things into groups. One pile may be enough, depending on how much there is to do. It's better to do too few things at once than too many." Did those statements make sense? Could you remember them easily? If you knew beforehand that they pertained to washing clothes, it would have helped (Bransford & Johnson, 1972; Smith, Adams, & Schorr, 1978). The label "washing clothes" evokes a schema. Instead of trying to remember strings of words, you'd fit the information to the organized structure. The structure helps the bits cohere and makes them easier to remember. One effect of schemas, then, is easier coding of new information.

Another effect of schemas comes from the fact that many events lack some information. If there's enough incoming information to identify a schema, you get more information *from memory.* You assume that what's in the schema is true of the new event, because it's been true in the past. For example, if you hear about Joe doing laundry, you're likely to assume he put soap in the washer, even if that's not mentioned. Indeed, later you may even recall that you'd been told about the soap, when you hadn't (Bransford & Franks, 1971; Cantor & Mischel, 1977). Something you assume is true unless you're told otherwise is called a **default.** A second effect of schemas, then, is to bring default information from memory to fill gaps.

A third effect of schemas concerns the fact that memory is selective. You don't remember everything you experience. What you remember is influenced by the schema you use. It tells where in the event to look for information. That is, you look for information that relates to the schema. If you change schemas, you change guidelines about what to look for. As a result, you notice and encode different things. As an example, Don and Sandy in the chapter opening looked at a house as potential buyers. They noticed and remembered things about appliances and room layouts. If they'd looked at a house from the viewpoint of a potential burglar, they'd instead notice and encode such things as jewelry, TVs, and stereos (Anderson & Pichert, 1978).

These schema-based biases can be self-perpetuating. That is, schemas don't just tell you where to look. They also suggest what you're going to find. As a result, you're more likely to remember information that *confirms* your expectation than information that doesn't. This can make the schema more solid in the future, and thus more resistant to disconfirmation or change (Hill, Lewicki, Czyzewska, & Boss, 1989).

Semantic Memory, Episodic Memory, and Scripts

Schemas are organizations among memories. But memories are organized in several ways (Tulving, 1972). **Semantic memory** is organized by meaning. It's categories of objects and concepts. As an example, most people have a schema for "boats," with images of what boats look like and words that describe their nature. This schema often has feeling qualities as well, if the person thinks of boats as a source of either fun or danger.

A second type of organization, **episodic memory,** is memory for events, or "episodes." It's memory for your experiences in space and time (Tulving, 1993). In episodic memory, elements of an event you experienced are strung together as they happened (Freyd, 1987). Some episodes are long and elaborate, for example, going to high school. Others are brief, for example, a screech of tires on pavement, followed by crashing metal and tinkling glass. A brief event can be stored both by itself and as a part of a longer event (e.g., a car crash may have been a vivid episode in your experience of high school).

If enough episodes of a given type are experienced, a schema for that class of episodes starts to form. This kind of schema is often called a **script** (Schank & Abelson, 1977). Scripts are prototypes of event categories. They're used partly to perceive and interpret common events such as going to the hardware store, mowing the lawn, and so on. Scripts provide perceptions with a sense of duration and a sense of flow and change through the event. As with all schemas, scripts have defaults, things you assume to be true.

An example is the script for "dining out" (Schank & Abelson, 1977). Read this description: "John went to a new Thai restaurant last night. He had chicken curry, very spicy. After paying his bill, he went home." You understood that description, using your "dining out" script. You probably added many details to what you read from your defaults. You probably assumed John drove to the restaurant (although you may have assumed he walked). You probably assumed he ordered the chicken before he ate it, rather than snatching it off someone else's table. And you probably assumed that the bill he paid was for his dinner, not for broken dishes or furniture. In all these cases, you supplied information to fill in gaps in the story. Scripts have room for lots

Scripts refer to well-defined sequences of behavior that tell us what to expect and what to do in certain situations, such as eating at a restaurant.

of diversity. Despite this, the basic structure of each is the same. Thus, when you encounter a new variation on it, you easily understand what's going on.

It's easy to distinguish between semantic and episodic memory, but a lot of experience is coded both ways at once. For example, conceptual categories (semantic) often develop through repeated exposures to regularities in experiences (episodic). If a young child tries to play with several animals and has varying degrees of success, it may help lead the child to discover that dogs and cats are two different categories of animals.

In recent years, theorists have become more aware that feelings play an important role in schemas of all kinds. The involvement of feelings has many implications, including the fact that the feeling quality itself can be an important cue for evoking a schema (Niedenthal, Halberstadt, & Innes-Ker, 1999). Incorporating feeling qualities in schemas seems especially likely when the feeling is one of threat (Crawford & Cacioppo, 2002). Presumably this is because sensing threat is so important for survival that we evolved a way to preferentially code information about it.

Socially Relevant Schemas

When cognitive psychologists began to study categories, personality psychologists soon began to study how these processes apply to socially meaningful stimuli, or **social cognition** (Fiske & Taylor, 1984; Higgins & Bargh, 1987; Kunda, 1999; Macrae & Bodenhausen, 2000; Schneider, 1991; Wyer & Srull, 1986). They found that people form categories of types of people (Brewer, Dull, & Lui, 1981; Dodge, 1986), gender roles (Bem, 1981; Deaux & Major, 1987; Lobel, 1994), environments (Brewer & Treyens, 1981; Tversky & Hemenway, 1983), social situations (Cantor, Mischel, & Schwartz, 1982; Schutte, Kenrick, & Sadalla, 1985), and types of social relations (Baldwin, 1992; Baldwin, Carrell, & Lopez, 1990; A. P. Fiske, 1992; Haslam, 1994). We even have schemas for the structure of music (Chew, Larkey, Soli, Blount, & Jenkins, 1982) and sets of emotions (Roseman, 1991; Shaver, Schwartz, Kirson, & O'Connor, 1987).

People differ in how readily they develop schemas (Moskowitz, 1993; Neuberg & Newsom, 1993). Schemas also differ from person to person in content and complexity. This is partly because people have different amounts of experience in any given domain. For example, some people have elaborate mental representations of the diversity among wines; others know only that some wine is red and some is white.

Another illustration of this diversity comes from research on how experienced probation officers differ from other people in their schemas about offenders (Lurigio & Carroll, 1985). Officers have detailed schemas, others don't. This influences how the different sets of people expect offenders to act. Participants read case files that portrayed schematic cases (burglar, drug addict, welfare fraud, and white-collar criminal) or cases of more mixed content. They then rated how likely the various offenders were to make it through probation successfully.

When the cases didn't fit a schema well, probation officers and clerical workers made similar ratings. When the cases fit a schema, though, differences emerged. Probation officers made sharp discriminations among the offenders (Figure 16.1). Clerical workers, in contrast, didn't see these differences. Thus, it seems that experience leads people to form rather distinct expectations about what behaviors to expect from a given category of people.

Self-Schemas

A particularly important schema is the one you form about yourself (Greenwald & Pratkanis, 1984; Markus, 1977; Markus & Wurf, 1987; T. B. Rogers, 1981), called the **self-schema.** This term is a little like *self-concept,* but it's also a little different. The self-schema acts like any schema. It makes it easier to remember things that fit it. It provides you with lots of default information. It also tells you where to look for new information. Your self-schema can even bias your recall of your past, twisting your recollections so they fit better with how you see yourself now (Ross, 1989).

Does the self-schema differ from other schemas? Well, it seems to be larger and more complex (Rogers, Kuiper, & Kirker, 1977). This makes sense, because you've probably spent more time noticing things about yourself than anything else in the world. It incorporates both trait labels and information about concrete behaviors (Fekken & Holden, 1992; Schell, Klein, & Babey, 1996), and it has more emotional elements than other schemas (Markus & Sentis, 1982). It even seems to be used as a default representation for people you don't know at all (Nickerson, 2001). There remain questions, though, about whether the self-schema is truly special. Features that seem

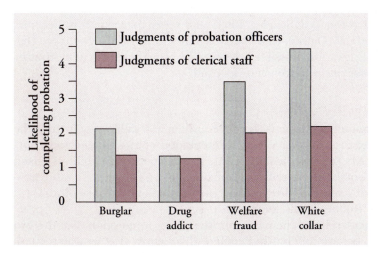

Figure 16.1

More experience creates more elaborate schemas. Participants read case files that portrayed offenders, then rated how likely the offenders would be to make it through probation successfully. Probation officers made sharp discriminations among cases that fit a schema, but clerical workers didn't (adapted from Lurigio & Carroll, 1985).

special in it are also there in other well-developed schemas (Greenwald & Banaji, 1989; Karylowski, 1990). Perhaps it seems special only because it's so well developed.

Although the self-schema is more complex than other schemas, there are individual differences in how complex it is (Linville, 1987). Some people keep their different self-aspects distinct from each other. Each role these people play, each goal they have, each activity they engage in, has its own existence in their self-image. These people are high in **self-complexity.** Other people's self-aspects are less distinct. These people are lower in self-complexity.

This difference has interesting implications. For people low in self-complexity, feelings relating to a bad event in one aspect of life tend to spill over into other aspects of the sense of self (Linville, 1987). Having trouble with a course may make you also feel bad about your social life. This doesn't happen as much for people high in self-complexity. Apparently their separations and boundaries between self-aspects prevents it (see also, Niedenthal, Setterlund, & Wherry, 1992; Showers & Ryff, 1996).

In the same way, thinking of the self in a contextualized way—even temporarily—can dampen emotional reactions to a specific failure (Mendoza-Denton, Ayduk, Mischel, Shoda, & Testa, 2001). Participants who were led to think of themselves in connections with particular classes of situations ("I am ___ when ___") were less affected emotionally by adverse outcomes than those who were led to think of themselves in broader terms ("I am ___").

How do people acquire (or fail to acquire) complexity in the self-schema? It may be partly a matter of how much you think about yourself. Nasby (1985) found that people who say they think about themselves a lot have self-schemas of greater complexity and detail than people who think about themselves less. Presumably the very process of thinking about yourself causes a continued growth and articulation of the self-schema.

Another way of viewing self-complexity is to see the self as a family of self-schemas, rather than one (e.g., Cantor & Kihlstrom, 1987; Markus & Nurius, 1986). In a sense, you're a different person when you're in different contexts (Andersen & Chen, 2002; Swann, Bosson, & Pelham, 2002). You make different assumptions about yourself, and you attend to different aspects of what's going on. When you go from your friends at college to your parents at home, it's as though you're putting aside one schema about yourself and taking up another one.

Self-schemas also vary in another way. Markus and her colleagues (e.g., Markus & Nurius, 1986) suggest that people develop diverse images of themselves. People have selves they'd like to become (Hewitt & Genest, 1990), selves they're afraid of becoming (Carver, Lawrence, & Scheier, 1999), and selves they expect to become. People have a disliked self (Ogilvie, 1987) and a self they think they ought to be (Higgins, 1987, 1990). These various **possible selves** can be brought to bear as motivators because they provide goals to approach or to avoid.

Entity and Incremental Schemas

Another difference among self-schemas is a difference in how stable people think the self is. The easiest example of this is the representation of an ability of some sort (Dweck & Leggett, 1988; see also Nicholls, 1984). To some people, an ability is a fixed *entity.* It's something you have more of or less of, but it doesn't change. To other people, ability is something you can *increment,* increase through experience. Both views are relatively stable (Robins & Pals, 2002).

Both of these views reflect schemas about the ability in question. But the two views lead people to behave differently. People with an entity view tend to see task

People who hold an incremental view of ability treat setbacks as challenges for future improvements.

performance as having the goal of *proving* their ability. If they do poorly, they're distressed and want to quit. People with an incremental view see their actions as having the goal of *extending* their ability. If they do poorly, they see this as an opportunity to increase their ability.

Are these views really schemas? They seem to act in ways schemas do. For example, they guide people's search for new information (Plaks, Stroessner, Dweck, & Sherman, 2001). When people hold an entity view, they attend to (and remember) information indicating consistency. When people hold an incremental view, they attend to (and remember) indications of change.

Much of the research on this topic has focused on naturally occurring differences among schemas. However, Wood and Bandura (1989) created the same difference experimentally, with much the same result. Participants were led to hold either an entity or an incremental view of decision-making skills. They then performed a hard managerial task. Holding the entity view caused a loss of confidence as the task proceeded, a loss of efficiency in strategies used, and poorer performance.

Attribution

An important aspect of construing events is judging their causes. Inferring the cause tells you what kind of event it was (e.g., intentional vs. accidental). It tells you something about how likely it is to occur again. Inferring the cause of an event is called **attribution** (Heider, 1944, 1958). It's apparently something people do spontaneously, without even being aware they're doing it (Hassin, Bargh, & Uleman, 2002). Attribution has been studied extensively, and several principles have been identified (Anderson & Weiner, 1992).

For one, people tend to interpret events they experience themselves (as actors) differently from events they see or hear about (as observers). Observers tend to see other people's behavior as reflecting their personality (Jones & Nisbett, 1971). The actors themselves, however, tend to see the very same acts as reflecting causal forces stemming from the situation. Thus, the same action can be construed in very different ways by two people. For example, if *you* get up in a disorganized meeting and take charge, *I* may think it's because you're pushy. If *I* do the same thing, I'd think it happened because the situation cried out for someone—anyone—to take charge. This attributional difference illustrates Kelly's principle of constructive alternativism (discussed in Chapter 15): the same action can be construed in multiple ways.

The process of making attributions doesn't occur in a vacuum. It relies on people's schemas about of the nature of social situations (Read, 1987). Default values provided by your schemas help you make inferences beyond the information that's there (Carlston & Skowronski, 1994). And using different schemas (different mental orientations) causes people to make different inferences. In this case, the inference is about the cause behind the event.

Another important aspect of attribution is the interpretations that people make for good and bad outcomes—successes and failures. Success and failure can have many causes, but special attention has been given to four causes: ability, effort, task difficulty, and luck or chance factors. The best-known analysis of this kind of attribution is that of Bernie Weiner (1979, 1986, 1990).

Weiner points out that these causes tend to form a dimension of *locus of causality:* either the cause is internal, a part of yourself (ability, effort), or it's external, outside yourself (chance factors, task difficulty). Causes also vary in *stability.* Some seem fairly stable (ability), whereas others vary from one time to another (effort). In general, people tend to see their success as having internal stable causes, specifically, their ability. (Perhaps this is because this view enhances self-esteem, as suggested in Chapter 14.) People tend to see their failures as having been caused by relatively *un*stable influences, bad luck or too little effort.

Although these general tendencies exist, people also differ in their attributional tendencies. This can have big implications. If you see failure as caused by unstable factors, there's no need to worry for the future. That is, if the cause is unstable, chances are the situation won't be the same next time. If the cause is stable, however, the picture is very different. If you failed because you don't have the ability, or because the world is permanently against you, you're going to face that same situation next time and every time. In that case, your expectation about the future will be for continued failure. Your behavior, thoughts, and feelings can be deeply affected by that expectation. Perceiving stable and permanent reasons for bad outcomes in life can lead to depression (e.g., Abramson, Alloy, & Metalsky, 1995; Abramson, Metalsky, & Alloy, 1989; Abramson, Seligman, & Teasdale, 1978; Weiner & Litman-Adizes, 1980) and perhaps even sickness and death (e.g., Buchanan, 1995; Peterson, 1995).

Activation and Use of Memories

We've devoted a lot of space here to people's knowledge structures. How do they actually operate in memory? One view is that memories form a network (Figure 16.2). Links between them reflect communication between **nodes,** areas of storage. Some links are semantic, linking attributes that contribute to a category (Figure 16.2, A). Others are episodic, linking events that made up an event (Figure 16.2, B). In this view, your knowledge is an elaborate web of associations of different strengths among an enormous number of nodes of information.

When a memory node is activated, the information in it is in conscious awareness. Nodes can be activated by an intentional search, but they can also become activated in other ways. As one node becomes active, a *partial* activation spreads to other nodes related to it. The closer and stronger the relation, the more the spread. Partial activation makes it easier for the related area to come all the way to consciousness. That is, because it's already partly activated, it takes less of a boost to make it fully active.

To use the examples in Figure 16.2, thinking of an orange partially activates related semantic nodes. Thinking of an orange tends to remind you of navel oranges, the color and flavor of oranges, orange trees, maybe the Orange Bowl. Since both orange groves and the Orange Bowl are in Florida, you may be slightly reminded of

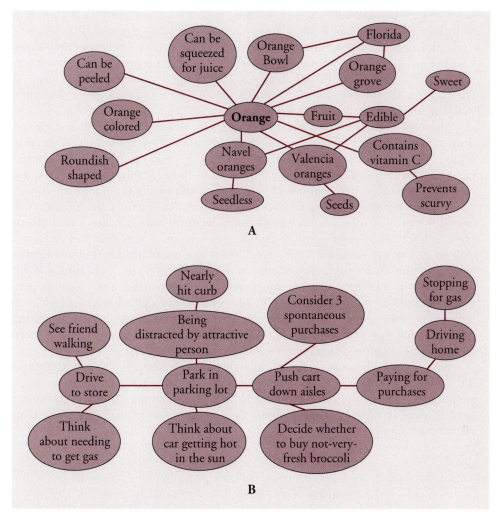

Figure 16.2

(A) Part of the network of semantic associations surrounding the concept "orange."
(B) Part of the network of episodic memories surrounding the event "going to the grocery store for broccoli, strawberries, and beer."

Florida, as well. In the same way, thinking about a bit of an episode partially activates related nodes. Thinking about being in the parking lot tends to remind you vaguely of the person you saw there, which in turn may remind you of the fact that you almost lost control over your driving and ran up over the curb.

These examples involve *partial* activation. The memory may not make it all the way to consciousness without another boost from somewhere. But it's more likely to get there than it was before. An extra boost sometimes comes from another source (e.g., seeing someone who looks a little like the person in the parking lot or hearing the song that was on the radio while you were parking). Given that extra boost, the node becomes active enough for its content (the image of the person) to pop into awareness. If the node hadn't already been partially active, the boost wouldn't have been enough.

The idea that partial activation causes easier access to memories has led to a technique called **priming.** Priming is activating a node of information in a task prior to the task of interest. It was first used to study two questions. One is whether *related* information thereby becomes more accessible. The other is whether the *same* information thereby is more accessible later on. That is, once priming has taken place, it takes a while for the activation to fade. This would leave the node more accessible than before, until the activation fades away.

The answer in each case is yes. For example, Srull and Wyer (1979) had people do a task that caused them to read words related to hostility. Later, in what was presented as a different study, they were more likely to see an ambiguously portrayed person as hostile (Figure 16.3). They rated him more negatively on other evaluative terms, as well, suggesting a spread of activation to related areas of memory.

Later research added complexity to this picture. For example, the effects occur only if the primed information can plausibly be applied to the later event (Herr, Sherman, & Fazio, 1983; Higgins & Brendl, 1995). If you prime "dishonest," it won't influence your judgments of athletic ability. On the other hand, priming seems to activate the full dimension, not just the end that's primed (Park, Yoon, Kim, & Wyer, 2001). If you prime "honest" and then present a target that might be *dis*honest, people are more likely to see dishonesty. (This finding fits Kelly's idea, discussed in Chapter 15, that constructs are bipolar dichotomies.) Other research shows that priming nonemotional aspects of a schema that has emotion makes its emotional quality more likely to be applied to neutral stimuli (Mikulincer et al., 2001).

When you think about what priming is, you realize that it happens constantly in life (Carver & Scheier, 2002). Whenever you hear something, read something, watch something, it makes the corresponding parts of your memories active. This in turn causes partial activation in related areas. That can have a wide range of subtle effects on behavior (see also Box 16.1).

Figure 16.3

Effects of priming. Participants read a set of items, 80 percent of which (or 20 percent of which) contained words related to hostility. Later, in what they thought was a different experiment, they read an ambiguous portrayal of a target person and rated him on two sets of scales, some pertaining to hostility and others evaluative but not directly related to hostility. Reading a larger number of hostile words caused the target person to be seen as more hostile and as less pleasant (adapted from Srull and Wyer, 1979, Experiment 1, immediate condition).

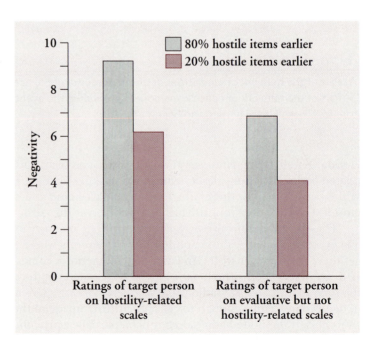

BOX 16.1

WHAT'S IN A NAME?

Priming is a funny process. It happens all the time when you don't realize it. And it can have some very unexpected effects on people's behavior. For example, consider your name. Your name is part of your self-schema. For most of us, our name marks family ties. But does your name have an impact on your life? Beyond the fact that some people are teased about having unusual names, most people would probably say no.

A series of studies has shown, however, that people's names are involved with several important life decisions. Pelham, Mirenberg, and Jones (2002) reported ten studies of people's names and how they related to where the people lived and what their businesses were. Five studies found that people were more likely to live in places whose names resembled their own than would happen by chance. For example, men named Jack live in Jacksonville in a greater proportion than in, say, Philadelphia. There are more than *twice* as many men named Louis in Louisiana than would be expected by chance. Women named Virginia are extra-likely to move to Virginia but not to Georgia, whereas the reverse is true of women named Georgia.

It's not just where people live. It's also what they do. People tend to have jobs that have the same first initial as their own names. Sherry's odds of owning a salon are greater than chance, but not Carol's. Carol is more likely to own a candle shop. People named Thompson have a greater than chance involvement in the travel business.

Pelham and his colleagues have also examined these effects in other areas of life. This work hasn't been published independently yet, but it was outlined by Pelham et al. (2002). In the 2000 presidential campaign, people whose last names start with B were more likely to give to the Bush campaign, those whose last names start with G were likely to give to Gore. Another study found that people are attracted to other people whose names resemble their own.

Why do these things happen? The explanation is that most people have positive feelings about themselves, as part of the self-schema. The positive feelings are evoked by anything that reminds them of themselves. This happens even if the reminding is very slight and even if it's unconscious. In effect, if you're named Ken and you live in Kentucky, you're surrounded by primes to your self-schema. People may gravitate slightly to anything that evokes that warm sense of self. We don't know if there's a Ken in Kentucky who owns a kennel and is married to a woman named Karen. But if there is, we'd bet he's probably a very contented man.

There's also evidence that people differ in what categories they have readily accessible (Bargh, Lombardi, & Higgins, 1988; Higgins, King, & Mavin, 1982; Lau, 1989). The categories that are most accessible are the ones they *use* the most. Thus, differences in *chronic* accessibility reflect people's readiness to use particular schemas in seeing the world (Bargh & Pratto, 1986).

As an example, children who grow up in violent neighborhoods are more likely than other children to develop social schemas with violent themes (Chen & Matthews, 2001). These schemas should be highly accessible for children from such neighborhoods, and thus more likely to be used. Consistent with this, children from poor neighborhoods perceive more hostile intent in ambiguous actions than other children (see also Flory, Matthews, & Owens, 1998).

Connectionist Views of Mental Organization

The view that cognition involves symbol processing (which has been implicit thus far) dominated cognitive psychology for many years. In the last twenty years or so, however, a split has developed. That split is now having reverberations in personality psychology. A different way to think about cognitive processes has taken hold. It has several labels, including *parallel distributed processing* (McClelland, Rumelhart, & PDP Research Group, 1986), *neural networks* (Anderson, 1995; Levine & Leven, 1992), and (perhaps most common) **connectionism** (McClelland, 1999).

This view uses neuronal processes, rather than computer processes, as a metaphor for cognitive processes. Because the nervous system processes information simultaneously along many pathways, parallel processing is one of its key features. It also holds that representations aren't centralized in specific nodes. Rather, this view says that a representation exists only in a pattern of activation of an entire network of neurons.

Connectionists describe cognition in terms of networks of simple neuronlike units, in which "processing" consists of passing activation from one unit to another (Figure 16.4). Each unit sums its inputs and passes its activation onward. Energy passes in only one direction for each connection, as in neurons. But connections are often assumed in which activation goes from a "later" unit back to influence an "earlier" one, which is also true of neurons. The network reacts to an input by generating a pattern of activity. This activity is transmitted through the layers of the network from the input side to the output side. The pattern that emerges on the output side is the response to the input stimulus.

The pattern of activations in the network is updated repeatedly. Potentially there are many cycles of updates. Gradually the system "settles" into a configuration and further cycling yields no more change. A common way to think about this is that the system *simultaneously satisfies multiple constraints* that the units place on each other (Thagard, 1989). For example, two nodes that inhibit each other can't both be highly active at the same time. Each is trying to constrain the other's activity. One would eventually inhibit the other enough to keep it from being active. Diverse constraints are settled out during the repeated updating of activations. The process is complicated, but here's the bottom line: the parallel constraint satisfaction process creates the greatest degree of organization and coherence across the network, given the constraints.

The literature of connectionism in cognitive psychology is large and growing rapidly (e.g., J. A. Anderson, 1995; Smolensky, Mozer, & Rumelhart, 1996). Several

Figure 16.4

Example of a connectionist network. The network consists of units that receive and send activation, with two connections (printed in color) that feed activation back to "earlier" units. A given activation can be either excitatory (+) or inhibitory (−). Each unit receives activation from all the units that project to it, and sends activation to all the units it projects to (adapted from Carver & Scheier, 1998).

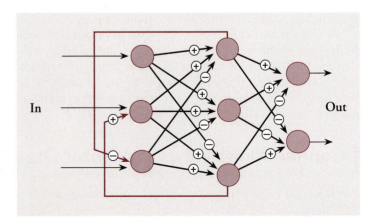

authors have also tried to indicate why these ideas are useful for other areas of psychology, including personality (Caspar, Rothenfluh, & Segal, 1992; Kunda & Thagard, 1996; Read & Miller, 1998, 2002; Read, Vanman, & Miller, 1997; Schultz & Lepper, 1996; Smith, 1996).

Of particular interest are social perception and decision making (Read et al., 1997; Thagard & Millgram, 1995). These are similar, in that each yields the selection of one possibility from among two or more available. When you view an ambiguous figure (Figure 16.5), you perceive one or the other of its possibilities, not a blend of the two. The perception of one or the other pops into mind. When you make a decision, you pick one option. You don't usually get to blend options. Again, even if you're trying to be rational, it's often the case that an answer seems to pop into your mind. Think back to Don and Sandy in the chapter opening, trying to find a house they liked. They were being rational and orderly, but a decision just suddenly appeared.

How would connectionists analyze such experiences? They would say that the experience is being constructed from bits of input information. These bits activate units in the network, and the units place constraints on each other. Activations get transferred from unit to unit, around and around. As the activation pattern is updated over and over, some constraints get stronger over cycles, some get weaker. The network as a whole settles into a pattern. The pattern is the perception or decision. Although there may be many cycles, the time involved can be very short. Subjectively, the pattern (perception, decision) emerges as a final product, sometimes abruptly.

One thing that's interesting about these networks is that it can be very hard to tell ahead of time how they will settle out. The pattern of constraints can be intricate. Constraints may relate to each other in ways that aren't obvious. The network doesn't care about the big picture. That's not how it works. Each unit just keeps sending out activations as a function of how active it is itself. In the pushing and pulling, perceptions and decisions can emerge that seem irrational. And they aren't rational, in a sense. The decision about a house isn't the algebraic sum of the ratings of the good and bad points of each house. It's more interwoven. This aspect of the connectionist approach in particular makes it feel very different from the symbolic approach.

Figure 16.5

An example of an ambiguous figure. This image can be seen either as a young woman turning aside or as an old woman with protruding nose and chin. Although your perception can easily shift from one to the other, you don't see a blend of images (adapted from Boring, 1930).

Another thing that's interesting about these networks is that they sometimes are very stable but sometimes reorganize abruptly (Read & Miller, in press). Sometimes constraints induce stability, so if you change one input, or more, nothing much changes. Sometimes, though, the change in an input is critically important. A change in this one can have profound reverberations over cycles, producing a drastic reorganization. Thus, if you're looking at a figure such as that in Figure 16.5, it can suddenly reorganize and become the alternate image. These ideas have been used to discuss how the self-concept is sometimes resistant to and sometimes responsive to information from outside (Nowak, Vallacher, Tesser, & Borkowski, 2000).

Dual Process Models

Cognitive psychologists have wrestled for some time with differences between the symbol-processing approach and the connectionist approach. In doing so, several have turned to the idea that cognition involves two kinds of thought rather than one. Smolensky (1988) argued that a *conscious processor* is used for effortful reasoning and following of programs of instructions. An *intuitive processor* manages intuitive problem solving, heuristic strategies, and skilled or automatic activities, using connectionist processes. This general view has also been expressed in several other theories (see Holyoak & Spellman, 1993; Sloman, 1996).

The subjective experiences of the two kinds of cognition differ. When doing controlled processing, the mind in effect says, "Find a rule, apply it to the situation, carry out its logical steps of inference and action, and make decisions as needed. If no rule is available, come up with whatever's closest." When the mind is in connectionist mode, the settling process goes on until the elements shake out and a pattern emerges. This mode fits the experience of insight: a pattern appears suddenly where none was before.

The idea that people experience the world through two different modes of processing also appears in the literature of personality. Depictions of two modes of processing bear a strong resemblance to an argument made first some time ago by Seymour Epstein (1985, 1990, 1994). Epstein's cognitive–experiential self-theory assumes we experience reality through two systems. The *rational* system operates mostly consciously, uses logical rules, and is fairly slow. This is the symbolic processor that we think of as our rational mind. The *experiential* system is intuitive. It's a "quick and dirty" way of assessing and responding to reality. It relies on shortcuts and information that's readily available. It functions automatically and quickly.

Epstein believes that both systems are always at work, and that they jointly determine behavior. Each can also be engaged to a greater degree by circumstances. For example, asking people to give strictly logical responses to hypothetical events tends to place them in the rational mode. Asking them how they would respond if the events happened to them tends to place them in the experiential mode (Epstein, Lipson, Holstein, & Huh, 1992). The more emotionally charged a situation is, the more thinking is dominated by the experiential system.

In Epstein's view, the experiential system is a system that resulted from eons of evolution. It's invoked when speed is needed (as when the situation is emotionally charged). You can't be thorough when you need to act fast (for example, to avoid danger). Maybe you can't even wait to form an intention. The rational system is more recent in origin. It provides a more cautious, analytic, planful way of proceeding. That also has advantages, of course, when there is enough time and freedom from pressure to think things through.

More recently the dual process idea has emerged several more times, in forms that are very similar to this. Metcalfe and Mischel (1999) proposed there is a "hot" system that's emotional, impulsive, and reflexive. It operates in a connectionist manner. A "cool" system is strategic, flexible, slower, and unemotional. This line of thought was derived in part from a long line of research on delay of gratification (see Box 16.2). But it obviously applies more broadly.

This idea has recently been applied to an interesting new topic: anger that arises in response to rejection (Ayduk, Mischel, & Downey, 2002). In this research, students recalled a situation in which they had been rejected or excluded. After bringing that situation to mind, some were told to focus on the feelings and sensations they had experienced, others were told to focus on the arrangement of people, objects, and lighting in the event. Then they wrote down what they had thought and felt while recalling the experience. Those who had taken a "cool" stance on the situation reported less anger and hurt than did the others.

BOX 16.2

DELAY OF GRATIFICATION
The Role of Cognitive Strategies

Several previous chapters have discussed people's ability to delay gratification, to wait for something good until a later time. From a psychoanalytic view (Chapter 8), this is a matter of ego processes holding the id in check until the time is right to fulfill its desires. From the view of ego psychology (Chapter 10), traits of ego control and resiliency determine this self-restraint. From the view of the learning perspective (Chapter 13), whether a person delays or not depends on the reward structure of the situation and the behavior of salient models.

The cognitive point of view suggests yet another angle on the process of delaying gratification. Specifically, an important influence on delay of gratification is the mental strategies people use (Kanfer, Karoly, & Newman, 1975; Mischel, 1974, 1979). What people think about—and *how* they think about it—can make delays easier or harder.

Early work showed that preschoolers will wait ten times longer for a desired food if it isn't visible than if it is (Mischel & Ebbesen, 1970). On the other hand, delays were easier to tolerate if pictures of the rewards were present (Mischel & Moore, 1973). Later research showed these effects can be changed by varying how children *think* about the desired object. In particular, thinking about consummatory aspects of a food reward, such as its taste, makes it nearly impossible for children to delay at all (Mischel & Baker, 1975). In contrast, attending to qualities of the food reward that aren't associated with eating makes it possible for children to tolerate delay quite easily (see also Kanfer et al., 1975; Moore et al., 1976; Toner & Smith, 1977).

Research on how these self-control strategies evolve shows that there's a natural progression over time (Mischel, 1979). At first, children attend to aspects of the reward that are most appealing (such as taste), which doesn't help (Yates & Mischel, 1979). Eventually they begin to generate cognitive strategies to keep these thoughts from their awareness. The result is increased self-restraint. As Mischel (1990) points out, it's not what's in front of the children that's important, but what's going on in their heads. This research thus reinforces one of Mischel's major theoretical points, and a theme that runs throughout this chapter: the importance of people's mental strategies in determining their behavior. As is indicated in the main text, this idea has since been expanded to talk about the notion of self-control more broadly.

The dual-process idea has also emerged in an analysis of attribution processes (Lieberman et al., in press). This version also includes an effort to link the two modes of functioning to different areas of the brain. It starts with the long-standing distinction in cognitive psychology between automatic and effortful processing. Effortful is consciously guided. Automatic occurs without conscious guidance. When something is done effortfully over and over, it starts to become automatic. Done often enough, it no longer requires attention, and the doing of it drops out of consciousness.

The interesting part is this: After a review of findings from several sources, Lieberman et al. (in press) asserted that the consciously controlled and automatic versions of a given behavior are managed by quite different parts of the brain. Partly on those grounds, they argued for two modes of functioning. As did Epstein, they assume the reflexive system is attuned to pressured and emotional demands of the world and that it acts very quickly. They assume that this system behaves in a connectionist fashion. The other system uses symbolic logic, and is slower. As did Epstein, they believe both systems are always at work and each can be induced to dominate by variations in the situation.

In Chapter 7 we mentioned the ideas of Liberman et al. in a different context. There we suggested the possibility that the two modes might relate to the personality trait of constraint. If behavior is dominated by controlled processing, the person may be constrained. If behavior is dominated by automatic processing, the person may be impulsive. In this chapter, the issue is different. The issue now is that the cognitive aspects of personality may be of two types, which have two different "feels." One of them is clearly recognizable as thinking. The other feels more like thoughtlessly reacting. Many people are inclined to see the former as more important, and more a part of personality. But the latter may be a far more potent determinant of behavior than most people realize, a point we take up in the next chapter.

Pulling the Pieces Together

Much of the cognitive view of personality examines specific mental processes underlying personality. This work tends to be tightly focused on particular issues. As a result, the cognitive approach is very fragmented (Funder, 2001). Attempts have been made, however, to make more integrative statements about cognition and personality. Two of the most influential statements were made by Walter Mischel, a theorist with a huge influence on today's cognitive view (see also Box 16.3). Interestingly, these statements were made nearly a quarter century apart.

Cognitive Person Variables

As is true of many who now hold a cognitive view on personality, Mischel earlier was identified with the *cognitive-social learning* view. The theoretical statement he made in 1973 represents a transition between Mischel the learning theorist and Mischel the cognitive theorist.

Mischel (1973) proposed that an adequate theory of personality must take into account five classes of cognitive variables in the person, all of which are influenced by learning. Given these criteria, Mischel gave them the long name of "cognitive social learning person variables." He intended them to take the place of traits (Mischel, 1990).

One class of variables is the person's *competencies*. These are the skills that people develop over their life's experiences. Just as people develop skills for manipu-

BOX 16.3

THE THEORIST AND THE THEORY
Mischel and His Mentors

Professional mentors influence their students in many ways. Most obviously, they impart a set of skills and a way of looking at the world, which the students then apply to domains of their own choosing. Sometimes, however, there is more than that. Sometimes an imprint on the mind of a student reverberates for a long time in that student's work. The student absorbs the essence of the mentor's view and recasts it in a new and more elaborated form. This seems to be the case in the career of Walter Mischel.

Mischel was born in Vienna in 1930 and lived within walking distance of Sigmund Freud's house. When Mischel was nine, his family fled to New York to escape Nazism. He grew up in New York and became a social worker, using Freud's theory of personality. His enthusiasm for psychoanalysis waned considerably, however, when he tried to apply its ideas to dealing with juvenile offenders in New York's Lower East Side.

After a stint as a social worker, Mischel set off to continue his education. At Ohio State University he came under the influence of two psychologists who were already making a mark on personality psychology, George Kelly and Julian Rotter. Kelly's ideas (described in Chapter 15) emphasized the im-

portance of personal constructs in people's handling of their social and physical worlds. Rotter's ideas (described in Chapter 13) concerned the important role played by people's expectations in determining their behavior. Both Kelly and Rotter were also skeptical about the wisdom of a purely dispositional approach to personality.

Mischel's work has incorporated all three of these themes, although Mischel has also taken each theme in directions of his own. For example, as discussed in Chapter 4, Mischel (1968) sparked a huge controversy in personality psychology over the question of whether behavior has enough cross-situational consistency to warrant believing in dispositions. He spent much of his career focusing on issues in the cognitive-social learning perspective, including the role played by various kinds of expectancies. In the past three decades his views have become increasingly cognitive, leading to what some see as a resolution of the controversy he sparked in 1968. As we noted at the start of this chapter, the emergence of today's cognitive view on personality has roots in several places other than Kelly's ideas. Surely, however, one reason for the emergence of this cognitive view is the impact that Kelly the mentor had on the young Walter Mischel.

lating the physical world, they develop social skills and problem-solving strategies, tools for analyzing the social world. Competencies aren't static knowledge. They're active processes that people can bring to bear on situations they confront. These competencies are much like what was discussed in Chapter 10, in the context of the idea that the ego functions to promote better adaptation.

Different people have different patterns of competencies, of course. People differ in how competent they are in a given area. Some people have the ability to empathize with others, some people have the skill to fix brakes, and some have the ability to make people laugh. Situations also vary in what competencies they call for (Shoda, Mischel, & Wright, 1993). Thus, different situations provide opportunities for different people to take advantage of.

The second class of variables is *encoding strategies and personal constructs*. This covers what Kelly said about the unique worldview that each person develops, and also the notion of schemas. You notice and categorize events and people differently, depending on the schema you're using. (You look at the house one way if you're a potential buyer, another way if you're a potential burglar.) It's not the objective situation that determines how you react, but how you construe it. Two people react to a situation differently because they literally experience it differently. Much of the work on the cognitive view of personality over the past three decades pertains to this class of variables.

Encoding strategies are ways of viewing the world. But to know what a person is going to *do* in that world, you need to know more. You need to know the person's *expectancies*. Two types of expectancies are important. One is the anticipation that one event typically is followed by another. For example, hearing a siren is often followed by seeing an emergency vehicle. Seeing dark clouds and hearing thunder are often followed by rain. These expectancies about what's connected to what provide continuity in experience. They play a large role in scripts.

The second expectancy is what Mischel called *behavior-outcome expectancy*. This is the belief that particular acts typically lead to particular outcomes. These are much like the outcome expectancies in Bandura's social cognitive learning theory (discussed in Chapter 13). Entering a restaurant (behavior) is usually followed by being greeted and seated by a host or waiter (outcome). Being friendly to other people (behavior) is usually followed by friendly responses (outcome). Entering the right set of codes into an automatic teller machine (behavior) usually leads to receiving money (outcome). If the rules you know match reality, your actions will be effective. If you've learned a set of behavior-outcome expectancies that don't fit the world, though, you'll be less effective.

Expectancies about links between actions and outcomes begin to specify what people do. They do things they think will produce outcomes. But what outcomes? The outcomes they *want*. The fourth part of the puzzle, then, is knowing what outcomes the person wants, the person's *subjective values*. These are the incentives that cause people to make use of their expectancies about links between behavior and outcome. If the outcome that's available isn't one the person cares about, all that knowledge will sit there unused.

The fifth set of cognitive variables that Mischel (1973) discussed is what he called *self-regulatory systems and plans*. People have to set goals, make plans, and do the various things that need to be done to see that the plans are realized in action. This category covers a lot of ground. Since the time Mischel proposed his five categories, this one has taken on something of a life of its own. In part for this reason, we'll talk about it separately, in Chapter 17.

Personality as a Cognitive–Affective Processing System

More recently, Mischel and Shoda (1995) proposed a model that extends and elaborates Mischel's earlier statement (we discussed this model briefly in Chapter 4). They described what they call a cognitive–affective processing system. The joining of *cognitive* to *affective* in this label reflects the increased recognition that emotion plays an important role in much of cognitive experience.

Mischel and Shoda said that people develop distinctive organizations of information about the nature of situations, other people, and the self. These organizations are more complex in one sense than what we've described thus far. Specifically, Mischel and Shoda said that people's schemas have a kind of *if . . . then,* property, a conditional quality. Saying someone is aggressive doesn't mean you think the person is aggressive every moment. It means you think he's more likely than most people to react aggressively to a certain class of situations. Evidence from several sources supports this view. For example, in describing others people often use "hedges," conditions under which the person acts a particular way (Wright & Mischel, 1988). This suggests that people normally think in conditional terms about each other.

Mischel and Shoda believe people also think in conditional terms about the self. That is, each person's own behavior also follows an *if . . . then* principle: Schemas to construe situations include information about appropriate behavior in those situations (Carver & Scheier, 1981). If a situation linked to a particular behavior is identified, then that behavior occurs.

In this view, individuality arises from two sources. First, people differ in the accessibility of their various schemas. Thus, different schemas are likely to pop up for different people in a given setting. People literally perceive different things in the same situation. People also differ in their *if . . . then* profiles. When a particular schema is active, the person will act in ways that fit its cognitive–affective elements. But it may be entirely different actions for different people.

For example, some people will view an ambiguous remark made by another person as a rejection, some as a provocation, some as an indication that a power play is underway, some as an indication that the other person was out too late last night and is hung over. If Marty sees a situation as a power play—even if no one else in the room sees it that way—he'll erupt in bluster and bravado. If he doesn't see it that way, he won't act that way. Ed is also sensitive to power plays, but he has a different *if . . . then* link: he gets very quiet and starts looking for cues about who's likely to win. If Ed sees the situation as a power play, just as Marty does, Ed will act quite differently than Marty will.

To predict consistency of action, then, you need to know two things. You need to know how the person construes the situation (which depends on the person's schemas and their accessibility). And you need to know the person's *if . . . then* profile. In this view, the unique profile of *if . . . then* relations is a "behavioral signature" for each person's personality (Shoda, Mischel, & Wright, 1994). Indeed, these profiles of *if . . . then* relations may in some sense *define* personality (Mischel et al., 2002). These *if . . . then* profiles are relatively stable over time (Shoda et al., 1994), and thus account for temporal consistency in behavior. Consistency over time, of course, is a key element in conceptions of personality.

This line of thought has been applied by Andersen and Chen (2002) to the key social relationships in a person's life. That is, they argue that we develop schematic knowledge of significant others early in life. When we encounter new people who resemble a significant other enough to activate that schema, it evokes the *if . . . then* profile associated with that significant other. You become more like the version of yourself that you display to that significant other.

This general viewpoint on behavior suggests that schemas are deeply interconnected to one another. That is, schemas about what people are like relate closely to schemas about the nature of situations. Both of these are tied to schemas for acting. Although you may focus on one of these at a time, the use of one implicitly involves the use of the others as well (Shoda et al., 1989).

Consistent with this general line of thought, there's evidence that some of the same brain structures are involved in both perception and cognition and related actions. Specifically, certain neurons that are active when a monkey does an action are also active when the same monkey sees the same action being done (Gallese, 2001; Rizzolatti, Fogassi, & Gallese, 2002). Evidence of the same process has been found in humans (Buccino et al., 2001). Later work extended this principle to the perceptual modality of sound. The neurons that are active when the monkey does or observes the action are also active when the monkey hears sounds associated with that action (Kohler, Keysers, Umiltà, Fogassi, Gallese, & Rizzolatti, 2002). Such findings have led to the idea that perceptual memories may actually be organized in terms of potentials for action (Fadiga, Fogassi, Gallese, & Rizzolatti, 2000).

Assessment

From the cognitive viewpoint, personality assessment emphasizes assessing people's mental structures. There are many ways to assess mental pictures of reality (e.g., Merluzzi, Glass, & Genest, 1981) called **cognitive assessment** techniques. They range from interviews and self-reports to think-aloud protocols, in which people say what comes into their minds while doing an activity. A variation on this is experience sampling, which is more intermittent. Another is retrospective thought listing, in which you think back to the event, rather than report on-line.

Think-Aloud, Experience Sampling, and Self-Monitoring

The technique used is often determined by the nature of the event of interest. For example, think-aloud approaches are used to assess cognition during problem solving (Ericsson & Simon, 1993). They're aimed at finding out what thoughts occur at various stages of problem solving. The intent is to examine such questions as which strategies are effective and which aren't, and how the strategies of experts and novices differ (Simon & Simon, 1987).

Experience sampling (or thought sampling) typically has somewhat different purposes. In this technique, people report at certain times what they've been thinking and doing. Sometimes the reports are made at scheduled times, sometimes people are randomly paged and asked to report (e.g., Csikszentmihalyi, 1978, 1982, 1990; Gable, Reis, & Elliot, 2000; Hormuth 1990; Laurenceau, Feldman Barrett, & Pietromonaco, 1998; Pietromonaco & Feldman Barrett, 1997). This procedure lets you sample across a wide range of events in the person's day. That way you can find out what cognitions and emotions go along with which kinds of events. The result is a clearer picture of what various events feel like to the people who are taking part in them.

For example, Csikszentmihalyi and Csikszentmihalyi (1988) paged people at irregular intervals and had them record their activities, thoughts, and feelings. As noted in Chapter 14, a focus of that work was on optimal experience. There were several interesting findings: positive feelings relate mostly to voluntary actions, not things people *have* to do. Satisfaction, freedom, alertness, and creativity relate to events in which people's attention is tightly focused on what they're doing (Csikszentmihalyi, 1978). Interestingly, positive feelings of immersion are very likely during work (see also Table 16.1).

More recent research has extended experience sampling methodology into many new domains. Further, it's now common to collect participants' reports of their thoughts and feelings on hand-held computers (Gable et al., 2000; Laurenceau et al., 1998; Pietromonaco & Feldman Barrett, 1997). This exciting development extends greatly the ease of collecting these sorts of cognitive assessments. This technique,

Table 16.1

Positive feelings of being deeply and pleasantly involved in one's activities are tied to a wide range of activities. People were given descriptions that expressed such feelings and were asked to indicate one context in which they themselves had had similar experiences in their own lives (adapted from Csikszentmihalyi, 1982).

Activity named	Percentage of people naming it
Work activities (working, being involved in challenging problems at work)	31
Hobbies and home activities (cooking, singing, photography, sewing, etc.)	22
Sports and outdoor activities (golf, dancing, swimming, etc.)	18
Social activities (spending time with spouse or children, parties, vacationing)	16
Passive attending activities (listening to music, reading, watching TV)	13

with its origins in the sampling of cognition, is now being used to study ideas derived from a variety of theoretical perspectives.

Another technique, termed event recording or self-monitoring, focuses not on particular moments or times of day, but on some particular class of events. In this technique, you record *instances of specific event types* (Ewart, 1978; Mahoney, 1977; Nelson, 1977). You note the particular behavior, emotion, or thought pattern, and record information about what was going on at the time (e.g., the time of day, whether you were with others or alone, what the situation was). Doing this lets you see regularities in the contexts that surround problem thoughts and emotions. You get a better understanding of what schemas you're automatically using.

Contextualized Assessment

Another element in the cognitive view on assessment is the idea that personality should be assessed regarding specific classes of contexts. This element is shared with the cognitive–social learning view. Several studies indicate that doing this adds important information.

Research on this issue by Wright and his colleagues has focused on assessment of children with problems. In one study (Wright, Lindgren, & Zakriski, 2001), teachers rated boys using two measures. One was a commonly used measure of problem behaviors (such as aggression and social withdrawal), but one that doesn't identify the context in which they happen. The other measure assesses how often the behaviors occur in response to specific situations. The broad measure was able to distinguish aggressive children from others, but didn't distinguish between two groups of boys whose aggression occurred in very different contexts. Thus, the contextualized measure provided fine-grained information that the other did not.

In another study (Wright, Zakriski, & Drinkwater, 1999), children were observed in a residential setting over a six-week period, with elaborate recordings made of their behaviors and the contexts in which they occurred. Each child was also rated on the same measure of problem behaviors, which doesn't note contexts. Each child was classified by that measure as being an externalizer (displaying behaviors such as aggression), an internalizer (displaying behaviors such as social withdrawal), a mixed case, or not a clinical case (i.e., not fitting a diagnosis).

The behavioral signatures of these groups differed in ways that would not have been predicted by the global ratings. When teased or threatened by a peer, externalizers tended to hit and boss, internalizers whined and withdrew. Other than these specific situations, their behavior wasn't different from children who weren't diagnosed with either problem. The mixed cases didn't do any of these things very much in response to teasing, but they did tend to both hit and withdraw socially in a context where a peer simply talked to them. Again, contextualized assessment gave much more information about those being assessed.

Diagnostic Categories as Prototypes

The cognitive approach has one more implication concerning assessment, which differs completely from anything we've said thus far. This point isn't about assessment methods, but about a result of some assessments. In particular, it concerns how clinicians organize their knowledge about the nature of people's problems.

People with psychological problems aren't just one big group. They fall into several diagnostic categories, based on symptoms. Categories once had defining characteristics. If a person had all of a specific set of qualities, he was in that category. If he didn't, he wasn't. An alternative strategy is suggested by a view on the nature of categories discussed earlier, in which categories don't have explicit definitions. Rather, the category is a fuzzy set, made up of a set of features that category members often have but sometimes don't. In the same way, a diagnostic category may be a collection of features that are *often* present in exemplars of that category, *but not always* (Cantor, Smith, French, & Mezzich, 1980).

Using the old strategy, if a person generally fits a diagnostic category but lacks a specific feature, the psychologist would hesitate to place the person in that category. With the newer strategy, the psychologist may be more willing to do so. Under this strategy, fit to the category is determined by the *proportion* of features that fit that category. This approach emphasizes the idea that diagnosis is probabilistic rather than exact (Cantor et al., 1980).

Problems in Behavior, and Behavior Change

The focus on cognitive structure that's been so apparent throughout this chapter is also involved in how this view conceptualizes psychological problems and therapeutic behavioral change.

Information-Processing Deficits

One implication of the cognitive view is that some problems reflect deficits in basic cognitive or memory functions: attending, extracting and organizing information, and so on. For example, people with schizophrenia require more time than other people to recognize stimuli such as letters (Miller, Saccuzzo, & Braff, 1979; Steronko & Woods, 1978). It isn't clear whether this implies a deeper problem, or whether it bears only on perceiving. Just by itself, however, this problem would account for some of the difficulty a schizophrenic person has in life.

Another simple idea from this view is that there's a limit on people's attentional capacity. If you use too much attention on other things, you become less efficient at what you're trying to do. It can also make it hard to learn. For example, anxiety takes up attention. For that reason alone, being anxious can impair your ability to process other information (Newman et al., 1993; Sorg & Whitney, 1992). People with test anxiety or social anxiety thus become less efficient when the anxiety is aroused. A related argument about overloaded attention has been used to explore deficits related to depression (Conway & Giannopoulos, 1993; Kuhl & Helle, 1986).

Some styles of *deploying* attention and processing cues may also create problems (Crick & Dodge, 1994). For example, children who are overly aggressive seem not to attend to cues of other children's intentions (Dodge, 1986; Dodge & Crick, 1990). As a result, they misjudge their intent and respond aggressively. Indeed, they develop the expectation that other children will be hostile and they strike out preemptively (Hubbard, Dodge, Cillessen, Coie, & Schwartz, 2001). This may also be true of violent adults (Holtzworth-Munroe, 1992).

Why do people deploy their attention in ineffective ways? Their *schemas* lead them to do so. Recall that one effect of schemas is to tell you where to look for information in a new event: you look for information that fits the schema. Thus, a biased or faulty schema can bias the search for cues, which can lead to misinferences and inappropriate actions.

Depressive Self-Schemas

A broader implication of the cognitive view is that many of people's problems stem from schemas that interfere with effective functioning. This reasoning has been applied to several problems, most notably depression. Theorists hold that people sometimes develop ideas about the world that are inaccurate or distorted. These ideas then have adverse effects for the person who has them (e.g., Beck, 1976; Ellis, 1987; Meichenbaum, 1977; Young & Klosko, 1993). Aaron Beck (1972, 1976; Beck, Rush, Shaw, & Emery, 1979) is one theorist who thinks that depression and other problems arise from such distortions. In effect, people with these problems use faulty schemas to interpret events. They rely on negative preconceptions (their schemas) and ignore information that's available in the environment (though see Box 16.4).

In Beck's view, the distorted schemas are used quickly and spontaneously. They produce a stream of what he calls **automatic thoughts.** These automatic thoughts (e.g., "I can't do this"; "What's the point of trying?"; "Everything's going to turn out wrong") influence feelings and behaviors. The pattern has a "run-on" quality, because the negative feelings lead to more use of negative schemas. This in turn leads to more negative affect (cf. Nolen-Hoeksema et al., 1993; Wenzlaff, Wegner, & Roper, 1988). Indeed, just expecting emotional distress makes distress more likely to arise (Kirsch, 1990; Kirsch, Mearns, & Catanzaro, 1990).

People who are prone to depression or anxiety seem to over-rely on information in memory and under-rely on the reality of the situation. This is problematic because the self-schemas of these people are negative (Kuiper & Derry, 1981; Segal, 1988). When people with problems use the negative schemas, they naturally expect bad outcomes. They don't look at the situation with an open mind but attend to and encode the worst side of what's happening (Gotlib, 1983).

Beck uses the term **cognitive triad** to refer to negative thinking about the self, the world, and the future. He thinks depressed people also use other distortions. They *overgeneralize* in a negative way from a single bad outcome to their overall sense of self-worth (Carver, 1998; Carver & Ganellen, 1983; Carver, La Voie, Kuhl, & Ganellen 1988). They make *arbitrary inferences,* jumping to negative conclusions when there isn't evidence to support them (Cook & Peterson, 1986). They *catastrophize,* anticipate that every problem will have a terrible outcome. They interpret bad

BOX 16.4

THEORETICAL CONTROVERSY
Whose Perceptions Are Distorted, Anyway?

Beck's theory of depression is based on the premise that people who get depressed make a variety of cognitive distortions. He sees these as leading to depressed feelings and to other symptoms of depression. However, research has raised questions about who's doing more distorting: people who are depressed or people who aren't.

In one research program bearing on this question (reviewed by Alloy & Abramson, 1988), participants were presented a series of problems. For some, there was a connection between their responses and the outcome of the problem. For others, there was no relation between response and outcome. The measure of interest was participants' estimates of the degree to which their responses had controlled the outcomes.

The results were surprising. The researchers found that depressed persons were in fact fairly *accurate* in their judgments. People who weren't depressed, on the other hand, tended to overestimate the control they'd had over good outcomes that in reality were random. No one was surprised that the depressed and nondepressed groups differed. What was surprising was that it was the *depressed* persons who apparently had the better grip on reality.

Another study made a similar case, using very different procedures (Lewinsohn, Mischel, Chaplin, & Barton, 1980). Participants were observed in social interaction and were rated on several dimensions by observers. The participants also rated themselves. The results revealed that people who weren't depressed saw themselves in a better light than the observers did. People who were depressed saw themselves pretty much as the observers saw them. Again, the depressed participants had a better grasp on reality than did the nondepressed.

What are the implications of these findings for Beck's theory of depression? In answering this question, it's important to keep in mind that depressed people *did* differ from nondepressed people, in the expected direction. Thus, Beck's argument that depression involves distortion—*in comparison with other people*—still holds. What was startling was that this distortion resulted in greater rather than less accuracy. Thus, if Beck's theory about depression is correct, it seems to need one additional assumption: that the perceptions of nondepressed people incorporate a rosy and unrealistic glow of optimism. A number of people have, in fact, reached precisely that conclusion (Taylor & Brown, 1988; Weinstein, 1989).

---

outcomes as permanent (Abramson et al., 1978; Abramson et al., 1989). The result of all this is a sense of low self-worth and hopelessness for the future (Haaga, Dyck, & Ernst, 1991; Roberts, Gotlib, & Kassel, 1996; Roberts & Monroe, 1994).

Cognitive Therapy

In Beck's view, therapy should get the person to put faulty schemas aside and build new ones. People must learn to recognize automatic self-defeating thoughts and substitute other self-talk for them. This is termed **cognitive restructuring** or **reframing.** They should also try to focus on the information in the situation and rely less on preconceptions. To put it differently, the person should become more *controlled* in processing what's going on, and less *automatic* (cf. Barber & DeRubeis, 1989; Kanfer & Busemeyer, 1982).

The procedures used for changing faulty schemas and their consequences are known broadly as **cognitive therapies** (Beck, 1976, 1991; Beck et al., 1979; DeRubeis, Tang, & Beck, 2001). There are several different techniques. One surprising one is

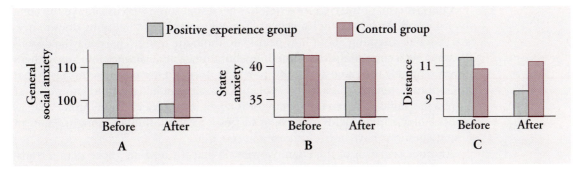

Figure 16.6

Scores before and after on three measures among socially anxious men who engaged in unpressured positive conversations with a woman on two different occasions, compared with scores of men who did not do so. The measures are (A) self-rated general social anxiety, (B) self-rated state anxiety (taken while in the presence of an attractive woman), and (C) distance from the woman while engaged in a cooperative task. The pleasant experiences improved participants' scores on all these variables (adapted from Haemmerlie & Montgomery, 1984).

getting people to go ahead and do things they expect (unrealistically) to have bad consequences. If the bad outcome doesn't happen, the people are thereby led to re-examine—and perhaps change—their expectations.

More generally, people are encouraged to view their thought patterns as hypotheses to be tested, instead of as certainties. They're also encouraged to test the hypotheses. For example, if you're a person who thinks a single failure means you can't do anything right, you might be told to examine your skills in other domains immediately after a failure. If you're a person who thinks everyone will despise you if you do anything wrong, you might be told to test this assumption by being with friends the next time you do something wrong.

Even a small amount of this sort of "reality testing" can have a large impact on how people view themselves. In one study (Haemmerlie & Montgomery, 1984), students with strong social anxiety were given a simple treatment for it. The treatment was a conversation with a member of the opposite sex, who'd been told to initiate conversation topics, use the pronoun *you* fairly often, and avoid being negative. These "biased interactions" were held twice, a week apart, for about an hour each time. The result was a large reduction in signs of anxiety (Figure 16.6).

Contemporary Cognitive Theories: Problems and Prospects

Some psychologists find the cognitive view on personality exciting. Others find it less so. It's seen by many as disorganized and not yet mature (Funder, 2001). Those who find it interesting acknowledge that its relatively recent origin leaves many loose ends dangling. Some critics of this view, on the other hand, think it's a passing fad, a misguided effort to graft a very different part of psychology someplace it just doesn't belong.

One criticism of the cognitive view has been that some who use it take the computer metaphor too literally. Knowing how a computer does something doesn't necessarily tell us anything about how people do the same thing. There may be dozens of ways to get a computer to do something, but there's no assurance that any of them is even remotely the same as the way a person does it. One response to this is that the computer metaphor is a useful conceptual tool, even if it's hard to know how far to press the analogy. When the metaphor is taken in its general form, rather than as a precise blueprint, it yields interesting suggestions about human thought. Many of these suggestions have been supported in research.

Another criticism of the cognitive view is that it's nothing more than a transplantation of cognitive psychology into the subject matter of personality. What's gained by knowing that a person's knowledge about the world (including the self) is schematically organized? What does it tell you about personality to know that these knowledge structures can be pulled into use by priming them?

One answer is that these aspects of the mind's functioning do seem to have important implications for day-to-day behaviors that we usually think of in terms of personality. People absorb new experiences in terms of their current understanding of the world. Thus, it's useful to know what biases are created by the current understanding (i.e., schemas). How people interpret their experiences is also influenced by the goals they have in mind. Because different people have different goals, they experience events in very different ways.

The fact that people's construals can be influenced by priming is of special interest, partly because it relates to an idea of Freud's, but with a very different spin. The idea is that people do things for reasons they're unaware of. Priming shows that this does happen, but the reason need not reside in the unconscious. The process may be far more superficial (and for that reason less ominous). But because it's superficial, it may also be far more common than previously realized (Carver & Scheier, in press).

The broadest answer to criticisms of the cognitive view, however, may be this: the cognitive viewpoint on personality is part of a broad attempt to understand the operating characteristics of the mind. A better understanding of those characteristics can't help but illuminate important aspects of personality. From this view, personality is a reflection of the complexities of the mind and its workings. We can't understand the former fully without understanding the latter.

SUMMARY

The cognitive orientation relates to Kelly's theory of personal constructs, to the social learning view, and to cognitive psychology. It considers how people attend to, process, organize, encode, store, and retrieve information. Schemas are mental organizations of information that develop over experience and are used to categorize new events. Some think schemas organize around prototypes (best members), some say that schemas have fuzzy, or inexact, definitions. Schemas facilitate coding of new events; they provide default information to fill in the gaps of events; they also orient you to new events, suggesting where to look for more information. Schemas can represent concepts (in semantic memory) and events (in episodic memory). Each aspect of memory holds exemplars and generalities. Stereotypic event categories are called scripts.

Social cognition refers to the cognitive processes that bear on stimuli relevant to social behavior. People develop schematic representations of other people, and environmental and social settings. People also develop self-schemas, representations of themselves. The self-schema is more elaborate than other schemas, but it seems to follow the same principles. Some social schemas imply permanence (entity), some imply potential for change (incremental).

Many psychologists view memory as a vast set of content nodes, linked to each other by various associations. Activating one node in memory causes partial activation of related nodes (priming), causing that information to become more accessible. Connectionist models view memory differently: as patterns in overall networks. The patterns reflect satisfaction of many constraints simultaneously. Some psychologists believe there are two distinct kinds of thought processes: one quick, emotional, and connectionist, the other slower, rational, and linear.

Broad statements on cognitive views of personality emphasize the importance of people's schemas, encoding strategies, personal competencies, expectancies about how things are related in the world, values or incentives, and self-regulatory systems. People's behavior is seen as following *if . . . then* contingencies, in which the *if* describes a situation, and the *then* describes a behavioral response. In this view, personality is a profile of these contingencies, forming a unique "behavioral signature" for each person.

Assessment from this viewpoint is the process of determining the person's cognitive tendencies and contents of consciousness. Cognitive assessment techniques include think-aloud procedures, thought sampling, and monitoring of the occurrence of particular categories of events. These procedures give a clearer idea of what sorts of thoughts are coming to mind in various kinds of situations, typically situations that are problematic. Also important is the idea that assessment be contextualized, to capture the person's *if . . . then* contingencies.

Problems in behavior can come from information-processing deficits (e.g., difficulty encoding, ineffective allocation of attention). Problems can also arise from development of negative self-schemas. In this view, depression results from various kinds of cognitive distortions, all of which cause events to seem more unpleasant or as having more negative implications than is actually true. Cognitive therapy involves, in part, attempting to get people to stop engaging in these cognitive distortions and develop more adaptive views of the events that they experience.

GLOSSARY

Attribution The process of making a judgment about the cause or causes of an event.

Automatic thoughts Self-related internal dialogue that often interferes with behavior.

Cognitive assessment Procedures used to assess cognitive processes and contents of consciousness.

Cognitive restructuring or **reframing** The process of taking a different and more positive view of one's experience.

Cognitive therapy Procedures aimed at reducing cognitive distortions and resulting distress.

Cognitive triad Negative patterns of thinking about the self, the world, and the future.

Connectionism Approach to understanding cognition based on metaphor of interconnected neurons.

Default Something assumed to be true until you learn otherwise.

Episodic memory Memory organized according to sequences of events.

Exemplar A specific example of a category member.

Fuzzy set A category defined by a set of attributes that aren't absolutely necessary for membership.

Node An area of memory storing some element of information.

Possible self An image of oneself in the future (expected, desired, feared, etc.).

Priming The process of activating an element in memory by using the information that's contained in it.

Prototype The representation of a category in terms of a "best" member of the category.

Schema An organization of knowledge in memory.

Script A memory structure used to represent a highly stereotyped category of events.

Self-complexity The degree to which one's self-schema is differentiated and compartmentalized.

Self-schema The schematic representation of the self.

Semantic memory Memory organized according to meaning.

Social cognition Cognitive processes focusing on socially meaningful stimuli.

Self-Regulation

■ **From Cognition to Behavior**

Schemas for Action
Automaticity in Action
Intentions
Implementation Intentions, and Deliberative
    and Implemental Mindsets
Goals and Goal Setting

■ **Self-Regulation and Feedback Control**

Feedback Control
Self-Directed Attention and the Action
    of the Comparator
Hierarchical Organization
Issues concerning Hierarchical Organization
Research on Hierarchies of Behavior
Emotion
Effects of Expectancies: Effort versus Disengagement

■ **Assessment**

Assessment of Self-Regulatory Qualities
Assessment of Goals

■ **Problems in Behavior,
    and Behavior Change**

Problems as Conflicts among Goals,
    and Lack of Goal Specifications
Problems from an Inability to Disengage
Self-Regulation and the Process of Therapy
Therapy Is Training in Problem Solving

■ **Self-Regulation Theories:
    Problems and Prospects**

SUMMARY

■ As Carolyn awakes, thoughts come to mind about the presentation she's to give this morning. While dressing, she rehearses the points she intends to make. She catches herself skipping too quickly from one to another, and makes a mental note to slow down in the middle section so she doesn't leave anything out. For the twentieth time she retraces her logic, looking for flaws. She wants this to be perfect, to nail down the recommendation for law school she's going to ask her professor for next week. She has planned what to wear to make the impression she wants to make, and just before leaving she checks her appearance in the hall mirror. A little poking and rearranging of her hair, and she turns to go. As she opens the door she runs a mental checklist of what she needs to have with her—notes for her presentation, money, purse, keys, and—oh, yeah—the photos she said she'd show Susan. Grab the photos. Check to see that the door's locked. Check to be sure there's enough gas in the car. Check to see if there's enough time to take the scenic route to campus. And she's off. Good, Carolyn thinks, things are going just the way I want them to. Everything's right on track.

People shift from one task to another as the day proceeds, yet there's usually continuity as well. Your days are usually planful (despite disruptions and side trips) and include many activities. How do you move so easily from one thing to another, keep it all organized, and make it all happen? These are some of the questions behind this chapter.

The approach to personality discussed here uses several metaphors, including person as robot. Robots extend computerlike functions into actions. Robotics is a young field, but it's made huge strides (Beer, 1995; Brooks, 1999, 2002; Brooks & Stein, 1994; Maes, 1990, 1994). Industrial robots weld car bodies and handle dangerous chemicals. Robots explore the far reaches of outer space and the inner slopes of volcanoes. The growth of robotics has also influenced the way some people think about human nature (Brooks, 2002). As more is learned about how to get machines to do things, suspicion has arisen that the ideas behind them may help us understand how human beings function.

Do people resemble robots? The idea may not seem odd when you think about arm and leg movements. It's harder, though, to see how the analogy could make sense for higher aspects of life. How can the aspirations, desires, and dreams of people relate to machines of silicon and wire? How could a robot have room for *emotions*—hopes and fears, joys and sorrows? It seems far-fetched. But several theorists over the past forty years or so have suggested it may not be (e.g., Carver & Scheier, 1981, 1998; Ford, 1987; MacKay, 1963, 1966; Miller, Galanter, & Pribram, 1960; Newell & Simon, 1972; Powers, 1973; Simon, 1967).

The easiest way to start exploring these ideas is to think of them as a view of motivation. Much of this chapter focuses on how people adopt, prioritize, and attain goals. In some ways these functions resemble what was discussed in Chapter 5 as motives.

From Cognition to Behavior

It will also help to recall the cognitive view of personality, discussed in Chapter 16. That view assumes a vast organized network of memories. As we continue, we'll as-

A basic assumption of the cognitive self-regulation perspective is that robots and people operate according to similiar principles.

sume the same general idea. Now, though, the focus is on how the cognitions and memories result in behavior.

Schemas for Action

As noted in Chapter 16, the schemas people use to understand events include information about behavior. This information serves two purposes. You use it to recognize what people are doing when you observe them, and you use it to guide *making of behavior*. Just as we have schemas for recognizing, we have schemas for moving, called **motor schemas** (Adams, 1976; Kelso, 1982; Rosenbaum, 1987, 1990; Salmoni, Schmidt, & Walter, 1984; Schmidt, 1976, 1988).

Motor schemas are for physical movement. But there's more to behavior than that. You also have schemas you use to *decide what to do* in a given situation (Burroughs & Drews, 1991; Dodge, 1986). They're not quite motor schemas, because they don't specify movement. Instead they specify a course of action (e.g., "go to the grocery store for some sugar and coffee"). Thus they *invoke* motor schemas ("stand," "walk," "unlock car," etc.). Because they're a starting point for behavior, these schemas can also be thought of as "behavior-specifying."

What's the relation between the information used to recognize acts and the information used to do acts? Schank and Abelson (1977) said scripts are used for both purposes. The dining out script lets you understand someone else's evening; it also reminds you what actions *you* are to take—order before you're served, and pay the bill before you leave.

It's not clear whether one script serves both purposes or whether there are two parallel forms, one for understanding and one for doing (Petri & Mishkin, 1994).

However, some of the brain structures involved in recognizing action seem also involved in the action itself. As we said in Chapter 16, evidence exists that the same neurons are active both when an action is being done and when the same action is being observed (Gallese, 2001; Rizzolatti, Fogassi, & Gallese, 2002). This suggests a very strong link between thinking and doing.

A different kind of evidence comes from studies that used priming techniques to activate cognitive schemas. Several studies have found that this influenced people's later behavior. In one study (Carver, Ganellen, Froming, & Chambers, 1983), participants had to form sentences from scrambled sets of words. Some read word sets with hostile content, others read word sets with no hostile content. Shortly afterward, all did a task in which they had to punish someone else in the course of teaching a concept. Those who'd been exposed to the words with hostile content gave stronger punishment than those exposed to less hostile content (Figure 17.1, A).

Another study used the scrambled-word task to prime the stereotype of the elderly (Bargh, Chen, & Burrows, 1996). Some participants had many words pertaining to the stereotype, some did not. Each then received credit for participation and left. The dependent measure was how long it took them to walk down the corridor on their way out. Those exposed to the stereotype of the elderly walked more slowly than did the others (Figure 17.1, B).

The interpretation for these effects goes like this: To form sentences from the words, you have to understand the words. Understanding the words requires activating nodes of meaning in memory. This activation spreads to nodes bearing on *be-*

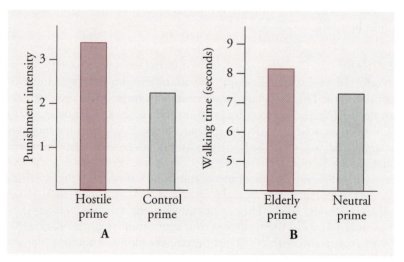

Figure 17.1

Effects of priming an *interpretive* schema on *behavior* that's related to that schema. (A) People who'd been exposed to hostile content in a sentence-formation task gave punishments of greater intensity in a later task than people exposed to less hostile content. (B) People who'd been exposed to elements of the elderly stereotype in a sentence-formation task took longer to walk to the elevator when leaving the experiment than people exposed to neutral words. (Panel A is based on data from Carver et al., 1983, Study 2; Panel B is based on data from Bargh et al., 1996, Experiment 2.)

havior. This quality then emerges in the person's own behavior (Bargh, 1997; D. A. Norman, 1981).

The idea that behavioral schemas are linked to schemas for understanding provides a simple way for behavioral qualities to become active. As you perceive (or think about) people you're with, situations you're in, and so on, you use certain memory nodes. Behavioral qualities linked to those nodes are partially activated (Dodge, 1986; Huesmann, 1988). The behavioral qualities thus become more likely. The activation is automatic, and the behavior emerges with little or no thought (Bargh, 1997). Indeed, it's argued that that's how habitual actions take place: situations activate strongly associated goals (Aarts & Dijksterhuis, 2000).

Automaticity in Action

Findings such as these are part of a large and growing literature on automaticity. Much of this work has been done by John Bargh and his colleagues (Bargh, 1997; Bargh & Chartrand, 1999; Bargh & Ferguson, 2000; Dijksterhuis & Bargh, 2001). Many studies now show that goals can be activated (and people pursue them) with no knowledge on people's part that it's happening. Indeed, some of the studies show that goals can be activated by **subliminal stimuli,** which are so brief that people aren't aware of what they are.

As an example, Chartrand and Bargh (1996) used the scrambled sentences procedure to prime some people with words about evaluation, others with words about memorizing. Participants then read about a target person. Finally, they reported their impressions and memories of the target. Those primed to evaluate formed more organized impressions of the target person than those primed to remember. This fits the view that they were evaluating that person. A second study found the same effect after a prime that was presented subliminally.

Another project (Bargh et al., 2001) extended the effects into the domains of achievement and cooperation. In one study, some participants were primed with performance words (*win, succeed*), others were not. All then did a word-search task. Those primed to achieve did better than those primed with neutral words. A second study created a dilemma to which participants could react by competing or cooperating with another person. It used a fishing scenario in which the lake needed to retain a minimum number of fish after each fishing season. After each "season," participants decided how many fish to return to restock the lake. Those primed by scrambled sentences to be cooperative returned more fish than those who weren't primed to cooperate (for more examples see Bargh & Ferguson, 2000).

The idea that behavioral qualities can be activated and emerge into the ongoing flow of behavior without your awareness is startling. Your actions can be influenced by things you hear on the radio or read in the paper, by conversations you have, by random stimuli you encounter, and you don't even know it. These ideas provide an interpretation of modeling (Chapter 13), in which people repeat things they observe others doing (Carver et al., 1983). People mimic, without realizing it, the posture and gestures of their interaction partners (Chartrand & Bargh, 1999). The pervasiveness of such effects is one factor leading some people to wonder whether behavior is best seen as "directed" or as "self-organizing" (Carver & Scheier, 2002; Vallacher & Nowak, 1997; Vallacher, Read, & Nowak, 2002).

Intentions

Behavioral qualities sometimes emerge automatically, with no conscious choice. Sometimes people act spontaneously and on the spur of the moment (Gibbons, Gerrard,

Blanton, & Russell, 1998). But not always. Sometimes behavior reflects intentions. Icek Ajzen and Martin Fishbein (Ajzen, 1985, 1988; Ajzen & Fishbein, 1980) have studied the process of forming intentions in some depth. They say it involves a kind of mental algebra leading to an action probability. If the probability is high enough, an intention is formed to do the act. Intending an act isn't the same as doing it (Gollwitzer, 1990), but it's an important step in that direction.

Ajzen and Fishbein suggested that when people are deciding whether to do something, they weigh several kinds of information (Figure 17.2). They think about the action's likely outcome, and how much they want it. For example, you might think that spending money on a Caribbean trip over spring break would result in a lot of fun, and you really want that fun. The outcome and its desirability merge to form an **attitude** about the behavior. Because they stem from your own wants, attitudes are *personal* orientations to the act.

Two other kinds of information pertain to the act's *social* meaning to you. One is whether people who matter to you want you to do the action. You might think about your parents, who don't want you to take the trip—they want you to come home for spring break. (Or you might think about your friends, who think the trip is a great idea.) The other element is how much you want to please the people you're thinking about. How much do you want to please your parents, or at least stay on their good side? (How much do you want to go along with your friends' wishes?) What the other people in your mind want you to do and how much that matters to you merge to form a **subjective norm** about the action.

The next step is the intention. This entails combining the attitude and the subjective norm. If they both favor the behavior, you'll form a strong intention to do it.

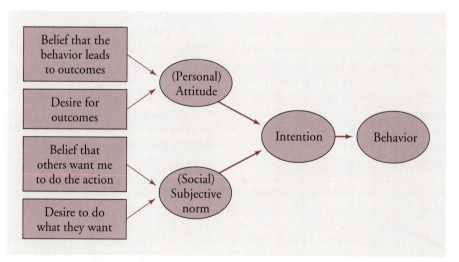

Figure 17.2

Foundations of intentions. The belief that an act will produce a particular outcome and the personal desirability of the outcome merge to form an attitude (a personal orientation to the act). The belief that other people want you to do the act and the desire to go along with their wishes merge to form a subjective norm (a social orientation to the act). The attitude and the subjective norm are weighted in forming the intention. The intention then influences the behavior (adapted from Ajzen, 1988).

If they both oppose the behavior, you'll form a strong intention *not* to do it. The process is more complex when attitude and subjective norm conflict. Sometimes you want the outcome, but you know your parents (or your friends) don't want you to do the behavior. In this case, the intention you form depends on which matters more, satisfying yourself or satisfying your parents (or friends).

Implementation Intentions, and Deliberative and Implemental Mindsets

A distinction has been made by Peter Gollwitzer and his colleagues (Brandstätter, Lengfelder, & Gollwitzer, 2001; Gollwitzer, 1999; Gollwitzer & Brandstätter, 1997) between two kinds of intentions. A **goal intention** is the intent to attain some particular outcome as an end. An **implementation intention** deals with the how, when, and where of the process. It's the intention to take specific actions given specific kinds of circumstances. The linking of the context to the action is very similar to what we described as *if . . . then* contingencies in Chapter 16 (Mischel & Shoda, 1995). *If . . . then* contingencies can be habitual (Brandstätter & Frank, 2002), but they can also be formed for particular intended paths of behavior.

Implementation intentions are subordinate to goal intentions. They serve the goal intentions. They're very important, because they help preempt problems that can arise in actually getting the behavior done. Most simply, people sometimes fail to act on their broad intentions because they haven't decided how to go about it. An implementation intention, being concrete and specific, jumps right past that roadblock. Sometimes people fail to act because they're distracted and brief opportunities pass them by. Having an implementation intention helps you recognize the opportunity quickly and act automatically (Brandstätter et al., 2001). Creating implementation intentions to do something hard (such as writing an assigned paper over Christmas break) greatly increases the likelihood of actually doing it (Gollwitzer & Brandstätter, 1997).

There's another issue that also matters here. Planning and doing are different activities. People engage in them with different kinds of mindsets. Forming an intention requires weighing possibilities, thinking of pros and cons, juggling options. This is called a **deliberative mindset** because the person is deliberating the decision to act. It is relatively unbiased, careful, and cautious, operating in the service of making the best choice (Taylor & Gollwitzer, 1995).

Once the intention has been formed, actually doing the behavior entails a different mindset (Heckhausen & Gollwitzer, 1987). People no longer consider. Now it's all about acting. This is called an **implemental mindset** because it focuses on implementing the intent to act. This mindset is optimistic about success and minimizes potential problems, in the service of trying as hard as possible to carry out the action (Taylor & Gollwitzer, 1995). Generally, it fosters persistence (Brandstätter & Frank, 2002).

There's evidence that these two mindsets may use different brain areas. Lengfelder and Gollwitzer (2001) studied patients with frontal-lobe damage and patients with damage in other areas. They found those with frontal damage were impaired in deliberating. However, if they were carefully provided with *if . . . then* implementation intentions, they weren't impaired at doing. This suggests that the planning is done in the frontal cortex, whereas the automatic handling of the action is done elsewhere. These findings would appear to be consistent with the two-mode models of thought that were discussed in Chapter 16.

Goals and Goal Setting

The ideas discussed thus far all imply that behavior is directed toward goals. Motor schemas have the goal of creating particular body movements. Forming an intention means setting up a goal for action to attain. Forming an implementation intention means establishing subgoals.

The idea that human experience is organized around goals has been discussed a lot in recent years (e.g., Austin & Vancouver, 1996; Elliott & Dweck, 1988; Freund & Baltes, 2002; Pervin, 1983, 1989). Theorists use diverse terms for goals, including *life tasks* (Cantor & Kihlstrom, 1987), *personal strivings* (Emmons, 1986), *current concerns* (Klinger, 1975, 1987), and *personal projects* (Little, 1983, 1989). Though labels differ, the core theme is largely the same. In each case, the point is that people's goals energize their activities, direct their movements, and even provide meaning for their lives (Baumeister, 1989). In this view, the self is made up partly of goals and organizations among them. Indeed, there's evidence that traits derive their meaning from the goals to which they relate (Read, Jones, & Miller, 1990; Roberts & Robins, 2000).

All these constructs assume both overall goals and subgoals. That is, a person's life tasks can be achieved in many ways. The way you choose depends on other aspects of your life. Strategies used for pursuing life tasks can differ a lot from one person to another (Langston & Cantor, 1989). For example, someone who's relatively shy will have different strategies for making friends than will a person who's more outgoing.

Many goals are nonevaluative. They represent intended and desired actions, but they don't imply a standard of attainment or excellence. The goal of going water skiing on a hot afternoon doesn't necessarily imply a goal of excellence (though it might). Forming an intention to go to the grocery store creates a guide for behavior, but it's not really very challenging.

On the other hand, performance level is clearly an issue in some areas. In many activities, the goal isn't just to perform, it's to do *well*. An example is a college course. The goal isn't just completing the course, it's getting a good grade. Another example is business performance. The goal isn't just to survive, but to excel. One question that arises in such contexts is this: does setting a particular goal level have an impact on how well you do?

There's considerable evidence that it does (Locke & Latham, 1990). Setting higher goals leads to higher performance. This is true when high goals are compared to easy goals, and it's also true when they're compared to a goal of "do your best." Apparently "do your best" isn't taken literally. It's taken as an instruction to try to do reasonably well. Thus, it leads to poorer performance than does a specific challenging goal.

Why do higher goals lead to better performance? There are three interrelated reasons. First, a higher goal causes you to *try* harder. For example, you know you won't solve fifty problems in ten minutes unless you push yourself. So you start out pushing yourself. Second, you're more *persistent*. A brief spurt of effort won't do; you'll have to push yourself the entire time. Third, high goals make you *concentrate* more, making you less susceptible to distractions. In all these respects, a lower goal causes people to ease back a little.

The positive effect of setting high goals is well documented. It does, however, have a very important limitation. In particular, if you're given a goal that's totally unrealistic, you won't adopt it. You won't really try for it. If you don't adopt the goal, it's as if the goal doesn't exist. The key, then, is taking up a goal that's high enough to sustain maximum effort, but not so high that it's rejected instead of adopted.

Self-Regulation and Feedback Control

So far we've discussed behavioral schemas, forming of intentions, the use of goals, and the impact of having lofty goals. But once a goal's set, an intention formed, or a motor schema activated, what makes sure the behavior you actually *do* is the one you *set out* to do? This question brings us to the concept of feedback control (Carver & Scheier, 1981, 1998; MacKay, 1963, 1966; Miller et al., 1960; Powers, 1973; Scheier & Carver, 1988; Wiener, 1948).

Feedback Control

A **feedback loop** is a system with four parts (Figure 17.3). The first is a value to self-regulate toward: a *goal,* or *standard of comparison,* or *reference value* for behavior (all these mean the same thing here). These can come from many places and can exist at many levels of abstraction. They can be motor schemas, plans, intentions, or "possible selves" (Markus & Nurius, 1986).

The second element is a perception of your present behavior and its effects. This simply means noting what you're doing and the effect it's having. Sometimes this is just a flicker of awareness, sensing in a vague way what you're doing. Sometimes it means thinking carefully about what you've been doing over a longer period. Sometimes people *literally* watch what they're doing (e.g., at exercise clubs or dance studios). Although it's easiest to talk about it in terms of thinking, this function doesn't require consciousness (Bargh & Ferguson, 2000).

These perceptions are *compared with the goal* (by a component termed a **comparator**). If you're doing what's intended, there's no discrepancy between the two, and you continue as before. If your behavior *differs* from what you intended, though, a final process kicks in. This process changes the behavior, adjusts it to bring it more in line with your intention. (For a subtle theoretical issue pertaining to this viewpoint see Box 17.1.)

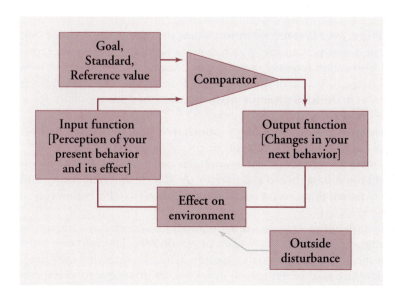

Figure 17.3

Diagram of a discrepancy-reducing feedback loop, which shows the basic processes presumed to underlie self-corrective behavioral self-regulation in both artificial and living systems.

BOX 17.1

THEORETICAL ISSUE
Feedback versus Reinforcement

It's long been known that people engaged in task-directed action benefit from knowing the results of their last efforts (Locke & Latham, 1990; Schmidt, 1988). But this evidence has been interpreted differently by different people. According to the view under discussion, knowledge of results is feedback, which people can use to adjust their behavior. It's sometimes argued, however, that the feedback is actually a *reinforcer* (Kulhavy & Stock, 1989). That's a rather different view of what's going on.

What's the role of reward and punishment in the self-regulation view? People whose work is discussed in this chapter don't entirely agree. Some see reward, particularly self-reward, as important. For example, Bandura (1986) holds that self-reward or self-praise that a person engages in after attaining a desired goal is a crucial aspect of self-regulation. A similar position has been taken by several others (Kanfer, 1977; Pervin, 1983).

On the other side of the disagreement, we've taken the position that this concept isn't needed (Carver & Scheier, 1981, 1990). In our view, it doesn't add anything to say that the person engages in self-praise after goal attainment. Although self-praise may occur, self-praise is a reaction to an event, but it's the

event that matters. The crucial events, in this view, are the goal attainment and the person's realization of how it was that the goal was reached.

The concept of reinforcement comes from learning theory. In thinking about this issue, it's of interest that learning theorists have long argued about the role of reinforcement in learning. Tolman (1932) believed that reward—even to a laboratory rat—doesn't stamp anything in, but just provides information that the animal can learn from. In particular, the animal learns what leads to what in the world, by experiencing the events in association with one another. Tolman said rewards and punishments aren't necessary for learning, but they can draw attention to aspects of the learning situation that are particularly relevant.

It's also been found that a simple social reinforcer such as saying "good" has more impact if you've been led to believe that the person saying "good" does so only rarely (Babad, 1973). Presumably this is because events that are rare provide more information than events that are common. That finding joins with Tolman in suggesting that it may be the *informational value* of the reinforcer that matters, rather than the reinforcer itself.

The word *feedback* is used because when you adjust the action, the result is "fed back" in the form of a new perception, which is rechecked against the reference value. This loop is also called a *control system,* partly because its overall effect is to nudge perceptions in the direction of the desired goal. The term *control* also reflects the fact that each event in the loop depends on the outcome of a previous one. Thus, each prior process "controls" what happens next.

The feedback loop idea has several implications. For one, it assumes that behavior is purposeful (as with the goal concepts discussed earlier). In this view, virtually all behavior involves trying to conform to some reference value. Life is a process of forming goals and intentions (broad and narrow, short-term and long-term), and adjusting behavior to match them, using feedback perceptions to tell whether you're doing as you've intended.

Another implication of this logic is that self-regulation is continuous and never-ending. Every change in output changes present conditions. The new one must be checked against the goal. Further, goals are often dynamic—evolving over time. For example, think of the goal of doing well in school, or making a good impres-

In order for feedback control to occur, people need to monitor what they are currently doing.

sion on someone (and maintaining it), or taking a vacation trip. You "do well in school" not by going to a particular end point, but by doing well at many tasks repeatedly over time. You "take a vacation trip" not by leaving and coming back, but by doing activities that constitute "vacationing." There's a continuous interplay between adjusting your action and moving forward to the next phase of a continually evolving goal.

Referring to something as a standard here means it's the value used as a guide. It doesn't *necessarily* mean a high standard of excellence (though it can). Think of a student who's regulating study behavior around the goal of making a C in a course, by looking over class notes the night before the exam but not doing much more. The *structure* of this behavior (setting a goal, checking, and adjusting as needed) is exactly the same as that of a student who's trying to make an A. They're just using two different comparison values.

Self-Directed Attention and the Action of the Comparator

Does human behavior follow the pattern of feedback control? One source of evidence is work concerning the effects of self-directed attention. It's been argued that when you have a goal or intention in mind, directing your attention toward yourself engages the comparator of the loop that's managing your behavior (Carver & Scheier, 1981, 1998).

In some research on self-directed attention, participants are exposed to manipulations that remind them of themselves (e.g., an audience, a TV camera, or a mirror that shows their image). In other studies, researchers measure the strength of people's dispositional tendency to be self-reflective, using the Self-Consciousness Scale (Fenigstein, Scheier, & Buss, 1975) or other related measures (e.g., Trapnell & Campbell, 1999).

The idea that self-directed attention engages a comparator leads to two kinds of predictions. First, self-focus should increase the tendency to compare goals with current behavior. It's hard to study this, but here's an indirect way. Create a situation in which people can't make the mental comparison between goal and ongoing behavior without getting some concrete information. Put people in that situation, then measure how much they seek the information. Presumably seeking the information implies more comparisons. In studies based on this reasoning, self-focused subjects sought comparison-relevant information more than those who were less self-focused (Scheier & Carver, 1983).

If self-directed attention engages a comparator, something else should also happen: behavior should be regulated more closely to the goal. It does. As an illustration, people in one project (Carver, 1975) said they either opposed or favored the use of punishment as a teaching tool. Later, all of them had to punish someone for errors in learning. All were told to use their own judgment about how much punishment to use. Only those who were self-aware actually acted in line with their opinions (Figure 17.4).

Many other studies also show that self-focus leads to goal matching. Various behaviors have been studied, ranging from aggression (Carver, 1975; Scheier, Fenigstein, & Buss, 1974) to clerical tasks (Carver & Scheier, 1981; Wicklund & Duval, 1971). The values in question include personal attitudes (Carver, 1975; Gibbons, 1978), social norms (Diener & Wallbom, 1976; Scheier et al., 1974), and experimental instructions (Carver, 1974; Wicklund & Duval, 1971). In each case, self-attention caused more conformity to the salient value.

Hierarchical Organization

These studies suggest that feedback processes might be involved in behavior. But a feedback loop is pretty simple. How do you actually get behavior out of it? One kind of answer is that feedback loops can be ordered in layers. William Powers (1973) has argued that this type of organization makes physical action possible, and others have made related arguments (e.g., Broadbent, 1977; Gallistel, 1980; Rosenbaum, 1987, 1990; Vallacher & Wegner, 1987).

The notion of a **feedback hierarchy** assumes there are both high-level and low-level goals. You have the goal of being a particular possible self, but you may also have the goal of having clean clothes to wear and the goal of making it to your psychology class on time. How do these things fit together? Recall the structure of the

Figure 17.4

Level of punishment given to another person, as a function of self-directed attention and participants' attitude toward the use of punishment. Those who favored punishment used more intense punishment than those who opposed it, but only if self-focus was high (adapted from Carver, 1975, Experiment 1).

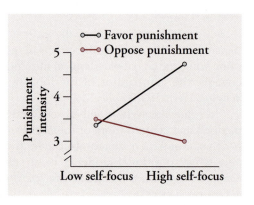

feedback loop from Figure 17.3. Powers says that in a hierarchy the *behavioral output* of a high-level loop consists of setting a goal for a lower-level loop (Figure 17.5). High-order loops don't "behave" by doing physical acts, but by providing guides to the loops below them. Only the very lowest loops actually create physical acts, by controlling muscle groups (Rosenbaum, 1987, 1990).

Powers proposed that human action involves nine levels of control. The levels most relevant to personality are shown in Figure 17.5. At the highest level are very abstract qualities he called **system concepts.** The easiest example is the broad sense of ideal self people try to maintain. Richard, the person whose behavior is outlined in Figure 17.5, is trying to live up to his ideal self-image. Fitting this value resembles the experience of self-actualization (Chapter 14). It promotes the sense of personal wholeness and integration.

People don't just go out and "be" their ideal selves, though. Trying to attain that ideal self means trying to live in accord with guiding **principles** it specifies. Thus, Powers gave the name *principle control* to the level below system-concept control. Principles are broad guidelines. They specify overriding qualities of behavior, which can be displayed in many ways. When they're active, principles help you decide what activities to begin and what choices to make as you do them (Verplanken & Holland, 2002). Principles tend to correspond to traits.

As Figure 17.5 shows, Richard's ideal self includes a principle of thoughtfulness. This principle can be used as a guide for many kinds of action, including taking this opportunity to buy flowers. As another example, the principle of honesty would lead a person to ignore an opportunity to cheat on an exam. The principle of frugality

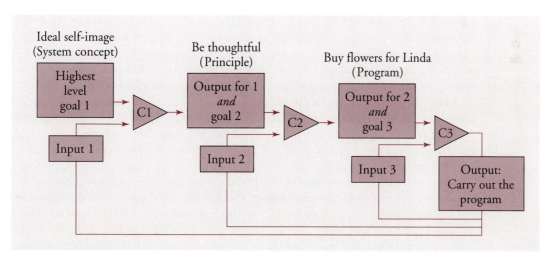

Figure 17.5

Diagram of a three-level hierarchy of feedback systems. This diagram shows the "cascade" of control that flows from higher-level loops to lower-level ones. High-level loops set the goals for the loops directly below them. The levels of control illustrated here are those at the top of the hierarchy proposed by Powers (1973). The diagram shows a cross section of the behavior of a man who is actively attempting to (1) match his self-perceptions to his idealized self, by (2) following the principle of thoughtfulness, which is being manifested (3) in the programmatic activity of buying flowers for his wife.

Calvin and Hobbes   **by Bill Watterson**

would lead a person to choose a moderate restaurant over an expensive one. If he was already at the expensive one, it would lead him toward less expensive choices on the menu.

What defines a principle isn't social acceptability. Rather, it's its abstractness and broad applicability to diverse behaviors. Thus, expedience is a principle, even though it's not a socially desirable one (see also Cartoon 17.1).

Just as people don't go out and "be" their ideal selves, neither do they just "do" principles. Principles act by specifying what Powers called **programs** (or by specifying decisions within programs). Thus, the next level in Figure 17.5 is *program control*. What's called a program there resembles what Schank and Abelson (1977) called a script. It specifies a course of action, but with many details left out. Enacting a program (or script) thus requires you to make many choices within a larger set of possibilities.

The principle of thoughtfulness led Richard in Figure 17.5 to enter the program of buying flowers. This program is partly specified: stop at the florist, pick out flowers, and pay for them. But which flowers he gets will depend on what's available; he can pay with cash or a credit card; and he may or may not have to put money into a parking meter.

Two more things about this example: both stem from the fact that there are several ways to conform to the principle of thoughtfulness. First, Richard might have chosen another program to embody this principle—making Linda a special dinner or washing her car. Choosing any of these programs would match his behavior to the same principle. Second, matching the principle of thoughtfulness didn't require *entering* a program; the principle might have come into play *during* a program. For example, suppose Linda had asked him to pick up flowers on his way home. Given this request, he would be buying flowers anyway. The thoughtfulness principle might have become active in the midst of the buying-flowers program, leading him to decide to buy Linda's favorite flower, even though it's out of season and expensive.

Much of what people do in their day-to-day lives seems programlike, or scriptlike. Most of the intentions you form in an average day involve programs. Doing the laundry, going to a store or the movies, preparing for an exam, fixing lunch, trying to get noticed by that person in class—all these are programs. They all have general

Much of what we do in our day-to-day lives, such as grocery shopping, has a programlike or scriptlike character.

courses of predictable acts and subgoals, but exactly what you do at a given point can vary, depending on the situation.

It probably is the case that there are well-learned habitual links between many principles and the programs to which they pertain. The habitual connections between programs and lower levels of control are probably even stronger. For example, there's evidence that when a person has a travel goal in mind, it automatically activates information about a plausible and common means to get there (Aarts & Dijksterhuis, 2000).

Issues concerning Hierarchical Organization

Several questions commonly come up when people think about hierarchies. For example, you might assume that all its levels are active all the time. Not necessarily. Sometimes behavior is guided not by the overall sense of self but by programs. To put it differently, lower levels may sometimes be *functionally superordinate.*

This is what happens, for example, when people do their routine "maintenance" activities of life: shopping for groceries, washing dishes, driving to school. At such times, people may lose sight of higher-order goals. In fact, programs inherently require decisions. This may cause them to be functionally superordinate more often than other levels. It's interesting that when people spontaneously describe themselves, they tend to describe things they *do,* rather than what they *are* (McGuire & McGuire, 1986). This suggests that the program level may be especially salient to people.

When low levels are functionally superordinate, it's almost as though the higher layers were temporarily disconnected. But the disconnect is rarely permanent. Goals at high levels can be affected by things that happen while lower levels are in charge. A program (buying shoes on sale) can help you conform to a principle (frugality), even if that's not why you engaged in the program (you just liked the shoes the moment you saw them). A program can also *increase* a discrepancy for a principle, if it violates the principle. Such an action is something you wouldn't have done if you'd been thinking about the principle. For example, many health-conscious people have a principle of eating low-fat foods. But if they get caught up in the action at a party (with lower levels in charge), they might eat lots of greasy food, which they'll later regret.

As we said earlier, this view assumes that goals can often be achieved in diverse ways. In a complementary way, any given concrete act can be done in the service of diverse principles. For example, Richard in Figure 17.5 could have been buying flowers not to be thoughtful but to be manipulative—to get on Linda's good side. Precisely the same physical motions would occur, but they'd be aimed at a very different higher-order goal.

Another point is that people often try to match several values at once. Not just low-level values within higher-level values. Rather, people often have several goals at the same time *at the same level.* Sometimes they're compatible (being frugal while being conscientious). In other cases they're less so (being frugal while dressing well; getting good grades while having an active social life). In such cases, matching one value creates a problem for the other (Emmons & King, 1988; Emmons, King, & Sheldon, 1993). This defines **conflict.**

Research on Hierarchies of Behavior

Is behavior organized hierarchically? Work by Robin Vallacher, Dan Wegner, and their colleagues suggests that it is (Vallacher & Wegner, 1985, 1987).

This research began by asking how people think about their actions, a process called **action identification.** Any behavior can be identified in a wide variety of ways. For example, taking class notes can be identified as "sitting in a room, making marks on paper with a pen," as "taking notes in a class," as "trying to do well in a course," as "getting an education," or even as "moving on my career path." Some of these identities are concrete, others are more abstract. Presumably how you think about your actions says something about the goals you're using as reference points for your behavior.

Vallacher and Wegner hold that when both a low-order identification and a higher-order identity are readily available, people tend to use the higher one. That is, people tend to regulate their actions in as high-level a way as they can. You're more likely to see your student behavior as "attending classes," "getting an education," or "listening to a lecture" than as "walking into a building, sitting down, and listening to someone talk."

But if people begin to struggle in performing an act at the high level, they tend to retreat to a lower-level identity for the act. In the term used in the previous section, difficulty at a high level causes a lower level to become functionally superordinate. Using that lower-level identity, the person irons out the problem. As the problem is resolved, the person tends to drift again to a higher-level identification.

For example, if you're in class taking notes and you're having trouble understanding the lecture, you may stop thinking of your behavior as "getting an education" and start thinking of it as "writing down as much as I possibly can so I can try to figure it out later." If the lecture gets easier to follow after a while, you may be able to start thinking of your behavior in more abstract terms again.

As another example, imagine you just met someone you're interested in and you're starting to talk. You're more likely to see what you're doing as "conveying the impression of someone who's cool and well worth knowing" than as "saying sentences and asking questions." On the other hand, if you find yourself struggling to carry it off, you may retreat to focusing on specific things to say and ask. If it starts to go better again, you can then drift back to the higher-order identification.

Emotion

At the beginning of the chapter we asked how the view under discussion (as cold and analytical as it is) could have a place in it for emotions. Nobel laureate Herb Simon (1967) made an early statement on this issue. He argued that emotions play a *crucial* role in information processing. He pointed out that people often have several goals, which they pursue sequentially (e.g., you go to a gas station, then stop for lunch, then drive to the beach, where you study for an exam while getting some sun, and then you go home and do some laundry if there's time). The order of things is partly a matter of their priorities—how important each goal is to you.

Priorities are subject to rearrangement. Simon argued that emotions are an internal call to rearrange. An emotion such as anxiety is a signal that you're not attending enough to personal well-being (an important goal) and that you should do so. Anger seems to be a signal that your autonomy (another goal that people value) needs to be given a higher priority.

It's implicit in Simon's theory that you monitor progress toward many goals outside awareness, while you focus on one goal at a time. As a problem arises for a secondary goal, emotion arises. If the problem gets big enough, the emotion becomes intense enough to interrupt you. For example, look back at the goals described two paragraphs earlier. If you decided to put off buying gas until after doing the other things, you might later start to feel anxious about maybe being stranded at the beach with an empty gas tank. If the anxiety got strong enough, you'd change your mind (reprioritize) and stop for the gas after all.

Simon's theory is compatible with the idea that emotions arise from a system that monitors rate of "progress" toward goals (Carver & Scheier, 1990, 1998). When progress is going well, you feel eager and happy (cf. Stotland, 1969b). When it's very rapid, you feel joy, even ecstasy. When things are going poorly, negative feelings arise: frustration, sadness, or anxiety. If you're actually losing ground instead of just failing to gain, the negative feelings intensify. In all these cases, the emotion is a subjective readout of how well you're doing.

Evidence fitting this has been reported by Hsee and Abelson (1991). Participants put themselves in hypothetical situations where they'd bet money on sports outcomes (Experiment 2). Each viewed a display on which progress toward winning was shown at different rates. They indicated how satisfied they'd be with each event they observed. Of special interest are events in which the starting and ending points were identical, but the rate of change differed. Participants were more satisfied with the faster change than the slower one.

Feelings also have implications for action. When things are going badly and negative feelings arise, the result is increased effort toward the goal the negative feeling relates to. If you're behind at something and feeling frustrated, you try harder. If you're scared of something, you try harder to get away from it. The role of positive feelings is less clear. It's been argued, though, that they also influence prioritization (Carver, 2003). When you feel good about some goal, you can "coast" a little about that one, and check to see if anything else needs your attention. This allows the priority of another goal to rise.

Emotions convey a lot of information. This idea in itself is useful to theorists. For example, as noted in Chapter 16, anxiety takes up space in consciousness. With less space available, performance deteriorates. Other theorists emphasize that emotion qualities are stored in memory just as other information is, and can be used as a retrieval cue like any other cue (Bower, 1981; Niedenthal, Halberstadt, & Innes-Ker, 1999; Schwarz, 1990).

In sum, it would be very wrong to assume that self-regulation views have no place for emotions. Certainly many questions remain to be answered. Yet theorists in this area are interested in emotions for several reasons. They are an important topic in this framework.

Effects of Expectancies: Effort versus Disengagement

Until the last section, we focused mostly on behavior *when there are no major difficulties.* However, things don't always work so well. People often encounter obstacles when they try to carry out their intentions, attain their goals. What happens then?

As just suggested, obstacles cause negative feelings. If the obstacles are serious, they also tend to interrupt action (Carver & Scheier, 1981, 1990, 1998; Simon, 1967). The interruption can be brief or long. It can occur before you start (if you anticipate trouble) or while acting (if snags arise along the way). These interruptions remove you temporarily from action and lead you to assess how likely you are to reach your goal, given the situation you're in.

Expectancy of success is an idea that's come up in other chapters. We discussed them in the motive viewpoint (Chapter 5). We also discussed them in the context of social learning theory (Chapter 13) and in describing Mischel's cognitive view (Chapter 16). The expectancy concept actually provides a major link between learning models and cognitive–self-regulation models.

The way expectancies function in self-regulation models is essentially the same as in the other theories. Confidence of overcoming obstacles leads people back into self-regulatory effort. With enough doubt, however, the person is more likely to **disengage,** reduce effort toward goal attainment—perhaps even abandon the goal altogether, temporarily or permanently (Klinger, 1975; Kukla, 1972; Wright, 1996).

Effort is a continuum. It can be useful, though, to think of variations in effort as forming a rough dichotomy (Figure 17.6). Think of it as the question of whether or not you keep trying or quit. In many cases people have only those two options (Carver

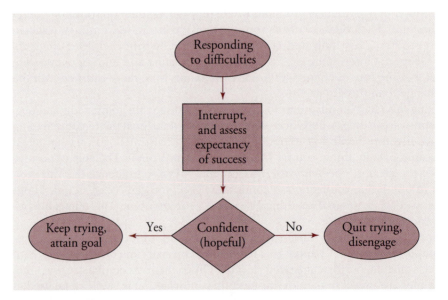

Figure 17.6

When people confront difficulties in moving toward their goals, they sometimes interrupt their efforts to assess the likelihood of succeeding. Sufficient confidence leads to renewed efforts, sufficient doubt leads to giving up. All responses seem ultimately to fall into one or the other of these classes.

& Scheier, 1998). This view of the impact of expectancies provides a way to talk about how people abandon one goal and turn to another (Wrosch, Scheier, Carver, & Schulz, in press). It creates a way for the person who's walked into a corner to back out of it and take up another goal.

Different people emphasize somewhat different expectancy qualities. Our work emphasizes confidence versus doubt of attaining desired outcomes, without focusing on the *reason* for the confidence or doubt (Carver & Scheier, 1998). Bandura, in contrast (described in Chapter 13), stresses self-efficacy expectancy: the belief that one has the personal capability of doing the action that needs to be done. He links confidence and doubt more explicitly to self-perceived capabilities. Whatever variation you prefer, there's evidence that expectancies play an important role in determining how hard people try and how well they do (see also Box 17.2). People who are confident

BOX 17.2

CONFIDENCE ABOUT LIFE:
The Impact of Generalized Optimism

In the main text, we say that expectancies are an important determinant of people's behavior. The expectancies we talk about there are mostly specific ones: confidence versus doubt about making a desired impression, achieving an academic goal, or carrying out a specific strategy. However, just as people have both specific and general goals, people also have both specific and generalized expectancies. What's been known for centuries as *optimism* is generalized confidence; what's been known as *pessimism* is generalized doubt—not about one specific outcome, but about life in general (Scheier & Carver, 1992; Scheier, Carver, & Bridges, 2001). This generalized confidence is very traitlike. It's quite stable over time and seems genetically influenced (Plomin et al., 1992).

Optimism as a dimension of personality has been studied for nearly two decades, and a lot is known about it (Scheier et al., 2001). For example, people who are optimistic about life are better liked than those who are more pessimistic (Carver, Kus, & Scheier, 1994). Probably for that reason, they're better at establishing social networks when they go to a new environment, such as starting college (Brissette et al., 2002). Consistent with the idea that they expect things to work out well for them, optimists also have more positive expected possible selves (Carver, Reynolds, & Scheier, 1994).

Much of the research on optimism deals with its influences on how people deal with stressful situations (Scheier et al., 2001). In general, optimists deal better with adversity than pessimists, in contexts ranging from experiencing missile attacks (Zeidner & Hammer, 1992) to confronting cancer (Carver, Pozo, Harris, et al., 1993; Stanton & Snyder, 1993) and heart disease (Scheier et al., 1989). They experience less distress, are more focused on moving forward, and are less likely to withdraw from their usual activities (Carver, Lehman, & Antoni, 2003). They seem more prepared to accept the reality of the stressful experience (Carver et al., 1993). They don't stick their heads in the sand and ignore threats to their well-being. They attend to risks in their lives, but only if the risk concerns a serious problem and also pertains to them (Aspinwall & Brunhart, 1996).

Most of what is known about optimism concerns people's actions and their subjective emotional experiences. At least a little research goes beyond that, however, looking at people's physical responses to adversity. For example, Scheier et al. (1999) found that after major heart surgery, pessimists were more likely than optimists to require rehospitalization. Optimists literally healed better. The possibility that this personality trait may have health benefits is one that is now being actively investigated.

about reaching their goals (or who hold perceptions of high efficacy) are more persistent and perform better than doubtful people. They do better in lots of ways.

A nice example of how confidence can influence behavior comes from a study by Ozer and Bandura (1990). Participants were women learning to protect themselves against sexual assault. They were taught physical skills needed for self-defense and verbal techniques to deal with dangerous situations before they escalate. At several points, the women rated their confidence that they could execute both the disabling maneuvers and the verbal tactics to deal with threats or harassment. They also rated their confidence that they could turn off thoughts about sexual assault and the extent to which they had such thoughts. The outcome was ratings of the extent to which they engaged in (or avoided) a range of activities outside the home.

The results are complex, but a broad theme shows through them. The sense of confidence was very important. The women's confidence that they could use their new coping skills related to perceptions of less vulnerability, to confidence that they could tell risky situations from safe ones, and ultimately to their behavior. Confidence about using the coping skills also related to confidence about being able to control thoughts about assault. That related to lower incidence of such thoughts, which also related to behavior. In sum, confidence in these areas helped the women cope more effectively with their social world.

Thus far we've distinguished sharply between continued effort and giving up. Sometimes, though, the line blurs. Sometimes a goal is unattainable, but another one can be substituted for it (Freund & Baltes, 2002; Wrosch et al., in press). For example, a person who enjoys sports but who becomes wheelchair-bound can't play football any more. But he can turn to sports that don't require the use of legs. Sometimes disengagement involves shifting from one activity to another. Sometimes it involves only scaling back from a lofty goal in a given domain to a less demanding one. This is disengagement, in the sense that the person is giving up the first goal while adopting the lesser one. It's more limited, in the sense that it doesn't entail leaving the domain. This partial disengagement keeps you engaged in the domain you had wanted to quit. By scaling back—giving up in a small way—you keep trying to move ahead—thus *not* giving up, in a larger way.

In discussing disengagement and giving up, we should reiterate that whether giving up is bad or good depends on the context (Wrosch et al., in press). In some cases, disengagement is bad. It's a poor way of coping with the ordinary difficulties of life. These are cases where being persistent would pay off in success. In such cases, the goal shouldn't be abandoned so easily.

On the other hand, it's often necessary to give up or defer goals when circumstances make it hard or impossible to reach them. For example, it's senseless to continue shopping once you realize you've left your money and credit cards at home. It's senseless to hold onto a lost love who will never return. Giving up is sometimes the right response. But sometimes when it's the right response it doesn't happen. There are times when it feels as if a goal *can't* be abandoned, when it seems so important it can't be left behind. In this case, the failure to disengage leads to continuing distress. We'll return to this point later on, when we consider problems in behavior.

Assessment

The self-regulation view on personality is fairly new. It's been far more theoretical than applied. Nevertheless, it offers a few suggestions concerning personality assessment.

Assessment of Self-Regulatory Qualities

The view on behavior described in this chapter emphasizes the existence of several processes within human experience. This emphasis suggests it may be useful to measure *individual differences in self-regulatory processes* (Williams, Moore, Pettibone, & Thomas, 1992).

For example, private self-consciousness (Fenigstein et al., 1975) is a tendency to be self-reflective—to think about your feelings, motives, actions, and so on. (The term *self-conscious* here doesn't mean embarrassment, just self-focus.) As was said earlier, self-focus seems to engage a feedback loop guiding behavior. It may follow that people high in self-consciousness are relatively careful and thorough self-regulators (maybe even "obsessive-compulsive" ones). They notice if their actions don't match their intentions and they adjust the actions accordingly. People with less self-consciousness are more random and less guided in their behavior (see also Box 17.3). There's also

BOX 17.3

THE REDUCTION OF SELF-REGULATION
Effects of Deindividuation and Alcohol

Earlier in the chapter we described how self-focused attention causes better self-regulation toward salient standards. If greater self-focus causes behavior to become better regulated, it follows that reduced self-focus causes behavior to become more *poorly* regulated. But what does this mean? It doesn't mean that the person stops behaving altogether. It means the behavior is more likely to fluctuate, to become random and less carefully thought out.

Two bodies of research have studied the effects of reduced self-awareness. Their origins are different, but the effects they've found are strikingly similar. One set of studies concerns deindividuation. The other concerns the effects of alcohol.

Deindividuation is an experience that people have when they become immersed in a group. In so doing, they often lose their sense of personal identity. This, in turn, makes them more likely to use obscenities (Festinger et al., 1952), to be aggressive (Mullen, 1986; Prentice-Dunn & Rogers, 1980, 1982), and to engage in childish and uninhibited acts such as playing in mud and sucking on baby bottles (Diener, 1979).

There's evidence that deindividuation involves loss of self-focus (Diener, 1979; Mullen, 1986; Prentice-Dunn & Rogers, 1982, 1989). It's easy to see its effects as reflecting poor self-regulation regarding programs and principles that normally guide behavior. Thus, there's a

tendency to act impulsively, to respond to cues of the moment rather than to use well-thought-out plans. Behavior becomes a string of spontaneous sequences rather than being guided by higher-order values.

These effects of deindividuation are remarkably similar to some of the effects of alcohol intoxication. People who've been drinking are often inappropriately aggressive and overly responsive to cues of the moment. Alcohol is widely regarded as a releaser of inhibitions, and it's sometimes used intentionally for precisely that purpose. Taken as a group, the behavioral manifestations of alcohol intoxication seem to reflect a loss of careful self-regulation regarding programs and principles. As with deindividuation, the result seems to be a string of sequences of spontaneous acts, rather than carefully planned activity.

Furthermore, behavioral effects of alcohol and deindividuation seem to have at least one process in common. Alcohol appears to act (at least partly) by reducing self-awareness (Hull, 1981; Hull & Rielly, 1986). As self-awareness diminishes, you stop monitoring your values and intentions. Behavior becomes more disorganized, impulsive, and fragmented. Thus, two distinct sets of phenomena—deindividuation and alcohol intoxication—can be interpreted by a single principle. Both seem to involve interference with a process that underlies the normal self-regulation of behavior.

suggestive evidence that this scale relates to conscientiousness from the five-factor model (Trapnell & Campbell, 1999).

Note that self-focus by itself is relatively content-free. That is, its self-regulatory effect is largely independent of the goal being used. Thus, an athlete who's self-conscious should be a little obsessive about working out. A self-conscious biology major should be sure she's always up to date in her biology homework. A self-conscious musician should be closely focused on reaching the music-related goals she's set for herself.

Trapnell and Campbell (1999) have distinguished two aspects of private self-consciousness. They think two motives underlie what the scale measures: the motives are curiosity, and the probing of negative feeling states. They found evidence that fit that idea, and developed their own measure, called the Rumination–Reflection Questionnaire, to focus more explicitly on it. Rumination items refer to being unable to put something behind you. Reflection items refer to being fascinated, philosophical, and inquisitive. Not surprisingly, reflection relates to openness to experience, and rumination relates to neuroticism.

Another self-regulatory function that might be useful to assess is whether people tend to view their behavior in high-level or lower-level terms. Vallacher and Wegner (1989) developed a measure called the Behavior Identification Form for that purpose. They argue that people who have similar trait patterns can differ greatly from each other if they think of their goals at different levels. This measure of action identification is also fairly content-free. That is, people who identify their actions at high levels tend to look at the "big picture" whether they're socializing, studying, or making music. People who identify their actions at lower levels tend to focus more on the "nuts and bolts" of what's going on, no matter the domain of the behavior.

Assessment of Goals

We don't mean to imply that the content of behavior doesn't matter to this viewpoint. As we said earlier, the self-regulation view emphasizes goals. It would seem useful, from this view, to assess people's goals and how they're organized (Emmons, 1986; Pervin, 1983). One might even want to assess what sort of "possible selves" the person has in mind (Markus & Nurius, 1986). Knowing what goals are salient to a person might be more informative than knowing other aspects of what the person is "like."

An example of this is the technique Emmons (1986) used to assess personal strivings. He asked people to describe their recurring personal goals in four areas: work/school, home/family, social relationships, and leisure/recreation. People were to think about their own intentions and goals and not to compare themselves with other people. Within these guidelines, they were free to write down any striving that seemed important to them. This produces an individualized picture of the goal values that occupy the person's mind over a given span of time.

Problems in Behavior, and Behavior Change

Given how recent the self-regulation point of view is, one might expect it to have had little or no impact on understanding either problems or therapy. This isn't so, however (see Hamilton, Greenberg, Pyszczynski, & Cather, 1993; Ingram, 1986; Merluzzi, Rudy, & Glass, 1981). Self-regulation models have a number of suggestions on those topics (see also Box 17.4).

BOX 17.4

REGULATING WITH THE WRONG FEEDBACK

A central theme of this chapter is that people act, then check to see whether they're doing what they intended to do. Just how fundamental is this principle? Research from health psychology suggests that informational feedback matters so much that people will seek it out and rely on it *even when it doesn't tell them anything.* They'll rely on it even when they're *told* it doesn't tell them anything. They'll rely on it even though relying on it creates *problems.*

Consider studies of the behavior of people being treated for hypertension—high blood pressure (Baumann & Leventhal, 1985; Meyer, Leventhal, & Gutmann, 1985). People with hypertension have no reliable symptoms. Yet most people with hypertension quickly come to believe that they *can* isolate a symptom of it. Indeed, the longer they're in treatment, the more likely they are to think they can tell when their blood pressure is up. More than 90 percent of those in treatment for more than three months claim to be able to tell (Meyer et al., 1985).

Can they? By and large, no. In one study (Baumann & Leventhal, 1985), self-reports of elevated blood pressure were well correlated with self-reports of symptoms and self-reported moods. But self-reported blood pressure elevation was virtually unrelated to actual elevation.

Unfortunately, people with hypertension use their symptoms as a guide to whether their blood pressure's up. They then make important decisions on the basis of those symptoms. In particular, they use the symptom to tell them whether to take their medication. If they think their blood pressure isn't up (because the symptom isn't there), they don't take the medication. When they feel no symptoms, they often drop out of treatment altogether. This can lead to serious medical problems, all because the people are relying on a faulty kind of feedback information to guide their decisions and actions.

This example concerns a physical problem rather than a psychological one. But the same pattern can also be seen in cases where people misinterpret others' reactions to them, or rely on the wrong kinds of cues from others. If you take someone's frown as a sign of rejection, when really he's remembering he forgot to put the cat out, you may behave in ways that create problems for you rather than help you attain your desired ends.

These examples also illustrate how much people rely on feedback to guide behavior. If the people with hypertension perceive a discrepancy between present state (symptom) and standard (no symptoms), they act in a way they think will reduce the discrepancy (take their medication). They're using feedback, just as the self-regulation approach suggests people do all the time. The problem is that the input channel is faulty. One interpretation of such phenomena is that people *need* feedback. The natural tendency to use feedback is so strong that people will continue to do so even when the feedback they're using is actually unrelated to what they're trying to control.

Problems as Conflicts among Goals, and Lack of Goal Specifications

The hierarchical model suggests several ways for problems to arise (Carver & Scheier, 1990, 1998). The simplest way stems from the idea of a deeply rooted conflict between goals. Conflict occurs when a person is committed to two goals that can't be attained easily at the same time (being a successful attorney while being a good wife and mother; having a close relationship while being emotionally independent). You may alternate between goals, but this can be exhausting. It requires a lot of effort to keep the conflict from reemerging. Another solution is to decide that one goal contributes more to your higher-order values than the other and to reorganize your hierarchy.

Conflict among goals creates problems. Emmons and King (1988) had participants report the personal strivings in their lives. Then they had them rate the extent to which success in one area tended to create problems for another one. They found that conflicts between strivings related to psychological distress and also to physical symptoms.

Another idea suggested by the hierarchical model is that people sometimes want abstract goals but lack the know-how to reach them. If specifications from level to level are missing, self-regulation falls apart. Thus, many people want to be "fulfilled," "successful," or "well liked"; many even have more-specific goals, such as "not arguing with my wife" or "being more assertive," but don't know how to attain them. They can't specify the concrete behavior that would move them in the right direction, so they can't make progress and are distressed.

Problems from an Inability to Disengage

A third source of problems stems from the idea that people who expect failure quit trying. As we noted earlier, sometimes this is the right response (when you realize you've forgotten your money, you quit shopping). Sometimes, though, it can't be done easily. Some goals are very hard to give up, even if you have extreme doubts about reaching them. Examples are doing well in your chosen work and having a fulfilling relationship with another person. Why is it so hard to give these up? The hierarchical view says it's because these goals are very high in your hierarchy (and thus central to your self) or represent paths to those higher goals. Sometimes abandoning a concrete goal means giving up on the person you want to be.

When people have serious doubts about attaining important goals, they show a predictable pattern. They stop trying, but soon confront that goal again. For example, having decided to give up on being in a fulfilling relationship, you see a movie about relationships, which reminds you that you want one. Having given up trying to get along with a coworker, you find you're assigned to work on a project together. Having given up on your calculus assignment, you see it's time for calculus class. Deep doubt about reaching an important goal can lead to a repeated cycle of sporadic effort, doubt, distress, disengagement, and reconfrontation with the goal.

Generally, when people fail at something, they want to ignore it, put it behind them and move on. After a failure most people avoid self-focus; after a success they seek it out (Gibbons & Wicklund, 1976; Greenberg & Musham, 1981). Seeking self-focus here presumably means focusing on the success. Avoidance of self-focus presumably means trying to avoid thinking about the failure. In contrast to this pattern, however, Pyszczynski and Greenberg (1985, 1987) found that people who are depressed show the *opposite* pattern. They are more likely to self-focus after a *failure* than after a success. What's going on? Apparently depressed people have difficulty giving up goals they haven't reached. Given a failure, they hang onto the goal, even if it wasn't important. They let success slide by without enjoying it.

It's not always bad to keep thinking about a failure. It can motivate you to try harder next time (if there is a next time). Sometimes it leads to ideas about how to do things differently next time (Martin & Tesser, 1996). But Pyszczynski and Greenberg (1985, 1987) argue that it's dangerous to do this when the failure (or loss) is one that can't be undone (see also Wrosch et al., in press). When people lose a core source of self-worth and focus too long on trying to regain it, major distress results. And doing this too often makes it a habit. Focusing on failure and ignoring success not only maintain depressive symptoms, they make the pattern self-perpetuating.

A similar point is made by Susan Nolen-Hoeksema and her colleagues. She argues that people who are prone to depression focus much of their attention on their sad feelings. This rumination acts to prolong the depressed state (Nolen-Hoeksema, Morrow, & Frederickson, 1993; Nolen-Hoeksema, Parker, & Larson, 1994).

Self-Regulation and the Process of Therapy

Control-process ideas have also been used by several theorists in addressing therapy issues. Fred Kanfer and his colleagues (e.g., Kanfer & Busemeyer, 1982; Kanfer & Hagerman, 1985; Kanfer & Schefft, 1988; see also Semmer & Frese, 1985) have depicted therapy in a way that's quite compatible with the self-regulatory ideas presented throughout this chapter, as well as with the cognitive principles discussed in Chapter 16.

One point they make is that much of human behavior isn't well monitored consciously but occurs automatically and habitually to certain cues. This is a point that was made early in this chapter, and has been made by many cognitive theorists as well (e.g., Beck, 1972, 1976; Dodge, 1986; Semmer & Frese, 1985). Therapy is partly an effort to break down the automaticity. The person must engage in more "controlled" or monitored processing of what's going on. Doing this should yield responses that are more carefully thought out.

Does this mean that people dealing with problems must spend the rest of their lives carefully monitoring their actions? Some think so (Kirschenbaum, 1987). If lifelong monitoring is to be avoided, therapy must find a way to make the desired responses automatic, in place of the problem responses. How do you substitute one set of automatic responses for another? Presumably it's an issue of how thoroughly coded the links are in memory. Kanfer argued that new responses become automatic by building them into memory very redundantly. This makes it more likely that they will be used later, when the person's on "automatic pilot." Techniques already in widespread use, such as imagery, role play, and practicing the therapeutic changes in real-life situations, probably do exactly this.

Another point made by Kanfer and Busemeyer (1982) is that the process of therapy is a dynamic feedback system. It's a series of stages in which clients repeatedly use feedback, both from therapy sessions and from actions outside therapy, to adjust their "movement" through a long-term plan of change. Thus, therapy itself is dynamic. The goals and issues that guide the process of changing behavior also keep changing. As you proceed, you must keep checking to make sure the concrete goals you're working toward support your higher-order goals.

Therapy Is Training in Problem Solving

A point that's been made by many people is that therapy is not just for the present. It should make the client a better problem solver, more equipped to deal with problems in the future (D'Zurilla & Goldfried, 1971; Kanfer & Busemeyer, 1982; Nezu, 1987; Schefft & Lehr, 1985). Being able to generate alternative behavior choices and select the most effective ones are important skills, whether you get them through therapy or on your own.

A useful way to do this is called **means–end analysis** (Newell & Simon, 1972). You begin a means–end analysis by determining the difference between your present state and your desired state (the "end"). You then think of an action that would reduce the difference (a "means"). At first, the things that come to mind are usually abstract, involving large-scale goals. You then examine each of the large steps and break it down into more restricted subgoals. If you keep breaking things down long enough, the means–end paths become sufficiently complete and concrete to get you from here to there.

This general line of thought has been used in a program designed to help low-income African American middle-school students develop an academic identity (Oyserman, Terry, & Bybee, 2002). Students in this program have difficulty creating possible selves that involve school as a pathway to adulthood. Oyserman et al. developed a small-group intervention to do that. They gave the students the experience of actively developing academic possible selves. Moreover, it tied those possible selves to clear strategies for achieving desired short-term goals and extended both of those to images of positive adult self-images. The program emphasized the solving of everyday problems, breaking them down by means–end analysis. The result was a stronger bonding to school and less trouble with authorities.

It's good to have goals broken down enough to be concrete and well specified. On the other hand, it's also possible to break things down too far (Kirschenbaum, 1985). In particular, too rigid a timetable can cause you to lose motivation. People seem to do best when they have flexibility. By being able to choose when to try to move forward, people can recognize better when certain kinds of efforts are counterproductive. They're also able to be "opportunistic," that is, take advantage of unexpected opportunities (Hayes-Roth & Hayes-Roth, 1979).

Finally, it's important to seek accurate feedback about the effects of your actions. If you get accurate feedback, it isn't necessary to make perfect choices. If you make continual adjustments from the feedback you get, you keep moving in the right direction. This principle, which is basic to the self-regulation approach, yields an important kind of freedom—the freedom from having to be right the first time.

Self-Regulation Theories: Problems and Prospects

As is true of the cognitive view, the self-regulation view on personality has led to mixed reactions. It shares some loose ends and unanswered questions with the cognitive view, and it has some of its own. It remains unclear whether these are fatal problems or just gaps remaining to be filled.

One criticism of this view derives from the robotics metaphor. The criticism is that such artificial systems can't possibly be adequate models for human behavior because they have limitations that humans don't have. Humans have free will and make their own decisions. Robots rely on the programs they've been given.

One response to this criticism is that it rests on the assumption that *people* have free will, and not everyone shares that assumption (Bargh & Ferguson, 2000; Wegner, 2002). Further, the behavior of "intelligent" artificial systems moves farther every year in the direction of what looks suspiciously like self-determination (Brooks, 2002). It seems clear that how humans and artificial systems resemble and differ from each other will continue to be debated well into the future. But as the behavior of artifacts becomes more and more personlike, the debate appears likely to focus on increasingly subtle points.

Another criticism sometimes made of the self-regulation approach is that a model based on feedback principles is merely a model of **homeostasis** (literally, "steady state"). Homeostatic mechanisms exist to control body temperature, the levels of various elements in the blood, and many other physical parameters of the body. But how much sense does it make to think this way about something we know is always *changing*? Human behavior isn't about steady states. Doesn't the self-regulation view imply that people should be immobile and stable, or just do the same thing over and over?

Actually, no. People do regulate some of their experiences in a recurrently homeostatic way, for example, the amount of affiliation they engage in across time (O'Connor & Rosenblood, 1996), but that's not always the case. As we noted earlier, many goals are dynamic (e.g., going on a vacation trip, having an interesting conversation with someone). Being dynamic doesn't make them any less goal-like. It just means that the whole process of matching behavior to the goal must be dynamic as well. If the goal is to create a flow of experiences rather than a state, the qualities of behavior being monitored will also have this changing quality. So there's no contradiction between the fact that humans keep changing what they're doing and the idea that behavior is embedded within a system of feedback control.

Greater difficulty is posed by another criticism, aimed specifically at the hierarchical model—that it fails to deal effectively with the "homunculus" problem. *Homunculus,* a term once used to explain how people act, refers to a hypothetical tiny man who sits inside your head and tells you what to do. That explains *your* behavior. But who tells the *little man* what to do? To return to the robot metaphor, robots are pretty stupid. When they do something, it's because an instruction has told them to. But if people are just fancy robots, where does the instruction come from? What tells the person what to do? Where do the *highest* goals come from, the ones that specify all the lower goals?

One response is that information-processing models often assume an "executive," or superordinate system, which coordinates other activities, makes decisions, and so on. The executive is manifest in subjective experience as consciousness. The executive presumably has control over many other systems and thus is the analogue of the homunculus. This reasoning is plausible, but it isn't altogether satisfying.

Another response is that people have built-in goals of survival, personal coherence, and so on. These goals are vague enough that they rarely appear in consciousness, but they're pervasive enough that they constantly influence in subtle ways people's decisions about what goals to take up. Thus, behavior is being guided by values that are built into the organism, but which aren't always apparent to the person. This line of reasoning is plausible too, but it's also less than fully satisfying. The homunculus problem thus remains a real one.

Another criticism of the self-regulation view (and the cognitive view of Chapter 16) is similar to a criticism made of the learning perspective: all this seems too much a description from the outside looking in. There's too little of the feel of what it means to *have* a personality. This approach describes the "self-regulation of behavior," but what does this really say about personality? This approach emphasizes structure and process, rather than content. For this reason, some see the ideas as dealing with an empty shell, programmed in ways that aren't well specified, for purposes and goals that are largely arbitrary (e.g., Deci & Ryan, 2000).

There is some merit to this criticism. We note, however, that these ideas weren't devised to focus directly on the concept of personality. Rather, they were intended to focus on issues that stand at a slight tangent from personality. Although these ideas don't form a full theory of personality, they provide a window on the nature of human experience that seems to have some implications for personality. Will these ideas evolve into a more complete picture of personality? It's too early to be sure.

Despite these criticisms, the self-regulation view on personality has proven to have some merit. It's had heuristic value, suggesting new places to look for information about how things work. Indeed, it makes some predictions that aren't intuitively suggested by other views. This value alone makes it likely that it will be around for a while. Only the test of time and further investigation will tell whether this approach will continue to emerge as a viable perspective on personality.

SUMMARY

Self-regulation models assume that behavior is directed from within the person. Behavior uses motor schemas, information about how to execute acts. These can be cued by interpretive schemas, if an interpretation is closely tied to an action quality. Many actions are triggered fairly automatically, even without the person's awareness. Sometimes actions instead follow from intentions. Intentions are products of a mental algebra in which personally desired outcomes and social considerations are weighed to yield a likelihood of acting. Some intentions are to attain end goals, others are about the implementing of action plans to reach those goals. The latter are important for ensuring that behavior actually gets done.

Theory concerning self-regulation emphasizes goals. The goals underlying behavior have a variety of labels, including life tasks, personal strivings, personal projects, and current concerns. This view treats the structure of the self as an organization among goals. Some goals are fairly neutral, but others imply a standard of excellence. In the latter case, setting higher goals results in higher performances. This is because committing oneself to a more demanding goal focuses one's efforts more fully. If the goal is too high, though, people don't adopt it.

Once a goal for behavior has been evoked, self-regulation reflects a process of feedback control. A reference value (or goal) is compared against present behavior. If the two differ, behavior is adjusted, leading to a new perception and comparison. Given that many goals are dynamic and evolving, this view emphasizes that self-regulation is a never-ending process. A feedback loop is too simple to account for the diversity in people's actions alone, but greater complexity is given by the fact that feedback systems can be organized in a hierarchy, in which one system acts by providing reference values to the system directly below it.

Emotions have been viewed within this framework as calls for reprioritizing one's goals. Emotions are also viewed as giving a subjective reading of how well you're progressing toward a goal. Emotion thus conveys information, which is stored in memory in the same way as any information.

When people encounter obstacles in their efforts, self-regulation is interrupted and the people consider whether success or failure is likely. If expectancies are positive enough, the person keeps trying; if not, the person may disengage from effort and give up. Disengagement is sometimes the adaptive response, but people sometimes give up too quickly. Sometimes disengagement is partial—goal substitution or scaling back. This keeps the person engaged, in one way, while disengaging in another.

Assessment from this view is partly a matter of assessing individual differences in self-regulatory functions, such as self-reflectiveness or the level of abstraction at which people view their goals. This view also suggests the value of assessing goals themselves. There are several ways to conceptualize problems from this view. One possibility focuses on conflict between incompatible goals; another points to a lack of specification of mid-level behavioral reference values to guide behavior. Another emphasizes that people sometimes are unable to disengage from behaviors that are necessary for the attainment of higher-order goals. There's evidence that people who are depressed display an exaggerated inability to disengage.

Just as behavior can be construed in terms of a hierarchy of feedback systems, so can the process of behavior change induced by therapy. People in therapy use feedback from decisions they've put into practice to make further decisions. They monitor the effects of changes in behavior to determine whether the changes have produced the desired effects. One long-term goal of therapy is to make people better problem solvers through techniques such as means–end analysis, so that they can make their own adjustments when confronting new problems.

GLOSSARY

Action identification The way one thinks of or labels whatever action one is performing.

Attitude A personal evaluation of the desirability of an action.

Comparator A mechanism that compares two values to each other.

Conflict An attempt to self-regulate toward two incompatible goals at the same time.

Deliberative mindset Careful mindset that is used while deciding whether to take an action.

Disengage To cease and put aside self-regulation with regard to some goal.

Feedback hierarchy An organization of feedback loops in which superordinate loops act by providing reference values to subordinate loops.

Feedback loop A self-regulating system that maintains conformity to some comparison value.

Goal intention The intention to attain some particular outcome.

Homeostasis Regulation around a constant steady state.

Implemental mindset Positively biased mindset used while implementing an intention to act.

Implementation intention Intention to take specific actions in specific contexts.

Means–end analysis The process of creating a plan to attain an overall goal (end) by breaking it into successively more concrete goals (means).

Motor schema A mental organization of information providing instructions for acting.

Principle A broad, abstract action quality that could be displayed in any of several programs.

Program A guideline for the actions that take place in some category of events (as a script).

Subjective norm A person's impression of how other people value an action.

Subliminal stimuli Stimuli presented too fast to be consciously recognized.

System concept A very abstract guide for behavior, such as an ideal sense of self.

PART nine

Personality in Perspective

18 Overlap and Integration

■ **Similarities among Perspectives**

Psychoanalysis and Evolutionary Psychology:
   The Structural Model
Psychoanalysis and Evolutionary Psychology:
   Fixations and Mating Patterns
Psychoanalysis and Conditioning
Psychoanalysis and Self-Regulation:
   The Structural Model
Psychoanalysis and Cognitive Processes
Social Learning and Cognitive
   Self-Regulation Views
Neoanalytic and Cognitive
   Self-Regulation Perspectives
Maslow's Hierarchy and Hierarchies
   of Self-Regulation

Self-Actualization and Self-Regulation
Dispositions and Their Equivalents in Other Models

■ **Recurrent Themes, Viewed
   from Different Angles**

Impulse and Restraint
Individual versus Group Needs

■ **Combining Perspectives**

Eclecticism
An Example: Biology and Learning as
   Complementary Influences on Personality

■ **Which Theory Is Best?**

SUMMARY

■   Six blind men from Indostan heard of a creature called an elephant. They went to investigate its nature. One of them bumped into the elephant's side, and concluded that elephants resemble walls. A second encountered a tusk, and decided elephants are much like spears. The third, grasping the wriggling trunk, decided that elephants are similar to snakes. Wrapping his arms around one of its legs, the fourth man concluded that elephants resemble trees. The fifth felt a floppy ear, and surmised that elephants are a type of fan. Coming upon its tail, the sixth decided that elephants are like ropes.

Each of these men was sure his investigation had led him to the truth. And, indeed, each of them was partly right. But all were partly wrong.

—Hindu fable

In the preceding chapters you encountered a series of viewpoints on the nature of personality. Each was rooted in its own assumptions about how best to view human nature. Each had its own way of thinking about how people function. Each had its own view of the sources of individual differences, as well as their meaning and importance. Each approach also had its drawbacks, places where things were left unexplained or even unexamined.

In writing about these perspectives on personality, we tried to give you a sense of what each one was like, from inside that perspective. In so doing, our emphasis tended to be on what makes each approach special, distinct from other approaches. The views do differ in important ways, and some points of conflict seem hard to resolve. For example, how can you reconcile the belief that people have free will (from the phenomenological perspective) with the belief that behavior is determined by patterns of prior outcomes (from the learning perspective) or the belief that behavior is determined by internal forces (from the psychoanalytic perspective)?

Our emphasis on each theory's uniqueness may have led you to see the theories as being quite different from one another. The diversity may even have led you to wonder whether the theorists were describing the same *creature*. (This would be true as well, of course, for anyone who listened to the blind men describe the elephant.) The diversity of ideas in earlier chapters raises questions. Do the various perspectives have anything in common? Is one perspective right, or better than the others? If so, which one? In this chapter, we consider these questions.

Do the theories you've read about have anything in common? Despite the differences, there's more in common than may have been apparent. The first part of this chapter describes several commonalities we think are interesting. You probably noticed some of them already, but others are more subtle and harder to spot.

The question of which view is "best" or "right" is harder to answer. One answer is that even big differences among theories may not mean that one is right and the others are wrong. It often happens that some issue, or some element of personality, seems very important from the view of one theory but is less important or even irrelevant from the view of another theory. As with the blind men, one theory grapples closely with an issue, but another theory doesn't even touch on it. To borrow Kelly's phrase, each theory has a "focus of convenience" that differs from those of other theories.

It may be, then, that the various perspectives on personality may reflect facets of a bigger picture. From this point of view, the perspectives would complement, rather than contradict, each other. Each may have some truth, but none by itself has the entire truth. The idea that different perspectives are facets of a broader picture is developed more fully in the last part of the chapter.

Similarities among Perspectives

Let's first consider some specific similarities among the views described earlier in the book. We won't point to every similarity there is. Rather, we want simply to give you a sense of some of the connections that can be made among perspectives.

We begin with commonalities between psychoanalysis and other views. Psychoanalysis is a natural starting point. It's been around for a very long time. Some people regard it as the only really comprehensive theory of personality ever devised. For both these reasons, it stands as a comparison point for every other approach.

On the other hand, psychoanalysis is also a particularly *unusual* theory. This suggests it should be hard to find similarities between it and other approaches. As we noted earlier in the book, even neoanalytic theories, which *derive* from psychoanalysis, don't seem to share a lot with it. Nonetheless, there are several similarities worth noting between psychoanalysis and other theories. In fact, parallels have been suggested between psychoanalytic ideas and ideas in at least three other perspectives: biological, learning, and cognitive self-regulation.

Psychoanalysis and Evolutionary Psychology: The Structural Model

How does psychoanalysis relate to the biological approach? Often overlooked is how strongly Freud was influenced by Darwin's view of evolution. Psychoanalytic theory is about beings that are deeply concerned with biological necessities: survival and reproduction. Attaining these goals is critical, because that's what biological life is all about. It should be no surprise, then, that the core of personality focuses closely on them. On the other hand, because humans live in a dangerous world, it's necessary to deal with complexities imposed by reality. Because we live in groups, it's eventually important to deal with another issue as well: the fact that people other than us also have needs.

This is the general line of thought that lies behind an attempt by Leak and Christopher (1982) to interpret some of Freud's ideas within the framework of evolutionary psychology. They note that the evolutionary view sees behavior as self-serving (with one exception, to which we turn momentarily). This self-serving quality in biological behavior resembles the selfish nature of Freud's concept of id. The id is primitive and single-minded about its desires. The id represents the self-interested animal that our genes cause us to be, as those genes try to continue their existence.

The id isn't rational, nor are the genes. Freud tied rationality to the ego, a mechanism to mediate between id and reality. Leak and Christopher suggested that the genes also need some help in dealing with the complexities of reality. They argued that the cortex of the brain evolved to serve this purpose. Evolution of the cortex in the species would parallel evolution of the ego in the person. Both structures—cortex and ego—permit greater planfulness and care in decision making. Both are adaptations that foster survival.

What about the superego? This is the trickiest part of Leak and Christopher's argument. To view the superego in evolutionary terms requires one more idea. Specifically, survival isn't only an individual matter. Humans evolved as highly social beings, living and surviving in groups. Because we're so interdependent, we sometimes do better in the long run by letting group needs override personal needs in the short run. As noted in Chapter 6, it's been argued that people in groups evolved mechanisms for inducing—even forcing—reciprocal altruism (Trivers, 1971). A genetic mechanism to do this would enhance the adaptive success of the group.

In psychological terms, evolving such a mechanism looks like developing a capacity to have a superego. Thus, having a superego confers an evolutionary advantage. People who adopt the values of their social group and conform to those values will be accepted as members of the group. They're more likely to get the benefits that follow from group membership (for example, having other members take care of you if you're sick). These benefits have survival value.

In sum, Leak and Christopher suggest that the ego (conscious rationality) is a behavioral management system, for which the id and the superego provide motivation. There are two types of motivation—selfish and group-related—but both have adaptive value. The id adapts to the physical environment, where competition for resources is intense and selfish. The superego is the tendencies that evolved in response to pressures from group living.

Psychoanalysis and Evolutionary Psychology: Fixations and Mating Patterns

We see one more similarity between psychoanalytic and evolutionary views, which is quite different from the points made by Leak and Christopher. Think back to the Oedipal conflict and the fixations that can emerge from it. Fixation in the phallic stage for a male is believed to cause an exaggerated attempt to demonstrate that he hasn't been castrated. He does this by having sex with as many women as possible and by seeking power and status. Female fixation in this stage involves a seductiveness that doesn't necessarily lead to sex.

These effects that Freud traced to an Oedipal conflict look remarkably similar to the mating strategies that evolutionary psychologists argue are part of our species. Recall from Chapter 6 the idea that men and women have different reproductive strategies, due to differing investment in offspring (Trivers, 1972). The male mating tactic is to create the appearance of power and status and to mate as frequently as possible. The female tactic is to appear highly desirable, but to hold out for the best mate available.

These tactics strongly resemble the fixations just described. We can't help but wonder whether Freud noticed a phenomenon that's biologically based, and ascribed psychodynamic properties to it in order to fit it better into his theory.

Psychoanalysis and Conditioning

Let's now turn to psychoanalysis and the learning perspective. We noted a relationship in Chapter 12, in passing, when discussing Miller and Dollard's (1941) effort to describe personality in terms of conditioning. In doing so, they were trying to translate psychoanalytic concepts into the ideas of learning. Thus, there's a built-in link between aspects of Freud's theory and Miller and Dollard's theory.

Of particular relevance is Miller and Dollard's analysis of repression. This concept is important in psychoanalysis, and it therefore was something of a focus for Miller and Dollard. They saw repression as a conditioned tendency to "*not-think*" about things that are distressing. By not-thinking about them, you avoid the pain. Escaping the pain reinforces the tendency to not-think. It thereby builds this tendency in more completely. In this way Miller and Dollard were able to account for a phenomenon that's central to the psychodynamic view, using very different language.

Though it may not be obvious, development of the not-thinking tendency also is a special case of extinction. That is, learning to "not-think" means that the tendency to "think" is getting weaker. If you're learning to not-think about a distressing topic, whatever stimulus formerly cued the thought no longer does so. Thus, the conditioned response (thinking) is extinguishing. It's only one more step to suggest that there may be a connection between *all* instances of extinction and repression, or anticathexis.

Freud said an anticathexis uses energy to keep an impulse or thought out of consciousness. If the restraining force isn't strong enough, the response leaks out. Recall that in Chapter 12 we described a phenomenon called spontaneous recovery after extinction. This phenomenon suggests that the behavioral tendency is still there. This in turn suggests that, at some level, extinction may involve creating an active restraint. Because a restraint presumably requires energy, it may be the same as an anticathexis.

Thinking about *anti*cathexes in conditioning terms leads us to consider *cathexes* as well. We noted in Chapter 8 that psychoanalytic theory distinguishes between id cathexes and ego cathexes. An id cathexis is binding energy in an activity or object that satisfies a need. An ego cathexis doesn't satisfy a need directly. Rather, it binds energy in an object or activity that's *associated* with the satisfying of a need.

There's a similarity between these ideas and conditioning concepts. Primary reinforcers in operant conditioning are things that directly satisfy a need (e.g., food or water). Obtaining a primary reinforcer might be equivalent to having an id cathexis. Secondary reinforcers are stimuli *associated* with primary reinforcers or which provide a way to *get* primary reinforcers. Getting (or anticipating) a secondary reinforcer seems similar to forming an ego cathexis.

A final similarity between conditioning and psychoanalytic views concerns the role of the unconscious in determining behavior. To behaviorists, behavior stems from prior conditioning. Conditioning occurs outside consciousness. In effect, this says that behavior results from unconscious influences. In this particular learning view, people do things for reasons they may not be aware of. This is consistent with one of Freud's beliefs. Obviously Freud had different dynamics in mind. Nonetheless, it's a potentially important link between the views.

Psychoanalysis and Self-Regulation: The Structural Model

The psychoanalytic approach to personality also has certain similarities to the cognitive self-regulation approach. One similarity derives from the notion of a self-regulatory hierarchy. The behavioral qualities involved range from very limited movements, through organized sequences, to abstract higher-level qualities. As pointed out in Chapter 17, attention can be diverted from the higher levels. When this happens, behavior is more spontaneous and responsive to cues of the moment. It's as though low-level action sequences, once triggered, run off by themselves. In contrast to this impulsive style of behavior, actions being regulated according to higher-order values (programs or principles) have a more carefully managed character.

Aspects of this description hint at similarities to Freud's three-part view of personality. Consider the spontaneity and responsiveness to situational cues in the self-regulation model when high-level control isn't being exerted. This resembles certain aspects of id functioning. An obvious difference is Freud's assumption that id impulses are primarily sexual or aggressive. The self-regulation model, in contrast, makes no such assumption. It's worth noting, though, that alcohol intoxication and deindividuation, which seem to reduce control at high levels (Chapter 17), often lead to sexual and/or destructive activity.

The link between id processes and low-level control is a bit tenuous. In contrast, there's quite a strong resemblance between program control in the self-regulation approach and ego functioning in the psychoanalytic approach. Program control involves planning, decision making, and behavior that's pragmatic, as opposed to either impulsive or principled. These qualities also characterize the ego's functioning.

Levels higher than program control resemble in some ways the functioning of the superego. Principle control, in some cases at least, induces people to conform to moral principles. Control at the highest level involves an effort to conform to your idealized sense of self. These efforts resemble in some respects the attempt to fit your behavior to the principles of the ego ideal and to avoid a guilty conscience for violating these principles.

The fit between models at this high level isn't perfect, partly because not all principles are moralistic. Yet, here's a question: why did Freud focus on morality and ignore other kinds of ideals? Was it perhaps because morality was so prominent an issue in his society at that time? Maybe the superego is really the capacity to follow rules *in general,* rather than just moral rules. If this were so—if the superego actually pushes behavior toward *other* principles as well as moral ones—the similarity between models would be even greater.

Psychoanalysis and Cognitive Processes

Several links exist between psychoanalytic themes and ideas from cognitive psychology (e.g., Westen, 1998). Matthew Erdelyi (1985) has even suggested that Freud's theory was largely a theory of cognition. Indeed, he said that Freud was straining toward an analogy between mind and computer, but never got there because the computer hadn't been invented yet.

Erdelyi argued that cognitive psychologists essentially reinvented many psychodynamic concepts. For example, Freud assumed a process that keeps threats out of awareness. This is similar in some ways to the filtering process by which the mind "preattentively" selects information to process more fully. Freud's concept of ego becomes "executive control processes." The strength of a cathexis is the amount of attention devoted to something. The topography of the mind becomes a matter of "levels of processing," and distortions become "biases in processing."

As an example of Erdelyi's approach, consider repression and denial (see also Paulhus & Suedfeld, 1988). When ideas, thoughts, or perceptions begin to arise that are threatening, repression and denial prevent them from reaching consciousness. This reaction can occur before a threatening stimulus is even experienced, a phenomenon termed **perceptual defense.** Or it can involve forgetting an event after it's been experienced. Erdelyi (1985) argued that these reflect a sequence of information-processing decisions (Figure 18.1).

He says information is partially analyzed preattentively. This yields an implicit estimate of how much anxiety would arise if the information reached awareness. If the estimate exceeds a threshold, processing stops and the information never goes farther. If the estimate is lower than the threshold, the information goes to a memory area corresponding to the preconscious. Similar decisions are made at other stages, with lower and lower criteria for moving to the next level of processing. This model treats repression, response suppression, and self-deception more generally (Chapter 9) as reflecting checks at several stages of information processing.

As implied by this description, today's cognitive view assumes that part of the mind is unconscious. Indeed, the study of unconscious processes is a very active area of work (Bargh, 1997; Kihlstrom, 1987). Today's cognitive view tends to equate consciousness with attention. Events that are unconscious are those that get little or no attention.

Figure 18.1

An information-processing picture of repression and denial. Input information (top)—whether perceptual or from a suppressed memory—is judged preattentively for its anxiety-inducing value. Then come a series of implicit decisions. First, does the anxiety the information would create (x) exceed a criterion of "unbearability" (u)? If so, processing stops; if not, the material goes to a memory area corresponding to the preconscious. Next, does the predicted anxiety exceed a "serious discomfort" criterion (v)? If so, processing ceases and the information stays in memory; if not, the information moves to consciousness. The final decision is whether to acknowledge openly the information that's now conscious, depending on whether the anxiety from doing so will exceed a final criterion (w). This sequence provides for information never to be stored in memory, to be stored but not reach consciousness, to reach consciousness but be suppressed, or to be acknowledged openly (adapted from Erdelyi, 1985).

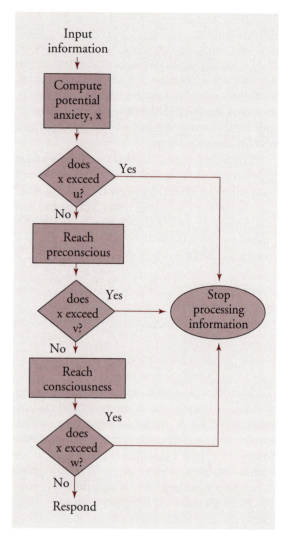

There are several reasons why an event might get little attention. It may be tagged preattentively as having too much potential for anxiety. Or it might occur in a part of the nervous system that attentional processes can't reach. Many cognitive scientists think of the nervous system as a set of special-purpose components, only some of which can be examined consciously (Gardner, 1985). Thus, the basic "wiring" of the system renders some aspects of experience inaccessible.

Events sometimes are unconscious because some behaviors are highly preprogrammed and automatic. Acts that are automatic require little or no monitoring. Highly automated sequences can be triggered by stimuli that are noted by the nervous system at some level but never reach consciousness (Bargh, 1997; Norman, 1981). Even elaborate actions drop mostly out of awareness as they become routine (which all experienced drivers discover at one time or other, as they arrive at home with no memory of how they got there).

Highly programmed acts, such as walking, can occur with little awareness. This suggests a possible point of contact between cognitive self-regulation ideas and psychodynamic theory.

These descriptions obviously differ in important ways from Freud's treatment of the unconscious. Only Erdelyi's example involving preattentive estimates of anxiety implies the sort of process that Freud assumed. All these ideas, however, suggest ways in which information can fail to reach consciousness.

Another body of work has linked cognitive processes to the psychoanalytic concept of *transference*. Transference occurs when a person in therapy displaces emotional reactions onto the therapist. Presumably these reactions were initially stimulated by significant others in the person's earlier life. Recent studies provide a cognitive explanation for such a turn of events (Andersen, Glassman, Chen, & Cole, 1995; Glassman & Andersen, 1999).

Specifically, the schemas people have of significant others seem chronically to be partially active (thus accessible). As with other instances of partial activation, this makes it easier for the schema to emerge and be used in perceiving and interpreting other stimuli. As a result, you may view many people through the lens of that schema, and not even realize it. If someone does something that reminds you vaguely of your mother's way of inducing guilt, you may use your mother schema and perceive that person as like your mother.

Indeed, when such schemas pop up, self-aspects relating to those significant others emerge as well (Hinkley & Andersen, 1996). Thus, if someone tends to induce guilt as your mother did, you may react just as you did to your mother (e.g., by becoming irrationally angry), even if the reaction isn't appropriate to the present situation. All this can happen in therapy, or anywhere.

Social Learning and Cognitive Self-Regulation Views

As newer theories were created over the years, personality psychologists were often influenced by ideas that were being used in other areas of psychology. Indeed, this cross-fertilization has become very common. Among the sources of ideas for personality psychologists during the past several decades were learning psychology and cognitive psychology. To a considerable extent, people who sampled from these sources sampled from both rather than just one.

One result of this pattern is a set of similarities between the social-cognitive learning approach (Chapter 13) and the cognitive self-regulation approaches (Chapters 16 and 17). One of these similarities is also shared with Kelly's personal construct theory (Chapter 15). These approaches have diverse histories, but their central concepts resemble one another more than just a little. Indeed, as you may have noticed, the work of several people pertains not just to one of these views but to two or more of them.

One area of overlap concerns the importance these approaches ascribe to cognitive processes in creating representations of the world and the self. Differences among theories on this issue stem largely from the fact that each has different *reasons* for emphasizing cognition. In discussing cognition from the social learning approach, Mischel (1973) said that if we want to understand learning, we have to look at people's mental representations of stimuli, not the stimuli themselves. People learn from what *they* think is there, not what an outsider sees. The way the stimuli are mentally represented and transformed determines how people will respond to them (see also Bandura, 1977a, 1986).

From the learning perspective, these statements emphasize that human learning is more complicated than it seems. An event doesn't lead automatically to conditioning that's the same for everyone. From the learning perspective, such statements are qualifications on theories of learning. They say to other learning theorists that the *person* has to be considered in analyzing learning. That's the point of such statements—*when they're made from the learning perspective.*

When embedded in Kelly's theory of personal constructs or today's cognitive view on personality, however, ideas about the role of cognition take on a broader life. From these views, cognitive processes are central to an understanding of *everything* about personality. When he's taking the cognitive view on personality, Mischel focuses not on the subtleties of learning but on how people organize their understanding. Note the difference of emphasis. In the cognitive view, the idea that people organize their experience is a key principle regarding the essence of personality. Learning per se is more peripheral, and it may even be disregarded altogether. Cognitive processes are also critical to the self-regulation view on personality, although once again there's a slight difference of emphasis. The focus in the self-regulation approach is mostly on the role cognitions play in creating behavior.

Another similarity between the social learning and cognitive self-regulation views concerns expectancies. (Indeed, expectancies also appear in the need-and-motive approach, and they're implicit in ego psychology.) All these approaches see expectancies as determinants of how hard people try to do things. Many people—Rotter (1954, 1966), Bandura (1977a, 1986), Kanfer (1977), Kirsch (1985, 1990), Mischel (1973, 1979), Carver and Scheier (1981, 1990, 1998), and others—have argued that people hold expectancies about effects their actions are likely to have and expectancies about whether they can do things they want to do. These expectations can influence how hard a person tries, and what the person learns from an event.

The social learning and cognitive self-regulation approaches also resemble each other in the structure they assume underlies behavior. (Kelly's theory becomes less relevant here, because Kelly didn't say much about behaving, as opposed to construing.) The social learning view says people have incentives, which draw them forward into action. Incentives are the same as goals, a concept that plays a large role in the self-regulation perspective. Indeed, other perspectives also have constructs that serve a comparable role in guiding behavior (see Table 18.1).

There is, however, one important difference of emphasis here between the learning and self-regulation views. It concerns the concept of reinforcement. The social learning view uses this concept explicitly. The concept is basic to the principle of instrumental learning. As we noted in Chapter 13, however, one theorist of the social learning view—Bandura—has consistently used the concept differently than did earlier theorists. To Bandura, reinforcers create mental representations of future incentives. They cause people to learn expectancies about what actions are useful in what situations. But reinforcers don't directly increase the tendency to do the acts that preceded them. The way Bandura used this concept raises questions about whether its meaning is compatible with that assumed by other learning theorists.

Keep in mind, though, that Bandura stands with one foot in the learning perspective and one in the cognitive self-regulation perspective. His view on reinforcement may reflect Bandura the self-regulation theorist more than Bandura the learning theorist. As we noted in Chapter 17, self-regulation theorists are divided on reinforcement as a concept. Some say that people self-reinforce after success. Others see the concept of self-reinforcement as less useful.

This may be a point where the personal histories of the theorists play a role in how their theories are constructed. Most self-regulation theorists who assume a role for self-reinforcement began their work in the learning perspective. Only gradually did they become identified with the emerging cognitive self-regulation view. Perhaps they retain a role for self-reinforcement from a psychological inertia, because it represents a comfortable tie to the past. It's also of interest that those theorists are more likely to talk about *self*-reinforcement than external reinforcement (e.g., Kanfer, 1977). It's the person's own goal representations that matter, after all. Only *you* can decide whether your goal's been met. Thus self-reinforcement, rather than external reinforcement, is at the heart of these discussions.

To others, introducing self-reinforcement as a concept simply raises questions. Certainly people often feel pride after success and sadness after failure. But do these reactions create the learning? Or are they just emotional reactions to informational

Table 18.1

Comparable behavioral concepts taken from four perspectives on personality.	
Concept	**Theoretical perspective**
Incentive	Social learning
Goal, reference value	Self-regulation
Motive	Need and motive
Ego cathexis	Psychoanalytic

events, with the latter being what really matters? This is an issue that's not settled in the self-regulation perspective (or, to some extent, even in the learning perspective; see Timberlake, 1993; Viken & McFall, 1994).

Neoanalytic and Cognitive Self-Regulation Perspectives

The learning and cognitive self-regulation perspectives arose in academic psychology, with an emphasis on controlled research. Early neoanalytic psychology, in contrast, derived mostly from clinical experiences of the theorists. Despite this difference, there's a surprising convergence across these views (cf. Westen, 1991).

Consider, for example, a series of conceptual similarities between self-regulation ideas and Adler's ideas. Recall that Adler saw people as motivated by feelings of inferiority, which make them strive for superiority. He referred to the continual struggle for greater competence as a great upward drive. As we said in Chapter 10, he believed that feelings of inferiority cause healthy people to work throughout life toward greater integration and perfection.

Adler also believed that people established long-term goals for their lives. He referred to this as the principle of *fictional finalism*. This term conveys the sense that people are motivated by views of their final outcomes and that those views are invented, or fictional. Future goals are always fictional in the sense that they aren't yet real. People act, however, as though they're headed toward these end points, and use them as guides for their efforts. To Adler these future-oriented goals (which he also called *guiding self-ideals*) are more important determinants of behavior than are events in the person's past.

These ideas resemble ideas from the cognitive self-regulation perspective in two ways. First, Adler's thinking placed considerable emphasis on goals, which are also a cornerstone of the self-regulation view of personality. Indeed, Adler's fictional life plans seem quite similar to the possible selves discussed by Markus and her colleagues.

The other similarity relates to the structure of people's strivings. Adler's account resembles the self-regulation approach in one way here, while differing from it in another. The similarity is Adler's belief that changes in behavior are prompted by discrepancies between where you are and where you want to be. When a person notices an inferiority (as Adler called it), there's an effort to overcome it. The structure of this process is very similar to that of the feedback loop described in Chapter 17. The difference is that Adler emphasized the role of subjective feelings of inferiority. The self-regulation model doesn't assume such feelings. It simply assumes that when goals have been set, the person tries to meet them.

Maslow's Hierarchy and Hierarchies of Self-Regulation

There are also similarities between elements of the phenomenological perspective and the cognitive self-regulation perspective. We noted earlier a strong thematic resemblance between Kelly's theory of personal constructs and today's cognitive theories. But this isn't the only similarity. Consider Maslow's hierarchy of motives (Chapter 14). There are at least two similarities between that hierarchy and the self-regulation hierarchy.

First, Maslow conceived of the motive qualities at the top of the hierarchy as more abstract and subtle, but also as more integrative, than those lower. The levels of the hierarchy of control also have this character. Second, Maslow saw the lower motives as more demanding than the higher ones, in the sense that a deficit or a problem lower in the hierarchy draws the person's attention to it and forces the person to deal with it. Similarly, in at least one version of the control hierarchy, if a problem develops at a low level, attention is brought to that level in an attempt to resolve the problem.

There are, however, differences between these views as well. The biggest difference concerns the "content" of the hierarchies. Maslow's analysis was explicitly an analysis of *motives,* intended to incorporate both biological needs and psychological motives. The control hierarchy, in contrast, focuses on the structure of *action,* with goals that relate to qualities of behavior. This difference means that the two hierarchies are very different at their low levels. Maslow's hierarchy points to survival needs, the other hierarchy points to muscle movements.

At higher levels, though, the two hierarchies are more similar. The highest level of control in the self-regulation view seems roughly equivalent to the concept of self-actualization used by Maslow and Rogers. There's still one difference, however. Woven through the writings of Maslow and Rogers on this topic is the sense that self-actualization is something that happens *to* you, if you can free yourself from the demands of motives at lower levels and just let yourself sense what your body is saying is right for you. It shouldn't involve an effort. If you're *trying* to self-actualize, you probably *aren't* self-actualizing.

The nature of self-regulation in the control hierarchy is ambiguous in that regard. It's by no means clear that such high-level self-regulation is free of effort. On the other hand, the nature of the goal at the highest level—an ideal self that relates to the many principles in force at the next lower level—is quite diffuse. It's so diffuse, in fact, that it isn't too hard to imagine that self-regulation toward it might also feel diffuse. Thus, the subjective experience of self-regulation at the highest level might *not* feel effortful in the same way as does self-regulation at lower levels.

Self-Actualization and Self-Regulation

Two other similarities between the self-actualization view and the self-regulation view of personality go beyond Maslow's hierarchy. One similarity is that both viewpoints use concepts corresponding to idealized and experienced qualities of self. The labels *real self* and *ideal self* are explicit in the phenomenological view of Rogers. The sense of an idealized self is also involved at the top of the control hierarchy, as is the experienced actual self that's compared with it.

The comparison process itself is also similar between the approaches. Rogers emphasized that people compare their current selves with their ideal selves and that they experience anxiety when there's incongruity between them. The comparison between a sensed condition and a standard, or reference point, is also intimately involved in the self-regulation perspective, not only with respect to an ideal self but at all levels of the hierarchy.

Dispositions and Their Equivalents in Other Models

Another resemblance among theories brings us full circle to an idea with which we began this book. We started with the concept of dispositions. We now return to it. As we noted in Chapter 1, a major theme of personality psychology is how people differ from one another, not just temporarily, but in an enduring way. This theme is the basis for the dispositional perspective on personality. Dispositions take a variety of forms: traits, enduring motive qualities, and (in a biological extension of this view) inherited temperaments.

The essence of dispositions, if not the concept itself, is also prominent in at least two more views on personality. The psychoanalytic view assumes that people derive stable personality qualities from childhood psychosexual crises. The neoanalytic view holds that early experience influences personality in other ways. Erikson assumed that childhood psychosocial crises shape adult personality, and object relations and attachment theories make similar assumptions.

These theories differ regarding the source of dispositions. Yet the theories share two assumptions: that something is stamped or etched into the individual early in life, and that this characteristic continues to influence the person from then on. The disposition has been viewed as a biological temperament, a transformation of sexual drives, a reflection of a psychosocial crisis, a learned motive quality, and simply a trait. Yet all these theories treat the disposition as having an enduring impact on the person's life experiences. This similarity among approaches, which is often overlooked, is not a trivial one.

Indeed, the disposition concept also has a place in other views. For example, one version of the learning approach assumes that people differ in locus of control, which helps determine how and what people learn. One aspect of the self-regulation approach assumes that people vary in the disposition to be self-reflective and, thus, carefully self-regulated. In both of these cases (and others as well), it's assumed that individual differences are stable dispositions that influence a broad range of the person's experiences.

Recurrent Themes, Viewed from Different Angles

Our emphasis in the preceding section has been on the notion that certain ideas in one theoretical perspective resemble ideas from another perspective. We also want to note another kind of similarity across perspectives. This is a similarity in the issues the theories consider. We said earlier in this chapter that different theories often address different issues. That's true. But at least a couple of themes recur across a wide range of perspectives.

Impulse and Restraint

One of these themes concerns what seems to be a basic distinction between *impulse* and *restraint*. This issue has been part of personality psychology for a long time, but it has become even more prominent in recent years. The issue is often introduced in the context of delay of gratification, where a choice must be made between a small reward now versus a larger reward later. In previous chapters we discussed delay of gratification from the angle of psychoanalysis (where we said the ego restrains id impulses), ego psychology (where we described variations in ego-control and ego-resiliency), social learning theory (where we considered effects of models), and the cognitive view (where the focus was on mental images that can foster restraint).

But the issue of impulse versus restraint is far broader than that. In some ways, it's fundamental to personality. As a result, its broader manifestations emerge in many views of personality:

■ It's there in trait psychology, in which a trait of conscientiousness is assumed to be defined partly by self-discipline and deliberation (McCrae & Costa, 1987). Indeed, another trait theory treats constraint as a basic dimension (Tellegen, 1985).

■ It comes up in temperament theories, where some argue that constraint is a basic temperament (Clark & Watson, 1999) and there are hints that impulsiveness may be genetically based.

■ It comes up in biological process models, where an argument is beginning to emerge that approach and avoidance systems are joined by a third system, which concerns restraint versus impulsiveness (Eysenck & Eysenck, 1976; Lieberman et al., in press; Zuckerman, 1994).

■ A core issue at the heart of psychoanalysis is the balance between the id's desires and the ego's restraint.

■ The issue also comes up in neoanalytic theories, where ego control (ranging from overcontrol to undercontrol) is a key dimension of personality (Block & Block, 1980).

■ It's there in cognitive theories, in the form of a contrast between rational and experiential systems (Epstein, 1994), and in a contrast between hot, incentive-related cognition and cool, restrained cognition (Metcalfe & Mischel, 1999).

■ It also appears in self-regulation theories, in the distinction between deliberative and implemental mindsets (Heckhausen & Gollwitzer, 1987).

Impulse versus restraint has emerged in the past decade as a key issue in several areas of personality psychology. This issue is one influence that's led a number of people to think about cognitive processing as occurring in two modes. In these theories, the management of behavior is seen as subject to two layers of influence, which may use two different parts of the brain. One system provides an automatic, intuitive, superficial, fast way of interacting with the world. It's believed to have evolved earlier. The other system provides a rational, deliberative, but slower way of interacting with the world. It's believed to be of more recent origin.

The question of how and why a person chooses to act quickly versus hold back from acting is basic. It's no wonder that many theories say something or other about this question. This issue undoubtedly will remain a focus of interest for many people in the years ahead.

Individual versus Group Needs

Another fundamental issue concerns the competing pressure of individualistic self-interest versus the needs arising from being involved in groups (or couples). In many specific cases, this issue is tangled up with the issue of action versus restraint. This is because the needs of others is often what urges restraint on one's own impulses. Conceptually, however, it's a separate issue.

Earlier in this chapter we noted that psychoanalytic theory and evolutionary psychology both confront the contrast between these pressures. In psychoanalysis, the ego deals with both social and physical reality, and the superego deals with other aspects of social needs. In evolutionary psychology, people have individualistic needs—survival, competition for mates. But they also have group-based needs—cooperation with a mate and with the larger society.

This distinction between individualistic and social goals also appears in other approaches. In trait psychology, in fact, it emerges in two places. One is the trait of agreeableness, which concerns maintaining positive relations with others. People high on this dimension are attuned to mutual well-being; those lower on the dimension are unconcerned with others' interests. The distinction also emerges in the trait of extraversion. Extraverts want to have social impact. Introverts are not concerned with group involvement, and follow more individualistic paths.

In the motive approach, this issue shows up in the motives to achieve and exert power versus affiliate and attain intimacy. The issue is also in the biological process approach, in unsocialized sensation seeking, with its disregard of others' needs. It's in the psychosocial approach, in the issue of separation-individuation versus merger. It's in the self-actualization approach, in the balance between the self-actualizing tendency and the need for positive regard.

In all these cases, people confront the need to balance the two competing pressures. Both pressures are important, in different ways. Given all this attention from theorists of so many different perspectives, this issue appears to be critically important in human experience.

Combining Perspectives

As should now be apparent, similarities do exist between seemingly unrelated approaches to personality. These similarities may, in time, allow integration of these approaches with one another. It's probably safe to say, though, that most personality psychologists view that as a distant goal. One reason is the sheer size and complexity of the job.

Theorists do sometimes try to integrate across boundaries. For example, Cattell (1985) tried to merge psychoanalytic elements of id, ego, and superego with physiological qualities of temperament and cognitive variables such as expectancy, all in a factor-analytic framework. It's hard, however, to fit all the pieces together in a way that people can easily use.

Theorists such as Eysenck and Zuckerman have tried to integrate across two or three perspectives. In describing Eysenck's work in earlier chapters, we treated it as two sets of ideas with separate focuses of convenience. Some of them are biological, dealing with brain function (and to some extent the heritability of differences). Others form a hierarchical model of relations among acts, habits, traits, and supertraits. Though we presented the ideas as separate, Eysenck viewed them as an integrated model with multiple facets. Zuckerman (1991b, 1994) has made a similar kind of statement, binding together—in a single model—trait, inheritance, and biological-process views.

Eclecticism

Another option, exercised by many psychologists, is to take an eclectic approach to personality. This involves drawing useful ideas from many theories, rather than being tied to just one or two. Essentially, it means saying that different ideas are useful for different purposes, and that there may be no approach that's best for all purposes. To understand a phenomenon, you may need to look at it from the angle of a theory that focuses on it, rather than a theory that doesn't. As Scarr (1985, p. 511) put it, "There is no need to choose a single lens for psychology when we can enjoy a kaleidoscope of perspectives."

This sort of approach suggests that views of personality from the various perspectives may be mutually supportive. It may not be necessary to integrate them into a single set of constructs or principles. As we said earlier, the "focus of convenience" of one theory differs from those of other theories. By taking bits of theory across several focuses of convenience, perhaps we can obtain a more well-rounded picture of what personality is really like.

Thus, many personality psychologists today accept the idea that personality was shaped by evolutionary pressures. Most assume there are inherited temperaments, and that the processes by which personality is reflected are biological. Several ideas from psychoanalytic theory are also widely accepted, for example, that determinants of behavior are sometimes outside awareness, and that mechanisms exist that protect us from things we don't want to deal with. Many personality psychologists accept the idea that early experiences have a big impact on what people are like. (Indeed, there's even evidence from the learning lab that associations conditioned first to a stimulus are more permanent than associations conditioned later; see Bouton, 1994.) Obviously learning has an impact on personality. People do seem to organize the experiences of their lives in idiosyncratic ways. People may well have an inner voice of self-actualization. Behavior may even reflect the operation of feedback loops.

All of these ideas may be true, or only some of them. All of them may be useful, or only some of them. Many psychologists pick and choose bits from various perspectives and use them where they seem reasonable. The choice among the available elements is an individual one.

An Example: Biology and Learning as Complementary Influences on Personality

Perhaps the simplest illustration of an eclectic approach is that psychologists almost universally acknowledge the importance to personality of both biology and learning. Everyone does this: people who focus on biology, people who focus on learning, and people who focus on some other part of personality. Early learning theorists claimed the mind is a "blank slate" on which any kind of personality can be sketched. It's clear, though, that this isn't true. There are biological constraints on learning.

In particular, some associations are learned more easily than others. A term used to describe this is **preparedness.** This term implies that organisms are prepared to condition certain links more easily than others (Öhman & Mineka, 2001; Seligman & Hager, 1972). Preparedness isn't all-or-nothing. It's a dimension of ease versus difficulty in learning connections. Presumably this is biologically influenced.

As an example, if you get sick to your stomach, you could in theory develop a conditioned aversive response toward any number of stimuli. If conditioning depended only on association between stimuli, you should condition aversions to *all* neutral stimuli that are present. However, you're more likely to develop an aversion to a *flavor* experienced just before getting sick than to other stimuli (Garcia & Koelling, 1966). Apparently the links are just easier to create in the nervous system for some pairs of events than others.

Preparedness also seems to be involved in instrumental learning. That is, some kinds of actions are easier for animals to learn than others, even if the same reward follows both. Rats learn more quickly to avoid a foot shock by jumping than by pressing a bar (Wickelgren, 1977). Pigeons quickly learn to peck a spot to obtain food, but it's hard to get them to learn to *refrain* from pecking to get food.

Just as it's clear the mind is not a blank slate, it's clear that expression of most biological tendencies depends on experience. Earlier in the book we talked about diathesis–stress models, in which a particular kind of stress produces a problem only if the person also has a particular vulnerability (which might be biological, though it doesn't have to be). Such models are widely accepted. One reason for this acceptance

Both biological and learning principles are needed to understand fully the phenomenon of preparedness—such as the biological readiness that chimps and people show in learning to use tools.

is that twin studies of serious disorders show two things at once. They show that serious disorders such as schizophrenia are genetically influenced. And they show just as clearly that genes aren't everything. That is, if you're the MZ twin of someone with schizophrenia, your chances of being schizophrenic are elevated, but still less than 100 percent. If genes were all that mattered, the figure would be 100 percent.

Thus, an eclectic acceptance of both biology and learning as important influences on personality seems well-founded. Perhaps other combinations will prove in the future to be similarly well-founded.

Which Theory Is Best?

As we said earlier, one answer to the question of which theory is best is that no theory is perfect, and you may benefit from using bits and pieces of many theories. We should point out, though, that this question is sometimes answered another way. This answer returns us to a point we made in the book's opening chapter. It may provide a fitting way to end, as well.

Over a century ago, William James wrote that theories must account reasonably well for the phenomena that people experience as real, but to be successful a theory needs to do more than that. He wrote (James, 1890, p. 312) that people will believe those theories which " . . . are most interesting, those which appeal most urgently to our aesthetic, emotional, and active needs." Put more simply, the theory that's best is the one you *like* best. The one that's best—for you—is the one that appeals to you most, the one you find most interesting and engaging. Edward Tolman (1959, p. 152) also put it pretty simply: "I have liked to think about psychology in ways that have proved congenial to me. . . . In the end, the only sure criterion is to have fun. And I have had fun."

SUMMARY

Although various perspectives on personality differ from one another in important ways, there are also similarities among theories. The psychoanalytic perspective has similarities to at least three alternative views. First, ideas about biological evolution in the species parallel Freud's ideas about the evolution of personality in the individual. That is, in each case a primitive force (the genes, the id) needs another force to help it deal with reality (the cortex, the ego), and eventually it also needs a force to keep it in contact with the social world (inherited sensitivity to social influence, the superego). Second, one branch of the conditioning view was devised to create a link between psychoanalytic concepts and the language of learning. Third, the psychoanalytic view and the cognitive self-regulation view resemble each other in two ways. The notion of a hierarchy of control echoes psychoanalytic theory's three components of personality. Work on cognition has also developed concepts that resemble in some ways those postulated years earlier by Freud.

A substantial overlap exists between the social learning and the cognitive self-regulation viewpoints. They share an emphasis on mental representations of the world (as does Kelly's theory of personal constructs), although the theories have somewhat different rationales for the emphasis. They also have similar views of the importance of people's expectancies and similar views on the basic structure of behavior.

A similarity also exists between self-regulation ideas and Adler's neoanalytic theory. Both assume that behavior is aimed at reducing discrepancies, and both emphasize the importance of people's long-term goals. The notion of a hierarchy in self-regulation also suggests a similarity between that view and the phenomenological view, especially Maslow's. Maslow's motive hierarchy deals with several motives that are ignored in the control hierarchy, but at their upper levels the models resemble each other more closely. The principle of self-actualization also resembles the self-regulation model in the concepts of ideal and actual self and the desire for congruity between them.

Another similarity among approaches concerns the concept of disposition. Obviously, this construct is central to the dispositional perspective. It's also important in the psychoanalytic and neoanalytic views. In all these cases (and by implication in others as well), the assumption is made that people have qualities that endure over time and circumstances and that influence their behaviors, thoughts, and feelings.

Although the various theories differ in their focus, certain issues do seem to recur across many of them. This represents another kind of similarity among the theories. One issue that many different theories address is the polarity between impulse versus restraint. Indeed, this issue has become increasingly prominent in recent years. Another is the competing pressures of individual self-interest and communal interest.

Thus, there are areas of overlap among theories. Yet the theories also differ. Which, then, is right? One answer is that all perspectives seem to have something of value to offer. Many psychologists prefer an eclectic position, taking elements and ideas from several views, rather than just one. At a minimum, people who operate within the framework of a given theory must take into account limitations imposed by other views. For example, temperament theorists believe much of personality is determined by genetics. Yet they also assume that temperaments are modified by learning. Learning theorists believe that personality is a product of a learning history. Yet it's clear that some kinds of learning are easier than others. Perhaps the future will see greater emphasis on this eclecticism, the sharing of ideas from one perspective to another.

GLOSSARY

Perceptual defense Responding to screen out a threatening stimulus before it enters awareness.

Preparedness The idea that some conditioning is easy because the animal is biologically "prepared" for it to happen.

Aarts, H., & Dijksterhuis, A. (2000). Habits as knowledge structures: Automaticity in goal-directed behavior. *Journal of Personality and Social Psychology, 78,* 53–63.

Abramson, L. Y., Alloy, L. B., & Metalsky, G. I. (1995). Hopelessness depression. In G. M. Buchanan & M. E. P. Seligman (Eds.), *Explanatory style* (pp. 113–134). Hillsdale, NJ: Erlbaum.

Abramson, L. Y., Metalsky, G. I., & Alloy, L. B. (1989). Hopelessness depression: A theory-based subtype of depression. *Psychological Review, 96,* 358–372.

Abramson, L. Y., Seligman, M. E. P., & Teasdale, J. D. (1978). Learned helplessness in humans: Critique and reformulation. *Journal of Abnormal Psychology, 87,* 49–74.

Adams, G. D., & Fastnow, C. (2000, November 10). A note on the voting irregularities in Palm Beach, Florida. Web posting. http://madison.hss.cmu.edu.

Adams, G. R., & Shea, J. A. (1979). The relationship between identity status, locus of control, and ego development. *Journal of Youth and Adolescence, 8,* 81–89.

Adams, J. A. (1976). Issues for a closed-loop theory of motor learning. In G. E. Stelmach (Ed.), *Motor control: Issues and trends* (pp. 87–107). New York: Academic Press.

Adams-Webber, J. R. (1979). *Personal construct theory: Concepts and applications.* New York: Wiley.

Adler, A. (1917). *Study of organ inferiority and its psychical compensation.* New York: Nervous and Mental Diseases Publishing.

Adler, A. (1927). *Practice and theory of individual psychology.* New York: Harcourt, Brace, & World.

Adler, A. (1929). *The science of living.* New York: Greenberg.

Adler, A. (1930). Individual psychology. In C. Murchison (Ed.), *Psychologies of 1930.* Worcester, MA: Clark University Press.

Adler, A. (1931). *What life should mean to you.* Boston: Little, Brown.

Adler, A. (1956). *The individual psychology of Alfred Adler: A systematic presentation of selections from his writings.* H. L.

Ansbacher & R. R. Ansbacher (Eds.). New York: Basic Books.

Adler, A. (1958). *What life should mean to you.* New York: Capricorn Books. (Originally published, 1931)

Adler, A. (1964). *Social interest: A challenge to mankind.* New York: Capricorn Books. (Originally published, 1933)

Agostinelli, G., Sherman, S. J., Presson, C. C., & Chassin, L. (1992). Self-protection and self-enhancement biases in estimates of population prevalence. *Personality and Social Psychology Bulletin, 18,* 631–642.

Agronick, G. S., & Duncan, L. E. (1998). Personality and social change: Individual differences, life path, and importance attributed to the women's movement. *Journal of Personality and Social Psychology, 74,* 1545–1555.

Ahadi, S., & Diener, E. (1989). Multiple determinants and effect size. *Journal of Personality and Social Psychology, 56,* 398–406.

Ainsworth, M. D. S. (1983). Patterns of infant–mother attachment as related to maternal care. In D. Magnusson & V. Allen (Eds.), *Human development: An interactional perspective.* New York: Academic Press.

Ainsworth, M. D. S., Blehar, M. C., Waters, E., & Wall, T. (1978). *Patterns of attachment.* Hillsdale, NJ: Erlbaum.

Ajzen, I. (1985). From intentions to actions: A theory of planned behavior. In J. Kuhl & J. Beckmann (Eds.), *Action control: From cognition to behavior.* Heidelberg & New York: Springer-Verlag.

Ajzen, I. (1988). *Attitudes, personality, and behavior.* Chicago: Dorsey.

Ajzen, I., & Fishbein, M. (1980). *Understanding attitudes and predicting social behavior.* Englewood Cliffs, NJ: Prentice-Hall.

Alexander, R. (1979). *Darwinism and human affairs.* Seattle: University of Washington Press.

Alicke, M. D. (1985). Global self-evaluation as determined by the desirability and controllability of trait adjectives. *Journal of Personality and Social Psychology, 49,* 1621–1630.

Allen, J. J., Iacono, W. G., Depue, R. A., & Arbisi, P. (1993). Regional electroencephalographic asymmetries in bipolar seasonal affective disorder before and after exposure to bright light. *Biological Psychiatry, 33,* 642–646.

Allen, L. S., & Gorski, R. A. (1992). Sexual orientation and the size of the anterior commissure in the human brain. *Proceedings of the National Academy of Sciences of the U.S.A., 89,* 7199–7202.

Allen, M. G. (1976). Twin studies of affective illness. *Archives of General Psychiatry, 33,* 1476–1478.

Alloy, L. B., & Abramson, L. Y. (1988). Depressive realism: Four theoretical perspectives. In L. B. Alloy (Ed.), *Cognitive processes in depression* (pp. 223–265). New York: Guilford.

Allport, G. W. (1937). *Personality: A psychological interpretation.* New York: Holt.

Allport, G. W. (1961). *Pattern and growth in personality.* New York: Holt, Rinehart, & Winston.

Allport, G. W., & Odbert, H. S. (1936). Trait-names: A psycho-lexical study. *Psychological Monographs, 47* (1, Whole No. 211).

Almagor, M., Tellegen, A., & Waller, N. G. (1995). The Big Seven model: A cross-cultural replication and further exploration of the basic dimensions of natural language trait descriptors. *Journal of Personality and Social Psychology, 69,* 300–307.

Amabile, T. M. (1985). Motivation and creativity: Effects of motivational orientation on creative writers. *Journal of Personality and Social Psychology, 48,* 393–399.

Amsel, A. (1967). Partial reinforcement effects on vigor and persistence: Advances in frustration theory derived from a variety of within-subject experiments. In K. W. Spence & J. T. Spence (Eds.), *The psychology of learning and motivation* (Vol. 1). New York: Academic Press.

Anastasi, A. (1988). *Psychological testing* (6th ed.). New York: Macmillan.

Andersen, S. M., & Chen, S. (2002). The relational self: An interpersonal social-cognitive theory. *Psychological Review, 109,* 619–645.

Andersen, S. M., & Cole, S. W. (1990). "Do I know you?": The role of significant others in general social perception. *Journal of Personality and Social Psychology, 59,* 384–399.

Andersen, S. M., Glassman, N. S., Chen, S., & Cole, S. W. (1995). Transference in social perception: The role of chronic accessibility in significant-other representations. *Journal of Personality and Social Psychology, 69,* 41–57.

Anderson, C. A., & Weiner, B. (1992). Attribution and attributional processes in personality. In G. Caprara &

G. Heck (Eds.), *Modern personality psychology: Critical reviews and new directions* (pp. 295–324). New York: Harvester Wheatsheaf.

Anderson, C., John, O. P., Keltner, D., & Kring, A. M. (2001). Who attains social status? Effects of personality and physical attractiveness in social groups. *Journal of Personality and Social Psychology, 81,* 116–132.

Anderson, J. A. (1995). *An introduction to neural networks.* Cambridge, MA: MIT Press.

Anderson, J. R. (1976). *Language, memory and thought.* Hillsdale, NJ: Erlbaum.

Anderson, J. R. (1985). *Cognitive psychology and its implications* (2nd ed.). New York: Freeman.

Anderson, J. R. (1991). The adaptive nature of human categorization. *Psychological Review, 98,* 409–429.

Anderson, J. W. (1988). Henry Murray's early career: A psychobiographical exploration. *Journal of Personality, 56,* 138–171.

Anderson, R. C., & Pichert, J. W. (1978). Recall of previously unrecallable information following a shift in perspective. *Journal of Verbal Learning and Verbal Behavior, 17,* 1–12.

Andrykowski, M. A., Brady, M. J., & Hunt, J. W. (1993). Positive psychosocial adjustment in potential bone marrow transplant recipients: Cancer as a psychosocial transition. *Psycho-oncology, 2,* 261–276.

Ardrey, R. (1966). *The territorial imperative.* New York: Dell.

Arkin, R. M., & Baumgardner, A. H. (1985). Self-handicapping. In J. H. Harvey & G. Weary (Eds.), *Attribution: Basic issues and applications.* New York: Academic Press.

Arndt, J., Greenberg, J., Schimel, J., Pyszczynski, T., & Solomon, S. (2002). To belong or not to belong: That is the question: Terror management and identification with gender and ethnicity. *Journal of Personality and Social Psychology, 83,* 26–43.

Arndt, J., Schimel, J., Greenberg, J., & Pyszczynski, T. (2002). The intrinsic self and defensiveness: Evidence that activating the intrinsic self reduces self-handicapping and conformity. *Personality and Social Psychology Bulletin, 28,* 671–685.

Arnett, P. A., Smith, S. S., & Newman, J. P. (1997). Approach and avoidance motivation in psychopathic criminal offenders during passive avoidance. *Journal of Personality and Social Psychology, 72,* 1413–1428.

Aron, E. N., & Aron, A. (1997). Sensory-processing sensitivity and its relation to introversion and emotionality. *Journal of Personality and Social Psychology, 73,* 345–368.

Asendorpf, J. B., & van Aken, M. A. G. (1999). Resilient, overcontrolled, and undercontrolled personality prototypes in childhood: Replicability, predictive power, and the trait-type issue. *Journal of Personality and Social Psychology, 77,* 815–832.

Asendorpf, J. B., & Wilpers, S. (1998). Personality effects on social relationships. *Journal of Personality and Social Psychology, 74,* 1531–1544.

Aserinsky, E., & Kleitman, N. (1953). Regularly occurring periods of eye motility, and concomitant phenomena during sleep. *Science, 118,* 273.

Ashton, M. C., Lee, K., & Son, C. (2000). Honesty as the sixth factor of personality: Correlations with Machiavellianism, primary psychopathy, and social adroitness. *European Journal of Personality, 14,* 359–368.

Aspinwall, L. G., & Brunhart, S. N. (1996). Distinguishing optimism from denial: Optimistic beliefs predict attention to health threats. *Personality and Social Psychology Bulletin, 22,* 993–1003.

Atkinson, J. W. (1957). Motivational determinants of risk-taking behavior. *Psychological Review, 64,* 359–372.

Atkinson, J. W., & Birch, D. (1970). *The dynamics of action.* New York: Wiley.

Atkinson, J. W., & Birch, D. (1978). *Introduction to motivation* (2nd ed.). New York: D. Van Nostrand.

Atkinson, J. W., Heyns, R. W., & Veroff, J. (1954). The effect of experimental arousal of the affiliation motive on thematic apperception. *Journal of Abnormal and Social Psychology, 49,* 405–410.

Atkinson, J. W., & McClelland, D. C. (1948). The projective expression of needs II. The effect of different intensities of the hunger drive on thematic apperception. *Journal of Experimental Psychology, 38,* 643–658.

Atkinson, J. W., & Raynor, J. O. (Eds.). (1974). *Motivation and achievement.* Washington, DC: V. H. Winston.

Austin, J. T., & Vancouver, J. B. (1996). Goal constructs in psychology: Structure, process, and content. *Psychological Bulletin, 120,* 338–375.

Avery, R. R., & Ryan, R. M. (1988). Object relations and ego development: Comparison and correlates in middle childhood. *Journal of Personality, 56,* 547–569.

Avia, M. D., & Kanfer, F. H. (1980). Coping with aversive stimulation: The effects of training in a self-management context. *Cognitive Therapy and Research, 4,* 73–81.

Avila, C. (2001). Distinguishing BIS-mediated and BAS-mediated disinhibition mechanisms: A comparison of disinhibition models of Gray (1981, 1987) and of Patterson and Newman (1993). *Journal of Personality and Social Psychology, 80,* 311–324.

Axelrod, R., & Hamilton, W. D. (1981). The evolution of cooperation. *Science, 211,* 1390–1396.

Axline, V. M. (1947). *Play therapy.* Boston: Houghton-Mifflin.

Axline, V. M. (1964). *Dibs: In search of self.* Boston: Houghton Mifflin.

Ayduk, O., Mischel, W., & Downey, G. (2002). Attentional mechanisms linking rejection to hostile reactivity: The role of "hot" versus "cool" focus. *Psychological Science, 13,* 443–448.

Ayllon, T., & Azrin, N. H. (1965). The measurement and reinforcement of behavior of psychotics. *Journal of the Experimental Analysis of Behavior, 8,* 357–383.

Ayllon, T., & Azrin, N. H. (1968). *The token economy.* New York: Appleton-Century-Crofts.

Babad, E. Y. (1973). Effects of informational input on the "social deprivation-satisfaction effect." *Journal of Personality and Social Psychology, 27,* 1–5.

Bailey, J. M., Dunne, M. P., & Martin, N. G. (2000). Genetic and environmental influences on sexual orientation and its correlates in an Australian twin sample. *Journal of Personality and Social Psychology, 78,* 524–536.

Bailey, J. M., Gaulin, S., Agyei, Y., & Gladue, B. A. (1994). Effects of gender and sexual orientation on evolutionarily relevant aspects of human mating psychology. *Journal of Personality and Social Psychology, 66,* 1081–1093.

Bailey, J. M., & Pillard, R. C. (1991). A genetic study of male sexual orientation. *Archives of General Psychiatry, 48,* 1089–1096.

Bailey, J. M., Pillard, R. C., Neale, M. C., & Agyei, Y. (1993). Heritable factors influence sexual orientation in women. *Archives of General Psychiatry, 50,* 217–223.

Bain, A. (1859). *The emotions and the will.* London: Longmans.

Baldwin, J. M. (1902). *Social and ethical interpretations in mental development* (3rd ed.). New York: Macmillan.

Baldwin, M. W. (1992). Relational schemas and the processing of social information. *Psychological Bulletin, 112,* 461–484.

Baldwin, M. W., Carrell, S. E., & Lopez, D. F. (1990). Priming relationship schemas: My advisor and the Pope are watching me from the back of my mind. *Journal of Experimental Social Psychology, 26,* 435–454.

Baldwin, M. W., Keelan, J. P. R., Fehr, B., Enns, V., & Koh-Rangarajoo, E. (1996). Social-cognitive conceptualization of attachment working models: Availability and accessibility effects. *Journal of Personality and Social Psychology, 71,* 94–109.

Balmary, M. (1979). *Psychoanalyzing psychoanalysis: Freud and the hidden fault of his father.* Baltimore, MD: Johns Hopkins University Press.

Baltes, P. B., & Staudinger, U. M. (1993). The search for a psychology of wisdom. *Current Directions in Psychological Science, 2,* 75–80.

Bandura, A. (1965). Influence of models' reinforcement contingencies on the acquisition of imitative response. *Journal of Personality and Social Psychology, 1,* 589–595.

Bandura, A. (1969). *Principles of behavior modification.* New York: Holt, Rinehart, & Winston.

Bandura, A. (1971). Vicarious and self-reinforcement processes. In R. Glaser (Ed.), *The nature of reinforcement.* New York: Academic Press.

Bandura, A. (1973). *Aggression: A social learning analysis.* Englewood Cliffs, NJ: Prentice-Hall.

Bandura, A. (1976). Self-reinforcement: Theoretical and methodological considerations. *Behaviorism, 4,* 135–155.

Bandura, A. (1977a). Self-efficacy: Toward a unifying theory of behavioral change. *Psychological Review, 84,* 191–215.

Bandura, A. (1977b). *Social learning theory.* Englewood Cliffs, NJ: Prentice-Hall.

Bandura, A. (1978). The self system in reciprocal determinism. *American Psychologist, 33,* 344–358.

Bandura, A. (1982a). The psychology of chance encounters and life paths. *American Psychologist, 37,* 747–755.

Bandura, A. (1982b). Self-efficacy mechanism in human agency. *American Psychologist, 37,* 122–147.

Bandura, A. (1986). *Social foundations of thought and action: A social cognitive theory.* Englewood Cliffs, NJ: Prentice-Hall.

Bandura, A. (1997). *Self-efficacy: The exercise of control.* New York: Freeman.

Bandura, A., Adams, N. E., & Beyer, J. (1977). Cognitive processes mediating behavioral change. *Journal of Personality and Social Psychology, 35,* 125–139.

Bandura, A., Adams, N. E., Hardy, A. B., & Howells, G. N. (1980). Tests of the generality of self-efficacy theory. *Cognitive Therapy and Research, 4,* 39–66.

Bandura, A., Grusec, J. E., & Menlove, F. L. (1967). Vicarious extinction of avoidance behavior. *Journal of Personality and Social Psychology, 5,* 16–23.

Bandura, A., & Jeffery, R. W. (1973). Role of symbolic coding and rehearsal processes in observational learning. *Journal of Personality and Social Psychology, 26,* 122–130.

Bandura, A., Jeffery, R., & Bachicha, D. L. (1974). Analysis of memory codes and cumulative rehearsal in observational learning. *Journal of Research in Personality, 7,* 295–305.

Bandura, A., & Menlove, F. L. (1968). Factors determining vicarious extinction of avoidance behavior through symbolic modeling. *Journal of Personality and Social Psychology, 8,* 99–108.

Bandura, A., & Mischel, W. (1965). Modification of self-imposed delay of reward through exposure to live and symbolic models. *Journal of Personality and Social Psychology, 2,* 698–705.

Bandura, A., & Rosenthal, T. L. (1966). Vicarious classical conditioning as a function of arousal level. *Journal of Personality and Social Psychology, 3,* 54–62.

Bandura, A., & Schunk, D. H. (1981). Cultivating competence, self-efficacy, and intrinsic interest through proximal self-motivation. *Journal of Personality and Social Psychology, 41,* 586–598.

Bandura, A., & Walters, R. (1963). *Social learning and personality development.* New York: Holt, Rinehart, & Winston.

Bannister, D. (Ed.). (1970). *Perspectives in personal construct theory.* London: Academic Press.

Bannister, D. (1985). *Issues and approaches in personal construct theory.* London: Academic Press.

Barash, D. P. (1977). *Sociobiology and human behavior.* New York: Elsevier.

Barash, D. P. (1986). *The hare and the tortoise: Culture, biology, and human nature.* New York: Penguin.

Barash, D. P. (2001). *Revolutionary biology: The new, gene-centered view of life.* London: Transaction.

Barber, J. P., & DeRubeis, R. J. (1989). On second thought: Where the action is in cognitive therapy for depression. *Cognitive Therapy and Research, 13,* 441–457.

Bargh, J. A. (1997). The automaticity of everyday life. In R. S. Wyer, Jr. (Ed.), *Advances in social cognition* (Vol. 10, pp. 1–61). Mahwah, NJ: Erlbaum.

Bargh, J. A., & Chartrand, T. L. (1999). The unbearable automaticity of being. *American Psychologist, 54,* 462–479.

Bargh, J. A., Chen, M., & Burrows, L. (1996). Automaticity of social behavior: Direct effects of trait construct and stereotype activation on action. *Journal of Personality and Social Psychology, 71,* 230–244.

Bargh, J. A., & Ferguson, M. J. (2000). Beyond behaviorism: On the automaticity of higher mental processes. *Psychological Bulletin, 126,* 925–945.

Bargh, J. A., Gollwitzer, P. M., Lee-Chai, A., Barndollar, K., & Trötschel, R. (2001). The automated will: Nonconscious activation and pursuit of behavioral goals. *Journal of Personality and Social Psychology, 81,* 1014–1027.

Bargh, J. A., Lombardi, W. J., & Higgins, E. T. (1988). Automaticity of chronically accessible constructs in person X situation effects on person perception: It's just a matter of time. *Journal of Personality and Social Psychology, 55*, 599–605.

Bargh, J. A., & Pratto, F. (1986). Individual construct accessibility and perceptual selection. *Journal of Experimental Social Psychology, 22*, 293–311.

Barkow, J. H., Cosmides, L., & Tooby, J. (1992). *The adapted mind: Evolutionary psychology and the generation of culture.* New York: Oxford University Press.

Barlow, D. H. (Ed.). (1981). *Behavioral assessment of adult disorders.* New York: Guilford.

Baron, R. A. (1974a). The aggression-inhibiting influence of heightened sexual arousal. *Journal of Personality and Social Psychology, 30*, 318–322.

Baron, R. A. (1974b). Sexual arousal and physical aggression: The inhibiting influence of "cheesecake" and nudes. *Bulletin of the Psychonomic Society, 3*, 337–339.

Baron, R. A. (1979). Heightened sexual arousal and physical aggression: An extension to females. *Journal of Research in Personality, 13*, 91–102.

Baron, R. A., & Bell, P. A. (1977). Sexual arousal and aggression by males: Effects of type of erotic stimuli and prior provocation. *Journal of Personality and Social Psychology, 35*, 79–87.

Baron, R. A., & Kempner, C. R. (1970). Model's behavior and attraction toward the model as determinants of adult aggressive behavior. *Journal of Personality and Social Psychology, 14*, 335–344.

Baron, R. A., & Richardson, D. R. (1994). *Human aggression* (2nd ed.). New York: Plenum.

Barrett, L., Dunbar, R., & Lycett, J. (2002). *Human evolutionary psychology.* Princeton, NJ: Princeton University Press.

Barron, F. (1953). An ego-strength scale which predicts response to psychotherapy. *Journal of Consulting Psychology, 17*, 327–333.

Bartholomew, K., & Horowitz, L. M. (1991). Attachment styles among young adults: A test of a four-category model. *Journal of Personality and Social Psychology, 61*, 226–244.

Bartholow, B. D., & Anderson, C. A. (2001). Effects of violent video games on aggressive behavior: Potential sex differences. *Journal of Experimental Social Psychology, 38*, 283–290.

Batson, C. D. (1990). How social an animal? The human capacity for caring. *American Psychologist, 45*, 336–346.

Batson, C. D. (1991). *The altruism question: Toward a social-psychological answer.* Hillsdale, NJ: Erlbaum.

Batson, C. D., Bolen, M. H., Cross, J. A., & Neuringer-Benefiel, H. E. (1986). Where is the altruism in the al-

truistic personality? *Journal of Personality and Social Psychology, 50*, 212–220.

Batson, C. D., Dyck, J. L., Brandt, J. R., Batson, J. G., Powell, A. L., McMaster, M. R., & Griffitt, C. (1988). Five studies testing two new egoistic alternatives to the empathy–altruism hypothesis. *Journal of Personality and Social Psychology, 55*, 52–77.

Batson, C. D., Fultz, J., & Schoenrade, P. A. (1987). Distress and empathy: Two qualitatively distinct vicarious emotions with different motivational consequences. *Journal of Personality, 55*, 19–39.

Battle, E., & Rotter, J. B. (1963). Children's feelings of personal control as related to social class and ethnic groups. *Journal of Personality, 31*, 482–490.

Bauer, J. J., & Bonanno, G. A. (2001). I can, I do, I am: The narrative differentiation of self-efficacy and other self-evaluations while adapting to bereavement. *Journal of Research in Personality, 35*, 424–448.

Baumann, L. J., & Leventhal, H. (1985). "I can tell when my blood pressure is up, can't I?" *Health Psychology, 4*, 203–218.

Baumeister, R. F. (1989). The problem of life's meaning. In D. M. Buss & N. Cantor (Eds.), *Personality psychology: Recent trends and emerging directions* (pp. 138–148). New York: Springer-Verlag.

Baumeister, R. F. (1994). The crystallization of discontent in the process of major life changes. In T. F. Heatherton & J. L. Weinberger (Eds.), *Can personality change?* (pp. 281–297). Washington, DC: American Psychological Association.

Baumeister, R. F. (2002). Ego depletion and self-control failure: An energy model of the self's executive function. *Self and Identity, 1*, 129–136.

Baumeister, R. F., Bratslavsky, E., Muraven, M., & Tice, D. M. (1998). Ego depletion: Is the active self a limited resource? *Journal of Personality and Social Psychology, 74*, 1252–1265.

Baumeister, R. F., & Campbell, W. K. (1999). The intrinsic appeal of evil: Sadism, sensational thrills, and threatened egotism. *Personality and Social Psychology Review, 3*, 210–221.

Baumeister, R. F., & Leary, M. R. (1995). The need to belong: Desire for interpersonal attachments as a fundamental human motivation. *Psychological Bulletin, 117*, 497–529.

Beck, A. T. (1972). *Depression: Causes and treatments.* Philadelphia: University of Pennsylvania Press.

Beck, A. T. (1976). *Cognitive therapy and the emotional disorders.* New York: International Universities Press.

Beck, A. T. (1991). Cognitive therapy: A 30-year retrospective. *American Psychologist, 46*, 368–375.

Beck, A. T., Rush, A. J., Shaw, B. F., & Emery, G. (1979). *Cognitive therapy of depression: A treatment manual.* New York: Guilford.

Becker, E. (1973). *The denial of death.* New York: Free Press.

Beer, R. D. (1995). A dynamical systems perspective on agent-environment interaction. *Artificial Intelligence, 72,* 173–215.

Bell, M., Billington, R., & Becker, B. (1986). A scale for the assessment of object relations: Reliability, validity, and factorial invariance. *Journal of Clinical Psychology, 42,* 733–741.

Belmont, L., & Marolla, F. A. (1973). Birth order, family size, and intelligence. *Science, 182,* 1096–1101.

Bem, D. J., & Allen, A. (1974). On predicting some of the people some of the time: The search for cross-situational consistencies in behavior. *Psychological Review, 81,* 506–520.

Bem, S. L. (1974). The measurement of psychological androgyny. *Journal of Consulting and Clinical Psychology, 42,* 155–162.

Bem, S. L. (1975). Sex role adaptability: One consequence of psychological androgyny. *Journal of Personality and Social Psychology, 31,* 634–643.

Bem, S. L. (1981). Gender schema theory: A cognitive account of sex-typing. *Psychological Review, 88,* 354–364.

Benet, V., & Waller, N. G. (1995). The Big Seven factor model of personality description: Evidence for its cross-cultural generality in a Spanish sample. *Journal of Personality and Social Psychology, 69,* 701–718.

Benet-Martínez, V., & John, O. P. (1998). Los Cinco Grandes across cultures and ethnic groups: Multitrait multimethod analyses of the Big Five in Spanish and English. *Journal of Personality and Social Psychology, 75,* 729–750.

Benjamin, J., Li, L., Patterson, C., Greenberg, B. D., Murphy, D. L., & Hamer, D. H. (1996). Population and familial association between the D4 dopamine receptor gene and measures of novelty seeking. *Nature Genetics, 12,* 81–84.

Bentler, P. M. (1990). Comparative fit indexes in structural models. *Psychological Bulletin, 107,* 238–246.

Benton, C., Hernandez, A., Schmidt, A., Schmitz, M., Stone, A., & Weiner, B. (1983). Is hostility linked with affiliation among males and with achievement among females? A critique of Pollak and Gilligan. *Journal of Personality and Social Psychology, 45,* 1167–1171.

Berant, E., Mikulincer, M., & Florian, V. (2001). Attachment style and mental health: A 1-year follow-up study of mothers of infants with congenital heart disease. *Personality and Social Psychology Bulletin, 27,* 956–968.

Berenbaum, S. A., & Hines, M. (1992). Early androgens are related to childhood sex-typed toy preferences. *Psychological Science, 3,* 203–206.

Berg, I. A. (Ed.). (1967). *Response set in personality assessment.* Chicago: Aldine.

Bergeman, C. S., Chipuer, H. M., Plomin, R., Pedersen, N. L., McClearn, G. E., Nesselrode, J. R., Costa, P. T., Jr., & McCrae, R. R. (1993). Genetic and environmental effects on openness to experience, agreeableness, and conscientiousness: An adoption/twin study. *Journal of Personality, 61,* 159–179.

Berger, S. M. (1961). Incidental learning through vicarious reinforcement. *Psychological Reports, 9,* 477–491.

Berger, S. M. (1962). Conditioning through vicarious instigation. *Psychological Review, 69,* 450–466.

Bergmann, M. S. (1980). Symposium on object relations theory and love: On the intrapsychic function of falling in love. *Psychoanalytic Quarterly, 49,* 56–77.

Berkowitz, L., & Alioto, J. T. (1973). The meaning of an observed event as a determinant of its aggressive consequences. *Journal of Personality and Social Psychology, 28,* 206–217.

Berkowitz, L., & Knurek, D. A. (1969). Label-mediated hostility generalization. *Journal of Personality and Social Psychology, 13,* 200–206.

Bernhardt, P. C., Dabbs, J. M., Jr., Fielden, J., & Lutter, C. (1998). Testosterone changes during vicarious experiences of winning and losing among fans at sporting events. *Physiology and Behavior, 65,* 59–62.

Bernstein, A., Newman, J. P., Wallace, J. F., & Luh, K. E. (2000). Left-hemisphere activation and deficient response modulation in psychopaths. *Psychological Science, 11,* 414–418.

Bernstein, D. A. (1973). Situational factors in behavioral fear assessment: A progress report. *Behavior Therapy, 4,* 41–48.

Bernstein, I. L. (1985). Learning food aversions in the progression of cancer and its treatment. *Annals of the New York Academy of Sciences, 443,* 365–380.

Berry, D. S., & Miller, K. M. (2001). When boy meets girl: Attractiveness and the five-factor model in opposite-sex interactions. *Journal of Research in Personality, 35,* 62–77.

Bertrand, S., & Masling, J. M. (1969). Oral imagery and alcoholism. *Journal of Abnormal Psychology, 74,* 50–53.

Berzonsky, M. D., & Neimeyer, G. J. (1994). Ego identity status and identity processing orientation: The moderating role of commitment. *Journal of Research in Personality, 28,* 425–435.

Bettelheim, B. (1982). Reflections: Freud and the soul. *New Yorker, 58,* 52–93.

Bettencourt, B. A., & Sheldon, K. (2001). Social roles as mechanisms for psychological need satisfaction within social groups. *Journal of Personality and Social Psychology, 81,* 1131–1143.

Binswanger, L. (1963). *Being-in-the-world: Selected papers of Ludwig Binswanger.* New York: Basic Books.

Bjorklund, D. F., & Pellegrini, A. D. (2002). *Origins of human nature: Evolutionary developmental psychology.* Washington, DC: American Psychological Association.

Black, A. E., & Deci, E. L. (2000). The effects of instructors' autonomy support and students' autonomous motivation on learning organic chemistry: A self-determination theory perspective. *Science Education, 84,* 740–756.

Blackburn, R. (1968a). Emotionality, extraversion and aggression in paranoid and non-paranoid schizophrenic offenders. *British Journal of Psychiatry, 115,* 1301–1302.

Blackburn, R. (1968b). Personality in relation to extreme aggression in psychiatry offenders. *British Journal of Psychiatry, 114,* 821–828.

Blake, R. R., & Mouton, J. S. (1980). *The versatile manager: A grid profile.* Homewood, IL: Dow Jones-Irwin.

Blanchard, E. B., & Epstein, L. H. (1978). *A biofeedback primer.* Reading, MA: Addison-Wesley.

Blanck, R., & Blanck, G. (1986). *Beyond ego psychology: Developmental object relations theory.* New York: Columbia University Press.

Blatt, S. J., Wein, S. J., Chevron, E., & Quinlan, D. M. (1979). Parental representations and depression in normal young adults. *Journal of Abnormal Psychology, 88,* 388–397.

Blatt, S. J., & Zuroff, D. C. (1992). Interpersonal relatedness and self-definition: Two prototypes for depression. *Clinical Psychology Review, 12,* 527–562.

Block, J. (1977). Advancing the science of personality: Paradigmatic shift or improving the quality of research? In D. Magnusson & N. S. Endler (Eds.), *Personality at the crossroads: Current issues in interactional psychology* (pp. 37–63). Hillsdale, NJ: Erlbaum.

Block, J. (1982). Assimilation, accommodation, and the dynamics of personality development. *Child Development, 53,* 281–295.

Block, J. (1995). A contrarian view of the five-factor approach to personality assessment. *Psychological Bulletin, 117,* 187–215.

Block, J. (2001). Millennial contrarianism: The five-factor approach to personality description 5 years later. *Journal of Research in Personality, 35,* 98–107.

Block, J. (2002). *Personality as an affect-processing system: Toward an integrative theory.* Mahwah, NJ: Erlbaum.

Block, J., & Kremen, A. M. (1996). IQ and ego-resiliency: Conceptual and empirical connections and separateness. *Journal of Personality and Social Psychology, 70,* 349–361.

Block, J., von der Lippe, A., & Block, J. H. (1973). Sex-role and socialization patterns: Some personality concomitants and environmental antecedents. *Journal of Consulting and Clinical Psychology, 41,* 321–341.

Block, J. H. (1961). *The Q-sort method in personality assessment and psychiatric research.* Springfield, IL: Charles C Thomas.

Block, J. H. (1973). Conceptions of sex role: Some cross-cultural and longitudinal perspectives. *American Psychologist, 28,* 512–526.

Block, J. H. (1979). Another look at sex differentiation in the socialization behaviors of mothers and fathers. In F. L. Denmark & J. Sherman (Eds.), *Psychology of women: Future directions for research.* New York: Psychological Dimensions.

Block, J. H., & Block, J. (1980). The role of ego-control and ego-resiliency in the organization of behavior. In W. A. Collins (Ed.), *Development of cognition, affect, and social relations* (Minnesota symposia on child psychology, Vol. 13, pp. 39–101). Hillsdale, NJ: Erlbaum.

Blum, G. S., & Miller, D. (1952). Exploring the psychoanalytic theory of the "oral character." *Journal of Personality, 20,* 287–304.

Blumer, H. (1969). *Symbolic interactionism: Perspective and method.* Englewood Cliffs, NJ: Prentice-Hall.

Bohman, M., Cloninger, R., Sigvardsson, S., & von Knorring, A.-L. (1987). The genetics of alcoholism and related disorders. *Journal of Psychiatric Research, 21,* 447–452.

Bolles, R. C. (1972). Reinforcement, expectancy, and learning. *Psychological Review, 79,* 394–409.

Bonarius, H., Holland, R., & Rosenberg, S. (Eds.). (1980). *Personal construct theory: Recent advances in theory and practice.* London: Macmillan.

Booth, A., & Dabbs, J. M., Jr. (1993). Testosterone and men's marriages. *Social Forces, 72,* 463–477.

Borgatta, E. F. (1964). The structure of personality characteristics. *Behavioral Science, 12,* 8–17.

Boring, E. G. (1930). A new ambiguous figure. *American Journal of Psychology, 42,* 444–445.

Borkenau, P., Riemann, R., Angleitner, A., & Spinath, F. M. (2001). Genetic and environmental influences on observed personality: Evidence from the German observational study of adult twins. *Journal of Personality and Social Psychology, 80,* 655–668.

Borkenau, P., Riemann, R., Angleitner, A., & Spinath, F. M. (2002). Similarity of childhood experiences and personality resemblance in monozygotic and dizygotic twins: A test of the equal environments assumption. *Personality and Individual Differences, 33,* 261–269.

Bornstein, R. F., & Masling, J. (1985). Orality and latency of volunteering to serve as experimental subjects: A replication. *Journal of Personality Assessment, 49,* 306–310.

Boss, M. (1963). *Psychoanalysis and Daseinsanalysis.* New York: Basic Books.

Bottome, P. (1939). *Alfred Adler: A biography.* New York: Putnam's.

Botwin, M. D., & Buss, D. M. (1989). Structure of act-report data: Is the five-factor model of personality recaptured? *Journal of Personality and Social Psychology, 56,* 988–1001.

Bouchard, T. J., Jr., Lykken, D. T., McGue, M., Segal, N. L., & Tellegen, A. (1990). Sources of human psychological differences: The Minnesota study of twins reared apart. *Science, 250,* 223–228.

Bouchard, T. J., Jr., & McGue, M. (1990). Genetic and rearing environmental influences on adult personality: An analysis of adopted twins reared apart. *Journal of Personality, 58,* 263–292.

Bourne, E. (1978a). The state of research on ego identity: A review and appraisal. Part I. *Journal of Youth and Adolescence, 7,* 223–251.

Bourne, E. (1978b). The state of research on ego identity: A review and appraisal. Part II. *Journal of Youth and Adolescence, 7,* 371–392.

Bouton, M. E. (1994). Context, ambiguity, and classical conditioning. *Current Directions in Psychological Science, 3,* 49–53.

Bouton, M. E. (2000). A learning theory perspective on lapse, relapse, and the maintenance of behavior change. *Health Psychology, 19,* 57–63.

Bower, G. H. (1981). Mood and memory. *American Psychologist, 36,* 129–148.

Bower, J. E., Kemeny, M. E., Taylor, S. E., & Fahey, J. L. (1998). Cognitive processing, discovery of meaning, CD4 decline, and AIDS-related mortality among bereaved HIV seropositive men. *Journal of Consulting and Clinical Psychology, 66,* 979–986.

Bowlby, J. (1969). *Attachment and loss: Vol. 1, Attachment.* New York: Basic Books.

Bowlby, J. (1988). *A secure base: Parent–child attachment and healthy human development.* New York: Basic Books.

Boyatzis, R. E. (1973). Affiliation motivation. In D. C. McClelland & R. S. Steele (Eds.), *Human motivation: A book of readings.* Morristown, NJ: General Learning Press.

Bradburn, N. M., & Berlew, D. E. (1961). Need for achievement and English industrial growth. *Economic Development and Cultural Change, 10,* 8–20.

Bradley, G. W. (1978). Self-serving biases in the attribution process: A reexamination of the fact or fiction question. *Journal of Personality and Social Psychology, 36,* 56–71.

Brady, J. P. (1972). Systematic desensitization. In W. S. Agras (Ed.), *Behavior modification: Principles and clinical applications.* Boston: Little, Brown.

Bramel, D., Taub, B., & Blum, B. (1968). An observer's reaction to the suffering of his enemy. *Journal of Personality and Social Psychology, 8,* 384–392.

Brandon, T. H., Tiffany, S. T., Obremski, K. M., & Baker, T. B. (1990). Postcessation cigarette use: The process of relapse. *Addictive Behaviors, 15,* 105–114.

Brandstätter, H. (1983). Emotional responses to other persons in everyday life situations. *Journal of Personality and Social Psychology, 45,* 871–883.

Brandstätter, V. & Frank, E. (2002). Effects of deliberative and implemental mindsets on persistence in goal-directed behavior. *Personality and Social Psychology Bulletin, 28,* 1366–1378.

Brandstätter, V., Lengfelder, A., & Gollwitzer, P. M. (2001). Implementation intentions and efficient action initiation. *Journal of Personality and Social Psychology, 81,* 946–960.

Bransford, J. D., & Franks, J. J. (1971). The abstraction of linguistic ideas. *Cognitive Psychology, 2,* 331–350.

Bransford, J. D., & Johnson, M. K. (1972). Contextual prerequisites for understanding: Some investigations of comprehension and recall. *Journal of Verbal Learning and Verbal Behavior, 11,* 717–726.

Braun, A. R., Balkin, T. J., Wesensten, N. J., Gwadry, F., Carson, R. E., Varga, M., Baldwin, P., Belenky, G., & Herscovitch, P. (1998). Dissociated pattern of activity in visual cortices and their projections during human rapid eye movement sleep. *Science, 279,* 91–95.

Breedlove, S. M. (1992). Sexual dimorphism in the vertebrate nervous system. *Journal of Neuroscience, 12,* 4133–4142.

Breedlove, S. M. (1994). Sexual differentiation of the human nervous system. *Annual Review of Psychology, 45,* 389–418.

Brehm, J. W. (1966). *A theory of psychological reactance.* New York: Academic Press.

Brehm, S. S., & Brehm, J. W. (1981). *Psychological reactance: A theory of freedom and control.* New York: Academic Press.

Breland, H. M. (1974). Birth order, family constellation, and verbal achievement. *Child Development, 45,* 1011–1019.

Breland, K., & Breland, M. (1961). The misbehavior of organisms. *American Psychologist, 16,* 681–684.

Brennan, K. A., Clark, C. L., & Shaver, P. R. (1998). Self-report measurement of adult attachment: An integrative overview. In J. A. Simpson & W. S. Rholes (Eds.), *Attachment theory and close relationships* (pp. 46–76). New York: Guilford.

Brenner, C. (1957). *An elementary textbook of psychoanalysis.* Garden City, NY: Doubleday.

Brewer, M. B., Dull, V., & Lui, L. (1981). Perceptions of the elderly: Stereotypes as prototypes. *Journal of Personality and Social Psychology, 41,* 656–670.

Brewer, W. F. (1974). There is no convincing evidence for operant or classical conditioning in adult humans. In W. B. Weimer & D. S. Palermo (Eds.), *Cognition and the symbolic processes.* Hillsdale, NJ: Erlbaum.

Brewer, W. F., & Treyens, J. C. (1981). Role of schemata in memory for places. *Cognitive Psychology, 13,* 207–230.

Bridger, W. H., & Mandel, I. J. (1964). A comparison of GSR fear responses produced by threat and electric shock. *Journal of Psychiatric Research, 2,* 31–40.

Briggs, S. R. (1989). The optimal level of measurement for personality constructs. In D. M. Buss & N. Cantor (Eds.), *Personality psychology: Recent trends and emerging directions* (pp. 246–260). New York: Springer-Verlag.

Brissette, I., Scheier, M. F., & Carver, C. S. (2002). The role of optimism in social network development, coping, and psychological adjustment during a life transition. *Journal of Personality and Social Psychology, 82,* 102–111.

Britt, T. W., & Shepperd, J. A. (1999). Trait relevance and trait assessment. *Personality and Social Psychology Review, 3,* 108–122.

Broadbent, D. E. (1977). Levels, hierarchies, and the locus of control. *Quarterly Journal of Experimental Psychology, 29,* 181–201.

Brody, N. (Ed.). (1987). Special issue on the unconscious. *Personality and Social Psychology Bulletin, 13,* 293–429.

Brokaw, D. W., & McLemore, C. W. (1983). Toward a more rigorous definition of social reinforcement: Some interpersonal clarifications. *Journal of Personality and Social Psychology, 44,* 1014–1020.

Brooks, R. A. (1999). *Cambrian intelligence: The early history of the new AI.* Cambridge, MA: MIT Press.

Brooks, R. A. (2002). *Flesh and machines: How robots will change us.* New York: Pantheon.

Brooks, R. A., & Stein, L. A. (1994). Building brains for bodies. *Autonomous Robots, 1,* 7–25.

Brown, I., Jr., & Inouye, D. K. (1978). Learned helplessness through modeling: The role of perceived similarity in competence. *Journal of Personality and Social Psychology, 36,* 900–908.

Brown, J. S. (1948). Gradients of approach and avoidance responses and their relation to level of motivation. *Journal of Comparative and Physiological Psychology, 41,* 450–465.

Brown, J. S. (1957). Principles of intrapersonal conflict. *Journal of Conflict Resolution, 1,* 135–154.

Bruhn, A. R., & Schiffman, H. (1982). Prediction of locus of control stance from the earliest childhood memory. *Journal of Personality Assessment, 46,* 380–390.

Bruner, J. S. (1957). On perceptual readiness. *Psychological Review, 64,* 123–152.

Brunstein, J. C., Schultheiss, O. C., & Grässmann, R. (1998). Personal goals and emotional well-being: The moderating role of motive dispositions. *Journal of Personality and Social Psychology, 75,* 494–508.

Brunswik, E. (1951). The probability point of view. In M. H. Marx (Ed.), *Psychological theory.* New York: Macmillan.

Buccino, G., Binkofski, F., Fink, G. R., Fadiga, L., Fogassi, L., Gallese, V., Seitz, R. J., Zilles, K., Rizzolatti, G., & Freund, H.-J. (2001). Action observation activates premotor and parietal areas in somatotopic manner: An fMRI study. *European Journal of Neuroscience, 13,* 400–404.

Buchanan, A., Brock, D. W., Daniels, N., & Wikler, D. (2000). *From chance to choice: Genetics and justice.* New York: Cambridge University Press.

Buchanan, G. M. (1995). Explanatory style and coronary heart disease. In G. M. Buchanan & M. E. P. Seligman (Eds.), *Explanatory style* (pp. 225–232). Hillsdale, NJ: Erlbaum.

Burger, J. M. (1989). Negative reactions to increases in perceived personal control. *Journal of Personality and Social Psychology, 56,* 246–256.

Burnstein, E., Crandall, C., & Kitayama, S. (1994). Some neo-Darwinian decision rules for altruism: Weighing cues for inclusive fitness as a function of the biological importance of the decision. *Journal of Personality and Social Psychology, 67,* 773–789.

Burroughs, W. J., & Drews, D. R. (1991). Rule structure in the psychological representation of physical settings. *Journal of Experimental Social Psychology, 27,* 217–238.

Bursik, K. (1991). Adaptation to divorce and ego development in adult women. *Journal of Personality and Social Psychology, 60,* 300–306.

Burt, S. A., McGue, M., Iacono, W., Comings, D., & MacMurray, J. (2002). An examination of the association between DRD4 and DRD2 polymorphisms and personality traits. *Personality and Individual Differences, 33,* 849–859.

Bushman, B. J. (2002). Does venting anger feed or extinguish the flame? Catharsis, rumination, distraction, anger, and aggressive responding. *Personality and Social Psychology Bulletin, 28,* 724–731.

Bushman, B. J., & Baumeister, R. F. (1998). Threatened egotism, narcissism, self-esteem, and direct and displaced aggression: Does self-love or self-hate lead to violence? *Journal of Personality and Social Psychology, 75,* 219–229.

Bushman, B. J., Baumeister, R. F., & Phillips, C. M. (2001). Do people aggress to improve their mood? Catharsis beliefs, affect regulation opportunity, and aggressive responding. *Journal of Personality and Social Psychology, 81,* 17–32.

Buss, A. H. (1983). Social rewards and personality. *Journal of Personality and Social Psychology, 44,* 553–563.

Buss, A. H. (1989). Personality as traits. *American Psychologist, 44,* 1378–1388.

Buss, A. H. (1995). *Personality: Temperament, social behavior, and the self.* Needham Heights, MA: Allyn & Bacon.

Buss, A. H., & Plomin, R. (1975). *A temperament theory of personality development.* New York: Wiley-Interscience.

Buss, A. H., & Plomin, R. (1984). *Temperament: Early developing personality traits.* Hillsdale, NJ: Erlbaum.

Buss, D. M. (1984). Toward a psychology of person-environment correlation: The role of spouse selection. *Journal of Personality and Social Psychology, 47,* 361–377.

Buss, D. M. (1985). Human mate selection. *American Scientist, 73,* 47–51.

Buss, D. M. (1988). The evolution of human intrasexual competition: Tactics of mate attraction. *Journal of Personality and Social Psychology, 54,* 616–628.

Buss, D. M. (1989). Sex differences in human mate preferences: Evolutionary hypotheses tested in 37 cultures. *Behavioral and Brain Sciences, 12,* 1–49.

Buss, D. M. (1991). Evolutionary personality psychology. *Annual Review of Psychology, 42,* 459–491.

Buss, D. M. (1994a). *The evolution of desire: Strategies of human mating.* New York: Basic Books.

Buss, D. M. (1994b). The strategies of human mating. *American Scientist, 82,* 238–249.

Buss, D. M. (1995). Evolutionary psychology: A new paradigm for psychological science. *Psychological Inquiry, 6,* 1–30.

Buss, D. M. (2001). Cognitive biases and emotional wisdom in the evolution of conflict between the sexes. *Current Directions in Psychological Science, 10,* 219–223.

Buss, D. M., Gomes, M., Higgins, D. S., & Lauterbach, K. (1987). Tactics of manipulation. *Journal of Personality and Social Psychology, 52,* 1219–1229.

Buss, D. M., Larsen, R. J., Westen, D., & Semmelroth, J. (1992). Sex differences in jealousy: Evolution, physiology, and psychology. *Psychological Science, 3,* 251–255.

Buss, D. M., & Schmitt, D. P. (1993). Sexual strategies theory: An evolutionary perspective on human mating. *Psychological Review, 100,* 204–232.

Buss, D. M., & Shackelford, T. K. (1997). From vigilance to violence: Mate retention tactics in married couples. *Journal of Personality and Social Psychology, 72,* 346–361.

Bussey, K., & Bandura, A. (1984). Influence of gender constancy and social power on sex-linked modeling. *Journal of Personality and Social Psychology, 47,* 1292–1302.

Bussey, K., & Bandura, A. (1999). Social cognitive theory of gender development and differentiation. *Psychological Review, 106,* 676–713.

Butcher, J. N. (Ed.). (1996). *International adaptations of the MMPI-2: Research and clinical applications.* Minneapolis: University of Minnesota Press.

Butcher, J. N., Dahlstrom, W., Graham, J., Tellegen, A., & Kaemmer, B. (1989). *Manual for administering and scoring the MMPI-2.* Minneapolis: University of Minnesota Press.

Butler, J. M., & Haigh, G. V. (1954). Changes in the relation between self-concepts and ideal concepts consequent upon client-centered counseling. In C. R. Rogers & R. F. Dymond (Eds.), *Psychotherapy and personality change: Co-ordinated research studies in the client-centered approach.* Chicago: University of Chicago Press.

Byrne, D., McDonald, R. D., & Mikawa, J. (1963). Approach and avoidance affiliation motives. *Journal of Personality, 31,* 21–37.

Cacioppo, J. T., Gardner, W. L., & Berntson, G. G. (1999). The affect system has parallel and integrative processing components: Form follows function. *Journal of Personality and Social Psychology, 76,* 839–855.

Cacioppo, J. T., & Petty, R. E. (1980). The effects of orienting task on differential hemispheric EEG activation. *Neuropsychologia, 18,* 675–683.

Cacioppo, J. T., & Petty, R. E. (1982). The need for cognition. *Journal of Personality and Social Psychology, 42,* 116–131.

Cacioppo, J. T., & Petty, R. E. (1983). *Social psychophysiology.* New York: Guilford.

Cacioppo, J. T., & Petty, R. E. (1984). The need for cognition: Relationship to attitudinal processes. In R. P. McGlynn, J. E. Maddux, C. Stoltenberg, & J. H. Harvey (Eds.), *Social perception in clinical and counseling psychology.* Lubbock: Texas Tech Press.

Cacioppo, J. T., Petty, R. E., Feinstein, J. A., & Jarvis, W. B. G. (1996). Dispositional differences in cognitive motivation: The life and times of individuals varying in need for cognition. *Psychological Bulletin, 119,* 197–253.

Cacioppo, J. T., Petty, R. E., Kao, C. F., & Rodriguez, R. (1986). Central and peripheral routes to persuasion:

An individual difference perspective. *Journal of Personality and Social Psychology, 51,* 1032–1043.

Cacioppo, J. T., Petty, R. E., & Morris, K. J. (1983). Effects of need for cognition on message evaluation, recall, and persuasion. *Journal of Personality and Social Psychology, 45,* 805–818.

Cacioppo, J. T., & Sandman, C. A. (1981). Psychophysiological functioning, cognitive responding, and attitudes. In R. E. Petty, T. M. Ostrom, & T. C. Brock (Eds.), *Cognitive responses in persuasion.* Hillsdale, NJ: Erlbaum.

Cain, D. J., & Seeman, J. (Eds.). (2002). *Humanistic psychotherapies: Handbook of research and practice.* Washington, DC: American Psychological Association.

Campbell, D. T. (1960). Recommendations for the APA test standards regarding construct, trait, and discriminant validity. *American Psychologist, 15,* 546–553.

Campbell, D. T., & Fiske, D. W. (1959). Convergent and discriminant validation by the multitrait-multimethod matrix. *Psychological Bulletin, 56,* 81–105.

Campbell, W. K. (1999). Narcissism and romantic attraction. *Journal of Personality and Social Psychology, 77,* 1254–1270.

Campbell, W. K., & Foster, C. A. (2002). Narcissism and commitment in romantic relationships: An investment model analysis. *Personality and Social Psychology Bulletin, 28,* 484–495.

Cannon, D. S., Baker, T. B., Gino, A., & Nathan, P. E. (1986). Alcohol-aversion therapy: Relation between strength of aversion and abstinence. *Journal of Consulting and Clinical Psychology, 54,* 825–830.

Cannon, W. B. (1932). *The wisdom of the body.* New York: Norton.

Cantor, N., & Kihlstrom, J. F. (1987). *Personality and social intelligence.* Englewood Cliffs, NJ: Prentice-Hall.

Cantor, N., & Mischel, W. (1977). Traits as prototypes: Effects on recognition memory. *Journal of Personality and Social Psychology, 35,* 38–48.

Cantor, N., Mischel, W., & Schwartz, J. C. (1982). A prototype analysis of psychological situations. *Cognitive Psychology, 14,* 45–77.

Cantor, N., Smith, E. E., French, R., & Mezzich, J. (1980). Psychiatric diagnosis as prototype categorization. *Journal of Abnormal Psychology, 89,* 181–193.

Caporeal, L. R. (2001). Evolutionary psychology: Toward a unifying theory and a hybrid science. *Annual Review of Psychology, 52,* 607–628.

Carey, G., Goldsmith, H. H., Tellegen, A., & Gottesman, I. I. (1978). Genetics and personality inventories: The limits of replication with twin data. *Behavior Genetics, 8,* 299–313.

Carlston, D. E., & Skowronski, J. J. (1994). Savings in the relearning of trait information as evidence for spontaneous inference generation. *Journal of Personality and Social Psychology, 66,* 840–856.

Carnelley, K. B., Pietromonaco, P. R., & Jaffe, K. (1994). Depression, working models of others, and relationship functioning. *Journal of Personality and Social Psychology, 66,* 127–140.

Carroll, L. (1987). A study of narcissism, affiliation, intimacy, and power motives among students in business administration. *Psychological Reports, 61,* 355–358.

Carter, B. L., & Tiffany, S. T. (1999). Meta-analysis of cue reactivity in addiction research. *Addiction, 94,* 327–340.

Carter, C. S. (1998). Neuroendocrine perspectives on social attachment and love. *Psychoneuroimmunology, 23,* 779–818.

Carver, C. S. (1974). Facilitation of physical aggression through objective self-awareness. *Journal of Experimental Social Psychology, 10,* 365–370.

Carver, C. S. (1975). Physical aggression as a function of objective self-awareness and attitudes toward punishment. *Journal of Experimental Social Psychology, 11,* 510–519.

Carver, C. S. (1996). Emergent integration in contemporary personality psychology. *Journal of Research in Personality, 30,* 319–334.

Carver, C. S. (1997a). Adult attachment and personality: Converging evidence and a new measure. *Personality and Social Psychology Bulletin, 23,* 865–883.

Carver, C. S. (1997b). The Internal–External scale confounds internal locus of control with expectancies of positive outcomes. *Personality and Social Psychology Bulletin, 23,* 580–585.

Carver, C. S. (1998). Generalization, adverse events, and development of depressive symptoms. *Journal of Personality, 66,* 609–620.

Carver, C. S. (2003). Pleasure as a sign you can attend to something else: Placing positive feelings within a general model of affect. *Cognition and Emotion,* in press.

Carver, C. S., & Baird, E. (1998). The American dream revisited: Is it *what* you want or *why* you want it that matters? *Psychological Science, 9,* 289–292.

Carver, C. S., & Ganellen, R. J. (1983). Depression and components of self-punitiveness: High standards, self-criticism, and overgeneralization. *Journal of Abnormal Psychology, 92,* 330–337.

Carver, C. S., Ganellen, R. J., Froming, W. J., & Chambers, W. (1983). Modeling: An analysis in terms of category accessibility. *Journal of Experimental Social Psychology, 19,* 403–421.

Carver, C. S., Kus, L. A., & Scheier, M. F. (1994). Effects of good versus bad mood and optimistic versus pessimistic outlook on social acceptance versus rejection. *Journal of Social and Clinical Psychology, 13,* 138–151.

Carver, C. S., LaVoie, L., Kuhl, J., & Ganellen, R. J. (1988). Cognitive concomitants of depression: A further examination of the roles of generalization, high standards, and self-criticism. *Journal of Social and Clinical Psychology, 7,* 350–365.

Carver, C. S., Lawrence, J. W., & Scheier, M. F. (1999). Self-discrepancies and affect: Incorporating the role of feared selves. *Personality and Social Psychology Bulletin, 25,* 783–792.

Carver, C. S., Lehman, J. M., & Antoni, M. H. (in press). Dispositional pessimism predicts illness-related disruption of social and recreational activities among breast cancer patients. *Journal of Personality and Social Psychology.*

Carver, C. S., Pozo, C., Harris, S. D., Noriega, V., Scheier, M.F., Robinson, D. S., Ketcham, A. S., Moffat, F. L., & Clark, K. C. (1993). How coping mediates the effect of optimism on distress: A study of women with early stage breast cancer. *Journal of Personality and Social Psychology, 65,* 375–390.

Carver, C. S., Reynolds, S. L., & Scheier, M. F. (1994). The possible selves of optimists and pessimists. *Journal of Research in Personality, 28,* 133–141.

Carver, C. S., & Scheier, M. F. (1981). *Attention and self-regulation: A control-theory approach to human behavior.* New York: Springer-Verlag.

Carver, C. S., & Scheier, M. F. (1986). Functional and dysfunctional responses to anxiety: The interaction between expectancies and self-focused attention. In R. Schwarzer (Ed.), *Self-related cognitions in anxiety and motivation.* Hillsdale, NJ: Erlbaum.

Carver, C. S., & Scheier, M. F. (1990). Principles of self-regulation: Action and emotion. In E. T. Higgins & R. M. Sorrentino (Eds.), *Handbook of motivation and cognition: Foundations of social behavior* (Vol. 2, pp. 3–52). New York: Guilford.

Carver, C. S., & Scheier, M. F. (1998). *On the self-regulation of behavior.* New York: Cambridge University Press.

Carver, C. S., & Scheier, M. F. (2000). Autonomy and self-regulation. *Psychological Inquiry, 11,* 284–291.

Carver, C. S., & Scheier, M. F. (2002). Control processes and self-organization as complementary principles underlying behavior. *Personality and Social Psychology Review, 6,* 304–315.

Carver, C. S., & White, T. L. (1994). Behavioral inhibition, behavioral activation, and affective responses to impending reward and punishment: The BIS/BAS scales. *Journal of Personality and Social Psychology, 67,* 319–333.

Caspar, F., Rothenfluh, T., & Segal, Z. (1992). The appeal of connectionism to clinical psychology. *Clinical Psychology Review, 12,* 719–762.

Caspi, A., Elder, G. H., Jr., & Bem, D. J. (1987). Moving against the world: Life-course patterns of explosive children. *Developmental Psychology, 23,* 308–313.

Caspi, A., Elder, G. H., Jr., & Bem, D. J. (1988). Moving away from the world: Life-course patterns of shy children. *Developmental Psychology, 24,* 824–831.

Caspi, A., & Herbener, E. S. (1990). Continuity and change: Assortative marriage and the consistency of personality in adulthood. *Journal of Personality and Social Psychology, 58,* 250–258.

Caspi, A., McClay, J., Moffitt, T. E., Mill, J., Martin, J., Craig, I. W., Taylor, A., & Poulton, R. (2002). Role of genotype in the cycle of violence in maltreated children. *Science, 297,* 851–854.

Cassidy, J., & Shaver, P. R. (Eds.). (1999). *Handbook of attachment: Theory, research, and clinical applications.* New York: Guilford.

Catania, A. C., & Harnad, S. (Eds.). (1988). *The operant behaviorism of B. F. Skinner: Comments and consequences.* New York: Cambridge University Press.

Cattell, H. E. P. (1993). Comment on Goldberg. *American Psychologist, 48,* 1302–1303.

Cattell, R. B. (1947). Confirmation and clarification of primary personality factors. *Psychometrica, 12,* 197–220.

Cattell, R. B. (1965). *The scientific analysis of personality.* Baltimore: Penguin.

Cattell, R. B. (1978). *The scientific use of factor analysis.* New York: Plenum.

Cattell, R. B. (1979). *Personality and learning theory, Volume 1. The structure of personality in its environment.* New York: Springer.

Cattell, R. B. (1985). *Human motivation and the dynamic calculus.* New York: Praeger.

Cattell, R. B., Eber, H. W., & Tatsuoka, M. M. (1977). *Handbook for the 16 personality factor questionnaire.* Champaign, IL: IPAT.

Cattell, R. B., & Kline, P. (1977). *The scientific analysis of personality and motivation.* New York: Academic Press.

Cervone, D. (1997). Social-cognitive mechanisms and personality coherence: Self-knowledge, situational beliefs, and cross-situational coherence in perceived self-efficacy. *Psychological Science, 8,* 43–50.

Chambliss, C. A., & Murray, E. J. (1979). Efficacy attribution, locus of control, and weight loss. *Cognitive Therapy and Research, 3,* 349–354.

Chance, S. E., Brown, R. T., Dabbs, J. M., Jr., & Casey, R. (2000). Testosterone, intelligence and behavior disorders in young boys. *Personality and Individual Differences, 28,* 437–445.

Chaplin, W. F., Phillips, J. B., Brown, J. D., Clanton, N. R., & Stein, J. L. (2000). Handshaking, gender, personality, and first impressions. *Journal of Personality and Social Psychology, 79,* 110–117.

Chapman, L. J. (1967). Illusory correlations in observational report. *Journal of Verbal Learning and Verbal Behavior, 6,* 151–155.

Chartrand, T. L., & Bargh, J. A. (1996). Automatic activation of impression formation and memorization goals: Nonconscious goal priming reproduces effects of explicit task instructions. *Journal of Personality and Social Psychology, 71,* 464–478.

Chartrand, T. L., & Bargh, J. A. (1999). The chameleon effect: The perception–behavior link and social interaction. *Journal of Personality and Social Psychology, 76,* 893–910.

Chatterjee, B. B., & Eriksen, C. W. (1962). Cognitive factors in heart rate conditioning. *Journal of Experimental Psychology, 64,* 272–279.

Cheek, J. (1982). Aggregation, moderator variables, and the validity of personality tests: A peer-rating study. *Journal of Personality and Social Psychology, 43,* 1254–1269.

Chen, E., & Matthews, K. A. (2001). Cognitive appraisal biases: An approach to understanding the relation between socioeconomic status and cardiovascular reactivity in children. *Annals of Behavioral Medicine, 23,* 101–111.

Chew, S. L., Larkey, L. S., Soli, S. D., Blount, J., & Jenkins, J. J. (1982). The abstraction of musical ideas. *Memory & Cognition, 10,* 413–423.

Chomsky, N. (1959). Review of *Verbal behavior* by B. F. Skinner. *Language, 35,* 26–58.

Christensen, A. J., Ehlers, S. L., Wiebe, J. S., Moran, P. J., Raichle, K., Ferneyhough, K., & Lawton, W. J. (2002). Patient personality and mortality: A 4-year prospective examination of chronic renal insufficiency. *Health Psychology, 21,* 315–320.

Church, A. T. (1994). Relating the Tellegen and five-factor models of personality structure. *Journal of Personality and Social Psychology, 67,* 898–909.

Church, A. T. (Ed.). (2001). Introduction: Culture and personality [Special issue]. *Journal of Personality, 69,* 787–801.

Church, A. T., & Burke, P. J. (1994). Exploratory and confirmatory tests of the big five and Tellegen's three- and four-dimensional models. *Journal of Personality and Social Psychology, 66,* 93–114.

Cialdini, R. B., Schaller, M., Houlihan, D., Arps, K., Fultz, J., & Beaman, A. L. (1987). Empathy-based helping: Is it selflessly or selfishly motivated? *Journal of Personality and Social Psychology, 52,* 749–758.

Ciminero, A. R., Calhoun, K. S., & Adams, H. E. (Eds.). (1977). *Handbook of behavioral assessment.* New York: Wiley.

Claridge, G. S. (1967). *Personality and arousal.* New York: Pergamon.

Clark, L. A., Kochanska, G., & Ready, R. (2000). Mothers' personality and its interaction with child temperament as predictors of parenting behavior. *Journal of Personality and Social Psychology, 79,* 274–285.

Clark, L. A., & Watson, D. (1999). Temperament: A new paradigm for trait psychology. In L. A. Pervin & O. P. John (Eds.), *Handbook of personality: Theory and research* (2nd ed., pp. 399–423). New York: Guilford.

Clark, R. A., & McClelland, D. C. (1956). A factor-analytic integration of imaginative and performance measures of the need for achievement. *Journal of General Psychology, 55,* 73–83.

Clark, R. D., & Hatfield, E. (1989). Gender differences in receptivity to sexual offers. *Journal of Psychology and Human Sexuality, 2,* 39–55.

Clark, W. R. (1996). *Sex and the origins of death.* New York: Oxford University Press.

Clausen, J. A. (1981). Men's occupational careers in the middle years. In D. H. Eichorn, J. A. Clausen, N. Haan, M. P. Honzik, & P. H. Mussen (Eds.), *Present and past in middle life* (pp. 321–351). New York: Academic Press.

Cleare, A. J., & Bond, A. J. (1997). Does central serotonergic function correlate inversely with aggression? A study using D-fenfluramine in healthy subjects. *Psychiatry Research, 69,* 89–95.

Cline, V. B., Croft, R. G., & Courrier, S. (1973). Desensitization of children to television violence. *Journal of Personality and Social Psychology, 27,* 360–365.

Cloninger, C. R. (1987). A systematic method of clinical description and classification of personality variants: A proposal. *Archives of General Psychiatry, 44,* 573–588.

Cloninger, C. R. (1988). A unified biosocial theory of personality and its role in the development of anxiety states: A reply to commentaries. *Psychiatric Developments, 2,* 83–120.

Clower, C. E., & Bothwell, R. K. (2001). An exploratory study of the relationship between the Big Five and inmate recidivism. *Journal of Research in Personality, 35,* 231–237.

Coccaro, E. F., Kavoussi, R. J., Cooper, T. B., & Hauger, R. L. (1997). Central serotonin activity and aggression: Inverse relationship with prolactin response to *d*-fenfluramine, but not CSF 5-HIAA concentration, in human subjects. *American Journal of Psychiatry, 154,* 1430–1435.

Cohen, A. R. (1957). Need for cognition and order of communication as determinants of opinion change. In C. I. Hovland (Ed.), *The order of presentation in persuasion.* New Haven, CT: Yale University Press.

Cohen, A. R., Stotland, E., & Wolfe, D. M. (1955). An experimental investigation of need for cognition. *Journal of Abnormal and Social Psychology, 51*, 291–294.

Cohn, L. D. (1991). Sex differences in the course of personality development: A meta-analysis. *Psychological Bulletin, 109*, 252–266.

Collins, N. L., & Read, S. J. (1990). Adult attachment, working models, and relationship quality in dating couples. *Journal of Personality and Social Psychology, 58*, 644–663.

Comings, D. E., Gade-Andavolu, R., Gonzalez, N., Wu, S., Muhleman, D., Blake, H., Mann, M. B., Dietz, G., Saucier, G., & MacMurray, J. P. (2000). A multivariate analysis of 59 candidate genes in personality traits: The temperament and character inventory. *Clinical Genetics, 58*, 375–385.

Conklin, C. A., & Tiffany, S. T. (2001). The impact of imagining personalized versus standardized urge scenarios on cigarette craving and autonomic reactivity. *Experimental and Clinical Psychopharmacology, 9*, 399–408.

Conklin, C. A., & Tiffany, S. T. (2002). Applying extinction research and theory to cue-exposure addiction treatments. *Addiction, 97*, 155–167.

Conley, J. J. (1985). Longitudinal stability of personality traits: A multitrait-multimethod-multioccasion analysis. *Journal of Personality and Social Psychology, 49*, 1266–1282.

Constantian, C. A. (1981). Attitudes, beliefs, and behavior in regard to spending time alone. Unpublished doctoral dissertation, Harvard University, Cambridge, MA.

Converse, J., & Presser, S. (1986). *Survey questions: Handcrafting the standardized questionnaire*. Newbury Park, CA: Sage.

Conway, M., & Giannopoulos, C. (1993). Dysphoria and decision making: Limited information use for evaluations of multiattribute targets. *Journal of Personality and Social Psychology, 64*, 613–623.

Cook, M. L., & Peterson, C. (1986). Depressive irrationality. *Cognitive Therapy and Research, 10*, 293–298.

Cook, W. L. (2000). Understanding attachment security in a family context. *Journal of Personality and Social Psychology, 78*, 285–294.

Cooley, C. H. (1902). *Human nature and the social order*. New York: Scribner's.

Cooley, E. J., & Spiegler, M. D. (1980). Cognitive versus emotional coping responses as alternatives to test anxiety. *Cognitive Therapy and Research, 4*, 159–166.

Coolidge, F. L., Moor, C. J., Yamazaki, T. G., Stewart, S. E., & Segal, D. L. (2001). On the relationship between Karen Horney's tripartite neurotic type theory and personality disorder features. *Personality and Individual Differences, 30*, 1387–1400.

Cooper, M. L., Shapiro, C. M., & Powers, A. M. (1998). Motivations for sex and risky sexual behavior among adolescents and young adults: A functional perspective. *Journal of Personality and Social Psychology, 75*, 1528–1558.

Corr, P. J., Pickering, A. D., & Gray, J. A. (1997). Personality, punishment, and procedural learning: A test of J. A. Gray's anxiety theory. *Journal of Personality and Social Psychology, 73*, 337–344.

Cortes, J. B., & Gatti, F. M. (1965). Physique and self-descriptions of temperament. *Journal of Consulting Psychology, 29*, 432–439.

Costa, P. T., Jr., & McCrae, R. R. (1980). Influence of extraversion and neuroticism on subjective well-being: Happy and unhappy people. *Journal of Personality and Social Psychology, 38*, 668–678.

Costa, P. T., Jr., & McCrae, R. R. (1985). *The NEO Personality Inventory manual*. Odessa, FL: Psychological Assessment Resources.

Costa, P. T., Jr., & McCrae, R. R. (1988a). From catalog to classification: Murray's needs and the five-factor model. *Journal of Personality and Social Psychology, 55*, 258–265.

Costa, P. T., Jr., & McCrae, R. R. (1988b). Personality in adulthood: A six-year longitudinal study of self-reports and spouse ratings on the NEO personality inventory. *Journal of Personality and Social Psychology, 54*, 853–863.

Costa, P. T., Jr., & McCrae, R. R. (1989). Personality continuity and the changes of adult life. In M. Storandt & G. R. VandenBos (Eds.), *The adult years: Continuity and change* (pp. 45–77). Washington, DC: American Psychological Association.

Costa, P. T., Jr., & McCrae, R. R. (1992). *Revised NEO Personality Inventory (NEO-PI-R) and NEO Five-Factor Inventory (NEO-FFI) professional manual*. Odessa, FL: Psychological Assessment Resources.

Costa, P. T., Jr., & McCrae, R. R. (1995). Domains and facets: Hierarchical personality assessment using the revised NEO Pesonality Inventory. *Journal of Personality Assessment, 64*, 21–50.

Costa, P. T., Jr. & Widiger, T. A. (Eds.). (2002). *Personality disorders and the five-factor model of personality* (2nd ed.). Washington, DC: American Psychological Association.

Couch, A., & Keniston, K. (1960). Yeasayers and naysayers: Agreeing response set as a personality variable. *Journal of Abnormal and Social Psychology, 60*, 151–174.

Coursey, R. D., Buchsbaum, M. S., & Frankel, B. L. (1975). Personality measures and evoked responses in chronic insomniacs. *Journal of Abnormal Psychology, 84*, 234–244.

Cozzarelli, C. (1993). Personality and self-efficacy as predictors of coping with abortion. *Journal of Personality and Social Psychology, 65*, 1224–1236.

Craig, K. D., & Weinstein, M. S. (1965). Conditioning vicarious affective arousal. *Psychological Reports, 17*, 955–963.

Craighead, W. E., Kazdin, A. E., & Mahoney, M. J. (1981). *Behavior modification: Principles, issues, and applications.* Boston: Houghton Mifflin.

Cramer, P. (2000). Defense mechanisms in psychology today: Further processes for adaptation. *American Psychologist, 55*, 637–646.

Crandall, R., McCown, D. A., & Robb, Z. (1988). The effects of assertiveness training on self-actualization. *Small Group Behavior, 19*, 134–145.

Crawford, C. B. (1989). The theory of evolution: Of what value to psychology? *Journal of Comparative Psychology, 103*, 4–22.

Crawford, C. B., Smith, M. S., & Krebs, D. (Eds.). (1987). *Sociobiology and psychology: Ideas, issues and applications.* Hillsdale, NJ: Erlbaum.

Crawford, L. E., & Cacioppo, J. T. (2002). Learning where to look for danger: Integrating affective and spatial information. *Psychological Science, 13*, 449–453.

Crews, F. (1996). The verdict on Freud. *Psychological Science, 7*, 63.

Crick, N. R., & Dodge, K. A. (1994). A review and reformulation of social information-processing mechanisms in children's social adjustment. *Psychological Bulletin, 115*, 74–101.

Crittenden, P. M. (1990). Internal representational models of attachment relationships. *Infant Mental Health Journal, 11*, 259–277.

Crocker, J. (1981). Judgment of covariation by social perceivers. *Psychological Bulletin, 90*, 272–292.

Crocker, J., & Wolfe, C. T. (2001). Contingencies of self-worth. *Psychological Review, 108*, 593–623.

Cronbach, L. J., & Meehl, P. E. (1955). Construct validity in psychological tests. *Psychological Bulletin, 52*, 281–302.

Crouse, B. B., & Mehrabian, A. (1977). Affiliation of opposite-sexed strangers. *Journal of Research in Personality, 11*, 38–47.

Crowne, D. P., & Marlowe, D. (1964). *The approval motive: Studies in evaluative dependence.* New York: Wiley.

Csikszentmihalyi, M. (1975). *Beyond boredom and anxiety.* San Francisco: Jossey-Bass.

Csikszentmihalyi, M. (1978). Attention and the holistic approach to behavior. In K. S. Pope & J. L. Singer (Eds.), *The stream of consciousness: Scientific investigations into the flow of human experience.* New York: Plenum.

Csikszentmihalyi, M. (1982). Toward a psychology of optimal experience. In L. Wheeler (Ed.), *Review of personality and social psychology* (Vol. 3, pp. 13–36). Beverly Hills, CA: Sage.

Csikszentmihalyi, M. (1990). *Flow: The psychology of optimal experience.* New York: Harper & Row.

Csikszentmihalyi, M., & Csikszentmihalyi, I. S. (Eds.). (1988). *Optimal experience: Psychological studies of flow in consciousness.* New York: Cambridge University Press.

Csikszentimihalyi, M., & LeFevre, J. (1989). Optimal experience in work and leisure. *Journal of Personality and Social Psychology, 56*, 815–822.

Cunningham, M. R., Barbee, A. P., & Pike, C. L. (1990). What do women want? Facialmetric assessment of multiple motives in the perception of male facial physical attractiveness. *Journal of Personality and Social Psychology, 59*, 61–72.

Cutter, H. S. G., Boyatzis, R. E., & Clancy, D. D. (1977). The effectiveness of power motivation training in rehabilitating alcoholics. *Journal of Studies on Alcohol, 38*, 131–141.

D'Zurilla, T., & Goldfried, M. (1971). Problem-solving and behavior modification. *Journal of Abnormal Psychology, 78*, 107–126.

Dabbs, J. M., Jr. (1992a). Testosterone and occupational achievement. *Social Forces, 70*, 813–824.

Dabbs, J. M., Jr. (1992b). Testosterone measurements in social and clinical psychology. *Journal of Social and Clinical Psychology, 11*, 302–321.

Dabbs, J. M., Jr. (1997). Testosterone, smiling, and facial appearance. *Journal of Nonverbal Behavior, 21*, 45–55.

Dabbs, J. M., Jr. (1998). Testosterone and the concept of dominance. *Behavioral and Brain Sciences, 21*, 370–371.

Dabbs, J. M., Jr., Alford, E. C., & Fielden, J. A. (1998). Trial lawyers: Blue collar talent in a white collar world. *Journal of Applied Social Psychology, 28*, 84–94.

Dabbs, J. M., Jr., Bernieri, F. J., Strong, R. K., Campo, R., & Milun, R. (2001). Going on stage: Testosterone in greetings and meetings. *Journal of Research in Personality, 35*, 27–40.

Dabbs, J. M., Jr., & Dabbs, M. G. (2000). *Heroes, rogues and lovers: Testosterone and behavior.* New York: McGraw-Hill.

Dabbs, J. M., Jr., de La Rue, D., & Williams, P. M. (1990). Testosterone and occupational choice: Actors, ministers, and other men. *Journal of Personality and Social Psychology, 59*, 1261–1265.

Dabbs, J. M., Jr., Frady, R. L., Carr, T. S., & Besch, N. F. (1987). Saliva testosterone and criminal violence in young adult prison inmates. *Psychosomatic Medicine, 49,* 174–182.

Dabbs, J. M., Jr., Hargrove, M. F., & Heusel, C. (1996). Testosterone differences among college fraternities: Well-behaved vs. rambunctious. *Personality and Individual Differences, 290,* 157–161.

Dabbs, J. M., Jr., Jurkovic, G. J., & Frady, R. L. (1991). Salivary testosterone and cortisol among late adolescent male offenders. *Journal of Abnormal Child Psychology, 19,* 469–478.

Dabbs, J. M., Jr., & Mallinger, A. (1999). High testosterone levels predict low voice pitch among men. *Personality and Individual Differences, 27,* 801–804.

Dabbs, J. M., Jr., & Mohammed, S. (1992). Male and female salivary testosterone concentrations before and after sexual activity. *Physiology and Behavior, 52,* 195–197.

Dabbs, J. M., Jr., & Morris, R. (1990). Testosterone, social class, and antisocial behavior in a sample of 4,462 men. *Psychological Science, 1,* 209–211.

Dabbs, J. M., Jr., Riad, J. K., & Chance, S. E. (2001). Testosterone and ruthless homicide. *Personality and Individual Differences, 31,* 599–603.

Dabbs, J. M., Jr., Ruback, R. B., Frady, R. L., Hopper, C. H., & Sgoutas, D. S. (1988). Saliva testosterone and criminal violence among women. *Personality and Individual Differences, 9,* 269–275.

Daitzman, R., & Zuckerman, M. (1980). Disinhibitory sensation seeking, personality and gonadal hormones. *Personality and Individual Differences, 1,* 103–110.

Daly, M., & Wilson, M. I. (1988). *Homicide.* New York: Aldine de Gruyter.

Daly, M., & Wilson, M. I. (1990). Killing the competition: Female/female and male/male homicide. *Human Nature, 1,* 81–107.

Daly, M., & Wilson, M. I. (1996). Violence agianst stepchildren. *Current Directions in Psychological Science, 5,* 77–81.

Daniels, D. (1986). Differential experiences of siblings in the same family as predictors of adolescent sibling personality differences. *Journal of Personality and Social Psychology, 51,* 339–346.

Daniels, D., & Plomin, R. (1985). Differential experience of siblings in the same family. *Developmental Psychology, 21,* 747–760.

Darley, J. M., & Goethals, G. R. (1980). People's analyses of the causes of ability-linked performances. In L. Berkowitz (Ed.), *Advances in experimental social psychology* (Vol. 13). New York: Academic Press.

Davidson, M. A., McInnes, R. G., & Parnell, R. W. (1957). The distribution of personality traits in seven-year-old children: A combined psychological, psychiatric, and somatotype study. *British Journal of Educational Psychology, 27,* 48–61.

Davidson, R. J. (1988). EEG measures of cerebral asymmetry: Conceptual and methodological issues. *International Journal of Neuroscience, 39,* 71–89.

Davidson, R. J. (1992). Prolegomenon to the structure of emotion: Gleanings from neuropsychology. *Cognition and Emotion, 6,* 245–268.

Davidson, R. J. (1995). Cerebral asymmetry, emotion, and affective style. In R. J. Davidson, & K. Hugdahl (Eds.), *Brain asymmetry* (pp. 361–387). Cambridge, MA: MIT Press.

Davidson, R. J., Ekman, P., Saron, C. D., Senulis, J. A., & Friesen, W. V. (1990). Approach–withdrawal and cerebral asymmetry: Emotional expression and brain physiology I. *Journal of Personality and Social Psychology, 58,* 330–341.

Davidson, R. J., Jackson, D. C., & Kalin, N. H. (2000). Emotion, plasticity, context, and regulation: Perspectives from affective neuroscience. *Psychological Bulletin, 126,* 890–909.

Davidson, R. J., Pizzagalli, D., Nitschke, J. B., & Putnam, K. (2002). Depression: Perspectives from affective neuroscience. *Annual Review of Psychology, 53,* 545–574.

Davidson, R. J., & Sutton, S. K. (1995). Affective neuroscience: The emergence of a discipline. *Current Opinion in Neurobiology, 5,* 217–224.

Davila, J., Burge, D., & Hammen, C. (1997). Why does attachment style change? *Journal of Personality and Social Psychology, 73,* 826–838.

Davis, C. G., Nolen-Hoeksema, S., & Larson, J. (1998). Making sense of loss and benefiting from the experience: Two construals of meaning. *Journal of Personality and Social Psychology, 75,* 561–574.

Davis, P. J. (1987). Repression and the inaccessibility of affective memories. *Journal of Personality and Social Psychology, 53,* 585–593.

Davis, P. J., & Schwartz, G. E. (1987). Repression and the inaccessibility of affective memories. *Journal of Personality and Social Psychology, 52,* 155–162.

Davis, W. N. (1969). Drinking: A search for power or for nurturance? Unpublished doctoral dissertation, Harvard University, Cambridge, MA.

Davison, G. C., & Wilson, G. T. (1973). Processes of fear reduction in systematic desensitization: Cognitive and social reinforcement factors in humans. *Behavior Therapy, 4,* 1–21.

Dawkins, R. (1976). *The selfish gene.* New York: Oxford University Press.

Dawson, M. E., & Furedy, J. J. (1976). The role of awareness in human differential autonomic classical conditioning: The necessary-gate hypothesis. *Psychophysiology, 13,* 50–53.

De Houwer, J., Thomas, S., & Baeyens, F. (2001). Associative learning of likes and dislikes: A review of 25 years of research on human evaluative conditioning. *Psychological Bulletin, 127,* 853–869.

Deaux, K., & Lewis, L. L. (1984). Structure of gender stereotypes: Interrelationships among components and gender label. *Journal of Personality and Social Psychology, 46,* 991–1004.

Deaux, K., & Major, B. (1987). Putting gender into context: An interactive model of gender-related behavior. *Psychological Review, 94,* 369–389.

Deci, E. L. (1975). *Intrinsic motivation.* New York: Plenum.

Deci, E. L., Koestner, R., & Ryan, R. M. (1999). A meta-analytic review of experiments examining the effects of extrinsic rewards on intrinsic motivation. *Psychological Bulletin, 125,* 627–668.

Deci, E. L., & Ryan, R. M. (1980). The empirical exploration of intrinsic motivational processes. In L. Berkowitz (Ed.), *Advances in experimental social psychology* (Vol. 13). New York: Academic Press.

Deci, E. L., & Ryan, R. M. (1985). *Intrinsic motivation and self-determination in human behavior.* New York: Plenum.

Deci, E. L., & Ryan, R. M. (1991). A motivational approach to self: Integration in personality. In R. Dienstbier (Ed.), *Nebraska symposium on motivation: Perspectives on motivation* (Vol. 38, pp. 237–288). Lincoln: University of Nebraska Press.

Deci, E. L., & Ryan, R. M. (2000). The "what" and "why" of goal pursuits: Human needs and the self-determination of behavior. *Psychological Inquiry, 11,* 227–268.

Deluty, R. H. (1985). Consistency of assertive, aggressive, and submissive behavior for children. *Journal of Personality and Social Psychology, 49,* 1054–1065.

Denney, D. R. (1974). Active, passive, and vicarious desensitization. *Journal of Counseling Psychology, 21,* 369–375.

Depue, R. A. (1979). *The psychobiology of the depressive disorders: Implications for the effect of stress.* New York: Academic Press.

Depue, R. A. (in press). *A neurobehavioral model of temperament and personality.* New York: Springer-Verlag.

Depue, R. A., & Collins, P. F. (1999). Neurobiology of the structure of personality: Dopamine, facilitation of incentive motivation, and extraversion. *Behavioral and Brain Sciences, 22,* 491–517.

Depue, R. A., & Iacono, W. G. (1989). Neurobehavioral aspects of affective disorders. *Annual Review of Psychology, 40,* 457–492.

Depue, R. A., Krauss, S. P., & Spoont, M. R. (1987). A two-dimensional threshold model of seasonal bipolar affective disorder. In D. Magnusson & A. Öhman (Eds.), *Psychopathology: An interactional perspective* (pp. 95–123). Orlando, FL: Academic Press.

Depue, R. A., Luciana, M., Arbisi, P., Collins, P., & Leon, A. (1994). Dopamine and the structure of personality: Relation of agonist-induced dopamine cativity to positive emotionality. *Journal of Personality and Social Psychology, 67,* 485–498.

DeRubeis, R. J., Tang, T. Z., & Beck, A. T. (2001). Cognitive therapy. In Dobson, K. S. (Ed.), *Handbook of cognitive-behavioral therapies* (2nd ed., pp. 349–392). New York: Guilford.

DeSteno, D., Bartlett, M. Y., Braverman, J., & Salovey, P. (2002). Sex differences in jealousy: Evolutionary mechanism or artifact of measurement? *Journal of Personality and Social Psychology, 83,* 1103–1116..

Detera-Wadleigh, S. D., Berrettini, W. H., Goldin, L. R., Boorman, D., Anderson, S., & Gershon, E. S. (1987). Close linkage of c-harvey-ras-1 and the insulin gene to affective disorder is ruled out in three North American pedigrees. *Nature, 325,* 806–808.

Deutsch, F. M., Ruble, D. N., Fleming, A., Brooks-Gunn, J., & Stangor, C. (1988). Information-seeking and maternal self-definition during the transition to motherhood. *Journal of Personality and Social Psychology, 55,* 420–431.

DeVellis, R. F., DeVellis, B. M., & McCauley, C. (1978). Vicarious acquisition of learned helplessness. *Journal of Personality and Social Psychology, 36,* 894–899.

DeVito, A. J. (1985). Review of Myers–Briggs Type Indicator. In J. V. Mitchell (Ed.), *The ninth mental measurements yearbook* (pp. 1029–1032). Lincoln, NE: Buros Institute of Mental Measurements.

Dick, D. M., & Rose, R. J. (2002). Behavior genetics: What's new? What's next? *Current Directions in Psychological Science, 11,* 70–74.

Dickens, W. T., & Flynn, J. R. (2001). Heritability estimates versus large environmental effects: The IQ paradox resolved. *Psychological Review, 108,* 346–369.

Di Blas, L., & Forzi, M. (1999). Refining a descriptive structure of personality attributes in the Italian language:

The abridged big three circumplex structure. *Journal of Personality and Social Psychology, 76,* 451–481.

DiClemente, C. C. (1981). Self-efficacy and smoking cessation. *Cognitive Therapy and Research, 5,* 175–187.

Diener, C. I., & Dweck, C. S. (1978). An analysis of learned helplessness: Continuous changes in performance, strategy, and achievement cognitions following failure. *Journal of Personality and Social Psychology, 36,* 451–462.

Diener, E. (1979). Deindividuation, self-awareness, and disinhibition. *Journal of Personality and Social Psychology, 37,* 1160–1171.

Diener, E., Sandvik, E., Pavot, W., & Fujita, F. (1992). Extraversion and subjective well-being in a U.S. national probability sample. *Journal of Research in Personality, 26,* 205–215.

Diener, E., & Wallbom, M. (1976). Effects of self-awareness on antinormative behavior. *Journal of Research in Personality, 10,* 413–423.

Digman, J. M. (1990). Personality structure: Emergence of the five-factor model. *Annual Review of Psychology, 41,* 417–440.

Digman, J. M. (1997). Higher-order factors of the Big Five. *Journal of Personality and Social Psychology, 73,* 1246–1256.

Digman, J. M., & Inouye, J. (1986). Further specification of the five robust factors of personality. *Journal of Personality and Social Psychology, 50,* 116–123.

Digman, J. M., & Shmelyov, A. G. (1996). The structure of temperament and personality in Russian children. *Journal of Personality and Social Psychology, 71,* 341–351.

Digman, J. M., & Takemoto-Chock, N. K. (1981). Factors in the natural language of personality: Re-analysis, comparison, and interpretation of six major studies. *Multivariate Behavioral Research, 16,* 149–170.

Dijksterhuis, A., & Bargh, J. A. (2001). The perception–behavior expressway. In M. P. Zanna (Ed.), *Advances in experimental social psychology* (Vol. 33, pp. 1–40). San Diego, CA: Academic Press.

Dijkstra, P., & Buunk, B. P. (1998). Jealousy as a function of rival characteristics: An evolutionary perspective. *Personality and Social Psychology Bulletin, 24,* 1158–1166.

DiLalla, L. F., & Gottesman, I. I. (1991). Biological and genetic contributors to violence—Widom's untold tale. *Psychological Bulletin, 109,* 125–129.

Diven, K. (1936). Certain determinants in the conditioning of anxiety reactions. *Journal of Psychology, 3,* 291–308.

Dixon, N. F. (1981). *Preconscious processing.* Chichester, England: Wiley.

Dodge, K. A. (1986). A social information-processing model of social competence in children. In M. Perlmutter (Ed.), *Minnesota symposium on child psychology* (Vol. 18). Hillsdale, NJ: Erlbaum.

Dodge, K. A., & Crick, N. R. (1990). Social information-processing bases of aggressive behavior in children. *Personality and Social Psychology Bulletin, 16,* 8–22.

Dollard, J., & Miller, N. E. (1950). *Personality and psychotherapy: An analysis in terms of learning, thinking, and culture.* New York: McGraw-Hill.

Dollinger, S. J., & Orf, L. A. (1991). Personality and performance in "personality": Conscientiousness and openness. *Journal of Research in Personality, 25,* 276–284.

Donnerstein, E. (1980). Aggressive erotica and violence against women. *Journal of Personality and Social Psychology, 39,* 269–277.

Donnerstein, E. (1983). Erotica and human aggression. In R. G. Geen & E. Donnerstein (Eds.), *Aggression: Theoretical and empirical reviews.* New York: Academic Press.

Donnerstein, E., & Berkowitz, L. (1981). Victim reactions in aggressive erotic films as a factor in violence against women. *Journal of Personality and Social Psychology, 41,* 710–724.

Donnerstein, E., Donnerstein, M., & Evans, R. (1975). Erotic stimuli and aggression: Facilitation or inhibition? *Journal of Personality and Social Psychology, 32,* 237–244.

Donnerstein, E., & Hallam, J. (1978). The facilitating effects of erotica on aggression toward females. *Journal of Personality and Social Psychology, 36,* 1270–1277.

Donovan, J. M. (1975). Identity status and interpersonal style. *Journal of Youth and Adolescence, 4,* 37–55.

Doob, A. N. (1970). Catharsis and aggression: The effect of hurting one's enemy. *Journal of Experimental Research in Personality, 4,* 291–296.

Dosamantes-Alperson, E., & Merrill, N. (1980). Growth effects of experiential movement psychotherapy. *Psychotherapy: Theory, Research, and Practice, 17,* 63–68.

Douglas, C. (1993). *Translate this darkness: The life of Christiana Morgan.* New York: Simon & Schuster.

Drabman, R. S., & Spitalnik, R. (1973). Training a retarded child as a behavioral teaching assistant. *Journal of Behavior Therapy and Experimental Psychiatry, 4,* 269–272.

Duck, S. W. (1973). *Personal relationships and personal constructs.* London: Wiley.

Duck, S. W. (1977). Inquiry, hypothesis, and the quest for validation: Personal construct systems in the development of acquaintance. In S. W. Duck (Ed.), *Theories of interpersonal attraction.* London: Academic Press.

Duck, S. W., & Allison, D. (1978). I liked you but I can't live with you: A study of lapsed friendships. *Social Behavior and Personality, 8,* 43–47.

Dulany, D. E. (1968). Awareness, rules and propositional control: A confrontation with S-R behavior theory. In T. R. Dixon & D. L. Horton (Eds.), *Verbal behavior and general behavior theory.* Englewood Cliffs, NJ: Prentice-Hall.

Dunn, J., & Plomin, R. (1990). *Separate lives: Why siblings are so different.* New York: Basic Books.

Dunning, D., & McElwee, R. O. (1995). Idiosyncratic trait definitions: Implications for self-description and social judgment. *Journal of Personality and Social Psychology, 68,* 936–946.

Dweck, C. S., & Leggett, E. L. (1988). A social-cognitive approach to motivation and personality. *Psychological Review, 95,* 256–273.

Eagle, M. N. (1984). *Recent developments in psychoanalysis: A critical evaluation.* New York: McGraw-Hill.

Eagly, A. H. (1987). *Sex differences in social behavior: A social-role interpretation.* Hillsdale, NJ: Erlbaum.

Eagly, A. H., & Wood, W. (1999). The origins of sex differences in human behavior: Evolved dispositions versus social roles. *American Psychologist, 54,* 408–423.

Eaves, L. J., Eysenck, H. J., & Martin, N. G. (1989). *Genes, culture, and personality: An empirical approach.* San Diego: Academic Press.

Ebbesen, E. B., Duncan, B., & Konecni, V. J. (1975). Effects of content of verbal aggression on future verbal aggression: A field experiment. *Journal of Experimental Social Psychology, 11,* 192–204.

Ebstein, R. P., Novick, O., Umansky, R., Priel, B., Osher, Y., Blaine, D., Bennett, E. R., Nemanov, L., Katz, M., & Belmaker, R. H. (1996). Dopamine D4 receptor (D4DR) exon III polymorphism associated with the human personality trait of novelty seeking. *Nature Genetics, 12,* 78–80.

Edwards, A. L. (1957). *The social desirability variable in personality assessment and research.* New York: Dryden.

Edwards, A. L. (1959). *Edwards Personal Preference Schedule manual.* New York: Psychological Corporation.

Egeland, J. A., Gerhard, D. S., Pauls, D. L., Sussex, J. N., & Kidd, K. K. (1987). Bipolar affective disorders linked to DNA markers on chromosome 11. *Nature, 325,* 783–787.

Einstein, D., & Lanning, K. (1998). Shame, guilt, ego development, and the five-factor model of personality. *Journal of Personality, 66,* 555–582.

Eisenberg, N., Fabes, R. A., Guthrie, I. K., & Reiser, M. (2000). Dispositional emotionality and regulation: Their role in predicting quality of social functioning. *Journal of Personality and Social Psychology, 78,* 136–157.

Eisenberg, N., Fabes, R. A., Murphy, B., Karbon, M., Maszk, P., Smith, M., O'Boyle, C., & Suh, K. (1994). The relations of emotionality and regulation to dispositional and situational empathy-related responding. *Journal of Personality and Social Psychology, 66,* 776–797.

Eisenberger, R. (1992). Learned industriousness. *Psychological Review, 99,* 248–267.

Eisenberger, R., Armeli, S., & Pretz, J. (1998). Can the promise of reward increase creativity? *Journal of Personality and Social Psychology, 74,* 704–714.

Eisenberger, R., & Rhoades, L. (2001). Incremental effects of reward on creativity. *Journal of Personality and Social Psychology, 81,* 728–741.

Eisenberger, R., & Selbst, M. (1994). Does reward increase or decrease creativity? *Journal of Personality and Social Psychology, 66,* 1116–1127.

Ekehammer, B. (1974). Interactionism in personality from a historical perspective. *Psychological Bulletin, 81,* 1026–1048.

Elder, G. H., Jr., Caspi, A., & Downey, G. (1986). Problem behavior and family relationships: Life course and intergenerational themes. In A. B. Sorenson, F. Weinert, & L. R. Sherrod (Eds.), *Human development and the life course: Multidisciplinary perspectives* (pp. 293–340). Hillsdale, NJ: Erlbaum.

Elder, G. H., Jr, & MacInnis, D. J. (1983). Achievement imagery in women's lives from adolescence to adulthood. *Journal of Personality and Social Psychology, 45,* 394–404.

Ellenberger, H. F. (1970). *The discovery of the unconscious.* New York: Basic Books.

Elliot, A. J., & Harackiewicz, J. M. (1994). Goal setting, achievement orientation, and intrinsic motivation: A mediational analysis. *Journal of Personality and Social Psychology, 66,* 968–980.

Elliot, A. J., & Harackiewicz, J. M. (1996). Approach and avoidance achievement goals and intrinsic motivation: A mediational analysis. *Journal of Personality and Social Psychology, 70,* 461–475.

Elliot, A. J., & McGregor, H. A. (2001). A 2 × 2 achievement goal framework. *Journal of Personality and Social Psychology, 80,* 501–519.

Elliot, A. J., & Sheldon, K. M. (1997). Avoidance achievement motivation: A personal goals analysis. *Journal of Personality and Social Psychology, 73,* 171–185.

Elliot, A. J., & Thrash, T. M. (2002). Approach–avoidance motivation in personality: Approach and avoidance temperaments and goals. *Journal of Personality and Social Psychology, 82,* 804–818.

Elliott, E. S., & Dweck, C. S. (1988). Goals: An approach to motivation and achievement. *Journal of Personality and Social Psychology, 54,* 5–12.

Ellis, A. E. (1987). The impossibility of achieving consistently good mental health. *American Psychologist, 42,* 364–375.

Elmore, A. M., & Tursky, B. (1981). A comparison of two psychophysiological approaches to the treatment of migraine. *Headache, 21,* 93–101.

Emmons, R. A. (1986). Personal strivings: An approach to personality and subjective well-being. *Journal of Personality and Social Psychology, 51,* 1058–1068.

Emmons, R. A., & Diener, E. (1986). Situation selection as a moderator of response consistency and stability. *Journal of Personality and Social Psychology, 51,* 1013–1019.

Emmons, R. A., Diener, E., & Larsen, R. J. (1986). Choice and avoidance of everyday situations and affect congruence: Two models of reciprocal interactionism. *Journal of Personality and Social Psychology, 51,* 815–826.

Emmons, R. A., & King, L. A. (1988). Conflict among personal strivings: Immediate and long-term implications for psychological and physical well-being. *Journal of Personality and Social Psychology, 54,* 1040–1048.

Emmons, R. A., King, L. A., & Sheldon, K. (1993). Goal conflict and the self-regulation of action. In D. M. Wegner & J. W. Pennebaker (Eds.), *Handbook of mental control* (pp. 528–551). Englewood Cliffs, NJ: Prentice-Hall.

Endler, N. S., & Magnusson, D. (1976). *Interactional psychology and personality.* Washington, DC: Hemisphere.

Entwisle, D. R. (1972). To dispel fantasies about fantasy-based measures of achievement motivation. *Psychological Bulletin, 77,* 377–391.

Epstein, L. H., Saelens, B. E., Myers, M. D., & Vito, D. (1997). Effects of decreasing sedentary behaviors on activity choice in obese children. *Health Psychology, 16,* 107–113.

Epstein, S. (1979). The stability of behavior: I. On predicting most of the people much of the time. *Journal of Personality and Social Psychology, 37,* 1097–1126.

Epstein, S. (1980). The stability of behavior: II. Implications for psychological research. *American Psychologist, 35,* 790–806.

Epstein, S. (1983). The unconscious, the preconscious, and the self-concept. In J. Suls & A. G. Greenwald (Eds.), *Psychological perspectives on the self* (Vol. 2). Hillsdale, NJ: Erlbaum.

Epstein, S. (1985). The implications of cognitive–experiential self theory for research in social psychology and personality. *Journal for the Theory of Social Behavior, 15,* 283–310.

Epstein, S. (1990). Cognitive–experiential self-theory. In L. Pervin (Ed.), *Handbook of personality: Theory and research* (pp. 165–192). New York: Guilford.

Epstein, S. (1994). Integration of the cognitive and the psychodynamic unconscious. *American Psychologist, 49,* 709–724.

Epstein, S., Lipson, A., Holstein, C., & Huh, E. (1992). Irrational reactions to negative outcomes: Evidence for two conceptual systems. *Journal of Personality and Social Psychology, 62,* 328–339.

Epting, F. R. (1972). The stability of cognitive complexity in construing social issues. *British Journal of Social and Clinical Psychology, 11,* 122–125.

Epting, F. R. (1980). *Personal construct theory psychotherapy.* New York: Wiley.

Erdelyi, M. H. (1985). *Psychoanalysis: Freud's cognitive psychology.* New York: Freeman.

Ericsson, K. A., & Simon, H. A. (1993). *Protocol analysis: Verbal reports as data* (Rev. ed.). Cambridge, MA: MIT Press.

Erikson, E. H. (1950). *Childhood and society* (1st ed.). New York: Norton.

Erikson, E. H. (1963). *Childhood and society* (2nd ed.). New York: Norton.

Erikson, E. H. (1964). *Insight and responsibility.* New York: Norton.

Erikson, E. H. (1968). *Identity: Youth and crisis.* New York: Norton.

Erikson, E. H. (1974). *Dimensions of a new identity.* New York: Norton.

Erikson, E. H. (1982). *The life cycle completed: A review.* New York: Norton.

Ernst, C., & Angst, J. (1983). *Birth order: Its influence on personality.* Berlin: Springer-Verlag.

Esterson, A. (1993). *Seductive mirage: An exploration of the work of Sigmund Freud.* Chicago: Open Court.

Esterson, A. (1998). Jeffrey Masson and Freud's seduction theory: A new fable based on old myths. *History of the Human Sciences, 11,* 1–21.

Esterson, A. (2001). The mythologizing of psychoanalytic history: Deception and self-deception in Freud's accounts of the seduction theory episode. *History of Psychiatry, 12,* 329–352.

Esterson, A. (2002). The myth of Freud's ostracism by the medical community in 1896–1905: Jeffrey Masson's assault on truth. *History of Psychology, 5,* 115–134.

Evans, R. I. (1989). *Albert Bandura: The man and his ideas—A dialogue.* New York: Praeger.

Ewart, C. K. (1978). Self-observation in natural environments: Reactive effects of behavior desirability and goal-setting. *Cognitive Therapy and Research, 2,* 39–56.

Exner, J. E., Jr. (1974). *The Rorschach systems.* New York: Grune & Stratton.

Exner, J. E., Jr. (1993). *The Rorschach: A comprehensive system*: Vol. 1. Basic foundations (3rd ed.). New York: Wiley.

Exner, J. E., Jr. (1996). A comment on "The comprehensive system for the Rorschach: A critical examination." *Psychological Science, 7,* 11–13.

Eysenck, H. J. (1952). *The scientific study of personality.* New York: Macmillan.

Eysenck, H. J. (1961). The effects of psychotherapy. In H. J. Eysenck (Ed.), *Handbook of abnormal psychology.* New York: Basic Books.

Eysenck, H. J. (1964a). *Crime and personality.* Boston: Houghton Mifflin.

Eysenck, H. J. (1964b). Involuntary rest pauses in tapping as a function of drive and personality. *Perceptual and Motor Skills, 18,* 173–174.

Eysenck, H. J. (1967). *The biological basis of personality.* Springfield, IL: Charles C Thomas.

Eysenck, H. J. (1970). *The structure of human personality* (3rd ed.). London: Methuen.

Eysenck, H. J. (1971). *Readings in extraversion-introversion: 3. Bearings on basic psychological processes.* New York: Wiley-Interscience.

Eysenck, H. J. (1975). *The inequality of man.* San Diego: EdITS.

Eysenck, H. J. (Ed.). (1981). *A model for personality.* Berlin: Springer-Verlag.

Eysenck, H. J. (1983). Psychopharmacology and personality. In W. Janke (Ed.), *Response variability to psychotropic drugs.* London: Pergamon.

Eysenck, H. J. (1986). Models and paradigms in personality research. In A. Angleitner, A. Furnham, & G. Van Heck (Eds.), *Personality psychology in Europe, Vol. 2: Current trends and controversies* (pp. 213–223). Lisse, Holland: Swets & Zeitlinger.

Eysenck, H. J. (1992). Four ways five factors are *not* basic. *Personality and Individual Differences, 13,* 667–673.

Eysenck, H. J. (1993). Comment on Goldberg. *American Psychologist, 48,* 1299–1300.

Eysenck, H. J., & Eysenck, M. W. (1985). *Personality and individual differences: A natural science approach.* New York: Plenum.

Eysenck, H. J., & Eysenck, S. B. G. (1975). *Manual of the Eysenck Personality Questionnaire.* San Diego, CA: EdITS.

Eysenck, H. J., & Eysenck, S. B. G. (1976). *Psychoticism as a dimension of personality.* London: Hodder & Stoughton.

Fadiga, L., Fogassi, L., Gallese, V., & Rizzolatti, G. (2000). Visuomotor neurons: Ambiguity of the discharge or 'motor' perception? *International Journal of Psychophysiology, 35,* 165–177.

Fagot, B. I. (1977). Consequences of moderate cross-gender behavior in preschool children. *Child Development, 48,* 902–907.

Fairbairn, W. R. D. (1952). *Psycho-analytic studies of the personality.* New York: Basic Books.

Fairbairn, W. R. D. (1954). *An object relations theory of personality.* New York: Basic Books.

Fairbanks, L. A. (2001). Individual differences in response to a stranger: Social impulsivity as a dimension of temperament in vervet monkeys (*Cercopithecus aethiops sabaeus*). *Journal of Comparative Psychology, 115,* 22–28.

Fairbanks, L. A., Melega, W. P., Jorgensen, M. J., Kaplan, J. R., & McGuire, M. T. (2001). Social impulsivity inversely associated with CSF 5-HIAA and fluoxetine exposure in vervet monkeys. *Neuropsychopharmacology, 24,* 370–378.

Falbo, T. (1981). Relationships between birth category, achievement, and interpersonal orientation. *Journal of Personality and Social Psychology, 41,* 121–131.

Feather, N. T. (1961). The relationship of persistence at a task to expectations of success and achievement-related motivation. *Journal of Abnormal and Social Psychology, 63,* 552–561.

Feather, N. T. (1968). Change in confidence following success and failure as a predictor of subsequent task performance. *Journal of Personality and Social Psychology, 9,* 38–46.

Feather, N. T. (Ed.). (1982). *Expectations and actions: Expectancy–value models in psychology.* Hillsdale, NJ: Erlbaum.

Feeney, B. C., & Collins, N. L. (2001). Predictors of caregiving in adult intimate relationships: An attachment theoretical perspective. *Journal of Personality and Social Psychology, 80,* 972–994.

Feeney, J. A., & Noller, P. (1990). Attachment style as a predictor of adult romantic relationships. *Journal of Personality and Social Psychology, 58,* 281–291.

Fehr, E., & Gächter, S. (2002). Altruistic punishment in humans. *Nature, 415,* 137–140.

Feij, J. A., Orlebeke, J. F., Gazendam, A., & van Zuilen, R. W. (1985). Sensation seeking: Measurement and psychophysiological correlates. In J. Strelau, F. H. Farley, & A. Gale (Eds.), *The biological bases of personality and behavior. Vol. 1. Theories, measurement techniques, and development.* Washington, DC: Hemisphere.

Feingold, A. (1992). Gender differences in mate selection preferences: A test of the parental investment model. *Psychological Bulletin, 112,* 125–139.

Fekken, G. C., & Holden, R. R. (1992). Response latency evidence for viewing personality traits as schema indicators. *Journal of Research in Personality, 26,* 103–120.

Feldman Barrett, L., Williams, N. L., & Fong, G. T. (2002). Defensive verbal behavior assessment. *Personality and Social Psychology Bulletin, 28,* 776–788.

Feldman, F. (1968). Results of psychoanalysis in clinic case assignments. *Journal of the American Psychoanalytic Association, 16,* 274–300.

Feldman, M. P., & MacCulloch, M. J. (1971). *Homosexual behavior: Therapy and assessment.* Oxford: Pergamon.

Fenichel, O. (1945). *The psychoanalytic theory of neurosis.* New York: Norton.

Fenigstein, A., & Buss, A. H. (1974). Association and affect as determinants of displaced aggression. *Journal of Research in Personality, 7,* 306–313.

Fenigstein, A., Scheier, M. F., & Buss, A. H. (1975). Public and private self-consciousness: Assessment and theory. *Journal of Consulting and Clinical Psychology, 43,* 522–527.

Fernando, C. K., & Basmajian, J. V. (1978). Biofeedback in physical medicine and rehabilitation. *Biofeedback and Self-regulation, 3,* 435–455.

Festinger, L., Pepitone, A., & Newcomb, T. (1952). Some consequences of deindividuation in a group. *Journal of Abnormal and Social Psychology, 47,* 382–389.

Findley, M. J., & Cooper, H. M. (1983). Locus of control and academic achievement: A literature review. *Journal of Personality and Social Psychology, 44,* 419–427.

Finkel, E. J., & Campbell, W. K. (2001). Self-control and accommodation in close relationships: An interdependence analysis. *Journal of Personality and Social Psychology, 81,* 263–277.

Fisher, S. (1973). *The female orgasm.* New York: Basic Books.

Fisher, S., & Greenberg, R. P. (1977). *The scientific credibility of Freud's theories and therapy.* New York: Basic Books.

Fiske, A. P. (1992). The four elementary forms of sociality: Framework for a unified theory of social relations. *Psychological Review, 99,* 689–723.

Fiske, D. W. (1949). Consistency of the factorial structures of personality ratings from different sources. *Journal of Abnormal and Social Psychology, 44,* 329–344.

Fiske, S. T., & Taylor, S. E. (1984). *Social cognition.* Reading, MA: Addison-Wesley.

Flanders, J. P. (1968). A review of research on imitative behavior. *Psychological Bulletin, 69,* 316–337.

Fleeson, W. (2001). Toward a structure- and process-integrated view of personality: Traits as density distributions of states. *Journal of Personality and Social Psychology, 80,* 1011–1027.

Fleeson, W., Malanos, A., & Achille, N. (in press). An intra-individual, process approach to the relationship between extraversion and positive affect: Is acting extraverted as "good" as being extraverted? *Journal of Personality and Social Psychology.*

Fletcher, G. J. O., Danilovics, P., Fernandez, G., Peterson, D., & Reeder, G. D. (1986). Attributional complexity: An individual differences measure. *Journal of Personality and Social Psychology, 51,* 875–884.

Flink, C., Boggiano, A. K., & Barrett, M. (1990). Controlling teaching strategies: Undermining children's self-determination and performance. *Journal of Personality and Social Psychology, 59,* 916–924.

Floderus-Myrhed, B., Pedersen, N., & Rasmuson, I. (1980). Assessment of heritability for personality, based on a short form of the Eysenck Personality Inventory: A study of 12,898 twin pairs. *Behavior Genetics, 10,* 153–162.

Florian, V., Mikulincer, M., & Hirschberger, G. (2002). The anxiety-buffering function of close relationships: Evidence that relationship commitment acts as a terror management mechanism. *Journal of Personality and Social Psychology, 82,* 527–542.

Flory, J. D., Matthews, K. A., & Owens, J. F. (1998). A social information processing approach to dispositional hostility: Relationships with negative mood and blood pressure elevations at work. *Journal of Social and Clinical Psychology, 17,* 491–504.

Fodor, E. M. (1984). The power motive and reactivity to power stresses. *Journal of Personality and Social Psychology, 47,* 853–859.

Ford, D. H. (1987). *Humans as self-constructing living systems: A developmental perspective on behavior and personality.* Hillsdale, NJ: Erlbaum.

Fowles, D. C. (1980). The three arousal model: Implications of Gray's two-factor learning theory for heart rate, electrodermal activity, and psychopathy. *Psychophysiology, 17,* 87–104.

Fox, N. A., & Davidson, R. J. (1988). Patterns of brain electrical activity during facial signs of emotion in 10-month-old infants. *Developmental Psychology, 24,* 230–236.

Fraley, R. C. (2002). Attachment stability from infancy to adulthood: Meta-analysis and dynamic modeling of developmental mechanisms. *Personality and Social Psychology Review, 6,* 123–151.

Fraley, R. C., Garner, J. P., & Shaver, P. R. (2000). Adult attachment and the defensive regulation of attention and memory: Examining the role of preemptive and postemptive defensive processes. *Journal of Personality and Social Psychology, 79,* 816–826.

Fraley, R. C., & Shaver, P. R. (1998). Airport separations: A naturalistic study of adult attachment dynamics in separating couples. *Journal of Personality and Social Psychology, 75,* 1198–1212.

Frank, E., & Brandstätter, V. (2002). Approach versus avoidance: Different types of commitment in intimate relationships. *Journal of Personality and Social Psychology, 82,* 208–221.

Frank, L. K. (1939). Projective methods for the study of personality. *Journal of Psychology, 8,* 389–413.

Frank, S., & Quinlan, D. M. (1976). Ego development and female delinquency: A cognitive-developmental approach. *Journal of Abnormal Psychology, 85,* 505–510.

Frankel, A., & Snyder, M. L. (1978). Poor performance following unsolvable problems: Learned helplessness or egotism? *Journal of Personality and Social Psychology, 36,* 1415–1423.

Frankl, V. E. (1969). *The doctor and the soul.* New York: Bantam.

Fransella, F. (1972). *Personal change and reconstruction.* New York: Academic Press.

Freedman, J. L. (1986). Television violence and aggression: A rejoinder. *Psychological Bulletin, 100,* 372–378.

French, E. G. (1955). Some characteristics of achievement motivation. *Journal of Experimental Psychology, 50,* 232–236.

French, E. G., & Lesser, G. S. (1964). Some characteristics of the achievement motive in women. *Journal of Abnormal and Social Psychology, 68,* 119–128.

Freud, A. (1966). *The ego and the mechanisms of defense* (Rev. ed.). New York: International Universities Press.

Freud, S. (1933). *New introductory lectures on psychoanalysis.* New York: Norton. (Translated by W. J. H. Sprott)

Freud, S. (1936). *The problem of anxiety.* New York: Norton. (Translated by H. A. Bunker; originally published, 1926)

Freud, S. (1949). *An outline of psychoanalysis.* New York: Norton. (Translated by J. Strachey; originally published, 1940)

Freud, S. (1953). Three essays on sexuality. In J. Strachey (Ed.), *The standard edition of the complete psychological works of Sigmund Freud* (Vol. 7). London: Hogarth. (Originally published, 1905)

Freud, S. (1955). Beyond the pleasure principle. In J. Strachey (Ed.), *The standard edition of the complete psychological works of Sigmund Freud* (Vol. 18). London: Hogarth. (Originally published, 1920)

Freud, S. (1959). Inhibitions, symptoms and anxiety. In J. Strachey (Ed.), *The standard edition of the complete psy-chological works of Sigmund Freud* (Vol. 20). London: Hogarth. (Originally published, 1926)

Freud, S. (1960a). *Jokes and their relation to the unconscious.* New York: Norton. (Translated by J. Strachey, originally published, 1905)

Freud, S. (1960b). Psychopathology of everyday life. In J. Strachey (Ed.), *The standard edition of the complete psychological works of Sigmund Freud* (Vol. 6). London: Hogarth. (Originally published, 1901)

Freud, S. (1961). The unconscious. In J. Strachey (Ed.), *The standard edition of the complete psychological works of Sigmund Freud* (Vol. 14). London: Hogarth. (Originally published, 1915)

Freud, S. (1962). *The ego and the id.* New York: Norton. (Originally published, 1923)

Freund, A. M., & Baltes, P. B. (2002). Life-management strategies of selection, optimization, and compensation. Measurement by self-report and construct validity. *Journal of Personality and Social Psychology, 82,* 642–662.

Freyd, J. J. (1987). Dynamic mental representations. *Psychological Review, 94,* 427–438.

Freyd, J. J. (1996). *Betrayal trauma: The logic of forgetting childhood abuse.* Cambridge, MA: Harvard.

Friedman, H. S., Tucker, J. S., Schwartz, J. E., Martin, L. R., Tomlinson-Keasey, C., Wingard, D. L., & Criqui, M. H. (1995). Childhood conscientiousness and longevity: Health behaviors and cause of death. *Journal of Personality and Social Psychology, 68,* 696–701.

Friedman, L. J. (1999). *Identity's architect: A biography of Erik H. Erikson.* New York: Scribner.

Fritz, H. L., & Helgeson, V. S. (1998). Distinctions of unmitigated communion from communion: Self-neglect and overinvolvement with others. *Journal of Personality and Social Psychology, 75,* 121–140.

Frodi, A. (1977). Sexual arousal, situational restrictiveness, and aggressive behavior. *Journal of Research in Personality, 11,* 48–58.

Fukuyama, F. (2002). *Our posthuman future: Consequences of the biotechnology revolution.* New York: Farrar, Straus, & Giroux.

Fultz, J., Schaller, M., & Cialdini, R. B. (1988). Empathy, sadness, and distress: Three related but distinct vicarious affective responses to another's suffering. *Personality and Social Psychology Bulletin, 14,* 312–325.

Funder, D. C. (1991). Global traits: A neo-Allportian approach to personality. *Psychological Science, 2,* 31–39.

Funder, D. C. (2001). Personality. *Annual Review of Psychology, 52,* 197–221.

Funder, D. C., & Block, J. (1989). The role of ego-control, ego-resiliency, and IQ in delay of gratification in adolescence. *Journal of Personality and Social Psychology, 57,* 1041–1050.

Funder, D. C., Block, J. H., & Block. J. (1983). Delay of gratification: Some longitudinal personality correlates. *Journal of Personality and Social Psychology, 44,* 1198–1213.

Funder, D. C., & Colvin, C. R. (1991). Explorations in behavioral consistency: Properties of persons, situations, and behaviors. *Journal of Personality and Social Psychology, 60,* 773–794.

Funder, D. C., & Ozer, D. J. (1983). Behavior as a function of the situation. *Journal of Personality and Social Psychology, 44,* 107–112.

Gable, S. L., Reis, H. T., & Elliot, A. J. (2000). Behavioral activation and inhibition in everyday life. *Journal of Personality and Social Psychology, 78,* 1135–1149.

Gacsaly, S. A., & Borges, C. A. (1979). The male physique and behavioral expectancies. *Journal of Psychology, 101,* 97–102.

Gallagher, W. (1994). How we become what we are. *Atlantic Monthly, 274,* 39–55.

Gallese. V. (2001). The 'shared manifold' hypthesis: From mirror neurons to empathy. *Journal of Consciousness Studies, 8,* 33–50.

Gallistel, C. R. (1980). *The organization of action: A new synthesis.* Hillsdale, NJ: Erlbaum.

Ganellen, R. J. (1996a). Comparing the diagnostic efficiency of the MMPMI, MCMI-II, and Rorschach: A review. *Journal of Personality Assessment, 67,* 219–243.

Ganellen, R. J. (1996b). *Integrating the Rorschach and MMPI-2 in personality assessment.* Hillsdale, NJ: Erlbaum.

Gangestad, S. W., & Simpson, J. A. (2000). The evolution of human mating: Trade-offs and strategic pluralism. *Behavioral and Brain Sciences, 23,* 573–587.

Gangestad, S. W., & Snyder, M. (1985). "To carve nature at its joints": On the existence of discrete classes in personality. *Psychological Review, 92,* 317–349.

Garcia, J., & Koelling, R. A. (1966). Relation of cue to consequence in avoidance learning. *Psychonomic Science, 4,* 123–124.

Gardner, H. (1985). *The mind's new science: A history of the cognitive revolution.* New York: Basic Books.

Gauthier, J., & Ladouceur, R. (1981). The influence of self-efficacy reports on performance. *Behavior Therapy, 12,* 436–439.

Geen, R. G. (1981). Behavioral and physiological reactions to observed violence: Effects of prior exposure to aggressive stimuli. *Journal of Personality and Social Psychology, 40,* 868–875.

Geen, R. G. (1984). Preferred stimulation levels in introverts and extraverts: Effects on arousal and performance. *Journal of Personality and Social Psychology, 46,* 1303–1312.

Geen, R. G. (1998). Aggression and antisocial behavior. In D. T. Gilbert, S. T. Fiske, & G. Lindzey (Eds.), *The handbook of social psychology* (Vol. 2, 4th ed., pp. 317–356). Boston: McGraw-Hill.

Geen, R. G., Stonner, D., & Shope, G. L. (1975). The facilitation of aggression by aggression: Evidence against the catharsis hypothesis. *Journal of Personality and Social Psychology, 31,* 721–726.

Gerst, M. S. (1971). Symbolic coding processes in observational learning. *Journal of Personality and Social Psychology, 19,* 7–27.

Gibbons, F. X. (1978). Sexual standards and reactions to pornography: Enhancing behavioral consistency through self-focused attention. *Journal of Personality and Social Psychology, 36,* 976–987.

Gibbons, F. X., Gerrard, M., Blanton, H., & Russell, D. W. (1998). Reasoned action and social reaction: Willingness and intention as independent predictors of health risk. *Journal of Personality and Social Psychology, 74,* 1164–1180.

Gibbons, F. X., & Wicklund, R. A. (1976). Selective exposure to self. *Journal of Research in Personality, 10,* 98–106.

Gibson, H. B. (1981). *Hans Eysenck: The man and his work.* London: Peter Owen.

Gigerenzer, G., & Goldstein, D. G. (1996). Reasoning the fast and frugal way: Models of bounded rationality. *Psychological Review, 103,* 650–669.

Gill, M. M. (1959). The present state of psychoanalytic theory. *Journal of Abnormal and Social Psychology, 58,* 1–8.

Gilovich, T. (1990). Differential construal and the false consensus effect. *Journal of Personality and Social Psychology, 59,* 623–634.

Glassman, N. S., & Andersen, S. M. (1999). Activating transference without consciousness: Using significant-other representations to go beyond what is subliminally given. *Journal of Personality and Social Psychology, 77,* 1146–1162.

Glueck, S., & Glueck, E. (1956). *Physique and delinquency.* New York: Harper.

Goldberg, A. (Ed.). (1985). *Progress in self psychology (Vol. 1).* New York: Guilford.

Goldberg, L. R. (1981). Language and individual differences: The search for universals in personality lexicons. In L. Wheeler (Ed.), *Review of personality and social psychology* (Vol. 2, pp. 141–165). Beverly Hills, CA: Sage.

Goldberg, L. R. (1982). From ace to zombie: Some explorations in the language of personality. In C. D. Spielberger & J. N. Butcher (Eds.), *Advances in personality assessment* (Vol. 1). Hillsdale, NJ: Erlbaum.

Goldberg, L. R. (1993a). The structure of personality traits: Vertical and horizontal aspects. In D. C. Funder, R. Parke, C. Tomlinson-Keasey, & K. Widaman (Eds.), *Studying lives through time: Approaches to personality and development* (pp. 169–188). Washington, DC: American Psychological Association.

Goldberg, L. R. (1993b). The structure of phenotypic personality traits. *American Psychologist, 48,* 26–34.

Goldenberg, J. L., Pyszczynski, T., Greenberg, J., & Solomon, S. (2000). Fleeing the body: A terror management perspective on the problem of human corporeality. *Personality and Social Psychology Review, 4,* 200–218.

Goldenberg, J. L., Pyszczynski, T., Greenberg, J., Solomon, S., Kluck, B., & Cornwell, R. (2001). I am *not* an animal: Mortality salience, disgust, and the denial of human creatureliness. *Journal of Experimental Psychology: General, 130,* 427–435.

Goldfield, G. S., & Epstein, L. H. (2002). Can fruits and vegetables and activities substitute for snack foods? *Health Psychology, 21,* 299–303.

Goldfried, M. R. (1971). Systematic desensitization as training in self-control. *Journal of Consulting and Clinical Psychology , 37,* 228–234.

Goldfried, M. R., & Davison, G. C. (1976). *Clinical behavior therapy.* New York: Holt, Rinehart, & Winston.

Goldfried, M. R., & Merbaum, M. (Eds.). (1973). *Behavior change through self-control.* New York: Holt, Rinehart, & Winston.

Goldiamond, I. (1976). Self-reinforcement. *Journal of Applied Behavior Analysis, 9,* 509–514.

Goldstein, J. H., & Arms, R. L. (1971). Effects of observing athletic contests on hostility. *Sociometry, 34,* 90–93.

Gollwitzer, P. M. (1990). Action phases and mind-sets. In E. T. Higgins & R. M. Sorrentino (Eds.), *Handbook of motivation and cognition: Foundations of social behavior* (Vol. 2, pp. 53–92). New York: Guilford.

Gollwitzer, P. M. (1999). Implementation intentions: Strong effects of simple plans. *American Psychologist, 54,* 493–503.

Gollwitzer, P. M, & Brandstätter, V. (1997). Implementation intentions and effective goal pursuit. *Journal of Personality and Social Psychology, 73,* 186–199.

Goranson, R. E. (1970). Media violence and aggressive behavior: A review of experimental research. In L.

Berkowitz (Ed.), *Advances in experimental social psychology* (Vol. 5). New York: Academic Press.

Gosling, S. D. (2001). From mice to men: What can we learn about personality from animal research? *Psychological Bulletin, 127,* 45–86.

Gotlib, I. H. (1983). Perception and recall of interpersonal feedback: Negative bias in depression. *Cognitive Therapy and Research, 7,* 399–412.

Gottesman, I. I., Carey, G., & Hanson, D. R. (1983). Pearls and perils in epigenetic psychopathology. In S. B. Guze, E. J. Earls, & J. E. Barrett (Eds.), *Childhood psychopathology and development* (pp. 287–300). New York: Raven.

Gottesman, I. I., & Shields, J. (1972). *Schizophrenia and genetics.* New York: Academic Press.

Gould, R. L. (1980). Transformations during early and middle adult years. In N. J. Smelser & E. H. Erikson (Eds.), *Themes of work and love in adulthood* (pp. 213–237). Cambridge, MA: Harvard University Press.

Grammer, K., & Thornhill, R. (1994). Human facial attractiveness and sexual selection: The role of symmetry and averageness. *Journal of Comparative Psychology, 108,* 233–242.

Gray, J. (1992). *Men are from Mars, women are from Venus: A practical guide for improving communication and getting what you want in your relationships.* New York: HarperCollins.

Gray, J. A. (1982). *The neuropsychology of anxiety: An enquiry into the functions of the septo-hippocampal system.* New York: Oxford University Press.

Gray, J. A. (1987). Perspectives on anxiety and impulsivity: A commentary. *Journal of Research in Personality, 21,* 493–509.

Gray, J. A. (1990). Brain systems that mediate both emotion and cognition. *Cognition and Emotion, 4,* 269–288.

Gray, J. A. (1991). The neuropsychology of temperament. In J. Strelau & A. Angleitner (Eds.), *Explorations in temperament: International perspectives on theory and measurement* (pp. 105–128). New York: Plenum.

Gray, J. A. (1994a). Personality dimensions and emotion systems. In P. Ekman & R. J. Davidson (Eds.), *The nature of emotion: Fundamental questions* (pp. 329–331). New York: Oxford University Press.

Gray, J. A. (1994b). Three fundamental emotion systems. In P. Ekman & R. J. Davidson (Eds.), *The nature of emotion: Fundamental questions* (pp. 243–247). New York: Oxford University Press.

Gray, J. D., & Silver, R. C. (1990). Opposite sides of the same coin: Former spouses' divergent perspectives in coping with their divorce. *Journal of Personality and Social Psychology, 59,* 1180–1191.

Graziano, W. G., & Eisenberg, N. H. (1999). Agreeableness as a dimension of personality. In R. Hogan, J. Johnson, & S. Briggs (Eds.), *Handbook of personality* (pp. 795–825). San Diego, CA: Academic Press.

Graziano, W. G., Jensen-Campbell, L. A., & Hair, E. C. (1996). Perceiving interpersonal conflict and reacting to it: The case for agreeableness. *Journal of Personality and Social Psychology, 70,* 820–835.

Green, J. D., & Campbell, W. K. (2000). Attachment and exploration in adults: Chronic and contextual accessibility. *Personality and Social Psychology Bulletin, 26,* 452–461.

Greene, D. L., & Winter, D. G. (1971). Motives, involvements, and leadership among Black college students. *Journal of Personality, 39,* 319–332.

Greenberg, J., & Musham, C. (1981). Avoiding and seeking self-focused attention. *Journal of Research in Personality, 15,* 191–200.

Greenberg, J., Pyszczynski, T., & Paisley, C. (1984). Effect of extrinsic incentives on use of test anxiety as an anticipatory attributional defense: Playing it cool when the stakes are high. *Journal of Personality and Social Psychology, 47,* 1136–1145.

Greenberg, J., Pyszczynski, T., & Solomon, S. (1982). The self-serving attributional bias: Beyond self-presentation. *Journal of Experimental Social Psychology, 18,* 56–67.

Greenberg, J., Pyszczynski, T., & Solomon, S. (1986). The causes and consequences of a need for self-esteem: A terror management theory. In R. F. Baumeister (Ed.), *Public self and private self* (pp. 189–212). New York: Springer-Verlag.

Greenberg, J., Solomon, S., & Pyszczynski, T. (1997). Terror management theory of self-esteem and social behavior: Empirical assessments and conceptual refinements. In M. P. Zanna (Ed.), *Advances in experimental social psychology* (Vol. 29, pp. 61–139). New York: Academic Press.

Greenfield, N. S., & Sternbach, R. A. (1972). *Handbook of psychophysiology.* New York: Holt, Rinehart, & Winston.

Greenwald, A. G., & Banaji, M. R. (1989). The self as a memory system: Powerful, but ordinary. *Journal of Personality and Social Psychology, 57,* 41–54.

Greenwald, A. G., & Pratkanis, R. A. (1984). The self. In R. S. Wyer, Jr., & T. K. Srull (Eds.), *Handbook of social cognition* (Vol. 3). Hillsdale, NJ: Erlbaum.

Greer, S., & Morris, T. (1975). Psychological attributes of women who develop breast cancer: A controlled study. *Journal of Psychosomatic Research, 19,* 147–153.

Griffin, D., & Bartholomew, K. (1994). Models of the self and other: Fundamental dimensions underlying measures of adult attachment. *Journal of Personality and Social Psychology, 67,* 430–445.

Grigsby, J., & Stevens, D. (2000). *Neurodynamics of personality.* New York: Guilford.

Grings, W. W. (1973). The role of consciousness and cognition in autonomic behavior change. In F. J. McGuigan & R. Schoonover (Eds.), *The psychophysiology of thinking.* New York: Academic Press.

Grolnick, W. S., & Ryan, R. M. (1989). Parent styles associated with children's self-regulation and competence in school. *Journal of Educational Psychology, 81,* 143–154.

Gruber, A. J., & Pope, H. G., Jr. (2000). Psychiatric and medical effects of anabolic-androgenic steroid use in women. *Psychotherapy and Psychosomatics, 69,* 19–26.

Gruen, R. J., & Mendelsohn, G. (1986). Emotional responses to affective displays in others: The distinction between empathy and sympathy. *Journal of Personality and Social Psychology, 51,* 609–614.

Guisinger, S., & Blatt, S. J. (1994). Individuality and relatedness: Evolution of a fundamental dialectic. *American Psychologist, 49,* 104–111.

Gurin, P., Gurin, G., Lao, R. C., & Beattie, M. (1969). Internal-external control in the motivational dynamics of Negro youth. *Journal of Social Issues, 25,* 29–53.

Gutierres, S. E., Kenrick, D. T., & Partch, J. J. (1999). Beauty, dominance, and the mating game: Contrast effects in self-assessment reflect gender differences in mate selection. *Personality and Social Psychology Bulletin, 25,* 1126–1134.

Haaga, D. A. F., Dyck, M. J., & Ernst, D. (1991). Empirical status of cognitive theory of depression. *Psychological Bulletin, 110,* 215–236.

Haan, N. (1981). Common dimensions of personality development: Early adolescence to middle life. In D. H. Eichorn, J. A. Clausen, N. Haan, M. P. Honzik, & P. H. Mussen (Eds.), *Present and past in middle life* (pp. 117–151). New York: Academic Press.

Haas, H. A. (2002). Extending the search for folk personality constructs: The dimensionality of the personality-relevant proverb domain. *Journal of Personality and Social Psychology, 82,* 594–609.

Hackett, G., & Horan, J. J. (1979). Partial component analysis of a comprehensive smoking program. *Addictive Behaviors, 4,* 259–262.

Haemmerlie, F. M., & Montgomery, R. L. (1984). Purposefully biased interactions: Reducing heterosocial anxiety through self-perception theory. *Journal of Personality and Social Psychology, 47,* 900–908.

Hall, C. S., & Van de Castle, R. L. (1963). An empirical investigation of the castration complex in dreams. *Journal of Personality, 33,* 20–29.

Hall, J. F. (1966). *The psychology of learning.* New York: Lippincott.

Hall, R. V., Lund, D., & Jackson, D. (1968). Effects of teacher attention on study behavior. *Journal of Applied Behavior Analysis, 1,* 1–12.

Halpern, J. (1977). Projection: A test of the psychoanalytic hypothesis. *Journal of Abnormal Psychology, 86,* 536–542.

Halverson, C. F., Jr., Kohnstamm, G. A., & Martin, R. P. (Eds.). (1994). *The developing structure of temperament and personality from infancy to adulthood.* Hillsdale, NJ: Erlbaum.

Hamer, D. H., Hu, S., Magnuson, V. L., Hu, N., & Pattatucci, A. M. L. (1993). A linkage between DNA markers on the X chromosome and male sexual orientation. *Science, 261,* 321–327.

Hamilton, J. C., Greenberg, J., Pyszczynski, T., & Cather, C. (1993). A self-regulatory perspective on psychopathology and psychotherapy. *Journal of Psychotherapy Integration, 3,* 205–248.

Hamilton, W. D. (1964). The genetical evolution of social behavior. *Journal of Theoretical Biology, 7,* 1–52.

Hampson, S. E., Andrews, J. A., Barckley, M., Lichtenstein, E., & Lee, M. E. (2000). Conscientiousness, perceived risk, and risk-reduction behaviors: A preliminary study. *Health Psychology, 19,* 496–500.

Hansenne, M., Pinto, E., Pitchot, W., Reggers, J., Scantamburlo, G., Moor, M., & Ansseau, M. (2002). Further evidence on the relationship between dopamine and novelty seeking: A neuroendocrine study. *Personality and Individual Differences, 33,* 967–977.

Harackiewicz, J. M. (1979). The effects of reward contingency and performance feedback on intrinsic motivation. *Journal of Personality and Social Psychology, 37,* 1352–1363.

Harmon-Jones, E., & Allen, J. J. (1997). Behavioral activation sensitivity and resting frontal EEG asymmetry: Covariation of putative indicators related to risk for mood disorders. *Journal of Abnormal Psychology, 106,* 159–163.

Harris, C. R. (2002). Sexual and romantic jealousy in heterosexual and homosexual adults. *Psychological Science, 13,* 7–12.

Harris, J. R. (1995). Where is the child's environment? A group socialization theory of development. *Psychological Review, 102,* 458–489.

Harrison, R. J., Connor, D. F., Nowak, C., Nash, K., & Melloni, R. H., Jr. (2000). Chronic anabolic-androgenic steroid treatment during adolescence increases ante-rior hypothalamic vasopressin and aggression in intact hamsters. *Psychoneuroendocrinology, 25,* 317–338.

Hart, D., Keller, M., Edelstein, W., & Hofmann, V. (1998). Childhood personality influences on social-cognitive development: A longitudinal study. *Journal of Personality and Social Psychology, 74,* 1278–1289.

Hart, H. M., McAdams, D. P., Hirsch, B. J., & Bauer, J. J. (2001). Generativity and social involvement among African Americans and white adults. *Journal of Research in Personality, 35,* 208–230.

Hartmann, H. (1958). *Ego psychology and the problem of adaptation.* New York: International Universities Press. (Originally published, 1939)

Hartmann, H. (1964). *Essays on ego psychology: Selected problems in psychoanalytic theory.* New York: International Universities Press.

Haslam, N. (1994). Mental representation of social relationships: Dimensions, laws, or categories? *Journal of Personality and Social Psychology, 67,* 575–584.

Hassin, R. R., Bargh, J. A., & Uleman, J. S. (2002). Spontaneous causal inferences. *Journal of Experimental Social Psychology, 38,* 515–522.

Hathaway, S. R., & McKinley, J. C. (1943). *MMPI manual.* New York: Psychological Corporation.

Haugtvedt, C. P., & Petty, R. E. (1992). Personality and persuasion: Need for cognition moderates the persistence and resistance of attitude changes. *Journal of Personality and Social Psychology, 63,* 308–319.

Hauser, S. T. (1976). Loevinger's model and measure of ego development: A critical review. *Psychological Bulletin, 83,* 928–955.

Haviland, J. M., McGuire, T. R., & Rothbaum, P. A. (1983). A critique of Plomin and Foch's "A twin study of objectively assessed personality in childhood." *Journal of Personality and Social Psychology, 45,* 633–640.

Hayes, S. C., Rincover, A., & Volosin, D. (1980). Variables influencing the acquisition and maintenance of aggressive behavior: Modeling versus sensory reinforcement. *Journal of Abnormal Psychology, 89,* 254–262.

Hayes-Roth, B., & Hayes-Roth, F. (1979). A cognitive model of planning. *Cognitive Science, 3,* 275–310.

Haynes, S. N., & O'Brien, W. H. (2000). *Principles and practice of behavioral assessment.* Amsterdam, The Netherlands: Kluwer.

Hazan, C., & Shaver, P. R. (1987). Romantic love conceptualized as an attachment process. *Journal of Personality and Social Psychology, 52,* 511–524.

Hazan, C., & Shaver, P. R. (1990). Love and work: An attachment-theoretical perspective. *Journal of Personality and Social Psychology, 59,* 270–280.

Hazan, C., & Shaver, P. R. (1994). Attachment as an organizational framework for research on close relationships. *Psychological Inquiry, 5,* 1–22.

Hazen, N. L., & Durrett, M. E. (1982). Relationship of security of attachment to exploration and cognitive mapping abilities in 2-year-olds. *Developmental Psychology, 18,* 751–759.

Heath, A. C., Neale, M. C., Kessler, R. C., Eaves, L. J., & Kendler, K. S. (1992). Evidence for genetic influences on personality from self-reports and informant ratings. *Journal of Personality and Social Psychology, 63,* 85–96.

Heckhausen, H. (1967). *The anatomy of achievement motivation.* New York: Academic Press.

Heckhausen, H., & Gollwitzer, P. M. (1987). Thought contents and cognitive functioning in motivational versus volitional states of mind. *Motivation and Emotion, 11,* 101–120.

Heckhausen, H., Schmalt, H. D., & Schneider, K. (1985). *Achievement motivation in perspective.* New York: Academic Press.

Heiby, E. M. (1982). A self-reinforcement questionnaire. *Behaviour Research and Therapy, 20,* 397–401.

Heider, F. (1944). Social perception and phenomenal causation. *Psychological Review, 51,* 358–374.

Heider, F. (1958). *The psychology of interpersonal relations.* New York: Wiley.

Heilbrun, K. S. (1980). Silverman's psychodynamic activation: A failure to replicate. *Journal of Abnormal Psychology, 89,* 560–566.

Helgeson, V. S. (1994). Relation of agency and communion to well-being: Evidence and potential explanations. *Psychological Bulletin, 116,* 412–428.

Helgeson, V. S., & Fritz, H. L. (1998). A theory of unmitigated communion. *Personality and Social Psychology Review, 2,* 173–183.

Helgeson, V. S., & Fritz, H. L. (1999). Unmitigated agency and unmitigated communion: Distinctions from agency and communion. *Journal of Research in Personality, 33,* 131–158.

Helgeson, V. S., & Sharpsteen, D. J. (1987). Perceptions of danger in achievement and affiliation situations: An extension of the Pollak and Gilligan versus Benton et al. debate. *Journal of Personality and Social Psychology, 53,* 727–733.

Heller, M. S., & Polsky, S. (1975). *Studies in violence and television.* New York: American Broadcasting Companies.

Helmreich, R. L., LeFan, J. H., Bakeman, R., Wilhelm, J., & Radloff, R. (1972). The Tektite 2 human behavior program. *JSAS Catalog of Selected Documents in Psychology, 2,* 13 (MS no. 70).

Helson, R., Kwan, V. S. Y., John, O. P., & Jones, C. (2002). The growing evidence for personality change in adulthood: Findings from research with personality inventories. *Journal of Research in Personality, 36,* 287–306.

Helson, R., & Moane, G. (1987). Personality change in women from college to midlife. *Journal of Personality and Social Psychology, 53,* 176–186.

Helson, R., & Roberts, B. W. (1994). Ego development and personality change in adulthood. *Journal of Personality and Social Psychology, 66,* 911–920.

Helson, R., & Srivastava, S. (2002). Creative and wise people: Similarities, differences, and how they develop. *Personality and Social Psychology Bulletin, 28,* 1430–1440.

Henderlong, J., & Lepper, M. R. (2002). The effects of praise on children's intrinsic motivation: A review and synthesis. *Psychological Bulletin, 128,* 774–795.

Henriques, J. B., & Davidson, R. J. (1990). Asymmetrical brain electrical activity discriminates between previously depressed subjects and healthy controls. *Journal of Abnormal Psychology, 99,* 22–31.

Henriques, J. B., & Davidson, R. J. (1991). Left frontal hypoactivation in depression. *Journal of Abnormal Psychology, 100,* 535–545.

Herbst, J. H., Zonderman, A. B., McCrae, R. R., & Costa, P. T., Jr. (2000). Do the dimensions of the temperament and character inventory map a simple genetic architecture? Evidence from molecular genetics and factor analysis. *American Journal of Psychiatry, 157,* 1285–1290.

Herr, P. M., Sherman, S. J., & Fazio, R. H. (1983). On the consequences of priming: Assimilation and contrast effects. *Journal of Experimental Social Psychology, 19,* 323–340.

Hersch, P. D., & Scheibe, K. E. (1967). Reliability and validity of internal-external control as personality dimensions. *Journal of Consulting Psychology, 31,* 609–613.

Hersen, M., & Bellack, A. (Eds.). (1976). *Behavioral assessment.* New York: Pergamon.

Heschl, A. (2002). *The intelligent genome: On the origin of the human mind by mutation and selection.* New York: Springer.

Hess, E. H. (1973). *Imprinting.* New York: Van Nostrand Reinhold.

Hewitt, P. L., & Genest, M. (1990). The ideal self: Schematic processing of perfectionistic content in dysphoric university students. *Journal of Personality and Social Psychology, 59,* 802–808.

Higgins, E. T. (1987). Self-discrepancy: A theory relating self and affect. *Psychological Review, 94,* 319–340.

Higgins, E. T. (1990). Personality, social psychology, and person–situation relations: Standards and knowledge activation as a common language. In L. A. Pervin (Ed.), *Handbook of personality: Theory and research* (pp. 301–338). New York: Guilford.

Higgins, E. T. (1997). Beyond pleasure and pain. *American Psychologist, 52,* 1280–1300.

Higgins, E. T., & Bargh, J. A. (1987). Social cognition and social perception. *Annual Review of Psychology, 38,* 369–425.

Higgins, E. T., Bond, R. N., Klein, R., & Strauman, T. (1986). Self-discrepancies and emotional vulnerability: How magnitude, accessibility and type of discrepancy influence affect. *Journal of Personality and Social Psychology, 51,* 1–15.

Higgins, E. T., & Brendl, C. M. (1995). Accessibility and applicability: Some "activation rules" influencing judgment. *Journal of Experimental Social Psychology, 31,* 218–243.

Higgins, E. T., King, G. A., & Mavin, G. H. (1982). Individual construct accessibility and subjective impressions and recall. *Journal of Personality and Social Psychology, 43,* 35–47.

Higgins, R. L., Snyder, C. R., & Berglas, S. (Eds.). (1990). *Self-handicapping: The paradox that isn't.* New York: Plenum.

Higgins, S. T., Wong, C. J., Badger, G. J., Haug Ogden, D. E., & Dantona, R. L. (2000). Contingent reinforcement increases cocaine abstinence during outpatient treatment and 1 year of follow-up. *Journal of Consulting and Clinical Psychology, 68,* 64–72.

Hilgard, E. R., & Hilgard, J. R. (1983). *Hypnosis in the relief of pain* (Rev. ed.). Los Altos, CA: Kaufman.

Hill, C. A. (1987). Affiliation motivation: People who need people . . . but in different ways. *Journal of Personality and Social Psychology, 52,* 1008–1018.

Hill, C. A. (1991). Seeking emotional support: The influence of affiliative need and partner warmth. *Journal of Personality and Social Psychology, 60,* 112–121.

Hill, T., Lewicki, P., Czyzewska, M., & Boss, A. (1989). Self-perpetuating development of encoding biases in person perception. *Journal of Personality and Social Psychology, 57,* 373–387.

Hillix, W. A., & Marx, M. H. (1960). Response strengthening by information and effect on human learning. *Journal of Experimental Psychology, 60,* 97–102.

Hilton, N. Z., Harris, G. T., & Rice, M. E. (2000). The functions of aggression by male teenagers. *Journal of Personality and Social Psychology, 79,* 988–994.

Hinkley, K., & Andersen, S. M. (1996). The working self-concept in transference: Significant-other activation and self change. *Journal of Personality and Social Psychology, 71,* 1279–1295.

Hiroto, D. S., & Seligman, M. E. P. (1975). Generality of learned helplessness in man. *Journal of Personality and Social Psychology, 31,* 311–327.

Hobfoll, S. E., Rom, T., & Segal, B. (1989). Sensation seeking, anxiety, and risk taking in the Israeli context. In S. Einstein (Ed.), *Drugs and alcohol use: Issues and factors* (pp. 53–59). New York: Plenum.

Hobson, J. A. (1988). *The dreaming brain.* New York: Basic Books.

Hodgins, H. S., Koestner, R., & Duncan, N. (1996). On the compatibility of autonomy and relatedness. *Personality and Social Psychology Bulletin, 22,* 227–237.

Hodgkinson, S., Sherrington, R., Gurling, H., Marchbanks, R., & Reeders, S. (1987). Molecular genetic evidence for heterogeneity in manic depression. *Nature, 325,* 805–806.

Hoffman, E. (1988). *The right to be human: A biography of Abraham Maslow.* Los Angeles: Jeremy P. Tarcher.

Hoffman, E. (1994). *The drive for self: Alfred Adler and the founding of individual psychology.* Reading, MA: Addison-Wesley.

Hoffman, L. W. (1991). The influence of the family environment on personality: Accounting for sibling differences. *Psychological Bulletin, 110,* 187–203.

Hofstee, W. K. B., de Raad, B., & Goldberg, L. R. (1992). Integration of the big five and circumplex approaches to trait structure. *Journal of Personality and Social Psychology, 63,* 146–163.

Hogan, R., DeSoto, C. B., & Solano, C. (1977). Traits, tests, and personality research. *American Psychologist, 32,* 255–264.

Hogan, R., & Nicholson, R. A. (1988). The meaning of personality test scores. *American Psychologist, 43,* 621–626.

Hogansen, J., & Lanning, K. (2001). Five factors in sentence-completion test categories: Toward rapprochement between trait and maturational approaches to personality. *Journal of Research in Personality, 35,* 449–462.

Hokanson, J. E., & Burgess, M. (1962a). The effects of status, type of frustration, and aggression on vascular processes. *Journal of Abnormal and Social Psychology, 65,* 232–237.

Hokanson, J. E., & Burgess, M. (1962b). The effects of three types of aggression on vascular processes. *Journal of Abnormal and Social Psychology, 64,* 446–449.

Hokanson, J. E., Burgess, M., & Cohen, M. F. (1963). Effects of displaced aggression on systolic blood pressure. *Journal of Abnormal and Social Psychology, 67,* 214–218.

Hokanson, J. E., & Edelman, R. (1966). Effects of three social responses on vascular processes. *Journal of Personality and Social Psychology, 3,* 442–447.

Hokanson, J. E., & Shetler, S. (1961). The effect of overt aggression on physiological arousal. *Journal of Abnormal and Social Psychology, 63,* 446–448.

Hokanson, J. E., Willers, K. R., & Koropsak, E. (1968). The modification of autonomic responses during aggressive interchanges. *Journal of Personality, 36,* 386–404.

Holden, K. B., & Rotter, J. B. (1962). A nonverbal measure of extinction in skill and chance situations. *Journal of Experimental Psychology, 63,* 519–520.

Holmes, D. (1972). Aggression, displacement and guilt. *Journal of Personality and Social Psychology, 21,* 296–301.

Holmes, D. S. (1981). Existence of classical projection and the stress-reducing function of attribution projection: A reply to Sherwood. *Psychological Bulletin, 90,* 460–466.

Holmes, D. S., & Houston, B. K. (1974). Effectiveness of situational redefinition and affective isolation in coping with stress. *Journal of Personality and Social Psychology, 29,* 212–218.

Holt, R. (1966). Measuring libidinal and aggressive motives and their controls by means of the Rorschach test. In D. Levine (Ed.), *Nebraska symposium on motivation.* Lincoln: University of Nebraska Press.

Holt, R. R. (1980). Loevinger's measure of ego development: Reliability and national norms for male and female short forms. *Journal of Personality and Social Psychology, 39,* 909–920.

Holtzworth-Munroe, A. (1992). Social skill deficits in maritally violent men: Interpreting the data using a social information-processing model. *Clinical Psychology Review, 12,* 605–617.

Holyoak, K. J., Koh, K., & Nisbett, R. E. (1989). A theory of conditioning: Inductive learning within rule-based default hierarchies. *Psychological Review, 96,* 315–340.

Holyoak, K. J., & Spellman, B. A. (1993). Thinking. *Annual Review of Psychology, 44,* 265–315.

Hopkin, K. (1995). Programmed cell death: A switch to the cytoplasm? *Journal of NIH Research, 7,* 39–41.

Hoppe, C. (1972). *Ego development and conformity behavior.* Unpublished doctoral dissertation, Washington University, St. Louis.

Hormuth, S. E. (1990). *The ecology of the self: Relocation and self-concept change.* Cambridge, England: Cambridge University Press.

Horner, M. S. (1973). A psychological barrier to achievement in women: The motive to avoid success. In D. C. McClelland & R. S. Steele (Eds.), *Human motivation: A book of readings.* Morristown, NJ: General Learning Press.

Horney, K. (1937). *Neurotic personality of our times.* New York: Norton.

Horney, K. (1939). *New ways in psychoanalysis.* New York: Norton.

Horney, K. (1942). *Self-analysis.* New York: Norton.

Horney, K. (1945). *Our inner conflicts.* New York: Norton.

Horney, K. (1950). *Neurosis and human growth.* New York: Norton.

Horney, K. (1967). *Feminine psychology.* New York: Norton.

Horowitz, M. J. (1986). *Stress response syndromes* (2nd ed.). New York: Aronson.

Horvath, P., & Zuckerman, M. (1993). Sensation seeking, risk appraisal, and risky behavior. *Personality and Individual Differences, 14,* 41–52.

Hovland, C. I. (1937). The generalization of conditioning responses. I. The sensory generalization of conditioned responses with varying frequencies of tone. *Journal of General Psychology, 17,* 125–148.

Howard, G. S. (1990). On the construct validity of self-reports: What do the data say? *American Psychologist, 45,* 292–294.

Howard, G. S., Maxwell, S. E., Weiner, R. L., Boynton, K. S., & Rooney, W. M. (1980). Is a behavioral measure the best estimate of behavioral parameters? Perhaps not. *Applied Psychological Measurement, 4,* 293–311.

Hsee, C. K., & Abelson, R. P. (1991). The velocity relation: Satisfaction as a function of the first derivative of outcome over time. *Journal of Personality and Social Psychology, 60,* 341–347.

Hubbard, J. A., Dodge, K. A., Cillessen, A. H. N., Coie, J. D., & Schwartz, D. (2001). The dyadic nature of social information processing in boys' reactive and proactive aggression. *Journal of Personality and Social Psychology, 80,* 268–280.

Hubbard, R. (1995). Genomania and health. *American Scientist, 83,* 8–10.

Huesmann, L. R. (1988). An information-processing model for the development of aggression. *Aggressive Behavior, 14,* 13–24.

Hull, C. L. (1943). *Principles of behavior.* New York: Appleton-Century-Crofts.

Hull, J. G. (1981). A self-awareness model of the causes and effects of alcohol consumption. *Journal of Abnormal Psychology, 90,* 586–600.

Hull, J. G., & Rielly, N. P. (1986). An information-processing approach to alcohol use and its consequences. In R. E. Ingram (Ed.), *Information processing approaches to clinical psychology.* New York: Academic Press.

Humphreys, L. G. (1939). The effect of random alteration of reinforcement on the acquisition and extinction of conditioned eyelid reactions. *Journal of Experimental Psychology, 15,* 141–158.

Hutchison, K. E., McGeary, J., Smolen, A., Bryan, A., & Swift, R. M. (2002). The DRD4 VNTR polymorphism moderates craving after alcohol consumption. *Health Psychology, 21,* 139–146.

Hy, L. X., & Loevinger, J. (1996). *Measuring ego development* (2nd ed.). Mahwah, NJ: Erlbaum.

Hyman, I. E., Husband, T. H., & Billings, F. J. (1995). False memories of childhood experiences. *Applied Cognitive Psychology, 9,* 181–197.

Hymbaugh, K., & Garrett, J. (1974). Sensation seeking among skydivers. *Perceptual and Motor Skills, 38,* 118.

Ingram, R. E. (Ed.). (1986). *Information-processing approaches to clinical psychology.* New York: Academic Press.

Isaacs, E. A., & Clark, H. H. (1987). References in conversation between experts and novices. *Journal of Experimental Psychology: General, 116,* 26–37.

Isabella, R. A., Belsky, J., & von Eye, A. (1989). Origins of infant–mother attachment: An examination of interactional synchrony during the infant's first year. *Developmental Psychology, 25,* 12–21.

Jacklin, C. N., Maccoby, E. E., & Doering, C. H. (1983). Neonatal sex-steroid hormones and timidity in 6–18-month-old boys and girls. *Developmental Psychobiology, 16,* 163–168.

Jackson, D. N. (1984). *Personality Research Form manual* (3rd ed.). Port Huron, MI: Research Psychologists Press.

Jackson, D. N., & Messick, S. (Eds.). (1967). *Problems in assessment.* New York: McGraw-Hill.

Jacob, S., McClintock, M. K., Zelano, B., & Ober, C. (2002). Paternally inherited HLA alleles are associated with women's choice of male odor. *Nature Genetics, 30,* 175–179.

James, W. (1890). *The principles of psychology* (Vol. 2). New York: Holt.

Jang, K. L., Hu, S., Livesley, W. J., Angleitner, A., Riemann, R., Ando, J., Ono, Y., Vernon, P. A., & Hamer, D. H. (2001). Covariance structure of neuroticism and agreeableness: A twin and molecular genetic analysis of the role of the serotonin transporter gene. *Journal of Personality and Social Psychology, 81,* 295–304.

Jang, K. L., Livesley, W. J., & Vernon, P. A. (1996). Heritability of the big five personality dimensions and their facets: A twin study. *Journal of Personality, 64,* 577–591.

Jang, K. L., McCrae, R. R., Angleitner, A., Riemann, R., & Livesley, W. J. (1998). Heritability of facet-level traits in a cross-cultural twin sample: Support for a hierar-chical model of personality. *Journal of Personality and Social Psychology, 74,* 1556–1565.

Janoff-Bulman, R. (1992). *Shattered assumptions: Towards a new psychology of trauma.* New York: Free Press.

Janoff-Bulman, R., & Leggatt, H. K. (2002). Culture and social obligation: When "shoulds" are perceived as "wants." *Journal of Research in Personality, 36,* 260–270.

Jeffery, R. W. (1976). The influence of symbolic and motor rehearsal on observational learning. *Journal of Research in Personality, 10,* 116–127.

Jenkins, H. M. (1962). Resistance to extinction when partial reinforcement is followed by regular reinforcement. *Journal of Experimental Psychology, 64,* 441–450.

Jenkins, S. R. (1987). Need for achievement and women's careers over 14 years: Evidence for occupational structure effects. *Journal of Personality and Social Psychology, 53,* 922–932.

Jenkins, S. R. (1994). Need for power and women's careers over 14 years: Structural power, job satisfaction, and motive change. *Journal of Personality and Social Psychology, 66,* 155–165.

Jensen, M. B. (1987). Psychobiological factors predicting the course of breast cancer. *Journal of Personality, 55,* 317–342.

Jensen-Campbell, L. A., Adams, R., Perry, D. G., Workman, K. A., Furdella, J. Q., & Egan, S. K. (2002). Agreeableness, extraversion, and peer relations in early adolescence: Winning friends and deflecting aggression. *Journal of Research in Personality, 36,* 224–251.

Jensen-Campbell, L. A., & Graziano, W. G. (2001). Agreeableness as a moderator of interpersonal conflict. *Journal of Personality, 69,* 323–362.

Jensen-Campbell, L. A., Graziano, W. G., & West, S. G. (1995). Dominance, prosocial orientation, and female preferences: Do nice guys really finish last? *Journal of Personality and Social Psychology, 68,* 427–440.

Jessor, R., Costa, F., Jessor, L., & Donovan, J. E. (1983). Time of first intercourse: A prospective study. *Journal of Personality and Social Psychology, 44,* 608–626.

Jessor, S. L., & Jessor, R. (1975). Transition from virginity to nonvirginity among youth: A social-psychological study over time. *Developmental Psychology, 11,* 473–484.

Jockin, V., McGue, M., & Lykken, D. T. (1996). Personality and divorce: A genetic analysis. *Journal of Personality and Social Psychology, 71,* 288–299.

John, O. P. (1990). The big-five factor taxonomy: Dimensions of personality in the natural language and in questionnaires. In L. Pervin (Ed.), *Handbook of personality theory and research* (pp. 66–100). New York: Guilford.

John, O. P., & Robins, R. W. (1994). Accuracy and bias in self-perception: Individual differences in self-enhancement and the role of narcissism. *Journal of Personality and Social Psychology, 66,* 206–219.

Johnson, D. J., & Rusbult, C. E. (1989). Resisting temptation: Devaluation of alternative partners as a means of maintaining commitment in close relationships. *Journal of Personality and Social Psychology, 57,* 967–980.

Johnson, G. B. (1966). Penis envy? Or pencil needing? *Psychological Reports, 19,* 758.

Johnson, J. A., & Ostendorf, F. (1993). Clarification of the five-factor model with the abridged big five dimensional circumplex. *Journal of Personality and Social Psychology, 65,* 563–576.

Johnson, J. A., Germer, C. K., Efran, J. S., & Overton, W. F. (1988). Personality as the basis for theoretical predilections. *Journal of Personality and Social Psychology, 55,* 824–835.

Johnson, W., & Kieras, D. (1983). Representation-saving effects of prior knowledge in memory for simple technical prose. *Memory & Cognition, 11,* 456–466.

Jonas, E., Schimel, J., Greenberg, J., & Pyszczynski, T. (2002). The Scrooge effect: Evidence that mortality salience increases prosocial attitudes and behavior. *Personality and Social Psychology Bulletin, 28,* 1342–1353.

Jones, A., & Crandall, R. (1986). Validation of a short index of self-actualization. *Personality and Social Psychology Bulletin, 12,* 63–73.

Jones, E. E., & Berglas, S. (1978). Control of attributions about the self through self-handicapping strategies: The appeal of alcohol and the role of underachievement. *Personality and Social Psychology Bulletin, 4,* 200–206.

Jones, E. E., & Nisbett, R. E. (1971). The actor and the observer: Divergent perceptions of the causes of behavior. In E. E. Jones et al. (Eds.), *Attribution: Perceiving the causes of behavior.* Morristown, NJ: General Learning Press.

Jones, E. E., & Pittman, T. S. (1982). Toward a general theory of strategic self-presentation. In J. Suls (Ed.), *Psychological perspectives on the self* (Vol. 1). Hillsdale, NJ: Erlbaum.

Jones, M. C. (1924). A laboratory study of fear. *Pedagogical Seminar, 31,* 308–315.

Jones, M. C. (1968). Personality correlates and antecedents of drinking patterns in adult males. *Journal of Consulting and Clinical Psychology, 32,* 2–12.

Jones, M. C. (1971). Personality antecedents and correlates of drinking patterns in women. *Journal of Consulting and Clinical Psychology, 36,* 61–69.

Jones, W. H., Hobbes, S. A., & Hockenberg, D. (1982). Loneliness and social skills deficits. *Journal of Personality and Social Psychology, 42,* 682–689.

Jöreskog, K. G., & Sörbom, D. (1979). *Advances in factor analysis and structural equations.* Cambridge, MA: Abt Associates.

Jorm, A. F., Henderson, A. S., Jacomb, P. A., Christensen, H., Korten, A. E., Rodgers, B., Tan, X., & Easteal, S. (1998). An association study of a functional polymorphism of the serotonin transporter gene with personality and psychiatric symptoms. *Molecular Genetics, 1,* 1–4.

Jourard, S. M. (1974). *Healthy personality: An approach from the viewpoint of humanistic psychology.* New York: Macmillan.

Jung, C. G. (1933). *Psychological types.* New York: Harcourt, Brace, & World.

Jung, C. G. (1960). *The structure and dynamics of the psyche, Collected works* (Vol. 8). Princeton, NJ: Princeton University Press. (Originally published in German, 1926)

Jung, C. G. (1968). *Analytical psychology: Its theory and practice.* New York: Pantheon.

Juni, S. (1981). Maintaining anonymity vs. requesting feedback as a function of oral dependency. *Perceptual and Motor Skills, 52,* 239–242.

Juni, S., & Fischer, R. E. (1985). Religiosity and preoedipal fixation. *Journal of Genetic Psychology, 146,* 27–35.

Juni, S., & Lo Cascio, R. (1985). Preference for counseling and psychotherapy as related to preoedipal fixation. *Psychological Reports, 56,* 431–438.

Juni, S., Masling, J., & Brannon, R. (1979). Interpersonal touching and orality. *Journal of Personality Assessment, 43,* 235–237.

Jussim, L. (1991). Social perception and social reality: A reflection–construction model. *Psychology Review, 98,* 54–73.

Kagan, J. (1994). *Galen's prophecy: Temperament in human nature.* New York: Basic Books.

Kahn, S., Zimmerman, G., Csikszentmihalyi, M., & Getzels, J. W. (1985). Relations between identity in young adulthood and intimacy at midlife. *Journal of Personality and Social Psychology, 49,* 1316–1322.

Kamin, L. J. (1968). Attention-like processes in classical conditioning. In M. R. Jones (Ed.), *Miami symposium on the prediction of behavior: Aversive stimuli* (pp. 9–32). Coral Gables, FL: University of Miami Press.

Kanayama, G., Gruber, A. J., Pope, H. G., Jr., Borowiecki, J. J., & Hudson, J. I. (2001). Over-the-counter drug use in gymnasiums: An underrecognized substance abuse problem? *Psychotherapy and Psychosomatics, 70,* 137–140.

Kanfer, F. H. (1977). The many faces of self-control, or behavior modification changes its focus. In R. B. Stuart (Ed.), *Behavioral self-management: Strategies, techniques, and outcomes.* New York: Brunner/Mazel.

Kanfer, F. H., & Busemeyer, J. R. (1982). The use of problem-solving and decision-making in behavior therapy. *Clinical Psychology Review, 2,* 239–266.

Kanfer, F. H., & Hagerman, S. (1981). The role of self-regulation. In L. P. Rehm (Ed.), *Behavior therapy for depression: Present status and future directions.* New York: Academic Press.

Kanfer, F. H., & Hagerman, S. M. (1985). Behavior therapy and the information-processing paradigm. In S. Reiss & R. R. Bootzin (Eds.), *Theoretical issues in behavior therapy.* New York: Academic Press.

Kanfer, F. H., Karoly, P., & Newman, A. (1975). Reduction of children's fear of the dark by competence-related and situational threat-related verbal cues. *Journal of Consulting and Clinical Psychology, 43,* 251–258.

Kanfer, F. H., & Marston, A. R. (1963). Human reinforcement: Vicarious and direct. *Journal of Experimental Psychology, 65,* 292–296.

Kanfer, F. H., & Saslow, G. (1965). Behavioral analysis: An alternative to diagnostic classification. *Archives of General Psychiatry, 12,* 519–538.

Kanfer, F. H., & Schefft, B. K. (1988). *Guiding the process of therapeutic change.* Champaign, IL: Research Press.

Kaplan, A. G., & Bean, J. P. (1976). *Beyond sex-role stereotypes: Readings toward a psychology of androgyny.* Boston: Little, Brown.

Kaplan, A. G., & Sedney, M. A. (1980). *Psychology and sex roles: An androgynous perspective.* Boston: Little, Brown.

Kaplan, J. R., Manuck, S. B., Fontenot, M. B., & Mann, J. J. (2002), Central nervous system monoamine correlates of social dominance in cynomolgus monkeys (*Macaca fascicularis*). *Neuropsychopharmacology, 26,* 431–443.

Karylowski, J. J. (1990). Social reference points and accessibility of trait-related information in self–other similarity judgments. *Journal of Personality and Social Psychology, 58,* 975–983.

Kasser, T. (2002). *The high price of materialism.* Cambridge, MA: Bradford Books.

Kasser, T., Koestner, R., & Lekes, N. (2002). Early family experiences and adult values: A 26-year, prospective longitudinal study. *Personality and Social Psychology Bulletin, 28,* 826–835.

Kasser, T., & Ryan, R. M. (1993). A dark side of the American dream: Correlates of financial success as a central life aspiration. *Journal of Personality and Social Psychology, 65,* 410–422.

Katigbak, M. S., Church, A. T., Guanzon-Lapeña, Ma. A., Carlota, A. J., & del Pilar, G. H. (2002). Are indigenous personality dimensions culture specific? Philippine inventories and the five-factor model. *Journal of Personality and Social Psychology, 82,* 89–101.

Katsuragi, S., Kunugi, H., Sano, A., Tsutsumi, T., Isogawa, K., Nanko, S., & Akiyoshi, J. (1999). Association between serotonin transporter gene polymorphism and anxiety-related traits. *Biological Psychiatry, 45,* 368–370.

Kazdin, A. E. (1974). Effects of covert modeling and reinforcement on assertive behavior. *Journal of Abnormal Psychology, 83,* 240–252.

Kazdin, A. E. (1975). Covert modeling, imagery assessment, and assertive behavior. *Journal of Consulting and Clinical Psychology, 43,* 716–724.

Kazdin, A. E. (1977). *The token economy: A review and evaluation.* New York: Plenum.

Keane, T. M., Kolb, L. C., Kaloupek, D. G., Orr, S. P., Blanchard, E. B., Thomas, R. G., Hsieh, F. Y., & Lavori, P. W. (1998). Utility of psychophysiological measurement in the diagnosis of posttraumatic stress disorder: Results from a Department of Veteran Affairs cooperative study. *Journal of Consulting and Clinical Psychology, 66,* 914–923.

Kelly, A. E., Klusas, J. A., von Weiss, R. T., & Kenny, C. (2001). What is it about revealing secrets that is beneficial? *Personality and Social Psychology Bulletin, 27,* 651–665.

Kelly, G. A. (1955). *The psychology of personal constructs* (Vols. 1 and 2). New York: Norton.

Kelly, G. A. (1962). Europe's matrix of decisions. In M. R. Jones (Ed.), *Nebraska symposium on motivation* (Vol. 10). Lincoln: University of Nebraska Press.

Kelly, G. A. (1969). In whom confide: On whom depend for what? In B. Maher (Ed.), *Clinical psychology and personality.* New York: Wiley.

Kelso, J. A. S. (Ed.). (1982). *Human motor behavior: An introduction.* Hillsdale, NJ: Erlbaum.

Kendler, K. S. (1997). Social support: A genetic–epidemiological analysis. *American Journal of Psychiatry, 154,* 1398–1404.

Kenford, S. L., Fiore, M. C., Jorenby, D. E., & Smith, S. S. (1994). Predicting smoking cessation: Who will quit with and without the nicotine patch. *Journal of the American Medical Association, 217,* 589–594.

Kenrick, D. T., Groth, G. E., Trost, M. R., & Sadalla, E. K. (1993). Integrating evolutionary and social exchange perspectives on relationships: Effects of gender, self-appraisal, and involvement level on mate selection criteria. *Journal of Personality and Social Psychology, 64,* 951–969.

Kenrick, D. T., & Keefe, R. C. (1992). Age preferences in mates reflect sex differences in human reproductive strategies. *Behavioral and Brain Sciences, 15,* 75–91.

Kenrick, D. T., Neuberg, S. L., Zierk, K. L., & Krones, J. M. (1994). Evolution and social cognition: Contrast effects as a function of sex, dominance, and physical attractiveness. *Personality and Social Psychology Bulletin, 20,* 210–217.

Kenrick, D. T., Sadalla, E. K., Groth, G., & Trost, M. R. (1990). Evolution, traits, and the stages of human courtship: Qualifying the parental investment model. *Journal of Personality, 58,* 97–116.

Kenrick, D. T., & Stringfield, D. O. (1980). Personality traits and the eye of the beholder: Crossing some traditional philosophical boundaries in the search for consistency in all of the people. *Psychological Review, 87,* 88–104.

Kenrick, D. T., Sundie, J. M., Nicastle, L. D, & Stone, G. O. (2001). Can one ever be too wealthy or too chaste? Searching for nonlinearities in mate judgment. *Journal of Personality and Social Psychology, 80,* 462–471.

Kernberg, O. (1976). *Borderline conditions and pathological narcissism.* New York: Jason Aronson.

Kernberg, O. (1980). *Internal world and external reality.* New York: Jason Aronson.

Kessler, R. C., Kendler, K. S., Heath, A., Neale, M. C., & Eaves, L. J. (1992). Social support, depressed mood, and adjustment to stress: A genetic epidemiologic investigation. *Journal of Personality and Social Psychology, 62,* 257–272.

Keyes, C. L. M., Shmotkin, D., & Ryff, C. D. (2002). Optimizing well-being: The empirical encounter of two traditions. *Journal of Personality and Social Psychology, 82,* 1007–1022.

Kihlstrom, J. F. (1987). The cognitive unconscious. *Science, 237,* 1445–1452.

Kimura, D. (1999). *Sex and cognition.* Cambridge, MA: MIT Press.

Kirkpatrick, L. A. (1998). God as a substitute attachment figure: A longitudinal study of adult attachment style and religious change in college students. *Personality and Social Psychology Bulletin, 24,* 961–973.

Kirkpatrick, L. A., & Davis, K. E. (1994). Attachment style, gender, and relationship stability: A longitudinal

analysis. *Journal of Personality and Social Psychology, 66,* 502–512.

Kirsch, I. (1985). Response expectancy as a determinant of experience and behavior. *American Psychologist, 40,* 1189–1202.

Kirsch, I. (1990). *Changing expectations: A key to effective psychotherapy.* Pacific Grove, CA: Brooks/Cole.

Kirsch, I., Mearns, J., & Catanzaro, S. J. (1990). Mood-regulation expectancies as determinants of dysphoria in college students. *Journal of Counseling Psychology, 37,* 306–312.

Kirschenbaum, D. S. (1985). Proximity and specificity of planning: A position paper. *Cognitive Therapy and Research, 9,* 489–506.

Kirschenbaum, D. S. (1987). Self-regulatory failure: A review with clinical implications. *Clinical Psychology Review, 7,* 77–104.

Kitcher, P. (1987). Précis of *Vaulting ambition: Sociobiology and the quest for human nature. Behavioral and Brain Sciences, 10,* 61–100.

Klein, G. S. (1970). *Perception, motives, and personality.* New York: Knopf.

Klein, G. S. (1972). The vital pleasures. In R. R. Holt & E. Peterfreund (Eds.), *Psychoanalysis and contemporary science: An annual of integrative and interdisciplinary studies* (Vol. I). New York: Macmillan.

Klein, J. (1987). *Our need for others and its roots in infancy.* London: Tavistock.

Klein, M. (1935). *The psychoanalysis of children.* New York: Norton.

Klein, M. (1955a). The psychoanalytic play technique. *American Journal of Orthopsychiatry, 112,* 418–422.

Klein, M. (1955b). The psychoanalytic play technique, its history and significance. In M. Klein, P. Heiman, & R. Money-Kyrle (Eds.), *New directions in psychoanalysis: The significance of infant conflict in the pattern of adult behavior.* New York: Basic Books.

Klinger, E. (1975). Consequences of commitment to and disengagement from incentives. *Psychological Review, 82,* 1–25.

Klinger, E. (1987). Current concerns and disengagement from incentives. In F. Halisch & J. Kuhl (Eds.), *Motivation, intention, and volition* (pp. 337–347). Berlin: Springer-Verlag.

Klion, R. E., & Leitner, L. M. (1991). Impression formation and construct system organization. *Social Behavior and Personality, 19,* 87–98.

Klohnen, E. C. (1996). Conceptual analysis and measurement of the construct of ego-resiliency. *Journal of Personality and Social Psychology, 70,* 1067–1079.

Klohnen, E. C., Vandewater, E. A., & Young, A. (1996). Negotiating the middle years: Ego-resiliency and successful midlife adjustment in women. *Psychology and Aging, 11,* 431–442.

Knapp, R. R. (1976). *Handbook for the Personal Orientation Inventory.* San Diego: EdITS.

Knee, C. R., Patrick, H., Vietor, N. A., Nanayakkara, A., & Neighbors, C. (2002). Self-determination as growth motivation in romantic relationships. *Personality and Social Psychology Bulletin, 28,* 609–619.

Knutson, B., Wolkowitz, O. M., Cole, S. W., Chan, T., Moore, E. A., Johnson, R. C., Terpstra, J., Turner, R. A., & Reus, V. I. (1998). Selective alteration of personalty and social behavior by serotonergic intervention. *American Journal of Psychiatry, 155,* 373–379.

Kobak, R. R., & Hazan, C. (1991). Attachment in marriage: Effects of security and accuracy of working models. *Journal of Personality and Social Psychology, 60,* 861–869.

Koestner, R., Zuckerman, M., & Koestner, J. (1987). Praise, involvement, and intrinsic motivation. *Journal of Personality and Social Psychology, 53,* 383–390.

Koffka, K. (1935). *Principles of Gestalt psychology.* New York: Harcourt, Brace.

Kohler, E., Keysers, C., Umiltà, M. A., Fogassi, L., Gallese, V., & Rizzolatti, G. (2002). Hearing sounds, understanding actions: Action representation in mirror neurons. *Science, 297,* 846–848.

Köhler, W. (1947). *Gestalt psychology.* New York: Liveright.

Kohut, H. (1977). *The restoration of the self.* New York: International Universities Press.

Konecni, V. J. (1975). Annoyance, type and duration of postannoyance activity, and aggression: The "cathartic effect." *Journal of Experimental Psychology: General, 104,* 76–102.

Koole, S. L., Jager, W., van den Berg, A. E., Vlek, C. A. J., & Hofstee, W. K. B. (2001). On the social nature of personality: Effects of extraversion, agreeableness, and feedback about collective resource use on cooperation in a resource dilemma. *Personality and Social Psychology Bulletin, 27,* 289–301.

Korchmaros, J. D., & Kenny, D. A. (2001). Emotional closeness as a mediator of the effect of genetic relatedness on altruism. *Psychological Science, 12,* 262–265.

Kornhaber, R. C., & Schroeder, H. E. (1975). Importance of model similarity on extinction of avoidance behavior in children. *Journal of Consulting and Clinical Psychology, 43,* 601–607.

Kotler, M., Cohen, H., Segman, R., Gritsenko, L., Nemanov, L., Lerer, B., Kramer, I., Zer-Zion, M., Kletz, I., &

Ebstein, R. P. (1997). Excess dopamine D_4 receptor (D4DR) exon III seven repeat allele in opioid-dependent subjects. *Molecular Psychiatry, 2,* 251–254.

Kotre, J. (1984). *Outliving the self: Generativity and the interpretation of lives.* Baltimore: Johns Hopkins University Press.

Kowaz, A. M., & Marcia, J. E. (1991). Development and validation of a measure of Eriksonian industry. *Journal of Personality and Social Psychology, 60,* 390–396.

Kramer, P. D. (1993). *Listening to Prozac: A psychiatrist explores anti-depressant drugs and the remaking of the self.* New York: Viking.

Krasner, L. (1970). Token economy as an illustration of operant conditioning procedures with the aged, with youth, and with society. In D. J. Lewis (Ed.), *Learning approaches to therapeutic behavior change.* Chicago: Aldine.

Kretschmer, E. (1925). *Physique and character.* New York: Harcourt, Brace.

Krieger, S. R., Epting, F. R., & Leitner, L. (1974). Personal constructs and attitudes toward death. *Omega, 5,* 299.

Kriegman, D., & Knight, C. (1988). Social evolution, psychoanalysis, and human nature. *Social Policy, 19,* 49–55.

Krueger, R. F., Schmutte, P. S., Caspi, A., Moffitt, T. E., Campbell, K., & Silva, P. A. (1994). Personality traits are linked to crime among men and women: Evidence from a birth cohort. *Journal of Abnormal Psychology, 103,* 328–338.

Kuhl, J., & Helle, P. (1986). Motivational and volitional determinants of depression: The degenerated-intention hypothesis. *Journal of Abnormal Psychology, 95,* 247–251.

Kuiper, N. A., & Derry, P. A. (1981). The self as a cognitive prototype: An application to person perception and depression. In N. Cantor & J. Kihlstrom (Eds.), *Cognition, social interaction, and personality.* Hillsdale, NJ: Erlbaum.

Kukla, A. (1972). Foundations of an attributional theory of performance. *Psychological Review, 79,* 454–470.

Kulhavy, R. W., & Stock, W. A. (1989). Feedback in written instruction: The place of response certitude. *Educational Psychology Review, 1,* 279–308.

Kunda, Z. (1999). *Social cognition: Making sense of people.* Cambridge, MA: MIT Press.

Kunda, Z., & Thagard, P. (1996). Forming impressions from stereotypes, traits, and behaviors: A parallel-constraint-satisfaction theory. *Psychological Review, 103,* 284–308.

La Greca, A. M., & Santogrossi, D. A. (1980). Social skills training with elementary school students: A behavioral group approach. *Journal of Consulting and Clinical Psychology, 48,* 220–227.

La Greca, A. M., Stone, W. L., & Bell, C. R., III (1983). Facilitating the vocational–interpersonal skills of mentally retarded individuals. *American Journal of Mental Deficiency, 88,* 270–278.

La Guardia, J. G., Ryan, R. M., Couchman, C. E., & Deci, E. L. (2000). Within-person variation in security of attachment: A self-determination theory perspective on attachment, need fulfillment, and well-being. *Journal of Personality and Social Psychology, 79,* 367–384.

Lakoff, G. (1987). *Women, fire, and dangerous things: What categories reveal about the mind.* Chicago: University of Chicago Press.

Lamiell, J. T. (1981). Toward an idiothetic psychology of personality. *American Psychologist, 36,* 276–289.

Landreth, G. L. (1991). *Play therapy: The art of the relationship.* Muncie, IN: Accelerated Development Publishers.

Landy, F. J. (1986). Stamp collecting versus science: Validation as hypothesis testing. *American Psychologist, 41,* 1183–1192.

Lane, R. D., & Nadel, L. (Eds.). (2000). *Cognitive neuroscience of emotion.* New York: Oxford.

Lang, P. J., & Lazovik, A. D. (1963). Experimental desensitization of a phobic. *Journal of Abnormal and Social Psychology, 66,* 519–525.

Langner, C. A., & Winter, D. G. (2001). The motivational basis of concessions and compromise: Archival and laboratory studies. *Journal of Personality and Social Psychology, 81,* 711–727.

Langston, C., & Cantor, N. (1989). Social anxiety and social constraint: When "making friends" is hard. *Journal of Personality and Social Psychology, 56,* 649–661.

Lanning, K. (1994). Dimensionality of observer ratings on the California Adult Q-set. *Journal of Personality and Social Psychology, 67,* 151–160.

Lansing, J. B., & Heyns, R. W. (1959). Need affiliation and frequency of four types of communication. *Journal of Abnormal and Social Psychology, 58,* 365–372.

Larsen, R. J., & Ketelaar, T. (1991). Personality and susceptibility to positive and negative emotional states. *Journal of Personality and Social Psychology, 61,* 132–140.

Larstone, R. M., Jang, K. L., Livesley, W. J., Vernon, P. A., & Wolf, H. (2002). The relationship between Eysenck's P-E-N model of personality, the five-factor model of personality, and traits delineating personality dysfunction. *Personality and Individual Differences, 33,* 25–37.

Lassiter, G. D., Briggs, M. A., & Bowman, R. E. (1991). Need for cognition and the perception of ongoing be-

havior. *Personality and Social Psychology Bulletin, 17,* 156–160.

Lassiter, G. D., Briggs, M. A., & Slaw, R. D. (1991). Need for cognition, causal processing, and memory for behavior. *Personality and Social Psychology Bulletin, 17,* 694–700.

Lau, R. R. (1989). Construct accessibility and electoral choice. *Political Behavior, 11,* 5–32.

Lauer, R. H., & Handel, W. H. (1983). *Social psychology: The theory and application of symbolic interactionism.* Englewood Cliffs, NJ: Prentice-Hall.

Laurenceau, J.-P., Feldman Barrett, L., & Pietromonaco, P. R. (1998). Intimacy as an interpersonal process: The importance of self-disclosure, and perceived partner responsiveness in interpersonal exchanges. *Journal of Personality and Social Psychology, 74,* 1238–1251.

Lazarus, R. S. (1966). *Psychological stress and the coping process.* New York: McGraw-Hill.

Lazarus, R. S., & Folkman, S. (1984). *Stress, appraisal, and coping.* New York: Springer.

Le Vay, S. (1991). A difference in hypothalamic structure between heterosexual and homosexual men. *Science, 253,* 1034–1037.

Le Vay, S. (1993). *The sexual brain.* Cambridge, MA: MIT Press.

Leak, G. K., & Christopher, S. B. (1982). Freudian psychoanalysis and sociobiology: A synthesis. *American Psychologist, 37,* 313–322.

Leary, M. R., & Baumeister, R. F. (2000). The nature and function of self-esteem: Sociometer theory. In M. P. Zanna (Ed.), *Advances in experimental social psychology* (Vol. 32, pp. 1–62). San Diego, CA: Academic Press.

Leary, T. (1957). *Interpersonal diagnosis of personality.* New York: Ronald.

Lee, L., & Snarey, J. (1988). The relationship between ego and moral development: A theoretical review and empirical analysis. In D. K. Lapsley & F. C. Power (Eds.), *Self, ego, and identity: Integrative approaches* (pp. 151–178). New York: Springer-Verlag.

Lefcourt, H. M. (1976). *Locus of control: Current trends in theory and research.* Hillsdale, NJ: Erlbaum.

Lefcourt, H. M. (Ed.). (1981). *Research with the locus of control construct. Vol. 1, Assessment methods.* New York: Academic Press.

Lefcourt, H. M., & Ludwig, G. W. (1965). The American Negro: A problem in expectancies. *Journal of Personality and Social Psychology, 1,* 377–380.

Lefcourt, H. M., Martin, R. A., Fick, C. M., & Saleh, W. E. (1985). Locus of control for affiliation and behavior in social interactions. *Journal of Personality and Social Psychology, 48,* 755–759.

Lefcourt, H. M., Von Baeyer, C. I., Ware, E. E., & Cox, D. J. (1979). The Multidimensional-Multiattributional Causality scale: The development of a goal specific locus of control scale. *Canadian Journal of Behavioral Science, 11,* 286–304.

Leit, R. A., Pope, H. G., Jr., & Gray, J. J. (2001). Cultural expectations of muscularity in men: The evolution of playgirl centerfolds. *International Journal of Eating Disorders, 29,* 90–93.

Leitner, L. M., & Cado, S. (1982). Personal constructs and homosexual stress. *Journal of Personality and Social Psychology, 43,* 869–872.

Lemann, N. (1994). Is there a science of success? *The Atlantic Monthly, 273,* 83–98.

Lengfelder, A., & Gollwitzer, P. M. (2001). Reflective and reflexive action control in patients with frontal brain lesions. *Neuropsychology, 15,* 80–100.

Lepper, M. R., & Greene, D. (1975). Turning play into work: Effects of adult surveillance and extrinsic rewards on children's intrinsic motivation. *Journal of Personality and Social Psychology, 31,* 479–486.

Lepper, M. R., & Greene, D. (1978). *The hidden costs of reward.* Hillsdale, NJ: Erlbaum.

Lesch, K-P., Bengel, D., Heils, A., Sabol, S. Z., Greenberg, B. D., Petri, S., et al. (1996). Association of anxiety-related traits with a polymorphism in the serotonin transporter gene regulatory region. *Science, 274,* 1527–1531.

Lesser, G. S. (1973). Achievement motivation in women. In D. C. McClelland & R. S. Steele (Eds.), *Human motivation: A book of readings.* Morristown, NJ: General Learning Press.

Levenson, H. (1973). Multidimensional locus of control in psychiatric patients. *Journal of Consulting and Clinical Psychology, 41,* 397–404.

Levenson, H. (1981). Differentiating among internality, powerful others, and chance. In H. F. Lefcourt (Ed.), *Research with the locus of control construct. Vol. 1, Assessment methods.* New York: Academic Press.

Levenson, R. W., & Ruef, A. M. (1992). Empathy: A physiological substrate. *Journal of Personality and Social Psychology, 63,* 234–246.

Levine, D. S., & Leven, S. J. (Eds.). (1992). *Motivation, emotion, and goal direction in neural networks.* Hillsdale, NJ: Erlbaum.

Levinson, D. J. (1978). *The seasons of a man's life.* New York: Alfred A. Knopf.

Lewin, D. I. (1990). Gene therapy nears starting gate. *The Journal of NIH Research, 2,* 36–38.

Lewin, K. (1951a). *Field theory in social science.* New York: Harper.

Lewin, K. (1951b). The nature of field theory. In M. H. Marx (Ed.), *Psychological theory.* New York: Macmillan.

Lewinsohn, P. M., Mischel, W., Chaplin, W., & Barton, R. (1980). Social competence and depression: The role of illusory self-perceptions. *Journal of Abnormal Psychology, 89,* 203–212.

Lewis, D. J., & Duncan, C. P. (1956). Effect of different percentages of money reward on extinction of a lever pulling response. *Journal of Experimental Psychology, 52,* 23–27.

Lewontin, R. C., Rose, S., & Kamin, L. J. (1984). *Not in our genes: Biology, ideology, and human nature.* New York: Penguin.

Li, N. P., Bailey, J. M., Kenrick, D. T., & Linsenmeier, J. A. W. (2002). The necessities and luxuries of mate preferences: Testing the tradeoffs. *Journal of Personality and Social Psychology, 82,* 947–955.

Li, T., Xu, K., Deng, H., Cai, G., Liu, J., Liu, X., Wang, R., Xiang, X., Zhao, J., Murray, R. M., Sham, P. C., & Collier, D. A. (1997). Association analysis of the dopamine D_4 gene exon III VNTR and heroin abuse in Chinese subjects. *Molecular Psychiatry, 2,* 413–416.

Lichtenstein, E., & Danaher, B. G. (1976). Modification of smoking behavior: A critical analysis of theory, research, and practice. In M. Hersen, R. M. Eisler, & P. M. Miller (Eds.), *Progress in behavior modification* (Vol. 3). New York: Academic Press.

Lieberman, M. D., Gaunt, R., Gilbert, D. T., & Trope, Y. (in press). Reflection and reflexion: A social cognitive neuroscience approach to attributional inference. In M. Zanna (Ed.), *Advances in Experimental Social Psychology.* San Diego, CA: Academic Press.

Lieberman, M. D., & Rosenthal, R. (2001). Why introverts can't always tell who likes them: Multitasking and nonverbal decoding. *Journal of Personality and Social Psychology, 80,* 294–310.

Liebert, R. M., & Baron, R. A. (1972). Some immediate effects of televised violence on children's behavior. *Developmental Psychology, 6,* 469–475.

Liebert, R. M., & Fernandez, L. E. (1970). Effects of vicarious consequences on imitative performance. *Child Development, 41,* 841–852.

Light, K. C., Smith, T. E., Johns, J. M., Brownley, K. A., Hofheimer, J. A., & Amico, J. A. (2000). Oxytocin responsivity in mothers of infants: A preliminary study of relationships with blood pressure during laboratory stress and normal ambulatory activity. *Health Psychology, 19,* 560–567.

Lilienfeld, S. O., Wood, J. M., & Garb, H. N. (2000). The scientific status of projective techniques. *Psychological Science in the Public Interest, 1,* 27–66.

Linder, D. E., & Crane, K. A. (1970). Reactance theory analysis of predecisional cognitive processes. *Journal of Personality and Social Psychology, 15,* 258–264.

Linder, D. E., Wortman, C. B., & Brehm, J. W. (1971). Temporal changes in predecision preferences among choice alternatives. *Journal of Personality and Social Psychology, 19,* 282–284.

Linville, P. W. (1987). Self-complexity as a cognitive buffer against stress-related illness and depression. *Journal of Personality and Social Psychology, 52,* 663–676.

Litt, M. D. (1988). Self-efficacy and perceived control: Cognitive mediators of pain tolerance. *Journal of Personality and Social Psychology, 54,* 149–160.

Little, B. R. (1983). Personal projects: A rationale and methods for investigation. *Environment and Behavior, 15,* 273–309.

Little, B. R. (1989). Personal projects analysis: Trivial pursuits, magnificent obsessions, and the search for coherence. In D. M. Buss & N. Cantor (Eds.), *Personality psychology: Recent trends and emerging directions* (pp. 15–31). New York: Springer-Verlag.

Lobel, T. E. (1994). Sex typing and the social perception of gender stereotypic and nonstereotypic behavior: The uniqueness of feminine males. *Journal of Personality and Social Psychology, 66,* 379–385.

Locke, E. A., & Latham, G. P. (1990). *A theory of goal setting and task performance.* Englewood Cliffs, NJ: Prentice-Hall.

Locurto, C. M., Terrace, H. S., & Gibbon, J. (Eds.). (1980). *Autoshaping and conditioning theory.* New York: Academic Press.

Loehlin, J. C. (1992). *Genes and environment in personality development.* Newbury Park, CA: Sage.

Loehlin, J. C., & Nichols, R. C. (1976). *Heredity, environment, and personality.* Austin: University of Texas Press.

Loehlin, J. C., Willerman, L., & Horn, J. M. (1985). Personality resemblances in adoptive families when the children are late-adolescent or adult. *Journal of Personality and Social Psychology, 48,* 376–392.

Loehlin, J. C., Willerman, L., & Horn, J. M. (1988). Human behavior genetics. *Annual Review of Psychology, 38,* 101–133.

Loevinger, J. (1966). The meaning and measurement of ego development. *American Psychologist, 21,* 195–206.

Loevinger, J. (1969). Theories of ego development. In L. Breger (Ed.), *Clinical–cognitive psychology: Models and integrations.* Englewood Cliffs, NJ: Prentice-Hall.

Loevinger, J. (1976). *Ego development: Conceptions and theories.* San Francisco: Jossey-Bass.

Loevinger, J. (1987). *Paradigms of personality.* New York: W. H. Freeman.

Loevinger, J. (1993). Measurement of personality: True or false? *Psychological Inquiry, 4,* 1–16.

Loevinger, J., & Knoll, E. (1983). Personality: Stages, traits, and the self. *Annual Review of Psychology, 34,* 195–222.

Loevinger, J., & Wessler, R. (1970). *Measuring ego development 1. Construction and use of a sentence-completion test.* San Francisco: Jossey-Bass.

Loftus, E. (Ed.). (1992). Science watch [Special section on the unconscious]. *American Psychologist, 47,* 761–809.

Loftus, E. F. (1997). Creating false memories. *Scientific American, 277,* 70–75.

Loftus, E. F., Coan, J. A., & Pickrell, J. E. (1996). Manufacturing false memories using bits of reality. In L. Reder (Ed.), *Implicit memory and metacognition* (pp. 195–220). Mahwah, NJ: Erlbaum.

Loftus, E. F., & Pickrell, J. E. (1995). The formation of false memories. *Psychiatric Annals, 25,* 720–725.

Lord, C. G. (1982). Predicting behavioral consistency from an individual's perception of situational similarities. *Journal of Personality and Social Psychology, 42,* 1076–1088.

Lovaas, O. I., Freitag, G., Gold, V. J., & Kassorla, I. C. (1965). Recording apparatus for observation of behaviors of children in free play settings. *Journal of Experimental Child Psychology, 2,* 108–120.

Lowell, E. L. (1952). The effect of need for achievement on learning and speed of performance. *Journal of Psychology, 33,* 31–40.

Lucas, R. E., & Diener, E. (2001). Understanding extraverts' enjoyment of social situations: The importance of pleasantness. *Journal of Personality and Social Psychology, 81,* 343–356.

Lucas, R. E., Diener, E., Grob, A., Suh, E. M., & Shao, L. (2000). Cross-cultural evidence for the fundamental features of extraversion. *Journal of Personality and Social Psychology, 79,* 452–468.

Lumsden, C., & Wilson, E. O. (1981). *Genes, mind, and culture.* Cambridge, MA: Harvard University Press.

Lundin, R. W. (1961). *Personality.* New York: Macmillan.

Lundy, A. C. (1985). The reliability of the Thematic Apperception Test. *Journal of Personality Assessment, 49,* 141–145.

Lurigio, A. J., & Carroll, J. S. (1985). Probation officers' schemata of offenders: Content, development, and impact on treatment decisions. *Journal of Personality and Social Psychology, 48,* 1112–1126.

Lütkenhaus, P., Grossmann, K. E., & Grossmann, K. (1985). Infant-mother attachment at twelve months and style of interaction with a stranger at the age of three years. *Child Development, 56,* 1538–1542.

Lykken, D. T., & Tellegen, A. (1993). Is human mating adventitious or the result of lawful choice? A twin study of mate selection. *Journal of Personality and Social Psychology, 65,* 56–68.

Lynn, R. (2001). *Eugenics: A reassessment.* Westport, CT: Praeger.

Lynn, S. J., Myers, B., & Malinoski, P. (1997). Hypnosis, pseudomemories, and clinical guidelines: A sociocognitive perspective. In J. D. Read & D. S. Lindsay (Eds.), *Recollections of trauma: Scientific studies and clinical practice.* New York: Plenum.

Maccoby, E. E., & Wilson, W. C. (1957). Identification and observational learning from films. *Journal of Abnormal and Social Psychology, 55,* 76–87.

MacKay, D. M. (1963). Mindlike behavior in artefacts. In K. M. Sayre & F. J. Crosson (Eds.), *The modeling of mind: Computers and intelligence.* Notre Dame, IN: University of Notre Dame Press.

MacKay, D. M. (1966). Cerebral organization and the conscious control of action. In J. C. Eccles (Ed.), *Brain and conscious experience.* Berlin: Springer-Verlag.

Macrae, C. N., & Boderhausen, G. V. (2000). Social cognition: Thinking categorically. *Annual Review of Psychology, 51,* 93–120.

Macrae, C. N., Milne, A. B., & Bodenhausen, G. V. (1994). Stereotypes as energy-saving devices: A peek inside the cognitive toolbox. *Journal of Personality and Social Psychology, 66,* 37–47.

Maddi, S. R. (1980). *Personality theories: A comparative analysis.* Homewood, IL: Dorsey.

Maes, P. (Ed.). (1990). *Designing autonomous agents: Theory and practice from biology to engineering and back.* Cambridge, MA: MIT Press.

Maes, P. (1994). Modeling adaptive autonomous agents. *Artificial Life, 1,* 135–162.

Magnus, K., Diener, E., Fujita, F., & Pavot, W. (1993). Extraversion and neuroticism as predictors of objective life events: A longitudinal analysis. *Journal of Personality and Social Psychology, 65,* 1046–1053.

Magnusson, D., & Endler, N. S. (Eds.). (1977). *Personality at the crossroads: Current issues in interactional psychology.* Hillsdale, NJ: Erlbaum.

Mahler, M. S. (1968). *On human symbiosis and the vicissitudes of individuation: Infantile psychosis.* New York: International Universities Press.

Mahler, M. S., Pine, F., & Bergman, A. (1975). *The psychological birth of the human infant: Symbiosis and individuation.* New York: Basic Books.

Mahone, C. H. (1960). Fear of failure and unrealistic vocational aspiration. *Journal of Abnormal and Social Psychology, 60,* 253–261.

Mahoney, M. J. (1977). Some applied issues in self-monitoring. In J. D. Cone & R. P. Hawkins (Eds.), *Behavioral assessment: New directions in clinical psychology.* New York: Brunner/Mazel.

Main, M., & Cassidy, J. (1988). Categories of response to reunion with the parent at age 6: Predictable from infant attachment classifications and stable over a 1-month period. *Developmental Psychology, 24,* 415–426.

Main, M., & Solomon, J. (1986). Discovery of an insecure-disorganized/disoriented attachment pattern. In T. B. Brazelton & M. W. Yogman (Eds.), *Affective development in infancy* (pp. 95–124). Norwood, NJ: Ablex.

Major, B., Cozzarelli, C., Sciacchitano, A. M., Cooper, M. L., Testa, M., & Mueller, P. M. (1990). Perceived social support, self-efficacy, and adjustment to abortion. *Journal of Personality and Social Psychology, 59,* 452–463.

Major, B., Richards, C., Cooper, M. L., Cozzarelli, C., & Zubek, J. (1998). Personal resilience, cognitive appraisals, and coping: An integrative model of adjustment to abortion. *Journal of Personality and Social Psychology, 74,* 735–752.

Malamuth, N. M., & Donnerstein, E. (Eds.). (1984). *Pornography and sexual aggression.* New York: Academic Press.

Malec, J., Park, T., & Watkins, J. T. (1976). Modeling with role playing as a treatment for test anxiety. *Journal of Consulting and Clinical Psychology, 44,* 679.

Mallick, S. K., & McCandless, B. R. (1966). A study of catharsis of aggression. *Journal of Personality and Social Psychology, 4,* 591–596.

Maltzman, I. (1968). Theoretical conceptions of semantic conditioning and generalization. In T. R. Dixon & D. L. Horton (Eds.), *Verbal behavior and general behavior theory.* Englewood Cliffs, NJ: Prentice-Hall.

Mancuso, J. C., & Adams-Webber, J. R. (Eds.) (1982). *The construing person.* New York: Praeger.

Maner, J. K., Luce, C. L., Neuberg, S. L., Cialdini, R. B., Brown, S., & Sagarin, B. J. (2002). The effects of perspective taking on motivations for helping: Still no evidence for altruism. *Personality and Social Psychology Bulletin, 28,* 1601–1610.

Manning, M. M., & Wright, T. L. (1983). Self-efficacy expectancies, outcome expectancies, and the persistence of pain control in childbirth. *Journal of Personality and Social Psychology, 45,* 421–431.

Mansfield, E. D., & McAdams, D. P. (1996). Generativity and themes of agency and communion in adult autobiography. *Personality and Social Psychology Bulletin, 22,* 721–731.

Manuck, S. B., Flory, J. D., Ferrell, R. E., Dent, K. M., Mann, J. J., & Muldoon, M. F. (1999). Aggression and anger-related traits associated with a polymorphism of the tryptophan hydroxylase gene. *Biological Psychiatry, 45,* 603–614.

Manuck, S. B., Flory, J. D., Ferrell, R. E., Mann, J. J., & Muldoon, M. F. (2000). A regulatory polymorphism of the monoamine oxidase-A gene may be associated with variability in aggression, impulsivity, and central nervous system serotonergic responsivity. *Psychiatry Research, 95,* 9–23.

Manuck, S. B., Flory, J. D., McCaffery, J. M., Matthews, K. A., Mann, J. J., & Muldoon, M. F. (1998). Aggression, impulsivity, and central nervous system serotonergic responsivity in a nonpatient sample. *Neuropsychopharmacology, 19,* 287–299.

Marangoni, C., Garcia, S., Ickes, W., & Teng, G. (1995). Empathic accuracy in a clinically relevant setting. *Journal of Personality and Social Psychology, 68,* 854–869.

Marcia, J. E. (1966). Development and validation of ego identity statuses. *Journal of Personality and Social Psychology, 3,* 551–558.

Marcia, J. E. (1976). Identity six years after: A follow-up study. *Journal of Youth and Adolescence, 5,* 145–160.

Marcia, J. E. (1980). Identity in adolescence. In J. Adelson (Ed.), *Handbook of adolescent psychology.* New York: Wiley.

Marcus, G. F. (1996). Why do children say "breaked"? *Current Directions in Psychological Science, 5,* 81–85.

Marcus-Newhall, A., Pedersen, W. C., Carlson, M., & Miller, N. (2000). Displaced aggression is alive and well: A meta-analytic review. *Journal of Personality and Social Psychology, 78,* 670–689.

Markus, H. (1977). Self-schemata and processing information about the self. *Journal of Personality and Social Psychology, 35,* 63–78.

Markus, H., & Nurius, P. (1986). Possible selves. *American Psychologist, 41,* 954–969.

Markus, H., & Sentis, K. (1982). The self and social information processing. In J. Suls (Ed.), *Psychological perspectives on the self* (Vol. 1, pp. 41–70). Hillsdale, NJ: Erlbaum.

Markus, H., & Wurf, E. (1987). The dynamic self-concept: A social psychological perspective. *Annual Review of Psychology, 38,* 299–337.

Martin, L. L., & Tesser, A. (1996). Some ruminative thoughts. In R. S. Wyer, Jr. (Ed.), *Advances in social cognition* (Vol. 9, pp. 1–47). Mahwah, NJ: Erlbaum.

Masling, J. M., & Bornstein, R. F. (Eds.). (1994). *Empirical perspectives on object relations theory.* Washington, DC: American Psychological Association.

Masling, J. M., Johnson, C., & Saturansky, C. (1974). Oral imagery, accuracy of perceiving others, and performance in Peace Corps training. *Journal of Personality and Social Psychology, 30,* 414–419.

Masling, J. M., O'Neill, R., & Jayne, C. (1981). Orality and latency of volunteering to serve as experimental subjects. *Journal of Personality Assessment, 45,* 20–22.

Masling, J. M., O'Neill, R., & Katkin, E. S. (1982). Autonomic arousal, interpersonal climate, and orality. *Journal of Personality and Social Psychology, 42,* 529–534.

Masling, J. M., Price, J., Goldband, S., & Katkin, E. S. (1981). Oral imagery and autonomic arousal in social isolation. *Journal of Personality and Social Psychology, 40,* 395–400.

Masling, J. M., Rabie, L., & Blondheim, S. H. (1967). Obesity, level of aspiration, and Rorschach and TAT measures of oral dependence. *Journal of Consulting Psychology, 31,* 233–239.

Masling, J. M., Weiss, L., & Rothschild, B. (1968). Relationships of oral imagery to yielding behavior and birth order. *Journal of Consulting and Clinical Psychology, 32,* 38–81.

Maslow, A. H. (1955). Deficiency motivation and growth motivation. In M. R. Jones (Ed.), *Nebraska symposium on motivation.* Lincoln: University of Nebraska Press.

Maslow, A. H. (1962). *Toward a psychology of being.* Princeton, NJ: Van Nostrand.

Maslow, A. H. (1968). *Toward a psychology of being* (2nd ed.). New York: Van Nostrand.

Maslow, A. H. (1970). *Motivation and personality* (Rev. ed.). New York: Harper & Row.

Maslow, A. H. (1971). *The farther reaches of human nature.* New York: Viking.

Maslow, A. H. (1979). *The journals of A. H. Maslow* (2 vols.). R. J. Lowry (Ed.). Monterey, CA: Brooks/Cole.

Mason, A., & Blankenship, V. (1987). Power and affiliation motivation, stress, and abuse in intimate relationships. *Journal of Personality and Social Psychology, 52,* 203–210.

Masson, J. M. (1984). *The assault on truth.* New York: Farrar, Straus, & Giroux.

Matas, L., Arend, R. A., & Sroufe, L. A. (1978). Continuity of adaptation in the second year: The relationship between quality of attachment and later competence. *Child Development, 49,* 547–556.

Matthews, K. A., Batson, C. D., Horn, J., & Rosenman, R. (1981). "Principles in his nature which interest him in the fortune of others . . .": The heritability of empathic concern for others. *Journal of Personality, 49,* 237–247.

Matthews, K. A., Owens, J. F., Kuller, L. H., Sutton-Tyrrell, K., & Jansen-McWilliams, L. (1998). Are hostility and anxiety associated with carotid atherosclerosis in healthy postmenopausal women? *Psychosomatic Medicine, 60,* 633–638.

Matthiesen, A-S., Ransjö-Arvidson, A-B., Nissen, E., & Uvnäs-Moberg, K. (2001). Postpartum maternal oxytocin release by newborns: Effects of infant hand massage and sucking. *Birth, 28,* 13–19.

May, R. (1953). *Man's search for himself.* New York: Norton.

May, R. (1958). The origins and significance of the existential movement in psychology. In R. May, E. Angel, & H. F. Ellenberger (Eds.), *Existence: A new dimension in psychiatry and psychology.* New York: Basic Books.

May, R. (Ed.). (1969). *Existential psychology* (2nd ed.). New York: Random House.

Mazur, A. (1985). A biosocial model of status in face-to-face primate groups. *Social Forces, 64,* 377–402.

Mazur, A., & Booth, A. (1998). Testosterone and dominance in men. *Behavior and Brain Sciences, 21,* 353–397.

Mazur, A., Booth, A., & Dabbs, J. M., Jr. (1992). Testosterone and chess competition. *Social Psychology Quarterly, 55,* 70–77.

McAdams, D. P. (1982). Experiences of intimacy and power: Relationships between social motives and autobiographical memory. *Journal of Personality and Social Psychology, 42,* 292–302.

McAdams, D. P. (1984). Human motives and personal relationships. In V. J. Derlaga (Ed.), *Communication, intimacy, and close relationships.* New York: Academic Press.

McAdams, D. P. (1985). *Power, intimacy, and the life story: Personological inquiries into identity.* New York: Guilford.

McAdams, D. P. (1989). *Intimacy: The need to be close.* New York: Doubleday.

McAdams, D. P. (1992). The five-factor model *in* personality: A critical appraisal. *Journal of Personality, 60,* 329–361.

McAdams, D. P. (1993). *The stories we live by: Personal myths and the making of the self.* New York: Morrow.

McAdams, D. P. (2001). The psychology of life stories. *Review of General Psychology, 5,* 100–122.

McAdams, D. P., & Bryant, F. B. (1987). Intimacy motivation and subjective mental health in a nationwide sample. *Journal of Personality, 55,* 395–413.

McAdams, D. P., & Constantian, C. A. (1983). Intimacy and affiliation motives in daily living: An experience sampling analysis. *Journal of Personality and Social Psychology, 45,* 851–861.

McAdams, D. P., & de St. Aubin, E. (1992). A theory of generativity and its assessment through self-report, behavioral acts, and narrative themes in autobiography. *Journal of Personality and Social Psychology, 62,* 1003–1015.

McAdams, D. P., Diamond, A., de St. Aubin, E., & Mansfield, E. (1997). Stories of commitment: The psychosocial construction of generative lives. *Journal of Personality and Social Psychology, 72,* 678–694.

McAdams, D. P., Healy, S., & Krause, S. (1984). Social motives and patterns of friendship. *Journal of Personality and Social Psychology, 47,* 828–838.

McAdams, D. P., Jackson, R. J., & Kirshnit, C. (1984). Looking, laughing, and smiling in dyads as a function of intimacy motivation and reciprocity. *Journal of Personality, 52,* 261–273.

McAdams, D. P., & Powers, J. (1981). Themes of intimacy in behavior and thought. *Journal of Personality and Social Psychology, 40,* 573–587.

McAdams, D. P., Reynolds, J., Lewis, M., Patten, A. H., & Bowman, P. J. (2001). When bad things turn good and good things turn bad: Sequences of redemption and contamination in life narrative and their relation to psychosocial adaptation in midlife adults and in students. *Personality and Social Psychology Bulletin, 27,* 474–485.

McAdams, D. P., & Vaillant, G. E. (1982). Intimacy motivation and psychosocial adjustment: A longitudinal study. *Journal of Personality Assessment, 46,* 586–593.

McArthur, L. Z. (1981). The role of attention in impression formation and causal attribution. In E. T. Higgins, C. P. Herman, & M. P. Zanna (Eds.), *Social cognition: The Ontario Symposium* (Vol. 1). Hillsdale, NJ: Erlbaum.

McClelland, D. C. (1961). *The achieving society.* Princeton, NJ: Van Nostrand.

McClelland, D. C. (1965). Toward a theory of motive acquisition. *American Psychologist, 20,* 321–333.

McClelland, D. C. (1977). The impact of power motivation training on alcoholics. *Journal of Studies on Alcohol, 38,* 142–144.

McClelland, D. C. (1979). Inhibited power motivation and high blood pressure in men. *Journal of Abnormal Psychology, 88,* 182–190.

McClelland, D. C. (1984). *Human motivation.* Glenview, IL: Scott, Foresman.

McClelland, D. C. (1985). How motives, skills, and values determine what people do. *American Psychologist, 40,* 812–825.

McClelland, D. C. (1989). Motivational factors in health and disease. *American Psychologist, 44,* 675–683.

McClelland, D. C., Atkinson, J. W., Clark, R. A., & Lowell, E. L. (1953). *The achievement motive.* New York: Appleton-Century-Crofts.

McClelland, D. C., & Boyatzis, R. E. (1982). Leadership motive pattern and long-term success in management. *Journal of Applied Psychology, 67,* 737–743.

McClelland, D. C., Davis, W. N., Kalin, R., & Wanner, E. (Eds.). (1972). *The drinking man.* New York: Free Press.

McClelland, D. C., Koestner, R., & Weinberger, J. (1989). How do self-attributed and implicit motives differ? *Psychological Review, 96,* 690–702.

McClelland, D. C., & Winter, D. G. (1969). *Motivating economic achievement.* New York: Free Press.

McClelland, J. L. (1999). Cognitive modeling, connectionist. In R. W. Wilson & F. C. Keil (Eds.), *The MIT encyclopedia of the cognitive sciences* (pp.137–139). Cambridge, MA: MIT Press.

McClelland, J. L., & Rumelhart, D. E. (1986). *Parallel distributed processing* (Vol. 2). Cambridge, MA: MIT Press.

McClelland, J. L., Rumelhart, D. E., & PDP Research Group. (Eds.). (1986). *Parallel distributed processing: Explorations in the microstructure of cognition: Vol. 2. Psychological and biological models.* Cambridge, MA: MIT Press.

McCrae, R. R. (1993). Moderated analyses of longitudinal personality stability. *Journal of Personality and Social Psychology, 65,* 577–585.

McCrae, R. R. (1996). Social consequences of experiential openness. *Psychological Bulletin, 120,* 323–337.

McCrae, R. R., & Costa, P. T., Jr. (1987). Validation of the five-factor model of personality across instruments and observers. *Journal of Personality and Social Psychology, 52,* 81–90.

McCrae, R. R., & Costa, P. T., Jr. (1989a). Reinterpreting the Myers–Briggs type indicator from the perspective of the five-factor model of personality. *Journal of Personality, 57,* 17–40.

McCrae, R. R., & Costa, P. T., Jr. (1989b). The structure of interpersonal traits: Wiggins's circumplex and the five-factor model. *Journal of Personality and Social Psychology, 56,* 586–595.

McCrae, R. R., & Costa, P. T., Jr. (1997). Personality trait structure as a human universal. *American Psychologist, 52,* 509–516.

McCrae, R. R., Costa, P. T., Jr., & Busch, C. M. (1986). Evaluating comprehensiveness in personality systems: The California Q-Set and the five factor model. *Journal of Personality, 54,* 430–446.

McCrae, R. R., Costa, P. T., Jr., Ostendorf, F., Angleitner, A., Hrebíčková, M., Avia, M. D., Sanz, J., Sánchez-Bernardos, M. L., Kusdil, M. E., Woodfield, R., Saunders, P. R., & Smith, P. B. (2000). Nature over nurture: Temperament, personality, and life span development. *Journal of Personality and Social Psychology, 78,* 173–186.

McCrae, R. R., & John, O. P. (1992). An introduction to the five-factor model and its implications. *Journal of Personality, 60,* 175–215.

McCrae, R. R., Zonderman, A. B., Costa, P. J., Jr., Bond, M. H., & Paunonen, S. V. (1996). Evaluating replicability of factors in the Revised NEO Personality Inventory: Confirmatory factor analysis versus procrustes rotation. *Journal of Personality and Social Psychology, 70,* 552–566.

McCullough, M. (2001). Freud's seduction theory and its rehabilitation: A saga of one mistake after another. *Review of General Psychology, 5,* 3–22.

McCullough, M. E., & Hoyt, W. T. (2002). Transgression-related motivational dispositions: Personality substrates of forgiveness and their links to the big five. *Personality and Social Psychology Bulletin, 28,* 1556–1573.

McFall, R., & Twentyman, C. T. (1973). Four experiments on relative contributions of rehearsal, modeling and coaching to assertion training. *Journal of Abnormal Psychology, 81,* 199–218.

McGregor, I., Zanna, M. P., Holmes, J. G., & Spencer, S. J. (2001). Compensatory conviction in the face of personal uncertainty: Going to extremes and being oneself. *Journal of Personality and Social Psychology, 80,* 472–488.

McGue, M., & Lykken, D. T. (1992). Genetic influence on risk of divorce. *Psychological Science, 3,* 368–373.

McGuire, W. (Ed.). (1974). *The Freud/Jung letters: The correspondence between Sigmund Freud and C. G. Jung.* Princeton, NJ: Princeton University Press.

McGuire, W. J., & McGuire, C. V. (1986). Differences in conceptualizing self versus conceptualizing other people as manifested in contrasting verb types used in natural speech. *Journal of Personality and Social Psychology, 51,* 1135–1143.

McKeachie, W. J. (1961). Motivation, teaching methods, and college learning. In M. R. Jones (Ed.), *Nebraska symposium on motivation.* Lincoln: University of Nebraska Press.

McMahan, I. D. (1973). Relationships between causal attributions and expectancy of success. *Journal of Personality and Social Psychology, 28,* 108–114.

Mead, G. H. (1934). *Mind, self, and society.* Chicago: University of Chicago Press.

Medin, D. L. (1989). Concepts and conceptual structure. *American Psychologist, 44,* 1469–1481.

Meehl, P. E. (1962). Schizotaxia, schizotypy, schizophrenia. *American Psychologist, 17,* 827–838.

Meehl, P. E. (1992). Factors and taxa, traits and types, differences of degree and differences in kind. *Journal of Personality, 60,* 117–174.

Megargee, E. I. (1966). Undercontrolled and overcontrolled personality types in extreme antisocial aggression. In E. I. Megargee & J. E. Moranson (Eds.), *Psychological Monographs*. New York: Harper & Row.

Megargee, E. I. (1971). The role of inhibition in the assessment and understanding of violence. In J. L. Singer (Ed.), *The control of aggression and violence*. New York: Academic Press.

Megargee, E. I., Cook, P. E., & Mendelsohn, G. A. (1967). Development and evaluation of an MMPI scale of assaultiveness in overcontrolled individuals. *Journal of Abnormal Psychology, 72,* 519–528.

Meichenbaum, D. (1971). Examination of model characteristics in reducing avoidance behavior. *Journal of Personality and Social Psychology, 17,* 298–307.

Meichenbaum, D. (1972). Cognitive modification of test anxious college students. *Journal of Consulting and Clinical Psychology, 39,* 370–379.

Meichenbaum, D. (1974). *Cognitive behavior modification*. Morristown, NJ: General Learning Press.

Meichenbaum, D. (1977). *Cognitve-behavior modification: An integrative approach*. New York: Plenum.

Meichenbaum, D. (1985). *Stress inoculation training*. New York: Pergamon.

Meichenbaum, D., & Goodman, J. (1971). Training impulsive children to talk to themselves: A means of developing self-control. *Journal of Abnormal Psychology, 77,* 115–126.

Melamed, B. G., & Siegel, L. J. (1975). Reduction of anxiety in children facing hospitalization and surgery by use of filmed modeling. *Journal of Consulting and Clinical Psychology, 43,* 511–521.

Melamed, B. G., Weinstein, D., Hawes, R., & Katin-Borland, M. (1975). Reduction of fear-related dental management problems using filmed modeling. *Journal of the American Dental Association, 90,* 822–826.

Meltzoff, A. N. (1985). Immediate and deferred imitation in fourteen- and twenty-four-month-old infants. *Child Development, 56,* 62–72.

Mendola, R., Tennen, H., Affleck, G., McCann, L., & Fitzgerald, T. (1990). Appraisal and adaptation among women with impaired fertility. *Cognitive Therapy and Research, 14,* 79–93.

Mendoza-Denton, R., Ayduk, O., Mischel, W., Shoda, Y., & Testa, A. (2001). Person × situation interactionism in self-encoding (*I am . . . when . . .*): Implications for affect regulation and social information processing. *Journal of Personality and Social Psychology, 80,* 533–544.

Merluzzi, T. V., Glass, C. R., & Genest, M. (Eds.). (1981). *Cognitive assessment*. New York: Guilford.

Merluzzi, T. V., Rudy, T. E., & Glass, C. R. (1981). The information-processing paradigm: Implications for clinical science. In T. V. Merluzzi, C. R. Glass, & M. Genest (Eds.), *Cognitive assessment*. New York: Guilford.

Mershon, B., & Gorsuch, R. L. (1988). Number of factors in the personality sphere: Does increase in factors increase predictability of real-life criteria? *Journal of Personality and Social Psychology, 55,* 675–680.

Metcalfe, J., & Mischel, W. (1999). A hot/cool-system analysis of delay of gratification: Dynamics of willpower. *Psychological Review, 106,* 3–19.

Meyer, D., Leventhal, H., & Gutmann, M. (1985). Common-sense models of illness: The example of hypertension. *Health Psychology, 4,* 115–135.

Meyer, J. P. (1980). Causal attribution for success and failure: A multivariate investigation of dimensionality, formation, and consequences. *Journal of Personality and Social Psychology, 38,* 708–718.

Meyer, J. P., & Pepper, S. (1977). Need compatibility and marital adjustment in young married couples. *Journal of Personality and Social Psychology, 35,* 331–342.

Meyers, S. A., & Berscheid, E. (1997). The language of love: The difference a preposition makes. *Personality and Social Psychology Bulletin, 23,* 347–362.

Michalski, R. L., & Shackelford, T. K. (2002). An attempted replication of the relationships between birth order and personality. *Journal of Research in Personality, 36,* 182–188.

Mickelson, K. D., Kessler, R. C., & Shaver, P. R. (1997). Adult attachment in a nationally representative sample. *Journal of Personality and Social Psychology, 73,* 1092–1106.

Mikulincer, M. (1998). Adult attachment style and individual differences in functional versus dysfunctional experiences of anger. *Journal of Personality and Social Psychology, 74,* 513–524.

Mikulincer, M., Florian, V., & Weller, A. (1993). Attachment styles, coping strategies, and posttraumatic psychological distress: The impact of the Gulf War in Israel. *Journal of Personality and Social Psychology, 64,* 817–826.

Mikulincer, M., Hirschberger, G., Nachmias, O., & Gillath, O. (2001). The affective component of the secure base schema: Affective priming with representations of attachment security. *Journal of Personality and Social Psychology, 81,* 305–321.

Mikulincer, M., & Horesh, N. (1999). Adult attachment style and the perception of others: The role of projective mechanisms. *Journal of Personality and Social Psychology, 76,* 1022–1034.

Mikulincer, M., & Nachshon, O. (1991). Attachment styles and patterns of self-disclosure. *Journal of Personality and Social Psychology, 61,* 321–331.

Mikulincer, M., & Shaver, P. R. (2001). Attachment theory and intergroup bias: Evidence that priming the secure base schema attenuates negative reactions to out-groups. *Journal of Personality and Social Psychology, 81,* 97–115.

Mill, J. S. (1962). "On liberty." In M. Warnock (Ed.), *John Stuart Mill: Utilitarianism, On liberty, Essay on Bentham, together with selected writings of Jeremy Bentham and John Austin.* Cleveland, OH: World. (Originally published, 1859)

Miller, G. A., Galanter, E., & Pribram, K. H. (1960). *Plans and the structure of behavior.* New York: Holt, Rinehart, & Winston.

Miller, I. W., & Norman, W. H. (1979). Learned helplessness in humans: A review and attribution-theory model. *Psychological Bulletin, 86,* 93–119.

Miller, L. C., Putcha-Bhagavatula, A., & Pedersen, W. C. (2002). Men's and women's mating preferences: Distinct evolutionary mechanisms? *Current Directions in Psychological Science, 11,* 88–93.

Miller, N. E. (1944). Experimental studies of conflict. In J. McV. Hunt (Ed.), *Personality and the behavior disorders* (Vol. 1, pp. 431–465). New York: Ronald.

Miller, N. E. (1948). Theory and experiment relating psychoanalytic displacement to stimulus–response generalization. *Journal of Abnormal and Social Psychology, 43,* 155–178.

Miller, N. E. (1951). Learnable drives and rewards. In S. S. Stevens (Ed.), *Handbook of experimental psychology.* New York: Wiley.

Miller, N. E., & Dollard, J. (1941). *Social learning and imitation.* New Haven: Yale University Press.

Miller, R. S. (1987). Empathic embarrassment: Situational and personal determinants of reactions to the embarrassment of another. *Journal of Personality and Social Psychology, 53,* 1061–1069.

Miller, S., Saccuzzo, D., & Braff, D. (1979). Information-processing deficits in remitted schizophrenics. *Journal of Abnormal Psychology, 88,* 446–449.

Mirels, H. (1970). Dimensions of internal versus external control. *Journal of Consulting and Clinical Psychology, 34,* 226–228.

Mischel, W. (1961). Delay of gratification, need for achievement, and acquiescence in another culture. *Journal of Abnormal and Social Psychology, 62,* 543–552.

Mischel, W. (1966). Theory and research on the antecedents of self-imposed delay of reward. In B. A. Maher (Ed.), *Progress in experimental personality research* (Vol. 3). New York: Academic Press.

Mischel, W. (1968). *Personality and assessment.* New York: Wiley.

Mischel, W. (1970). Sex typing and socialization. In P. H. Mussen (Ed.), *Carmichael's manual of child psychology* (Rev. ed.). New York: Wiley.

Mischel, W. (1973). Toward a cognitive social learning reconceptualization of personality. *Psychological Review, 80,* 252–283.

Mischel, W. (1974). Processes in delay of gratification. In L. Berkowitz (Ed.), *Advances in experimental social psychology* (Vol. 7). New York: Academic Press.

Mischel, W. (1977). The interaction of person and situation. In D. Magnusson & N. S. Endler (Eds.), *Personality at the crossroads: Current issues in interactional psychology.* Hillsdale, NJ: Erlbaum.

Mischel, W. (1979). On the interface of cognition and personality: Beyond the person–situation debate. *American Psychologist, 34,* 740–754.

Mischel, W. (1990). Personality dispositions revisited and revised: A view after three decades. In L. A. Pervin (Ed.), *Handbook of personality: Theory and research* (pp. 111–134). New York: Guilford.

Mischel, W., & Baker, N. (1975). Cognitive transformations of reward objects through instructions. *Journal of Personality and Social Psychology, 31,* 254–261.

Mischel, W., & Ebbesen, E. (1970). Attention in delay of gratification. *Journal of Personality and Social Psychology, 16,* 329–337.

Mischel, W., Ebbesen, E., & Zeiss, A. (1973). Selective attention to the self: Situational and dispositional determinants. *Journal of Personality and Social Psychology, 27,* 129–142.

Mischel, W., & Liebert, R. M. (1966). Effects of discrepancies between observed and imposed reward criteria on their acquisition and transmission. *Journal of Personality and Social Psychology, 3,* 45–53.

Mischel, W., & Metzner, R. (1962). Preference for delayed reward as a function of age, intelligence, and length of delay interval. *Journal of Abnormal and Social Psychology, 64,* 425–431.

Mischel, W., & Moore, B. (1973). Effects of attention to symbolically presented rewards upon self-control. *Journal of Personality and Social Psychology, 28,* 172–179.

Mischel, W., & Peake, P. K. (1982). Beyond déjà vu in the search for cross-situational consistency. *Psychological Review, 89,* 730–755.

Mischel, W., & Shoda, Y. (1995). A cognitive–affective system theory of personality: Reconceptualizing situations, dispositions, and invariance in personality structure. *Psychological Review, 102,* 246–268.

Mischel, W., Shoda, Y., & Mendoza-Denton, R. (2002). Situation–behavior profiles as a locus of consistency in personality. *Current Directions in Psychological Science, 11,* 50–54.

Monson, T., Hesley, J., & Chernick, L. (1982). Specifying when personality traits can and cannot predict behavior: An alternative to abandoning the attempt to predict single-act criteria. *Journal of Personality and Social Psychology, 43,* 385–399.

Moore, B., Mischel, W., & Zeiss, A. (1976). Comparative effects of the reward stimulus and its cognitive representation in voluntary delay. *Journal of Personality and Social Psychology, 34,* 419–424.

Moore, J. W. (1972). Stimulus control: Studies of auditory generalization in rabbits. In A. H. Black & W. F. Prokasy (Eds.), *Classical conditioning II: Current research and theory.* New York: Appleton-Century-Crofts.

Morf, C. C., & Rhodewalt, F. (1993). Narcissism and self-evaluation maintenance: Explorations in object relations. *Personality and Social Psychology Bulletin, 19,* 668–676.

Morgan, C. D., & Murray, H. A. (1935). A method for investigating fantasies. *Archives of Neurology and Psychiatry, 34,* 289–306.

Morris, J. L. (1966). Propensity for risk taking as a determinant of vocational choice: An extension of the theory of achievement motivation. *Journal of Personality and Social Psychology, 3,* 328–335.

Morris, L. W., Davis, M. A., & Hutchings, C. H. (1981). Cognitive and emotional components of anxiety: Literature review and a revised worry–emotionality scale. *Journal of Educational Psychology, 73,* 541–555.

Morrone, J. V., Depue, R. A., Scherer, A. J., & White, T. L. (2000). Film-induced incentive motivation and positive activation in relation to agentic and affiliative components of extraversion. *Personality and Individual Differences, 29,* 199–216.

Moskowitz, D. S. (1994). Cross-situational generality and the interpersonal circumplex. *Journal of Personality and Social Psychology, 66,* 921–933.

Moskowitz, G. B. (1993). Individual differences in social categorization: The influence of personal need for structure on spontaneous trait inferences. *Journal of Personality and Social Psychology, 65,* 132–142.

Motley, M. T. (1985). Slips of the tongue. *Scientific American, 253,* 116–127.

Mowrer, O. H., & Mowrer, W. M. (1938). Enuresis—A method for its study and treatment. *American Journal of Orthopsychiatry, 8,* 436–459.

Mueller, C. M., & Dweck, C. S. (1998). Praise for intelligence can undermine children's motivation and performance. *Journal of Personality and Social Psychology, 75,* 33–52.

Mullen, B. (1986). Atrocity as a function of lynch mob composition: A self-attention perspective. *Personality and Social Psychology Bulletin, 12,* 187–197.

Muraven, M., & Baumeister, R. F. (2000). Self-regulation and depletion of limited resources: Does self-control resemble a muscle? *Psychological Bulletin, 126,* 247–259.

Muraven, M., Tice, D. M., & Baumeister, R. F. (1998). Self-control as a limited resource: Regulatory depletion patterns. *Journal of Personality and Social Psychology, 74,* 774–789.

Murray, E. J. (1985). Coping and anger. In T. M. Field, P. M. McCabe, & N. Schneiderman (Eds.), *Stress and coping.* Hillsdale, NJ: Erlbaum.

Murray, H. A. (1938). *Explorations in personality.* New York: Oxford University Press.

Murray, S. L., & Holmes, J. G. (1993). Seeing virtues in faults: Negativity and the transformation of interpersonal narratives in close relationships. *Journal of Personality and Social Psychology, 65,* 707–722.

Murray, S. L., Holmes, J. G., & Griffin, D. W. (2000). Self-esteem and the quest for felt security: How perceived regard regulates attachment processes. *Journal of Personality and Social Psychology, 78,* 478–498.

Murray, S. L., Holmes, J. G., Griffin, D. W., Bellavia, G., & Rose, P. (2001). The mismeasure of love: How self-doubt contaminates relationship beliefs. *Personality and Social Psychology Bulletin, 27,* 423–436.

Myers, M. B., & McCaulley, M. H. (1985). *Manual: A guide to the development and use of the Myers–Briggs Type Indicator.* Palo Alto, CA: Consulting Psychologists Press.

Nasby, W. (1985). Private self-consciousness, articulation of the self-schema, and the recognition memory of trait adjectives. *Journal of Personality and Social Psychology, 49,* 704–709.

Neale, M. C., & Stevenson, J. (1989). Rater bias in the EASI temperament scales: A twin study. *Journal of Personality and Social Psychology, 56,* 446–455.

Neary, R. S., & Zuckerman, M. (1976). Sensation seeking, trait and state anxiety, and the electrodermal orienting reflex. *Psychophysiology, 13,* 205–211.

Neimeyer, G. J., & Neimeyer, R. A. (1981). Personal construct perspectives on cognitive assessment. In T. V. Merluzzi, C. R. Glass, & M. Genest, Eds., *Cognitive assessment.* New York: Guilford.

Neimeyer, R. A. (1985). Personal constructs in clinical practice. In P. C. Kendall (Ed.), *Advances in cognitive-behavioral research and therapy* (Vol. 4, pp. 275–339). New York: Academic Press.

Nell, V. (2002). Why young men drive dangerously: Implications for injury prevention. *Current Directions in Psychological Science, 11,* 75–79.

Nelson, R. O. (1977). Methodological issues in assessment via self-monitoring. In J. D. Cone & R. P. Hawkins (Eds.), *Behavioral assessment: New directions in clinical psychology.* New York: Brunner/Mazel.

Neuberg, S. L., & Newsom, J. T. (1993). Personal need for structure: Individual differences in the desire for simple structure. *Journal of Personality and Social Psychology, 65,* 113–131.

Newcomb, M. D., & McGee, L. (1991). Influence of sensation seeking on general deviance and specific problem behaviors from adolescence to young adulthood. *Journal of Personality and Social Psychology, 61,* 614–628.

Newell, A. (1990). *Unified theories of cognition.* Cambridge, MA: Harvard University Press.

Newell, A., & Simon, H. A. (1972). *Human problem solving.* Englewood Cliffs, NJ: Prentice-Hall.

Newman, D. L., Tellegen, A., & Bouchard, T. J., Jr. (1998). Individual differences in adult ego development: Sources of influence in twins reared apart. *Journal of Personality and Social Psychology, 74,* 985–995.

Newman, J. P., Wallace, J. F., Strauman, T. J., Skolaski, R. L., Oreland, K. M., Mattek, P. W., Elder, K. A., & McNeeley, J. (1993). Effects of motivationally significant stimuli on the regulation of dominant responses. *Journal of Personality and Social Psychology, 65,* 165–175.

Newman, L. S., Duff, K. J., & Baumeister, R. F. (1997). A new look at defensive projection: Thought suppression, accessibility, and biased person perception. *Journal of Personality and Social Psychology, 72,* 980–1001.

Nezu, A. M. (1987). A problem-solving formulation of depression: A literature review and proposal of a pluralistic model. *Clinical Psychology Review, 7,* 121–144.

Nicholls, J. G. (1984). Achievement motivation: Conceptions of ability, subjective experience, task choice, and performance. *Psychological Review, 91,* 328–346.

Nickerson, R. S. (2001). The projective way of knowing: A useful heuristic that sometimes misleads. *Current Directions in Psychological Science, 10,* 168–172.

Niedenthal, P. M., Halberstadt, J. B., & Innes-Ker, A. H. (1999). Emotional response categorization. *Psychological Review, 106,* 337–361.

Niedenthal, P. M., Setterlund, M. B., & Wherry, M. B. (1992). Possible self-complexity and affective reactions to goal-relevant evaluation. *Journal of Personality and Social Psychology, 63,* 5–16.

Nielsen, T. A. (2000). A review of mentation in REM and NREM sleep: "Covert" REM sleep as a possible reconciliation of two opposing models. *Behavioral and Brain Sciences, 23,* 851–866.

Nigg, J. T. (2000). On inhibition/disinhibition in developmental pychopathology: Views from cognitive and personality psychology as a working inhibition taxonomy. *Psychological Bulletin, 126,* 220–246.

Nisbett, R. E., & Cohen, D. (1996). *Culture of honor.* Boulder, CO: Westview.

Nisbett, R. E., & Ross, L. (1980). *Human inference: Strategies and shortcomings of social judgment.* Englewood Cliffs, NJ: Prentice-Hall.

Nisbett, R. E., & Wilson, T. D. (1977). Telling more than we can know: Verbal reports on mental processes. *Psychological Review, 84,* 231–259.

Nolen-Hoeksema, S., Morrow, J., & Frederickson, B. L. (1993). Response styles and the duration of episodes of depressed mood. *Journal of Abnormal Psychology, 102,* 20–28.

Nolen-Hoeksema, S., Parker, L., & Larson, J. (1994). Ruminative coping with depressed mood following loss. *Journal of Personality and Social Psychology, 67,* 92–104.

Norman, D. A. (1981). Categorization of action slips. *Psychological Review, 88,* 1–15.

Norman, W. T. (1963). Toward an adequate taxonomy of personality attributes: Replicated factor structure in peer nomination personality ratings. *Journal of Abnormal and Social Psychology, 66,* 574–583.

Novaco, R. W. (1978). Anger and coping with stress: Cognitive behavioral interventions. In J. P. Foreyt & D. P. Rathjen (Eds.), *Cognitive behavior therapy: Research and application.* New York: Plenum.

Nowak, A., Vallacher, R. R., Tesser, A., & Borkowski, W. (2000). Society of self: The emergence of collective properties in self-structure. *Psychological Review, 107,* 39–61.

Nunnally, J. C., Duchnowski, A. J., & Parker, R. K. (1965). Association of neutral objects and rewards: Effects on verbal evaluation, reward expectancy, and selective attention. *Journal of Personality and Social Psychology, 1,* 270–274.

O'Connor, B. P., & Dyce, J. A. (2001). Rigid and extreme: A geometric representation of personality disorders in five-factor model space. *Journal of Personality and Social Psychology, 81,* 1119–1130.

O'Connor, S. C., & Rosenblood, L. K. (1996). Affiliation motivation in everyday experience: A theoretical comparison. *Journal of Personality and Social Psychology, 70,* 513–522.

O'Donnell, M. C., Fisher, R., Rickard, M., & McConaghy, N. (2000). Emotional suppression: Can it predict cancer outcome in women with suspicious screening mammograms? *Psychological Medicine, 30,* 1079–1088.

O'Donohue, W., & Kitchener, R. (Eds.). (1999). *Handbook of behaviorism.* San Diego, CA: Academic Press.

O'Leary, K. D., & Becker, W. C. (1967). Behavior modification of an adjustment class: A token reinforcement program. *Exceptional Children, 33,* 637–642.

Ogilvie, D. M. (1987). The undesired self: A neglected variable in personality research. *Journal of Personality and Social Psychology, 52,* 379–385.

Öhman, A., & Mineka, S. (2001). Fears, phobias, and preparedness: Toward an evolved module of fear and fear learning. *Psychological Review, 108,* 483–522.

Oliver, M. B., & Hyde, J. S. (1993). Gender differences in sexuality: A meta-analysis. *Psychological Bulletin, 114,* 29–51.

Olson, J. M., Vernon, P. A., Harris, J. A., & Jang, K. L. (2001). The heritability of attitudes: A study of twins. *Journal of Personality and Social Psychology, 80,* 845–860.

Oring, E. (1984). *The jokes of Sigmund Freud: A study in humor and Jewish identity.* Philadelphia: University of Pennsylvania Press.

Orlofsky, J. L., Marcia, J. E., & Lesser, I. M. (1973). Ego identity states and the intimacy versus isolation crisis of young adulthood. *Journal of Youth and Adolescence, 27,* 211–219.

Orr, S. P., Lasko, N. B., Metzger, L. J., Berry, N. J., Ahern, C. E., & Pitman, R. K. (1998). Psychophysiologic assessment of women with posttraumatic stress disorder resulting from childhood sexual abuse. *Journal of Consulting and Clinical Psychology, 66,* 906–913.

Osher, Y., Hamer, D., & Benjamin, J. (2000). Association and linkage of anxiety-related traits with a functional polymorphism of the serotonin transporter gene regulatory region in Israeli sibling pairs. *Molecular Psychiatry, 5,* 216–219.

Overmier, J. B., & Seligman, M. E. P. (1967). Effects of inescapable shock upon subsequent escape and avoidance learning. *Journal of Comparative and Physiological Psychology, 63,* 28–33.

Oyserman, D., Terry, K., & Bybee, D. (2002). A possible selves intervention to enhance school involvement. *Journal of Adolescence, 25,* 313–326.

Ozer, D. J. (1986). *Consistency in personality: A methodological framework.* New York: Springer-Verlag.

Ozer, D. J., & Reise, S. P. (1994). Personality assessment. *Annual Review of Psychology, 45,* 357–388.

Ozer, E. M., & Bandura, A. (1990). Mechanisms governing empowerment effects: A self-efficacy analysis. *Journal of Personality and Social Psychology, 58,* 472–486.

Panksepp, J. (1998). *Affective neuroscience.* New York: Oxford University Press.

Park, J-W., Yoon, S-O., Kim, K-H., & Wyer, R. S., Jr. (2001). Effects of priming a bipolar attribute concept on dimension versus concept-specific accessibility of semantic memory. *Journal of Personality and Social Psychology, 81,* 405–420.

Parke, R. D. (1969). Effectiveness of punishment as an interaction of intensity, timing, agent nurturance, and cognitive structuring. *Child Development, 40,* 211–235.

Parnell, R. W. (1957). Physique and mental breakdown in young adults. *British Medical Journal, 1,* 1485–1490.

Patterson, C. M., & Newman, J. P. (1993). Reflectivity and learning from aversive events: Toward a psychological mechanism for the syndromes of disinhibition. *Psychological Review, 100,* 716–736.

Paul, G. L. (1966). *Insight vs. desensitization in psychotherapy: An experiment in anxiety reduction.* Stanford, CA: Stanford University Press.

Paulhus, D. L. (1983). Sphere-specific measures of perceived control. *Journal of Personality and Social Psychology, 44,* 1253–1265.

Paulhus, D. L. (1998). Interpersonal and intrapsychic adaptiveness of trait self-enhancement: A mixed blessing? *Journal of Personality and Social Psychology, 74,* 1197–1208.

Paulhus, D. L., & Christie, R. (1981). Spheres of control: An interactionist approach to assessment and perceived control. In H. F. Lefcourt (Ed.), *Research with the locus of control construct. Vol. 1, Assessment methods.* New York: Academic Press.

Paulhus, D. L., & Suedfeld, P. (1988). A dynamic complexity model of self-deception. In J. S. Lockard & D. L. Paulhus (Eds.), *Self-deception: An adaptive mechanism?* Englewood Cliffs, NJ: Prentice-Hall.

Paulhus, D. L., Trapnell, P. D., & Chen, D. (1999). Birth order effects on personality and achievement within families. *Psychological Science, 10,* 482–488.

Paunonen, S. V. (1989). Consensus in personality judgments: Moderating effects of target–rater acquaintanceship and behavior observability. *Journal of Personality and Social Psychology, 56,* 823–833.

Paunonen, S. V. (1998). Hierarchical organization of personality and prediction of behavior. *Journal of Personality and Social Psychology, 74,* 538–556.

Paunonen, S. V., & Ashton, M. C. (2001a). Big Five factors and facets and the prediction of behavior. *Journal of Personality and Social Psychology, 81,* 524–539.

Paunonen, S. V., & Ashton, M. C. (2001b). Big Five predictors of academic achievement. *Journal of Research in Personality, 35,* 78–90.

Paunonen, S. V., & Jackson, D. N. (2000). What is beyond the Big Five? Plenty! *Journal of Personality, 68,* 821–835.

Paunonen, S. V., Jackson, D. N., Trzebinski, J., & Forsterling, F. (1992). Personality structure across cultures: A multimethod evaluation. *Journal of Personality and Social Psychology, 62,* 447–456.

Pavlov, I. P. (1927). *Conditioned reflexes.* Oxford, England: Oxford University Press.

Pavlov, I. P. (1955). *Selected works.* New York: Foreign Languages.

Peabody, D. (1984). Personality dimensions through trait inferences. *Journal of Personality and Social Psychology, 46,* 384–403.

Peabody, D., & Goldberg, L. R. (1989). Some determinants of factor structures from personality-trait descriptors. *Journal of Personality and Social Psychology, 57,* 552–567.

Pedersen, N. L., Plomin, R., McClearn, G. E., & Friberg, L. (1988). Neuroticism, extraversion, and related traits in adult twins reared apart and reared together. *Journal of Personality and Social Psychology, 55,* 950–957.

Peirson, A. R., Heuchert, J. W., Thomala, L., Berk, M., Plein, H., & Cloninger, C. R. (1999). Relationship between serotonin and the temperament and character inventory. *Psychiatry Research, 89,* 29–37.

Pelham, B. W., Mirenberg, M. C., & Jones, J. T. (2002). Why Susie sells seashells by the seashore: Implicit egotism and major life decisions. *Journal of Personality and Social Psychology, 82,* 469–487.

Pennebaker, J. W. (1989). Confession, inhibition, and disease. In L. Berkowitz (Ed.), *Advances in Experimental Social Psychology* (Vol. 22, pp. 211–244). San Diego: Academic Press.

Pennebaker, J. W. (1993). Putting stress into words: Health, linguistic, and therapeutic implications. *Behaviour Research and Therapy, 31,* 539–548.

Pennebaker, J. W., & Beall, S. K. (1986). Confronting a traumatic event: Toward an understanding of inhibition and disease. *Journal of Abnormal Psychology, 95,* 274–281.

Pennebaker, J. W., & Graybeal, A. (2001). Patterns of natural language use: Disclosure, personality, and social integration. *Current Directions in Psychological Science, 10,* 90–93.

Pennebaker, J. W., Kiecolt-Glaser, J. K., & Glaser, R. (1988). Disclosure of traumas and immune function: Health implications for psychotherapy. *Journal of Consulting and Clinical Psychology, 56,* 239–245.

Peplau, L. A. (1976). Impact of fear of success and sex-role attitudes on women's competitive achievement. *Journal of Personality and Social Psychology, 34,* 561–568.

Peplau, L. A., & Perlman, D. (Eds.). (1982). *Loneliness: A sourcebook of current theory, research, and therapy.* New York: Wiley.

Perkins, K. A. (1999). Nicotine self-administration. *Nicotine and Tobacco Research, 1* (suppl.), 133–137.

Pervin, L. A. (1983). The stasis and flow of behavior: Toward a theory of goals. In M. M. Page & R. Dienstbier (Eds.), *Nebraska symposium on motivation* (Vol. 31). Lincoln: University of Nebraska Press.

Pervin, L. A. (1985). Personality: Current controversies, issues, and directions. *Annual Review of Psychology, 36,* 83–114.

Pervin, L. A. (Ed.). (1989). *Goal concepts in personality and social psychology.* Hillsdale, NJ: Erlbaum.

Pervin, L. A. (1994). A critical analysis of current trait theory. *Psychological Inquiry, 5,* 103–113.

Peterson, C. (1995). Explanatory style and health. In G. M. Buchanan & M. E. P. Seligman (Eds.), *Explanatory style* (pp. 233–246). Hillsdale, NJ: Erlbaum.

Peterson, L. M. (1980). Why men have pockets in their pants: A feminist insight (or, If Freud had been a woman). *Society for the Advancement of Social Psychology Newsletter, 6,* 19.

Petri, H. L., & Mishkin, M. (1994). Behaviorism, cognitivism, and the neuropsychology of memory. *American Scientist, 82,* 30–37.

Petry, N. M., Martin, B., Cooney, J. L., & Kranzler, H. R. (2000). Give them prizes, and they will come: Contingency management for treatment of alcohol dependence. *Journal of Consulting and Clinical Psychology, 68,* 250–257.

Phares, E. J. (1957). Expectancy changes in skill and chance situations. *Journal of Abnormal and Social Psychology, 54,* 339–342.

Phares, E. J. (1976). *Locus of control in personality.* Morristown, NJ: General Learning Press.

Piedmont, R. L., McCrae, R. R., & Costa, P. T., Jr. (1992). An assessment of the Edwards Personal Preference Schedule from the perspective of the five-factor model. *Journal of Personality Assessment, 58,* 67–78.

Pierce, T., & Lydon, J. E. (2001). Global and specific relational models in the experience of social interactions. *Journal of Personality and Social Psychology, 80,* 613–631.

Pietromonaco, P. R., & Carnelley, K. B. (1994). Gender and working models of attachment: Consequences for perception of self and romantic relationships. *Personal Relationships, 1,* 3–26.

Pietromonaco, P. R., & Feldman Barrett, L. (1997). Working models of attachment and daily social interactions. *Journal of Personality and Social Psychology, 73,* 1409–1423.

Plaks, J. E., Stroessner, S. J., Dweck, C. S., & Sherman, J. W. (2001). Person theories and attention allocation: Preferences for stereotypic versus counterstereotypic information. *Journal of Personality and Social Psychology, 80,* 876–893.

Plomin, R. (1974). *A temperament theory of personality development: Parent–child interactions.* Unpublished doctoral dissertation, University of Texas at Austin.

Plomin, R. (1981). Ethnological behavioral genetics and development. In K. Immelmann, G. W. Barlow, L. Petrinovich, & M. Main (Eds.), *Behavioral development: The Bielefeld interdisciplinary project.* Cambridge, England: Cambridge University Press.

Plomin, R. (1989). Environment and genes: Determinants of behavior. *American Psychologist, 44,* 105–111.

Plomin, R. (1995). Molecular genetics and psychology. *Current Directions in Psychological Science, 4,* 114–117.

Plomin, R. (1997). *Behavioral Genetics.* New York: Freeman.

Plomin, R., & Caspi, A. (1999). Behavioral genetics and personality. In L. A. Pervin & O. P. John (Eds.), *Handbook of personality: Theory and research* (2nd ed., pp. 251–276). New York: Guilford.

Plomin, R., & Crabbe, J. (2000). DNA. *Psychological Bulletin, 126,* 806–828.

Plomin, R., & Daniels, D. (1987). Why are children in the same family so different from one another? *Behavioral and Brain Sciences, 10,* 1–60.

Plomin, R., DeFries, J. C., Craig, I. W., & McGuffin, P. (Eds.). (2003). *Behavioral genetics in the postgenomic era.* Washington, DC: American Psychological Association.

Plomin, R., DeFries, J. C., & Loehlin, J. C. (1977). Genotype–environment interaction and correlation in the analysis of human behavior. *Psychological Bulletin, 84,* 309–322.

Plomin, R., DeFries, J. C., & McClearn, G. E. (1990). *Behavioral genetics: A primer* (2nd ed.). New York: W. H. Freeman.

Plomin, R., & Foch, T. T. (1980). A twin study of objectively assessed personality in childhood. *Journal of Personality and Social Psychology, 39,* 680–688.

Plomin, R., & Rende, R. (1991). Human behavioral genetics. *Annual Review of Psychology, 42,* 161–190.

Plomin, R., & Rowe, D. C. (1977). A twin study of temperament in young children. *Journal of Psychology, 97,* 107–113.

Plomin, R., Scheier, M. F., Bergeman, C. S., Pedersen, N. L., Nesselroade, J. R., & McClearn, G. E. (1992). Optimism, pessimism, and mental health: A twin/adoption analysis. *Personality and Individual Differences, 13,* 921–930.

Poldrack, R. A., & Gabrieli, J. D. E. (2001). Characterizing the neural mechanisms of skill learning and repetition priming: Evidence from mirror-reading. *Brain, 124,* 67–82.

Pollak, S., & Gilligan, C. (1982). Images of violence in Thematic Apperception Test stories. *Journal of Personality and Social Psychology, 42,* 159–167.

Pool, R. (1993). Evidence for homosexuality gene. *Science, 261,* 291–292

Posner, M. I., & DiGirolamo, G. J. (2000). Cognitive neuroscience: Origins and promise. *Psychological Bulletin, 126,* 873–889.

Postman, L. (1951). Toward a general theory of cognition. In J. H. Rohrer & M. Sherif (Eds.), *Social psychology at the crossroads.* New York: Harper.

Powell, J., & Azrin, N. (1968). The effects of shock as a punisher for cigarette smoking. *Journal of Applied Behavior Analysis, 1,* 63–71.

Powell, R. A., & Boer, D. P. (1994). Did Freud mislead patients to confabulate memories of abuse? *Psychological Reports, 74,* 1283–1298.

Powers, W. T. (1973). *Behavior: The control of perception.* Chicago: Aldine.

Prager, K. J. (1982). Identity development and self-esteem in young women. *Journal of Genetic Psychology, 141,* 177–182.

Pratt, M. W., Danso, H. A., Arnold, M. L., Norris, J. E., & Filyer, R. (2001). Adult generativity and the socialization of adolescents: Relations to mothers' and fathers' parenting beliefs, styles, and practices. *Journal of Personality, 69,* 89–120.

Pratto, F., & Hegarty, P. (2000). The political psychology of reproductive strategies. *Psychological Science, 11,* 57–62.

Prentice-Dunn, S., & Rogers, R. W. (1980). Effects of deindividuating situational cues and aggressive models on subjective deindividuation and aggression. *Journal of Personality and Social Psychology, 39,* 104–113.

Prentice-Dunn, S., & Rogers, R. W. (1982). Effects of public and private self-awareness on deindividuation and aggression. *Journal of Personality and Social Psychology, 43,* 503–513.

Prentice-Dunn, S., & Rogers, R. W. (1989). Deindividuation and the self-regulation of behavior. In P. B. Paulus (Ed.), *Psychology of group influence* (2nd ed., pp. 87–109). Hillsdale, NJ: Erlbaum.

Preston, K. L., Umbricht, A., Wong, C. J., & Epstein, D. H. (2001). Shaping cocaine abstinence by successive approximation. *Journal of Consulting and Clinical Psychology, 69,* 643–654.

Price, M. A., Tennant, C. C., Smith, R. C., Butow, P. N., Kennedy, S. J., Kossoff, M. B., & Dunn, S. M. (2001).

The role of psychosocial factors in the development of breast carcinoma: Part I. The cancer-prone personality. *Cancer, 91,* 679–685.

Privette, G., & Landsman, T. (1983). Factor analysis of peak performance: The full use of potential. *Journal of Personality and Social Psychology, 44,* 195–200.

Pyszczynski, T., & Greenberg, J. (1985). Depression and preference for self-focusing stimuli after success and failure. *Journal of Personality and Social Psychology, 49,* 1066–1075.

Pyszczynski, T., & Greenberg, J. (1987). Self-regulatory perseveration and the depressive self-focusing style: A self-awareness theory of reactive depression. *Psychological Bulletin, 102,* 122–138.

Pyszczynski, T., Greenberg, J., & Solomon, S. (2000). Proximal and distal defense: A new perspective on unconscious motivation. *Current Directions in Psychological Science, 9,* 156–160.

Pyszczynski, T., Solomon, S., & Greenberg, J. (2002). *In the wake of 9/11: The psychology of terror.* Washington, DC: American Psychological Association.

Pytlik Zillig, L. M., Hemenover, S. H., & Dienstbier, R. A. (2002). What do we assess when we assess a Big 5 trait? A content analysis of the affective, behavioral, and cognitive processes represented in Big 5 personality inventories. *Personality and Social Psychology Bulletin, 28,* 847–858.

Quinn, S. (1987). *A mind of her own: The life of Karen Horney.* New York: Summit.

Rabin, A. I., Zucker, R. A., Emmons, R. A., & Frank, S. (Eds.). (1990). *Studying persons and lives.* New York: Springer.

Rachlin, H. (1977). Reinforcing and punishing thoughts. *Behavior Therapy, 8,* 659–665.

Rachman, J., & Teasdale, J. (1969). *Aversion therapy and behaviour disorders: An analysis.* Coral Gables, FL: University of Miami Press.

Rachman, S. (Ed.). (1978). *Advances in behaviour research and therapy* (Vol. 1). Oxford: Pergamon.

Rapaport, D. (1960). *The structure of psychoanalytic theory: A systematizing attempt* (Psychological Issues Monograph 6). New York: International Universities Press.

Raskin, P. A., & Israel, A. C. (1981). Sex-role imitation in children: Effects of sex of child, sex of model, and sex-role approriateness of modeled behavior. *Sex Roles, 7,* 1067–1076.

Razran, G. H. S. (1940). Conditioned response changes in rating and appraising sociopolitical slogans. *Psychological Bulletin, 37,* 481.

Read, S. J. (1987). Constructing causal scenarios: A knowledge structure approach to causal reasoning. *Journal of Personality and Social Psychology, 52,* 288–302.

Read, S. J., & Miller, L. C. (Eds.). (1998). *Connectionist models of social reasoning and social behavior.* Mahwah, NJ: Erlbaum.

Read, S. J., & Miller, L. C. (2002). Virtual personalities: A neural network model of personality. *Personality and Social Psychology Review, 6,* 357–369.

Read, S. J., Jones, D. K., & Miller, L. C. (1990). Traits as goal-based categories: The importance of goals in the coherence of dispositional categories. *Journal of Personality and Social Psychology, 58,* 1048–1061.

Read, S. J., Vanman, E. J., & Miller, L. C. (1997). Connectionism, parallel constraint satisfaction processes, and Gestalt principles: (Re)introducing cognitive dynamics to social psychology. *Review of Personality and Social Psychology, 1,* 26–53.

Reason, J., & Mycielska, K. (1982). *Absent-minded? The psychology of mental lapses and everyday errors.* Englewood Cliffs, NJ: Prentice-Hall.

Redmore, C., & Waldman, K. (1975). Reliability of a sentence completion measure of ego development. *Journal of Personality Assessment, 39,* 236–243.

Reese, E. P. (1966). The analysis of human operant behavior. In J. A. Vernon (Ed.), *Introduction to psychology: A self-selection textbook.* Dubuque, IA: Brown.

Reinisch, J. M. (1981). Prenatal exposure to synthetic progestins increases potential for aggression in humans. *Science, 211,* 1171–1173.

Repetti, R. L. (1989). Effects of daily workload on subsequent behavior during marital interactions: The role of social withdrawal and spouse support. *Journal of Personality and Social Psychology, 57,* 651–659.

Rescorla, R. A. (1972). Informational variables in Pavlovian conditioning. In G. H. Bower (Ed.), *The psychology of learning and motivation* (Vol. 6, pp. 1–46). New York: Academic Press.

Rescorla, R. A. (1987). A Pavlovian analysis of goal-directed behavior. *American Psychologist, 42,* 119–129.

Rescorla, R. A. (1988). Pavlovian conditioning: It's not what you think it is. *American Psychologist, 43,* 151–160.

Rescorla, R. A. (1997). Response-inhibition in extinction. *Quarterly Journal of Experimental Psychology: Comparative and Physiological Psychology, 50B,* 238–252.

Rescorla, R. A. (1998). Instrumental learning: Nature and persistence. In M. Sabourin, F. Craik, et al. (Eds.), *Advances in psychological science, Vol. 2: Biological and cognitive aspects* (pp. 239–257). Hove, England: Psychology Press.

Reynolds, S. K., & Clark, L. A. (2001). Predicting dimensions of personality disorder from domains and facets of the five-factor model. *Journal of Personality, 69,* 199–222.

Rhawn, J. (1980). Awareness, the origin of thought, and the role of conscious self-deception in resistance and repression. *Psychological Reports, 46,* 767–781.

Rhee, S. H., & Waldman, I. D. (2002). Genetic and environmental influences on antisocial behavior: A meta-analysis of twin and adoption studies. *Psychological Bulletin, 128,* 490–529.

Rhodewalt, F., & Morf, C. C. (1998). On self-aggrandizement and anger: A temporal analysis of narcissism and affective reactions to success and failure. *Journal of Personality and Social Psychology, 74,* 672–685.

Rholes, W. S., Simpson, J. A., & Oriña, M. M. (1999). Attachment and anger in an anxiety-provoking situation. *Journal of Personality and Social Psychology, 76,* 940–957.

Riedel, W. (1970). An investigation of personal constructs through nonverbal tasks. *Journal of Abnormal Psychology, 76,* 173–179.

Riordan, C. A., & Tedeschi, J. T. (1983). Attraction in aversive environments: Some evidence for classical conditioning and negative reinforcement. *Journal of Personality and Social Psychology, 44,* 683–692.

Risley, T. R. (1968). The effects and side effects of punishing the autistic behaviors of a deviant child. *Journal of Applied Behavior Analysis, 1,* 21–34.

Ritvo, L. B. (1990). *Darwin's influence on Freud: A tale of two sciences.* New Haven, CT: Yale University Press.

Rizzolatti, G., Fogassi, L., & Gallese, V. (2002). Motor and cognitive functions of the ventral premotor cortex. *Current Opinion in Neurobiology, 12,* 149–154.

Roberts, B. W., Caspi, A., & Moffitt, T. E. (2001). The kids are alright: Growth and stability in personality development from adolescence to adulthood. *Journal of Personality and Social Psychology, 81,* 670–683.

Roberts, B. W., & DelVecchio, W. F. (2000). The rank-order consistency of personality traits from childhood to old age: A quantitative review of longitudinal studies. *Psychological Bulletin, 126,* 3–25.

Roberts, B. W., & Robins, R. W. (2000). Broad dispositions, broad aspirations: The intersection of personality traits and major life goals. *Personality and Social Psychology Bulletin, 26,* 1284–1296.

Roberts, J. E., & Monroe, S. M. (1994). A multidimensional model of self-esteem in depression. *Clinical Psychology Review, 14,* 161–181.

Roberts, J. E., Gotlib, I. H., & Kassel, J. D. (1996). Adult attachment security and symptoms of depression: The mediating roles of dysfunctional attitudes and low self-esteem. *Journal of Personality and Social Psychology, 70,* 310–320.

Robins, R. W., Fraley, R. C., Roberts, B. W., & Trzesniewski, K. H. (2001). A longitudinal study of personality change in young adulthood. *Journal of Personality, 69,* 617–640.

Robins, R. W., John, O. P., Caspi, A., Moffitt, T. E., & Stouthamer-Loeber, M. (1996). Resilient, overcontrolled, and undercontrolled boys: Three replicable personality types. *Journal of Personality and Social Psychology, 70,* 157–171.

Robins, R. W., & Pals, J. L. (2002). Implicit self-theories in the academic domain: Implications for goal orientation, attributions, affect, and self-esteem change. *Self and Identity, 1,* 313–336.

Robinson, F. G. (1992). *Love's story told: A life of Henry A. Murray.* Cambridge, MA: Harvard University Press.

Roccas, S., Sagiv, L., Schwartz, S. H., & Knafo, A. (2002). The Big Five personality factors and personal values. *Personality and Social Psychology Bulletin, 28,* 789–801.

Rogers, C. R. (1951). *Client-centered therapy: Its current practice, implications and theory.* Boston: Houghton Mifflin.

Rogers, C. R. (1959). A theory of therapy, personality and interpersonal relationships, as developed in the client-centered framework. In S. Koch (Ed.), *Psychology: A study of a science* (Vol. 3). New York: McGraw-Hill.

Rogers, C. R. (1961). *On becoming a person.* Boston: Houghton Mifflin.

Rogers, C. R. (1965). *Client-centered therapy: Its current practice, implication, and theory.* Boston: Houghton Mifflin.

Rogers, C. R., & Dymond, R. F. (Eds.). (1954). *Psychotherapy and personality change: Co-ordinated research studies in the client-centered approach.* Chicago: University of Chicago Press.

Rogers, C. R., & Stevens, B. (1967). *Person to person: The problem of being human.* New York: Simon & Schuster.

Rogers, T. B. (1981). A model of the self as an aspect of the human information-processing system. In N. Cantor & J. F. Kihlstrom (Eds.), *Personality, cognition and social interaction.* Hillsdale, NJ: Erlbaum.

Rogers, T. B., Kuiper, N. A., & Kirker, W. S. (1977). Self-reference and the encoding of personal information. *Journal of Personality and Social Psychology, 35,* 677–688.

Rorer, L. G. (1965). The great response-style myth. *Psychological Bulletin, 63,* 129–156.

Rorschach, H. (1942). *Psychodiagnostics.* Berne, Switzerland: Huber.

Rosch, E., & Mervis, C. (1975). Family resemblances: Studies in the internal structure of categories. *Cognitive Psychology, 7,* 573–605.

Rosekrans, M. A. (1967). Imitation in children as a function of perceived similarity and vicarious reinforcement. *Journal of Personality and Social Psychology, 7,* 307–315.

Roseman, I. J. (1991). Appraisal determinants of discrete emotions. *Cognition and Emotion, 5,* 161–200.

Rosen, C. M. (1987). The eerie world of reunited twins. *Discover, 8,* 36–46.

Rosenbaum, D. A. (1987). Hierarchical organization of motor programs. In S. Wise (Ed.), *Neural and behavioral approaches to higher brain function* (pp. 45–66). New York: Wiley.

Rosenbaum, D. A. (1990). *Human motor control.* San Diego: Academic Press.

Rosenthal, T. L., & Reese, S. L. (1976). The effects of covert and overt modeling on assertive behavior. *Behavior Research and Therapy, 14,* 463–469.

Rosenwald, G. C. (1972). Effectiveness of defenses against anal impulse arousal. *Journal of Consulting and Clinical Psychology, 39,* 292–298.

Ross, D. M., Ross, S. A., & Evans, T. A. (1971). The modification of extreme social withdrawal by modeling with guided participation. *Journal of Behavior Therapy and Experimental Psychiatry, 2,* 273–279.

Ross, M. (1989). Relation of implicit theories to the construction of personal histories. *Psychological Review, 96,* 341–357.

Ross, M., & Fletcher, G. J. O. (1985). Attribution and social perception. In G. Lindzey & E. Aronson (Eds.), *The handbook of social psychology* (3rd. ed., pp. 73–122). Reading, MA: Addison-Wesley.

Roth, S. (1980). A revised model of learned helplessness in humans. *Journal of Personality, 48,* 103–133.

Rotter, J. B. (1954). *Social learning and clinical psychology.* New York: Prentice-Hall.

Rotter, J. B. (1966). Generalized expectancies for internal versus external control of reinforcement. *Psychological Monographs, 80* (1, Whole No. 609).

Rotter, J. B. (1982). *The development and applications of social learning theory: Selected papers.* New York: Praeger.

Rotter, J. B. (1990). Internal versus external control of reinforcement: A case history of a variable. *American Psychologist, 45,* 489–493.

Rotter, J. B., Seeman, M., & Liverant, S. (1962). Internal versus external control of reinforcement: A major variable in behavior theory. In N. F. Washburne (Ed.), *Decisions, values, and groups* (Vol. 2). New York: Pergamon.

Rowe, D. C. (1994). *The limits of family influence: Genes, experience, and behavior.* New York: Guilford.

Rowe, D. C. (2001). *Biology and crime.* Los Angeles, CA: Roxbury.

Rozsnafszky, J. (1981). The relationship of level of ego development to Q-sort personality ratings. *Journal of Personality and Social Psychology, 41,* 99–120.

Rubin, R. T., Reinisch, J. M., & Haskett, R. F. (1981). Postnatal gonadal steroid effects on human behavior. *Science, 211,* 1318–1324.

Runck, B. (1980). *Biofeedback—Issues in treatment assessment.* Rockville, MD: National Institute of Mental Health.

Rushton, J. P. (1988). Genetic similarity, mate choice, and fecundity in humans. *Ethology and Sociobiology, 9,* 329–335.

Rushton, J. P. (1989a). Genetic similarity, human altruism, and group selection. *Behavioral and Brain Sciences, 12,* 503–559.

Rushton, J. P. (1989b). Genetic similarity in male friendships. *Ethology and Sociobiology, 10,* 361–373.

Rushton, J. P., Brainerd, C. J., & Pressley, M. (1983). Behavioral development and construct validity: The principle of aggregation. *Psychological Bulletin, 94,* 18–38.

Rushton, J. P., Fulker, D. W., Neale, M. C., Nias, D. K. B., & Eysenck, H. J. (1986). Altruism and aggression: The heritability of individual differences. *Journal of Personality and Social Psychology, 50,* 1192–1198.

Rushton, J. P., Russell, R. J. H., & Wells, P. A. (1984). Genetic similarity theory: Beyond kin selection. *Behavior Genetics, 14,* 179–193.

Ryan, R. M. (1982). Control and information in the intrapersonal sphere: An extension of cognitive evaluation theory. *Journal of Personality and Social Psychology, 43,* 450–461.

Ryan, R. M. (1993). Agency and organization: Intrinsic motivation, autonomy, and the self in psychological development. In J. Jacobs (Ed.), *Nebraska symposium on motivation: Developmental perspectives on motivation* (Vol. 40, pp. 1–56). Lincoln: University of Nebraska Press.

Ryan, R. M., & Connell, J. P. (1989). Perceived locus of causality and internalization: Examining reasons for acting in two domains. *Journal of Personality and Social Psychology, 57,* 749–761.

Ryan, R. M., & Deci, E. L. (2001). On happiness and human potentials: A review of research on hedonic and eudaimonic well-being. *Annual Review of Psychology, 52,* 141–166.

Ryan, R. M., Rigby, S., & King, K. (1993). Two types of religious internalization and their relations to religious orientations and mental health. *Journal of Personality and Social Psychology, 65,* 586–596.

Ryan, R. M., Sheldon, K. M., Kasser, T., & Deci, E. L. (1996). All goals are not created equal: An organismic perspective on the nature of goals and their regulation. In P. M. Gollwitzer & J. A. Bargh (Eds.), *The psychology of action: Linking cognition and motivation to behavior* (pp. 7–26). New York: Guilford.

Sadalla, E. K., Kenrick, D. T., & Vershure, B. (1987). Dominance and heterosexual attraction. *Journal of Personality and Social Psychology, 52,* 730–738.

Salmoni, A. W., Schmidt, R. A., & Walter, C. B. (1984). Knowledge of results and motor learning: A review and critical reappraisal. *Psychological Bulletin, 95,* 355–386.

Sarason, I. G. (1975). Test anxiety and the self-disclosing coping model. *Journal of Consulting and Clinical Psychology, 43,* 148–153.

Saucier, G. (1992). Benchmarks: Integrating affective and interpersonal circles with the big-five personality factors. *Journal of Personality and Social Psychology, 62,* 1025–1035.

Saucier, G., & Goldberg, L. R. (1998). What is beyond the Big Five? *Journal of Personality, 66,* 495–524.

Saucier, G., & Ostendorf, F. (1999). Hierarchical subcomponents of the Big Five personality factors: A cross-language replication. *Journal of Personality and Social Psychology, 76,* 613–627.

Saudino, K. J., McGuire, S., Reiss, D., Hetherington, E. M., & Plomin, R. (1995). Parent ratings of EAS temperaments in twins, full siblings, half siblings, and step siblings. *Journal of Personality and Social Psychology, 68,* 723–733.

Saudino, K. J., Pedersen, N. L., Lichtenstein, P., McClearn, G. E., & Plomin, R. (1997). Can personality explain genetic influences on life events? *Journal of Personality and Social Psychology, 72,* 196–206.

Scarr, S. (1985). Constructing psychology: Making facts and fables for our time. *American Psychologist, 40,* 499–512.

Scarr, S., & Carter-Saltzman, L. (1979). Twin method: Defense of a critical assumption. *Behavior Genetics, 9,* 527–542.

Scarr, S., & McCartney, K. (1983). How people make their own environments: A theory of genotype -> environment effects. *Child Development, 54,* 424–435.

Schank, R. C., & Abelson, R. P. (1977). *Scripts, plans, goals, and understanding.* Hillsdale, NJ: Erlbaum.

Schefft, B. K., & Lehr, B. K. (1985). A self-regulatory model of adjunctive behavior change. *Behavior Modification, 9,* 458–476.

Scheier, M. F., & Carver, C. S. (1983). Self-directed attention and the comparison of self with standards. *Journal of Experimental Social Psychology, 19,* 205–222.

Scheier, M. F., & Carver, C. S. (1988). A model of behavioral self-regulation: Translating intention into action. In L. Berkowitz (Ed.), *Advances in experimental social psychology* (Vol. 21, pp. 303–346). New York: Academic Press.

Scheier, M. F., & Carver, C. S. (1992). Effects of optimism on psychological and physical well-being: Theoretical overview and empirical update. *Cognitive Therapy and Research, 16,* 201–228.

Scheier, M. F., Carver, C. S., & Bridges, M. W. (2001). Optimism, pessimism, and psychological well-being. In E. C. Chang (Ed.), *Optimism and pessimism: Implications for theory, research, and practice* (pp. 189–216). Washington, DC: American Psychological Association.

Scheier, M. F., & Fenigstein, A., & Buss, A. H. (1974). Self-awareness and physical aggression. *Journal of Experimental Social Psychology, 10,* 264–273.

Scheier, M. F., Matthews, K. A., Owens, J. F., Magovern, G. J., Lefebvre, R. C., Abbott, R. A., & Carver, C. S. (1989). Dispositional optimism and recovery from coronary artery bypass surgery: The beneficial effects on physical and psychological well-being. *Journal of Personality and Social Psychology, 57,* 1024–1040.

Scheier, M. F., Matthews, K. A., Owens, J. F., Schulz, R., Bridges, M. W., Magovern, G. J., Sr., & Carver, C. S. (1999). Optimism and rehospitalization following coronary artery bypass graft surgery. *Archives of Internal Medicine, 159,* 829–835.

Scheirer, M. A., & Kraut, R. E. (1979). Increasing educational achievement via self-concept change. *Review of Educational Research, 49,* 131–150.

Schell, T. L., Klein, S. B., & Babey, S. H. (1996). Testing a hierarchical model of self-knowledge. *Psychological Science, 7,* 170–173.

Schiedel, D. G., & Marcia, J. E. (1985). Ego identity, intimacy, sex-role orientation, and gender. *Journal of Personality and Social Psychology, 21,* 149–160.

Schimek, J. G. (1987). Fact and fantasy in the seduction theory: A historical review. *Journal of the American Psychoanalytic Association, 35,* 937–965.

Schimel, J., Arndt, J., Pyszczynski, T., & Greenberg, J. (2001). Being accepted for who we are: Evidence that social validation of the intrinsic self reduces general defensiveness. *Journal of Personality and Social Psychology, 80,* 35–52.

Schlenker, B. R., Dlugolecki, D. W., & Doherty, K. (1994). The impact of self-presentations on self-appraisals and behavior: The power of public commitment. *Personality and Social Psychology Bulletin, 20,* 20–33.

Schmidt, L. A. (1999). Frontal brain electrical activity in shyness and sociability. *Psychological Science, 10,* 316–320.

Schmidt, R. A. (1976). The schema as a solution to some persistent problems in motor learning theory. In G. E. Stelmach (Ed.), *Motor control: Issues and trends.* New York: Academic Press.

Schmidt, R. A. (1988). *Motor control and learning: A behavioral emphasis* (2nd ed.). Champaign, IL: Human Kinetics Publishers.

Schmitt, D. P., & Buss, D. M. (1996). Strategic self-promotion and competitor derogation: Sex and context effects on the perceived effectiveness of mate attraction tactics. *Journal of Personality and Social Psychology, 70,* 1185–1204.

Schmitt, D. P., & Buss, D. M. (2001). Human mate poaching: Tactics and temptations for infiltrating existing mateships. *Journal of Personality and Social Psychology, 80,* 894–917.

Schmitt, W. A., Brinkley, C. A., & Newman, J. P. (1999). Testing Damasio's somatic marker hypothesis with psychopathic individuals: Risk takers or risk averse? *Journal of Abnormal Psychology, 108,* 538–543.

Schneider, D. J. (1991). Social cognition. *Annual Review of Psychology, 42,* 527–561.

Schneider, K. J., Bugental, J. F. T., & Pierson, J. F. (Eds.). (2001). *The handbook of humanistic psychology: Leading edges in theory, research, and practice.* Thousand Oaks, CA: Sage.

Schneiderman, N., & Gormezano, I. (1964). Conditioning of the nictitating membrane of the rabbit as a function of the CS–US interval. *Journal of Comparative and Physiological Psychology, 57,* 188–195.

Schober, M. F., & Clark, H. H. (1989). Understanding by addressees and overhearers. *Cognitive Psychology, 21,* 211–232.

Schriesheim, C. A., & Hill, K. D. (1981). Controlling acquiescence response bias by item reversals: The effect on questionnaire validity. *Educational and Psychological Measurement, 41,* 1101–1114.

Schuckit, M. A., & Rayses, V. (1979). Ethanol ingestion: Differences in blood acetaldehyde concentrations in relatives of alcoholics and controls. *Science, 203,* 54–55.

Schultheiss, O. C. (2002). An information-processing account of implicit motive arousal. In P. R. Pintrich & M. L. Maehr (Eds.), *Advances in motivation and achievement: New directions in measures and methods* (Vol. 12, pp. 1–41). Amsterdam, The Netherlands: Elsevier.

Schultheiss, O. C., & Brunstein, J. C. (2001). Assessment of implicit motives with a research version of the TAT: Picture profiles, gender differences, and relations to other personality measures. *Journal of Personality Assessment, 77,* 71–86.

Schultheiss, O. C., & Brunstein, J. C. (2002). Inhibited power motivation and persuasive communication: A lens model analysis. *Journal of Personality, 70,* 553–582.

Schultheiss, O. C., Campbell, K. L., & McClelland, D. C. (1999). Implicit power motivation moderates men's testosterone responses to imagined and real dominance success. *Hormones and Behavior, 36,* 234–241.

Schultheiss, O. C., & Rohde, W. (2002). Implicit power motivation predicts men's testosterone changes and implicit learning in a contest situation. *Hormones and Behavior, 41,* 195–202.

Schultz, C. B., & Pomerantz, M. (1976). Achievement motivation, locus of control, and academic achievement behavior. *Journal of Personality, 44,* 38–51.

Schultz, T. R., & Lepper, M. R. (1996). Cognitive dissonance reduction as constraint satisfaction. *Psychological Review, 103,* 219–240.

Schutte, N. S., Kenrick, D. T., & Sadalla, E. K. (1985). The search for predictable settings: Situational prototypes, constraint, and behavioral variation. *Journal of Personality and Social Psychology, 49,* 121–128.

Schwartz, B. (1989). *Psychology of learning and behavior* (3rd ed.). New York: Norton.

Schwarz, N. (1990). Feelings as information: Informational and motivational functions of affective states. In E. T. Higgins and R. M. Sorrentino (Eds.), *Handbook of motivation and cognition: Foundations of social behavior* (Vol. 2, pp. 527–561). New York: Guilford.

Sears, D. O. (1986). College sophomores in the laboratory: Influences of a narrow data base on social psychology's view of human nature. *Journal of Personality and Social Psychology, 51,* 515–530.

Sears, R. R. (1943). *Survey of objective studies of psychoanalytic concepts* (Bulletin 51). New York: Social Sciences Research Council.

Sears, R. R., Rau, L., & Alpert, R. (1965). *Identification and child rearing.* Stanford, CA: Stanford University Press.

Sechrest, L. (1977). Personal constructs theory. In R. J. Corsini (Ed.), *Current personality theories.* Itasca, IL: Peacock.

Sederer, L., & Seidenberg, R. (1976). Heiress to an empty throne: Ego-ideal problems of contemporary women. *Contemporary Psychoanalysis, 12,* 240–251.

Segal, N. L. (1993). Twin, sibling, and adoption methods: Tests of evolutionary hypotheses. *American Psychologist, 48,* 943–956.

Segal, N. L. (1999). *Entwined lives: Twins and what they tell us abut human behavior.* New York: Dutton.

Segal, Z. V. (1988). Appraisal of the self-schema construct in cognitive models of depression. *Psychological Bulletin, 103,* 147–162.

Seifer, R., Sameroff, A. J., Barrett, L. C., & Krafchuk, E. (1994). Infant temperament measured by multiple observations and mother report. *Child Development, 65,* 1478–1490.

Seligman, M. E. P., & Hager, J. L. (Eds.). (1972). *Biological boundaries of learning*. New York: Appleton-Century-Crofts.

Seligman, M. E. P., & Maier, S. F. (1967). Failure to escape traumatic shock. *Journal of Experimental Psychology, 74*, 1–9.

Seltzer, R. A. (1973). Simulation of the dynamics of action. *Psychological Reports, 32*, 859–872.

Semmer, N., & Frese, M. (1985). Action theory in clinical psychology. In M. Frese & J. Sabini (Eds.), *Goal directed behavior: The concept of action in psychology*. Hillsdale, NJ: Erlbaum.

Shapiro, D. (1965). *Neurotic styles*. New York: Basic Books.

Shapiro, D., & Surwit, R. S. (1979). Biofeedback. In O. F. Pomerleau & J. P. Brady (Eds.), *Behavioral medicine: Theory and practice*. Baltimore: Williams & Wilkins.

Shaver, P. R., & Brennan, K. A. (1992). Attachment styles and the "big five" personality traits: Their connections with each other and with romantic relationship outcomes. *Personality and Social Psychology Bulletin, 18*, 536–545.

Shaver, P. R., & Rubenstein, C. (1980). *Childhood attachment experience and adult loneliness*. In L. Wheeler (Ed.), *Review of personality and social psychology* (Vol. 1, pp. 42–73). Beverly Hills, CA: Sage.

Shaver, P. R, Schwartz, J., Kirson, D., & O'Connor, C. (1987). Emotion knowledge: Further exploration of a prototype approach. *Journal of Personality and Social Psychology, 52*, 1061–1086.

Shedler, J., & Block, J. (1990). Adolescent drug use and psychological health: A longitudinal inquiry. *American Psychologist, 45*, 612–630.

Shedler, J., Mayman, M., & Manis, M. (1993). The *illusion* of mental health. *American Psychologist, 48*, 1117–1131.

Sheldon, K. M., & Elliot, A. J. (1998). Not all personal goals are personal: Comparing autonomous and controlled reasons for goals as predictors of effort and attainment. *Personality and Social Psychology Bulletin, 24*, 546–557.

Sheldon, K. M., & Elliot, A. J. (1999). Goal striving, need satisfaction, and longitudinal well-being: The self-concordance model. *Journal of Personality and Social Psychology, 76*, 482–497.

Sheldon, K. M., Elliot, A. J., Kim, Y., & Kasser, T. (2001). What is satisfying about satisfying events? Testing 10 candidate psychological needs. *Journal of Personality and Social Psychology, 80*, 325–339.

Sheldon, K. M., & Houser-Marko, L. (2001). Self-concordance, goal attainment, and the pursuit of happiness: Can there be an upward spiral? *Journal of Personality and Social Psychology, 80*, 152–165.

Sheldon, K. M., & Kasser, T. (1998). Pursuing personal goals: Skills enable progress but not all progress is beneficial. *Personality and Social Psychology Bulletin, 24*, 1319–1331.

Sheldon, K. M., Ryan, R. M., & Reis, H. (1996). What makes for a good day? Competence and autonomy in the day and in the person. *Personality and Social Psychology Bulletin, 22*, 1270–1279.

Sheldon, W. H. (with the collaboration of S. S. Stevens) (1942). *The varieties of temperament: A psychology of constitutional differences*. New York: Harper.

Sher, K. J., Bartholow, B. D., & Wood, M. D. (2000). Personality and substance use disorders: A prospective study. *Journal of Consulting and Clinical Psychology, 68*, 818–829.

Sherwood, G. G. (1981). Self-serving biases in person perception: An examination of projection as a mechanism of defense. *Psychological Bulletin, 90*, 445–459.

Shibutani, T. (1961). *Society and personality: An interactionist approach to social psychology*. Englewood Cliffs, NJ: Prentice-Hall.

Shipley, T. E., & Veroff, J. (1952). A projective measure of need for affiliations. *Journal of Experimental Psychology, 43*, 349–356.

Shoda, Y., Mischel, W., & Wright, J. C. (1989). Intuitive interactionism in person perception: Effects of situation–behavior relations on dispositional judgments. *Journal of Personality and Social Psychology, 56*, 41–53.

Shoda, Y., Mischel, W., & Wright, J. C. (1993). The role of situational demands and cognitive competencies in behavior organization and personality coherence. *Journal of Personality and Social Psychology, 65*, 1023–1035.

Shoda, Y., Mischel, W., & Wright, J. C. (1994). Intraindividual stability in the organization and patterning of behavior: Incorporating psychological situations into the idiographic analysis of personality. *Journal of Personality and Social Psychology, 67*, 674–687.

Shostrom, E. L. (1964). An inventory for the measurement of self-actualization. *Educational and Psychological Measurement, 24*, 207–218.

Shostrom, E. L. (1974). *Manual for the Personal Orientation Inventory*. San Diego: EdITS.

Showers, C. J., & Ryff, C. D. (1996). Self-differentiation and well-being in a life transition. *Personality and Social Psychology Bulletin, 22*, 448–460.

Shubsachs, A. P. W. (1975). To repeat or not to repeat? Are frequently used constructs more important to the subject? *British Journal of Medical Psychology, 48*, 31–37.

Sidanius, J., Pratto, F., & Bobo, L. (1994). Social dominance orientation and the political psychology of gender: A case of invariance? *Journal of Personality and Social Psychology, 67,* 998–1011.

Silverman, L. H. (1976). Psychoanalytic theory: "The reports of my death are greatly exaggerated." *American Psychologist, 31,* 621–637.

Silverman, L. H. (1983). The subliminal psychodynamic activation method: Overview and comprehensive listing of studies. In J. Masling (Ed.), *Empirical studies of psychoanalytic theories* (Vol. 1, pp. 69–100). Hillsdale, NJ: Erlbaum.

Silverman, L. H., Ross, D. L., Adler, J. M., & Lustig, D. A. (1978). Simple research paradigm for demonstrating subliminal psychodynamic activation: Effects of Oedipal stimuli on dart-throwing accuracy in college men. *Journal of Abnormal Psychology, 87,* 341–357.

Simon, D. P., & Simon, H. A. (1978). Individual differences in solving physics problems. In R. S. Siegler (Ed.), *Children's Thinking: What develops?* (pp. 325–348). Hillsdale, NJ: Erlbaum.

Simon, H. A. (1967). Motivational and emotional controls of cognition. *Psychological Review, 74,* 29–39.

Simpson, J. A. (1990). Influence of attachment styles on romantic relationships. *Journal of Personality and Social Psychology, 59,* 971–980.

Simpson, J. A., & Rholes, W. S. (Eds.). (1998). *Attachment theory and close relationships.* New York: Guilford.

Simpson, J. A., Rholes, W. S., & Nelligan, J. S. (1992). Support seeking and support giving within couples in an anxiety-provoking situation: The role of attachment styles. *Journal of Personality and Social Psychology, 62,* 434–446.

Simpson, J. A., Rholes, W. S., Oriña, M. M., & Grich, J. (2002). Working models of attachment, support giving, and support seeking in a stressful situation. *Personality and Social Psychology Bulletin, 28,* 598–608.

Singh, D. (1995). Female judgment of male attractiveness and desirability for relationships: Role of waist-to-hip ratio and financial status. *Journal of Personality and Social Psychology, 69,* 1089–1101.

Skinner, B. F. (1938). *The behavior of organisms.* New York: Appleton-Century-Crofts.

Skinner, B. F. (1948). "Superstition" in the pigeon. *Journal of Experimental Psychology, 38,* 168–172.

Skinner, B. F. (1953). *Science and human behavior.* New York: Macmillan.

Skinner, B. F. (1974). *About behaviorism.* New York: Knopf.

Skinner, B. F. (1987). Whatever happened to psychology as the science of behavior? *American Psychologist, 42,* 780–786.

Skinner, B. F. (1989). The origins of cognitive thought. *American Psychologist, 44,* 13–18.

Skowronski, J. J., Carlston, D. E., Mae, L., & Crawford, M. T. (1998). Spontaneous trait transference: Communicators take on the qualities they describe in others. *Journal of Personality and Social Psychology, 74,* 837–848.

Sloman, S. A. (1996). The empirical case for two forms of reasoning. *Psychological Bulletin, 119,* 3–22.

Small, M. F. (1993). *Female choices: Sexual behavior of female primates.* Ithaca, NY: Cornell University Press.

Smith, A. (1969). *The theory of moral sentiments.* New Rochelle, NY: Arlington House. (Originally published in 1759)

Smith, C. P. (Ed.). (1992). *Motivation and personality: Handbook of thematic content analysis.* New York: Cambridge University Press.

Smith, E. E., Adams, N., & Schorr, D. (1978). Fact retrieval and the paradox of interference. *Cognitive Psychology, 10,* 438–464.

Smith, E. E., Shoben, E. J., & Rips, L. J. (1974). Structure and process in semantic memory: A featural model for semantic decisions. *Psychological Review, 81,* 214–241.

Smith, E. R. (1996). What do connectionism and social psychology offer each other? *Journal of Personality and Social Psychology, 70,* 893–912.

Smith, E. R., Murphy, J., & Coats, S. (1999). Attachment to groups: Theory and measurement. *Journal of Personality and Social Psychology, 77,* 94–110.

Smith, G. M. (1967). Usefulness of peer ratings of personality in educational resarch. *Educational and Psychological Measurement, 27,* 967–984.

Smith, K. D., Keating, J. P., & Stotland, E. (1989). Altruism reconsidered: The effect of denying feedback on a victim's status to empathic witnesses. *Journal of Personality and Social Psychology, 57,* 641–650.

Smith, M. L., & Glass, G. V. (1977). Meta-analysis of psychotherapy outcome studies. *American Psychologist, 32,* 752–760.

Smith, M. L., Glass, G. V., & Miller, T. I. (1980). *The benefits of psychotherapy.* Baltimore: Johns Hopkins Press.

Smith, R. E. (1989). Effects of coping skills training on generalized self-efficacy and locus of control. *Journal of Personality and Social Psychology, 56,* 228–233.

Smith, T. W., Snyder, C. R., & Handelsman, M. M. (1982). On the self-serving function of an academic wooden leg: Test anxiety as a self-handicapping strategy. *Journal of Personality and Social Psychology, 42,* 314–321.

Smolensky, P. (1988). On the proper treatment of connectionism. *Behavioral and Brain Sciences, 11,* 1–23.

...ds.). ...Mah-

...n: Effects... ...bles. *Journal of Consulting and Clinical Psychology*, ..., ...-184.

Snyder, C. R., & Higgins, R. L. (1988). Excuses: Their effective role in the negotiation of reality. *Psychological Bulletin, 104,* 23–35.

Snyder, M. (1974). The self-monitoring of expressive behavior. *Journal of Personality and Social Psychology, 30,* 526–537.

Snyder, M. (1987). *Public appearances/private realities: The psychology of self-monitoring.* New York: W. H. Freeman.

Snyder, M., & Gangestad, S. (1982). Choosing social situations: Two investigations of the self-monitoring process. *Journal of Personality and Social Psychology, 43,* 123–135.

Snyder, M. L., Stephan, W. G., & Rosenfield, D. (1976). Egotism and attribution. *Journal of Personality and Social Psychology, 33,* 435–441.

Snyder, M. L., Stephan, W. G., & Rosenfield, D. (1978). Attributional egotism. In J. H. Harvey, W. Ickes, & R. F. Kidd (Eds.), *New directions in attributional research* (Vol. 2). Hillsdale, NJ: Erlbaum.

Sobotka, S. S., Davidson, R. J., & Senulis, J. A. (1992). Anterior brain electrical asymmetries in response to reward and punishment. *Electroencephalography and Clinical Neurophysiology, 83,* 236–247.

Solms, M. (2000). Dreaming and REM sleep are controlled by different brain mechanisms. *Behavioral and Brain Sciences, 23,* 843–850.

Solomon, R. L. (1964). Punishment. *American Psychologist, 19,* 239–253.

Somer, O., & Goldberg, L. R. (1999). The structure of Turkish trait-descriptive adjectives. *Journal of Personality and Social Psychology, 76,* 431–450.

Sorg, B. A., & Whitney, P. (1992). The effect of trait anxiety and situational stress on working memory capacity. *Journal of Research in Personality, 26,* 235–241.

Sorrentino, R. M., & Field, N. (1986). Emergent leadership over time: The functional value of positive motivation. *Journal of Personality and Social Psychology, 50,* 1091–1099.

Spacapan, S., & Cohen, S. (1983). Effects and aftereffects of stressor expectations. *Journal of Personality and Social Psychology, 45,* 1243–1254.

Spangler, W. D., & House, R. J. (1991). Presidential effectiveness and the leadership motive profile. *Journal of Personality and Social Psychology, 60,* 439–455.

Spanos, N. P. (1996). *Multiple identities and false memories.* Washington, DC: American Psychological Association.

Sperling, M. B., & Berman, W. H. (Eds.). (1994). *Attachment in adults: Clinical and developmental perspectives.* New York: Guilford.

Spetch, M. L., Wilkie, D. M., & Pinel, J. P. J. (1981). Backward conditioning: A reevaluation of the empirical evidence. *Psychological Bulletin, 89,* 163–175.

Spielberger, C. D., & DeNike, L. D. (1966). Descriptive behaviorism versus cognitive theory in verbal operant conditioning. *Psychological Review, 73,* 309–326.

Spooner, A., & Kellogg, W. N. (1947). The backward conditioning curve. *American Journal of Psychology, 60,* 321–334.

Sprecher, S., Sullivan, Q., & Hatfield, E. (1994). Mate selection preferences: Gender differences examined in a national sample. *Journal of Personality and Social Psychology, 66,* 1074–1080.

Sroufe, L. A., & Fleeson, J. (1986). Attachment and the construction of relationships. In W. W. Hartup & Z. Rubin (Eds.), *Relationships and development* (pp. 51–71). Hillsdale, NJ: Erlbaum.

Srull, T. K., & Wyer, R. S., Jr. (1979). The role of category accessibility in the interpretation of information about persons: Some determinants and implications. *Journal of Personality and Social Psychology, 37,* 1660–1672.

St. Clair, M. (1986). *Object relations and self psychology: An introduction.* Monterey, CA: Brooks/Cole.

Staats, A. W. (1996). *Behavior and personality: Psychological behaviorism.* New York: Springer.

Staats, A. W., & Burns, G. L. (1982). Emotional personality repertoire as cause of behavior. *Journal of Personality and Social Psychology, 43,* 873–881.

Staats, A. W., & Staats, C. K. (1958). Attitudes established by classical conditioning. *Journal of Abnormal and Social Psychology, 57,* 37–40.

Staats, A. W., Staats, C. K., & Crawford, H. L. (1962). First-order conditioning of meaning and the parallel conditioning of a GSR. *Journal of General Psychology, 67,* 159–167.

Staats, C. K., & Staats, A. W. (1957). Meaning established by classical conditioning. *Journal of Experimental Psychology, 54,* 74–80.

Stanton, A. L., Danoff-Burg, S., Sworowski, L. A., Collins, C. A., Branstetter, A. D., Rodriguez-Hanley, A., Kirk, S. B., & Austenfeld, J. L. (2002). Randomized, controlled trial of written emotional expression and benefit finding in breast cancer patients. *Journal of Clinical Oncology, 20,* 4160–4168.

Stanton, A. L., & Snider, P. R. (1993). Coping with a breast cancer diagnosis: A prospective study. *Health Psychology, 12,* 16–23.

Steele, C. M. (1988). The psychology of self-affirmation: Sustaining the integrity of the self. In L. Berkowitz (Ed.), *Advances in experimental social psychology,* (Vol. 21, pp. 261–302). New York: Academic Press.

Steele, C. M. (1997). A threat in the air: How stereotypes shape intellectual identity and performance. *American Psychologist, 52,* 613–629.

Sternberg, R. J. (Ed.). (1982). *Handbook of human intelligence.* New York: Cambridge University Press.

Steronko, R. J., & Woods, D. J. (1978). Impairment in early stages of visual information processing in nonpsychotic schizotypic individuals. *Journal of Abnormal Psychology, 87,* 481–490.

Stevens, R. (1983). *Erik Erikson: An introduction.* New York: St. Martin's Press.

Stevenson, H. W., Hale, G. A., Hill, K. T., & Moely, B. E. (1967). Determinants of children's preferences for adults. *Child Development, 38,* 1–14.

Stewart, A. J. (1980). Personality and situation in the prediction of women's life patterns. *Psychology of Women Quarterly, 5,* 195–206.

Stewart, A. J., & Vandewater, E. A. (1999). "If I had it to do over again . . . " Midlife review, midcourse corrections, and women's well-being in midlife. *Journal of Personality and Social Psychology, 76,* 270–283.

Stock, G. (2002). *Redesigning humans: Our inevitable genetic future.* Boston: Houghton Mifflin.

Stolar, D., & Fromm, E. (1974). Activity and passivity of the ego in relation to the superego. *International Review of Psycho-Analysis, 1,* 297–311.

Stolberg, S. (1994, March 27). Genetic bias: Held hostage by heredity. *Los Angeles Times,* p. 1A.

Stone, L. J., & Hokanson, J. E. (1969). Arousal reduction via self-punitive behavior. *Journal of Personality and Social Psychology, 12,* 72–79.

Stotland, E. (1969a). Exploratory investigation of empathy. In L. Berkowitz (Ed.), *Advances in experimental social psychology* (Vol. 4). New York: Academic Press.

Stotland, E. (1969b). *The psychology of hope.* San Francisco: Jossey-Bass.

Straub, R. E., Jiang, Y., MacLean, C. J., Ma, Y., Webb, B. T. et al. (2002). Genetic variation in the 6p22.3 gene *DTNBP1,* the human ortholog of the mouse dysbindin gene, is associated with schizophrenia. *American Journal of Human Genetics, 71,* 337–348.

Strauman, T. J. (1989). Self-discrepancies in clinical depression and social phobia: Cognitive structures that underlie emotional disorders? *Journal of Abnormal Psychology, 53,* 14–22.

Strauman, T. J., & Higgins, E. T. (1987). Automatic activation of self-discrepancies and emotional syndromes: When cognitive structures influence affect. *Journal of Personality and Social Psychology, 53,* 1004–1014.

Strong, R. K., & Dabbs, J. M., Jr. (2000). Testosterone and behavior in normal young children. *Personality and Individual Differences, 28,* 909–915.

Strube, M. J. (1989). Evidence for the *type* in Type A behavior: A taxometric analysis. *Journal of Personality and Social Psychology, 56,* 972–987.

Stucke, T. S., & Sporer, S. L. (2002). When a grandiose self-image is threatened: Narcissism and self-concept clarity as predictors of negative emotions and aggression following ego-threat. *Journal of Personality, 70,* 509–532.

Stumpf, H. (1993). The factor structure of the Personality Research Form: A cross-national evaluation. *Journal of Personality, 61,* 27–48.

Stumphauzer, J. S. (1972). Increased delay of gratification in young prison inmates through imitation of high delay peer models. *Journal of Personality and Social Psychology, 21,* 10–17.

Sulloway, F. J. (1996). *Born to rebel: Birth order, family dynamics, and creative lives.* New York: Pantheon.

Suppes, P., Pavel, M., & Falmagne, J-Cl. (1994). Representations and models in psychology. *Annual Review of Psychology, 45,* 517–544.

Sutton, S. K., & Davidson, R. J. (1997). Prefrontal brain asymmetry: A biological substrate of the behavioral approach and inhibition systems. *Psychological Science, 8,* 204–210.

Swann, W. B., Jr. (1987). Identity negotiation: Where two roads meet. *Journal of Personality and Social Psychology, 53,* 1038–1051.

Swann, W. B., Jr. (1990). To be adored or to be known: The interplay of self-enhancement and self-verification. In E. T. Higgins & R. M. Sorrentino (Eds.), *Handbook of motivation and cognition* (Vol. 2, pp. 408–448). New York: Guilford.

Swann, W. B., Jr., Bosson, J. K., & Pelham, B. W. (2002). Different partners, different selves: Strategic verification of circumscribed identities. *Personality and Social Psychology Bulletin, 28,* 1215–1228.

Swann, W. B., Jr., Pelham, B. W., & Krull, D. S. (1989). Agreeable fancy or disagreeable truth? Reconciling self-enhancement and self-verification. *Journal of Personality and Social Psychology, 57,* 782–791.

Swann, W. B., Jr., Wenzlaff, R. M., & Tafarodi, R. W. (1992). Depression and the search for negative evaluations: More evidence of the role of self-verification strivings. *Journal of Abnormal Psychology, 101,* 314–317.

Tajfel, H., & Turner, J. C. (1986). The social identity theory of intergroup behavior. In S. Worchel & W. G. Austin (Eds.), *Psychology of intergroup relations* (2nd ed., pp. 7–24). Chicago: Nelson-Hall.

Tannen, D. (1990). *You just don't understand: Women and men in conversation.* New York: Ballantine.

Tavris, C., & Wade, C. (1984). *The longest war: Sex differences in perspective* (2nd ed.). New York: Harcourt Brace Jovanovich.

Taylor, M. C., & Hall, J. A. (1982). Psychological androgyny: Theories, methods and conclusions. *Psychological Bulletin, 92,* 347–366.

Taylor, S. E. (1983). Adjustment to threatening events: A theory of cognitive adaptation. *American Psychologist, 38,* 1161–1173.

Taylor, S. E. (2002). *The tending instinct: How nurturing is essential to who we are and how we live.* New York: Henry Holt.

Taylor, S. E., & Brown, J. D. (1988). Illusion and well-being: A social psychological perspective on mental health. *Psychological Bulletin, 103,* 193–210.

Taylor, S. E., & Fiske, S. T. (1978). Salience, attention, and attribution: Top of the head phenomena. In L. Berkowitz (Ed.), *Advances in experimental social psychology* (Vol. 11). New York: Academic Press.

Taylor, S. E., & Gollwitzer, P. M. (1995). Effects of mindset on positive illusions. *Journal of Personality and Social Psychology, 69,* 213–226.

Taylor, S. E., Klein, L. C., Lewis, B. P., Gruenewald, T. L., Gurung, R. A. R., & Updegraff, J. A. (2000). Biobehavioral responses to stress in females: Tend-and-befriend, not fight-or-flight. *Psychological Review, 107,* 411–429.

Taylor, S. E., Lichtman, R. R., & Wood, J. V. (1984). Attributions, beliefs in control, and adjustment to breast cancer. *Journal of Personality and Social Psychology, 46,* 489–502.

Tedeschi, R. G., & Calhoun, L. G. (1995). *Trauma and transformation: Growing in the aftermath of suffering.* Thousand Oaks, CA: Sage.

Tellegen, A. (1985). Structure of mood and personality and their relevance to assessing anxiety, with an emphasis on self-report. In A. H. Tuma & J. D. Maser (Eds.), *Anxiety and the anxiety disorders* (pp. 681–706). Hillsdale, NJ: Erlbaum.

Tellegen, A., Lykken, D. T., Bouchard, T. J., Jr., Wilcox, K. J., Segal N. L., & Rich, S. (1988). Personality similarity in twins reared apart and together. *Journal of Personality and Social Psychology, 54,* 1031–1039.

Tesch, S. A., & Whitbourne, S. K. (1982). Intimacy status and identity status in young adults. *Journal of Personality and Social Psychology, 43,* 1041–1051.

Tesser, A. (1971). Evaluative and structural similarity of attitudes as determinants of interpersonal attraction. *Journal of Personality and Social Psychology, 18,* 92–96.

Tesser, A. (1986). Some effects of self-evaluation maintenance on cognition and action. In R. M. Sorrentino & E. T. Higgins (Eds.), *The handbook of motivation and cognition: Foundations of social behavior.* New York: Guilford.

Tesser, A. (1988). Toward a self-evaluation maintenance model of social behavior. In L. Berkowitz (Ed.), *Advances in experimental social psychology,* (Vol. 21, pp. 181–227). New York: Academic Press.

Tesser, A. (1991). Social vs. clinical approaches to self psychology: The self-evaluation maintenance model and Kohutian object relations theory. In R. Curtis (Ed.), *The relational self: Theoretical convergences in psychoanalysis and social psychology* (pp. 257–281). New York: Guilford.

Tesser, A. (1993). The importance of heritability in psychological research: The case of attitudes. *Psychological Review, 100,* 129–142.

Tesser, A., & Campbell, J. (1983). Self-definition and self-evaluation maintenance. In J. Suls & A. G. Greenwald (Eds.), *Psychological perspectives on the self* (Vol. 2). Hillsdale, NJ: Erlbaum.

Thagard, P. (1989). Explanatory coherence. *Behavioral and Brain Sciences, 12,* 435–467.

Thagard, P., & Millgram, E. (1995). Inference to the best plan: A coherence theory of decision. In A. Ram & D. B. Leake (Eds.), *Goal-driven learning* (pp. 439–454). Cambridge, MA: MIT Press.

Theios, J. (1962). The partial reinforcement effect sustained through blocks of continuous reinforcement. *Journal of Experimental Psychology, 64,* 1–6.

Thelen, M. H., & Rennie, D. L. (1972). The effect of vicarious reinforcement on imitation: A review of the literature. In B. Maher (Ed.), *Progress in experimental personality research* (Vol. 6). New York: Academic Press.

Thiessen, D., & Gregg, B. (1980). Human assortative mating and genetic equilibrium: An evolutionary perspective. *Ethology and Sociobiology, 1,* 111–140.

Thomas, A., & Chess, S. (1977). *Temperament and development.* New York: Brunner/Mazel.

Thomas, M. H., Horton, R. W., Lippincott, E. C., & Drabman, R. S. (1977). Desensitization to portrayals of real-life aggression as a function of exposure to television violence. *Journal of Personality and Social Psychology, 35,* 450–458.

Thompson, G. C. (1968). George Alexander Kelly (1905–1967). *Journal of General Psychology, 79,* 19–24.

Thompson, S. C. (1985). Finding positive meaning in a stressful event and coping. *Basic and Applied Social Psychology, 6,* 279–295.

Thompson, S. C. (1991). The search for meaning following a stroke. *Basic and Applied Social Psychology, 12,* 81–96.

Thompson, S. C., & Janigian, A. S. (1988). Life schemes: A framework for understanding the search for meaning. *Journal of Social and Clinical Psychology, 7,* 260–280.

Thorndike, E. L. (1898). Animal intelligence: An experimental study of the associative processes in animals. *Psychological Monographs, 2* (Whole No. 8).

Thorndike, E. L. (1905). *The elements of psychology.* New York: A. G. Seiler.

Thorndike, E. L. (1933). *An experimental study of rewards.* New York: Columbia University Teachers College Press.

Thorne, A. (1987). The press of personality: A study of conversations between introverts and extraverts. *Journal of Personality and Social Psychology, 53,* 718–726.

Thrash, T. M., & Elliot, A. J. (2002). Implicit and self-attributed achievement motives: Concordance and predictive validity. *Journal of Personality, 70,* 729–755.

Thronquist, M. H., Zuckerman, M., & Exline, R. V. (1991). Loving, liking, looking, and sensation seeking in unmarried college couples. *Personality and Individual Differences, 12,* 1283–1292.

Timberlake, W. (1993). Behavior systems and reinforcement: An integrative approach. *Journal of the Experimental Analysis of Behavior, 60,* 105–128.

Tobin, R. M., Graziano, W. G., Vanman, E. J., & Tassinary, L. G. (2000). Personality, emotional experience, and efforts to conrtrol emotions. *Journal of Personality and Social Psychology, 79,* 656–669.

Tolman, E. C. (1932). *Purposive behavior in animals and men.* New York: Appleton-Century-Crofts.

Tolman, E. C. (1959). Principles of purposive behavior. In S. Koch (Ed.), *Psychology: A study of a science* (Vol. 2, pp. 92–157). New York: McGraw-Hill.

Tomich, P. T., & Helgeson, V. S. (2002). Five years later: A cross-sectional comparison of breast cancer survivors with healthy women. *Psycho-Oncology, 11,* 154–169.

Toner, I. J., & Smith, R. A. (1977). Age and overt verbalization in delay-maintenance behavior in children. *Journal of Experimental Child Psychology, 24,* 123–128.

Tooby, J., & Cosmides, L. (1989). Evolutionary psychology and the generation of culture, Part I. *Ethology and Sociobiology, 10,* 29–49.

Tooby, J., & Cosmides, L. (1990). On the universality of human nature and the uniqueness of the individual. *Journal of Personality, 58,* 17–67.

Trapnell, P. D., & Campbell, J. D. (1999). Private self-consciousness and the five-factor model of personality: Distinguishing rumination from reflection. *Journal of Personality and Social Psychology, 76,* 284–304.

Trapnell, P. D., & Wiggins, J. S. (1990). Extension of the interpersonal adjective scales to include the big five dimensions of personality. *Journal of Personality and Social Psychology, 59,* 781–790.

Tresemer, D. W. (1977). *Fear of success.* New York: Plenum.

Triandis, H. C., Hui, H., Albert, R. D., Leung, S., Lisansky, J., Diaz-Loving, R., Plasencia, L., Marin, G., Betancourt, H., & Loyola-Cintron, L. (1984). Individual models of social behavior. *Journal of Personality and Social Psychology, 46,* 1389–1404.

Trivers, R. L. (1971). The evolution of reciprocal altruism. *Quarterly Review of Biology, 46,* 35–57.

Trivers, R. L. (1972). Parental investment and sexual selection. In B. Campbell (Ed.), *Sexual selection and the descent of man: 1871–1971* (pp. 136–179). Chicago: Aldine.

Trobst, K. K., Herbst, J. H., Masters, H. L., III, & Costa, P. T., Jr. (2002). Personality pathways to unsafe sex: Personality, condom use, and HIV risk behaviors. *Journal of Research in Personality, 36,* 117–133.

Trope, Y. (1975). Seeking information about one's own ability as a determinant of choice among tasks. *Journal of Personality and Social Psychology, 32,* 1004–1013.

Trope, Y. (1979). Uncertainty-reducing properties of achievement tasks. *Journal of Personality and Social Psychology, 37,* 1505–1518.

Trope, Y. (1980). Self-assessment, self-enhancement, and task preference. *Journal of Experimental Social Psychology, 16,* 116–129.

Truax, C. B., & Mitchell, K. M. (1971). Research on certain therapist interpersonal skills in relation to process and outcome. In A. E. Bergin & S. L. Garfield (Eds.), *Handbook of psychotherapy and behavior change.* New York: Wiley.

Tse, W. S., & Bond, A. J. (2001). Serotonergic involvement in the psychosocial dimension of personality. *Journal of Psychopharmacology, 15,* 195–198.

Tsuang, M. T., & Faraone, S. V. (1990). *The genetics of mood disorders.* Baltimore: Johns Hopkins Press.

Tulving, E. (1972). Episodic and semantic memory. In E. Tulving & W. Donaldson (Eds.), *Organization of memory.* New York: Academic Press.

Tulving, E. (1993). What is episodic memory? *Current Directions in Psychological Science, 2,* 67–70.

Turk, D. (1978). Cognitive behavioral techniques in the management of pain. In J. P. Foreyt & D. P. Rathjen (Eds.), *Cognitive behavior therapy: Research and application.* New York: Plenum.

Turkheimer, E. (1998). Heritability and biological explanation. *Psychological Review, 105,* 782–791.

Turner, J. L., Foa, E. B., & Foa, U. G. (1971). Interpersonal reinforcers: Classification, interrelationship, and some differential properties. *Journal of Personality and Social Psychology, 19,* 168–170.

Turner, R. A., Altemus, M., Enos, T., Cooper, B., & McGuinness, T. (1999). Preliminary research on plasma oxytocin in normal cycling women: Investigating emotion and interpersonal distress. *Psychiatry, 62,* 97–113.

Tversky, B., & Hemenway, K. (1983). Categories of environmental scenes. *Cognitive Psychology, 15,* 121–149.

Twenge, J. M. (2000). The age of anxiety? Birth cohort change in anxiety and neuroticism, 1952–1993. *Journal of Personality and Social Psychology, 79,* 1007–1021.

Twenge, J. M. (2001). Birth cohort changes in extraversion: A cross-temporal meta-analysis, 1966–1993. *Personality and Individual Differences, 30,* 735–748.

Twenge, J. M. (2002). Birth cohort, social change, and personality: The interplay of dysphoria and individualism in the 20th century. In D. Cervone & W. Mischel (Eds.), *Advances in personality science* (pp. 196–218). New York: Guilford.

Twenge, J. M., Baumeister, R. F., Tice, D. M., & Stucke, T. S. (2001). If you can't join them, beat them: Effects of social exclusion on aggressive behavior. *Journal of Personality and Social Psychology, 81,* 1058–1069.

Twenge, J. M., & Campbell, W. K. (2001). Age and birth cohort differences in self-esteem: A cross-temporal meta-analysis. *Personality and Social Psychology Review, 5,* 321–344.

Tyner, S. D., Venkatachalam, S., Choi, J., Jones, S., Ghebranious, N., Igelmann, H., Lu, X., Soron, G., Cooper, B., Brayton, C., Park, S. H., Thompson, T., Karsenty, G., Bradley, A., & Donehower, L. A. (2002). p53 mutant mice that display early ageing-associated phenotypes. *Nature, 415,* 45–53.

Udry, J. R., & Talbert, L. M. (1988). Sex hormone effects on personality at puberty. *Journal of Personality and Social Psychology, 54,* 291–295.

Underwood, B. J. (1975). Individual differences as a crucible in theory construction. *American Psychologist, 30,* 128–134.

Vaillant, G. E. (1977). *Adaptation to life.* Boston: Little, Brown.

Vallacher, R. R., & Nowak, A. (1997). The emergence of dynamical social psychology. *Psychological Inquiry, 8,* 73–99.

Vallacher, R. R., Read, S. J., & Nowak, A. (Eds.). (2002). The dynamical perspective in personality and social psychology. [Special issue]. *Personality and Social Psychology Review, 6* (4).

Vallacher, R. R., & Wegner, D. M. (1985). *A theory of action identification.* Hillsdale, NJ: Erlbaum.

Vallacher, R. R., & Wegner, D. M. (1987). Action identification theory: The representation and control of behavior. *Psychological Review, 94,* 3–15.

Vallacher, R. R., & Wegner, D. M. (1989). Levels of personal agency: Individual variation in action identification. *Journal of Personality and Social Psychology, 57,* 660–671.

Vallerand, R. J. (1997). Toward a hierarchical model of intrinsic and extrinsic motivation. In M. P. Zanna (Ed.), *Advances in experimental social psychology* (Vol. 29, pp. 271–360). San Diego, CA: Academic Press.

Van Maanen, J. (1973). Observations on the making of policemen. *Human Organization, 32,* 407–418.

Van Maanen, J. (1975). Police socialization: A longitudinal examination of job attitudes in an urban police department. *Administrative Science Quarterly, 20,* 207–228.

Vandenberg, S. G., Singer, S. M., & Pauls, D. L. (1986). *The heredity of behavior disorders in adults and children.* New York: Plenum.

Vandewater, E. A., Ostrove, J. M., & Stewart, A. J. (1997). Predicting women's well-being in midlife: The importance of personality development and social role involvements. *Journal of Personality and Social Psychology, 72,* 1147–1160.

Vaughan, K. B., & Lanzetta, J. T. (1980). Vicarious instigation and conditioning of facial expressive and autonomic responses to a model's expressive display of pain. *Journal of Personality and Social Psychology, 38,* 909–923.

Vernon, D. T. A. (1974). Modeling and birth order in responses to painful stimuli. *Journal of Personality and Social Psychology, 29,* 794–799.

Vernon, P. E. (1964). *Personality assessment: A critical survey.* New York: Wiley.

Veroff, J. (1957). Development and validation of a projective measure of power motivation. *Journal of Abnormal and Social Psychology, 54,* 1–8.

Verplanken, B. (1991). Persuasive communication of risk information: A test of cue versus message processing effects in a field experiment. *Personality and Social Psychology Bulletin, 17,* 188–193.

Verplanken, B., & Holland, R. W. (2002). Motivated decision making: Effects of activation and self-centrality of values on choices and behavior. *Journal of Personality and Social Psychology, 82,* 434–447.

Vertes, R. P., & Eastman, K. E. (2000). The case against memory consolidation in REM sleep. *Behavioral and Brain Sciences, 23,* 867–876.

Viken, R. J., & McFall, R. M. (1994). Paradox lost: Implications of contemporary reinforcement theory for behavior therapy. *Current Directions in Psychological Science, 3,* 121–125.

Viken, R. J., Rose, R. J., Kaprio, J., & Koskenvuo, M. (1994). A developmental genetic analysis of adult personality: Extraversion and neuroticism from 18 to 59 years of age. *Journal of Personality and Social Psychology, 66,* 722–730.

Wagner, A. R., Siegel, S., Thomas, E., & Ellison, G. D. (1964). Reinforcement history and the extinction of a conditioned salivary response. *Journal of Comparative and Physiological Psychology, 58,* 354–358.

Wahlsten, D. (1990). Insensitivity of the analysis of variance to heredity–environment interaction. *Behavioral and Brain Sciences, 13,* 100–161.

Wahlsten, D. (1999). Single-gene influences on brain and behavior. *Annual Review of Psychology, 50,* 599–624.

Walker, E. F., & Diforio, D. (1997). Schizophrenia: A neural diathesis-stress model. *Psychological Review, 104,* 667–685.

Walker, R. N. (1962). Body build and behavior in young children. Body build and nursery school teacher ratings. *Monographs of the Society for Research on Child Development, 27* (Serial No. 84).

Wallace, H. M., & Baumeister, R. F. (2002). The performance of narcissists rises and falls with perceived opportunity for glory. *Journal of Personality and Social Psychology, 82,* 819–834.

Walls, R. T., & Cox, J. (1971). Expectancy of reinforcement in chance and skills tasks under motor handicaps. *Journal of Clinical Psychology, 27,* 436–438.

Wallston, B. S., & Wallston, K. A. (1978). Locus of control and health: A review of the literature. *Health Education Monographs, 6,* 107–117.

Wallston, K. A., & Wallston, B. S. (1981). Health locus of control scales. In H. F. Lefcourt (Ed.), *Research with the locus of control construct. Vol. 1, Assessment methods.* New York: Academic Press.

Walters, R. H., & Parke, R. D. (1964). Influence of response consequences to a social model on resistance to deviation. *Journal of Experimental Child Psychology, 1,* 269–280.

Walther, E. (2002). Guilty by mere association: Evaluative conditioning and the spreading attitude effect. *Journal of Personality and Social Psychology, 82,* 919–934.

Waterman, A. S. (1982). Identity development from adolescence to adulthood: An extension of theory and a review of research. *Developmental Psychology, 18,* 341–358.

Watson, D., & Clark, L. A. (1984). Negative affectivity: The disposition to experience aversive emotional states. *Psychological Bulletin, 96,* 465–490.

Watson, D., & Clark, L. A. (1994). Introduction to the special issue on personality and psychopathology. *Journal of Abnormal Psychology, 103,* 3–5.

Watson, D., & Clark, L. A. (1997). Extraversion and its positive emotional core. In R. Hogan, J. Johnson, & S. Briggs (Eds.), *Handbook of personality psychology* (pp. 767–793). San Diego, CA: Academic Press.

Watson, D., Clark, L. A., McIntyre, C. W., & Hamaker, S. (1992). Affect, personality, and social activity. *Journal of Personality and Social Psychology, 63,* 1011–1025.

Watson, D., & Tellegen, A. (1985). Toward a consensual structure of mood. *Psychological Bulletin, 98,* 219–235.

Watson, D., Wiese, D., Vaidya, J., & Tellegen, A. (1999). The two general activation systems of affect: Structural findings, evolutionary considerations, and psychobiological evidence. *Journal of Personality and Social Psychology, 76,* 820–838.

Watson, J. B., & Raynor, R. (1920). Conditioned emotional reactions. *Journal of Experimental Psychology, 3,* 1–14.

Watt, J. D., & Blanchard, M. J. (1994). Boredom proneness and the need for cognition. *Journal of Research in Personality, 28,* 44–51.

Wegner, D. M. (1989). *White bears and other unwanted thoughts: Suppression, obsession, and the psychology of mental control.* New York: Viking Penguin.

Wegner, D. M. (1994). Ironic processes of mental control. *Psychological Review, 101,* 34–52.

Wegner, D. M. (2002). *The illusion of conscious will.* Cambridge, MA: MIT Press.

Wegner, D. M., Schneider, D. J., Carter, S. R., III, & White, T. L. (1987). Paradoxical effects of thought suppression. *Journal of Personality and Social Psychology, 53,* 5–13.

Wegner, D. M., Shortt, J. W., Blake, A. W., & Page, M. S. (1990). The suppression of exciting thoughts. *Journal of Personality and Social Psychology, 58,* 409–418.

Wegner, D. M., & Wheatley, T. (1999). Apparent mental causation: Sources of the experience of will. *American Psychologist, 54,* 480–492.

Weijers, H.-G., Wiesbeck, G. A., Jakob, F., & Böning, J. (2001). Neuroendocrine responses to fenfluramine and its relationship to personality in alcoholism. *Journal of Neural Transmission, 108,* 1093–1105.

Weinberger, D. A., Schwartz, G. E., & Davidson, R. J. (1979). Low-anxious, high-anxious, and repressive coping styles: Psychometric patterns and behavioral and physiological responses to stress. *Journal of Abnormal Psychology, 88,* 369–380.

Weinberger, J. L., & Hardaway, R. (1990). Separating science from myth in subliminal psychodynamic activation. *Clinical Psychology Review, 10,* 727–756.

Weinberger, J. L., & Silverman, L. H. (1987). Subliminal psychodynamic activation: A method for studying psychoanalytic dynamic propositions. In R. Hogan & W. H. Jones (Eds.), *Perspectives in personality* (Vol. 2, pp. 251–287). Greenwich, CT: JAI Press.

Weiner, B. (1979). A theory of motivation for some classroom experiences. *Journal of Educational Psychology, 71,* 3–25.

Weiner, B. (1986). *An attributional theory of motivation and emotion.* New York: Springer-Verlag.

Weiner, B. (1990). Attribution in personality psychology. In L. A. Pervin (Ed.), *Handbook of personality: Theory and research* (pp. 465–485). New York: Guilford.

Weiner, B., Heckhausen, H., Meyer, W., & Cook, R. E. (1972). Causal ascriptions and achievement behaviors: A conceptual analysis of effort and reanalysis of locus of control. *Journal of Personality and Social Psychology, 21,* 239–248.

Weiner, B., & Litman-Adizes, T. (1980). An attributional, expectancy–value analysis of learned helplessness and depression. In J. Garber & M. E. P. Seligman

(Eds.), *Human helplessness: Theory and applications.* New York: Academic Press.

Weiner, B., Nierenberg, R., & Goldstein, M. (1976). Social learning (locus of control) versus attributional (causal stability) interpretations of expectancy of success. *Journal of Personality, 44,* 52–68.

Weinstein, N. D. (1989). Optimistic biases about personal risks. *Science, 246,* 1232–1233.

Weisberg, P., & Waldrop, P. B. (1972). Fixed-interval work habits of congress. *Journal of Applied Behavioral Analysis, 5,* 93–97.

Weiss, L., & Masling, J. (1970). Further validation of a Rorschach measure of oral imagery: A study of six clinical groups. *Journal of Abnormal Psychology, 76,* 83–87.

Weiss, R. S. (Ed.). (1973). *Loneliness: The experience of emotional and social isolation.* Cambridge, MA: MIT Press.

Wenzlaff, R. M., & Wegner, D. M. (2000). Thought suppression. *Annual Review of Psychology, 51,* 59–91.

Wenzlaff, R. M., Wegner, D. M., & Roper, D. W. (1988). Depression and mental control: The resurgence of unwanted negative thoughts. *Journal of Personality and Social Psychology, 55,* 1–11.

Westen, D. (1991). Social cognition and object relations. *Psychological Bulletin, 109,* 429–455.

Westen, D. (1998). The scientific legacy of Sigmund Freud: Toward a psychodynamically informed psychological science. *Psychological Bulletin, 124,* 333–371.

Westenberg, P. M., & Block, J. (1993). Ego development and individual differences in personality. *Journal of Personality and Social Psychology, 65,* 792–800.

Westmaas, J. L., & Silver, R. C. (2001). The role of attachment in responses to victims of life crises. *Journal of Personality and Social Psychology, 80,* 425–438.

Wheeler, R. E., Davidson, R. J., & Tomarken, A. J. (1993). Frontal brain asymmetry and emotional reactivity: A biological substrate of affective style. *Psychophysiology, 30,* 82–89.

Whitam, F. L., Diamond, M., & Martin, J. (1993). Homosexual orientation in twins: A report on 61 pairs and three triplet sets. *Archives of Sexual Behavior, 22,* 187–206.

Whitbeck, L. B., Hoyt, D. R., Simons, R. L., Conger, R. D., Elder, G. H., Jr., Lorenz, F. O., & Huck, S. (1992). Intergenerational continuity of parental rejection and depressed affect. *Journal of Personality and Social Psychology, 63,* 1036–1045.

Whitbourne, S. K., Zuschlag, M. K., Elliot, L. B., & Waterman, A. S. (1992). Psychosocial development in adulthood: A 22-year sequential study. *Journal of Personality and Social Psychology, 63,* 260–271.

White, K. M., Houlihan, J., Costos, D., & Speisman, J. C. (1990). Adult development in individuals and relationships. *Journal of Research in Personality, 24,* 371–386.

White, R. W. (1959). Motivation reconsidered: The concept of competence. *Psychological Review, 66,* 297–333.

White, R. W. (1963). *Ego and reality in psychoanalytic theory: A proposal regarding independent ego energies* (Psychological Issues Monograph 11). New York: International Universities Press.

Wickelgren, W. A. (1977). *Learning and memory.* Englewood Cliffs, NJ: Prentice-Hall.

Wicker, F. W., Brown, G., Wiehe, J. A., Hagen, A. S., & Reed, J. L. (1993). On reconsidering Maslow: An examination of the deprivation/domination proposition. *Journal of Research in Personality, 27,* 118–133.

Wicklund, R. A., & Duval, S. (1971). Opinion change and performance facilitation as a result of objective self-awareness. *Journal of Experimental Social Psychology, 7,* 319–342.

Widiger, T. A., Trull, T. J., Clarkin, J. F., Sanderson, C., & Costa, P. T, Jr. (2002). A description of the DSM-IV personality disorders with the five-factor model. In P. T. Costa, Jr. & T. A. Widiger (Eds.), *Personality disorders and the five-factor model of personality* (2nd ed., pp. 89–99). Washington, DC: American Psychological Association. Rohde

Wiedenfeld, S. A., O'Leary, A., Bandura, A., Brown, S., Levine, S., & Raska, K. (1990). Impact of perceived self-efficacy in coping with stressors on components of the immune system. *Journal of Personality and Social Psychology, 59,* 1082–1094.

Wiener, N. (1948). *Cybernetics: Control and communication in the animal and the machine.* Cambridge, MA: MIT Press.

Wiggins, J. S. (1973). *Personality and prediction: Principles of personality assessment.* Reading, MA: Addison-Wesley.

Wiggins, J. S. (1979). A psychological taxonomy of trait-descriptive terms: The interpersonal domain. *Journal of Personality and Social Psychology, 37,* 395–412.

Wiggins, J. S. (Ed.). (1996). *The five-factor model of personality: Theoretical perspectives.* New York: Guilford.

Wiggins, J. S., Phillips, N., & Trapnell, P. (1989). Circular reasoning about interpersonal behavior: Evidence concerning some untested assumptions underlying diagnostic classification. *Journal of Personality and Social Psychology, 56,* 296–305.

Willerman, L., Loehlin, J. C., & Horn, J. M. (1992). An adoption and a cross-fostering study of the Minnesota Multiphasic Personality Inventory (MMPI) Psychopathic Deviate scale. *Behavior Genetics, 22,* 515–529.

Williams, G. C., & Deci, E. L. (1996). Internalization of biopsychosocial values by medical students: A test of self-determination theory. *Journal of Personality and Social Psychology, 70,* 767–779.

Williams, G. C., Grow, V. M., Freedman, Z. R., Ryan, R. M., & Deci, E. L. (1996). Motivational predictors of weight loss and weight-loss maintenance. *Journal of Personality and Social Psychology, 70,* 115–126.

Williams, R. L., Moore, C. A., Pettibone, T. J., & Thomas, S. P. (1992). Construction and validation of a brief self-report scale of self-management practices. *Journal of Research in Personality, 26,* 216–234.

Wilson, E. O. (1975). *Sociobiology: The new synthesis.* Cambridge, MA: Harvard University Press.

Wilson, J. Q., & Herrnstein, R. J. (1985). *Crime and human nature.* New York: Simon & Schuster.

Wilson, M. I., & Daly, M. (1985). Competitiveness, risk-taking, and violence: The young male syndrome. *Ethology and Sociobiology, 6,* 59–73.

Wilson, M. I., & Daly, M. (1996). Male sexual proprietariness and violence against wives. *Current Directions in Psychological Science, 5,* 2–7.

Wink, P., & Helson, R. (1993). Personality change in women and their partners. *Journal of Personality and Social Psychology, 65,* 597–605.

Winson, J. (1985). *Brain and psyche: The biology of the unconscious.* Garden City, NY: Doubleday.

Winson, J. (1990). The meaning of dreams. *Scientific American, 263,* 86–96.

Winter, D. G. (1972). The need for power in college men: Action correlates and relationship to drinking. In D. C. McClelland, W. N. Davis, R. Kalin, & E. Wanner (Eds.), *The drinking man.* New York: Free Press.

Winter, D. G. (1973). *The power motive.* New York: Free Press.

Winter, D. G. (1988). The power motive in women—and men. *Journal of Personality and Social Psychology, 54,* 510–519.

Winter, D. G. (1993). Power, affiliation, and war: Three tests of a motivational model. *Journal of Personality and Social Psychology, 65,* 532–545.

Winter, D. G. (1996). *Personality: Analysis and interpretation of lives.* New York: McGraw-Hill.

Winter, D. G., & Barenbaum, N. B. (1985). Responsibility and the power motive in women and men. *Journal of Personality, 53,* 335–355.

Winter, D. G., John, O. P., Stewart, A. J., Klohnen, E. C., & Duncan, L. E. (1998). Traits and motives: Toward an integration of two traditions in personality research. *Psychological Bulletin, 105,* 230–250.

Winter, D. G., Stewart, A. J., & McClelland, D. C. (1977). Husband's motives and wife's career level. *Journal of Personality and Social Psychology, 35*, 159–166.

Wispé, L. (1986). The distinction between sympathy and empathy: To call forth a concept, a word is needed. *Journal of Personality and Social Psychology, 50*, 314–321.

Woike, B. A. (1995). Most-memorable experiences: Evidence for a link between implicit and explicit motives and social cognitive processes in everyday life. *Journal of Personality and Social Psychology, 68*, 1081–1091.

Wolberg, L. R. (1967). *The technique of psychotherapy*. New York: Grune & Stratton.

Wolfe, J. B. (1936). Effectiveness of token-rewards for chimpanzees. *Comparative Psychology Monographs, 12* (Whole No. 60).

Wolfe, R. N., & Kasmer, J. A. (1988). Type versus trait: Extraversion, impulsivity, sociability, and preferences for cooperative and competitive activities. *Journal of Personality and Social Psychology, 54*, 864–871.

Wolpe, J. (1961). The systematic desensitization treatment of neuroses. *Journal of Nervous and Mental Disorders, 132*, 189–203.

Wolpe, J. (1981). Behavior therapy versus psychoanalysis: Therapeutic and social implications. *American Psychologist, 36*, 159–164.

Wong, M. M., & Csikszentmihalyi, M. (1991). Affiliation motivation and daily experience: Some issues on gender differences. *Journal of Personality and Social Psychology, 60*, 154–164.

Wood, J. M., Nezworski, M. T., & Stejskal, W. J. (1996a). The comprehensive system for the Rorschach: A critical examination. *Psychological Science, 7*, 3–10.

Wood, J. M., Nezworski, M. T., & Stejskal, W. J. (1996b). Thinking critically about the comprehensive system for the Rorschach: A reply to Exner. *Psychological Science, 7*, 14–17.

Wood, R., & Bandura, A. (1989). Impact of conceptions of ability on self-regulatory mechanisms and complex decision making. *Journal of Personality and Social Psychology, 56*, 407–415.

Wood, W., & Eagly, A. H. (2002). A cross-cultural analysis of the behavior of women and men: Implications for the origins of sex differences. *Psychological Bulletin, 128*, 699–727.

Woodruffe, C. (1985). Consensual validation of personality traits: Additional evidence and individual differences. *Journal of Personality and Social Psychology, 48*, 1240–1252.

Wortman, C. B., & Brehm, J. W. (1975). Responses to uncontrollable outcomes: An integration of reactance theory and the learned helplessness model. In L. Berkowitz (Ed.), *Advances in experimental social psychology* (Vol. 8). New York: Academic Press.

Wright, J. C., Lindgren, K. P., & Zakriski, A. L. (2001). Syndromal versus contextualized personality assessment: Differentiating environmental and dispositional determinants of boys' aggression. *Journal of Personality and Social Psychology, 81*, 1176–1189.

Wright, J. C., & Mischel, W. (1988). Conditional hedges and the intuitive psychology of traits. *Journal of Personality and Social Psychology, 55*, 454–469.

Wright, J. C., Zakriski, A. L., & Drinkwater, M. (1999). Developmental psychopathology and the reciprocal patterning of behavior and environment: Distinctive situational and behavioral signatures of internalizing, externalizing, and mixed-syndrome children. *Journal of Consulting and Clinical Psychology, 67*, 95–107.

Wright, R. A. (1996). Brehm's theory of motivation as a model of effort and cardiovascular response. In P. M. Gollwitzer & J. A. Bargh (Eds.), *The psychology of action: Linking cognition and motivation to behavior* (pp. 424–453). New York: Guilford.

Wrosch, C., Scheier, M. F., Carver, C. S., & Schulz, R. (in press). The importance of goal disengagement in adaptive self-regulation: When giving up is beneficial. *Self and Identity*.

Wulfert, E., Block, J. A., Santa Ana, E., Rodriguez, M. L., & Colsman, M. (2002). Delay of gratification: Impulsive choices and problem behaviors in early and late adolescence. *Journal of Personality, 70*, 533–552.

Wyer, R. S., Jr., & Srull, T. K. (1986). Human cognition in its social context. *Psychology Review, 93*, 322–359.

Wylie, R. (1979). *The self concept* (Vol. 2). Lincoln: University of Nebraska Press.

Yates, B. T., & Mischel, W. (1979). Young children's preferred attentional strategies for delaying gratification. *Journal of Personality and Social Psychology, 37*, 286–300.

Yates, J., & Taylor, J. (1978). Stereotypes for somatotypes: Shared beliefs about Sheldon's physiques. *Psychological Reports, 43*, 777–778.

York, K. L., & John, O. P. (1992). The four faces of Eve: A typological analysis of women's personality at midlife. *Journal of Personality and Social Psychology, 63*, 494–508.

Young, J. E., & Klosko, J. S. (1993). *Reinventing your life*. New York: Plume.

Young, P. A., Eaves, L. J., & Eysenck, H. J. (1980). Intergenerational stability and change in the causes of variation in personality. *Personality and Individual Differences, 1*, 35–55.

Zadeh, L. (1965). Fuzzy sets. *Information and Control, 8,* 338–353.

Zald, D. H., & Depue, R. A. (2001). Serotonergic functioning correlates with positive and negative affect in psychiatrically healthy males. *Personality and Individual Differences, 30,* 71–86.

Zanna, M. P., Kiesler, C. A., & Pilkonis, P. A. (1970). Positive and negative attitudinal affect established by classical conditioning. *Journal of Personality and Social Psychology, 14,* 321–328.

Zeidner, M., & Hammer, A. L. (1992). Coping with missile attack: Resources, strategies, and outcomes. *Journal of Personality, 60,* 709–746.

Zeldow, P. B., Daugherty, S. R., & McAdams, D. P. (1988). Intimacy, power, and psychological well-being in medical students. *Journal of Nervous and Mental Disease, 176,* 182–187.

Zelenski, J. M., & Larsen, R. J. (1999). Susceptibility to affect: A comparison of three personality taxonomies. *Journal of Personality, 67,* 761–791.

Zener, K. (1937). The significance of behavior accompanying conditioned salivary secretion for theories of the conditioned response. *American Journal of Psychology, 50,* 384–403.

Zentall, T. R., Sutton, J. E., & Sherburne, L. M. (1996). True imitative learning in pigeons. *Psychological Science, 7,* 343–346.

Zern, D. (1973). Competence reconsidered: The concept of secondary process development as an explanation of "competence" phenomena. *Journal of Genetic Psychology, 122,* 135–162.

Zillmann, D. (1971). Excitation transfer in communication-mediated aggressive behavior. *Journal of Experimental Social Psychology, 7,* 419–434.

Zillmann, D. (1998). *Connections between sexuality and aggression* (2nd ed.). Mahwah, NJ: Erlbaum.

Zimmerman, B. J., & Rosenthal, J. T. (1974). Observational learning of rule-governed behavior by children. *Psychological Bulletin, 81,* 29–42.

Zimmerman, D. W. (1957). Durable secondary reinforcement: Method and theory. *Psychological Review, 14,* 373–383.

Zinbarg, R. E., & Mohlman, J. (1998). Individual differences in the acquisition of affectively valenced associations. *Journal of Personality and Social Psychology, 74,* 1024–1040.

Zucker, A. N., Ostrove, J. M., & Stewart, A. J. (2002). College-educated women's personality development in adulthood: Perceptions and age differences. *Psychology & Aging, 17,* 236–244.

Zuckerman, M. (1971). Dimensions of sensation seeking. *Journal of Consulting and Clinical Psychology, 36,* 45–52.

Zuckerman, M. (1979). *Sensation seeking: Beyond the optimal level of arousal.* Hillsdale, NJ: Erlbaum.

Zuckerman, M. (1985). Biological foundations of the sensation-seeking temperament. In J. Strelau, F. H. Farley, & A. Gale (Eds.), *The biological bases of personality and behavior. Vol. 1. Theories, measurement techniques, and development.* Washington, DC: Hemisphere.

Zuckerman, M. (1991a). Biotypes for basic personality dimensions? "The twilight zone" between genotype and social phenotype. In J. Strelau & A. Angleitner (Eds.), *Explorations in temperament: International perspectives on theory and measurement* (pp. 129–146). New York: Plenum.

Zuckerman, M. (1991b). *The psychobiology of personality.* New York: Cambridge University Press.

Zuckerman, M. (1992). What is a basic factor and which factors are basic? Turtles all the way down. *Personality and Individual Differences, 13,* 675–681.

Zuckerman, M. (1993). P-impulsive sensation seeking and its behavioral, psychophysiological and biochemical correlates. *Neuropsychobiology, 28,* 30–36.

Zuckerman, M. (1994). *Behavioral expression and biosocial bases of sensation seeking.* New York: Cambridge University Press.

Zuckerman, M. (1995). Good and bad humors: Biochemical bases of personality and its disorders. *Psychological Science, 6,* 325–332.

Zuckerman, M. (1996). The psychobiological model for impulsive unsocialized sensation seeking: A comparative approach. *Neuropsychobiology, 34,* 125–129.

Zuckerman, M., Bernieri, F., Koestner, R., & Rosenthal, R. (1989). To predict some of the people some of the time: In search of moderators. *Journal of Personality and Social Psychology, 57,* 279–293.

Zuckerman, M., Kieffer, S. C., & Knee, C. R. (1998). Consequences of self-handicapping: Effects on coping, academic performance, and adjustment. *Journal of Personality and Social Psychology, 74,* 1619–1628.

Zuckerman, M., Koestner, R., DeBoy, T., Garcia, T., Maresca, B. C., & Sartoris, J. M. (1988). To predict some of the people some of the time: A reexamination of the moderator variable approach in personality theory. *Journal of Personality and Social Psychology, 54,* 1006–1019.

Zuckerman, M., Kuhlman, D. M., & Camac, C. (1988). What lies beyond E and N? Factor analyses of scales believed to measure basic dimensions of personality. *Journal of Personality and Social Psychology, 54,* 96–107.

Zuckerman, M., Kuhlman, D. M., Joireman, J., Teta, P., & Kraft, M. (1993). A comparison of three structural models for personality: The big three, the big five, and the alternative five. *Journal of Personality and Social Psychology, 65,* 757–768.

Zuckerman, M., Murtaugh, T. M., & Siegel, J. (1974). Sensation seeking and cortical augmenting-reducing. *Psychophysiology, 11,* 535–542.

Zuckerman, M., & Neeb, M. (1980). Demographic influences in sensation seeking and expressions of sensation seeking in religion, smoking, and driving habits. *Personality and Individual Differences, 1,* 197–206.

Zuroff, D. C. (1986). Was Gordon Allport a trait theorist? *Journal of Personality and Social Psychology, 51,* 993–1000.

Name Index

Note: **Bold** type indicates profiles.

Aarts, H., 475, 485
Abbott, R. A., 489
Abelson, R. P., 445, 473, 484, 487
Abramson, L. Y., 76, 370, 450, 465–466
Achille, N., 80
Adams, G. D., 26
Adams, G. R., 270–271
Adams, H. E., 334
Adams, J. A., 473
Adams, N. E., 371–373, 444
Adams, R., 70
Adams-Webber, J. R., 415
Adler, A., 259–261, 272–273, **273**, 275, 281
Adler, J. M., 230, 231
Affleck, G., 433
Agostinelli, G., 392
Agronick, G. S., 75
Agyei, Y., 135, 144, 145
Ahadi, S., 79
Ahern, C. E., 335
Ainsworth, M. D. S., 285
Ajzen, I., 476
Akiyoshi, J., 136, 163
Albert, R. D., 426
Alexander, R., 138
Alford, E. C., 176
Alicke, M. D., 392
Alioto, J. T., 206
Allen, A., 77–78
Allen, J. J., 161, 163, 180, 182
Allen, L. S., 173
Allen, M. G., 149
Allison, D., 425
Alloy, L. B., 370, 450, 465–466
Allport, G. W., 5–6, 58, 62, 82, 128, 256
Almagor, M., 72
Alpert, R., 364

Altemus, M., 179
Amabile, T. M., 398
Amico, J. A., 179
Amsel, A., 331, 332
Anastasi, A., 36, 239
Andersen, S. M., 282, 283, 448, 461, 509
Anderson, C., 70
Anderson, C. A., 206, 449
Anderson, J. A., 454
Anderson, J. R., 443, 444
Anderson, J. W., 91
Anderson, R. C., 445
Anderson, S., 149
Ando, J., 136
Andrews, J. A., 70
Andrykowski, M. A., 433
Angleitner, A., 127, 132–134, 136, 137
Angst, J., 261
Ansseau, M., 162
Antoni, M. H., 489
Arbisi, P., 162, 163, 182
Ardrey, R., 138
Arend, R. A., 295
Arkin, R. M., 393
Armeli, S., 334
Arndt, J., 402, 408
Arnett, P. A., 170, 182
Arnold, M. L., 302
Aron, A., 167
Aron, E. N., 167
Arps, K., 351
Asendorpf, J. B., 69, 264, 265
Aserinsky, E., 235
Ashton, M. C., 73
Aspinwall, L. G., 489
Atkinson, J. W., 98, 99, 101, 109–111
Austenfeld, J. L., 433
Austin, J. T., 478
Avery, R. R., 269
Avia, M. D., 133, 372
Avila, C., 170
Axelrod, R., 140
Axline, V. M., 306, 309

Ayduk, O., 448, 457
Ayllon, T., 342
Azrin, N. H., 340, 342

Babad, E. Y., 480
Babey, S. H., 447
Bachicha, D. L., 360
Badger, G. J., 341
Baeyens, F., 323, 324
Bailey, J. M., 135, 143–145
Bain, A., 277
Baird, E., 388
Bakeman, R., 259–260
Baker, N., 457
Baker, T. B., 339, 340
Baldwin, J. M., 427, 446
Baldwin, M. W., 290, 446
Baldwin, P., 235
Balkin, T. J., 235
Balmary, M., 214
Baltes, P. B., 304
Banaji, M. R., 447–448
Bandura, A., 349, 350, 352, 354, 355, 357, **358**, 359, 360, 361, 363, 364, 365, 366, 369, 371, 372, 373, 376, 449, 460, 480, 490, 510
Bannister, D., 415
Barash, D. P., 138, 142, 150–151
Barbee, A. P., 143
Barber, J. P., 466
Barckley, M., 70
Barenbaum, N. B., 104–105
Bargh, J. A., 194, 217, 411, 446, 449, 453, 474, 475, 479, 496, 507–508
Barkow, J. H., 138
Barlow, D. H., 335–336
Barndollar, K., 194, 475
Baron, R. A., 204, 206, 366
Barrett, L. C., 130
Barrett, M., 387
Barron, F., 200
Bartholomew, B. D., 84, 206

Bartholomew, K., 289, 290, 305
Bartlett, M. Y., 145
Barton, R., 466
Basmajian, J. V., 343
Batson, C. D., 140, 351, 440
Batson, J. G., 351
Battle, E., 356
Bauer, J. J., 302, 359
Baumann, L. J., 493
Baumeister, R. F., 202, 205, 207, 229, 241, 265–266, 285, 307, 388, 395–396, 410, 478
Baumgardner, A. H., 393
Beall, S. K., 243
Beaman, A. L., 351
Bean, J. P., 365
Beattie, M., 357
Beck, A. T., 465–467, 495
Becker, B., 305
Becker, E., 401, 402
Becker, W. C., 336
Beer, R. D., 472
Belenky, G., 235
Bell, C. R., III, 369
Bell, M., 305
Bell, P. A., 204
Bellack, A., 334
Bellavia, G., 391
Belmaker, R. H., 135–136, 162
Belmont, L., 261
Belsky, J., 286
Bem, D. J., 75, 77–78
Bem, S. L., 365, 446
Benet, V., 67, 72
Benet-Martinez, V., 67
Bengel, D., 136, 163
Benjamin, J., 135–136, 162, 163
Bennett, E. R., 135–136, 162
Bentler, P. M., 59
Benton, C., 108
Berant, E., 309

Berenbaum, S. A., 174
Berg, I. A., 45
Bergeman, C. S., 132, 133, 489
Berger, S. M., 352
Berglas, S., 393, 394
Bergman, A., 282
Bergmann, M. S., 196
Berk, M., 163, 171
Berkowitz, L., 204, 206, 324
Berlew, D. E., 100
Berman, W. H., 287
Bernhardt, P. C., 177
Bernieri, F. J., 78, 177, 183
Bernstein, A., 182
Bernstein, D. A., 336
Bernstein, I. L., 321
Berntson, G. G., 164
Berrettini, W. H., 149
Berry, D. S., 70
Berry, N. J., 335
Berscheid, E., 422
Bertrand, S., 209
Berzonsky, M. D., 300
Besch, N. F., 175
Bettelheim, B., 201, 231
Bettencourt, B. A., 388
Beyer, J., 371–373
Billings, F. J., 225
Billington, R., 305
Binkofski, F., 462
Binswanger, L., 401
Birch, D., 98, 99, 109, 110
Bjorklund, D. F., 138
Black, A. E., 406
Blackburn, R., 205
Blaine, D., 135–136, 162
Blake, A. W., 223
Blake, H., 171–172
Blake, R. R., 57
Blanchard, E. B., 335, 343
Blanchard, M. J., 257
Blanck, G., 282
Blanck, R., 282
Blankenship, V., 104
Blanton, H., 475–476
Blatt, S. J., 140–141, 305, 306, 308, 309
Blehar, M. C., 285
Block, J., 72, 79, 86, 197, 262–263, 266, 270, 271, 275–276, 515
Block, J. A., 197
Block, J. H., 197, 262, 405, 515
Blondheim, S. H., 209
Blount, J., 446
Blum, B., 206
Blum, G. S., 209
Blumer, H., 427
Bobo, L., 143

Bodenhausen, G. V., 443
Boer, D. P., 216
Boggiano, A. K., 387
Bohman, M., 149
Bolen, M. H., 351
Bolles, R. C., 355
Bonanno, G. A., 359
Bonarius, H., 415
Bond, A. J., 171, 184
Bond, M. H., 67
Bond, R. N., 407
Boorman, D., 149
Booth, A., 176–178
Borgatta, E. F., 66, 68
Borges, C. A., 126
Boring, E. G., 455
Borkenau, P., 127, 133, 137
Borkowski, W., 456
Bornstein, R. F., 209, 281
Borowiecki, J. J., 176
Boss, A., 445
Boss, M., 401
Bosson, J. K., 448
Bothwell, R. K., 70
Bottome, P., 273
Botwin, M. D., 67
Bouchard, T. J., Jr., 132, 133, 266
Bourne, E., 299
Bouton, M. E., 323, 329, 340, 517
Bower, G. H., 487
Bower, J. E., 433
Bowlby, J., 285, 289
Bowman, P. J., 302, 304
Bowman, R. E., 257
Boyatzis, R. E., 102, 105, 108, 114
Boynton, K. S., 43
Böning, J., 163, 171
Bradburn, N. M., 100
Bradley, A., 203
Bradley, G. W., 392
Brady, J. P., 339
Brady, M. J., 433
Braff, D., 464
Brainerd, C. J., 74
Bramel, D., 206
Brandon, T. H., 340
Brandstätter, H., 78
Brandstätter, V., 102, 477
Brandt, J. R., 351
Brannon, R., 209
Bransford, J. D., 444–445
Branstetter, A. D., 433
Bratslavsky, E., 202
Braun, A. R., 235
Braverman, J., 145
Brayton, C., 203
Breedlove, S. M., 172
Brehm, J. W., 370, 389–390

Brehm, S. S., 389–390
Breland, H. M., 261
Breland, K., 344
Breland, M., 344
Brendl, C. M., 452
Brennan, K. A., 289, 292
Brenner, C., 232–234
Brewer, M. B., 446
Brewer, W. F., 355, 446
Bridger, W. H., 355
Bridges, M. W., 489
Briggs, M. A., 257
Briggs, S. R., 67, 73
Brinkley, C. A., 182
Brissette, I., 134, 489
Britt, T. W., 58
Broadbent, D. E., 482
Brock, D. W., 148
Brody, N., 194
Brokaw, D. W., 349
Brooks, R. A., 472, 496
Brooks-Gunn, J., 432
Brown, G., 396
Brown, I., Jr., 359, 370
Brown, J. D., 70, 392, 466
Brown, J. S., 337
Brown, R. T., 183
Brown, S., 351, 359
Brownley, K. A., 179
Bruhn, A. R., 272
Bruner, J. S., 389, 443
Brunhart, S. N., 489
Brunstein, J. C., 108, 111, 113, 389
Brunswik, E., 354
Bryan, A., 150
Bryant, F. B., 107
Buccino, G., 462
Buchanan, A., 148
Buchanan, G. M., 450
Buchsbaum, M. S., 168
Bugental, J. F. T., 383
Burge, D., 289
Burger, J. M., 373
Burgess, M., 205, 206
Burke, P. J., 67
Burns, G. L., 323
Burnstein, E., 140
Burroughs, W. J., 473
Burrows, L., 474
Bursik, K., 271
Burt, S. A., 162
Busch, C. M., 66–67
Busemeyer, J. R., 466, 495
Bushman, B. J., 205, 206, 307
Buss, A. H., 87, 128–131, 133, 151, 349, 481, 482, 491
Buss, D. M., 67, 70, 78, 138, 143–146

Bussey, K., 364, 365
Butcher, J. N., 45, 48
Butler, J. M., 409
Butow, P. N., 243
Buunk, B. P., 145
Bybee, D., 496
Byrne, D., 105

Cacioppo, J. T., 161, 164, 257, 323, 335, 446
Cado, S., 432
Cai, G., 150
Cain, D. J., 408
Calhoun, K. S., 334
Calhoun, L. G., 433
Campbell, D. T., 42–44
Campbell, J., 392
Campbell, J. D., 481, 491–492
Campbell, K., 182
Campbell, K. L., 105
Campbell, W. K., 137, 202, 291, 307, 410
Campo, R., 177, 183
Cannon, D. S., 339, 340
Cannon, W. B., 178–179
Cantor, N., 444–446, 448, 464, 478
Caporael, L. R., 138
Carey, G., 132, 150
Carlota, A. J., 67
Carlson, M., 207
Carlston, D. E., 323, 450
Carnelley, K. B., 291, 309
Carr, T. S., 175
Carrell, S. E., 446
Carroll, J. S., 447
Carroll, L., 104
Carson, R. E., 235
Carter, B. L., 340
Carter, C. S., 179
Carter, S. R., III, 223
Carter-Saltzman, L., 127
Carver, C. S., 102, 134, 164–166, 217, 291–292, 305, 357, 369, 373, 388, 411, 448, 452, 454, 461, 465, 468, 472, 474, 475, 479–482, 487–490, 493, 494, 510
Casey, R., 183
Caspar, F., 455
Caspi, A., 57, 75, 78, 162, 182, 264, 265, 275–276, 309
Cassidy, J., 286, 287
Catania, A. C., 333
Catanzaro, S. J., 465
Cather, C., 492
Cattell, H. E. P., 73
Cattell, R. B., 48, 62, 63, 65

Cervone, D., 79
Chambers, W., 474, 475
Chambliss, C. A., 373
Chan, T., 184
Chance, S. E., 175, 183
Chaplin, W., 466
Chaplin, W. F., 70
Chapman, L. J., 20–21
Chartrand, T. L., 475
Chassin, L., 392
Chatterjee, B. B., 355
Cheek, J., 74
Chen, D., 261
Chen, E., 453
Chen, M., 474
Chen, S., 282, 283, 448, 461, 509
Chernick, L., 76
Chess, S., 130
Chevron, E., 305, 306
Chew, S. L., 446
Chipuer, H. M., 132, 133
Choi, J., 203
Chomsky, N., 333
Christensen, A. J., 70
Christensen, H., 136, 163
Christie, R., 357
Christopher, S. B., 504–505
Church, A. T., 67, 172
Cialdini, R. B., 351
Cillessen, A. H. N., 465
Ciminero, A. R., 334
Clancy, D. D., 114
Clanton, N. R., 70
Claridge, G. S., 159
Clark, C. L., 289
Clark, H. H., 426
Clark, K. C., 489
Clark, L. A., 69, 70, 84, 161, 166, 168–169, 515
Clark, R. A., 98, 99
Clark, R. D., 144
Clark, W. R., 203
Clarkin, J. F., 84
Clausen, J. A., 303
Cleare, A. J., 171
Cline, V. B., 366
Cloninger, C. R., 160–163, 171
Cloninger, R., 149
Clower, C. E., 70
Coan, J. A., 225
Coats, S., 290
Coccaro, E. F., 170–171
Cohen, A. R., 257
Cohen, D., 177
Cohen, H., 150
Cohen, M. F., 205, 206
Cohen, S., 355
Cohn, L. D., 269
Coie, J. D., 465

Cole, S. W., 184, 509
Collier, D. A., 150
Collins, C. A., 433
Collins, N. L., 288, 290, 291, 305
Collins, P. F., 160–163, 166, 170
Colsman, M., 197
Colvin, C. R., 79
Comings, D. E., 162, 171–172
Conger, R. D., 309
Conklin, C. A., 340
Conley, J. J., 79
Connell, J. P., 406
Connor, D. F., 176
Constantian, C. A., 105–106
Converse, J., 46
Conway, M., 465
Cook, M. L., 465
Cook, P. E., 205
Cook, R. I., 357
Cook, W. L., 290
Cooley, C. H., 427
Cooley, E. J., 372
Coolidge, F. L., 308
Cooney, J. L., 341
Cooper, B., 179, 203
Cooper, H. M., 356
Cooper, M. L., 95–96, 359
Cooper, T. B., 170–171
Copernicus, 192
Cornwell, R., 403
Corr, P. J., 163
Cortes, J. B., 126
Cosmides, L., 138
Costa, F., 263
Costa, P. T., Jr., 66–70, 72, 73, 75, 83, 84, 112, 132, 133, 163, 165, 303, 514
Costos, D., 270
Couch, A., 46
Couchman, C. E., 290
Courrier, S., 366
Coursey, R. D., 168
Cox, D. J., 357
Cox, J., 356
Cozzarelli, C., 359
Crabbe, J., 135, 136, 147–148
Craig, I. W., 135, 148, 182
Craig, K. D., 352
Craighead, W. E., 336
Cramer, P., 229
Crandall, C., 140
Crandall, R., 406
Crane, K. A., 390
Crawford, C. B., 138
Crawford, H. L., 323, 324
Crawford, L. E., 446

Crawford, M. T., 323
Crews, F., 217
Crick, N. R., 465
Criqui, M. H., 70
Crittenden, P. M., 290
Crocker, J., 20–21, 386
Croft, R. G., 366
Cronbach, L. J., 42
Cross, J. A., 351
Crouse, B. B., 105
Crowne, D. P., 47
Csikszentmihalyi, I. S., 400, 462
Csikszentmihalyi, M., 106, 108, 300, 301, 400, 462, 463
Cunningham, M. R., 143
Cutter, H. S. G., 114
Czyzewska, M., 445

D'Zurilla, T., 495
Dabbs, J. M., Jr., 175–178, 183
Dabbs, M. G., 175, 183
Dahlstrom, W., 48
Daitzman, R., 177
Daly, M., 146, 147
Danaher, B. G., 340
Daniels, D., 137, 323
Daniels, N., 148
Danilovics, P., 257
Danoff-Burg, S., 433
Danso, H. A., 302
Dantona, R. L., 341
Darley, J. M., 392
Darwin, C., 188, 192
Daugherty, S. R., 108
Davidson, M. A., 126
Davidson, R. J., 160–163, 180, 182, 184, 230
Davila, J., 289
Davis, C. G., 433
Davis, K. E., 291
Davis, M. A., 368
Davis, P. J., 230
Davis, W. N., 104, 114
Davison, G. C., 338, 339, 369
Dawkins, R., 138
Dawson, M. E., 355
de La Rue, D., 176, 177
de Raad, B., 67
de St. Aubin, E., 301–302
Deaux, K., 364, 446
DeBoy, T., 78
Deci, E. L., 290, 387, 388, 406, 407, 408, 410, 497
DeFries, J. C., 78, 125, 127, 135, 148
DeGirolamo, G. J., 184
DeHouwer, J., 323, 324

del Pilar, G. H., 67
Deluty, R. H., 79
DelVecchio, W. F., 75
Deng, H., 150
DeNike, L. D., 355
Denney, D. R., 371
Dent, K. M., 171
Depue, R. A., 160–163, 165, 166, 170, 171, 182, 183
DeRubeis, R. J., 466–467
DeSoto, C. B., 79
DeSteno, D., 145
Deters-Wadleigh, S. D., 149
Deutsch, F. M., 432
DeVellis, B. M., 370
DeVellis, R. F., 370
DeVito, A. J., 254
Di Blas, L., 67
Diamond, A., 302
Diamond, M., 135
Dick, D. M., 149
Dickens, W. T., 136–137
DiClemente, C. C., 372
Diener, C. I., 357
Diener, E., 69, 78, 79, 165, 166, 482, 491
Dienstbier, R. A., 67, 71
Dietz, G., 171–172
Diforio, D., 183
Digman, J. M., 66–69, 72, 133
Dijksterhuis, A., 145, 475, 485
DiLalla, L. F., 150
Diven, K., 353
Dlugolecki, D. W., 427
Dodge, K. A., 446, 465, 473, 495
Doering, C. H., 174
Doherty, K., 427
Dollard, J., 325, 327–328, 333, 337, 341
Dollinger, S. J., 69
Donehower, L. A., 203
Donnerstein, E., 204
Donnerstein, M., 204
Donovan, J. E., 263
Donovan, J. M., 300
Doob, A. N., 206
Dosamantes-Alperson, E., 406
Douglas, C., 91
Downey, G., 309, 457
Drabman, R. S., 326, 366, 367
Drews, D. R., 473
Drinkwater, M., 463
Duchnowski, A. J., 324
Duck, S. W., 425
Duff, K. J., 229

Dulany, D. E., 355
Dull, V., 446
Duncan, B., 206
Duncan, C. P., 331
Duncan, L. E., 75, 113
Duncan, N., 388
Dunn, J., 137
Dunn, S. M., 243
Dunne, M. P., 135
Dunning, D., 58
Durrett, M. E., 295, 296
Duval, S., 482
Dweck, C. S., 334, 357, 448, 449, 478
Dyck, J. L., 351
Dyck, M. J., 466
Dymond, R. F., 405

Eagle, M. N., 281
Eagly, A. H., 364, 365
Easteal, S., 136, 163
Eaves, L. J., 131–134
Ebbesen, E., 197, 457
Ebbesen, E. B., 206
Eber, H. W., 62
Ebstein, R. P., 135–136, 150, 162
Edelman, R., 206
Edelstein, W., 262
Edwards, A. L., 47, 111
Efran, J. S., 9
Egan, S. K., 70
Egeland, J. A., 149
Ehlers, S. L., 70
Einstein, D., 268, 271
Eisenberg, N. H., 69, 264, 275, 351
Eisenberger, R., 332, 334, 387
Ekehammer, B., 76
Ekman, P., 163
Elder, G. H., Jr., 75, 101, 309
Elder, K. A., 464–465
Ellenberger, H. F., 191–193, 242
Elliot, A. J., 102–103, 165, 385, 387, 389, 397, 406, 462
Elliot, L. B., 304
Elliott, E. S., 478
Ellison, G. D., 322–323
Elmore, A. M., 343
Emery, G., 465, 466
Emmons, R. A., 78, 111, 478, 486, 492, 494
Endler, N. S., 76, 81
Enns, V., 290
Enos, T., 179
Entwisle, D. R., 111
Epstein, D. H., 341

Epstein, L. H., 341, 343
Epstein, S., 74, 80, 194, 422, 456, 515
Epting, F. R., 431, 434
Erdelyi, M. H., 191, 229–230, 243, 507, 508
Ericsson, K. A., 462
Eriksen, C. W., 355
Erikson, E. H., 110–111, 292, 294, 297–298, **298,** 300, 302–305, 306, 309, 310
Ernst, C., 261
Ernst, D., 466
Esterson, A., 216, 217, 242
Evans, R., 204
Evans, R. I., 358
Evans, T. A., 369
Ewart, C. K., 463
Exline, R. V., 166–167
Exner, J. E., Jr., 239, 240
Eysenck, H. J., 58, 62, 64, 65, 69, 71, 72, 131–135, 140, 149, 150, 156, **157,** 158, 159, 245, 515
Eysenck, M. W., 131, 132
Eysenck, S. B. G., 62, 64, 65, 515

Fabes, R. A., 264, 275, 351
Fadiga, L., 462
Fagot, B. J., 365
Fahey, J. L., 433
Fairbairn, W. R. D., 255, 281
Fairbanks, L. A., 166, 171
Falbo, T., 261
Falmagne, J-Cl., 444
Faraone, S. V., 149
Fastnow, C., 26
Fazio, R. H., 452
Feather, N. T., 99, 354, 356
Feeney, B. C., 290
Feeney, J. A., 288
Fehr, B., 290
Fehr, E., 140, 141
Feij, J. A., 167–168
Feingold, A., 143, 145
Feinstein, J. A., 257
Fekken, G. C., 447
Feldman Barrett, L., 107, 227, 462
Feldman, F., 245
Feldman, M. P., 339
Fenichel, O., 215
Fenigstein, A., 481, 482, 491
Ferguson, M. J., 194, 411, 475, 479, 496
Fernandez, G., 257
Fernandez, L. E., 352, 362–363

Fernando, C. K., 343
Ferneyhough, K., 70
Ferrell, R. E., 167, 171
Festinger, L., 491
Fick, C. M., 357, 369
Field, N., 105
Fielden, J. A., 176, 177
Filyer, R., 302
Findley, M. J., 356
Fink, G. R., 462
Finkel, E. J., 202
Fiore, M. C., 340
Fischer, R. E., 211
Fisher, R., 243
Fisher, S., 166, 209, 245
Fiske, A. P., 446
Fiske, D. W., 43–44, 66, 68
Fiske, S. T., 360, 446
Fitzgerald, T., 433
Flanders, J. P., 359
Fleeson, J., 285
Fleeson, W., 80, 82
Fleming, A., 432
Fletcher, G. J. O., 227, 257
Flink, C., 387
Floderus-Myrhed, B., 131
Florian, V., 291, 309, 403
Flory, J. D., 164, 167, 171, 453
Flynn, J. R., 136–137
Foa, E. B., 349
Foa, U. G., 349
Foch, T. T., 130, 147
Fodor, E. M., 103
Fogassi, L., 462, 474
Folkman, S., 60, 417
Fong, G. T., 227
Fontenot, M. B., 162, 171
Ford, D. H., 472
Forsterling, F., 67, 112
Forzi, M., 67
Foster, C. A., 307
Fowles, D. C., 161, 182
Fox, N. A., 161
Frady, R. L., 175
Fraley, R. C., 75, 289, 291, 292
Frank, E., 102, 477
Frank, L. K., 237
Frank, S., 111, 271
Frankel, A., 370
Frankel, B. L., 168
Frankl, V. E., 401
Franks, J. J., 444–445
Fransella, F., 434
Frederickson, B. L., 465, 495
Freedman, J. L., 366
Freedman, Z. R., 408
Freitag, G., 336
French, E. G., 99, 101

French, R., 464
Frese, M., 495
Freud, A., 221, 222, 228–229, 253–255, 298
Freud, S., 8, 11, 12, 188–196, 198–204, 207–208, 212, **214,** 215–216, 221, 224, 227, 231, 234, 235, 236, 237, 240–242, 245, 246, 250, 253, 254, 266, 267, 269, 271, 277, 281, 284, 292, 293, 295–296, 298, 342, 459, 468
Freund, A. M., 478, 490
Freund, H.-J., 462
Freyd, J. J., 224, 445
Friberg, L., 131, 133
Friedman, H. S., 70
Friedman, L. J., 298
Friesen, W. V., 163
Fritz, H. L., 260, 310
Frodi, A., 204
Froming, W. J., 474, 475
Fromm, E., 199
Fujita, F., 78, 165
Fukuyama, F., 148
Fulker, D. W., 140
Fultz, J., 351
Funder, D. C., 36, 73, 74, 79, 197, 263, 458, 467
Furdella, J. Q., 70
Furedy, J. J., 355

Gable, S. L., 462
Gabrieli, J. D. E., 169
Gacsaly, S. A., 126
Gade-Andavolu, R., 171–172
Galanter, E., 472, 479
Galen, 57, 62, 125
Gallagher, W., 128
Gallese, V., 462, 474
Gallistel, C. R., 482
Ganellen, R. J., 240, 465, 474, 475
Gangestad, S. W., 57, 78, 142
Garb, H. N., 111, 239–240, 274
Garcia, J., 517
Garcia, S., 351
Garcia, T., 78
Gardner, H., 508
Gardner, W. L., 164
Garner, J. P., 292
Garrett, J., 166
Gatti, F. M., 126
Gaulin, S., 144
Gächter, S., 140
Gaulin, S., 145

Gaunt, R., 169, 458, 515
Gaunzon-Lapeña, M. A., 67
Gauthier, J., 372
Gazendam, A., 167–168
Gächter, S., 141
Geen, R. G., 158, 205, 206, 366
Genest, M., 448, 462
Gerhard, D. S., 149
Germer, C. K., 9
Gerrard, M., 475–476
Gershon, E. S., 149
Gerst, M. S., 360
Getzels, J. W., 300, 301
Ghebranious, N., 203
Giannopoulos, C., 465
Gibbon, J., 317
Gibbons, F. X., 475–476, 482, 494
Gibson, H. B., 157
Gigerenzer, G., 443
Gilbert, D. T., 169, 458, 515
Gill, M. M., 256
Gillath, O., 291, 452
Gilligan, C., 101, 102, 108
Gilovich, T., 426
Gino, A., 339, 340
Gladue, B. A., 144, 145
Glaser, R., 243
Glass, C. R., 462, 492
Glass, G. V., 245, 409
Glassman, N. S., 509
Gleuck, E., 126
Glueck, S., 126
Goethals, G. R., 392
Gold, V. J., 336
Goldband, S., 209
Goldberg, A., 283
Goldberg, L. R., 62, 66, 67, 68, 69, 71, 72, 73
Goldenberg, J. L., 403
Goldfield, G. S., 341
Goldfried, M. R., 339, 369, 495
Goldiamond, I., 350
Goldin, L. R., 149
Goldsmith, H. H., 132
Goldstein, D. G., 443
Goldstein, M., 357
Gollwitzer, P. M., 194, 475, 476, 477, 515
Gomes, M., 78
Gonzalez, N., 171–172
Goodman, J., 373, 374
Goranson, R. E., 206
Gormezano, I., 320
Gorski, R. A., 173
Gorsuch, R. L., 73
Gosling, S. D., 67

Gotlib, I. H., 465, 466
Gottesman, I. I., 132, 149, 150
Gould, R. L., 303
Graham, J., 48
Grammer, K., 145
Gray, J., 145, 160–162, 163, 165–166
Gray, J. A., 163
Gray, J. D., 392
Gray, J. J., 176
Graybeal, A., 243
Graziano, W. G., 69, 70, 143
Grässman, R., 389
Green, J. D., 291
Greenberg, B. D., 135–136, 162, 163
Greenberg, J., 224, 392, 394, 402, 403, 408, 492, 494
Greenberg, R. P., 209, 245
Greene, D., 387
Greene, D. L., 103
Greenfield, N. S., 335
Greenwald, A. G., 447–448
Greer, S., 243
Gregg, B., 142
Grich, J., 290, 292
Griffin, D., 305
Griffin, D. W., 391
Griffitt, C., 351
Grigsby, J., 217
Grings, W. W., 355
Gritsenko, L., 150
Grob, A., 69, 166
Grolnick, W. S., 387
Grossmann, K., 296
Grossmann, K. E., 296
Groth, G. E., 143–145
Grow, V. M., 408
Gruber, A. J., 176
Gruen, R. J., 351
Gruenewald, T. L., 179
Gruser, J. E., 364, 372
Guisinger, S., 140–141
Gurin, G., 357
Gurin, P., 357
Gurling, H., 149
Gurung, R. A. R., 179
Guthrie, I. K., 264, 275
Gutierres, S. E., 144
Gutmann, M., 493
Gwadry, E., 235

Haaga, D. A. F., 466
Haan, N., 303
Haas, H. A., 67
Hackett, G., 339
Haemmerlie, F. M., 467
Hagen, A. S., 396

Hager, J. L., 517
Hagerman, S. M., 350, 495
Haigh, C. V., 409
Hair, E. C., 69
Halberstadt, J. B., 446, 487
Hale, G. A., 365
Hall, C. S., 213
Hall, J. A., 365
Hall, J. F., 319
Hall, R. V., 349
Hallam, J., 204
Halpern, J., 229
Halverson, C. F., Jr., 133
Hamaker, S., 69
Hamer, D. H., 135–136, 162, 163
Hamilton, J. C., 492
Hamilton, W. D., 138–140
Hammen, C., 289
Hammer, A. L., 489
Hampson, S. E., 70
Handel, W. H., 427
Handelsman, M. M., 394
Hansenne, M., 162
Hanson, D. R., 150
Harackiewicz, J. M., 102, 161, 387
Hardaway, R., 231
Hardy, A. B., 372
Hargrove, M. F., 177
Harmon-Jones, E., 161, 163, 180
Harnad, S., 333
Harris, C. R., 145
Harris, G. T., 146, 147
Harris, J. A., 134
Harris, J. R., 137
Harris, S. D., 489
Harrison, R. J., 176
Hart, D., 262
Hart, H. M., 302
Hartmann, H., 255, 256
Haskett, R. F., 172
Haslam, N., 446
Hassin, R. R., 449
Hatfield, E., 143, 144
Hathaway, S. R., 48
Haug Ogden, D. E., 341
Hauger, R. L., 170–171
Haugtvedt, C. P., 257
Hauser, S. T., 269
Haviland, J. M., 152
Hawes, R., 372
Hayes, S. C., 326
Hayes-Roth, B., 496
Hayes-Roth, F., 496
Haynes, S. N., 335–336
Hazan, C., 285–288, 290, 309
Hazen, N. L., 295, 296
Healy, S., 104, 106

Heath, A. C., 131–134
Heckhausen, H., 98, 357, 477, 515
Hegarty, P., 152
Heiby, E. M., 350
Heider, F., 416, 443, 449
Heilbrun, K. S., 231
Heils, A., 136, 163
Helgeson, V. S., 108, 260, 310, 433
Helle, P., 465
Heller, M. S., 366
Helmreich, R. L., 259–260
Helson, R., 75, 266, 268, 271, 304
Hemenover, S. H., 67, 71
Hemenway, K., 446
Henderlong, J., 355, 387
Henderson, A. S., 136, 163
Henriques, J. B., 182
Herbener, E. S., 78
Herbst, J. H., 70, 163
Hernandez, A., 108
Herr, P. M., 452
Herrnstein, R. J., 150
Hersch, P. D., 357
Herscovitch, P., 235
Hersen, M., 334
Heschl, A., 138
Hesley, J., 76
Hess, E. H., 138
Hetherington, E. M., 130, 134, 147
Heuchert, J. W., 163, 171
Heusel, C., 177
Hewitt, P. L., 448
Heyns, R. W., 98, 105–106
Higgins, D. S., 78
Higgins, E. T., 102, 407, 425, 446, 448, 452, 453
Higgins, R. L., 392–394
Higgins, S. T., 341
Hilgard, E. R., 194
Hilgard, J. R., 194
Hill, C. A., 105, 106
Hill, K. D., 46
Hill, K. T., 365
Hill, T., 445
Hillix, W. A., 352
Hilton, N. Z., 146, 147
Hines, M., 174
Hinkley, K., 509
Hippocrates, 57, 62, 125
Hiroto, D. S., 370
Hirsch, B. J., 302
Hirschberger, G., 291, 403, 452
Hobbes, S. A., 301
Hobfoll, S. E., 166–167
Hobson, J. A., 235
Hockenberg, D., 301

Hodgins, H. S., 388
Hodgkinson, S., 149
Hoffman, E., 273, 395
Hoffman, L. W., 137
Hofheimer, J. A., 179
Hofmann, V., 262
Hofstee, W. K. B., 67, 70–71
Hogan, R., 42–43, 79
Hogansen, J., 271
Hokanson, J. E., 205, 206
Holden, K. B., 356
Holden, R. R., 447
Holland, R. W., 415, 483
Holmes, D. S., 207, 229, 417
Holmes, J. G., 228, 391, 402–403, 408, 421
Holstein, C., 456
Holt, R. R., 209, 268
Holtzworth-Munroe, A., 465
Holyoak, K. J., 321, 456
Hopkin, K., 203
Hoppe, C., 270
Hopper, C. H., 175
Horan, J. J., 339
Horesh, N., 226
Hormuth, S. E., 462
Horn, J. M., 131, 132, 140, 149, 150
Horner, M. S., 101
Horney, K., 212, 283, **284,** 305, 307–308
Horowitz, L. M., 289, 290, 305
Horowitz, M. J., 433
Horton, R. W., 366, 367
Horvath, P., 166
Houlihan, D., 351
Houlihan, J., 270
House, R. J., 100, 103
Houser-Marko, L., 389
Houston, B. K., 417
Hovland, C. I., 322
Howard, G. S., 43
Howells, G. N., 372
Hoyt, D. R., 309
Hoyt, W. T., 70
Hrebíčková, M., 133
Hsee, C. K., 487
Hsieh, F. Y., 335
Hu, N., 135
Hu, S., 135, 136
Hubbard, J. A., 465
Hubbard, R., 148
Huck, S., 309
Hudson, J. I., 176
Huesmann, L. R., 475
Huh, E., 456
Hui, H., 426

Hull, C. L., 328
Hull, J. G., 491
Humphreys, L. G., 331
Hunt, J. W., 433
Husband, T. H., 225
Hutchings, C. H., 368
Hutchison, K. E., 150
Hy, L. X., 274
Hyde, J. S., 144
Hyman, I. E., 225
Hymbaugh, K., 166

Iacono, W. G., 160–162, 182
Ickes, W., 351
Igelmann, H., 203
Ingram, R. E., 492
Innes-Ker, A. H., 446, 487
Inouye, D. K., 359, 370
Inouye, J., 66, 68, 69
Isaacs, E. A., 426
Isabella, R. A., 286
Isogawa, K., 136, 163
Israel, A. C., 365

Jacklin, C. N., 174
Jackson, C. D., 160–161, 184
Jackson, D., 349
Jackson, D. N., 45, 67, 73, 111, 112
Jackson, R. J., 107
Jacob, S., 141
Jacomb, P. A., 136, 163
Jaffe, K., 309
Jager, W., 70–71
Jakob, F., 163, 171
James, W., 9, 518
Jang, K. L., 84, 132–134, 136
Janigian, A. S., 433
Janoff-Bulman, R., 386, 433
Jansen-McWilliams, L., 243
Jarvis, W. B. G., 257
Jayne, C., 209
Jeffery, R. W., 360
Jenkins, H. M., 332
Jenkins, J. J., 446
Jenkins, S. R., 101, 104
Jensen, M. B., 243
Jensen-Campbell, L. A., 69, 70, 143
Jessor, L., 263
Jessor, R., 263
Jessor, S. L., 263
Jiang, Y., 149
Jockin, V., 134
John, O. P., 57, 67, 70, 73, 75, 113, 264, 265, 275–276, 307

Johns, J. M., 179
Johnson, C., 209
Johnson, D. J., 419
Johnson, G. B., 213
Johnson, J. A., 9, 67
Johnson, M. K., 444
Johnson, R. C., 184
Johnson, W., 361
Joireman, J., 71, 168
Jonas, E., 402
Jones, A., 406
Jones, C., 75
Jones, D. K., 478
Jones, E. E., 17, 393, 449
Jones, J. T., 453
Jones, M. C., 263
Jones, W. H., 301
Jöreskog, K. G., 59
Jones, M. C., 338, 371
Jones, S., 203
Jorenby, D. E., 340
Jorm, A. F., 136, 163
Jourard, S. M., 404
Jung, C. G., 57, 62, 91, 254
Juni, S., 209, 211
Jurkovic, G. J., 175
Jussim, L., 415, 444

Kaemmer, B., 48
Kagan, J., 128
Kahn, S., 300, 301
Kalin, N. H., 160–161, 184
Kalin, R., 114
Kaloupek, D. G., 335
Kamin, L. J., 152, 321
Kanayama, G., 176
Kanfer, F. H., 334, 349, 350, 352, 354, 362–363, 372, 457, 466, 480, 495, 510, 511
Kao, C. F., 257
Kaplan, A. G., 365
Kaplan, J. R., 162, 171
Kaprio, J., 131–133
Karbon, M., 351
Karoly, P., 457
Karsenty, G., 203
Karylowski, J. J., 447–448
Kasmer, J. A., 73
Kassel, J. D., 466
Kasser, T., 387–389, 397, 407
Kassorla, I. C., 336
Katigbak, M. S., 67
Katin-Borland, M., 372
Katkin, E. S., 209
Katsuragi, S., 136, 163
Katz, M., 135–136, 162
Kazdin, A. E., 336, 342, 369

Keane, T. M., 335
Keating, J. P., 351
Keefe, R. G., 143, 144
Keelan, J. P. R., 290
Keller, M., 262
Kellogg, W. N., 320
Kelly, A. E., 244
Kelly, G. A., 12, 415–437, **421,** 443, 452, 459–460
Kelso, J. A. S., 473
Keltner, D., 70
Kemeny, M. E., 433
Kempner, C. R., 366
Kendler, K. S., 131–134
Kenford, S. L., 340
Keniston, K., 46
Kenny, C., 244
Kenny, D. A., 140
Kenrick, D. T., 76, 78, 143–146, 446
Kernberg, O., 307
Kessler, R. C., 131–134, 292
Ketcham, A. S., 489
Ketelaar, T., 164–165
Keyes, C. L. M., 70
Keysers, C., 462
Kidd, K. K., 149
Kiecolt-Glaser, J. K., 243
Kieras, D., 361
Kiesler, C. A., 324
Kihlstrom, J. F., 194, 448, 478, 507
Kim, K-H., 452
Kim, Y., 387, 397
Kimura, D., 174
King, G. A., 425, 453
King, K., 406
King, L. A., 486, 494
Kirk, S. B., 433
Kirker, W. S., 447
Kirkpatrick, L. A., 290, 291
Kirsch, I., 354–355, 364, 465, 510
Kirschenbaum, D. S., 495, 496
Kirshnit, C., 107
Kirson, D., 446
Kitayama, S., 140
Kitchener, R., 328
Kitcher, P., 152
Klein, G. S., 196, 256
Klein, J., 281
Klein, L. C., 179
Klein, M., 306, 309
Klein, R., 407
Klein, S. B., 447
Kleitman, N., 235
Kletz, I., 150
Kline, P., 62, 65
Klinger, E., 478, 488

Klion, R. E., 425
Klohnen, E. C., 113, 262
Klosko, J. S., 465
Kluck, B., 403
Klusas, J. A., 244
Knafo, A., 71
Knapp, R. R., 406
Knee, C. R., 388
Knight, C., 140–141
Knoll, E., 265
Knurek, D. A., 324
Knutson, B., 184
Kobak, R. R., 290
Kochanska, G., 70
Koelling, R. A., 517
Koestner, J., 387
Koestner, R., 78, 111, 387, 388
Koffka, K., 443
Koh, K., 321
Koh-Rangarajoo, E., 290
Kohler, E., 462
Kohnstamm, G. A., 133
Kohut, H., 283
Kolb, L. C., 335
Konecni, V. J., 206
Koole, S. L., 70–71
Korchmaros, J. D., 140
Kornhaber, R. C., 371
Koropsak, E., 206
Korten, A. E., 136
Köhler, W., 443
Kohut, H., 307
Korten, A. E., 163
Koskenvuo, M., 131–133
Kotler, M., 150
Kotre, J., 301, 302
Kowaz, A. M., 297
Krafchuk, E., 130
Kraft, M., 71, 168
Kramer, I., 150
Kramer, P. D., 183–184
Kranzler, H. R., 341
Krasner, L., 342
Krause, S., 104, 106
Krauss, S. P., 161
Kraut, R. E., 22–23
Krebs, D., 138
Kremen, A. M., 262–263
Kretschmer, E., 126
Krieger, S. R., 431
Kriegman, D., 140–141
Kring, A. M., 70
Krones, J. M., 144
Krueger, R. F., 182
Krull, D. S., 393
Kuhl, J., 465
Kuhlman, D. M., 71, 168
Kuiper, N. A., 447
Kukla, A., 488
Kulhavy, R. W., 480

Kuller, L. H., 243
Kunda, Z., 446, 455
Kunugi, H., 136, 163
Kus, L. A., 489
Kusdil, M. E., 133
Kwan, V. S. Y., 75

La Greca, A. M., 369
La Guardia, J. G., 290
Ladouceur, R., 372
Lakoff, G., 444
Lamiell, J. T., 58
Landreth, G. L., 309
Landsman, T., 400
Landy, F. J., 42–43
Lane, R. D., 184
Lang, P. J., 336
Langner, C. A., 104, 105
Langston, C., 478
Lanning, K., 66–67, 268, 271
Lansing, J. B., 105–106
Lanzetta, J. T., 352
Lao, R. C., 357
Larkey, L. S., 446
Larsen, R. J., 78, 145, 164–166, 171
Larson, J., 433, 495
Larstone, R. M., 84
Lasko, N. B., 335
Lassiter, G. D., 257
Latham, G. P., 478, 480
Lau, R. R., 453
Lauer, R. H., 427
Laurenceau, J.-P., 107, 462
Lauterbach, K., 78
LaVoie, L., 465
Lavori, P. W., 335
Lawrence, J. W., 102, 448
Lawton, W. J., 70
Lazarus, R. S., 60, 417
Lazovik, A. D., 336
Leak, G. K., 504–505
Leary, M. R., 285, 388, 395–396
Leary, T., 65
Lee, K., 73
Lee, L., 269
Lee, M. E., 70
Lee-Chai, A., 194, 475
LeFan, J. H., 259–260
Lefcourt, H. M., 356, 357, 369
Lefebvre, R. C., 489
LeFevre, J., 400
Leggatt, H. K., 386
Leggett, E. L., 448
Lehman, J. M., 489
Lehr, B. K., 495
Leit, R. A., 176
Leitner, L. M., 425, 431, 432

Lekes, N., 388
Lemann, N., 114
Lengfelder, A., 477
Leon, A., 162, 163
Lepper, M. R., 355, 387, 455
Lerer, B., 150
Lesch, K-P., 136, 163
Lesser, G. S., 101
Lesser, I. M., 300
Leung, S., 426
Leven, S. J., 454
Levenson, H., 357
Levenson, R. W., 351
Leventhal, H., 493
Levine, D. S., 454
Levine, S., 359
Levinson, D. J., 303
Lewicki, P., 445
Lewin, D. I., 148
Lewin, K., 354, 443
Lewinsohn, P. M., 466
Lewis, B. P., 179
Lewis, D. J., 331
Lewis, L. L., 364
Lewis, M., 302, 304
Lewontin, R. C., 152
Li, L., 135–136, 162
Li, N. P., 143, 145
Li, T., 150
Lichtenstein, E., 70, 340
Lichtenstein, P., 134
Lichtman, R. R., 433
Lieberman, M. D., 166, 169, 458, 515
Liebert, R. M., 352, 362–364, 366
Light, K. C., 179
Lilienfeld, S. O., 111, 239–240, 274
Linder, D. E., 390
Lindgren, K. P., 463
Linsenmeier, J. A. W., 143, 145
Linville, P. W., 448
Lippincott, E. C., 366, 367
Lipps, T., 193
Lipson, A., 456
Lisansky, J., 426
Litman-Adizes, T., 450
Litt, M. D., 359
Little, B. R., 478
Liu, J., 150
Liu, X., 150
Liverant, S., 356
Livesley, W. J., 84, 132, 133, 136
Lo Cascio, R., 211
Lobel, T. E., 446
Locke, E. A., 478, 480
Locurto, C. M., 317

Loehlin, J. C., 78, 127, 131–133, 149, 150
Loevinger, J., 265–269, 271, 274, 277
Loftus, E. F., 194, 225
Lombardi, W. J., 453
Lopez, D. F., 446
Lord, C. G., 429
Lorenz, F. O., 309
Lovaas, O. I., 336
Lowell, E. L., 98, 99
Lu, X., 203
Lucas, R. E., 69, 166
Luce, C. L., 351
Luciana, M., 162, 163
Ludwig, G. W., 356
Luh, K. E., 182
Lui, L., 446
Lumsden, C., 138
Lund, D., 349
Lundin, R. W., 330
Lundy, A. C., 111
Lurigio, A. J., 447
Lustig, D. A., 230, 231
Lutter, C., 177
Lütkenhaus, P., 296
Lydon, J. E., 290
Lykken, D. T., 132–134, 142
Lynn, R., 148
Lynn, S. J., 225

Ma, Y., 149
Maccoby, E. E., 174, 365
MacCulloch, M. J., 339
MacInnis, D. J., 101
MacKay, D. M., 472, 479
MacKean, C. J., 149
MacMurray, J. P., 162, 171–172
Macrae, C. N., 443
Maddi, S. R., 7, 9, 10
Mae, L., 323
Maes, P., 472
Magnus, K., 78
Magnuson, V. L., 135
Magnusson, D., 76, 81
Magovern, G. J., 489
Mahler, M. S., 282
Mahone, C. H., 98–99
Mahoney, M. J., 336, 463
Maier, S. F., 370
Main, M., 286, 287
Major, B., 359, 446
Malamuth, N. M., 204
Malanos, A., 80
Malec, J., 372
Malinoski, P., 225
Mallick, S. K., 206
Mallinger, A., 177
Maltzman, I., 353

Mancuso, J. C., 415
Mandel, I. J., 355
Maner, J. K., 351
Manis, M., 226
Mann, J. J., 162, 164, 167, 171
Mann, M. B., 171–172
Manning, M. M., 359
Mansfield, E. D., 302
Manuck, S. B., 162, 164, 167, 171
Marangoni, C., 351
Marchbanks, R., 149
Marcia, J. E., 297, 299, 300
Marcus, G. F., 353–354
Marcus-Newhall, A., 207
Maresca, B. C., 78
Markus, H., 397, 447, 448, 479, 492
Marlowe, D., 47
Marolla, R. A., 261
Marston, A. R., 349, 352, 362–363
Martin, B., 341
Martin, J., 135, 182
Martin, L. L., 494
Martin, L. R., 70
Martin, N. G., 134, 135, 144
Martin, R. A., 357, 369
Martin, R. P., 133
Marx, M. H., 352
Masling, J. M., 209, 281
Maslow, A., 394–400, **395,** 409–411, 512–513
Mason, A., 104
Masson, J., 242
Masters, H. L., III, 70
Maszk, P., 351
Matas, L., 295
Mattek, P. W., 464–465
Matthews, K. A., 140, 164, 171, 243, 453, 489
Matthiesen, A-S., 179
Mavin, G. H., 425, 453
Maxwell, S. E., 43
May, R., 401, 402
Mayman, M., 226
Mazur, A., 176–178
McAdams, D. P., 86, 104–108, 111, 116, 295, 301–302, 304
McArthur, L. Z., 360
McCaffery, J. M., 164, 171
McCandless, B. R., 206
McCann, L., 433
McCartney, K., 78
McCauley, C., 370
McCaulley, M. H., 254
McClay, J., 182

McClearn, G. E., 125, 127, 131–134, 489
McClelland, D. C., 92, 98–100, 104, 105, 108–116
McClelland, J. L., 321, 454
McClintock, M. K., 141
McConaghy, N., 243
McCown, D. A., 406
McCrae, R. R., 66–69, 72, 73, 75, 83, 112, 132–134, 163, 165, 303, 514
McCullough, M., 242
McCullough, M. E., 70
McDonald, R. D., 105
McElwee, R. O., 58
McFall, R. M., 369, 512
McGeary, J., 150
McGee, L., 166
McGregor, H. A., 102
McGregor, I., 402–403, 408, 421
McGue, M., 132, 134, 162
McGuffin, P., 135, 148
McGuinnes, T., 179
McGuire, C. V., 485
McGuire, S., 130, 134, 147
McGuire, T. R., 152
McGuire, W. J., 254, 485
McInnes, R. G., 126
McIntyre, C. W., 69
McKeachie, W. J., 104
McKinley, J. C., 48
McLemore, C. W., 349
McMahan, I. D., 357
McMaster, M. R., 351
McNeely, J., 464–465
Mead, G. H., 427
Mearns, J., 465
Medin, D. L., 444
Meehl, P. E., 42, 57, 85
Megargee, E. I., 205
Mehrabian, A., 105
Meichenbaum, D., 371, 373, 374, 465
Melamed, B. G., 372
Melloni, R. H., Jr., 176
Meltzoff, A. N., 359
Mendelsohn, G. A., 205, 351
Mendola, R., 433
Mendoza-Denton, R., 79, 448, 461
Menlove, F. L., 364, 372
Merbaum, M., 339
Merluzzi, T. V., 462, 492
Merrill, N., 406
Mershon, B., 73
Mervis, C., 444
Messick, S., 45

Metalsky, G. I., 370, 450, 465–466
Metcalfe, J., 457, 515
Metzger, L. J., 335
Metzner, R., 197
Meyer, D., 493
Meyer, J. P., 106, 357
Meyer, W., 357
Meyers, S. A., 422
Mezzich, J., 464
Michalski, R. L., 261
Mickelson, K. D., 292
Mikawa, J., 105
Mikulincer, M., 226, 291, 301, 309, 403, 452
Mill, J. S., 182, 277
Miller, D., 209
Miller, G. A., 472, 479
Miller, I. W., 370
Miller, K. M., 70
Miller, L. C., 152, 455, 456, 478
Miller, N., 207
Miller, N. E., 325, 327–328, 333, 337, 341
Miller, R. S., 351
Miller, S., 464
Miller, T. I., 245
Millgram, E., 455
Milne, A. B., 443
Milun, R., 177, 183
Mineka, S., 517
Mirels, H., 357
Mirenberg, M. C., 453
Mischel, W., 74–77, 79, 80, 86, 197, 350, 354, 364, 365, 368, 444–446, 448, 457–461, **459,** 466, 477, 510, 515
Mishkin, M., 473–474
Mitchell, K. M., 409
Moane, G., 75
Moely, B. E., 365
Moffat, F. L., 489
Moffitt, T. E., 57, 75, 182, 264, 265, 275–276
Mohammed, S., 177
Mohlman, J., 161, 163
Monroe, S. M., 466
Monson, T., 76
Montgomery, R. L., 467
Moor, C. J., 308
Moor, M., 162
Moore, B., 457
Moore, C. A., 491
Moore, E. A., 184
Moore, J. W., 322
Moran, P. J., 70
Morf, C. C., 307
Morgan, C. D., 97
Morris, J. L., 98–99

Morris, K. J., 257
Morris, L. W., 368
Morris, R., 175
Morris, T., 243
Morrone, J. V., 165
Morrow, J., 465, 495
Moskowitz, D. S., 79
Moskowitz, G. B., 446
Motley, M. T., 232, 233
Mouton, J. S., 57
Mozer, M. C., 454
Mueller, C. M., 334
Mueller, P. M., 359
Muhleman, D., 171–172
Muldoon, M. F., 164, 167, 171
Mullen, B., 491
Muraven, M., 202
Murphy, B., 351
Murphy, D. L., 135–136, 162
Murphy, J., 290
Murray, E. J., 206, 373
Murray, H. A., 17–18, 90–95, **91,** 97, 110, 113, 116–117, 298
Murray, R. M., 150
Murray, S. L., 228, 391
Murtaugh, T. M., 168
Musham, C., 494
Mycielska, K., 231
Myers, B., 225
Myers, M. B., 254
Myers, M. D., 341

Nachmias, O., 291, 452
Nachshon, O., 301
Nadel, L., 184
Nanayakkara, A., 388
Nanko, S., 136, 163
Nasby, W., 448
Nash, K., 176
Nathan, P. E., 339, 340
Neale, M. C., 130–135, 140
Neary, R. S., 167–168
Neeb, M., 166
Neighbors, C., 388
Neimeyer, G. J., 431, 443
Neimeyer, R. A., 431, 443
Nell, V., 146
Nelligan, J. S., 290
Nelson, R. O., 463
Nemanov, L., 135–136, 150, 162
Nesselroade, J. R., 132, 133, 489
Neuberg, S. L., 144, 351, 446
Neuringer-Benefiel, H. E., 351
Newcomb, M. D., 166

Newcomb, T., 491
Newell, A., 444, 472, 495
Newman, A., 457
Newman, D. L., 266
Newman, J. P., 169, 170, 182, 464–465
Newman, L. S., 229
Newsom, J. T., 446
Nezu, A. M., 495
Nezworski, M. T., 240
Nias, D. K. B., 140
Nicastle, L. D., 143
Nicholls, J. G., 448
Nichols, R. C., 127, 131, 132
Nicholson, R. A., 42–43
Nickerson, R. S., 447
Niedenthal, P. M., 446, 448, 487
Niemeyer, G. J., 300
Nierenberg, R., 357
Nigg, J. T., 170
Nisbett, R. E., 17, 177, 194, 321, 443, 449
Nissen, E., 179
Nitschke, J. B., 182
Nolen-Hoeksema, S., 433, 465, 495
Noller, P., 288
Noriega, V., 489
Norman, D. A., 475, 508
Norman, W. H., 370
Norman, W. T., 66, 68
Norris, J. E., 302
Novaco, R. W., 374
Novick, O., 135–136, 162
Nowak, A., 456, 475
Nowak, C., 176
Nunnally, J. C., 324
Nurius, P., 397, 448, 479, 492

O'Boyle, C., 351
O'Brien, W. H., 335–336
O'Connor, C., 446
O'Connor, S. C., 497
O'Donnell, M. C., 243
O'Donohue, W., 328
O'Leary, A., 359
O'Leary, K. D., 336
O'Neill, R., 209
Ober, C., 141
Obremski, K. M., 340
Odbert, H. S., 62
Ogilvie, D. M., 102, 448
Oliver, M. B., 144
Olson, J. M., 134
Ono, Y., 136
Oreland, K. M., 464–465
Orf, L. A., 69
Oriña, M. M., 290, 292

Oring, E., 236
Orlebeke, J. F., 167–168
Orlofsky, J. L., 300
Orr, S. P., 335
Osher, Y., 135–136, 162, 163
Ostendorf, F., 67, 133
Ostrove, J. M., 302
Overmier, J. B., 370
Overton, W. F., 9
Owens, J. F., 243
öhman, A., 517
Owens, J. F., 453, 489
Oyserman, D., 496
Ozer, D. J., 67, 74, 76
Ozer, E. M., 490

Page, M. S., 223
Paisley, C., 394
Pals, J. L., 448
Panksepp, J., 172–173, 179
Park, J-W., 452
Park, S. H., 203
Park, T., 372
Parke, R. D., 352, 364
Parker, L., 495
Parker, R. K., 324
Parnell, R. W., 126
Partch, J. J., 144
Patatucci, A. M. L., 135
Patrick, H., 388
Patten, A. H., 302, 304
Patterson, C., 135–136, 162
Patterson, C. M., 169, 182
Paul, G. L., 336
Paulhus, D. L., 229–230, 261, 307, 357, 507
Pauls, D. L., 149, 150
Paunonen, S. V., 36, 67, 73, 112
Pavel, M., 444
Pavlov, I. P., 317, 322
Pavot, W., 78, 165
Peabody, D., 67–69, 72
Peake, P. K., 75
Pedersen, N. L., 131–134, 489
Pedersen, W. C., 152, 207
Peirson, A. R., 163, 171
Pelham, B. W., 393, 448, 453
Pellegrini, A. D., 138
Pennebaker, J. W., 243
Pepitone, A., 491
Peplau, L. A., 101, 300
Pepper, S., 106
Perkins, K. A., 340
Perlman, D., 300
Perry, D. G., 70
Pervin, L. A., 76, 86, 478, 480, 492

Peterson, C., 450, 465
Peterson, D., 257
Peterson, L. M., 212
Petri, H. L., 473–474
Petri, S., 136, 163
Petry, N. M., 341
Pettibone, T. J., 491
Petty, R. E., 161, 257, 335
Phares, E. J., 356
Phillips, C. M., 205
Phillips, J. B., 70
Phillips, N., 65, 66
Piaget, J., 265
Pichert, J. W., 445
Pickering, A. D., 163
Pickrell, J. E., 225
Piedmont, R. L., 112
Pierce, T., 290
Pierson, J. F., 383
Pietromonaco, P. R., 107, 291, 309, 462
Pike, C. L., 143
Pilkonis, P. A., 324
Pillard, R. C., 135
Pine, F., 282
Pinel, J. P. J., 320
Pinto, E., 162
Pitchot, W., 162
Pitman, R. K., 335
Pittman, T. S., 393
Pizzagalli, D., 182
Plaks, J. E., 449
Plein, H., 163, 171
Plomin, R., 78, 125, 127–139, 147, 148, 149, 151, 162, 323, 489
Poldrack, R. A., 169
Pollak, S., 101, 102, 108
Polsky, S., 366
Pomerantz, M., 99
Pool, R., 135
Pope, H. G., Jr., 176
Posner, M. I., 184
Postman, L., 354, 359
Poulton, R., 182
Powell, A. L., 351
Powell, J., 340
Powell, R. A., 216
Powers, A. M., 95–96
Powers, J., 106, 107
Powers, W. T., 472, 479, 482, 483
Pozo, C., 489
Prager, K. J., 299
Pratkanis, R. A., 447
Pratt, M. W., 302
Pratto, F., 143, 152, 453
Prentice-Dunn, S., 491
Presser, S., 46
Pressley, M., 74
Presson, C. C., 392

Preston, K. L., 341
Pretz, J., 334
Pribram, K. H., 472, 479
Price, J., 209
Price, M. A., 243
Priel, B., 135–136, 162
Privette, G., 400
Putcha-Bhagavatula, A., 152
Putnam, K., 182
Pyszczynski, T., 224, 392, 394, 402, 403, 408, 492, 494
Pytlik Zillig, L. M., 67, 71

Quinlan, D. M., 271, 305, 306
Quinn, S., 284

Rabie, L., 209
Rabin, A. I., 111
Rachlin, H., 333
Rachman, J., 326, 339–340
Rachman, S., 373
Radloff, R., 259–260
Raichle, K., 70
Ransjö-Arvidson, A-B., 179
Rapaport, D., 256
Raska, K., 359
Raskin, P. A., 365
Rasmuson, I., 131
Rau, L., 364
Raynor, J. O., 98, 111
Raynor, R., 323, 336–338
Rayses, V., 149
Razran, G. H. S., 323, 324
Read, S. J., 288, 290, 291, 305, 450, 455, 456, 475, 478
Ready, R., 70
Reason, J., 231
Redmore, C., 274
Reed, J. L., 396
Reeder, G. D., 257
Reeders, S., 149
Reese, E. P., 330
Reese, S. L., 369
Reggers, J., 162
Reinisch, J. M., 172–174
Reis, H., 406
Reis, H. T., 462
Reise, S. P., 67
Reiser, M., 264, 275
Reiss, D., 130, 134, 147
Rende, R., 125, 149
Rennie, D. L., 362–363
Repetti, R. L., 179
Rescorla, R. A., 317, 320, 321, 329
Reus, V. I., 184
Reynolds, J., 302, 304

Reynolds, S. K., 84
Reynolds, S. L., 489
Rhawn, J., 193
Rhee, S. H., 150
Rhoades, L., 334, 337, 387
Rhodewalt, F., 307
Rholes, W. S., 287, 290, 292
Riad, J. K., 175
Rice, M. E., 146, 147
Rich, S., 132, 133
Richards, C., 359
Richardson, D. R., 206
Rickard, M., 243
Riedel, W., 424
Rielly, N. P., 491
Riemann, R., 127, 132–134, 136, 137
Rigby, S., 406
Rincover, A., 326
Riordan, C. A., 323, 324
Rips, L. J., 444
Risley, T. R., 326
Ritvo, L. B., 188
Rizzolatti, G., 462, 474
Robb, Z., 406
Roberts, B. W., 70, 71, 75, 266, 268, 271, 478
Roberts, J. E., 466
Robins, R. W., 57, 70, 71, 75, 264, 265, 275–276, 307, 448, 478
Robinson, D. S., 489
Robinson, F. G., 91
Roccas, S., 71
Rodgers, B., 136, 163
Rodriguez, M. L., 197
Rodriguez, R., 257
Rodriguez-Hanley, A., 433
Rogers, C. R., 383–386, **385**, 391, 392, 395, 405, 407, 408, 409, 411
Rogers, R. W., 491
Rogers, T. B., 447
Rohde, W., 105
Rom, T., 166–167
Rooney, W. M., 43
Roper, D. W., 465
Rorer, L. G., 45
Rorschach, H., 238
Rosch, E., 444
Rose, P., 391
Rose, R. J., 131–133, 149
Rose, S., 152
Rosekrans, M. A., 362–363
Roseman, I. J., 446
Rosen, C. M., 129
Rosenbaum, D. A., 473, 482, 483
Rosenberg, S., 415
Rosenblood, L. K., 497

Rosenfield, D., 370, 392
Rosenman, R., 140
Rosenthal, J. T., 360
Rosenthal, R., 78, 166
Rosenthal, T. L., 352, 369
Rosenwald, G. C., 211
Ross, D. L., 230, 231
Ross, D. M., 369
Ross, L., 443
Ross, M., 227, 272, 447
Ross, S. A., 369
Roth, S., 370
Rothbaum, P. A., 152
Rothenfluh, T., 455
Rothschild, B., 209
Rotter, J. B., 349, 354–357, 510
Rowe, D. C., 130, 137, 149, 150, 167, 182
Rozsnafszky, J., 270
Ruback, R. B., 175
Rubenstein, C., 300
Rubin, R. T., 172
Ruble, D. N., 432
Rudy, T. E., 492
Ruef, A. M., 351
Rumelhart, D. E., 321, 454
Runck, B., 343
Rusbult, C. E., 419
Rush, A. J., 465, 466
Rushton, J. P., 74, 140, 141, 152
Russell, D. W., 475–476
Russell, R. J. H., 141
Ryan, R. M., 269, 290, 387, 388, 406, 407, 408, 410, 497
Ryff, C. D., 70, 448

St. Clair, M., 281
Sabol, S. Z., 136, 163
Saccuzzo, D., 464
Sadalla, E. K., 76, 143, 144, 145, 446
Saelens, B. E., 341
Sagarin, B. J., 351
Sagiv, L., 71
Saleh, W. E., 357, 369
Salmoni, A. W., 473
Salovey, P., 145
Sameroff, A. J., 130
Sanderson, C., 84
Sandman, C. A., 323
Sandvik, E., 165
Sano, A., 136, 163
Santa Ana, E., 197
Santogrossi, D. A., 369
Sanz, J., 133
Sarason, I. G., 372
Saron, C. D., 163
Saslow, G., 334

Saturansky, C., 209
Sánchez-Bernardos, M. L., 133
Sartoris, J. M., 78
Saucier, G., 67, 72, 73, 171–172
Saudino, K. J., 130, 134, 147
Saunders, P. R., 133
Scantamburlo, G., 162
Scarr, S., 78, 127, 516
Schaller, M., 351
Schank, R. C., 445, 473, 484
Schefft, B. K., 495
Scheibe, K. E., 357
Scheier, M. F., 102, 134, 369, 373, 411, 448, 452, 454, 461, 468, 472, 475, 479–482, 487–491, 493, 494, 510
Scheirer, M. A., 22–23
Schell, T. L., 447
Scherer, A. J., 165
Schiedel, D. G., 300
Schiffman, H., 272
Schimek, J. G., 242
Schimel, J., 402, 408
Schlenker, B. R., 427
Schmalt, H. D., 98
Schmidt, A., 108
Schmidt, L. A., 163
Schmidt, R. A., 473, 480
Schmitt, D. P., 70, 143, 144, 145
Schmitt, W. A., 182
Schmitz, M., 108
Schmutte, P. S., 182
Schneider, D. J., 223, 446
Schneider, K., 98
Schneider, K. J., 383
Schneiderman, N., 320
Schober, M. F., 426
Schoenrade, P. A., 351
Schorr, D., 444
Schriesheim, C. A., 46
Schroeder, H. E., 371
Schuckit, M. A., 149
Schultheiss, O. C., 105, 108, 111, 112, 113, 389
Schultz, C. B., 99
Schultz, T. R., 455
Schulz, R., 489, 490, 494
Schunk, D. H., 372
Schutte, N. S., 76, 446
Schwartz, B., 317, 487
Schwartz, D., 465
Schwartz, G. E., 230
Schwartz, J., 446
Schwartz, J. C., 446
Schwartz, J. E., 70

Schwartz, S. H., 71
Schwarz, N., 443
Sciacchitano, A. M., 359
Sears, D. O., 20
Sears, R. R., 216, 364
Sechrest, L., 421–422
Sederer, L., 198
Sedney, M. A., 365
Seeman, J., 408
Seeman, M., 356
Segal, B., 166–167
Segal, D. L., 308
Segal, N. L., 129, 132, 133, 138, 149
Segal, Z., 455, 465
Segman, R., 150
Seidenberg, R., 198
Seifer, R., 130
Seitz, R. J., 462
Selbst, M., 334
Seligman, M. E. P., 76, 370, 450, 465–466, 517
Seltzer, R. A., 92, 495
Semmelroth, J., 145
Sentis, K., 447
Senulis, J. A., 161, 163
Setterlund, M. B., 448
Sgoutas, D. S., 175
Shackelford, T. K., 145, 261
Sham, P. C., 150
Shao, L., 69, 166
Shapiro, C. M., 95–96
Shapiro, D., 211, 343
Sharpsteen, D. J., 108
Shaver, P. R., 285–292, 300, 309, 446
Shaw, B. F., 465, 466
Shea, J. A., 270–271
Shedler, J., 226, 263
Sheldon, K. M., 102–103, 385, 387–389, 397, 406, 407, 486
Sheldon, W. H., 126
Shepperd, J. A., 58
Sher, K. J., 84
Sherburne, L. M., 363
Sherman, J. W., 449
Sherman, S. J., 392, 452
Sherrington, R., 149
Sherwood, G. G., 229
Shetler, S., 206
Shibatuni, T., 427
Shields, J., 149
Shipley, T. E., 105
Shmelyov, A. G., 133
Shmotkin, D., 70
Shoben, E. J., 444
Shoda, Y., 79, 80, 86, 448, 459–461, 477
Shope, G. L., 205, 206

Shortt, J. W., 223
Shostrom, E. L., 406
Showers, C. J., 448
Shubsachs, A. P. W., 431
Sidanius, J., 143
Siegel, J., 168
Siegel, S., 322–323
Sigvardsson, S., 149
Silva, P. A., 182
Silver, R. C., 291, 392
Silverman, L. H., 216, 230, 231
Simon, D. P., 462
Simon, H. A., 462, 472, 486–487, 495
Simons, R. L., 309
Simpson, J. A., 142, 287, 288, 290, 291, 292, 305
Singer, S. M., 149, 150
Singh, D., 143
Skinner, B. F., 324–325, 328, 333–335, 355
Skolaski, R. L., 464–465
Skowronski, J. J., 323, 450
Slaw, R. D., 257
Sloman, S. A., 456
Small, M. F., 142
Smith, A., 277
Smith, C. P., 111
Smith, E. E., 444, 464
Smith, E. R., 290, 455
Smith, G. M., 66
Smith, K. D., 351
Smith, M., 351
Smith, M. L., 245, 409
Smith, M. S., 138
Smith, P. B., 133
Smith, R. A., 457
Smith, R. C., 243
Smith, R. E., 374
Smith, S. S., 170, 182, 340
Smith, T. E., 179
Smith, T. W., 394
Smolen, A., 150
Smolensky, P., 454, 456
Smyth, J. M., 243
Snarey, J., 269
Snider, P. R., 489
Snyder, C. R., 392–394
Snyder, M., 57, 77, 78
Snyder, M. L., 370, 392
Sobotka, S. S., 161
Solano, C., 79
Soli, S. D., 446
Solomon, J., 286
Solomon, R. L., 326
Solomon, S., 224, 392, 402, 403
Somer, O., 67
Son, C., 73
Sophocles, 211

Sörbom, D., 59
Sorg, B. A., 464–465, 465
Soron, G., 203
Sorrentino, R. M., 105
Spacapan, S., 355
Spangler, W. D., 100, 103
Spanos, N. P., 225
Speisman, J. C., 270
Spellman, B. A., 456
Spencer, S. J., 402–403, 408, 421
Sperling, M. B., 287
Spetch, M. L., 320
Spiegler, M. D., 372
Spielberger, C. D., 355
Spinath, F. M., 127, 133, 137
Spitalnik, R., 326
Spooner, A., 320
Spoont, M. R., 161
Sporer, S. L., 307
Sprecher, S., 143
Srivastava, S., 304
Sroufe, L. A., 285, 295
Srull, T. K., 446, 452
Staats, A. W., 317, 323, 324, 334–336
Staats, C. K., 323, 324
Stangor, C., 432
Stanton, A. L., 433, 489
Staudinger, U. M., 304
Steele, C. M., 224, 392
Stein, J. L., 70
Stein, L. A., 472
Stejskal, W. J., 240
Stephan, W. G., 370, 392
Sternbach, R. A., 335
Sternberg, R. J., 133–134
Steronko, R. J., 464
Stevens, B., 408
Stevens, D., 217
Stevens, R., 294
Stevenson, H. W., 365
Stevenson, J., 130
Stewart, A. J., 101, 104, 113, 302, 303
Stewart, S. E., 308
Stock, G., 148
Stock, W. A., 480
Stolar, D., 199
Stolberg, S., 148
Stone, A., 108
Stone, G. O., 143
Stone, L. J., 206
Stone, W. L., 369
Stonner, D., 205, 206
Stotland, E., 257, 351, 487
Stouthamer-Loeber, M., 57, 264, 265, 275–276
Straub, R. E., 149
Strauman, T. J., 407, 464–465

Stringfield, D. O., 78
Stroessner, S. J., 449
Strong, R. K., 177, 183
Strube, M. J., 57
Stucke, T. S., 207, 307
Stumpf, H., 67, 112
Stumphauzer, J. S., 364
Suedfeld, P., 229–230, 507
Suh, E. M., 69, 166
Suh, K., 351
Sullivan, Q., 143
Sulloway, F. J., 261
Sundie, J. M., 143
Suppes, P., 444
Surwit, R. S., 343
Sussex, J. N., 149
Sutton, J. E., 363
Sutton, S. K., 161, 163, 180
Sutton-Tyrrell, K., 243
Swann, W. B., Jr., 393, 448
Swift, R. M., 150
Sworowski, L. A., 433

Tafarodi, R. W., 393
Tajfel, H., 419
Takemoto-Chock, N. K., 69
Talbert, L. M., 177
Tan, X., 136, 163
Tang, T. Z., 466–467
Tannen, D., 145
Tassinary, L. G., 70
Tatsuoka, M. M., 62
Taub, B., 206
Tavris, C., 172
Taylor, A., 182
Taylor, J., 126
Taylor, M. C., 365
Taylor, S. E., 179, 360, 392, 433, 446, 466, 477
Teasdale, J. D., 76, 326, 339–340, 370, 450, 465–466
Tedeschi, J. T., 323, 324
Tedeschi, R. G., 433
Tellegen, A., 48, 72, 132, 133, 142, 161, 164, 166, 168–169, 266, 514
Teng, G., 351
Tennant, C. C., 243
Tennen, H., 433
Terpstra, J., 184
Terrace, H. S., 317
Terry, K., 496
Tesch, S. A., 300
Tesser, A., 134, 283, 392, 425, 456, 494
Testa, A., 448
Testa, M., 359
Teta, P., 71, 168
Thagard, P., 454, 455
Theios, J., 332

Thelen, M. H., 362–363
Thiessen, D., 142
Thomala, L., 163, 171
Thomas, A., 130
Thomas, E., 322–323
Thomas, M. H., 366, 367
Thomas, R. G., 335
Thomas, S., 323, 324
Thomas, S. P., 491
Thompson, G. C., 421
Thompson, S. C., 433
Thompson, T., 203
Thorndike, E. L., 325, 326
Thorne, A., 78
Thornhill, R., 145
Thrash, T. M., 165, 406
Thronquist, M. H., 166–167
Tice, D. M., 202, 207
Tiffany, S. T., 340
Timberlake, W., 512
Tobin, R. M., 70
Tolman, E. C., 354, 480, 518
Tomarken, A. J., 161
Tomich, P. T., 433
Tomlinson-Keasey, C., 70
Toner, I. J., 457
Tooby, J., 138
Trapnell, P. D., 65, 66, 72, 261, 481, 491–492
Tresemer, D. W., 101
Treyens, J. C., 446
Triandis, H. C., 426
Trivers, R. L., 140, 142, 504, 505
Trötschel, R., 194
Trope, Y., 169
Trost, M. R., 143
Trötschel, R., 475
Trobst, K. K., 70
Trope, Y., 99, 100, 458, 515
Trost, M. R., 144, 145
Truax, C. B., 409
Trull, T. J., 84
Trzebinski, J., 67, 112
Trzesniewski, K. H., 75
Tse, W. S., 184
Tsuang, M. T., 149
Tsutsumi, T., 136, 163
Tucker, J. S., 70
Tulving, E., 445
Turk, D., 374
Turkheimer, E., 137
Turner, J. C., 419
Turner, J. L., 349
Turner, R. A., 179, 184
Tursky, B., 343
Tversky, B., 446
Twenge, J. M., 137, 207
Twentyman, C. T., 369
Tyner, S. D., 203

Udry, J. R., 177
Uleman, J. S., 449
Umansky, R., 135–136, 162
Umbricht, A., 341
Umiltà, M. A., 462
Underwood, B. J., 31
Updegraff, J. A., 179
Uvnäs-Moberg, K., 179

Vaidya, J., 161, 164
Vaillant, G. E., 107, 303
Vallacher, R. R., 456, 475, 482, 486, 492
Vallerand, R. J., 387
van Aken, M. A. G., 264, 265
Van de Castle, R. L., 213
van den Berg, A. E., 70–71
Van Maanen, J., 432
van Zuilen, R. W., 167–168
Vancouver, J. B., 478
Vandenberg, S. G., 149, 150
Vandewater, E. A., 262, 302, 303
Vanman, E. J., 70, 455
Varga, M., 235
Vaughan, K. B., 352
Venkatachalam, S., 203
Vernon, D. T. A., 372
Vernon, P. A., 84, 132–134, 136
Vernon, P. E., 74
Veroff, J., 98, 104, 105
Verplanken, B., 257, 483
Vershure, B., 143
Vietor, N. A., 388
Viken, R. J., 131–133, 512
Vito, D., 341
Vlek, C. A. J., 70–71
Volosin, D., 326
Von Baeyer, C. L., 357
von der Lippe, A., 197
von Eye, A., 286
von Knorring, A.-L., 149
von Weiss, R. T., 244

Wade, C., 172
Wagner, A. R., 322–323
Wahlsten, D., 136, 152
Waldman, I. D., 150
Waldman, K., 274
Waldrop, P. B., 331
Walker, E. F., 183
Walker, R. N., 126
Wall, T., 285
Wallace, H. M., 307
Wallace, J. F., 182, 464–465

Wallbom, M., 482
Waller, N. G., 67, 72
Walls, R. T., 356
Wallston, B. S., 357
Wallston, K. A., 357
Walter, C. B., 473
Walters, R., 363
Walters, R. H., 352
Walther, E., 324
Wang, R., 150
Wanner, E., 114
Ware, E. E., 357
Waterman, A. S., 299, 304
Waters, E., 285
Watkins, J. T., 372
Watson, D., 69, 84, 161, 164, 166, 168–169, 515
Watson, J. B., 323, 336–338
Watt, J. D., 257
Webb, B. T., 149
Wegner, D. M., 223, 390, 465, 482, 486, 492, 496
Weijers, H.-G., 163, 171
Wein, S. J., 305, 306
Weinberger, D. A., 230
Weinberger, J. L., 111, 230, 231
Weiner, B., 108, 357, 449, 450
Weiner, R. L., 43
Weinstein, D., 372
Weinstein, M. S., 352
Weinstein, N. D., 466
Weis, L., 209
Weisberg, P., 331
Weiss, L., 209
Weiss, R. S., 300
Weller, A., 291
Wells, P. A., 141
Wenzlaff, R. M., 223, 393, 465
Wesensten, N. J., 235
Wessler, R., 274
West, S. G., 143
Westen, D., 145, 507, 512
Westenberg, P. M., 270, 271
Westmaas, J. L., 291
Wheatley, T., 390
Wheeler, R. E., 161
Wherry, M. B., 448
Whitam, F. L., 135
Whitbeck, L. B., 309
Whitbourne, S. K., 300, 304
White, K. M., 270
White, R. W., 256, 357
White, T. L., 164–165, 223
Whitney, P., 464–465

Wickelgren, W. A., 517
Wicker, F. W., 396
Wicklund, R. A., 482, 494
Widiger, T. A., 84
Wiebe, J. S., 70
Wiedenfeld, S. A., 359
Wiehe, J. A., 396
Wiener, N., 479
Wiesbeck, G. A., 163, 171
Wiese, D., 161, 164
Wiggins, J. S., 65, 66, 72, 84
Wikler, D., 148
Wilcox, K. J., 132, 133
Wilhelm, J., 259–260
Wilkie, D. M., 320
Willerman, L., 131, 132, 149, 150
Willers, K. R., 206
Williams, G. C., 388, 408
Williams, N. L., 227
Williams, P. M., 176, 177
Williams, R. L., 491
Wilpers, S., 69
Wilson, E. O., 138
Wilson, G. T., 338, 339
Wilson, J. Q., 150
Wilson, M. I., 146, 147
Wilson, T. D., 194
Wilson, W. C., 365
Wingard, D. L., 70
Wink, P., 75
Winson, J., 235
Winter, D. G., 103–105, 108, 109, 111, 113–115
Wispé, L., 351
Woike, B. A., 112
Wolberg, L. R., 255
Wolf, H., 84
Wolfe, C. T., 386
Wolfe, D. M., 257
Wolfe, J. B., 326
Wolfe, R. N., 73
Wolkowitz, O. M., 184
Wolpe, J., 245, 338
Wong, C. J., 341
Wong, M. M., 106, 108
Wood, J. M., 111, 239–240, 274
Wood, J. V., 433
Wood, M. D., 84
Wood, R., 359, 449
Wood, W., 364, 365
Woodfield, R., 133
Woodruffe, C., 78, 79
Woods, D. J., 464
Workman, K. A., 70

Wortman, C. B., 370, 390
Wright, J. C., 79, 459, 461, 463
Wright, R. A., 488
Wright, T. L., 359
Wrosch, C., 489, 490, 494
Wu, S., 171–172
Wulfert, E., 197
Wundt, W., 62
Wurf, E., 447
Wyer, R. S., Jr., 446, 452
Wylie, R., 22–23

Xiang, X., 150
Xu, K., 150

Yamazaki, T. G., 308
Yates, B. T., 457
Yates, J., 126
Yoon, S-O., 452
York, K. L., 57
Young, A., 262
Young, J. E., 465
Young, P. A., 131

Zadeh, L., 444
Zakriski, A. L., 463
Zald, D. H., 163, 171
Zanna, M. P., 324, 402–403, 408, 421
Zeidner, M., 489
Zeiss, A., 197, 457
Zelano, B., 141
Zeldow, P. B., 108
Zelenski, J. M., 165, 166, 171
Zener, K., 320
Zentall, T. R., 363
Zer-Zion, M., 150
Zern, D., 196
Zhao, J., 150
Zierk, K. L., 144
Zilles, K., 462
Zillmann, D., 204
Zimmerman, B. J., 360
Zimmerman, D. W., 326
Zimmerman, G., 300, 301
Zinbarg, R. E., 161, 163
Zonderman, A. B., 67, 163
Zubek, J., 359
Zucker, A. N., 302
Zucker, R. A., 111
Zuckerman, M., 71, 72, 78, 162, 166–170, 177, 182, 387
Zuroff, D. C., 82, 308, 309
Zuschlag, M. K., 304

Subject Index

Accidents, 233–234
Achievement motivation, 96, 98–103
    divergent motives, 101–103
    effects of, 99–101
    ego psychology and, 268
    increasing, 114–115, 116
    individual differences in, 98–103
Acquiescence, 46–47
Acquisition, performance versus,
        361–363
Action identification, 486
Activity level, 129
Actual self, 391, 393, 407, 513
Adaptation, 235
    in ego psychology, 254, 255,
        256–259, 262–265
Adoption studies, 128
    on alcohol abuse, 149–150
    environmental effects and, 136
    temperament and, 131
Adrenal glands, 174
Advanced stages of ego development,
        268–269
Affiliation motivation, 96, 105–106,
        109
Aggregation, 74–75
Aggression
    adaptation and, 256
    anabolic steroids and, 176
    catharsis and, 205–206
    impulsivity and, 171
    media and modeling of, 366–367
    in psychoanalytic perspective, 192
    sexual drives and, 204, 207
    testosterone and, 173–174, 175,
        176
    verbal, 208–209
    young male syndrome and,
        146–147
Agreeableness
    in five-factor model, 68, 69, 70–71,
        72, 75, 132, 133, 136
    heritability of, 132
AIDS/HIV, 433

Alcohol abuse
    adoption studies on, 149–150
    deindividuation and, 491
    ego control and, 263
    need for power and, 114
    oral stage and, 209
    twin studies on, 149–150
Alienation scale, 305
Alleles, 135–136, 139
Altruism, 138–140, 351
Ambivalent (resistant) attachment,
        285–292
    of adults, 287–292
    of children, 285–287
American Psychoanalytic Association,
        246
Amish families, 149
Anabolic steroids, 176
Anal expulsive traits, 210
Anal retentive traits, 211
Anal stage, 210–211, 213, 228
Anal triad, 211
Analysis of variance model, 76–78
Androgens, 174, 179
Androgyny, 365
Anticathexes, 202, 222, 240
Anticipatory learning, 320
Antidepressants, 183–184
Antisocial personality
    biological bases of, 150, 175,
        182–183
    testosterone and, 175
    twin studies and, 150
Anxiety
    basic, 283–284, 307–308
    in biological perspective, 163–165,
        182, 183–184
    castration, 211–213
    in cognitive psychology, 465
    dealing with, 433–434
    in ego psychology, 256, 273,
        275–276
    in humanistic psychology, 407–408
    intellectualization and, 227

personal constructs and, 431–432,
        433–434
    pharmacotherapy for, 183
    in psychoanalytic perspective,
        211–213, 221–222, 245
    verbal slips and, 232–233
Apoptosis, 203
Apperception, 97–98
Approach and avoidance motivation,
        102–103
Arbitrary inferences, 465–466
Archetypes, 254
Ascending reticular activating system
        (ARAS), 156–157
Assessment, 35–51
    of autonomy and control, 406
    behavioral, 335–336
    in biological perspective, 147–148,
        180–181
    in cognitive psychology, 462–464
    contextualized, 463–464
    defined, 36
    diagnostic categories as prototypes
        in, 464
    in dispositional perspective, 82–84,
        111–113
    in ego psychology, 271–274
    electroencephalogram (EEG), 180
    empirical approach to, 48–49
    experience sampling in, 462–463
    improving, 49–50
    interviews in, 404
    in learning perspective, 334–336,
        367–368
    of level of ego development, 274
    of lifestyles, 272–273
    of motives, 96–98, 111–113
    nature of, 13
    of needs, 111–113
    neuro-imaging, 180–181, 184
    in phenomenological perspective,
        404–406, 429–431
    physiological, 335
    projective techniques, 237–240

Assessment *(continued)*
in psychoanalytic perspective, 237–240
in psychosocial approach, 305–307
rational (theoretical) approach to, 47–48
reliability of measurement in, 38–41
Role Construct Repertory Test (Rep Test), 429–431
of self-actualization, 406
self-concept and Q-sort, 404–406
self-monitoring in, 463
in self-regulation, 490–492
sources of information for, 36–38
think-aloud approaches, 462
validity of measurement in, 41–47, 239–240
Associative techniques, 238
Assortative mating, 142
Attachment theory, 285–292
adult, 287–292
assessment and, 305–306
childhood, 285–287
five-factor model and, 291–292
number of patterns in, 289
oxytocin and, 179
specificity in, 290
stability in, 289
Attention, in observational learning, 359–360
Attentional capacity, 464–465
Attitudes
classical conditioning and, 324
forming, 476
Attraction effect, 141–142
Attribution, 449–450
Augmenters, 168
Autoeroticism, 211
Automaticity, 475
Automatic thoughts, 465
Autonomous stage of ego development, 266, 269
Autonomy
in ego psychology, 256
in humanistic psychology, 387–390, 406
measuring, 406
Autonomy versus shame and doubt, 295
Aversion therapy, 339–340
Avoidance, 86
Avoidant attachment, 285–292
of adults, 287–292, 308–309
of children, 285–287
Awareness, in conditioning, 355

Balance, in structural model of personality, 199–200
BAS (behavioral approach system), 160–162, 164–165, 170, 171–172, 182
Basic anxiety, 283–284, 307–308
Basic trust versus basic mistrust, 294–295
Behavior, 108–110. *See also* Motives; Needs
evolution and, 138–147
expectancy and, 110
incentive value and, 109–110
reinforcement of dimensions of, 334
reliability in measuring, 74–75
traits and, 73–75, 79–82, 84–86
Behavioral approach system (BAS), 160–162, 164–165, 170, 171–172, 182
Behavioral assessment, 335–336
Behavioral genetics, 125, 152
Behavioral inhibition system (BIS), 162–165, 170, 171–172, 182
Behavioral record, 307
Behavior change, 14
in biological perspective, 151, 183–184
in cognitive self-regulation perspective, 466–467
cognitive therapy and, 466–467
in dispositional perspective, 85–86, 113–115
in ego psychology, 276
in humanistic psychology, 408–409
in learning perspective, 336–343
motives and, 92–93, 114–115
in neoanalytic perspective, 276
personal constructs and, 434–435
pharmacotherapy and, 183–184
problem solving and, 495–496
in psychoanalytic perspective, 241–245
in psychosocial theory, 309–310
self-regulation and, 495
Behavior genetics, 149–150
Behavior Identification Form, 492
Behavior modification, 336
Behavior-outcome expectancies, 460
Behavior problems, 14
in biological perspective, 148–151, 181–184
cognitive distortions, 465–466
in cognitive self-regulation perspective, 464–466, 492–496
conceptualizing, 368–369
depressive self-schemas, 465–466

in dispositional perspective, 84–86, 113–115
evolution and, 150–151
in humanistic psychology, 407–410
information-processing deficits, 464–465
interactionism and, 84–85
in learning perspective, 336–343
origins of, 240–241
personal constructs and, 431–434
in psychoanalytic perspective, 215–217, 240–241, 431–434
in psychosocial theories, 307–309
Behavior therapy, 336
Biofeedback, 342–343
Biological needs, 92, 116
Biological perspective, 11, 121–186
assessment in, 147–148, 180–181
behavioral approach and, 160–162, 164–165, 170, 171–172, 182
behavioral inhibition and, 162–165, 170, 171–172, 182
environmental effects in, 136–137
evolutionary psychology and, 138–147, 151–153
extraversion and cortical arousal, 156–159, 165–166
impulsiveness in, 169–172
inheritance in, 125–136, 151–153
learning perspective and, 517–518
neuroticism, 160
problems and prospects of, 151–153, 184–185
problems in behavior, and behavior change in, 148–151, 181–184
sensation seeking in, 166–169
sex hormones and, 172–179
themes and underlying assumptions of, 122–123
Bipolar disorder (manic depression), pharmacotherapy for, 183
Bipolor disorder (manic-depression), behavior genetics and, 149
Birth order, 261, 273
BIS (behavioral inhibition system), 162–165, 170, 171–172, 182
Blaming, 392
Body building, 176
Body type, 126
Bonding, 179
Brain
behavioral approach system (BAS), 160–162, 164–165, 170, 171–172, 182
behavioral inhibition system (BIS), 162–165, 170, 171–172, 182

in cognitive psychology, 458, 461–462
electroencephalograms, 180
extraversion/introversion and, 156–159, 165–166
impulsiveness and, 169–172
neuro-imaging techniques, 180–181, 184
pharmacotherapy and, 183–184
sensation seeking and, 166–169
sex hormones and, 172–179
temperaments or traits and, 164–165

California Psychological Inventory (CPI), 131, 132
Cancer, 243, 321, 433, 489
Case studies, 17–19
defined, 18
nature of, 18–19
Castration anxiety, 211–213
Catastrophizing, 465–466
Catharsis, 204–207
Cathexes, 202–203, 216, 281, 506
Causality, 25–30
defined, 25
in experimental research, 27–30
limitation on inference, 25–27
locus of, 450
Central tendency, 290
Cerebrotonia, 126
Child sexual abuse, 242
Circularity problem, 86
Clarification of feelings, 409
Classical conditioning, 317–324, 336–341
as anticipatory learning, 320
attitudes and, 324
of aversion, 339–340
basic elements of, 317–320
conceptualizing behavior problems and, 368
context and, 340
developments in, 321
discrimination and, 320–322
emotional conditioning, 323
of emotional responses, 336–341
extinction and, 322–323, 340
generalization and, 320–322
Client-centered therapy, 408–409
Clinical significance, 25
Cognitive-affective processing system, 460–462
Cognitive assessment, 462–464
Cognitive behavioral modification, 373–374

Cognitive psychology, 435–436, 442–470
assessment in, 462–464
connectionist approach in, 321, 453–458
person variables in, 458–462
problems and prospects of, 467–468
problems in behavior, and behavior change in, 464–467
psychoanalytic perspective and, 507–509
schemas in, 443–453
Cognitive restructuring, 466–467
Cognitive self-regulation perspective, 12, 194, 244, 439–499. *See also* Cognitive psychology; Self-regulation
assessment in, 462–464, 490–492
neoanalytic perspective and, 512
problems and prospects of, 467–468, 496–498
problems in behavior, and behavior change in, 464–467, 492–496
themes and underlying assumptions of, 440–441
Cognitive-social learning view, 458
Cognitive therapies, 466–467
Cognitive triad, 465–466
Collective unconscious, 254
Comparators, 479, 481–482
Competence motivation, 256–260, 387, 406
nature of, 256–259
in psychosocial development, 293
striving for superiority, 259–261
Competencies, 297, 458–459
Competition
in mate selection, 142–145
young male syndrome and, 147
Completion techniques, 238
Conceptual definitions, 41–42
Concordance, 149
Condensation, 236
Conditional positive regard, 385
Conditional self-regard, 385–386
Conditioned/conditional response (CR), 319–324
Conditioned/conditional stimulus (CS), 318–324
Conditioned courage, 332
Conditioning theories, 163, 316–346, 370, 375
assessment and, 334–336
classical conditioning, 317–324, 336–341

elaborations on, 348–359
instrumental conditioning, 324–334, 341–343
problems and prospects of, 343–344
problems in behavior, and behavior change, 336–343
psychoanalytic perspective and, 505–506
Conditions of worth, 385–386
Conduct disorders, in ego psychology, 276
Conflict
defined, 341, 486
among goals, 493–494
instrumental conditioning of, 341–342
Conflict-free sphere, 255
Conflict sphere, 255
Conformist stage of ego development, 266, 267–268
Conformity, 268
Congruence, 383–384, 393
Connectionism, 321, 453–458
Conscience, 198
Conscientiousness
in five-factor model, 68, 69, 70, 71, 72, 75, 132, 133, 166
heritability of, 132
Conscientious stage of ego development, 266, 268
Conscious, 193–195, 217
Conscious processors, 456
Consistency
individual differences in, 77–78
internal, 38–40
personal constructs and, 428–429
of personality, 4
predicting, 461
in trait psychology, 87
Consolidation, 235
Constraint, 168–169, 171, 458
Constructive alternativism, 416
Constructive techniques, 238
Construct validity, 42–43
Contamination themes, 305
Content, in Rorschach inkblot responses, 239
Content analysis, 404
Context
in assessment, 463–464
classical conditioning and, 340
interactionism and, 79–82
Continuity, of personality, 4
Continuous reinforcement, 330

Control, 480. *See also* Feedback
    control
    experimental, 27–28
    measuring personal, 406
Convergent validity, 43–44
Cooperation, 138–141
Coping model, 371, 373–374, 417
Core roles, 427–428
Correlation, 59, 60–61, 136
Correlational studies, 21–27
    advantages and disadvantages of,
        30–31
    causality and, 25–27
    correlation, defined, 21–22
    experiments versus, 30–31
    limitation on inference in, 25–27
    significance in, 25
Correlation coefficient, 24–25
Counterconditioning, 338, 340
Covariation, 59
Criterion keying, 48
Criterion validity, 43
Cultural differences
    language in psychoanalytic
        perspective, 201
    validity and, 45
Culture
    genetic attraction and, 141–142
    importance of, in identity, 298
Current concerns, 234

Dasein, 401–402
Death
    death instincts, 203, 216
    existential psychology and,
        400–403
Default, 445
Defense mechanisms, 222–231
    denial, 224–226, 391, 507–508
    displacement, 207, 228, 244
    intellectualization, 227
    problems and prospects of,
        245–247
    projection, 226
    rationalization, 226–227, 391
    reaction formation, 227–228
    regression, 228
    repression. *See* Repression
    research on, 229–230
    self and process of defense,
        390–394
    sublimation, 207–208, 229
    unconscious conflict and,
        230–231
Defensive reappraisal, 417
Deficiency-based motives, 397
Definition, 420–422

Definitions
    conceptual, 41–42
    operational, 41–42
Deindividuation, 491
Delay of gratification
    in cognitive psychology, 457
    in ego psychology, 263
    modeling and, 364
    in psychoanalytic perspective, 197
Deliberative mindset, 477
Denial, 224–226, 391, 507, 508
Dependent variables, 28–29
Depression
    attachment theory and, 308–309
    biological bases of, 182, 183–184
    in ego psychology, 275–276
    pharmacotherapy for, 183–184
    projective techniques and, 240
    in psychoanalytic perspective, 240,
        245
    self-schemas based on, 465–466
    as unconscious conflict, 230
Descriptive statistics, 26
Desensitization, 366–367
Determinant, in Rorschach inkblot
        responses, 239
Diagnostic categories, 464
Diagnostic Council, 110
Diagnosticity, 99
Diathesis-stress model, 85
Directional selection, 139
Discriminant validity, 44
Discrimination
    in classical conditioning, 320–322
    in instrumental conditioning,
        327–329, 352
Discriminative stimulus, 327–329, 332
Disengagement, 488, 490, 494–495
Disorganization, 391–392
Disorganized/disoriented
        attachment, 286
Displacement, 207, 228, 244
Dispositional needs, 94–95, 98–108,
        111
Dispositional perspective, 11, 53–119,
        157, 513–514
    assessment in, 82–84, 111–113
    individual differences in, 98–108
    interactionism in, 76–82
    motives in, 92–93, 94–98, 112–113,
        114–115
    multiple determinants of behavior
        in, 108–110
    needs in, 90–92, 95–96, 98–108,
        110
    personology in, 17–18, 110–111
    press in, 93–94

problems and prospects of, 86–87,
        115–117
    problems in behavior, and behavior
        change in, 84–86, 113–115
    situationism and, 74
    themes and underlying
        assumptions of, 54–55
    traits in, 57–66, 73–74, 79–82,
        86–87, 113
    types in, 57–58
Distancing, 291
Divorce
    genetic influences on risk of, 134
    sense of identity and, 300
Dizygotic (DZ) twins, 126–127,
        130–131
DNA, 135
Dominance. *See* Power motivation
Dopamine, 135–136, 150
    behavioral approach system (BAS)
        and, 162, 171–172
    schizophrenia and, 183
Dreams, 234–236, 237
Dream work, 236, 237
Drives, 200–208, 328
Drug therapy, 183–184
Drug use
    ego control and, 263
    heroin addiction, 150
Dual process models, 456–458
Dynamic feedback system, 495

Early stage of ego development,
        266–267
Eclecticism, 516–517
Ectomorphy, 126
Edwards Personal Preference
        Schedule, 111
Effectance motivation, 256–258
Efficacy expectancies, 357–359,
        372–373, 375, 489–490
Effortfulness, 334
Ego, 196–197, 216, 241, 504, 505. *See
        also* Defense mechanisms
    attachment and, 290
    cathexes and, 202–203, 216, 281,
        506
    conflict with id, 197, 198, 234
    delay of gratification and, 197
    overcontrolled aggressors and, 205
    shifting emphasis from id, 255–256
    symbolization and, 236
Ego cathexes, 202
Egocentricity, 305
Ego control, 262–265
    five-factor model and, 264–265
    nature of, 262–264

Ego-defensiveness, 392
Ego development, 265–271, 277
  advanced stages of, 268–269
  assessment of level of, 274
  early stage of, 266–267
  and five-factor model, 271
  middle stages of, 267–268
  research on, 269–271
Ego ideal, 198
Ego identity, 292
Ego integrity versus despair, 302–304
Ego psychology
  assessment in, 271–274
  ego development in, 265–271, 277
  emergence of, 253
  principles of, 253–265
  problems and prospects for,
    276–277
  problems in behavior, and
    behavior change, 275–276
Ego quality, 294
Ego resiliency, 262–265
  five-factor model and, 264–265
  life challenges and, 271
  nature of, 262–264
Ego strength, 200, 294
Egotism, 392
Electra, 211
Electroencaphalogram (EEG), 180
Emergent poles, 418
Emotion, in self-regulation, 486–487
Emotional arousal, 373
Emotional conditioning, 323
Emotional isolation, 300–301
Emotionality, 130
  biological basis of, 160, 164–165
  in five-factor model, 68, 69, 71, 72,
    132, 133, 136
  heritability of, 132
  negative, 163
  neurotic needs and, 307–308
  positive, 161
  in supertrait analysis, 62–65
Empathy, 350–352
Empirical approach, to scale
    development, 48–49
Emptiness, 402
Encoding strategies, 460
Endomorphy, 126
Entitlement, 307
Entity schemas, 448–449
Environmental effects, 136–137
  nature of, 137
  size of, 136–137
Epigenesis, 304–305
Epiphenomena, 333
Episodic memory, 445

Erogenous zones, 203
Eros, 201, 203
Error
  defined, 38
  sources of, 38, 39
Estrogen, 179
Ethology, 138
Events, 416
Evolutionary psychology, 138–147
  aggression, 146–147, 178
  behavior problems and, 150–151
  genetic similarity and attraction,
    141–142
  mate retention, 145–146, 147
  mate selection, 142–145
  problems and prospects of,
    151–153
  psychoanalytic perspective and,
    504–505
  sociobiology, 138–141, 152
  testosterone and, 178
Exemplars, 443–444
Existential guilt, 401–402
Existential psychologists, 401
Existential psychology, 400–403
  dilemma of, 401–402
  emptiness and, 402
  terror management and, 402–403,
    408
Expectancies, 110, 354–359, 460
  concerning outcomes, 354–355
  efficacy, 357–359, 372–373, 375,
    489–490
  locus-of-control, 356–357
  in self-regulation, 488–490
Experience sampling, 462–463
Experiential mode of processing, 194
Experiential systems, 456
Experimental control, 27–28
Experimental method, 27–30
  advantages and disadvantages of,
    30–31
  correlational studies versus, 30–31
  dependent variable in, 28–29
  experimental control and, 27–28
  independent variable in, 27–29
  multifactor studies, 31–33
  random assignment in, 28, 29
Experimental personality research,
    32
Extension, 420–422
External locus of control, 358–359
Extinction, 505–506
  in classical conditioning, 322–323,
    340
  in instrumental conditioning, 329,
    330, 331–332

Extraversion
  behavioral approach/inhibition
    systems and, 165–166
  cortical arousal and, 156–159,
    165–166
  defined, 57
  in five-factor model, 67–69, 70–71,
    72, 132, 133, 137
  heritability of, 132–133
  multitasking and, 166
  need for intimacy and, 113
  principle of opposites and, 254
  in supertrait analysis, 62–65
Eysenck Personality Questionnaire
    (EPQ), 64

Face validity, 44–45
Factor analysis, 59–62
Factor extraction, 59–60
Factor loadings, 59–61
Factors, 59–61
Failure, 392, 393–394, 450
False memories, 225
Fear
  modeling and responses to,
    371–372
  phobias, 336–339
Feedback control, 479–490
  emotion and, 486–487
  expectancies and, 488–490
  feedback versus reinforcement
    and, 480
  hierarchical organization and,
    482–486
  incorrect feedback and, 493
  nature of, 479–481
  self-directed attention and,
    481–482
  in therapy process, 495
Feedback hierarchy, 482–486, 494
  issues in, 485–486
  research on hierarchical behavior,
    486
Feedback loops, 479–482
Feelings of inferiority, 259–261
Feminism, 284
Fenfluramine, 164
Fictional finalism, 512
Fidelity, 299
Fight or flight response, 178–179
Firstborn children, 261
Five-factor model, 66–73
  attachment and, 291–292
  cautions and further variations in,
    72–73
  dispositional perspective, 66–73
  ego control and, 264–265

Five-factor model *(continued)*
  ego resiliency and, 264–265
  heritability of traits and, 132–134
  motives and, 112
  nature of factors in, 67–69
  other models and, 71–72
  personality disorders and, 84
  reflections on factors in, 70–71
  supertraits in, 62–65, 73, 132–133, 152
  temperaments and, 133–134
Fixation, 208, 213, 240–241, 246, 505
Fixed interval schedule of reinforcement, 331
Fixed ratio schedule of reinforcement, 331
Fixed role therapy, 434–435
Focus of convenience, 419–420
Foreclosure, 299
Forgetting, 231–232, 322
Fraternal (dizygotic) twins, 126–127, 130–131
Free association, 241–244
Free will, 389–390, 411, 503
Freudian slips, 191, 232–233
Friendship
  feelings of inferiority and, 260
  genetic attraction and, 141–142
  need for affiliation and, 105
  need for power and, 103–104
  tend and befriend response, 179
Fully functioning person, 384, 409–410
Functional autonomy, 256
Functional MRI (fMRI), 181, 184
Functional superordinacy, 485
Fundamental ego function, 281
Fuzzy sets, 444

Gender
  achievement motivation and, 100–101
  attachment and, 290–291
  intimacy needs and, 107–108, 113
  mate retention and, 145–146, 147
  mate selection and, 142–145
  modeling and sex role acquisition, 364–365
  oxytocin and, 178–179
  phallic stage and, 211–213
  power motivation and, 104–105
  testosterone and, 178
  young male syndrome and, 146–147
Generality (generalizability), 19–20, 45

Generalization
  in classical conditioning, 320–322
  in cognitive psychology, 465–466
  in instrumental conditioning, 329
  semantic, 353
Generativity versus stagnation, 301–302, 304–305
Genetic counseling, 148
Genetic similarity theory, 141–142
Genital stage, 215
Genome, 135–136, 148
Goals
  assessment of, 492
  goal intention, 477, 478
  problems as conflicts among, 493–494
Grandiosity, 283, 307
Growth-based motives, 397, 409–410
Guiding self-ideals, 512
Guilt
  core roles and, 428
  existential, 401–402
  initiative versus, 295–296

Habit hierarchy, 325–326
Harm avoidance, 171–172
Health problems
  human genome and, 148
  incorrect feedback and, 493
  organ inferiority and, 259
  repression and, 243
Helplessness, 369, 370
Heredity. *See* Inheritance and personality
Heritability, 127. *See also* Inheritance and personality
  agreeableness, 132
  temperaments and, 130–131
Heroin addiction, 150
Hierarchy of needs (Maslow), 394–400, 512–513
Higher-order conditioning, 320, 324
HIV/AIDS, 433
Holocaust survivors, 225–226, 243
Homeostasis, 496–497
Homicide, young male syndrome and, 146–147
Homosexuality
  heritability of, 134–135
  reaction formation and, 228
Homunculus problem, 497
Honesty, 73
Hostility, 236
Human genome, 135–136, 148
Humanistic psychology, 382–413
  assessment in, 404–406
  existential psychology in, 400–403

hierarchy of motives in, 394–400, 512–513
  problems and prospects of, 410–411
  problems in behavior, and behavior change in, 407–410
  self-actualization in, 383–386, 394–400, 406, 411
  self and processes of defense in, 390–394
  self-determination in, 387–390
  self discrepancies in, 407
Human potential movement. *See* Humanistic psychology
Humor, 236
Hypertension, 493
Hypnosis, 194
  behavior change through, 241, 242
  traumatic childhood memories and, 225

Id, 195–196, 216, 255, 504
  cathexes and, 202–203
  conflict with ego, 197, 198, 234
  overcontrolled aggressors and, 205
  repression of, 223
  shifting emphasis to ego, 255–256
Ideal self, 391, 393, 407, 483–484, 513
Identical twins. *See* Monozygotic (MZ) twins
Identification, 203, 211–212, 388
Identity achievement, 299
Identity crisis, 299–300
Identity diffusion, 299–300
Identity statuses, 299–300
Identity versus role confusion, 297–300
Idiographic view of personality, 58–59, 80
If . . . then principle, 460–461, 477
Imaginal coding, 360–361
Implemental mindset, 477
Implementation intention, 477
Implicit motives, 111–112
Implicit poles, 418
Imprinting, 138
Impulsive stage, 266, 267
Impulsive unsocialized sensation seeking (IUSS), 168–169
Impulsivity, 169–172, 514–515
  as basic versus resultant property, 170
  personality scales and, 171–172
  processes involved in, 169
  punishment for, 222
  sensation seeking and, 169
  serotonin function and, 170–171
  as temperament, 131–132

Incentives, 109–110, 160–162, 354
Inclusive fitness, 139
Incongruity, 391–392, 393
Incremental schemas, 448–449
Independent variable, 27–29
Individual differences. *See also*
    Interactionism
  in consistency, 77–78
  defined, 6
  in dopamine reactivity, 162
  in multifactor studies, 31–32
  personal constructs and, 423–426
  in self-regulation, 491–492
  in self-schemas, 447–448
  species-wide adaptations to, 139
  in specific needs, 98–108
  testosterone and, 177
Individualistic stage of ego
    development, 268
Individualist stage of ego
    development, 266, 269
Industry versus inferiority, 296–297
Inference
  arbitrary, 465–466
  description versus, 26
  limitation on, 25–27
Inferential statistics, 26
Inferiority complexes, 275
Inferiority feelings, 259–261
Information-processing deficits,
    464–465
Inheritance and personality, 125–136
  adoption studies and, 128, 131,
    136, 149–150
  problems and prospects of,
    151–153
  temperaments and, 128–134
  twin studies and, 125–128,
    129–136, 149–150
Inhibited power motivation, 108, 109
Initiative versus guilt, 295–296
Insecure attachment, 285–292, 305
  of adults, 287–292
  of children, 285–287
Insight, 244, 245
Instrumental conditioning, 324–334,
    341–343
  biofeedback and, 342–343
  of conflict, 341–342
  discrimination in, 327–329, 352
  extinction in, 329, 330, 331–332
  generalization in, 329
  law of effect and, 325–326
  learning "irrational" behavior,
    332–334
  motives in, 328
  persistence and, 330, 332

phobias and, 337
punishment and, 326–327,
    329–330, 342, 352
reinforcement and, 326–327, 328,
    330–332, 334, 342, 348–350,
    352–353, 355
shaping in, 329–330
successive approximation in,
    329–330
thoughts in, 333
token economies and, 342
Integrated stage of ego development,
    266, 269
Intellect
  in five-factor model, 68, 69, 70, 71,
    133
  heritability of, 133
Intellectualization, 227
Intelligence
  correlation between genetic and
    environmental influences,
    136–137
  as temperament, 131–132
Intentions, 475–477
  implementing, 477
  nature of, 475–476
Interaction, 32–33
Interactionism, 76–82. *See also*
    Individual differences
  behavior problems and, 84–85
  context and, 79–82
  incentive value and, 109–110
  moving beyond analysis of variance
    in, 78
  nature of, 76–77
Internalization, 282
Internal reliability (consistency), 38–40
Interpersonal circle, 65–66
Inter-rater reliability, 40, 239
Interval schedule of reinforcement,
    330
Interviews, in assessment process, 404
Intimacy motivation, 106–108, 111,
    113
Intimacy versus isolation, 300–301
Intrapersonal functioning, defined,
    6–7
Introjected regulation, 387–388
Introjection, 198
Introspection, 268
Introversion
  defined, 57
  in five-factor model, 70–71
  multitasking and, 166
  need for intimacy and, 113
  principle of opposites and, 254
  in supertrait analysis, 62–65

Intuitive processors, 456
Inventories, described, 37
Irrational behavior, 332–334
  phobias as, 336–339
  superstitions and, 333–334
Isolation, 209, 300–301

Jealousy, 145
Jungian theory, 254

Kin selection, 139

Labeling, 86
Latency period, 214–215, 296–297
Latent content, 234–236
Latent needs, 96–98
Law of effect, 325–326
Leadership, inhibited power
    motivation and, 108, 109
Learned helplessness, 369, 370
Learning perspective, 11, 313–378,
    503. *See also* Conditioning
    theories; Social-cognitive
    learning theories
  assessment in, 334–336, 367–368
  biological perspective and,
    517–518
  classical conditioning, 317–324,
    336–341
  elaborations on conditioning
    processes, 348–359
  instrumental conditioning,
    324–334, 341–343
  manifestations of cognitive and
    social learning, 363–367
  observational learning in,
    359–363
  problems in behavior, and
    behavior change in, 336–343,
    368–374
  problems and prospects of,
    343–344, 374–376
  social regulation and, 510–512
  themes and underlying
    assumptions of, 314–315
Lexical criterion, 62
Libido, 203, 204, 211, 215–216,
    246–247
Life instincts, 203
Lifestyles, 260
  assessment of, 272–273
Lithium, 183
Location, in Rorschach inkblot
    responses, 239
Locus of causality, 450
Locus-of-control expectancies,
    356–357

Love
  mental models of, 288
  mirroring in, 283
  self-concept and, 284

Magnetic resonance imaging (MRI),
    180–181
Main effect, 32
Manic depression (bipolar disorder).
    See Bipolar disorder (manic
    depression)
Manifest content, 234–236
Manifest needs, 96–98
MAO (monoamine oxidase), 167,
    170, 182–183
Marriage
  achievement motivation and, 101
  affiliation motivation and, 106
  competition for mates and,
    142–145
  genetic influences on risk of
    divorce, 134
  genetic similarity and, 141–142
  intimacy needs and, 107–108
  mate retention and, 145–146, 147
  power motivation and, 104
Masturbation, 237
Mate selection, 505
  competition for mates and, 142–145
  genetic similarity and, 141–142
  mate retention and, 145–146, 147
Means-end analysis, 495–496
Mechanism of opposites, 236
Media, symbolic models and, 365,
    366–367
Memories, 444–446, 450–453
  activation and use of, 450–453
    episodic memory, 445
    semantic memory, 445
Mesomorphy, 126
Metatheory, 10–12
Middle stages of ego development,
    267–268
Midlife crisis, 303
Minnesota Center for Twin and
    Adoption Research, 129
Minnesota Multiphasic Personality
    Inventory (MMPI), 48–49, 240
Mirroring, 283, 307
Mistaken lifestyles, 260
Modeling, 364–367
  of aggression, 366–367
  and delay of gratification, 364
  interpretation of, 475
  participant, 372–373
  and responses to fear, 371–372
  and sex role acquisition, 364–365

Molecular genetics, 135–136
Monoamine oxidase (MAO), 167,
    170, 182–183
Monozygotic (MZ) twins, 125–126
  separation at birth, 129
  temperament and, 130–131
  traits of, 132
Moral anxiety, 222
Moral-reasoning capabilities, 269–270
Moratorium, 299
Mortality, 402–403
Mother-infant bonding, 179
Motivation, 200–208
  aggressive energies in, 204
  catharsis in, 204–207
  cathexes in, 202–203, 216, 281, 506
  competence, 256–261, 293, 387,
    406
  death instincts in, 203, 216
  displacement in, 207, 228, 244
  effectance, 256–258
  libidinal energies in, 204
  life instincts in, 203
  sublimation in, 207–208, 229
Motives
  analysis of, 513
  changing, 92–93, 114–115
  dispositional needs and, 94–95
  in dispositional perspective, 92–93,
    94–98, 112–113, 114–115
  five-factor model and, 112
  influence on behavior, 110
  in instrumental conditioning, 328
  Maslow's hierarchy of, 394–400
  measuring, 96–98, 111–113
  nature of, 92–93
  needs versus, 94
  theoretical problems and
    prospects, 115–117
  traits versus, 113
Motor schemas, 473–475, 478
Multifactor studies, 31–33
  nature of, 31–32
  reading results of, 32–33
Myers-Briggs Type Indicator, 254

Names, self-schemas and, 453
Narcissism, 283, 307
Natural selection, 139
Nazi persecution, 225–226, 243
Need for achievement, 96, 98–103
  divergent motives, 101–103
  effects of, 99–101
  ego psychology, 268
  increasing, 114–115, 116
  individual differences in, 98–103
Need for affiliation, 96, 105–106, 109

Need for cognition, 257
Need for intimacy, 106–108, 111, 113
Need for nurturance, 96
Need for power, 96, 103–105, 108,
    114, 175–178, 212–213, 261,
    295–296
Needs
  assessment of, 111–113
  in dispositional perspective, 90–92,
    95–96, 98–108, 110
  individual differences in, 98–108
  individual versus group, 515–516
  influence on behavior, 110
  Maslow's hierarchy of, 394–400,
    512–513
  motives versus, 94
  Murray's approach to, 95–96, 106,
    109, 112, 114, 115–117
  nature of, 90–92
  theoretical problems and
    prospects, 115–117
  types of, 91–92
Negative reinforcement, 326
Negativity emotionality, 163
Neoanalytic perspective, 11, 110–111,
    249–312. *See also* Ego psychology;
    Psychosocial theories
  cognitive self-regulation
    perspective and, 512
  themes and underlying
    assumptions of, 250–251
NEO Personality Inventory (NEO-PI),
    72, 73, 83, 112
Neural networks, 454
Neuro-imaging, 180–181, 184
Neurotic anxiety, 221–222, 408
Neuroticism. *See* Emotionality
Neurotic needs, 307–308
Neurotransmitters
  assessing function of, 164
  behavioral approach system (BAS)
    and, 162
  behavioral inhibition system (BIS)
    and, 163
Nodes, 450–452, 454
Nomothetic view of personality,
    58–59
Nurturance need, 96

Obesity
  instrumental conditioning and,
    341
  oral stage and, 209
Objective measures, 37–38
Object relations theories, 281–284
  assessment and, 305–306
  basic anxiety and, 283–284

behavior change and, 309–310
self psychology and, 283
Observational learning, 359–363
attention in, 359–360
performance in, 360, 361–363
production in, 360–361
retention in, 360–361
Observer ratings, 270
described, 36
subjectivity/objectivity of, 37–38
Oedipus complex, 211, 213, 214, 216,
217, 230, 231, 241, 254, 505
Only children, 261
Openness to experience
in five-factor model, 68, 69, 70, 71,
72, 133–134
heritability of, 133
Operant conditioning. *See*
Instrumental conditioning
Operational definitions, 41–42
Optimism, 410–411, 489–490
Oral incorporative phase, 208
Oral sadistic phase, 208–209
Oral stage, 208–210, 213, 228
Organ inferiority, 259
Organismic valuing process, 384
Ought self, 407
Overcontrol, 262–264, 275–276
Overcontrolled aggressors, 205
Overgeneralization, 465–466
Overregularization, 353–354
Oxytocin, 178–179

Parallel distributed processing, 454
Parapraxes, 231–232
Parenting style, 302
Parsimony, 9
Partial reinforcement, 330
Partial reinforcement effect, 331–332
Participant modeling, 371–373
Patterns of construals, 426
Pavlovian conditioning. *See* Classical
conditioning
Peak experience, 400
Penis envy, 212–213
Perceptual defense, 507
Performance, in observational
learning, 360, 361–363
Permeability, 419
Persistence, in instrumental
conditioning, 330, 332
Personal constructs, 414–437, 460,
510
appraisal and stress in, 417
behavioral consistency and,
428–429
bipolar nature of, 418–419

extension of, 420–422
focus of convenience of, 419–420
individuality of, 423–426
nature of, 416
organization among, 422–423
psychological distress and,
431–432
range of convenience of, 419
role of recurrences in, 419
role taking and, 426–428
similarities and differences
between people, 425–426
using, 417–418
Personal efficacy, 258–259, 375
Personality, 3–7
as concept, 3–5
individual differences and, 6
intrapersonal functioning and,
6–7
perspectives on, 10–13
stability over time, 75
study of. *See* Study of personality
working definition of, 5–6
Personality coefficient, 74
Personality disorders
five-factor model and, 84
narcissism, 283, 307
Personality profiles, 82–84
Personality psychology, 7–10. *See also*
Study of personality
Personality Research Form (PRF),
111, 112
Personality scales, 171–172
Personal Orientation Inventory
(POI), 406
Person-centered therapy, 408–409
Personology
defined, 17–18
methods of, 110–111
Perspective of the generalized other,
427
Persuasion, 108, 257
Pessimism, 489–490
Phallic stage, 211–213
Pharmacotherapy, 183–184
Phenomenological perspective,
11–12, 503. *See also* Humanistic
psychology; Personal constructs
assessment in, 404–406, 429–431
phenomenology, defined, 380
problems and prospects of,
410–411, 435–436
problems in behavior, and
behavior change in, 407–410,
431–435
themes and underlying
assumptions of, 380–381

Phobias, 336–339
classical conditioning and, 336–339
instrumental conditioning and, 337
list of common, 337
Physiological assessment, 335
Play, in assessment, 306–307
Play therapy, 309
Pleasure principle, 195–196
Positive affect, 166
Positive emotionality, 161
Positive regard, 384–386, 395, 408
Positive reinforcement, 326
Positron emission tomography (PET),
180, 181, 184
Possible selves, 448
Post-Freudian psychodynamic
theorists. *See* Neoanalytic
perspective
Power motivation, 96, 103–105, 108,
114
anabolic steroids and, 176
birth order and, 261, 273
initiative versus guilt, 295–296
penis envy and, 212–213
testosterone and, 175, 176–178
Practical significance, 25
Precondition for acceptance, 386
Preconscious, 193, 195
Prediction, theories and, 7, 8
Predictive efficiency, 417–418, 424
Predictive validity, 43
Pregnancy, androgens and, 174
Preparedness, 517–518
Press, nature of, 93–94
Primary appraisal, 417
Primary ego autonomy, 256
Primary needs, 91–92
Primary process, 196, 236
Primary reinforcers, 326
Priming, 452, 453, 474, 475
Principle control, 483
Principle of opposites, 254
Principles, 483
Production, in observational
learning, 360–361
Programs, 484–485
Projection, 226
Projective techniques, 237–240
Prototypes, 444
Psyche, 201
Psychoanalysis, 191–193
behavior change through, 241–245
defense mechanisms and, 246
effectiveness of, 245, 385
free association in, 241–244
in historical context, 192
insight through, 244, 245

Psychoanalytic perspective, 11,
    187–248, 503
  anxiety and, 211–213, 221–222, 245
  assessment in, 237–240
  cognitive psychology and, 507–509
  conditioning theories and,
    505–506
  defense mechanisms in, 222–231,
    245–247
  evolutionary psychology and,
    504–505
  motivation and, 200–208
  problems and prospects of,
    215–217, 245–247
  problems in behavior, and
    behavior change in, 240–245
  psychoanalysis and, 191–193,
    241–245
  psychosexual development and,
    208–215
  self-regulation and, 506–507
  structural model of personality
    and, 195–200, 506–507
  themes and underlying
    assumptions of, 188–189
  topographical model of mind and,
    193–195, 217
  unconscious in, 193–195, 231–237,
    240–244, 246–247
Psychodynamic approach, 188
Psychogenic needs, 91
Psychopathology of everyday life,
    231–234, 358
Psychosexual development, 208–215,
    246–247
  anal stage, 210–211, 213, 228
  genital stage, 215
  latency period, 214–215, 296–297
  oral stage, 208–210, 213, 228
  phallic stage, 211–213
Psychosocial crisis (conflict), 293
Psychosocial development, 292–305
  adolescent stage, 297–300
  adulthood stage, 301–302
  competence and, 293
  early childhood stage, 295
  ego identity and, 292
  epigenetic principle in, 304–305
  Erikson versus other theorists, 305
  identity as life story in, 304–305
  infancy stage, 294–295
  old age stage, 302–304
  preschool stage, 295–296
  psychosocial crisis or conflict in,
    293
  school age stage, 296–297
  young adulthood stage, 300–301

Psychosocial theories, 280–312
  assessment of, 305–307
  attachment theory, 285–292,
    305–306, 310
  object relations theories, 281–284,
    305–306, 309–310
  problems in behavior, and
    behavior change, 307–310
  problems and prospects of, 310
  psychosocial development theory,
    292–305
Psychoticism, 65, 168, 240, 408
Punishers, 326
Punishment
  for impulsivity, 222
  in instrumental conditioning,
    326–327, 329–330, 342, 352

Q-sort, 66–67, 404–406, 429

Radical behaviorism, 328
Random assignment, 28, 29
Range of convenience, 419
Rapid eye movement (REM), 235
Rational approach, to scale
    development, 47–48
Rationalization, 226–227, 391
Rational systems, 456
Reactance, 389–390
Reaction formation, 227–228
Reality anxiety, 221
Reality principle, 196–197
Reality testing, 196–197, 467
Real self, 391, 393, 407, 513
Reciprocal altruism, 140
Redemption themes, 304–305
Reducers, 168
Reflexes, 317–318
Reframing, 466–467
Regression, 228
Reinforcement, 511
  feedback versus, 480
  instrumental conditioning and,
    326–327, 328, 330–332, 334, 342,
    348–350, 352–353, 355
Reinforcers, 326
Rejection, 457, 461
Relatedness, 387, 388–389
Relaxation, 339
Reliability, 38–41
  defined, 38
  internal, 38–40
  inter-rater, 40, 239
  in measuring behavior,
    74–75
  split-half, 39–40
  test-retest, 40–41, 75, 239

Repression, 202, 241, 505, 507
  breakdown of, 225
  denial compared with, 226, 508
  forgetting as, 231–232
  impact of disclosure on health, 243
  nature of, 222–224
  research on, 230
Rep Test (Role Construct Repertory
    Test), 429–431
Resiliency. *See* Ego resiliency
Resistance, 244
Response sets, 45–47
Restatement of content, 409
Restraint, 514–515
Retention, in observational learning,
    360–361
Rewards
  in instrumental conditioning,
    329–330
  problems of, 387
Reward sensitivity, 166
Role confusion, 297–300
Role Construct Repertory Test (Rep
    Test), 429–431
Role taking, 426–428
Rorschach inkblot test, 238–240
Rule-based learning, 353–354
Rules, 267–268
Rumination-Reflection
    Questionnaire, 492

Sadism, 204, 208–209
Satisfying, 327
Scatterplots, 22–25
Schedules of reinforcement, 330–332
Schemas, 443–453
  for action, 473–475, 478
  attribution and, 449–450
  behavioral, 474–475
  defined, 443
  development of, 443–444
  effects of, 444–445
  entity, 448–449
  incremental, 448–449
  memories and, 444–446, 450–453
  scripts and, 445–446, 473–474,
    484–485
  self-schemas, 447–448, 453,
    465–466
  socially relevant, 446–447
Schizophrenia
  behavior genetics and, 149–150
  pharmacotherapy for, 183
Scrambled sentences procedure,
    474–475
Scripts, 445–446, 473–474, 484–485
Secondary appraisal, 417

Secondary ego autonomy, 256
Secondary elaboration, 236
Secondary needs, 91
Secondary process, 196
Secondary reinforcers, 326
Second-born children, 261, 273
Second-order factors, 65
Secure attachment, 285–292
   of adults, 287–292
   of children, 285–287
Seduction theory, 241, 242
Selective serotonin reuptake
     inhibitors (SSRIs), 183–184
Self-acceptance, 385–386
Self-actualization, 383–386, 410–411,
     483
   application of concept of, 399
   assessment of, 406
   characteristics of self-actualizers,
      397–399
   defined, 383–384
   Maslow and, 394–400
   need for positive regard and,
      384–386
   peak experience and, 400
   Rogers and, 383–386
Self-affirmation, 392
Self-attributed motives, 112
Self-aware stage of ego development,
     266, 268
Self-complexity, 448
Self-concept, 391, 404–406, 447–448
Self-concordance, 389
Self-consciousness, 491–492
Self-Conscious Scale, 481
Self-control, 364
Self-defense, 490
Self-determination, 387–390
   free will and, 389–390, 411, 503
   identification in, 388
   introjection in, 387–388
   need for relatedness and, 388–389
   self-concordance and, 389
   self-regulation versus, 496
Self-disclosure
   in assessment interviews, 404
   health impact of, 243
   intimacy motivation and, 106–107
Self-efficacy, 357–359, 489–490
Self-enhancement, 307
Self-esteem
   low, 391
   maintenance and enhancement of,
      392–393
Self-evaluation, 392
Self guides, 407
Self-handicapping, 393–394

Self-instructions, 373–374
Self-monitoring, 77, 463
Selfobject, 283
Self-protective stage of ego
     development, 266, 267
Self psychology, 283
Self-ratings, 270
Self-reflection, 491–492
Self-regulation, 460, 471–499
   assessment of, 490–492
   automaticity in action, 475
   feedback control and, 479–490,
      493
   goals and goal setting in, 477, 478
   hierarchy of needs and, 512–513
   intentions and, 475–477
   learning perspective and, 510–512
   problems in behavior, and
      behavior change in, 492–496
   problems and prospects of,
      496–498
   psychoanalytic perspective and,
      506–507
   schemas for action in, 473–475
Self-reinforcement, 350
Self-reports, 28–29, 111–112, 367, 493
   described, 36–37
   personality profiles, 82–84
   reliability of, 39, 40
   response sets and, 46
   subjectivity/objectivity of, 37–38
Self-schemas, 447–448, 453, 465–466
Self-talk, 466–467
Self theory, 390–391
Self-verification, 393
Semantic generalization, 353
Semantic memory, 445
Sensation seeking, 166–169
   function of, 167–169
   impulsivity and, 169
Sensory stimulation, 234
Sentence Completion Test for Ego
     Development, 274
Separation anxiety, 282
Separation-individuation, 282, 283
Serotonin, 136
   gene involved in, 163
   impulsivity and, 170–171
   sensitivity variations, 164
Sex hormones, 172–179
   androgen, 174, 179
   early exposure to, 173–174
   estrogen, 179
   oxytocin, 178–179
   role of, 172–173
   testosterone, 172, 174–177
Sex role acquisition, 364–365

Sexual arousal, aggression and, 204,
     207
Sexual instincts, 203
Sexuality
   adaptation and, 256
   ego control and, 263
   in psychoanalytic perspective, 192,
      237
   terror management and, 403
Sexual orientation
   heritability of, 134–135
   reaction formation and, 228
Shaping, 329–330
Shyness, 75
Siblings
   birth order and, 261, 273
   environmental influences on,
      137
   twins as, 127
Significance, 25
Significant others, 384–386
Simplification, 344
Situationism, 74, 79–80
16 Personality Factor inventory
     (16PF), 62, 65, 66
Skill deficits
   defined, 369
   modeling-based therapy for,
      369–371
Sleep
   dreams and, 234–236, 237
   function of, 235
Slips of the tongue and pen, 191,
     232–233
Smell, 141
Smoking relapse, 340
Sociability, 129–130, 139, 165–166
Social cognition, 446–447
Social-cognitive learning theories,
     347–378
   assessment and, 367–368
   elaborations on conditioning
      processes and, 348–359
   manifestations of cognitive and
      social learning, 363–367
   observational learning, 359–363
   problems in behavior, and
      behavior change in, 368–374
   problems and prospects of,
      374–376
Social desirability, 46–47
Social incompetence, 305–306
Social isolation, 209, 300–301
Socialization, 72, 104, 182
Socially relevant schemas, 446–447
Social reinforcement, 348–350
Sociobiology, 138–141, 152

Socioeconomic status (SES),
    testosterone and, 175
Somatotonia, 126
Somatotype, 126
Sources of information
    for assessment, 36–38
    about personality, 17
Specificity
    of attachment, 290
    case studies and, 17–19
Split-half reliability, 39–40
Spontaneous performance, 362–363
Spontaneous recovery, 506
Stability
    of attachment, 289
    of personality, 75
    in supertrait analysis, 62–65
Stabilizing selection, 139
Stage theories
    of ego development, 265–271
    of psychosexual development,
        208–215
    of psychosocial development,
        292–305
Statistical significance, 25
Strange situation, 285
Stress
    appraisal and, 417
    optimism and, 489
    oxytocin and, 178–179
Stress inoculation, 374
Striving for superiority, 259–261
Structural model of personality,
    195–200, 506–507
    balancing forces in, 199–200
    ego, 196–197, 198
    id, 195–196, 197
    superego, 198–199
Structured self-reports, 305
Studies of many people, 19–20
Study of personality, 16–34. *See also*
        Biological perspective; Cognitive
        self-regulation perspective;
        Dispositional perspective;
        Learning perspective;
        Neoanalytic perspective;
        Phenomenological perspective;
        Psychoanalytic perspective
    information-gathering, 17–20
    relationships among variables,
        20–33
Subjective measures, 37–38
Subjective norms, 476
Subjective values, 460
Sublimation, 207–208, 229
Subliminal stimuli, 230, 231, 475
Successive approximation, 329–330

Superego, 198–199, 222, 241, 255,
    504–505
    cathexes and, 202–203
    overcontrolled aggressors and, 205
    symbolization and, 236
Superiority complexes, 275
Superstitious behavior, 333–334
Supertrait analysis, 62–65, 73,
    132–133, 152
Suppression, 222, 223, 243
Symbiosis, 282
Symbiotic stage, 266–267
Symbolic association, 235
Symbolic interactionism, 427
Symbolic models, 365, 366–367
Symbolization, 236
Systematic desensitization, 338–339
System concepts, 483

Temper, 75
Temperament, 128–134
    activity level, 129
    aspects of, 126
    behavioral approach/inhibition
        systems and, 164–165
    defined, 128–129
    emotionality, 130
    and five-factor model, 133–134
    heritability of, 130–131, 133–134
    impulsivity, 131–132
    intelligence, 131–132
    modifying, 151
    problems and prospects of,
        151–152
    sociability, 129–130
Tend and befriend response, 179
Territorial markers, 138
Terror management, 402–403, 408
Testability, of theories, 8
Testosterone
    adult personality and, 174–177
    aggression and, 173–174, 175, 176
    cycle of action and, 177
    evolutionary psychology and, 178
    influence on behavior, 174
    role of, 172
Test-retest reliability, 40–41, 75, 239
Thanatos, 203
Thematic Apperception Test (TAT),
    96–98, 99, 103, 111–113, 238
Theoretical approach. *See* Rational
        approach
Theories
    defined, 7
    evaluating, 8
    grand-scale, 12–13
    groupings among, 10–12

    in personality psychology, 7–10
    purposes of, 7
    qualities of good, 8–10
Think-aloud technique, 223, 462
Third variable problem, 26–27
Thoughts, in conditioning, 333
Thought suppression, 222, 223
Threat
    dealing with, 433–434
    personal constructs and, 432,
        433–434
    sources of, 224
Threat sensitivity, 163
Thurstone Temperament Schedule
    (TTS), 131, 132
Time competence, 406
Time out, 326–327
Toilet training, 295
Token economies, 342
Topographical model of mind,
    193–195, 217
    conscious in, 193, 195
    preconscious in, 193, 195
    unconscious in, 193–195
Trait psychology, 57–88
    assessment in, 82–84
    behavioral approach/inhibition
        systems and, 164–165
    behaviors and, 73–75, 79–82, 84–86
    Cattell's approach to, 62, 63, 65,
        66, 73
    Eysenck's approach to, 62–65, 73,
        84
    factor analysis in, 59–62
    five-factor model in, 66–73, 152
    inheritance of traits, 132–133
    interactionism and, 76–82
    interpersonal circle and, 65–66
    motives versus, 113
    problems and prospects of, 86–87
    situationism and, 74, 79–80
    traits, defined, 57
Transcendent self-actualizers, 399
Transference, 244, 283, 509
Transpersonal, 399
Trauma
    false memories of childhood, 225
    reconstruing world after, 433
    self-disclosure of, 243
    as source of behavior problems,
        241
Trust, 294–295
    attachment and, 290
    narcissism and, 307
Twin studies, 125–128
    on alcohol abuse, 149–150
    environmental effects and, 136

five-factor model and, 133
heritability of sexual orientation,
134–135
separation at birth, 129
temperament and, 130–131
traits and, 132
Types, 57–58

Unconditional positive regard,
384–385, 408, 409–410
Unconditioned/unconditional
response (UR), 318–324
Unconditioned/unconditional
stimulus (US), 318–324
Unconscious, 231–237, 240, 244,
246–247
current views of, 194
dreams and, 234–236, 237
in ego psychology, 271
free association and, 241–244
humor and, 236
nature of, 193–195
in psychopathology of everyday
life, 231–234
Undercontrol, 264, 275–276

Vagina envy, 212
Validity, 41–47, 239–240
construct, 42–43
convergent, 43–44
criterion, 43
culture and, 45
defined, 41
discriminant, 44
face, 44–45
predictive, 43
response sets and loss of,
45–47
Variable interval schedule of
reinforcement, 331
Variable ratio schedule of
reinforcement, 331
Variables, 20–33
causality and, 25–30
cognitive person, 458–462
correlation between, 21–27
defined, 20
dependent, 28–29
independent, 27–29
significance and, 25
Verbal coding, 360–361

Verbal persuasion, 373
Vicarious classical conditioning,
351–352
Vicarious emotional arousal,
350–352
Vicarious experiences,
372–373
Vicarious reinforcement,
352–353
Vicious cycle, 284
Violence
social schemas and, 453
young male syndrome and, 147
Virtue, 294
Viscerotonia, 126

War, 108, 109
Will, 295
Wisdom, 304
Wish fulfillment, 196, 234

X chromosomes, 135

Youngest child, 261
Young male syndrome, 146–147

Photo Credits